W9-CBG-978

DATE DUE

GAYLORD

PRINTED IN U.S.A.

HANDBOOK OF PSYCHOLOGICAL ASSESSMENT

THIRD EDITION

with WAIS-III Supplement

Gary Groth-Marnat

BENEDICTINE UNIVERSITY LIBRARY
IN THE KINDLON HALL OF LEARNING
5700 COLLEGE ROAD

WITHDRAWN

John Wiley & Sons, Inc.
New York • Chichester • Weinheim • Brisbane • Singapore • Toronto

150.287
G881h
1999

To Barbara, Rudy, Gabrielle,
Dawn, and Katrina

This text is printed on acid-free paper. ∞

Copyright © 1997, 1999 by John Wiley & Sons, Inc.

Published by John Wiley & Sons, Inc.

All rights reserved. Published simultaneously in Canada.
Reproduction or translation of any part of this work beyond
that permitted by Section 107 or 108 of the 1976 United
States Copyright Act without the permission of the copyright
owner is unlawful. Requests for permission or further
information should be addressed to the Permissions Department,
John Wiley & Sons, Inc.

This publication is designed to provide accurate and authoritative
information in regard to the subject matter covered. It is sold
with the understanding that the publisher is not engaged in
rendering professional services. If legal, accounting, medical,
psychological, or any other expert assistance is required, the
services of a competent professional person should be sought.

Library of Congress Cataloging-in-Publication Data:
Groth-Marnat, Gary.
    Handbook of psychological assessment / Gary Groth-Marnat. — 3rd
ed.
      p.   cm.
    Includes bibliographical references and index.
    ISBN 0-471-05220-5 (cloth : alk. paper)
    1. Psychological tests. 2. Personality assessment. I. Title.
    BF176.G76   1997
    150'.28'7—dc20   96-23803

Printed in the United States of America

10 9 8 7

Contents———————————————————

Preface

My dear readers, colleagues, friends, collaborators, and reviewers: We have arrived at another edition of the *Handbook of Psychological Assessment.* I would like to thank you for making it all possible. Your enthusiasm, support, help, and yes, even your criticisms, have all made this possible. I now give this part of myself back to you. I believe the Handbook will continue to be a useful, practical, comprehensive guide to understanding people. Although much of the material in this edition is technical, I hope I have also captured the human side of writing the book, as well as the very human side of conducting assessment. At some point, every effective assessment must go beyond the scores, data, profiles, and norms and reach out with a willingness to engage the person. Without this connection, a report is likely to feel cool, distant, and lacking in substance. I hope that between each technical line, my readers will simultaneously feel that the purpose is still to reach out and connect with the other. In constructing the book, I have attempted to give credence and respect to the technical as well as the art; to the unique individual as well as the larger system; to both acturial and clinical approaches.

To those readers familar with previous editions and who now peruse the current one, much will be the same but much will be different. The book reflects the changes that have occurred both in my thinking and in the field. Most noticeably, this revision includes three new chapters. Perhaps the most important of these (and yet the shortest), is Chapter 13, which deals with treatment planning. I strongly believe that psychologists conducting assessment will progressively need to direct more of their efforts toward treatment planning. Over the past 5 to 10 years, empirical support for such efforts has dovetailed with increasing demands for cost-effectiveness and accountability. The systematic treatment selection model presented in Chapter 13 is, in my view, the most extensive, conceptually sound, and empirically validated model to date. A new chapter also is devoted to the Millon Clinical Multiaxial Inventory (MCMI; Chapter 7). The MCMI is an efficient, well-designed, contemporary inventory that provides valuable information about a client. Accordingly, it is one of the few tests to have "risen through the ranks" of frequently administered tests to the extent that a relatively high proportion of practitioners are currently using it. This growth in the instrument looks likely to continue. In the 1999 revision of the third edition, there is a supplement to update readers on the recent (1997) WAIS-III. Finally, Chapter 12 provides an overview and integration of a variety of strategies for neuropsychological assessment. Because general psychologists increasingly need to be conversant with many of the skills involved in neuropsychological assessment, knowledge of one or two single screening instruments simply will no longer be sufficient. Therefore, a number of the most frequently used instruments have been included and organized around different functional domains.

The book also has numerous smaller changes: There are sections on the ethics of testing; test selection; an expanded, fully integrated interpretive system for the Wechsler Scales (including several new worksheets and tables); integration of the new WISC-III with the WAIS-R; material on the MMPI-A; expansion of the discussion of the Rorschach to include all of Exner's scoring and interpretation categories; the inclusion of Bellak's interpretive system for the Thematic Apperception Test; a new objective interpretation system by Naglieri for human figure drawings; and two new examples of psychological reports. In response to the development and increasing emphasis on neuropsychological assessment, I have added relevant material to sections on the Wechsler scales, MMPI, and interviewing. Whenever possible, I have included treatment planning information in the interpretation sections of the tests. Most noticeably, the scale interpretations for the MMPI and the MCMI both have new treatment planning sections.

Finally, all areas have been thoroughly updated to reflect a multitude of events and movements in the field as well as the numerous articles continually being published. Major events include the impact of managed care, new ethical guidelines (1992), release of the WISC-III (1991), three new editions of Exner's three volumes on the Rorschach (1991, 1993, 1995), advances in identifying the empirical relationships between interventions and treatment planning, a new version of the MCMI (1994), new surveys of test usage, updated or newly released software, new developments in the theory and practice of ability testing, and advances in neuropsychological assessment. It would be most convenient if all publications would stop until this third edition gets published; however, even now I know that numerous articles and chapters are on the way too late for inclusion. My goal has been to display the utmost in conscientiousness but to fall just short of obsessiveness.

No one can write a handbook like this one without the support of colleagues. I feel particularly pleased to have had such an encouraging and supportive group. First, I want to again thank my original collaborator, Dorothy (Gita) Morena. We set out on the first edition nearly 15 years ago now. Her thoughts, time, creativity, and friendship have been much appreciated and enjoyed. I also owe special thanks to Herb Reich, Senior Editor at John Wiley & Sons who humored, cajoled, informed, networked, suggested, faxed, supported, and inspired me through the second edition and the first portion of the third edition. I have come to think of him as both friend and colleague. Herb's successor, Jo Ann Miller, Executive Editor at John Wiley & Sons, along with her team, has also provided valuable assistance in completing the third edition. This has included the production manager, Joseph Mills and the editorial assistant, Elizabeth Skrapits. In addition the crew at Publications Development Company are to be commended for their careful attention to detail, patience, and professionalism—Nancy Marcus Land, Pam Blackmon, and Maryan Malone.

Numerous colleagues have generously contributed their time to review drafts of chapters and generally share their ideas with me. Perhaps the most influential of these have been the two formal reviewers of the second edition, John Rosen and Jerold Gold. Their numerous favorable comments have been deeply appreciated. Even more helpful, however, have been their suggestions on how to improve the book. I have carefully thought over each of their ideas and worked to integrate them into this now released third edition. Colleagues who have reviewed additional chapters include Hank Andrews, Larry Beutler, James Choca, Dan Fisher, Michael Hunt, Alan Kaufman, Ian Kneebone, Pat Lacks, Richard Lewak, George Prigatano, Paul Retzlaff, Clare Roberts, Jeff Richards, Don Thompson, and Jennifer Thornton. In particular, Larry Beutler at the University of California, Santa Barbara, was extremely helpful and generous in sharing his time, students, facilities, and ideas with me while I was on a 1995 sabbatical that enabled me to write major sections of the third edition.

Several research assistants were invaluable in responding (amazingly) to endless requests to chase up obscure articles, proofread barely intelligible material, create tedious tables (i.e., Lynne, Internet Cybersurfer extraordinaire), and make last-minute dashes to PsychLit (i.e., thanks, Nigel). My thanks, then, to Kate Oliier, Lynne Roberts, Nigel Spurgeon, and Darin Cairns.

Special thanks also go to several of my students, who provided me with valuable feedback when they "test-drove" drafts of third edition chapters or provided me with additional resources. These include Mary Baker, Ron Baker, Daniella Barbuzza, Kirsten Bouse, Gregg Ebsworthy, Sharon Hooper, Craig Nichols, Nigel Spurgeon, Roger Summers, Katie Thomas, and Leiza van der Zanden.

My thanks to all these persons; without their help and support, the third edition of *Handbook of Psychological Assessment* would not have been possible.

Chapter 1

INTRODUCTION

The *Handbook of Psychological Assessment* has been designed to develop a high level of practitioner competence by providing relevant practical as well as some theoretical material. It can serve as both a reference and instructional guide. As a reference book, it can aid in test selection and the development of a large number and variety of interpretive hypotheses. As an instructional text, it provides students with the basic tools for conducting an integrated psychological assessment. The significant and overriding emphasis in this book is on assessing areas that are of practical use in evaluating individuals within a clinical context. It is applied in its orientation, and for the most part, I have kept theoretical discussions to a minimum. Many books written on psychological testing—and the courses organized around these books—focus primarily on test theory, with a brief overview of a large number of tests. In contrast, my intent is to focus on the actual processes that practitioners go through during assessment. I begin with such issues as role clarification and evaluation of the referral question and end with treatment planning and the actual preparation of the report itself. Although I have included some material on test theory, my purpose is to review those areas that are most relevant in evaluating tests before including them in a battery.

One of the crucial skills that I hope readers of this text will develop, or at least have enhanced, is a realistic appreciation of the assets and limitations of assessment. This includes an appraisal of psychological assessment as a general strategy as well as an awareness of the assets and limitations of specific instruments and procedures. A primary limitation of assessment lies in the incorrect handling of the data, which is not integrated within the context of other sources of information (behavioral observations, history, other test scores). Also, the results are not presented in a way that helps solve the unique problems clients or referral sources are confronting. To counter these limitations, the text continually provides practitioners with guidelines for integrating and presenting the data in as useful a manner as possible. The text is thus not so much a book on test interpretation (although this is an important component) but on test integration within the wider context of assessment. As a result, psychologists should be able to create reports that are accurate, effective, concise, and highly valued by the persons who receive them.

ORGANIZATION OF THE HANDBOOK

My central organizational plan for the *Handbook of Psychological Assessment* replicates the sequence practitioners follow when performing an evaluation. They are initially concerned with clarifying their roles, ensuring that they understand all the implications of the referral question, deciding which procedures would be most appropriate for the assessment, and reminding themselves of the potential problems associated with clinical judgment (Chapter 1). They also need to understand the context in which they will conduct the assessment. This understanding includes appreciating the issues, concerns, terminology, and likely roles of the persons from these contexts. Practitioners also must have clear ethical guidelines, know how to work with possible test bias, and recognize issues related to computer-assisted assessment and the ways that the preceding factors might influence their selection of procedures (see Chapter 2).

Once practitioners have fully understood the preliminary issues discussed in Chapters 1 and 2, they then must select different strategies of assessment. The three major strategies are interviewing, observing behavior, and psychological testing. An interview is likely to occur during the initial phases of assessment and is also essential in interpreting test scores and understanding behavioral observations (see Chapter 3). The assessment of actual behaviors might also be undertaken (see Chapter 4). Behavioral assessment might be either an end in itself or an adjunct to testing. It might involve a variety of strategies such as the measurement of overt behaviors, cognitions, alterations in physiology, or relevant measures from self-report inventories.

The middle part of the book (Chapters 5 through 12) provides a general overview of the most frequently used tests. Each chapter begins with an introduction to the test in the form of a discussion of its history and development, current evaluation, and procedures for administration. The main portions of these chapters provide a guide for interpretation, which includes such areas as the meaning of different scales, significant relations between scales, frequent trends, and the meaning of unusually high or low scores. When appropriate, there are additional subsections. For example, Chapter 5, "Wechsler Intelligence Scales," includes a discussion of the nature of intelligence because it is especially crucial for a practitioner to understand the theoretical construct of "intelligence" before attempting to interpret IQ scores. Likewise, Chapter 10, "The Thematic Apperception Test," includes a summary of Murray's theory of personality because a knowledge of his concepts is a prerequisite for understanding and interpreting the test. Chapter 12, "Screening and Assessing for Neuropsychological Impairment," varies somewhat from the preceding format in that it is more a compendium and interpretive guide to some of the most frequently used short neuropsychological tests along with a section on the special considerations in conducting a neuropsychological interview. This organization reflects the current emphasis on and strategies for assessing patients with possible neuropsychological dysfunction.

Several of the chapters on psychological tests are quite long, particularly those for the Wechsler scales, Minnesota Multiphasic Personality Inventory, and neuropsychological screening and assessment. These chapters include extensive summaries of a wide variety of interpretive hypotheses intended for reference purposes when practitioners must generate interpretive hypotheses based on specific test scores. To gain initial familiarity with the tests, I recommend that practitioners or students carefully read the initial sections (history and development, psychometric properties, etc.) and then skim through the interpretation sections more quickly. This will provide the reader with a basic familiarity with the procedures and types of data obtainable from the tests. As practical test work progresses, clinicians can then study the interpretive hypotheses in greater depth and will gradually develop more extensive knowledge of the scales and their interpretation.

Based primarily on current frequency of use, the following tests are covered in this text: the Wechsler intelligence scales, Minnesota Multiphasic Personality Inventory (MMPI), Millon Clinical Multiaxial Inventory (MCMI), Bender Visual Motor Gestalt Test (along with other frequently used neuropsychological tests), Rorschach, Thematic Apperception Test (TAT), and the Draw-A-Person (or House-Tree-Person; Piotrowski & Zalewski, 1993; Watkins, 1991; Watkins, Campbell, Nieberding, & Hallmark, 1995). I chose the Wechsler Adult Intelligence Scale-Revised (WAIS-R) and the Wechsler Intelligence Scale for Children-III (WISC-III) instead of the Stanford-Binet because the WAIS-R and WISC-III are both used more frequently and also tend to be more helpful in evaluating personality and providing useful clinical information. The Millon Clinical Multiaxial Inventory and the California Personality Inventory (CPI) were selected because of their excellent technical development (Anastasi, 1988, 1996; Baucom, 1985; Millon, 1992; Wetzler, 1990), numerous research studies based on them, and the finding that, except for the MMPI, they are the most frequently used objective personality inventories used in clinical practice (Piotrowski & Keller, 1984; Piotrowski & Zalewski, 1993; Watkins et al., 1995). The preceding instruments represent the core assessment devices used by most practitioners.

Finally, the clinician must generate relevant treatment recommendations and integrate the assessment results into a psychological report. Chapter 13 provides a systematic approach for working with assessment results to develop practical, empirically supported treatment recommendations. Chapter 14 presents guidelines for report writing, a report format, and four sample reports representative of the four common types (psychiatric, legal, academic, personality) from the most frequently encountered referral sources (medical setting, legal context, educational context, psychological clinic). Thus the chapters follow a logical sequence and provide useful, concise, and practical knowledge.

ROLE OF THE CLINICIAN

The central role of clinicians conducting assessments should be to answer specific questions and aid in making relevant decisions. To fulfill this role, clinicians must integrate a wide range of data and bring into focus diverse areas of knowledge. Thus, they are not merely administering and scoring tests. A useful distinction to highlight this point is the contrast between a psychometrist and a clinician conducting psychological assessment (Maloney & Ward, 1976; Matarazzo, 1990). Psychometrists tend to use tests merely to obtain data, and their task is often perceived as emphasizing the clerical and technical aspects of testing. Their approach is primarily data oriented, and the end product is often a series of traits or ability descriptions. These descriptions are typically unrelated to the person's overall context and do not address unique problems the person may be facing. In contrast, psychological assessment attempts to evaluate an individual in a problem situation so that the information derived from the assessment can somehow help with the problem. Tests are only one method of gathering data, and the test scores are not end products, but merely means of generating hypotheses. Psychological assessment, then, places data in a wide perspective, with its main focus being problem solving and decision making.

The distinction between psychometric testing and psychological assessment can be better understood and the ideal role of the clinician more clearly defined by briefly elaborating on the historical and methodological reasons for the development of the psychometric approach. When psychological tests were originally developed, group measurements of intelligence met with early and noteworthy success, especially in military and industrial settings where individual interviewing and case histories were too expensive and time consuming. An advantage of the data-oriented intelligence tests was that they appeared to be objective, which would reduce possible interviewer bias. More important, they were quite successful in producing a relatively high number of true positives when used for classification purposes. Their predictions were generally accurate and usable. However, this created the early expectation that all assessments could be performed using the same method and would provide a similar level of accuracy and usefulness. Later assessment strategies often tried to imitate the methods of earlier intelligence tests for such variables as personality and psychiatric diagnosis.

A further development consistent with the psychometric approach was the strategy of using a "test battery." It was reasoned that, if a single test could produce accurate descriptions of an ability or trait, then administering a series of tests could create a total picture of the person. The goal, then, was to develop a global, yet definitive, description for the person using purely objective methods. This goal encouraged the idea that the tool (psychological test) was the best process for achieving the goal, rather than being merely one technique in the overall assessment procedure. Behind this approach were the concepts of *individual differences* and *trait psychology*. These assume that one of the best ways to describe the differences among individuals is to measure their strengths and weaknesses with respect to various traits. Thus, the clearest approach to the study of personality involved developing a relevant taxonomy of traits and then creating tests to measure these traits. Again, there was an emphasis on the tools as primary, with a deemphasis on the input of the clinician. These trends created a bias toward administration and clerical skills. Within this context, the psychometrist requires little, if any, clinical expertise other than administering, scoring, and interpreting tests. According to such a view, the most preferred tests would be machine scored—true-false or multiple choice—constructed so that the normed scores rather than the psychometrist provide the interpretation.

The objective psychometric approach is most appropriately applicable to ability tests such as those measuring intelligence or mechanical skills. Its usefulness decreases, however, when users attempt to assess personality traits such as dependence, authoritarianism, or anxiety. Personality variables are far more complex and therefore need to be validated within the context of history, behavioral observations, and interpersonal relationships. For example, a T score of 70 on the MMPI-2 scale 9 (Mania) takes on an entirely different meaning for a high-functioning physician than for an individual with a poor history of work and interpersonal relationships. When the purely objective psychometric approach is used for the evaluation of problems in living (neurosis, psychosis, etc.), its usefulness is questionable.

Psychological assessment is most useful in the understanding and evaluation of personality and especially of problems in living. These issues involve a particular problem situation having to do with a specific individual. The central role of the clinician performing psychological assessment is that of an expert in human behavior who must deal with complex processes and understand test scores within the context of a person's life. The clinician must have knowledge concerning problem areas and, on the basis of this knowledge, form a general idea regarding behaviors to observe and areas in which to collect relevant data. This involves an awareness and appreciation of multiple causation, interactional influences, and multiple relationships. As Woody (1980) has stated, "Clinical assessment is individually oriented, but it always considers social existence; the objective is usually to help the person solve problems."

In addition to an awareness of the role suggested by psychological assessment, clinicians should be familiar with test construction and basic statistics, and should possess other specific areas of knowledge (e.g., personality theory, abnormal psychology, the psychology of adjustment). Furthermore, clinicians should know the main interpretive hypotheses in psychological testing and be able to identify, sift through, and evaluate a series of hypotheses to determine which are most relevant and accurate. For each assessment device, clinicians must understand conceptually what they are trying to test. Thus, rather than merely knowing the labels and definitions for various types of anxiety or thought disorders, clinicians should also have in-depth operational criteria for them. For example, the concept of intelligence, as represented by the IQ score, can sometimes appear misleadingly straightforward. Intelligence test scores can be complex, however, involving a variety of cognitive abilities, the influence of cultural factors, varying performance under different conditions, and issues related to the nature of intelligence. Unless clinicians are familiar with these areas, they are not adequately prepared to handle IQ data. A problem in many training programs is that, although students frequently have a knowledge of abnormal psychology, personality theory, and test construction, they usually have insufficient training to integrate their knowledge into the interpretation of test results. Their training focuses on developing competency in administration and scoring, rather than on knowledge relating to what they are testing.

The approach in this book is consistent with that of psychological assessment: Clinicians not only should be knowledgeable about traditional content areas in psychology and the nature of what is being tested, but also should be able to integrate the test data into a relevant description of the person. This description, although focusing on the individual, should take into account the complexity of his or her social environment, personal history, and behavioral observations. Yet, the end goal is not merely to describe the person, but rather to develop relevant answers to specific questions, aid in problem solving, and facilitate decision making.

PATTERNS OF TEST USAGE IN CLINICAL ASSESSMENT

Psychological assessment is crucial to the definition, training, and practice of professional psychology. Fully 91% of all practicing psychologists engage in assessment (Watkins et al., 1995), and a recent survey indicated that 64% of all nonacademic advertisements listed assessment as an important prerequisite (Kinder, 1994). Assessment skills are also strong prerequisites for internships and postdoctoral training. The theory and instruments of assessment can be considered the very foundation of clinical investigation, applied research, and program evaluation. In many ways, psychological assessment is professional psychology's unique contribution to the wider arena of clinical practice. The early professional psychologists even defined themselves largely within the context of their role as psychological testers. Practicing psychologists currently spend 10% to 25% of their time conducting psychological assessment (Watkins, 1991; Watkins et al., 1995).

Even though assessment has always been a core, defining feature of professional psychology the patterns of use and relative importance of assessment have changed with time. During the 1940s and 1950s, psychological testing was frequently the single most important activity of professional psychologists. In contrast, the past 50 years have seen psychologists become involved in a far wider diversity of activities. Lubin and his colleagues (Lubin, Larsen, & Matarazzo, 1984; Lubin, Larsen, Matarazzo, & Seever, 1985, 1986) found that the average time spent performing assessment across five treatment settings was 44% in 1959, 28% in 1969, and only 22% in 1982. The average time spent in 1982 performing assessments in the five different settings ranged from 14% in counseling centers to 31% in psychiatric hospitals (Lubin et al., 1984, 1985, 1986). A recent survey indicated that clinical psychologists spend 12% of their time in personality assessment and 8% performing intellectual assessment (Watkins et al., 1995). The gradual decrease in the total time spent in assessment is due in part to the widening role of psychologists. Whereas in the 1940s and 1950s a practicing psychologist was almost synonymous with a tester, professional psychologists currently are increasingly involved in administration, consultation, organizational development, and many areas of direct treatment (Bamgbose, Smith, Jesse, & Groth-Marnat, 1980; Groth-Marnat, 1988). Decline in testing has also been attributed to disillusionment with the testing process based on criticisms about the reliability and validity of most assessment devices (Ziskin & Faust, 1995). In addition, psychological assessment has come to include a wide variety of activities beyond merely the administration and interpretation of traditional tests. These include conducting structured and unstructured interviews, behavioral observations in natural settings, observations of interpersonal interactions, neuropsychological assessment, and behavioral assessment.

The relative popularity of different traditional psychological tests has been surveyed since 1935 in many settings such as academic institutions, psychiatric hospitals, counseling centers, veterans administration centers, institutions for the developmentally disabled, private practice, and various APA memberships and professional organizations. Surveys of test usage have found that the 10 most frequently used tests are the Wechsler intelligence scales, Minnesota Multiphasic Personality Inventory, Bender Visual Motor Gestalt Test, Rorschach, Sentence Completion Test (all kinds), Thematic Apperception Test, Projective drawings (Draw-A-Person, House-Tree-Person), Millon Clinical Multiaxial Inventories, California Psychological Inventory, and the Beck Depression Inventory (Lubin et al., 1985; Piotrowski & Zalewski, 1993; Watkins, 1991; Watkins et al., 1995). The pattern for the first seven tests has remained quite stable since 1969. The pattern of test usage varies somewhat across different studies and will obviously vary considerably from setting to setting. Schools and centers for the intellectually disabled will emphasize tests of intellectual abilities such as the WISC-R/WISC-III; counseling centers might be more likely to use vocational interest inventories; and psychiatric settings would emphasize tests assessing level of pathology such as the MMPI/MMPI-2.

One clear change in testing practices has been a relative decrease in the status of projective techniques. Criticisms have been wide ranging but have centered on overly complex scoring systems, subjectivity of scoring, poor predictive utility, and inadequate or even nonexistent validity (Pruitt, Smith, Thelen, Lubin, 1985; Ziskin & Faust, 1995). Further criticisms include the extensive time required to effectively learn the techniques, greater cost-effectiveness, greater empirical validity of many objective tests (MMPI, CPI, etc.), and the heavy reliance of projective techniques on psychoanalytic theory. These criticisms have usually occurred from within the academic community where they are used less and less for research purposes (Piotrowski & Zalewski, 1993; Watkins, 1991). Despite these criticisms, the standard projective tests have not decreased within the context of actual practice; the Rorschach, TAT, House-Tree-Person, and Draw-A-Person are still among the 10 most frequently used clinical assessment techniques (Piotrowski & Keller, 1989b; Piotrowski & Zalewski, 1993; Watkins et al., 1995). Tests such as the Rorschach continue to be used even though other potentially better instruments have been developed such as the Holtzman Inkblot Technique (Holtzman, 1988). The continued strong use of projectives within clinical settings might be attributed to lack of time available for practitioners to learn new techniques, expectations that students in internships know how to use them (Durand, Blanchard, & Mindell, 1988; Piotrowski & Zalewski, 1993), unavailability of other practical alternatives, and the fact that clinical experience is usually given more weight by practitioners than empirical evidence (Beutler, Williams, Wakefield, & Entwistle, 1995). This suggests distance between the quantitative, theoretical world of the academic and the practical, problem-oriented world of the practitioner. In fact, assessment practices in professional settings seem to have little relationship to the number of research studies done on assessment tools, attitudes by academic faculty (Piotrowski, 1984; Piotrowski & Zalewski, 1993), or the psychometric quality of the test (Reynolds, 1979). Interestingly, even one-third of all behavior therapists, who have traditionally kept closer links to empirical research, reported using standard projective devices such as the TAT, Rorschach, and Human Figure Drawings (Piotrowski & Keller, 1984).

The earliest form of assessment was through clinical interview. Clinicians such as Freud, Jung, and Adler used unstructured interaction to obtain information regarding history, diagnosis, or underlying structure of personality. Later clinicians taught interviewing by providing outlines of the areas that should be discussed. During the 1960s and 1970s, much criticism was directed toward the interview leading many psychologists to perceive interviews as unreliable and lacking empirical validation. Tests, in many ways, were designed to counter the subjectivity and bias of interview techniques. More recently, a wide variety of structured interview techniques have been gaining popularity and have often been found to be reliable and valid indicators of a client's level of functioning. Structured interviews such as the Diagnostic Interview Schedule (DIS; Robins, Helzer, Cottler, & Goldring, 1989), Structured Clinical Interview for the DSM-III-R (SCID; Spitzer, Williams, & Gibbon, 1987), and Renard Diagnostic Interview (Helzer, Robins, Croughan, & Welner, 1981) are often given preference over psychological tests. These interviews, however, are very different from the traditional unstructured approaches. They have the advantage of being psychometrically sound even though they might lack important elements of rapport, idiographic richness, and flexibility that characterize less structured interactions.

A further trend has been the development of neuropsychological assessment. The discipline is a synthesis between behavioral neurology and psychometrics and was created from a need to answer such questions as the nature of a person's organic deficits, severity of deficits, localization, and differentiating between functional versus organic impairment. The pathognomonic sign approach and the psychometric approaches are two clear traditions that have developed within the discipline. Clinicians relying primarily on a pathognomonic sign approach are more likely to interpret specific behaviors such as perseverations or weaknesses on one side of the body, which are highly indicative of the presence and nature of organic impairments. These clinicians tend to rely on the tradition of assessment associated with Luria (Bauer, 1995; Luria, 1973) and base their interview design and tests on a flexible method of testing possible hypotheses for different types of impairment. In contrast, the more quantitative tradition represented by Reitan and his colleagues (Reitan & Wolfson, 1993; Russell, 1995) is more likely to rely on critical cutoff scores, which distinguish between normal and brain-damaged persons. Reitan and Wolfson (1985, 1993) have recommended using an "impairment index," which is the proportion of brain-sensitive tests that fall into the brain-damaged range. In actual practice, most clinical neuropsychologists are more likely to combine the psychometric and pathognomonic sign approaches. The two major neuropsychological test batteries currently used in the United States are the Luria-Nebraska Neuropsychological Battery (Golden, Purisch, & Hammeke, 1985) and the Halstead Reitan Neuropsychological Test Battery (Reitan & Wolfson, 1993). A typical neuropsychological battery might include tests specifically designed to assess organic impairment along with tests such as the MMPI, Wechsler intelligence scales, and the Wide Range Achievement Test (WRAT-III). As a result, extensive research over the past 10 to 15 years has been directed toward developing a greater understanding of how the older and more traditional tests relate to different types and levels of cerebral dysfunction.

During the 1960s and 1970s, behavior therapy was increasingly used and accepted. Initially, behavior therapists were concerned with an idiographic approach to the functional analysis of behavior. As their techniques became more sophisticated, formalized methods of behavioral assessment began to arise. These techniques arose in part from dissatisfaction with the *Diagnostic and Statistical Manual of Mental Disorders* (*DSM-II*) methods of diagnosis as well as from a need to have assessment relate more directly to treatment and its outcomes. There was also a desire to be more accountable for documenting behavior change over time. For example, if behaviors related to anxiety decreased after therapy, then the therapist should be able to demonstrate that the treatment had been successful. Behavioral assessment could involve measurements of movements (behavioral checklists, behavioral analysis), physiological responses (GSR, EMG) or self-reports (self-monitoring, Beck Depression Inventory, assertiveness scales). Whereas the early behavioral assessment techniques showed little concern with the psychometric properties of their instruments, there has been an increasing push to have them meet adequate levels of reliability and validity (First, Francis, Widiger, Pincus, & Davis, 1992; Follette & Hayes, 1992). Despite the many formalized techniques of behavioral assessment, many behavior therapists feel that an unstructured idiographic approach is most appropriate. Furthermore, many behavior therapists still feel it is important for practitioners to be competent with standard objective and projective instruments (Piotrowski & Keller, 1984; Piotrowski & Zalewski, 1993).

Traditional means of assessment, then, have decreased due to an overall increase in other activities of psychologists and an expansion in the definition of assessment. Currently, a psychologist doing assessment might include such techniques as interviewing, administering and interpreting of traditional psychological tests (MMPI, WAIS-R, etc.), naturalistic observations, neuropsychological assessment, and behavioral assessment. In addition, professional psychologists might be required to assess areas that were not given much emphasis before the 1980s: personality disorders (borderline personality, narcissism), stress and coping (life changes, burnout, existing coping resources), hypnotic responsiveness, psychological health, adaptation to new cultures, and the changes associated with increasing modernization (Dana, 1984). Additional areas might include family systems interactions, relation between a person and his or her environment (social climate, social supports), cognitive processes related to behavior disorders, and level of personal control (self-efficacy). All these require clinicians to be continually aware of new and more specific assessment devices and to maintain flexibility in the approaches they take.

The future of psychological assessment will probably be most influenced by the trends toward computerized assessment and adaptation to managed healthcare. Computerized assessment is likely to enhance efficiency through rapid scoring, complex decision rules, reduction in client-practitioner contact, and generation of interpretive hypothesis. Future assessments are also likely to tailor the presentation of items based on the client's previous responses. Unnecessary items will not be given with one result being that a larger amount of information will be obtained through the presentation of relatively fewer items. This time efficiency is in part stimulated by the cost savings policies of managed care, which will require psychologists to demonstrate the cost-effectiveness of their services (Butcher, in press; Groth-Marnat, 1995; Groth-Marnat & Edkins, 1996). Within assessment, this will mean linking assessment with treatment planning. Thus, psychological reports of the future are likely to spend relatively less time on client dynamics and more time on details related to specific intervention strategies. Whereas considerable evidence supports the cost-effectiveness of using psychological tests in organizational contexts, healthcare will similarly need to demonstrate that assessment can increase the speed of treatment as well as optimize treatment outcome (see Butcher, in press).

Evaluating Psychological Tests

Prior to using a psychological test, clinicians should investigate and understand the theoretical orientation of the test, practical considerations, the appropriateness of the standardization sample, and the adequacy of its reliability and validity. Often, helpful descriptions and reviews that relate to these issues can be found in the *Mental Measurements Yearbook* (Conoley & Kramer, 1989; Kramer & Conoley, 1992), *Tests in Print* (1994), *Test Critiques* (Keyser & Sweetland, 1985), *Tests: A Comprehensive Reference for Assessment in Psychology, Education, and Business* (Sweetland & Keyser, 1983, 1991), and *Measures for Clinical Practice: A Sourcebook* (Corcoran & Fischer, 1994). Reviews can often be found in assessment-related journals such as the *Journal of Personality Assessment, Journal of Psychoeducational Assessment,* and *Educational and Psychological Measurement.* Test users will also need to carefully review the manual

Table 1–1.   Evaluating a psychological test

Theoretical Orientation

1. Do you adequately understand the theoretical construct the test is supposed to be measuring?

2. Do the test items correspond to the theoretical description of the construct?

Practical Considerations

1. If reading is required by the examinee, does his or her ability match the level required by the test?

2. How appropriate is the length of the test?

Standardization

1. Is the population to be tested similar to the population the test was standardized on?

2. Was the size of the standardization sample adequate?

3. Have specialized subgroup norms been developed?

4. How adequately do the instructions permit standardized administration?

Reliability

1. Are reliability estimates sufficiently high (generally around .90 for clinical decision making and around .70 for research purposes)?

2. What implications do the relative stability of the trait, the method of estimating reliability, and the test format have on reliability?

Validity

1. What criteria and procedures were used to validate the test?

2. Will the test produce accurate measurements within the context and purpose for which you would like to use it?

---

accompanying the test. Table 1–1 outlines the more important questions that should be answered. The issues outlined in this table will be discussed further. The discussion reflects the practical orientation of this text by focusing on problems that clinicians using psychological tests are likely to confront. It is not intended to provide a comprehensive coverage of test theory and construction; if a more detailed treatment is required, the reader is referred to one of the many texts on psychological testing (e.g., Anastasi, 1996; Kaplan & Sacuzzo, 1993).

Theoretical Orientation

Before clinicians can effectively evaluate whether a test is appropriate, they must understand its theoretical orientation. Clinicians should research the construct that the test is supposed to measure and then examine how the test approaches this construct (see Haynes, Richard, & Kubany, 1995). This information can usually be found in the test manual. If for any reason the information in the manual is insufficient, clinicians should seek it elsewhere. Clinicians can frequently obtain useful information regarding the construct being measured by carefully studying the individual test items. Usually the manual provides an individual analysis of the items, which can help the potential test user evaluate whether or not they are relevant to the trait being measured.

Practical Considerations

A number of practical issues relate more to the context and manner in which the test will be used than to its construction. First, tests vary in terms of the level of education (especially reading skills) that examinees must have to understand them adequately. The examinee must be able to read, comprehend, and respond appropriately to the test. Second, some tests are too long, which can lead to a loss of rapport with, or extensive frustration on the part of, the examinee. Administering short forms of the test may reduce these problems, provided these forms have been properly developed and are treated with appropriate caution. Finally, clinicians have to assess the extent to which they will need training to administer and interpret the instrument. If further training is necessary, then a plan must be developed for acquiring this training.

Standardization

Another central issue relates to the adequacy of norms (see Cicchetti, 1994). Each test has norms that reflect the distribution of scores by a standardization sample. The basis on which individual test scores have meaning relates directly to the similarity between the individual being tested and the sample. If a similarity exists between the group or individual being tested and the standardization sample, then adequate comparisons can be made. For example, if the test was standardized on college students between the ages of 18 to 22, then useful comparisons can be made for college students in that age bracket (if one assumes that the test is otherwise sufficiently reliable and valid). The more dissimilar the person is from this standardization group (e.g., over 70 years of age with low educational achievement), the less useful the test is for evaluation. The examiner may need to consult the literature to determine whether research that followed the publication of the test manual has developed norms for different groups. This is particularly important for tests such as the MMPI and the Rorschach where norms for younger populations have been published.

Three major questions that relate to the adequacy of norms must be answered. The first is whether or not the standardization group is representative of the population on which the examiner would like to use the test. The test manual should include sufficient information to determine the representativeness of the standardization sample. If this information is insufficient or in any way incomplete, it greatly reduces the degree of confidence with which clinicians can use the test. The ideal and current practice is to use stratified random sampling. However, because this can be an extremely costly and time-consuming procedure, many tests are quite deficient in this respect. The second question is whether the standardization group is large enough. If the group is too small, the results may not give stable estimates because of too much random fluctuation. Finally, a good test will have specialized subgroup norms as well as broad national norms. Knowledge relating to subgroup norms will give examiners greater flexibility and confidence if they are using the test with similar subgroup populations (see Kehoe & Tenopyr, 1994). This is particularly important when subgroups produce significantly different sets of scores from the normal standardization group. These subgroups can be based on such factors as sex, geographic location, age, level of education, socioeconomic status, or urban versus rural environment. Knowledge of each of these subgroup norms allows for a more appropriate and meaningful interpretation of scores.

Standardization can also refer to administration procedures. A well-constructed test should have instructions that permit the examiner to give the test in a structured manner similar to that of other examiners and also to maintain this standardized administration between one testing session and the next. Research has demonstrated that varying the instructions between one administration and the next can alter the types and quality of responses the examinee makes, thereby compromising the test's reliability. Standardization of administration should refer not only to the instructions, but also to ensuring adequate lighting, quiet, no interruptions, and good rapport.

Reliability

The reliability of a test refers to its degree of stability, consistency, predictability, and accuracy. It addresses the extent to which scores obtained by a person will be the same if the person is reexamined by the same test on different occasions. Underlying the concept of reliability is the possible range of error, or error of measurement, of a single score. This is an estimate of the range of possible random fluctuation that can be expected in an individual's score. It should be stressed however, that a certain degree of error or noise will always be present in the system, from such factors as a misreading of the items, poor administration procedures, or the changing mood of the client. If there is a large degree of random fluctuation, the examiner cannot place a great deal of confidence in an individual's scores. The goal of a test constructor is to reduce, as much as possible, the degree of measurement error, or random fluctuation. If this is achieved, the difference between one score and another for a measured characteristic is more likely to be due to some true difference than to some chance fluctuation.

Two main issues relate to the degree of error in a test. The first is the inevitable, natural variation in human performance. Usually the variability is less for measurements of ability than for those of personality. Whereas ability variables (intelligence, mechanical aptitude, etc.) show gradual changes resulting from growth and development, many personality traits are much more highly dependent on factors such as mood. This is particularly true in the case of a characteristic like anxiety. The practical significance of this in evaluating a test is that certain factors outside the test itself can serve to reduce the reliability that the test can realistically be expected to achieve. Thus, an examiner should generally expect higher reliabilities for an intelligence test than for a test measuring a personality variable like anxiety. It is the examiner's responsibility to know what is being measured, especially the degree of variability to be expected in the measured trait.

The second important issue relating to reliability is that psychological testing methods are necessarily imprecise. For the hard sciences, researchers can make direct measurements such as the concentration of a chemical solution, the relative weight of one organism compared with another, or the strength of radiation. In contrast, many constructs in psychology are often measured indirectly. For example, intelligence cannot be perceived directly; it must be inferred by measuring behavior that has been defined as being intelligent. Variability relating to these inferences is likely to produce a certain degree of error due to the lack of precision in defining and observing inner psychological constructs. Variability in measurement will also occur simply because people have true (not due to test error) fluctuations in performance between one testing session and the next. Whereas it is impossible to control for the natural variability in human performance, adequate test construction can attempt to reduce the imprecision that is a function of the test itself. Natural human variability and test imprecision make the task of measurement extremely difficult. Although some error in testing is inevitable, the goal of test construction is to keep testing errors within reasonably accepted limits. A high correlation is generally .80 or more, but the variable being measured will also change the expected strength of the correlation. Likewise, the method of determining reliability will alter the relative strength of the correlation. Ideally, clinicians should hope for correlations of .90 or higher in tests that will be used to make decisions about individuals, whereas a correlation of .70 or more is generally adequate for research purposes.

The purpose of reliability is to estimate the degree of test variance caused by error. The four primary methods of obtaining reliability involve determining (a) the extent to which the test produces consistent results on retesting (test-retest), (b) the relative accuracy of a test at a given time (alternate forms), (c) the internal consistency of the items (split half), and (d) the degree of agreement between two examiners (interscorer). Another way to summarize this is that reliability can be time to time (test-retest), form to form (alternate forms), item to item (split half), or scorer to scorer (interscorer). Although these are the main types of reliability, there is a fifth type, the Kuder-Richardson; like the split half, it is a measurement of the internal consistency of the test items. However, because this method is considered appropriate only for tests that are relatively pure measures of a single variable, it is not covered in this book.

Test-Retest Reliability   Test-retest reliability is determined by administering the test and then repeating it on a second occasion. The reliability coefficient is calculated by correlating the scores obtained by the same person on the two different administrations. The degree of correlation between the two scores indicates the extent to which the test scores can be generalized from one situation to the next. If the correlations are high, then the results are less likely to be due to random fluctuations in the condition of the examinee or the testing environment. Thus, when the test is being used in actual practice, the examiner can be relatively confident that differences in scores are the result of an actual change in the trait being measured rather than random fluctuation.

A number of factors must be considered in assessing the appropriateness of test-retest reliability. One is that the interval between administrations can affect reliability. Thus, a test manual should specify the interval as well as any significant life changes that the examinees may have experienced such as counseling, career changes, or psychotherapy. For example, tests of preschool intelligence often give reasonably high correlations if the second administration is within several months of the first one. However, correlations with later childhood or adult IQ results are generally low due to innumerable intervening life experiences. One of the major difficulties with test-retest reliability is the effect that practice and memory may have on performance, which can produce improvement between one administration and the next. This is a particular problem for speeded and memory tests such as those found on the Digit Symbol and Arithmetic subtests of the WAIS-R. Additional sources of variation may be the result of random, short-term fluctuations in the examinee, or of variations in the testing conditions. In general, test-retest reliability is the preferred method only if the variable being measured is relatively stable. If the variable is highly changeable (e.g., anxiety), then this method is usually not adequate.

Alternate Forms   The alternate forms method avoids many of the problems encountered with test-retest reliability. The logic behind alternate forms is that, if the trait is measured several times on the same individual by using parallel forms of the test, then the different measurements should produce similar results. The degree of similarity between the scores represents the reliability coefficient of the test. As in the test-retest method, the interval between administrations should always be included in the manual as well as a description of any significant intervening life experiences. If the second administration is given immediately after the first, then the resulting reliability is more a measure of the correlation between forms and not across occasions. Correlations determined by tests given with a wide interval, such as two months or more, provide a measure of both the relation between forms and the degree of temporal stability.

The alternate forms method eliminates many carryover effects, such as the recall of previous responses the examinee has made to specific items. However, there is still likely to be some carryover effect in that the examinee can learn to adapt to the overall style of the test even when the specific item content between one test and another is unfamiliar. This is most likely when the test involves some sort of problem-solving strategy in which the same principle in solving one problem can be used to solve the next one. An examinee, for example, may learn to use mnemonic aids to increase his or her performance on an alternate form of the WAIS-R Digit Symbol.

Perhaps the primary difficulty with alternate forms lies in determining whether the two forms are actually equivalent. For example, if one test is more difficult than its alternate form, then the difference in scores may represent actual differences in the two tests rather than differences due to the unreliability of the measure. Since the test constructor is attempting to measure the reliability of the test itself and not the differences between the tests, this could confound and lower the reliability coefficient. Alternate forms should be independently constructed tests that use the same specifications including the same number of items, type of content, format, and manner of administration.

A final difficulty is encountered primarily when there is a delay between one administration and the next. With such a delay, the examinee may perform differently due to short-term fluctuations such as mood, stress level, or the relative quality of the previous night's sleep. Thus, an examinee's abilities may vary somewhat from one examination to another, thereby affecting test results. Despite these problems, alternate forms reliability has the advantage of at least reducing, if not eliminating, many carryover effects of the test-retest method. A further advantage is that the alternate test forms can be useful for other purposes, such as assessing the effects of a treatment program or monitoring a patient's changes over time by administering the different forms on separate occasions.

Split Half Reliability   The split half method is the best technique for determining reliability for a trait with a high degree of fluctuation. Because the test is given only once, then the items are split in half, and the two halves are correlated. Since there is only one administration, it is not possible for the effects of time to intervene as they might with the test-retest method. Thus, the split half method gives a measure of the internal consistency of the test items rather than the temporal stability of different administrations of the same test. To determine split half reliability, the test is often split on the basis of odd and even items. This method is usually adequate for most tests. Dividing the test into a first half and second half can be effective in some cases, but is often inappropriate due to the cumulative effects of warming up, fatigue, and boredom, all of which can result in different levels of performance on the first half of the test compared with the second.

As is true with the other methods of obtaining reliability, the split half method has limitations. When a test is split in half, there are fewer items on each half, which results in wider variability because the individual responses cannot stabilize as easily around a mean. As a general principle, the longer a test is, the more reliable it will be because the larger the number of items, the easier it is for the majority of items to compensate for minor alterations in responding to a few of the other items. As with the alternate forms method, differences in content may exist between one half and another.

Interscorer Reliability   In some tests, scoring is based partially on the judgment of the examiner. Since judgment may vary between one scorer and the next, it may be important to assess the extent to which reliability might be affected. This is especially true for projectives and even for some ability tests where hard scorers may produce somewhat different results than easy scorers. This variance in interscorer reliability may apply for global judgments based on such test scores as brain damaged versus normal, or for small details of scoring such as whether a person has given a shading versus a texture response on the Rorschach. The basic strategy for determining interscorer reliability is to obtain a series of responses from a single client and to have these responses scored by two different individuals. A variation is to have two different examiners test the same client using the same test and then to determine how close their scores or ratings of the person are. The two sets of scores can then be correlated to determine a reliability coefficient. Any test that requires even partial subjectivity in scoring should provide information on interscorer reliability.

The best form of reliability is dependent on both the nature of the variable being measured and the purposes for which the test will be used. If the trait or ability being measured is highly stable, the test-retest method is preferable, whereas split half is more appropriate for characteristics that are highly subject to fluctuations. When using a test to make predictions, the test-retest method is preferable since it gives an estimate of the dependability of the test from one administration to the next. This is particularly true if, when determining reliability, an increased time interval existed between the two administrations. If, on the other hand, the examiner is concerned with the internal consistency and accuracy of a test for a single, one-time measure, then either the split half or the alternate forms would be best.

Another consideration in evaluating the acceptable range of reliability is the format of the test. Longer tests will usually have higher reliabilities than shorter ones. Also, the format of the responses will affect reliability. For example, a true-false format is likely to have a lower reliability than multiple choice because each true-false item has a 50% possibility of the answer being correct due to chance. In contrast, each question in a multiple choice format having five possible choices has only a 20%

possibility of being correct due to chance. A final consideration is that tests with various subtests or subscales should report the reliability for the overall test as well as for each of the subtests. In general, the overall test score will have a significantly higher reliability than its subtests. In estimating the confidence with which test scores can be interpreted, the examiner should take into account the lower reliabilities of the subtests. For example, a Full Scale IQ score on the WAIS-R can be interpreted with more confidence than the specific subscale scores.

Most test manuals include a statistical index of the amount of error that can be expected for test scores, which is referred to as the standard error of measurement (SEM). The logic behind the standard error of measurement is that test scores consist of both truth and error. Thus, there will always be noise or error in the system, and the standard error of measurement provides a range to indicate how extensive that error is likely to be. The range depends on the test's reliability so that the higher the reliability, the narrower the range of error. The standard error of measurement is a standard deviation score so that, for example, a SEM of 5 on an intelligence test would indicate that an individual's score has a 68% chance of being ± 5 IQ points from the estimated true score. This is because the SEM of 5 represents a band extending from -1 to $+1$ standard deviations above and below the mean. Likewise there would be a 95% chance that the individual's score would fall within a range of ± 10 points from the estimated true score. From a theoretical perspective, the standard error of measurement is a statistical index of how a person's repeated scores on a specific test would fall around a normal distribution. Thus, it is a statement of the relationship among a person's obtained score, his or her theoretically true score, and the test reliability. Since it is an empirical statement of the probable range of scores, the standard error of measurement has more practical usefulness than a knowledge of the test reliability. This band of error is also referred to as a confidence interval.

The acceptable range of reliability is difficult to identify and depends partially on the variable being measured. In general, unstable aspects (states) of the person produce lower reliabilities than stable ones (traits). Thus, in evaluating a test, the examiner should expect higher reliabilities on stable traits or abilities than on changeable states. For example, a person's general fund of vocabulary words is highly stable and will therefore produce high reliabilities. In contrast, a person's level of anxiety is often highly changeable. This means examiners should not expect nearly as high reliabilities for anxiety as for an ability measure such as vocabulary. A further consideration, also related to the stability of the trait or ability, is the method of reliability that is used. Alternate forms are considered to give the lowest estimate of the actual reliability of a test, while split half provide the highest estimate. Another important way to estimate the adequacy of reliability is by comparing the reliability derived on other similar tests. The examiner can then develop a sense of the expected levels of reliability, which will provide a baseline for comparisons. In the example of anxiety, a clinician may not know what is an acceptable level of reliability. A general estimate can be made by comparing the reliability of the test under consideration with other tests measuring the same or a similar variable. The most important thing to keep in mind is that lower levels of reliability usually suggest that less confidence can be placed in the interpretations and predictions based on the test data. However, clinical practitioners are less likely to be concerned with low statistical reliability if they have some basis for believing the test is a valid measure of the client's state at the time of testing. The main consideration is that the sign or test score does not mean one thing at one time and something different at another.

Validity

The most crucial issue in test construction is validity. Whereas reliability addresses issues of accuracy and consistency, validity assesses what the test is to be accurate about. A test that is valid for clinical assessment should measure what it is intended to measure and should also produce information useful to clinicians. A psychological test cannot be said to be valid in any abstract or absolute sense, but more practically it must be valid within a particular context and for a specific group of people (Messick, 1995). Although a test can be reliable without being valid, the opposite is not true; a necessary prerequisite for validity is that the test must have achieved an adequate level of reliability. Thus, a valid test is one that accurately measures the variable it is intended to measure. For example, a test comprising questions about a person's musical preference might erroneously state that it is a test of creativity. The test might be reliable in the sense that if it is given to the same person on different occasions, it will produce similar results each time. However, it would not be reliable in that an investigation might indicate it does not correlate with other more valid measurements of creativity.

Establishing the validity of a test can be extremely difficult, primarily because psychological variables are usually abstract concepts such as intelligence, anxiety, and personality. These concepts have no tangible reality, so their existence must be inferred through indirect means. In addition, conceptualization and research on constructs undergo change over time requiring that test validation go through continual refinement (Smith & McCarthy, 1995). In constructing a test, a test designer must follow two necessary, initial steps. First, the construct must be theoretically evaluated and described; second, specific operations (test questions) must be developed to measure it (Haynes et al., 1995). Even when the designer has followed these steps closely and conscientiously, it is sometimes difficult to determine what the test really measures. For example, IQ tests are good predictors of academic success, but many clinicians question whether they adequately measure the concept of intelligence as it is theoretically described. Another hypothetical test that, based on its item content, might seem to measure what is described as musical aptitude, may in reality be highly correlated with verbal abilities. Thus, it may be more a measure of verbal abilities than of musical aptitude.

Any estimate of validity is concerned with relationships between the test and some external independently observed event. The *Standards for Educational and Psychological Testing* (AERA, APA, NCME, 1985) list the three main methods of establishing validity as content-related, criterion-related, and construct-related.

Content Validity   During the initial construction phase of any test, the developers must first be concerned with its content validity. This refers to the representativeness and relevance of the assessment instrument to the construct being measured (Haynes et al., 1995). During the initial item selection, the constructors must carefully consider the skills or knowledge area of the variable they would like to measure. The items are then generated based on this conceptualization of the variable. At some point, it might be decided that the item content overrepresents, underrepresents, or excludes specific areas, and alterations in the items might be made accordingly. If experts on subject matter are used to determine the items, then the number of these experts and their qualifications should be included in the test manual. The instructions they received and the extent of agreement between judges should also be provided. A good test will cover not just the subject matter being measured, but additional variables as well. For example, factual knowledge may be one criterion, but the application of that knowledge and the ability to analyze data are also important. Thus, a test with high content validity must cover all major aspects of the content area and must do so in the correct proportion.

A concept somewhat related to content validity is face validity. These terms are not synonymous, however, since content validity pertains to judgments made by experts, whereas face validity has to do with judgments made by the test users. The central issue in face validity is test rapport. Thus, a group of potential mechanics who are being tested for basic skills in arithmetic should have word problems that relate to machines rather than to business transactions. Face validity, then, is present if the test looks good to the persons taking it, to policymakers who decide to include it in their programs, and to other untrained personnel. Despite the potential importance of face validity in regard to test-taking attitudes, disappointingly few formal studies on face validity are performed and/or reported in test manuals (Nevo, 1985; Nevo & Sfez, 1985).

In the past, content validity has been conceptualized and operationalized as being based on the subjective judgment of the test developers. As a result, it has been regarded as the least preferred form of test validation albeit necessary in the initial stages of test development. In addition, its usefulness has been primarily focused at achievement tests (how well has this student learned the content of the course?) and personnel selection (does this applicant know the information relevant to the potential job?). More recently, it has become used more extensively in personality and clinical assessment (Butcher, Graham, Williams, & Ben-Porath, 1989; Haynes et al., 1995; Millon, 1994). This has paralleled more rigorous and empirically based approaches to content validity along with a closer integration to criterion and construct validation.

Criterion Validity   A second major approach to determining validity is criterion validity, which has also been called empirical or predictive validity. Criterion validity is determined by comparing test scores with some sort of performance on an outside measure. The outside measure should have a theoretical relation to the variable that the test is supposed to measure. For example, an intelligence test might be correlated with grade point average, an aptitude test with independent job ratings, or general maladjustment scores with other tests measuring similar dimensions. The relation between the two measurements is usually expressed as a correlation coefficient.

Criterion-related validity is most frequently divided into either concurrent or predictive validity. Concurrent validity refers to measurements taken at the same, or approximately the same, time as the test. For example, an intelligence test might be administered at the same time as assessments of a group's level of academic achievement. Predictive validity is used to refer to outside measurements that were taken some time after the test scores were derived. Thus, predictive validity might be evaluated by correlating the intelligence test scores with measures of academic achievement a year after the initial testing. Concurrent validation is often used as a substitute for predictive validation because it is simpler, less expensive, and not as time consuming. However, the main consideration in deciding whether concurrent or predictive validation is preferable depends on the test's purpose. Predictive validity is most appropriate for tests used for selection and classification of personnel. This may include hiring job applicants, placing military personnel in specific occupational training programs, screening out individuals who are likely to develop emotional disorders, or identifying which category of psychiatric populations would be most likely to benefit from specific treatment approaches. These situations all require that the measurement device provide a prediction of some future outcome. In contrast, concurrent validation is preferable if an assessment of the client's current status is required, rather than a prediction of what might occur to the client at some future time. The distinction can be summarized by asking, Is Mr. Jones maladjusted? (concurrent validity) rather than, Is Mr. Jones likely to become maladjusted at some future time? (predictive validity).

An important consideration is the degree to which a specific test can be applied to a unique work-related environment (see Hogan, Hogan, & Roberts, 1996). This relates more to the social value and consequences of the assessment than the formal validity as reported in the test manual (Messick, 1995). In other words, can the test under consideration provide accurate assessments and predictions for the environment in which the examinee is working? To answer this question adequately, the examiner must refer to the manual and assess the similarity between the criteria used to establish the test's validity and the situation to which he or she would like to apply the test. For example, can an aptitude test that has adequate criterion validity in the prediction of high school grade point average also be used to predict academic achievement for a population of college students? If the examiner has questions regarding the relative applicability of the test, he or she may need to undertake a series of specific tasks. The first is to identify the required skills for adequate performance in the situation involved. For example, the criteria for a successful teacher may include such attributes as verbal fluency, flexibility, and good public speaking skills. The examiner then must determine the degree to which each skill contributes to the quality of a teacher's performance. Next, the examiner has to assess the extent to which the test under consideration measures each of these skills. The final step is to evaluate the extent to which the attribute that the test measures is relevant to the skills the examiner needs to predict. Based on these evaluations, the examiner can estimate the confidence that he or she will place in the predictions developed from the test. This approach is sometimes referred to as *synthetic validity* since examiners must integrate or synthesize the criteria reported in the test manual with the variables they will encounter in their clinical or organizational setting.

The strength of criterion validity will depend in part on the type of variable being measured. Usually, intellectual or aptitude tests give relatively higher validity coefficients than personality tests because there are generally a greater number of variables influencing personality than intelligence. As the number of variables that influence the trait being measured increases, it becomes progressively more difficult to account for them. When a large number of variables are not accounted for, the trait can be affected in unpredictable ways. This can create a much wider degree of fluctuation in the test scores, thereby lowering the validity coefficient. Thus, when evaluating a personality test, the examiner should not expect as high a validity coefficient as for intellectual or aptitude tests. A helpful guide is to look at the validities found in similar tests and compare them with the test being considered. For example, if an examiner wants to estimate the range of validity to be expected for the extraversion scale on the Myers Briggs Type Indicator, he or she might compare it with the validities for similar scales found in the California Personality Inventory and Eysenck Personality Questionnaire. The relative level of validity, then, will depend both on the quality of the construction of the test and on the variable being studied.

An important consideration is the extent to which the test accounts for the trait being measured or the behavior being predicted. For example, the typical correlation between intelligence tests and academic performance is around .50 (Neisser et al., 1996). Since no one would say that grade point average is entirely the result of intelligence, the relative extent to which intelligence determines grade point average has to be estimated. This can be calculated by squaring the correlation coefficient and changing it into a percentage. Thus, if the correlation of .50 was squared, it would come out to 25%, indicating that 25% of academic achievement can be accounted for by IQ as measured by the intelligence test. The remaining 75% may include such factors as motivation, quality of instruction, and past educational experience. The problem facing the examiner is to determine whether 25% of the variance is sufficiently useful for the intended purposes of the test. This ultimately depends on the personal judgment of the examiner.

The main problem confronting criterion validity is finding an agreed on, definable, acceptable, and feasible outside criterion. Whereas for an intelligence test the grade point average might be an acceptable criterion, it is far more difficult to identify adequate criteria for most personality tests. Even with so-called intelligence tests, many researchers argue that it is more appropriate to consider them tests of scholastic aptitude rather than of intelligence. Yet another difficulty with criterion validity is the possibility that the criterion measure will be inadvertently biased. This is referred to as criterion contamination and occurs when knowledge of the test results influences an individual's later performance. For example, a supervisor in an organization who receives such information about subordinates may act differently toward a worker placed in a certain category after being tested. This situation may set up negative or positive expectations for the worker, which could influence his or her level of performance. The result is likely to artificially alter the level of the validity coefficients. To work around these difficulties, especially in regard to personality tests, a third major method must be used to determine validity.

Construct Validity   The method of construct validity was developed in part to correct the inadequacies and difficulties encountered with content and criterion approaches. Early forms of content validity relied too much on subjective judgment, while criterion validity was too restrictive in working with the domains or structure of the constructs being measured. Criterion validity had the further difficulty in that there was often a lack of agreement in deciding on adequate outside criteria. The basic approach of construct validity is to assess the extent to which the test measures a theoretical construct or trait. This assessment involves three general steps. Initially the test constructor must make a careful analysis of the trait. This is followed by a consideration of the ways in which the trait should relate to other variables. Finally, the test designer needs to test whether or not these hypothesized relationships actually exist (Foster &

Cone, 1995). For example, a test measuring dominance should have a high correlation with the individual accepting leadership roles and a low or negative correlation with measures of submissiveness. Likewise, a test measuring anxiety should have a high positive correlation with individuals who are measured during an anxiety-provoking situation, such as an experiment involving some sort of physical pain. As these hypothesized relationships are verified by research studies, the degree of confidence that can be placed in a test increases.

There is no single, best approach for determining construct validity; rather, a variety of different possibilities exist. For example, if some abilities are expected to increase with age, then correlations can be made between a population's test scores and age. This may be appropriate for such variables as intelligence or motor coordination, but it would not be applicable for most personality measurements. Even in the measurement of intelligence or motor coordination, this approach may not be appropriate beyond the age of maturity. Another method for determining construct validity is to measure the effects of experimental or treatment interventions. Thus, a posttest measurement may be taken following a period of instruction to see if the intervention affected the test scores in relation to a previous pretest measure. For example, after an examinee completes a course in arithmetic, it would be predicted that scores on a test of arithmetical ability would increase. Often, correlations can be made with other tests that supposedly measure a similar variable. However, a new test that correlates too highly with existing tests may represent needless duplication unless it incorporates some additional advantage such as a shortened format, ease of administration, or superior predictive validity. Factor analysis is of particular relevance to construct validation because it can be used to identify and assess the relative strength of different psychological traits. Factor analysis can also be used in the design of a test to identify the primary factor or factors measured by a series of different tests. Thus, it can be used to simplify one or more tests by reducing the number of categories to a few common factors or traits. The factorial validity of a test is the relative weight or loading that a factor has on the test. For example, if spatial organization has a weight of .72 on a picture arrangement type of test, then the factorial validity is .72.

Another method used in construct validity is to estimate the degree of internal consistency by correlating specific subtests with the test's total score. For example, if a subtest on an intelligence test does not correlate adequately with the overall or Full Scale IQ, then it should be either eliminated or altered in a way that will increase the correlation. A final method for obtaining construct validity is for a test to converge or correlate highly with variables that are theoretically similar to it. The test should not only show this convergent validity but should also have discriminate validity, in which it would demonstrate low or negative correlations with variables that are dissimilar to it. Thus, scores on reading comprehension should show high positive correlations with performance in a literature class and low correlations with performance in a class involving mathematical computation.

Related to discriminant and convergent validity is the degree of sensitivity and specificity an assessment device demonstrates in identifying different categories. Sensitivity refers to the percentage of true positives that the instrument has identified, whereas specificity is the relative percentage of true negatives. A structured clinical interview might be quite sensitive in that it would accurately identify 90% of schizophrenics in an admitting ward of a hospital. However, it may not be sufficiently specific in that 30% of schizophrenics would be incorrectly classified as either normal or having some other diagnosis. The difficulty in determining sensitivity and specificity lies in developing agreed on, objectively accurate outside criteria for such categories as psychiatric diagnosis, intelligence, or personality traits.

As is indicated by the variety of approaches discussed, no single, quick, efficient method exists for determining construct validity. It is similar to testing a series of hypotheses where the results of the studies determine the meanings that can be attached to later test scores (Foster & Cone, 1995; Hogan & Nicholson, 1988; Messick, 1995). Almost any data can be used, including material from the content and criterion approaches. The greater the amount of supporting data, the greater is the level of confidence with which the test can be used. In many ways, construct validity represents the strongest and most sophisticated approach to test construction. Hogan and Nicholson (1988) argue that all types of validity should be considered as subcategories of construct validity. It involves theoretical knowledge of the trait or ability being measured, knowledge of other related variables, hypothesis testing, and statements regarding the relationship of the test variable to a network of other variables that have been investigated. Thus, construct validation is a never-ending process in which new relationships always can be verified and investigated.

VALIDITY IN CLINICAL PRACTICE

Although a test may have been found to have a high level of validity during its construction, it does not necessarily follow that the test will also be valid within a specific situation with a particular client. A test can never be valid in any absolute sense because, in practice, numerous variables might affect the test results. A serious issue, then, is the degree of validity generalization that is made. In part, this generalization will depend on the similarity between the population used during various stages of test construction and the population and situation that it is being used for in practice. Validity in clinical practice also depends on the extent to which tests can work together to improve each other's accuracy. Some tests thus show incremental validity in that they improve accuracy in increments as increasing numbers of data sources are used. Incremental validity, then, refers to the ability of tests to produce information above what is already known. Another important consideration is the ability of the clinician to generate hypotheses, test these hypotheses, and blend the data derived from hypothesis testing into a coherent, integrated picture of the person. Maloney and Ward (1976) refer to this latter approach to validity as conceptual validity since it involves creating a conceptually coherent description of the person.

Incremental Validity

For a test to be considered useful and efficient, it must be able to produce accurate results above and beyond the results that could be obtained with greater ease and less expense. If equally accurate clinical descriptions could be obtained through such basic information as biographical data and knowing the referral question, then there would be no need for psychological tests. Incremental validity also needs to be evaluated in relation to cost-effectiveness. A psychological test might indeed demonstrate incremental validity by increasing the relative proportions of accurate diagnoses, or hit rates, by 2%. However, practitioners need to question whether this small increase in accuracy is worth the extra time involved in administering and interpreting the test. Clinicians might direct their time more productively toward direct treatment.

In the 1950s, one of the theoretical defenses for tests having low reliabilities and validities was that, when used in combination, their accuracy could be improved. In other words, results from a series of different tests could provide checks and balances to correct for inaccurate interpretations. A typical strategy used to empirically test for this was to first obtain biographical data, make interpretations/decisions based on this data, and then test its accuracy based on some outside criterion. Next, a test such as the MMPI could be given; then, the interpretations and decisions based on it could likewise be assessed for accuracy. Finally, clinicians could be given both sets of data to assess any improvements in the accuracies of interpretation/decisions between either of the first two conditions and the combined information.

It would seem logical that the greater the number of tests used, the greater would be the overall validity of the assessment battery. However, research on psychological tests used in clinical practice has often demonstrated that they have poor incremental validity. An older but representative study by Kostlan (1954) on male psychiatric outpatients compared the utility of a case history, Rorschach, MMPI, and a sentence completion test. Twenty experienced clinicians interpreted different combinations of these sources of test data. Their conclusions were combined against criterion judges who used a lengthy checklist of personality descriptions. The conclusions were that, for most of the data, the clinicians were no more accurate than if they had used only age, occupation, education, marital status, and a basic description of the referral question. The exception was that the most accurate descriptions were based on a combination of social history and the MMPI. In contrast, psychological tests have sometimes clearly demonstrated their incremental validity. Schwartz and Wiedel (1981) demonstrated that neurological residents gave more accurate diagnoses when an MMPI was used in combination with history, EEG, and physical exam. This was probably due not so much to a specific MMPI neurological profile, but rather that the MMPI increased diagnostic accuracy by enabling the residents to rule out other possible diagnoses.

Often clinical psychologists will attempt to make a series of behavioral predictions based on complex psychological tests. Although these predictions may show varying levels of accuracy, a simpler and more effective means of achieving this information might be to simply ask the clients to predict their own behaviors. In some circumstances self-prediction has been found to be more accurate than psychological tests whereas in others tests have been found to be more accurate (Mabe & West, 1982; Shrauger & Osberg, 1981). Advantages of self-assessment are that it can be time-efficient, cost-effective, and facilitate a colleagial relationship between assessor and client. In contrast, difficulties are that, compared with formal testing, self-assessment may be significantly more susceptible to social desirability, attributional errors, distortions due to poor adjustment, and the relative self-awareness of the client. These factors need to be carefully considered before deciding to use self-assessment versus formal psychological tests. Although the incremental validity of using self-assessment in combination with formal testing has not been adequately researched, it would seem that this is conceptually a potentially useful strategy for future research.

Reviews of studies on incremental validity (Garb, 1984, 1994a) have provided a number of general conclusions. The addition of an MMPI to background data has consistently led to increases in validity although the increases were quite small when the MMPI was added to extensive data. The addition of projective tests to a test battery did not generally increase incremental validity. Lanyon and Goodstein (1982) have argued that case histories are generally preferable to psychological test data. Furthermore, a single test in combination with case history data is generally as effective as a large number of tests with case history data. The MMPI alone was generally found to be preferable to a battery containing the MMPI, Rorschach, and Sentence Completion (Garb, 1984, 1994a).

In defense of the poor incremental validity of many of the traditional clinical tests are weaknesses and unanswered questions relating to the preceding research. First, few studies have looked at statistically derived predictions and interpretations based on optimal multiple cutoff scores or multiple regression equations. However, more recent research, particularly on such tests as the MMPI and CPI, has emphasized this approach. For example, combined weightings on such variables as specific CPI scores, Scholastic Aptitude Test (SAT) scores, grade point average (GPA), and IQ can be combined to predict success in specific programs (see Chapter 8). Further research using this approach may yield greater incremental validity for a wide number of assessment techniques. Second, few studies on incremental validity have investigated the ways in which different tests might show greater incremental validity in specific situations for specific populations. Instead, most research has focused on the validity of global personality descriptions, perhaps without tying these descriptions to the unique circumstances or contexts persons might be involved in. Finally, since most previous studies have focused on global personality descriptions, certain tests will demonstrate greater incremental validity when predicting highly specific traits and behaviors.

Conceptual Validity

A further method for determining validity that is highly relevant to clinical practice is conceptual validity (Maloney & Ward, 1976). In contrast to the traditional methods (content validity, etc.), which are primarily concerned with evaluating the theoretical constructs within the test itself, conceptual validity focuses on individuals with their unique histories and behaviors. It is a means of evaluating and integrating test data so that the clinician's conclusions make accurate statements about the examinee. There are similarities with construct validity in that construct validity also tries to test specific hypothesized relationships between constructs. Conceptual validity is likewise concerned with testing constructs, but in this case the constructs relate to the individual rather than to the test itself.

In determining conceptual validity, the examiner generally begins with individuals for whom no constructs have been developed. The next phase is to observe, collect data, and form a large number of hypotheses. If these hypotheses are confirmed through consistent trends in the test data, behavioral observations, history, and additional data sources, then the hypotheses can be considered to represent valid constructs regarding the person. The focus is on an individual in his or her specific situation, and the data are derived from a variety of sources. The conceptual validity of the constructs is based on the logicalness and internal consistency of the data. Unlike construct validity, which begins with previously developed constructs, conceptual validity produces constructs as its end product. Its aim is for these constructs to provide valid sources of information that can be used to help solve the unique problems that an individual may be facing.

CLINICAL JUDGMENT

Any human interaction involves mutual and continually changing perceptions. Clinical judgment is a special instance of perception in which the clinician attempts to use whatever sources are available to create accurate descriptions of the client. These sources may include test data, case history, medical records, personal journals, and verbal and nonverbal observations of behavior. Relevant issues and processes involved in clinical judgment include data gathering, data synthesis, the relative accuracy of clinical versus statistical/actuarial descriptions, and judgment in determining what to include in a psychological report. This sequence also parallels the process clinicians go through when assessing a client.

Data Gathering and Synthesis

Most of the research related to the strengths and weaknesses of data gathering and synthesis has focused on the assessment interview (see Chapter 3). However, many of the issues and problems related to clinical judgment during interviewing also have implications for the gathering and synthesis of test data. One of the most essential elements in gathering data from any source is the development of an optimum level of rapport. Rapport increases the likelihood that clients will give their optimum level of performance. If rapport is not sufficiently developed, it is increasingly likely that the data obtained from the person will be inaccurate.

Another important issue is that the interview itself is typically guided by the client's responses and the clinician's reaction to these responses. A client's responses might be nonrepresentative because of such factors as a transient condition (stressful day, poor night's sleep, etc.) or conscious/unconscious faking. The client's responses also need to be interpreted by the clinician. These interpretations can be influenced by a combination of personality theory, research data, and the clinician's professional and personal experience. The clinician typically develops hypotheses based on a client's responses and combines his or her observations with his or her theoretical understanding of the issue. These hypotheses can be further investigated and tested by interview questions and test data, which can result in confirmation, alteration, or elimination of the hypotheses. Thus, bias can potentially enter into this process from a number of different directions, including the types of questions asked, initial impressions, level of rapport, or theoretical perspective.

The clinician typically collects much of the initial data regarding a client through unstructured or semistructured interviews. Unstructured approaches in gathering and interpreting data provide flexibility, focus on the uniqueness of the person, and are ideographically rich. In contrast, an important disadvantage of unstructured approaches is that a clinician, like most other persons, can be influenced by a number of personal and cultural biases. For example, clinicians might develop incorrect hypotheses based on first impressions (primacy effect). They might end up seeking erroneous confirmation of incorrect hypotheses by soliciting expected responses rather than objectively probing for possible disconfirmation. Thus clinicians might be unduly influenced by their preferred theory of personality, halo effects, self-fulfilling prophecies, expectations, and cultural stereotypes. These areas of potential sources of error have led to numerous questions regarding the dependability of clinical judgment.

Accuracy of Clinical Judgments

After collecting and organizing their data, clinicians then need to make final judgments regarding the client. Determining the relative accuracy of these judgments is crucial. In some cases, clinical judgment is clearly in error whereas in others it can be quite accurate. To increase accuracy, clinicians need to know how errors might occur, how to correct these errors, and the relative advantages of specialized training.

A possible source of inaccuracy is that clinicians frequently do not take into account the base rate, or the rate at which a particular behavior, trait, or diagnosis occurs in the general population (Faust, 1991; Hawkins & Hastie, 1990; Wedding & Faust, 1989). For example, an intake section of a psychiatric hospital might evaluate a population of whom 50% could be considered to be schizophrenic. A clinician who would randomly diagnosis patients as either schizophrenic or nonschizophrenic would be correct 50% of the time. Thus, even a 60% correct diagnosis of schizophrenia would only exceed the base rate (or chance occurrence) by 10%. It is also rare for clinicians to receive feedback regarding either the accuracy of their diagnoses or other frequently used judgments such as behavioral predictions, personality traits, or the relative success of their recommendations (Garb, 1989, 1994a). Thus it is possible for inaccurate strategies for arriving at conclusions to be continued with little likelihood of correction.

A further source of error is that information obtained earlier in the data collection process is frequently given more importance than information received later (primacy effect). This means that different starting points in the decision-making process may result in different conclusions. This can be further reinforced if clinicians make early judgments and then work to confirm these judgments through seeking supporting information. This confirmatory bias can be especially likely to occur in a hypothesis-testing situation where clinicians do not adequately seek information that could disconfirm as well as confirm their hypothesis (Haverkamp, 1993). The most problematic examples occur when clinicians interpret a client's behavior and then work to persuade the client that their interpretation is correct (Loftus, 1993).

Research on person perception accuracy indicates that, even though no two persons are uniformly accurate, some persons are much better at accurately perceiving others. Taft (1955) and Vernon (1964) summarize the early research on person perception accuracy by pointing out that accuracy is not associated with age (in adults), there is little difference in accuracy between males and females (although females are slightly better), and accurate perceptions of others are positively associated with intelligence, artistic/dramatic interests, social detachment, and good emotional adjustment. Authoritarian personalities tend to be poor judges. In most instances, accuracy is related to similarity in race and cultural backgrounds (Malpass & Kravitz, 1969; Shapiro & Penrod, 1986). In some cases, accuracy by psychologists may be only slightly related to their amount of clinical experience (Garb, 1989, 1992, 1994a), and for some judgments psychologists may be no better than certain groups of nonprofessionals, such as physical scientists and personnel workers (Garb, 1992, 1994a; Taft, 1955). Relatively higher rates of accuracy were achieved when clinical judgments based on interviews were combined with formal assessments and when statistical interpretive rules were used. When subjective test interpretation was combined with clinical judgment, it was questionable whether any increase in accuracy was obtained (Garb, 1984, 1989).

It would be logical to assume that the more confidence clinicians feel regarding the accuracy of their judgments, the more likely it would be that their judgments would be accurate. In several studies, however, confidence was often not related to accuracy (Kelly & Fiske, 1951; Kleinmuntz, 1990). Kelly and Fiske (1951) even found that degree of confidence was inversely related to predicting the success of trainees in a VA training program. Several studies (Kareken & Williams, 1994; Lichtenstein & Fischoff, 1977) concluded that persons were generally overconfident regarding judgments, and when outcome knowledge was made available, clinicians typically overestimated what they thought they knew prior to having received outcome knowledge (Hawkins & Hastie, 1990). This is usually referred to as hindsight bias ("I would have known it all along") and is usually accompanied by a denial that the outcome knowledge has influenced judgment. Paradoxically, as knowledge and experience in an area increase, there is generally a decrease in confidence regarding judgments. This observation was found to be true unless the clinicians were very knowledgeable, in which case they were likely to have a moderate level of confidence (Garb, 1989). Thus, the more experienced clinicians were able to more accurately rate their level of confidence.

Crucial to clinical judgment is whether clinicians can make judgments better than laypersons and whether amount of clinical training can increase accuracy. This is a particularly important issue if psychologists are offering their services as expert witnesses to the legal justice system. Research reviews generally support the value of clinical training, but this is dependent on the domain being assessed. For example, Garb (1982) has concluded, "Clinicians are able to make reliable and valid judgments for many tasks, and their judgments are frequently more valid than judgments by laypersons" (p. 451). In particular, clinicians have been found to make more accurate judgments relating to relatively complex technical areas such as clinical diagnosis, ratings of mental status, many domains related to interview information, short-term (and possibly long-term) predictions of violence, psychological test interpretation (WAIS, MMPI), forensic knowledge, competency evaluations, neuropsychological test results, psychotherapy data, and biographical data (see primarily Garb, 1992 but also 1984, 1989, 1994a). In contrast, trained clinicians were no better than laypersons in making judgments based on projective test results and in making personality descriptions based on face-to-face interaction.

The preceding material indicates that errors in clinical judgment can and do occur. It is thus crucial, especially when appearing as an expert witness, that clinicians are familiar with the relevant literature on clinical judgment and, based on this information, take steps to improve their accuracy. Accordingly, Garb (1994a) and Wedding and Faust (1989) have made the following recommendations:

1. To avoid missing crucial information, clinicians should use comprehensive, structured or at least semistructured approaches to interviewing. This is especially important in cases where urgent clinical decisions (danger to self or others) may need to occur.

2. Clinicians should not only consider the data that supports their hypotheses, but also carefully consider or even list evidence which does not support their hypotheses. This will be likely to reduce the likelihood of hindsight and confirmatory bias.

3. Diagnoses should be based on careful attention to the specific criteria contained in the *DSM-IV* (or *ICD-10*). In particular, this means not making errors due to inferences biased by gender and ethnicity.

4. Since memory can be a reconstructive process subject to possible errors, clinicians should avoid relying on memory and rather refer to careful notes as much as possible.

5. In making predictions, clinicians should attend to base rates as much as possible. Such a consideration will potentially provide a rough estimate of how frequently the behavior will occur within a given population or context. Any clinical predictions then, will be guided by this base rate occurrence and are likely to be improvements on the base rate.

6. Clinicians should seek feedback whenever possible regarding the accuracy and usefulness of their judgments. For example, psychological reports should ideally be followed up with rating forms (that can be completed by the referral sources) relating to the clarity, precision, accuracy, and usefulness of the information and recommendations contained in the reports (see Ownby & Wallbrown, 1983).

7. Clinicians should learn as much as possible regarding the theoretical and empirical material relevant to the person or group they are assessing. This would potentially help to develop strategies for obtaining comprehensive information, allow clinicians to make correct estimates regarding the accuracy of their judgments, and provide them with appropriate base rate information.

8. Familiarity with the literature on clinical judgment should be used to continually update practitioners on past and emerging trends.

Sometimes in court proceedings, psychologists are challenged regarding the difficulties associated with clinical judgment. If the preceding steps are taken, then they can justifiably reply that they are familiar with the literature and have taken appropriate steps to guard against inaccuracies in clinical judgment. More importantly, the quality of service related to clients and referral sources is also likely to be enhanced.

Clinical versus Actuarial Prediction

Over 40 years ago, Meehl (1954) published a review of research comparing the relative accuracy of clinical judgment versus statistical formulas when used on identical sets of data (life history, demographic data, test profiles). The clinical approach used clinicians' judgment, whereas the actuarial approach used empirically derived formulas, such as single/multiple cutoffs and regression equations, to come to decisions regarding a client. His review covered a large number of settings including military placement, college success, criminal recidivism, and benefit from psychotherapy. He concluded that statistical decisions consistently outperformed clinical judgments (Meehl, 1954, 1965). This resulted in some lively debate in the journals, with Meehl's conclusions generally being supported (Garb, 1994b; Goldberg, 1965; Kleinmuntz, 1990; Wiggins, 1973). Dawes and Corrigan (1974) even found that an actuarial formula based on specific clinicians' own decision-making processes yielded more valid future predictions than the clinicians' own predictions. This was probably due to the formula reducing the influence of uncontrolled errors in the clinicians' procedures.

Despite the empirical support for an actuarial approach, several practical and theoretical issues need to be considered. A clinical approach to integrating data and arriving at conclusions allows a clinician to explore, probe, and deepen his or her understanding in many areas. These frequently involve areas that tests or statistical formulas cannot measure. Often an interview is the only means of obtaining observations of behavior and unique aspects of history. Idiosyncratic events with a low frequency of occurrence may significantly alter a clinician's conclusions although no formulas take these events into account. It is quite common for unique, rare events to have occurred at some time in a client's life, and during the process of assessment, they are frequently relevant and can often alter the conclusions of many, if not most, clinical assessments. Not only do unique aspects of a person change interpretations, but typically an assessment for a person needs to be focused for a specific context and specific situation that he or she is involved in. When the focus changes from institutional to individual decision making, the relevance of statistical rules becomes less practical (Vane & Guarnaccia, 1989). Not only are individuals too multifaceted, but their unique situations, contexts, and the decisions facing them are even more multifaceted.

A further difficulty with a purely actuarial approach is that development of both test reliability and validity, as well as actuarial formulas, requires conceiving the world as stable and static. For such approaches to be useful, the implicit assumption is that neither people nor criteria change. In contrast, the practitioner must deal with a natural world that is imperfect, constantly changing, does not necessarily follow rules, is filled with constantly changing perceptions, and is subject to chance or at least impossible to predict events. Thus, even when statistical formulas are available, they may not apply. This distinction between the statistical orientation of the psychometrician and the natural environment of the practitioner underlies the discrepancy between their two worlds. Practitioners must somehow try to combine these two modes of analysis, but often find the task difficult. It may be true that controlled studies generally favor a statistical approach over a clinical one but, at the same time, that truth is seldom useful to the practitioner involved in the changing and unique world of practice (Bonarius, 1984). Often, there is no alternative other than to rely on clinical judgment to combine a wide variety of relevant information. This return to a pre-Meehl perspective is unfortunate and is accepted by most clinicians with hesitation.

Bonarius (1984) presents a conceptual alternative to this dilemma. The first step is to alter mechanistic views of prediction. Instead, clinicians might avoid the term prediction altogether and use anticipation. Anticipating future possibilities implies a cognitive con-structional process rather than a mechanical process. It admits that the world can never be perfect in any mechanistic sense and that there is no such thing as an average person in an average situation engaged in an average interaction. Furthermore, the creation of future events is shared by coparticipants. Clients take an active part in formulating and evaluating their goals. The success of future goals depends on the degree of effort they are willing to put into them. The coparticipants share responsibility for the future. Thus, the likelihood that future events will occur is related to both cognitive constructions of an idiosyncratic world, and interaction between participants.

Ideally, clinicians need to be aware of and to use, whenever available, actuarial ap-proaches such as multiple cutoffs and regression equations. Future computer-assisted analysis of assessment results can increasingly provide actuarial predictions especially from multiple sources (i.e., Bank & Patterson, 1992; Kane & Kay, 1992). The conclu-sions reached from actuarial approaches also need to be integrated with data and infer-ences obtainable only through clinical means. If unusual details regarding a client are discovered and result in altering an interpretation, then the basis for this alteration should be noted in the psychological report. Clinicians should also be sensitive to indi-vidual differences in person perception accuracy between one practitioner and the next. These differences may depend on experience, training, knowledge, personality, and the amount and quality of feedback regarding the perceptions of different clinicians. In ad-dition, clinicians must recognize possible increases and decreases in test interpretation and clinical judgment resulting from the incremental validity of their instruments since more information does not necessarily increase the accuracy of clinically based predic-tions (Garb, 1994b; Kleinmuntz, 1990). While it is unlikely that actuarial prediction rules will replace clinical judgment, formal prediction rules can and should be used more extensively as a resource to improve the accuracy of clinical decision making.

The Psychological Report

An accurate and effective psychological report requires that clinicians clarify their thinking and crystallize their interpretations. The report ties together all sources of in-formation, often combining complex interprofessional and interpersonal issues. All the advantages and limitations involved with clinical judgment either directly or indirectly affect the report. The focus should be a clear communication of the clinician's inter-pretations, conclusions, and recommendations. Chapter 14 provides in-depth informa-tion on the psychological report as it relates to relevant research, guidelines, format, and sample reports.

PHASES IN CLINICAL ASSESSMENT

An outline of the phases of clinical assessment can provide both a conceptual frame-work for approaching an evaluation and a summary of some of the points already dis-cussed. Although the steps in assessment will be isolated for conceptual convenience, in actuality they often occur simultaneously and interact with one another. Through-out these phases, the clinician should integrate data and serve as an expert on human behavior rather than merely an interpreter of test scores. This is consistent with the belief that a psychological assessment can be most useful when it addresses specific individual problems and provides guidelines for decision making regarding these problems.

Evaluating the Referral Question

Many of the practical limitations of psychological evaluations are due to an inadequate clarification of the problem. Since clinicians are aware of the assets and limitations of psychological tests and since clinicians are responsible for providing useful information, it is their duty to clarify the requests they receive. Furthermore, they cannot assume that initial requests for an evaluation will be adequately stated. Clinicians may need to uncover hidden agendas, unspoken expectations, and complex interpersonal relationships, as well as to explain the specific limitations of psychological tests. One of the most important general requirements is that clinicians understand the vocabulary, conceptual model, dynamics, and expectations of the referral setting in which they will be working.

Clinicians rarely are asked to give a general or global assessment, but instead are asked to answer specific questions. To address these questions, it is sometimes helpful to contact the referral source at different stages in the assessment process. For example, it is often important in an educational evaluation to observe the student in the classroom environment. The information derived from such an observation might be relayed back to the referral source for further clarification or modification of the referral question. Likewise, an attorney may wish to somewhat alter his or her referral question based on preliminary information derived from the clinician's initial interview with the client.

Acquiring Knowledge Relating to the Content of the Problem

Before beginning the actual testing procedure, examiners should carefully consider the problem, the adequacy of the tests they will be using, and the specific applicability of that test to an individual's unique situation. This preparation may require referring both to the test manual and to additional outside sources. Clinicians should be familiar with operational definitions for such problems as anxiety disorders, psychoses, personality disorders, or organic impairment so that they can be alert to their possible expression during the assessment procedure. Competence in merely administering and scoring tests is insufficient to conduct effective assessment. For example, the development of an IQ score does not necessarily indicate that an examiner is aware of differing cultural expressions of intelligence or of the limitations of the assessment device. It is essential that clinicians have in-depth knowledge about the variables they are measuring or their evaluations are likely to be extremely limited.

Related to this is the relative adequacy of the test in measuring the variable being considered. This includes evaluating certain practical considerations, the standardization sample, and reliability and validity (see Table 1–1). It is important that the examiner also considers the problem in relation to the adequacy of the test and decides whether a specific test or tests can be appropriately used on an individual or group. This demands knowledge in such areas as the client's age, race, educational background, motivation for testing, anticipated level of resistance, social environment, and interpersonal relationships. Finally, clinicians need to assess the effectiveness or utility of the test in aiding the treatment process.

Data Collection

After clarifying the referral question and obtaining knowledge relating to the problem, clinicians can then proceed with the actual collection of information. This may come from a wide variety of sources, the most frequent of which are test scores, personal history, behavioral observations, and interview data. Clinicians may also find it useful to obtain school records, previous psychological observations, medical records, police reports, or discuss the client with parents or teachers. It is important to realize that the tests themselves are merely a single tool, or source, for obtaining data. The case history is of equal importance since it provides a context for understanding the client's current problems and, through this understanding, renders the test scores meaningful. In many cases, a client's history is of even more significance in making predictions and in assessing the seriousness of his or her condition than his or her test scores. For example, a high score on depression on the MMPI is not as helpful in assessing suicide risk as are historical factors like the number of previous attempts, age, sex, details regarding any previous attempts, and length of time the client has been depressed. Of equal importance is that the test scores themselves will usually not be sufficient to answer the referral question. For specific problem solving and decision making, clinicians must rely on multiple sources and, using these sources, check to assess the consistency of the observations they make.

Interpreting the Data

The end product of assessment should be a description of the client's present level of functioning, considerations relating to etiology, prognosis, and treatment recommendations. Etiologic descriptions should avoid simplistic formulas and should instead focus on the influence exerted by several interacting factors. These factors can be divided into primary, predisposing, precipitating, and reinforcing causes, and a complete description of etiology should take all of these into account. Further elaborations may also attempt to assess the person from a systems perspective in which the clinician evaluates patterns of interaction, mutual two-way influences, and the specifics of circular information feedback. An additional crucial area is to use the data to develop an effective plan for intervention (see Beutler & Clarkin, 1990; Gaw & Beutler, 1995; Jongsma & Peterson, 1995). Clinicians should also pay careful attention to research on, and the implications of, incremental validity and continually be aware of the limitations and possible inaccuracies involved in clinical judgment. If actuarial formulas are available, they should be used whenever possible. These considerations indicate that the description of a client should not be a mere labeling or classification, but should rather provide a deeper and more accurate understanding of the person. This understanding should allow the examiner to perceive new facets of the person in terms of both his or her internal experience and his or her relationships with others.

To develop these descriptions, clinicians must make inferences from their test data. Although such data is objective and empirical, the process of developing hypotheses, obtaining support for these hypotheses, and integrating the conclusions is dependent on the experience and training of the clinician. This process generally follows a sequence of developing impressions, identifying relevant facts, making inferences, and supporting these inferences with relevant and consistent data. Maloney and Ward (1976) have conceptualized a seven-phase approach (Figure 1–1) toward evaluating data. They note that, in actual practice, these phases are not as clearly defined as indicated in Figure 1–1, but often occur simultaneously. For example, when a clinician reads a referral question or initially observes a client, he or she is already developing hypotheses about that person and checking to assess the validity of these observations.

Phase 1   The first phase involves collecting data about the client. It begins with the referral question and is followed by a review of the client's previous history and records. At this point, the clinician is already beginning to develop tentative hypotheses and to

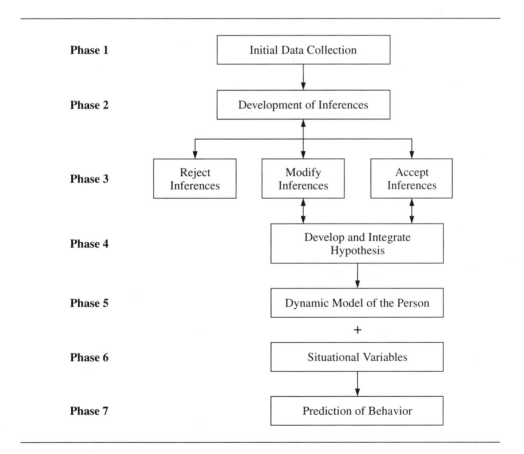

Figure 1–1.   Conceptual model for interpreting assessment data

Adapted from Maloney and Ward, 1976, p. 161. Reprinted by permission from *Psychological Assessment: A Conceptual Approach,* by M. P. Maloney and M. P. Ward, New York: Oxford University Press, 1976.

clarify questions for investigation in more detail. The next step is actual client contact, in which the clinician conducts an interview and administers a variety of psychological tests. The client's behavior during the interview, as well as the content or factual data, are noted. Out of this data, the clinician begins to make his or her inferences.

Phase 2   Phase 2 focuses on the development of a wide variety of inferences about the client. These inferences serve both a summary and explanatory function. For example, an examiner may infer that a client is depressed, which also may explain his or her slow performance, distractibility, flattened affect, and withdrawn behavior. The examiner may then wish to evaluate whether this depression is a deeply ingrained trait or more a reaction to a current situational difficulty. This may be determined by referring to test scores, interview data, or any additional sources of available information. The emphasis in the second phase is on developing multiple inferences that should initially be tentative. They serve the purpose of guiding future investigation to obtain additional information that is then used to confirm, modify, or negate later hypotheses.

Phase 3   Since the third phase is concerned with either accepting or rejecting the inferences developed in Phase 2, there is constant and active interaction between these phases. Often, in investigating the validity of an inference, a clinician will alter either the meaning or the emphasis of an inference, or will develop entirely new ones. Rarely is an inference entirely substantiated, but rather the validity of that inference is progressively strengthened as the clinician evaluates the degree of consistency and the strength of data that support a particular inference. For example, the inference that a client is anxious may be supported by WAIS-R subscale performance, MMPI scores, and behavioral observations, or it may only be suggested by one of these sources. The amount of evidence to support an inference directly affects the amount of confidence a clinician can place in this inference.

Phase 4   As a result of inferences developed in the previous three phases, the clinician can move in Phase 4 from specific inferences to general statements about the client. This involves elaborating each inference to describe trends or patterns of the client. For example, the inference that a client is depressed may be due to self-verbalizations in which the client continually criticizes and judges his or her behavior. This may also be expanded to give information regarding the ease or frequency with which a person might enter into the depressive state. The central task in Phase 4 is to develop and begin to elaborate on statements relating to the client.

Phases 5, 6, 7   The fifth phase involves a further elaboration of a wide variety of the personality traits of the individual. It represents an integration and correlation of the client's characteristics. This may include describing and discussing such general factors as cognitive functioning, affective and mood levels, and interpersonal-intrapersonal level of functioning. Although Phases 4 and 5 are similar, Phase 5 provides a more comprehensive and integrated description of the client than Phase 4. Finally, Phase 6 places this comprehensive description of the person into a situational context and Phase 7 makes specific predictions regarding his or her behavior. Phase 7 is the most crucial element involved in decision making and requires that the clinician take into account the interaction between personal and situational variables.

Establishing the validity of these inferences presents a difficult challenge for clinicians since, unlike many medical diagnoses, psychological inferences cannot usually be physically documented. Furthermore, clinicians are rarely confronted with feedback about the validity of these inferences. Despite these difficulties, psychological descriptions should strive to be reliable, have adequate descriptive breadth, and possess both descriptive and predictive validity. Reliability of descriptions refers to whether the description or classification can be replicated by other clinicians (interdiagnostician agreement) as well as by the same clinician on different occasions (intradiagnostician agreement). The next criterion is the breadth of coverage encompassed in the classification. Any classification should be broad enough to encompass a wide range of individuals and yet specific enough to provide useful information regarding the individual being evaluated. Descriptive validity involves the degree to which individuals who are classified are similar on variables external to the classification system. For example, are individuals with similar MMPI profiles also similar on other relevant attributes such as family history, demographic variables, legal difficulties, or alcohol abuse? Finally, predictive validity refers to the confidence with which test inferences can be used to evaluate future outcomes. These may include academic achievement, job performance, or the outcome of treatment. This is one of the most crucial functions of testing. Unless inferences can be made that effectively enhance decision making, the scope and relevance of testing are significantly reduced. Although these criteria are difficult to achieve and to evaluate, they represent the ideal standard for which assessments should strive.

RECOMMENDED READING

Anastasi, A. (1996). *Psychological testing* (7th ed.). New York: Macmillan.

Garb, H. N. (1994). Judgment research: Implications for clinical practice and testimony in court. *Applied and Preventive Psychology, 3,* 173–183.

Kaplan, R. M., & Sacuzzo, D. (1993). *Psychological testing: Principles, applications, and issues* (2nd ed.). Pacific Grove, CA.: Wadsworth.

Matarazzo, J. D. (1990). Psychological assessment versus psychological testing: Validation from Binet to the school, clinic, and courtroom. *American Psychologist, 45,* 999–1017.

McReynolds, P. (1989). Diagnosis and clinical assessment: Current status and major issues. *Annual Review of Psychology, 40,* 83–108.

Chapter 2 ——————————————————————————————

THE CONTEXT OF
CLINICAL ASSESSMENT

Although general knowledge regarding tests and test construction is essential, practitioners must consider a wide range of additional issues to place testing procedures and test scores in an appropriate context. These considerations include clarifying the referral question, determining who will read the final report, following ethical guidelines, identifying and working with test bias, selecting the most appropriate instrument for the variable or problem being studied, and making appropriate use of computer-assisted interpretation.

TYPES OF REFERRAL SETTINGS

Throughout the assessment process, practitioners should try to understand the unique problems and demands encountered in different referral settings. Otherwise, examiners—despite being skilled in administering and interpreting tests—may provide much useless information to their referral source and perhaps even administer a needless series of tests. That is, a thorough investigation of the underlying motive for a referral can sometimes lead to the discovery that evaluation through testing is not warranted.

Errors in test interpretation frequently occur because clinicians do not respond to the referral question in its broadest context (Levine, 1981). In turn, requests for psychological testing are often worded vaguely: "I would like a psychological evaluation on Mr. Smith," or "Could you evaluate Jimmy because he is having difficulties in school?" The request seldom states a specific question that must be answered or a decision that must be made, when in fact this is almost always the position that the referral source is in. For example, a school administrator may need testing to support a placement decision, a teacher may want to prove to parents that their child has a serious problem, or a psychiatric resident may not be comfortable with the management of a patient. An organization's surface motive for testing may be as vague as a statement that the procedure is a matter of policy. Greater clarification is necessary before clinicians can provide useful problem-solving information. Furthermore, many of these situations have hidden agendas that may not be adequately handled through psychological testing alone.

It must be stressed that the responsibility for exploring and clarifying the referral question lies with the clinician who should actively work with the referral source to place the client's difficulty within a practicable context. Clinicians must understand the decisions that the referral source is facing, as well as the available alternatives and the relative usefulness of each of these alternatives. Clinicians also need to specify the relevance of the psychological evaluation in determining different alternatives and their possible outcomes. They should make clear the advantages and usefulness of psychological testing, but should also explain the limitations inherent in test data.

To help clarify the referral question as well as develop a relevant psychological evaluation, clinicians should become familiar with the types of environments in which they will be working. The most frequent environments are the psychiatric setting, the general medical setting, the legal context, the educational context, and the psychological clinic.

The Psychiatric Setting

Levine (1981) has summarized the important factors for a psychologist to be aware of in a psychiatric setting. These referrals typically come from a psychiatrist, who may be asking the referral question in the role of administrator, psychotherapist, or physician. Each role presents unique issues for the psychiatrist, and clinicians have a primary responsibility to develop evaluations that directly address the problems at hand.

One of the main roles a psychiatrist fills is as an administrator in a ward. Ward administrators frequently must make decisions about such problems as suicide risk, admission/discharge, and the suitability of a wide variety of medical procedures. While retaining primary responsibility, a psychiatrist often will use information from other persons to help with decisions. This represents a change from the typical role of psychiatrists 30 years ago when psychiatrists were mainly concerned with diagnosis and treatment. Currently, issues about custody, freedom of the patient, and the safety of society have taken over as the primary focus. From the perspective of psychologists performing assessments, this means that making a formal *DSM-IV* psychiatric diagnosis is not sufficient in and of itself. For example, a patient may be diagnosed manic-depressive, but this label does not indicate the level of dangerousness that the patient poses to him- or herself or to others. Once patients have been admitted to a psychiatric setting, many practical questions have to be answered, such as the type of ward in which to place them, the activities in which they should be involved, and the method of therapy that would be most likely to benefit them.

Initially, the psychologist must determine exactly what information the ward administrator is looking for, particularly in regard to any decisions that must be made about the patient. Psychologists in psychiatric settings who receive vague requests for "a psychological" sometimes develop a standard evaluation based on their preconception of what this term implies. They may evaluate the patient's defense mechanisms, diagnosis, cognitive style, and psychosocial history without addressing the specific decisions that have to be made or perhaps only covering two or three relevant issues and omitting others. To maximize the usefulness of an evaluation, examiners must be especially aware of, and sensitive to, psychiatric administrators' legal and custodial responsibilities.

In contrast to the concerns of ward administrators, the standard referral questions from psychiatrists evaluating a patient for possible psychotherapy involve the appropriateness of the client for such therapy, the strategies that are most likely to be effective, and the likely outcome of therapy. These assessments are usually clear-cut and typically do not present any difficulties. Such an evaluation can elaborate on likely problems that may occur during the course of therapy, defenses, capacity for insight, cognitive styles, affective level, and diagnosis (see Chapter 13). If a referral is made during therapy, however, a number of problem areas may exist that are not readily apparent from the referral question. The assessor must investigate these complicating factors along with potential decisions derived from the assessment information.

An area of potential conflict arises when psychiatrists are attempting to fulfill roles of both administrator (caretaker) and psychotherapist, and yet have not clearly defined these roles either for themselves or for their patients. The resulting ambiguity may cause the patient to feel defensive and resistant and the psychiatrist to feel that the patient is not living up to the therapist's expectations. Elaboration of a specific trait or need within the patient cannot resolve this conflict, but must occur in the context of interactions between the therapist and the patient. A standard psychological evaluation investigating the internal structure of the patient will not address this issue.

A second possible problem area for clients referred in the midst of therapy can be the result of personal anxiety and discomfort on the therapist's part. Thus, such issues as countertransference and possibly the therapist's unreasonable expectations may be equally or even more important than looking at a patient's characteristics. If role ambiguity, countertransference, or unreasonable expectations are discovered, they must be elaborated and communicated in a sensitive manner.

When psychiatrists are acting in the role of physician, they and the psychologist may have different conceptual models for describing a patient's disorder. Whereas psychiatrists function primarily from a disease or medical model, psychologists may speak in terms of difficulties in living with people and society. In effectively communicating the results of psychological evaluations, examiners must bridge this conceptual difference. For example, a psychiatrist may ask whether a patient is schizophrenic, whereas a psychologist may not believe that the label "schizophrenia" is useful or even a scientifically valid concept. The larger issue, however, is that the psychiatrist is still faced with some practical decisions. In fact, the psychiatrist may share some of the same concerns regarding the term schizophrenia, but this conceptual issue may not be particularly relevant in dealing with the patient. Legal requirements or hospital policies might require that the patient be given a traditional diagnosis. The psychiatrist may also have to decide whether to give antipsychotic medication, electroconvulsive therapy, or psychotherapy. For a patient who is diagnosed as schizophrenic rather than brain damaged or personality disordered, then, (given a hospital's current and economic policy considerations), the psychiatrist may decide on antipsychotic medication. An effective examiner should be able to see beyond possible conceptual differences and instead address practical considerations. A psychiatrist may refer a defensive patient who cannot or will not verbalize his or her concerns and ask whether this person is schizophrenic. Beyond this are such factors as the quality of the patient's thought processes and whether the person poses a danger to him- or herself or to others. Thus, the effective examiner must translate his or her findings into a conceptual model that is both understandable by a psychiatrist and useful from a task-oriented point of view.

The General Medical Setting

It has been estimated that as many as two-thirds of patients seen by physicians have primarily psychosocial difficulties, and of those with clearly established medical diagnoses, between 25% to 50% have specifically psychological disorders in addition to medical ones (Cummings, 1991; Sartorius et al., 1990). Most of these psychological difficulties are neither diagnosed nor referred for treatment (Borus, Howes, Devins, & Rosenberg, 1988; Quill, 1985). In addition, many traditionally "medical" disorders such as coronary heart disease, asthma, allergies, rheumatoid arthritis, ulcers, and headaches have been found to possess a significant psychosocial component (Friedman & Booth-Kewley, 1987; Groth-Marnat & Edkins, 1996; Schwartz, 1982). Not only are psychological factors related to disease, of equal importance, they are related to the development and maintenance of health. In addition, the treatment and prevention of psychosocial aspects of "medical" complaints has been demonstrated to be cost-effective for such areas as preparation for surgery, smoking cessation, rehabilitation of chronic pain patients, obesity, interventions for coronary heart disease, and patients who are somatizing psychosocial difficulties (Groth-Marnat & Edkins, 1996; Groth-Marnat, Edkins, & Schumaker, 1995). A complete approach to the patient, then, involves an awareness of the interaction between physical, psychological, and social variables (Schwartz, 1982). Thus psychologists have the potential to make an extremely important contribution. To adequately work in general medical settings, psychologists must become familiar with medical descriptions, which often means learning a complex and extensive vocabulary. Another possible limitation is that, even though physicians often draw information from several sources to aid in decision making, they must take ultimate responsibility for their decisions.

The most frequent situations in which physicians might use the services of a psychologist involve possible emotional factors associated with medical complaints, assessment for neuropsychological deficit, psychological treatment for chronic pain, and the treatment of chemical dependency (Bamgbose, Jesse, Smith, & Groth-Marnat, 1980; Groth-Marnat, 1988). Although a medical exam may not suggest any physical basis for the patient's complaints, the physician still has to devise some form of treatment or at least an appropriate referral. This is crucial in that a significant portion of patients referred to physicians do not have any detectable physical difficulties and their central complaint is likely to be psychological (Borus et al., 1988; Cummings, 1991; Jencks, 1985). The psychologist can then elaborate and specify how a patient can be treated for possible psychosocial difficulties (Wickramasekera, 1995).

Another area that has greatly increased in importance is the psychological assessment of a patient's neuropsychological status (see Chapter 12). Whereas physicians attempt to detect physical lesions in the nervous system, the neuropsychologist has traditionally been more concerned with the status of higher cortical functions. Another way of stating this: Physicians evaluate how the *brain* is functioning, whereas the neuropsychologist evaluates how the *person* is functioning as a result of possible brain abnormalities. The typical areas of assessment focus primarily on the presence of possible intellectual deterioration in such areas as memory, sequencing, abstract reasoning, spatial organization, or executive abilities (Lezak, 1995; Reitan & Wolfson, 1993). Such referrals, or at least screening for neuropsychological deficit typically account for 30% of all psychological referrals in psychiatric and medical settings (Craig, 1979). In the past, neuropsychologists have been asked to help determine whether a patient's complaints were "functional" or "organic." The focus now is more on whether the person has neuropsychological deficits that may contribute to or account for observed behavioral difficulties than on either/or distinctions (Loenberger, 1989). Physicians often want to know whether a test profile suggests a specific diagnosis, particularly malingering, conversion disorder, hypochondriasis, organic brain syndrome, or depression with pseudoneurological features. Further issues that neuropsychologists often address include the nature and extent of identified lesions, localization of lesions, emotional status of neurologically impaired patients, extent of disability, and suggestions for treatment planning such as recommendations for cognitive rehabilitation, vocational training, and readjustment to family and friends.

A physician might also request a psychologist to conduct a presurgical evaluation to assess the likelihood of a serious stress reaction to surgery. Finally, physicians, particularly pediatricians, are often concerned with detecting early signs of serious psychological disorder, which may have been brought to their attention by parents, other family members, or teachers. In such situations, the psychologist's evaluation should assess not only the patient's present psychological condition, but also the contributing factors in his or her environment, and should provide a prediction of the patient's status during the next few months or years. When the patient's current condition, current environment, and future prospects have been evaluated, the examiner can then recommend the next phase in the intervention process. A psychologist may also consult with physicians to assist them in effectively discussing the results of an examination with the patient or the patient's family.

The Legal Context

During the past 15 years, the use of psychologists in legal settings has become more prevalent, important, and accepted. Psychologists might be called in at any stage of legal decision making. During the investigation stage, they might be consulted to assess the reliability of a witness or to help evaluate the quality of information by a witness. The prosecuting attorney might also need to have a psychologist evaluate the quality of another mental health professional's report, evaluate the accused person's competency, or help determine the specifics of a crime. A defense attorney might use a psychologist to help in supporting an insanity plea, to help in jury selection, or to document that brain damage has occurred. A judge might use a psychologist's report as one of a number of factors to help determine a sentence, a penal officer might wish consultation to help determine the type of confinement or level of dangerousness, or a parole officer might need assistance to help plan a rehabilitation program. Even though a psychologist might write a legal report, he or she is likely to actually appear in court in only about one in every ten cases.

Over the past 10 or 20 years, psychologists have become increasingly accepted within the legal-justice system. This has resulted in a gradual clarification of their roles (Blau, 1984). However, acclimatizing to the courtroom environment is often difficult due to the quite different roles between courtroom and clinic as well as the need to become familiar with specialized legal terms such as diminished capacity and insanity. In addition, many attorneys are familiar with the same professional literature that psychologists read and may use this information to attack a psychologist's qualifications, methods of assessment, or conclusions (Faust, Ziskin, & Hiers, 1991; Ziskin & Faust, 1995).

Each psychologist appearing in court must have his or her qualifications approved. Important areas of consideration are the presence of clinical expertise in treating specialty disorders and relevant publication credits. Evaluation of legal work by psychologists indicates they are generally viewed favorably by the courts and may have reached parity with psychiatrists (Hall, Catlin, Boissevain, & Westgate, 1984; Sales & Miller, 1994).

As outlined by the American Board of Forensic Psychology, the practice of forensic psychology includes training/consultation with legal practitioners, evaluation of populations likely to come into contact with the legal system, and the translation of relevant technical psychological knowledge into usable information. Psychologists are used most frequently in child custody cases, competency of a person to dispose of property, juvenile commitment, and personal injury suits in which the psychologist documents the nature and extent of the litigant's suffering or disability (stress, anxiety, cognitive deficit). In contrast, psychiatrists are far more likely to be used in assessing a person's competency to stand trial, degree of criminal responsibility, and the presence of mental defectiveness. Although psychologists can testify in these cases, physicians need to sign any commitment certificates and are therefore more likely to be used.

An essential requirement when working in the legal context is for psychologists to modify their language. Many legal terms have exact and specific meanings that, if misunderstood, could lead to extremely negative consequences. Words such as "incompetent," "insane," or "reasonable certainty" may vary within different judicial systems or from state to state. Psychologists must familiarize themselves with this terminology and the different nuances involved in its use. Psychologists may also be requested to explain in detail the meaning of their conclusions and how these conclusions were reached. Whereas attorneys rarely question the actual data that psychologists generate, the inferences and generalizability of these inferences are frequently placed under scrutiny or even attacked. Often this questioning can seem rude or downright hostile, but in most cases, attorneys are merely doing their best to defend their client. Proper legal protocol also requires that the psychologist answer questions directly rather than respond to the implications or underlying direction suggested by the questions. Furthermore, attorneys (or members of the jury) may not be trained in or appreciate the scientific method, which is the mainstay of a psychologist's background. In contrast, attorneys are trained in legal analysis and reasoning, which subjectively focuses on the uniqueness of each case rather than on a comparison of the person to a statistically relevant normative group.

Two potentially problematic areas lie in evaluating insanity and evaluating competency. Even though physicians are more typically called on to testify in these areas, psychologists can also become involved. Although the insanity plea has received considerable publicity, very few people make the appeal and, of those who do, few have it granted. It is usually difficult for an expert witness to evaluate such cases because of the problem of possible malingering to receive a lighter sentence and the possible ambiguity of the term "insanity." Usually a person is considered insane in accordance with the McNaughton Rule, which states that persons are not responsible if they did not know the nature and extent of their actions and if they cannot distinguish that what they did was wrong according to social norms. In some states, the ambiguity of the term is increased because defendants can be granted the insanity plea if it can be shown they were insane at the time of the incident. Other states include the clause of an "irresistible impulse" to the definition of insanity. Related to insanity is whether the defendant is competent to stand trial. Competence is usually defined as whether or not the person can cooperate in a meaningful way with the attorney, understand the purpose of the proceedings, and understand the implications of the possible penalties. To increase the reliability and validity of competency and insanity evaluations, specialized assessment techniques have been developed such as the Competency Screening Test (Lipsitt, Lelos, & McGarry, 1971; Nottingham & Mattson, 1981) and the Rogers Criminal Responsibility Scales (Rogers, 1984).

The prediction of dangerousness has also been a problematic area. Since actual violent or self-destructive behavior is a relatively unusual behavior (low base rate), any cut-off criteria typically are going to produce a high number of false positives. Thus, people incorrectly identified may potentially be detained and understandably be upset. However, the negative result of failure to identify and take action against people who are potentially violent makes erring on the side of caution more acceptable. Attempts to use special scales on the MMPI (Overcontrolled Hostility Scale; Megargee & Mendelsohn, 1962) or a 4-3 code type (see Chapter 6) have not been found to be sufficiently accurate for individual decision making. However, significant improvements have been made in predicting dangerousness and reoffending by using actuarial strategies, formal ratings, and summed ratings which include relevant information on developmental influences, possible events that lower thresholds, arrest record, life situation, and situational triggers such as interpersonal stress and substance intoxication (Apperson, Mulvey, & Lidz, 1993; Fisher & Thornton, 1993; Hall et al., 1984; Klassen & O'Connor, 1989; Mulvey & Lidz, 1995). The legal/justice system is most likely to give weight to those individual assessment strategies that combine recidivism statistics, tests specifically designed to predict dangerousness, summed ratings, and double administrations of psychological tests to assess change over time. Clinical judgment combined with a single administration of tests is usually considered to be only mildly useful (Hall et al., 1984).

Psychologists are sometimes requested to help with child custody decisions. The central consideration is to determine which arrangement will be in the child's best interest. Areas to be considered include the mental health of the parent, the quality of love and affection between the parent and child, the nature of the parent-child relationship, and the long-term effect of the different decisions on the child. Often, psychological evaluations are conducted on each member of the family using traditional testing instruments. Specific tests have also been developed, such as the Bricklin Perceptual Scales (Bricklin, 1984).

A final, frequently requested service is to aid in the classification of inmates in correctional settings. One basic distinction is between merely managing the person versus attempting a program of rehabilitation. Important management considerations are levels of suicide risk, appropriateness of dormitory versus a shared room, possible harassment from other inmates, or degree of dangerousness to others. Rehabilitation recommendations may need to consider the person's educational level, interests, skills, abilities, and personality characteristics related to employment.

The Educational Context

Psychologists are frequently called on to assess children who are having difficulty in or may need special placement within the school system. Sattler (1992) has summarized school assessments into these relevant areas: evaluating the nature and extent of a child's learning difficulties, measuring intellectual strengths and weaknesses, assessing behavioral difficulties, creating an educational plan, estimating a child's responsiveness to intervention, and recommending changes in a child's program or placement. Any educational plan should be sensitive to the interactions among a child's abilities, the child's personality, the characteristics of the teacher, and the needs and expectations of the parents.

An assessment should first include a visit to the classroom for observation of a child's behavior under natural conditions. A valuable aspect of this is to observe the interaction between the teacher and child. Typically, any behavioral difficulty is closely linked with the child-teacher interaction. Sometimes the teacher's style of responding to a student can be as much a part of the problem as the student. Consequently, classroom observations can cause discomfort to teachers and should be handled sensitively.

Observing the child in a wider context is, in many ways, contrary to the tradition of individual testing. However, individual testing all too frequently provides a relatively limited and narrow range of information. If it is combined with a family or classroom assessment, additional crucial data may be collected, but there is also likely to be significant resistance. This resistance may result from legal or ethical restrictions regarding the scope of the services the school can provide or the demands that a psychologist can make on the student's parents. Often there is an initial focus on, and need to perceive, the student as a "problem child" or "identified patient." This may obscure larger, more complex, and yet more significant issues such as marital conflict, a disturbed teacher, misunderstandings between teacher and parents, or a conflict between the school principal and the parents. All or some of these individuals may have an investment in perceiving the student as the person with the problem rather than acknowledging that a disordered school system or significant marital turmoil may be responsible. An individually oriented assessment may be made with excellent interpretations, but unless wider contexts are considered, understood, and addressed, the assessment may very well be ineffective in solving both the individual difficulties and the larger organizational or interpersonal problems.

A typical assessment of children within a school context will include behavioral observations, a test of intellectual abilities such as the WISC-III, Stanford Binet, Woodcock-Johnson Psychoeducational Battery-Revised or Kaufman Assessment Battery for Children (K-ABC), and tests of personality functioning. In the past, assessment of children's personality generally relied on projective techniques. However, many projectives have failed to meet psychometrically accepted standards for adults, and this difficulty is magnified with children. Projectives that have been found to meet more scientific standards with children are the Blacky Pictures Test (Blum, 1968), Rotter Incomplete Sentences (Rotter & Rafferty, 1950), and Incomplete Sentences Test (Lanyon & Lanyon, 1980). In contrast to older projective techniques, a variety of sound objective instruments have also been developed such as the Personality Inventory for Children (PIC; Wirt, Lachar, Klinedinst, & Seat, 1977). The inventory was designed along similar lines as the MMPI, but is completed by a child's parent. It produces four validity scales to detect faking and 12 clinical scales, such as Depression, Family Relations, Delinquency, Anxiety, and Hyperactivity. The scale was normed on 2,400 children, empirically developed, extensively researched, and has yielded good reliability. Additional well-designed scales that show excellent promise within a school context are the Child Behavior Check List/Child Behavior Profile (Achenbach, 1978; Achenbach & Edelbrock, 1979), Adaptive Behavior Inventory for Children (Mercer & Lewis, 1978), Vineland Adaptive

Behavior Scales (Sparrow, Balla, & Cicchetti, 1984), and the Revised Behavior Problem Checklist (Hogan, Quay, Vaughn, & Shapiro, 1989; Quay & Peterson, 1987).

Any report written for an educational setting should focus not only on a child's weaknesses, but also on his or her strengths. Understanding a child's strengths can potentially be used to increase a child's self-esteem as well as to create change within a wide context. Recommendations should be realistic and practical. This can most effectively be developed when the clinician has a thorough understanding of relevant resources in the community, the school system, and the classroom environment. This understanding is particularly important since the quality and resources available between one school or school system and the next can vary tremendously. Recommendations typically specify which skills need to be learned, how these can be learned, a hierarchy of objectives, and possible techniques for reducing behaviors that make learning difficult. Recommendations for special education should only be made when a regular class would clearly not be equally beneficial. However, the recommendations are not the end product. They are beginning points that should be elaborated and modified depending on the initial results. Ideally, a psychological report should be followed up with continuous monitoring.

Messick (1984) suggests that the assessment of children should be carried out in two phases. The first phase should assess the nature and quality of the child's learning environment. If the child is not exposed to adequate quality instruction, then he or she cannot be expected to perform well. Thus it must first be demonstrated that a child has not been learning even with appropriate instruction. The second phase involves a comprehensive assessment battery, which includes measures of intellectual abilities, academic skills, adaptive behavior, and screening out any biomedical disorders that might disrupt learning. Intellectual abilities might involve memory, spatial organization, abstract reasoning, and sequencing. Regardless of students' academic and intellectual abilities, they will not perform well unless they have relevant adaptive abilities, such as social skills, adequate motivation, and ability to control impulses. Assessing a child's values and attitudes toward education may be particularly important since they determine whether the student is willing to use whatever resources he or she may have. Likewise, the person's level of personal efficacy helps to determine whether the person is able to perform behaviors leading toward attaining the goals he or she values. Physical difficulties that might interfere with learning include poor vision, poor hearing, hunger, malnutrition, or endocrine dysfunction.

The preceding considerations clearly place the assessment of children in educational settings into a far wider context than merely the interpretation of test scores. Relationships among the teacher, family, and student need to be assessed, along with the relative quality of the learning environment. Furthermore, the child's values, motivation, and sense of personal efficacy need to be taken into consideration, along with possible biomedical difficulties. Examiners need to become knowledgeable regarding the school and community resources as well as to learn new instruments that have demonstrated relatively high levels of reliability and validity.

The Psychological Clinic

In contrast to the medical, legal, and educational institutions where the psychologist serves only as a consultant to the decision maker, the psychologist working in a psychological clinic is often the decision maker. A number of typical referrals come into the psychological clinic. Perhaps the most common ones are individuals who are self-referred and are seeking relief from psychological turmoil. For most of these individuals, psychological testing is not relevant and, in fact, may be contraindicated because the delay between the time of testing and the feedback of the results is usually time that could best be applied toward treatment. There may be certain groups of self-referred clients about whom the psychologist may question whether the treatment available in a psychological clinic is appropriate. These clients can include persons with extensive medical problems, individuals with legal complications that need additional clarification, and persons who may require inpatient treatment. With these cases, it might be necessary to obtain additional information through psychological testing. However, the main purpose of the testing would be to aid in decision making rather than to serve as a direct source of help for the client.

Two other situations in which psychological assessment may be warranted involve children who are referred by their parents for school or behavioral problems and referral from other decision makers. Where referrals are made for poor school performance or behavioral problems involving legal complications, special precautions must be taken prior to testing. Primarily, the clinician must develop a complete understanding of the client's social network and the basis for the referral. This may include a history of previous attempts at treatment and a summary of the relationship among the parents, school, courts, and child. Usually a referral comes at the end of a long sequence of events, and it is important to obtain information regarding these events. Once the basis of the referral has been clarified, the clinician may decide to have a meeting with different individuals who have become involved in the case such as the school principal, previous therapists, probation officer, attorney, or teacher. This meeting may uncover a myriad of issues that require decisions, such as referral for family therapy, placement in a special education program, a change in custody agreements between divorced parents, individual therapy of other members of the family, and a change in school. All of these may affect the relevance of, and approach to, testing, but these issues may not be apparent if the initial referral question is taken at face value. Sometimes psychologists are also confronted with referrals from other decision makers. For example, an attorney may want to know if an individual is competent to stand trial. Other referrals may involve a physician who wants to know whether a head-injured patient can readjust to his or her work environment or drive a car, or the physician may need to document changes in a patient's recovery.

So far, this discussion on the different settings in which psychological testing is used has focused on when to test and how to clarify the manner in which tests can be most helpful in making decisions. Several additional summary points must be stressed. As has been discussed previously, a referral source sometimes will be unable to adequately formulate the referral question. In fact, the referral question will usually be neither clear nor concise. It is the clinician's responsibility to look beyond the referral question and determine the basis for the referral in its widest scope. Thus, an understanding must be developed of the complexity of the client's social setting including interpersonal factors, family dynamics, and the sequence of events leading to the referral. In addition to clarifying the referral question, a second major point is that psychologists are responsible for developing knowledge about the setting for which they are writing their reports. This includes learning the proper language, the roles of the individuals working in the setting, the choices facing decision makers, and the philosophical and theoretical beliefs they adhere to. It is also important that clinicians understand the values underlying the setting and assess whether these values coincide with their own. For example, psychologists who do not believe in aversion therapy, capital punishment, or electroconvulsive therapy may come into conflict while working in certain settings. Psychologists thus should clearly understand how the information they give their referral source will be used. It is essential for them to appreciate that they have a significant responsibility, since decisions made regarding their clients, which are often based on assessment results, can frequently be major changing points in a client's life. If the possibility exists for the information to be used in a manner that will conflict with the clinician's value system, then he or she should reconsider, clarify, or possibly change his or her relationship to the referral setting.

A final point is that clinicians should not allow themselves to be placed into the role of a "testing technician" or psychometrist. This role ultimately does a disservice to the client, the practitioner, and the profession. Clinicians should not merely administer, score, and interpret tests, but should also understand the total referral context in its broadest sense. This means they also take on the role of an expert who can integrate data from a variety of sources. Tests, by themselves, are limited in that they are not flexible or sophisticated enough to address themselves to complex referral questions. Levine (1981) writes:

> [The formal research on test validity is] not immediately relevant to the practical use of psychological tests. The question of the value of tests becomes not "Does this test correlate with a criterion?" or "Does the test accord with a nomological net?" but rather "Does the use of the test improve the success of the decision making process?" by making it either more efficient, less costly, more accurate, more rational, or more relevant. (p. 292)

All of these concerns are consistent with the emphasis on an examiner fulfilling the role of an expert clinician performing psychological assessment rather than a psychometrist acting as a technician.

THE ETHICAL PRACTICE OF ASSESSMENT

During the approximately 80 years that psychologists have been conducting formal assessment, a number of ethical guidelines have gradually evolved to ensure that appropriate professional relationships and procedures are developed and maintained. These guidelines have largely evolved through careful considerations of what constitutes ideal practice. Many of these considerations have been highlighted and refined due to difficulties surrounding assessment procedures. Criticism has been directed at the use of tests in inappropriate contexts, cultural bias, invasion of privacy, and the continued use of tests that are inadequately validated. This has resulted in restrictions on the use of certain tests, greater clarification within the profession regarding ethical standards, and increased skepticism from the public. To deal with these potential difficulties as well as conduct useful and accurate assessments, clinicians need to be aware of the ethical use of assessment tools. The American Psychological Association (APA) and other professional groups have published guidelines for examiners in their *Standards for Educational and Psychological Tests* (1985), *Ethical Principles of Psychologists and Code of Conduct* (1992), and *Guidelines for Computer-Based Test Interpretations* (APA, 1986). The following section outlines the most important of these guidelines along with additional related issues.

Developing a Professional Relationship

Assessment should only be conducted within the context of a clearly defined professional relationship. This means that the nature, purpose, and conditions of the relationship are discussed and agreed upon. Usually, the clinician provides relevant information, which is then followed by the client's signed consent. Information conveyed to the client usually relates to the type and length of assessment, alternative procedures, details relating to appointments, the nature and limits of confidentiality, financial requirements, and additional general information that might be relevant to the unique context of an assessment (see Handelsman & Galvin, 1988 and Zuckerman & Guyett, 1992 for specific guidelines, formats, and forms for informed consent).

An important area to be aware of is the impact the quality of the relationship can have on both assessment results as well as the overall working relationship. It is the examiner's responsibility to recognize the possible influences he or she may exert on the client and to optimize the level of rapport. For example, enhanced rapport with older children (but not younger ones) involving verbal reinforcement and friendly conversation has been shown to increase WISC-R scores by an average of 13 IQ points compared with an administration involving more neutral interactions (Feldman & Sullivan, 1971). This is a difference of nearly one full standard deviation. It has also been found that mildly disapproving comments such as "I thought you could do better than that" resulted in significantly lowered performance when compared with either neutral or approving ones (Witmer, Bornstein, & Dunham, 1971). In a review of 22 studies, Fuchs and Fuchs (1986) concluded that, on the average, IQ scores were four points higher when the examiner was familiar with the child being examined than when he or she was unfamiliar with the child. This trend was particularly pronounced for lower socioeconomic status children. Whereas there is little evidence (Lefkowitz & Fraser, 1980; Sattler, 1973a, 1973b, 1988; Sattler & Gwynne, 1982) to support the belief that African American students have lower performance when tested by European American examiners, it has been suggested that African American students are more responsive to tangible reinforcers (money, candy) than European American students, who generally respond better to verbal reinforcement (Schultz & Sherman, 1976). However, in a later study, Terrell, Taylor, and Terrell (1978) demonstrated that the main factor was the cultural relevance of the response. They found a remarkable 17.6 point increase in IQ scores when African American students were encouraged by African American examiners with culturally relevant comments such as "nice job, blood" or "good work, little brother." Thus the rapport and feedback, especially if that feedback is culturally relevant, can significantly improve test performance. As a result, the feedback and level of rapport should, as much as possible, be held constant from one test administration to the next.

A variable extensively investigated by Rosenthal and his colleagues is that a researcher/examiner's expectations can influence another person's level of performance (Rosenthal, 1966). This has been demonstrated with humans as well as laboratory rats. For example, when an experimenter was told to expect better performances from rats who were randomly selected from the same litter as "maze bright" (compared with "maze dull"), the descriptions of the rats' performance given by the experimenter conformed to the experimenter's expectations (Rosenthal & Fode, 1963). Despite criticisms that have been leveled at his studies and the finding that the magnitude of the effect was not as large as originally believed (Barber & Silver, 1968; Elashoff & Snow, 1971; Thorndike, 1968), Rosenthal maintains that an expectancy effect exists in some situations and suggests that the mechanisms are through minute nonverbal behaviors (Cooper & Rosenthal, 1980). He maintains that the typical effects on an individual's performance are usually small and subtle, and occur in some situations but not others. The obvious implication for clinicians is that they should continually question themselves regarding their expectations of clients and check to see whether they may in some way be communicating these expectations to their clients in a manner which confounds the results.

An additional factor that may affect the nature of the relationship between the client and the examiner is the client's relative emotional state. It is particularly important to assess the degree of the client's motivation and his or her overall level of anxiety. There may be times in which it would be advisable to discontinue testing because situational emotional states may significantly influence the results of the tests. At the very least, examiners should consider the possible effects of emotional factors and incorporate these into their interpretations. For example, it might be necessary to increase the estimate of a client's optimal intellectual functioning if the client was extremely anxious during administration of an intelligence test.

A final consideration, which can potentially confound both the administration and more commonly the scoring of responses, is the degree to which the examiner likes the client and perceives him or her as warm and friendly. Several studies (Sattler, Hillix, & Neher, 1970; Sattler & Winget, 1970) have indicated that the more the examiner likes the client, the more likely he or she will be to score an ambiguous response in a direction favorable to the client. Higher scores can occur even on items in which the responses are not ambiguous (Donahue & Sattler, 1971; Egeland, 1969; Simon, 1969). Thus, "hard" scoring, as opposed to more lenient scoring, can occur at least in part due to the degree of subjective liking the examiner feels toward the client. Again, examiners should continually check themselves to assess whether their relationship with the client is interfering with the objectivity of the test administration and scoring.

Invasion of Privacy

One of the main difficulties examinees can encounter in relation to psychological tests is that the examiner might discover aspects of the client that he or she would rather keep secret. Also of concern is that this information may be used in ways that are not in the best interest of the client. The Office of Science and Technology (1967), in a report entitled *Privacy and Behavioral Research,* has defined privacy as "the right of the individual to decide for him/herself how much he will share with others his thoughts, feelings, and facts of his personal life" (p. 2). This right is considered to be "essential to insure dignity and freedom of self determination" (p. 2). The invasion of privacy issue usually becomes most controversial with personality tests since items relating to motivational, emotional, and attitudinal traits are sometimes disguised. Thus, persons may unknowingly reveal characteristics about themselves that they would rather keep private. Similarly, many persons consider their IQ scores to be highly personal.

Public concern over this issue culminated in an investigation by the Senate Subcommittee on Constitutional Rights and the House Subcommittee on Invasion of Privacy. Neither of these investigations found evidence of deliberate or widespread misuse of psychological tests (Brayfield, 1965). Dahlstrom (1969) has argued that public concern over the invasion of privacy is based on two basic issues. The first is that tests have been oversold to the public, with a resulting exaggeration of their scope and accuracy. The public is usually not aware of the limitations of test data and may often feel that tests are more capable of discovering hidden information than they actually are. The second misconception is that it is not necessarily wrong to obtain information about persons that they either are unaware of themselves or would rather keep private. The more important issue is the use to which the information will be put. Furthermore, the person who controls where or how this information will be used is generally the client. The ethical code of the APA (1992) specifically states that information derived by a psychologist from any source can be released only with the permission of the client. Although there may be exceptions regarding the rights of minors, or when clients are a danger to themselves or others, the ability to control the information is usually clearly defined as being held by the client. Thus, the public is often uneducated regarding its rights and typically underestimates the power it has in determining how the test data will be used.

Despite ethical guidelines relating to invasion of privacy, dilemmas sometimes arise. For example, during personnel selection, applicants may feel pressured into revealing personal information on tests because they aspire to a certain position. Also, applicants may unknowingly reveal information due to subtle, nonobvious test questions, and, perhaps more important, they have no control over the inferences that examiners will make about the test data. Lovell (1967), in referring to the function of tests in personnel selection, argues that they are unacceptable based on ethical, scientific, and community service reasons. He states that, ethically, psychological tests often have no place in a free society, scientifically they do not have adequate validity for special institutional settings, and in the long run, they do not serve the public's best interests. However, if a position requires careful screening and if serious negative consequences may result from poor selection, then it is necessary to evaluate an individual as closely as possible. Thus, the use of testing for personnel in the police, delicate military positions, or important public duty overseas may warrant careful testing.

In a clinical setting, obtaining personal information regarding clients usually does not present problems. The agreement that the information will be used to help clients develop new insights and change their behavior is generally clear and straightforward. However, should legal difficulties arise relating to such areas as child abuse, involuntary confinement, or situations in which clients may be a danger to themselves or others, then ethical questions often arise. Usually, there are general guidelines regarding the manner and extent to which information should be disclosed. These are included in the APA's *Ethical Principles of Psychologists and Code of Conduct* (1992), and test users are encouraged to familiarize themselves with these guidelines.

Adequate handling of the issue of an individual's right to privacy involves both a clear explanation of the relevance of the testing and obtaining informed consent. Examiners should always have a clear conception of the specific reasons for giving a test. Thus, if personnel are being selected based on their mechanical abilities, then tests measuring such areas as general maladjustment should not ordinarily be administered. Examiners must continually evaluate whether a test, or series of tests, is valid for a particular purpose, and whether each set of scores has been properly interpreted in relation to a particular context. Furthermore, the general rationale for test selection should be provided in clear, straightforward language that can be understood by the client. Informed consent involves communicating not only the rationale for testing, but also the kinds of data obtained and the possible uses of the data. This does not mean the client should be shown the specific test subscales themselves beforehand, but rather that the nature and intent of the test should be described in a general way. For example, if a client is told that a scale measures "sociability," this foreknowledge might alter the test's validity in that the client may answer questions based on popular, but quite possibly erroneous, stereotypes. Introducing the test format and intent in a simple, respectful, and forthright manner will significantly reduce the chance that the client will perceive the testing situation as an invasion of privacy.

Inviolacy

Whereas concerns about invasion of privacy relate to the discovery and misuse of information that clients would rather keep secret, inviolacy involves the actual negative feelings created when clients are confronted with the test or test situation. Inviolacy is particularly relevant when clients are requested to discuss information they would rather not think about. For example, the MMPI contains questions about many ordinarily taboo topics relating to sexual practices, toilet behavior, bodily functions, and personal beliefs about human nature. Such questions may produce anxiety by making the examinees more aware of deviant thoughts or repressed unpleasant memories. Many individuals obtain a certain degree of security and comfort by staying within familiar realms of thought. Even to be asked questions that may indicate the existence of unusual alternatives can serve as an anxiety-provoking challenge to personal rules and norms. This problem is somewhat related to the issue of invasion of privacy and it, too, requires one-to-one sensitivity as well as providing clear and accurate information about the assessment procedure.

Labeling and Restriction of Freedom

When individuals are given a medical diagnosis for physical ailments, the social stigmata are usually relatively mild. In contrast are the potentially damaging consequences of many psychiatric diagnoses. A major danger is the possibility of creating a self-fulfilling prophecy based on the expected roles associated with a specific label. Many of these expectations are communicated nonverbally and are typically beyond a person's immediate awareness (Cooper & Rosenthal, 1980; Rosenthal, 1966). Other self-fulfilling prophecies may be less subtle; for example, the person who is labeled as a chronic schizophrenic is therefore only given minimal treatment because chronic schizophrenics rarely respond and then does not improve perhaps mainly because of having received suboptimal treatment. Another negative consequence of labeling is the social stigma attached to different disorders. Thus, largely due to the public's misconceptions of such terms as schizophrenia, labeled individuals may be socially avoided.

Just as labels imposed by others can have negative consequences, self-acceptance of labels can likewise be detrimental. Clients may use their label to excuse or deny responsibility for their behavior. This is congruent with the medical model, which usually assumes that a "sick" person is the victim of an "invading disorder." Thus, in our society, "sick" persons are not considered to be responsible for their disorders. However, the acceptance of this model for behavioral problems may perpetuate behavioral disorders because persons see themselves as helpless, passive victims under the power of mental health "helpers" (Szasz, 1987). This sense of helplessness may serve to lower their ability to deal effectively with new stress. In contrast to this is the belief that clients require an increased sense of responsibility for their lives and actions to effectively change their behavior.

A final difficulty associated with labeling is that it may unnecessarily impose limitations on either an individual or a system by restricting progress and creativity. For example, an organization may conduct a study to determine the type of person who has been successful at a particular type of job and may then develop future selection criteria based on this study. This can result in the future selection of relatively homogeneous employees, which in turn could prevent the organization from changing and progressing. There may be a narrowing of the "talent pool," in which people with new and different ideas are never given a chance. In other words, what has been labeled as adaptive in the past may not be adaptive in the future. One alternative to this predicament is to look at future trends and develop selection criteria based on these trends. Furthermore, diversity might be incorporated into an organization so that different but compatible types can be selected to work on similar projects. Thus, clinicians should be sensitive to the potential negative impact resulting from labeling by outside sources or by self-labeling, as well as to the possible limiting effects that labeling might have.

Competent Use of Assessment Instruments

To correctly administer and interpret psychological tests, an examiner must have proper training, which generally includes adequate graduate course work, combined with lengthy supervised experience. Clinicians should have a knowledge of tests and test limitations, and should be willing to accept responsibility for competent test use. Intensive training is particularly important for individually administered intelligence tests and for the majority of personality tests. Students who are taking or administering tests as part of a class requirement are not adequately trained to administer and interpret tests professionally. Thus, test results obtained by students have questionable validity, and they should clearly inform their subjects that the purpose of their testing is for training purposes only.

In addition to the preceding general guidelines for training, examiners should also acquire a number of specific skills (see Moreland, Eyde, Robertson, Primoff, & Most,

1995). These include the ability to evaluate the technical strengths and limitations of a test, the selection of appropriate tests, and a knowledge of issues relating to the test's reliability and validity. Examiners need to be aware of the material in the test manual as well as relevant research both on the variable the test is measuring and the status of the test since its publication. This is particularly important with regard to newly developed subgroup norms and possible changes in the meaning of scales as a result of further research. Once examiners evaluate the test itself, they must also be able to evaluate whether the purpose and context for which they would like to use it are appropriate. Sometimes an otherwise valid test can be used for purposes it was not intended for, resulting in either invalid or useless inferences based on the test data. Examiners must also be continually aware of, and sensitive to, conditions affecting the examinee's performance. These conditions may include expectations on the part of the examiner, minor variations from the standardized instructions, degree of rapport, mood of the examinee, or timing of the test administration in relation to an examinee's life changes. To help develop accurate conclusions, examiners should have a general knowledge of human behavior. Particularly relevant areas include personality theory, abnormal psychology, and the psychology of adjustment. Furthermore, interpretations should only be made after evaluating other relevant information beyond the mere test scores. A final consideration is that, if interns or technicians are administering the tests, then an adequately trained psychologist should be available as a consultant or supervisor.

Specific data-based guidelines for test user qualifications have been developed by relevant professional organizations (American Psychological Association, 1988; Moreland et al., 1995) and these guidelines have been incorporated by most organizations selling psychological tests. Qualification forms request information regarding the purpose for using tests (counseling, research, personnel selection), area of professional expertise (marriage and family, social work, school), level of training (degrees, licenses), specific courses taken (descriptive statistics, career assessment), and quality control over test use (test security, appropriate tailoring of interpretations). Persons completing the forms certify that they possess appropriate training and competencies and agree to adhere to ethical guidelines and legal regulations regarding test use.

In addition to being appropriately trained to use tests themselves, psychologists should not promote the use of psychological techniques by persons who are not qualified. This does not mean that all psychological tests should be used exclusively by psychologists since some tests are available to other professionals. However, psychologists should be generally aware which tests require a high level of training (i.e., individually administered IQ tests) and those which are more generally available.

One of the important aspects of competent test use is that the tests should only be used for the purposes they were designed for. Typically, tests being extended beyond what they were designed for has been done in good faith and with good intentions. For example, an examiner might use a TAT or Rorschach as the primary means of inferring an individual's IQ. Similarly, the MMPI, which was designed to assess the extent of psychopathology in an individual, might be inappropriately used to assess a normal person's level of functioning. Although some conclusions can be drawn from the MMPI relating to certain aspects of a normal person's functioning, or although IQ estimates based on projectives can be made, they should be considered extremely tentative. These tests were not designed for these purposes and, as a result, such inferences do not represent their strengths. A somewhat more serious misuse can occur when a test such as the MMPI is used to screen applicants for some types of personnel selection. Results from MMPI type tests are likely to be irrelevant for assessing most job-related skills. Of equal importance is that the information derived from the MMPI is typically of a highly personal nature and, if used in many types of personnel selection, is likely to represent an invasion of privacy.

Interpretation and Use of Test Results

Interpreting test results should never be considered a simple, mechanical procedure. Accurate interpretation means not simply using norms and cuttoff scores, but also taking into consideration unique characteristics of the person combined with relevant aspects of the test itself. For example, a high level of situational anxiety on the part of the examinee might have resulted in certain test results being compromised or exaggerated. Another issue might arise if there is little resemblance between the person being examined and the norms developed for the tests. If there are significant reservations regarding the test interpretation, this should be communicated usually in the psychological report itself.

A further issue is that test norms and stimulus materials eventually become outdated. As a result, interpretations based on these tests may become inaccurate. This means that clinicians need to stay current on emerging research and new versions of tests. A rule of thumb is that if a clinician has not updated his or her test knowledge in the past 10 years, they are probably not practicing competently.

Part of remaining current means that psychologists should select their testing instruments as well as any scoring and interpretation services based on evidence related to the validity of the programs or tests. Part of this will require a knowledge of the context of the situation. A well-validated test might have been found to be quite valid in one context or population but not for another. Another issue that might compromise the validity of test results is conversion to a computerized administration (Faust & Ziskin, 1989). Research should be available to document that different scores are not achieved as a result of the computerized administration (Watson, Thomas, & Anderson, 1991). Ultimately, any interpretations and recommendations regarding a client are the responsibility of the clinician. Placing a signature on a report means that the clinician is taking responsibility for the contents of the report. Indeed, an important difference between an actuarial formula or automated report and a practitioner is that the practitioner ultimately will be held accountable.

Communicating Test Results

Psychologists should ordinarily give feedback to the client and referral source regarding the results of assessment (see Pope, 1992 for specific guidelines and responsibilities). If the psychologist is not the person giving the feedback, then this should be agreed on in advance and the psychologist should ensure that the person providing the feedback presents the information in a clear, competent manner. Unless the results are communicated effectively, the purpose of the assessment is likely to not be achieved. This involves understanding the needs and vocabulary of the referral source, client, and other persons who may be affected by the test results such as parents or teachers. Initially, there should be a clear exploration of the rationale for testing and the nature of the tests being administered. This may include the general type of conclusions that will be drawn, the limitations of the test, and common misconceptions surrounding the test or test variable. If a child is being tested in an educational setting, a meeting should be arranged with the school psychologist, parents, teacher, and other relevant persons. Such an approach is crucial for IQ tests, which are more likely to be misinterpreted, than for achievement tests. Feedback of test results should be given in terms that are clear and understandable to the receiver. Descriptions are generally most meaningful when performance levels are clearly indicated along with behavioral references (Ownby, 1987). For example, in giving IQ results to parents, it will only be minimally relevant to say that their child has an IQ of 130 with relative strengths in spatial organization, even though this may be appropriate language for a formal psychological evaluation. A more effective description might be that their child is currently functioning in the top 2% when compared with his or her peers and is particularly good at organizing nonverbal material such as piecing together puzzles, putting together a bicycle, or building a playhouse.

In providing effective feedback, the clinician should also consider the personal characteristics of the receiver, such as his or her general educational level, relative knowledge regarding psychological testing, and possible emotional response to the information. The emotional reaction is especially important when a client is learning about his or her personal strengths or shortcomings. Facilities should be available for additional counseling, if needed. If properly given, feedback is not merely informative but can actually serve to reduce symptomatic distress and enhance self-esteem (Finn & Tonsager, 1992). Thus, providing feedback can actually be part of the intervention process itself. Since psychological assessment is often requested as an aid in making important life decisions, the potential impact of the information should not be underestimated. Clinicians are usually in positions of power and with that comes responsibility in that the information that clients receive and the decisions they make based on this information will often be with them for many years.

Maintenance of Test Security

If test materials were widely available, it would be easy for persons to review the tests, learn the answers, and respond according to the impression they would like to make. Thus the materials would lose their validity. This means that psychologists should make all reasonable efforts to ensure that test materials are secure. Specifically, all tests should be kept locked in a secure place and no untrained persons should be allowed to review them. Any copyrighted material should not be photoduplicated. In addition, raw data from tests should not ordinarily be released to clients or other persons who may misinterpret them. However, clients have a right to the reports themselves should they request them. They also have the right to have the information released to a person they designate but such a request should be in writing (see Zuckerman & Guyett, 1992, for forms and guidelines).

Sometimes in legal contexts, the court or the opposing council may wish to see either raw data or the actual test materials. Under these conditions, the court should be informed that ethical guidelines as well as agreements made with the test distributor require that this information not be released to untrained persons. An acceptable alternative would be for the psychologist to designate a person with appropriate training to whom the information might be given who could then explain the data or describe the test material (Tranel, 1994).

TEST BIAS AND USE WITH MINORITY GROUPS

Bias in testing refers to the presence of systematic error in the measurement of certain factors (e.g., academic potential, intelligence, psychopathology) among certain individuals or groups (see Suzuki, Meller, & Ponterotto, 1996). The possible presence of bias toward minority groups has resulted in one of the most controversial issues in psychological testing. More specifically, critics believe that psychological tests are heavily biased in favor, and reflect the values of, European American, middle-class society. They argue that such tests cannot adequately assess intelligence or personality when applied to minority groups. Whereas the greatest controversy has arisen from the use of intelligence tests, the presence of cultural bias is also relevant in the use of personality testing. For example, some populations of African Americans have usually scored significantly higher than European Americans on MMPI scales F, 8, and 9 (Greene, 1980; Pritchard & Rosenblatt, 1980), and controversy has arisen over whether interpretations based on these elevations are accurate (Greene, 1987, 1991; Green & Kelly, 1988; Timbrook & Graham, 1994). Thus, the possibility exists that personality tests, such as the MMPI, may also have discriminatory bias.

The basic issue lies in determining whether tests are as valid for minority groups as for nonminorities. Undoubtedly, differences exist; however, the meaning that can be attributed to these differences has been strongly debated. A further question lies in identifying the cause of these differences. Some theorists believe that the differences are primarily the result of environmental factors (Kamin, 1974; Rosenthal & Jacobson, 1968), whereas others stress hereditary determination (Jensen, 1969, 1972; Rushton, 1994). Even though the debate is far from resolved, guidelines have been established by the Equal Employment Opportunity Commission (EEOC) for the use of psychological tests with minority groups in educational and industrial settings. The basic premise is that a screening device (psychological test) can have an adverse impact if it screens out a proportionally larger number of minorities than nonminorities. Furthermore, it is the responsibility of the employer to demonstrate that the procedure produces valid inferences for the specific purposes for which the employer would like to use it. If an industrial or educational organization does not follow the guidelines as defined by the EEOC (1978), the Office of Federal Contract Compliance has the direct power to cancel any government contract that the institution might have.

The degree of test validity when used with ethnic minorities is of central importance to the legal issues, research data, and guidelines for the individual clinician. If investigated from the perspective of content validity, popular individual intelligence tests appear on the surface to be culturally biased. This conclusion is based largely on early intuitive observations that many African American children and other minorities usually do not have the opportunity to learn the types of material contained in many of the test items (Kagan, Moss, & Siegel, 1963; Lesser, Fifer, & Clark, 1965). Thus, their lower scores may represent not a lack of intelligence, but merely a lack of familiarity with European American, middle-class culture. Critics of the tests point out that it would clearly be unfair to assess a European American's intelligence based on whether he or she knows what the "funky chicken" is or what "blood" means, or for that matter, to ask him or her the meaning of British terms such as "shilling" or "lorrie." Low scores would simply measure an individual's relative unfamiliarity with a specific culture rather than his or her specific mental strengths. If one uses this reasoning, many IQ and aptitude tests may appear on the surface to be culturally biased. However, studies in which researchers, to the best of their ability, eliminated biased test items or items that statistically discriminate between minorities and nonminorities, have not been successful in altering overall test scores. In a representative study, 27 items were removed from the Scholastic Aptitude Test (SAT) that consistently differentiated minorities from nonminorities. This did little to change either the test takers' individual scores, or the differences between the two groups (Flaugher & Schrader, 1978). Thus, the popular belief, based on a superficial appraisal of many psychological tests that biased items are responsible for test differences, does not appear to be supported by research.

Although test differences between minority and nonminority groups have frequently been found, the meaning and causes of these differences is open to debate. It has been demonstrated that African Americans consistently score lower than European Americans on the WISC-R (Jensen & Reynolds, 1982; Neisser et al., 1996), WAIS-R (Kaufman, McLean, & Reynolds, 1988), and SAT (Temp, 1971) although these differences may be decreasing (Vincent, 1991). However, when African Americans and European Americans of equal socioeconomic status were compared, the differences in IQ scores were greatly reduced (Loehelin, 1989). Likewise, the 5 T-score point differences found on MMPI scales F, 8, and 9 were also decreased or even insignificant when African Americans and European Americans were comparable in age, education, and other relevant demographic characteristics (Dahlstrom, Lachar, & Dahlstrom, 1986; Timbrook & Graham, 1994). This suggests that many differences in test scores may be primarily due more to factors such as socioeconomic status rather than to ethnicity.

Another consideration is the adequacy of the predictive validity of various tests when used with minority groups. Since one of the main purposes of these tests is to predict later performance, it is essential to evaluate the extent to which the scores in fact adequately predict such areas as a minority's performance in college. A representative group of studies indicates that the SAT actually overpredicts how well minorities will perform in college (Jensen, 1984; Kallingal, 1971; Pfeifer & Sedlacek, 1971; Reynolds, 1986). Furthermore, both the WISC and the WISC-R are equally as effective in predicting the academic achievement of both African Americans and European Americans in primary and secondary school (Neisser et al., 1996; Reynolds & Hartlage, 1979). In actually working with minority groups, however, it is important to become familiar with different subgroup norms and to know the confidence with which predictions can be made based on the scores of these subgroups.

The preceding discussion of content and predictive validity represents the traditional defense of psychological tests. For many individuals, these defenses are still not sufficient. The two main choices, then, are either to outlaw all psychological tests for minority groups or to develop more appropriate psychological assessment approaches. A half-serious attempt toward a more appropriate measuring device is the Dove Counterbalance General Intelligence Test (Dove, 1968). It has since become referred to as the "Chitling Test" and includes items relevant for a African American inner-city culture, such as "a handkerchief head" is: (a) a cool cat, (b) a porter, (c) an Uncle Tom, (d) a haddi, (e) a preacher. A similar attempt by Williams (1974) is his development of the Black Intelligence Test of Cultural Homogeneity (BITCH). Although neither test has been standardized and validated, both contain vocabulary words and experiences with which most African American children would be familiar but with which European American children would be unfamiliar.

A number of additional tests have been developed with the partial intent of using them in the assessment of ethnic minorities. These tend to emphasize nonverbal tasks and include the Leiter International Performance Scale, Culture Fair Intelligence Test, Raven's Progressive Matrices, and the Goodenough-Harris Drawing Test. Available research indicates that most of these "culture-fair" tests do not show greater validity for minorities as compared with nonminorities (Sattler, 1992). One relatively recent development that does show good potential for the assessment of minorities is the Kaufman Assessment Battery for Children (K-ABC; Kaufman & Kaufman, 1983). Mean IQ scores for European Americans, African Americans, and Hispanics are relatively close, and there is some evidence that reliability and concurrent validity is comparable for different ethnic populations (Kaufman & Kaufman, 1983; Xitao, Willson, & Reynolds, 1995). The test is based on empirical developments in cognitive psychology and has a good record of reliability and validity.

The System of Multicultural Pluralistic Assessment (SOMPA; Mercer, 1979; Mercer & Lewis, 1978) provides an alternative and more complex method of evaluating minorities by using traditional assessment tools but correcting the bias involved with these tools. The assumption underlying this approach is that all cultural groups have the same average potential and any adequate assessment device should be able to accurately test this potential for a particular individual. One of its primary goals is to differentiate between members of minorities who have been incorrectly labeled mentally retarded due to test bias and those who are in fact mentally retarded. The SOMPA method involves medical, social system, and pluralistic components. The "medical component" assesses whether students have any physical disorders that may be interfering with their level of performance. This assessment includes tests of hearing, vision, and motor function. The rationale for the medically oriented assessment is that children from lower socioeconomic groups are both more likely to have medical difficulties, due to their harsher environment, and less likely to obtain treatment for these difficulties, due to financial constraints. The "social system" component uses traditional assessment tools, such as the WISC-R, to measure whether the student is functioning at a level consistent with social norms. The problem with this component is that it provides a narrow definition of successful functioning because the criteria are based on the dominant culture's definition of success. Thus, the final "pluralistic" component attempts to correct for the narrow approach in the social system component by evaluating an individual's test scores against a culturally similar group, thereby it is hoped adjusting for such variables as socioeconomic status and cultural background. Thus, comparisons are made between performances within a specific subgroup, rather than with the performance, values, and criteria of the dominant culture. The resulting adjusted scores are referred to as an individual's Estimated Learning Potentials (ELPs).

SOMPA has had many critics, most of whom argue that the criterion for judging it should be the adequacy with which it can predict school performance (Brown, 1979; Johnson & Danley, 1981; Oakland, 1980). Studies indicate that, whereas WISC-R scores correlate at a level of .60 with grade point average, SOMPA scores have a correlation of only .40 (Oakland, 1980). ELPs have also been found to have lower correlations with other forms of achievement than traditional IQ measures (Wurtz, Sewell, & Manni, 1985), and it is difficult to relate ELP results to specific applications in the classroom (Brooks & Hosie, 1984). Mercer refutes these criticisms by pointing out that her intent was not so much to predict school performance, as to identify students who have been falsely classified as mentally retarded. Proponents of SOMPA have been so persuasive that it has been adopted by several states. Many people hoped that SOMPA would create more accurate labeling of mentally retarded students. However, students who are now labeled "normal" through the SOMPA approach, but were previously labeled "mentally retarded" or "learning disabled," might still require some additional form of special instruction. In fact, reclassifying students as normal through a calculation of ELPs may bar access of these students from special educational services. In addition, studies indicate that a high proportion of students classified as mentally retarded using the SOMPA are still likely to be minorities (Heflinger, Cook, & Thackrey, 1987) and that scores may be biased in favor of urban children, regardless of their ethnicity (Taylor, Sternberg, & Partenio, 1986). Due to the above difficulties, SOMPA has probably not achieved its goal of equalizing educational opportunities for ethnic minority children, and thus should be used with caution for individual educational decision making.

As is true for ability tests and tests of scholastic aptitude, personality tests also have the potential to be biased. The main research in this area has been performed on the MMPI and has consistently indicated that minority groups do score differently than nonminorities. In general, African Americans scored higher than European Americans on scales F, 8, and 9 (Green & Kelly, 1988; Gynther & Green, 1980), but this pattern was not consistent across all populations (Greene, 1987, 1991). Even if consistent score differences were found, this does not mean these differences will be of sufficient magnitude to alter a clinician's interpretations, nor does it mean that predictions based on empirical criteria will be different. Studies using empirical criteria for prediction indicate that the MMPI does not result in greater descriptive accuracy for European Americans than African Americans (Elion & Megargee, 1975; Green & Kelly, 1988). In a review of MMPI performance for Asian Americans, African Americans, Hispanics, and Native Americans, Greene (1987) concluded that "the failure to find a consistent pattern of scale differences between any two ethnic groups in any publication suggests that it is premature to begin to develop new norms for ethnic groups" (p. 509). What seems to affect MMPI profiles more than ethnicity are moderator variables such as socioeconomic status, intelligence, and education. Furthermore, the existing differences may be due to true differences in behavior and personality caused by the greater stresses often encountered by minorities. Graham (1987) suggests that, when MMPI scores are deviant, the clinician should tentatively accept these scores but make special efforts to explore the person's life situation and level of adjustment, and integrate this information with the test scores.

From this discussion, it should be obvious that the problems are both complicated and far from being resolved. Several general solutions have been suggested (see Suzuki, Meller, & Ponterotto, 1996). These include improving selection devices, developing different evaluation criteria, and changing social environments. Improving the use of selection devices would involve paying continual attention to, and obtaining greater knowledge of, the meaning of different scores for different subgroups. This may include tailoring specific test scores to the types of decisions individuals may make in their lives. For example, African Americans typically achieve scores equal to European Americans on the verbal portion of the SAT, but their average scores on math are lower. This suggests that African American students have a greater development in their verbal skills than in their quantitative ones. This conclusion is further reflected by, and consistent with, the fact that African Americans are more likely to choose verbally oriented majors in college. Based on this, it may be more accurate to predict the future college performances of African Americans from their SAT verbal scores than their SAT math scores.

Another approach toward solving the problem of potential test bias is to develop different and more adequate criterion measures. For example, it has been found that WISC-R scores correlate highly with teacher/classroom ratings for nonminorities, but not for minorities (Goldman & Hartig, 1976). This indicates that using teacher/classroom ratings as a criterion of academic achievement is not appropriate for minorities. In contrast, the WISC-R accurately predicts grade point average for both minorities and nonminorities, which suggests that grade point average is a better criterion measure. Perhaps of greater relevance is the actual prediction of an individual's career performance. Current test predictors for graduate schools (Law School Aptitude Test, Medical School Aptitude Test, etc.) give generally satisfactory predictions for later academic performance, but do not predict whether an individual will be, for example, a good attorney or physician. In fact, it has been shown that medical school grades themselves are not associated with later success as a physician (Loughmiller, Ellison, Taylor, & Price, 1970). This issue may become particularly pronounced in comparing the relative effectiveness of minorities and nonminorities when working in different cultural settings. For example, if a European American and a Hispanic attorney are both placed in settings in which they will be working with Hispanics, it is probable that the Hispanic attorney would be more effective because he or she will have increased rapport and greater familiarity with the language and values of his or her clientele.

Another solution involves changing the social environment. Part of the rationale for emphasizing this approach is the belief held by many researchers that the differences in test scores between minorities and nonminorities are not due to test bias but rather because tests accurately reflect the effects of an unequal environment and unequal opportunities (Flaugher, 1978; Green, 1978). Even though, in some situations, different minority norms and additional predictive studies on minority populations are necessary, the literature suggests that tests are not as biased as they have been accused of being. Removal of seemingly biased or discriminating SAT items still results in the same mean scores, the WISC-R provides accurate predictions of grade point average for both minorities and nonminorities, and the MMPI is usually equally as accurate for making behavioral predictions for African Americans as for European Americans. Tests themselves are not the problem but merely the means of establishing that, often, inequalities exist between ethnic groups. The goal should be to change unequal environments that can ideally increase a population's skills as measured by current tests of aptitude, IQ, and achievement. Whereas improving selection devices and developing different criterion measures are still important, future efforts should also stress more equal access to educational and career opportunities.

All of these solutions can give some direction to the profession in general, but it is the responsibility of individual clinicians to keep abreast of research relating to minority groups and to incorporate this knowledge into the interpretations they make of test scores. As Mercer (1979) has emphasized, test scores are neither valid nor invalid, but inferences by clinicians based on these scores are.

SELECTING PSYCHOLOGICAL TESTS

The most important factor in test selection is the extent to which the test is useful in answering the referral question. An assessment of neurological patients might use tests sensitive to cerebral deficit, depressed patients might be given the Beck Depression Inventory (Beck, 1967a, 1967b), and pain patients might be given the McGill Pain Questionnaire (Melzack, 1975), MMPI, or Illness Behavior Questionnaire (Pilowski, Spence, Cobb, & Katsikitis, 1984). Another important factor in test selection is a particular practitioner's training, experience, personal preferences, and familiarity with relevant literature. For example, a clinician who has received training in the MMPI might be concerned about its ability to assess personality disorders (Widiger & Frances, 1987) and may rather choose to use an instrument such as the Millon Clinical Multiaxial Inventory (Millon, 1994). Clinicians might also select an instrument because it has practical efficiency in terms of time and economy. Thus, they may wish to use simple behavioral predictions made by the client rather than use more expensive, time consuming, and, quite possibly, less accurate tests (Shrauger & Osberg, 1981). Computer-assisted instruments may also help to lower the costs of assessment primarily by reducing direct practitioner time and achieving greater speed for scoring and hypothesis generation.

The most frequently used assessment techniques are included in the following chapters. Various combinations of these tests typically constitute a core battery used by clinicians. However, it is often necessary to expand such a core battery depending on the specifics of the referral question. Table 2–1 provides a listing of the domain for assessment along with relevant tests. While some of these tests are thoroughly described in specific chapters dedicated to them, some may be relatively unfamiliar and practitioners will need to obtain additional information on them. Various sources are available for finding information about these and other tests. Such sources can provide important information for deciding whether to obtain the tests and incorporate them into a battery. Probably the most useful is the *Mental Measurements Yearbook,* which contains a collection of critical test reviews that include evaluations of the meaning of the available research on each test. The tenth *Mental Measurements Yearbook* was published in 1989 (Conoley & Kramer, 1989) with the eleventh becoming available in 1992 (Kramer & Conoley, 1992). The reviews are available in book form as well as online computer (*Mental Measurement Database*). *Tests in Print IV* (Buros, 1994) is associated with the *Mental Measurements Yearbook* but, rather than focusing on evaluating tests, lists information

Table 2–1.   Assessment instruments relevant for specific response domains

Cognitive Functioning
  General functioning
    Mental Status Examination
    Mini-Mental Status Examination (MMSE)
  Intellectual functioning
    Wechsler Adult Intelligence Scale-Revised
    Wechsler Intelligence Scale for Children-III
    Stanford-Binet (4th ed.)
    Kaufman Assessment Battery for Children
    Woodcock-Johnson Psychoeducational Battery-Revised
  Memory functions
    Wechsler Memory Scale-Revised
    Rey Auditory Verbal Learning Test
    California Verbal Learning Test
    Benton Visual Retention Test
  Visuoconstructive abilities
    Bender Visual Motor Gestalt Test
    Drawing tests
  Content of thought processes
    Thematic Apperception Test
    Children's Apperception Test

Emotional Functioning and Level of Psychopathology
  General patterns and severity
    Minnesota Multiphasic Personality Inventory
    Millon Clinical Multiaxial Inventory
    Millon Adolescent Personality Inventory
    Rorschach
    Symptom Checklist 90-Revised
    Brief Symptom Inventory
    Personality Inventory for Children
  Depression
    Beck Depression Inventory
    Hamilton Rating Scale for Depression
    Children's Depression Inventory
  Anxiety
    State-Trait Anxiety Inventory
    Fear Survey Schedule
    Anxiety Disorders Interview Schedule
  Sexual disturbance
    Derogatis Sexual Functioning Inventory
  Marital/family disturbance
    Dyadic Adjustment Scale
    Family Environment Scale
    Marital Satisfaction Inventory
    Draw-A-Family/Kinetic Family Drawing

(continued)

Table 2–1.   *(continued)*

Interpersonal patterns
  California Psychological Inventory
  Rathus Assertiveness Schedule
  Therapeutic Reactance Scale
General personality measures
  Sixteen Personality Factors
  NEO-PI-R
  Myers Briggs Type Indicator
  Adjective Checklist
  Taylor Johnson Temperament Analysis
  Sentence completion tests
Academic/school adjustment
  Achenbach Child Behavior Checklist
  Vineland Social Maturity Scale
  Connors Behavior Rating Scale
  Kinetic School Drawing
Academic achievement
  Wide Range Achievement Test-III
  Peabody Individual Achievement Test
Adaptive Level
  AAMD Adaptive Behavior Scale
  Vineland Adaptive Behavior Scale
Vocational interests
  Self-Directed Search
  Strong Interest Inventory
  Kuder Occupational Interest Survey
Alcohol abuse
  Michigan Alcoholism Screening Test
  Alcohol Use Inventory
Diagnosis
  Diagnostic Interview Schedule
  Schedule for Affective Disorders and Schizophrenia
  Structured Clinical Interview for DSM
  Structured Interview for DSM Personality Disorders
  Diagnostic Interview for Children and Adolescents
Prognosis and risk
Suicide potential
  Scale of Suicide Ideation
  Beck Hopelessness Scale
Schizophrenia prognosis
  Camberwell Family Interview

on each test such as its title, population it was designed for, available subtests, updating, author(s), and publisher. Similar publications are Sweetland and Keyser's (1991) *Tests: A Comprehensive Reference for Assessment in Psychology, Education, and Business,* which provides descriptive information on over 3,500 tests, and *Test Critiques* (Keyser & Sweetland, 1985), which reviews specific topics related to psychological testing.

Practitioners interested in obtaining information on rating scales and other measures used in clinical practice might consult *Measuring Mental Illness: Psychometric Assessment for Clinicians* (Wetzler, 1989) or *Measures for Clinical Practice: A Sourcebook* (Corcoran & Fischer, 1994). Neuropsychological tests are reviewed in the preceding resources as well as Lezak's (1995) *Neuropsychological Assessment,* Spreen and Strauss's (1991) *A Compendium of Neuropsychological Tests* and specialty journals in neuropsychology particularly *Neuropsychology Review.* A careful review of the information included in these references will frequently answer questions clinicians might have related to a test's psychometric properties, usefulness, appropriateness for different populations, details for purchasing, and strengths and limitations. Most of the questions listed in Table 1–1 (see Chapter 1) can be answered by consulting the preceding resources.

An important and current trend in research and practice on psychological assessment is to use tests to generate a treatment plan (Beutler & Clarkin, 1990; Jongsma & Peterson, 1995; Nezu & Nezu, 1993; Norcross & Beutler, in press). Indeed, a basic objective of psychological assessment is that it should provide useful information regarding the planning, implementation, and evaluation of treatment. With the increased specificity of both treatment and assessment, this goal is becoming possible. For example, oppositional, resistant clients have been found to have optimal treatment outcomes when either self-directed or paradoxical interventions have been used (Beutler, Sandowicz, Fisher, & Albanese, 1996). In addition, a problem's severity has clear implications for the restrictiveness of treatment (inpatient, outpatient) as well as treatment duration and intensity. Thus, clinicians should not select tests based simply on their diagnostic accuracy or psychometric properties, but they should also be concerned with the functional utility of the tests in treatment planning. Accordingly, Chapter 13 presents a systematic, integrated approach to transforming assessment results into a series of clear treatment recommendations.

Two special concerns in selecting tests are faking and the use of short forms. In many situations, clinicians might be concerned that persons will either consciously or unconsciously provide inaccurate responses. Thus, these clinicians may want to be sure to include and pay particular attention to such tests as the MMPI, MCMI, and CPI, which have validity scales incorporated into them. Although controversial, many projective techniques may be resistant to attempts at faking. Concerns regarding the time required for assessment may cause examiners to consider selecting short forms of such instruments as the WAIS-R, WISC-III, or MMPI. Although many short forms for cognitive tests seem sufficiently valid for screening purposes, their use as substitutes for the longer forms is not acceptable (Kaufman, 1990, 1994; Kaufman, Kaufman, Balgopal, & McLean, 1996). Attempts to develop short forms for the longer objective personality tests such as the MMPI have not been found to be successful and have been discouraged by experts in the field (Butcher & Hostetler, 1990; Butcher & Williams, 1992; Smith & McCarthy, 1995).

During the evaluation of single cases, such as in clinical diagnoses and counseling, clinicians do not usually use formal combinations of test scores. Rather, they rely on their past judgment, clinical experience, and theoretical background to interpret and integrate test scores. However, for personnel decisions, academic predictions, and some clinical decisions (recidivism rate, suicide risk), clinicians may be advised to use statistical formulas (Garb, 1994b). The two basic approaches for combining test results are multiple regression equations and multiple cutoff scores. Multiple regression equations are developed by correlating each test or subtest with a criterion. The higher the correlation, the greater the weight in the equation. The correlation of the entire battery with the criterion measure gives an indication of the battery's highest predictive validity. For example, high school achievement can be predicted with the following regression equation, which combines IQ and CPI subtests:

$$\text{Achievement} = .786 + .195 \text{ Responsibility} + .44 \text{ Socialization}$$
$$- 130 \text{ Good Impression} + .19 \text{ Achievement via Conformance}$$
$$+ .179 \text{ Achievement Imagery} + .279 \text{ IQ}$$

This equation raises the correlation with grade point average (GPA) to .68 as compared with .60 when using IQ alone (Megargee, 1972). This correlation indicates that academic achievement is dependent not only on intellectual factors, but also on psychosocial ones, such as responsibility, socialization, achievement imagery, and achievement via conformance, all of which are measured by the CPI. The second strategy, multiple cutoff scores, involves developing an optimum cutoff for each test or subtest. If the person is above a certain specified score (i.e., above the brain damaged or schizophrenic range), then the score can be used to indicate the presence of a certain characteristic. Although not all tests have equations or cutoffs developed for them, the decision to include a test in a battery may in part depend on the presence of such formal extensions of the tests. In addition, many of the computer-assisted interpretive packages use various actuarial formulas (usually in combination with expert interpretations) to develop their interpretations.

COMPUTER-ASSISTED ASSESSMENT

During the past 30 years, computer-assisted assessment has grown exponentially. By 1990, 17% of practicing psychologists frequently used computer-generated narratives with an additional 36% using them on an occasional basis (Piotrowski & Keller, 1989b; Speilberger & Piotrowski, 1990). In excess of 400 software packages are available and listed in such publications as Krug's (1993) *Psychware Sourcebook (4th ed.),* the American Psychological Association's *Computer Use in Psychology: A Directory of Software* (Stoloff & Couch, 1992), and Butcher's (1987) *Computerized Psychological Assessment: A Practitioner's Guide.* It has been estimated that by the year 2001 the vast majority of psychological tests will be automated and many will include such features as speech analyzers, physiological monitoring devices, and verbal and pictorial stimulus presentations. Computing in mental health has included not only computer-assisted assessment but also computer interviews, computerized diagnosis, computer-aided instruction, direct treatment intervention, clinical consultation, and simulated psychiatric interviews (Ager, 1991).

Computer-assisted administration and interpretation in neuropsychology has seen a number of particular advances (see review by Kane & Kay, 1992). Batteries have mainly been developed within large organizational contexts (military, Federal Aviation Authority) and focused on specialized types of problems. For example, the Neurobehavioral Evaluation System is particularly sensitive to the impact of environmental toxins (Groth-Marnat, 1993), COGSCREEN has been used in the selection of airline pilots, and the military's UTCPAB was originally developed to assess the impact of drugs in the workplace. Despite these developments, they currently do not have the extensive validation studies associated with the more traditional tests such as the Halstead Reitan Neuropsychological Test Battery (Reitan & Wolfson, 1993). Although the computer-assisted programs show considerable promise, they are currently not being used nearly as much as the more familar individually administered neuropsychological tests or test batteries (Butler, Retzlaff, & Vanderploeg, 1991; Lezak, 1995).

Computer-assisted assessment has a number of advantages. Computers can save valuable professional time, potentially improve test-retest reliability, reduce possible tester bias, and reduce the cost to the consumer by improving efficiency. Even greater benefits may someday be realized by incorporating more complicated decision rules in interpretation, collecting data on response latency and key pressure, incorporating computer-based models of personality, tailoring future questions to a client based on past responses, and estimating the degree of certainty of various interpretations (Ager, 1991; Butcher, 1987; Yossef, Slutsky, & Butcher, 1989).

Nevertheless, computer-assisted assessment has resulted in considerable controversy within mental health publications (Faust & Ziskin, 1989; Groth-Marnat & Schumaker, 1989; Matarazzo, 1986), the popular media (Hall, 1983), and professional publications outside the mental health area (Groth-Marnat, 1985). A primary issue is untested validity. It has been assumed that, if a paper-and-pencil version of the test is valid, then a computerized version will also have equal validity. However, a computer administration may change the nature of the task and alter a subject's responses to the task, thereby resulting in questionable validity. Even though computer acceptance has been well documented (French & Beaumont, 1987), patients who are given computer administrations may alter their level of truthfulness (Lockshin & Harrison, 1991; Lucas, Mullin, Luna, & McInroy, 1977), and African Americans have been found to score better on computer-administered ability tests (Johnson & Mihal, 1973). Many other studies have suggested equivalence between computer administered and conventionally administered tests (Lee, Moreno, & Sympson, 1986; Lukin, Down, Plake, & Kraft, 1985). Watson, Thomas, and Anderson (1992) concluded their meta-analysis on computerized versus conventional administration of the MMPI by noting that there was usually less that one T score point between the two modes of administration with the greatest difference being 1.33 T scores for the Hysteria scale. Of greater concern is that little consideration has been given to the differences between test validity and either the validity of either individually computer-generated interpretations or computer-generated narrative reports. The studies which have been done have been performed almost exclusively on MMPI-assisted reports. Evaluating computer-generated validity is further complicated by software manuals that typically have not provided enough information to judge the adequacy of their decision rules. One concern is that computer-generated reports might be given more credibility than they deserve due to their objective, scientific appearance (Matarazzo, 1986; Walker & Myrick, 1985). However, current research indicates that whether or not a narrative report is computer- or clinician-generated makes little difference in terms of consumer ratings (Andrews & Gutkin, 1991).

A further concern is that many software packages are available to persons who do not possess appropriate professional qualifications. In some cases, no agreed-on and enforced standards are in place to determine who is a qualified user. Ideally, qualified persons should be those who meet the requirements for using psychological tests in general.

The American Psychological Association (1986) has attempted to clarify these standards in their *Guidelines for Computer-Based Test Interpretation* and "Guidelines for Test User Qualifications" (American Psychological Association, 1988), but Krug's (1993) *Psychware Sourcebook (4th ed.)* indicated that approximately a fifth of the programs could be sold to the general public. The American Psychological Association guidelines specify that users "have an understanding of psychological or educational measurement, validation problems, and test research" and that practitioners "will limit their use of computerized testing to techniques which they are familiar and competent to use" (American Psychological Association, 1986, p. 8). Users should also "be aware of the method used in generating the scores and interpretation and be able to evaluate its applicability to the purpose for which it will be used" (American Psychological Association, 1986, pp. 8–9).

A further problem is that clinicians may subtly be encouraged to take the role of a technician without properly integrating the test results into a client's overall situation. Similarly, a narrative report is unsigned, and therefore the results do not have the same legal and professional accountability that a signature might have. Matarazzo (1986) equates this with a physician randomly selecting another physician from the phone book and accepting an unsigned report of a consultation from this physician. Thus, clinicians need to critically analyze and evaluate the results derived from a narrative report to such an extent that they feel legally and professionally comfortable in signing it. Finally, there are few mechanisms for correcting obsolete software. As a result, incorrect interpretations might continue to be generated indefinitely.

The preceding difficulties associated with computer-assisted instruction suggest a number of guidelines for users (Groth-Marnat & Schumaker, 1989). First, practitioners should not blindly accept computer-based narrative statements, but rather should ensure, to the best of their ability, that the statements are both linked to empirically based research and placed within the context of the unique history and unique situation of the client. Computers have, among other benefits, the strong advantage of offering a wide variety of possible interpretations to the clinician, but these interpretations still need to be critically evaluated. Far greater research needs to be performed on both the meaning of computer-administered test scores and on the narrative interpretations based on these scores. The developers of software should also be encouraged to provide enough information in the manual to allow proper evaluation of the programs and should develop mechanisms to ensure the updating of obsolete programs.

RECOMMENDED READING

Blau, T. (1984). *The psychologist as expert witness.* New York: Wiley. (new edition expected in 1997/1998)

Groth-Marnat, G., & Schumaker, J. (1989). Computer-based psychological testing: Issues and guidelines. *American Journal of Orthopsychiatry, 59,* 257–263.

Zuckerman, E. L., & Guyett, I. P. R. (1992). *The paper work office: The tools to make your small psychotherapy practice work ethically, legally, and profitably—forms, guidelines, and resources.* Pittsburgh, PA: Three Wishes Press.

Chapter 3

THE ASSESSMENT INTERVIEW

Probably the single most important means of data collection during psychological evaluation is the assessment interview. Without interview data, most psychological tests are meaningless. The interview also provides potentially valuable information that may be otherwise unobtainable, such as behavioral observations, idiosyncratic features of the client, and the person's reaction to his or her current life situation. In addition, interviews are the primary means for developing rapport and can serve as a check against the meaning and validity of test results.

Sometimes an interview is mistakenly thought to be simply a conversation. In fact, the interview and conversation differ in many ways. An interview will typically have a clear sequence and be organized around specific, relevant themes because it is meant to achieve defined goals. Unlike a normal conversation, the assessment interview may even require that the interviewer and interviewee discuss unpleasant facts and feelings. Its general objectives are to gather information that cannot easily be obtained through other means, establish a relationship that is conducive to obtaining the information, develop greater understanding in both the interviewer and interviewee regarding problem behavior, and provide direction and support in helping the interviewee deal with problem behaviors. The interviewer not only must direct and control the interaction to achieve specific goals, but also must have knowledge about the areas to be covered in the interview.

A basic dimension of interviews is their degree of structure. Some interviews allow the participants to freely drift from one area to the next, whereas others are highly directive and goal oriented, often using structured ratings and checklists. The more unstructured formats offer flexibility, possibly high rapport, the ability to assess how clients organize their responses, and the potential to explore unique details of a client's history. Unstructured interviews, however, have received frequent criticism, resulting in widespread distrust of their reliability and validity. As a result, highly structured and semistructured interviews have been developed that provide sound psychometric qualities, the potential for use in research, and the capacity to be administered by less trained personnel.

Regardless of the degree of structure, any interview needs to accomplish specific goals, such as assessing the client's strengths, level of adjustment, the nature and history of the problem, diagnosis, and relevant personal and family history. Techniques for accomplishing these goals vary from one interviewer to the next. Most practitioners use at least some structured aids, such as intake forms that provide identifying data and basic elements of history. Obtaining information through direct questions on intake forms frees the clinician to investigate other aspects of the client in a more flexible, open-ended manner. Clinicians might also use a checklist to help ensure that they have covered all relevant areas. Other clinicians continue the structured format throughout most of the interview by using one of the formally developed structured interviews, such as the Schedule for Affective Disorders and Schizophrenia (SADS) or Structured Clinical Interview for the *DSM-IV* (SCID).

HISTORY AND DEVELOPMENT

Early Developments

The earliest form of obtaining information from clients was through clinical interviewing. At first, these interviews were modeled after question-and-answer medical formats, but later the influence of psychoanalytic theories resulted in a more open-ended, free-flowing style. Parallel to the appearance of the psychoanalytically oriented interview was the development of the more structured and goal-oriented mental status examination originally formulated by Adolf Meyer in 1902. The mental status examination assessed relevant areas of a client's current functioning, such as general appearance, behavior, thought processes, thought content, memory, attention, speech, insight, and judgment. Professionals also expressed early interest in the relationship between biographical data and the prediction of occupational success or prognosis for specific disorders.

Regardless of the style used, the interviews all had these common objectives: to obtain a psychological portrait of the person, to conceptualize what is causing the person's current difficulties, to make a diagnosis, and to formulate a treatment plan. The difficulty with unstructured interviews is that they were (and still are) considered to have questionable reliability, validity, and cost-effectiveness. The first standardized psychological tests were developed to overcome these limitations. Tests could be subjected to rigorous psychometric evaluation and were more economical because they required less face-to-face contact with the person(s) being evaluated.

Developments during the 1940s and 1950s

During the 1940s and 1950s, researchers and clinicians began conceptualizing and investigating the following critical dimensions of interviews:

1. Content versus process.
2. Goal orientation (problem solving) versus expressive elements.
3. Degree of directiveness.
4. Amount of structure.
5. The relative amount of activity expressed by the participants.

These issues have been the focus of numerous research studies. A representative and frequently cited study on interviewer style was reported by Snyder (1945), who found that a nondirective approach was most likely to create favorable changes and self-exploration in clients. In contrast, a directive style using persuasion, interpretation, and interviewer judgments typically resulted in clients being defensive and resistant to expressing difficulties. Strupp (1958) investigated the experience-inexperience dimension and found, among other things, that experienced interviewers expressed more warmth, a greater level of activity, and a greater number of interpretations. Level of empathy did not alter, regardless of the interviewer's degree of experience. Further, representative studies include Porter's (1950) in-depth evaluation of the effects of different types of responses (evaluative, probing, reassuring) and Wagner's (1949) early review, which questioned the reliability and validity of employment interviews.

Developments during the 1960s

A considerable amount of research in the 1960s was stimulated by Rogers (1961), who emphasized understanding the proper interpersonal ingredients necessary for an optimal therapeutic relationship (warmth, positive regard, genuineness). Elaborating on Roger's ideas, Truax and Carkhuff (1967) developed a 5-point scale to measure interviewer understanding of the client. This scale was used for research on interviewing, therapist training, and as support for a client-centered theoretical orientation. Additional research efforts were also directed toward listing and elaborating on different categories of interactions such as clarification, summarizing, and confrontation.

Other investigators conceptualized interviewing as an interactive system in which the participants simultaneously influenced each other (Matarazzo, 1965; Watzlawick, Beavin, & Jackson, 1966). This emphasis on an interactive, self-maintaining system became the core for most early and later formulations of family therapy. The 1960s also saw the development and formalization of behavioral assessment, primarily in the form of goal-directed interviews that focused on understanding current and past reinforcers as well as on establishing workable target behaviors. Proponents of behavioral assessment also developed formal rating instruments and self-reports for such areas as depression, assertiveness, and fear.

Some attempts were made at integrating different schools of thought into a coherent picture, such as Beier's (1966) conceptualization of unconscious processes being expressed through nonverbal behaviors that could then be subject to covert social reinforcement. However, the 1960s (and part of the 1970s) was mostly characterized by a splintering into different schools of conflicting and competing ideologies. For example, client-centered approaches emphasized the importance of staying with the client's self-exploration; behavioral interviews emphasized antecedents and consequences of behavior; and family therapy focused on interactive group processes. Parallel progress was made within each of these different schools and within different disciplines, but little effort was devoted to cross-fertilization and/or integration.

Throughout the 1950s and 1960s, child assessment was primarily conducted through interviews with parents. Direct interviews with the child were considered to be for therapeutic purposes rather than for assessment. Differential diagnosis was unusual; almost all children referred to psychiatric clinics were either undiagnosed or diagnosed as "adjustment reactions" (Rosen, Bahn, & Kramer, 1964). Early research by Lapouse and Monk (1958, 1964), using structured interviews, indicated that mothers were more likely to report overt behaviors that are bothersome to adults (thumbsucking, temper tantrums), but children were more likely to reveal covert difficulties (fears, nightmares). Somewhat later, Graham and Rutter (1968), using structured interviews of children (rather than a parent), found interrater agreement was high for global psychiatric impairment (.84); moderate for attentional deficit, motor behavior, and social relations (.61–.64); and low for more covert difficulties such as depression, fears, and anxiety (.30).

Developments during the 1970s

Assessment with adults and children during the 1970s saw a further elaboration and development of the trends of the 1960s, as well as increased emphasis on structured interviews. The interest in structured interviews was fueled largely by criticisms about the poor reliability of psychiatric diagnosis. A typical structured interview would be completed by the interviewer either during or directly after the interview, and the data would be transformed into such scales as organicity, disorganization, or depression-anxiety.

Initial success with adult structured interviews (e.g., Present State Examination, Renard Diagnostic Interview) encouraged thinking regarding the further development of child structured interviews both for global ratings as well as for specific content areas. Child assessment became concerned not only with information derived from parents, but also with the child's own experience. There was a trend toward direct questioning of the child, greater emphasis on differential diagnosis, and the development of parallel versions of structured interviews for both the parent(s) and child.

Behavioral strategies of interviewing for both children and adults not only emphasized the interviewee's unique situation, but also provided a general listing of relevant areas for consideration. Kanfer and Grimm (1977) outlined the areas an interviewer should assess as:

1. Behavioral deficiencies.
2. Behavioral excesses.
3. Inappropriate environmental stimulus control.
4. Inappropriate self-generated stimulus.
5. Problem reinforcement contingencies.

In a similar categorization, Lazarus (1973) developed his BASIC-ID model, which describes a complete assessment as involving behaviors (B), affect (A), sensation (S), imagery (I), cognition (C), interpersonal relations (I), and need for pharmacological intervention/drugs (D).

Additional themes in the 1970s included interest in biographical data, online computer technology, and the training of interviewer skills. Specifically, efforts were made to integrate biographical data for predicting future behavior (suicide, dangerousness, prognosis for schizophrenia) and for inferring current traits. Johnson and Williams (1977) were instrumental in developing some of the earliest online computer technology to collect biographical data and to integrate it with test results. Although training programs were devised for interviewers, a central debate was whether interview skills could actually be significantly learned or improved (Wiens, 1976).

Whereas most reviews of the literature in the 1970s emphasized the advantages of a comprehensive structured format, family therapists were dealing with group processes in which formal interview structure was typically deemphasized. Since most family therapists were observing fluid interactional processes, they needed to develop a different vocabulary than that used in traditional psychiatric diagnosis. In fact, *DSM* categories were usually considered irrelevant since they described static characteristics of individuals rather than ongoing group processes. Few, if any, structured formats were available to assess family relationships.

Developments during the 1980s

Many of the trends, concepts, and instruments developed in the 1960s and 1970s were further refined and adapted for the 1980s. One important effort was the adaptation of many instruments to the *DSM-III* (1980) and *DSM-III-R* (1987). In addition, the increased delineation of childhood disorders required greater knowledge related to differential diagnosis and greater demand for structured interviews as adjuncts to assessment. Many of the efforts were consistent with the use of specific diagnostic criteria along with a demand for efficiency, cost-effectiveness, and accountability. Despite concerns regarding computer-based interpretations (Groth-Marnat & Schumaker, 1989), some of these functions were beginning to be performed by specific computer programs. Since interviews were becoming increasingly structured, with the inclusion of scales and specific diagnostic strategies, the distinction between tests and interviews was becoming less clear. In some contexts, aspects of interviewing were even replaced with computer-requested and computer-integrated information and combined with fairly simple programs to aid in diagnosis, such as DIANO III (Spitzer, Endicott, & Cohen, 1974) and CATEGO (Wing, Cooper, & Sartorius, 1974). During the mid and late 1980s, most clinicians, particularly those working in large institutions, used a combination of structured interviews along with open-ended unstructured approaches. Some research focused on the importance of the initial interview regarding clinical decision making and later therapeutic outcome (Hoge, Andrews, Robinson, & Hollett, 1988; Turk & Salovey, 1985). There was also a greater appreciation and integration of the work from different disciplines and from differing theoretical persuasions (Hersen, 1988). Finally, greater emphasis was placed on the impact and implications of culture and gender on the assessment process (Brown, 1990).

The 1990s and Beyond

Two of the defining features of psychology in the 1990s are managed healthcare and the controversy over the validity of repressed memories. Both these issues have had significant implications for interviewing. Managed healthcare emphasizes the cost-effectiveness of providing health services, and for interviewing, this means developing the required information in the least amount of time. This may mean streamlining interviews by maximizing computer-derived information or paper-pencil forms. This brings up the larger issue of the extent to which practitioners need to spend face-to-face time with the client versus deriving information through other means. The recent emphasis on single-session therapy (Hoyt, 1994) illustrates the potential brevity of information that might be required prior to making therapeutic interventions. There is also recognition that precise patient-treatment matching can optimize the treatment and potentially the cost-effectiveness of psychosocial interventions (Beutler & Clarkin, 1990).

The controversy over repressed memories has forced interviewers to clarify the extent to which the information they derive from clients represents literal as opposed to narrative truth. Research has consistently indicated that client self-reports are reconstructions of events (Henry, Moffitt, Caspi, Langley, & Silva, 1994; Lindsay & Read, 1995; Loftus, 1993) and are likely to be particularly questionable for retrospective reports of psychosocial variables (Henry et al., 1994). The even greater challenge to interviewers is to ensure that their interviewing style and method of questioning are not distorting the information derived from clients. This issue becomes intensely highlighted during interviews to investigate the possibility of childhood sexual abuse (see guidelines in White & Edelstein, 1991).

Further continuing themes in the 1990s are the impact of gender and cultural issues and the further development of structured interviews. In some cases, the preceding issues have produced tension. For example, the greater demands for brief focused interventions contradict the emphasis of structured interviews on detailed and often time-consuming procedures. In addition, there has been greater clinical and political importance attached to detecting and treating childhood abuse and yet research and media coverage of recovered memories has suggested that some if not many of these memories are of questionable validity. The themes related to cost-effectiveness, patient-treatment matching, recovered memories, use of structured interviews, and cultural and gender issues are far from resolved and will likely continue to be defining issues in interviewing and assessment throughout the 1990s.

ISSUES RELATED TO RELIABILITY AND VALIDITY

Although the interview is not a standardized test, it is a means of collecting data and, as such, can and should be subjected to some of the same types of psychometric considerations as a formal test. This is important since interviews might introduce numerous sources of bias, particularly if the interviews are relatively unstructured. Reliability of interviewers is usually discussed in relation to interrater (interviewer) agreement. Wagner's (1949) early review of the literature found tremendous variation, ranging from .23 to .97 ($Mdn = .57$) for ratings of personal traits and $-.20$ to .85 ($Mdn = .53$) for ratings of overall ability. Later reviews have generally found similar variations in interrater agreement (Arvey & Campion, 1982; Ulrich & Trumbo, 1965). The problem then becomes how to determine which ratings to trust and which to view with skepticism. Of particular relevance is why some interviewers focus on different areas and have different biases. A consistent finding is that, when interviewers were given narrow areas to assess and were trained in interviewer strategies, interrater reliability increased (Dougherty, Ebert, & Callender, 1986; Zedeck, Tziner, & Middlestadt, 1983). The consensus was that highly structured interviews were more reliable. However, increased structure undermines one of the greatest strengths of interviews—

their flexibility. In many situations, a free-form, open-ended approach may be the only way to obtain some types of information (Morrison, 1993; Wiens, 1983).

Research on interview validity has typically focused on sources of interviewer bias. For example, halo effects result from the tendency of an interviewer to develop a general impression of a person and then infer other seemingly related characteristics. For example, clients who are considered to express warmth may be seen as more competent or mentally healthy than they actually are. This clustering of characteristics may be incorrect, thereby producing distortions and exaggerations. Similarly, first impressions have been found to bias later judgments (Cooper, 1981). Confirmatory bias might occur when an interviewer makes an inference about a client and then directs the interview to elicit information that confirms the original inference. For example, a psychoanalytically oriented interviewer might direct questions related to early childhood traumas possibly incorrectly confirming traditional psychoanalytic explanations of current adult behaviors. Similar to halo effects is the finding that one specific outstanding characteristic (educational level, physical appearance, etc.) can lead an interviewer to judge other characteristics that he or she incorrectly believes are related to the outstanding one. For example, physical attractiveness has been found to create interviewer bias in job applicants (Gilmore, Beehr, & Love, 1986). Within a clinical context, physical attractiveness may result in practitioners either deemphasizing pathology or, on occasion, exaggerating pathology due to discomfort the interviewer may feel over his or her feelings of attraction (Brown, 1990). Interviewers also may focus incorrectly on explanations of behavior that emphasize traits rather than situational determinants (Ross, 1977). This error is particularly likely when the interpretation of interview data relies heavily on psychological tests, since tests, by their nature, conceptualize and emphasize static characteristics of the person rather than ongoing interactional processes.

In addition to the interviewer having perceptual and interactional biases, the interviewees may distort their responses. For example, they may present an overly favorable view of themselves, particularly if they are relatively naive regarding their motivations. Distortions are most likely in such sensitive areas as sexual behavior. Some specific areas of distortions are represented by the finding that victims of automobile accidents typically exaggerated the amount of time they lost from work, 40% of respondents provided overestimates of their contributions to charity, and 17% of respondents reported their ages incorrectly (Kahn & Cannell, 1961). More extreme cases of falsification occur with outright (conscious) lies, delusions, confabulations, and lies by pathological (compulsive) liars that they partially believe themselves (Kerns, 1986). Inaccuracies based on retrospective accounts have been found to most likely occur related to psychosocial information (e.g., family conflict, onset of psychiatric symptoms) compared with variables such as change of residence, reading skill, height, and weight (Henry et al., 1994).

Reviews of interview validity, in which interviewer ratings were compared with outside criterion measures, have, like reliability measures, shown tremendous variability ranging from −.05 to +.75 (Arvey & Campion, 1982; Henry et al., 1994; Ulrich & Trumbo, 1965). The data, however, refer mainly to unstructured types of interviews. A brief review of reliability and validity on selected structured interviews is provided at the end of this chapter. The information on relatively unstructured interviews strongly suggests that the information derived from them enables the development of tentative hypotheses that need to be supported by other means. Interviewers should also continually question the extent to which their particular style, attitudes, and expectations might be compromising interview validity.

ASSETS AND LIMITATIONS

Both structured and unstructured interviews allow clinicians to place test results in a wider, more meaningful context. In addition, biographical information from interviews can be used to help predict future behaviors; what a person has done in the past is an excellent guide to what he or she is likely to continue doing in the future. Factors for predicting suicide risk, success in certain occupations, and prognosis for certain disorders can usually be most effectively accomplished by attending to biographical data rather than test scores. Since tests are almost always structured or "closed" situations, the unstructured or semistructured interview is typically the only time during the assessment process when the clinician can observe the client in an open, ambiguous situation. Observations can be made regarding how persons organize their responses, and inferences can be derived from subtle, nonverbal cues. These inferences can be followed up with further, more detailed questioning. This flexibility inherent in unstructured and semistructured interviews is frequently their strongest advantage over standardized tests. The focus during unstructured interviews is almost exclusively on the individual rather than on how that individual does or does not compare with a larger normative comparison group. Some types of information can only be obtained through this flexible, person-centered approach, which allows the interviewer to pay attention to idiosyncratic factors. In crisis situations when relatively rapid decisions need to be made, it can be impractical to take the time required to administer and interpret tests, leaving interviews and rapid screening devices as the only means of assessment. Finally, interviews allow clinicians to establish rapport and encourage client self-exploration. Rarely will clients reveal themselves nor will they perform optimally on tests unless they first sense trust, openness, and a feeling of being understood.

The greatest difficulty with unstructured interviews is interviewer bias from such perceptual and interactional processes as the halo effect, confirmatory bias, and the primacy effect. This bias typically results in considerable variability for both reliability and validity as well as in difficulty comparing one subject with the next. An early but seminal article by Ward, Beck, Mendelson, Mock, and Erbaugh (1961) found that the main reasons for diagnostic disagreement were variations in the information they obtained ("information variance") and variations in the criteria ("criterion variance") they used to conclude the presence or absence of a condition. In more concrete terms, this means that different practitioners will develop and ask a wide variety of questions and apply standards for the presence of a condition such as depression in an inconsistent fashion. A further difficulty is the high cost of using trained interviewers for large-scale epidemiological studies.

Structured interviews have many distinct advantages over unstructured approaches. Since structured interviews have more psychometric precision, the results enable comparability between one case or population and the next. The standardized presentation allows for the development of reliable ratings, reduces information variance, and uses consistent diagnostic criteria (Rogers, 1995). In addition, the comprehensiveness of many structured interviews reduces the likelihood of missing a diagnosis or set of relevant symptomology. Partially as a result of these advantages, structured clinical interviews have progressed from being used primarily for research to use in a number of clinical settings. At issue, however, is the time required for structured interviews. The more recently developed computer-assisted programs offer a potential method of countering this difficulty (First, Gibbon, Williams, & Spitzer, 1995, 1996). In addition instruments such as the Diagnostic Interview Schedule and Diagnostic Interview for Children and Adolescents have been designed for administration by lay interviewers thereby reducing the time required by professionals.

Even though structured interviews generally have higher psychometric properties than unstructured formats, they tend to overlook the idiosyncracies and richness of the person. In many cases, these unique aspects may go undetected and yet may make a significant difference in interpreting test scores or making treatment recommendations. Although still somewhat controversial (Helzer & Robins, 1988), another criticism of many clinicians and researchers is that a highly structured approach may not create enough rapport for the client to feel sufficiently comfortable about revealing highly personal information. This is more true for the highly structured interviews such as the Diagnostic Interview Schedule than for a semistructured instrument such as the Schedule for Affective Disorders and Schizophrenia, which includes an initial, relatively unstructured component. However, Rosenthal (1989) has noted that rapport with structured instruments can be enhanced through carefully educating the client as to the importance and procedures of these more structured approaches.

Although many of the structured interviews have demonstrated adequate reliability, studies relating to validity have primarily focused on the general level of impairment or simple discriminations between psychiatric and nonpsychiatric populations. There has been considerable controversy over what exactly is an acceptable outside criterion measure regarding the "true" diagnosis. In-depth studies of construct validity or incremental validity have yet to be performed. Furthermore, far more work needs to be done on the treatment utility of structured interviews in such areas as prognosis, selection of treatment, and likely response to specific forms of pharmacological or psychotherapeutic interventions.

THE ASSESSMENT INTERVIEW AND CASE HISTORY

General Considerations

The previously mentioned historical and psychometric considerations indicate that no single correct way exists to conduct an unstructured or semistructured interview. Interviewer style will be strongly influenced by theoretical orientation and by practical considerations. Persons strongly influenced by client-centered theories will tend to be nondirective and avoid highly structured questions. This is consistent with the underlying belief that persons have the inner ability to change and organize their own behaviors. The goal of a client-centered interview, then, would be to create the type of interpersonal relationship most likely to enhance this self-change. In contrast, a behavioral interview is more likely to be based on the assumption that change occurs as a result of specific external consequences. As a result, behavioral interviews will be relatively structured since they will be directed toward obtaining specific information that would help to design strategies based on altering external conditions. In addition, different interviewing styles and strategies will work well with some clients but may be relatively ineffective with others.

A useful distinction is between a diagnostic interview versus one that is more informal and exploratory. The goal of a diagnostic interview is to develop a specific diagnosis usually based on the multiaxial *DSM-IV* model (see Othmer & Othmer, 1994; Rogers, 1995). This might follow a five-step process in which the clinician develops diagnostic clues, considers these in relation to diagnostic criteria, takes a psychiatric history, and, based on this information, develops a multiaxial diagnosis with corresponding estimates of prognosis (Othmer & Othmer, 1994). Such an interview is likely to be directive with a careful consideration of inclusion and exclusion criteria for different disorders. It is most likely to occur within a psychiatric or general medical setting. In contrast, many practitioners do not believe in the value of formal diagnosis and, accordingly, do not pursue a formal *DSM-IV* diagnosis. They might be more concerned with such areas as a client's coping style, social supports, family dynamics, or the nature of their disability. As such, their interview might be less directive and more flexible. Again, neither style is right or wrong but instead may be appropriate and effective in one context (or client), whereas it is ineffective or inappropriate within another context.

Often, interviewers might wish to construct a semistructured interview format by listing in sequence the types of questions they would like to ask the person. To construct such a list, interviewers might consult Table 3–1 to note possibly relevant areas. Each of these areas might then be converted into specific questions. For example, the first few areas might be converted into the following series of questions:

- "What are some important concerns that you have?"
- "Could you describe the most important of these concerns?"
- "When did the difficulty first begin?"
- "How often does it occur?"
- "Have there been any changes in how often it has occurred?"
- "What happens after the behavior(s) occurs?"

Since clients vary regarding their personal characteristics (age, educational level, degree of cooperation) and type of presenting problem (childhood difficulties, legal problems, psychosis), the questions will necessarily need to vary from person to person. Furthermore, any series of questions should not be followed rigidly, but with a certain degree of flexibility, to allow exploring unique but relevant areas that arise during the interview.

Good interviewing is difficult to define, partly because different theoretical perspectives exist regarding clinician-client interaction. Furthermore, clinicians achieve successful interviews not so much by what they do or say, but by making sure they express the proper attitude. Whereas clinicians from alternative theoretical persuasions might differ regarding such areas as their degree of directiveness or the type of information they should obtain, they would all agree that certain aspects of the relationship

Table 3–1.   Checklist for an assessment interview and case history

History of the Problem

Description of the problem	Intensity and duration
Initial onset	Previous treatment
Changes in frequency	Attempts to solve
Antecedents/consequences	Formal treatment

Family Background

Socioeconomic level	Cultural background
Parent's occupation(s)	Parent's current health
Emotional/medical history	Family relationships
Married/separated/divorced	Urban/rural upbringing
Family constellation	

Personal History

Infancy

Developmental milestones	Early medical history
Family atmosphere	Toilet training
Amount of contact with parents	

Early and Middle Childhood

Adjustment to school	Peer relationships
Academic achievement	Relationship with parents
Hobbies/activities/interests	Important life changes

Adolescence

All areas listed for early and middle childhood	Early dating
	Reaction to puberty
Presence of acting out (legal, drugs, sexual)	

Early and Middle Adulthood

Career/occupational	Marriage
Interpersonal relationships	Medical/emotional history
Satisfaction with life goals	Relationship with parents
Hobbies/interests/activities	Economic stability

Late Adulthood

Medical history	Reaction to declining abilities
Ego integrity	Economic stability

Miscellaneous

Self-concept (like/dislike)	Somatic concerns (headaches, stomach-
Happiest/saddest memory	aches, etc.)
Earliest memory	Events that create happiness/sadness
Fears	Recurring/noteworthy dreams

are essential (Patterson, 1989). These include the interviewer's expression of sincerity, acceptance, understanding, genuine interest, warmth, and a positive regard for the worth of the person. If clinicians do not demonstrate these qualities, they are unlikely to achieve the goals of the interview, no matter how these are defined.

Patient ratings of the quality of interviews have been found to be dependent on the extent to which interviewers can understand the patient's emotions and detect emotional messages that are only partially expressed, particularly since these emotions are likely to be indirect and conveyed through nonverbal behaviors (Dimatteo & Taranta, 1976). This is especially relevant in clinical interviews that focus on a client's personal difficulties. Typically, words are inadequate to accurately describe problem emotions, so interviewers must infer them from paraverbal or nonverbal expression. This is highlighted by the assumption that nonverbal aspects of communication are likely to be a more powerful method of conveying information. For example, eye contact is most likely to convey involvement, rigidity of posture might suggest client defensiveness, and hand movements often occur beyond the person's conscious intent suggesting nervousness, intensity, or relaxation. Mehrabian (1972) has supported this perspective with his estimates that the message received is 55% dependent on facial expression, 38% by tone, and only 7% by the content of what is said.

Interviewers vary in the extent to which they take notes during the interview. Some argue that note taking during an interview might increase a client's anxiety, raise questions regarding anonymity, increase the likelihood that he or she will feel like an object under investigation, and might create an unnatural atmosphere. In contrast, many interviewers counter these arguments by pointing out that a loss of rapport is rarely due solely to note taking during the interview, assuming, of course, that the interviewer can still spend a sufficient amount of time attending to the client. Ongoing note taking is also likely to capture more details and result in less memory distortion than recording material after the interview has been completed. Thus, an intermediate amount of note taking during the interview is recommended. If the interview is audio- or videotaped, the reasons for this procedure need to be fully explained, along with the assurance of confidentiality and the procuring of a signed agreement. Although audio- or videotape recording is often awkward at first, usually the interviewer and client quickly forget that it is occurring.

Interview Tactics

Numerous tactics or types of statements have been proposed and studied. These include the clarification statement, verbatim playback, probing, confrontation, understanding, active listening, reflection, feedback, summary statement, random probing, self-disclosure, perception checking, use of concrete examples, and therapeutic double binds. Additional relevant topics are the importance of eye contact, self-disclosure, active listening, and touch. These areas are beyond the scope of this chapter, but the interested reader is referred to excellent discussions by Cormier and Cormier (1990), Morrison (1993), Sattler (1992), and Wiens (1983). The most relevant skills for interviewing do not so much come from memorizing interviewing tactics, but develop from reviewing actual live or taped interview sessions. However, several important tactics of interviewing will be described since they provide a general interviewing strategy.

Preliminaries

During the initial phase of the interview, practitioners need to ensure that they deal adequately with the following issues:

1. Organize the physical characteristics of the interview situation so that the room looks used but not untidy and lighting is optimal; seating is arranged so that the interviewer and client will be neither too close nor too far and so that eye level will be approximately equal.

2. Introduce yourself and indicate how you prefer to be addressed (Doctor, first name, etc.) and clarify how the client prefers to be addressed.

3. State the purpose of the interview, check the client's understanding of the interview, and clarify any discrepancies between these two understandings.

4. Explain how the information derived from the interview will be used.

5. Describe the confidential nature of the information, the limits of confidentiality, and special issues related to confidentiality (e.g., how the information might be obtained and used by the legal justice system). Further explain that the client has the right not to discuss any information he or she does not wish to disclose. If the information will be sent to other persons, obtain a signed release of information.

6. Explain the role and activities you would like the client to engage in, the instruments that are likely to be used in the assessment, and the total length of time required. In some circumstances, this may be formalized into a written contract (Handelsman, Galvin, Zuckerman, & Guyett, 1992).

7. Make sure that any fee arrangements have been clarified including the hourly rate, total estimated cost, the amount the client versus a third party is likely to need to pay, and the interval between billing and the expected payment.

With the possible exception of fee arrangement (item 7), the preceding issues should be handled by a mental health practitioner rather than a secretary or receptionist. Covering these areas during the preliminary stages of the interview is likely to reduce the likelihood of miscommunications and later difficulties.

Directive versus Nondirective Interviews

The degree to which clinicians choose to be structured and directive during an interview will depend on both theoretical and practical considerations. If time is limited, the interviewer will need to be direct and to the point. The interviewer will use a different approach for assessing a person who has been referred and will be returning to the referring person than for a person prior to conducting therapy with him or her. An ambiguous, unstructured approach will probably make an extremely anxious person even more anxious, while a direct approach may prove more effective. A passive, withdrawn client will also be likely to initially require a more direct question-and-answer style. As stated previously, a less structured style often encourages deeper client self-exploration, enables clinicians to observe the client's organizational abilities, and may result in greater rapport, flexibility, and sensitivity to the client's uniqueness.

Frequently, behavioral interviews are characterized as being structured and directed toward obtaining a comprehensive description of actual behaviors and relevant cognitions, attitudes, and beliefs (see Chapter 4). This is often contrasted with the more unstructured psychodynamic approach, which investigates underlying motivations and hidden dynamics, and assesses information that may not be within the person's ordinary awareness. Typically, these approaches are perceived as competing and mutually exclusive. Haas, Hendin, and Singer (1987) point out that this either/or position is not only unnecessary, but unproductive, because each style of interviewing provides different types of information that could potentially compensate for the other's weaknesses. Using both approaches might increase interview breadth and validity. This is similar to basing client descriptions on direct behavioral data (public communication), self-description, and private symbolization (Leary, 1957). Each of these levels may be useful for different purposes, and the findings from each level might be quite different from one another.

Sequence of Interview Tactics

Most authors recommend that interviewers begin with open-ended questions and, after observing the client's responses, then use more direct questions to fill in gaps in their understanding (Beutler, 1995a; Maloney & Ward, 1976; Morrison, 1993; Othmer & Othmer, 1994). Although this sequence might begin with open-ended questions, it should typically lead to interviewer responses that are intermediate in their level of directiveness such as facilitating comments, requesting clarification, and possibly confronting the client with inconsistencies.

An important advantage of open-ended questions is that they require clients to comprehend, organize, and express themselves with little outside structure. This is perhaps the only occasion in the assessment process that makes this requirement of clients, since most tests or structured interviews provide guidance in the form of specific, clear stimuli. When clients are asked open-ended questions, they will be most likely to express significant but unusual features about themselves. Verbal fluency, level of assertiveness, tone of voice, energy level, hesitations, and areas of anxiety can be noted. Hypotheses can be generated from these observations and further open-ended or more direct questions used to test these hypotheses. In contrast to these advantages, open-ended questions can potentially provide an overabundance of detailed, vague, and tangential information.

Interviewer responses that show an intermediate level of directiveness are facilitation, clarification, empathy, and confrontation. Facilitation of comments will maintain or encourage the flow of conversation. This might be accomplished verbally ("Tell me more . . . ," "Please continue . . .") or nonverbally (eye contact, nodding). These requests for clarification might be used when clients indicate, perhaps through subtle cues, that they have not fully expressed something regarding the topic of discussion. Requests for clarification can bring into the open material that was only implied. In particular, greater clarification might be achieved by requesting the client to be highly specific, such as asking him or her to provide concrete examples (a typical day or a day that best illustrates the problem behavior). Empathic statements ("It must have been difficult for you") can also facilitate client self-disclosure.

Sometimes interviewers might wish to confront or at least comment on inconsistencies in a client's information or behavior. Carkhuff (1969) has categorized the potential types of inconsistencies as being between what a person is versus what he or she wants to be, what he or she is saying versus what he or she is doing, and between the person's self-perception versus the interviewer's experience of the person. A confrontation might also challenge the improbable content of what he or she is reporting ("tall" stories).

The purpose of confrontations during assessment is to obtain more in-depth information about the client. In contrast, therapeutic confrontations are used to encourage client self-exploration and behavior change. If a practitioner is using the initial interview and assessment as a prelude to therapy, then this distinction is less important. However, a confrontational style can produce considerable anxiety, which should only be created if sufficient opportunity exists to work through the anxiety. Usually, a client will be most receptive to confrontations when they are posed hypothetically as possibilities to consider rather than as a direct challenge. Confrontations also require a sufficient degree of rapport in order to be sustained; unless this rapport is present, confrontations will probably result in client defensiveness and a deterioration of the relationship.

Finally, direct, close-ended questions can be used to fill in gaps in what the client has stated. Thus, a continual flow can be formed between client-directed or client-organized responses and clinician-directed responses. This sequence beginning with open-ended questions, then moving to intermediately structured responses (facilitation, clarification, confrontation), and finally ending in directive questions should not be rigid but should vary throughout the interview.

Comprehensiveness

The basic focus of an assessment interview should be to define the problem behavior (nature of the problem, severity, related affected areas) and its causes (conditions that worsen or alleviate it, origins, antecedents, consequences). Interviewers might wish to use a checklist, such as the one in Table 3–1, to ensure they are covering most relevant areas. In using such a checklist, the interviewer might begin with a general question, such as "How were you referred here?" or "What are some areas that concern you?" Observations and notes can then be made about the way the client organizes his or her responses, what he or she says, and the way he or she says it. The interviewer could use facilitating, clarifying, and confronting responses to obtain more information. Finally, the interviewer could review the checklist on family background to see if all relevant areas were covered sufficiently. If some areas or aspects of areas weren't covered, then the interviewer might ask direct questions, such as "What was your father's occupation?" or "When did your mother and father divorce?" The interviewer could then begin the same sequence for personal history related to infancy, middle childhood, and so on. Table 3–1 is not comprehensive, but is intended as a general guide for most interview situations. If practitioners generally evaluate specific client types (child abuse, suicide, brain impaired), then this checklist may need additional guidelines and/or be used as an adjunct to commercially available structured interviews, such as the Personality Disorder Examination (Loranger, 1988), Neuropsychological Status Examination (Schinka, 1983) or Lawrence Psychological-Forensic Examination (Lawrence, 1984).

Avoidance of "Why" Questions

It is best to avoid "why" questions since they are likely to increase client defensiveness. A "why" question typically sounds accusatory or critical and thus forces the client to account for his or her behavior. In addition, clients are likely to become intellectual in this situation, thereby separating themselves from their emotions. An alternative approach is to preface the question with either "What is your understanding of . . ." or "How did it occur that . . ." rather than "why?" These options are more likely to result in a description rather than a justification and to keep clients more centered on their emotions.

Nonverbal Behaviors

Interviewers should also be aware of their own as well as their client's nonverbal behaviors. In particular, interviewers might express their interest by maintaining eye contact, being facially responsive, and attending verbally and nonverbally, such as through occasionally leaning forward.

Concluding the Interview

Any interview will be bound by time constraints. An interviewer might help to ensure observance of these constraints by alerting the client when only 5 or 10 minutes remain until the arranged completion of the interview. This allows the client or interviewer to obtain final relevant information. There should also be an opportunity for the client to ask any questions or provide comments. At the end of an interview or assessment session, the interviewer should summarize the main themes of the interview and, if appropriate, make any recommendations.

MENTAL STATUS EXAMINATION

The mental status exam was originally modeled after the physical medical exam; just as the physical medical exam is designed to review the major organ systems, the mental status exam reviews the major systems of psychiatric functioning. Since its introduction into American psychiatry by Adolf Meyer in 1902, it has become the mainstay of patient evaluation in most psychiatric settings. The data derived from the mental status exam are handled by psychiatrists in much the same way as psychological test results are handled by psychologists. The mental status exam "raw" data are selectively integrated with general background information to present a coherent portrait of the person and arrive at a diagnosis. Whereas psychiatry has placed considerable emphasis on the mental status exam (and more recently on structured clinical interviews), psychology and other related mental health disciplines have chosen to focus more on psychological tests and case histories.

It is rare for a psychological report to include a traditional mental status examination. However, it is included and outlined in this chapter since it is such an essential means of interviewing within the broader mental health field. Most psychiatrists consider it to be as essential to their practice as the physical examination is in general medicine (Rodenhauser & Fornal, 1991). Despite its popularity among psychiatrists, this form of interviewing is not typically used by psychologists partly because many areas reviewed by the mental status exam are already covered during the assessment interview and through the interpretation of psychological test results. Many psychological tests cover these areas in a more precise, in-depth, objective, and validated manner with scores being compared to appropriate norms. A client's appearance, affect, and mood are usually noted by attending to behavioral observations. A review of the history and nature of the problem is likely to pick up such areas as delusions, misinterpretations, and perceptual disorders (hallucinations). Likewise, interview data and psychological test results typically assess a client's fund of knowledge, attention, insight, memory, abstract reasoning, and level of social judgment. However, the mental status examination reviews all of the preceding areas in a relatively brief, systematic manner. Furthermore, there are situations, such as intakes in an acute medical or psychiatric hospital, where insufficient time is available to evaluate the client with psychological tests.

Numerous sources in the psychiatric literature provide thorough guidelines for conducting a mental status exam (Crary & Johnson, 1981; Othmer & Othmer, 1994; Strub & Black, 1993; Taylor, 1993), and Rogers (1995) has provided a review of the more structured mental status exams. This literature indicates that practitioners vary widely in how they conduct the mental status examination. The most unstructured versions merely involve the clinician using the mental status examination as a set of general guidelines. The more structured versions range between comprehensive instruments that assess both general psychopathology and cognitive impairment to those that focus primarily on cognitive impairment. For example, the comprehensive North Carolina Mental Status Examination (Ruegg, Ekstrom, Evans, & Golden, 1990) includes 36 items that are rated on a 3-point scale (not present, slight or occasional, marked or repeated) to cover the important clinical dimensions of physical appearance, behavior, speech, thought processes, thought content, mood, affect, cognitive functioning, orientation, recent memory, immediate recall, and remote memory. Another similar comprehensive instrument is the Missouri Automated Mental Status Examination Checklist (Hedlund, Sletten, Evenson, Altman, & Cho, 1977), which requires the examiner to make ratings on the following nine areas of functioning: general appearance, motor behavior, speech and thought, mood and affect, other emotional reactions, thought content, sensorium, intellect, and insight and judgment. The checklist includes a total of 119 possible ratings, but the examiner makes ratings in only those areas he or she judges to be relevant. Despite extensive development, the more comprehensive mental status examinations have not gained wide acceptance. In contrast, the narrower structured mental status examinations that focus more exclusively on cognitive impairment are used quite extensively. One of the most popular has been the Mini Mental Status Examination (Folstein, Folstein, & McHugh, 1975). It comprises 11 items designed to assess orientation, registration, attention, calculation, and language. It has excellent interrater and test-retest reliabilities (usually well above .80), correlates with WAIS IQs (.78 for verbal IQ), and is sensitive to global and left hemisphere deficits (but not right hemisphere impairment; Rogers, 1995; Tombaugh, McDowell, Kristjansson, & Hubley, 1996). Clinicians who wish to develop knowledge and skills in conducting mental status examinations are encouraged to consult the preceding sources.

The following descriptions of the typical areas covered will serve as a brief introduction to this form of interviewing. The outline is organized around the categories recommended by Crary and Johnson (1981), and a checklist of relevant areas is included in Figure 3–1. Interviewers can answer the different areas on the checklist either during or after a mental status examination. The tabled information can then be used to answer relevant questions relating to the referral question, to help in diagnosis, or to add to other test data. Such a checklist is important since clinicians not using similar checklists have been found to omit frequently crucial information (Ruegg et al., 1990).

			No Data	Present	Absent
Name _____ **Observer's Name** _____					
APPEARANCE		1. unkempt, unclean, disheveled.............			
		2. clothing and/or grooming atypical........			
		3. unusual physical characteristics.........			
COMMENTS RE APPEARANCE:					
BEHAVIOR	Posture	4. slumped.................................			
		5. rigid, tense............................			
	Facial Expression Suggests	6. anxiety, fear, apprehension.............			
		7. depression, sadness.....................			
		8. anger, hostility........................			
		9. absence of feeling, blandness...........			
		10. atypical, unusualness...................			
	General Body Movements	11. accelerated, increased speed............			
		12. decreased, slowed.......................			
		13. atypical, unusual.......................			
		14. restlessness, fidgetiness...............			
	Speech	15. rapid speech............................			
		16. slowed speech...........................			
		17. loud speech.............................			
		18. soft speech.............................			
		19. mute....................................			
		20. atypical quality, slurring, stammer.....			
BEHAVIOR	Therapist-Patient Relationship	21. domineering, controlling................			
		22. submissive, overly compliant, dependent..			
		23. provocative, hostile, challenging.......			
		24. suspicious, guarded, evasive............			
		25. uncooperative, non-compliant............			
COMMENTS RE BEHAVIOR:					
FEELING (AFFECT AND MOOD)		26. inappropriate to thought content........			
		27. increased lability of affect............			
		predominant mood is:			
		28. blunted, dull, bland....................			
		29. euphoria, elation......................			
		30. anger, hostility.......................			
		31. anxiety, fear, apprehension............			
		32. depression, sadness....................			
COMMENTS RE FEELING:					
PERCEPTION		33. illusions..............................			
		34. auditory hallucinations................			
		35. visual hallucinations..................			
		36. other types of hallucinations..........			
COMMENTS RE PERCEPTION:					
THINKING	Intellectual Functioning	37. impaired level of consciousness.........			
		38. impaired attention span, distractible....			
		39. impaired abstract thinking.............			
		40. impaired calculation ability...........			
		41. impaired intelligence..................			
	Orientation	42. disoriented to person..................			
		43. disoriented to place...................			
		44. disoriented to time....................			
	Memory	45. impaired recent memory.................			
		46. impaired remote memory.................			
	Insight	47. denies presence of psychological problems.............................			
		48. blames others or circumstances for problems.............................			
	Judgment	49. impaired ability to make routine decisions................................			
		50. impaired impulse control...............			
THINKING	Thought Content	51. obsessions.............................			
		52. compulsions............................			
		53. phobias................................			
		54. depersonalization......................			
		55. suicidal ideation......................			
		56. homicidal ideation.....................			
		57. delusions..............................			
	Stream of Thought	58. associational disturbance..............			
COMMENTS RE THINKING:					

DIAGNOSIS:_____
   as manifested by the following M.S.E. items

_____   _____   _____   _____   _____

_____   _____   _____   _____   _____

Figure 3–1. Format for mental status and history

Reproduced by permission of MTP Press LTD., Lancaster, England, from Crary, W. G., & Johnson, C. W. (1981). Mental status examination. In Johnson, C. W., Snibbe, J. R., & Evans, L. A. (Eds.), *Basic Psychopathology: A Programmed Text* (2nd ed.). Lancaster: MIP Press, pp. 55–56.

General Appearance and Behavior

This area assesses similar material as that requested in the "behavioral observations" section of a psychological report (see Chapter 14). A client's clothing, posture, gestures, speech, personal care/hygiene, and any unusual physical features such·as physical handicaps, tics, or grimaces are noted. Attention is given to the degree to which his or her behavior conforms to social expectations, but this is placed within the context of his or her culture and social position. Additional important areas are facial expressions, eye contact, activity level, degree of cooperation, physical attractiveness, and attentiveness. Is the client friendly, hostile, seductive, or indifferent? Do any bizarre behaviors or significant events occur during the interview? In particular, speech might be fast or slow, loud or soft, or include a number of additional unusual features. Figure 3–1 includes a systematic checklist of relevant areas of behavior and appearance.

Feeling (Affect and Mood)

A client's mood refers to the dominant emotion expressed during the interview, whereas affect refers to the client's range of emotions. This is inferred from the content of the client's speech, facial expressions, and body movements. The type of affect can be judged according to such variables as its depth, intensity, duration, and appropriateness. The client might be cold or warm, distant or close, labile and, as is characteristic of schizophrenia, his or her affect might be blunted or flattened. The client's mood might also be euphoric, hostile, anxious, or depressed.

Perception

Different clients perceive themselves and their world in a wide variety of ways. It is especially important to note whether there are any illusions or hallucinations. The presence of auditory hallucinations are most characteristic of schizophrenics, whereas vivid visual hallucinations are more characteristic of persons with organic brain syndromes.

Thinking

Intellectual Functioning

Any assessment of higher intellectual functioning needs to be made within the context of a client's educational level, socioeconomic status, and familiarity and identification with a particular culture. If a low level of intellectual functioning is consistent with a general pattern of poor academic and occupational achievement, then a diagnosis of intellectual disability might be supported. However, if a person performs poorly on tests of intellectual functioning and yet has a good history of achievement, then organicity might be suspected.

Intellectual functioning typically involves reading and writing comprehension, general fund of knowledge, ability to do arithmetic, and the degree to which the client can interpret the meaning of proverbs. Throughout the assessment, clinicians typically note the degree to which the client's thoughts and expressions are articulate versus incoherent. Sometimes clinicians might combine assessments of intellectual functioning with some short, formal tests such as the Bender, with an aphasia screening test, or even with portions of the WAIS-R or WISC-III.

Orientation

The ability of clients to be oriented can vary in the degree to which they know who they are (person), where they are (place), and when current and past events have occurred or are occurring (time). Clinical observation indicates the most frequent type of disorientation is for time, whereas disorientation for place and person occur less frequently. When disorientation does occur for place, and especially for person, the condition is relatively severe. Disorientation is most consistent with organic conditions. If a person is oriented in all three spheres, this is frequently abbreviated as "oriented X3."

Related to the orientation of clients is their sensorium, which refers to how intact their physiological processes are to receiving and integrating information. Sensorium might refer to hearing, smell, vision, and touch and might range from being clouded to clear. Can the client attend to and concentrate on the outside world or are these processes interrupted? The client might experience unusual smells, hear voices, or have the sense that his or her skin is tingling. Sensorium can also refer to the client's level of consciousness, which may vary from hyperarousal and excitement to drowsiness and confusion. Disorders of a client's sensorium often reflect organic conditions, but may also be consistent with psychosis.

Memory, Attention, and Concentration

Since memory retrieval or acquisition requires attention and concentration, these three functions are frequently considered together. Long-term memory is often assessed by requesting information regarding the client's general fund of information (e.g., important dates, major cities in a country, three major heads of state since 1900). Some clinicians include the Information or Digit Span subtests from the WAIS-R/WISC-III or other formal tests of a similar nature. Recall of a sentence or paragraph might be used to assess short-term memory for longer, more verbally meaningful information. In addition, clients' long-term memory might be evaluated by measuring recall of their major life events and the accuracy of their recall can be compared with objective records of these events (e.g., year graduated from high school, date of marriage). It is often useful to record any significant distortions of selective recall in relation to life events as well as to note the client's attitudes toward his or her memory.

Short-term memory might be assessed by either requesting that clients recall recent events (most recent meal, how they got to the appointment) or by having them repeat digits forward and backward. Again, the WAIS-R/WISC-III Digit Span subtest might be used or at least a similar version of it. Serial sevens (counting forward by adding seven each time) can be used to assess how distractible or focused they are. Persons who are anxious and preoccupied will have a difficult time with serial sevens as well as with repeating digits forward and especially digits backward.

Insight and Judgment

Clients vary in their ability to interpret the meaning and impact of their behavior on others. They also vary widely in their ability to provide for themselves, evaluate risks, and make future plans. Adequate insight and judgment involves developing and testing hypotheses regarding their own behavior and the behavior of others. Clients also need to be assessed to determine why they believe they were referred for evaluation and, in a wider context, their attitudes toward their difficulties. How do they relate their past history to current difficulties, and how do they explain these difficulties? Where do they place the blame for their difficulties? Based on their insights, how effectively can they solve problems and make decisions?

Thinking

A client's speech can often be considered to be a reflection of his or her thoughts. The client's speech may be coherent, spontaneous, and comprehensible or may contain unusual features. It may be slow or fast, be characterized by sudden silences, or be loud or unusually soft. Is the client frank or evasive, open or defensive, assertive or passive, irritable, abusive, or sarcastic? Consideration of a person's thoughts is often divided into thought content and thought processes. Such thought contents as delusions might suggest a psychotic condition, but delusions may also be consistent with certain organic disorders, such as dementia. The presence of compulsions or obsessions should be followed up with an assessment of the client's degree of insight into the appropriateness of these thoughts and behaviors. Such thought processes as the presence of rapid changes in topics might reflect flighty ideas. The client might also have difficulty producing a sufficient number of ideas, include an excessive number of irrelevant associations, or ramble aimlessly.

INTERPRETING INTERVIEW DATA

Interpreting and integrating interview data into the psychological report inevitably involves clinical judgment. Even with the use of structured interviews, the clinician still must determine which information to include or exclude. Thus, all the potential cautions associated with clinical judgment need to be taken into account (see Chapter 1). This is particularly important since life decisions and the success of later treatment may be based on conclusions and recommendations described in the report.

Several general principles can be used to interpret interview data. The interview is the primary instrument that clinicians use to develop tentative hypotheses regarding their clients. Thus, interview data can be evaluated by determining whether these hypotheses are supported by information outside the interview. Interview data that is supported by test scores can be given greater emphasis in the final report if it is relevant to the referral question. Even material that is highly supported throughout different phases of the interview process should not be included unless it relates directly to the purpose of the referral.

Enelow and Wexler (1966) suggest reducing interview data into short phrases and categorizing them into either process or content areas. Process areas might include unusual behaviors, tone of voice, or level of tension. Content areas might include a client's thoughts, preoccupations, interests, or significant life events. A convenient summary can be reached by listing key phrases under each category. For example, the following list might summarize some of the data recorded during a legal evaluation:

Process	Content
1. Excited	1. Fearful of imprisonment
2. Poorly focused	2. Arrested for burglary
3. Disheveled appearance	3. Abused as a child
4. Loud	4. Dropped out of school
5. Two previous arrests	

The data can then be more easily screened and placed into appropriate sections of the report. A worksheet like the one shown might be used in conjunction with Ownby's (1987) recommendation to list the topic for consideration (e.g., learning difficulties, depression) followed by relevant data (test scores, behavioral observations, relevant biographical details) leading to a listing of possible constructs, diagnoses, or conclusions and finally to treatment recommendations (see Chapter 14, Figure 14–1). The previous listing of interview data into either process or content areas can be used as one source of information that might be included in a worksheet such as Figure 14–1.

Interview data might also be organized and interpreted based on the presence of different themes. For example, one person's history might be characterized by frequent difficulties with authority figures. Specific details relating to these difficulties might emerge, such as the client feeling like a martyr and eventually inappropriately expressing extreme anger toward the authority figure(s). A careful review of the client's history might reveal how he or she becomes involved in these recurring relationships and how he or she typically attempts to resolve them. Other persons who are frequently depressed might distance themselves from others by their behavior and then be confused about why relationships seem to be difficult. Often these themes will emerge during a carefully conducted interview, yet aspects of the themes (or the entire themes themselves) will not be apparent to the interviewee.

There is no one strategy for sensitizing interviewers to the types and patterns of recurring themes they may encounter during interviews. Inevitably, clinical judgment will be a significant factor. The accuracy and types of judgments will depend on the theoretical perspective of the interviewer, knowledge regarding the particular difficulty the interviewer is investigating, past experience, types of questions asked, and purpose of the interview.

STRUCTURED CLINICAL INTERVIEWS

Standardized psychological tests and structured interviews were developed to reduce the problems associated with open-ended interviews. They both serve to structure the stimuli presented to the person and reduce the role of clinical judgment. Since structured interviews generate objective ratings on the same areas, they have the advantage of making possible comparisons between one case or population and the next. Typically, these interviews vary in their degree of structure, the relative expertise required to administer them, and the extent to which they serve as screening procedures designed for global measurement or as tools used to obtain specific diagnoses.

Before structured interviews could be developed, clear, specific criteria needed to be created relating to symptom patterns and diagnoses. This ideally helped to reduce the amount of error caused by vague guidelines for exclusion or inclusion in different categories (criterion variance). These criteria then needed to be incorporated into the interview format and interview questions. Information variance refers to the variability in amount and type of information derived from interviews with patients. In most unstructured interviews, information variance is caused by the wide differences in content and phrasing due to such factors as the theoretical orientation of the interviewer. Structured interviews correct for this by requesting the same or similar questions from each client.

The first popular system of specific criterion-based diagnosis was developed by Feighner et al. (1972) and provided clear, behaviorally oriented descriptions of 16 psychiatric disorders based on the *DSM-II*. Clinicians using the Feighner criteria were found to have an immediate and marked increase in interrater diagnostic reliability. The descriptions of and relevant research on the Feighner criteria were published in Woodruff, Goodwin, and Guze's (1974) book, *Psychiatric Diagnosis*. Several interviews such as the Renard Diagnostic Interview (Helzer, Robins, Croughan, & Welner, 1981) incorporated the Feighner criteria. Spitzer, Endicott, and Robins (1978) further altered and elaborated the Feighner criteria to develop the Research Diagnostic Criteria. Simultaneous with the development of the Research Diagnostic Criteria, Endicott and Spitzer (1978) developed the Schedule for Affective Disorders and Schizophrenia (SADS), which was based on the new Research and Diagnostic Criteria. When new versions of the *Diagnostic and Statistical Manual* were published (1980, 1987, 1994), revisions of previous interviews typically incorporated the most recent *DSM* criteria along with elements of the Feighner criteria and/or the Research Diagnostic Criteria.

As noted earlier, the reliability of structured interviews has been found to vary depending on the specificity or precision of the rating or diagnosis. Whereas the highest reliabilities have been found for global assessment (presence/absence of psychopathology), much lower reliabilities have generally been found for the assessment of specific types of behaviors or syndromes. Likewise, high reliabilities have been found for overt behaviors, but reliability has been less satisfactory for more covert aspects of the person such as obsessions, fears, and worries. Reliability also tends to be lower when clinicians are requested to attempt exact estimates regarding behavioral frequencies and for inferences of multifaceted aspects of the person derived from complex clinical judgments.

Most early studies on validity were based on item content (content validity) or degree of accuracy in distinguishing between broad areas of psychopathology (psychiatric/nonpsychiatric). More recent trends have attempted to assess the accuracy of far more specific areas. However, most validity studies have suffered from an absence of clear, commonly agreed-on criteria. Even though structured interviews were attempts to improve on previous, imperfect instruments (unstructured interviews, standardized tests), the structured interviews themselves could not be compared with anything better. For example, the "procedural validity" strategy is based on comparing lay interviewers' diagnoses with diagnoses derived from trained psychiatrists. Even though the psychiatrist's diagnosis may be better than the layperson's, diagnoses by trained psychiatrists still cannot be said to be an ultimate, objective, and completely accurate standard. Furthermore, there is confusion about whether actual validity is being measured (which would assume psychiatrists' diagnoses are the true, accurate ones) or merely a version of interrater reliability.

Future studies need to involve aspects of what has previously been discussed as construct validity. This means looking more carefully at structured interviews in relationship to etiology, course, prognosis, and treatment utility relating to such areas as the appropriate selection of types of treatments and the likelihood of favorable responses to these treatments. Validity studies also need to look at the interaction between and implications of multiple criterion measures, including behavioral assessment, checklists, rating scales, self-report inventories, biochemical indices, and neuropathological alterations.

Since the mid-1970s, there has been a proliferation of structured interviews for a wide range of areas. Clinicians working in specific areas will often select structured interviews directed toward diagnosing the disorders they are most likely to encounter. For example, some situations might benefit from using the Anxiety Disorders Interview Schedule (Brown, DiNardo, & Barlow, 1994) to make clear distinctions between anxiety disorders and substance abuse, and between psychosis and major affective disorders. Other contexts might be best served by the Eating Disorder Examination (EDE; Cooper & Fairburn, 1987) or the Structured Interview for *DSM-IV*-Dissociative Disorders (SCID-D; Steinberg, 1993). Three categories of structured interviews with representative frequently used instruments are included in Table 3–2 and have been extensively reviewed in Roger's (1995) *Diagnostic and Structured Interviewing: A Handbook for Psychologists.* One consideration in selecting these instruments is that, since most structured interviews are undergoing continuous revisions, the most up-to-date research should be consulted to ensure that practitioners obtain the most

Table 3–2.   Frequently used structured interviews by categories

I. Assessment of Axis I disorders

   Schedule of Affective Disorders and Schizophrenia (SADS)and Schedule of
      Affective Disorders and Schizophrenia for School-Age Children (K-SADS)
   Diagnostic Interview Schedule (DIS) and Diagnostic Interview for Children (DISC)
   Structured Clinical Interview for *DSM-III-R* (SCID)
   Diagnostic Interview for Children and Adolescents (DICA)

II. Assessment of Axis II disorders

   Structured Interview for *DSM-III* Personality Disorders (SIDP)
   Personality Disorder Examination (PDE)
   Structured Clinical Interview for *DSM-III-R* Personality Disorders (SCID-II)

III. Focused structured interviews

   Anxiety Disorders Interview Schedule (ADIS)
   Diagnostic Interview for Borderlines (DIB)
   Psychopathy Checklist (PCL)
   Structured Interview for *DSM-IV*-Dissociative Disorders (SCID-D)
   Structured Interview of Reported Symptoms (SIRS)
   Psychosocial Pain Inventory (PSPI)
   Comprehensive Drinker Profile (CDP)
   Eating Disorder Examination (EDE)
   Structured Interview of Sleep Disorders (SIS-D)
   Substance Use Disorders Diagnostic Schedule (SUDDS)

recently revised versions. The following pages provide an overview of the most frequently used and most extensively researched structured interviews.

Schedule for Affective Disorders and Schizophrenia

The Schedule for Affective Disorders and Schizophrenia (Endicott & Spitzer, 1978), an extensive semistructured interview, has been the most widely used structured interview for clinical research purposes. Even though it was originally designed for differential diagnosis between affective disorders and schizophrenia, it actually covers a much wider range of symptoms and allows the interviewer to consider many different diagnostic categories. A wide range of disorders are considered within the SADS, but its primary strength lies in obtaining fine detail regarding different subtypes of affective disorders and schizophrenia. The interview rates clients on six gradations of impairment from which diagnoses are reached using the clear, objective categories derived from Spitzer, Endicott, and Robins' (1978) Research Diagnostic Criteria (RDC). The SADS is divided into adult versions for current symptoms, occurrence of lifetime symptoms, and degree of change. There is a further version for the assessment of children's difficulties. Two more recent modifications for the SADS have been the inclusion of anxiety disorders (SADS-LA; Fyer, Endicott, Manuzza, & Klein, 1985) and eating disorders (EAT-SADS-L; Herzog, Keller, Sacks, Yeh, & Lavori, 1992).

Adult Version

The adult version of the Schedule for Affective Disorders and Schizophrenia (SADS; Endicott & Spitzer, 1978) is designed to be administered in two different parts, the first focusing on the client's present illness and the second on past episodes. This division roughly corresponds with the three different versions of the SADS. The first is the regular version (SADS), the second is the lifetime version (SADS-L, which is actually the second half of the SADS), and the third is the SADS-C, which measures changes in the client. The SADS-L is directed toward diagnosing the possible presence of psychiatric disturbance throughout the person's life. The SADS and SADS-L are the most extensively used. Since the questions in the SADS are directed toward current symptoms and those symptoms experienced one week before the illness, it is most appropriate for administration when the client is having current difficulties. In contrast, the SADS-L is most appropriate when there is no current illness. To make accurate ratings, interviewers are allowed to use a wide range of sources (client's family, medical records) and ask a number of different questions. Final ratings are made on a 6-point Likert-type scale. Administration involves over 200 items and takes from 1.5 to 2 hours and should only be conducted by a psychiatrist, psychologist, or psychiatric social worker. The end product is the following eight Summary Scales:

1. Mood and ideation.
2. Endogenous features.
3. Depressive-associated features.
4. Suicidal ideation and behavior.
5. Anxiety.

6. Manic syndrome.

7. Delusions-hallucinations.

8. Formal thought disorder.

Interrater reliabilities for the specific diagnostic categories have been found to be quite high, with the exception being the Formal Thought Disorder Scale (Endicott & Spitzer, 1978). The low reliability of this scale may have been because few of the patients in the Endicott and Spitzer (1978) sample showed clear patterns of disordered thoughts, which resulted in high variability for the ratings. Test-retest reliabilities were likewise good, ranging from .88 for Manic Disorders to .52 for Chronic and Intermittent Depressive Disorder (Spiker & Ehler, 1984). The exception was a low reliability for Schizoaffective, Depressed (.24), but this was probably due to the small number of patients included in this category, which resulted in limited variance. Using a different and possibly more appropriate statistical method, reliability increased to .84. Overall, the SADS has demonstrated excellent reliability particularly for interrater and test-retest reliabilities related to current episodes of psychiatric disturbance.

Validity studies have been encouraging in that expected relationships have been found between SADS scores and external measures of depression, anxiety, and psychosis. For example, Johnson, Margo, and Stern (1986) found that relevant SADS measures could effectively discriminate between patients with depression, and paranoid and nonparanoid schizophrenia. In addition, the SADS depression measures effectively rated the relative severity of a patient's depression. A further representative study by Coryell et al. (1994) found clear consistency between different locations using the SADS to assess major depression. The authors suggest that incremental validity might be increased by having clients referred for a medical examination to screen out physical difficulties that might be resulting in central nervous system dysfunction. The authors also recommend that interviewers try to increase validity by always including the best available information (family history, structured tests, other rating schedules) prior to making final ratings.

Child Version

The SADS for School-Age Children (Kiddie-SADS-P, K-SADS-P; Puig-Antich & Chambers, 1978) and the K-SADS-III-R (Ambrosini, Metz, Prabucki, & Lee, 1989) is a semistructured interview developed for children between 6 and 17. The test is scored using the Research Diagnostic Criteria and focuses on current level of pathology according to how it was at its worst and how it has been during the past week. Although much of the K-SADS-P is based on research with major depressive disorders of prepubertal children, it also covers a wide range of disorders such as phobias, conduct disorders, obsessive-compulsive disorders, and separation anxiety.

The interview should be administered by a professional clinician who has been trained in the use of the K-SADS and is familiar with *DSM-III-R* criteria. Administration time is approximately one hour, but usually takes longer with younger children. Separate interviews are given to the parent and then the child, and any discrepancies between the two sources of information are clarified before final ratings are made. The first phase is a 15- to 20-minute unstructured interview in which rapport is developed as well as an overview of relevant aspects of history, including the frequency and duration of presenting symptoms, their onset, and whether the parents have sought previous treatment. This is followed by structured questions regarding symptoms, which are rated on a Likert scale, with 1 representing "not at all" and 7 indicating that they are "extreme." A skip structure is built into the format so that interviewers can omit irrelevant questions. Interviewers are allowed to use their judgment regarding the wording and the type and number of questions. Finally, ratings are made regarding behavioral observations (appearance, attention, affect). Interviewers are also requested to rate the completeness and reliability of the interview and to make a global assessment of pathology (degree of symptomatology and level of impairment).

Test-retest reliability on the K-SADS has been good for conduct disorders and symptoms related to depression, but poor for anxiety disorders. Overall reliabilities have been lower for the K-SADS (and K-SADS-III-R) than for the adult SADS, but this is to be expected given the relative changeableness and less well-developed language skills found with children (Ambrosini et al., 1989; Chambers et al., 1985). Validity studies indicate that relevant K-SADS measures correlated highly with diagnoses for conduct disorders, schizophrenia, and depression (Apter, Bleich, Plutchik, Mendelsohn, & Tyrano, 1988). Additional expected correlations have been found between SADS measures and ratings of adolescent mood (Costello et al., 1991) and the Child Behavior Checklist (Achenbach & Edelbrock, 1983).

Collectively, the different versions of the SADS provide a thorough, well-organized structured interview that has been well accepted in research as well as clinical settings. Rogers (1995) has summarized its strengths as being excellent interrater reliability and provision of ratings of symptom severity, measures of associated symptoms, guidelines for possible malingering, and evidence of convergent validity. In contrast, its weaknesses are that it has a relatively narrow band of diagnosis compared with some of the other available instruments such as the SCID or DIS. In addition, the diagnoses are based on Research Diagnostic Criteria (RDC) rather than the more recent *DSM-III-R* or *DSM-IV* criteria. This criticism is somewhat moderated, however, by many of the RDC and *DSM-III/DSM-IV* criteria being nearly the same, especially for childhood disorders. Finally, administration and interpretation of the SADS requires extensive training (usually a week) as well as a good working knowledge of differences between the SADS/RDC and *DSM-III-R/DSM-IV* criteria.

Diagnostic Interview Schedule

In contrast to the SADS, which is semistructured and requires administration by trained professionals, the Diagnostic Interview Schedule (DIS; Robins, Helzer, Croughan, & Ratcliff, 1981) is highly structured and was designed specifically by the National Institute of Mental Health (Division of Biometry and Epidemiology) to be administered by nonprofessional interviewers for epidemiological studies (see Helzer & Robins, 1988). An updated version has been developed for *DSM-III-R* (DIS-III-R; Robins, Helzer, Cottler, & Goldring, 1989) and a *DSM-IV* version should be available in the near future (Robins & Helzer, 1994). Clinical judgment is reduced to a minimum through the use of verbatim wording, specific guidelines, and a clear flow from one question to the next. Thus, the DIS is far more economical to administer than the SADS. Studies have generally indicated that results are comparable between trained clinicians and nonprofessional interviewers (Helzer, Spitznagel, & McEvoy, 1987).

Adult Version

The original version of the DIS was derived from the format of the earlier Renard Diagnostic Interview. Diagnosis is currently based on both the *DSM-III* and Research Diagnostic Criteria. Initially, questions are directed toward obtaining information regarding the client's life, and information is also requested regarding more current symptoms based on the past two weeks, past month, past six months, and past year. Specific probe questions distinguish whether a symptom is clinically significant. A total of 470 potential clinical ratings are made and organized around 24 major categories. Administration time is approximately 60 to 90 minutes.

Computerized administration and scoring programs are available that can generate diagnoses based on the *DSM-III,* Research Diagnostic Criteria, or Feighner criteria. Computer administration is available and this has been found to generate an average of 5.5 possible diagnoses compared with an average of 2.6 for nonstructured interviews (Wyndowe, 1987). Patient acceptance for the computer administration has been found to be high, although the average administration time of 111.6 minutes is somewhat longer than the clinician-interviewed version. An abbreviated paper-pencil version (DISSA or DIS Self-Administration; Kovess & Fournier, 1990) is available, which is limited to depressive disorders, anxiety disorders, and alcoholism.

Studies of the reliability and validity of the DIS have been both variable and controversial. The comparability of diagnosis by professionals and nonprofessionals using the DIS has generally been supported. This suggests that nonprofessionals can effectively use it to help gather data for large epidemiological studies. For example, Robins et al. (1981) found diagnostic agreement between psychiatrists and nonprofessional interviewers to be .69. The sensitivity (percent interviewees correctly identified) of the DIS varied according to type of diagnosis, but had a mean of 75% with a mean specificity (percent noncases correctly identified) of 94%. However, data on sensitivity and specificity were based on using psychiatrists' diagnoses as the true index of diagnostic accuracy. The difficulties in considering psychiatrists' ratings as the truly accurate or "gold standard" criterion for validity have already been noted, so it is probably best to consider the preceding data on sensitivity and specificity as forms of interrater reliability rather than concurrent validity. In contrast to this study, Vandiver and Sheer (1991) found somewhat modest median test-retest reliabilities ranging between .37 to .46.

Although many of the ratings between professional and lay interviewers were equivalent, Helzer et al. (1985) found that, when compared with psychiatrists, nonprofessional interviewers tended to overdiagnose major depression. In contrast to Helzer et al. (1987), Folstein et al. (1985) did not find a sufficiently high rate of agreement between diagnoses by a panel of psychiatrists and diagnoses by the DIS to warrant its use in epidemiological studies. Specifically, it was found that the DIS generated more cases of depression and schizophrenia and fewer cases of alcoholism and antisocial personality (Cooney, Kadden, & Litt, 1990; Folstein et al., 1985). However, determining the relative accuracy of the psychiatrists or the DIS is more difficult. The DIS has also been found to be comparable with other commonly used psychiatric rating devices such as the Psychiatric Diagnostic Interview, but both of these may contain inaccuracies and, as in the Folstein et al. (1985) study, it is difficult to tell in which areas these inaccuracies occurred (Weller et al., 1985). The DIS has had the greatest difficulty accurately diagnosing borderline conditions and patients in remission, but this is to be expected since these are the most problematic diagnoses for many other assessment strategies (Robins & Helzer, 1994). In contrast, Swartz et al. (1989) were able to find quite respectable sensitivities (85.7%) and specificities (86.2%) for borderline conditions using a DIS borderline index.

Child Version

The Diagnostic Interview Schedule for Children (DISC; Costello, Edelbrock, Duncan, & Kalas, 1984) is similar to the adult version in that it is highly structured and designed for nonprofessional interviewers. It differs in that it is designed to be given as both a child interview (DISC-C) having 264 items and parent interview (DISC-P) involving 302 items. Ratings are coded as 0 (not true), 1 (somewhat true), or 2 (very often true). *DSM-III* diagnoses are generated based on the combined ratings for the child and parent interviews. Some of the more problematic diagnoses (autism, pervasive developmental disorder, pica) are based on an interview with the parent only. The entire interview usually takes one hour, but an explicit skip structure can enable some interviews to be somewhat shorter. The most recent modification of the DISC (DISC-Version 2.3 or DISC-2.3; NIMH, 1991) was developed in 1991 and was designed to be compatible with the *DSM-III-R* and anticipated *DSM-IV.* The DISC-2.3 comprises the following six modules: Anxiety Disorders, Miscellaneous Disorders, Affective Disorders, Schizophrenia and Other Disorders, Disruptive Behavior Disorders, and Alcohol and Other Substance Abuse Disorders.

DISC test-retest reliability for *DSM-III* diagnoses and symptom scores were .84 for parent interviews and .75 for child interviews (Edelbrock, Costello, Duncan, Kalas, & Conover, 1985). More recent evaluations of interrater reliability and test-retest reliability have been strongly supportive (Schwab-Stone et al., 1993; Shaffer et al., 1993). Children's reliability increased with age which would be expected considering their increase in intellectual abilities, greater memory, and improved language comprehension and expression. In contrast, reliabilities based on ratings from interviews with the parents decreased with the child's age, probably due to the parents having progressively less contact with their child. Comparisons between psychiatric and pediatric referrals indicated that psychiatric referrals had more symptom scores and more psychiatric diagnoses than pediatric referrals (Costello, Edelbrock, & Costello, 1985). Discriminations between psychiatric and pediatric groups were good for children with severe diagnoses and severe symptoms but not for children with a mild-to-moderate level of difficulties. Discriminations based on interviews with parents were generally more accurate than those based on child interviews (Costello et al., 1985). The DISC has also been found to identify risk factors for suicide attempts (Borst, Noam, & Bartok, 1991) and substance abuse (Greenbaum, Prange, Friedman, & Silver, 1991). In summary, the weakest validity for the DISC is for comparisons with other tests such as the Child Behavior Checklist, whereas the strongest is moderate-to-good support for diagnostic validity related to the presence of general psychopathology. However, there is currently insufficient data to assess the validity of the DISC for many specific disorders (Rogers, 1995).

Diagnostic Interview for Children and Adolescents

The Renard Diagnostic Interview (Helzer et al., 1981) inspired both the DIS and the Diagnostic Interview for Children and Adolescents (DICA; Herjanic, 1983; Herjanic & Campbell, 1977). It has been through several revisions, which have incorporated the *DSM-III, DSM-III-R,* and elements of the DIS. Similar to the DIS, the DICA has been designed for administration by lay interviewers. The most recent version (DICA-R) was published in 1991 and is available in child (Reich, Shayka, & Taibleson, 1991a) parent (Reich, Shayka, & Taibleson, 1991b), and adolescent versions (Reich, Shayka, & Taibleson, 1991c). The DICA can be administered to children between 6 and 17 years. The format is highly structured and primarily organized around different themes, such as behavior at home, behavior at school, and interpersonal relationships with peers. Additional content areas are substance abuse and the presence of such syndromes as anxiety disorders, mania, and affective disorders. Elaborate instructions are given for skipping irrelevant items, and total administration time is between 60 and 90 minutes. The administration begins with an interview of both the parent and child, which is designed to establish baseline behaviors and to obtain relevant chronological information. The parent is then questioned about the child to determine the possible appropriateness of 18 *DSM-III-R* diagnostic categories. The final step is to administer a "Parent Questionnaire," which requests additional medical and developmental history and addresses possible diagnoses that have not been covered by previous questioning.

Reliability of the DICA has been quite variable. Test-retest reliability has been quite good ranging between .76 and .90 (Bartlett, Schleifer, Johnson, & Keller, 1991; Earls, Reich, Jung, & Cloninger, 1988). In contrast, most cross-informant (parent-child) agreement related to specific symptoms has been disappointingly low (.19–.54; Herjanic & Reich, 1982; Sylvester, Hyde, & Reichler, 1987). The highest level of agreement was for the oldest children and the lowest for younger groups. Whereas mothers reported more behavioral symptoms, children were more likely to report subjective complaints.

Validity studies on the DICA indicate that it can accurately make the somewhat gross distinction between middle to older aged children who were referred to a general psychiatric clinic from those referred to a pediatric clinic (Herjanic & Campbell, 1977). However, there was considerable overlap for children between six and eight, thus suggesting that a greater possibility of misdiagnosis exists for children in this age range. The interview was found to be most effective for assessing relationship problems, less effective for academic difficulties, and least effective for assessing school problems, somatic complaints, and neurotic symptoms (Herjanic & Campbell, 1977). In addition, adolescents diagnosed with depression on the DICA also had corresponding elevations on the Beck Depression Inventory (Marton, Churchard, Kutcher, & Korenblum, 1991). In summary, the psychometric properties of the DICA have been variable with more studies needed to substantiate its validity, particularly concurrent validity (Rogers, 1995).

The Structured Clinical Interview for the *DSM-III*

The Structured Clinical Interview for the *DSM-III* (SCID; Spitzer, Williams, & Gibbon, 1987) is a comprehensive broad-spectrum instrument that adheres closely to the *DSM-III-R/DSM-IV* decision trees for psychiatric diagnosis. A certain degree of flexibility is built in so that administration can be tailored to different populations and contexts. Thus, slightly different forms are used for psychiatric inpatients (SCID-P), outpatients (SCID-OP), and nonpatients (SCID-NP). Whereas these versions of the SCID are directed toward Axis I diagnoses, a separate version has been developed for the diagnosis of Axis II disorders (SCID-II; Spitzer, Williams, Gibbon, & First, 1990). A further variation, the SCID-D (Steinberg, 1993), has been developed using *DSM-IV* criteria for the assessment of dissociative disorders. The SCID and its variations include several open-ended questions as well as a skip structure, which enables the interviewer to branch into new areas dependent on the client's previous responses. Since clinical judgment is essential throughout the interview, it should only be administered by trained professionals. To increase incremental validity, the authors encourage the inclusion of relevant additional data in making final diagnostic decisions.

The SCID, along with its variations, is the most comprehensive structured interview available. As a result, administration time can be considerable even with the inbuilt screening questions and skip structure. Many individual clinicians and treatment sites deal with this by primarily administering the modules they are most concerned with. For example, a treatment center specializing in substance abuse might administer the module for Psychoactive Substance Use Disorders along with the SCID-II when the comorbidity of personality disorders is suspected. Administration time might also be reduced by administering the computerized mini-SCID (First et al., 1995) which has been designed to screen for possible Axis I disorders. In addition, a computerized SCID-II (AutoSCID-II; First et al., 1996) is available which can also potentially reduce clinician time.

The SCID and its variations have not been subjected to near the level of reliability and validity studies as the SADS or DIS. This might be partially due to the considerable breadth of coverage encompassed by the SCID making it a daunting task to cover all areas. The reliability studies that have been performed have resulted in overall moderate but quite variable test-retest and interrater reliabilities. For example, interrater agreement using the SCID-II for common diagnostic categories to range between .40 to .86 with a mean of .59 (First, Spitzer, Gibbon, & Williams, 1995). Riskind, Beck, Berchick, Brown, and Steer (1987) found that several difficult-to-distinguish diagnostic categories had relatively good levels of interrater agreement. These included generalized anxiety disorders (.79, 86% agreement), depressive disorders (.72, 82% agreement; Riskind et al., 1987), panic disorders ($k = .86$), and major depression ($k = .81$; Reich & Noyes, 1987).

For the most part, validity studies of the SCID have assumed that *DSM-III-R* and *DSM-IV* diagnoses are the benchmark for making comparisons of diagnostic accuracy. Thus, "procedural validity" has often been assumed since the SCID has closely paralleled the diagnostic criteria derived from the *DSM-III-R/DSM-IV* (Rogers, 1995). A representative validity study found good agreement ($k = .83$) between interviewer ratings and cross ratings of interviewer videotapes by two senior psychiatrists (Maziade et al.,

1992). Other studies have found considerable diagnostic overlap within Axis I disorders and between Axis I and Axis II disorders (Alnacs & Torgerson, 1989; Brawman-Mintzer et al., 1993). However, evaluating the meaning of this overlap is difficult since the extent to which it is due to instrument error versus true comorbidity (i.e., the frequent occurrence of anxiety and depression) is difficult to determine. In summary, the strength of the SCID is its impressive breadth of coverage, use of modules targeted toward specific areas, and close parallel with the *DSM-III-R/DSM-IV.* Its weaknesses are its wide variation in reliability and its need for further validity studies particularly relating it to other diagnostic measures.

RECOMMENDED READING

Cormier, W. H., & Cormier, L. S. (1990). *Interviewing strategies for helpers* (3rd ed.). Monterey, CA: Brooks-Cole.

Morrison, J. (1993). *The first interview: A guide for clinicians.* New York: Guilford.

Othmer, E., & Othmer, S. C. (1994). *The clinical interview using DSM-IV: Vol.1: Fundamentals.* Washington, DC: American Psychiatric Press.

Rogers, R. (1995). *Diagnostic and structured interviewing: A handbook for psychologists.* Odessa, FL: Psychological Assessment Resources.

Chapter 4 ———————————————

BEHAVIORAL ASSESSMENT

Behavioral assessment is one of a variety of assessment traditions such as projective testing, neuropsychological assessment, and objective techniques. Behavioral assessment distinguishes itself by being a set of specific techniques as well as a way of thinking about behavior disorders and how these disorders can be changed. One of its core assumptions is that behavior can be most effectively understood by focusing on preceding events and resulting consequences. Out of this core assumption has come a surprisingly diverse number of assessment methods, including behavioral interviewing, several strategies of behavioral observation, measurement of relevant cognitions, psychophysiological assessment, and a variety of self-report inventories.

Behavioral assessment can be most clearly defined by contrasting it with traditional assessment (see Table 4–1). One of the most important comparisons is the emphasis that behavioral assessment places on situational determinants of behavior. This emphasis means that behavioral assessment is concerned with a full understanding of the relevant antecedents and consequences of behavior. In contrast, traditional assessment is often perceived as more likely to view behavior as the result of enduring, underlying traits. It is this underlying difference in conceptions of causation that explains most of the other contrasts between the two traditions. An extension of this conceptual difference is that behavioral assessment goes beyond the attempt to understand the contextual or situational features of behavior and, more importantly, concerns itself with ways to change these behaviors. There is a close connection between assessment itself and its implications for treatment. Thus, behavioral assessment is more direct, utilitarian, and functional.

The perceived limitations of traditional assessment were a major factor in stimulating the development of behavioral assessment. Specifically, traditional assessment was considered to focus too extensively on abstract, unobservable phenomena that were distant from the actual world of the client. In addition, behaviorists felt that traditional clinical psychology had stagnated because its interventions were not sufficiently powerful and too much emphasis was placed on verbal therapy. The concepts of traditional assessment seemed to exist in an abstract world divorced from the immediate realities and requirements of behavior change. The result of many traditional procedures seemed to be a large quantity of information that had little direct relevance to treatment intervention and outcome. However, this is a stereotyped, somewhat polarized view of traditional (and behavioral) assessment in that there has been considerable and increasing emphasis on the treatment implications and situational context of information derived from traditional methods of assessment. This stereotyped view is meant to

Table 4–1. Aims, assumptions, and applications of the behavioral and traditional approaches to assessment

	Behavioral Approaches	Traditional Approaches
I. Aims	To assist in the identification of problem behaviors and their maintaining conditions To assist in the selection of an appropriate treatment To assist in the evaluation of treatment effectiveness To assist in the revision of treatment	To assist in the diagnostication or classification of problem conditions To assist in the identification of etiological factors To assist in prognostication
II. Assumptions		
1. Causes of performance	Performance is thought to be a function of situational variables or the interaction of situational and person variables	Performance is thought to be a function of intrapsychic or person variables
2. Meaning of performance	Test performance is viewed as a sample of a person's repertoire in a specific situation	Test performance is viewed as a sign of an enduring, underlying state or trait or person variable
III. Applications		
1. Instrument construction	Adequate representation of the contextual features of the setting of interest is emphasized (in that performance is seen as situationally determined) Adequate representation of the repertoire of interest is emphasized (in that the test performance is seen as a sample of the repertoire)	Little emphasis on the representation of contextual features (in that performance is seen as consistent across time and settings) Adequate representation of the underlying state or trait or person variable of interest is emphasized (in that test performance is seen as sign of the underlying variable)
2. Scope of assessment	Broad focus encompassing the problem behaviors and their maintaining conditions, treatment prerequisites, treatment administration, treatment outcome, etc.	Narrow focus encompassing the problem condition
3. Schedule of assessment	Repeated assessment: at key junctures in the course of treatment or throughout the course of treatment	Infrequent assessment: typically prior to and after treatment
4. Method of assessment	Preference for direct methods of measurement	Methods of measurement are by definition indirect (in that test performance is seen as a sign of an underlying state or trait)

Source: Adapted from Barrios & Hartman (1986) and Barrios, Hartman, Roper, & Bradford (1979). Entire table reprinted, with permission, from *Behavioral Assessment: A Practical Approach.* A. S. Bellack & M. Hersen (Eds.), 1988, p. 5, Pergamon Press PLC.

highlight differences between the two strategies rather than to capture the complexities and similarities between them.

A further contrast between behavioral and traditional assessment is that behavioral assessment is concerned with clearly observable aspects in the way a person interacts with his or her environment. A typical behavioral assessment might include specific *measures of behavior* (overt and covert), *antecedents* (internal and external), *conditions surrounding behaviors,* and *consequences.* This knowledge can then be used to specify methods for changing relevant behaviors. Even though some behavioral assessers might take selected personality traits into account, these traits would only be considered relevant if they had direct implications for therapy. For example, locus of control has been found to predict success in self-regulation training (Carlson, 1982) and introversion/extroversion can help predict response to different types of therapy (Eysenck, 1976). This focus on the person and his or her unique situation is quite different from psychodynamic, biochemical, genetic, or normative trait models.

The behavioral approach stresses that different behavior disorders are typically expressed in a variety of modes. These might include overt behaviors, cognitions, changes in physiological states, and patterns of verbal expressions. This implies that different assessment strategies should be used for each of these modes (Lazarus, 1989). An inference based on one mode will not necessarily generalize to another. For example, depression for one person may be caused and maintained primarily by the person's cognitions and only minimally by poor social skills. Another person might have few cognitions relating to depression but be depressed largely because of inadequate social skills. The person with inadequate social skills would be most effectively treated through social skills training and only minimally helped through approaches that alter irrational thoughts (McKnight, Nelson, Hayes, & Jarrett, 1984). Furthermore, altering a person's behavior in one mode is likely to affect other modes, and these effects might have to be taken into account.

Whereas the preceding information presents a relatively rigid and stereotyped distinction between traditional and behavioral assessment, most practicing clinicians, including those who identify themselves as behavior therapists, typically combine and adopt techniques from both traditions (Fernandez-Ballesteros & Staats, 1992; Haynes & Uchigakiuchi, 1993). This was demonstrated by Piotrowski and Keller (1984) who surveyed members of the American Association of Behavior Therapy and found that 70% used the MMPI, 34% used the Rorschach, and 38% used the TAT. Thus, behavioral assessment has become increasingly eclectic and now is usually perceived as part of mainstream assessment, not as a new and contrasting alternative. Traditional and behavioral approaches have now come to resemble each other in many areas. In particular, behavioral assessment has gone through both a turning inward as well as a turning outward toward traditional psychometric approaches. The turning inward is most apparent in that internal behavioral repertoires and aspects of cognition are seen as essential for a complete understanding of the person (Fernandez-Ballesteros & Staats, 1992). Specific cognitive techniques include having the person think aloud as he or she is involved in a specific situation, sampling thoughts when a beeper goes off, and using a wide variety of self-statement inventories. Second, behavioral assessment has turned outward in that it has become increasingly concerned with traditional psychometric considerations. This has included evaluating the reliability and validity of behavioral observations, self-report inventories, and diagnoses (First et al., 1992; Follette & Hayes, 1992).

The assumptions and perspectives of behavioral assessment have resulted in an extremely diverse number of approaches and an even wider variety of specific techniques. These approaches and their corresponding techniques can be organized into the areas of behavioral interviewing, behavioral observation, cognitive behavioral assessment, psychophysiological assessment, and self-report inventories. Each of these areas was developed within a wider historical context extending over several decades.

HISTORY AND DEVELOPMENT

Treatment based on behavioral principles has a long history, dating back to the days of Little Albert and his fear of white, furry objects (Jones, 1924; Watson & Raynor, 1920). However, extensive, well-defined behavioral assessment strategies that were consistent with behavioral therapy were relatively slow to develop. The earliest formal use of behavioral assessment occurred in industrial and organizational settings (Hartshorne & May, 1928; OSS Assessment Staff, 1948), but behavioral assessment did not become popular within the clinical context until the mid-to-late 1960s. This was probably due to the powerful influence of psychodynamic approaches among clinicians who were taught to "look beneath the surface" to understand the "true" causes of behavior. Perhaps in part as a reaction to this indirect and inferential approach to understanding the person, the earliest forms of behavioral assessment focused almost exclusively on observable behaviors. Although organismic variables such as cognitions, feelings, and psychophysiological responses were acknowledged, they were not considered important influences on behavior and, as a result, were not stressed in assessment and treatment. Instead, behavioral assessment was consistent with the then dominant operant conditioning paradigm in that it focused on identifying discrete behavioral responses, target behaviors, and reinforcers that could change specific behaviors. Measurement of these areas typically quantified the frequency, rate, and duration of relevant behaviors (Ullman & Krasner, 1965). The result was numerous, highly innovative assessments of overt behaviors. Typically, interventions involved single cases, which was consistent with their idiographic approach.

Early definitions of behavioral assessment were created partially by making contrasts with traditional psychodynamic approaches. Each had different aims (identification of problem behaviors vs. classification), assumptions (behavior is caused by situations vs. enduring traits), and applications (direct observation vs. indirect inferences). In particular, Mischel (1968) attacked the very nature of traits by arguing that they were fictions based on distortions of language (a preponderance of static descriptions), the result of consistency of roles and situations (not inner traits), perceptual bias based on needs for predictability, and the rarity of disconfirmation when traits are (incorrectly) inferred. This attack fueled a lengthy controversy, which was relevant to behavioral assessment in that Mischel's perspective was used to argue for a focus on situational determinants of behavior. Proponents of behavioral assessment (along with psychiatry itself) were also dissatisfied with traditional *DSM-II* diagnosis, which had poor reliability and validity and did not seem to relate to the real world of the client or have direct treatment utility.

During the 1970s, there was a much greater emphasis on a wider approach. The typical single case study format gave way to assessment within a much larger context such as schools, businesses, families, and differing sociocultural frameworks. This assessment approach was based partially on the observation that these larger contexts could have considerable influence on the person, so that effective individual change often required change in these wider contexts. A refocusing on larger contexts was also motivated by challenges to the strict operant paradigm in that, while effective in controlled situations (hospital ward, Skinner box, prison), it had questionable social validity and doubtful long-term clinical impact (Goldfried, 1983; Milne, 1984). Assessment was also widened by arguments to focus on the wider aspects of the person, which meant not only behavior, but also feelings, sensations, internal imagery, cognitions, interpersonal relations, and psychophysiological functioning (Lazarus, 1973). This emphasis on a multimodal or multifaceted approach forced the mainstream of behavioral assessment to accept a number of indirect measures such as self-reports, ratings by significant others, and cognitions (Cone, 1977, 1978). Relevant publications were the first editions of *Behavioral Assessment: A Practical Handbook* (Hersen & Bellack, 1976), *Handbook of Behavioral Assessment* (Ciminero, Calhoun, & Adams, 1977), and the journals *Behavioral Assessment* and the *Journal of Behavioral Assessment,* both of which began in 1979.

The 1980s and 1990s have seen a proliferation of publications within the field of behavioral assessment, a dramatic reevaluation of some of its most basic assumptions, and the incorporation of influences from other traditions and disciplines. In particular, psychiatry had similar difficulties with the *DSM-II* as behavioral assessment, and began to develop strategies quite similar to those of behavioral assessment. The Problem Oriented Record (Weed, 1968) was introduced into many general hospital and psychiatric settings to improve diagnostic and treatment practices by providing behavior-specific databases, problem lists, treatment plans, and follow-up data. It thereby more effectively tied in the relationship between assessment and treatment, and more clearly delineated diagnostic issues. Perhaps of greater importance, *DSM-III-R,* and *DSM-IV* were similar to the efforts of behavioral assessment in that each diagnostic category was developed using behavior-specific descriptions. Numerous publications have worked to integrate behavioral assessment with traditional psychiatric diagnosis (First et al., 1992; Follette & Hayes, 1992; Hersen, 1988; Hersen & Bellack, 1988b) in such areas as depression (Nelson & Maser, 1988), the diagnosis of childhood disorders (Kazdin, 1988), and understanding different models of causation (Haynes & O'Brien, 1988). The perspectives of psychiatry and behavioral assessment have been further linked by the *Journal of Behavior Therapy* and *Experimental Psychiatry.*

The development and expansion of behavioral medicine has also drawn extensively on behavioral assessment strategies in the evaluation of headaches, coronary heart disease, Reynaud's disease, asthma, chronic pain, sleep disturbances, and eating disorders (Williamson, Davis, & Prather, 1988). More recently, behavioral assessment strategies have begun to focus on unstable, transitional behaviors in part motivated by new conceptual developments based on chaos theory (Haynes, 1995; Heiby, 1995). Thus, not only has behavioral assessment increasingly accepted the contributions of other disciplines and alternative models of conceptualizing behavior, but many of the most honored behavioral techniques have been challenged (Goldfried, 1983). For example, clinical judgment within the context of structured interviews has been accepted, diagnostic classification is now considered potentially useful, reliance solely on behavioral observations is perceived in some contexts as inappropriate, and indirect measurement is seen as essential.

In essence, the 1980s and 1990s have witnessed a significant reappraisal and expansion of what is involved in behavioral assessment. Birchler (1989) summarizes his review by noting, "Behavioral assessment as we may have known it in the recent past is in a rapidly changing process of (choose one): disarray, revision, broad expansion, advancement, confusion, and/or extinction" (p. 385). Since there has clearly been a significant blurring and cross-fertilization between behavioral assessment and other forms of assessment, the future may eventually result in behavioral assessment and traditional assessment being indistinguishable. This integration and overlap seems to be partially based on the belief (realization) that predicting behavior and optimizing treatment outcomes is probably most effective when the strengths of both traditions are utilized; that each contains complementary types of information.

ISSUES RELATED TO RELIABILITY AND VALIDITY

Traditional psychometric considerations for behavioral assessment are difficult to summarize due to the wide diversity of techniques and to the differences in assumptions regarding the focus, nature, and causes of behavior. Whereas traditional assessment stresses the relative stability of various characteristics, behavioral assessment assumes variability based largely on environmental factors. A finding such as low test-retest reliability is more likely to be interpreted within the behavioral context as being due to true variance resulting from environmental conditions rather than error within the data collection procedure. Furthermore, behavioral assessment stresses the importance of individually tailored approaches emphasizing the client's idiosyncracies. Within this context, normative comparisons are frequently seen as both irrelevant and inappropriate. Despite these issues, many from within the area of behavioral assessment have successfully argued for evaluating behavioral assessment techniques with traditional psychometric approaches (Anderson, Cancelli, & Kratochwill, 1984; Gresham, 1984). For example, interobserver agreement for behavioral observations is essential before the data gathered from this approach can be trusted. This is typically determined by calculating the percentage of interrater agreement (Cooper, Heron, & Heward, 1987). Likewise, data derived from self-reports in such areas as assertiveness and fear needs to demonstrate that the findings can be generalized to other situations such as role plays, simulations, and especially daily life.

The earliest forms of behavioral assessment relied primarily on behavioral observation and assumed that the direct observation of specific behaviors was sufficiently clear, reliable, and accurate. The emphasis was primarily on determining a functional analysis between behavior and its antecedents and consequences. In an activity such as pressing a bar for reinforcement, the behavior could be easily recorded by an electronic detector and therefore the reliability of the measure could be considered to be quite high. However, with behaviors that are more difficult to define, the reliability of measurement, especially when based on behavioral observation, cannot be assumed. For example, fingernail-biting might be defined merely by the person touching his or her face, or it may involve touching the mouth, actually chewing the nail, or removing part of the nail or perhaps the entire nail. The issue of precise definition and accurate measurement of the behavior becomes even more problematic when dealing with internal cognitions, where the clinician is completely dependent on self-reports rather than on direct observation.

The level of reliability across different observational strategies has been found to vary. In general, material derived from behavioral observation during behavioral assessment can be influenced by observer expectations in similar ways, as has been found by experimental research (Cooper & Rosenthal, 1980; Orne, 1962; Rosenthal, 1966). Consistent with this is that interrater agreement has been quite variable for such areas as overt difficulties and underlying mechanisms (Persons, Mooney, & Padesky, 1995). In such situations as natural observation where observer bias, outside factors such as interference from nontarget persons, and a lack of clear definitions are likely to create variability in observer responses reliability can be expected to be relatively low. Further sources of observer error include halo effects, primacy effects, failure to score a behavior that has occurred, rating toward the center of the scale, and leniency or generosity of scoring. When bias is reduced through the use of highly structured procedures, then reliability has increased. Thus, a procedure such as systematic sampling in which clear strategies are used to determine when and how the behavior will be measured has generally been found to be more reliable and accurate than naturalistic observation (Cunningham & Thorp, 1981). Although reliability has been found to increase in controlled situations where the observers know that they, themselves, are being evaluated for accuracy (Romanczyk, Kent, Diament, & O'Leary, 1973), this outside monitoring of observers rarely occurs in clinical situations. Thus, the reliability found in clinical situations cannot be assumed to be as high as for controlled studies in which evaluators are themselves being evaluated. General guidelines for increasing reliability in clinical situations include having two observers compare their results, providing careful instructions when a client is requested to monitor his or her own behavior, specifying target behaviors, clearly wording items on self-reports, taking care in the construction of instruments, and thoroughly training observers such as parents or teachers. Reliability of ratings is also likely to be increased by paying closer attention to contextual variables (Beck, 1994; Durand, 1990; Persons, et al., 1995).

During the 1960s and 1970s, the validity of various assessment procedures depended primarily on informal content validity. Questionnaires and observational strategies were based on rational considerations regarding what was to be studied and how these measurements were to be made. Few efforts were made to develop empirically derived categories. For example, the assessment of depression might have been based on knowledge about the typical thoughts depressed people seem to have as well as additional variables that seem important regarding social supports and typical antecedent events. The various areas of observation were mostly selected based on what rationally seemed to be the most critical considerations. Since the early 1980s, increased work has gone into assessing the validity of various methods of behavioral assessment. In general, few validity studies have been performed on behavioral interviews and naturalistic observations, whereas much more has been done on behavioral questionnaires (Morrison, 1988). Most validity studies have been conducted by using relevant outside criteria. Many of the same issues have come up with criterion validity for behavioral assessment as for traditional assessment, including difficulty generalizing to different populations, settings, and methods of administration.

The early behavioral self-report questionnaires relied on content and face validity. Since these questionnaires represented new techniques with a different underlying philosophy, it was believed that they did not have to be judged using the same criteria as the older and more traditional psychometric tests. They were considered to be direct reports of client behaviors and thus little psychometric validity was reported. Kaplan and Sacuzzo (1993) criticize this by stating that behavioral self-reports may be "repeating history and reinventing the wheel" (p. 493). They further point out that the "early paper-and-pencil structured personality tests which were finally abandoned in the 1930s are indeed difficult to distinguish from many present-day (behavioral) self-report procedures" (p. 494). The problems of response bias, questionable reliability and validity, no norms, and assumed client truthfulness need to be addressed for any standardized instrument, including behavioral procedures. Many behavioral self-report questionnaires might be best referred to as "idiosyncratic clinical tools" rather than psychometrically sound tests. The familiar argument used for traditional tests is that different assessment procedures serve to provide checks and balances for one another. Although it is often argued that self-reports are supported by other sources of data (direct observation, psychophysiological measurement, internal dialogue), few actual studies on the incremental validity of these procedures have been conducted.

Many behavioral self-report inventories have been developed but have had widely varying degrees of success demonstrating acceptable psychometric qualities. For example, the Rathus Assertiveness Schedule (RAS; Rathus, 1973) has been subjected to traditional psychometric procedures and illustrates the difficulties encountered in this as well as other similar behavioral inventories. Whereas Heimberg, Harrison, Goldberg, Desmarais, and Blue (1979) did not find a very high correspondence between scores on the RAS and observational reports of role plays in an inmate population, the RAS did relate to nonassertiveness in a group of dental students (Rathus, 1972) and communicator apprehension (Kearney, Beatty, Plax, & McCroskey, 1984). However, a difficulty with relating assertiveness in role-play situations, which most of the preceding studies used, is that assertiveness in role plays may not relate to assertiveness in naturalistic situations (Bellack, Hersen, & Turner, 1979). Perhaps when subjects are requested to role-play, they can alter their daily level of assertiveness to "act the part" correctly (Higgins, Alonso, & Pendleton, 1979). The RAS similarly has poor criterion validity based on instructor evaluations of observed assertive behavior and grades in a communication course (Tucker, Weaver, Duran, & Redden, 1983). Thus, even though the RAS is a frequently used device in both research and clinical settings, the meaning of the scores might be difficult to evaluate. Other behavioral self-report questionnaires have experienced similar problems.

ASSETS AND LIMITATIONS

Probably the greatest advantage of behavioral assessment is that its practitioners have continually paid attention to its relevance toward treatment. Any measurement of problem behaviors is usually directly tied to how these behaviors can be changed. Furthermore, relevant behaviors are given an empirical functional analysis, which enables clinicians to make baseline measurements of behavior and to assess the antecedents and consequences of these behaviors. An initial functional analysis can then allow clinicians to evaluate whether change has actually occurred during or after treatment. Even though many techniques have not been through rigorous traditional validity studies, the emphasis on treatment validity has proven to be attractive to many practitioners. Thus, behavioral assessment is particularly useful for persons using a hypothesis-testing approach and for those who wish to have clear accountability that change has actually taken place. In some situations, however, behavioral assessment can be tied too closely to treatment, particularly in legal assessments or other situations where assessment and therapy are separate.

A further asset is that behavioral assessment offers a wide range of possible techniques for use in extremely varied contexts. These strategies include self-reports, naturalistic observation, physiological monitoring, structured observation, and self-monitoring. Variations in techniques are consistent with the view that a complete understanding of the person requires multiple modes of assessment. The different assessment modes might involve relevant aspects of person-situation interaction, physiological changes, cognitions, interpersonal relationships, overt behaviors, feelings, imagery, and aspects of the person's larger social system. Many behavioral assessment models organize their approach around stimulus, organism, response, and contingencies (Goldfried, 1982). Other approaches rely on Lazarus BASIC-ID (Lazarus, 1989), or on Kanfer and Saslow's (1969) functional analysis of behavioral excesses and deficits. These approaches place the person in a much wider context than traditional assessment procedures.

Behavioral assessment is particularly appropriate when a presenting problem is determined primarily by environmental factors. In most cases, a clear, functional relationship (environmental interaction) can be established for such disorders as phobias, marital difficulties, acting out, temper tantrums, and inappropriate classroom behavior. Behavioral assessment is somewhat less relevant when environmental factors account for a smaller portion of the variance. Organic factors may be more important than environmental ones in chronic schizophrenia, certain types of headaches, and head injuries. Although behavioral assessment and intervention can still be effective for such problems, greater difficulties are involved, since the environment is relatively less important.

A previously described but extremely important drawback of many behavioral assessment strategies is that they have poor or at least untested psychometric properties. Often the attempts to establish reliability and validity have been disappointing. In addition, the accuracy of behavioral observation and interviewing can be distorted due to such factors as observer bias, halo effects, primacy effects, low interobserver agreement, and confirmatory bias.

Although cognitive behavioral assessment has been given increased importance, in many ways it is contrary to the original spirit of behavioral assessment's emphasis on direct observation. Cognitive assessment is necessarily unobservable and relies on client self-reports. Difficulties might include differences in meaning between the client and the clinician, response biases, assumed honesty of reporting, and assumptions about the equivalence of internal dialogues and their verbal descriptions.

A final limitation of behavioral assessment is that it often requires extensive resources in terms of time, personnel, and equipment. This is particularly true for psychophysiological and observational methods. Wade, Baker, and Hartman (1979) surveyed 257 behaviorally oriented professionals, and 43.8% felt that behavioral assessment was impractical in applied settings. This probably explains why only 12% of the members of the American Association of Behavior Therapy recommend the use of behavioral analysis and only 20% endorsed the use of observation (Piotrowski & Keller, 1984). As a result, behavioral assessment is frequently limited to interviews and questionnaires (Bornstein, Bridgewater, Hickey, & Sweeney, 1980). An additional drawback is that many behavioral instruments have not been designed to deal with problems frequently encountered in clinical practice, such as dissociative disorders, paranoia, and hypochondriasis.

STRATEGIES OF BEHAVIORAL ASSESSMENT

Behavioral assessment has given rise to numerous and highly varied techniques, many of which have been described in Hersen and Bellack's (1988a) *Dictionary of Behavioral Assessment Techniques.* Barrios and Hartman (1988) found over 100 instruments for assessing children's fears and anxieties. Despite this diversity, behavioral assessment strategies can be organized into the general categories of behavioral interviewing, behavioral observation, cognitive behavioral assessment, psychophysiological assessment, and self-report inventories. Each of these approaches varies in the degree to which it emphasizes direct versus indirect measures of the person, as well as in the extent to which it relies on inference. For example, cognitive assessment is more indirect than behavioral observation and relies much more on inferences regarding the degree to which cognitions affect and interact with overt behavior. However, all of these techniques stress developing a functional analysis of behavior through understanding person-environment interaction. They also emphasize that each aspect of assessment is directly relevant to treatment planning and evaluation.

Behavioral Interviewing

Behaviorally oriented interviews generally focus on describing and understanding the relationships between antecedents, behaviors, and consequences (ABC). In addition, a baseline or pretreatment measure of behavior is developed through a systematic consideration of the frequency, intensity, and duration of relevant behaviors. Behaviors might also be provided with a description of specific behavioral excesses and deficits (Kanfer & Saslow, 1969). Any goal must be able to be measured and tested in an objective and reliable way, and the client should agree on its relevance (Gresham, 1984). Although the behavioral approach might seem long and involved, the process is simplified by considering only areas that are relevant for treatment.

  Despite this emphasis on treatment utility, it is essential to place each aspect of the information derived from a behavioral interview into a wide context. A basic description of a target behavior is simplistic since it does not take into account an interactionist model. For example, a phobia is likely to create difficulties in the client's relationships, which could undermine the person's sense of competence. The person might then react by becoming highly dependent on a primary relationship, reinforcing the sense of helplessness. The helplessness might then reinforce a fear of not being able to cope, which can then interact with and quite possibly exacerbate the phobia. Thus, a complete interview would evaluate not only the existence of and nature of the phobia, but also the effect of the phobia on relationships, work effectiveness, and self-statements. Whereas the earlier behavioral interviews of the 1960s and 1970s often had a narrow focus, current models of behavioral assessment emphasize taking this wider context into consideration.

The general purpose of the behavioral interview is multifaceted. It might help identify relevant target behaviors or select additional behavioral assessment procedures. It also provides an opportunity to obtain informed consent, obtain a history of the problem, identify causal factors related to the presenting problem, develop a functional analysis of the problem behavior, increase client motivation, design intervention programs, and evaluate the effectiveness of previously attempted interventions.

The initial phase of a behavioral interview needs to include many of the elements relevant for traditional interviews. A sufficient degree of rapport needs to be established, a statement needs to be developed of the general and specific purposes of the interview, and a review should be made of the client's relevant history. However, history tends to be deemphasized in favor of current behaviors because the main cause of client behavior is considered to be situational rather than historical. Common clinician approaches involve reflective comments, probing, understanding, and expressed empathy. Open-ended questions can be followed up with more direct questioning. However, the extensive use of nondirective techniques is inappropriate in that the clinician must set a clear direction and have the client answer direct questions relevant to a behaviorally oriented approach.

Sometimes clients provide excellent descriptions of their problems and can specify relevant antecedent and consequent conditions. Other clients experience difficulty describing the events surrounding the decision to seek treatment, elaborating on their feelings, stating who referred them, or providing information about how other people might be perceiving their problem. Since a careful behavioral analysis requires a complete description of problem behaviors, the client and therapist must work to establish the extent of the difficulty, where it occurs, when it occurs, and its effects on relationships. Sometimes it is helpful to have the client keep a diary of relevant events and observations. Often clients will describe and define their difficulties by relying extensively on general trait descriptions rather than on more behaviorally oriented ones. A behavioral interviewer, then, needs to work with the client to develop specific and easily observable descriptions. For example, if a client says he or she is a "depressed type of person," this might translate into specific types of behaviors (slow movement, spending too much time in bed, avoiding people, being nonassertive), cognitions (that he or she is no good, a failure), and feelings (hopelessness, apathy). The belief in an underlying permanent trait (illness) needs to be reframed as a group of specific behaviors that are potentially changeable. This reframing process, in itself, is likely to be beneficial to clients because they will be better able to see specific things they can do to change how they feel. Speaking in concrete behavioral terms rather than abstractions is also likely to increase mutual understanding between client and therapist.

A wide-based behavioral assessment should describe not only the specific presenting problem, but also the manner in which the problem has generalized into other areas. In particular, this assessment might involve information about the larger social system. Often, the client's school, work, or family situation can be incorporated into the assessment and treatment program to ensure both immediate and long-term success. In contrast, if a narrow approach to change is taken, the client may attempt to express his or her newly acquired behavior in contexts that will not be supportive of it. As a result, previous problem behavior might once again develop to the exclusion of newer, more adaptive behavior. This might be true if the client developed new effective behaviors that were learned only within the narrow context of the practitioner's office.

An interview should end by providing the client with a summary of the information that has been obtained, an explanation of additional information that is required, and an estimate of the likely success of treatment (Morganstern, 1988). If further information is required, the clinician and client need to agree on what is needed and how to obtain it. This might involve instructions for keeping an effective diary, requests for observations from other people, or techniques for self-monitoring of different behaviors. If the interview is a prelude to therapy, additional information should be given about possible strategies for intervention, the length of treatment, possible financial and emotional costs, and assurances that the client will have input into all decisions.

Because most interviews tend to be somewhat informal and haphazard, they frequently provide information with low reliability and validity. For example, Wilson and Evans (1983) found a low level of reliability among clinicians trying to specify appropriate target behaviors. Some authors urge that behavioral interviews be structured and standardized. Kratochwill (1985) has suggested that interviews be planned around a four-stage problem-solving process. The first stage is *problem identification* in which the problem is specified and explored, and procedures are established to measure current performance and desired target behaviors. The vague and generalized descriptions that clients typically come in with are developed into specific behavioral descriptions. Next, a *problem analysis* is performed by assessing the client's resources, and by noting the relevant environmental conditions influencing behavior and the context in which the behavior excesses or deficits occur. An interview also needs to establish how a *plan might be implemented,* which would also include ongoing procedures for collecting data relevant to the progress of the treatment. Finally, strategies for *treatment evaluation* should be specified by considering the pre- and posttreatment measures to determine whether the intervention was successful.

Witt and Elliott (1983) provide the following somewhat similar outline of expected accomplishments for any behavioral interview:

1. Initially, provide the client with an overview of what needs to be accomplished and why a clear and detailed specification of the problem behavior is important.

2. Identify the target behavior(s) and articulate them in precise behavioral terms.

3. Identify the problem frequency, duration, and intensity ("How many times has it occurred today," "How long has it been going on," etc.).

4. Identify conditions in which the problem occurs in terms of its antecedents, behaviors, and consequences.

5. Identify the desired level of performance and consider an estimate of how realistic this is and possible deadlines.

6. Identify the client's strengths.

7. Identify the procedures for measuring relevant behaviors. What will be recorded, who will record it, how will it be recorded, when and where will it be recorded?

8. Identify how the effectiveness of the program will be evaluated.

9. After completing discussion of the preceding areas, summarize it to ensure that the client understands and agrees.

This outline should not be followed rigidly, but should be used as a general guideline. However, each behavioral assessment should have accomplished all nine areas prior to completion.

Behavioral Observation

In some cases, the behavioral interview is itself sufficient to obtain an adequate assessment. However, some form of actual behavioral observation is usually required before, during, and/or after treatment. The particular method for observing behavior is usually decided on during the initial interview. Whereas the interview is primarily directed toward obtaining verbal information from the client, behavioral observation is used to decide on and actually carry out specific strategies and techniques of measuring the relevant areas of behavior discussed during the interview. In some cases such as assessing the developmentally disabled, resistant clients, or very young children, behavioral observation may become one of the most important means of assessment. These observations might be made by the professional who is actually conducting the treatment or by someone else who is more involved in the client's life such as a teacher, parent, spouse, or self-monitoring by the client. The most frequent approaches are narrative recording, interval recording, event recording, and ratings recording.

The first behavioral observation task is to select relevant target behaviors, which can vary from a single response set to a larger interactive unit. The target behavior should either involve the problem behavior itself or relate to it in a meaningful way. Decisions must be made regarding the number of behaviors to record and the relative complexity of the recording method. Both the recording method and the target behavior need to be manageable and should avoid being overly complex. The target behavior can best be clarified by beginning with a narrative description of the client's difficulty and then further specified by considering the antecedents and consequences related to the problem behavior.

All behaviors to be measured must have objective, complete definitions that allow clear observations of the measures of the behavior. In particular, the definition should avoid abstract and highly inferential terms, such as "apathy" or "sadness," and instead translate such terms into specific behaviors. Any description of the target behavior should involve an easy-to-read dictionary-type definition, an elaboration of the behavior, and specifications regarding precisely when the behavior occurs as well as descriptions of borderline examples and clear nonexamples (Foster, Bell-Dolan, & Burge, 1988). In measuring behavioral frequencies, the practitioner must clearly define when the behavior begins and ends. This might be easy for measuring the number of cigarettes a person smokes or number of times a child bangs his or her head, but is more difficult when measuring less clearly defined behaviors, such as the number of aggressive acts a person makes or frequency of nonassertive behaviors. Recordings also need to measure the duration of behaviors and their intensity. For example, how hard a child bangs his or her head and the total time engaged in the activity have implications for the urgency and strength of the treatment approach.

The different devices used to make recordings might include various combinations of golf counters, stopwatches, pencil-and-paper forms, or electromechanical devices such as an event recorder with buttons that can be pressed when various categories of behaviors occur. Sometimes the recordings of behaviors might be entered into a computer and summarized or audio and video recordings might be made for later review.

The settings of behavioral observation can range from those that are natural to those that are highly structured. Natural, or in vivo, settings might include the home, classroom, business, or playground. Observations made from these types of settings are likely to be directly relevant to and reflective of the client's life. Natural settings are most effective when assessing high-frequency behaviors and/or more global behaviors, such as attentional deficits, social withdrawal, or depressive behaviors. They are also useful when measuring the amount of change the client has made following intervention. However, natural settings present difficulties due to the extensive time required to make observations. Furthermore, natural settings are problematic when trying to measure infrequently occurring behaviors (aggression, nonassertiveness) or behaviors that occur only in the absence of others (fire setting, suicide). To counter the difficulties inherent in naturalistic observation, practitioners may wish to create structured environments (role plays, work simulations) that elicit specific types of behaviors. Such environments are especially important for infrequent behaviors. However, inferences need to be derived cautiously from observations in these structured or analogue situations, since they may not generalize into the client's actual life.

When clinicians are concerned that observations made by a person outside the client's environment might contaminate the results, they may wish to train persons who are already a part of the client's natural setting such as parents, teachers, or spouses. This might help prevent subjects from changing their behaviors simply because they are aware that they are being observed (reactivity). These more natural observers can be much less obtrusive than an outside professional. The training of observers needs to include a clear rationale for measuring the behavior with emphasis on making accurate and objective recordings. Observers need to memorize the recording code, practice making the recordings, and receive feedback about the relative accuracy of their recordings. Precautions should be taken to avoid observer error, such as through observer bias, leniency, lapses in concentration, and discussion of data with other observers. Sometimes reliability might be checked by comparing the degree of agreement between different observers rating the same behaviors. Caution should be made when using trained observers since widely varying levels of interobserver agreement have been noted (Margolin, Hattem, John, & Yost, 1985).

A system of coding behaviors usually needs to be developed so that recordings are abbreviated and simplified. If too many codes are used, it will be difficult for recorders to recall them, especially if behaviors occur in rapid succession. Both the type of recording method (narrative recording, event recording, etc.) and the coding system will depend largely on the goals of assessment. A coding system that is clear, simple, and closely connected to the presenting problem is likely to be both useful and reliable. Important considerations in selecting a recording and coding system are the number of times the behavior needs to be observed, the length of observation periods, when to make the recording, the type of recording to be made, and the target behaviors to be recorded (Sattler, 1992). The following sections describe the most frequently used recording systems along with examples of different methods of coding.

Narrative Recording

Narrative recording requires that the observer simply make note of behaviors of interest. There is little quantification and the observations can vary in the degree of inferences made. For example, an observer may stick close to direct descriptions of behavior, such as noting that someone frequently laughs and smiles at his or her friends, or may infer from these behaviors that the client has good peer relations. The primary value of narrative recordings is that they may help define future, more specific areas, which can then be measured in a more quantitative manner. Thus, narrative recording is usually a precursor to alternative forms of measurement. It has the advantages of potentially discovering relevant behaviors; it can elaborate on these behaviors; it requires little, if any, equipment; and numerous hypotheses can be generated from the narrative descriptions. Limitations are that it doesn't enable the observer to quantify the observations, may have questionable validity, and the usefulness of the observations depends largely on the individual skill of the observer.

Interval Recording

A clinician may choose to record whether or not selected aspects of behavior occur within predetermined intervals. As a result, this technique is also referred to as time sampling, interval sampling, or interval time sampling. Usually the intervals vary from 5 to 30 seconds and may be based either on set schedules for each observation period (e.g., every 5 minutes) or may be selected randomly. Interval recording is most appropriately used when measurements of overt behaviors with moderate frequencies (e.g., once every 5 to 20 seconds) are required and when these behaviors do not have any clear beginning or end. This might include such behaviors as walking, listening, playing, reading, or looking up and down.

When developing a strategy for interval recording, clinicians must decide on the length of time between each observation, the method of recording, and the length of the observation period. This will depend largely on the type of behavior. For example, different types of verbal interaction may vary in length and, as such, the observation periods must be adjusted to take this into account. Some strategies might require the observer to alternate back and forth between recording (e.g., for 10 seconds), then observing (e.g., for 20 seconds), and then going back to recording the observation that has just been made. Cues regarding the beginning and end of each behavior must be specified. The target behaviors for observation will be derived from information based from such sources as the initial interview, self-report inventories, narrative observations, and especially from descriptions of the presenting problem. The focus of observation may also vary between different people such as the husband, wife, teacher, child, or client. Sometimes clinicians or researchers arrange to have an outside person observe the same client behaviors. The interrater reliability of the observations can then be established by calculating the percentage of agreement between the two raters

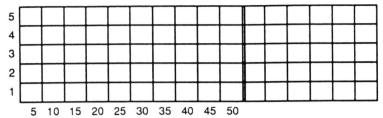

a. Graph paper with series of columns, each five blocks high. Double heavy line marks off 10 columns, for a 50-minute period.

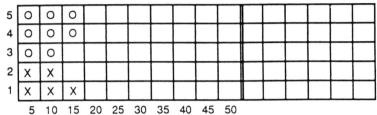

b. Chart after 13 minutes of monitoring pupil's behavior. First two columns are completed and the third is partially completed. If the pupil behaves appropriately during the next (14th) minute, the observer will mark an "X" in the third column just above the other "X." If the pupil misbehaves, the observer will mark an "O" in that column just under the other two "Os."

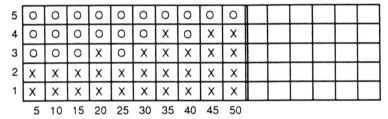

c. Chart after observer has completed the 50-minute period.

Figure 4–1. Example of interval recording

To set up a self-graphing data recording system, start with a piece of graph paper. Mark 2 heavy lines across the paper so that 5 blocks are between the lines. You have now a series of columns, all 5 blocks high. Each block will represent an interval (e.g., minute) of observation time. Mark off the number of 5-block columns needed for the scheduled observation period: a 50-minute period would need 10 columns of 5 blocks; a 30-minute period would need 6 columns; a 45-minute period would need 9 columns; and a 5-minute period would need only 1 column of 5 blocks. For now, let's assume you have scheduled a 50-minute period for your observation, as shown in Figure 4–1 a–c. You have marked off 10 columns on your paper, each 5 blocks high, for a total of 50 blocks: 1 block for each minute scheduled.

For each interval (minute) in which the behavior occurs, you will place an "X" in a box. For each interval in which the behavior does not occur, you will place an "O" in a box. Start with the left column and work toward the right. In each column, work from the bottom up with the "Xs," but from the top down with the "O" marks. When the "Xs" and "Os" meet in the middle, the column is filled. Move to the next column to the right and continue: "Xs" from the bottom, "Os" from the top down, until they meet. As you move across the row of 5 columns, the data recorded will automatically form a graph without any extra effort on your part. With this methods, trends in data across the session can be easily identified and shared with school personnel or parents. By focusing on the "Xs" in Figure 4–1c, it is clear that the amount of "on task" behavior by the pupil is steadily increasing during the observation session (i.e., there are fewer "Xs" in the first column, and more "Xs" in the later columns).

Source: From "Behavioral Observation for the School Psychologist: Responsive-Discrepancy Model" by G. J. Alessi, 1980, *School Psychology Review,* p. 40. All explanatory material is verbatim from Alessi (1980).

114

(see Cooper, Heron, & Heward, 1987). A representative interval recording chart, with instructions on how to develop such a chart, are provided in Figure 4–1.

Interval recording is time-efficient, highly focused on specific behaviors, and has the potential to measure almost any behavior. Interval recording is not designed to assess the quality of the target behaviors, however, and can be artificial or may overlook other additional important behaviors.

Event Recording

Whereas interval recording depends on measurements defined by units of time that are imposed on target behaviors, event recording depends on the occurrence of the behavior itself. The observer must wait for the target behavior to occur, and then record relevant details of the behavior. Examples of behaviors most appropriate for event recording are aggressive actions, greetings, or use of such verbal expressions as assertion or profanity.

The basic design of event recording systems is to note the behavior's frequency, duration, and intensity, and to record the behavior on such devices as a checklist, golf counter, or hand counter. Although the main emphasis is on quantifying the frequency of responding, its duration also can be measured with a stopwatch. The intensity of the behavior can be noted by simply specifying whether it was slight, moderate, or strong. A representative example of an event-recording chart is included in Figure 4–2.

Event recording is especially good for recording behaviors having low frequencies, measuring changes in behaviors over time, and for use in studying many different types of behavior. However, event recording is relatively poor at measuring behaviors that do not have clear beginnings and endings, and presents difficulties in keeping the attention of observers for behaviors of long durations. Since event recording does not

| | | | Intervals in minutes | | | | | |
Behavior	Totals	Person Observed	5	10	15	20	25	30
Getting out of seat	27	Subject	□	⌐'	□	⦙	·	··
	8	Comparison	··	,	⸬ ,	·		·
Requesting help	5	Subject		·		⦙ ··		,
	11	Comparison	··	⦙ ··	⦙ ·	,	,	·

Figure 4–2.   Example of event recording within 5-minute intervals

Figure 4–2 illustrates an event recording for two different types of behaviors, the first of which (getting out of seat) the subject's teacher would like to see less of and the second (requesting help) the subject's teacher would like to see more of. In addition to recording the subject's behavior, another student was selected as a basis for comparison. The coding of the number of responses was developed by Tukey (1977) and uses dots and lines to indicate the number of responses which were made. One dot equals one response. Any number above four responses is indicated by a line connecting two dots. For example, in the first 5-minute block for "getting out of seat," the subject got out of his seat eight times. By noting the increases and decreases in the different recordings, observers can be alerted to possible environmental events that might have caused these changes. In this example, there was both a decrease in "getting out of seat" and an increase in "requesting help" beginning at the 20-minute interval.

Name __Bill__ Rater __Mark__ Date __7/16/88__

Behavior Description __Hitting objects (e.g., tops of tables) with his hand.__

Setting Description __One-to-one instructional settings in school__

Instructions: The **Motivation Assessment Scale** is a questionnaire designed to identify those situations in which an individual is likely to behave in certain ways. From this information, more informed decisions can be made concerning the selection of appropriate reinforcers and treatments. To complete the **Motivation Assessment Scale,** select one behavior that is of particular interest. It is important that you identify the behavior *very specifically.* *Aggressive,* for example, is not as good a description as *hits his sister.* Once you have specified the behavior to be rated, read each question carefully and circle the *one* number that best describes your observations of this behavior.

QUESTIONS	Never	Almost Never	Seldom	Half the Time	Usually	Almost Always	Always
1. Would the behavior occur continuously, over and over, if this person was left alone for long periods of time? (For example, several hours.)	(0)	1	2	3	4	5	6
2. Does the behavior occur following a request to perform a difficult task?	0	1	2	3	4	(5)	6
3. Does the behavior seem to occur in response to your talking to other persons in the room?	0	(1)	2	3	4	5	6
4. Does the behavior ever occur to get a toy, food, or activity that this person has been told that he or she can't have?	0	1	2	(3)	4	5	6
5. Would the behavior occur repeatedly, in the same way, for very long periods of time, if no one was around? (For example, rocking back and forth for over an hour.)	(0)	1	2	3	4	5	6
6. Does the behavior occur when *any* request is made of this person?	0	1	2	3	(4)	5	6
7. Does the behavior occur whenever you stop attending to this person?	0	(1)	2	3	4	5	6
8. Does the behavior occur when you take away a favorite toy, food, or activity?	0	1	2	3	(4)	5	6
9. Does it appear to you that this person enjoys performing the behavior? (It feels, tastes, looks, smells, and/or sounds pleasing.)	0	(1)	2	3	4	5	6
10. Does this person seem to do the behavior to upset or annoy you when you are trying to get him or her to do what you ask?	0	1	2	3	4	(5)	6
11. Does this person seem to do the behavior to upset or annoy you when you are not paying attention to him or her? (For example, if you are sitting in a separate room, interacting with another person.)	0	1	(2)	3	4	5	6
12. Does the behavior **stop** occurring shortly after you give this person the toy, food or activity he or she has requested?	0	1	2	3	(4)	5	6
13. When the behavior is occurring, does this person seem calm and unaware of anything else going on around him or her?	(0)	1	2	3	4	5	6

Figure 4–3. A completed Motivation Assessment Scale for Bill's object hitting in one-to-one instructional settings

Source: From *Severe Behavior Problems: A Functional Communication Training Approach* (pp. 80–82), by V. M. Durand, 1990, New York: Guilford: Copyright © 1990 by Guilford Press. Reprinted by permission.

QUESTIONS   ANSWERS

14. Does the behavior **stop** occurring shortly after (one to five minutes) you stop working or making demands of this person?

	Never	Almost Never	Seldom	Half the Time	Usually	Almost Always	Always
	0	1	2	3	4	5	(6)

15. Does this person seem to do the behavior to get you to spend some time with him or her?

	Never	Almost Never	Seldom	Half the Time	Usually	Almost Always	Always
	0	(1)	2	3	4	5	6

16. Does the behavior seem to occur when this person has been told that he or she can't do something he or she had wanted to do?

	Never	Almost Never	Seldom	Half the Time	Usually	Almost Always	Always
	0	1	2	(3)	4	5	6

	Sensory		Escape		Attention		Tangible
1.	O	2.	5	3.	I	4.	3
5.	O	6.	4	7.	I	8.	4
9.	I	10.	5	11.	2	12.	4
13.	O	14.	6	15.	I	16.	3
Total score =	I		20		5		14
Mean score =	0.25		5.0		1.25		3.5
Relative ranking =	4		1		3		2

Figure 4–3.   *(continued)*

provide information regarding sequences of behaviors, it is difficult to make inferences about how and why behaviors occur.

Ratings Recording

Rather than recording direct observations of behaviors, clinicians may wish to obtain general impressions of relevant dimensions of behaviors and have these impressions rated on a checklist or scale. Such measures tend to be more global and may involve more abstract terms, such as the client's level of cooperativeness or ability to maintain self-care. Typically, ratings recordings are made after a period of observation. A typical format might request the evaluator to rate, on a scale from one to five or one to seven, the client's frequency of temper tantrums, quality of peer relations, or conscientiousness. For example, the Motivation Assessment Scale (MAS; Durand, 1990) is a 16-item questionnaire that evaluates the functional significance of behavior related to the dimensions of sensory, escape/avoidance, social attention, and tangible rewards. Interrater reliability for the MAS ranged between .80 and .95 with test-retest reliability (30 days apart) ranging between .89 and .98. Validity has been supported through such means as determining that teacher's ratings on the MAS predicted student's behavior in analogue situations (Durand, 1990). An example of a completed MAS is illustrated in Figure 4–3.

Ratings recordings potentially can be used for a wide variety of behaviors. Other advantages are that the data can be subjected to statistical analysis, the ratings can be made either for individuals or groups, and due to the time efficiency of ratings recordings, they are likely to be cost-effective. Disadvantages include possibly low interrater agreement due to the subjectivity of the ratings, little information regarding antecedent and consequent events, and possibly inaccurate ratings, especially if much time elapses between making the observations and making the ratings.

Cognitive Behavioral Assessment

Over the past 20 years, considerable research has been conducted on understanding the cognitive processes underlying behavior disorders. Relevant areas include the self-statements associated with different disorders, the underlying structure or cognitive organization related to these disorders, differences between cognitive distortions in pathological versus normal behavior, and cognitive alterations that occur during therapy. This research has considerably influenced and altered the nature of behavioral assessment. In particular, researchers have developed specific techniques for assessing cognitive processes, such as having the person think aloud, listing different thoughts, thought sampling at various intervals, and a wide variety of self-statement inventories.

This internal perspective is quite different from the early emphasis of behavioral assessment, which focused almost exclusively on observable overt behavior. This transition has come about due to persuasive evidence for the relationship between behavior and cognitions (Bandura, 1986; Haaga, Dyck, & Ernst, 1991; Kendall & Hollon, 1981; Schwartz & Garamoni, 1989). Cognitive processes not only change during the course of effective therapy, but may be causally related to both the development as well as the maintenance of different types of disorders (Brewin, 1996; Ingram, Kendall, Siegle, Guarino, & McLaughlin, 1995; Westling & Ost, 1995). Some approaches assume that altering cognitions can be sufficiently powerful to change behaviors. However, there are also a number of significant limitations with cognitive behavioral assessment. All material is necessarily derived from the client's self-reports of his or her internal processes and, as such, may be subject to a number of distortions. Clients usually can recall and describe the results of their cognitive processes, but they have much greater difficulty describing how they arrived at these conclusions (Nisbett & Wilson, 1977). The actual processes may need to be inferred based on complicated analyses of the results derived from intricate assessment strategies. In addition, remembering events seems to be a reconstructive process in which each successive recall can be altered based on the person's needs, biases, and expectations (Henry et al., 1994; Lindsay & Read, 1995; Loftus, 1993). These inherent difficulties have led some traditional behaviorists to question the theoretical and practical appropriateness of cognitive assessment.

A relevant finding is that the popular belief in the "power of positive thinking" is simplistic in that it is not a very good predictor of adjustment. What seems more important is the absence of negative statements or, what Kendall and Hollon (1981) have referred to as "the power of nonnegative thinking." Furthermore, the effect of negative self-talk is greater than the ability of positive thinking to counter negative internal dialogue. As might be expected, gains in therapy have been associated with reductions in negative self-statements (Beck, 1994). Another issue is that relevant cognitions such as self-efficacy vary across situations. For example, a particular client might have cognitions quite consistent with competency in employment situations yet feel quite incompetent within family or other interpersonal situations. This means that clinicians conducting cognitive and other forms of assessments need to take these contextual variables into consideration (Beck, 1994; Persons et al., 1995).

Specific Content Areas

Theories of the cognitive processes of *depression* suggest that it is maintained by characteristic and repetitive thoughts that are self-perpetuating. For example, Beck (1967a,

1967b) listed the cognitions associated with depression as involving *arbitrary inference* (making inferences without substantiating evidence), *selective abstraction* (making a broad judgment based on a minor aspect of an event), *overgeneralization* (extrapolating in an unjustified fashion from a minor event), and *magnification/minimization* (overemphasizing negative events; minimizing positive ones). Although these processes seem to be related to depression, a simple cause-effect model between depression and specific cognitions does not appear to be warranted and further clarification is required (Brewin, 1985; Haaga et al., 1991).

A wide number of self-report inventories have been developed for the cognitive assessment of *depression.* The most time-honored and frequently used of these is the Beck Depression Inventory (BDI; Beck, Rush, Shaw, & Emery, 1979). A more complete coverage of the BDI is included in the section on self-report inventories. A further test based on Beck's theory of depression is the Dysfunctional Attitudes Scale (Weissman & Beck, 1978) which requests the extent to which people endorse the attitudes and beliefs held by persons subject to depression. The Cognitive Bias Questionnaire (Hammen, 1978; Hammen & Krantz, 1976), is a fairly well developed endorsement inventory that measures the likelihood of distorted thinking. It presents a series of vignettes, and requests the client to answer depressed/nondepressed and distorted/nondistorted options. Both child and adult versions are available. Persons who have been diagnosed as depressed are more likely to endorse "depressotypic distortions" (Michael & Funabiki, 1985), and scores have been found to change as depression lifts (Miller & Norman, 1986).

Several additional cognitive self-report inventories have also become frequently used in research and clinical practice. The Attributional Styles Questionnaire (Seligman, Abramson, Semmel, & von Baeyer, 1979) is based on the relationship between self-attribution and learned helplessness. Since causal attributions which are internal, stable, and global in their relationship to negative outcomes are related to depression, the Attributional Styles Questionnaire systematically assesses the occurrence of these attributions. The Automatic Thoughts Questionnaire (Hollon & Kendall, 1980) is a 30-item endorsement inventory that shows good reliability, can discriminate between the severity of different pathological states, is sensitive to alterations in affective states, and shows good discriminate and convergent validity (Ingram et al., 1995). The Cognitive Response Test (Watkins & Rush, 1983) uses an open-ended sentence format (incomplete sentences) and requests the person to respond to vignettes relating to occupation, family, marriage, and friendships.

The main cognitions that seem to characterize *social phobias* are interpersonal threat along with beliefs that positive interpersonal feedback is incorrect (Sewitch & Kirsch, 1984). The importance of a cognitive assessment of social phobias is underscored by research suggesting that cognitive deficits and distortions are more important in causing and maintaining the difficulty than deficits in social skills (Galassi & Galassi, 1979; Heimberg, 1994). Social phobics are more likely to recall negative information, interpret ambiguous feedback negatively, underestimate their own performance, expect more negative evaluations from others, and have more negative self-statements prior to interactions (Cacioppo, Glass, & Merluzzi, 1979; Hope & Heimberg, 1993; Smith & Sarason, 1975). Assessment of the relative rate of occurrence of each of these areas can provide specific treatment suggestions regarding which processes need to be modified. The most frequent instruments in the cognitive assessment of social phobias are the Social Avoidance and Distress Scale (SADS; Watson & Friend, 1969), Fear of Negative Evaluation Scale (FNE; Watson & Friend, 1969), and the Social Interaction Self-statement Test (Glass, Merluzzi, Biever, & Larson, 1982). Many of the self-statements described by research on social phobias and measured by such tests as the Social Interaction Self-statement Test are quite similar to the ones described by Beck (1967a) as being characteristic of depression. These similarities raise the still unresolved issue of whether specific irrational beliefs are related to specific disorders, or whether there is a nonspecific (yet generally negative) effect of irrational beliefs (see Heimberg, 1994).

Although less work has been done on *generalized anxiety,* two relevant assessment devices have been developed. The Irrational Beliefs Test (Jones, 1969) provides the client with 100 items that cover 10 different categories of irrational beliefs. The test has demonstrated adequate psychometric properties that suggest satisfactory validity because scores have been found to change when a person is under distress (Jones, 1969; Nelson, 1977) and are correlated with other measures of anxiety and depression (Cook & Peterson, 1986). In support of the nonspecificity view of irrational beliefs, test scores have not been found to relate to specific problem areas. The somewhat similar 70-item Rational Behavior Inventory (Shorkey, Reyes, & Whiteman, 1977) has also been used in the assessment of irrational beliefs and their relationship to anxiety.

Several strategies have been used in the assessment of eating disorders based on the observations that this class of disorders involve considerable cognitive distortions (Mizes & Christiano, 1994). Some authors have taken a previously developed scale such as the Cognitive Error Questionnaire (Lefebvre, 1981) and modified it to evaluate the cognitive distortions specific to eating disorders (Dritschel, Williams, & Cooper, 1991). Another approach has been to have eating-disordered persons monitor their self-statements in their natural environment (Zotter & Crowther, 1991). The value of such strategies is that they indicate that cognitive behavioral instruments can be tailored toward specific disorders and the information derived from these strategies has direct relevance for treatment in that it provides clinicians with specific cognitions to work with.

Self-efficacy has received considerable interest, particularly since it has been related to a variety of different predictions relevant to treatment (Bandura, 1986). A person having a high level of self-efficacy is likely to have positive expectations about his or her effectiveness to judge and deal effectively with situations. Self-efficacy is determined by the attainments someone has achieved in the past, vicarious (observational) experiences, verbal persuasion, and physiological states. An assessment of self-efficacy is especially important in understanding the antecedent and retrospective accounts of the effect and quality of the behavior. The relative level of self-efficacy has been found to predict a wide number of variables, including general therapy outcome (O'Leary, 1985), the prediction of success in the treatment of smoking (Baer, Holt, & Lichtenstein, 1986; Baer & Lichtenstein, 1988; DiClemente, 1986), and relapse rate from self-regulatory training (Carlson, 1982). Useful distinctions should be made between the level of strength of self-efficacy and its generalizability from one situation to the next. Since some question exists regarding the degree to which self-efficacy can be related from one situation to the next, specific measurements are often used for different areas (depression, assertion, smoking, etc.).

An area needing further development is the *clinical assessment of imagery*. It has frequently been observed that a person's presenting problem is significantly related to his or her fantasies or daydreams and different dreaming states. A depressed person may continually repeat images of being criticized, the anxious person might replay scenes of danger, and the paranoid might frequently review images of persecution. Knowing a person's relative ability to produce and control images may be important in predicting response to treatment that requires the formation of images such as systematic desensitization, covert desensitization, covert aversive conditioning, and certain types of relaxation procedures. Extensive experimental work has been conducted on imagery in such areas as the different dimensions of imagery (Parks, 1982), differences between waking and nonwaking imagery (Cartwright, 1986), and the effects of conscious and unconscious images on behavior (Horowitz, 1985). However, little material has been published regarding the clinical assessment of imagery. Of studies that have been published, most have related to measures of imagery ability (Sheehan, Ashton, & White, 1983) rather than to the effect of clinically relevant images on the person. Persons wishing to assess both clinical imagery and other aspects of cognitions might use one or several of the following strategies that have been developed to assess cognitions.

Recording Cognitions

In addition to the many self-report inventories available, a number of strategies have been developed for recording cognitions in a less-structured manner. Parks and Hollon (1988) have listed and summarized the following methods used by previous researchers:

Thinking Aloud.   Clients are requested to verbalize their ongoing thoughts, with these verbalizations usually extending for 5 to 10 minutes. A similar technique is free association, where the client is asked to simply say whatever comes to mind rather than report on his or her ongoing inner thoughts. A potential problem is that the procedure may feel unnatural and therefore provide a sample different from normally occurring internal thoughts. Also, the client may have no opportunity to verbalize competing thoughts with the result that the reported thoughts will most likely be a limited portion of the total cognitions. In addition, clients may not report everything honestly. A factor that is likely to make the verbally reported thoughts different from actual ongoing processes is that typically people change the topic of ongoing internal dialogues every 5 to 6 seconds, whereas verbal reports of these dialogues may only have topic changes on the average of every 30 seconds.

Private Speech.   Sometimes, children's cognitions can be assessed by paying close attention to barely audible speech they make while engaged in various activities. It is believed that these private verbalizations are closely aligned to inner thoughts.

Articulated Thoughts.   Clinicians may wish to create structured situations or simulations that parallel the problems the client reports. For example, a situation may be created that demands the client to be assertive or be exposed to criticism or phobic stimuli. The person can then be requested to articulate the thoughts he or she is experiencing during these situations. Typical thoughts can be noted and inferences made regarding how they relate to the problem behaviors.

Production Methods.   Instead of requesting clients to articulate their thoughts during a simulation, an actual naturalistic situation can occur (criticism, phobic stimuli, etc.), with clients then noting and recording the typical thoughts they have related to these situations. As such, these methods might also be referred to as in vivo self-reports.

Endorsement Method.   The client might be presented with either a standardized (e.g., Irrational Beliefs Test, Cognitive Bias Questionnaire) or an informally developed list of items and then is requested to rate their frequency of occurrence, strength of belief, and how the item might be uniquely represented in the person's cognitions. These items might include ratings of the frequency of such thoughts as "What's the use" or "I can't do anything right." Potential difficulties with this technique are the effects of the demand characteristics of the situation and social desirability. An underlying and questionable assumption behind the technique is that the relevant cognitions are within the client's conscious awareness.

Thought Listing.   Instead of developing a continuous description of ongoing thoughts, clients might be requested simply to summarize their relevant thoughts. The thoughts to be listed might be elicited by a specific stimulus, problem area, or by merely attending to or anticipating a stimulus.

Thought Sampling.   A sample of a person's thoughts might be obtained by setting a prompt (e.g., a beep on a timer), then having the client describe the thoughts he or she was having just prior to being interrupted by the prompt.

Event Recording.   The client might be requested to wait until a relevant event occurs (e.g., handwashing for an obsessive-compulsive), at which point, the thoughts related to these events are written down. Instead of merely waiting for a problem or spontaneously occurring behavior, a client might also be requested to describe the thoughts related to the expression of new and desired behaviors, such as assertion. The relevant thoughts about these behaviors might then be used to increase the likelihood of their continued occurrence.

Psychophysiological Assessment

A complete understanding of the person involves an assessment of not only behavioral, affective, and cognitive modes, but also of the ways these interact with and are dependent on physiological functioning. Such psychophysiological assessments have recently become easier to make due to increased interest and knowledge regarding instrumentation (electronics, computers), operant conditioning of behaviors that at one time were considered involuntary, physiological and neurochemical aspects of behavior, and behavioral medicine (Haynes, 1991; Sturgis & Gramling, 1988). The most frequently assessed physiological responses are heart rate, blood pressure, skin temperature, muscle tension, vasodilation, galvanic skin response (GSR), and brain activity as measured by electroencephalograms (EEGs). By quantifying data gathered through these areas, psychological problems can be translated into more precise physiological indices.

One of the first relevant studies to relate psychological and physiological modes indicated that fear and anger had different physiological responses in blood pressure and skin conductance (Ax, 1953). This result suggested that these and other psychological variables might be measured in ways other than through self-report inventories. More recently, it has been found that persons scoring high on psychological indices of intelligence had relatively small pupillary dilations (Ahern & Beatty, 1979), lower heart-rate variability, and less skin conductance when requested to perform tasks (Geiselman, Woodward, & Beatty, 1982). This suggests not only that persons with higher intelligence require less effort to complete a task but that, potentially, intellectual assessment might increasingly be based on psychophysiological measurement. A further representative area of research has involved the relationship between different personality variables and psychophysiological measurement (Iacono, 1991). Schizophrenics (when unmedicated) and persons with anxiety disorders have been found to have a relatively higher level of sympathetic responsiveness compared with parasympathetic responsiveness. In contrast, antisocial personalities are characterized by parasympathetic dominance and low levels of sympathetic responsiveness (Iacono, 1991; Porges & Fox, 1986; Wenger, 1966). Physiological indicators to detect lying, while still in extensive use, have not been found to have adequate psychometric properties (Kleinmuntz & Szucko, 1984; Saxe, Dougherty, & Cross, 1985). Greater promise has been demonstrated differentiating true from faked memory loss using event-related potentials (Allen, Iacono, & Danielson, 1992). While most of the previously mentioned studies represent very general correlations among such variables as emotions, intelligence, and behavioral disorders, they show considerable potential for future assessment should these measures become more refined. Physiological baseline measures for an area such as anxiety can and have been used to monitor the effectiveness of treatment for social phobias, generalized anxiety disorders, and obsessive-compulsive disorders (Turpin, 1991).

In addition to the usual knowledge relating to psychological assessment, clinicians who obtain and interpret psychophysiological data must have knowledge in anatomy, electronics, and the physiology of cardiovascular, musculoskeletal, neurological, respiratory, electrodermal, ocular, and gastrointestinal response systems. This extensive background is particularly important since instrumentation presents a number of special problems. A variety of confounding factors may be present, such as the effect of slowing respiratory rate to alter cardiac output or the effect of eye roll on measured brain activity. Filters might be necessary to exclude noise in the system. The techniques are also intrusive, thereby making the situation artificial and, partially as a result, generalizations to outside aspects of the client's life or between different response modes may be inappropriate. A wide variety of difficulties may arise regarding meaningful psychological interpretations based on the physiological data. In the future, the development of better instruments and improved methods of computer analysis is likely to increase the utility of psychophysiological assessment and overcome many of these difficulties.

SELF-REPORT INVENTORIES

An extremely wide number of self-report inventories have been developed for behavioral assessment. Typically, they involve between 20 and 100 items, with respondents requested to indicate their degree of endorsement to each item on a Likert-type scale. Most of these instruments have been developed for a specific topic such as assertiveness, depression, anxiety, fear, dysfunctional attitudes, control of visual imagery, ability to resolve conflict, or irrational thoughts. Many of these inventories have poor or even nonexistent psychometric properties. Also, normative data is rarely provided. In contrast to many behavioral inventories, the following inventories on depression, assertiveness, and fear have been selected because they have been extensively used in clinical and research settings and because they have had relatively extensive evaluations of their psychometric properties.

The Beck Depression Inventory

The Beck Depression Inventory (BDI) was introduced in 1961 by Beck, Ward, Mendelson, Mock, and Erbaugh (1961), was revised in 1971, and was copyrighted in 1978 (Beck, Rush, Shaw, & Emery, 1979). Although the later version involved a clarification and modification of the items, the two versions were found to be highly correlated (.94; Lightfoot & Oliver, 1985). The BDI has been widely used for the assessment of cognitions associated with depression for both psychiatric patients (Marton, Churchard, Kutcher, & Korenblum, 1991; Piotrowsky, Sherry, & Keller, 1985) as well as depression in normals (Steer, Beck, & Garrison, 1986). It has been found to detect depression as effectively as longer and more costly structured interviews (Stukenberg, Dura, & Kiecolt-Glaser, 1990). The popularity of this instrument is amply demonstrated in that, in the 35 years since its introduction, well over 1,000 research studies have been performed either on or using it.

The items in the BDI were originally derived from observing and summarizing the typical attitudes and symptoms presented by depressed psychiatric patients (Beck et al., 1961). However, most of these items were developed to reflect Beck's cognitive views on depression (see Haaga et al., 1991). A total of 21 symptoms were included; respondents were requested to rate the intensity of these symptoms on a scale from 0 to 3. Typical questions relate to such areas as sense of failure, guilt feelings, irritability, sleep disturbance, and loss of appetite. The inventory is self-administered and takes from 5 to 10 minutes to complete.

Several forms have been developed, including a card form (May, Urquhart, & Tarran, 1969), several computerized forms, a normal 21-item form, and a 13-item short form (Beck & Beck, 1972). Correlations between the short and long forms have ranged from .89 to .97 (Beck, Rial, & Rickels, 1974). A fifth- to sixth-grade reading level is required to adequately comprehend the items. The total possible range of scores extends from a low of 0 to a theoretical high of 63. However, only the most severe levels of depression are reflected by scores of 40 or 50. More typically, clinically depressed or maladaptively nonclinical populations will score in the 10 to 30 range (Beck, 1967a; Tanaka-Matsumi & Kameoka, 1986).

Reliability and Validity

Since its initial development in 1961, the BDI has been subjected to extensive psychometric evaluation. A meta-analysis of the different efforts to establish internal consistency has shown them to range from .73 to .92 with a mean of .86 (Beck, Steer, & Garbin, 1988). Similar reliabilities have been found with the 13-item short form (Leahy, 1992). Test-retest reliabilities have ranged from .48 to .86, depending on the interval between retesting and type of population (Beck et al., 1988). However, some controversy exists over whether the variable(s) the BDI is measuring is a state or trait. The practical implication of this is that, if the variable measures a state, then relatively wide fluctuations can be expected and thus the lower test-retest reliabilities would be more acceptable.

Evaluation of content, concurrent, and discriminant validity as well as factor analysis has generally been favorable. The content of the BDI items was derived by consensus from clinicians regarding symptoms of depressed patients (Beck et al., 1961), and six of the nine *DSM-III* categories for the diagnosis of depression are included. Concurrent validity is suggested by high to moderate correlations (.55 to .96, *Mdn r* = .72) with clinical ratings for psychiatric patients (Beck et al., 1988; Finer, Beebe, & Holmbeck, 1994; Marton et al., 1991). In addition, moderate correlations have been found with similar scales that also rate depression, such as the Hamilton Psychiatric Rating Scale for Depression (.73), Zung Self Reported Depression Scale (.76), and the MMPI Depression Scale (.76; Beck et al., 1988; Brown, Schulberg, & Madonia, 1995; Finer et al., 1994). The BDI has been able to discriminate psychiatric from nonpsychiatric populations (Byerly & Carlson, 1982; Marton et al., 1991) as well as discriminate the level of adjustment in seventh graders (Albert & Beck, 1975). Although Delay, Pichot, Lemperiere, and Mirouze (1963) were unable to make fine distinctions between endogenous, involutional, and psychogenic depression, Steer, Beck, Brown, and Berchick (1987) reported that patients with major depressive disorders had relatively higher scores than those with dysthymic disorders. Furthermore, the BDI has been used to discriminate persons who were lonely (Gould, 1982), under stress (Hammen & Mayol, 1982), persons self-reporting anxiety (Baker & Jessup, 1980), and those reporting general distress (Finer et al., 1994). Factor analytic studies indicate that the BDI clearly measures a primary factor variously referred to as a general depressive factor (Welch, Hall, & Walkley, 1990) or a cognitive/depressive one (Louks, Hayne, & Smith, 1989). However, the existence of strong additional factors remains controversial. Brown et al. (1995) found that whereas the BDI seems to measure primarily cognitive and affective aspects of depression (negative self focus, anhedonia, functional impairment), the Hamilton Rating Scale for Depression measures predominantly somatic symptoms (anxiety, weight, sleep, anhedonia/energy).

Interpretation

An ipsative interpretation of BDI responses can be used to specify irrational beliefs and relevant symptoms that are likely to be related to a person's depression. Identification of these beliefs and symptoms can be useful in specifying those which need to be worked on in therapy. Any of the following can be assumed to be an area of difficulty if a score of 3 is indicated on the numbered item:

1. Sadness
2. Pessimism
3. Sense of failure
4. Dissatisfaction
5. Guilt
6. Expectation of punishment
7. Dislike of self
8. Self-accusation
9. Suicidal ideation
10. Episodes of crying
11. Irritability
12. Social withdrawal
13. Indecisiveness
14. Change in body image
15. Retardation in work
16. Insomnia
17. Fatigability
18. Loss of appetite
19. Loss of weight
20. Somatic preoccupation
21. Low level of energy

The following scores can be used to indicate the general level of depression:

5 to 9	No or minimal depression
10 to 18	Mild to moderate depression
19 to 29	Moderate to severe depression
30 to 63	Severe depression
Below 4	Possible denial of depression, faking good; lower than usual scores for normals.
Above 40	Significantly above even severely depressed persons, suggesting possible exaggeration of depression; possibly characteristic of histrionic or borderline personality disorders. Significant levels of depression are still possible.

Fear Survey Schedule

The Fear Survey Schedule (FSS; Wolpe & Lang, 1964, 1969, 1977) is one of the most thoroughly researched behavioral instruments and has been used for a variety of purposes, including the measurement of the types of fears in children and adults, the evaluation of phobic disorders, and as an index of pre- and posttreatment change. In particular, the FSS has been used as an ipsative instrument to identify the typical situations that result in avoidance so effective treatment can be based on the identified fears. The first version of the FSS was a 50-item inventory by Akutagawa (1956), but several variations have since been developed of which the most frequently used (Caldwell-Colbert & Robinson, 1984) is the 78-item FSS-III by Wolpe and Lang (1964). Ratings on the different Fear Survey Schedules are made either on a 5- or 7-point Likert scale that indicates the extent of fear to such situations or stimuli as snakes, open places, surgery, dead animals, or speaking in public. The different fear categories were selected based on clinical observation, actual cases, and laboratory experiments (Geer, 1965; Wolpe & Lang, 1964).

At least seven variations of the FSS have been developed (Tasto, 1977). One noteworthy version is the Fear Questionnaire (Marks & Mathews, 1979), a shortened 20-item scale developed to produce scores on a person's main phobia, global phobia, total phobia, and overall level of anxiety and depression. An 80-item version was developed for children (Fear Survey Schedule for Children; Scherer & Nakamura, 1968) and later modified as the Revised Fear Survey Schedule for Children (FSSC-R; Ollendick, 1978). A 100-item version is the Temple Fear Survey Inventory (Braun & Reynolds, 1969), which includes items from previously developed surveys. The 108-item FSS (Wolpe & Lang, 1969) is probably the most readily available and frequently used form. It is not known which of the many versions is best. There is also no unified standardized administration for the different forms and no clear procedures for scoring and interpretation.

Reliability and Validity

Due to the many variations of the FSS, it is difficult to evaluate as a unitary instrument. Furthermore, authors have sometimes not specified which variation they used in their studies. Internal consistency of the original Wolpe and Lang (1964) scale was reported as greater than .90 (Geer, 1965; Spinks, 1980). The following subscales based on FSS items answered by college students have likewise demonstrated satisfactory internal consistencies: Hostile-dependent (males, .91; females, .90), Body Assault (.97 for both males and females), Developmental Fear (males, .83; females, .66), Performance Evaluation (males, .80; females, .69), Death Evasion (males, .80; females, .73), and Nuisance Animals (.81 for both males and females; Gulas, McClanahan, & Poetter, 1975). A somewhat different categorization of subscales based on the responses of agoraphobics likewise indicated adequate internal consistency ranging from .62 to .76 (Arrindell, 1980). A review of FSS test-retest (3 to 10 weeks) reliability studies indicated a range of .72 to .90, with shorter intervals generally producing higher reliabilities (Arrindell, Emmelkamp, & van der Ende, 1984).

Content validity by Wolpe and Lang (1964) based on a rational consideration of the items indicated the following six, broad, fear-related categories:

1. Animal fears.
2. Tissue damage, illness, death, or associated stimuli.
3. Classical phobias.
4. Social stimuli.
5. Noises.
6. Miscellaneous (Wolpe & Lang, 1964).

Some of the meanings behind responses to the items might be clarified by improved wording. For example, if a respondent reports anxiety related to flying in an airplane, a wide variety of reasons are possible, including excessive noise, being in an enclosed place, height, fear related to travel/transport, or a combination of these factors (Arrindell, Emmelkamp, & van der Ende, 1984). More formal factor analytic studies have often served to confuse the FSS's underlying factors due to the wide number of often overlapping categories. Frequently, different factors have been found according to patient versus nonpatient populations. A representative factor analysis done on a large sample of phobics using a 76-item FSS-III listed social fears (9.7% of the variance), agoraphobia (9.1%), fears relating to bodily injury, death, and illness (8.2%), fears relating to the display of sexual or aggressive themes (7.2%), and fears relating to harmless animals (7.0%; Arrindell, 1980; Arrindell, Emmelkamp, & van der Ende, 1984). Adequate, concurrent validity of the FSS is suggested by high scores being related to a person's sensitivity to becoming anxious (Reiss, Peterson, Gursky, & McNally, 1986) and FSS results being able to predict phobic avoidance behaviors (Lick, Sushinsky, & Malow, 1977). Similarly, Oei, Moylan, and Evans (1991) found that the FSS can aid in the differential diagnosis of various anxiety disorders.

Relatively extensive psychometric data is available for the 80-item Fear Survey Schedule for Children-Revised (FSSC-R; Ollendick, 1978, 1983). Internal consistency was .94, and test-retest reliability over a one-week interval was .82, but this dropped to a low of .55 after a three-month retesting period (Ollendick, 1978, 1983). Validity studies indicate a relationship between trait anxiety, high self-concept (in girls), and the ability to discriminate school-phobic children from normals (Ollendick, 1983). Factor analysis suggests the following five factors: fear of failure (giving an oral report, being teased, failing a test), fear of the unknown (mystery movie, dark places, nightmares), fear of injury and small animals (lizards, sharp objects, getting in a fight), fear of danger and death (earthquakes, being hit by a car, death, or dead people), and medical fears, (going to the dentist, riding in a car, getting carsick; McCathie & Spence, 1991; Ollendick, 1983).

Research using the FSSC-R indicates that girls have consistently reported more fears and a greater intensity to their fears (McCathie & Spence, 1991; Ollendick, 1983). However, the following seven greatest reported fears (rank ordered) were the same for both girls and boys: a burglar breaking into house, being sent to the principal, bombing attacks, being hit by a car or truck, falling from high places, being in earthquakes, and not being able to breathe (Ollendick, 1983). In contrast, anxious adult female patients reported that the five most frequent fears were, in rank order, the prospect of a surgical operation, speaking in public, losing control of self, feeling rejected by others, and failure (Thyer, Tomlin, Curtis, Cameron, & Nesse, 1985). The five most frequent fears of anxious adult male patients were speaking in public, losing control of self, failure, feeling rejected by others, and looking foolish (Thyer et al., 1985). However, McCathie and Spence (1991) clarify that the fear survey schedules may not be necessarily measuring the actual frequency of these fears in a person's daily life since many of the items on the surveys are very unlikely to occur (e.g., sharks, earthquakes). It is more likely that the surveys are measuring the intensity of the person's actual affective response to the item when the survey is presented to them.

Interpretation

Most clinicians use an ipsative analysis of client responses to determine clusters of self-reported fears. Some clients might have a preponderance of medical fears such as having surgery, getting sick, or going to the dentist. Others might report concerns related to social situations such as speaking in public, interpersonal rejection, or social disapproval. By knowing the specific fears or clusters of fears, the clinician can help focus the interview toward developing more information regarding the antecedents and consequences of these concerns. Client scores can also later be used as baseline measures for evaluating the effectiveness of interventions.

Although they provide less specific information, FSS total fear scores can also be used diagnostically to compare client scores. Tomlin et al. (1984) reported that the overall mean for patients with diagnosed anxiety disorders was 108.6 ($SD = 61.5$). Scores for specific anxiety subgroups were provided for simple phobias ($M = 89.9$, $SD = 53.5$), social phobias ($M = 86.9$, $SD = 63.5$), agoraphobias ($M = 152$, $SD = 58.9$), obsessive-compulsives ($M = 117.6$, $SD = 43.1$), and panic disorder ($M = 113.5$, $SD = 61.4$). Although some researchers have reported higher scores for females, the Tomlin et al. (1984) study did not find significant differences. Fischer and Turner (1978), using a normal college population, have reported extensive normative data for individual items, but no means and standard deviations are available for total scores for normal populations.

Rathus Assertiveness Schedule

The assessment of assertiveness is typically measured by either observing role-play situations or through self-report inventories. A wide variety of self-report inventories have been developed, including the Wolpe-Lazarus Assertion Inventory (Wolpe & Lazarus, 1966), Gambrill Assertion Inventory (Gambrill & Richey, 1975), Bakker Assertiveness Inventory (Bakker, Bakker-Rabdau, & Breit, 1978), and the Conflict Resolution Inventory (McFall & Lillesand, 1971). However, the Rathus Assertiveness Schedule (RAS; Rathus, 1973) has been the most extensively used, and relevant normative data are available for normal college students (Quillan, Besing, & Dinning, 1977) as well as for psychiatric populations (Rathus & Nevid, 1977). The 30 items on the schedule were derived from diaries kept by the author's undergraduate students, from the Wolpe-Lazarus Assertion Inventory and, to a lesser extent, from relevant items from Allports's A-S Reaction Study and Guilford and Zimmerman's Temperament Survey (1956). Respondents are requested to rate, on a 6-point scale, how descriptive each statement is of themselves. A -3 indicates that the statement is "very uncharacteristic of me" and a $+3$ indicates that it is "very characteristic." Sixteen items have been reversed to reduce the likelihood of response bias. Scores can theoretically range between -90 to $+90$, with higher scores indicating high levels of assertiveness.

In addition to the original 30-item schedule, two other versions have been developed for special populations. The modified RAS (MRAS; Del Greco, Breitbach, & McCarthy, 1981) was developed for young adolescents. Moderate test-retest reliability (.74; three-week interval) has been reported with means of 8.58 ($SD = 19.42$) for adolescent males and $-.29$ ($SD = 19.70$) for adolescent females (Del Greco, Breitbach, Rumer, McCarthy, & Suissa, 1986). A simplified version of the RAS is available that requires a minimum sixth-grade reading skills level in contrast to the tenth-grade reading level required for the regular version (SRAS; McCormick, 1984). The simplified version has high correlations with the regular RAS (.94) and produces similar means and standard deviations.

Reliability and Validity

Moderate levels of internal consistency have been reported, ranging from .59 to .86 with a mean of .78 (Beck & Heimberg, 1983). Test-retest reliabilities have been moderately high (.80; Norton & Warnick, 1976). A number of criterion validity studies have been reported that suggest adequate concurrent and predictive validities. A moderate correlation (.72) was reported with the Wolpe-Lazarus Assertion Inventory (Henderson & Furnham, 1983), although this would be expected given that the RAS and Wolpe-Lazarus Assertion Inventory share nine items in common. A positive correlation has been reported with communicator apprehension (Kearney et al., 1984) and an inverse relationship with depression (Sanchez & Lewinsohn, 1980). The relation with depression is particularly associated with RAS items that deal with inhibited social expression (Culkin & Perrotto, 1985). A decrease in RAS scores has been reported following successful treatment (Rathus, 1972, 1973) as well as high correspondence between RAS scores and the frequency of assertive responses in role plays (Futch & Lisman, 1977).

The different components of assertive behavior that Gambrill (1977) has described include positive assertion (complimenting others, expressing affection), negative assertion (expressing annoyance or irritation), behavior initiation (beginning a conversation with a stranger), and responding to another (participating in a conversation started by another). Assertive skills may not generalize from one area to the next—a person may be able to freely express compliments but have difficulty dealing with conflict. Most factor analytic studies of the RAS indicate that it emphasizes negative situations that require assertion and responding to another, and focuses to a much lesser extent on behavior initiation and positive situations requiring assertion. A representative factor analytic study by Henderson and Furnham (1983) indicated that the strongest factor (22.4% of the total variance) was "standing up for rights in a public place." This factor was most related to items 25, 3, 27, and 28, which deal with making complaints about poor service, making complaints about food in a restaurant, and asking noisy theater patrons for quiet. The second most important factor, accounting for only 6.6% of the variance, was "initiating and maintaining interaction with nonintimate others." Relevant items for this factor were 10, 2, 11, and 5, which relate to enjoying a conversation with a stranger and hesitating over dates through shyness. However, the number of different factors that have been isolated has ranged from 3 to 12, and this variation along with the different, often imprecise and overlapping categories, has often added to confusion rather than simplification of the underlying factors. A further difficulty is that the RAS often seems to confuse aggression and assertion, as represented by the lack of clarity in "Most people seem to be more aggressive and assertive than I am."

Interpretation

As with previously discussed behavioral self-report inventories, the RAS can be used as an ipsative instrument as well as for normative comparisons. If used ipsatively, the client's responses on the specific items can be interpreted based on their content. These responses can be used to provide information for treatment planning or evaluation. Such information might be particularly important if a client's difficulties with assertion are restricted to a specific area. The result might be responses indicating low assertiveness for certain items, yet the overall score might still be within normal limits. Thus, in certain cases, simply noting their total scale score may be misleading.

Normative data derived from a normal college population found that males had a mean of 9.68 ($SD = 22.36$) and females had a mean of 8.35 ($SD = 18.65$; Brenner & Bertsch, 1983). Although these means are quite similar, differences in specific items indicated that males tend to be more assertive in public situations and more willing to question high-status persons, but are shier in dating situations. In contrast, females reported being more assertive in private interpersonal settings (Brenner & Bertsch, 1983). A similar normative study of normal college students by Quillin et al. (1977) revealed the following percentile rankings for overall RAS raw scores:

Score	Ranking (%)	Score	Ranking (%)
35	95	−4	45
25	90	−5	40
21	85	−9	35
15	75	−13	30
11	70	−14	25
10	65	−19	20
6	60	−20	15
2	55	−25	10
0	50	−35	5

RECOMMENDED READING

Alessi, G. J. (1980). Behavioral observation for the school psychologist: Responsive-discrepancy model. *School Psychology Review, 9,* 31–45.

Bellack, A. S., & Hersen, M. (Eds.). (1988). *Behavioral assessment: A practical handbook* (3rd ed.). New York: Pergamon.

Cooper, J. O., Heron, T. B., & Heward, W. L. (1987). *Applied behavior analysis.* Columbus, OH: Merrill.

Durand, V. M. (1990). *Severe behavior problems: A functional communication training approach.* New York: Guilford.

Hersen, M., & Bellack, A. S. (Eds.). (1988a). *Dictionary of behavioral assessment techniques.* New York: Pergamon.

Chapter 5 ———————————————————————————————

THE WECHSLER INTELLIGENCE SCALES

The Wechsler Adult Intelligence Scale-Revised (WAIS-R) and Wechsler Intelligence Scale for Children-Revised (WISC-III) are individually administered, composite intelligence tests in a battery format. They assess different areas of intellectual abilities and create a situation in which aspects of personality can be observed. Both the WAIS-R and the WISC-III provide three different IQ scores: an overall or Full Scale IQ, a Verbal IQ, and a Performance IQ. The WAIS-R Verbal IQ and Performance IQ are derived from averaged scores on 11 subtests: Six are verbal and primarily measure a verbal comprehension factor; five are performance and measure visual-spatial abilities. The WISC-III has essentially the same subtests as the WAIS-R, except that the content of the items is designed for children and two additional optional performance subtests (Symbol Search and Mazes) are included, which brings the total number of potentially administered WISC-III subtests to 13. A further downward extension of the Wechsler scales has been the Wechsler Preschool and Primary Scale of Intelligence (WPPSI/WPPSI-R) for use with children between the ages of 4 and 6.5 years. Although the Wechsler intelligence scales have several limitations, they have become the most frequently used tests in clinical practice (Piotrowski & Zalewski, 1993; Watkins et al., 1995) and are considered to be a model to which other assessment instruments aspire.

THE NATURE OF INTELLIGENCE

Attempts to develop an accurate definition for "intelligence" have been fraught with difficulty and controversy (see Sternberg, 1994; Weinberg, 1989). This is largely because intelligence is an abstract concept and has no actual basis in concrete, objective, and physical reality. It is a general label for a group of processes that are inferred from more observable behaviors and responses. For example, it is possible to observe problem-solving techniques and to measure the results of these techniques objectively, but the intelligence assumed to produce these techniques cannot be observed or measured directly. Thus, the concept of intelligence is somewhat like the term "force" in physics: it can be known by its effects, yet its presence must be inferred. Both intelligence and force provide terms that allow a person to approach, discuss, and generalize certain types of objective events. However, the ambiguity in the term "intelligence" has also enabled it to become influenced by and framed within the context of different philosophical assumptions, political agendas, social issues, and legal restrictions.

Numerous attempts have been made to define intelligence. One of the earliest was that of Binet and Simon (1916) who conceptualized it as:

. . . judgement, otherwise called good sense, practical sense, initiative, the faculty of adapting one's self to circumstances. To judge well, to comprehend well, to reason well, these are the essential activities of intelligence. (pp. 42–43)

One of the most frequently used definitions of intelligence was developed by Wechsler in 1958. He considered intelligence to be a global concept that involved an individual's ability to act purposefully, think rationally, and deal effectively with the environment. He further emphasized that "general intelligence cannot be equated with intellectual ability, however broadly defined, but must be regarded as a manifestation of the personality as a whole" (in Matarazzo, 1972, p. 79). Thus, for Wechsler, intelligence can be social, practical, or abstract, but it cannot be measured or even considered independently from certain nonintellectual aspects of functioning such as persistence, drive, interests, or need for achievement. A review of most definitions of intelligence reveals that they all imply, include, or elaborate on the following five areas:

1. Abstract thinking.
2. Learning from experience.
3. Solving problems through insight.
4. Adjusting to new situations.
5. Focusing and sustaining one's abilities to achieve a desired goal.

The practical significance of a clear conceptualization of intelligence is to allow clinicians to fully appreciate the complexity of what they are attempting to evaluate. Such an appreciation should allow them to estimate more adequately which aspects of a client's intelligence have been measured and which have not. It should also help them evaluate the assets and limitations involved in using a specific test by contrasting the test items with the theoretical nature of intelligence. For example, an "intelligence" test that emphasizes verbal abilities will be limited because it will not assess such areas as nonverbal problem solving or adjusting to new situations. A thorough overview of the history and nature of intelligence is beyond the scope of this chapter, but interested readers can find excellent discussions in Sattler (1992), Sternberg (1982, 1992, 1994b) or Neisser et al. (1996). Most of the different discussions of intelligence focus on four major traditions that have emerged over the past 80 years. These include:

1. The psychometric approaches.
2. Neurological-biological approaches.
3. Developmental theories.
4. Information processing.

Psychometric Approaches

The psychometric approach assumes that intelligence is a construct or trait in which there are individual differences. Although the early psychometrists such as Binet, Ebinghaus, and Wernicke were concerned with a theoretical understanding of intelligence, the tests they actually constructed were more concerned with the practical issues of correct classification and prediction. Thus, there was an early division between a practical orientation that was oriented toward solving problems and another more conceptual approach concerned with theory. The following summary focuses primarily on the development of theoretical concepts relating to the nature of intelligence. However, a pressing concern, which will be discussed later is, and has been, whether IQ is a scientifically valid construct and whether intelligence tests actually measure intelligence as it is theoretically understood.

In 1904, Binet petitioned the French government for a grant for funds to develop a tool that could distinguish those capable of learning at normal rates from those in need of a slower paced, specially designed educational program. His basic task was one of correct classification, and it was not necessary for him to develop a theoretical understanding of that which he sought to measure. His early scales (1905, 1908) were based on the premise that each individual possesses both a "chronological age" (CA) or actual age in years, and a "mental age" (MA), indicative of the average intellectual abilities present within a specific age group. After computing a student's mental age, a comparison could be made with his or her chronological age to determine his or her relative standing in relation to persons with similar chronological ages.

Binet was already an accomplished lawyer, playwright, psychologist, and hypnotist, and after creating his intelligence test, he became one of the world's first psychometrists. He began the development of his initial scales by selecting a large number of problems that, at face value, seemed to test a student's ability to benefit from instruction. Next, he tested these items with a random sample of students to determine which were "good" items and which were "poor." Good items were those for which, as the age of the student increased, the number of items answered correctly also increased. Thus, as the students within the sample became chronologically older, they were able to obtain progressively higher scores since they could answer more and more of the items correctly. Poor items, on the other hand, were questions that did not demonstrate a relationship between the number of correct answers and chronological age. A poor item might be a question that all the students, regardless of age, answered incorrectly or which, as the students grew older, fewer and fewer of them answered correctly. By compiling and organizing the good items, and discarding the poor ones, Binet was able to develop a test that ranked questions by age so that the student's mental age could be determined. For example, at age 7 or 8, relatively few children can define the word "connection." At 10 years of age, 10% can, and at 13 years, 60% are able to do so correctly. Therefore, a student's ability to define "connection" indicates a mental ability comparable to that of the average 13-year-old and would be one of several items reflecting a mental age of 13. The student's mental age could then be compared with his or her chronological age to determine the extent to which the person is ahead of, equal to, or behind his or her age-related peers.

Binet's original scale, which was first used in 1905, has gone through numerous revisions, the most significant ones being in 1916, 1937, 1960, and 1986, when the most recent (fourth) edition was published. One of the more important changes was the reconceptualization of the intelligence quotient, or IQ, by Terman in 1916. The problem with Binet's early IQ (the difference between MA and CA) was its differing meaning for various age groups. A one-year lag for a child of 3 has a quite different meaning from that for a child of 14. This is because the greatest absolute change in intelligence occurs in the early years, so that a one-year lag for a 3-year-old is much more severe than a one-year lag for a 14-year-old. This problem was countered to a certain extent by Terman's (1916) computation of IQ as being equal to MA/CA × 100. If one uses this formula, a child of 3 with a one-year lag would have an IQ of 66, whereas a 14-year-old with a one-year lag would have a relatively higher IQ of 93. Thus, Terman's revision more adequately reflected the severity of a lower MA than CA for different age groups. It was assumed, however, that mental age reaches a peak around the age of 16. Difficulties would then occur when evaluating adult IQs since adults' chronological ages would be greater than their mental ages. Furthermore, decreases in mental age due to aging or adult brain damage could not be estimated accurately. For this reason, the 1960 and 1986 revisions of the Stanford-Binet used Wechsler's concept of the deviation IQ. This is simply a standard score on an ability test that can be compared with the performances of others in an age group. The result is that more meaningful comparisons can be made between persons of different ages.

Whereas Binet did not specifically develop a theory of intelligence, Spearman (1927) became concerned with what it was that intelligence tests were supposed to be measuring. He stated that a general factor, or "g factor," is common to all types of intellectual activity, in addition to specific factors, or "s factors," which are unique to particular problems. Spearman stressed that the different tests of intelligence were highly correlated and further observed that persons who dealt effectively in one area generally were effective in others as well. This led him to believe that the g factor serves to integrate and enhance most, if not all, of a person's abilities. Although Spearman's work has often been referred to as a two-factor theory, he emphasized the importance of a single global factor (g) and attempted to assess the relative importance of g within any single test of intelligence.

Thurstone (1938) developed a theory that was a radical departure from Spearman's in that he did not believe in the existence of a unifying g factor. Rather, he believed that intelligence was made up of specific and separate abilities. This theory was developed through the factor analysis of different tasks in which Thurstone attempted to conceptualize and isolate the different skills required for the performance of these tasks. His factor analytic studies suggested that intellect comprises seven components, which he referred to as "Primary Mental Abilities":

1. Verbal ability.
2. Verbal fluency.
3. Numerical ability.
4. Spatial ability.
5. Perceptual ability.
6. Inductive reasoning.
7. Memory.

Some vivid examples suggest a specific factor can exist without a corresponding unifying g factor. So-called idiot savants typically show the extreme development of only one ability, whereas in other areas of their lives they may be functioning at an extremely low level. Cases have been documented in which an idiot savant could correctly and almost immediately compute the day of the week on which a certain date occurred several years ago or could reproduce a long piece of music after hearing it one time. Such a specific differentiation of abilities gives some support to Thurstone's contention that, at least potentially, *s* factors can exist without a globally unifying *g* factor. However, Thurstone's seven factors have been found to be highly correlated. This suggests that Thurstone's factors are not completely independent and that a *g* factor also is common throughout the seven primary abilities.

A more recent conceptualization of specific intellectual factors by Gardner (1983, 1993) has expanded intelligence into a much wider scope than that encompassed by most other theorists. He has described the following seven relatively independent competencies:

1. Linguistic.
2. Musical.
3. Logical-mathematical.
4. Spatial.
5. Bodily-kinesthetic.
6. Interpersonal.
7. Intrapersonal.

He has included not only the traditional types of competencies assessed by IQ tests (verbal, mathematical, spatial abilities) but also gives credence to intelligence as encompassing athletic ability, knowledge of self and others, and musical talent. Thus, an outstanding gymnast or keyboard player who performs poorly in school (or on IQ tests) might still be considered to be extremely intelligent. Gardner (1993) has developed what he refers to as "Schema" which comprises 15 measures to assess his multiple intelligences. These measures are not traditional paper-and-pencil tests but are rather based on naturalistic assessments of thinking skills within the context of classroom environments. While Gardner's system has had significant impact on conceptualizations of intelligence and, in many cases, educational practice, his work is currently lacking a strong empirical basis (Lubinski & Benbow, 1995; Sternberg, 1994a).

For many years, the main issue in conceptualizing intelligence was whether it could be best represented by Spearman's single, unitary, generalized factor or Thurstone's multiple-factor theory (so called lumpers vs. splitters). Vernon (1950) took an intermediate position, stating that intelligence is integrated and unitary but also comprises a number of both large and small specific abilities. His model (Figure 5–1) is basically hierarchical, with the *g* factor at the top to indicate that it unifies all the abilities occurring at lower levels. The next level is composed of verbal-educational and spatial-mechanical abilities. Smaller subdivisions at lower levels refer to increasingly more specific and discrete abilities such as verbal fluency, numerical reasoning, and creativity. Blaha and Wallbrown (1984) have indicated that the WISC and WISC-R (and, by extension, the WISC-III) ability arrangement can be categorized using Vernon's model. They have found that a general factor seemed to unify most abilities, with more specific minor abilities being organized by Verbal Comprehension, Perceptual Organization, and Freedom from Distractibility. A similar hierarchical model by Horn (1985) emphasized a developmental hierarchy (sensory reception, association processing, perceptual organization,

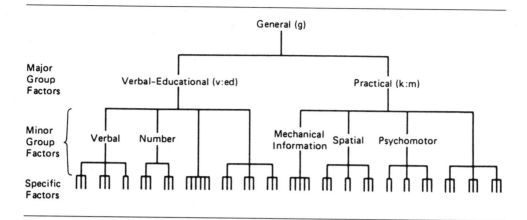

Figure 5-1.   **Vernon's hierarchical model of intelligence**

Adapted from Vernon, 1960, p. 22. Reprinted by permission from *The Structure of Human Abilities* by P. E. Vernon, Methuen & Co., Ltd., 1960.

relation education) based on distinct functions, such as short-term acquisition and retrieval, clerical ability, broad auditory thinking, and fluid ability.

Guilford (1967, 1988) used a highly sophisticated series of factor analytic techniques to develop a conceptualization of intelligence around specific interactions among different factors (Structure of Intellect, or SOI). He examined a far larger and more varied number of test items than previous researchers and broke down intelligence into 120 different factors (later increased to 150). He reasoned that each intellectual skill involved a particular operation, on a particular type of content, to yield a particular product or outcome. Thus, Guilford believed that intelligent behavior involves an interaction of operations, contents, and products. Through his factor analytic techniques, he determined five operations or cognitive processes (Recognition, Memory, Divergent Production, Convergent Production, and Evaluation), four contexts (Figures, Symbols, Semantics, and Behaviors), and six outcomes or products (Units, Classes, Relations, Systems, Transformations, and Implications). Each specific intellectual skill involves one of the operations, performed on one of the types of contexts, to produce one of the outcomes. The total ($5 \times 4 \times 6$) possible interactions yields Guilford's 120 specific intellectual skills, which he uses to define the structure of intellect. Guilford (1988) has slightly modified his theory by excluding Figural content and replacing it with Auditory and Visual contents. The operation of Memory was similarly further divided into Memory Recording (long term) and Memory Retention (short term).

While Guilford's conceptualization of intelligence appears highly theoretical, it demonstrates a wide variety of intellectual skills and can potentially give insight into practical difficulties. For example, it can help educators determine which skills are emphasized in an educational system and which are neglected. In general, most educational systems train students to deal with the physical world far more than the social world and to approach problems with logical thinking more than creative thinking. Using Guilford's terminology, students are usually far better trained to "converge" from a number of possible answers to one externally defined "correct" answer, than to "diverge" from one question to a number of possible answers. In addition, different intelligence tests, particularly the WAIS-R and WISC-III have been more fully described using Guilford's SOI (see Kaufman, 1990, 1994).

Although Binet began the study of intelligence from a global and somewhat poorly defined concept, the understanding of cognitive functioning has become increasingly specific and complex. This progression started with Binet's (1908) implied global factor and proceeded to the contrasting views of Spearman's (1927) two-factor theory, with an emphasis on *g,* as opposed to Thurstone's (1938) multiple-factor theory. A resolution was attempted with Vernon's (1950) and Horn's (1985) hierarchical models, which described specific abilities arranged according to increasing specificity or developmental complexity. One of the more current major theories is Guilford's (1967, 1988) classification of 120 separate abilities. From a practical standpoint, the views of intelligence presented here can help clinicians to understand and describe more precisely a client's intellectual abilities. However, a significant limitation of the psychometric approach is that, even though theories relating to the nature of intelligence have been expounded, most of the tests of intelligence that have been developed may not actually measure these constructs. This discrepancy between theory and practicality should be taken into consideration when interpreting IQ test scores. Thus, IQ tests are generally quite effective when used to predict later academic performance, but they may not actually measure "intelligence." Sternberg (1992) comments, "Our testing of intelligence has been and continues to be inadequate, in part because tests have been only partial operationalizations of the theories upon which they are based" (p. 1).

This is not to say that theories of intelligence are useless; they serve the important function of enabling practitioners to perceive and discuss aspects of the client that were not accessible before they were conceptualized. Such theories potentially increase the depth and breadth of understanding. Likewise, IQ tests have relevance and usefulness in relation to specific types of predictions. The apparent discrepancy between theories of intelligence and tests of intelligence also suggests that this gap must be narrowed, and indicates future directions for research and test construction. So far, the traditional psychometrically based tests (Stanford-Binet and Wechsler scales) have dominated intelligence assessment. More recently, however, a number of tests have been developed that more closely operationalize theories of intelligence. An example is the K-ABC (Kaufman & Kaufman, 1983), which has its theoretical foundations in Luria's neurological theories, especially sequential versus simultaneous information processing and knowledge related to cerebral specialization. Similarly, the Das Naglieri Cognitive Assessment System (Das & Naglieri, 1994), Woodcock-Johnson-Revised (WJ-R; Woodcock & Johnson, 1989), and Kaufman Adolescent and Adult Intelligence Test (KAIT; Kaufman & Kaufman, 1993) are based on Luria's Planning-Attention-Successive-Simultaneous (PASS) model. In addition, assessment instruments based on practical or common sense problem solving have been developed (Sternberg, Wagner, Williams, & Horvath, 1995) such as the Tacit Knowledge Inventory for Managers (Wagner & Sternberg, 1991).

Neurological-Biological Approaches

All four of the general approaches to understanding intelligence assume that there is an underlying neurological substrate on which intelligence is ultimately dependent. It is therefore important to somehow conceptualize and search for the neuroanatomic and neurophysiological processes underlying the behaviors that are referred to as intelligent. This might include a greater understanding of anatomic structures, electrophysiological processes, or the extent of cerebral blood flow to different portions of the brain during various cognitive processes. The most simplistic approach might be to study the relationship between brain size and measurements of intelligence, which have indicated modest correlations ranging between .10 and .35 for specific brain structures (Detterman, 1994). This type of theorizing has been the general trend, but it has been conducted in a far more complex and theoretical manner.

Halstead (1961) has proposed a theory of biological intelligence. He stated that a number of brain functions relating to intelligence are relatively independent of cultural considerations. They are biologically based and pertain to the brain functions of all individuals. The four factors he delineates are central integrative (C), abstraction (A), power (P), and directional (D). These are summarized as follows:

1. The *central integrative* (C) factor involves one's ability to organize experience. A person's background of familiar experiences and past learning works with and integrates new incoming experiences; its main purpose is adaptive.

2. The *abstraction* (A) factor is the ability to group things into different categories, and to perceive similarities and differences among objects, concepts, and events.

3. The *power* (P) factor refers to cerebral power, which is the undistorted strength of the brain. It involves the ability to suspend affect so that rationality and intellectual abilities can grow and develop.

4. The *directional* (D) factor provides direction or focus to a person's abilities; it specifies the manner in which intellect and behaviors will be expressed.

Two other contributions to biological approaches are from Horn and Cattell (1963) and Hebb (1972). There are sufficient similarities in Horn and Cattell's conceptualization of fluid and crystallized intelligence and Hebb's A and B intelligence to discuss them together. Both Horn and Cattell and Hebb emphasized the existence of certain areas of intelligence that are directly tied to brain function. Hebb refers to this as intelligence A and stresses that it is innate and biological, requires an intact nervous system, relates to problem-solving abilities, and cannot be measured by psychological tests. Horn and Cattell's fluid intelligence (*Gf*) is similar and enables a person to solve new problems, and perceive relations, similarities, and parallels. It is dependent on the brain's efficiency and relative intactness, and is sensitive to the effects of brain damage. Furthermore, it is primarily nonverbal independent of formal schooling, culture free, and can be measured by such tests as progressive matrices and figural analyses. It has been claimed that the Performance subtests of the WAIS-R and WISC-III also measure fluid intelligence. Fluid intelligence increases until around the age of 14, at which time it levels off until age 20, when it shows a gradual decline.

In addition to the more fluid, biologically based aspects of intelligence, Horn and Cattell and Hebb also refer to more environmentally determined, content-oriented dimensions. Hebb labels this "intelligence B" and indicates that it is based on experience and can be reflected in the extent of a person's accumulated knowledge. It is this dimension of intelligence that most intelligence tests measure. Horn and Cattell's term "crystallized" intelligence suggests that it is relatively permanent and generally less susceptible to the effects of brain damage. It is developed from the interaction between a person's innate fluid intelligence and such environmental factors as culture and education. Cattell states that it grows and develops until the age of 40, at which time it generally shows a slow decline. Representative tests that measure crystallized intelligence are those that relate to acquired skills and knowledge such as vocabulary and general information. However, Horn and Cattell differ from Hebb in that they believe both fluid (Gf) and crystallized (Gc) intelligence can be measured, whereas Hebb believes that psychometric tests cannot adequately measure intelligence A.

Another extremely influential approach has been the work of Luria (1980), who conceptualized the brain as comprising differentiated systems of functional units. These units are coordinated to form an integrated whole. The three main units are for *arousal* (brain stem and midbrain structures), *sensory-inputs* (temporal, parietal, and occipital lobes), and the *executive* unit which initiates, organizes, and plans behavior (the frontal lobes). Luria further conceptualized the different cognitive functions as involving Planning-Attention-Successive-Simultaneous means of information processing. In particular, the Successive (sequential) and Simultaneous means of information processing corresponds well with the left versus right hemispheric areas of specialization.

Moderate success has been achieved in relating intelligence to different types of psychophysiological responses. For example, Ahern and Beatty (1979) found that more intelligent subjects showed smaller pupillary dilations while performing tasks. Similarly, more intelligent subjects required less effort and energy (as measured by skin conductance and heart-rate variability) while performing a cognitive task (Geiselman, Woodward, & Beatty, 1982). Studies on the relationship between brain-wave patterns and intelligence have also been found to correlate with patterns of visual evoked potentials (speed at which EEG readings respond to a visual stimulus) for children (Engel & Fay, 1972; Henderson & Engel, 1974), most adults (Hendrickson & Hendrickson, 1980), but not to the intelligence levels of older persons (Engel & Fay, 1972; Henderson & Engel, 1974; Perry, McCoy, Cunningham, Falgout, & Street, 1976). However, the preceding studies are merely correlates of intelligence and, while implying an underlying neurological process, do not help explain either its nature or structure.

Biological approaches to intelligence generally have serious methodological and theoretical difficulties. So far, no specific neurological substrates have been found that clearly relate to intelligence. Also, it is extremely difficult to actually separate the effects of learning and culture from a hypothesized underlying biological structure. However, other theories depend on this underlying neurological structure. It is hoped that, as the techniques of psychological measurement parallel increases in knowledge relating to neuroanatomy and neurophysiology, this approach will become better integrated and the actual links between intelligent brain-behavior relationships will become more adequately understood (see Eysenck & Barrett, 1985; Vernon, 1987).

Developmental Theory

One criticism directed at the psychometric approach is that test constructors have been more concerned with quantitative scores than the quality of, or reasoning behind, an examinee's responses (Embretson, 1986; Sigel, 1963; Siegler & Richards, 1982). In contrast, Piaget studied the incorrect responses of children to different questions or tasks as a means of understanding their internal processes. He was not so much concerned with whether the answers were right or wrong as with why they were right or wrong. Piaget soon noticed that certain patterns of responses characterized different age groups. Further studies suggested to him that qualitative differences existed in the thinking of persons of certain ages. This led him to the following general conclusions regarding cognitive abilities:

- Mental growth follows definite patterns and is nonrandom.
- There are qualitative differences in the thinking of younger as opposed to older children.
- As a person develops, there is corresponding development in new cognitive structures and abilities.
- Mental growth is complete somewhere during late adolescence.

Piaget (1950) viewed intelligence as a special form of biological adaptation between a person and his or her environment. It involves an interaction in which a person must somehow fit his or her personal needs into some workable relationship with environmental demands. As persons grow and develop, they are in a continual process of reorganizing their psychological structures to deal more effectively with the environment. Piaget believes that this process occurs through both "assimilation" and "accommodation." Assimilation is primarily an inward process in which a person incorporates input from his or her environment into some sort of internal organized structure. It is a relatively active process beyond merely coping with the environment. Assimilation also involves a certain degree of independence from the environment, which allows for the growth and development of internal cognitive structures. For example, make-believe play with objects requires that a child act as if the objects are something else. This necessitates a certain degree of independence from the object, an active interaction with it, and the use and growth of new cognitive structures in relation to it. Whereas assimilation is inward and active, accommodation looks outward to adapt and change cognitive structures in accordance with external demands. Thus, the changing or "accommodating" mental constructions must have a direct correspondence with the real world. Piaget stressed that both assimilation and accommodation occur simultaneously, independently of age, but also within all age groups. However, within these general processes there are specific age-related differences. Horn (1985) has further drawn and elaborated on some of these principles to conceptualize that the earliest forms of "intelligence" depend on sensory reception followed by association processing and perceptual organization. During adolescence and adulthood, understanding relations and implications becomes most important (relation education).

Piaget described four major stages of cognitive development:

1. *Sensorimotor Period* (Birth to approx. 2 years). The child passes through six different stages. These begin with simple reflex actions and grow in complexity until simple mental schemas are developed to more effectively deal with the world. The stage ends with the first sign of internal or symbolic constructs.

2. *Preoperational Period* (Approx. 2 to 7 years). The child develops language and basic symbolic constructs. The child can begin to think internally; is aware of the past, present, and future; can engage in symbolic play, can search for hidden objects; and can engage in delayed imitation.

3. *Concrete Operational Period* (Approx. 7 to 11 years). At this stage, the child acquires conservation skills (in which independence from the stimulus properties of objects is developed, and the child is not fooled by mere perceptual transformations). He or she can add, subtract, classify, and serialize, and is less egocentric and more social. The child still has difficulty performing operations independently from his or her environment.

4. *Formal Operations Period* (Approx. 11+ years). This stage marks the development of adult thinking in which the child can think abstractly, form and test hypotheses, use deductive reasoning, and evaluate solutions.

The preceding cognitive stages are action-oriented in that a developing person actively operates on the environment and develops internal constructs based on these interactions. Piaget also emphasized the qualitative changes that occur in a person's cognitive processes. He believed that it is more important to describe the nature and style of these changes than to quantitatively measure them. The different stages also occur within all cultures, and the sequence cannot be varied. The later stages are dependent on earlier ones. However, even though the sequence cannot be changed, there is some variability in the ages at which these stages occur between one individual and another, and from culture to culture. Thus, it may be important to determine what variables slow these stages down or accelerate them. In summary, Piaget's central theme is that intelligence is a developmental phenomenon of adaptation in which a person moves toward constructing reality in progressively more symbolic terms.

Information-Processing Approaches

The greater cognitive emphasis in psychology that began during the late 1970s has resulted in models of intelligence with a focus on ongoing processes rather than contents. This has involved an understanding of operations, mental processes, transformations, manipulations, and the different stages of acquisition and retrieval. An information-processing model usually considers the manner in which information is received, stored, and retrieved and the ways these processes eventually result in a response. The combinations and transformations that occur at various stages in this procedure are defined and elaborated. Most information-processing models include both structural (memory storage, short- and long-term memory, sensory reception) as well as functional (transformations, processes) components.

A representative information-processing theory is the work of Campione and Brown (1978), which was later elaborated by Borkowski (1985). Their theory includes both an architectural and an executive system. The architectural system refers to and depends on an intact central and peripheral nervous system. Its three components are *capacity* (the amount of memory that can be stored and worked with), *durability* (the hardiness of the system, resistance to disruption, time taken to lose information), and *efficiency* (speed of processing; rate of encoding/decoding). Whereas the architectural system relates to relatively fixed abilities or structures, the executive system is more concerned with ongoing fluid processes. Within the executive system, the *knowledge base* encompasses not only stored information, but how that information is received. *Schemas* are used in much the same way as described by Piaget (framework for incoming information) and *control processes* are the strategies and rules used to focus, monitor, and rehearse for a task. Finally, *metacognition* is the ability to stand back and observe one's thoughts. It involves retracing various cognitive processes and understanding why these processes were effective or ineffective in problem solving. It is through the effective functioning of both control processes (focusing, concentration, monitoring) and metacognition (self-reflection, retracing, puzzlement) that new solutions are developed.

Another example of an information-processing approach is Sternberg's (1985) triarchic theory, which is composed of:

1. Metacomponents.
2. Performance.
3. Knowledge.

Like other theorists, he has emphasized that intelligence must be purposeful, goal oriented, and relevant, and must also involve the development of effective information processing. An important aspect of his theory is its focus on the internal experience of the person (particularly novelty) as well as the social context of the experience. In particular, intelligence is a sociocultural phenomenon; what is considered adaptive within one culture may not be considered adaptive in another culture. Furthermore, intellectual assessment is importantly a "folk concept" in that day-to-day human interaction (at a party, in the office) involves intuitively evaluating the level of intelligence of each other. These considerations have led to measures of real world or practical intelligence particularly directed toward managerial contexts (Sternberg et al., 1995). A future somewhat related research area with important practical implications for personnel selection is the further investigation of creativity (Sternberg & Lubant, 1996). A final contribution to human information-processing approaches has been made by Das and his colleagues (Das & Naglieri, 1994; Jarman & Das, 1977) who have elaborated and operationalized Luria's *simultaneous processing* (integrated, semispatial) versus *successive processing* (orderly sequence, recall of numbers, reading).

Over the past 15 years, significant developments have occurred in understanding the processes underlying intelligence. This has resulted in a number of tests designed around these theories such as the Kaufman Assessment Battery for Children (K-ABC; Kaufman & Kaufman, 1983), Kaufman Adolescent and Adult Intelligence Test (KAIT; Kaufman & Kaufman, 1993), Woodcock-Johnson Psychoeducational Battery-Revised (WJ-R; Woodcock & Johnson, 1989), and the Das-Naglieri Cognitive Assessment System (Das & Naglieri, 1994). Each of these have drawn on various aspects of psychometric, neurological-biological, developmental, and information-processing theories both for their development, as well as their interpretation. In addition, theoretical approaches have been used to further understand older tests particularly the Wechsler intelligence scales.

Specifically, the WAIS-R and WISC-III can be analyzed from the perspective of fluid-crystallized intelligence, simultaneous-sequential processing, Guilford's Structure of Intellect, and the information-processing components of input, integration/storage, and output (see Kaufman, 1990, 1994). Although the process of integrating theory with assessment techniques often seems slow and frequently tradition bound, change does seem to be occurring in that several options are available for practitioners wishing to use scales other than the older, time-honored ones. However, it remains to be seen how extensively these newer techniques are utilized and the accuracy they will have in decisions regarding clients and educational programs (Kline, Snyder, & Castellanos, 1996).

THE TESTING OF INTELLIGENCE: PRO AND CON

The testing of intelligence has had a consistent history of misunderstanding, controversy, and occasional misuse (Houts, 1977; Weinberg, 1989). Criticisms have ranged from moral indictments against labeling individuals, to cultural bias, and even to accusations of flagrant abuse of test scores. Although valid criticisms can be made against testing intelligence, such procedures also have a number of advantages.

One of the main assets of intelligence tests is their accuracy in predicting future behavior. Initially, Binet was able to achieve a certain degree of predictive success with his scales, and, since that time, test procedures have become progressively more refined and accurate. More recent studies indicate that the Wechsler intelligence scales can predict an extremely wide number of variables (Appelbaum & Tuma, 1982; Grossman & Johnson, 1982; Kitson & Vance, 1982; Matarazzo & Herman, 1984; Reilly, Drudge, Rosen, Loew, & Fischer, 1985; Ryan & Rosenberg, 1983; Sutter & Bishop, 1986). In particular, IQ tests are excellent predictors of academic achievement (Appelbaum & Tuma, 1982; Grossman & Johnson, 1982; Neisser et al., 1996; Ryan & Rosenberg, 1983). However, certain liabilities are also associated with these successes. First, intelligence tests can be used to classify children into stereotyped categories, that limit their freedom to choose fields of study. Furthermore, IQ tests are quite limited in predicting nontest or nonacademic activity, yet they are sometimes incorrectly used to make these inferences (Snyderman & Rothman, 1987). It should also be stressed that intelligence tests are measures of a person's present level of functioning and, as such, can only provide short-term predictions. Long-term predictions, although attempted frequently, are less accurate because there are many uncontrolled, influencing variables. Similarly, even short-term academic placements made solely on the basis of an IQ score have a high chance of failure since all the variables that may be crucial for success are not and cannot be measured by an intelligence test (Zigler & Farber, 1985). It can sometimes be tempting for test users to extend the meaning of test scores beyond their intended scope, especially in relation to the predictions they can realistically be expected to make.

In addition to predicting academic achievement, IQ scores have also been correlated with occupation ranging from highly trained professionals having mean IQs of 125 to unskilled workers with mean IQs of 87 (Mitchell, Grandy, & Lupo, 1986; Reynolds, Chastion, Kaufman, & McLean, 1987). Correlations between job proficiency and general intelligence have been highest in predicting relatively more complex jobs rather than less demanding occupations. Hunter (1986) reported moderately high correlations between general intelligence and success for managers (.53), salespersons (.61) and clerks (.54). For intellectually demanding tasks, nearly half the variance related to performance criteria can be accounted for by general intelligence (Schmidt, Ones, & Hunter, 1992).

Another important asset of intelligence tests, particularly the WAIS-R and WISC-III, is that they provide valuable information about a person's cognitive strengths and weaknesses. They are standardized procedures whereby a person's performance in various areas can be compared with that of age-related peers. In addition, useful comparisons can be made regarding a person's pattern of strengths and weaknesses. The WAIS-R, WISC-III, and other individually administered tests provide the examiner with a structured interview within which a variety of tasks can be used to observe the unique and personal ways in which the examinee approaches cognitive tasks. Through a client's interactions with both the examiner and the test materials, an initial impression can be made of the individual's self-esteem, behavioral idiosyncrasies, anxiety, social skills, and motivation, while also obtaining a specific picture of intellectual functioning.

Intelligence tests often provide clinicians, educators, and researchers with baseline measures for use in determining either the degree of change that has occurred in an individual over time or how an individual compares with other persons in a particular area or ability. This may have important implications for evaluating the effectiveness of an educational program or for assessing the changing abilities of a specific student. In cases involving recovery from a head injury or readjustment following neurosurgery, it may be extremely helpful for clinicians to measure and follow the cognitive changes that occur within a patient. Furthermore, IQ assessments may be important in researching and understanding more adequately the effect on cognitive functioning of environmental variables such as educational programs, family background, and nutrition. Thus, these assessments can provide useful information about cultural, biological, maturational, or treatment-related differences among individuals.

A criticism leveled at intelligence tests is that almost all have an inherent bias toward emphasizing convergent, analytical, and scientific modes of thought. Thus, a person who emphasizes divergent, artistic, and imaginative modes of thought may be at a distinct disadvantage. Guilford (1967, 1988) has specifically stated that the single IQ score does not do justice to the multidimensional nature of intelligence. Some critics have even stressed that the current approach to intelligence testing has become a social mechanism used by people with similar values to pass on educational advantages to children who resemble themselves. Not only might IQ tests tend to place creative individuals at a disadvantage, but they are limited in assessing nonacademically oriented intellectual abilities (Frederiksen, 1986; Snyderman & Rothman, 1987). Thus, social acumen, success in dealing with people, the ability to handle the concrete realities of one's daily world, social fluency, and specific tasks such as purchasing merchandise are not measured by any intelligence test. More succinctly, people are capable of many more cognitive abilities than can possibly be measured on an intelligence test.

Misunderstanding and potential misuse of intelligence tests frequently occur when scores are treated as measures of innate capacity. The IQ is not a measure of an innate fixed ability, nor is it representative of all problem-solving situations. It is a specific and limited sample, made at a certain point in time, of abilities that are subject to numerous alterations. It reflects, to a large extent, the richness of an individual's past experiences. Although interpretation guidelines are quite clear in pointing out the limited nature of a test score, there is a tendency to look at test results as absolute facts reflecting permanent characteristics within an individual. People often want a quick, easy, and reductionist method to quantify, understand, and assess cognitive abilities, and the IQ score has become the most widely misused test score to fill this need.

An important limitation of intelligence tests is that, for the most part, they are not concerned with the underlying processes involved in problem solving. They focus on the final product or outcome rather than on the steps involved in reaching the outcome. They look at the "what" rather than the "how" (Embretson, 1986; Sigel, 1963). Thus, if a person gives the correct response to the question "How are a desk and couch similar?" the examiner does not know if the response results from past learning, perceptual discrimination, syllogistic reasoning, or a combination of these (Sigel, 1963). The extreme example of this "end product" emphasis is the global IQ score. When the examiner looks at the myriad assortment of intellectual abilities as a global ability, the complexity of cognitive functioning may be simplified to the point of being almost useless. The practitioner can apply labels quickly and easily, without attempting to examine the specific strengths and weaknesses that might make precise therapeutic interventions or knowledgeable recommendations possible. Such thinking detracts significantly from the search for a wider, more precise, and more process-oriented understanding of mental abilities (Siegler & Richards, 1982).

A further concern about intelligence tests involves their limited usefulness in assessing minority groups with divergent cultural backgrounds. It has been stated that intelligence-test content is strongly biased in favor of European American, middle-class values. Critics stress that minorities tend to be at a disadvantage when taking the tests due to deficiencies in motivation, lack of practice, lack of familiarity with culturally loaded items, and difficulties in establishing rapport. Numerous arguments against using intelligence tests for the assessment and placement of minorities have culminated in legal restrictions on the use of IQ scores. However, traditional defenses of IQ scores suggest that they are less biased than has been accused. For example, the removal of biased items has done little to alter overall test scores, and IQs still provide mostly accurate predictions for many minorities (see Chapter 2 for a further discussion). The issue has certainly not been resolved, but clinicians should continue to be aware of this dilemma, pay attention to subgroup norms, and interpret minority group IQ scores cautiously.

Finally, many people feel that their IQs are deeply personal pieces of information. They would prefer that others, even a psychologist who is expected to observe confidentiality, not be allowed access to this information. This problem is further compounded when IQ scores might be given to several different persons, such as during legal proceedings or personnel selection.

Intelligence tests provide a number of useful and well-respected functions. They can adequately predict short-term scholastic performance, assess an individual's relative strengths and weaknesses, reveal important personality variables, and permit the researcher, educator, or clinician to trace possible changes within an individual or population. However, these assets are only helpful if the limitations of intelligence tests are adequately understood and appropriately taken into consideration. They are limited in predicting certain types of occupational success and such nonacademic skills as creativity, motivational level, social acumen, and success in dealing with people. Furthermore, IQ scores are not measures of an innate, fixed ability, and their use in classifying minority groups has been questioned. Finally, there has been an overemphasis on understanding the end product of cognitive functioning and a relative neglect in appreciating underlying cognitive processes.

HISTORY AND DEVELOPMENT

During the 1930s, Wechsler began studying a number of standardized tests and selected 11 different subtests to form his initial battery. His search for subtests was in part guided by his conception that intelligence is global in nature and represents a part of the greater whole of personality. Several of his subtests were derived from portions of the 1937 revision of the Stanford-Binet (Comprehension, Arithmetic, Digit Span, Similarities, and Vocabulary). The remaining subtests came from the Army Group Examinations (Picture Arrangement), Koh's Block Design (Block Design), Army Alpha (Information, Comprehension), Army Beta (Digit Symbol, Coding), Healy Picture Completion (Picture Completion) and the Pinther-Paterson Test (Object Assembly). These subtests were combined and published in 1939 as the Wechsler-Bellevue Intelligence Scale. The Wechsler-Bellevue had a number of technical deficiencies primarily related to both the reliability of the subtests and the size and representativeness of the normative sample. Thus, it was revised to form the Wechsler Adult Intelligence Scale (WAIS) in 1955, and another revised edition (WAIS-R) was published in 1981. The 1981 revision was based on 1,880 individuals who were generally representative of the 1970 census and categorized into nine different age groups. A revision of the WAIS-R (the WAIS-III) is anticipated to be available in August, 1998.

The original Wechsler-Bellevue Scale was developed for adults, but in 1949 Wechsler developed the Wechsler Intelligence Scale for Children (WISC) so that children down to the age of 5 years, 0 months could be assessed in a similar manner. Easier items, designed for children, were added to the original scales and standardized on 2,200 European American boys and girls selected to be representative of the 1940 census. However, some evidence shows that Wechsler's sample may have been overrepresentative of children in the middle and upper socioeconomic levels. Thus, ethnic minorities and children from lower socioeconomic levels may have been penalized when compared with the normative group. The WISC was revised in 1974 and standardized on a new sample that was more accurately representative of children in the United States. The WISC-III (Wechsler, 1991) was released in 1991 with the major changes being the inclusion of four factor/index scores (Verbal Comprehension, Perceptual Organization, Freedom from Distractibility, and Processing Speed). The new Processing Speed factor has involved the inclusion of the new subtest of Symbol Search along with the older Coding subtest. As with the earlier WISC-R and WISC, the standardization and reliability are excellent. The scales were standardized on 2,200 children between the ages of 6 and 16 who closely matched the 1988 census. The sample consisted of 100 boys and 100 girls for each of the different age groups. The new materials are colorful, contemporary, and easy to administer (see review by Little, 1992).

In 1967, the Wechsler Preschool and Primary Scale of Intelligence (WPPSI) was first published for the assessment of children between the ages of 4 and 6 years, 6 months. Just as the WISC is a downward extension of the WAIS, so the WPPSI is generally a downward extension of the WISC in which easier but similar items are used. Although most of the scales are similar in form and content to the WISC, a number of them are unique to the WPPSI. The WPPSI was revised in 1989 to form the WPPSI-R (Wechsler, 1989). It has retained the same subtests as the WPSSI, but there has been a greater emphasis on speeded performance.

RELIABILITY AND VALIDITY

WAIS-R Reliability and Validity

Reliabilities for the three IQ scores of the WAIS-R have generally been quite high. Wechsler (1981) reported that the split-half reliability for the Full Scale IQ was .97; Verbal IQ, .97; and Performance IQ, .93. The specific subtests were far more variable (*Mdn r* = .83), with the highest split-half reliability being for Vocabulary (.96) and the lowest for Object Assembly (.52). Similar to the WISC-R, the split-half reliabilities were higher for the Verbal subtests than for the Performance subtests.

Test-retest reliabilities over a one- to seven-week interval were quite high. Full Scale IQ reliabilities averaged .97; Verbal IQ, .97; and Performance IQ, .93. The specific subtests were somewhat less satisfactory with an average low of .67 reported for Object Assembly and a high of .94 for Vocabulary.

The mean increase in scores during a two- to seven-week interval was 6.2 for the Full Scale IQ, 3.3 for the Verbal IQ, and 8.4 for the Performance IQ (Matarazzo & Herman, 1984). As is also true for the WISC-III, the increase was primarily due to short-term practice effects; these expected increases should be taken into consideration when making interpretations of clients' abilities over a short (2–6 months) retesting interval. One practical implication is that since there are relatively greater gains in the Performance Scale, this will result in either decreasing subject's Verbal-Performance differences for those with initial V > P scores or increasing it for those with initial P > V scores. Matarazzo, Carmody, and Jacobs (1980) suggest that a 15-point increase for both Full Scale and Verbal IQs is required to indicate a "true" (significant) improvement in functioning but a 20- to 25-point gain is required for the Performance IQ. It is very unusual to find any decreases in IQ on retesting. However, caution should be exercised due to the wide range that was recorded; although the average scores were higher, some persons also showed significant losses.

This general pattern of average gains was found for both a normal population as well as for various clinical (Ryan, Georgemiller, Geisser, & Randall, 1985) and head-injured patients (Moore et al., 1990). It is noteworthy that the practice effects in these latter two studies occurred even after retesting intervals of 9 months. Similar practice effects might be expected for normal persons as well although it is likely that any practice effects will be far less pronounced after one year.

Standard error of measurements (SEMs) for the WAIS-R scales indicate that the greatest confidence can be placed in the Full Scale and Verbal Scale IQs (SEMs for IQ points = 2.53 and 2.74 respectively). Somewhat lesser confidence can be placed in the

Performance IQ (4.14) and specific subtests (SEMs range between .61 and .25 sub-scale points). The lowest standard error of measurement was found for the Verbal sub-tests (.61 to 1.24) with the narrowest range of error for Vocabulary (.61) and the widest for Information (.93). The Performance subtests ranged from .98 for Block Design to 1.54 for Object Assembly.

When the WAIS-R was first published, the extensive and impressive validity studies on the WAIS were used as support for the validity of the newer revision. This seemed reasonable given that the two tests were conceptually quite similar and shared many of the same items. As would be expected, correlations between the two tests were quite high. Median WAIS/WAIS-R correlations reported by Sattler (1992) were .94 for the Full Scale IQ, .94 for the Verbal IQ, and .86 for the Performance IQ. These high correlations were used as one of the strongest sources of support for the validity of the WAIS-R. However, Kaufman (1983) indicated that the WAIS-R norms were quite different than the norms used for the WAIS. As a result, the assumed validity of the WAIS-R may have been accepted prematurely. In particular, mean IQs obtained by most populations have produced lower scores on the WAIS-R than on the WAIS (Ryan, Nowak, & Geisser, 1987). The median WAIS-R lowerings were 6.6 for the Full Scale IQ, 6.4 for the Verbal IQ, and 6.8 for the Performance IQ (Sattler, 1992). However, this lowering for obtained WAIS-R IQs may occur only for the midranges of intelligence and not for IQs derived from either extreme (Mitchell, Grandy, & Lupo, 1986; Spitz, 1986). Spruill and Beck (1988) found that WAIS/WAIS-R IQs were equal for a mildly retarded population, but WAIS-R scores were actually higher for moderately retarded persons. Thus, the WAIS and WAIS-R are not fully interchangeable and comparisons related to validity or individually derived scores should take the differences between the two tests into consideration.

Since the publication of the WAIS-R, a sufficient number of validity studies on the WAIS-R have been specifically published to establish the validity of the newer revision without having to rely on research from the older version. Full Scale WAIS-R IQs have been found to correlate with a wide number of criterion measures, including the Stanford-Binet (.85), WRAT (Reading, .62; Spelling, .60; Arithmetic, .76), Slosson Intelligence Test (.78), and number of years of education (.54; Sattler, 1992). Furthermore, the construct validity has been found to be strong. For example, factor analytic studies have indicated that nearly all the subtests have moderate to high correlations with general intelligence. The factor structure also supports the basic distinction originally made by Wechsler between the Verbal IQ (Verbal Comprehension factor) and the Performance IQ (Perceptual Organization factor; Leckliter, Matarazzo, & Silverstein, 1986; Naglieri & Kaufman, 1983). Factor analytic studies also support two- and three-factor solutions for normal as well as various clinical populations (Allen & Thorndike, 1995; Atkinson et al., 1990; Burgess, Flint, & Adsheed, 1992; Ryan, Paolo, & Brungardt, 1993). Theoretical predictions related to scores that decline with age have also been supported in that verbal abilities are relatively stable throughout the life span, which is consistent with the view that Verbal Scales primarily measure crystallized intelligence. In contrast, performance abilities, which are associated more with fluid intelligence, show a slow decline with age until after age 70, at which time the decline becomes much sharper (Ivnik et al., 1992; Kaufman, 1990; Kaufman, Reynolds, & McLean, 1989; Ryan, Paolo, & Brungardt, 1990).

WISC-III Reliability and Validity

The WISC-III has generally excellent reliability. The average WISC-III internal consistency reported by Wechsler (1991) across all 11 age groups was .96 for the Full Scale IQ, .95 for the Verbal Scale, and .91 for the Performance Scale. Internal consistency for the specific subtests was far more variable, ranging from a low for Object Assembly of .69 to a high of .87 for Vocabulary. The average reliabilities for Verbal subtests ranged between .77 to .87 (*Mdn r* = .83), while the Performance subtests were somewhat lower, ranging between .69 and .89 (*Mdn r* = .78). However, the reliabilities vary somewhat according to different age levels with the younger subgroups having lower reliabilities than older groups.

Test-retest reliabilities are likewise quite high for the three IQ scores and somewhat lower for the specific subtests. Full Scale IQ reliability for all ages over a 23-day (median) retesting was .94 and the Verbal and Performance Scales were .94 and .87 respectively (Wechsler, 1991). The average increase in scores for retesting over the 23-day interval was 7 to 8 points for the Full Scale IQ, 2 to 3 points for the Verbal IQ, and 11 to 13 points for the Performance IQ. This can mainly be accounted for by practice effects that seem to be particularly pronounced for the Performance Scale. The practical implication for this is that clinicians should incorporate the meaning of these short-term increases into their interpretations. Specifically, moderate short-term increases in scores of 5 to 10 points should not usually be considered to indicate true improvement in ability. Longer term retesting for the WISC-R over a two-year interval (which is more typical in clinical settings) has shown somewhat more stability with less than an average three-point difference in Full Scale IQ (Haynes & Howard, 1986). This suggests similar long-term test-retest stability for the WISC-III although no longer term studies are currently available. Test-retest reliabilities for the specific subtests ranged from a high of .89 for Vocabulary to a low of .69 for Object Assembly with an overall median of .76.

The standard error of measurement (indicated in IQ points) for the Full Scale IQ was 3.20, Verbal IQ was 3.53, and Performance IQ was 4.54. The standard error of measurement (given in subscale scores) for the Verbal subtests ranged from 1.08 to 1.45, with the narrowest range of error for Vocabulary (1.08) and the widest for Comprehension (1.45). The Performance subtests ranged from 1.11 to 1.67, with the narrowest range for Block Design (1.11) and widest for Object Assembly (1.67) and Mazes (1.64). Further information for incorporating specific standard error of measurement scores into WISC-III (and WAIS-R) interpretations is included in the section "Interpretation Procedures."

Given the high degree of item overlap, subtest correlations, and IQ score correlations between the WISC-R and WISC-III, much of the extensive validity research on the WISC-R can be generalized to the WISC-III (Dixon & Anderson, 1995). This validity relates primarily to extensive correlations with relevant criterion measures, including other ability tests, school grades, and achievement tests. Selected median correlations reviewed and reported by Sattler (1992) include those for the Stanford-Binet: Fourth Edition (.78), K-ABC (.70), group IQ tests (.66), WRAT (.52 to .59), Peabody Individual Achievement Test (.71), item overlap with the WPPSI-R (Sattler & Atkinson, 1993), and school grades (.39). The underlying factor structure has supported Wechsler's conceptualization of abilities into a Verbal Comprehension factor that roughly corresponds with the Verbal Scale, and a Perceptual Organizational factor that generally corresponds with the Performance Scale (Allen & Thorndike, 1995; Blaha & Wallbrown, 1996; Kaufman, 1975, 1994). A less strongly supported factor, variously referred to as Freedom from Distractibility, Memory, or Sequencing (Allen & Thorndike, 1995; Bannatyne, 1974; Burgess, Flint, & Adshead, 1992; Kaufman, 1975, 1994), has also typically emerged along with a relatively pure factor for Perceptual Speed (Blake & Wellbrown, 1996). Thus, the WISC-III has been found both to predict relevant variables in the subject's life and to be based on a conceptually sound framework.

ASSETS AND LIMITATIONS

Since their initial publication, the Wechsler intelligence scales have been used in numerous research studies and have become widely used throughout the world. Thus, they are familiar to both researchers and practitioners and also have a long and extensive history of continued evaluation. This enormous research base allows practitioners to make relatively accurate predictions regarding clients. Inconsistencies between an individual's performance and relevant research can also be noted alerting the practitioner that they need to develop and pursue further hypotheses. Furthermore, the subtests are relatively easy to administer, and the accompanying manual(s) provide clear instructions, concise tables, and excellent norms.

Perhaps of even more practical importance to the clinician is the clear, precise data obtained regarding the person's cognitive functioning from the pattern of responses to the subtests. It is relatively easy for an examiner to develop hypotheses related to a person's psychological strengths and weaknesses by comparing the results of each subtest. For example, relatively high scores on Block Design and Object Assembly suggest that the person is strong in perceptual organization, whereas an individual with relative peaks on Arithmetic and Digit Span most likely has strengths in short-term memory and is not easily distracted. A clinician can become extremely sensitive to the different nuances and limitations of each of these subtests and the pattern of their results. In addition, a quick review of a person's Verbal, Performance, and Full Scale IQs on the three WAIS-R or four WISC-III factor/index scores can point to areas of concern that may need further evaluation.

A final, but extremely important, asset of the Wechsler scales is their ability to aid in assessing personality variables. This can be done by directly observing the individual as he or she interacts with the examiner, studying the content of test item responses, or evaluating information inferred from the individual's pattern of subtest scores. For example, a person scoring low on Digit Span, Arithmetic, and Digit Symbol is likely to be experiencing anxiety, attentional deficit, or both. On the other hand, it might be hypothesized that a person who scores high in both Comprehension and Picture Arrangement is likely to have good social judgment. Despite attempts to establish descriptions of how different clinical groups perform on the Wechsler intelligence scales, few clear findings have emerged (Piedmont, Sokolove, & Fleming, 1989a, 1989b). Thus, the Wechsler scales should not be likened to "personality scales" or "clinical scales." Rather, the subject's behavior surrounding the test and qualitative responses to the items should be considered as a means of generating hypotheses related to personality. Within this context, the Wechsler intelligence scales are noteworthy in the degree to which they can provide personality variables and clinical information.

Perhaps the most significant criticism leveled at the Wechsler scales has been the lack of enough data related to their validity (Anastasi, 1988). Although they have been correlated with other measures, including the Stanford-Binet and academic achievement, for the most part there has been a notable lack of comparisons with behavior external to the scales themselves. This is despite the belief that many significant areas of a person's functions, such as adaptive behavior, or need for achievement are separate (but related) constructs (Keith, Fehrmann, Harrison, & Pottebaum, 1987). In particular, the meanings associated with subtest scores should be investigated in far more depth. For example, Picture Completion has traditionally been considered to be a measure of a person's ability to distinguish relevant from irrelevant details in his or her environment, yet this assumption has not been adequately tested. Likewise, no studies have been made to determine if high or low Digit Span scores relate to actual day-by-day behaviors, such as recalling telephone numbers, facility with computer programming sequences, or following directions.

A further weakness is that the Wechsler intelligence scales do not adequately measure extreme ranges of intelligence (below 40 and above 160) when compared with such tests as the Stanford-Binet (Carvajal, Gerber, Hewes, & Weaver, 1987). This is particularly true for individuals at the extreme age ranges. The lowest WISC-III IQ score a 6–0 year old child can obtain is 46, whereas the highest for adolescents aged 16–8 years is 154. It is only with the average and moderately below or above-average ranges that the Wechsler scales and the Stanford-Binet provide means that are comparable. Thus, the Stanford-Binet and WISC-III are closely correlated for the average or moderately below-average child or adult, but to a lesser extent for the child of either superior intelligence or extremely low intelligence (Spruill, 1991). Despite this seeming advantage, the Stanford-Binet has achieved its larger range by extrapolating perhaps too much from the scores of midrange subjects rather than actually using extremely high and low IQ subjects in the norming process.

A peculiar feature of the WAIS-R was its development of scaled scores from the age group between 20 and 34 ($N = 500$) and the subsequent use of these as the comparison for all other age groups. This age group produced scaled scores with a mean of 10 and an average standard deviation of 3. When the 16- to 17-year-olds and 18- to 19-year-olds included in the standardization sample are compared with the 20- to 34-year-olds, their scores are surprisingly low, especially on the verbal subtests. The mean Vocabulary score for 16- to 17-year-olds was only 7.8, whereas the 18- to 19-year-olds scored only slightly higher, with a mean of 8.1. It might be reasoned that their knowledge was not yet fully developed, but even this does not explain the substantial increase in scores within the 20- to 34-year-old group. Thus, there may be some bias in the sample perhaps due to its being unrepresentative of the overall population in some unknown way (Gregory, 1987). The practical implication for practitioners is that the validity of WAIS-R results (and especially subtest scores) may not be as high for persons under 20 as for other age groups. It also suggests that for the overlapping age range of 16 to 17, the WISC-III should be used instead of the WAIS-R. The WISC-III choice also has the additional advantage of having more updated norms.

Another related area of caution relates to the use of WAIS-R profile analysis for older persons, particularly if they are 70 or older. A clear finding is that subtest scores decrease with age but do so quite differently for different subtests. For example, the mean subtest scores for Block Design and Digit Symbol for 70- to 74-year-olds is only 6.4 and 4.9 respectively. In contrast, the mean Vocabulary score is 9.2. A practitioner might be tempted to incorrectly interpret this normal subscale scatter as being abnormal and thus reach erroneous conclusions regarding an elderly person's strengths and weaknesses. A partial solution is the use of conversions based on age-corrected scaled scores (see Table 21 in Wechsler's 1981 Manual) or the subtest means for 61- to 91-year-olds available in Quereshi and Erstad (1990) or individuals 75 years and older in Ryan et al. (1990) or Ivnik et al. (1992). However, this may make the protocol unwieldy and increase the risk of clerical errors. Despite this, practitioners should always use these age-corrected scores when making subscale comparisons for older persons.

There are several additional limitations to the Wechsler scales. Some critics believe that norms may not be applicable for ethnic minorities or persons from lower socioeconomic backgrounds. Furthermore, there is a certain degree of subjectivity when scoring many of the items on Comprehension, Similarities, and Vocabulary. Thus, a "hard" scorer may develop a somewhat lower score than an "easy" scorer. This is particularly true for Similarities, Comprehension, and Vocabulary, where scoring criteria are less clear than for other subtests. The Wechsler scales, like other tests of intelligence, are also limited in the scope of what they can measure. They do not assess such important factors as need for achievement, motivation, creativity, or success in dealing with people.

THE MEANING OF IQ SCORES

Since only a weak and vague relation exists between theories of intelligence and the tests themselves, it is important for all persons involved with testing to understand the meaning of IQ scores. Untrained persons are particularly likely to misinterpret IQ scores, which may result in poor decisions or negative attitudes related to the client. The meaning of IQ scores can be partially clarified by elaborating on some of the more common misinterpretations. IQ is often incorrectly believed to be fixed, unchangeable, and innate. IQ scores, however can be subject to a wide variety of environmental influences. Second, IQ scores are not exact, precise measurements; rather, they are estimates in which there is an expected range of fluctuation between one performance and the next. Furthermore, such tests as the Wechsler scales measure only a limited range of abilities, and a large number of variables usually considered to be "intelligent" are beyond the scope of most intelligence tests. No test or battery of tests can ever give a complete picture; they can only assess various areas of functioning. In summary, an IQ is an estimate of a person's current level of functioning as measured by the various tasks required in a test.

An assumption of any global IQ score is that it derives from a wide array of interacting abilities. A subtest such as Information will assess specific areas of a person's range of knowledge and is related to general intelligence. IQ scores are also influenced by achievement orientation, curiosity, culture, and the person's interests. More general prerequisites are that the client must comprehend what has been requested, follow directions, provide a response, and understand English. Factors such as persistence and drive are also likely to influence any type of task presented to the person. The tasks included in IQ tests are those, based on judgments by psychometrists, most valued by Western society. In other words, they relate to and are predictive of relevant skills outside the testing situation. It is certainly possible to test a much wider range of areas (as in Guilford's Structure of Intelligence), but many of these would be of little relevance to the practical aspects of work and academic achievement.

Despite the many relevant areas measured by IQ tests, practitioners need to observe some humility when making predictions based on them. Many persons with quite high IQs achieve little or nothing. Having a high IQ is in no way a guarantee of success, but merely means that one important condition has been met. In contrast, persons with relatively low IQs will have more severe limitations placed on them. As a result of their relatively narrower range of options, predictions regarding their behavior tend to be more accurate.

Regardless of the person's IQ range, clinicians should be clear regarding the likely band of error (standard error of measurement). It is often useful to include the standard error of measurement into a report. For example, the WAIS-R Full Scale IQ has an average standard error of measurement of 2.53. Thus, a particular IQ will have a 95% chance of being within ± 5 IQ points of a person's obtained IQ. The WISC-III has a slightly higher average standard error of measurement of 3.20 for the Full Scale IQ, 3.53 for the Verbal IQ, and 4.54 for the Performance IQ (Wechsler, 1991). Error can also be the result of unforeseen events beyond the context of IQ tests. Even though 50% to 75% of the variance of children's academic success is dependent on nonintellectual factors (persistence, personal adjustment, curiosity), most of a typical assessment is spent evaluating IQ. Some of these nonintellectual areas might be quite difficult to assess and others might even be impossible to account for. For example, a student might unexpectedly develop an excellent relationship with a teacher, which significantly changes his or her attitude toward school thereby stimulating his or her interest to passionately pursue a specific area. Thus, any meaning attached to an IQ score should acknowledge the possible effects of uncertainty both within the measurement itself as well as from the wider context of the person's life.

Another important aspect of IQ is the statistical meaning of the different scores. Binet originally conceptualized intelligence as the difference between a person's mental age and his or her chronological age. This was found to be inadequate and has been replaced by the use of the deviation IQ. The assumption behind the deviation IQ is that intelligence falls around a normal distribution (see Figure 5–2). The interpretation of an IQ score, then, is straightforward in that it gives the relative position of a person compared with his or her age-related peers. The IQ can thus be expressed in deviation units away from the norm. Each of the three Wechsler IQs (Full Scale, Verbal, Performance) has a mean of 100 and a standard deviation of 15. Scores also can be easily translated into percentile equivalents. For example, an IQ of 120 is 1.33 standard deviations above the mean and places an individual in the ninety-first percentile (see Appendix A). Thus, this person's performance is better than 91% of his or her age-related peers. The IQ cutoff for mental retardation is 70, which indicates that such individuals are functioning in the lowest 2% when compared with their age-related peers. Appendix A can be used to convert Wechsler IQ scores ($M = 100$, $SD = 15$) into percentile rankings.

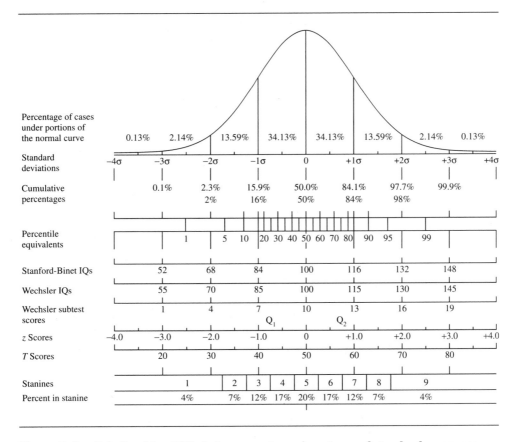

Figure 5–2. Relationship of Wechsler scores to various types of standard measures

A final consideration is the different classifications of intelligence. Table 5–1 lists commonly used diagnostic labels and compares them with IQ ranges and percentages. These terms are taken from the 1991 WISC-III manual and the designations for high average, low average, and intellectually deficient correspond to the earlier 1955 WAIS manual terms of bright normal, dull normal, and mental defective, respectively. Thus, an IQ can be expressed conceptually as an estimate of a person's current level of ability, statistically as a deviation score that can be transformed into percentile equivalents, and diagnostically using common terms for classification.

CAUTIONS AND GUIDELINES IN ADMINISTRATION

By most testing standards, the Wechsler manuals provide quite clear guidelines for administration and scoring. Despite this clarity, the number of administration and scoring errors on the part of trainee and experienced clinicians is far higher than they should be (Slate & Hunnicutt, 1988; Slate, Jones, & Murray, 1991). Even with repeated administration of the Wechsler scales, often examiners end up "practicing their mistakes" rather than correcting them (Slate et al., 1991). The causes of these errors include lack of proper instruction, lack of clarity between academic versus clinical site regarding where

Table 5–1.   Intelligence classifications

WAIS-R/WISC-III	More Value-Neutral Terms	Corresponding IQ Range
Very superior	Higher extreme above average	130+
Superior	Well above average	120–129
High average	High average	110–119
Average	Average	90–109
Low average	Low average	80–89
Borderline	Well below average	70–79
Mentally retarded (WAIS-R) or Intellectually deficient (WISC-III)	Lower extreme	69 and below

Source: The classification systems of the WAIS-R are from Wechsler (1981, Table 9) and for the WISC-III are from Wechsler (1991, Table 2.8). Percentile ranks can be calculated by consulting Appendix A.

training is supposed to occur, carelessness, variations in the quality of the examiner-examinee relationship, and work overload for clinicians (Slate & Hunnicutt, 1988). One approach to reducing errors is awareness regarding the most frequent *general* categories of errors. These have been investigated by Slate et al. (1991), and the most common errors, in order of frequency, are as follows (Slate et al., 1991):

1. Failure to record examinee responses, circle scores, or record times (error of administration).
2. Assigning too many points to an examinee's response (leniency by examiner).
3. Failing to question when required by test manual (poor reading and recalling of information in the manual).
4. Questioning examinee inappropriately (poor reading and/or incorrect integration of the manual).
5. Assigning too few points when required by test manual (examiner too hard).
6. Incorrect conversion of raw score to standard score (clerical error).
7. Failure to assign correct points for Performance items (clerical and timing error).
8. Incorrect calculation of raw score for subtest totals (clerical error).
9. Incorrect calculation of chronological age (clerical error).

Whereas the preceding list covers quite general categories, the following list, adapted from Moon, Blakey, Gorsuch, and Fantuzzo (1991), includes a series of recommendations based on the most frequently occurring errors but does so by listing concrete and specific recommendations:

1. Recite digits (on Digit Span) at the rate of one per second with the pitch of the voice dropping on the last digit of each trial.
2. State during the introduction that each task begins with easy questions and ends with difficult ones. Examiners may also note that not everyone is expected to succeed on all problems.

3. Record responses verbatim on Vocabulary.

4. Properly orient blocks (on Block Design) at examinee's midline.

5. The first time the examinee points out a nonessential part on Picture Completion, the examiner should comment, "Yes, but what is the most important thing missing?"

6. Attempt to elicit the examinee's perception of the testing situation and correct any misconceptions.

7. Check to see if the examinee is comfortable.

Despite clear guidelines in the manual as well as awareness of frequent errors, examiners are still likely to make mistakes. Thus, optimal training guidelines should be incorporated into graduate programs and continuing education. A recommended format is the Mastery Model which involves the following steps: (a) 1–2 hours studying the manual, (b) viewing a videotape of a flawless WAIS-R/WISC-III administration, (c) viewing a videotaped lecture of major pitfalls of administration, (d) successfully detecting errors in a videotaped flawed WAIS-R/WISC-III administration, (e) actually administering the WAIS-R/WISC-IIIs to be evaluated by a rating device such as Fantuzzo and Moon's (1984) *Criteria for Competent WAIS-R Administration* and Blakey, Fantuzzo, Gorsuch, and Moon's (1987) *Criteria for Competent WAIS-R Scoring*. A training manual that includes many of the components of the Mastery Model (e.g., guidelines, rating forms) is available from the Psychological Corporation (Fantuzzo, Blakey, & Gorsuch, 1989). Such procedures are likely to significantly shorten the length of training time, number of training administrations, and yet significantly increase the level of competence related to Wechsler scale administration and scoring (Blakey et al., 1987; Fantuzzo & Moon, 1984; Moon, Fantuzzo, & Gorsuch, 1986; Slate et al., 1991).

WAIS-R/WISC-III SUCCESSIVE LEVEL INTERPRETATION PROCEDURE

The following successive-level approach to interpreting Wechsler scores represents an integration and synthesis of the approaches outlined by Kamphaus (1993), Kaufman (1990, 1994), Kramer (1993), Naglieri (1993), and Sattler (1992). This approach provides clinicians with a sequential, five-level format for working with and discussing a person's performance. The underlying purpose for each of these steps should be based on confirming, disconfirming, or altering hypotheses derived from the referral question and any available background information. The next section of this chapter ("The Wechsler subtests") covers descriptions of the Wechsler subtests including the more frequently encountered abilities associated with these subtests. This section can serve as a summary and quick reference for clinicians, especially in analyzing test profiles (Levels II and III).

Examiners who are relatively unfamiliar with the Wechsler scales are likely to find the level of detail in the following interpretation procedure and Wechsler subtest sections somewhat daunting due to its complexity. It is thus recommended that they initially read through the interpretation procedures to gain familiarity with the material. It might be particularly helpful to review the summary of these procedures in

Table 5–2.   Summary of successive five-level WAIS-R/WISC-III interpretive procedures

Level I. Interpret the Full Scale IQ

Determine percentile rankings and IQ classification (see Appendix A and Table 5–1)

Level II. Interpret Verbal-Performance, Factor Scores, and Additional Groupings

a. Verbal-Performance IQs

Interpret if V-P discrepancy is 12 or more points

b. Factor Scores: Verbal Comprehension, Perceptual Organization, Freedom from Distractibility, Processing Speed (WISC-III only).

Interpret if significant discrepancies occur between the mean of the three WAIS-R or four WISC-III scores/indexes and relevant factor scores.

c. Additional Groupings: Bannatyne's Categories, ACID/SCAD profiles, Horn groupings, Fuld profile (see Appendixes B and C).

Interpret if significant differences occur between means of groupings and individual grouping/category.

Level III. Interpret Subtest Variability (Profile Analysis)

a. Determine whether subtest fluctuations are significant:

1. Decide appropriateness of using full scale versus verbal and/or performance subtest means; calculate relevant means.
2. Calculate the difference scores between subtests and relevant means.
3. Determine whether the difference between subtest score and scale means is significant (see Appendix D).
4. Indicate on profile as either a strength or a weakness.
5. Repeat steps 1–5 for each relevant subtest.

b. Develop hypotheses related to the meaning of subtest fluctuations (Appendix E).

c. Integrate subtest hypotheses with additional information.

Level IV. Analyze Intrasubtest variability.

Level V. Conduct a Qualitative analysis.

Table 5–2, both prior to and after reading this section. Table 5–2 can also serve as a useful future quick reference guide when actually working with Wechsler protocols. After perusing the "Interpretation Procedures" section, student examiners should next obtain a completed WAIS-R/WISC-III profile, preferably one they themselves have administered, and then work through the levels of interpretation in a sequential manner. This should then add the required level of clarity and integration of the material to begin to work more confidently with future protocols.

The following are principles to keep in mind when working through the interpretation procedures:

• The interpretation procedures outlined here require a number of clerical calculations. While these calculations are fairly simple and straightforward, they need to be checked and rechecked for accuracy, particularly for examiners who are relatively unfamiliar with testing procedures. This is highlighted by an extensive literature documenting that the frequency of clerical errors in the development of scores for the Wechsler scales is surprisingly and worrisomely high (Moon et al., 1986; Moon et al., 1991; Slate & Hunnicutt, 1988; Slate, Jones, & Murray, 1991).

- The successive steps begin with the most general aspects of the WAIS-R/WISC-III (Full Scale IQ) and gradually work their way to more specific aspects of the person's performance (subtest scatter, qualitative responses to individual items, etc.).

- Examiners can interpret the more global measures (Full Scale, Verbal, and Performance IQs) with greater meaning, usefulness, and certainty if there is not a high degree of subtest scatter. With increasing subtest scatter, the purity of the global measures becomes contaminated so that interpretations of these global measures becomes less meaningful. For example, if the Verbal scales display a pattern in which Arithmetic and Digit Span are significantly higher or lower than the other Verbal scales, then it makes more sense to interpret the Verbal scales according to the two factors of Verbal Comprehension and Freedom from Distractibility.

- To determine whether scores (factor scores, additional groupings, subtests) are significantly high or low, a consistent, uniform approach is used. This involves first calculating the means of all relevant scores, groupings, or subtests and then calculating the difference which a score in question varies from the relevant mean. The exception to this is the Verbal versus Performance IQ discrepancy, which is traditionally determined by simply noting the difference between the two.

- For the purposes of the following interpretive system, the level set to establish significant difference is the .05 level. This is true for differences through all levels of interpretation including Verbal-Performance, factor scores, additional grouping, and subtest differences. It was felt that this level of significance is sufficiently rigorous for clinical purposes. If either less stringent ($p = .15$) or more stringent ($p = .01$) levels are desired, relevant tables can be found in such sources such as Naglieri (1993), Kamphaus (1993), Kaufman and Kaufman (1990, 1993), Kramer (1993), Silverstein (1982a), or Wechsler (1991). Whenever possible, Bonferroni corrections have been included to correct for the possible statistical error resulting from significant results being inflated due to the number of comparisons.

- Any interpretations, especially those related to the more specific levels (Levels III, IV, and V), should be considered as tentative hypotheses requiring support from additional sources of information (behavioral observations, school records, etc.). Preferably, each hypothesis should be supported by at least two additional sources. This process of hypothesis generation, confirmation/disconfirmation, and integration with other sources is not merely a statistical procedure but also involves considerable clinical wisdom and judgment.

Level I. The Full Scale IQ

An examinee's Full Scale IQ should be considered first since it provides the basis and context for evaluating other cognitive abilities. It is generally the single most reliable and valid score. The Full Scale IQ gives the person's relative standing in comparison with his or her age-related peers and provides a global estimate of his or her overall mental abilities. It is often useful to transform the Full Scale IQ into a percentile rank (see Appendix A) or intelligence classification (see Table 5–1). This is especially important when relating test results to untrained persons since both percentile rank and intelligence classifications are usually less subject to misinterpretation than IQ scores. Many examiners also prefer to include the standard error of measurement (*SEM*) as an estimate of the confidence that can be placed in the obtained score. For example, a WAIS-R Full Scale IQ of 110 has a 95% probability of falling between 105 and 115 IQ points. This clarifies that the IQ score is not a precise number but is rather a range with an expected margin of error.

Two areas that might potentially be areas of misinterpretation are the intelligence classifications of "Borderline" and "Mentally Retarded." The former term might be confused with the *DSM-IV* psychiatric diagnosis of Borderline Personality. Examiners might counter this by clarifying in parentheses that the "Borderline" range can also be described as "Well below Average" (Kaufman, 1990). Similarly, the "Mentally Retarded" intelligence classification might lead a reader to conclude that a diagnosis of mental retardation has been made. However, such a diagnosis cannot be made unless there has also been a thorough assessment of the examinee's level of adaptive behavior. Furthermore, some referral sources and other readers of a psychological report may feel that the term "mentally retarded" might be objectionable. An examiner may wish to clarify this issue or provide the alternate term of "Lower Extreme" or "Significantly below Average" range of intelligence (Kaufman, 1990).

Although the Full Scale IQ is the most stable and well-validated aspect of the Wechsler scales, its significance becomes progressively less important as the fluctuations increase between Verbal and Performance IQs, with high fluctuations between the factor scores, or when there is a high degree of subtest scatter. When such fluctuations occur, then it is incumbent on the examiner to work in more detail to extract the significance of these relative strengths and weaknesses. The next four successive levels of interpretation will provide a sequential method of accomplishing this goal.

Level II. Verbal-Performance IQs, Factor Scores, and Additional Grouping

The second level of interpretation is to consider Verbal and Performance IQs, factor scores, and additional groupings. During each of these subsections, procedures for determining the significance (.05 level) of the scores in relation to relevant means will be provided. In addition, formulas will be listed for the Bannatyne categories, ACID/SCAD profiles, and additional groupings that will enable examiners to convert the scores into the familiar and IQ-related standard scores having a mean of 100 and standard deviation of 15. Each of these formulas is listed for quick reference in Appendix B for the WAIS-R and Appendix C for the WISC-III.

Step IIa. Verbal-Performance IQs

The Verbal IQ is an index of an individual's verbal comprehensive abilities, while the Performance IQ provides an estimate of his or her perceptual organizational abilities. However, clinicians should be aware that a pure test of verbal comprehension or perceptual organization does not exist. A seemingly simple task, such as repeating numbers, involves not only verbal comprehension but also adequate rapport, ability to concentrate, number facility, and adequate short-term memory.

One of the central principles behind interpreting Verbal and Performance IQs is that there needs to be a significant difference between them. If such a difference occurs, then an explanation for these differences should be developed. An area of difficulty (and controversy) lies in deciding what should be considered an interpretable difference between Verbal and Performance scores. On both the WAIS-R and WISC-III, a 12-point difference is significant at the .05 level (and a 15-point difference is significant at the .01 level). Thus, a difference of 12 points or greater (95% chance of a significant difference) should be investigated further. It should still be noted that a full 20% of the WAIS-R and 24% of the WISC-III standardization samples obtained Verbal-Performance differences of 15 points or greater (Grossman, 1983; Wechsler, 1981, 1991). Among bright, healthy, elderly ($M = 71$) populations, the 15-point Verbal-Performance discrepancy was found in 25% of the cases (Mitrushina & Satz, 1995). This means that, although a 12-point difference is statistically significant, it is still a fairly common occurrence (see also Crawford & Allan, 1996). The difference, then, may represent merely useful information rather than "lurking pathology." The possibility of pathology is far more likely with a 25-point or more difference, which only occurred in 5% of the WAIS-R/WISC-III standardization samples.

Interpreting the magnitude of and meaning behind Verbal-Performance differences should always occur within the context of what is known about the person (particularly age and education) as well as his or her condition. For example, persons from higher socioeconomic backgrounds or with higher IQs are likely to have verbal scores significantly higher than their performance scores (Bornstein, Suga, & Prifitera, 1989). In contrast, unskilled workers are more likely to have higher performance scores relative to verbal. If these trends are reversed (e.g., an attorney with higher performance scores), then the importance of such a result becomes greater. The major variables influencing and possible meanings behind Verbal-Performance score differences are summarized in the sections "Verbal Scales" and "Performance Scales" as well as in the sections on special populations. However, Sattler (1992) has summarized the possible general meanings associated with such differences as relating to cognitive style, patterns of interests, sensory deficits, psychopathology (such as emotional disturbance or brain damage), deficiencies/strengths in information processing, or deficiencies/strengths in ability to work under pressure. Once an interpretation has been made, practitioners can eventually work to develop implications and instructional recommendations for high and low scores (for Full Scale, Verbal, and Performance IQs, and Freedom from Distractibility; see section "Instructional Recommendations" and Appendixes H and I).

Under certain conditions, even statistically significant differences between Verbal and Performance IQs can be considered meaningless. The first condition is when Arithmetic and Digit Span are both either quite low or quite high compared with the rest of the Verbal subtests. This is because these subtests are more associated with the third Freedom from Distractibility Factor (Kaufman, 1990, 1994). Thus, it may make more sense to interpret the results according to a three-factor solution (see next section) rather than Wechsler's Verbal and Comprehension factors. This approach is further supported if Digit Symbol is similar to scores on Arithmetic and Digit Span and similarly quite high or low compared with other Performance subtests. This is because the WAIS-R Digit Symbol subtest, like Arithmetic and Digit Span, is more associated with the Freedom from Distractibility Factor for adults.

A further condition that might render the Verbal and/or Performance IQs meaningless occurs when there is a high degree of subtest scatter in general (WAIS-R Verbal subtest range 9+ points, Performance 9+ points; WISC-III Verbal range 7+ points, Performance range 9+ points). This is because the intent of the three IQs is that they represent a unitary construct in which the person's Full, Verbal, or Performance IQs are general, integrated means of functioning. In contrast, high subtest scatter attacks the unitary, integrated nature of the IQs. It is then the examiner's task to work with the relative high and low combinations of subtests to make sense of the person's intellectual strengths and weaknesses. These steps are outlined in Levels IIb, IIc, and III. However, before continuing to an interpretation of subtest scatter, important clusters of subtests might be found through a consideration of factor scores or additional groupings.

Step IIb. Factor Scores

An alternative to interpreting Verbal-Performance differences is to consider the meaning associated with factor scores. The factor structure of the Wechsler scales has been controversial, with different researchers coming up with somewhat different numbers and types of factors. Most authors, however, refer to Verbal Comprehension, Perceptual Organization, and Freedom from Distractibility (see Allen & Thorndike, 1995; Blaha & Wallbrown, 1996; Burgess et al., 1992; Gregory, 1987; Kaufman, 1990, 1994; Leckliter et al., 1986; Reynolds & Ford, 1994; Sattler, 1992; Waller & Waldman, 1990). A fourth Processing Speed factor or "index score" emerged from the WISC-III due to the inclusion of the new Symbol Search subtest which could then be paired with the older Coding subtest (Blaha & Wallbrown, 1996; Wechsler, 1991).

The *Verbal Comprehension* factor on both the WAIS-R and WISC-III comprises Information, Similarities, Vocabulary, and Comprehension and represents a somewhat purer measure of verbal abilities than the Verbal Scale itself. The *Perceptual Organization* factor is likewise a somewhat purer measure of perceptual abilities. On the WISC-III, Perceptual Organization comprises Picture Completion, Picture Arrangement, Block Design, and Object Assembly. On the WAIS-R, Picture Completion, Block Design, and Object Assembly make up the Perceptual Organization factor but, unlike the WISC-III, Picture Arrangement is not included. Perceptual Organization has been found to be the factor that is least related to educational level (Kaufman, McLean, & Reynolds, 1988).

The *Freedom from Distractibility* factor, a more complex and controversial construct, has been extensively studied with children but much less so with adults. It comprises Arithmetic and Digit Span on the WISC-III. The WAIS-R subtests of Arithmetic and Digit Span are likewise related to Freedom from Distractibility, but Digit Symbol (the WAIS-R equivalent of Coding) has been found to be related to Freedom from Distractibility only for certain age groups (18–19 and 45–54; Parker, 1983a).

In many ways, the term "Freedom from Distractibility" is a misnomer since this factor measures a much wider range of abilities than merely distractibility. It has primarily been related to concentration, attention, and short-term memory and is believed to be lowered by poor number facility, anxiety, difficulty making mental shifts, and poor self-monitoring. Bannatyne (1974) has stressed the importance of sequencing since each of the relevant subtests requires that the respondent place numbers and symbols in their proper order. Wielkiewicz (1990) has suggested that the low concentration, memory, and sequencing reflected on this factor is often due to a poorly functioning executive ability. Specifically, the person experiences difficulty attending to stimuli and simultaneously performing other mental tasks (e.g., listening to spoken digits and storing them while simultaneously reversing them and then repeating them backward). As a result of these diverse functions, a low Freedom from Distractibility factor is also likely to lower performances in other areas, and this should be taken into account when estimating the person's overall potential.

The *Processing Speed* factor (WISC-III only) includes Symbol Search and Coding. It reflects the mental and motor speed with which a person can solve nonverbal problems. Further subtest support for this factor can be found if the person also has correspondingly high (or low) performances on the timed nonverbal tests of Object Assembly and Block Design. In addition to mental and motor speed, the Processing Speed factor is also a measure of a person's ability to plan, organize, and develop relevant strategies. Low scores on Processing Speed can also reflect poor motor control. Since speed and concentration require good test-taking attitudes, Processing Speed (as well as Freedom from Distractibility) can also be lowered by poor motivation to perform well. For this reason, these two factors are sometimes referred to as "validity" factors. Whether or not a lowered performance is the result of poor motivation can often best be assessed by behavioral observations in combination with clarification and consideration of the presenting problem. An overly reflective problem-solving style could also lower the Processing Speed factor since the person would take too much time cautiously considering his or her response to each item.

To determine standard scores ($M = 100$, $SD = 15$) for each of the WAIS-R factor scores, the following formulas can be used (Kaufman, 1990):

$$\text{Verbal Comprehension: } 1.4 (I + V + C + S) + 44$$

$$\text{Perceptual Organization: } 2.0 (PC + BD + OA) + 40$$

$$\text{Freedom from Distractibility: } 2.8 (DSp + A) + 44$$

To calculate the preceding formulas, *age-corrected scaled scores must be used*. To determine whether the factor-related standard scores differ significantly, use the following steps:

1. Find the mean for all three of the factor-based standard scores.
2. Calculate the difference between each of the three factor-related standard scores and the mean for the total factor-based standard scores.
3. Determine whether the difference scores vary from the mean.

To vary at the .05 level, the following difference values have been provided by Kaufman (1990):

- *Verbal Comprehension:* 8 (ages 16–19) or 7 (ages 20–74)
- *Perceptual Organization:* 11 (ages 16–19) or 9 (ages 20–74)
- *Freedom from Distractibility:* 11 (ages 16–19) or 9 (ages 20–74)

In some cases, there will be an extensive degree of factor subtest scatter (highest minus lowest subtest). When this occurs, it indicates that the factors are not unitary but are rather composed of quite different clusters of abilities. As a result, factor interpretations should either not be made or made with considerable caution. Scatter of 7 for Verbal Comprehension, 8 for Perceptual Organization, and 4 for Freedom from Distractibility should be considered too large to safely interpret any of these factors.

The WISC-III has made calculating the factor scores easier in that conversion into standard scores (or "Indexes") has been incorporated into the normal scoring procedure. However, examiners still need to determine what are significant (interpretable) differences between the combinations of factor scores. As with the previous WAIS-R calculations, first find the means for all four of the factor-based standard scores. Then calculate the difference between each of the four factor-related standard scores and the mean for the total factor-based standard scores. To vary at the .05 level, Naglieri (1993) has provided the following values to determine whether discrepancies are significant:

- *Verbal Comprehension:* 9.1 points.
- *Perceptual Organization:* 10.4 points.
- *Freedom from Distractibility:* 11.5 points.
- *Processing Speed:* 12.0 points.

As with the WAIS-R, extensive factor subtest scatter suggests that factor interpretation should either not be made at all, or done with extreme caution. Cutoffs for this should be 7 for Verbal Comprehension, 8 for Perceptual Organization, 4 for Freedom from Distractibility, and 4 for Processing Speed.

Factor scores can be used for interpreting a person's relative strengths and weaknesses. However, the actual factor-based standard scores should not be presented in the psychological report since readers may confuse them with IQ scores. In addition, including both IQ scores and factor-based standard scores would make the report unnecessarily cluttered with too many numbers. Once interpretations have been made, practitioners can then work to develop appropriate instructional recommendations if an educational or rehabilitation plan needs to be developed (see section "Instructional Recommendations").

Step IIc. Additional Groupings: Bannatyne's Categories,
ACID/SCAD Profiles, Horn Groupings

Four additional factors or groupings can often yield useful interpretations. These are optional and should be calculated when, on initially appraising the pattern of subtest scatter, it seems they might be relevant to investigate more formally. For example, if subtests which are highly loaded on spatial abilities (Picture Completion, Block Design, Object Assembly) appear significantly higher than sequencing subtests (Digit Span, Arithmetic, Digit Symbol), a formal calculation of Bannatyne's categories will serve to confirm or disconfirm initial impressions related to the subtest profiles. Another reason to calculate the groupings listed in Level IIc occurs when an examiner wishes to see if a person's subtest profile is similar or dissimilar to a person from an actual or suspected client population (e.g., learning disabled, Alzheimer's disease).

Bannatyne's Categories   Bannatyne's categories comprise subtest patterns in which *Spatial* abilities are relatively higher than *Verbal Conceptualization,* which is in turn higher than *Sequential* abilities, with *Acquired Knowledge* typically being the lowest (Spatial > Verbal Conceptualization > Sequential > Acquired Knowledge). These categories were originally developed as a means of detecting and understanding learning-disabled populations (Bannatyne, 1974). However, it has been found that many learning-disabled persons do not necessarily have this pattern, and many non-learning-disabled populations do have the pattern (Groff & Hubble, 1981; Katz, Goldstein, Rudisin, & Bailey, 1993; Kavale & Forness, 1984; Thompson, 1981; see subsection "Learning Disabilities"). The result has been that Bannatyne's categories have been used to further understand Wechsler scale profiles in general and not for the diagnosis of specific conditions.

The traditional method of determining the relative magnitudes of these categories is simply to determine the subtest mean for each category and compare them to see which are highest, intermediate, or lowest (Bannatyne, 1974; Katz et al., 1993). In addition, the following formulas for calculating standard scores ($M = 100$, $SD = 15$) on the four categories are provided by Kaufman (1990, 1994):

> WAIS-R and WISC-III Spatial: 2.0 (PC + BD + OA) + 40
>
> WAIS-R and WISC-III Verbal Conceptualization: 1.9 (V + C + S) + 43
>
> WAIS-R Sequential: 2.1 (DSp + A + DSy) + 37
>
> WISC-III Sequential: 2.3 (DSp + A + Coding) + 31
>
> WAIS-R and WISC-III Acquired Knowledge: 1.9 (I + V + A) + 43

Picture Arrangement has been excluded from the categories since it is a maverick subtest that doesn't clearly load on any of the four categories. For each of these formulas *age-corrected subtest scores must be used.* The standard scores then need to be contrasted to determine whether or not they are significant at the .05 level. To calculate this, first find the mean for the four standard scores from each of the categories. Then calculate the degree of difference which the four standard scores vary from the mean. The following values are required for the scores to vary at the .05 level:

- *Spatial:* WAIS-R; 11 (ages 16–19) or 10 (ages 20–74) and WISC-III; 10 (average for all ages)
- *Verbal Conceptualization:* WAIS-R; 9 (ages 16–19) or 8 (ages 20–74) and WISC-III; 8.5 (average for all ages)
- *Sequential:* WAIS-R; 11 (ages 16–19) or 9 (ages 20–74) and WISC-III; 12 (average for all ages)
- *Acquired Knowledge:* WAIS-R; 8 (ages 16–19) or 7 (ages 20–74) and WISC-III; 8.5 (average for all ages)

An interpretive warning is perhaps advisable. Only about 20% to 25% of learning-disabled persons will actually demonstrate the classic sequence of Bannatyne's Spatial > Verbal Conceptualization > Sequential > Acquired Knowledge pattern (Groff & Hubble, 1981; Katz et al., 1993; Thompson, 1981). A noteworthy exception from the Bannatyne profile is that sometimes a bright, highly motivated learning-disabled person with poor sequencing abilities will compensate by developing a high level of acquired knowledge. Thus, the Acquired Knowledge category might be outstandingly high even though Sequential abilities might still be quite low (Ackerman, McGrew, & Dykman, 1987). Another less bright and/or less motivated learning-disabled person might experience the disruption of poor sequencing to a greater extent and may have then become correspondingly alienated from academic learning. This would then be reflected in an outstandingly low Acquired Knowledge category. This is consistent with the finding that learning disabilities are a heterogeneous group of disorders with sometimes well-defined subtypes (Anderson & Gilandas, 1994; Rourke, 1991). This means that examiners need to take a flexible approach toward interpreting the relation and implications between the Bannatyne categories.

The ACID/SCAD Profiles   The *ACID* and *SCAD* profiles are similar to those of Bannatyne's categories. Low scores on each of these profiles has been found to occur more frequently among learning-disabled populations (Ackerman et al., 1987; Cordoni et al., 1981; Kaufman, 1990, 1994; Prifitera & Dersh, 1993). The *ACID* profile comprises **A**rithmetic, **C**oding (Digit Symbol for the WAIS-R), **I**nformation, and **D**igit Span. Note that three of the subtests (Arithmetic, Coding/Digit Symbol, Digit Span) comprise Bannatyne's Sequential Category and one (Information) is included in Bannatyne's Acquired Knowledge category. As with the Bannatyne categories, an exception to the pattern is that often learning-disabled university students who have academically compensated for their learning disabilities have relatively good performances on Information (Ackerman et al., 1987).

A WAIS-R standard score ($M = 100$, $SD = 15$) can be calculated for the ACID profile by using the following formula (Kaufman, 1990):

$$\text{ACID (WAIS-R): } 1.6(A + DSy + I + DSp) + 36$$

Note that *age-corrected scores must be used.*

For the WISC-III, Kaufman (1994) recommends deleting Information and instead inserting Symbol Search. The profile is then composed of **S**ymbol Search, **C**oding, **A**rithmetic, and **D**igit Span and can then be appropriately renamed the *SCAD* profile. These four subtests are a merging of the WISC-III's Freedom from Distractibility (Arithmetic and Digit Span) and Perceptual Speed (Symbol Search and Coding) factors. To convert the SCAD profile into a standard score, the following formula can be used (Kaufman, 1994):

$$\text{SCAD (WISC-III): } 1.7 (SS + C + A + DSp) + 32$$

As for previous and similar formulas, *age-corrected scores must be used.*

To vary from the Full Scale IQ (standard score for all subtests) at the .05 level, the following values must be achieved:

- *ACID* profile (WAIS-R): 11 points (ages 16–19), 9 points (ages 20–74)
- *SCAD* profile (WISC-III): 9.5 points

  Note: If there is a significant difference (16 or more points) between the Processing Speed (Symbol Search and Coding) and Freedom from Distractibility (Arithmetic and Digit Span) Index (standard) scores, then the SCAD profile should not be interpreted.

Horn Groupings   Horn and Cattell's (1966) fluid versus crystallized intelligence have been used to organize many of the WAIS-R/WISC-III subtests (Kaufman, 1990, 1994; Woodcock, 1990). On the WAIS-R, *Fluid Intelligence* includes Digit Span, Similarities, Picture Completion, Picture Arrangement, Block Design, and Object Assembly. In contrast, *Crystallized Intelligence* is measured by Information, Vocabulary, Comprehension, and Similarities. A third WAIS-R Horn grouping has also been developed for *Retention* which includes Information, Digit Span, and Arithmetic. Formulas to convert the sum of subtest scores into standard scores ($M = 100$, $SD = 15$) for each of these groupings are as follows:

WAIS-R Fluid Intelligence: 1.1 (DSp + S + PC + PA + BD + OA) + 34

WAIS-R Crystallized Intelligence: 1.4 (I + V + C + S) + 44

WAIS-R Retention: 2.0 (I + DSp + A) + 40

Age-corrected scores must be used in calculating the sums.

The Horn groupings on the WISC-III are somewhat different from the WAIS-R in that *Fluid Intelligence* includes Picture Arrangement, Block Design, Object Assembly, Similarities, and Arithmetic. *Crystallized Intelligence* includes Information, Similarities, Vocabulary, Comprehension, and Picture Arrangement. Because Picture Arrangement and Similarities include skills related to both crystallized and fluid intelligence, they are included on both groupings. An additional grouping is *Achievement* which is a composite of all tests most influenced by academic learning. This grouping includes Information, Similarities, Arithmetic, Vocabulary, Comprehension, and Picture Arrangement. To convert the WISC-III Horn groupings into standard scores ($M = 100$, $SD = 15$), the following formulas can be used (Kaufman, 1994):

WISC-III Fluid Intelligence: 1.3 (S + A + PA + BD + OA) + 35

WISC-III Crystallized Intelligence: 1.3 (I + S + V + C + PA) + 35

WISC-III Achievement: 0.85 (I + S + A + V + C + PA) + 49

Age-corrected scores must be used when calculating the preceding formulas.

Comparisons should be made between each of the three standard scores to determine whether they are significantly different. To do this, first calculate the mean for the total subtests used in the three Horn groupings by summing the three standard scores and dividing by three. Then calculate the difference that each of the three standard scores varies from the mean. To be significant at the .05 level, the following values must be achieved:

- *Fluid Intelligence:* WAIS-R; 9 points (ages 16–19), 9 points (ages 20–74), and WISC-III; 8.5
- *Crystallized Intelligence:* WAIS-R; 7 points (ages 16–19), 6 (ages 20–74), and WISC-III; 9 points
- *Retention:* WAIS-R only; 9 points (ages 16–19), 7 points (ages 20–74)
- *Achievement:* WISC-III only; 8.5 points

Level III. Interpreting Subtest Variability

The third step is to consider the degree to which the individual subtests deviate from the full scale, verbal, or performance subtest means and to determine the meaning associated with the subtest fluctuations. The outcome should be a description of a person's relative cognitive strengths and weaknesses. A listing and discussion of the meaning of each subtest and the abilities it measures is provided in the next major section of this chapter ("The Wechsler Subtests"). Clinicians can refer to this section, as well as to information on how to assess special populations in developing their own hypotheses about important dimensions of intersubtest scatter. Readers may also wish to refer to Kamphaus (1993), Kaufman (1990, 1994), Kramer (1993), Naglieri (1993), Sattler (1992), and Wechsler (1991), who have provided a detailed list of hypotheses and useful tables for various combinations of high and low subtest scores. However, Level III interpretation is only necessary if there is sufficient subtest scatter. If all the subtests are fairly even, then its not necessary to attempt subtest profile interpretation.

Clinicians need to be aware that interpreting subtest variability involves clinical judgment guided by theory, observation, and an integration of the specifics of each case. Because there is little research base to support this process, it should be approached with caution. As a general rule, the more subtests that can be combined to make inferences based on their shared abilities, the more support can be found for such an inference. At one extreme would be a series of subtests that combine to make up one of the previously discussed factors. The opposite would be the use of only one subtest to make an inference. In general, inferences based on only a single subtest should be treated with the most caution. While these single subtest-based inferences can be viable, it is incumbent upon the clinician to obtain as much supporting evidence as possible.

The following three steps are recommended in interpreting subtest variability: (a) Determine whether subtest fluctuations are significant, (b) develop hypotheses related to the meaning of any subtest fluctuations, and (c) integrate these hypotheses with additional relevant information regarding the examinee. For profile interpretation, *age-corrected scores should be used at all times.* For the WAIS-R (ages 16–74), these can be located in Table 21 (pp. 142–150) of the WAIS-R manual. Age-corrected subtest scores for individuals 75+ have been developed by Ryan et al. (1990) and Ivnik et al. (1992), and clinicians should use these two sets of norms in the assessment of elderly patients with Alzheimer's disease or other populations of dementing patients (see McCurry, Fitz, & Terri, 1994). The WISC-III has conveniently incorporated age-corrected scores into the standard scoring procedure making it unnecessary to look them up separately.

Step IIIa. Determine Whether Subtest Fluctuations Are Significant

The first step in profile analysis is to account for the implications of the mostly modest reliabilities associated with the different subtests. This means each clinician needs to seriously consider whether the variability is due to reliably measured strengths or weaknesses, or merely due to chance error inherent in the subtest. This issue has caused some authors to question whether profile analysis should even be undertaken (Faust, Ziskin, & Hiers, 1991; Hanson, Hunsley, & Parker, 1988; McDermott, Fantuzzo, & Glutting, 1990; McDermott et al., 1992; Ziskin & Faust, 1995). At the center of this controversy is the importance of determining what should be considered a significant deviation from mean subtest scores on the Full Scale, Verbal, and Performance Scales (Matarazzo, Daniel, Prifitera, & Herman, 1988; Piedmont, Sokolove, & Fleming, 1989a, 1989b). Silverstein (1982a) has provided tables for the WAIS-R (also reproduced in Gregory, 1987) as Kaufman (1994), Kramer (1993), and Wechsler (1991) have for the WISC-III that take into account each subtest's relative reliability (and therefore, band of error). For example, the WAIS-R Vocabulary, with a high reliability of .96, would only need to deviate by a scaled score of 1.9 to achieve a .05 level of significance. In contrast, Object Assembly, with a relatively low reliability of .68, would need to have a much larger deviation of 4.1 scaled score points to achieve the same .05 level of significance.

To determine whether or not a subtest varies significantly (at the .05 level), follow the procedures detailed in Appendix D, which includes a Worksheet for Determining Magnitude of WAIS-R Subtest Fluctuations and a second Worksheet for Determining Magnitude of WISC-III Subtest Fluctuations. This will establish whether or not the subtests actually fluctuate from the Verbal, Performance, or Full Scale means to a significant extent.

This procedure should be undertaken with an awareness of the frequency with which subtest fluctuations occur. Similar to Verbal-Performance discrepancies, a moderately high range (highest minus lowest subtest score) is a fairly common occurrence. The *average* range on the WISC-III standardization sample was 8.5 points (*SD* = 2.3) for the Full Scale (13 subtests), 5.5 (*SD* = 2.1) points for the Verbal Scale (6 subtests), and 7.1 points (*SD* = 2.4) for the Performance Scale (7 subtests; Wechsler, 1991). Approximately two thirds of the WISC-III standardization sample had subscales that ranged between seven to eight points. Similarly, a subtest range of 9 points on the WAIS-R Full Scale (and 7 points on the Verbal and Performance Scales) was not unusual (Crawford & Allan, 1996; Matarazzo et al., 1988) even among a general population of brain-damaged patients (Ryan, Paolo, & Smith, 1992). Well-educated, elderly populations have been found to have a particularly high level of subtest scatter (Mitrushina & Satz, 1995). Persons with low obtained WAIS-R IQs are less likely to have a high amount of subtest scatter than persons with high IQs. Thus, the diagnostic significance would be greater for low IQ persons who have a high amount of subscale scatter. However, a high range of subtest scatter may merely indicate cognitive style rather than pathology or exceptionality. The criteria for an unusually high range on the WAIS-R/WISC-III is 7 points for the Verbal subtests, 9 points for the Performance subtests, and 10 points if the comparison is made for the total highest and lowest subtests used to calculate the Full Scale IQ. It should also be noted that this procedure is used to make comparisons relative *only* to the clients themselves (ipsative comparisons).

Often it will be found that there are no significant subtest fluctuations. In these cases, do not proceed to Steps IIIb and IIIc. Instead, focus on interpreting the profile based on information derived from Levels I and II and possibly Levels IV and V if these are relevant.

Step IIIb. Develop Hypotheses Related to the Meaning of Subtest Fluctuations

Just because a subtest or group of subtests has been designated as a relative strength or weakness does not then mean that it is clear which of the various functions involved with the subtest is a strength or weakness. For example, Picture Arrangement involves planning (sequencing), visual organization, distinguishing essential from nonessential detail, and comprehending social situations. For one person, scoring high in Picture Arrangement might reflect excellent planning/sequencing abilities, for another it might reflect good social skills, and a third person might be high in both. It is the examiner's responsibility to become actively engaged with the pattern of subtests and any other relevant sources of information to determine which ability or abilities are high and low for the person. Interpreters who merely list the subtest's abilities as they are listed in a book are quite likely to make incorrect and even potentially damaging conclusions about the examinee. This cookbook type of approach should be strongly discouraged.

The underlying principle in uncovering the actual subtest strengths or weaknesses is to initially consider a significantly high or low subtest score within the context of scores on other subtests. If a person has scored high on Picture Arrangement and this might reflect good planning/sequencing, then an examiner would expect other subtests that also measured planning/sequencing to be at least within the average range if not higher. Thus, they might make sure that other sequencing-oriented tasks, primarily Digit Span and Arithmetic, were also high.

The difficulty with such a procedure is that it requires an in-depth knowledge of each subtest's abilities, familiarity with frequent clusters of subtests, and an overreliance on intuition in terms of noticing and testing out different patterns. This is a particularly daunting task for beginning and even experienced clinicians. Thus, a formal step-by-step procedure of comparing and contrasting relative strengths and weaknesses is recommended. This can be accomplished by completing Appendix E ("Guidelines for Determining Subtest Strengths and Weaknesses"). These guidelines use the same underlying principle in that consistencies and inconsistencies among patterns of subtests are determined. However, these patterns are investigated in a thorough and systematic pattern. The directions are adapted from Kaufman (1990, 1994) and the listed subtest abilities were adapted from those described by a wide variety of sources including Bannatyne (1974), Gregory (1987), Horn (1985), Kamphaus (1993), Kaufman (1990, 1994), Lezak (1995), and Sattler (1992). After completing Appendix E, the clinician will have arrived at a series of empirically derived and partially tested hypotheses.

An important consideration in this strategy of subtest interpretation is that it should not be a rigid, mechanical process. For example, a client who presents with subjective complaints related to poor sequencing (e.g., difficulty following directions, placing things in the wrong order) may not have all the expected WAIS-R/WISC-III quite within the statistically interpretable range. However, given the quite clear symptom reports (and possibly behavioral observations), practitioners may still choose to interpret the sequencing-related subtests. Somewhat similarly, a client might have sequencing subtests that are in the statistically interpretable range (according to calculations on Appendix D) along with a similar portrayal of symptom complaints as the preceding client. However, the interpretive process described in Appendix E may have "neutralized" this interpretation. Due to the strength of the symptom pattern combined with the statistically significant clustering of subtests, the practitioner may still conclude that sequencing was a problem for the person. The outlined procedure, then, should be used for hypothesis generation in which other factors beyond the mechanical interpretation procedure can confirm or disconfirm these hypotheses.

Step IIIc. Integrate Subtest Hypotheses with Additional Information

Before finally accepting or rejecting the step-by-step empirically derived hypotheses from Steps IIIa and IIIb, examiners should consider additional sources of relevant information. This might include behavioral observations, medical records, school records, teacher's reports, other test data, or qualitative responses that examinees have made to the test items (see Level V). For example, an examiner might be trying to decide whether low scores on Arithmetic and Digit Span reflect poor attention or poor sequencing. If the examinee was observed to have attended well to the tasks but had difficulty following a series of directions, then it suggests sequencing is more likely to be the difficulty. Or an examiner might be trying to decide whether the examinee prefers a simultaneous or sequential style of processing information. A relevant behavioral observation would be to have carefully observed how the person worked on Block Design. Did he or she proceed in a step-by-step sequence trying to match up each block with a segment of the picture, or rather try to understand the design as a whole while attempting to complete the task? A final relevant example might be low scores on Arithmetic, Digit Span, Coding/Digit Symbol, and Symbol Search. Each of these subtests requires a high level of motivation. Indeed, they have sometimes been referred to as validity scales since they are likely to be lowered as a result of poor motivation (Kaufman, 1994). Rather than work to decipher the examinee's low *abilities* as reflected in these subtests, the examiner might decide that behavioral observations more accurately suggest the person was not expending a sufficient amount of effort.

A focus on additional sources of information, particularly behavioral observations, also has relevance for determining the significance of subtest fluctuations (Step IIIa) and developing hypotheses (Step IIIb). As was stressed previously, sometimes a subtest fluctuation may not quite achieve formal statistical significance, yet because of additional information, the practitioner feels justified in giving the score greater clinical importance and considering it for interpretation. Similarly, generating hypotheses by formally putting the data through Step IIIb may not have confirmed a suspected hypothesis. However, if clinicians have additional information that might justify accepting the suspected hypothesis, they may be persuaded to accept it even though some of the formal procedures have not quite supported it. This highlights an essential underlying philosophy of Wechsler scale and subtest interpretation: It is not merely a statistical and empirical exercise but, more importantly, involves the use of clinical skills and judgment.

Level IV. Intrasubtest Variability

A further, potentially important area of analysis involves looking at the patterns of performance within the items of each subtest. These items are arranged in sequences that become progressively more difficult. Thus, a normal and expected pattern would be for the examinee to pass the initial items and slowly but evenly begin to fail more difficult ones. A more sporadic pattern, in which the examinee misses initial easier items but passes later more difficult ones, may suggest an attentional deficit or specific memory losses. If performance is highly sporadic, the reason for this should be explored further. For example, clients might be consciously faking if they miss every other item, miss extremely easy items, and/or appear much more alert than their obtained IQ. Sporadic performance might also be characteristic of brain-damaged patients with diffuse cortical involvement (Mittenberg, Hammeke, & Rao, 1989). An analysis of the intrasubtest scatter can thus provide a type of information different from that obtained by merely looking at the quantitative-scaled scores.

Level V. Qualitative Analysis

The final step is to look at the content of responses, especially on Information, Vocabulary, Comprehension, and Similarities. Frequently, the presence of unique, highly personal, or unusual responses can suggest some important dimensions of an individual's intellectual or personality functioning. For example, some responses may reflect aggressive tendencies, concrete thinking, or unusual associations. A highly aggressive person might provide unusual responses on the Vocabulary item of knife, or a person with paranoid personality characteristics might provide rigid, cautious, and legalistic responses. Similarly, impulsivity might be suggested by persons who draw lines that extend beyond the walls of the Mazes or by persons who say they would "yell" if they noticed a fire in a theater.

THE WECHSLER SUBTESTS

To interpret the Wechsler scales adequately, it is essential to understand the various abilities that each subtest measures. This section presents the different abilities involved in each of the 11 WAIS-R and 13 WISC-III subtests, followed by a discussion of their relevant features, including the possible meanings associated with high or low scores. Descriptions of the subtest abilities and data on factor loadings presented for most of the WISC-III subtests are derived from Kamphaus (1993) and Kaufman (1975, 1979, 1994). Subtest abilities and factor loadings for the WAIS-R are based on research reviewed by Gregory (1987), Kaufman (1990), and Sattler (1992). Some citing of relevant and usually recent sources is also provided.

In keeping with the overall approach of this book, any interpretations suggested in the discussion of the subtests should be considered tentative. They are merely beginning possibilities that must be explored further and placed in a proper context. In addition, no subtest is a pure measurement of any single intellectual ability; rather, each represents a combination of skills. It is important to emphasize that a low or high score on a specific subtest can occur for a variety of reasons, which the examiner must consider in interpreting the overall profile. This section will be most helpful only after practitioners are familiar with the subtest stimuli and administration procedure outlined in the WAIS-R and WISC-III manuals.

Verbal Scales

The Wechsler Verbal Scales assess an individual's proficiency in the following areas:

- The ability to work with abstract symbols.
- The amount and degree of benefit a person has received from his or her educational background.
- Verbal memory abilities.
- Verbal fluency.

The WAIS-R and WISC-III Verbal Scales are generally more subject to cultural influences, whereas the Performance Scales are considered to be somewhat more culture free. If an individual does significantly better (12 points or more) on the Verbal Scales compared with the Performance subtests, this difference may indicate a number of interpretative possibilities, including a relatively high level of education, a tendency toward overachieving, psychomotor slowing due to depression, difficulty working with practical tasks, deficits in performance abilities, poor visual-motor integration, a slow, deliberate, reflective work style that results in relatively lower scores on timed tests (but higher scores on verbal tests), or a quick, impulsive work style resulting in relatively more errors on Performance subtests (see Gregory, 1987; Kaufman, 1990, 1994; Sattler, 1992). In addition, persons from professional occupations, high educational attainment, and high IQs in general are likely to have quite high Verbal IQs. Also, psychiatric populations (5–6 point V > P discrepancy), persons with Alzheimer's disease, and persons with motor coordination problems tend to have higher verbal scores relative to their performance scores.

Studies have typically found that persons with right hemisphere lesions have, on average, a 9-point higher Verbal than Performance IQ (Kaufman, 1990, 1994; Reitan & Wolfson, 1993; Sattler, 1992). However, a V > P (e.g., depressed Performance IQ) should never be *diagnostic of* right hemisphere brain damage but rather *consistent with* this condition in some cases. It should be stressed that there is a complex interaction with a wide number of variables. A V > P effect is likely to be most pronounced among adult, educated (12+ years), caucasian males with acute lesions who have strokes, tumors, or other focal lesions toward the posterior (versus anterior/frontal) regions. These variables have been extensively reviewed by Kaufman (1990, 1994) and are summarized in the following list:

- *Age.* Whereas the V > P effect has been clearly and consistently found for most adult populations, studies with children have been met with numerous contradictions. This is because there are a greater number of intervening variables for children and their brains are more symmetrical and characterized by greater plasticity. Thus, neurological inferences related to Verbal-Performance discrepancies should *not* be made for children.

- *Education.* Because persons with higher education (and generally persons with higher IQs) typically score higher on verbal subtests, a further lowering in performance abilities due to a right hemisphere lesion will serve to exaggerate the V > P discrepancy to an even greater extent. Persons from lower educational backgrounds often have higher Performance IQs relative to their Verbal IQs so that a lowering in their Performance IQ due to a right hemisphere lesion may either not produce the expected V > P effect, or the difference may not be as wide as for persons with higher educational attainment.

- *Race.* European-American and African-Americans are more likely to have the V > P discrepancy following right hemisphere damage than either Hispanics or Native-Americans. This is because Hispanics and Native-Americans are more likely to have higher Performance than Verbal IQs prior to their injury/illness.

- *Gender.* The V > P discrepancy following right hemisphere lesions is more pronounced in males (11.8 points) than females (6.7 points; Kaufman, 1990). This is due to greater cerebral assymetry in males. It is also possibly due to more verbally mediated strategies for Performance subtests by females which serves to partially compensate for organically lowered performance abilities.

- *Recency of Lesion.* Acute (less than 12 months) right hemisphere lesions produce greater V > P effects than chronic lesions. This is because, over time, patients are able to improve their performance abilities due to both natural recovery of function and compensatory techniques. Even with chronic lesions, there is still an expected V > P discrepancy but it is not as extreme as for acute lesions.

- *Type and Location of Lesion.* Especially right hemisphere strokes, but also tumors and, to a lesser extent, right temporal lobe epilepsy results in the expected V > P effect. Frontal lobe lesions have little effect on V > P, whereas posterior lesions do result in the expected V > P discrepancy.

Information[1]

Range of general factual knowledge.*

Old learning or schooling.

Intellectual curiosity or urge to collect knowledge.

Alertness to day-to-day world.

Long-term memory.

The Information subtest samples the type of knowledge that average persons with average opportunities should be able to acquire (Matarazzo, 1972). This knowledge is usually based on habitual, overlearned material, particularly in the case of older

---

[1] Abilities followed by an asterisk (*) indicate specific abilities and traits strongly associated with the subtest under discussion.

children and adults. Both Information and Vocabulary are highly resistant to neurological deficit and psychological disturbance (Lezak, 1995; Reitan & Wolfson, 1993), and are two of the most stable subtests on the WAIS-R. Due to this stability, Wechsler referred to them as "hold" tests as opposed to "no-hold" tests, which he theorized are more sensitive to deterioration and such situational variables as anxiety and fatigue (i.e., Arithmetic, Digit Symbol/Coding, Block Design). Furthermore, both these subtests are good measures of general intelligence and are highly correlated with educational level (Kaufman, McLean, & Reynolds, 1988) and WISC-R and WAIS-R Full Scale IQs. The WAIS-R Information and Vocabulary subtests have also been found to predict college grade point average as accurately as well-established college aptitude tests (Feingold, 1983). It is for these reasons that Information (along with Vocabulary and Arithmetic) is included in Bannatyne's Acquired Knowledge category. It also loads most strongly (56% of variance) on the Verbal Comprehension factor.

Although performance on the Information subtest involves remote memory and alertness to the environment, it is only influenced to a small extent by conscious effort and is believed to be only minimally affected by such factors as anxiety. To score well, the individual must have been exposed to a highly varied past environment, have an intact long-term memory, and possess a wide range of interests.

A high score on this subtest suggests that the examinee has good long-term memory, cultural interests, strong educational background, positive attitude toward school, good verbal ability, and possibly intellectualization as his or her most frequently used defense mechanism. Low scorers may show superficiality of interests, lack of intellectual curiosity, cultural deprivation, or lack of familiarity with Western (primarily American) culture (however, note the availability of numerous foreign country adaptations). Failing initial easy items combined with success on more difficult ones (high intrasubtest variability; see Level IV procedure) suggests difficulties with retrieval or possibly malingering or poor motivation.

Digit Span

Immediate rote recall.*

Reversibility; ability to shift thought patterns (from digits forward to digits backward).*

Concentration and attention.

Auditory sequencing.

Rote learning.

Digit Span is considered to be a test of short-term memory and attention. The subject must recall and repeat auditory information in the proper sequence. Bannatyne (1974) has further described this as "auditory vocal sequencing memory." Correct responses require a two-step process. First, the information must be accurately received, which requires attention and encoding. Persons who are easily distractible have difficulty in this phase. Second, the examinee must accurately recall, sequence, and vocalize the information. Persons who can perhaps receive the information correctly may still have difficulty at this phase if they have short-term memory difficulties because they cannot hold the memory trace long enough. Sometimes, the previous digit is forgotten as they are attempting to vocalize a present one. Whereas Digits Forward is a simpler, more straightforward task requiring rote memory, Digits Backward is more complex. The examinee must usually hold the memory longer and also transform it prior to making a restatement. Thus, a good performance on Digits Backward is likely to reflect a person who is flexible, can concentrate, and is tolerant of stress. High Digits Backward scores may also involve the ability to form, maintain, and scan visual mental images formed from the auditory stimulus (Lezak, 1995; Wielkiewicz, 1990).

Passive, anxiety-free individuals seem to do best on this test. It requires an effortless and relatively unhampered contact with reality, which is characterized by open receptivity to incoming information. Performance is greatly hampered by increased anxiety or tension, and the Digit Span subtest is considered to be the most susceptible to the effects of anxiety. In addition to Digit Span, the other two subtests that are sensitive to the effects of anxiety are Arithmetic and Digit Symbol/Coding. These three subtests are sometimes referred to as the "anxiety triad." Digit Span, along with Digit Symbol/Coding, is one of the most sensitive tests to brain damage, mental retardation, and learning disabilities (Lezak, 1995; Mishra, Ferguson, & King, 1985).

Persons who score high have good auditory short-term memory and excellent attention, and may be relatively unaffected by stress and anxiety. However, just because a person has good short-term auditory memory for digits does not necessarily mean that his or her memory for more complicated information, such as music or verbally relevant information, will also be good. These more complex features of memory may have to be assessed by other means. When Digits Backward is longer than Digits Forward, this rare event (3%–10% of children's protocols; Wechsler, 1991) suggests that the individual has excellent numerical abilities. Low scores on Digit Span indicate difficulty concentrating, which may be the result of anxiety or unusual thought processes. A large discrepancy (5+ digits) in favor of Digits Forward versus Digits Backward can suggest the presence of an organic deficit, particularly if the overall backward Digit Span score is below scores for such tests as Information and Vocabulary. Whereas Digits Forward is fairly stable and resistant to deterioration, Digits Backward is a far more difficult task and is quite sensitive to deterioration (see subsection on estimating premorbid IQ in the section "Assessing Brain Damage"). Whereas Digits Forward is more likely to be lowered by left hemisphere lesions, lowered Digits Backward is more consistent with either diffuse or right frontal involvement (Lezak, 1995; Swierchinsky, 1978). Lowered performance for Both Digit Span backward, and Digit Symbol occur with the diffuse damage associated with exposure to solvents (Groth-Marnat, 1993; Morrow, Furman, Ryan, & Hodgson, 1988).

Vocabulary

Language development.*

Word knowledge.*

General verbal intelligence.

Language usage and accumulated verbal learning ability.

Rough measure of the subject's optimal intellectual efficiency.

Educational background.

Range of ideas, experiences, or interests that a subject has acquired.

The Vocabulary subtest is a test of accumulated verbal learning, and represents an individual's ability to express a wide range of ideas with ease and flexibility. It may also involve one's richness of ideas, long-term memory, concept formation, and language development. Vocabulary is noteworthy in that it is the most reliable verbal subtest (WAIS-R test-retest reliability = .96; WISC-III test-retest reliability = .89) and, like Information, it is highly resistant to neurological deficit and psychological disturbance (Lezak, 1995; Reitan & Wolfson, 1993). Although the Vocabulary subtest holds up with age, it tends to fall off with those people for whom visual-spatial skills are far more important than verbal abilities. Vocabulary generally reflects the nature and level of sophistication of one's schooling and cultural learning. Vocabulary is primarily dependent on the wealth of early educational environment, but it is susceptible to improvement by later experience or schooling. It is the least variable of all the subtests, and subtest scores below the Vocabulary level sometimes imply a drop of efficiency in that function. Vocabulary is the best single indicator of general intelligence, with 86% of its variance accounted for by g on the WAIS-R and 80% of its variance accounted for by g on the WISC-III. Because of its high degree of stability, Vocabulary is often used as an indicator of a person's intellectual potential and to make an estimate of their premorbid level of functioning (see precise method in section "Assessing Brain Damage").

The Vocabulary responses are similar to Comprehension and Similarities in that a qualitative analysis often provides useful information relating to the examinee's thought processes, background, life experiences, and response to frustration. It is often important to explore incorrect responses to determine whether they were guesses, clang associations (e.g., "ponder" meaning "to pound" or "assemble" meaning to "resemble"), concrete thinking, bizarre associations, or overinclusive reasoning. Even when a response is correct, a consideration of the style used to approach the word and specific content can be helpful.

High scores suggest high general intelligence, and indicate that the examinee can adequately recall past ideas and form concepts relating to these ideas. Persons with high scores have a wide range of interests, a good fund of general information, and may have high needs for achievement. Clinical populations who score high on Vocabulary may use compulsive or intellectualizing defense mechanisms. Low scores suggest a limited educational background, low general intelligence, poor language development, lack of familiarity with English, and/or poor motivation.

Arithmetic

Computational skill.*

Auditory memory.

Sequencing ability.

Numerical reasoning and speed of numerical manipulation.

Concentration and attention/low distractibility.

Reality contact and mental alertness; that is, active relationship to the outside world.

School learning (earlier items)/acquired knowledge.

Logical reasoning, abstraction, and analysis of numerical problems (later items).

The Arithmetic subtest requires a focused concentration as well as basic mathematical skills and an ability to apply these skills. The skills required to complete this test are usually acquired by the time a person reaches junior high school, so that low scores are more likely to be the result of poor concentration. Arithmetic is likely to be more challenging and stressful than such tests as Information and Vocabulary both because the task itself is more demanding and because it is timed. Thus, persons who are susceptible to the disruptive effects of anxiety are likely to be adversely affected. However, examiners may want to establish whether the person simply lacked the necessary skills or rather had difficulty concentrating. This can be assessed by giving the person previously missed items a second time, but allowing the use of a paper and pencil without a time limit. Under these circumstances, persons with adequate mathematical knowledge who are distractible should be able to complete the items correctly.

Individuals from higher socioeconomic backgrounds, obedient teacher-oriented students, and persons with intellectualizing tendencies usually do well on this subtest. A helpful formula is that Information plus Arithmetic equals school achievement. Since numbers come from the outside environment, and create rule and direction, some individuals react rebelliously. This is particularly true for antisocial personalities. Histrionic personalities, who do not readily accept outside direction and generally refuse to take responsibility for their behaviors, may likewise do poorly. This is not to suggest that lowered Arithmetic scores are diagnostic of these clinical groups, but rather that this lowering may at times be consistent with the way these individuals interact with their environment.

High scorers show alertness, capacity for concentration, freedom from distractibility, and good short-term auditory memory, and may use intellectualizing defenses. Low scorers show poor mathematical reasoning, lack of capacity to concentrate, distractibility, and poor auditory short-term memory. A poor educational background in which adequate mathematical skills have not been developed can also account for lowered performance.

Comprehension

Demonstration of practical knowledge.*

Social maturity.*

Knowledge of conventional standards of behavior.*

Ability to evaluate past experience; that is, proper selection, organization, and emphasis of facts and relationships.*

Abstract thinking and generalization (later items only).*

Social judgment, common sense, or judgment in practical social situations.

Grasp of one's social milieu; for example, information and knowledge of moral codes, social rules, and regulations.

Reality awareness, understanding, and alertness to the day-to-day world.

Comprehension has often been considered to reflect the extent to which an examinee adheres to conventional standards, has benefited from past cultural opportunities, and has a well-developed conscience. This is somewhat supported in that Comprehension (and Picture Arrangement) have been found to be related to measures of social intelligence on the CPI (Sipps, Berry, & Lynch, 1987). In contrast, other research has noted that the preceding interpretation, along with other personality-related Wechsler interpretations needs to be made with caution (Lipsitz, Dworkin, & Erlenmeyer-Kimling, 1993; Nobo & Evans, 1986; Piedmont, Sokolove, & Fleming, 1989). Comprehension is also, at least in part, a test of information, which is supported by its high correlation (low- to mid-70s, depending on age) with the Information and Vocabulary subtests. Comprehension involves an adaptive response by the individual to a situation that requires him or her to select the most efficient way of dealing with a specific problem. The examinee not only must possess relevant information but must appropriately use this information for decision making. In this sense, the Comprehension subtest goes one step beyond the degree of complexity and synthesis required for the Information subtest. Like Vocabulary and Information, it measures general verbal ability which is reflected in that 50% of its WAIS-R variance and 42% of its WISC-III variance is attributed to the Verbal Comprehension factor. The examinee must not only have the necessary information, but must apply it in a coherent, problem-oriented manner. Thus, a Comprehension score significantly below the Information score suggests that an examinee is not effectively using his or her knowledge.

In assessing an examinee's responses, it can be important to distinguish between actually dealing with the material to develop an original response and merely repeating overlearned concepts. For example, parroting answers to "forest," "bad company," or the proverbs does not indicate full comprehension and may simply be based on past experience rather than on accurate problem solving, good judgment, or abstract reasoning (Gibbs & Beitel, 1995). Thus, basic rule-of-thumb answers can significantly increase the total number of correct responses. However, in the later items, a correct response requires higher-level problem solving, and these items, therefore, can still be a good measure of general intelligence instead of merely rote memorization.

Personality variables, especially those relating to judgment, are important areas to consider in this subtest. In particular, poor levels of adjustment can lower scores on Comprehension. Clinicians should note the pattern of responses, cliches, literalness, and any circumscribed responses. In contrast, good judgment involves the ability to engage in discriminative activity. Failure on the easy items indicates impaired judgment, even though later, more difficult items are passed. It is important to note emotional implications on this subtest since emotional responsiveness influences the way in which a person evaluates environmental events. For example, individuals who are highly analytical and use these analytical abilities to avoid emotions may have difficulty understanding the social components of situations as presented in Comprehension.

High scorers show reality awareness, capacity for social compliance, good judgment, and emotionally relevant use of information. Low scorers, especially if they have four subscale points or more below Vocabulary, might have poor judgment, impulsiveness, and hostility against their environment. Mentally disturbed persons often do poorly on Comprehension, which may be the result of disturbed perceptions, idiosyncratic thinking, impulsiveness, or antisocial tendencies.

Similarities

Logical abstract reasoning.*

Verbal concept formation or conceptual thinking.

Distinguishing essential from nonessential details.

Associative ability combined with language facility.

The Similarities subtest requires verbal concept formation and abstract reasoning ability. These functions mediate for the individual an awareness of the belonging-togetherness of objects and events of the day-to-day world. An essential aspect of adjusting to one's environment is the use of these abilities to clarify, reduce, and classify the style and manner to which a response will be made. Inductive reasoning is required since the examinee must move from particular facts to a general rule or principle. Implicit in the test is the ability of individuals to use long-term memory and to apply elegant expressions in their responses. The more precise and abstract the expression, the higher the score, which indicates that verbal fluency is an important determinant. Correct responses to the last few items indicate a particularly high level of abstraction. Individuals with a good ability for insight and introspection tend to perform highly on this subtest; thus it may be used as an indicator of favorable prognosis for psychotherapy. Scores decrease significantly in schizophrenics, rigid or inflexible thinkers, and patients with senile conditions. Examiners can therefore use this subtest to gain further information regarding the nature of an examinee's idiosyncratic or pathological form of concept formation.

High scorers show good verbal concept formation, which, if unusually high, may reflect intellectualizing tendencies. Low scorers show poor abstraction abilities, literalness, and inflexible thinking. Similarities in adult protocols is the most sensitive subtest to left hemisphere lesions particularly the lesions to the left temporal and/or left frontal regions (Dobbins & Russell, 1990).

Performance Scales

The performance scales reflect:

- The individual's degree and quality of nonverbal contact with the environment.
- The ability to integrate perceptual stimuli with relevant motor responses.
- The capacity to work in concrete situations.
- The ability to work quickly.
- The ability to evaluate visuospatial information.

The Performance subtests are generally less affected by educational background than are the Verbal Scales. If an individual does significantly better (.05 level = 12 points or more; .01 level = 15 points or more) on the Performance Scales than on the Verbal subtests (P > V), this may indicate a number of interpretive possibilities including superior perceptual organizational abilities, ability to work under time pressure, a tendency toward low academic achievement, possible acting out (juvenile delinquency), an individual who could be described as a doer rather than a thinker, a person from a relatively low socioeconomic background, presence of a language deficit, poorly developed auditory conceptual/processing skills, or that immediate problem solving is better developed than problem solving based on accumulated knowledge.

A number of studies have found that a higher Performance than Verbal IQ (P > V) is consistent with left hemisphere lesions (Kaufman, 1990). There is, however, a complex relation between a number of relevant variables and P > V for left lesion patients. One issue is that the average Verbal IQ superiority of 4 points for left lesion patients across studies is not nearly as pronounced as the 9-point average for V > P with right hemisphere lesions.

Since the P > V effect is not as strong as the V > P discrepancy found with right hemisphere lesions, interpretations need to be quite tentative. In general, P > V discrepancies are most likely to occur for adult male patients with low educational attainment who have lesions in the posterior (versus frontal) regions (see Kaufman, 1990). These variables can be summarized as follows:

- *Age.* The P > V difference for left lesion adults is relatively small but has been found not to occur for children. Therefore, inferences regarding lateralization should be restricted to adults.
- *Gender.* The laterality effect for P > V following left hemisphere lesions has been found to be greater for males (6.2 points) than for females (only 1.6 points; Kaufman, 1990; see also previous section on gender for V > P following right hemisphere lesions).
- *Education.* Individuals having less than a high school education generally score 2 to 3 points higher on their Performance IQ than Verbal IQ. Clinically, this means that persons with low educational attainment are more likely to have even greater P > V following left hemisphere lesions than persons with more education.
- *Type and Location of Lesion.* Posterior left lesions are likely to show the expected P > V difference. Frontal lesions, no matter what the cause, are not likely to demonstrate any V > P differences. Left hemisphere strokes tend to produce the clearest P > V effect and, to a lesser extent, left temporal lobe epilepsy. Left hemisphere tumors, as well as the relative recency of the lesion (acute versus chronic), have little effect on V > P discrepancies.

A further consideration related to P > V difference is that certain population groups are likely to score higher on Performance subtests. In particular, children, adolescents, adult Native Americans and Hispanics (especially if bilingual) have Performance scores which can be an average of nearly 15 points above their Verbal scores. Kaufman (1990, 1994) recommends not interpreting their Full Scale IQs since these scores may not be valid for the above, or other bilingual groups. Instead, the Verbal and Performance IQs should be considered separately. Additional correlates of P > V are autism, mental retardation, learning disabilities, illiteracy, delinquency, conduct disorder or psychopathy, bilingual populations, and individuals from occupations (especially blue-collar) emphasizing visual-spatial skills. Possible explanations for these differences include the challenges involved in learning two languages, the level to which the test instructions have been understood, attitudes and experience working within time constraints, degree of cerebral lateralization, and cultural or subcultural differences (i.e., extent that nonverbal communication is emphasized). Each of these correlates should be taken into account when making interpretations related to lateralization of brain lesions or any of the other possible interpretations consistent with P > V discrepancies.

Picture Completion

Visual alertness.*

Visual recognition and identification (long-term visual memory).*

Awareness of environmental detail; reality contact.

Perception of the whole in relation to its parts; visual conceptual ability.

Ability to differentiate essential details from nonessential details.

Visual concentration combined with an ability to visually organize material.

The Picture Completion subtest is a measure of visual concentration and is a nonverbal test of general information. It involves discovering consistency and inconsistency by paying close attention to the environment and accessing remote memory. It is dependent on, and also draws on, an individual's experience with his or her culture. Thus, a person who is unfamiliar with common features of American society will often make errors due to a lack of experience rather than a lack of intelligence. A person will also make errors if he or she is unable to detach him- or herself emotionally from the material, thereby making accurate discriminations difficult. For example, passive, dependent personalities might make errors because they notice the absence of people controlling the actions in the pictures. Typical responses might be that "there's nobody holding the pitcher," "there are no people rowing the boat," or "there's no flagpole." Schizophrenic patients also make certain characteristic responses, such as responding to number 4 (playing card) with "the other 48 cards are missing" or to number 12 (crab) with "there's no scales" (Weiner, 1966), which is consistent with their frequently scoring quite low on Picture Completion (Crookes, 1984). Sometimes negative, inflexible, oppositional individuals will state that there is nothing missing in the pictures.

High scorers are able to recognize essential visual information, are alert, and demonstrate good visual acuity. Low scores indicate poor concentration and inadequate visual organization. Impulsiveness can often produce lowered performance since the examinee may make a quick response without carefully analyzing the whole picture.

Picture Arrangement

Planning ability (comprehending and sizing up a total situation).*

Anticipation of consequences.*

Temporal sequencing and time concepts.*

Accurately understanding nonverbal interpersonal situations.

Ability to comprehend a total situation and evaluate its implications.

Visual organization and perception of essential visual cues.

Speed of associating and planning information.

The Picture Arrangement test is primarily a test of the ability to plan, interpret, and accurately anticipate social events within a given cultural context. Thus, an individual's cultural background can affect his or her performance on the test; normal subjects with poor or different cultural backgrounds often do poorly. This means that scores derived from such persons should be treated with caution. Wechsler (1958) has stated that the test requires an examinee to use general intelligence in nonverbal social situations. In fact, each of the items requires a person to respond to some practical interpersonal interaction. Solving the correct sequence also requires at least some sense of humor. However, interpretive caution should be exercised in that, even though Picture Arrangement has been found to be related to social intelligence on the CPI (Sipps et al., 1987), other authors have not found expected relationships using different measures of social functioning (Lipsitz et al., 1993; Nobo & Evans, 1986; Ramos & Die, 1986). Both Picture Arrangement and Block Design are measures of nonverbal intelligence. However, Picture Arrangement is far more dependent on cultural variables than is Block Design. Picture Arrangement also requires the person to grasp or "size up" the complete situation before proceeding to a correct response. In contrast, persons can achieve good scores on Block Design by approaching the task in small segments and then contrasting their performance on each segment with the whole design.

Picture Arrangement is somewhat sensitive to the effects of brain damage, especially for those injuries that disrupt nonverbal social skills (Golden, 1979; Lezak, 1995). An unusually low Picture Arrangement score in a protocol in which there is little difference between Verbal and Performance IQs implies an organic impairment consistent with a static lesion to the right anterior temporal lobe (Reitan, 1974; Reitan & Wolfson, 1993). More generalized right hemisphere lesions are likely to lower not only scores on Picture Arrangement, but also performance on Block Design, and Object Assembly (Russell, 1979). There is also some evidence that patients with frontal lobe impairment do poorly on Picture Arrangement due to their tendency to respond impulsively and without considering the entire problem (Walsh, 1987).

Two approaches can be followed to obtain additional qualitative information from Picture Arrangement. The first is to observe and record how the person attempts to solve the problem. Does the client carefully consider the overall problem or rather impulsively begin altering the cards? Is the client easily discouraged or does he or she demonstrate a high degree of persistence? Once the entire subtest has been completed, an examiner may also want to obtain a subject's description of the stories related to the pictures. This might be initiated by simply asking the examinee to "tell me what is happening in the pictures" or "make up a story about the cards." The cards that usually produce the richest information on the WAIS-R are 2, 8, and 10. The following questions are especially important: Are the stories logical, fanciful, or bizarre? Are they original or rather stereotyped and conventional? Do examinees reveal any emotional attitudes relating either to themselves or to their interpersonal relationships? Were errors the result of incorrectly perceiving specific details or rather of neglect in even considering certain details? Did the examinee consider all the different relationships in the pictures or were important aspects omitted?

The above information on Picture Arrangement applies primarily to the WAIS-R rather than the WISC-III because a substantial amount of extra credit for speed was given for the WISC-III revision of Picture Arrangement. The result has been that it relates quite closely to the Processing Speed factor (along with Coding and Symbol Search; Hishinuma & Yamakawa, 1993; Wechsler, 1991). Psychometrically, WISC-III Picture Arrangement correlates only .35 with the WAIS-R Picture Arrangement and .42 with the earlier WISC-R Picture Arrangement. The practical implication of this is that WISC-III interpretation of Picture Arrangement scores should emphasize the speed component above or at least within the context of Picture Arrangement's other aspects (e.g., understanding nonverbal interpersonal situations).

Persons who score high on Picture Arrangement are usually sophisticated, have a high level of social intelligence, and demonstrate an ability to quickly anticipate the consequences of initial acts. Low scorers may have a paucity of ideas, have difficulty planning ahead, slow processing of information, a poor sense of humor, difficulty in interpersonal relationships, and poor rapport.

Block Design

Analysis of whole into component parts.*

Spatial visualization.*

Nonverbal concept formation.

Visual-motor coordination and perceptual organization.

Capacity for sustained effort; concentration.

Visual-motor-spatial coordination; manipulative and perceptual speed.

The Block Design subtest involves nonverbal problem-solving skills due to its emphasis on analyzing a problem into its component parts and then reintegrating these parts into a cohesive whole. The examinee must apply logic and reasoning in a manner that will solve spatial relationship problems. As a test of nonverbal concept formation, Block Design demands skills in perceptual organization, spatial visualization, and abstract conceptualization. The Block Design subtest is sturdy and reliable, correlating highly with general intelligence, and is not likely to be lowered except by the effects of depression or organic impairment (Schorr, Bower, & Kiernan, 1982). To perform well, examinees must be able to demonstrate a degree of abstraction that is free from literal concreteness. They must also make a distinction between part and whole by demonstrating both analytic and synthetic skills. This test involves an ability to shift the frame of reference while maintaining a high degree of flexibility. The examinee must also be able to inhibit his or her impulsive tendencies and to persist in a designated task.

An important feature of Block Design is that it enables an examiner to actually observe the examinee's response. Some subjects are easily discouraged and give up, while others insist on completing the task even if they have to work beyond the time limit. In approaching the task, one might impulsively place the blocks together in a nonrandom sequence, whereas another subject might demonstrate a meticulous sequential style thereby revealing preferences for either a holistic simultaneous or a more sequential problem-solving style. Additional observations can reveal such factors as hand preference, motor coordination, speed of information processing, frustration tolerance, and ability to benefit from feedback. A highly reflective or compulsive style can lower scores due to the resulting extended time completing the task. Thus, potentially valuable information can be obtained by observing and recording differences in solving the Block Design tasks.

Block Design is also a nonverbal, relatively culture-free test of intelligence. It is reliable in that it correlates highly with general intelligence (approximately 53% of its variance may be attributed to g), but it has a relatively low correlation with education (.40–.46). Thus, the Block Design subtest is only minimally biased by an examinee's cultural or educational background. Block Design scores can, therefore, be an important tool in assessing the intellectual potential of persons from divergent cultural and intellectual backgrounds.

Block Design is an excellent indicator of right hemisphere brain damage and is especially sensitive to right parietal lesions (Lezak, 1995; Reitan & Wolfson, 1992, 1993). Right lesion patients tend to make errors in that they might distort the designs, misperceive aspects of them, or become disoriented when attempting to complete them. In contrast, left lesion patients, particularly if the lesions are in the parietal lobes, are not nearly as likely to have a poor Block Design score. However, when they do, it is likely to be expressed in design simplification, confusion, and a concrete approach to reproducing the design (Lezak, 1995). Inattention (neglect) can be reflected by the examinee failing to complete the right or left portion of the design. For example, only two or three of the blocks might be used for a four-block design (Lezak, 1995). Block Design is typically the lowest subtest in Alzheimer's patients. It is sensitive to the early phases of the disease and thus can be useful in differentiating between Alzheimer's and pseudodementing conditions such as depression (Fuld, 1984; La Rue & Jarvik, 1987).

High scorers show a good capacity for visual-spatial perception, visual-motor speed, a good ability to concentrate, and excellent nonverbal concept formation. Low scores suggest poor perceptual abilities, difficulties with visual integration, and problems in maintaining a sustained effort.

Object Assembly

Ability to benefit from sensory-motor feedback.*

Anticipation of relationships among parts.*

Visual-motor organization.

Simultaneous (holistic) processing.

Synthesis; putting things together in a familiar configuration.

Ability to differentiate familiar configurations.

Manipulative and perceptual speed in perceiving the manner in which unknown objects relate to each other.

Object Assembly is a good test of motor coordination and control, as are Digit Symbol (Coding) and Block Design. It measures the ability to differentiate familiar configurations, and also involves some anticipation and planning. However, scores are subject to a high degree of fluctuation, primarily due to the potential for accidentally fitting together parts. A related area that may create some confusion is that persons who are in the lower ranges of intelligence (60–75) sometimes do quite well, whereas persons with above-average IQs can do quite poorly. The preceding difficulties have resulted in rather low test-retest reliabilities ranging between .66 and .71. In addition, Object

Assembly is only a moderate measure of general intelligence (38%–40% of its variance may be attributed to *g*) and is not highly correlated with Full Scale IQ scores (.56–.65). Furthermore, its correlation with other subtests is generally low (.30–.69). Thus, it is psychometrically one of the poorest subtests, and scores should be treated with caution. In addition, it lacks a sufficient amount of subtest specificity (WAIS-R = 23%, WISC-III = 26%) for adequate interpretation of the test's underlying abilities.

Despite these difficulties, an advantage of Object Assembly is that, as with Block Design and Picture Arrangement, an examiner can directly observe a person's problem-solving style and reactions to success or failure. The test presents an "open" situation, and those who can work freely within this context usually do well. However, those with rigid visual organizations will stick with one clue without allowing themselves to change their frame of reference. This inflexibility is often seen with obsessive-compulsives. On the other hand, a flexible visual organization permits a rapid integration of new clues and an adaptation of these clues toward completing the task. The same observations relevant for Block Design are appropriate for Object Assembly. These include persistence, concentration, hand preference, frustration tolerance, speed of processing information, reflectivity, impulsiveness, ability to benefit from feedback, and preference for a simultaneous versus a sequential problem-solving style. In particular, an overly cautious, reflective, and/or obsessive approach is likely to lower performances due to the loss of bonus points resulting from their slow completion of the task.

Persons scoring high on Object Assembly show good perceptual-motor coordination, have superior visual organization, and can maintain a flexible mental outlook. Low scorers show visual-motor disorganization, concreteness, and difficulties with visual concept formation. Like Block Design, Object Assembly is sensitive to right, especially right posterior, lesions (Lezak, 1995; Reitan & Wolfson, 1993). However, given the test's inadequate test specificity and low reliabilities, these interpretations should be somewhat more tentative than for other subtests.

Digit Symbol/Coding

Psychomotor speed.*

Ability to follow directions.*

Clerical speed and accuracy.*

Visual short-term memory.*

Ability to follow directions.*

Paper-pencil skills.*

Ability to learn an unfamiliar task; capacity for learning and responding to new visual material.

Some degree of flexibility; ability to shift mental set.

Capacity for sustained effort, attention, concentration, and mental efficiency.

Associative learning and ability to imitate newly learned visual material.

Sequencing ability.

Visual-motor integration is implied by good performance on Digit Symbol. However, the most important function necessary for a high score is psychomotor speed. This test involves appropriately combining the newly learned memory of the digit with the symbol, as well as adequate spatial-motor orientation followed by executing the half-habituated activity of drawing the symbol. The subtest also requires the ability to learn an unfamiliar task, accuracy of eye-hand coordination, attentional skills, short-term memory, and the ability to work under pressure. This is a delicate and complex interaction, which can be disturbed due to difficulties with any of the preceding skills. In contrast to Vocabulary, which is a highly stable subtest, Digit Symbol is extremely sensitive to the effects of either organic or functional impairment. In particular, depressed and brain-damaged patients have a difficult time with this subtest. It is also the subtest that is most influenced by age with the mean ranging from 10.5 for the age group 20–24 but decreasing to nearly half that to a mean of only 5.5 for ages 70–74.

For the most part, Digit Symbol is relatively independent from the other subtests with a full 45% of its variance being accounted for by abilities other than the three WAIS-R factors. However, for the age groups 18–19 and 45–54, Digit Symbol has been found to relate to the Freedom from Distractibility factor (Parker, 1983a). This means that sometimes Digit Symbol should be used to give support to the Freedom from Distractibility factor, but it should be given far less weight than either Arithmetic or Digit Span. A new feature of the WISC-III is that Coding pairs up with the new Symbol Search subtest to make up the Processing Speed factor. It is therefore only minimally associated with the WISC-III Freedom from Distractibility Factor.

Since visual-motor coordination, (particularly visual acuity and motor activity) is implied, it is not surprising to find that those individuals with high reading and writing experience are among the high scorers. Functions that are implicit in the task are rapid visual, spatial, and motor coordination, as well as the executive action of drawing the symbol. Since this task requires sustained attention and quick decision making, anxious hesitancy, obsessiveness, deliberation, and perfectionism will significantly lower scores. This difficulty might be somewhat counteracted by informing persons who appear perfectionistic and reflective that they need only make their responses legibly but not perfectly. Persons who are extremely competitive but also become highly anxious in competitive situations may also be adversely affected. Not only can Digit Symbol/Coding scores be lowered by anxiety, but the psychomotor slowing found in depressive states or the confused orientation of schizophrenics likewise produces a decrease in performance. Thus, a rough index of the severity of a person's depression can be assessed by comparing the relative lowering of Digit Symbol with other more stable subtests. Of particular significance is that Digit Symbol/Coding is one of the most sensitive subtests to the effects of any type of organic impairment (Lezak, 1995; Reitan & Wolfson, 1993; Swiercinsky, 1978), and it tends to be one of the lower scores found in learning-disabled individuals (Ackerman et al., 1987; Bannatyne, 1974; Kaufman, 1994). Even with minimal brain damage, Digit Symbol/Coding is still likely to be the lowest subtest overall (Lezak, 1995; Reitan & Wolfson, 1993). In addition, patients with rapidly growing tumors are more likely to have lower scores than those with slow-growing tumors (Reitan & Wolfson, 1993).

Since Digit Symbol/Coding requires such a diverse range of abilities, high or low scores can potentially indicate a wide number of possibilities. This means that clinicians need to work particularly hard to extract the significance of scores by integrating scores with other relevant measures, behavioral observations, and medical/personal history. High scorers potentially have excellent visual-motor ability, mental efficiency, capacity for rote learning of new material, and quick psychomotor reactions. Lower scorers may have reduced capacity for visual associative learning, impaired visual-motor functioning, and poor mental alertness.

Symbol Search (WISC-III only)

Speed of visual search.*

Speed of processing information.

Planning.

Encoding information in preparation for further processing.

Visual-motor coordination.

Learning ability.

Symbol search is a new subtest that has been added to the WISC-III (and is also likely to be on the upcoming WAIS-III). It was designed to be as pure a test as possible of information-processing speed. It pairs nicely with Coding because conceptually they assess similar areas, as is more formally indicated by a relatively high .53 correlation between the two subtests. Together, they form the WISC-III Processing Speed factor. However, Symbol Search is psychometrically superior to Coding in that it correlates relatively highly with both Full Scale ($r = .56$ vs. only .33 for Coding) as well as Performance IQs ($r = .58$ vs. .32 for Coding). Future research will continue to provide more information related to Symbol Search.

High scores suggest that the individual can rapidly absorb information as well as integrate and respond to this information. In addition, it suggests good levels of visual-motor coordination, short-term visual memory, planning, general learning, and a high level of attention and concentration. Low scores suggest slow mental processes, visual perceptual difficulties, possibly poor motivation and/or anxiety, difficulties with short-term visual memory, and a reflective, perfectionistic, or obsessive problem-solving style.

Mazes (WISC-III only)

Planning ability or foresight.

Perceptual organization.

Visual-motor coordination and speed.

Nonverbal reasoning.

The Mazes subtest is an optional portion of the WISC-III and is not extensively used. Its correlation with the Full Scale IQ is unimpressive ($r = .31$), and it is also a poor measure of g (9% of its variance may be attributed to g). Despite these significant limitations, Mazes can at times provide an additional useful test, particularly with nonverbally oriented children or when a further assessment of planning, sequencing, and perceptual organization is required. Its main advantage is that it is a relatively pure measure of perceptual planning ability.

Individuals with high scores may have an efficient ability to plan ahead and maintain a flexible mental orientation, which further suggests an excellent ability to delay impulsive action (Ireland-Galman, Padilla, & Michael, 1980). Low scores reflect impulsivity and poor visual-motor coordination. Often, unusually low scores may suggest poor reality orientation or organic cerebral impairment, particularly to the frontal areas (Waugh & Bush, 1971).

ASSESSING BRAIN DAMAGE

General Principles

The WAIS-R and WISC-III measure many abilities that are likely to be lowered by brain damage. These include memory, learning, perceptual organization, problem solving, and abstract reasoning. As a result, the Wechsler intelligence scales are typically a core feature of any neuropsychological battery. At one time, it was hoped that the Wechsler intelligence scales, along with other more specialized psychological tests, could be used in the actual diagnosis of brain damage. Despite some noteworthy success in this area, it is currently more typical for psychological tests to be used in the assessment (and often localization) of the effects a known lesion is likely to have on a person's cognitive and adaptive functioning. This further highlights the point that the WAIS-R and WISC-III, along with other specific tests of neurocognitive ability, are not tests specifically sensitive to brain damage. Rather, they are tests that can reflect the effects of brain damage as well as a variety of other conditions.

During the earlier development of the WAIS and WISC, Wechsler (1958) hoped that brain damage could be discriminated based on relative lowerings in subtests that were most sensitive to neurological impairment. He referred to these brain-sensitive tests as "no-hold" tests (Digit Span, Digit Symbol, Similarities, Block Design) and contrasted them with "hold" tests, which were believed to be far more resistant to impairment (Information, Object Assembly, Picture Completion, Vocabulary). Although the distinction between hold and no-hold tests has some truth, the use of such a distinction in diagnosing brain damage has been found to result in too many misclassifications. Vogt and Heaton (1977) have summarized the reasons for this lack of success by pointing out:

- There is no single pattern of brain damage, so it would be expected that highly variable test responses would occur.
- The hold/no-hold distinction does not account for other significant factors, such as the age when the brain damage occurred, environmental variables, education, location of the lesion, and whether the lesion is recent versus chronic.
- Many important abilities related to brain damage still are not measured by the WAIS-R or WISC-III.

More recent work supports that there is no specific brain damage profile (Aram & Ekelman, 1986; Bornstein, 1983; Lezak, 1995; Todd, Coolidge, & Satz, 1977). Some persons with brain damage produce low IQs, whereas for others, IQs are still high. Sometimes there is a high level of subtest scatter, and at other times the scores on the subtests are quite even. Some brain-damaged persons produce a high Verbal-Performance split and others do not. This is further complicated because a Verbal-Performance split is more likely to occur for males than for females (Bornstein &

Matarazzo, 1982; Kaufman, 1990; Lezak, 1995) and for adults but not for children (Kaufman, 1990, 1994; Lezak, 1995). Brain damage may cause a general lowering on all or most subtests and, at other times, there may only be a lowering of specific subtests. The most general indicator for the detection of brain damage is whether a person's scores (either general or specific) are lower than expected given his or her socioeconomic status, age, education, occupation, and other relevant areas of his or her history.

One of the older conventional wisdoms about brain damage is that left hemisphere involvement is more likely to lower the Verbal Scales, whereas right hemisphere involvement results in relatively lower scores on the Performance Scales (see previous discussions under Verbal/Performance IQs, Verbal Scales, and Performance Scales). Reviews of this hypothesis have shown that sometimes this laterality effect has occurred and at other times it has not (Aram & Ekelman, 1986; Bornstein, 1983; Kaufman, 1990; Larrabee, 1986; Lezak, 1995). On average, right hemisphere lesions produce a V > P discrepancy of 9 points, whereas left hemisphere lesions produce a less marked P > V difference of 4 points (see review by Kaufman, 1990). Probably the safest approach is that a Verbal-Performance split is not *diagnostic* of either brain damage in general or, more specifically, damage to one or the other hemisphere. However, a Verbal-Performance split (especially if 15 points or greater) can at times be *consistent with* this hypothesis. This is especially true if the Verbal-Performance difference is 25 points or greater. More specifically, a lowered Verbal Scale (15 points or greater) suggests the possibility of language impairment. Noteworthy subtests within the Verbal Scales are Arithmetic and Digit Span, which, if lowered, suggest difficulties with attending and concentrating. A Performance Scale that is 15 or more points lower than the Verbal Scale suggests impaired perceptual organization abilities. Appropriate caution should be taken to avoid the risk of overinterpreting a person's results and to use further means of investigation including knowledge of health status, medical history, and additional specialized psychological tests.

Another frequent belief is that brain damage is more likely to lower Performance than Verbal tests. Some good reasons can be given to suggest this may be true. The Performance subtests are timed and, since many persons with brain damage tire easily and have difficulties with concentration and attention, they would be expected to have a particularly difficult time with these tests. From a theoretical perspective, fluid intelligence is more tied to an intact brain structure and is also more clearly assessed by the ongoing problem-solving tasks presented in the Performance subtests. Thus, a destruction of brain tissue would be more likely to lower fluid intelligence, which would be reflected in lowered Performance subtest scores. This hypothesis can be further assessed by calculating Horn's WAIS-R or WISC-III subtest groupings for fluid intelligence (see "WAIS-R/WISC-III Successive Level Interpretation Procedure" section, Level II, Step c). Although there is some basis for accepting the preceding assumptions, there are also many exceptions. Russell (1979) and Zilmer, Waechtler, Harris, Khan, and Fowler (1992) found that left hemisphere damage caused a lowering in both WAIS/WAIS-R Performance *and* Verbal subtests, whereas right hemisphere and diffuse damage resulted in the expected lowering primarily in Performance subtests.

Kaufman (1990) suggests that an important reason for this relatively small V > P effect for left lesion patients is that different hemispheres do not so much process different *types* of information (verbal content versus visual-spatial content), but more that the left hemisphere processes information *sequentially* whereas the right hemisphere processes information *simultaneously.* This is supported by the observation that adult left lesion patients do worst on Arithmetic, Digit Span, and Digit Symbol, all of which require sequencing (and compose the Freedom from Distractibility factor). The WAIS-R difference between left lesion patients' average subtest scores on Perceptual Organization (8.7) and Freedom from Distractibility (6.8) is nearly 2 subscale points. Thus, it might be more useful to assess the relative extent of lowering on left lesion patients Freedom from Distractibility than to merely assess the extent of their P > V difference.

Many of the inferences related to brain damage depend on profile analysis. Useful material relevant to brain damage can be found in the discussion of Levels II through V under "Interpretation Procedure" and in the relevant discussions for each subtest in "The Wechsler Subtests" section of this chapter. Much of this interpretation depends on hypothesis testing in which the practitioner integrates knowledge about the person, brain function, Wechsler subtests, and past clinical experience. Often, no clear, empirically based guidelines exist. Accuracy of any inferences are based partially on whether they make neuropsychological sense. However, one generally accepted principle is that intersubtest scatter is most likely to occur with focal lesions of recent origin (Kaufman, 1990). In contrast, general lowering of all abilities (low subtest scatter) is more likely with either chronic lesions or with diffuse degenerating diseases (e.g., exposure to neurotoxins; Groth-Marnat, 1993; Miller, 1993).

When the preceding cautions and principles are taken into account, clinicians can generate and test useful hypotheses developed from different patterns of subtest scores. The following list summarizes some of the most frequently supported hypotheses about specific subtests or patterns of subtests:

- Digit Symbol/Coding is the most brain-sensitive Wechsler subtest and can be lowered by lesions in any location. A lowering implies difficulties with speed of information processing and/or learning, sequencing, rote learning, concentration (especially with lowerings in Digit Span and Arithmetic), visual-motor abilities, and speed of processing or speed of learning (Lezak, 1995; Reitan & Wolfson, 1992).

- Block Design is also brain sensitive, especially to either left or right parietal lesions (Golden, 1979; Lezak, 1995; McFie, 1960, 1969). A lowering implies visual-spatial problems (especially combined with a lowering in Object Assembly) and possible difficulty in constructing objects (constructional apraxia: note quality of drawings; Zilmer, Bell, Fowler, Newman, & Stutts, 1991).

- Picture Arrangement lowering is consistent with right anterior temporal and possibly right frontal lesions (Reitan, 1974b; Reitan & Wolfson, 1993; Russell, 1979). In some cases, Picture Arrangement might also be lowered by left hemisphere lesions if there is a resulting impairment in following directions and/or conceptual skills.

- Both Digit Span and Arithmetic are frequently lowered in brain-damaged populations, particularly with left hemisphere lesions (Kaufman, 1990; Lezak, 1995; McFie, 1960, 1969). It suggests poor concentration and attention and, if Digits

Backward is significantly lower than Digits Forward (generally 5 or more digits), a significantly reduced level of mental flexibility and/or difficulty forming and maintaining a visual image of the digits. It may also suggest difficulties in a person's executive functions related to selecting a key stimulus, attending to it, and maintaining the information in short-term storage, while simultaneously performing other mental tasks (Wielkiewicz, 1990).

- Vocabulary, Information, and Picture Completion have often been used as a rough estimate of a person's premorbid level of functioning since they are relatively unaffected by lesions. An important exception is that brain-damaged children often score lowest on the Vocabulary subtest (Boll, 1974; Reitan, 1974b; Reitan & Wolfson, 1992). In addition, Information and Vocabulary are generally lowered (especially relative to Similarities) in patients with left temporal damage suggesting difficulties with word comprehension, retrieval, and language expression (Dobbins & Russell, 1990). Another hold test, Picture Completion, while usually resistant to brain damage, might be lowered due to difficulties involving vision, especially visual agnosia (difficulty recognizing objects). Thus, always considering Vocabulary, Information, and Picture Completion as indicators of premorbid functioning can potentially result in incorrect inferences and should be interpreted in relation to what is known about brain-behavior relationships.

- Similarities, especially in relation to Information and Vocabulary, is most likely to be lowered with left frontal lesions and suggests difficulty with verbal reasoning and verbal concept formation (Dobbins & Russell, 1990).

- Qualitative responses on the subtests (even when the subtests are not lowered) can provide useful information related to brain damage. Some responses might suggest poor judgment and impulsivity, whereas others might indicate concrete thinking in which the person is bound by the stimulus value of the item (e.g., winter defined as "wet, cold" rather than the more abstract reference to a season; or the "clang" response that "ponder" means "to pound"). Other persons might report they once knew the answer but have forgotten. Diffuse brain damage (but not focal) might also be consistent with a high degree of intratest scatter in which the client misses easy items but correctly answers later, more difficult ones (Mittenberg et al., 1989). This suggests retrieval failure and/or the random loss of previously stored information. This intrasubtest scatter is most likely to occur on Vocabulary, Comprehension, Information, Similarities, and Picture Completion.

Estimating Premorbid IQ

Neuropsychologists are frequently confronted with the need to estimate a client's premorbid level of functioning. This requires taking into account both factors outside the WAIS-R/WISC-III (previous work history, age, size of the lesion, etc.) as well as indicators from within the scales themselves. A rough estimate can be obtained by considering the performance on tests most resistant to neurological impairment (Information, Picture Completion, and especially Vocabulary). These subtests can be considered to reflect the person's past level of functioning. However, for subgroups whose premorbid Performance Scales are likely to have been greater than Verbal

Scales (i.e., Native-Americans, Hispanics, bilinguals, persons with low educational attainment, blue-collar workers) this method would most likely result in an underestimate of their premorbid level. A related technique is to consider the person's two or three highest subtests (regardless of whether the subtests are brain-sensitive or non-brain-sensitive) and then use these to estimate the person's premorbid level of functioning. Despite their occasional usefulness, the preceding procedures are likely to result in a high number of misclassifications since they do not take into account such crucial factors as the person's age, educational level, or location of the lesion (Matarazzo & Prifitera, 1989).

A more accurate and sophisticated technique for determining premorbid WAIS-R IQ is the Barona Index (Barona, Reynolds, & Chastain, 1984). It was developed through a stepwise multiple-regression procedure to create formulas that take into account a person's relevant demographic characteristics. The following formula can be used to estimate premorbid Full Scale IQ:

$$\text{Estimated Full Scale IQ} = 54.96 + 0.47 \text{ (age)} + 1.76 \text{ (sex)} + 4.71 \text{ (race)}$$
$$+ 5.02 \text{ (education)} + 1.89 \text{ (occupation)}$$
$$+ 0.59 \text{ (region)}$$

The specific codes to complete the formula are as follows:

Age: 16 to 17 = 1, 18 to 19 = 2, 20 to 24 = 3, 25 to 34 = 4,
35 to 44 = 5, 45 to 54 = 6, 55 to 64 = 7,
65 to 69 = 8, 70 to 74 = 9
Sex: male = 2, female = 1
Race: African American = 1, other ethnicity = 2,
European American = 3
Education: 0 to 7 years of school = 1, 8 years = 2, 9 to 11 years = 3,
12 years = 4, 13 to 15 years = 5,
16 or more years = 6.

Occupation: professional and technical = 6; managers, officials, proprietors, clerical and sales workers = 5; craftspersons and forepersons (skilled workers) = 4; not in the labor force = 3; operatives, service workers, farmers, and farm managers (semiskilled) = 2; farm laborers, farm forepersons, and laborers (unskilled workers) = 1
Region (U.S.): South = 1, North Central = 2,
West = 3, Northeast = 4.

Barona et al. (1984) also provide formulas for estimating Verbal and Performance premorbid IQs (also reproduced in Eppinger, Craig, Adams, & Parsons, 1987, and Gregory, 1987).

The following similar formula (Reynolds & Gutkin, 1979) was developed for use with the WISC-R:

$$\text{Estimated Full Scale IQ} = 126.9 - 3.65 \text{ (SES)} - 9.72 \text{ (race)} - 1.79 \text{ (sex)} - 1.20$$
$$\text{(residence)} - 0.41 \text{ (region)}.$$

The specific codes to complete the formula are as follows:

SES: (based on father's occupational group): upper = 1, upper middle = 2, middle = 3, lower middle = 4, lower = 5

Race: European-American= 1, African-American= 2, other = 3
Sex: male = 1, female = 2
Residence: urban = 1, rural = 2
Region (U.S.): Northeast = 1, North Central = 2, South = 3, West = 4.

Reynolds and Gutkin (1979) also provide formulas for estimating WISC-R Verbal and Performance IQs.

The formulas should be used with caution since less accuracy is likely with either extremely high (above 120) or extremely low (below 69) IQs (Barona et al., 1984) and the formulas are likely to overestimate most premorbid IQ levels (Eppinger, Craig, Adams, & Parsons, 1987). In addition, these formulas produce a relatively wide band of error (*SEM* = 12.14 for the WAIS-R and 13.50 for the WISC-R). Despite this, formulas have been found to be generally more accurate than clinical judgment since clinicians consistently overestimate the confidence of their judgments partially because they incorrectly believe that progressively more information will increase accuracy (Kareken & Williams, 1994). In contrast, actuarial formulas such as the Barona Index use consistent decision-making rules, correct values associated with the magnitude of relevant relationships, and provide accurate estimates regarding the margin of error.

Alzheimer's Disease

The initial symptoms of Alzheimer's disease are characterized by apathy, a decline in short-term memory, and difficulties with problem solving. Underlying these changes are reductions in cholinergic activity. Currently, neuropsychological assessment, particularly with the WAIS-R, is one of a variety of diagnostic procedures to enhance diagnosis. A specific WAIS-R profile developed by Fuld (Fuld, 1983, 1984) has been reported to reflect the pattern of performance of many patients with Alzheimer's disease. It uses *age-corrected subtest scores* from seven of the WAIS-R subtests. These are grouped and titled as A, B, C, D and, for the purposes of calculating the profile, the first three groupings (A, B, C) are divided by two:

A = Information + Vocabulary/2
B = Similarities + Digit Span/2
C = Digit Symbol + Block Design/2
D = Object Assembly

The ordering of the profile is as follows:

$$A > B > C \leq D \text{ and } A > D$$

Information and Vocabulary are relatively resistant to deterioration, reflect crystallized abilities, and are correspondingly the highest subtests in the profile. In contrast, Digit

Symbol and Block Design are relatively sensitive to deterioration, reflect areas of fluid intelligence and, along with Object Assembly are the lowest subtests in the profile.

Initial support for the profile came from seven studies that were reviewed by Kaufman (1990). He summarized that 38% of Alzheimer's disease patients had the profile whereas it was only found in 6% of multi-infarct dementias, 10% of head-injured patients, 17% of nondementia patients, 7% of elderly patients, and 9% in patients with AIDS/ARC (AIDS-Related Complex; van Gorp, Tulin, Evans, & Satz, 1990). In addition, the neuropharmacological basis of the profile was supported in that normal college students who had an experimentally induced deficiency in acetycholine demonstrated the Fuld profile to a greater extent than students given a placebo (53% vs. 18%; Fuld, 1984). Since Alzheimer's disease patients have decreases in acetycholine, this study was considered to be an experimental analogue of Alzheimer's disease. However, a more recent and extensive review of 18 studies concluded that sensitivity (proportion of true positives) to Alzheimer's disease was a very low 24.1% (Massman & Bigler, 1993). In contrast, the profile's specificity (proportion of true negatives) was 93.3%. They caution that more adequate means of differential diagnosis such as memory indices are likely to lead to greater diagnostic accuracy.

ASSESSING ADDITIONAL SPECIAL POPULATIONS

Learning Disabilities

Learning disabilities make up a complex, heterogeneous, loosely defined disorder with a wide variety of manifestations and many different theories regarding causation (Hammill, 1990; Myers & Hammill, 1982; Rourke, 1991; Sattler, 1992). A central component of all definitions is that learning disabilities involve difficulties in developing skills in reading (most commonly), writing, listening, speaking, reasoning, spelling, or math. This is sometimes summarized as poor information processing. Further essential features are that learning-disabled persons have adequate intelligence, show a significant discrepancy between achievement and intellectual ability, and have a disorder that is considered primarily intrinsic to the person, presumably due to central nervous system dysfunction. The underachievement cannot be primarily the result of an intellectual disability (mental retardation), brain damage, behavior problems, sensory handicaps, or environmental disadvantage.

The major purpose of learning disability assessment is to identify a client's strengths and weaknesses in order to decide on an appropriate placement and to design an optimal program. Relevant areas to assess include developmental-cognitive processes, achievement, environmental demands, reactions of others to the client's difficulties, and the possible interaction of additional factors, such as fear of failure, overall level of interpersonal adjustment, and family history of similar difficulties (Anderson & Gilandas, 1994). The Wechsler scales are typically considered essential as a means of identifying the client's overall level of functioning, and specific cognitive strengths and weaknesses, and to eliminate the possibility of intellectual disability (mental retardation). Other tests are usually required such as achievement tests, measures of adaptive behavior, visual-motor tests, assessments of auditory and visual processing, and measures of emotional and behavioral problems.

Considerable effort has been placed into searching for a specific Wechsler scale profile that is unique to learning-disabled populations. There is some evidence that approximately 20% of persons who have been diagnosed as being learning disabled have lowered performance on **A**rithmetic, **C**oding/Digit Symbol, **I**nformation, and **D**igit Span (the so-called ACID profile; Ackerman et al., 1987; Cordoni, O'Donnell, Ramaniah, Kurtz, & Rosenshein, 1981; Kaufman, 1990, 1994; Prifitera & Dersh, 1993; Wechsler, 1991). A somewhat similar WISC-III profile substitutes the new Symbol Search subtest for Information resulting in the SCAD (**S**ymbol Search, **C**oding, **A**rithmetic, **D**igit Span) profile (see Level IIIb in "Interpretation Procedure" section). These four subtests emphasize the functions of speed of information processing, visual short-term memory, and visual-motor coordination (Symbol Search and Coding) as well as number ability and sequencing (Arithmetic and Digit Span). These are specifically the types of functions that many learning-disabled individuals (as well many other types of persons with brain dysfunctions) have difficulty with. Accordingly, children with learning disabilities and attention deficit disorder have been found to score particularly low on the SCAD profile (Kaufman, 1994; Prifitera & Dersh, 1993). Similarly, children diagnosed with attention-deficit hyperactivity disorder (ADHD) have performed relatively poorly on the WISC-III Freedom from Distractibility factor (Anastopoulos, Spisto, & Maher, 1994). This finding should be used with caution, however, since a relatively large proportion of ADHD children still do not have this profile. It has been speculated that future research will find that a high proportion of students with reading disabilities will be found to have low scores on the Processing Speed Factor (Blaha & Wallbrown, 1996).

A more refined and multifaceted approach to understanding learning disabilities and related disorders are Bannatyne's categories, which conceptualize learning-disabled performances as highest on subtests requiring spatial abilities (Object Assembly, Block Design, Picture Completion) in which little or no sequencing is required (Bannatyne, 1974). Conceptual skills are intermediate (Comprehension, Similarities, Vocabulary), and subtests requiring sequencing abilities (Digit Span, Digit Symbol/Coding, Picture Arrangement) are lowest. Thus, their spatial abilities are believed to be greater than their conceptual abilities, which in turn are greater than their sequential abilities. A fourth category, Acquired Knowledge (Information, Arithmetic, Vocabulary) is also sometimes used as a rough index of the extent to which the person has accumulated school-related facts and skills (see Level IIIc of "Interpretation Procedures" section).

Collectively, the preceding profiles suggest that many learning-disabled individuals perform best on tasks requiring holistic, right brain, simultaneous processing (Object Assembly, Picture Completion, Block Design) and worst on those requiring sequential processing (Digit Span, Digit Symbol/Coding, Picture Arrangement), which is expressed in difficulties with planning, reading, and numerical ability. Wielkiewicz (1990) has further suggested that these subtests indicate a poorly functioning executive ability in which the individual experiences difficulty attending to stimuli while simultaneously performing other mental tasks.

Reviews and cross-validation of Bannatyne's and ACID/SCAD profiles have produced inconsistent results. Only some groups of learning-disabled students in some studies showed the Bannatyne Spatial > Conceptual > Sequential pattern (Ackerman et al., 1987; Katz et al., 1993; Kaufman, 1990, 1994; Kavale & Forness, 1984). This is not surprising given the many different modes of expression found under the umbrella term of "learning disabilities" (Rourke, 1991). In addition, Bannatyne's pattern has not been found to be unique to learning disabilities, but frequently occurs in a diverse number of groups including juvenile delinquents (Culbertson, Feral, & Gabby, 1989; Groff & Hubble, 1981) and emotionally handicapped children (Thompson, 1981). Although only minimal support exists for Bannatyne's categories as a diagnosis for learning disabilities, they are far from useless. The four categories (Spatial, Conceptual, Sequential, Acquired Knowledge) can be invaluable for interpreting relative strengths and weaknesses for learning-disabled persons as well as for other groups. While research has not been able to produce a unique "learning-disabled profile," the research invested in this effort has resulted in a useful means of analyzing Wechsler scale profiles.

Mental Retardation (Intellectual Disability)

Mental retardation (intellectual disability) is a nonspecific, heterogeneous disorder that occurs during a person's early developmental stages (birth–18 years; Luckasson et al., 1992). It is defined in part as involving subaverage general intellectual performance, which in turn is defined as less than 2 standard deviations below average. Of equal importance are difficulties in adaptive behavior, and any assessment of intellectual disability must demonstrate *both* a low intelligence level (2 standard deviations below the mean) *and* that the person cannot function independently or deal effectively with day-to-day life problems (American Psychiatric Association, 1994). This must include at least two adaptive skill areas including communication, self-care, home living, social skills, community use, self-direction, health and safety, functional academics, leisure, and work (Luckasson et al., 1992). Classification of mental retardation (intellectual disabilities) should identify the person's psychological and emotional strengths and weaknesses, overall physical health, and current environmental placement. The American Association of Mental Retardation (AAMR) guidelines (Luckasson et al., 1992) stress that this should lead to a profile that places less emphasis on describing the level of disability (mild, moderate, severe) and more on identifying the types and intensities of supports required by the person. These might be intermittent, limited, extensive, or pervasive. Thus there has been a recent move away from describing the disability in favor of using information about the person to identify how the person's functioning could best be optimized by the best support available for the person. With appropriate supports, the person's functioning should be able to improve over time. In addition, assessment should take into consideration cultural and linguistic diversity, the context of the community environment, and balance out the individual's adaptive limitations with his or her adaptive skills and personal capabilities (see Schalock et al., 1994).

The AAMR guidelines emphasize the interaction of the person with the environment and in particular they encourage any assessment to focus on the level and intensity of required support with a philosophy of empowering the person. As such, there has been a relative deemphasis on the global IQ score along with the elimination of person-oriented levels of disability. This does not mean that IQ scores are not important, but there is more of a focus on treatment and community-oriented descriptions. In somewhat of a contrast to this trend are the guidelines in the *DSM-IV* (American Psychiatric Association, 1994), which continue to classify the degree of severity (and corresponding diagnostic code) based on the following IQ ranges: 50–55 to 70 (mild), 35–40 to 50–55 (moderate), 20–25 to 35–40 (severe), below 20–25 (profound) and severity unspecified (mental retardation is presumed to exist but intelligence is untestable by standard tests). The implications of this are that, for most contexts, clinicians should follow the AAMR guidelines since they are more useful, more clearly tied to recommendations, represent the most current thinking within the field, and are in accordance with national recommendations. However, there may be certain situations in some contexts where *DSM-IV* guidelines might be required.

Although mental retardation (intellectual disability) is a heterogeneous disorder, there is consensus that it consists of two general categories. *Nonorganic,* (or *familial*), *retardation* is caused by low genetic inheritance, poor environment, and possibly some organic factors. Persons with familial retardation constitute the upper realms of intelligence (50 to 69) and adaptive functioning among persons with intellectual disabilities and can be educated. *Organic retardation* is frequently severe (IQ less than 50) and is more closely associated with neurological dysfunction and genetic impairment. Persons with this disorder typically require more supervision and care but are typically able to be taught to manage some routine day-to-day activities.

A typical assessment battery for the diagnosis and assessment of mental retardation (intellectual disability) includes the WISC-III or other individually administered intelligence tests (K-ABC, Stanford Binet), an achievement test (Wide Range Achievement Test-III, Wechsler Individual Achievement Test, Kaufman Test of Educational Achievement), and measures of adaptive functioning (AAMD Adaptive Behavior Scale, Vineland Adaptive Behavior Scales). Further information from interviews, behavioral observations, and medical records is also essential. An important purpose of a test such as the WISC-III is to establish the client's general intelligence level so this can be placed into the context of other relevant information. The AAMR guidelines point out that, when determining the cutoff IQ for diagnosis, the range of error of the test should be taken into account. This means that the IQ cutoff criteria will be somewhere between 70 and 75. The most difficult subtests for mentally retarded persons are Information, Arithmetic, and Vocabulary (primarily the Verbal Comprehension factor), while the easiest subtests are Picture Completion and Object Assembly (primarily the Perceptual Organization factor; Mueller, Dash, Matheson, & Short, 1984).

Gifted Children

Gifted children are frequently defined as having Verbal or Performance IQs of 130 or higher. Children who have a single outstanding ability such as in art, music, or math are also frequently classified as gifted even though their IQs may not necessarily be above 130. Although the WISC-III might be frequently used to identify giftedness, the Stanford-Binet may be somewhat more effective since it has a higher ceiling than the WISC-III. However, neither may be particularly good if a single outstanding ability is used to determine whether a particular child is gifted. Additional assessment strategies for children should include samples of their work, achievement tests, rating forms, or designation by a highly qualified person.

An essential goal of assessing for giftedness is to optimize (rather than "normalize") the child's abilities so that a greater likelihood exists that the child will eventually make a significant contribution to society. This implies that the assessment will be able to recommend an appropriate educational placement and provide general guidelines for program planning. IQ, in itself, is in many ways a limited definition of giftedness. Many persons with extremely high IQs do not accomplish anything of significance. A high IQ (or outstanding talent in a specific area) is merely one of a variety of prerequisites. The interactions of internal motivation, discipline, and environmental opportunities such as appropriate instruction are of equal importance.

Caution should also be used when using a test such as the WISC-III to assess gifted persons who demonstrate high creativity. Often, highly intelligent people are not particularly creative, which is supported by the low correlation between intelligence tests and creativity (Amabile, 1983). For such abilities as artistic or musical creativity, measures outside IQ testing may prove to be of greater importance. These might include a list of creative achievements, nomination by a qualified person, and specific tests of creativity.

Ethnic Minorities

Intelligence tests have frequently been criticized for being limited in assessing ethnic minorities. A detailed discussion of this issue is included in Chapter 2 (see section "Test Bias and Use with Minority Groups"). However, several additional guidelines should be noted. Often, it is essential to be familiar with the values and beliefs of the client's culture as well as relevant research. This is underscored by the observation that the degree of cultural difference between an interviewer and client has been found to be related to the amount of inaccurate perceptions (Malpass & Kravitz, 1969; Shapiro & Penrod, 1986). A clinician should determine the language most familiar to the client and establish the extent and manner in which any language difference might bias the test results. Of related and equal importance is the degree to which clients have assimilated into the dominant culture. Directions and pronunciation should be particularly clear. The examiner also needs to pay particular attention to the importance of rapport and motivation.

Probably the most important strategy is to maintain a flexible attitude combined with the use of alternative assessment strategies. This strategy might include a variety of nonverbal techniques, such as the Draw-A-Person, Raven's Progressive Matrices Test, or emphasis on the Performance Scales of the WAIS-R/WISC-III. Material beyond merely tests should also have a greater significance (teacher reports, discussions with parents, history, behavioral observations).

Delinquency

Delinquent, acting-out persons usually score significantly higher on Performance subtests (especially Object Assembly, Picture Completion, Picture Arrangement) than on Verbal ones (Culbertson et al., 1989; Sacuzzo & Lewandowski, 1976; Wickham, 1978). In particular, scores on subtests that reflect academic achievement (Information, Vocabulary, and Arithmetic) are likely to be low, with difficulties in judgment often reflected by a lowered performance in Comprehension (Brandt, 1982). Although most Verbal subtests will tend to be lower, Similarities, which is a test of abstract thinking relatively independent of education, may still be relatively elevated. This pattern reflects the difficulty these individuals have in adapting and conforming to a structured academic environment, which results in a general lowering in tests that depend on an adequate assimilation of traditional academic information.

SHORT FORMS

Dozens of short forms for the WAIS-R and WISC-III/WISC-R have been developed to provide a more time-efficient means of estimating IQ. These short forms reduce administration time by either giving selected subtests or deleting specific items (early easy ones, odd or even items). Although time-efficient, these short forms tend to provide less information about a person's cognitive abilities, produce a wider band of error than a full administration, result in less clinical information, and are often of questionable accuracy when used for intelligence classifications (Silverstein, 1990). However, short forms can serve appropriately as screening devices, which are best used when the purpose of evaluation is other than for intellectual assessment. The results can either be used as a rough indicator of intelligence, or as a basis for determining whether a more complete cognitive assessment is necessary. None of the short forms should be confused with a full intellectual assessment or even with a valid indicator of IQ (Watkins, 1986). For this reason, it is important to clearly specify on the report that a "brief WAIS-R/WISC-III" was given. If this is not specified, the IQ derived from the short form may be confused with a full administration and later decisions may be incorrectly based on the misleadingly described results.

The basic requirement for any short form is a minimum correlation of .90 with the full administration. Even at the .90 level, the band of error will be considerably wider than for an IQ derived from a full administration. Schwartz and Levitt (1960) calculated that, with a .90 correlation, two-thirds of the IQs will fall within 9 points of a person's actual IQ and a full one-third will be 10 or more points away from the actual IQ.

Most clinicians calculate short form IQs by prorating the subtest scores. This is done by calculating the mean subtest score for the subtests that were given. This mean can then be multiplied by the total number of Performance, Verbal, or Full Scale subtests to derive the equivalent of the Verbal, Performance, and/or Full Scale sum of scaled scores. Once this estimate of sum of scaled scores has been determined, relevant tables in the manual(s) can be consulted to determine the estimated IQs. Unfortunately, prorating may produce error by failing to take into account the relative reliabilities of the different subtests that were used. Clinicians who wish to reduce this source of potential error for the WAIS-R might consult conversion tables developed by Silverstein (1982b) and by Brooker and Cyr (1986). Similarly, Sattler (1992) has provided a formula (see Sattler, 1992, p. 138, Exhibit 6–3) for obtaining deviation IQs from short forms in combination with WAIS-R and WISC-III conversion tables (see also Sattler's tables; C-37–40, pp. 851–854 and L-12–15, pp. 1171–1176).

Best Two- and Three-Subtest Short Forms

One of the most frequently used two-subtest WAIS-R/WISC-III short forms uses Vocabulary and Block Design. Mean administration time is 20 minutes (Kaufman, 1990) and correlations with the full-administration Full Scale IQ are generally in the .90 range

(Brooker & Cyr, 1986; Hoffman & Nelson, 1988; Silverstein, 1982b). In two-thirds of the cases, IQs will fall within seven points of a person's actual IQ, and one-third of the scores will have an error of eight points or greater. Conceptually, Vocabulary and Block Design are good tests to use since they are both good measures of *g*, are quite stable, and represent a sample subtest from both the Performance and Verbal scales. However, they may potentially underestimate the IQs from African Americans since these two subtests are typically their lowest scores (Kaufman, McLean, & Reynolds, 1988). Furthermore, persons with high IQs are likely to have a greater margin of error when short forms are used to estimate their IQs due to the greater degree of subtest scatter among this subgroup (Matarazzo et al., 1988). If examiners wish to add a third subtest, the inclusion of Similarities, Information, Comprehension, Picture Arrangement, and Picture Completion have each been found to increase correlations into the low .90s (McNemar, 1974). An "amazingly short" form made up of the very short administration time subtests of Information and Picture Completion (conversion to standard score = 2.9 (I + PC) + 42; Kaufman, Kaufman, Ramaswamy, & McLean, 1996) has been found to have correlations in the high .80s to low .90s (McCusker, 1994; Nagle & Bell, 1995).

Best Four-Subtest Short Forms

A frequently used WAIS-R tetrad comprises Vocabulary, Arithmetic, Block Design, and Picture Arrangement (Silverstein, 1982b). Mean WAIS-R administration time is 36 minutes (Kaufman, 1990). Correlations with the full administration range from .93 to .95 for the WAIS-R, WISC-III, and WISC-R (McNemar, 1974; Sattler, 1992; Silverstein, 1982b). These four subtests are usually excellent in detecting abnormal cognitive functioning (Ryan, Georgemiller, & McKinney, 1984). The inclusion of Arithmetic with Vocabulary and Block Design provides an assessment of auditory attention along with an important indicator of how effectively the person functions in the real world. Picture Arrangement provides information on a person's knowledge of sequencing and his or her relative perceptiveness about common social situations. An important caution is that any short-form combination of Vocabulary, Block Design, Arithmetic, or Picture Arrangement is likely to overestimate the IQs of patients referred for neuropsychological evaluation (Roth, Hughes, Mankowski, & Crosson, 1984). Additional short forms using any four combinations of Vocabulary, Block Design, Arithmetic, Picture Arrangement, Information, Comprehension, Similarities, or Picture Completion are also likely to produce correlations in the low to mid .90s (McNemar, 1974; Sattler, 1992). Kaufman et al. (1996) and Ward and Ryan (1996) have suggested an extremely brief four WAIS-R subtest form comprising Arithmetic, Similarities, Picture Completion, and Digit Symbol (conversion to standard score: 1.6 (A + S + PC + DSy) + 36) with reliabilities with the Full Scale IQ ranging from .92 to .95 (McCusker, 1994). However, a comparison of different popular short forms (prior to 1990) found that the traditional Vocabulary, Arithmetic, Block Design, and Picture Arrangement tetrad estimated Full Scale WAIS-R IQ with greater accuracy than other variations (Boone, 1990).

Kaufman et al. (1996) evaluated WISC-III four-subtest short forms based on clinical, practical, and psychometric considerations and recommended that the overall best tetrad was composed of Similarities-Arithmetic-Picture Completion-Block Design. Total administration time was approximately 27 minutes, scoring time was relatively brief, and it was found to be as psychometrically sound as other combinations.

Conversion formulas to estimate Full Scale IQs utilize the sum of the four scaled scores (S + A + PC + BD; abbreviated as simply Xc) but vary according to the following age groups: ages 6, 8–14, 16, and total sample (1.6 Xc + 36); age 7 (1.7 Xc + 32); and age 15 (1.5 Xc + 40).

Seven-Subtest Short Forms

A more recent strategy is to delete the most time-consuming subtests and give as many of the shorter subtests as possible (Ward & Ryan, 1996). Ward (1990) developed a seven-subtest short form (Information, Digit Span, Arithmetic, Similarities, Picture Completion, Block Design, Digit Symbol), which takes 35 minutes to administer. The scores can be prorated prior to using Wechsler's Table 20 to calculate IQ scores by using the following procedure: Verbal sum of scaled scores = 2 (I + S) + (DSp + A) and Performance sum of scaled scores = 2 (PC + BD) + (DSy). Correlations with the WAIS-R Full Scale IQ have been in the high 90s with 99% of subjects obtaining estimates of their Full Scale IQ within 8 points of their actual full administration IQs (Benedict, Schretlen, & Bobholz, 1992). Performance and Full Scale IQ scores have been found to be nearly as reliable as for full-administration IQs with the average Full Scale standard error of measurement being 3.07 vs. 2.58 for the Full WAIS-R administration (Axelrod, Woodard, Shretten, & Benedict, 1996). This would increase the 95% confidence interval for the seven-subtest Full Scale IQ to plus or minus 6.2 points (vs. the 5.5 average for the full administration standard error of measurement). Thus, the psychometric properties of the seven-subtest short form are excellent and administration times are only marginally longer than the more traditional Silverstein (1982b) four-subtest short form.

The Satz-Mogel and Yudin Approaches

An alternative to administering various combinations of subtests is to use every subtest but limit the number of items from each of the subtests. The most frequently used variation is the Satz and Mogel (1962) approach, which was originally developed for the WAIS but has been updated for the WAIS-R (Adams, Smigielski, & Jenkins, 1984). The procedure is to administer every third item for Information and Vocabulary and multiply the scores by three to obtain the raw scores. Only odd items are administered for Similarities, Arithmetic, Comprehension, Block Design, Object Assembly, and Picture Completion and each score is multiplied by two to obtain the respective scaled scores. Full administrations are given for Digit Span and Digit Symbol. The entire procedure takes approximately 30 minutes and the derived IQs have correlations similar to the best four subtest variations. A distinct advantage over four subtest variations is that the Satz-Mogel approach samples a wider range of areas. This is likely to increase the stability of scores over a wider variety of populations and also allows clinicians to develop inferences over a larger number of behaviors. For example, results of the Satz-Mogel and a full administration were comparable for an elderly demented population (Osato, van Gorp, Kern, Satz, & Steinman, 1989). Intelligence classifications using the Satz-Mogel method have been found to be 93% accurate and 97% of IQs were found to be within 15 IQ points of IQs derived from a full administration (Watkins, Edinger, & Shipley, 1986). A caution is that, even though a score is provided for each subtest, it is inappropriate to attempt a profile analysis since the individual subtests will not be sufficiently reliable (Silverstein, 1990).

A WISC-R/WISC equivalent of the Satz-Mogel approach was developed by Yudin (1966) and has the same advantages and disadvantages and follows a nearly identical procedure. The main difference is that Digit Span and Mazes are not administered since they are optional subtests, but Coding, like Digit Symbol on the WAIS-R, is given in its entirety. Directions for the WISC-III would be the same with the added omission of the optional Symbol Search subtest. However, if examiners did decide to use the Symbol Search subtest due to its good psychometric properties or clinical relevance, then it would need to be given in its entirety.

Modified Format

A final approach is the elimination of early, easy items on each of the subtests. This is most appropriate for relatively bright subjects but should be used cautiously with persons of below-average intelligence. Cella (1984) has provided guidelines for the number of items to be omitted based on a subject's performance on the Information subtest. Such a procedure has been found to have an almost exact correlation (.99) with a full administration and yet can reduce the total administration time by 25%. Despite this high correlation, some caution should be exercised toward Cella's Modified Format and the Satz-Mogel approaches. First, lowered internal consistency is likely to reduce subtest reliabilities sufficiently to render profile analysis questionable. Second, examinees are disadvantaged since they are not able to have as many previous subtest items to practice on (since items are skipped) before being administered more difficult items. The result may be that the norms for the full administration may not necessarily apply to the shortened versions.

PROFILE FORMS

The forms in Appendixes F and G may be used to plot WAIS-R or WISC-III scores so that an individual's test results can be quickly and easily observed. The abilities required for the 11 WAIS-R and the 13 WISC-R subtests are summarized on the far right side, and the scaled scores are plotted in the center. This provides persons reviewing the test results with a listing of the three IQs as well as a summary of relative strengths and weaknesses. This should be done cautiously, however, due to the previously discussed difficulties with profile analysis. The profiles should not be perceived as interpretations but as hypotheses that may or may not be confirmed through comparisons with other subtests (see Level III of "Interpretation Procedures" section) and additional sources of information.

INSTRUCTIONAL RECOMMENDATIONS

Once a WAIS-R or WISC-III has been scored and interpreted, an examiner must still develop practical recommendations. Appendix H gives the interpretive rationales, implications of high and low scores, and possible instructional recommendations for persons scoring low on either the Full Scale, Verbal, or Performance IQ Appendix I has a similar format but enables a clinician to develop instructional recommendations (activities) for commonly occurring groups of subtests. Although these tables were originally developed for the analysis of children's (WISC-R/WISC-III) scores, a clinician can utilize the recommendations for adult (WAIS-R) scores by developing tasks that are similar but somewhat more difficult. In addition, clinicians should not merely make these recommendations in a cookbook fashion. They should carefully consider the needs of the client along with the resources available in the community and expand on or tailor them accordingly. Instructional and other recommendations should not be based on tests and tables, but should rather be guided by the wisdom and experience of the clinician who uses the tests and tables as useful tools to guide their development of recommendations.

RECOMMENDED READING

Kamphaus, R. W. (1993). *Clinical assessment of children's intelligence: A handbook for professional practice.* Boston: Allyn & Bacon.

Kaufman, A. S. (1990). *Assessing adolescent and adult intelligence.* Boston: Allyn & Bacon.

Kaufman, A. S. (1994). *Intelligent testing with the WISC-III.* New York: Wiley.

Sattler, J. M. (1992). *Assessment of children* (3rd ed., rev.). San Diego: Author.

Wechsler, D. (1991). *Manual for the Wechsler Intelligence Scale for Children* (3rd. ed.). New York: Psychological Corporation.

Wechsler, D. (1981). *Manual for the Wechsler Adult Intelligence Scale-Revised.* New York: Psychological Corporation.

Weinberg, R. A. (1989). Intelligence and IQ: Landmark issues and great debates. *American Psychologist, 44,* 98–104.

Chapter 6

THE MINNESOTA MULTIPHASIC PERSONALITY INVENTORY

The Minnesota Multiphasic Personality Inventory (MMPI)[1] is a standardized questionnaire that elicits a wide range of self-descriptions scored to give a quantitative measurement of an individual's level of emotional adjustment and attitude toward test taking. Since its original development by Hathaway and McKinley in 1940, the MMPI has become the most widely used clinical personality inventory, with over 10,000 published research references (Archer, 1992; Graham & Lilly, 1984; Lubin et al., 1985; Piotrowski & Keller, 1989a; Piotrowski & Zalewski, 1993; Watkins et al., 1995). Thus, in addition to its clinical usefulness, the MMPI has stimulated a vast amount of literature.

The 1943 MMPI test format consisted of 504 affirmative statements that could be answered "True" or "False." The number of items was later increased to 566 through the inclusion of repeat items and Scales 5 (Masculinity-Femininity) and 0 (Social Introversion). The 1989 restandardization retained the same basic format but altered, deleted, and/or added a number of items that resulted in a total of 567. The different categories of responses can be either hand or computer scored and summarized on a profile sheet. An individual's score as represented on the profile form can then be compared with the scores derived from different normative samples.

The original MMPI had 13 standard scales of which 3 related to validity and 10 to clinical or personality indices. The more recent MMPI-2 and MMPI-A have maintained the original 10 clinical/personality scales as well as the original 3 validity scales but the total number of validity scales has been increased (see Table 6–1). The clinical and personality scales are known both by their scale numbers and by scale abbreviations. Additional options are available to refine the meaning of the clinical scales as well as provide additional information. These include scales based on item content (content scales), subscales for the clinical and personality scales based on clusters of content related-items (Harris-Lingoes subscales), assessment of items and item clusters that relate to relevant dimensions (critical items) and empirically derived new scales (supplementary scales). New scales are still being researched and reported in the literature. The result of these developments is an extremely diverse and potentially useful test which can be interpreted, refined, and expanded from a variety of different perspectives.

---

[1] Items from the MMPI-2 are reproduced, by permission, from Starke R. Hathaway and J. Charnley McKinley, *The Minnesota Multiphasic Personality Inventory,* by University of Minnesota Press, Minneapolis, MN.

Table 6–1.   Basic Minnesota Multiphasic Personality Inventory Scales

Name	Abbreviation	Scale No.	MMPI-2 No. of Items
Original Validity Scales			
Cannot say	?		
Lie	L		15
Infrequency	F		60
Correction	K		30
New Validity Scales			
Variable Response Inconsistency	VRIN		98
True Response Inconsistency	TRIN		40
F back	Fb		40
Clinical Scales			
Hypochondriasis	Hs	1	32
Depression	D	2	57
Hysteria	Hy	3	60
Psychopathic-Deviate	Pd	4	50
Masculinity-Femininity	Mf	5	56
Paranoia	Pa	6	40
Psychasthenia	Pt	7	48
Schizophrenia	Sc	8	78
Hypomania	Ma	9	46
Social Introversion	Si	0	69

The contents for the majority of MMPI questions are relatively obvious and deal largely with psychiatric, psychological, neurological, or physical symptoms. However, some of the questions are psychologically obscure in that the underlying psychological process they are assessing is not intuitively obvious. For example, item 68, "I sometimes tease animals" is empirically answered "False" more frequently by depressed subjects than normals. Thus, it was included under Scale 2 (Depression) even though it does not, on the surface, appear to directly assess an individual's degree of depression. For the most part, however, the statements are more direct and self-evident, such as item 56, "I wish I could be as happy as others seem to be" (True) or 146, "I cry easily" (True), both of which also reflect an examinee's level of depression. The overall item content is extremely varied and relates to such areas as general health, occupational interests, preoccupations, morale, phobias, and educational problems.

Once a test profile has been developed, the scores are frequently arranged or coded in a way that summarizes and highlights significant peaks and valleys. However, to accurately interpret the test, both the overall configuration of the different scales and the relevant demographic characteristics of the client must be taken into consideration. In many instances, the same scaled score on one test profile can mean something quite different on another person's profile when the elevations or lowerings of other scales are also considered. For example, an elevated Scale 3 (Hysteria) may indicate an individual who denies conflict, demands support from others, expresses optimism, and is somewhat interpersonally naive. However, if this elevation is also accompanied by a high 4 (Psychopathic

Deviate), there is likely to be a strong undercurrent of repressed anger. This anger is usually expressed indirectly, and any negative effects on others are likely to be strongly denied. Thus, it is important for the clinician to avoid the use of purely quantitative or mechanical formulas for interpreting the profile and instead examine the scores within the overall context of the other scale elevations and lowerings. Not only should a particular scale be examined within the context of the overall test configuration, but additional sources such as demographic characteristics (age, education, socioeconomic status, ethnicity), behavioral observations, other psychometric devices, and relevant history can often increase the accuracy, richness, and sensitivity of personality descriptions.

A further important, general interpretive consideration is that the scales represent measures of personality traits rather than simply diagnostic categories. Although the scales were originally designed to differentiate normal from abnormal behavior, it is generally regarded as far more useful to consider that the scales indicate clusters of personality variables. For example, Scale 2 (Depression) may suggest such characteristics as mental apathy, self-depreciation, and a tendency to worry over even relatively small matters. This approach characterizes the extensive research performed on the meanings of the two highest scales (two-point code types), which are summarized later in this chapter. Rather than merely labeling a person, this descriptive approach creates a richer, more in-depth, and wider assessment of the individual being tested.

HISTORY AND DEVELOPMENT

The original development of the MMPI was begun in 1939 at the University of Minnesota by Starke R. Hathaway and J. Charnley McKinley. They wanted an instrument that could serve as an aid in assessing adult patients during routine psychiatric case workups and that could accurately determine the severity of their disturbances. Furthermore, Hathaway and McKinley were interested in developing an objective estimate of the change produced by psychotherapy or other variables in a patient's life.

The most important approach taken during construction of the MMPI was empirical criterion keying. This refers to the development, selection, and scoring of items within the scales based on some external criterion of reference. Thus, if a clinical population was given a series of questions to answer, the individuals developing the test would select questions for inclusion or exclusion based on whether this clinical population answered differently from a comparison group. Even though a theoretical approach might be used initially to develop test questions, the final inclusion of questions would not be based on this theoretical criterion. Instead, test questions would be selected based on whether they were answered in a direction different from a contrasted group. For example, a test constructor may believe that an item such as "sometimes I find it almost impossible to get up in the morning" is a theoretically sound statement to use in assessing depression. However, if a sample population of depressed patients did not respond to that question differently from a normative group, then the item would not be included. Thus, if a person with hysterical traits answers "True" to the statement "I have stomach pains," whether he or she actually does have stomach pains is less important—from an empirical point of view—than that the individual *says* he or she does. In other words, the final criterion for inclusion of items within an inventory is based on whether or not these items are responded to in a significantly different manner by a specified population sample.

Using this method, Hathaway and McKinley began with an original item pool of over 1,000 statements derived from a variety of different sources, including previously developed scales of personal and social attitudes, clinical reports, case histories, psychiatric interviewing manuals, and personal clinical experience. Of the original 1,000 statements, many were eliminated or modified. The result was 504 statements that were considered to be clear, readable, not duplicated, and balanced between positive and negative wording. The statements themselves were extremely varied and were purposely designed to tap as wide a number of areas in an individual's life as possible. The next step was to select different groups of normal and psychiatric patients to whom the 504 questions could be administered. The normals were primarily friends and relatives of patients at the University of Minnesota hospitals who were willing to complete the inventory. They consisted of 226 males and 315 females who were screened with several background questions about age, education, marital status, occupation, residence, and current medical status. Individuals who were under the care of a physician at the time of the screening were excluded from the study. This group was further augmented by the inclusion of other normal subjects, such as recent high school graduates, Work Progress Administration workers, and medical patients at the University of Minnesota hospitals. This composite sample of 724 individuals was closely representative in terms of age, sex, and marital status of a typical group of individuals from the Minnesota population, as reflected in the 1930 census. The clinical group comprised patients who represented the major psychiatric categories being treated at the University of Minnesota hospitals. These patients were divided into clear subgroups of approximately 50 in each category of diagnosis. If a patient's diagnosis was at all in question, or if a person had a multiple diagnosis, then he or she was excluded from the study. The resulting subgroups were hypochondriasis, depression, hysteria, psychopathic deviate, paranoia, psychasthenia, schizophrenia, and hypomania.

Once the normals and psychiatric patients had been administered the 504-item scale, Hathaway and McKinley could then compare their responses. Each item that correctly differentiated between these two groups was included in the resulting clinical scale. For example, item 40, "Much of the time my head seems to hurt all over," was answered "True" by 12% of the sample of hypochondriacs and by only 4% of the normals. It was thus included in the clinical scale for hypochondriasis. The comparisons, then, were between each clinical group and the group of normals rather than among the different clinical groups themselves. This was the selection procedure used to develop tentative clinical scales.

Still another step was included in the scale constructions. The fact that an item was endorsed differently by the group of 724 Minnesota normals than by the patients from various clinical populations did not necessarily indicate that it could be used successfully for clinical screening purposes. Thus, an attempt was made to cross-validate the scales by selecting a new group of normals and comparing their responses with a different group of clinical patients. The items that still provided significant differences between these groups were selected for the final version of the scales. It was reasoned, then, that these items and the scales comprising these items would be valid for differential diagnosis in actual clinical settings.

Whereas this procedure describes how the original clinical scales were developed, two additional scales that used slightly different approaches were also included. Scale 5 (Masculinity-Femininity) was originally intended to differentiate male homosexuals from males with a more exclusively heterosexual orientation. However, few items were found that could effectively perform this function. The scale was then expanded to distinguish items that were characteristically endorsed in a certain direction by the majority of males from those that were characteristically endorsed in a certain direction by females. This was accomplished in part by the inclusion of items from the Terman and Miles I Scale (1936). The second additional scale, Social Introversion *(Si),* was developed by Drake in 1946. It was initially developed by using empirical criterion keying in an attempt to differentiate female college students who participated extensively in social and extracurricular activities from those who rarely participated. It was later generalized to reflect the relative degree of introversion for both males and females.

It soon became apparent to the test constructors that persons could alter the impression they made on the test due to various test-taking attitudes. Hathaway and McKinley thus began to develop several scales that could detect the types and magnitude of the different test-taking attitudes most likely to invalidate the other clinical scales. Four scales were developed: the Cannot say (?), the Lie *(L),* the Infrequency *(F),* and the Correction *(K).* The Cannot say scale (?) is simply the total number of unanswered questions. If a high number of these are present, it would obviously serve to reduce the validity of the overall profile. High scores on the Lie scale indicate a naive and unsophisticated effort on the part of the examinee to create an overly favorable impression. The items selected for this scale were those that indicated a reluctance to admit to even minor personal shortcomings. The *F* scale is composed of those items endorsed by less than 10% of normals. A high number of scorable items on the *F* scale, then, reflects that the examinee is endorsing a high number of unusually deviant responses.

K, which reflects an examinee's degree of psychological defensiveness, is perhaps the most sophisticated of the validity scales. The items for this scale were selected by comparing the responses of known psychiatric patients who still produced normal MMPIs (clinically defensive) with "true" normals who also produced normal MMPIs. Those items that differentiated between these two groups were used for the *K* scale. Somewhat later, the relative number of items endorsed on the *K* scale was used as a "correction" factor. The reasoning behind this was that, if some of the scales were lowered due to a defensive test-taking attitude, then a measure of the degree of defensiveness could be added into the scale to compensate for this. The result would theoretically be a more accurate appraisal of the person's clinical behavior. The scales that are not given a *K* correction are those whose raw score still produced an accurate description of the person's actual behavior. However, there have been some questions regarding the effectiveness of the *K* correction in some settings. As a result, clinicians have the choice of whether they wish to use MMPI-2 profile sheets with or without the *K* correction, and the MMPI-A has omitted the use of the *K* correction altogether.

Since the publication of the original MMPI, special scales and numerous adjunctive approaches to interpretation have been developed. A primary strategy has been content interpretation. The most frequently used are the Harris and Lingoes subscales, Wiggins Content Scales, and several different listings of critical items whose contents can potentially provide important qualitative information regarding an examinee. In addition, many supplementary scales have been developed, such as the Anxiety Scale, the MacAndrew Scale to assess the potential for substance abuse, and the Ego Strength Scale to estimate the extent to which a person will benefit from insight-oriented therapy. Each of these approaches can be used as an adjunct in interpreting the traditional clinical scales and/or experimental scales for assessing or researching specific populations (see Butcher, Graham, Williams, & Ben-Porath, 1990; Caldwell, 1988; Williams, Butcher, Ben-Porath, & Graham, 1992).

In addition to innovations in scales and interpretations, the MMPI has been used within a wide number of settings for extremely diverse areas. Most studies have focused on the identification of medical and psychiatric disorders as well as on uses in forensic contexts (Greene, 1988; Pope, Butcher, & Seelen, 1993), and on expanding or further understanding the psychometric properties of the MMPI. Other frequent topics include alcoholism, aging, locus of control, computer-based interpretation, chronic pain, and the assessment of different occupational groups. The MMPI has been translated into a number of different languages and has been used in a wide range of different cross-cultural contexts (Butcher & Pancheri, 1976; Cheung & Song, 1989; Cheung, Zhao, & Wu, 1992; Greene, 1987; Strassberg, Tilley, Bristone, & Oei, 1992).

Criticisms of the original MMPI have primarily centered on its growing obsolescence, difficulties with the original scale construction, inadequacy of its standardization sample, and difficulties with many of the items (Butcher & Pope, 1989; Helmes & Reddon, 1993). Problems with the items included sexist wording, possible racial bias, archaic phrases, and objectionable content. In addition, the original norms had poor representation of minorities and are inappropriate in making comparisons with current test takers. Further problems have related to inconsistent meanings associated with T score transformations.

These criticisms led to an extensive restandardization of the MMPI, which began in 1982. Despite the need to make major changes, the restandardization committee wanted to keep the basic format and intent of the MMPI as intact as possible so that the extensive research base collected over the past 50 years would still be applicable to the restandardized version. The result was that the following six goals were established (Butcher & Pope, 1989):

1. The deletion of obsolete or objectionable items.
2. Continuation of the original validity and clinical scales.
3. The development of a wide, representative normative sample.
4. Norms that would most accurately reflect clinical problems and would result in a uniform percentile classification.
5. The collection of new clinical data that could be used in evaluating the items and scales.
6. The development of new scales.

The restandardization used a special research form consisting of the original 550 items (of which 82 were modified) and additional 154 provisional items used for the development of new scales. Even though 82 of the original items were reworded, their psychometric properties apparently were not altered (Ben-Porath & Butcher, 1989). The resulting 704-item form (Form AX) was administered to 1,138 males and 1,462 females from seven different states, several military bases, and a Native American reservation. The subjects were between the ages of 18 and 90 and were contacted by requests through direct mail, advertisements in the media, and special appeals. The resulting restandardization sample was highly similar to the 1980 U.S. census in almost all areas with the exception that they were somewhat better educated than the overall population.

The new MMPI-2 (Butcher, Dahlstrom, Graham, Tellegen, & Kaemmer, 1989) differs from the older test in a number of ways. The T scores that subjects obtain are generally not as deviant as those from the earlier version. In addition, the T scores were designed to produce the same range and distribution throughout the traditional clinical scales (except for Scales 5 and 0). The practical result is that T scores of 65 or greater are considered to be in the clinical range (versus a cutoff score of 70 for the MMPI). Also, the percentile distributions are uniform throughout the different clinical scales (whereas they were unequal for the MMPI). The test booklet itself contains 567 items, but the order has been changed so that the traditional scales (3 validity and 10 clinical) can be derived from the first 370 items. The remaining 197 items (371 to 567) provide different supplementary, content, and research measures. A number of new scales have been included along with new, subtle, adjunctive measures of test validity, separate measures of masculinity and femininity, and 15 additional content scales measuring specific personality factors (Anxiety, Health concerns, Cynicism, etc.). An extensive research base is accumulating related to such areas as the validity of MMPI/MMPI-2 codetypes, use with special populations, the ability to distinguish over- or underreporting of symptoms, and comparability between the original MMPI, MMPI-2, and MMPI-A.

Early on, it was noticed that the original MMPI produced different scale elevations for adolescents than for adults. This resulted in the development of different sets of recommended norms for use with adolescent populations (Archer, 1987; Colligan & Offord, 1989; Klinefelter, Pancoast, Archer, & Pruitt, 1990; Marks, Seeman, & Haller, 1974). However, many practitioners and researchers felt that, even with the use of adolescent norms, there were still considerable difficulties. Specifically, it was too long, the reading level was too high, there was a need for contemporary norms, more of the content needed to assess problems specifically related to adolescents, and some of the language was outmoded and/or inappropriate (Archer, Maruish, Imhof, & Piotrowski, 1991). In response to these issues, the restandardization committee for the MMPI-2 decided in 1989 to develop the MMPI-Adolescent (MMPI-A) which was first made available in 1992 (Butcher et al., 1992). It was normed against a generally representative group of 805 males and 815 females between the ages of 14 and 18. The main discrepancy between the normative group and comparison with U.S. census data was that the parents of the normative group were better educated. Despite the similarity with the MMPI and MMPI-2, there are several important differences. Fifty-eight items were deleted from the original standard scales, some of the wording of items was changed, and new items relevant to adolescent concerns were included. The result has been the inclusion of four new validity scales (VRIN, TRIN, F1, F2) in addition to the earlier validity scales *(L, F, K)*. There are also six supplementary scales (e.g., Immaturity Scale, Anxiety, Repression) and additional newly developed content scales (e.g., A-dep/Adolescent Depression). To counter claims that the MMPI is too long, especially for adolescents, the new MMPI-A contains 478 items, thereby shortening the administration time. This can be shortened even further by administering only the first

350 items, still sufficient to obtain the validity and standard clinical scales. Thus, the MMPI-A is both strongly related to the MMPI and MMPI-2 (and their respective databases) but also has a number of important distinctive features of its own.

RELIABILITY AND VALIDITY

Reliability studies on the MMPI indicate that it has moderate levels of temporal stability and internal consistency. For example, Hunsley, Hanson, and Parker (1988) performed a meta-analysis of studies performed on the MMPI between 1970 and 1981, and concluded, "all MMPI scales are quite reliable, with values that range from a low of .71 (Scale *Ma*) to a high of .84 (Scale *Pt*)" (p. 45). Their analysis was derived from studies that included a wide range of populations, intervals that ranged from one day to two years, and a combined sample size exceeding 5,000. In contrast to Hunsley et al. (1988), some authors have reported that the fluctuations in some of the scales are sufficiently wide to question their reliabilities (Hathaway & Monachesi, 1963; Mauger, 1972). Proponents of the MMPI counter that some fluctuation in test scores are to be expected. This is especially true for psychiatric populations since the effects of treatment or stabilization in a temporary crisis situation are likely to be reflected in a patient's test performance (Graham, Smith, & Schwartz, 1986). Bergin (1971) has demonstrated that Scale 2 (Depression) is particularly likely to be lowered after successful treatment. Similarly, Scale 7 (Psychasthenia) would be likely to alter according to a person's external situation. Thus, test-retest reliability may actually be an inappropriate method of evaluating these scales for certain populations. This defense of the test's reliability is somewhat undermined by the observation that test-retest reliability is actually slightly more stable for psychiatric populations than for normals. Whereas the median range for psychiatric patients is around .80, median reliabilities for normals are around .70. Split-half reliabilities are likewise moderate, having an extremely wide range from .05 to .96, with median correlations in the .70s (Hunsley et al., 1988).

Reliability reported in the MMPI-2 manual indicates moderate test-retest reliabilities. However, test-retest reliabilities were calculated for a narrow population over short-term retesting intervals. Reliabilities for normal males over an average interval of 8.58 days (*Mdn* = 7 days) ranged from a low of .67 for Scale 6 to a high of .92 for Scale 0 (Butcher et al., 1989). A parallel sample of females over the same retesting interval produced similar reliabilities ranging from .58 (Scale 6) to .91 (Scale 0). Standard error of measurements for the different scales ranged from 2 to 3 raw score points (Butcher et al., 1989; Munley, 1991). Future studies will no doubt provide a further evaluation of the MMPI-2's reliability over longer intervals and for various population groups.

One difficulty with the MMPI lies in the construction of the scales themselves. The intercorrelations between many of the scales are quite high, which is primarily due to the extensive degree of item overlap. Sometimes, the same item will be simultaneously used for the scoring of several different scales, and most of the scales have a relatively high proportion of items common to other scales. For example, Scales 7 (Psychasthenia) and 8 (Schizophrenia) have fairly high overlap, which is reflected in correlations ranging from .64 to .87, depending on the population sampled (Butcher et al., 1989; Dahlstrom & Welsh, 1960). Scale 8, which has the highest number of items (78), has only 16 items that are unique to it (Dahlstrom, Welsh, & Dahlstrom, 1972). Similarly, Scale *F* (Infrequency) is highly correlated with Scales 7 *(Pt)*, 8 *(Sc),* and the Bizarre Mentation content scale. The practical implication of this is that interpreters need to be quite cautious about inferring a "fake bad" profile if profile *F* is elevated along with 7 *(Pt),* 8 *(Sc),* and Bizarre Mentation. Several factor analytic studies have been conducted that were motivated in part by a need to further understand the high intercorrelations among scales. These studies have not found any consistent numbers and types of factors. The numbers of factors range between 2 (Dahlstrom et al., 1972, 1975) and 9 (Costa, Zonderman, Williams, & McCrae, 1985; Reddon, Marceau, & Jackson, 1982) and even up to 21 (Johnson, Null, Butcher, & Johnson, 1984). This suggests that these factors are not highly differentiated.

The different scales correlate so highly, in part, because the original selection of the items for inclusion in each scale was based on a comparison of normals with different clinical groups. The items, then, were selected based on their differentiation of normals from various psychiatric populations, rather than on their differentiation of one psychiatric population from another. Even though the psychiatric groups varied from the normals on several traits, this manner of scale construction did not develop accurate measurements of these different traits. Rather, the scales are filled with many heterogeneous items and measure multidimensional, often poorly defined attributes. This approach has also led many items to be shared with other scales. In contrast, an approach in which specific psychiatric groups had been compared with one another would have been more likely to have resulted in scales with less item overlap and with the ability to measure more unidimensional traits.

A partial defense of item overlap is that for complex, multidimensional variables such as pathological syndromes, important relationships would be expected with other similar constructs. If these other constructs were being measured on the same test, it would further be expected that there would be scale overlap on these theoretically and clinically related syndromes (Dahlstrom et al., 1972). For example, depression is a common feature among several categories of psychopathology. Thus it would be theoretically related to such conditions as hypochondriasis, schizophrenia, and anxiety. This in turn would result in expected intercorrelations between scales, and would produce scales that, while intercorrelated, would still have subtle and clinically different meanings (Broughton, 1984). Thus the multidimensionality of the scales combined with their item overlap would not so much be a weaknesses of the MMPI/MMPI-2/MMPI-A, but would be expected, given the nature of the constructs. Accurate interpretation, however, would need to include an awareness of the subtle differences and similarities between scales.

An issue related to MMPI/MMPI-2/MMPI-A scale multidimensionality is that elevations can often occur for a variety of reasons. For example, an elevation on 4 (Psychopathic Deviance) might occur due to family discord, poor peer relations, alienation from self and society, and/or acting out associated with legal difficulties. This means that a person interpreting an elevated Scale 4 (Psychopathic Deviance) might potentially infer antisocial acting out when family discord is the major reason for the scale elevation. To enhance the likelihood of accurate interpretations, practitioners need to carefully evaluate the meanings of scale elevations. This might include looking at the content of selected items (critical items), scoring the Harris-Lingoes subscales, considering the meanings of content or supplementary scales, referring to published MMPI research, and integrating the results from the client's history and relevant behavioral observations. Differentiating which of these scale dimensions is most relevant can be quite challenging for the practitioner.

A further difficulty relating to scale construction is the imbalance in the number of true and false items. In the *L* scale, all the items are scorable if answered "False"; on the *K* scale, 29 of 30 items are scored if answered "False"; and Scales 7, 8, and 9 have a ratio of approximately 3 to 1 of true compared with false items. The danger of this imbalance is that persons having response styles of either acquiescing ("yea-saying") or disagreeing ("nay-saying") may answer according to their response style rather than to the content of the items. A more theoretically sound approach to item construction would have been to include an even balance between the number of true and false answers. Some authors (Edwards, 1957, 1964; Jackson, 1986) have even suggested that test results do not reflect psychological traits as much as generalized test-taking attitudes. Thus, a controversy has arisen over "content variance," in which an examinee is responding to the content of the items in a manner that will reflect psychological traits rather than "response style variance," in which responses reflect more the examinee's tendency to respond in a certain biased direction. In a review of the literature, Koss (1979) concluded that, although response sets can and do exist, the examinee's tendency to respond accurately to the item content is far stronger. The MMPI-2 restandardization committee has also developed the Variable Response Inconsistency (VRIN) and True Response Inconsistency (TRIN) scales to help detect invalid profiles caused by inconsistent or contradictory responding. These scales have been specifically designed to detect either response acquiescence or response nonacquiescence and thus should help counter the potential complications due to imbalanced keying.

The difficulties associated with reliability and scale construction have led to challenges to the MMPI's validity. Rodgers (1972) has even referred to the MMPI as a "psychometric nightmare." However, even though the strict psychometric properties present difficulties, this has been somewhat compensated by extensive validity studies. More specifically, the meanings of two- and three-point profile code types have been extensively researched, as have the contributions that the MMPI can make toward assessing and predicting specific problem areas. Dahlstrom et al. (1975), in Volume 2 of their revised MMPI handbook, cite 6,000 studies investigating profile patterns. This number is continually increasing (see, e.g., Archer, Gordon, Giannetti, & Singles, 1988; DuAlba & Scott, 1993; Galluci, 1994; Sheppard, Smith, & Rosenbaum, 1988), and past studies provide extensive evidence of the MMPI's construct validity. For example, elevations on Scales 4 *(Pd)* and 9 *(Ma)* have been associated with measures of impulsivity, aggression, substance abuse, and sensation seeking among adolescent inpatients (Gallucci, 1994). Somewhat similarly, alcoholics with elevations on Scales 4 and 9 (49/94 code type) have been found to be more likely to drop out of a residential alcoholism treatment program than other code types (Sheppard et al., 1988). Finally, high scores on Scale 0 *(Si)* have been associated with persons who have low self-esteem, social anxiety, and low sociability (Sieber & Meyers, 1993). Individual clinicians can consult research on code types to obtain specific personality descriptions and learn of potential problems to which a client may be susceptible. The extensiveness and strength of these validity studies have proven to be a major asset of the MMPI and help to explain its continued popularity.

In addition to studying the correlates of code type, another approach to establishing validity is to assess the accuracy of inferences based on the MMPI. Early studies by Kostlan (1954) and Little and Shneidman (1959) indicated that the MMPI is relatively more accurate than other standard assessment instruments, especially when the MMPI was combined with social case history data. This incremental validity of the MMPI has been supported in later reviews by Garb (1984) and Graham and Lilly (1984). For example, the accuracy of neurologists' diagnoses was found to increase when they added an MMPI to their patient data (Schwartz & Wiedel, 1981). Garb (1984) concluded that the MMPI was more accurate than social history alone, was superior to projectives, and that the highest incremental validity was obtained when the MMPI was combined with social history. In addition, incremental validity of the new MMPI-2 content scales has been found in that they both expanded on and increased the validity of the standard clinical scales (Ben-Porath, McCully, & Almagor, 1993).

ASSETS AND LIMITATIONS

The previous discussion on reliability and validity highlights several issues associated with the MMPI. These include moderate levels of reliability, extensive length, and problems related to the construction of the scales such as item overlap, high intercorrelations among scales, and multidimensional poorly defined variables. Some of the criticisms of the original MMPI relating to obsolete norms, offensive items, and poorly worded items have been largely corrected with the publication of the MMPI-2 and MMPI-A. The MMPI also has a number of strengths along with other weaknesses.

One caution stemming from the construction of the original MMPI is that it generally does not provide much information related to normal populations. The items were selected on the basis of their ability to differentiate a bimodal population of normals from psychiatric patients. Thus, extreme scores can be interpreted with a fairly high degree of confidence, but moderate elevations must be interpreted with appropriate caution. An elevation in the range of one standard deviation above the mean is more likely to represent an insignificant fluctuation of a normal population than would be the case if a normally distributed group had been used for the scale construction. This is in contrast to a test like the California Personality Inventory (CPI), which used a more evenly distributed sample (as opposed to a bimodal one) and, as a result, can make meaningful interpretations based on moderate elevations. The MMPI-2 partially addresses this difficulty in that it has used broad contemporary norms for its comparisons combined with uniform T scores (Tellegen & Ben-Porath, 1992). However, evaluation of normals is sometimes complicated by the observation that normal persons often achieve high scores. Despite these difficulties, the use and understanding of nonclinical populations has been increasing (Graham & McCord, 1985; Keiller & Graham, 1993). In particular, uses have included screening personnel for sensitive jobs such as air traffic controllers, police officers, and nuclear plant operators.

Even though there have been a number of notable improvements with the MMPI-2, issues have been raised regarding comparability between the two versions. In defense of their comparability are the many similarities in format, scale descriptions, and items. In particular, Ben-Porath and Butcher (1989a) found that the effects of rewriting 82 of the MMPI items for inclusion in the MMPI-2 were minimal. The rewritten items had no effect on any of the validity, clinical, or special scales when comparisons were made between administrations of the original and restandardized versions using college students. This provided some support for Butcher and Pope's (1989) contention that the MMPI-2 validity and clinical scales measure "exactly what they have always measured (p. 11)." Further studies have generally found that there are few differences based on individual scale comparisons (Ben-Porath & Butcher, 1989b; Chojnacki & Walsh, 1992; Harrell, Honaker, & Parnell, 1992; Ward, 1991). Similarly, number of elevated scales between the two forms does not seem to be significantly different and there has been 75% agreement regarding whether a subject's profile was considered to be within normal limits (Ben-Porath & Butcher, 1989a).

Despite these similarities, the use of the restandardization norms and the use of uniform T scores have created differences in two-point codes among different population samples including differences among 31% of the code types derived from general psychiatric patients (Butcher et al., 1989), 22% of peace officers (Hargrave, Hiatt, Ogard, & Karr, 1994), 39%–42% of psychiatric inpatients (Edwards, Morrison, & Weissman, 1993; Weissman, 1992), and a full 50% of both university students (Weissman, 1992) and forensic populations (Humphrey & Dahlstrom, 1995). The greatest level of disagreements were for poorly defined code types (low elevations combined with more than two "competing" scales). In contrast, well defined code types (highly elevated and without "competing" third or fourth most elevated scales) had considerably higher concordance (Tellegen & Ben-Porath, 1993). These results seem to question the exact comparability of past MMPI research performed on the code types since a sizable proportion of code types derived from the MMPI-2 have been found to be different. However, the most important unanswered question is whether the MMPI or MMPI-2 (or MMPI-A) most accurately describes an individual's relevant behaviors. Initial research does seem to support comparability between MMPI and MMPI-2 code type descriptors (Archer, Griffin, & Aiduk, 1995). Until further research clarifies the meaning and difference in patterns between these changes, interpretations based on code types derived from the MMPI-2 should be made with caution. One important guideline would be to take special care regarding poorly defined code types and, if more than two scales are elevated, then the meanings of the relatively high scales not included in the code should be given particular interpretive attention.

In both versions of the MMPI, the scale labels can be misleading since they use traditional diagnostic categories. A person might read a scale such as "schizophrenia" and infer that a person with a peak on that scale therefore fits the diagnosis of schizophrenia. Although it was originally hoped that the MMPI could be used to make differential psychiatric diagnoses, it was soon found that it could not adequately perform this function. Thus, even though schizophrenics score high on Scale 8, so do other psychotic and nonpsychotic groups. Also, moderate elevations can occur for some normal persons. With the publication of the third and fourth editions of the *Diagnostic and Statistical Manual of Mental Disorders* (American Psychiatric Association, 1980, 1987, 1994), the traditional labels on which the scale names were based have become progressively more outdated. This causes further confusion related to diagnosis since the scales reflect older categories. For example, Scales 1, 2, and 3 are called the "neurotic triad," and Scale 7 is labeled Psychasthenia; yet clinicians are often faced with the need to translate these outdated designations into *DSM-IV* terminology. This difficulty has been somewhat alleviated through research focusing on the frequencies of *DSM-III* and *DSM-III-R* classifications, which are related to different code types (Morey, Blashfield, Webb, & Jewell, 1988; Vincent et al., 1983). *DSM-III* translations have been further aided through the use of different content and supplementary scales that allow for broader descriptions of symptom patterns (Butcher, Graham, Williams, & Ben-Porath, 1990; Caldwell, 1988).

To compensate for the difficulties related to scale labels, clinicians should become aware of the current meanings of the scales based on research rather than the meanings implied by the often misleading scale titles. This approach can be aided in part through the use of scale numbers rather than titles. For example, Scale 8 suggests such attributes as apathy, feelings of alienation, philosophical interests, poor family relations, and unusual thought processes rather than "schizophrenia." It is the clinician's responsibility to determine which of these attributes are most characteristic of the person being evaluated. Clinicians should also be aware of the relationships among scales as represented by the extensive research performed on two- and three-point code types. Usually, the patterns or profiles of the scales are far more useful and valid than merely considering individual scale elevations. The extensiveness of research in this area represents what is probably the strongest asset of the MMPI. This volume of work has prevented the MMPI from becoming obsolete and has been instrumental in transforming it from a test of psychiatric classification into a far more wide-band personality inventory.

A further significant asset is the MMPI's immense popularity and familiarity within the field. Extensive research has been performed in a variety of areas, and new developments have included abbreviated forms, new scales, the use of critical items, and computerized interpretation systems (Archer, 1992). The MMPI has been translated into over 50 languages and is available in numerous countries. Normative and validity studies have been conducted on several different cultural groups (Butcher & Pancheri, 1976; Cheung & Song, 1989; Cheung et al., 1992), which makes possible the comparison of data collected from varying cultures. In contexts where no norms have been developed, at least the test format lends itself to the development of more appropriate norms that can then be used in these contexts.

A complicating aspect of the MMPI is that interpretations often need to take into account many demographic variables. It has been demonstrated that age, sex, race, place of residence, intelligence, education, and socioeconomic status are all related to the MMPI scales. Often the same relative elevation of profiles can have quite different meanings when corrections are made for demographic variables. Some of the more important and well researched of these will be discussed.

Age

Typically, elevations occur on Scales 1 and 3 for older normal populations (Leon, Gillum, Gillum, & Gouze, 1979). On the other hand, MMPI Scales *F* 4, 6, 8, and 9 are commonly elevated for adolescent populations (Marks, Seeman, & Haller, 1974). These patterns have been accounted for in the MMPI-A in that separate norms have been used. As the sampled population becomes older, the deviations of the latter group of scales tend to decrease. A further finding has been that Scale 9 is more commonly elevated in younger persons but decreases with age until it becomes the most frequent low point in older populations (Gynther & Shimkuras, 1966). As a general rule, the left side of the profile (Scales 1, 2, and 3) increases with age, which parallels the trend in older persons toward greater concern with health (Scales 1 and 3) and depression (Scale 2). Conversely, the right side of the profile decreases with age, which parallels a decrease in energy level (Scale 9), increased introversion (Scale 0 as well as 2), and decreased assertiveness (Scale 4). In specific cases, however, there may also be a complex interaction with gender, health, socioeconomic status, and ethnicity. In addition to considering scale elevations related to aging, it may be helpful to evaluate individual item content. Swensen, Pearson, and Osborne (1973) provide a list of 30 items that are likely to be affected by aging, such as MMPI item 9, "I am about as able to work as I ever was" (False) and MMPI item 261, "If I were an artist I would like to draw flowers" (True). An analysis of these items indicates that older persons generally express a decrease in hostility (MMPI items 39, 80, 109, 282, and 438), have more stereotypically "feminine" interests (MMPI items 132 and 261), and are more dutiful, placid, and cautious (Gynther, 1979).

As noted earlier, a significant feature of adolescent populations is a general elevation in many of the MMPI scales. This has led to considerable controversy over whether adolescents have more actual pathology (based on external behavioral correlates) or whether they merely have higher scores without correspondingly higher pathology (Archer, 1984, 1987, 1992). The controversy has encouraged efforts to more clearly understand behavioral correlates of adolescent profiles (Archer & Jacobson, 1993; Archer, Gordon, Giannetti, & Singles, 1988; Basham, 1992; Spirito, Faust, Myers, & Bechtel, 1988). Most authors have encouraged the use of specific adolescent norms, such as those developed by Marks, Seeman, and Haller (1974). A problem with the Marks et al. (1974) norms is that they may have been adequate for past assessment of adolescents (before and shortly after 1974), but current adolescent populations may require the use of more recently developed norms (Archer, Pancoast, & Klinefelter, 1989; Pancoast & Archer, 1988; Williams & Butcher, 1989a, 1989b), particularly the norms developed for the MMPI-A (Archer, 1992; Butcher et al., 1992). A specific problem is that the older Marks et al. (1974) norms produce a high percentage of false negatives for contemporary populations, and descriptors based on adult norms may actually be more accurate than descriptors based on the Mark et al. (1974) norms. Furthermore, Scale 5 (Masculinity-Femininity) does not seem to have external correlates for adolescents, and many of the more frequent adolescent code types have received only limited recent support (Williams & Butcher, 1989a, 1989b). Current researchers make the somewhat awkward recommendation that both adolescent and adult descriptors should be used for developing interpretations of adolescent profiles if using the MMPI or MMPI-2 (Archer, 1984, 1987). It was these and related issues that led to the development of the MMPI-A. As with the MMPI-2, the major issue is whether or not the new norms more accurately predict behavior more accurately than the older norms. Whereas initial MMPI-A research indicates the accuracy of behavioral predictions within the contexts studied (Archer, 1992; Butcher et al., 1992; Weed, Butcher, & Williams, 1994), such research will need to be extended into a wider number of areas to more fully address this issue.

Ethnicity

Although the MMPI has been used in the assessment of persons from different cultural contexts, such assessments should be made with caution. Cultural differences are likely to be especially pronounced if a clinician used the original Minnesota norms rather than ones developed for the particular group being evaluated (Butcher & Pancheri, 1976). When interpreting the profiles of culturally divergent groups, clinicians should have a knowledge of the beliefs and values of that culture and should consult appropriate norms and relevant research when available. There are a wide variety of possible reasons why persons from different cultural groups might score in a certain direction. Although scores may be due to the accurate measurement of different personality traits, they may also be the result of cultural tendencies to acquiesce by giving socially desirable responses, differing beliefs about modesty, role conflicts, or varying interpretations of the meaning of items. Profiles may also reflect the results of racial discrimination in that scales associated with anger, impulsiveness, and frustration may be elevated.

A number of different research efforts have attempted to study the effects of ethnicity on MMPI performance. Most of this work has centered on differences between African versus European Americans and the use of the MMPI within different cross-cultural contexts. Research on African American versus European American's MMPI performance has frequently indicated that African Americans are more likely to score higher on Scales F, 8, and 9 (Green & Kelley, 1988; Gynther & Green, 1980; Smith & Graham, 1981). This has resulted in considerable controversy over whether these differences indicate higher levels of actual pathology or merely reflect differences in perceptions and values without implying greater maladjustment. If the differences did not reflect greater actual pathology, then specialized subgroup norms would be required to correct for this source of error. However, reviews by Greene (1987, 1991) demonstrated that, although African versus European American differences could be found for some populations, there was no consistent pattern to these differences across all populations. What seemed of greater significance was the role of moderator variables, such as education, income, age, and type of pathology. When African American and European American psychiatric patients were compared according to level of education and type of pathology, their MMPI/MMPI-2 performances were the same (Davis, Beck, & Ryan, 1973; Timbrook & Graham, 1994). The issue of actual behavioral correlates of African American MMPI performances has received little research, and the results of those studies generally have not found differences between African American and European Americans. For example, the main behavioral features of 68/86 code types between African American and European Americans were the same (Clark & Miller, 1971). Furthermore, predictions based on African American and European American juvenile delinquents' MMPI scores were equally accurate for African Americans and European Americans (Green & Kelley, 1988; Timbrook & Graham, 1994). Based on the preceding findings, Greene (1987, 1991) and Pritchard and Rosenblatt (1980) concluded that it would be premature to develop and use separate norms for African Americans. However, it would still be important for clinicians to continually be aware of the many possible factors that could cause differences in African American versus European American's MMPI scores and correct for these factors when appropriate.

Similar to African American versus European American comparisons, no consistent patterns have been found across different populations for Native American, Hispanics, and Asian Americans. For example, normal Native Americans scored higher than European Americans on most clinical scales but these differences did not occur among psychiatric or substance abusing populations (Greene, 1987, 1991). Differences between

Hispanics and European Americans have generally been found to be less than African American or European American differences (Greene, 1991; Whitworth & McBlaine, 1993). There is also some indication that Hispanics may score higher than European Americans on Scale *L* but lower on *K,* 3 *(Hy),* and 4 *(Pd*; Whitworth & McBlaine, 1993). In addition, Hispanic workers compensation cases may be more likely to somatize psychological distress as reflected by greater elevations on 1 *(Hs),* 2 *(D),* and 3 *(Hy)* than European Americans (DuAlba & Scott, 1993). Greene (1987, 1991) concluded his reviews of ethnicity and MMPI performance with four major points and recommendations:

1. It is premature to develop new norms for ethnic groups, particularly since moderator variables (education, intelligence, socioeconomic status) seem to explain most of the variance in performance.
2. Future research needs to take into account the subject's degree of identification with his or her ethnic group.
3. More research needs to address actual empirical correlates of ethnicity and MMPI performance rather than merely reporting small mean differences.
4. More research needs to study the relationship between ethnicity and the many MMPI supplementary and content scales.

It should be further noted that the standardization sample for the MMPI-2 had representative samples of ethnic groups so that use of the MMPI-2 with these groups should be less problematic than the original MMPI.

Although African American versus European American scale differences within the United States are more frequently encountered in the literature, research has also been conducted, and norms developed, for using the MMPI within a cross-national context. This is at least partially because it is more efficacious to adapt and validate the MMPI rather than go to the far more extensive effort of developing a whole new test for the culture. Examples of countries where adaptations have occurred include such diverse areas as China (Cheung, 1986; Cheung & Song, 1989; Cheung et al., 1992), Israel (Merbaum & Hefetz, 1976), Pakistan (Mirza, 1977), South Africa (Lison & Van der Spuy, 1977), Chile (Rissetti et al., 1979), Mexico (Lucio, Reyes-Lagunes, & Scott, 1994), and Japan (Tsushima & Onorato, 1982). Whenever clinicians work with different cross-national groups, they should consult the specific norms that have been developed for use with these groups, as well as become familiar with any research that may have been carried out with the MMPI on these groups. Useful sources are Butcher and Pancheri's (1976) handbook for cross-national MMPI research and reviews of cross-cultural research by Butcher and Clark (1979), Butcher (1985), and Greene (1987, 1991, pp. 338–354).

Social Class and Education

The original MMPI was standardized on a group that, by today's standards, would be considered to be poorly educated. There were also additional differences including no or few ethnic groups, relatively lower endorsement of "unusual" item content, and the impact of considerable social changes over the past five decades. The result was that social class, in particular, had to be taken into account when interpreting the original MMPI since it seemed to influence Scales *L, F, K,* and 5 quite extensively. However, the MMPI-2's more representative sample means that, for most educational levels, education does not need to be taken into account. However, for persons with quite low educational levels (less than 11 years), *K* and 5 *(Mf)* may have lower overall scores so that they need to be interpreted with caution.

The advantages and cautions for using the MMPI, MMPI-2, and MMPI-A indicate that a considerable degree of psychological sophistication is necessary. Both their assets and limitations need to be understood and taken into account. The limitations for the original MMPI are numerous and include moderately adequate reliability, problems related to scale construction, excessive length, offensive items, limited usefulness for normal populations, misleading labels for the scales, inadequacy of the original normative sample, and the necessity of considering demographic variables. Some of these limitations have been corrected by the MMPI-2 and MMPI-A, including an option to decrease the length (by giving only the first 370 items for the MMPI-2 or first 350 items for the MMPI-A), increased appropriateness for normal populations, rewording of 82 of the items, and the use of a larger, more broad-based, modern normative sample. The limitations of the MMPI are also balanced by a number of significant assets, especially the extensive research relating to the meanings of the different scales and the relationships among scales. Extensive strategies are also in place to help refine and expand the meanings of scale elevations by using alternative scales (content, Harris-Lingoes, supplementary). Further assets are the MMPI's familiarity in the field, the development of subgroup norms, and extensive research in specific problem areas. Of central importance is that the MMPI has repeatedly proven itself to have practical value for clinicians, especially because the variables that the scales attempt to measure are meaningful and even essential areas of clinical information. Butcher (1979) has poignantly summarized the status of the MMPI by calling it "an outmoded but as yet unsurpassed psychopathology inventory" (p. 34). The over 10,000 studies on or using it, combined with its extensive clinical use provide ample evidence of its popularity. The 1989 restandardization should ensure that it not only continues to achieve the status of being an "unsurpassed psychopathology inventory" but will also be a more modern clinical tool.

ADMINISTRATION

The MMPI/MMPI-2 can be administered to persons who are 16 years of age or older with an eighth-grade reading level. As noted, it is possible to administer the MMPI/MMPI-2 to persons between 16 and 18, but adolescent norms need to be used. However, the preferred option for individuals between 14 and 18 is to have them take the MMPI-A. It is often helpful to augment the standard instructions on the MMPI-2 and MMPI-A booklets. In particular, examiners should give clients an explanation of the reason for testing and how the results will be used. It might also be pointed out that the test was designed to determine whether or not someone has either presented him- or herself in an unrealistically positive or exaggeratedly disturbed manner. Thus their best strategy is to be as honest and as clear as possible. Finally, it might be clarified that some or even many of the questions might seem a bit unusual.

They have been developed to assess individuals with a wide range of personality styles and problem presentations. If they don't apply to the person taking the test, then this should be indicated with either a true or a false response. Including this additional information is likely to result in less anxiety, more accurate responses, and greater rapport. Completion times for all persons taking the test should be noted.

The MMPI-2 and MMPI-A have only one booklet form although these are available in either softcover or hardcover. Completion of the first 370 items on the MMPI-2 and first 350 items on the MMPI-A allows for the scoring of the basic validity and standard clinical scales. The final 197 MMPI-2 and 128 MMPI-A items are used for scoring different supplementary and content scales. An online computer administration is available through National Computer Systems. For persons who have special difficulties, an individual (Box) form and a tape-recorded form have been developed. The Box form is most appropriate for persons who have difficulties concentrating and/or reading. Each item is presented on a card which the person is requested to place into one of three different sections to indicate a "true," "false," or "cannot say" response. The tape-recorded form is used for persons who have reading difficulties due to such factors as illiteracy, blindness, or aphasia.

The sometimes prohibitive length of the MMPI has encouraged the development of numerous short forms. However, none is sufficiently reliable or valid to be considered a substitute for the complete administration (Butcher & Hostetler, 1990; Butcher & Williams, 1992; Graham, 1993). The only acceptable abbreviated form is to administer all the items necessary for scoring only the basic validity and standard clinical scales (e.g., the first 370 MMPI-2 items or the first 350 MMPI-A items).

Some clinicians allow the client to take the MMPI under unsupervised conditions (such as at home). Butcher and Pope (1989) stress that this is not recommended, for the following reasons:

- The conditions are too dissimilar from those used for the normative samples and any significant change in proceedings might alter the results.
- Clients might consult others to determine which answers to make.
- The clinician cannot be aware of possible conditions that might have compromised reliability and validity.
- There is no assurance that the client actually completed the protocol him- or herself.

Thus, any administration should closely follow the administration procedures used for the normative samples. This means providing clear, consistent instructions, ensuring that the directions are understood, providing adequate supervision, and making sure the setting will enhance concentration by limiting noise and potential interruptions.

INTERPRETATION PROCEDURE

The following eight steps are recommended for interpreting MMPI-2/MMPI-A profiles. These steps should be followed with a knowledge and awareness of the implications of demographic variables such as age, culture, intellectual level, education, social class, and occupation. A summary of the relationship between MMPI profiles and some of the main demographic variables including age, culture, and intellectual level has already been provided. While looking at the overall configuration of the test (Steps 4, 5, and 6), clinicians can elaborate on the meanings of the different scales and the relationships among scales by consulting the interpretive hypotheses associated with them. These can be found in later sections of this chapter on validity scales, clinical scales, and two-point codes as well as sections on supplementary scales and content scales. The discussion of the various scales and codes represents an integration and summary of both primary sources as well as the following MMPI-2/MMPI-A resources: Archer (1992, 1994); Butcher et al. (1989); Butcher et al. (1990); Caldwell (1988); Dahlstrom et al. (1972); Graham (1993); Greene (1991); Greene and Clopton (1994); Keiller and Graham (1993); Lewak, Marks, and Nelson (1990); and Marks et al. (1974). In particular, the subsections on treatment implications have drawn on the work of Butcher (1990), Greene and Clopton (1994), and Lewak et al. (1990). Occasionally, additional quite recent material and/or relevant reviews/meta-analysis have been cited to either update material related to scale descriptions or highlight important areas of research.

Step 1. Completion Time

The examiner should note the length of time required to complete the test. For a mildly disturbed person who is 16 years or older with an average IQ and eighth-grade education, the total completion time for the MMPI-2 should be approximately 90 minutes. Computer administrations are usually 15 to 30 minutes shorter (60 to 75 minutes in total). The MMPI-A usually takes 60 minutes to complete with computer administrations taking 15 minutes less time (45 minutes in total). If two or more hours are required for the MMPI-2 or 1.5 or more for the MMPI-A, the following interpretive possibilities must be considered:

- Major psychological disturbance, particularly a severe depression or functional psychosis.
- Below-average IQ or poor reading ability resulting from an inadequate educational background.
- Cerebral impairment.

If, on the other hand, an examinee finishes in less than an hour, one should suspect an invalid profile, an impulsive personality, or both.

Note any erasures or pencil points on the answer sheet. The presence of a few of these signs may indicate that the person took the test seriously and reduces the likelihood of random marking; a great number of erasures may reflect obsessive-compulsive tendencies.

Step 2. Score and Plot the Profile

Complete the scoring and plot the profile. Specific directions for tabulating the MMPI-2 raw scores and converting them into profiles are provided in Appendix J. If examiners would like to score and profile the MMPI-2/MMPI-A content scales, Harris-Lingoes and *Si,* or the most frequently used supplementary scales, additional keys and profile forms may be obtained through National Computer Systems. In addition to the possibility of scoring alternative scales, clinicians should also compile further information, including IQ scores, relevant history, demographic variables, and observations derived from Steps 1 and 2.

Score the critical items (see Appendix K) and note which ones indicate important trends. It is often helpful at some point to review these items with the client and obtain elaborations. In particular, it would be essential to determine whether the person understood what the item was asking. Similarly, it can sometimes be helpful to examine the answer sheet and note which, if any, questions were omitted. A discussion with the client about why he or she chose not to respond might shed additional light on how he or she is functioning psychologically and what areas are creating conflict for him or her.

Step 3. Organize the Scales and Identify the Code Type

There are several options in arranging the test scores:

a. Simply list the scores according to the order in which they appear on the profile sheet (*L, F, K,* 1, 2, 3, etc.) with their *T* scores to the right of these scales. For the purposes of communicating scale scores, *T scores rather than raw scores should be used.*

b. Arrange the 10 clinical scales in order of descending elevation and place the three validity scales last. This makes it somewhat easier to determine the code type.

c. The following Welsh code symbols can be used to indicate the relative elevation of each scale. Note that this system has been slightly modified following the suggestion of Butcher and Williams (1992) by indicating a "+" for scores between 65 and 69. This enables clinicians to note when scores have first increased above the MMPI-2 cutoff of 65 (indicated by the upper darkened line on the profile sheet). Correspondingly, the "−" symbol which was used previously to denote scores between 60 and 69 has been reduced to a range indicating scores between 60 and 64.

Range	Elevation Symbol
100+	**
90–99 T	*
80–89 T	"
70–79 T	'
65–69 T	+
60–64 T	−
50–59 T	/
40–49 T	:
30–39 T	#
Under 29 T	No Symbol

In other words, all *T* scores above 100 have two asterisks (**) after them, all *T* scores between 90 and 99 have one asterisk after them, and so on. The following example shows how to Welsh code a set of *T* scores:

Before Welsh Coding:

No.	8	7	9	6	1	3	4		2		0		5
Scale	*Sc*	*Pt*	*Ma*	*Pa*	*Hs*	*Hy*	*Pd*	*F*	*D*	*L*	*Si*	*K*	*Mf*
T score	92	85	83	80	75	66	65	63	60	56	50	46	43

Note: The preceding *T* scores are arranged in descending magnitude, which makes it easier to assign them their correct Welsh code.

After Welsh Coding:

8*796"1'34 + F2 − LO/K5:

The coding procedure provides a shorthand method of recording MMPI-2/MMPI-A results. In addition, the abbreviations make it easy to determine code types. Code types can be determined by simply looking at the two highest scale elevations. For example, the code type in the above example would be a 87/78. The 87/78 code type can then be looked up in the "Two-Point Codes" section to obtain various descriptions relating to that code type. Note that Scales 5 (Masculinity-Femininity) and 0 (Social introversion) are not strictly clinical scales so they are not used in determining code type. Examiners should keep in mind that only well-defined code types can be safely interpreted (Butcher & Williams, 1992; Edwards et al., 1993; Graham, 1993; Tellegen & Ben-Porath, 1993). A well-defined code type is considered one in which the elevated scales are above 65 and the scales used to determine the code type are 5 or more *T* score points above the next highest scales. Less well-defined profiles should be interpreted by noting each scale that is elevated and then integrating the meanings derived from the different descriptors.

Step 4. Determine Profile Validity

Assess the validity of the profile by noting the pattern of the validity scales. There are a number of indicators suggesting invalid profiles which are described in the next section. However, the basic patterns include a defensive style in which pathology is minimized (elevated *L* and/or *K* on the MMPI-2 and MMPI-A) an exaggeration of pathology (elevated *F* and/or *Fb* on the MMPI-2 or *F*, *F*1, or *F*2 on the MMPI-A), or an inconsistent response pattern (elevated VRIN or TRIN on the MMPI-2 or MMPI-A). However, note that scoring and profiling for the VRIN and TRIN scales are not part of the standard procedures for the MMPI-2 although they are incorporated into the MMPI-A. In addition, clinicians should consider the context of the assessment to determine whether a defensive, fake bad, or inconsistent response style supports what is known about the client. In particular, the examiner should determine the likelihood that the examinee would potentially gain by over- or underreporting psychopathology.

Step 5. Determine Overall Level of Adjustment

Note the number of scales over 65 and the relative elevation of these scales. The degree to which F is elevated can also be an excellent indicator of the extent of pathology (assuming that it is not so high as to indicate an invalid profile). The greater the number and relative elevation of these scales, the more the individual is likely to have difficulties carrying out basic responsibilities and experience social and personal discomfort.

Step 6. Describe Symptoms, Behaviors, and Personality Characteristics

This step represents the core process in interpretation. Mild elevations on individual scales ($T = 60$–65) represent tendencies or trends in the individual's personality. Interpretations should be treated cautiously with the more extreme descriptors being deleted or rephrased to represent milder characteristics. Scores in this range on the MMPI-A are highlighted by being shaded, thereby designating a marginal or transitional zone between normality and pathology. Elevations above 65 on the MMPI-2 and MMPI-A are more strongly characteristic of the individual and, with progressively greater increases, are more likely to represent core features of personality functioning. However, basing interpretations solely on specific T score elevations may be misleading since a client's demographic characteristics often exert a strong influence. For example, persons with lower educational backgrounds usually score lower on K and Mf so that interpretations need to take this into account. Furthermore, different authors use different criteria for determining high and low scores. Some authors have used T score ranges (e.g., $T = 70$–80); others have defined elevated scores as being in the upper quartile; and still others have defined a high score as being the highest in a profile regardless of other T score elevations. This issue is further complicated because two persons with the same elevation on a scale but with quite different personal histories (e.g., psychiatric vs. adequate level of functioning) will have different interpretations that are appropriate for them. As a result, the descriptors in the following sections on interpretation do not designate specific T score elevations. Instead, more general descriptions associated with high and low scores have been provided. Clinicians will need to interpret the accuracy of these potential meanings by taking into consideration not merely the elevations, but other relevant variables as well. In addition, each of the descriptions are modal. They should be considered as *possible* interpretations that will not necessarily apply to all persons having a particular score. They are merely hypotheses in need of further verification. The exception to not providing specific scores is in the subsection on validity scales. The reason for the inclusion of validity T and sometimes raw scores is that there is extensive research on optimal cutoff scores.

During the interpretive process, do not merely note the meanings of the individual scales but also examine the overall pattern or configuration of the test and note the relative peaks and valleys. Typical configurations, for example, might include the "conversion V" reflecting a possible conversion disorder or elevated Scales 4 and 9, which reflect a high likelihood of acting-out behavior. Note especially any scales greater than 65 or less than 40 as being particularly important for the overall interpretation. The meaning of two-point code configurations can be determined by consulting the corresponding section in this chapter ("Two-Point Codes"). When working to understand the meaning of a profile with two or more elevated clinical scales, it is recommended that clinicians read the descriptors for the individual scales, as well as relevant two-point code descriptions. It is also recommended that, when reading about elevations on single scales, clinicians should read the meanings of high and low elevations, as well as the more general information on the relevant scale. Further elaboration on the meaning of the scale elevations and code types can be obtained by scoring and interpreting the content scales, Harris-Lingoes and Si subscales, supplementary scales, and/or the critical items; these scales are discussed later in this chapter. Graham (1993) recommends that, whenever possible, descriptions related to the following areas should be developed: symptoms, major needs (e.g., dependency, autonomy, achievement, responsibility), perceptions of the environment (e.g., significant people), reactions to stress including coping strategies and defenses, self-concept, emotional control, interpersonal relationships, and psychological resources. When interpretive information is available, clinicians can examine an individual's profile in combination with the requirements of the referral questions to determine relevant descriptions for each of these areas.

Profile Definition

As noted previously, a clearly defined code type is indicated by both a high elevation and either single scales which are elevated with no other "competing" scale elevations (so-called spike profiles) or clear code types in which the elevated scales in the code types similarly do not have competing scales that are close to the degree of elevations of the scales in the code. Well-defined elevations indicate greater validity of the relevant descriptors. In addition, they are more likely to be stable over time (high test-retest reliability).

Poorly Defined Profiles

If the elevation is not particularly high (generally $T = 60-65$), then the interpretations need to be modified by either toning down the descriptors to a more normal level, or deleting the more extreme descriptors. Often the content, Harris-Lingoes, and supplementary scales can be useful in understanding the meaning of elevations in the $T = 60-64$ range. If the profile is poorly defined because there are additional scales that "compete" with the scales in the code type (e.g., 27/72 code type but with Scales 1 and 8 also elevated nearly as high as Scales 2 and 7), then several strategies need to be used. The safest and most conservative strategy is that descriptors which occur in common among all the different elevated scales can be considered to be the most valid (e.g., anxiety is likely to be a common descriptor for elevations on Scales 1, 2, 7, and 8; this is strengthened if 7 is the most highly elevated scale). In addition, examiners need to make an effort to understand and integrate the interpretations given under each of the individual scale descriptions. Furthermore, the meanings of alternative code type combinations need to be considered and integrated (e.g., if Scales 2, 7, 1, and 8 are all elevated, then the following code type descriptors need to be considered: 27/72, 18/81, 87/78, 12/21, 17/71, and 28/82). Finally, with poorly defined elevations, it becomes increasingly important to use the content, Harris-Lingoes, critical items, and supplementary scales to more fully understand and refine the meanings of the clinical scale elevations.

Use of Content Scales

The content scales can be used to supplement, extend, confirm, and refine interpretations derived from the basic validity and standard clinical scales. Furthermore, some of the content scales (e.g., TPA/Type A, WRK/Work Interference) provide additional information not included in the clinical scales. The adult content scales are divided into the clusters of internal symptoms, external aggressive tendencies, negative self-view, and general problem areas. Similarly, the adolescent content scales are divided into scales reflecting interpersonal functioning, treatment recommendations, and academic difficulties (see section entitled "Content Scales").

Harris-Lingoes and Si Subscales

To understand which personality and clinical variables of a person might have been responsible for elevating the clinical scales, clinicians might wish to selectively use the rationally devised Harris-Lingoes and Social Introversion subscales. These scales (or subscales) organize clusters of content-related items so that the different dimensions of the scales can be more clearly differentiated. For example, it might be found that an elevation on Scale 4 (Psychopathic Deviate) was due primarily to family discord. In contrast, criminal acting out might be suggested by subscale elevations on authority conflict and social imperturbability. This would then have implications for both interpretations as well as case management (see section "Harris-Lingoes Scales").

Critical Items

Clinicians may also wish to evaluate the meanings of content related to specific items the client has endorsed by investigating critical items (see section "Critical Items").

Supplementary Scales

The empirically derived supplementary scales can also be used to both refine the meanings of the clinical scales, as well as add additional information not included in the clinical scales (see section "Supplementary Scales").

Low Scale Scores

For the most part, low scale scores (below *T* score of 35 or 40) are likely to represent strengths and these may serve to modify any high scale elevations.

Specific Interpretive Guidelines Organized Around Symptom Domains

Suppression (constriction). Scales 5 *(Mf)* and 0 *(Si)* are sometimes referred to as suppressor scales in that, if either or both are elevated, they tend to suppress or "soften" the expression of characteristics suggested by other elevated scores.

Acting Out (impulsivity). In contrast to Scales 5 *(Mf)* and 0 *(Si)*, Scales 4 *(Pd)*, and 9 *(Ma)* are sometimes referred to as "releaser" or "excitatory scales," and if one or both are elevated, this reflects that the person is likely to act out difficulties. This hypothesis is further strengthened if 0 *(Si)* is also quite low.

Internalizing Coping Style. Similar to the preceding two guidelines are indicators of internalizing versus externalizing coping styles. If the combined scores for Scales 4 *(Pd)*, 6 *(Pa)*, and 9 *(Ma)* are lower than the combined scores for 2 *(D)*, 7 *(Pt)*, and 0 *(Si)*, then the individual can be considered to have an internalizing coping style.

Externalizing Coping Style. In contrast to the preceding, an individual who has combined scores on 4 *(Pd)*, 6 *(Pa)*, and 9 *(Ma)* that are greater than his or her combined scores on 2 *(D)*, 7 *(Pt)*, and 0 *(Si)* can be considered to have an externalizing coping style.

Overcontrol (repression). Rigid overcontrol of impulses, particularly hostility, is suggested by elevations on 3 *(Hy)* and the O-H (Overcontrolled Hostility) supplementary scale.

Anger (loss of control). Angry loss of control is suggested by elevations on the ANG (Anger) content scale.

Subjective Distress. A general check on the degree of subjective stress a person is encountering can be determined by noting the degree to which scales 2 *(D)* and 7 *(Pt)* are elevated.

Anxiety. Elevations on Scale 7 *(Pt)*, especially if 7 *(Pt)* is greater than 8 *(Sc)*, suggest anxiety.

Depression. A high score on 2 *(D)* combined with a low score on 9 *(Ma)* is particularly indicative of depression.

Mania. A high score on 9 *(Ma)* combined with a low score on 2 *(D)* suggests mania.

Psychosis. A high score on 8 *(Sc)* especially if 8 *(Sc)* is 10 points or more higher than 7 *(Pt)* suggests psychosis.

Confusion and Disorientation. Elevations above $T = 80$ on F, 8 *(Sc)*, and 7 *(Pt)* suggest a confused, disoriented state. Confusion can also be suggested if the mean for all 8 clinical scales (this excludes Scales 5 and 0 since these are not strictly clinical scales) is greater than $T = 70$.

Suspicion Mistrust. If 6 *(Pa)* is moderate to highly elevated and, especially if 6 is the highest scale, then suspicion and mistrust is strongly indicated.

Dominance. Dominance is suggested by elevations on the *Do* supplementary scale.

Introversion. Introversion is indicated by elevations on the 0 *(Si)* scale.

Obsessiveness. Obsessiveness is indicated by elevations on 7 *(Pt*; especially when this is the highest point) and elevations on the OBS/Obsessiveness content scale.

Cynicism. Cynicism is indicated by elevations on the CYN (Cynicism) content scale.

Drug or Alcohol Problems. Elevations on Scales 4 *(Pd)*, 2 *(D)*, and 7 *(Pt)* are consistent with (although not diagnostic of) drug- and alcohol-related problems. Lifestyle and personality patterns consistent with, and suggesting proneness to drug and alcohol patterns, are indicated by elevations on MAC-R and the Alcohol

Potential Scale (APS). Clear awareness of and open discussion of alcohol and/or drug problems are indicated by elevations on the Alcohol Acknowledgment Scale (AAS).

Quality and Style of Interpersonal Relations.   Scales that are most useful for understanding the patterns of interpersonal relations include the following: 0 (*Si*; level of sociability, shyness, social avoidance, alienation), Social Discomfort Scale (SDS; social discomfort), 1 (*Hs*; complaining, critical, demanding, indirect expression of hostility, passive, preoccupied with self), 4 (*Pd*; good first impressions but use others for their own needs, outgoing, talkative, energetic but also shallow and superficial, and impulsive), 6 (*Pa*; moralistic, suspicious, hypersensitive, resentful, guarded), 8 (isolated from social environment, seclusive, withdrawn, inaccessible, feels misunderstood), Marital Distress Scale (MDS; presence of marital distress), and Dominance (*Do*; assertive, dominant, takes the initiative, confident).

The preceding topic areas and interpretive strategies are intended to be basic, rule-of-thumb approaches to help guide hypothesis generation around specific areas. There are certainly other relevant areas but the ones listed can generally be considered to be the most important. While these guidelines will serve to alert clinicians to specific areas, they will still need to investigate these areas in far more depth by consulting relevant scale descriptors and patterns between scales. Clinicians may also wish to consult one of the MMPI-2/MMPI-A resources listed in the recommended readings to further extend and expand on the meanings of different profiles.

Step 7. Provide Diagnostic Impressions

Although the original MMPI as well as the MMPI-2/MMPI-A have not been successful in leading directly to diagnosis, they can often contribute considerable information relevant to diagnostic formulations. In the section on code types, possible *DSM-IV* diagnoses consistent with each code type have been included. Clinicians should consider these, along with additional available information, to help make an accurate diagnosis. In some contexts and for some types of referral questions this will be relevant, but for other contexts and referral questions, formal diagnosis will neither be required nor will it be appropriate (e.g., employment screening). A further review of the considerations and guidelines described in Step 6 might be useful in extracting relevant information for diagnosis.

Step 8. Elaborate on Treatment Implications and Recommendations

Often, one of the most valuable services a practitioner can provide is to predict the client's likelihood of benefiting from interventions. This typically means elaborating on the person's strengths and weaknesses, level of defensiveness, ability to form a treatment relationship, predicted response to psychotherapy (note especially Es and TRT scales), antisocial tendencies, and level of insight. Much of this information is summarized at the ends of the subsections on scale elevations and code types. If doing extensive work with specific types of clients, clinicians might need to expand on the knowledge relating to types and outcome of treatments by referring to the extensive research base that is available (e.g., chronic pain, substance abuse, outcomes related to specific code types). Butcher's (1990) *MMPI-2 in Psychological Treatment* can be particularly helpful in this regard. Treatment responsiveness might be further extended into providing suggestions for tailoring specific interventions for client profiles and types of problems. Reviewing the areas, considerations, and guidelines described in Step 6 might be useful in extracting information relevant to treatment planning. Further useful resources in this process are Greene (1994) and Clopton and Archer's (1994) chapters, both of which are in Maruish's (1994) *The Use of Psychological Testing for Treatment Planning and Outcome Assessment.* Lewak et al. (1990) not only provide implications for treatment but also outline a step-by-step procedure for translating MMPI-2 results into feedback for the client. These steps include specific issues for the client (e.g., "Working on a single task may be difficult for you"), background and early life experiences (e.g., "People with your profile have always had a lot of energy and ambition"), and self-help suggestions ("Do not make any changes in your life or goals until you have discussed these and thought them through with someone else").

COMPUTERIZED INTERPRETATION

Computerized interpretation systems are an important and frequently used adjunct to MMPI interpretation. The number of such services has grown considerably since 1965 when the first system was developed by the Mayo Clinic. Major providers are National Computer Systems, Roche Psychiatric Service Institute (RPSI), Clinical Psychological Services, Inc. (using the Caldwell Report), Western Psychological Services, and Behaviordyne Psychodiagnostic Laboratory Service. A description and evaluation of many of these services is included in the *Mental Measurements Yearbook* (9th, 10th, 11th eds.; 1985, 1989, 1992). Lists and descriptions of software packages available for personal computers can be found in Krug's (1993) *Psychware Sourcebook* (4th ed.) or Stoloff and Couch's (1992) *Computer Use in Psychology: A Directory of Software* (3rd ed.).

Caution in the use of different computer-based interpretive systems is important since the interpretive services and software packages are highly varied in terms of quality, and most of them have untested or only partially tested validity. Many do not specify the extent to which they were developed using empirical guidelines versus clinical intuition. Each computerized system has a somewhat different approach. Some provide screening, descriptive summaries, and cautions relating to treatment, whereas others provide extensive elaborations on interpretations or may provide optional interpretive printouts for the clients themselves.

The rationale behind computerized systems is that they are efficient and can accumulate and integrate large amounts of information derived from the vast literature on the MMPI, which even experienced clinicians cannot be expected to recall. However, serious questions have been raised regarding misuse (Groth-Marnat, 1985; Groth-Marnat & Schumaker, 1989; Matarazzo, 1986). In particular, computerized services are limited to standard interpretations and are not capable of integrating the unique variables usually encountered in dealing with clinical cases. This is a significant factor, which untrained personnel may be more likely to either overlook or inadequately evaluate. In response to these issues, the American Psychological Association developed a set of guidelines to ensure the proper use of computerized interpretations (APA, 1986, 1994). It should be stressed that, although computerized systems can offer information from a wide variety of accumulated data, their interpretations are still not end products. Like all test data, they need to be placed in the context of the client's overall background and current situation, and integrated within the framework of additional test data.

VALIDITY SCALES

The MMPI was one of the first tests to develop scales to detect whether or not respondents were answering in such a manner as to invalidate the overall results. This tradition has continued and been expanded into the newer MMPI-2 and MMPI-A. Meta-analyses of studies on the various validity scales generally indicates that they are able to effectively detect faking. Probably the most effective strategy is the *F* scale's ability to detect overreporting of pathology (Bagby, Buis, & Nicholson, 1995; Bagby, Rogers, & Buis, 1994; Berry, Baer, & Harris, 1991; Graham, Watts, & Timbrook, 1991; Iverson, Franzen, & Hammond, 1995) and the *K* scale, while still useful, is somewhat less effective in detecting underreporting (Baer, Wetter, & Berry, 1992; Graham et al., 1991). However, adding two supplementary validity scales (Social Desirability scale, Superlative scale) to *L* and *K* can serve to increase the detection of underreporting (Baer, Wetter, Nichols, Greene, & Berry, 1995). Despite the consensus related to the accuracy of detection, a concern is that a wide range of cutoff scores are recommended depending on the group being assessed (Bagby et al., 1994; Bagby et al., 1995; Stein, Graham, & Williams, 1995). For example, optimal cutoffs scores for normals faking bad are lower than psychiatric patients faking bad (Berry et al., 1991; Graham et al., 1991). An unresolved issue is whether normals who are motivated to fake bad as well as given information on how to fake (e.g., symptom patterns of individuals with posttraumatic stress disorder, paranoid schizophrenia, schizophrenia) can avoid detection. Some research indicates that, even with motivation and a clear strategy, they still cannot avoid detection (Sivec, Hilsenroth, & Lynn, 1995; Wetter, Baer, Berry, Robinson, & Sumpter, 1993), whereas other research suggests that strategic (informed) fakers can consistently produce profiles that are indistinguishable from true patients (Rogers, Bagby, & Chakraborty, 1993; Wetter & Deitsch, 1996). Attempts to fake bad might be particularly likely to succeed if subjects are given information on the design and intent of the validity scales (Lamb, Berry, Wetter, & Baer, 1994).

The standard MMPI-2 profile sheets (validity and clinical scales) include only the original *L, F,* and *K* validity scales. The more recent *Fb,* VRIN, and TRIN validity scales have been included on the profile sheet for the supplementary scales. In contrast, the MMPI-A has included the newer VRIN, TRIN, *F*1, and *F*2 validity scales on the same profile sheet as the standard clinical scales. A further difference between the original MMPI and the MMPI-2 is that the MMPI-2 provides the option of profile sheets that can either include *K* corrections or sheets that omit this procedure. The MMPI-A does not include the *K* correction on its profile sheets. This is because, in some contexts, particularly those for adolescents, the *K* correction is not appropriate (Colby, 1989).

The ? "Scale" (Cannot Say; *Cs*)

The ? scale (abbreviated by either ? or *Cs*) is not actually a formal scale but merely represents the number of items left unanswered on the profile sheet. The MMPI-2 does not even include a column for profiling a ? *(Cs)* scale, but merely provides a section to include the total number of unanswered questions. The usefulness of noting the total number of unanswered questions is to provide one of several indices of a protocol's validity. If 30 or more items are left unanswered, the protocol is most likely invalid and no further interpretations should be attempted. This is simply because an insufficient number of items have been responded to, which means less information is available for scoring the scales. Thus, less confidence can be placed in the results. To minimize the number of "cannot say" responses, the client should be encouraged to answer all questions.

A high number of unanswered questions can occur for a variety of reasons. It might indicate difficulties with reading, psychomotor retardation, indecision, confusion, or extreme defensiveness. These difficulties might be consistent with severe depression, obsessional states, extreme intellectualization, or unusual interpretations of the items. Defensiveness might stem from legalistic overcautiousness or a paranoid condition. High *Cs* might also occur due to the perception that the unanswered items are irrelevant.

The *L* Scale

The *L* or "lie" scale consists of 15 items that indicate the extent to which a client is attempting to describe him- or herself in an unrealistically positive manner. Thus, high scorers describe themselves in an overly perfectionistic and idealized manner. The items consist of descriptions of relatively minor flaws to which most people are willing to admit. Thus, a person scoring high on the *L* Scale might answer "False" to item 102, "I get angry sometimes." However, persons from uneducated, lower socioeconomic backgrounds are likely to score somewhat lower on *L* than those from higher socioeconomic backgrounds with more education. On the original MMPI, the *L* score is scored by counting the total number of false responses to items 15, 45, 75, 135, 165, 195, 225, 255, 285, 30, 60, 90, 120, and 150. The MMPI-2 and MMPI-A provide separate scoring keys.

High Scores on L

Evaluating whether an *L* scale is elevated requires that the person's demographic characteristics first be considered. A raw score of 4 or 5 would be a moderate score for lower-class persons or persons from the middle class who are laborers. In contrast, a raw score of 4 or 5 would be considered high for college-educated persons unless it can be explained based on their occupation (e.g., clergy). If the client's score is considered high, then it may indicate the person is describing him- or herself in an overly favorable light. This may be due to conscious deception or, alternatively, might be due to an unrealistic view of him- or herself. Such clients may be inflexible, unoriginal, unaware of the impressions they make on others, and perceive their world in a rigid, self-centered manner. As a result of their rigidity, they may have a low tolerance to stress. Since they will deny any flaws in themselves, their insight will be poor. This is likely to make them poor candidates for psychotherapy. Extremely high scores would suggest that they are ruminative, extremely rigid, and will experience difficulties in relationships. This may be consistent with many paranoids who place considerable emphasis on denying their personal flaws and instead project them onto others. Extremely high scores might also be the result of conscious deception by antisocial personalities.

Low Scores on L

Low scores suggest that clients were frank and open regarding their responses to the items. They are able to admit minor faults in themselves and may also be articulate, relaxed, socially ascendant, and self-reliant. Low scorers might also indicate clients who are somewhat sarcastic and cynical.

The *F* Scale (Infrequency)

The *F* (Infrequency) scale measures the extent to which a person answers in an atypical and deviant manner. The MMPI and MMPI-2 *F* scale items were selected based on their being endorsed by less than 10% of the population. Thus, from a statistical definition, they reflect nonconventional thinking. For example, a response is scored if the client answers "True" to item 49, "It would be better if almost all laws were thrown away" or "False" to 64, "I like to visit places where I have never been before." However, the items do not cohere around any particular trait or syndrome. This indicates that a client who scores high is answering in a scorable direction to a wide variety of unusual characteristics. As might be expected, high scores on *F* are typically accompanied by high scores on many of the clinical scales. High scores can often be used as a general indicator of pathology. In particular, high scores can reflect unusual feelings due to some specific life circumstance to which the person is reacting. This might include grieving, job loss, or divorce. A person scoring high may also be "faking bad," which could serve to invalidate the protocol. No exact cutoff score is available to determine whether a profile is invalid or is accurately reflecting pathology. Even *T* scores from 70 to 90 do not necessarily reflect an invalid profile particularly among prison or inpatient populations. In general, moderate elevations represent an openness to unusual experiences and possible psychopathology, but it is not until more extreme elevations that an invalid profile is suspected. Further information can be obtained by consulting the *F-K* index and *F* back scale (see sections on *F-K* index and *F* back or *Fb*).

The 66-item MMPI-A *F* scale was constructed in a similar manner as the MMPI-2 *F* scale. However, since adolescents are more likely to endorse unusual experiences, a more liberal criterion of 20% endorsement was used for inclusion. The MMPI-A *F* scale was further divided into *F*1 scales to assess validity for the first portion of the booklet (clinical scales) and *F*2 to assess the last portion of the book (supplementary and content scales; see sections on *F-K* index, *F*1 and *F*2).

High Scores on F

Scores approximating 100 or greater suggest an invalid profile. This might have been caused by clerical errors in scoring, random responding, false claims by the client regarding symptoms, or distortions caused by a respondent's confused and delusional thinking. If, in the rare cases where psychiatric scores of 100 do reflect a valid assessment, it indicates hallucinations, delusions of reference, poor judgment, and/or extreme withdrawal. Because of the variations in scores between normals and psychiatric patients, different recommendations for indicating an invalid profile have been provided for each of these groups. For normal adult populations faking bad, an MMPI-2 raw cutoff score of 18 (male $T = 95$; female $T = 99$) is recommended, whereas for psychiatric patients faking bad, a higher raw cutoff score of 29 ($T = 120+$) is recommended for males and 27 ($T = 119+$) for females (Graham et al., 1991). No optimal cutoff scores for the MMPI-A have yet been developed.

In evaluating the possibility of an invalid profile, T scores of 80 to 99 suggest malingering, an exaggeration of difficulties, resistance to testing, or significant levels of pathology. In those cases where this range accurately reflects pathology, clients should have corresponding histories and behavioral observations indicating they are disoriented, restless, moody, and dissatisfied. Scores of 70 to 80 suggest the client has unconventional and unusual thoughts and may be rebellious, antisocial, and/or having difficulties in establishing a clear identity. Scores from 70 to 90 might represent a "cry for help" in which persons are being quite open regarding their difficulties in an attempt to indicate they need assistance. If a client scores from 65 to 75, but does not seem to be pathological, he or she might be curious, complex, psychologically sophisticated, opinionated, unstable, and/or moody.

Low Scores on F

Low scores on *F* indicate that clients perceive the world like most other people. However, if their history suggests pathology, they might be denying difficulties ("faking good"). This distinction might be made by noting the relative elevation on *K* and interpreting the significance of the *F-K* index.

Fb (*F* back) Scale (MMPI-2); *F*1 and *F*2 (MMPI-A)

The 40-item MMPI-2 *Fb* was developed in conjunction with the restandardization of the MMPI. It was designed to identify a "fake bad" mode of responding for the last 197 items. This might be important since the traditional *F* scale was derived only from items taken from what are now the first 370 questions on the MMPI-2. Without the *Fb* scale, no check on the validity of the later questions would be available. It might be possible for a person to answer the earlier items accurately and later change to an invalid mode of responding. This is important for the supplementary and content scales since many of them are derived either partially or fully from the last 197 questions. The *Fb* scale was developed in the same manner as the earlier *F* scale in that items with low endorsement frequency (less than 10% of nonpatient adults) were included. Thus, a high score suggests the person was answering the items in an unusual mode. As with the *F* scale, this could indicate either generalized pathology or that the person was attempting to exaggerate his or her level of symptomatology.

Somewhat similar to the MMPI-2, the MMPI-A includes a 66-item *F* scale that is divided into *F*1 and *F*2 subscales. The *F*1 scale is composed of 33 items, all of which appear on the first half (initial 236 items) of the MMPI-A booklet, and relates to the standard clinical scales. In contrast, the 33-item *F*2 scale is composed of items on the last half of the booklet (final 114 items) and relates to the supplementary and clinical scales. The *F*1 and *F*2 scales can be interpreted in much the same way as for

F and *Fb* on the MMPI-2. The optimal MMPI-2 *Fb* raw cutoff for normal males faking bad has been recommended as being 19 ($T = 120$), and for normal females the recommended raw score is 22 ($T = 120+$; Graham et al., 1991). In contrast, optimal raw cutoffs for adult psychiatric patients were a somewhat higher 23 ($T = 120+$) for males and 24 ($T = 120+$) for females. No optimal cutoff scores have yet been developed for the MMPI-A. However, the *Fb* scale has not been found to be as effective a predictor of malingering as the *F* scale (Iverson et al., 1995).

Useful interpretive information can sometimes be obtained by noting the following relationships between *F* and *Fb* and between *F*1 and *F*2:

- **Highly elevated MMPI-2 *F* and *Fb* or highly elevated MMPI-A *F*, *F*1, and *F*2 inclusive (generally above 100).** No further interpretation since both clinical and content scales will not be valid.

- **Moderate to low MMPI-2 *F* but elevated *Fb* or moderate to low MMPI-A *F*1 but elevated *F*2 (*F*/*F*1 below 89; *Fb*/*F*2 above 90).** The clinical scales are probably valid and can be interpreted but the content and supplementary scales should be considered invalid, possibly the result of boredom or fatigue when taking the later portion of the test. However, if the *F* or *F*2 scales are in the 75 to 89 range, then it would be expected that there would also be a corresponding psychiatric history to explain these elevations.

- **Moderate to low MMPI-2 *F* and *Fb* or moderate to low MMPI-A *F*1 and *F*2 (F and Fb both below 89).** All scales can be considered to not be invalidated due to over reporting of pathology. Again note that, for the 75 to 89 range, there should also be a history of psychological difficulties which is consistent with these elevations.

The *K* Scale

The *K* scale was designed to detect clients who are describing themselves in overly positive terms. It therefore has a similarity with the *L* scale. The *K* scale, however, is more subtle and effective. Whereas only naive, moralistic, and unsophisticated individuals would score high on *L*, more intelligent and psychologically sophisticated persons might have somewhat high *K* scores and yet be unlikely to have any significant elevation on *L*. Persons from low socioeconomic and educational backgrounds score somewhat lower on *K* so, for these groups, this might need to be taken into account during interpretation.

Moderate scorers often have good ego strength, effective emotional defenses, good contact with reality, and excellent coping skills. Typically, they are concerned with and often skilled in making socially acceptable responses. As might be expected, *K* scores are inversely related to scores on Scales 8, 7, and 0. Elevations on *K* can also represent ego defensiveness and guardedness. This might occur with persons who avoid revealing themselves due to personality style or because something might be gained by conveying a highly favorable impression (e.g., employment). There is no clear cutoff for differentiating between positive ego strength (adjustment), ego defensiveness, or faking good. A general guideline is that the more ego-defensive the person is, the more likely it is that some of the clinical scales might also be elevated. Helpful information can also be obtained through the *F-K* index, relevant history, and the context of the testing (legal proceedings, employment evaluation, etc.).

Since a defensive test-taking approach is likely to suppress the clinical scales, a *K* correction is added to five of the MMPI-2 clinical scales (1/*Hs*, 4/*Pd*, 7/*Pt*, 8/*Sc*, 9/*Ma*) to compensate for this defensiveness. This correction is obtained by taking a designated fraction of *K* and adding it to the relevant scale (see directions in Appendix J). However, the basis of the *K* correction has been called into question. It has been omitted from the MMPI-A and the MMPI-2 contains separate scoring sheets with and without the *K* correction so that examiners can decide whether they wish to use it or not.

High Scores on K

Scores that are much higher than would be expected (generally above *T* = 65 or 70) given the person's history suggest that clients are attempting to describe themselves in an overly favorable light or deny their difficulties, or that they answered false to all items (nay-saying). If the profile is considered to be valid, high scores indicate such persons are presenting an image of being in control and functioning effectively, but they will overlook any faults they might have. They will have poor insight and resist psychological evaluation. Since they will resist being in a patient role, their ability to benefit from psychotherapy will be limited. They will be intolerant of nonconformity in others and perceive them as weak. Their typical defense will be denial and, due to their poor insight, will be unaware of the impression they make on others. They might also be shy, inhibited, and have a low level of social interaction.

Moderate Scores on K

Moderate scores (*T* = 56–64) suggest moderate levels of defensiveness, as well as a number of potential positive qualities. These clients may be independent, self-reliant, express an appropriate level of self-disclosure, and have good ego strength. Their verbal ability and social skills might also be good. Even though they might admit to some "socially acceptable" difficulties, they might minimize other important conflicts. They would be unlikely to seek help. Moderate scores in adolescents contraindicates acting out.

Low Scores on K

Low scores suggest a fake bad profile in which the person exaggerates his or her pathology. It might also suggest a protocol in which all the responses have been marked true. In an otherwise valid profile, the client might be disoriented and confused, extremely self-critical, cynical, skeptical, dissatisfied, and have inadequate defenses. He or she would be likely to have a poor self-concept with a low level of insight. Low scores among adolescents are not uncommon and may reflect a greater level of openness and sensitivity to their problems. It might be consistent with their undergoing a critical self-assessment related to establishing a clear sense of identity. Low scores are also quite common among clients from lower socioeconomic levels and, as such, would not be as likely to suggest difficulties with adjustment.

The *F-K* Index (Dissimulation Index)

The difference between scores on *F* and *K* can provide an index of the likelihood that a person is producing an invalid profile. This index can be determined by subtracting the raw score (not *T* scores) on *K* from the raw score on *F*. At the present time, *F-K* should be used cautiously for the MMPI-2 since not only have some of the items on *F* and *K* been worded differently from the MMPI, but 4 of the original 64 MMPI items have been removed from the *F* scale. This may result in subtle distortions of the meaning of the *F-K* index. Because not enough is known about the *F-K* index for adolescents, it should not be used on the MMPI-A.

F-K = +12 (Normal Females) or +17 (Normal Males)/+25 (Female Psychiatric Patients) or +27 (Male Psychiatric Patients)

The values provided are optimal cutoff points based on gender and psychiatric status. Note that, since many of the clinical scales are highly correlated with *F* (and are likely to be elevated among psychiatric patients), it takes a much higher *F-K* index among psychiatric patients to indicate a fake bad profile. The values given are minimum cut-off scores so values of increasing magnitude further reinforce the interpretation of an invalid profile consistent with malingering. These scores are higher than the previously recommended cutoff of 11. This earlier more liberal cutoff might help to explain many examiners' clinical experience of having a high number of potentially invalid profiles among patient populations. The current more stringent cutoffs should significantly reduce the number of questionable profiles among this group. Note, however, that persons might have elevated *F-K* indexes (approaching or even exceeding the optimal cut-off scores) for a number of reasons including a cry for help consistent with persons who are experiencing a wide number of symptomlike behaviors due to a temporary re-action to situational stress. An elevated *F-K* index might also occur in persons who overdramatize their difficulties. They would then be expected to be self-indulgent, self-pitying, unstable, narcissistic, or histrionic. They might be using and even exploit-ing their current difficulties to manipulate others and/or gain attention (a "psycho-chondriac"). Elevated *F-K* scores might also be found in severely disturbed psychiatric patients who have distorted self-perceptions and, a wide range of symptoms, and who therefore provide deviant responses to the items.

F-K = −11 or Less

Low *F-K* indexes have traditionally been used to indicate minimization of difficulties and defensiveness in which the client is attempting to present an overly favorable image. Interpretations of the rest of the clinical scales will thus have been made with extreme caution. However, the *F-K* index (or K elevation) for detecting a fake good profile has not been nearly as effective as for detecting fake bad profiles (Baer et al., 1992; Berry et al., 1991; Graham et al., 1991). Thus, interpretation of underreporting of symptomology (fake good) should be made with caution.

F-K = −20 or Less

An index this low indicates extreme defensiveness. This may be due either to conscious deception or to the inability of persons to admit to any personal inadequacies. Their approach to evaluation will be extremely negative to the extent that they may refuse to cooperate. Since they will have a distorted image with low levels of insight, they would be poor candidates for psychotherapy. However, note the earlier caution relating to the interpretation of the *F-K* index for detecting fake good profiles.

VRIN (Variable Response Inconsistency Scale)

The VRIN scale is a new MMPI-2 and MMPI-A validity scale designed to complement the existing validity scales. It comprises pairs of selected questions that would be expected to be answered in a consistent manner if the person is approaching the testing in a valid manner. Each pair of items is either similar or opposite in content. It would be expected that similar items would be answered in the same direction. If a person answers in the opposite direction, then it indicates an inconsistent response and is therefore scored as one raw score on the VRIN scale. Pairs of items with opposite contents would be expected to be answered in opposite directions. If instead, these pairs are answered in the same direction, this would represent inconsistent responding, which would also be scored as one raw score point on the VRIN scale.

High VRIN (MMPI-2 T = 80; *MMPI-A* T = 75)

A high number of inconsistent responses suggests indiscriminate responding. Thus, the profile would be considered to be invalid and should not be interpreted. *T* scores 5 to 10 points below this (MMPI-2 70-79; MMPI-A 70-74) also raise the possibility that the profile is invalid. If VRIN is high along with a high *F,* this further suggests that the person has answered in a random manner. In contrast, a low or moderate VRIN accompanied by high *F* suggests that the person was either severely disturbed, or was intentionally attempting to exaggerate symptoms.

TRIN (True Response Inconsistency Scale)

The MMPI-2 and MMPI-A TRIN scales are like the VRIN scale in comprising pairs of items. However, only pairs with opposite contents are included. This means there would be two ways for a person to obtain a response that would be scored on the VRIN scale. A "True" response to both items would indicate inconsistency and would therefore be scored as plus one raw score point. A "False" response to both pairs would also indicate inconsistency but would be scored as minus one point (negative scores are avoided by adding a constant).

Very High Scores (MMPI-2 T = 80+ *; MMPI-A* T = 75+ *)*

Scores in this range indicate that the person is indiscriminately answering "True" to the items (acquiescence or yea-saying). However, *T* scores 5 to 10 points (MMPI-2 70-79; MMPI-A 70-74) below the indicated cutoffs can still raise the possibility of an invalid profile. Thus an elevated TRIN is interpreted in much the same way as elevated VRIN profiles. Correspondingly, a high *F* accompanied by a high TRIN suggests indiscriminate responding whereas a high *F* and a low to moderate TRIN suggests either excessive pathology or an exaggeration of symptoms.

CLINICAL SCALES

Scale 1. Hypochondriasis *(Hs)*

Scale 1 was originally designed to distinguish hypochondriacs from other types of psychiatric patients. Although it can suggest a diagnosis of hypochondriasis, it is most useful as a scale to indicate a variety of personality characteristics that are often consistent with but not necessarily diagnostic of hypochondriasis. High scorers not only show a high concern with illness and disease, but are also likely to be egocentric, immature, pessimistic, sour, whiny, and passive aggressive. They rarely act out directly but rather express hostility indirectly and are likely to be critical of others. Their complaints are usually related to a wide variety of physical difficulties. An important purpose of these complaints is to manipulate and control others. Low scores suggest an absence of these complaints.

Scale 1 may also be elevated along with Scales 2, 3, and 7. This would reflect corresponding levels of depression, denial, conversions, or anxiety states. However, persons who score high on 1 typically experience little overt anxiety. A conversion V occurs when there are elevations on Scales 1 and 3 along with a significant lowering (10 or more points) on 2. This profile suggests that the person converts psychological conflicts into bodily complaints (see 13/31 code type).

High Scores on Scale 1

Persons with high scores on Scale 1 are described as stubborn, pessimistic, narcissistic, and egocentric. Symptom complaints typically include epigastric complaints, pain, fatigue, and headaches. While they will have a reduced level of efficiency, they are rarely completely incapacitated. Others might perceive them as dull, unenthusiastic, ineffective, and unambitious. They will use their symptom-related complaints to manipulate others and, as a result, will make others around them miserable. Their symptom-related complaints are vague and diffuse and will often shift to various locations on their bodies. They often overuse the medical system and their histories might reveal numerous visits to a wide variety of practitioners. However, they refuse to believe assurances that their difficulties have no organic basis. Each time they visit a physician, they will recite a long series of symptom complaints (sometimes referred to as an "organ recital"). Their symptoms are usually not reactions to situational stress but more of long-standing duration. Persons with moderate scores may have a true organic basis for their difficulties. However, even moderately high scorers will be likely to exaggerate their physical difficulties. If Scale 7 is also elevated, this may indicate a better prognosis for psychotherapy since clients' level of anxiety is high enough to motivate them to change. Extremely high scores might suggest that the person has a wide variety of symptom-related complaints and will probably be extremely constricted. This might be consistent with a person with psychotic like features (schizoid, schizoaffective, schizophrenic, psychotic depression) who is having bodily delusions (check elevations on Scales 6, 7, 8, and 9).

Treatment Implications   Individuals with elevations on Scale 1 have often rejected and criticized the "help" that has been offered to them. They would be likely to resent any suggestion that their difficulties are even partly psychologically based. Since their level of insight is quite poor, they typically do not make good candidates for psychotherapy. They are generally pessimistic about being helped and, as a result, might be argumentative with professional staff (confirm/disconfirm this by checking the TRT/Negative Treatment Indicators content scale). They need to be assured that they have been well understood and that their symptoms will not be ignored. Often framing interventions with biomedical terminology may make interventions more acceptable (e.g., biofeedback procedures might be described as "neurological retraining").

MMPI-A Considerations   The preceding descriptors are relevant for adolescent profiles. However, they also suggest school-related difficulties. Girls are likely to experience family problems (marital disagreements, financial concerns) and eating disorders. However, elevations on this scale are relatively rare among adolescents.

Low Scores on Scale 1

Low scores for females (but not males) suggest an absence of physical complaints and health-related concerns. They might also be generally alert, capable, responsible, and conscientious perhaps even to the point of being moralistic.

Scale 2. Depression *(D)*

Scale 2 comprises 60 items on the MMPI and 57 items on the MMPI-2. The Harris-Lingoes recategorization of the scale content suggests that these items are organized around the areas of brooding, physical slowness, subjective feelings of depression, mental apathy, and physical malfunctioning. Thus, high scores may indicate difficulties in one or more of these areas. Patients seeking inpatient psychiatric treatment are most likely to have Scale 2 as the highest point on their profiles. As would be expected, elevations on 2 typically decrease after successful psychotherapy. The relative elevation on Scale 2 is the single best predictor of a person's level of satisfaction, sense of security, and degree of comfort. Persons who score high on 2 are usually described as self-critical, withdrawn, aloof, silent, and retiring.

Any interpretation of scores on 2 needs to take into account the person's age and the implications of possible elevations on other scales. Adolescents typically score 5 to 10 points lower than nonpatient adults. In contrast, elderly persons usually score 5 to 10 points higher. A frequent pattern often referred to as the "neurotic triad" occurs when 1, 2, and 3 are all elevated. This suggests that the person has a wide variety of complaints, including not only depression, but also somatic complaints, irritability, difficulties with interpersonal relationships, work-related problems, and general dissatisfaction (see code types 12/21, 13/31, 23/32). An accompanying elevation on Scale 7 suggests that the self-criticalness and intropunitiveness of the depression also includes tension and nervousness. In some ways, moderate elevations on Scales 2 and 7 are a favorable sign for psychotherapy. Such elevations indicate that persons are motivated to change due to the discomfort they experience and they are also likely to be introspective and self-aware. Scales 2 and 7 are often referred to as the "distress scales" since they provide an index of the degree of personal pain, anxiety, and discomfort the person is experiencing (see code types 27/72). If an elevation on Scale 2 is accompanied by an elevation on Scale 8, it suggests that the depression is characterized by unusual thoughts, disaffiliation, isolation, and a sense of alienation (see code type 28/82).

High Scores on Scale 2

Moderate elevations on 2 might suggest a reactive depression, particularly if 2 is the only high point. The person would likely be confronting his or her difficulties with a sense of pessimism, helplessness, and hopelessness. These may even be characteristic personality features that become exaggerated when the person is confronted by current problems. He or she may have a sense of inadequacy, poor morale, and difficulty concentrating, which may be severe enough to create difficulties in working effectively. The person might be described as retiring, shy, aloof, timid, inhibited but also irritable, high-strung, and impatient. Since such persons are highly sensitive to criticism, they might attempt to avoid confrontations at all costs. This may result in their avoiding interpersonal relationships in general. Others may perceive them as being conventional, cautious, passive, and unassertive. Increasingly higher scores on 2 indicate an exaggeration of these trends. They may worry excessively over even minor problems, and their ability to deal effectively with interpersonal problems could be impaired. Their sense of discouragement might result in psychomotor retardation, lethargy, and withdrawal. Often they have a variety of somatic complaints (check for corresponding elevations on 1, HEA, and Harris-Lingoes D3/Physical Malfunctioning). In particular this might include feeling sluggish, tense, and having a low level of energy. They are also likely to have a preoccupation with death and suicide. Decisions may need to be made to determine whether they would require inpatient or outpatient treatment. Such decisions center on determining whether or not these clients are a danger to themselves.

Treatment Implications   An important consideration is whether external (reactive) or internal (endogenous) factors are responsible for the depression. In addition, clients should be further assessed to determine the relative contribution of cognitions, social support, and the prevalence of vegetative symptoms. Treatment should be planned taking these considerations into account. An elevation on 2 raises the possibility of suicide. This is particularly true if the elevations are high to extremely high and if there are corresponding elevations on 4, 7, 8, and/or 9. Even though these elevations might raise the possibility of suicide, no clear "suicidal profile" has been found to be an accurate predictor. Any suggestion of suicidal behavior on the profile should be investigated further through a careful assessment of additional relevant variables (demographics; presence, clarity, lethality of plan, etc.). More specific information might also be obtained by noting relevant critical items (see Appendix K) and then discussing these with the client. The presence of a moderate level of depression can be a positive sign for psychotherapy since they are likely to be highly motivated (but check possible negative indicators with elevations on TRT/Negative Treatment Indicators, *L*, *K*, and 1). In contrast, an extremely high score suggests they may be too depressed to experience sufficient motivation to change.

MMPI-A Considerations   The preceding MMPI-2 descriptors and use of the Harris-Lingoes scales are also relevant for adolescents, particularly for girls. In addition, high adolescent scores on 2 suggest school-related difficulties (check A-sch/School Problems content scale) and a worsening of arguments between their parents (check A-fam/Family Problems content scale). They are less likely to act out but more likely to report eating problems (especially females), somatic complaints, and low self-esteem. Interpersonally, they will be introverted with few friends.

Low Scores on Scale 2

Low scores generally indicate not only an absence of depression, but that the person is likely to be cheerful, optimistic, alert, active, and spontaneous. They report few difficulties trying to sleep, and do not appear to worry over their health. They may also be undercontrolled, self-seeking, and even prone to self-display. Males are likely to be confident, curious, able to easily make decisions, and relatively unconcerned what others think of them. Females are described as being cheerful, report few physical ailments, and unlikely to worry or become nervous. Sometimes a low 2 score might indicate a person who is denying significant levels of underlying depression.

Scale 3. Hysteria *(Hy)*

Scale 3 was originally designed to identify patients who had developed a psychogenically based sensory or motor disorder. The 60 items primarily involve specific physical complaints and a defensive denial of emotional or interpersonal difficulties. The types of physical complaints are generally quite specific and include such areas as fitful sleep, nausea, vomiting, headaches, and heart or chest pains (check HEA). The important feature of persons who score high on this scale is that they simultaneously report specific physical complaints but also use a style of denial in which they may even express an exaggerated degree of optimism. One of the important and primary ways in which they deal with anxiety and conflict is to channel or convert these difficulties onto the body. Thus, their physical complaints serve as an indirect expression of these conflicts. Their traits might be consistent with a histrionic personality in that they will demand affection and social support but do so in an indirect and manipulative manner. They are also likely to be socially uninhibited and highly visible. They can easily initiate relationships, yet their relationships are likely to be superficial. They will approach others in a self-centered and naive manner. They might act out sexually or aggressively, but have a convenient lack of insight into either their underlying motives or their impact on others. However, Scale 3 is quite heterogeneous in its item composition. The Harris-Lingoes item analysis has divided these into denial of social anxiety, need for affection, lassitude-malaise, somatic complaints, and inhibition of aggression. If Scale 3 is clearly elevated and a clinician is unclear regarding the meaning of the elevation, it can often be useful to formally score the Harris-Lingoes subscales (see section on Harris-Lingoes subscales).

An elevated Scale 3 is frequently found, with corresponding elevations on Scales 1 and 2 (see code types 12/21, 13/31, and 23/32). If *K* is also elevated, the person is likely to be inhibited, affiliative, overconventional, and to have an exaggerated need to be liked and approved of by others. This is particularly true if scales *F* and 8 are also low. A high score on 3 reduces the likelihood the person will be psychotic, even though Scales 6 and 8 might be relatively high.

High Scores on Scale 3

High scorers are likely to have specific functionally related somatic complaints. They will use a combination of denial and dissociation. They usually experience low levels of anxiety, tension, and depression and rarely report serious psychopathology such as hallucinations, delusions, and suspiciousness. Their insight about their behavior will be low since they both deny difficulties and have a strong need to see themselves in a favorable light. Persons with moderate scores, especially if educated and from higher socioeconomic groups, may have good levels of adjustment. Scale 3 might also be somewhat elevated in persons wishing to present a favorable impression for employment, thereby reflecting the endorsement of specific items denying any abnormality. With increasing scores, however, there is an exaggeration of denial, somatization, dissociation, immaturity, and low levels of insight. In particular, they may be perceived as highly conforming, immature, naive, childishly self-centered, and impulsive. They will have strong needs for approval, support, and affection but will attempt to obtain these through indirect and manipulative means. Thus they are interpersonally indirect, with difficulty expressing hostility and resentment. Often, they will communicate with others to create an impact rather than to convey specific information. They will perceive events globally rather than attend to specific and often relevant details of a situation. Their physical difficulties typically worsen in response to increases in stress levels. The complaints can be either quite vague or quite specific and are of unknown origins. When their level of stress decreases, their physical difficulties will be likely to disappear very quickly. This is particularly true for persons with *T* scores over 80.

Treatment Implications   Initial response to therapy is likely to be enthusiastic and optimistic, at least in part because the clients have strong needs to be liked. However, they will be slow to gain insight into the underlying motives for their behavior since they use extensive denial and repression typically denying the presence of any psychological problems. Often they will look for simplistic, concrete, and naive solutions to their problems. They would be likely to attempt to manipulate the therapist into a supportive and nonconfrontive role. As their defenses become challenged, they might become more manipulative, perhaps resorting to complaints of mistreatment and not being understood. At times, they may even become verbally aggressive. Their core conflicts are usually centered around issues of dependence versus independence. Often direct suggestion focusing on short-term goals is effective in creating change.

MMPI-A Considerations   While the interpretations for adults with elevated Scale 3 can also be made with adolescents, they should be done with caution due to questions related to questionable validity with this population. In particular, the Harris-Lingoes subscales can help to clarify the meanings of scale elevations. Females (but not males) are still likely to have somatic complaints in response to stress. Males were more likely to have both school problems (check A-sch/School Problems content scale) and a history of suicidal ideation and gestures. However, Scale 3 is rarely a high point among adolescent males.

Low Scores on Scale 3

Low scores might be consistent with persons who are narrow-minded, cynical, socially isolated, conventional, constricted, and controlled. They might also have a difficult time trusting others and be difficult to get to know. Males are likely to be shy and more likely to report being worn out.

Scale 4. Psychopathic Deviate *(Pd)*

The purpose of Scale 4 is to assess the person's general level of social adjustment. The questions deal with such areas as degree of alienation from family, social imperviousness, difficulties with school and authority figures, and alienation from self and society (see ANG/Anger and FAM/Family Problems content scales). The original purpose of the scale was to distinguish those persons who had continuing legal difficulties yet were of normal intelligence and did not report having experienced cultural deprivation. They were people who seemed unconcerned about the social consequences of their behavior and yet did not appear to suffer from neurotic or psychotic difficulties. An important rationale for developing the scale is that high scorers might not be engaged in acting out at the time of testing. In fact, they may often make an initial good impression, which could sometimes be described as "charming." Recent friends and acquaintances may not believe that they could even be capable of antisocial behavior. However, under stress or when confronted with a situation that demands consistent, responsible behavior, they would be expected to act out in antisocial ways. Even though they might get caught, these persons would still have a difficult time learning from their mistakes.

Different relatively normal groups will often have somewhat elevated Scale 4 profiles. This might include counterculture groups, which reflects their relative disregard for the values and beliefs of mainstream culture. Similarly, African Americans often score higher, which might reflect their feelings that many of the rules and laws of the dominant culture are unfair and serve to disadvantage them. Normal persons who are graduate students in the humanities and social sciences often have somewhat elevated scores. More positive characteristics to be found with moderate elevations include frankness, deliberateness, assertion, sociability, and individualism. In addition, normal persons who are extraverted, risk takers, and have unconventional lifestyles (skydivers, police officers, actors) are also likely to have somewhat elevated Scale 4 profiles.

Relating Scale 4 with other corresponding scales can help to make more precise and accurate interpretations. If Scales 4 and 9 are elevated, it indicates that the persons not only have an underlying sense of anger and impulsiveness, but also have the energy to act on these feelings (see 49/94 code type and ASP/Antisocial Practices and ANG/Anger content scales). Their histories will almost always reveal extensive impulsive behavior. This acting out has frequently been done in such a way as to damage their family's reputation. They may also have been involved in criminal activity. However, moderate elevations on Scales 4 and 9 might suggest that the behaviors were less extreme and the person may have even been able to develop a good level of adjustment (see 49/94 code type). A psychotic expression of antisocial behavior might be consistent with elevations on both 4 and 8 (see 48/84 code type). A high 4 accompanied by a high 3 suggests that antisocial behavior might be expressed in covert or disguised methods or that the person might even manipulate another person into acting out for him or her (see 34/43 code type). Elevations on Scales 4 and 2 suggest that the person has been caught performing antisocial behavior and is feeling temporary guilt and remorse for his or her behaviors (see 24/42 code type).

High Scores on Scale 4

High scorers typically have problems with persons in authority, frequent marital and work difficulties, and poor tolerance for boredom. They can be described as having an angry disidentification with their family, society, or both. Even though they might have been frequently caught for episodes of acting out, they are slow to learn from the consequences of their behavior. When confronted with the consequences of their actions, these individuals may feel genuine remorse, but this is usually short-lived. Their difficulty in profiting from experience also extends to difficulties in benefiting from psychotherapy. Usually, their relationships are shallow and characterized by recurrent turmoil and they have difficulty forming any long-term loyalties. They are likely to blame others, particularly their families, when things go wrong. Others often perceive these individuals as angry, alienated, impulsive, and rebellious (see ASP/Antisocial Practices content scale) but also outgoing, extraverted, talkative, active, and self-centered. They usually have a history of involvement with the legal system as well as extensive alcohol or drug abuse. Since they resent rules and regulations, they will also have a history of work-related difficulties. Although they may often make an initial good impression, eventually they will have an outbreak of irresponsible, untrustworthy, and antisocial behavior.

Extremely high scorers might be aggressive or even assaultive. In addition, they will be unstable, irresponsible, self-centered, and most will have encountered legal difficulties as a result of their antisocial behaviors. In contrast, persons scoring in the moderate ranges might be described as adventurous, pleasure-seeking, sociable, self-confident, assertive, unreliable, resentful, and imaginative.

Treatment Implications   Since persons scoring high on 4 are usually verbally fluent, energetic, and intelligent, they might initially be perceived as good candidates for psychotherapy. However, their underlying hostility, impulsiveness, and feelings of alienation eventually surface. They are also likely to blame others for the problems they have encountered. As a result, they will eventually resist therapy and terminate as soon as possible (see *TRT*/Negative Treatment Indicators content scale). Part of their resistance is that they have difficulty committing themselves to any, including the therapeutic, relationship. If they are not feeling any subjective distress (low Scales 2 and 7), then their motivation for change is likely to be particularly low. In addition, their original motivation for therapy may not have been to actually change, but rather to avoid some form of punishment, such as jail. Thus, their long-term prognosis in therapy is poor. Short-term goals that focus on documenting clear behavior change (rather than merely verbalizing it) would be indicated. Some sort of external motivation for therapy (e.g., condition of parole or continued employment) might also increase the likelihood that they will follow through on treatment.

MMPI-A Considerations   Adolescents frequently have elevations on Scale 4 and it will be their highest overall scale. A full one third of the clinical sample used in the development of the MMPI-A had elevations of 65 or more. These generally high scores most likely reflect their often turbulent attempts to form a sense of identity and achieve independence from their parents. Thus, the elevation might be part of a temporary phase of development rather than a permanent enduring trait. However, high or extremely high scores will still reflect significant levels of pathology. Such scores are associated with delinquents who commit antisocial acts (see A-ang/Anger and A-con/Conduct Problems scales), are in conflict with their families (see A-fam/Family Problems), school-related difficulties (see A-Sch/School Problems), and are involved with drugs and/or alcohol (see MAC-R, ACK/Alcohol Drug Acknowledgment, and PRO/Alcohol Proneness supplementary scales). Often they report little guilt for this acting out and appear impervious to punishment. Additional difficulties might include externalizing behavior problems (lying, cheating, stealing, temper outbursts, jealousy), and school dropout. Boys frequently report physical abuse and having run away and girls similarly report physical abuse but also having been sexually abused. They are also likely to be sexually active. Often they are not particularly motivated to become involved in therapy. Since Scale 4 is quite heterogeneous with a correspondingly high number of descriptors, a formal scoring and inspection of the Harris-Lingoes scales can often be extremely useful in determining which of the scale descriptors is most appropriate.

Low Scores on Scale 4

Scores below 45 reflect persons who are overcontrolled, self-critical, rigid, conventional, and overidentified with social status. They might also be balanced, cheerful, persistent, and modest, but are somewhat passive and have difficulties asserting themselves. Males are less likely to become annoyed, less likely to resent being told what to do, less likely to be moody, and rarely report having been in trouble with the law. Females are more likely to be cooperative, pleasant, and relaxed but less likely to have the following characteristics: temper tantrums, resent being told what to do, act stubbornly, feel that others don't care about them, argue about minor things, be envious, talk back to others, nag, be overly sensitive, be irritable, and to tell people off for having made mistakes.

Scale 5. Masculinity-Femininity *(Mf)*

This scale was originally designed to identify males who were having difficulty with homosexual feelings and gender-identity confusion. However, it has been largely unsuccessful in that a high score does not seem to clearly and necessarily relate to a persons's sexual preference. Instead, it relates to the degree to which a person endorses items related to traditional masculine or feminine roles or interests. A high score for males is also positively correlated with intelligence and education. Thus, males who have completed university degrees will usually score an average of 5 T scores above ($T = 60-65$) the standardization sample and those with less than a high school education will score, on average, 5 T scores lower. This means that interpretations need to take the influence of education into account. The item content seems to be organized around the following five dimensions: personal and emotional stability, sexual identification, altruism, feminine occupational identification, and denial of masculine occupations. The items are scored in the opposite direction for females. Thus, high scores for males have traditionally been used to suggest a nonidentification with stereotyped masculine roles, whereas a high score for females has traditionally been used to suggest an identification with these masculine roles.

Since the original development of Scale 5, considerable change has occurred in society regarding the roles and behaviors of males and females. This, as well as other factors in scale construction, has caused some challenges to the current validity of 5 (Wong, 1984). Despite these challenges, the most recent study done on college students indicated that the behavioral correlates now were quite similar to what they were a generation ago (Todd & Gynther, 1988). However, there is insufficient research to fully understand the behavioral correlates of Scale 5, and there are still unanswered questions about its original development. These concerns were sufficient to result in the restandardization committee considering deleting it from the MMPI-2 and MMPI-A (Butcher & Williams, 1992; Williams & Butcher, 1989b). The practical implication is that clinicians must make Scale 5 interpretations quite cautiously, particularly for females.

An important consideration regarding Scale 5 is that it is not an actual clinical scale in the same sense as most of the other scales. It does not actually assess any pathological syndromes and thus does not provide clinical information. However, it can be useful in providing color or tone to the other scales. This means interpretations should first be made of the other scales and then the meaning of the relative score on 5 should be taken into consideration. For example, an elevation on Scale 4 (Pd) would indicate that the person is impulsive, might act out under stress, and feels alienated from his or her self or society. If the person scoring a high 5 is a male and also scores low on Scale 4, then he would be likely to express his dissatisfaction through action, have low insight into his behavior, and place emphasis on physical strength. In contrast, a high scale on 4 accompanied by an elevated 5 suggests that the person will be more introspective, sensitive, articulate, and may channel his or her antisocial feelings toward creating social change. However, in deciding what should be considered to be a high or low 5, the person's level of education and socioeconomic status should always be taken into account.

A high score on 5 for males should never be used to diagnose homosexuality. Instead, high-scoring males are more likely to suggest that the person has aesthetic interests, sensitivity to others, a wide range of interests, tolerance, passivity, and is capable of expressing warmth. Males with moderate scores would be inner directed, curious, clever, and have good judgment and common sense. In some cases, extremely high scores might suggest homosexuality, but this is only raised as a possibility: The scores themselves are not diagnostic. The scale is also quite susceptible to faking since the meanings of the items are fairly transparent. Thus, a person wishing to conceal his or her gender-identity confusion could easily alter the items. In contrast, males with low scores could be expected to endorse traditional masculine interests and be described as easygoing, adventurous, but also sometimes coarse.

Females who lack much education and score low on Scale 5 are usually described as fulfilling traditionally feminine roles and occupations. They will be passive, submissive, modest, sensitive, and yielding. In contrast, highly educated females who score in the same ranges are likely to be intelligent, forceful, considerate, insightful, conscientious, and capable. Females who score high are more likely to be involved in more traditionally male roles and occupational areas such as mechanics and science. They are frequently described as aggressive, competitive, confident, adventurous, and dominating.

Sometimes, males have elevations on both 4 and 5. Such a profile is likely to reflect a person who is not only unconventional, but will also be flamboyant about expressing this unconventionality. Thus, he may enjoy openly defying and challenging conventional modes of appearance and behavior (see 45/54 code type). In contrast, males who score low on 5 and high on 4 will be likely to make an obvious, perhaps even compulsive, display of their masculinity. Females with a high 5 and 4 will rebel against traditional expressions of femininity. As the elevation on 4 becomes progressively higher, this rebellion is likely to become correspondingly more deviant. Females having a profile with a high 4 and low 5 will similarly feel angry and hostile but will find it very difficult to express these feelings. This is likely to produce a considerable inner tension and turmoil. Sometimes, males have high scores on 5 with corresponding high scores on 2 and 7, and occasionally on 4. These males will present themselves as self-effacing, weak, submissive, inferior, and guilty. In high school or college, they may have taken on either the role of the self-critical school clown or a withdrawn "egghead." Females expressing these qualities would be likely to have the same pattern of scores, except they would have a valley rather than an elevation on 5.

High Scores on Scale 5 (Males)

High scores for males have traditionally been interpreted as suggesting that they are likely to be undemanding, shy, emotional, curious, and creative, with a wide range of intellectual interests. Extremely high scores might suggest males who are not only involved in traditional feminine interests but also have gender-identity confusion. They might be effeminate, passive, experience homoerotic feelings, and have difficulty asserting themselves. Due to their passivity, they may experience marital problems since they have difficulty assertively fulfilling their partner's needs. In rare cases, some high-scoring males might develop a reaction formation against their passivity and display an exaggerated expression of masculinity. Thus, they would be outwardly similar to low-scoring males on Scale 5 although their inner experience of these behaviors would be quite different. In contrast, moderate scorers will be expressive, demonstrative, empathic, individualistic, express interpersonal sensitivity, have aesthetic interests, be self-controlled, nurturant, and exercise good common sense. They should be able to communicate their ideas effectively and are psychologically sophisticated, idealistic, and inner directed. College and seminary students usually score within the moderate ranges.

Treatment Indications Moderate scores suggest that the individual is insightful, sensitive, and introspective, all of which are qualities conducive to psychotherapy. A high 5 reduces the likelihood that any existing pathology will be acted out. However, with increasing elevations, there is likely to be important issues related to passivity, dependency, impracticality, problems dealing with anger, and difficulties with heterosexual adjustment. In contrast, low scoring men may have difficulties with psychotherapy since they have low verbal skills, are not psychologically minded, have a narrow range of interests, and tend to be action oriented. The most successful approaches for working with low scoring males would be to involve clear behavioral descriptions with concrete, short-term goals.

MMPI-A Considerations Scale 5 elevations for males were rare on both the MMPI-A clinical and normative samples. While many of the descriptions for high-scoring adult males should be considered for adolescents, any interpretations should be made with caution. However, they will seem interested in stereotypically feminine interests, deny stereotypically masculine interests, and are less likely to act out. If there are correspondingly high elevations on other scales suggesting acting out (Scales 4, 9, *F*), then these should be given more consideration than the suppression value of an elevated Scale 5.

Low Scores on Scale 5 (Males)

Low-scoring males will be domineering and impersonal. Their interests might be somewhat narrow and they will lack originality. They will show little interest in understanding the underlying motivation behind their own behavior or the behavior of others. In contrast, they will prefer action over contemplation and will be generally uncomfortable with their feelings. They will place considerable emphasis on athletic prowess and physical strength. Thus, they will act in a traditionally masculine manner. They might also be described as self-indulgent, independent, and narcissistic. Sometimes their masculine strivings might even be overdone and expressed in a rigid, almost compulsive manner. Extremely low scorers might even be expressing exaggerated masculine behavior to conceal serious doubts regarding their own masculinity.

High Scores on Scale 5 (Females)

Since the scoring for females is reversed, a high score will mean the opposite for females as it would for males. Thus, high-scoring females would be endorsing traditionally masculine interests and activities, and may be involved in occupations which are more frequently occupied by males. They will often be described as confident, spontaneous, bold, unsympathetic, competitive, logical, and unemotional. When compared with low-scoring females, their physical health is likely to be better and they will more frequently be involved in active hobbies and interests. As the scale elevation increases, they correspondingly might be more aggressive, tough-minded, and domineering. They may often be rebelling against the traditional female role and feel uncomfortable in heterosexual relations.

Treatment Implications   High-scoring females might be difficult to engage in traditional psychotherapy since they usually do not value introspection and insight and have difficulty articulating their problems and expressing emotions. In contrast, low-scoring females who are well educated will be articulate, sensitive, have a wide range of interests, and can clearly express their emotions, thus making them good candidates for psychotherapy. However, low-scoring females with low levels of education might be difficult to work with since they are likely to be extremely passive, superficially compliant, but have difficulty actually implementing change.

MMPI-A Considerations   Further research needs to be conducted on the behavioral correlates of both high and low scoring adolescent females. However, tentative interpretations would indicate that high scoring females have stereotypically masculine interests.

Low Scores on Scale 5 (Females)

College-educated females with low scores on 5 will be tender, emotional, have a balanced view of gender role behavior, express aesthetic interests, and be capable, competent, and conscientious. They may still endorse many traditionally feminine roles and behaviors. They are more likely to have a greater number of health-related complaints than high-scoring females, and their hobbies and interests will be more passive. In contrast to low-scoring educated females, low-scoring females with limited education are typically described quite differently. They may be caricatures of traditionally feminine behavior. They are likely to be modest, passive, constricted, and yielding. They may attempt to make others feel guilty by taking on an excessive number of burdens. As a result, they might be complaining and self-pitying, and might spend time finding faults in others. It is not unusual to have a low 5 accompanied by elevations on the "neurotic triad" (Scales 1, 2, and 3). A low 5 accompanied by elevations on Scales 4 and 6 has been referred to as the "Scarlett O'Hara" profile because the person is likely to express an exaggerated degree of femininity combined with covert manipulations, underlying antisocial feelings, and hypersensitivity.

Scale 6. Paranoia *(Pa)*

Scale 6 was designed to identify persons with paranoid conditions or paranoid states. It measures a person's degree of interpersonal sensitivity, self-righteousness, and suspiciousness. Many of the 40 items center on such areas as ideas of reference, delusional beliefs, pervasive suspiciousness, feelings of persecution, grandiose self-beliefs, and interpersonal rigidity. Whereas some of the items deal with overt psychotic content, other less extreme questions ask information related to perceived ulterior motives. The Harris-Lingoes subscales divide the items in Scale 6 into ideas of external influence, poignancy (feelings of being high-strung, sensitive, having stronger feelings than others, and a sense of interpersonal distance), and naivete (overly optimistic, high morality, denial of hostility, overly trusting, and vulnerability to being hurt).

Mild elevations on Scale 6 suggest that the person is emotional, soft-hearted, and experiences interpersonal sensitivity. As the elevation increases, a person's suspicion and sensitivity become progressively more extreme and consistent with psychotic processes. He or she may have delusions, ideas of self-reference, a grandiose self-concept, and disordered thought processes. In contrast, low-scoring persons are seen as being quite balanced. However, there are some differences between the descriptions given for low-scoring males as opposed to low-scoring females. Low-scoring males are described as cheerful, decisive, self-centered, lacking in a strong sense of conscience, and having a narrow range of interests. Females are somewhat differently described as mature and reasonable. Persons scoring extremely low might actually be paranoid but are attempting to hide their paranoid processes. Thus, they would actually have characteristics quite similar to high-scoring persons.

In some ways, Scale 6 is quite accurate in that high-scoring persons will usually have significant levels of paranoia. However, the contents of most of the 40 items are fairly obvious. Thus, a person wanting to conceal his or her paranoia, due to fear over the imagined consequences of detection, could do so quite easily. This means it might be possible for low or moderate scores to still be consistent with paranoia. This is especially true for bright and psychologically sophisticated persons. They might mask their paranoia not only on the test, but also in real life. Thus, they might be a member of some extreme political group or religious cult that provides some degree of social support for their underlying paranoid processes. However, if the scale is clearly elevated, it is an excellent indication of paranoia.

A pronounced elevation on Scales 6 and 8 is highly suggestive of paranoid schizophrenia, regardless of the elevations on the other scales (see 68/86 code type). Another frequent combination is a corresponding elevation on 3. Such persons would then repress their hostile and aggressive feelings and appear naive, positive, and accepting. They might easily enter into superficial relationships, but once these relationships deepen, their underlying suspiciousness, hostility, ruthlessness, and egocentricity would become more openly expressed (see 36/63 code type).

High Scores on Scale 6

Extremely high scores on 6 indicate persons who are highly suspicious, vengeful, brooding, resentful, and angry. They will feel mistreated and typically misinterpret the motives of others, feeling that they have not received a fair deal in life. They are likely to have a thought disorder with accompanying ideas of reference, delusional thinking, fixed obsessions, compulsions, and phobias. Their thinking will be extremely rigid and they will be quite argumentative.

Moderate elevations are much less likely to reflect overtly psychotic trends. However, the person is still likely to be suspicious, argumentative, potentially hostile, and quite sensitive in interpersonal relationships. They might easily misinterpret the benign statements of others as personal criticisms. They would then enlarge on and brood over these partially or wholly invented criticisms. It would be difficult to discuss emotional problems with them. Although they might have underlying feelings of anger, they are likely to deny these in a rigidly moralistic and intellectual manner. They would also be likely to defend themselves from anxiety through intellectualization and would use projection to deny underlying feelings of hostility. They might then express their own hostility through indirect means and yet appear outwardly self-punishing. They will feel as if they have gotten an unfair deal from life and feel particular resentment toward family members.

Persons with mild elevations on 6 are usually described in relatively favorable terms. These include hardworking, industrious, moralistic, sentimental, softhearted, peaceable, generous, and trusting unless betrayed. They are also likely to be intelligent, poised, rational, fair-minded, and have a broad range of interests. However, they might also tend to be submissive, prone to worry, high strung, dependent, and lacking in self-confidence. The preceding descriptions are particularly likely among nonpatient groups. Psychiatric patients with the same elevations are described somewhat differently as being oversensitive, slightly paranoid, suspicious, and feeling as if their environment is not sufficiently supportive.

Treatment Implications   Considering the relative elevation of this scale can be extremely important since it provides an index of the degree to which clients can develop a trusting relationship, their attitudes toward authority figures, and their degree of flexibility. Very high scores suggests psychotic processes possibly requiring medication (check BIZ/Bizarre Mentation and critical item clusters related to mental confusion and persecutory ideas subscales). Psychotherapy with individuals scoring high on Scale 6 would be extremely difficult due to their rigidity, poor level of insight, and suspiciousness (check TRT/Negative Treatment Indicators Content scale). In addition, they do not like to discuss emotional issues, overvalue rationality, and are likely to blame others for their difficulties. They frequently will not return following the initial session and leave feeling that they have not been understood. Thus, a major challenge with an intake is to make sure that they feel understood. During subsequent sessions, they might attempt to manipulate the therapist by implicitly suggesting they will terminate. They are often argumentative, cynical, and resentful thereby making it difficult to establish a relationship of mutual trust, empathy, and respect. If brooding and resentment are particularly pronounced, it might be important to assess for potential dangerousness toward others.

MMPI-A Considerations   Elevations are consistent with academic problems including poor grades and suspension (check A-sch/School Problems content scale). Clinical girls report significant disagreements with their parents (check A-fam/Family Problems content scale). Clinical boys are described as hostile, withdrawn, immature, and argumentative; they feel persecuted and are not well liked by their peers. In addition, they are perceived as being overly dependent on adults, attention-seeking, resentful, anxious, and obsessed; they feel as if they are bad and deserving of punishment. Since the items between the MMPI, MMPI-2, and MMPI-A are the same, the Harris-Lingoes scales can be used to understand possible patterns of item endorsement.

Low Scores on Scale 6

Most persons with low scores on 6 are described as being quite balanced. Males tend to be cheerful, decisive, lacking in a sense of conscience, self-centered, can effectively control their emotions, and have a narrow range of interests. Females are somewhat more favorably described as being not only balanced, but also mature and reasonable. Both males and females are likely to be able to accept the challenges of life and are trusting, loyal, decisive, and self-controlled. Whereas the preceding descriptions tend to be true for nonpatient groups, persons having the same scores among patient groups are described as oversensitive, uninsightful, introverted, undependable, touchy, and rough, with poorly developed consciences and a narrow range of interests. Persons with extremely low scores might be paranoids who are attempting to hide their thought processes. Thus, they would be similar to high-scoring persons and could be described as guarded, defensive, shy, secretive, evasive, and withdrawn. This would be particularly likely if the following conditions are present: The validity scales indicate a defensive pattern of underreporting psychopathology (L and K are above 60 and above F), at least one of the T scores on one of the other clinical scales is above 65, and Scale 1 is less than 35 and is the lowest on the profile.

Scale 7. Psychasthenia *(Pt)*

The 48 items on Scale 7 were originally designed to measure the syndrome of psychasthenia. Although psychasthenia is no longer used as a diagnosis, it was current when the MMPI was originally developed. It consisted of compulsions, obsessions, unreasonable fears, and excessive doubts. Thus, it is quite similar to what today would be an anxiety disorder with obsessive-compulsive features. However, there are important differences. Scale 7 measures more overt fears and anxieties that the person might be experiencing (check also ANX/Anxiety). In contrast, persons having an obsessive-compulsive disorder could potentially score quite low on 7 because their behaviors and obsessions are effective in reducing their levels of anxiety (check the OBS/Obsessiveness content scale). Even though an elevation on 7 may suggest the possibility of an obsessive-compulsive disorder, other anxiety-related disorders or situational states could also produce an elevation.

Scale 7 is the clinical scale that most clearly measures anxiety and ruminative self-doubt. Thus, along with elevations on Scale 2, it is a good general indicator of the degree of distress the person is undergoing. High scorers are likely to be tense, indecisive, obsessionally worried, and have difficulty concentrating. Within a medical context, they are prone to overreact to even minor medical complaints. They are usually rigid, agitated, fearful, and anxious. The most frequent complaints will be related to cardiac problems as well as difficulties related to their gastrointestinal or genitourinary systems. Within nonmedical and more normal populations, high scorers are likely to be high-strung, articulate, individualistic, and perfectionistic, with extremely high standards of morality.

If both Scales 7 and 2 are moderately elevated, it suggests a good prognosis for therapy since these individuals are sufficiently uncomfortable to be motivated to change. They are likely to stay in treatment longer than most other groups. Although their progress will be slow, there is likely to be progressive improvement (see 27/72 code type). If their scores are extremely high, they might require antianxiety medication to enable them to relax sufficiently to be able to coherently discuss their difficulties. It might also be important to note the elevation of 7 in relationship to 8. If 7 is significantly higher than 8, it indicates the person is still anxious about and struggling with an underlying psychotic process. However, if 7 is quite low (10 T score points or more) in comparison with 8, the person is likely to have given up attempting to fight the disorder and his or her psychotic processes are either of a chronic nature or likely to become more chronic (see 78/87 code type).

High Scores on Scale 7

Elevations on Scale 7 suggest persons who are apprehensive, worrying, perfectionistic, and tense, and who may have a wide variety of superstitious fears. Mild elevations suggest that, in addition to a certain level of anxiety, these persons will be orderly, conscientious, reliable, persistent, and organized although they will also lack originality. Even minor problems might become a source of considerable concern. They will overreact and exaggerate the importance of events. Although they might attempt to use rationalization and intellectualization to reduce their anxiety, these defenses are rarely successful. With increasing elevations, they are likely to experience greater levels of self-doubt and be progressively more rigid, meticulous, apprehensive, uncertain, and indecisive. They are shy and experience social difficulties frequently worrying regarding their degree of acceptance and popularity. They may be rigid and moralistic with high standards for themselves and others. Defenses against their anxiety could be expressed in a variety of rituals and difficulty in concentrating. They will be highly introspective, self-critical, self-conscious, and feel a generalized sense of guilt. Extremely high scores might indicate a disruption in a person's ability to perform daily activities.

Treatment Implications   Since persons scoring high on Scale 7 experience clear, overt levels of discomfort, tension, and cognitive inefficiency, they are highly motivated to change. Thus they will usually stay in therapy. Progress tends to be slow although steady. The immediate task is to work directly with their anxiety, which might be accomplished through such procedures as cognitive restructuring, hypnosis, relaxation, or systematic desensitization. For some clients, their anxiety may be sufficiently high that a short-term regimen of antianxiety medication might be considered to help them work more constructively in a therapeutic context and function in their daily activities. Insight-oriented therapy should be used with caution since they will have a tendency to intellectualize and ruminate indefinitely without making any concrete changes. A further potential difficulty is that they may be overly perfectionistic and rigid, thereby making it difficult to either accept insights or to think in a flexible, problem-solving manner.

MMPI-A Considerations   Few descriptors have been found for adolescents with high scores on *Pt*. This has been speculated to be in part because an early (adolescent) rigid personality style may not become problematic until later in adult life. Girls from clinical populations are likely to be depressed, may make suicidal threats, are more likely to steal, and report significant disagreements with their parents. Boys from clinical populations are likely to have low self-confidence and may have been sexually abused. However, more research needs to be performed to more clearly understand the behavioral correlates of high 7 scoring adolescents.

Low Scores on Scale 7

Low scorers are likely to be relaxed, warm, cheerful, friendly, alert, and self-confident. They will approach their world in a balanced manner and are often described as efficient, independent, placid, and secure. Both males and females are less likely to be critical of others and typically have few fears. Males are also less likely to worry about health concerns. Females are unlikely to be nervous, critical of themselves or others, have bad dreams, and worry over minor issues or events. It is rare for persons referred for treatment to have low scores on this scale.

Scale 8. Schizophrenia *(Sc)*

Scale 8 was originally designed to identify persons who were experiencing schizophrenic or schizophrenic like conditions. It has been partially successful in this goal in that a diagnosis of schizophrenia is raised as a possibility in the case of persons who score extremely high. However, even persons scoring quite high would not necessarily fulfill the criteria for schizophrenia, in part because the items in the scale cover a highly diverse number of areas. Thus, elevations can occur for a variety of reasons, which means that the descriptions of high scorers would also be quite varied. The items assess such areas as social alienation, apathy, poor family relations, unusual thought processes, and peculiarities in perception. Other questions are intended to measure reduced efficiency, difficulties in concentration, general fears and worries, inability to cope, and difficulties with impulse control. Because of the many scale items, heterogeneity of their content, and the resulting numerous potential descriptors for individuals scoring high on Scale 8, it would be advisable to consult the Harris-Lingoes subscales to more fully understand the meanings of elevations. The following six different content areas have been described by Harris and Lingoes: social alienation, emotional alienation, lack of ego mastery-cognitive (strange thought processes, fear of losing their mind, difficulty concentrating, feelings of unreality), lack of ego mastery-cognitive (difficulty coping with everyday life, low interest in life, hopelessness, depression), lack of ego mastery-defective inhibition (impulsive, hyperactive, sense of being out of control, impulsive, laughing or crying spells) and bizarre sensory experiences.

In general, an elevated score on 8 suggests the person feels alienated, distant from social situations, and misunderstood. He or she might have a highly varied fantasy life and, when under stress, will withdraw further into fantasy. Others will most likely perceive the person as eccentric, seclusive, secretive, and inaccessible. He or she will often have a difficult time maintaining a clear and coherent line of thought. Communication skills will be poor; often, other people will feel they are missing some important component of what this individual is trying to say. The person will typically not make clear and direct statements and often will have difficulty focusing on one idea for very long.

Age and race are important when deciding what should be considered a high versus a low score on 8. Many populations of African Americans score somewhat higher on 8, which might reflect their greater level of social alienation and estrangement. However, this may be more related to education and socioeconomic status than ethnicity (Greene, 1987, 1991). Adolescents also score higher on Scale 8, which might be consistent with their greater openness to unusual experiences, turmoil in establishing a solid sense of identity, and greater feelings of alienation. Some groups of relatively normal persons might have mild elevations on 8. These might include individuals developing sensory impairments, persons with organic brain disorders, or unconventional persons who identify with the counterculture. Persons who have had a variety of drug experiences may score somewhat higher on 8. This may reflect the direct effects of the drugs themselves rather than suggest greater levels of pathology.

Simultaneous elevations on 4 and 8 indicate persons who feel extremely distrustful and alienated from their world. They perceive their environment as dangerous and are likely to react to others in a hostile and aggressive fashion (see 48/84 code type). Another important but unusual profile is an elevation on 8 along with an elevation on 9. Such persons will be likely to constantly deflect the direction of conversation, frequently diverting it to unusual tangents. They are likely to not only have a distorted view of their world, but also to have the energy to act on these distorted perceptions (see 89/98 code type). Another important pattern is the prognostic significance associated with the relative height of 7 and 8 (see 78/87 code type) and the schizoid profile of elevated *F,* 2, 4, 8, and 0 (see Scale 2).

High Scores on Scale 8

A high score suggests persons who have unusual beliefs, are unconventional, and may experience difficulties concentrating and focusing their attention. Within moderately elevated protocols, they might merely be aloof, different, and approach tasks from an innovative perspective. They may have philosophical, religious, or abstract interests, and care little about concrete matters. Others might describe them as shy, aloof, and reserved. Progressively higher scores would be likely to reflect individuals with greater difficulties in organizing and directing their thoughts. They might have aggressive, resentful, and/or hostile feelings yet cannot express these feelings. At their best, they might be peaceable, generous, sentimental, sharp-witted, interesting, creative, and imaginative. Very high elevations suggest persons with bizarre mentation, delusions, highly eccentric behaviors, poor contact with reality, and possibly hallucinations (see BIZ/Bizarre Mentation content scale). They will feel incompetent, inadequate, and be plagued by a wide variety of sexual preoccupations, self-doubts, and unusual religious beliefs. However, extremely high scores rarely occur, even among diagnosed schizophrenics. These extremes are likely to reflect unusual experiences reported by unusually anxious patients, adolescent adjustment reactions, prepsychotics, borderline personalities, or relatively well-adjusted persons who are malingering.

Treatment Implications   Since high-scoring persons have difficulty trusting others and developing relationships, therapy might be difficult especially during its initial stages. However, such individuals tend to stay in therapy longer than many other types of clients and may eventually develop a relatively close and trusting client/therapist relationship. Due to the often chronic nature of their difficulties, their prognosis is frequently poor. If their thought processes are extremely disorganized, referral for medication might be indicated.

MMPI-A Considerations   Both boys and girls report a higher rate of having several school-related problems with boys frequently being suspended and girls being unlikely to report having had any significant achievements (check A-sch/School Problems content scale). In addition, the possibility of sexual abuse should be investigated. Girls are likely to report increased disagreements with their parents (check A-fam/Family Problems content scale) and, among clinical populations, may be aggressive, threaten suicide, act out, and have outbursts of temper. In contrast, clinical boys are described as having behaviors such as being guilt-prone, shy, withdrawn, fearful, and perfectionistic; showing low self-esteem; being "clingy"; and having somatic complaints (nausea, headaches, dizziness, stomach pains). Clinical boys with quite high elevations might also have psychotic features including delusions, hallucinations, ideas of reference, grandiose beliefs, or peculiar speech and mannerisms (check A-biz/Bizarre Mentation content scale).

Low Scores on Scale 8

Persons scoring low are likely to be cheerful, good-natured, friendly, trustful, and adaptable. However, they are also likely to be overly accepting of authority, restrained, submissive, unimaginative, and avoid deep and involved relationships with others.

Scale 9. Hypomania *(Ma)*

The 46 items on Scale 9 were originally developed to identify persons experiencing hypomanic symptoms. These symptoms might include cyclical periods of euphoria, increased irritability, and excessive unproductive activity that might be used as a distraction to stave off an impending depression. Thus, the items are centered around such topics as energy level, irritability, egotism, and expansiveness. The Harris and Lingoes subscales classify the content of the items under amorality, psychomotor acceleration, imperturbality, and ego inflation. However, hypomania occurs in cycles. Thus persons in the acute phase were unable to be tested due to the seriousness of their condition. Further, some persons might score quite low on Scale 9, which might reflect the depressive side of their cycle. These low scorers, then, might still develop a hypomanic state and may have actually been hypomanic in the past.

The scale is effective not only in identifying persons with moderate manic conditions (extreme manic patients would be untestable) but also in identifying characteristics of nonpatient groups. A full 10%–15% of normals have elevations on this scale suggesting such characteristics as an unusually high drive level. Males with moderate to mild elevations and with no history of psychiatric disturbance might be described as warm, enthusiastic, outgoing, and uninhibited. They would most likely be able to expend a considerable amount of energy over a sustained period of time. They might also be easily offended, hyperactive, tense, and prone to periods of worry, anxiety, and depression. Others might describe them as expressive, individualistic, generous, and affectionate. Nonpatient females are likely to be frank, courageous, talkative, enthusiastic, idealistic, and versatile. Their husbands are likely to describe them as making big plans, wearing strange or unusual clothes, stirring up excitement, becoming very excited for no reason, being risk takers, and telling people off. High-scoring males were described by their wives as demanding excessive attention, being bossy, talking back to others without thinking, whining, and taking nonprescription drugs.

Age and race are important when evaluating what should be considered a high or low score. Some studies have indicated that certain populations of African Americans score higher than European Americans. Also, younger populations (adolescents and college-age students) score somewhat higher than nonpatient adults. In contrast, elderly persons often score quite low on Scale 9.

Useful information can often be obtained by interpreting the significance of corresponding scores on 9, 2, 7, and *K*. Usually 9 and 2 are negatively correlated. Sometimes, however, they may both be elevated, reflecting an agitated state in which the person is attempting to defend or distract him- or herself from underlying hostile and aggressive impulses. Sometimes such persons are highly introspective and narcissistically self-absorbed. Scales 9 and 2 can also be elevated for certain types of organically impaired patients. Profiles in which 2 and 7 are low (suggesting a minimum of psychological distress) combined with an elevation on 9, might be consistent with males who have an almost compulsive need to seek power and place themselves in narcissistically competitive situations. If the profile is accompanied by an elevation on *K,* then these males are likely to be managerial, autocratic, and power hungry, and expend a considerable degree of effort in organizing others. Their self-esteem would often be dependent on eliciting submission and weakness from others. What they usually receive from others is a grudging deference rather than admiration. Females having this profile are likely to be prone to exhibitionistic self-display and be extremely concerned with their physical attractiveness.

High Scores on Scale 9

Extremely high scores are suggestive of a moderate manic episode. These individuals will be maladaptively hyperactive and poorly focused, and will have flightive ideas, an inflated sense of self-importance, and low impulse control. They might make an initial good impression since they are enthusiastic, friendly, and pleasant. However, they also tend to be deceptive, manipulative, and unreliable, ultimately causing interpersonal difficulties. While others might perceive them as creative, enterprising, and ingenious, a high 9's appraisal of what he or she can actually accomplish is unrealistic. Thus these clients have an unwarranted sense of optimism. They are likely to become irritable at relatively minor interruptions and delays. Although they expend a considerable amount of energy, their activity usually will be unproductive since it is unfocused. Others might also perceive them as restless and agitated. They will quickly develop relationships with others, but these relationships will be superficial.

Persons with more moderate elevations are often more able to focus and direct their energy in productive directions. Nonpatients will be direct, energetic, enthusiastic, sociable, independent, optimistic, and have a wide range of interests. They might also be somewhat guileful, overactive, impulsive, persuasive, and prefer action to thought. They sometimes show mood difficulties and experience elation without cause. They are also described as being self-centered and impulsive. Sometimes scores alone are not sufficient to distinguish a person who is energetic, optimistic, and focused from a person who is scattered, ineffective, and hyperactive. Useful information might be obtained by noting relevant critical items, interpreting the Harris and Lingoes subscales, or integrating relevant historical information.

Treatment Implications   Since elevation on 9 indicates distractibility and overactivity, these clients might be difficult to work with. They might resist focusing on problems by diverging onto irrelevant tangents and object to psychological interpretations of their behavior. The client might attempt to persuade the therapist into believing in their grandiose plans for change but these are seldom followed through with. They also tend to use denial and avoid self-examination. Since they have a low frustration for tolerance and become easily irritated, therapy sessions might become dramatic. Frequently they show disregard for prearranged appointment times and cancel because they are too busy. This generally resistive stance suggests they might optimally benefit from non- or self-directive interventions or paradoxical strategies. They might need to be formally evaluated for the possibility of a bipolar disorder with follow-up for appropriate medication. Further assessment should also be made regarding alcohol or drug abuse (check MAC-R, AAS/Addiction Acknowledgment scale, and APS/Addiction Potential scale). Clients with low scores on 9 are likely to be apathetic, depressed, fatigued, inadequate, and pessimistic. As a result, they might have difficulty becoming motivated and require a concrete action program with a high degree of structure.

MMPI-A Considerations   Moderate elevations suggest that the individual is enthusiastic, animated, and takes an interest in things. However, higher elevations suggest underachievement in school and problems at home (check A-sch/School Problems and A-fam/Family Problems content scales). Scale 9 elevations might also reflect irrational, manic behaviors and antisocial acts (check A-con/Conduct Problems content scale). Among boys, amphetamine use is relatively common. They are typically insensitive to criticism, do not like to reflect on their behavior, and are therefore unmotivated to become involved in therapy. They may also believe that they know more than authority figures, and feel that such persons punish people unjustly. They might be self confident, oppositional, take advantage of others, and deny any social discomfort.

Low Scores on Scale 9

Persons scoring low on 9 are likely to have low levels of energy and activity. They are often described as dependable, responsible, conventional, practical, and reliable, but may also lack self-confidence. For example, they would be unlikely to dress in strange or unusual clothes, curse, stir up excitement, or talk back to others. They might be seclusive, withdrawn, quiet, modest, overcontrolled, and humble. Low scores are more frequently found among the elderly than among younger populations. Extremely low scores suggest serious depression, even if Scale 2 is within normal limits.

Scale 0. Social Introversion *(Si)*

This scale was developed from the responses of college students on questions relating to an introversion-extraversion continuum. It was validated based on the degree to which the students participated in social activities. High scores suggest that the respondent is shy, has limited social skills, feels uncomfortable in social interactions, and withdraws from many interpersonal situations. In particular, these individuals may feel uncomfortable around members of the opposite sex. They would prefer to be alone or with a few close friends than with a large group. One cluster of items deals with self-depreciation and neurotic maladjustment, whereas the other group deals with the degree to which the person participates in interpersonal interactions. The different item contents have been further organized around the areas of shyness/self-consciousness, social avoidance, and the extent that a person feels alienated from self and others (Ben-Porath, Hostetler, & Butcher, 1989). These contents form subscales that can be used in conjunction with the Harris-Lingoes subscales to help determine the different variables related to why a person had an elevation on Scale 0 (see section on Harris-Lingoes and *Si* subscales).

Scale 0 is similar to 5 in that it is used to "color" or provide a different emphasis to the other clinical scales. Thus, interpretations should first be made without considering 5 and 0 and, later, the implications of these scales should be included. As a result, code types involving 0 have not been included in the section on two-point codes. Elevations on 0 help provide information on the other scales by indicating how comfortable persons are with interactions, their degree of overt involvement with others, the effectiveness of their social skills (check SOD/Social Discomfort content scale), and the likelihood that they will have a well-developed social support system. A low score on 0 will often reduce the degree of pathology that might otherwise be suggested by elevations on the other scales. A low 0 also suggests that, even if persons have a certain level of pathology, they are able to find socially acceptable outlets for these difficulties. In contrast, a high 0 suggests an exaggeration of difficulties indicated by the other scales. This is particularly true if 0, 2, and 8 are all elevated. This suggests that the person feels socially alienated, withdrawn, is self-critical, and has unusual thoughts. However, he or she is not likely to have an adequate social support group to help in overcoming these difficulties. Although an elevated 0 can suggest an increase in personal difficulties, it often reflects a decreased likelihood of acting out. This is further supported by corresponding elevations on 2 and 5 (for males or a lowering for females). As a result 0, 2, and 5 are often referred to as inhibitory scales.

High Scores on Scale 0

Persons scoring high on Scale 0 will feel uncomfortable in group interactions and may have poorly developed social skills. They may be self-effacing, lacking in self-confidence, submissive, shy, and timid. Others might experience them as cold, distant, rigid, and difficult to get to know. Extremely high scorers are described as withdrawn, ruminative, indecisive, insecure, and retiring. They are both uncomfortable regarding their lack of interaction with others and sensitive to the judgments others make of them. Often they will not have a well-developed social support group to help them overcome difficulties. Persons with moderate scores on 0 are dependable, conservative, cautious, unoriginal, serious, and overcontrolled. Normal males who score high on 0 are described as modest, inhibited, lacking in self-confidence, and generally deficient in poise and social presence. Normal females who score moderately high are somewhat similarly described as modest, shy, self-effacing, sensitive, and prone to worry.

Treatment Implications The relative elevation on 0 is potentially quite useful in treatment planning since it provides an index of the individual's degree of social comfort, inhibition, and control in relationships. It also indicates the degree to which the person is able to become engaged in interpersonal relationships. Thus, high scorers would have difficulty engaging in therapy because they are shy, withdrawn and anxious, whereas low scorers would have difficulties as well but this would be due to a superficial orientation and disinclination to reflect inwardly. High scorers would take time to develop a therapeutic relationship and expect the therapist to be directive and dominate. A therapist who was somewhat withdrawn and nondirective might increase such a client's anxiety and the person might then discontinue therapy. On the surface they might appear to be unmotivated and passive but internally they are likely to feel high-strung and anxious (check LSE/Low Self-Esteem, A-lse/Low Self Esteem, SOD/Social Discomfort, and A-sod/Social Discomfort content scales). They are also likely to be overcontrolled and experience considerable difficulties in making changes. Group treatment and social skills training are often appropriate interventions. However, the group should be supportive and accepting thereby increasing the likelihood that they would experiment with new behaviors.

MMPI-A Considerations Among adolescents, high scores on 0 are a clear indication of difficulties in social relationships particularly related to low self-esteem and social withdrawal. The behavioral correlates for girls suggest that they are withdrawn, shy, fearful, depressed, may have had suicidal ideation and/or gestures, have eating problems, are socially withdrawn, and have only a few friends. Elevations also suggest an inhibitory effect in that they are unlikely to actually act out on their pathology. Thus, they rarely report difficulties with drugs or alcohol, delinquency, sexual acting out, and have little interest in heterosexual relationships. There are less behavioral correlates for boys, but high scores do suggest that they are unlikely to participate in school activities.

Low Scores on Scale 0

Low scorers are described as warm, outgoing, assertive, self-confident, verbally fluent, and gregarious. They will have strong needs to be around other people. They are likely to be concerned with power, recognition, and status. They may even be opportunistic, exhibitionistic, manipulative, and self-indulgent. In some cases, they might be immature, self-indulgent and superficial in their relationships with others. Normal males who score low are often perceived as being sociable, expressive, socially competitive, and verbally fluent. Normal females are similarly described as sociable, talkative, assertive, enthusiastic, and adventurous. Extremely low scores suggest persons who have highly developed social techniques, but behind their external image, they may have feelings of insecurity with a strong need for social approval. They may also be hypersensitive and may have difficulties dealing with feelings of dependency. They are likely to have a large number of superficial friends, but probably do not feel close to anyone.

TWO-POINT CODES

Code-type interpretation often produces more accurate and clinically useful interpretations than merely interpreting individual scales. The basis of code-type interpretation depends on empirical correlations among various classes of nontest behavior. The two-point codes included in the following section have been selected based on their frequency of occurrence, the thoroughness of the research performed on them, and their relative clinical importance. Thus, some combinations of code types will not be discussed.

Code-type interpretation is most appropriate for disturbed populations in which T score elevations are at least 65 on the MMPI-2 or MMPI-A. The descriptions are clearly oriented around the pathological dimensions of an individual. The two-point code descriptions, then, do not have the same divisions into low, moderate, and high elevations as the individual scores but are directed primarily toward discussions of high elevations. When considering two-point codes that are in the moderate range (MMPI-2 $T = 60$–70), interpretations should be made with caution and the more extreme descriptions should be considerably modified or excluded.

Usually, the elevation of one scale in relationship to the other does not make much difference as long as the elevations are still somewhat similar in magnitude. A general approach is that, if one scale is 10 points or more higher than the other, then the higher one gives more color to, or provides more emphasis for, the interpretation. Specific elaborations are made for scales in which a significant difference between their relative elevations is especially important. If the scales have an equal magnitude, they should be given equal emphasis.

In some cases, more than two scales will be equally elevated, thereby making it difficult to clearly establish which scales represent the two-point code. In these cases, clinicians should look at the descriptions provided for other possible combinations. For example, if scales 2, 7, and 8 are elevated for a particular profile, then the clinician should look up the 27/72 code as well as codes 78/87 and 28/82. The descriptions for the code type with the highest elevations and those descriptors that are common between the different code descriptions are most likely to be valid. However, multiple elevations also raise the issue of the generalizability of the MMPI descriptors (which the majority of research has been derived from) and the MMPI-2 (Butcher et al., 1990; Butcher & Williams, 1992; Edwards et al., 1993; Humphrey & Dahlstrom, 1995; Tellegen &

Ben-Porath, 1993; Weissman, 1992). Up to 50% of the code types have been found to differ and this is particularly true for poorly defined code types. This would potentially
compromise the validity of the code type descriptions. A more cautious approach would
be to then rely more on the single-scale descriptors.

In developing meaningful interpretations, it is important to continually consider the
underlying significance of elevated scales. This requires taking into account such factors as the manner in which the scales interact, the particular category of psychopathology they suggest, and their recurring patterns or themes. Whenever possible,
DSM-IV classifications have been used, but the term "neurosis" is used occasionally
due to its ability to summarize a wide variety of disorders and/or its ability to refer to
a cluster of related scales (e.g., "neurotic triad"). Some characteristics described in
the code types will be highly accurate for a specific person, whereas others will not be
particularly relevant or accurate. Clinicians, then, will need to continually reflect on
their data to develop descriptions and diagnoses that are both accurate and relevant.

Use of the code types from the MMPI-A should be made with considerable caution
since there is currently insufficient research on the behavioral correlates of these code
types. In contrast, there is considerable research on the correlates of individual MMPI-
A scale elevations. With this caution in mind, it is recommended that clinicians tentatively use the code types described in the following pages to help generate hypotheses
concerning adolescent functioning. This is partially justified in that many of the MMPI
code type correlates are common for both adults and adolescents (Archer, 1992). In addition, the majority of the code types derived from the MMPI will also be the same for
the MMPI-A, especially if these code types are well defined. If there are differences
between adult and adolescent descriptors, or if no adolescent descriptors are available,
this will be noted in the following code type descriptions.

12/21

Symptoms and Behaviors

Difficulties experienced by patients with the 12/21 code type revolve around physical
symptoms and complaints that can be either organic or functional (check the
HEA/Health Concerns content scale). Common complaints relate to pain, irritability,
anxiety, physical tension, fatigue, and overconcern with physical functions. In addition
to these symptoms a significant level of depression is present. These individuals characteristically handle psychological conflict through repression and by attending to real,
exaggerated, or imagined physical difficulties. Regardless of whether these physical difficulties are organically based, these individuals will exaggerate their symptoms and
use them to manipulate others. In other words, they elaborate their complaints beyond
what can be physically confirmed, often doing so by misinterpreting normal bodily
functions. Typically, they have learned to live with their complaints and use them to
achieve their own needs. This code pattern is more frequently encountered in males and
older persons.

The three categories of patients that this code is likely to suggest are the generalized hypochondriac, the chronic pain patient, and persons having recent and severe accidents. General hypochondriacs are likely to have significant depressive features and
to be self-critical, indirect, and manipulative. If their difficulties are solely functional,

they are more likely to be shy and withdrawn, whereas persons with a significant organic component are likely to be loud complainers. Furthermore, complaints are usually focused around the trunk of the body and involve the viscera. This is in contrast to the 13/31 code in which complaints are more likely to involve the central nervous system and peripheral limbs. When the 12/21 code is produced by chronic pain patients with an organic basis, they are likely to have given in to their pain and learned to live with it. Their experience and/or expression of this pain is likely to be exaggerated, and they use it to manipulate others. They may have a past history of drug or alcohol abuse, which represents attempts at "self-medication." The most common profile associated with heavy drinkers consists of elevations in Scales 1, 2, 3, and 4. Such persons will experience considerable physical discomfort, digestive difficulties, tension, depression, and hostility, and will usually have poor work and relationship histories. The third category associated with the 12/21 code type involves persons who are responding to recent, severe accidents. Their elevations on Scales 1 and 2 reflect an acute, reactive depression that occurs in response to the limiting effects of their condition.

Personality Characteristics

They are typically described as introverted, shy, self-conscious, and passive dependent. They may harbor resentment against persons for not providing them with sufficient attention and emotional support. Interpersonally, they are likely to be extremely sensitive and manipulate others through references to their symptoms.

Treatment Implications

They lack insight, are not psychologically sophisticated, and resent any implications that their difficulties may be even partially psychological (check the TRT/Negative Treatment Indicators scale). It is difficult for them to take responsibility for their behavior. They somatize stress with one result being that they are able to tolerate high levels of discomfort before being motivated to change. Thus they are not good candidates for psychotherapy, especially if the therapy is insight oriented. Typically, they seek medical explanations and solutions for their difficulties.

13/31

Symptoms and Behaviors

The 13/31 code type is associated with the classic conversion V, which occurs when Scale 2 is significantly lower (10 points or more) than Scales 1 or 3. As 2 becomes lower in relation to 1 and 3, the likelihood of a conversion disorder increases. This type of difficulty is strengthened in males who have correspondingly high Scales 4 and 5, and in females with a correspondingly high 4 but lowered 5. However, the 13/31 code type is more frequent in females and the elderly than in males and younger persons. Typically, very little anxiety is experienced by individuals with these profiles since they are converting psychological conflict into physical complaints. This can be checked by looking at the corresponding elevations of Scales 2 and 7. If these are also high, it indicates that they are experiencing anxiety and depression, perhaps because their conversions are currently unable to effectively eliminate their conflicts. Persons with conversion Vs will typically engage in extensive complaining about physical difficulties. Complaints may involve problems related to eating, such as obesity, nausea, anorexia nervosa, or bulimia, and there may be the presence of vague "neurological" difficulties, such as dizziness, numbness, weakness, and fatigue. There is often a sense of indifference and a marked lack of concern regarding these symptoms. These individuals have a strong need to appear rational and socially acceptable, yet nonetheless control others through histrionic and symptom-related means. They defensively attempt to appear hypernormal, which is particularly pronounced if the *K* scale is also elevated. Regardless of the actual, original cause of the complaints, a strong need exists to exaggerate them. Even if their complaints were originally caused by an organic impairment, there will be a strong functional basis to their problems.

If Scale 3 is higher than Scale 1, this allows for the expression of a certain degree of optimism, and their complaints will most likely be to the trunk of the body. Thus, patients might complain of such difficulties as gastrointestinal disorders, or diseases of the lungs or heart. Furthermore, a relatively higher 3 suggests the strong use of denial and repression. These people are passive, sociable, and dependent; they manipulate others through complaints about their "medical" problems. Conversely, if Scale 3 is lower than Scale 1, the person tends to be significantly more negative, and any conversion is likely to be to the body extremities such as the hands or legs. If scores are very high on Scale 8, a corresponding peak on Scale 1 is associated with somatic delusions.

Under stress, their symptom-related complaints will usually increase. However, once the stress level decreases, their symptoms will often disappear.

The most frequent diagnoses with 13/31 codes are major affective disorders (major depression, dysthymic disorder) hypochondriasis, conversion disorder, passive aggressive personality, and histrionic personality. Anxiety may be present if either Scale 7 or 8 is also elevated, but these corresponding elevations are rare. The 13/31 profile is also found in pain patients with an organic injury whose symptoms typically worsen under stress.

Personality Characteristics

Interpersonal relationships will be superficial, with extensive repression of hostility, and often their interactions will have an exhibitionistic flavor. Others describe them as selfish, immature, and egocentric but also as being outgoing, extraverted, and with strong needs for affection. They typically lack insight into their problems, use denial, and will often blame others for their difficulties (check the Repression/*R* scale). Usually, they are extremely threatened by any hint that they are unconventional and tend to organize themselves around ideals of service to others. However, their relationships and actual degree of involvement tend to be superficial. They may also feel resentment and hostility toward persons they feel have not provided them with sufficient attention and emotional support. When the conversion V is within the normal range (1 and 3 at or slightly below 65 on the MMPI-2), persons will be optimistic but somewhat immature and tangential. They can be described as responsible, helpful, normal, and sympathetic.

Treatment Implications

Since they lack insight and need to appear hypernormal, they typically make poor candidates for psychotherapy. They prefer simple, concrete answers to their difficulties and avoid introspection. However, they might respond to either direct suggestions or placebos, especially if the placebos are given within a medical context. Interventions to reduce their stress such as stress inoculation might also be helpful. A potentially useful technique would be to describe any psychosocial interventions using medical terminology. Thus biofeedback or other stress reduction techniques might be referred to as "neurological retraining." Often, however, they will terminate treatment prematurely, especially if their defenses are challenged. This issue becomes all the more difficult if there is a personality disorder since this would require a lengthier commitment to therapy.

14/41

Symptoms and Behaviors

The 14/41 code is encountered somewhat rarely, but is important since persons with these elevations will be severely hypochondriacal. They will be egocentric, will demand attention, and will express continuous concern with their physical complaints. There will be some similarities to other high-scoring 4s in that these individuals may have a history of alcohol abuse, drug addiction, and poor work and personal relationships (check WRK/Work Interference, MAC-R/MacAndrew Alcoholism scale, APS/Addiction Potential scale, and AAS/Addiction Acknowledgment scale) to refine interpretations). They may also be indecisive and rebellious.

The two most frequently encountered diagnoses will be hypochondriasis and a personality disorder, especially antisocial personality. Differentiation between these two can be aided by noting the relative strength of either Scale 1 or 4, as well as other related scales. Profiles involving "neurotic" features (anxiety, somatoform, dissociative, and dysthymic disorders) are characterized by a relatively higher Scale 1 with 2 and/or 3 also elevated. Personality disorders are more strongly suggested when Scale 4 is the primary high point.

Personality Characteristics

A core feature of this code type is likely to be ongoing personality difficulties. They are likely to act out and use poor judgment. Interpersonal interactions will be extremely manipulative but rarely will they be extremely antisocial. They might feel a sense of rebelliousness toward their homes and parents although these feelings are not likely to be expressed openly. Although they will be able to maintain control over their impulses, they will do so in a way that is bitter, pessimistic, self-pitying, and resentful of any rules and limits that are imposed on them. They are likely to be described by others as demanding, grouchy, and dissatisfied (check the CYN/Cynicism, ASP/Antisocial Practices, and FAM/Family Problems scales).

Treatment Implications

Usually, they will be resistant to therapy, although they may have a satisfactory response to short-term, symptom-oriented treatment. However, long-term therapy will be difficult and characterized by sporadic participation. Sessions may become somewhat tense due to their level of resentment and hostility which is likely to be sometimes expressed toward the therapist (check the TRT/Negative Treatment Indicators and ANG/Anger scales).

18/81

Symptoms and Behaviors

Peaks on Scales 1 and 8 are found with persons who present a variety of vague and unusual complaints (check the HEA/Health Concerns scale). They may also experience confusion, disorientation, and difficulty in concentrating. They focus on physical symptoms as a way to organize their thoughts, although the beliefs related to these symptoms may represent delusions. Their ability to deal effectively with stress and anxiety is extremely limited. They will experience interpersonal relationships with a considerable degree of distance and alienation. Often, they will feel hostile and aggressive but will keep these feelings inside. However, when such feelings are expressed, the expressions will be made in an extremely inappropriate, abrasive, and belligerent manner. Others will perceive these individuals as eccentric or even bizarre. They will distrust others and may disrupt their relationships due to difficulty in controlling their hostility. There may even be paranoid ideation, which will probably, but not necessarily, be reflected in an elevated Scale 6. They might be confused, distractible, and disoriented.

Common scales that are elevated along with 1 and 8 are 2, 3, and/or 7. These serve to color or give additional meaning to 18/81. Thus, an elevated Scale 2 will emphasize self-critical, pessimistic dimensions; 7, the presence of fears and anxiety (check the ANX/Anxiety, A/Anxiety, FRS/Fears, and OBS/Obsessions scales); and 3, the likelihood of conversions and/or somatic delusions.

The 18/81 code is frequently diagnosed as schizophrenia, especially if the *F* scale is also high. With a normal *F*, hypochondriasis is an important possibility, but if Scale 7 is elevated, an anxiety disorder is also strongly suggested.

Personality Characteristics

Personality difficulties of a long-standing nature are likely to be a significant factor. They are low in interpersonal trust and feel socially inadequate. They will feel socially isolated and alienated. Consistent with this, their past histories will often reveal a nomadic lifestyle with poor work histories (check the WRK/Work Interference scale).

Treatment Implications

Engaging them in therapy will be difficult since their level of insight will be poor. In addition, they will be distrustful, pessimistic, alienated, and hostile (check the TRT/Negative Treatment Indicators scale).

19/91

Symptoms and Behaviors

The 19/91 code is rarely encountered but is important because it may suggest organic difficulties relating to endocrine dysfunction or the central nervous system. Complaints are likely to include gastrointestinal difficulties, exhaustion, and headaches. There will be extensive complaining and overconcern with physical difficulties, but these patients may paradoxically attempt to deny and conceal their complaints at the same time. In other words, they may invest significant energy in avoiding confrontations relating to their complaints, yet will make a display of these techniques of avoidance. They will typically be extraverted, talkative, and outgoing, but also tense and restless. They might be in a state of turmoil and experience anxiety and distress. The expectations they have of themselves will be extremely high, yet their goals will be poorly defined and often unobtainable. If their complaints have no organic basis, then their behavior may be an attempt to stave off an impending depression. Often, this depression will be related to strong but unacceptable dependency needs.

Both hypochondriasis and manic states are frequent diagnoses and may occur simultaneously. These may be in response to, and exacerbated by, an underlying organic condition, an impending depression, or both. Corresponding elevations on Scales 4 and 6 make the possibility of a passive aggressive personality an important diagnostic consideration.

Personality Characteristics

Superficially, these clients might appear outgoing, assertive, and ambitious. However, they are likely to have an underlying passive dependent core to their personalities.

Treatment Implications

Psychotherapy will be difficult since these individuals are reluctant to accept a psychological explanation for their complaints (check the TRT/Negative Treatment Indicators scale).

23/32

Symptoms and Behaviors

Persons with elevations on Scales 2 and 3 will be lacking in energy, weak, apathetic, listless, depressed, anxious, and frequently report gastrointestinal complaints. They feel inadequate and have difficulty accomplishing their daily activities. Much of their energy is invested in excessively controlling their feelings and behavior. Although situational stress may serve to increase their depression, usually this depression is long-standing, and they have learned to live with their unhappiness and general lack of satisfaction. They are not very involved or interested in life and experience a difficult time initiating activities.

Some important male-female differences exist in the expression of this code type. Males are more ambitious, industrious, serious, and competitive, but also are immature and dependent. They strive for increased responsibilities, yet also fear them. They want to appear normal and receive recognition for their accomplishments, yet they often feel ignored and their level of work adjustment is often inadequate. In contrast, females are more apathetic and weak, and experience significant levels of depression. They have usually resigned themselves to long-term unhappiness and a lack of satisfaction. Although there is often significant marital strife (check the FAM/Family Problems scale), they rarely seek divorce.

Affective disorders represent the most frequent category of diagnosis given to this code. Corresponding elevations on Scales 4, 6, and 0 may provide additional information relating to the personality of these persons. With a high Scale 4, there is more likely to be an angry, brooding component to their depression, with underlying antisocial thoughts, yet their external behavior is usually overcontrolled. An elevated Scale 6 suggests that their depression relates to extreme interpersonal sensitivity and distrust, whereas a high 0 indicates they are socially withdrawn and introspective. An additional diagnosis that should be considered is a major depression with psychotic features, especially if Scales *F* and/or 8 are also elevated. Many patients with this code type are diagnosed as having a somatoform disorder. A 23/32 code type is frequently seen with chronic pain patients, especially if Scale 1 is also elevated.

Personality Characteristics

Individuals having this code type are often perceived as passive, docile, and dependent, and therefore often obtain nurturance from others. By keeping their relationships superficial, they achieve a certain level of security. Their behavior often elicits nurturance from others. They are uncomfortable around members of the opposite sex and may experience sexual maladjustment including impotence or frigidity. Interpersonally, they appear immature, childish, and socially inadequate. In terms of work, they feel the need to achieve and be successful, but are afraid of the added pressure this might produce. Although they might appear as if they are driven to succeed, they are anxious regarding competitive situations. Despite this avoidance of competition, they feel that their achievements are not adequately recognized.

Treatment Implications

These individuals will rarely volunteer for psychotherapy, their level of insight is poor, and they usually do not show significant improvement during treatment. This is primarily because their main dynamic is denial and situations such as therapy represent a threat to their avoidant style. Any conflicts are likely to be somatized and they are highly invested in medical explanations for their complaints. Accordingly, they might seek medical "solutions" to interpersonal conflicts through such methods as tranquilizers and pain medications. A further area that makes treatment difficult is that they are able to tolerate a considerable amount of discomfort and seem resigned to live with their unhappiness. However, since their level of distress is usually quite high, some method of symptom relief is indicated possibly through antidepressant medication. In addition, supportive (rather than insight-oriented) psychotherapy is often beneficial.

24/42

Symptoms and Behaviors

The most significant aspect of the 24/42 code is that these persons have an underlying antisocial trend to their personality, with difficulty maintaining control over their impulses. However, once they act on their underlying antisocial impulses, they experience guilt and anxiety regarding the consequences of their actions. This anxiety usually occurs too late to serve as an effective deterrent, and these individuals are unable to plan ahead effectively. The depression they experience is probably situational, and the distress they feel may reflect a fear of external consequences rather than an actual internalized moral code. Once the situation has subsided, there is usually further acting out. For this reason, the 24/42 code is sometimes considered to reflect an antisocial personality who has been caught.

The history of persons with high Scales 2 and 4 is often characterized by heavy drinking and/or drug abuse, which serves as a form of self-medication for their depression (check the MAC-R, ACK/Alcohol Acknowledgment, and APS/Alcohol Potential scales). Their interpersonal relationships are poor, which is reflected in numerous family difficulties (check the FAM/Family Problems scale) and sporadic employment. Their prospects for long-term employment are rarely favorable (check the WRK/Work Interference scale). These problems have often resulted in numerous legal complications (check the ASP/Antisocial Practices scale).

The hostility that is present with the 24/42 code may be expressed either directly or indirectly. A more direct expression is suggested if Scale 6 is high, since these individuals may feel justified in externalizing their anger due to real or imagined wrongs that have been committed against them. In contrast, a low 6 may reflect a suppression or unconscious denial of hostility. If high energy levels are suggested by a high Scale 9, the person may be extremely dangerous and volatile, and may have committed violent behaviors.

The 24/42 code is associated with personality disorders, especially passive aggressive or antisocial personalities. This is further strengthened if Scale 6 is also high. However, this code frequently reflects an adjustment disorder with a depressed mood. An important distinction to make is whether the depression is reactive or chronic. If chronic, then difficulties related to anxiety, conversions, and depression (neurotic features) will more likely be predominant, especially if Scales 1 and 3 are also high. A reactive depression is more likely to represent an antisocial personality who has been apprehended for his or her impulsive acting out. Substance abuse may be either the primary difficulty or may occur in addition to the other disorders suggested earlier. If Scale 4 is extremely elevated (above 90), a psychotic or prepsychotic process may be present, especially if *F* and 8 are also high.

Personality Characteristics

The initial impression may be friendliness or even charm, and, in a hospital setting, these patients may attempt to manipulate the staff. At their best, they can appear sociable, competent, and enthusiastic. Others might perceive them as sociable and outgoing. However, in the long term they are likely to produce resentment in interpersonal relationships. While appearing superficially competent and confident, they are likely to experience an underlying sense of dissatisfaction and feel self-conscious. Such persons respond to their failures with pessimism, self-criticism, and self-doubt. In an attempt to deal with these feelings, they will often develop passive-dependent relationships.

Treatment Implications

A 24/42 code type is the most frequent pattern found in alcohol and drug treatment programs. As a result, persons with this code type should always be assessed for substance abuse, regardless of the setting or reason for referral. Often an acknowledgment by clients that they indeed do have a drug or alcohol problem and an appraisal into its impact on their lives is an essential initial step (check the AAS/Addiction Acknowledgment scale). This profile also suggests long-standing personality difficulties that often make therapy difficult. Although such people may promise to change and their guilt is generally authentic, their acting out is usually resistant to change. Effective therapy must include clear limits, a change in environment, warm supports, and continual contact. However, the prognosis for long-term success in therapy is poor and the individuals will be likely to terminate when confronted with situational stress or when external motivators (e.g., legal) have been eliminated. Thus, some sort of external monitoring (i.e., legal or work-related) of their treatment, perhaps even conducting their treatment in a controlled environment, is advisable. Since peer influences are likely to have considerable impact, group interventions are likely to be more effective than individual treatment.

26/62

Symptoms and Behaviors

The most significant feature of the 26/62 code is extreme sensitivity to real or imagined criticism. These individuals will sometimes interpret the statements of others in a way that creates rejection, yet their conclusions will be based on insufficient data. Even minor criticism is brooded over and elaborated on. Usually, they have long histories of difficulties with interpersonal relationships. Others describe them as resentful, aggressive, and hostile. To protect themselves from the impending rejection of others, they will often reject others first, which results in other people avoiding them. When they are avoided, these individuals then have evidence that they are being rejected which gives them a justification for feeling and expressing anger. They can then blame others for their difficulties. This cycle is thus self-fulfilling and self-perpetuating, yet such people have difficulty understanding the part they play in creating the interpersonal responses directed toward them.

If Scales 7, 8, and possibly 9 are also high, a greater likelihood of a psychotic or prepsychotic condition exists, especially paranoid schizophrenia. A more controlled, well-defined paranoid system with a generally adequate level of adjustment may be suggested when Scales 2, 6, and *F* are only moderately elevated. Further possible diagnoses with the 26/62 code are a dysthymic disorder and, if Scale 4 is also elevated, a passive aggressive personality.

Personality Characteristics

Since persons with this code type are openly hostile and hypersensitive, they are likely to have poor interpersonal relationships (check the FAM/Family Problems and CYN/Cynicism scales). They are blaming, resentful, hostile, and are likely to have passive aggressive qualities. These patterns are usually of a long-standing nature and are difficult to alter.

Treatment Implications

The major challenge will be to effectively develop and maintain their rapport and trust. This will mean continually disengaging from their hostility and suspiciousness (check the ANG/Anger scale). An important area of further assessment would be to determine the extent of possible underlying psychotic processes.

27/72

Symptoms and Behaviors

The 27/72 code is extremely common in psychiatric populations and reflects persons who are depressed, agitated, restless, and nervous. Their behavior may be accompanied by slowed speech and movements, as well as by insomnia and feelings of social and sexual inadequacy. They generally spend a good deal of time anticipating problems before they actually occur and are vulnerable to actual or imagined threats. They worry excessively, often overreacting to minor events. Scales 2 and 7 reflect the relative degree of subjective turmoil the person is experiencing and they are thus often referred to as the "distress scales" (check the ANX/Anxiety, A/Anxiety, FRS/Fears, and OBS/Obsessiveness scales). Physical complaints may include weakness, fatigue, chest pain, constipation, and dizziness (check the HEA/Health Concerns scale).

Moderate elevations on Scales 2 and 7 can indicate a good prognosis for therapy, since this suggests that the person is introspective and is experiencing a sufficient amount of distress to be motivated to change. However, extreme elevations are likely to reflect a high level of disruption in their abilities to cope. The most frequent diagnoses are affective disorders, particularly major affective disorder, although they might also have an adjustment disorder with depressed mood. Anxiety disorders are also a possibility, particularly obsessive-compulsive disorder. Possible personality disorders might be avoidant, compulsive, or passive aggressive. However, with only moderate elevations, they may be normals who are fatigued and exhausted, with a high degree of rigidity and excessive worry. This code occurs more frequently with males 27 years or older from higher educational backgrounds. If 4 is elevated along with 2 and 7 (274/427/724), the meaning of the profile is changed. It then suggests persons who are anxious and depressed due to poor judgment related to self indulgence, particularly related to problem alcohol or drug use (check the MAC-R, AAS/Addiction Acknowledgment, and the APS/Addiction Potential scales).

Personality Characteristics

They can be characterized as perfectionistic and meticulous, and as having a high need for recognition. Their thinking is often obsessive and they experience a wide variety of phobias and fears (check the FRS/Fears scale). Interpersonally, they have difficulty asserting themselves and will be self-blaming, self-punishing, and passive dependent (check the SOD/Social Discomfort scale). They will rarely be argumentative or provocative. Their consciences are strong and inflexible, and they will often be extremely religious in a rigidly fundamental manner. Most are married and their courtships were fairly brief, many marrying within one month of their initial dating. They are described by others as docile and dependent, and typically elicit nurturance from others. They frequently rely on their friends and family to an excessive extent. Internally, they feel inadequate, insecure, and deal with feelings of hostility in an intropunitive manner.

Treatment Implications

Even though 27/72 persons usually express a great deal of pessimism regarding treatment and the future in general, their psychological distress is ordinarily reactive, and in time, they can be expected to improve. For most patients having this profile, the disorder takes between one month and one year to develop, and, if they report for treatment, it will be their first need for such intervention. If these scales are extremely high, the person may be too agitated to focus and concentrate. In such cases, medication may be necessary to relax them sufficiently to function in a psychotherapeutic context. The presence of suicidal thoughts is a definite possibility, especially if Scales 6 and 8 are also elevated, and the suicidal potential of these patients must be carefully evaluated. They can often be extremely self-critical during therapeutic sessions and require considerable emotional support. They are prone to being perfectionistic and guilty, which frequently leads to unproductive periods of rumination. While obsessive about the possibility of change, they often have a difficult time actually attempting new behaviors. However, they generally establish new relationships relatively easily and these relationships are frequently deep and of a long duration.

When working with persons with 274/427/724 code types, their drinking patterns might be of a long-standing nature therefore complicating any interventions. The possible presence of these difficulties should be determined early in the treatment sessions. In contrast to the pure 27/72 code type, they do not do well in individual insight-oriented therapy and are likely to terminate prematurely. There may be an initial "honeymoon" effect in which changes have apparently been made, but during times of stress, they are likely to act out and undermine any progress. They would be most likely to benefit from group interventions with a focus on clear specific goals that would include, among other things, environmental changes.

28/82

Symptoms and Behaviors

Persons with the 28/82 code complain of depression, anxiety, insomnia, fatigue, and weakness, as well as mental confusion, memory impairments, and difficulties in concentrating. They may also feel withdrawn, alienated, agitated, tense, and jumpy. Their motivation to achieve is characteristically low, as is their overall level of efficiency. They are likely to be unoriginal, stereotyped, apathetic, and indifferent. Often, they will have fears relating to an inability to control their impulses, including suicide. They are suspicious and extremely sensitive to the criticisms of others. Delusions and hallucinations may also be present, especially if Scale 8 is greater than 85. This list of complaints presents a highly diverse description of attributes, only some of which may be present in any specific case. The presence or absence of these complaints must be determined by examining data other than mere scale elevations. This may include the investigation of critical items, clinical interview data, personal history, and the use of the Harris-Lingoes and content scales (particularly BIZ/Bizarre Mentation, FRS/Fears, OBS/Obsessions, LSE/Low Self-Esteem, and SOD/Social Discomfort).

Differential diagnosis can be extremely important to determine. Most persons with this code type are diagnosed as having a major affective disorder (bipolar-depressed or major depression). Schizophrenia or schizoaffective disorder is also a possibility. Personality disorders might include borderline, avoidant, obsessive-compulsive, or schizoid. These personality patterns might feature lability, emotional instability, and acting out.

Personality Characteristics

Relevant personality descriptors include resentful, unassertive, dependent, and irritable. They often feel excessive guilt and are self-punitive. They justifiably have a fear of losing control of their emotions. A typical coping strategy is to deny unacceptable impulses, but this sometimes results in dissociative periods of acting out.

Treatment Implications

These clients are likely to have multiple problems related to expressing their anger, relationship difficulties, and social withdrawal. In particular, they might lose control over their feelings of anger and this might be directed toward the therapist during times of stress. They are also likely to feel ambivalence toward relationships in general and this may express itself in resistance to therapy. This ambivalence will also make it difficult to experiment with new strategies learned in therapy. Thus therapy tends to be long term. The therapist potentially can provide a point of stability in an otherwise chaotic and unpredictable life. An important area that should be assessed both during the initial session(s) and throughout treatment is the potential for suicide. During times of crises, many persons with this profile might require medication to control their thoughts and feelings.

29/92

Symptoms and Behaviors

Although anxiety and depression are present with the 29/92 code, a high level of energy also predominates. This energy may be associated with a loss of control, or it may also serve to defend against experiencing underlying depressive feelings. By speeding up their level of activity, these individuals can distract themselves from unpleasant depressive experiences. At times, this will be successful, but they may also use alcohol either to relax or to decrease their depression. With moderate elevations, this code will at the very least reflect tension and restlessness. Often, these persons will ruminate on feelings of worthlessness. They are typically perceived as self-absorbed and self-centered. Somatic complaints (especially upper-gastrointestinal) and sporadic alcohol abuse are common. They have high needs for achievement but may paradoxically set themselves up for failure. When this code type occurs among younger persons, it might reflect a vocational crisis with a resulting loss of identity. Sometimes brain-injured persons have this profile, which reflects that they feel a loss of control over their thoughts and feelings but are attempting to compensate for this by speeding up their level of activity.

If both scales are in the higher elevations, this suggests a mixed bipolar depression. However, both scales can change according to the particular phase the patient is in. This code can also reflect certain types of brain-injured patients or a cyclothymic disorder.

Personality Characteristics

The core feelings will be a sense of inadequacy and worthlessness. However, the person may deny these feelings and defend against them through the use of excessive activity.

Treatment Implications

Since alternating periods of intense activity followed by exhaustion and depression often occur, a major challenge of treatment is to stabilize these mood and activity swings. This might be further complicated by a long-standing history of alcohol or drug abuse. In addition, suicide potential should be carefully monitored. During initial assessment, depression may not be immediately apparent. However, a careful consideration of the client's background will reveal long-term but sporadic phases of depression.

34/43

Symptoms and Behaviors

Persons having peaks on Scales 3 and 4 are immature and self-centered, with a high level of anger that they have difficulty expressing. Thus, their anger will often be expressed in an indirect, passive-aggressive style. Outwardly, such individuals are continually trying to conform and please other people, but they still experience a considerable degree of anger and need to find ways of controlling or discharging it. This anger stems from a sense of alienation and rejection by family members. They might at times vicariously act out their aggression by developing a relationship with an individual who directly and spontaneously expresses his or her hostility. Such a relationship might be characterized by the 34/43 individual's covertly encouraging and fueling the other person's angry expressions, yet on a more superficial social level, disapproving of the other person. Typically, these individuals will have poor insight regarding their own behavior. If Scale 6 is also high, their lack of insight will be even more pronounced since their hostility will be projected onto others. Usually, past interpersonal relationships have been difficult. There may be a history of acting out, marital discord, and alcohol abuse (check the MAC-R, AAS/Addiction Acknowledgment Scale, APS/Addiction Potential Scale, and MDS/Marital Distress scales). Females are more likely than males to have vague physical complaints such as headaches, blackouts, and upper-gastrointestinal complaints. Despite such complaints, these females are generally free from extensive levels of anxiety. Furthermore, their relationships will be superficial, and will be characterized by naive expectations and a perfectionistic view of the world, which they maintain by glossing over and denying conflicts.

The 34/43 code most clearly fits the pattern of a passive-aggressive interactional style. However, histrionic or borderline personalities are also common. Persons with 34/43 code types are also frequently diagnosed as having an adjustment disorder with depressed mood or mixed emotional features. If both scales are extremely elevated (T greater than 85), then there may be fugue states in which aggressive and/or sexual impulses will be acted out.

Personality Characteristics

Conflicts relating to dependence versus independence are significant since both of these needs are intense. They tend to demand approval and affection from others. However, they will also have underlying feelings of anger that can easily become activated by criticism. Superficially, they might appear conforming but underneath they have strong feelings of rebelliousness.

Treatment Implications

Treatment sessions are likely to be stormy since the client will treat the therapeutic relationship similar to other relationships. Central issues will be self-control and difficulty with taking responsibility for their behaviors. The major resistance to therapy will be that they project blame onto others and have low levels of insight regarding this coping style. Often, they terminate therapy out of anger and frustration. Sometimes internal motivation to seek therapy is lacking, and they have been forced into treatment through external pressures from their spouse, work, or the legal justice system. Since they are relatively more responsive to peer (versus authority) pressures, group therapy can be quite effective. It is often useful to arrange for some external monitoring and external motivation to keep them in treatment.

36/63

Symptoms and Behaviors

A 36/63 code type indicates that the person is extremely sensitive to criticism, and re-presses his or her hostile and aggressive feelings. These individuals are fearful, tense, and anxious, and may complain of physical difficulties such as headaches or stomach problems. Overtly, they might deny suspiciousness and competitiveness, and might even see the world in naively accepting, positive, and perfectionistic terms. They can quickly and easily develop comfortable, superficial relationships. However, as a rela-tionship's depth and closeness increases, their underlying hostility, egocentricity, and even ruthlessness become more apparent.

If Scale 6 is higher than Scale 3 (by more than 5 points), these individuals will at-tempt to develop some sense of security in their lives by seeking power and prestige. If Scale 3 is higher than Scale 6 (by more than 5 points), their tendency to blame will be reduced, and such people will be more likely to deny any conflicts or problems. This will be consistent with a tendency to idealize both themselves and their world. They will be more likely to develop somatic complaints rather than paranoid ideation, and the chance of a psychotic process is significantly reduced.

Personality Characteristics

They will harbor feelings of resentment and hostility especially toward family mem-bers although they are unlikely to express these feelings directly. At times, they can be naive and gullible.

Treatment Implications

Their ability to acquire personal insight is limited since they are psychologically unso-phisticated and resent suggestions that their difficulties may be even partially psycho-logical (check the TRT/Negative Treatment Indicators scale). They will usually blame their personal problems on others, which creates one of their major difficulties in rela-tionships. In therapy, they will typically terminate abruptly and unexpectedly. They can be ruthless, defensive, and uncooperative. A central issue will be having them take responsibility for their feelings and behaviors.

38/83

Symptoms and Behaviors

This somewhat rare code involves symptoms of anxiety, depression, and such complaints as headaches, gastrointestinal disturbances, and numbness. They may have a series of obscure, intractable somatic complaints. If Scale 8 is significantly higher than Scale 3, these individuals may also have thought disturbances including mental confusion, disori-entation, difficulties with memory, and at times, delusional thinking (check the

BIZ/Bizarre Mentation scale). They often experience considerable turmoil and feel tense, fearful, and worried. Outwardly, they might appear apathetic and withdrawn. Although they have unusual experiences related to their thought processes and feel socially alienated, they also have strong needs to appear normal and strong needs for affection. They feel that, if others knew how unusual their experiences were, they would be rejected. Thus, they are extremely afraid of dependent relationships. To protect themselves, they use extensive denial, which makes their capacity for insight poor. They typically will describe their difficulties in a vague, guarded, and nonspecific manner.

An important variation from the 38/83 code occurs when elevated Scales 3 and 8 are also accompanied by elevations on *K,* with a low *F.* Persons with this profile are likely to be affiliative, inhibited, and overconventional, and to have an exaggerated need to be liked and approved of by others. Frequently, they maintain an unrealistic yet unassailable optimism. They emphasize harmony, perhaps even at the cost of sacrificing their own needs, attitudes, and beliefs. Furthermore, individuals who have high 3s with low *F* scores are extremely uncomfortable with anger and will avoid it at all costs. Typically, they will also avoid independent decision making and many other situations in which they must exert their power. Since they have an exaggerated sense of optimism and deny their personal conflicts, these individuals rarely appear in mental health clinics. It is almost as if any feelings of anger, tension, or defeat are intolerable. Such feelings seem to represent both a personal failure and, perhaps more importantly, a failure in their attempts at controlling their world by developing an overconventional, exaggeratedly optimistic, and inhibited stance.

When Scale 3 is relatively higher than Scale 8, and 8 and/or *F* is less than 70, somatoform or dissociative disorders are important considerations. If 8 and *F* are both highly elevated, the person might be schizophrenic.

Personality Characteristics

Persons with this profile can be described as having strong needs for attention and affection and are also immature and dependent. On the surface they might seem conventional, stereotyped, and unoriginal. Despite having a number of unusual internal experiences, they are uncomfortable with these processes and tend to limit them by being intropunitive.

Treatment Implications

Since they are typically apathetic and uninvolved in life activities, it is similarly difficult to engage them in therapy. Treatment is further complicated in that their level of insight is low. Specifically, they place considerable effort into appearing normal despite considerable unusual underlying processes. Thus, individual insight-oriented therapy is contraindicated. However, they may be responsive to a more supportive and directive approach.

45/54

Symptoms and Behaviors

High scores on Scales 4 and 5 reflect persons who have difficulty incorporating societal values. For the most part they can control antisocial feelings, but they may have brief episodes of acting out associated with low frustration tolerance and underlying anger and resentment. Their usual coping style is through passive-aggressive means. Overt homosexuals who make obvious displays of their orientation may have this code, especially if Scales 4 and 5 are the only peaks in an otherwise normal profile. The 45/54 code should in no way be considered diagnostic of homosexuality but simply, at times, is consistent with a subgroup of persons who have this orientation. To obtain further information associated with this or any profile in which Scale 5 is a high point, it is extremely helpful to interpret the third-highest scale and give it the degree of importance usually associated with the second highest point. Thus, a profile in which 4, 5, and 6 are all high might be interpreted as though it were a 46/64 code type.

Some important differences exist between males and females who have this code. First of all, it occurs much more frequently among men. Males with this code type will be openly nonconformist, but if they are from higher educational levels, they will be more likely to direct their dissatisfaction into social causes and express organized dissent toward the mainstream culture. If 9 is correspondingly high, they will be dissatisfied with their culture, sensitive, and aware, but will also have the energy to attempt to create change. They are often psychologically sophisticated, and can communicate clearly and openly. In contrast, elevated Scales 4 and 9 accompanied by a low Scale 5 suggest a high probability of sexual acting out and the probable development of a "Don Juan" personality. These men are self-centered and have difficulty delaying their gratification. Behind their overt display of affection is an underlying current of hostility.

Females with the 45/54 code will be openly rebelling against the traditional feminine role. Often, this rebellion is motivated by an intense fear related to developing dependent relationships. A further alternative interpretation is that these women are merely involved in a subculture or occupation that emphasizes traditionally male-oriented activities.

Personality Characteristics

Persons with this profile are immature, self-centered, and inner-directed, and are not only nonconformist but likely to openly express this nonconformity in a challenging, confrontive manner. They may also have significant problems with sexual identity and experience sexual dysfunction. A further area of conflict revolves around ambivalence relating to strong but unrecognized dependency needs.

Treatment Implications

Although persons with this profile are guarded and defensive about revealing themselves, they are also capable of thinking clearly and have good insight into their behavior. They rarely report for treatment because they typically are satisfied with themselves and their behavior. They usually do not report being emotionally distressed. When they do seek treatment, issues are likely to center around dominance and dependence. Significant change is unlikely due to the chronic, ingrained nature of their personality.

46/64

Symptoms and Behaviors

Persons with the 46/64 code type are hostile, brooding, distrustful, irritable, immature, self-centered, and usually unable to form close relationships. They have significant levels of social maladjustment often related to continually blaming others for their personal faults. This style of blaming prevents them from developing insight into their own feelings and behavior, since they are constantly focusing on the behavior of others rather than their own. They lack self-criticism, and are highly defensive and argumentative, especially if *L* and *K* are also high. Although they lack self-criticism, they are highly sensitive to real or imagined criticism from others, often inferring hostility or rejection when this was not actually intended. To avoid rejection and maintain a certain level of security, they become extremely adept at manipulating others. Often, they will have a history of drug addiction or alcohol abuse (check the MAC-R, AAS/Addiction Acknowledgment, and APS/Addiction Potential scales).

Frequent corresponding high points are on Scales 2, 3, and/or 8. Males with high 8s are often psychotic, especially paranoid schizophrenic or prepsychotic, but with 2 and/or 3 also elevated, the chances of a borderline condition are significantly increased. These men are likely to be angry and to have significant conflicts relating to their own denied, but strong, needs for dependency. They are likely to rebel against authority figures and may use suicidal threats to manipulate others. Females with a 46/64 code type may be psychotic or prepsychotic, but they are more often passive-aggressive personalities. If Scale 3 is also elevated, they will have intense needs for affection and will be egocentric and demanding. However, they will be resentful of the demands placed on them by others.

Personality Characteristics

A core issue is often passive dependency. These individuals frequently have adjustment difficulties associated with their hostility, anger, mistrust, and a tendency to blame others. They tend to avoid deep involvement. People perceive them as sullen, argumentative, obnoxious, and resentful of authority (check the ANG/Anger scale).

Treatment Implications

Persons with this profile are generally suspicious and even antagonistic towards treatment. When they do appear for treatment, it is at the insistence of someone else. As a result, they are mistrustful, suspicious, and project the blame for any difficulties onto someone else. Treatment plans should be concrete, clear, realistic, and described in such a way as to not arouse suspicion or antagonism. A therapeutic relationship is difficult to establish and, once established, is likely to be somewhat turbulent. The possibility of angry acting out should be carefully monitored.

47/74

Symptoms and Behaviors

Persons with high scores on Scales 4 and 7 experience guilt over their behavior, and are brooding and resentful. Although they are frequently insensitive to the feelings of others, they are intensely concerned with their own responses and feelings. They justify this insensitivity because they feel rejected or restricted by others. Their behavioral and interpersonal difficulties follow a predictable cycle in which they will alternately express anger and then feel guilty over their behavior. While they feel angry, they may have little control over their behavior, which results in impulsive acting out (check the ASP/Antisocial Practices and ANG/Anger scales). This is then followed by a phase of excessive overcontrol accompanied by guilt, brooding, and self-pity (check the O-H/Over-Controlled Hostility scale). Frustrated by these feelings, they may then attempt to selfishly meet their needs through such means as alcohol abuse, promiscuity, or aggressive acting out. Thus, the cycle continues and is usually fairly resistant to change. This frequently leads to legal problems and to difficulties in their work and home relationships. Although they do feel genuine and even excessive guilt and remorse, their self-control is still inadequate and their acting out continues.

Diagnostically, the 47/74 type is most likely to be either an antisocial personality or an anxiety disorder. This profile is frequently seen in alcohol, drug (check the MAC-R, AAS/Alcohol Acknowledgment, or APS/Alcohol Potential scales), or other treatment settings to which individuals with impulsive-compulsive styles are referred (e.g., eating disorder programs for persons with bulimia).

Personality Characteristics

Core difficulties relate to feelings of insecurity and ambivalence regarding dependency. Clients need frequent reassurances that they are worthy.

Treatment Implications

During the early stages of treatment, clients typically show remorse and express the need to change. This might seem sincere but as their guilt diminishes, they will again act out. Thus, therapists should be suspicious of early "easy" gains. Frequently, the person will respond to limit-setting with anxiety and resentfulness, often either testing the limits or completely ignoring them. The style of acting out followed by guilt is a chronic pattern, and therapeutic attempts to decrease anxiety may actually result in an increase in acting out because the control created by guilt and remorse might be diminished. These individuals may respond well to reassurance and support. However, long-term, fundamental change will be difficult to achieve.

48/84

Symptoms and Behaviors

Persons with the 48/84 code are strange, eccentric, emotionally distant, and have severe problems with adjustment. Their behavior is unpredictable and erratic, and may involve strange sexual obsessions and responses. Usually, there will be antisocial behavior resulting in legal complications (check the ASP/Antisocial Practices scale). These individuals also lack empathy, and are nonconforming and impulsive. Sometimes, they will be members of strange religious cults or unusual political organizations. In their early family histories, they learned that relationships were dangerous due to constant confrontation with intense family conflicts. They were rejected and, as a result, felt alienated and hostile, sometimes attempting to compensate with counterrejection and other forms of retaliation. Their academic and later work performance has usually been erratic and characterized by underachievement. In interpersonal relationships, their judgment is generally poor and their style of communication is likely to be inadequate. Often, others feel as if they are missing important elements or significant connotations of what the 48/84 individual is saying, but they cannot figure out exactly what or why.

If *F* is elevated with a low Scale 2, these individuals are typically aggressive, cold, and punitive, and have a knack for inspiring guilt and anxiety in others. Often, they take on roles in which such behavior is socially sanctioned, for example, a rigid law enforcement officer, overzealous member of the clergy, or a strict school disciplinarian. Their behavior may range all the way from merely stern, punitive, and disapproving, to actual clinical sadism. Underneath these overt behaviors, they usually have a deep sense of alienation, vulnerability, and loneliness, which may give rise to feelings of anxiety and discomfort.

Criminal behavior occurs frequently in males with a 48/84 code type, especially when Scale 9 is also elevated. The crimes are likely to be bizarre, and often extremely violent, involving homicide and/or sexual assault. These behaviors are usually impulsive, poorly planned, without apparent reason, and generally self-defeating, eventually resulting in self-punishment. Females are less likely to act criminally, but their relationships will usually be primarily sexual and they will rarely become emotionally close. Often, they will form relationships with men who are significantly inferior to themselves and who could be described as losers.

The most likely diagnosis is a schizoid or paranoid personality. However, a psychotic reaction, often paranoid schizophrenia is also common, especially with elevations on Scale 6.

Personality Characteristics

Although these individuals have deep needs for attention and affection, they frequently set themselves up for rejection and failure. They have deep feelings of insecurity and a poor self-concept.

Treatment Implications

Since the client will be aloof and unconventional, it will be difficult to establish a therapeutic relationship. The sessions are likely to be chaotic with a difficulty focusing on relevant areas. Thus they may seem relatively unproductive. There will often be so many different problems to work on, that it is difficult to know where to begin and easy to get sidetracked. Treatment may be further complicated by long-standing drug- and alcohol-related problems. Acting out may further complicate the picture. Since these clients are also likely to be mistrustful, they are likely to terminate prematurely.

49/94

Symptoms and Behaviors

Persons with 49/94 codes not only feel alienated and have antisocial tendencies, but also have the energy to act on these tendencies. They can be described as self-indulgent, sensation seeking, impulsive, oriented toward pleasure, irritable, extraverted, violent, manipulative, and energetic. They have poorly developed consciences, with a marked lack of concern for rules and conventions. Since they are free from anxiety, talkative, and charming, they can often make a good initial impression. However, their relationships are usually shallow because any sort of deeper contact with them brings out the more problematic sides of their personality. An investigation of their past history typically reveals extensive legal, family, and work-related difficulties (check the ASP/Antisocial Practices and WRK/Work Interference scales). The 49/94 code, when found in persons over age 30, suggests that this pattern is highly resistant to change. In adolescent males, it is associated with delinquency.

With a correspondingly low 0, this code is likely to reflect a person with highly developed social techniques, who will use these skills to manipulate others. Thus, he or she may be involved in elaborate, antisocial "con" games. If Scale 3 is correspondingly high, it decreases the chance of acting out. In these cases, the expression of hostility is likely to be similar to that of the 34/43 code in that it will be indirect and often passive-aggressive. When Scale 6 is elevated along with Scales 4 and 9, extreme caution should be taken since these individuals will be very dangerous and have poor judgment. Their acting out will often be violent and bizarre, and will appear justified to themselves due to strong feelings of resentment toward others.

The most likely diagnosis is an antisocial personality, although caution should be made, especially when categorizing adolescents since these scales are more commonly elevated for both normal and abnormal adolescents. If Scale 8 is also high, it may reflect either a manic state or schizophrenia.

Personality Characteristics

They will often produce an external facade of being confident and secure but underneath they will be immature, dependent, and insecure. They are likely to be narcissistic and incapable of deep emotional closeness. They will have a difficult time delaying gratification and often exercise poor judgment. Others will perceive them as being extraverted, talkative, uninhibited, restless, and needing emotional stimulation and excitement. Initially they might make a good impression, but their antisocial style will soon become apparent. In particular, they will rationalize their own shortcomings and blame their problems on others.

Treatment Implications

There are numerous difficulties encountered in therapy with individuals having 49/94 code types. They have difficulty focusing for any length of time and are constantly embarking on often irrelevant tangents. Despite this, they can be quite articulate. They have difficulty delaying gratification and usually do not learn from experience but are more concerned with self-gratification (often at the expense of others). They are frequently irritable and, if confronted by a therapist, will express their fairly extensive hostility. In addition, their typical coping strategy is through conning other people. Manipulation may involve a combination of charm laced with occasional belligerence. When this behavior occurs, it is advisable to confront it as soon as possible. Thus, treatment is likely to be slow, frustrating, and often unproductive. These individuals rarely volunteer for therapy but are rather referred by the court system or at the insistence of someone else (e.g., employer, spouse). External monitoring and motivation are usually required to keep them in treatment. However, since their anxiety level is quite low, they will not be motivated to change. Group treatment has been reported to be relatively helpful and behavioral modification can often help them develop better coping styles. Despite this, termination is usually premature and associated with the client feeling bored with the sessions, acting out, or a combination of the two.

68/86

Symptoms and Behaviors

The key features of people with the 68/86 code type are suspiciousness and distrustfulness, and they often perceive the intentions of others as suspect and questionable. They will be extremely distant from others, with few or no friends. They can be described as inhibited, shy, resentful, anxious, and unable to accept or appropriately respond to the demands that are made of them. This is because they are highly involved in their fantasy world, uncooperative, and apathetic, and because they have poor judgment and experience difficulty concentrating. Their sense of reality is poor, and they often experience guilt, inferiority, and mental confusion; sometimes their affect will be flat. The content of their thoughts can be expected to be unusual if not bizarre, frequently containing delusions of grandeur and/or self-reference. While their affect might be blunt, they are still internally quite anxious. Surprisingly, their past work history is often adequate provided the elevations on 6 and 8 are not extremely high. However, an intensification of their symptoms brought on by stress will usually disrupt their ability to work. Persons with this code are more often single and younger than 26 years of age. If they are married, their spouses are frequently also emotionally disturbed.

The most frequent diagnosis is paranoid schizophrenia, especially if Scale 4 is also elevated and 8 is relatively higher than 7. These persons will experience depression, inappropriate affect, phobias, and paranoid delusions. If Scale 7 is 10 points or more lower than Scales 6 and 8, this pattern is referred to as the "paranoid valley" and emphasizes the presence of paranoid ideation. A highly elevated *F* with Scales 6 and 8 above 80 does not necessarily indicate an invalid profile. A paranoid state is also a frequent diagnosis with the 68/86 code; less frequently, organic brain disorders or severe anxiety disorders may be diagnosed.

Personality Characteristics

Persons with this code type will be insecure with low self-confidence and poor self-esteem. Others perceive them as being unfriendly, negativistic, moody, and irritable. Since their level of social discomfort is high, they will feel most relaxed when alone and will generally avoid deep emotional ties. Their defenses will be poorly developed and, when under stress, are likely to regress (check the LSE/Low Self-Esteem and SOD/Social Discomfort scales).

Treatment Implications

Since a significant level of psychopathology is present with this profile, clinicians must be aware of a number of different issues related to further assessment and case management. In particular, treatment on either an inpatient or an outpatient basis needs to be decided. One of the major factors in this decision is a further assessment of the extent to which the client is a danger to themselves or others. A further consideration is whether psychopharmacological intervention and maintenance will help control psychotic thinking. In addition, basic daily living skills will be an issue. Clients might require training in basic social skills, assertiveness, job interviewing, and knowledge of resources to resort to when their symptoms increase. Insight-oriented therapy is often contraindicated since self-reflection might result in further regression. Instead, a concrete, behaviorally oriented method of intervention is likely to be more successful. One difficulty might be that these clients have unusual or even bizarre belief systems with quite different sets of logic than the therapist (check the BIZ/Bizarre Mentation scale). This might pose particular problems for attempts at cognitively based interventions. Furthermore, their level of suspicion and projection of blame will present further challenges. Due to their high level of mistrust, poor social skills, and social discomfort, they are likely to have difficulty forming a relationship with a therapist. Often sessions will seem slow, unproductive, and characterized by long periods of silence. Impulsivity and regression are also likely to provide further treatment challenges.

69/96

Symptoms and Behaviors

Persons with 69/96 profiles are likely to be excited, oversensitive, mistrustful, energetic, and irritable. They may have difficulty thinking and exercise poor judgment. They feel extremely vulnerable to real or imagined threats and experience anxiety much of the time. Their typical response to stress is to withdraw into fantasy. They may have clear or subtle signs of a thought disorder including delusions, difficulty concentrating, hallucinations, tangential associations, incoherent speech, and appear perplexed and disoriented. They are likely to be obsessional, ruminative, and overideational. Diagnosis is likely to be either schizophrenia (paranoid type) or a mood disorder.

Personality Characteristics

Individuals with this profile can be described as mistrustful and suspicious. They also have high needs for affection and their relationships will often be passive-dependent. There is likely to be a clear discrepancy between how they describe themselves and how others perceive them. Whereas they describe themselves as calm, easygoing, happy, and in good health, others are likely to describe them as hostile, angry, and overreactive to even minor stress. These reactions to stress can result in their either becoming overly excited or apathetic and withdrawn. Thus, they have difficulties modulating their expression of emotions.

Treatment Implications

This code type is characteristic of inpatient populations. Psychopharmacological interventions to help control disorganized thinking or regulate mood can often be extremely effective. Due to their disorganized, regressive, and ruminative thought processes, insight-oriented therapy is usually not effective. In addition, their lack of trust and suspiciousness often makes it difficult to form a therapeutic relationship. If a trusting relationship can be developed, then concrete, problem-focused approaches are most effective.

78/87

Symptoms and Behaviors

The 78/87 code often occurs among psychiatric patients and reflects a level of agitation sufficiently intense to disrupt their daily activities. Usually, this profile represents a reaction to a specific crisis. They may have been previously functioning at a fairly adequate level until some event or series of events triggered a collapse in their defenses ("nervous breakdown"). Their style of relating to others is passive, and they have difficulty developing and sustaining mature heterosexual relationships. They are lacking in self-confidence, often experience insomnia, and may have hallucinations and delusions. Common feelings include guilt, inferiority, confusion, worry, and fear, and they may have difficulties related to sexual performance.

The extent of elevations on Scales 7 and 8, and the relative heights between them, have important implications both diagnostically and prognostically. If Scale 7 is higher than Scale 8, the person's psychological condition is more susceptible to improvement and tends to be more benign. This has a tendency to be true regardless of the elevation of 8, as long as 7 maintains its relatively higher position. The higher Scale 7 suggests that the person is still actively fighting his or her problem and has some of his or her defenses still working. It also suggests an anxiety disorder rather than psychosis. Thus, ingrained bizarre thought patterns and withdrawn behavior have not yet become established. A relatively higher Scale 8, on the other hand, reflects more fixed patterns and is therefore more difficult to treat. This is particularly true if Scale 8 is over 75. If Scales 7 and 8 are both greater than 75 (with Scale 8 relatively higher), this suggests an established schizophrenic pattern, especially if the "neurotic triad" is low (check the BIZ/Bizarre Mentation scale). Even if schizophrenia can be ruled out, the condition tends to be extremely resistant to change, as, for example, with a severe, alienated personality disorder. If Scale 2 is also elevated, this raises the possibility of either a dysthymic or obsessive-compulsive disorder.

Personality Characteristics

Persons with 78/87 code types are likely to feel inferior, inadequate, indecisive, and insecure. Their relationships will often be passive-dependent and they will have difficulties asserting themselves in heterosexual relationships. They might be preoccupied in excessive and unusual sexual fantasies. They will feel extremely uncomfortable in most social relationships and are likely to defend themselves with excessive withdrawal (check SOD/Social Discomfort scale).

Treatment Implications

There may be a significant suicidal risk, which can be further evaluated by looking at the relative elevation of Scale 2, checking relevant critical items, taking a careful history, and asking relevant questions related to the client's thought processes.

89/98

Symptoms and Behaviors

The 89/98 code suggests persons who are highly energetic, perhaps to the point of hyperactivity. They will be emotionally labile, tense, and disorganized, with the possibility of delusions of grandeur sometimes with a religious flavor, especially if Scale 6 is also elevated. Their thought processes are likely to be tangential and speech bizarre, possibly characterized by neologisms, clang associations, and echolalia (check the BIZ/Bizarre Mentation scale). Their goals and expectations will be unrealistic; they often make extensive plans that are far beyond their ability to accomplish. Thus, their aspirations will be significantly higher than their actual achievements. Usually, they will have severe symptoms related to insomnia. Serious psychopathology is likely to be present.

The most frequent diagnosis is schizophrenia, or possibly a schizoaffective disorder with manic states. In addition, a severe personality disorder is a diagnostic consideration. Sometimes, the relative elevation of *F* can be used as an index of the relative severity of the disorder.

Personality Characteristics

Their interpersonal relationships are childish and immature, and they will usually be fearful, distrustful, irritable, and distractible. Although they might be highly talkative and energetic, they will also prefer to withdraw from interpersonal relationships. They will resist any deep involvement with other people. While on the one hand they are grandiose and boastful, underneath they will have feelings of inferiority and inadequacy. When they do become involved with people, they demand considerable attention and become hostile and resentful when their needs are not met (check the ANG/Anger scale).

Treatment Implications

Since they are highly distractible and tangential, psychotherapeutic approaches with them are extremely difficult. Furthermore, their level of insight is poor, they resist psychological interpretations of their behavior, and they cannot focus on any one area for any length of time. A frequent defense is denial of any psychological problems along with grandiose thoughts and an inflated sense of their self-worth. Challenging these defenses is likely to provoke irritability, anger, or even aggression. If extensive delusions and hallucinations are present, antipsychotic medication may be indicated. Lithium may be useful if the mood component of their disorder predominates.

MMPI-2 CONTENT SCALES

The first formal attempt to develop a series of MMPI content scales was by Wiggins (1966, 1971) who organized scales based on an overall analysis of the contents of the MMPI items. He began with item clusters that were based on such areas as authority conflicts and social maladjustment. These clusters were revised and refined using factor analysis and evaluations of internal consistency. During the 1989 restandardization of the MMPI, many of the items relating to the Wiggins scales were altered or deleted. As a result, Butcher et al. (1990) developed a new set of 15 different content scales. At first, provisional content scales were developed by rationally sorting the items into different content categories. These categories were then refined statistically by making item-scale correlations with psychiatric inpatients and correlations between the scales. Further validity studies have confirmed that they are at least as valid as the MMPI/ MMPI-2/MMPI-A empirically derived scales (Ben-Porath, Butcher, & Graham, 1991; Ben-Porath, McCulley, & Almagor, 1993; Butcher & Williams, 1992). A further advantage over the clinical scales is that they measure single dimensions. The practical significance of this is that they can be relatively easily interpreted using rational, intuitive strategies. In contrast, the MMPI clinical and validity scales are multidimensional. Thus, they require clinicians to work with them to extract the most useful and valid interpretations, often from a wide variety of possible descriptors.

An important function of the content scales is that they can be used to refine the meanings of the clinical scales. For example, if an individual obtains an elevation on 4 (Psychopathic Deviance), clinicians can note possible corresponding elevations on FAM (Family Problems) and ASP (Antisocial Practices). If FAM is elevated but not ASP, this suggests that the reason for the elevated 4 has more to do with family alienation and conflict than criminal and other forms of antisocial behavior. Thus, the content scales can incrementally increase the validity of the clinical scales (Ben-Porath, McCulley, & Almagor, 1993).

In addition to clarifying the meanings of the scales, their interpretations and implications can also be extended. For example, elevations on 1, 2, and 3 are consistent with pain patients. However, in considering their prognosis for rehabilitation programs, it would also be important to assess their attitudes toward returning to work by noting the scores on WRK (Work Interference) and responsiveness to treatment by noting scores on TRT (Negative Treatment Indicators; Clark, 1996). Elevations above 65 on the content scales indicate that many of the descriptors for the scale apply to the person. Scales which are mildly elevated (60–64 inclusive) suggest that several of the behaviors apply to the person. Thus the inclusion of the new MMPI-2 and MMPI-A content scales represent potentially important and easily interpreted dimensions of assessment. The MMPI-2 content scales can be divided into the following clusters relating to internal symptoms, external aggression, negative self-views, and general problem areas.

Internal Symptomatic Behaviors

ANX/Anxiety Generalized anxiety, somatic difficulties, worries, insomnia, ambivalence, tension, a feeling that life is a strain, fears of losing one's minds, pounding heart and shortness of breath, concentration problems, difficulties making decisions; symptoms clearly perceived and admitted to by the client.

FRS/Fears Multiple specific fears (nuisance animals, blood, dirt, leaving home, natural disasters, mice, snakes, etc.).

OBS/Obsessiveness Ruminates, difficulty with decision making, resistant to change, needless repetitive counting, may have compulsive behaviors such as counting or alphabetizing one's experience; worried, sometimes overwhelmed by one's own thoughts; others become easily impatient with the person.

DEP/Depression High number of depressive thoughts, uninterested in life; feeling of emptiness; feeling of having committed unpardonable sins; cries easily; unhappy; possible suicidal ideation; sense that other people are not sufficiently supportive; sensitive to rejection, tense, passive feeling of hopelessness; helplessness about the future.

HEA/Health Concerns Numerous physical complaints regarding gastrointestinal, neurological, sensory, skin, cardiovascular and/or respiratory difficulties; problems of adjustment; worried and nervous; lacking in energy.

BIZ/Bizarre Mentation Psychotic thought processes, hallucinations (auditory, visual, olfactory), paranoid beliefs, strange thoughts, delusions.

External Aggressive Tendencies

ANG/Anger   Difficulties in controlling anger, irritable, impatient, annoyed, stubborn, may swear; episodes of loss of control, possibly breaking objects or actually being physically abusive.

CYN/Cynicism   Distrust of other people; fear of being used, or that others will lie and cheat them; belief that the only reason for others not lying or cheating is fear of being caught; negativity toward friends and associates, belief that people are friendly only for selfish reasons.

ASP/Antisocial Practices   Past legal and/or academic problem behaviors; expectation that others will lie, support of illegal behavior; enjoyment of criminal behavior of others; thought patterns that characterize criminal behavior, whether or not such behavior actually occurs.

TPA/Type A   Driven, hardworking, competitive, hostile, irritable with time constraints, overbearing, annoyed with interruptions, tries to do more and more in less and less time, blunt and direct, petty regarding minor details (this scale is a better construct for use with males than females).

Negative Self-View

LSE/Low Self-Esteem   Low self-confidence, feeling of insignificance, negative beliefs regarding self (clumsy, inept, unattractive), acutely aware of faults, feeling of being disliked by others, sometimes overwhelmed by one's own faults, difficulty accepting compliments from others.

General Problem Areas Cluster

SOD/Social Discomfort   Shy, withdrawn, uneasy with others, introverted, dislikes social events, prefers to be alone.

FAM/Family Problems   Family discord, unhappy childhood, difficult and unhappy marriages, families that do not express much love but are rather quarrelsome and unpleasant, possibly an abusive childhood.

WRK/Work Interference   Personal difficulties that interfere with work; tension, worry, obsessiveness, difficulty concentrating, career indecision and/or dissatisfaction, poor concentration, dislike of coworkers; difficulty initiating work-related activities; little family support for career choice; easily defeated by difficulties.

TRT/Negative Treatment Indicators   Dislike or distrust of helping professionals, discomfort in discussing difficulties, resistance to change, disbelief in the possibility of change, belief that no one can really understand or help them, preference for giving up rather than facing a crisis (Clark, 1996).

MMPI-A CONTENT SCALES

The MMPI-A content scales were developed and refined in much the same way as the MMPI-2 content scales. Some of the items were changed to be more relevant for adolescent populations. In addition, some new scales were added such as the Adolescent-School Problems scale (instead of the adult WRK/Work Interference scale) and others were dropped such as the TPA (Type A) scale since they were not considered relevant for adolescents. Elevations above 65 indicate that there has been extensive endorsement of the problems indicated in the scales whereas a mild elevation (60–64 inclusive) suggests that several of the descriptors apply to the person.

A-anx/Adolescent-Anxiety   High scores suggest tension, nervousness, worry, sleep-related difficulties (nightmares, difficulty with sleep onset, early morning awakening); life feels like a strain; problems seem as if they are insurmountable; there will be feelings of impending doom, fears of losing one's mind, confusion and difficulty concentrating, increase in family discord; girls in clinical settings report feeling depressed and have somatic complaints.

A-obs/Adolescent-Obsessiveness   High scores suggest excessive worry, ruminations, obsessive counting of objects, extreme fear regarding making changes, difficulty making decisions, obsessing over past events or behaviors; others lose patience with them; boys in clinical settings are described as anxious, overly concerned with the future, dependent, worried, preoccupied, resentful, feel as if they deserve punishment; girls in clinical settings may have suicidal ideation and/or have actually made suicidal gestures.

A-dep/Adolescent-Depression   High scores suggest fatigue, crying spells, self-criticism, feelings of being condemned and unworthy, feelings of hopelessness; life is uninteresting, suicidal ideation is present; there is difficulty initiating activities, dissatisfaction; boys in clinical settings might be further assessed for a history of abuse; girls in clinical settings have depression and low self-esteem; girls in school settings are likely to have poor grades, are unlikely to have noteworthy personal achievements, and are likely to be concerned about being overweight.

A-hea/Adolescent-Health   Elevations indicate the presence of health problems that result in school absence and limit their physical activities; complaints cover several different physical areas including gastrointestinal (nausea, vomiting, constipation, stomach trouble), sensory problems (poor eyesight, hearing difficulty), neurological complaints (convulsions, paralysis, numbness, dizzy spells, fainting), cardiovascular problems (heart or chest pains), skin disorders, respiratory problems, excessive worry over health and belief that all related problems would be fine if their health difficulties could be solved; in clinical settings they are likely to report being afraid of school; in school settings they are likely to have academic and behavioral difficulties (school suspensions, course failures, low grades); girls in clinical settings are likely to report an increase in disagreements with parents; boys in clinical settings are described as anxious, worried, guilt prone, accident prone, perfectionistic (but less bright), clinging, fearful, and more likely to have lost weight.

A-aln/Adolescent-Alienation   High scores indicate a high level of emotional distance, a feeling that no one really understands or cares for them, a sense that they are getting a raw deal from life, difficulty getting along with others, not liked, others are unkind and even out to get them; there is a belief that others have more fun than they do, low self-disclosure is likely; others interfere with their attempts to succeed; they feel anxious when talking to a group and are likely to have poor grades in school; girls may have a problem with weight gain; girls in clinical settings have few or no friends, increase in disagreements with parents; boys in clinical populations have low self-esteem and poor social skills.

A-biz/Adolescent-Bizarre Mentation   High scores indicate very strange thoughts and experiences, possibly auditory, olfactory, and visual hallucinations, paranoid thoughts (plotted against, someone is trying to kill them), possible beliefs that evil spirits or ghosts are trying to control them; girls in clinical settings probably come from dysfunctional families, parents and/or siblings might have arrest records; boys in clinical settings are likely to have been under the supervision of a child protective worker, likely to exhibit bizarre and possibly psychotic behavior; individuals from school settings are likely to have numerous difficulties including poor grades, suspensions, and course failures.

A-ang/Adolescent-Anger   High scores indicate that the person finds it difficult controlling anger, feels like breaking or smashing things, sometimes yelling to make a point and throwing tantrums to get his or her way; feels like getting into fist fights; shows irritability when others try to hurry him or her, impatient, especially likely to get into fights when drinking, likely to act out in school and/or home; adolescents in clinical settings are extremely interested in violence and aggression, histories of assault, described as angry, resentful, impulsive, moody, externalize behaviors; boys in clinical settings are described as attention seeking, resentful, anxious, self-condemning but also dependent and clinging, may have a history of sexual abuse; girls in clinical settings are likely to be aggressive, delinquent, have been arrested, act out sexually (promiscuity), are flirtatious, wear provocative clothes, need to be supervised around boys.

A-con/Adolescent-Conduct Problems   Elevations suggest that the client is oppositional, has legal problems, peer group is often in trouble; behavior problems including lying, stealing, shoplifting, swearing, vandalism; likely to enjoy other people's criminal behavior, might also enjoy making other people afraid of them; uses drugs and alcohol, has record of poor academic performance and school-related behavior problems (course failures, suspensions, lying and cheating), disobedient, impulsive; clinical girls are described as impulsive, angry, unpredictable, sexually active, provocative, resentful, impatient, require supervision around boys, unlikely to be depressed.

A-lse/Adolescent-Low Self-Esteem   High scores indicate that the individual feels unattractive, useless, has little ability, many faults, low self confidence, unable to do anything particularly well including planning own future, confused and forgetful, difficulty accepting compliments, susceptible to social pressure, passive; high-scoring boys should be further assessed for the possibility of sexual abuse; girls are likely to report weight gain, poor grades, and no noteworthy personal achievements; boys in clinical settings are described as having poor social skills; girls in clinical settings will be depressed, are likely to have learning disabilities, have increasing numbers of conflicts with their parents, suicidal thoughts, and possibly suicidal gestures.

A-las/Adolescent-Low Aspirations   High scores indicate a low level of interest, especially academically; the person dislikes studying, reading, listening to lectures (especially science); has problems initiating activities, gives up easily, dislikes facing difficult situations; has low expectations for achievement, and little interest in continuing on to college; described by others as lazy, has poor grades, little interest in school activities; clinical girls are likely to report sexual acting out, very unlikely to report having won a prize or award; clinical boys are likely to have been truant in school and run away from home.

A-sod/Adolescent-Social Discomfort   High scores indicate that the person is shy, prefers to be alone, difficulty making friends, extremely uncomfortable when addressing a group, dislikes parties and crowds, difficult to get to know, uncomfortable meeting new people, dislikes initiating conversations, might actively avoid others, unlikely to report using drugs or alcohol; boys are likely to avoid school activities; girls in clinical settings are unlikely to be involved in acting out, are uninterested in boys, have few friends, may be depressed, have eating difficulties, may be fearful, withdrawn, physically weak, and are not likely to be involved with drugs, alcohol, or irresponsible behavior.

A-fam/Adolescent-Family Problems   High scorers are likely to have extensive difficulties with parents and other family members including fault-finding, jealousy, little love, serious arguments, poor communication; they long for the day when they can finally leave home, feel that parents punish them unfairly, show little acceptance of responsibility around home, feel that they cannot depend on their family in times of need; beatings and runaways are possible, however, problems usually do not extend into the legal justice system; there may be some school-related difficulties (low grades, suspensions); may reflect marital difficulties of parents; girls in school settings report possible exam failure and/or weight gain; in clinical settings there may be more externalizing behaviors including lying, cheating, stealing as well as somatic complaints, crying, guilt, timidity, and withdrawal; boys in clinical settings are described as sad, secretive, uncommunicative, disliked, self-conscious, unloved, dependent, resentful, attention seeking, and self-blaming; girls in clinical settings are typically described as immature, likely to fight, cruel, destructive, secretive, self-conscious, hyperactive, provocative, sexually acting out (promiscuity), and preoccupied with sex; further assessment should include possible sexual abuse for girls and possible physical abuse for boys.

A-sch/Adolescent-School   High scores indicate a wide number of school-related difficulties including low grades, truancy, easily upset by school events, learning disabilities, low level of social competence, boredom, suspensions, dislike of school, disciplinary actions, difficulty concentrating, probations, and negative attitudes toward teachers; feels that school is a waste of time; often school-related difficulties are specific to school

itself and do not spill over into other areas; boys from clinical populations are likely to
have run away, been irresponsible, and have a history of drug, particularly amphetamine,
use, they should be further evaluated for the possibility of sexual abuse; girls from clinical populations may have learning disabilities and/or academic underachievement.

A-trt/Adolescent-Negative Treatment Indicators   High scores indicate negative attitudes and feelings toward health care professionals; they do not like to share personal
information with others; they feel that they can never really be understood and others
do not really care what happens to them; they will have anxiety related to people asking them personal questions; they have difficulty planning for the future and are unwilling to take responsibility for the negative things in their lives; they feel that they
have many secrets they need to keep to themselves.

HARRIS-LINGOES AND Si SUBSCALES

One of the more popular developments has been the reorganization by Harris and
Lingoes (1955/1968) of the standard scales into more homogeneous content categories.
These subscales were constructed by intuitively grouping together items that seemed to
reflect single traits or attitudes contained within the already existing MMPI Scales 2, 3,
4, 6, 8, and 9. Ben-Porath, Hostetler, Butcher, and Graham (1989) further developed subscales similar to the Harris-Lingoes subscales for Scale 0. No subscales were developed
for 1 and 7 since these were considered to be relatively homogeneous in their item content. These same subscales have been carried over for use with the MMPI-A. The subscales and a brief summary of the meanings associated with high scores are provided in
this section. These summaries are derived from material by Harris and Lingoes (1968),
and extensions of these materials as summarized by Butcher et al. (1990), Butcher and
Williams (1992), Graham (1993), Greene (1991), and Levitt and Gotts (1995). Scoring
templates and profile sheets for the MMPI-2 and MMPI-A Harris-Lingoes subscales are
available from National Computer Systems.

Although the Harris and Lingoes subscales show high intercorrelations with the parent scales (Harris & Lingoes, 1968), the internal consistency of the subscales is somewhat low (.04 to .85; Gocka, 1965). Several initial validity studies are available
(Boerger, 1975; Calvin, 1975; Gordon & Swart, 1973) that demonstrate the potential
clinical usefulness of these subscales. The Social Introversion subscales have been found
to account for 90% of the variance of the *Si* scale, and convergent and discriminant
validity was demonstrated based on an analysis of spouses' ratings of one another (Ben-
Porath et al., 1989). The practical importance of both sets of subscales is that they provide a useful supplement for interpreting the original scales. For example, a clinician can
assess whether a person scoring high on Scale 4 (Psychopathic Deviate) achieved that elevation primarily due to family discord (*Pd* 1) authority problems (*Pd* 2) or social imperturbability (*Pd* 3). This breakdown is likely to be quite helpful in interpreting why a
client received a high score that was unexpected based on the person's history. It might
also be quite useful in interpreting the significance associated with moderate elevations
($T = 60$–65). A further situation to score and interpret the Harris-Lingoes scales would
be to understand the possible reasons for contradictory descriptions such as might

emerge if both Scales 2 and 9 were elevated. However, if the clinical scales are either within the normal range, or quite high, the Harris-Lingoes scales are not particularly useful. Only Harris-Lingoes and *Si* subscale elevations of $T = 65$ or greater should be interpretated.

The Harris-Lingoes and *Si* subscales should not be used for routine interpretations since they are quite time consuming to hand-score. Rather than scoring all the Harris-Lingoes and *Si* subscales, clinicians can select and score only those that are relevant for refining and clarifying the meanings of clinical scales that are in question. Despite some validity efforts, the amount of research available is still inadequate, and in many cases, the internal consistency of the subscales is insufficient (Friedman, Webb, & Lewak, 1989). Thus, any interpretations should be made cautiously and be considered as hypotheses in need of further support. This is particularly true for the MMPI-A where there has been even less investigation using the Harris-Lingoes and *Si* subscales than for the MMPI/MMPI-2. Furthermore, item deletions and alterations between the MMPI/MMPI-2 and MMPI-A, primarily for the *Si* scale, bring into question the transferability of the Harris-Lingoes and *Si* scales with the adolescent version of the MMPI.

Scale 2. Depression

D1/Subjective Depression   Unhappy, low energy, sense of inferiority, low self-confidence, socially uneasy, few interests.

D2/Psychomotor Retardation   Low energy, immobilized, socially withdrawn, listless.

D3/Physical Malfunctioning   Reports wide variety of physical symptoms, preoccupied with health, denial of good health.

D4/Mental Dullness   Low energy, pessimistic, little enjoyment of life; difficulties with concentration, attention, and memory; apathetic.

D5/Brooding   May feel as if he or she is losing control of his or her thoughts; broods, cries, ruminates, feels inferior, and is hypersensitive.

Scale 3. Hysteria

Hy1/Denial of Social Anxiety   Extraverted, comfortable with social interaction, minimally influenced by social standards.

Hy2/Need for Affection   Strong needs for affection with fears that these needs will not be met, denies negative feelings toward others.

Hy3/Lassitude-Malaise   Subjective, discomfort, poor health, fatigued, poor concentration, insomnia, unhappiness.

Hy4/Somatic Complaints   Wide variety of physical complaints, denial of hostility toward others.

Hy5/Inhibition of Aggression   Denial of hostility and anger, interpersonally hypersensitive.

Scale 4. Psychopathic Deviate

Pd1/Familial Discord   Family that was critical, unsupportive, and interfered with independence.

Pd2/Authority Conflict   Rebellion against societal rules, beliefs of right/wrong that disregard societal norms, legal/academic difficulties.

Pd3/Social Imperturbability   Opinionated, socially confident, outspoken.

Pd4/Social Alienation   Isolated from others, feels poorly understood.

Pd5/Self-Alienation   Unhappy with self, guilt and regret regarding past behavior.

Scale 6. Paranoia

Pa1/Persecutory Ideas   Perceives world as dangerous, feels poorly understood, distrustful.

Pa2/Poignancy   Feels lonely, tense, hypersensitive, possibly high sensation-seeking.

Pa3/Naivete   Overly optimistic, extremely high moral standards, denial of hostility.

Scale 8. Schizophrenia

Sc1/Social Alienation   Feels unloved, mistreated, and possibly persecuted.

Sc2/Emotional Alienation   Depression, fear, possible suicidal wishes.

Sc3/Lack of Ego Mastery, Cognitive   Strange thoughts, sense of unreality, poor concentration and memory, loss of mental control.

Sc4/Lack of Ego Mastery, Conative   Depressed, worried, fantasy withdrawal, life is too difficult, possible suicidal wishes.

Sc5/Lack of Ego Mastery, Defective Inhibition   Sense of losing control of impulses and feelings, labile, hyperactive, cannot control or recall certain behaviors.

Sc6/Bizarre Sensory Experiences   Hallucinations, peculiar sensory and motor experiences, strange thoughts, delusions.

Scale 9. Hypomania

Ma1/Amorality   Selfish, poor conscience, manipulative; justifies amoral behavior by believing others are selfish and opportunistic.

Ma2/Psychomotor Acceleration   Restless, hyperactive, accelerated thoughts and behaviors, seeks excitement to reduce boredom.

Ma3/Imperturbability   Unaffected by concerns and opinions of others, denies feeling socially anxious.

Ma4/Ego Inflation   Unrealistic perception of abilities, resentful of demands placed on him- or herself.

Scale 0. Social Introversion

(*Note:* The Social Introversion subscales are scored on the MMPI-2 Supplementary Scales Profile sheet; scoring templates are available from National Computer Systems.)

Si1/Shyness   Easily embarrassed, reluctant to initiate relationships, socially uncomfortable, shy.

Si2/Social Avoidance   Dislike and avoidance of group activities, parties, social activities.

Si3/Self/Other Alienation   Poor self-esteem, self-critical, low self-confidence, sense of ineffectiveness.

CRITICAL ITEMS

An alternative to content analysis other then scoring and interpreting actual scales, is to interpret the meanings of single items or clusters of items that seem, based on their content, to relate to different areas of psychopathology (depressed suicidal ideation, mental confusion, etc.). Several attempts have been made to isolate those items considered critical to the presence of psychopathology. Answering in a significant direction on these items could represent serious pathology, regardless of how the person responded on the remainder of the inventory. These items have been referred to as "pathognomonic items," "stop items," or, more frequently, "critical items." It has been assumed that the direction in which a person responds represents a sample of the person's behavior and acts like a short scale that indicates the client's general level of functioning. Two early lists of critical items were Grayson's (1951) list of 38 items and Caldwell's (1969) more comprehensive list of 69 items. Both of these were intuitively derived and have been found to be useful in differentiating which category of crisis a particular patient is in (acute anxiety, depressed-suicidal, mental confusion, etc.). The Grayson items have been able to indicate a person in crisis, but they were primarily used to specify the presence of psychotic complaints (mental confusion, persecutory ideas). Attempts to establish an efficient cutoff score for differentiating normals from psychiatric patients have met with only minimal success due to the extensive response overlap between the two groups (Koss, Butcher, & Hoffman, 1976).

Two more recent and comprehensive lists of critical items have been developed by Koss, Butcher, and Hoffman (1976) and Lachar and Wrobel (1979). They were developed through a combination of intuitive and empirical procedures. Although both sets are somewhat longer and have considerable item overlap with scales F and 8, they are generally more valid than the Grayson (1951) and Caldwell (1990) lists. The Koss-Butcher list has been revised and updated for the MMPI-2 (Butcher et al., 1990) and is listed, along with the direction of their scoring, in Appendix K. The critical items will be most useful if clinicians look at the individual item content in relationship to the specific types of information that the item reveals. This information might be used to guide further interviewing. In addition, the items themselves, along with the responses ("True" or "False") might be included in the psychological report to provide qualitative information regarding the client. However, some caution needs to be taken in their interpretation, since they are both subject to an acquiescing response set (most items are keyed in the "True" direction) and faking bad. They should not be considered to be scales but rather direct communications to the clinician about areas specific to the item content.

While the Koss-Butcher and Lachar-Wrobel lists of critical items have been included in standard interpretive guides for the MMPI-A (Archer, 1992; Butcher & Williams, 1992), clinicians should use these lists with adolescents with caution. First of all, normal adolescents as well as clinical populations of adolescents endorse, on average, twice the number of critical items as normal adults (Archer & Jacobson, 1993). In addition, normal adolescents and clinical populations endorse item frequencies about equally, thereby suggesting that the items themselves should not be used to differentiate between these two groups. This means that empirical attempts to develop critical item lists for adolescents might be quite difficult. As for the MMPI/MMPI-2, clinicians should not treat the different clusters of critical items as rough scales to be interpreted. Rather, the individual item content should be used to develop specific interview questions, and the relative deviancy of these items should be handled with appropriate tolerance.

MMPI-2 AND MMPI-A SUPPLEMENTARY SCALES

Since the initial publication of the MMPI, over 450 new scales have been developed (see Levitt & Gotts, 1995). Some of these have been developed for normals and are unrelated to pathology, such as dominance *(Do)* and social status *(St)*. Other scales relate more directly to pathological dimensions, and often use the data from Hathaway and McKinley's original standardization sample or the more recent restandardization group. Scoring is only possible if the entire 567 MMPI-2 or 478 MMPI-A items are given. Although exact cutoffs for determining high scores have not been specified, they are generally $T = 65$. Scoring templates and profile sheets are available through National Computer Systems. The scales selected for inclusion on this profile sheet are considered to be most useful, have been most extensively researched, or show promise in terms of future usefulness and/or are likely to be researched more extensively in the future. The following lists provide their names and interpretations surrounding scale elevations.

MMPI-2 Supplementary Scales

A/Anxiety   High scores indicate that the person is upset, shy, retiring, insecure, has low self-confidence, is inhibited, uncertain, hesitant, conforming, under stress, and has extreme difficulty making decisions. Low scores indicate that the individual is extraverted, energetic, competitive, and generally has an absence of emotional difficulties.

R/Repression   High scorers tend to be submissive, overcontrolled, slow, clear thinking, conventional, formal, cautious, use denial and rationalization, and go to great lengths to avoid unpleasant interpersonal situations. Low scorers are likely to be dominant, enthusiastic, excitable, impulsive, self-indulgent, and outspoken.

Es/Ego Strength   Assesses the degree to which a client is likely to benefit from psychotherapy but it is probably specific to predicting the response of neurotic patients to insight-oriented therapy; it is probably not useful for other types of patients or other kinds of treatments (Graham, 1978). High scores suggest these persons can benefit from psychotherapy since they are likely to be adaptable and possess personal resources, have good reality contact, are tolerant, balanced, alert, have a secure sense of reality, will seek help due to situational difficulties, possess strongly developed interests, are persistent, can deal effectively with others, have a sense of personal adequacy, can easily gain social acceptance, and have good physical health. Persons with low scores reflect that the person is generally maladjusted. They are likely to have low self-esteem, a poor self-concept, lack personal resources, feel insecure, be rigid and moralistic, have chronic physical problems, possess fears and phobias, are confused and helpless, have chronic fatigue, may be withdrawn and seclusive, inhibited, have personality rather than situational problems, and poor work histories, and will therefore have difficulty benefiting from psychotherapy.

MAC-R/MacAndrew Alcoholism Scale/Revised   The MAC-R scale is best considered a measure of the potential for substance abuse; it differentiates between outpatient alcoholics and nonalcoholic psychiatric outpatients, identifies persons who are at risk of later developing alcohol-related problems (current alcohol use is not assessed but rather the *potential* to develop or be involved in these problems; also the scale has difficulty differentiating alcohol abusers from other substance abusers); high scores on the MAC-R scale primarily suggest actual or potential substance abuse but may also suggest extraversion, affiliation, confidence, assertiveness, risk taking, sensation seeking, past school behavior problems, the possibility of having experienced blackouts and possible difficulties in concentration; low scores are not only a contraindication of substance abuse but may also suggest introversion, conformity, and low self-confidence; if low scores in a known substance abuser do occur, this suggests that the abuse is more based on psychological disturbance than typical addictive processes; the recommended *raw* score cutoff to indicate the initial point of drug and/or alcohol problems for males is 26 to 28, whereas for females it is a lower 23 to 25; the scale is not particularly effective with African Americans and other non-Caucasian respondents; high scorers are likely to be extraverted, impulsive risk takers who will benefit from a group-oriented, confrontive treatment approach; low scorers are more likely to be introverted, withdrawn, depressed risk avoiders who will be more likely to benefit from a supportive and relatively nonconfrontational treatment approach.

AAS/Addiction Acknowledgment Scale   High scores suggest a conscious awareness of and willingness to share information related to drug and/or alcohol-related problems; low scores merely clarify that the person has not acknowledged these problems (although there is still the possibility that they do have drug and/or alcohol-related difficulties).

APS/Addiction Potential Scale   High scores indicate that the person has a considerable number of lifestyle and personality factors consistent with those who abuse alcohol and/or drugs; the scale does not necessarily measure the extent of current use but more the potential for developing such problems; if the person scores in the normal to low range but history reveals that they have a drug and/or alcohol problem, it suggests that this problem is based primarily on psychological maladjustment (drug/alcohol use as self medication) than a typical addictive pattern (harmful habits, peer group issues, physiological impact of the drug); this scale is quite similar to the MAC-R scale but used more of the newer MMPI-2 item pool than the MAC-R; there is some indication that it measures the same factors as the MAC-R but may do so more effectively (Greene, 1992; Weed, 1992).

MDS/Marital Distress Scale   High scores indicate the person is experiencing marital distress; this scale is more specifically related to marital difficulties than either the FAM content scale or Scale 4 (both of which assess relationship difficulties not necessarily specific to marriage); MDS should only be interpreted for persons who are married, separated, or divorced.

O-H/Overcontrolled Hostility Scale   High scores suggest that the person is emotionally constricted, bottles up anger, and may overreact possibly becoming physically or verbally aggressive; the aggressiveness usually occurs as rare incidents in a person who is otherwise extremely well controlled; the scale is most useful in understanding past behavior rather than predicting the likelihood of future hostility; some persons who score high are not actively struggling to control dangerous hostility but are very well controlled and highly socialized. Thus the scale is more directly a measure of persons who deny aggressive actions and are somewhat constricted; therapy, at least initially might seem superficial and lacking in affect.

Do/Dominance   Elevations indicate that the individual is self-confident, realistic, task oriented, feels a sense of duty toward others; is competent to solve problems, socially dominant, poised, and self-assured in working with groups; takes the initiative in relationships, possesses strong opinions, perseveres at tasks, and has a good ability to concentrate; the scale is useful and frequently used in personnel selection (e.g., police officer selection).

Re/Responsibility   High scores suggest that the individual possesses high standards, a strong sense of justice and fairness, strong (even rigid) adherence to values, is self-confident, dependable, trustworthy; the scale is a general index of positive personality characteristics; often useful in personnel screening.

Mt/College Maladjustment   High scores indicate general maladjustment among college students; they are likely to be worried, anxious, and procrastinate; they are pessimistic, ineffectual, somatize stress, and feel that, much of the time, life is a strain.

GM/Masculine Gender Role   Persons who score high (both males and females) are likely to be self-confident, deny feeling afraid or worried, and be persistent in pursuing their goals; females scoring high are likely to be honest, unworried, and have a willingness to explore new things; high scores on GM with correspondingly low scores on Gf indicate stereotypic male interests and orientations; high scores on both GM and Gf suggest androgyny (the person has both masculine and feminine characteristics); low scores on GM along with high scores on Gf suggest stereotypic feminine interests and orientation; low scores on both scales suggest an undifferentiated masculine/feminine orientation; this is still an experimental scale in need of further research.

GF/Feminine Gender Role   High scores suggest the endorsement of stereotypically feminine interests and orientations; may also suggest religiosity and possibly abuse of alcohol and/or nonprescription drugs; males scoring high may be hypercritical, express religiosity, avoid swearing but be bossy, and have a difficult time controlling their temper; this is still an experimental scale in need of further research.

PK/Posttraumatic Stress Disorder Scale   High scores indicate emotional distress, depression, anxiety, sleep disturbances, guilt, loss of control over thinking, a feeling of being misunderstood and mistreated by others; the scale does not determine that trauma has actually occurred but indicates that the symptoms reported are consistent with persons exposed to traumatic events; the existence of a trauma still needs to be determined through other means.

PS/Posttraumatic Stress Disorder Scale   This is a second trauma-related scale that is listed on the supplementary scale profile sheet but is currently an experimental scale under development.

Si1, Si2, Si3/Shyness, Social Avoidance, Self-Other Alienation   (These are listed here for clarification; they occur on the supplementary scale profile sheet but actually refer to the Social Introversion content subscales described in the previous section on Harris-Lingoes and *Si* subscales.)

MMPI-A Supplementary Scales

MAC-R/MacAndrew Alcoholism Scale   High scores suggest that the person is similar to others who have alcohol or drug problems; dominant, assertive, egocentric, self-indulgent, impulsive, unconventional; risk taker and sensation seeker; increased possibility of conduct disorder and legal difficulties; low scores suggest that the person is dependent, conservative, avoids sensation seeking activities, is overcontrolled, and indecisive.

ACK/Alcohol Drug Acknowledgment Scale   Persons who score high have a conscious awareness of and willingness to admit to alcohol- and/or drug-related problems;

includes problem use, reliance on alcohol to cope or as a means of freely expressing feelings, harmful substance abuse habits; friends or acquantainces may tell them that they have alcohol and/or drug problems; they may get into fights while drinking.

PRO/Alcohol Drug Proneness Scale   A high score suggests that the person is prone to developing drug- and/or alcohol-related problems, school and home behavior problems; no obvious items related to drugs and alcohol are included on the scale so the scale more measures personality and lifestyle patterns consistent with alcohol- and drug-related problems; the scale does not so much measure current alcohol or drug use patterns (although they may still be present; quite similar to the MMPI-2 APS scale).

IMM/Immaturity Scale   High scorers are untrustworthy, undependable, boisterous; quickly become angry, are easily frustrated, may tease or bully others; are resistant, defiant, and are likely to have background of school and interpersonal difficulties.

A/Anxiety   General maladjustment, anxiety, distress, emotionally upset, experiences discomfort.

R/Repression   Submissive, conventional, works hard to avoid unpleasant or disagreeable situations.

RECOMMENDED READING

Archer, R. A. (1992). *MMPI-A: Assessing adolescent psychopathology.* Hillsdale, NJ: Erlbaum.
Butcher, J. N. (1990). *The MMPI-2 in psychological treatment.* New York: Oxford University Press.
Butcher, J. N., & Williams, C. L. (1992). *Essentials of MMPI-2 and MMPI-A interpretation.* Minneapolis: University of Minnesota Press.
Graham, J. R. (1993). *MMPI-2: Assessing personality and psychopathology* (2nd ed.). New York: Oxford University Press.
Keller, L. S., & Butcher, J. N. (1991). *Assessment of chronic pain patients with the MMPI-2.* Minneapolis: University of Minnesota Press.
Lewak, R. W., Marks, P. A., & Nelson, G. E. (1990). *Therapist guide to the MMPI & MMPI-2.* Muncie, IN: Accelerated Development.
Levitt, E. E., & Gotts, E. E. (1995). *The clinical application of MMPI special scales* (2nd ed.). Hillsdale, NJ: Erlbaum.

Chapter 7

MILLON CLINICAL MULTIAXIAL INVENTORY

The Millon Clinical Multiaxial Inventory (MCMI) is a standardized, self-report questionnaire that assesses a wide range of information related to a client's personality, emotional adjustment, and attitude toward taking tests. It has been designed for adults (18 years and older) who have a minimum of an eighth-grade reading level. The MCMI is unique among tests in that it focuses on personality disorders along with symptoms that are frequently associated with these disorders. Originally developed in 1977 (Millon, 1977), it has since been through two revisions (MCMI-II; Millon, 1987; MCMI-III; Millon, 1994). Since its original publication, it has stimulated over 600 published papers on or using it and has become one of the more frequently used tests in clinical practice (Piotrowski & Zalewski, 1993; Watkins et al., 1995). Indeed, it is one of the few tests that has "risen through the ranks" of test usage over the past 30 years. Among objective personality tests for clinical trainees to be familiar with, directors of clinical training programs ranked it second only to the MMPI/MMPI-2 in importance (Piotrowski & Zalewski, 1993). Its popularity is further supported by its use in several different countries and its translation into a number of different languages.

The current version, MCMI-III, is comprised of 175 items that are scored to produce 28 scales divided into the following categories: Modifying Indices, Clinical Personality Patterns, Severe Personality Pathology, Clinical Syndromes, and Severe Syndromes (see Table 7–1). The scales, along with the items that comprise the scales, are closely aligned to both Millon's theory of personality and the DSM-IV. For example, an item endorsing a person's belief in his or her own superiority would be part of the Narcissistic scale, because the content clearly relates to components of Millon's and the DSM-IV's conceptualization of the narcissistic personality. Many of the scales have both theoretical and item overlap—an important fact to keep in mind when conceptualizing the client and interpreting the scales. Thus, an elevation on both the Antisocial and Sadistic scales which would reflect a person who has sadistic features along with legal difficulties and impulsiveness, and who is interpersonally exploitive. Similarly, a person scoring high on the Antisocial scale might have a corresponding elevation on the Alcohol Dependence scale. The corresponding elevations on conceptually related scales allow for a more complete understanding of the client.

In some ways, the MCMI is an alternative or even a competitor to the MMPI. Both instruments cover a wide range of adult pathology—long-standing personality patterns as well as clinical symptomatology. In other ways, the MCMI nicely complements the MMPI in that the MMPI focuses primarily on Axis I disorders whereas the MCMI was

Table 7–1.   MCMI-III scale categories, abbreviations, number of items, and reliabilities

Scale Category/Name	Abbreviation	No. of Items	Alpha
Modifying Indices			
Disclosure	X	na	NA
Desirability	Y	21	.85
Debasement	Z	33	.95
Validity	V	4	NA
Clinical Personality Patterns			
Schizoid	1	16	.81
Avoidant	2A	16	.89
Depressive	2B	15	.89
Dependent	3	16	.85
Histrionic	4	17	.81
Narcissistic	5	24	.67
Antisocial	6A	17	.77
Aggressive (Sadistic)	6B	20	.79
Compulsive	7	17	.66
Passive-Aggressive (Negativistic)	8a	16	.83
Self-Defeating	8B	15	.87
Severe Personality Pathology			
Schizotypal	S	16	.85
Borderline	C	16	.85
Paranoid	P	17	.84
Clinical Syndromes			
Anxiety	A	14	.86
Somatoform	H	12	.86
Bipolar: Manic	N	13	.71
Dysthymia	D	14	.88
Alcohol Dependence	B	15	.82
Drug Dependence	T	14	.83
Posttraumatic Stress Disorder	PT	16	.89
Severe Syndromes			
Thought Disorder	SS	17	.87
Major Depression	CC	17	.90
Delusional Disorder	PP	13	.79

Adapted from Millon (1994).

specifically designed to assist in diagnosing Axis II disorders. One important advantage of the MCMI is that it is considerably shorter than the MMPI-2 (175 vs. 567 items) and yet provides a wide range of information. The MCMI takes only 20 to 30 minutes to complete; however, the research base, validity studies, and options for interpretations are clearly more extensive for the MMPI than for the MCMI. Neither instrument should be considered to provide diagnosis. Instead, they provide considerable information relevant to diagnosis. In this sense, they place the clinician in the right "diagnostic ballpark," but the clinician must then integrate this with other information in order to make the final diagnosis. In other words, tests (or computer reports) don't diagnose (or make decisions); only practitioners can perform this function.

Factors that greatly assist in useful interpretation are familiarity with the theoretical constructs as well as experience with relevant clinical populations. Theoretical knowledge can be greatly assisted through familiarity with Millon and Davis's (1996) *Disorders of Personality* (2nd ed.) as well as the diagnostic criteria of the DSM-IV. The above emphasis on clinical populations also focuses on the principle that the MCMI is intended for psychiatric populations and should not be used with normal persons or those who are merely mildly disturbed. Interpretations should be restricted to persons who scored at or above the designated cutoff scores (75 and 85). Practitioners should resist the temptation to attempt interpretations of persons who have mild "elevations" on the scale but who are still clearly below the formal cutoff.

HISTORY AND DEVELOPMENT

Development of the Original MCMI

Shortly after Millon published his 1969 text, *Modern Psychopathology,* fellow professionals urged him to develop an instrument that would operationalize and measure the dimensions of personality as outlined in the book. By 1972, an initial form was developed: the Millon–Illinois Self-Report Inventory (MI-SRI). Over the next five years, the items were further developed, refined, and coordinated with the upcoming personality disorders that were later to be incorporated into DSM-III. Once the initial refinements were completed, the test was published and renamed the Millon Clinical Multiaxial Inventory (MCMI; Millon, 1977).

The formal development of the original MCMI used a combination of rational theory-based as well as empirical procedures. The first step was the development of a large pool of face valid questions—a total of 3,500 items derived from Millon's (1969) theories. These were then rationally grouped into 20 different scales. The number of items was initially reduced by the test developers by rewording those that were poorly worded and removing those that were redundant. Further refinement was done empirically by having patients rate the clarity and difficulty of the items. A further procedure involved having clinicians regroup the items into scales, to evaluate the extent to which these scales related to those originated by the test developers. Based on the above procedures, the items were then grouped into two equivalent provisional research forms, with 556 items in each form. The forms were administered to 200 patients, and their responses were evaluated for their endorsement frequency and item-scale intercorrelations. The highest within-scale item intercorrelations were retained, and items that were either very frequently (>85%) or very rarely (<15%) endorsed were eliminated. The research form was thereby reduced to a test comprised of 289 items.

The 289-item research form was given to 167 clinicians who blindly rated a total of 682 of their patients on 20 different variables after having given them the form. The amount of endorsement frequency and the degree of scale overlap were then used to reduce the items from 289 to 154. Based on the above initial validation procedure, three scales were dropped (Sociopathy, Hypochondriasis, and Obsession-Compulsion), and three new scales were developed and added (Drug Abuse, Alcohol, and Hypomania). This brought the total number of surviving items to 175, with a total of 733 different keyings on the 20 different scales.

The scales were initially standardized on 1,591 clinical subjects used in the construction phase of the test. This sample was used to establish the optimal cutoff scores for determining the presence or absence of certain characteristics. A group of 297 nonclinical subjects was used to establish the responses of a normal comparison group. In 1981, the MCMI responses of 43,218 patients were reviewed to further refine and recalculate the cutoff scores.

One feature of the MCMI and its revisions is the use of cutoffs related to Base Rate (BR) scores to designate the presence or absence of a particular characteristic. The BR score, like the more familiar T score, is essentially a means of transforming a raw score into a more meaningful score for interpretation. However, BR scores are derived from the percentage of a population that has been deemed to have a certain characteristic or syndrome. For example, 17% of a psychiatric population can be considered to have clear characteristics of a Dependent personality whereas only 1% are considered to have clear features of a Sadistic personality. This means that decisions regarding client characteristics are made when a client scores in a range that is consistent with either of the above two syndromes. However, the relatively more frequent psychiatric disorders with high base rates (i.e., Dependent) will require relatively lower cutoff points than those rare disorders with low base rates (i.e., Sadistic). Millon arbitrarily set a BR score of 85 as indicating that the characteristic(s) in question was definitely present. A lower BR score of 75 indicated that some of the features were present. Additional cutoff or anchor points were set at 35, to represent the median score for normal or nonpsychiatric groups, and at 60, the median for psychiatric populations. The above base rate approach has been theoretically encouraged by a number of authors (Finn, 1982; Widiger & Kelso, 1983) and empirically demonstrated to increase diagnostic accuracy when compared with the more frequently used T score approach (Duthie & Vincent, 1986).

Development of the MCMI-II

The MCMI-II (Millon, 1987) maintained most of the features of the original MCMI. Its development was motivated by a need to incorporate additional research and theory on personality disorders while remaining aligned with the criteria outlined in DSM-III and DSM-III-R. In addition, between 40 and 50 of the original MCMI items were found to be expendable. Items were developed for two new scales, in part by dividing the previous Negativistic scale into separate scales for Passive-Aggressive (Negativistic) and Self-Defeating. Similarly, the earlier Antisocial-Aggressive scale was divided into an Antisocial scale and an Aggressive/Sadistic scale. Additional items were generated with procedures similar to those used for the original MCMI. This resulted in an MCMI-II Provisional Form of 368 items, which was given to 184 patients who had been carefully diagnosed using DSM-III-R criteria. Items were retained or deleted based on the extent to which they could differentiate relevant diagnostic criterion groups. Like the earlier MCMI, the MCMI-II totaled 175 items, but they were keyed on 22 (as opposed to only 20) different scales. In an attempt to reduce scale intercorrelation, individual items were given weightings of 1, 2, or 3 points, based on their relative importance for the specific scales they were being keyed on. Optimal BR cutoff scores were based on a standardization group of 1,292 patients who had a wide variety of presenting problems.

Development of the MCMI-III

Ongoing research, new conceptual developments, and the publication of the DSM-IV contributed to the MCMI-II's revision into its latest version, the MCMI-III (Millon, 1994). With procedures similar to those used for the MCMI and MCMI-II, a provisional 325-item test was developed; Depressive and PTSD scales were added. The Self-Defeating and Sadistic personality disorder scales were maintained, even though these diagnoses were eliminated from the DSM-IV. The final MCMI-III still totaled 175 items, but 90 of the items from the MCMI-II were "changed" (85 remained the same). Actually, most of the changed items remained essentially the same in their primary content; the alterations related mostly to increasing the severity of the symptoms. This was done to decrease the number of people endorsing particular items, in the hope that the MCMI-III would be more selective in suggesting pathology. In addition, the items per scale were reduced by half, and the number of keyings was reduced from 953 on the MCMI-II to only 440 for the MCMI-III. The possible ratings per item were reduced from 1, 2, or 3 to either 1 or 2. The resulting 28 scales are divided into the categories shown in Table 7–1. Optimal BR cutoff scores were derived from a standardization sample of 1,079 clinical patients who had come from a wide diversity of backgrounds and treatment settings.

Theoretical Considerations

The development of the three versions of the MCMI has been partially guided by Millon's theories of personality. One of his core principles is the use of the polarities of pleasure-pain, active-passive, and self-other (Millon & Davis, 1996). Each of these polarities can be used to describe differences in personality organization for normal persons as well as those with personality disorders. For example, normal levels of functioning can occur on the active-passive dimension but, when these are exaggerated, they become dysfunctional. Thus, schizoid and avoidant personality disorders are extreme in the direction of passivity. Within the self-other dimension, dependent and histrionic personalities are highly oriented toward others, whereas the narcissistic personality is extremely self-oriented. Many of the personality styles can be simultaneously portrayed on each of the three polarities. For example, the histrionic style is quite active and is both other (dependent) and pleasure-oriented. In some cases, the person is ambivalent on one or more of these dimensions, thereby resembling a person with a passive-aggressive style who is overtly passive and compliant but covertly expresses conflict and anger. Considerably more detail on the above polarities, along with other aspects of personality disorders, can be found in Millon and Davis's (1996) *Disorders of Personality: DSM-IV Axis II and Beyond* (2nd ed.).

Another important point relates to both the test's development and its implications for interpretation: The personality styles are not mutually exclusive. For example, a person with an antisocial style might be frequently uncomfortable with underlying anger and antisocial impulses and thus express them in passive-aggressive modes. This expected overlap among characteristics is one reason why the test developers were not overly concerned that many of the scales were highly correlated. Also, the overlap that was present seemed to occur in theoretically consistent patterns. From a practical perspective, this means that combinations of scale elevations can be used to give added meaning to each other. For example, a high score on the Antisocial scale, in combination with an elevation on the Sadistic scale, clearly suggests that the person will act out his or her antisocial feelings in a predictable and potentially dangerous manner. This activity would have very clear implications for case management and treatment planning.

A further consideration is that scale elevations should always be placed into the context of the person's life. A high score is not diagnostic of a personality disorder in and of itself. If a person can find an appropriate niche where the expression of his or her personality style is not dysfunctional, then that person should not be considered to be "disordered." Thus, the distinction between a personality "style" versus an actual personality "disorder" should be stressed. For example, a salesman with a narcissistic antisocial style might be able to optimize these traits in a way that makes him quite occupationally successful. The diagnostic criteria for personality disorders specifically state that there must be an enduring pattern leading to "clinically significant distress or impairment in social, occupational, or other important areas of functioning" (American Psychiatric Association, 1994, p. 630). If there is no or little distress or impairment, then a personality disorder should not be diagnosed. Thus, it is crucial for clinicians to determine whether a given personality style suggested by the MCMI has actually led to distress and/or impairment.

Finally, the different categories of scales (Clinical Personality Patterns, Severe Personality Pathology, Clinical Syndrome, Severe Syndrome) are conceptually and clinically related (see Table 7–1). The first two categories relate to Axis II diagnoses but are separated to designate the greater levels of severity for the schizotypal, borderline, and paranoid conditions. As was previously pointed out, however, any of the personality styles are not disorders unless there is distress and impairment. The second categories are intended to measure the type and level of distress and thus relate more to Axis I levels of diagnoses. They represent the expression of personality styles that are not working well for the person. For example, if the narcissistic antisocial salesman mentioned previously tries to act toward his spouse as he does toward his business contacts, she may file for divorce. His means of coping with this outcome might be abuse of alcohol. In contrast, an individual with a dependent avoidant style who is undergoing a divorce would be likely to respond with a major depression. This difference underlies the essential interrelationship between Axis I and Axis II diagnoses. It also points out that the MCMI can help to establish the presence of an Axis II diagnosis by noting the type and degree of distress and impairment as expressed in elevations on the scales in the Clinical Syndrome and Severe Syndrome categories.

RELIABILITY AND VALIDITY

Reliability and validity studies on the MCMI indicate that it is generally a well-constructed psychometric instrument. Measures of internal consistency have been particularly strong. For the MCMI-III, alpha coefficients exceed .80 for 20 of the 26 scales, with a high of .90 for Depression and a low of .66 for Compulsive (Millon, 1994). Similarly, high test-retest reliabilities have been reported for the MCMI-III with a median of .91 (the high is .96 for Somatoform and the low is .82 for Debasement). These are excellent test-retest reliabilities, but the interval ranged only between 5 and 14 days (Millon, 1994). Given the theoretically long-term stability of personality styles, it would be desirable to test this out by developing test-retest reliabilities over a longer interval. Although this has not yet been done for the MCMI-III, the original MCMI was found to have test-retest reliabilities, over an average of a 379-day interval, of a mean of .69 for the personality scales and a mean of .67 for the clinical scales (Overholser, 1989). These results suggest a moderate level of long-term stability.

One consideration is that, because the personality scales theoretically represent enduring, ingrained characteristics, they should have greater stability than the clinical scales, which are based on more changeable symptomatic patterns. In some cases, this has been found to be true; in others, little difference has been found. Studies on the MCMI-I have indicated the theoretically expected higher stability for the personality scales as opposed to the clinical scales (Millon, 1982; Piersma, 1986). In contrast, the previously cited Overholser (1989) study found very little difference between the mean personality and clinical scales, despite an extended retesting interval. Similarly, the MCMI-III manual reported a mean of .89 for the personality scales and a slightly greater mean of .91 for the clinical scales. This suggests that the original MCMI may have had the theoretically higher temporal stability for the personality scales versus the clinical scales, but later versions have roughly equivalent temporal stabilities between the two categories of scales.

One central issue, when evaluating the validity of the MCMI, is the extent to which validity studies on previous versions can be generalized to the newer versions. With appropriate caution, some transferability is probable because the correlation between the MCMI-II and MCMI-III scales is moderately high. Specifically, the correlations range from a high of .94 for Debasement to a low of .59 for Dependent, with 12 of the 25 scale comparisons being above .70. Comparisons between the Depressive and Post-Traumatic Stress Disorder scales could not be made because they were uniquely developed for the MCMI-III. Future studies will enable researchers and practitioners to better evaluate the MCMI-III on its own, without having to refer to previous research on the MCMI-II and its presumed transferability to the MCMI-III. In the meantime, practitioners performing forensic evaluations or assessments in other contexts requiring maximum accountability might be advised to use the MCMI-II until the validity of the MCMI-III becomes better documented. Given the above considerations, the following selective and representative overview of validity will draw on material from both the more recent MCMI-III and the MCMI-II.

Factor analysis of the MCMI-II has generally supported the organization of the scales. The most extensive published factor analysis involved 769 cases and resulted in an 8-factor solution (Millon, 1987). The largest factor accounted for 31% of the variance, was related to general Maladjustment, and involved depressed affect, impaired interpersonal relationships, low self-esteem, and unusual cognition and self-behavior. The next two largest factors were Acting Out/Self-Indulgent (13% of the variance) and Anxious and Depressed Somatization (8% of the variance). The final factors, listed according to progressively decreasing proportions of the variance, were Compulsively

Defended/Delusional Paranoid, Submissive/Aggressive Sadistic, Addictive Disorders, Psychoticism, and Self and Other Conflictual/Erratic Emotionality. Over 17 factor-analytic studies have been performed on the various MCMI versions, and these have generally supported the keying of the items (Retzlaff, Lorr, & Hyer, 1989) as well as the clustering of the factors around Millon's conceptualization of psychopathology (see Choca, Shanley, & Van Denburg, 1996; McCann, 1991). However, most of the latter factor-analytic studies have been somewhat limited because of significantly lower sample sizes.

A variety of correlations have been made between the MCMI and various related instruments, including the Beck Depression Inventory, General Behavior Inventory, Michigan Alcoholism Screening Test, State-Trait Anxiety Inventory, Symptom Checklist-90, and the MMPI (Millon, 1994). These are reported in detail in the MCMI-III manual. Representative findings include expected correlations between the Beck Depression Inventory and the MCMI-III Major Depression (.74) and Dysthymia (.71) scales. Similarly, high correlations were found between the MMPI-2 Depression scale and the MCMI-III Depression (.71) and Dysthymia (.68) scales. As would be expected, negative correlations were found between the Beck Depression Inventory and MCMI-III scales related to denying pathology (Histrionic, −.49; Narcissistic, −.40; and Compulsive, −.30). An additional representative finding was a .55 correlation between the MCMI-III Somatoform scale and the Symptom Checklist-90-Revised scale for Somatization. One puzzling finding was a low correlation of .29 between the MCMI-III Paranoid scale and the MMPI-2 Paranoia scale. Similar surprising results were moderate correlations between the MMPI-2 Psychopathic deviate scale and the MCMI-III scales for Self-Defeating (.45), Schizotypal (.43), and Depressive (.41). For the most part, however, correlations between the MCMI and external criterion instruments have been in the expected direction.

One of the important and relatively unique contributions of the MCMI has been the development and availability of data on its diagnostic efficiency. This is usually calculated by designating Base Rate scale scores of 75 and/or 85 as *test positives* and comparing these with clinician ratings of whether the characteristics predicted by the scale scores actually matched these clinician ratings. Based on the above procedure, calculations were made on the percentage of agreement (or *hit rate*) between the test prediction and clinician ratings (Millon, 1994). The MCMI-III cutoff score of 75 produced hit rates with a high of 90.4% for Aggressive (Sadistic) and a low of 61.3% for Avoidant. Somewhat greater hit rates were reported using the more stringent cutoff of 85: a high of 97.8% (Aggressive; Sadistic) and a low of 74.8% (Dependent).

The above data on hit rates are provided in the MCMI-III manual, but there may be situations where the prevalence of a disorder is substantially different from the sample used to determine hit rates in the manual. In these settings, the hit rates will not be as useful an index of diagnostic accuracy. For example, forensic and/or substance abuse treatment facilities usually have high numbers of persons with antisocial personality styles. In these cases, calculation of the *positive predictive power* of the MCMI for the particular setting is recommended. Essentially, positive predictive power is a calculation of the probability that a test score accurately indicates the presence of a characteristic or diagnosis based on some other measure such as clinical ratings. Such a calculation involves a formula (Gibertini, Brandenberg, & Retzlaff, 1986; see Millon, 1994, pp. 41–43) in which prevalence rates must be inserted (derived from knowledge regarding a specific client population) along with sensitivity and specificity data (available in the MCMI-III manual). Such a calculation provides practitioners with an estimate of the extent to which the instrument performs above and beyond merely base rate levels. For example, if the prevalence or base rate of antisocial personalities is .25 but the positive predictive power of the MCMI is .76, then the difference (.76 − .25) of .56 indicates that the incremental validity of the instrument is .56 above merely base rate (prevalence) or chance predictions. This emphasis on levels of certainty, with its implications for actual clinical decision making, is one of the strong features of the MCMI.

Calculations of the positive predictive power of the MCMI-II indicated impressive predictive power ranging between .30 and .80 (Millon, 1987). Although the calculations of positive predictive powers for the MCMI-III were encouraged in the manual, these were not actually provided. When these were calculated by Retzlaff (in press), they were only half as high as those reported for the MCMI-II. Predictive powers for the personality disorders only ranged between .0 and .30, with the Sadistic scale having no predictive power at all. It is unlikely that this is due to poor MCMI-III test development. There has been theoretical continuity in the development of all versions; moderately high correlations exist between the MCMI-II and MCMI-III scales; scale reliabilities themselves are quite high; and traditional methods of validity (criterion measures with other tests) are good. Based on this description, Retzlaff (in press) argues that the reason for the low predictive power of the MCMI-III was the poor MCMI-III diagnostic validity studies. Specifically, clinicians making the diagnoses in the study were probably not sufficiently familiar with the DSM-IV diagnostic criteria, did not have extensive knowledge of the clients themselves, were provided with minimal criteria for diagnosis, and conducted no interrater reliability checks on single clinicians' diagnoses. Further studies need to be performed in this area of validity, and will no doubt be forthcoming.

ASSETS AND LIMITATIONS

The strategy of developing the MCMI has been commendable and innovative. The history and development section outlines how this has involved a combination of theoretical-conceptual, internal-structural, and external criterion procedures. Each of the procedures has progressed in a stepwise manner; only those items that survived the previous steps were retained. The result has been an instrument that adheres closely to theory, demonstrates good reliability, and has shown excellent promise regarding internal and external validity. The use of base rate scores has been a noteworthy innovation and has probably resulted in increases in diagnostic accuracy. However, difficulties have been noted related to the need for greater test-retest intervals for the MCMI-III and the generally low level of interdiagnostician agreement among clinicians using methods such as structured interviews and the MMPI.

As has been pointed out previously, the MCMI is a relatively time-efficient test that potentially produces a wide range of information. Of central importance, this information focuses not only on clinical symptomatology (Axis I), but also on the more enduring and potentially more problematic personality disorders (Axis II). These personality disorders can frequently be overlooked. Practitioners might overlook them because (a) the client is more likely to express concern over more overt symptoms and (b) personality styles are often more hidden and must be inferred. Clients themselves may be unaware of personality styles that have become so automatic that it is difficult to recognize them. They can feel the emotional pain of symptoms, but are rarely aware of the recurring patterns of behaviors and cognitions that frequently are at the core of the development and maintenance of these symptoms. Thus, the MCMI inhabits a crucial niche in objective assessment in that it has been designed to better understand personality dysfunction.

Despite the above assets of the MCMI, there are a number of inherent difficulties in the assessment of personality disorders. One central issue is that there is no "benchmark" or "gold standard" to compare the MCMI assessments to. Individual clinicians relying on interview information generally have low interdiagnostician agreement even when using the more recent DSM criteria (American Psychiatric Association, 1980; Hyler, Skodol, Andrew, Kellman, & Oldham, 1990). Similarly, formal instruments such as the MMPI, MCMI, and structured interviews have shown little agreement (Miller, Streiner, & Parkinson, 1992; Streiner & Miller, 1990), which makes it difficult to judge the "true" accuracy of MCMI personality disorder assessment. A related issue is that some of the diagnostic criteria incorporated into the MCMI items are closely tied to the DSM criteria, whereas others are more closely linked to Millon's theories. In some cases, these criteria are similar; in others, the criteria are different. This has led to some controversy regarding the relative advantages and disadvantages of having different criteria (Flynn, McCann, & Fairbank, 1995). One disadvantage is that, in many cases, the MCMI should not be considered a DSM measure even though the titles of the scales may lead practitioners to think that it is (Wetzler & Marlowe, 1992; Widiger, Williams, Spitzer, & Francis, 1985). However, this may actually be an advantage for some of the scales/disorders because the DSM criteria have been criticized as being both insufficiently related to theory and clearly inadequate in some areas. Because the MCMI has not strictly adhered to the DSM criteria, it can work to remedy some of the DSM's perceived inadequacies. For example, the DSM-III-R/DSM-IV diagnosis for Antisocial personality has attained high interrater reliability but has done so by sticking closely to clear behavioral criteria primarily related to overt acts against society. The more intangible but crucial issue of poor conscience development has not been sufficiently addressed, which has led to accusations that the DSM criteria relate more to a "criminal" disorder than to a "personality" disorder. The theory behind the MCMI antisocial personality disorder items stresses both overt behaviors and the relative lack of conscience, and this conceptualization is reflected in the item content.

One further issue relevant to the diagnosis of personality disorders is the difficulty in distinguishing state and trait. Theoretically, Axis I disorders relate primarily to states, and Axis II characteristics relate to traits. In reality, they are highly interdependent and it is often difficult to separate them. State (clinical) MCMI elevations seem to be closely related to scores on trait (personality) scales. For example, Reich and Noyes (1987) found a 50% decrease in MCMI personality disorder prevalence estimates when the MCMI was given during the recovery phase as opposed to measures during the acute phase. Elevations in MCMI-II personality scales have also been demonstrated to increase the more state-related MMPI-2 F (and other validity) scales (Grillo, Brown, Hilsabeck, Price, & Lees-Haley, 1994). Given this state/trait distinction, it would be predicted that the trait/personality scales would be more stable than the clinical/state scales; yet, in many cases, this has not been demonstrated to be so. A number of sources, including the MCMI-III manual (Millon, 1994), have demonstrated little difference in the test-retest reliabilities between the two categories of scales. Collectively, these observations indicate that state and trait measures are quite interdependent. To account for this, Millon has developed, for some of the MCMI-II and MCMI-III scales, a number of adjustments that work similar to the K correction on the MMPI. Also, as with the MMPI K correction, it is unclear and controversial as to how effectively they achieve their purpose.

Because of the MCMI's reliance on the DSM, efforts have been made to incorporate changes that parallel the ongoing developments of the DSM. This has the advantage of keeping current with changing diagnostic criteria, but it has also meant that the MCMI has been relatively frequently revised (1977, 1987, 1994). In contrast, the MMPI and CPI have been through far fewer revisions. As a result, the MCMI (and particularly the MCMI-II) has not been in an unchanged version long enough for it to be fully evaluated. With the introduction of the MCMI-III in 1994, researchers and practitioners must now wait until sufficient research has been performed to decide such crucial questions as whether the MCMI-III has sufficient validity, when (or whether) to continue with the previous MCMI-II, or whether the interpretations developed for the MCMI-I and MCMI-II should now be used with the MCMI-III.

An important consideration is whether the MCMI measures actual personality "disorders" or, rather, personality "style." Choca, Shanley, and Van Denburg (1992, 1996) prefer to think of the various scales as referring to personality "style" because the inference to disorder requires more information than can realistically be found in scale elevations. Persons with certain personality styles may have been able to find an occupational and/or interpersonal niche that allows them to function fairly adequately. For example, a schizoid or avoidant personality may work quite well as a night watchperson. Thus, the inference from style to disorder must be made by the individual practitioner and not by the test. Practitioners who look for the test to include actual diagnosis are overextending its use beyond realistic expectations.

A further issue with the MCMI has been extensive *item overlap*. The original MCMI (MCMI-I) had its 175 items arranged on 733 different keyings, and the MCMI-II had an even greater 953 keyings. Thus, because many of the items were used to score numerous scales, there were frequently high scale correlations. For example, the MCMI-I's Borderline and Dysthymic scales shared 65% of their items and were highly correlated (.95). Given these characteristics, practitioners might be justifiably concerned that some of the scales were measuring constructs that were too similar and therefore redundant. The defense of the high scale intercorrelation has been that many of the constructs are theoretically and clinically similar, and the similarity would therefore be psychometrically reflected in many high scale correlations. Practitioners would then need to look at the relationships between the different scale elevations as a means of "fine tuning" their interpretations. For example, Avoidant and Schizoid personalities are similar in their passivity and interpersonal distance. Clinical lore suggests that many persons initially believed to be Schizoids appear more similar to Avoidants as more information is obtained from them. Given the theory and intent of the MCMI, the two scales measuring these styles would be expected to have similar items and to be elevated. Notwithstanding this defense, the recently revised MCMI-III has attempted to reduce the item scale overlap (and resulting intercorrelations) by reducing the number of items per scale, providing item weightings depending on their relative importance for a scale, and reducing the number of keyings to 440 (Millon, 1994). This seems to have been successful in that none of the interscale correlations reported in the manual were above .90 and only three were .80 (the rest were lower). This suggests that the MCMI-III scales, compared to the previous versions, are measuring somewhat more independent domains.

When interpreting the MCMI, it is sometimes difficult to know where the interpretive information was derived. It is based on a combination of theory and empirical relationships determined specifically through validity studies of the MCMI itself. Each of these two interpretive sources has developed over a number of years, during which three versions of the MCMI have appeared. It is often difficult to know whether the interpretations have been empirically-versus-theory-based or whether they have been derived from validity studies done on previous versions of the MCMI. If they have been done on previous versions, it can be rightfully argued that most of the interpretations can be transferred from these earlier versions because there has been continuity in theory and scale development. This is particularly reflected in the moderate-to-high correlations between the new and the older scales. However, practitioners must struggle with which of the interpretations have been empirically versus conceptually derived as well as which are obsolete versus still current. This problem is relevant for the MCMI as well as other similar instruments (i.e. MMPI, CPI), and it highlights the importance of clinicians' working with the test results and integrating them with additional sources. Millon (1992) summarizes that the quality of the interpretive information is dependent on "the overall validity of the inventory, the adequacy of the theory that provides the logic underlying the separate scales, the skill of the clinician, and the interpreter's experience with relevant populations" (p. 424).

A criticism related to the above issue is that the MCMI overdiagnoses and overpathologizes (Flynn et al., 1995). For example, Wetzler (1990) has noted that MCMI-related diagnoses of personality disorder were 60% higher than diagnoses based on structured interviews. One of the reasons for at least the potential for overdiagnosis among practitioners is the possibly misleading name of the personality scales. They create the external appearance of clear DSM diagnostic categories when they are probably best conceptualized as styles that may or may not reflect an actual disorder. This does not mean that the MCMI cannot be extremely useful in diagnosing personality disorders; but it should be more accurately perceived as placing the practitioner in the correct domain or coming half (or more) of the way toward diagnosis. A further problem is that the MCMI does not perform well on normal or only mildly disturbed populations. Such persons might have moderate elevations that are still below the BR 75 cutoff, but practitioners might be tempted to interpret these "elevations." This confusion is complicated further if correlations derived from the modifying indices "bump up" the personality or clinical scales into the interpretable range. Unfortunately, the MCMI NCS computer interpretations tend to both reinforce interpretations of moderate "elevations" and suggest that DSM diagnoses can be made based on MCMI scores. Thus, the MCMI should be used only with clinical populations. A related difficulty is that the scales and their related interpretations tend to emphasize a client's deficiencies without balancing these out with the client's strengths. The result is likely to be an overly negative description of a client's functioning.

INTERPRETATION PROCEDURE

Effective interpretation of the MCMI requires considerable sophistication and knowledge related to psychopathology in general and personality disorders in particular. At a minimum, practitioners should be familiar with issues related to personality disorders along with the DSM-IV criteria. Ideally, practitioners should also have read Millon and Davis's (1996) definitive *Disorders of Personality: DSM-IV and Beyond* (2nd ed.), worked with clients with personality disorders, and administered the MCMI to a number of such clients. Clinicians should also be aware of the previously outlined assets and limitations of the MCMI so that they can most appropriately work with the data. In particular, the MCMI does not provide DSM-IV diagnosis; it should be used only with clinical populations; it is not particularly helpful in assessing a person's strengths; and there is a possibility that it might overdiagnose personality disorders and be overinterpreted by clinicians.

One consideration in interpreting the MCMI is the possible influence of gender, age, and ethnicity. Gender influences have been minimized in that separate norms are used for scoring the profiles of males and females. The gender differences that have emerged on the MCMI are also consistent with prevalence rate estimates. For example, the greater rate of antisocial personalities among males is reflected in the BR scores, which take this greater prevalence rate into account. Some differences between European American and African American psychiatric patients have been found on 9 of the 20 MCMI-II scales. African Americans scored especially higher on Antisocial, Narcissistic, Paranoid, Hypomania, and Drug Abuse (Choca, Shanley, Peterson, & Van Denburg, 1990). As with the MMPI, ethnic differences have been noted, but the meaning attributed to these is less clear. For example, the greater elevations on the above MCMI-II scales may mean that these scores are accurate representations of the more difficult circumstances many African Americans encounter. In contrast, the higher scores might be distortions based on error in the specific scales. This controversy should alert practitioners to be cautious and conservative when making interpretations for African American or other ethnic groups. Finally, there do seem to be age-related differences on the MCMI-II: older persons score higher on Dependent but lower on Compulsive and Borderline (Choca, Van Denburg, Bratu, & Meagher, 1995). This means that interpretations among older persons should take these age-related variables into account.

The set of procedures outlined below is recommended for interpreting the MCMI. The discussion of the various scales and codes represents an integration and summary of current research as well as material included in the MCMI-III manual (Millon, 1994) and interpretive guides developed by Choca et al. (1992, 1996) and Craig (1993, 1995). The subsections related to treatment planning have summarized material from Goncalves, Woodward, and Millon (1994), Retzlaff (1995), and Millon and Davis (1996). Each of the 28 MCMI-III scales is discussed in relation to interpretation, possible interaction with other scales, and implications for treatment planning.

The formal elaboration and separate listing of two- and three-point code types are not discussed, for several reasons. First, research on the MCMI does not have the well-developed code-type validity literature found for the MMPI. Instead, many of the MCMI code-type descriptions are based on a conceptual integration of the implications of clusters of scale elevations. In many ways, this is a task that individual practitioners can do themselves by rationally considering the meanings of associated scale elevations.

For example, an elevation on Antisocial, combined with a corresponding elevation on Aggressive (Sadistic), would clearly indicate the abusive, combative, and impersonal expression of the person's antisocial tendencies. Second, given that there are fully 28 MCMI-III scales, the total number of possible code types is both unwieldy to list and unrealistic to fully research. However, a short subsection ("frequent code types") under most of the scale descriptions does briefly describe the meanings attached to some of the more important associated scale elevations. Readers are encouraged to read these descriptions and to expand on their meanings by reading the longer interpretive descriptions for the entire associated scale.

1. Determine Profile Validity

Before interpreting the personality and clinical scales, practitioners must be assured that the client has not over- or underreported symptoms or responded in a random manner. The profile validity can be assessed by noting the pattern of scores on the Modifying Indices (validity indicators):

> *Random responding* is suggested by scores of one or more on the three items of the MCMI-III Validity scale ("True" on items 65, 110, and 157).
>
> *Underreporting of difficulties* on the MCMI-III is suggested by low scores (raw score less than 34) on Disclosure (X) and Debasement (Z) and a high score (BR over 75) on Desirability (Y; an "arrow" profile on the Modifying Indices). However, it is sometimes difficult to differentiate persons who are faking good (underreporting) from those who actually have the positive qualities of being cooperative, self-confident, and conscientious. The client's history is often the best tool for making this distinction.
>
> *Fake bad* profiles are suggested by a high score (raw score above 178) on Disclosure (X) and a high score (BR above 75) on Debasement (Z; a "valley" profile on the Modifying Indices). With moderate elevations, this might be a "cry for help" but with progressively higher scores (BR above 85) the likelihood of an invalid profile is increased.

It should be noted that base rate adjustments for certain scales have been made in an effort to increase MCMI-III profile validity. The adjustments serve as correction scores in much the same way as the K correction serves for the MMPI. These adjustments are part of the standard scoring (see Appendix D in the manual) and involve adjustments for Disclosure (if either high or low), Anxiety/Depression, Inpatient, and Denial/Complaint.

2. Interpret the Personality Disorder Scales

Retzlaff (1995) recommends that, when interpreting the personality disorder scales, practitioners should first check to see whether any of the Severe Personality Disorder scales are elevated. If so, this will strongly suggest that one or more of the Clinical Personality Pattern scales will also be elevated. However, the high scale(s) on the Severe Personality Disorder section should take precedence over equivalently elevated scales on the Clinical Personality Pattern scales. The Clinical Personality Pattern scales will then serve to color or elaborate on the elevation(s) on the Severe Personality Disorder scale(s). The primary focus for diagnosis, then, should be to rely on the Severe Personality Disorder elevation unless elevations on other categories of scales were extremely elevated compared to the Severe Personality Disorder scales. When that occurs, the extremely elevated scales would take on greater interpretive meaning compared to the more moderately elevated Severe Personality Disorder scale(s). (Interpretive descriptions of each of these scales can be found in the next section.) If there are no elevations on the Severe Personality Disorder scales, then practitioners should interpret any elevations on the Clinical Personality Pattern scales.

The interpretive sections under the personality disorder scales are divided into general interpretive descriptions, frequent code types, and treatment implications. Often, the descriptors are fairly severe and negative. Interpreters will need to determine whether these apply to the individual client, based on how high the scale is elevated, implications of associated scale elevations, and additional data available on the client. For example, some of the descriptors might need to be "softened" if they are in the marginally elevated range (BR 75–80). More severe interpretations might be appropriate for extremely elevated scores or if the elevations are from either the Severe Personality Pathology or Severe Syndromes categories. Millon (1994) specifies that scores in the 75–84 range indicate the syndrome or pattern is present, whereas scores of 85 or above indicate that it is prominent. The general rule, then, is: The higher the elevation, the more likely that the interpretive descriptions are accurate. Another consideration is the height of elevated scales relative to other elevated scales. If they are approximately the same height, they should be given equal interpretive weight. On the other hand, if there are 20 or more BR points between scales, the lower scale's influence is likely to be so subtle that it can be minimized or even ignored.

The general interpretive descriptions for the Clinical Personality Pattern scales (but not the Severe Personality Disorder) also include paragraphs on possible strengths or positive descriptions. These will provide a means of partially balancing the primarily negative descriptions associated with scale elevations. The subsection listed as "frequent code types" will give a brief description of the meanings attached to frequently associated elevations. Any code types that have been described previously will refer the reader back to these earlier descriptions.

3. Interpret Clinical Syndrome Scales

Similar to step 2, Retzlaff (1995) recommends that precedence be given to interpreting any elevations on the Severe Clinical Syndrome scales. Sometimes, all or most of these scales will be elevated, which should not be considered contradictory; rather, these elevations can be used to complement one another. Any elevations on the Severe Clinical Syndrome scales will usually be accompanied by complementary elevations on the Basic Clinical Syndrome scales as well as the personality disorder scales. For example, an elevation on the Severe Clinical Syndrome scale of Major Depression might also have corresponding elevations on Drug Dependence, Anxiety, and Avoidant. Interpretations would clearly center around depression but would also include fear of interpersonal involvement, anxiety, and the distinct likelihood that the person is using alcohol as a means of coping with these difficulties. Another example might be a person with an elevation on Anxiety but with a corresponding elevation on Avoidant and Dependent, which suggests he or she will be experiencing the anxiety due to a conflict between wanting to be accepted and cared for by others, and being terrified of criticism and humiliation. In contrast, another person with an elevation on Anxiety but with a corresponding elevation on Narcissistic will most likely be experiencing anxiety because of significant challenges to his or her self-inflated sense of importance and superiority. This careful interplay between the scales is crucial for accurate and effective profile interpretation.

One of the unique features of the MCMI is that it is an objective test that measures personality styles/patterns relevant to Axis II disorders. The sections describing each of these scales include subsections on frequent code types (including possible relations with clinical syndrome scales) and treatment implications. In contrast, the clinical syndrome scale descriptions include only descriptions of the scales, without material on frequent code types or treatment implications. This is partially because relevant relations with the personality scales have already been mentioned in the previous section. In addition, there is already a well-developed clinical literature (and extensive time is spent in most training programs) on treating these clinical syndromes (anxiety, depression, and so on). Practitioners who wish to develop detailed treatment procedures for difficulties measured by the clinical syndrome scales can consult resources such as Barlow's (1993) *Clinical Handbook of Psychological Disorders* (3rd ed.) or Kaplan and Sadock's (1996) *Comprehensive Textbook of Psychiatry.*

4. Review Noteworthy Responses (Critical Items)

The MCMI-III manual has listed a series of Noteworthy Responses in Appendix M (pp. 149–150). These are organized around the topics of Health Preoccupation, Interpersonal Alienation, Emotional Dyscontrol, Self-Destructive Potential, Childhood Abuse, and Eating Disorder(s). Similar to the MMPI critical items, the MCMI's Noteworthy Responses are not so much formal scales as they are rationally categorized items that might be important for a clinician to more fully understand. Accordingly, they can be used to organize a semistructured interview around relevant responses. They can also be selectively inserted into a psychological report to provide a more concrete qualitative portrayal of the client's attitudes, affect, and behavior.

5. Provide Diagnostic Impressions

Given the above interpretive descriptions of a client's profile (steps 2, 3, and 4), along with any other relevant information, clinicians can formulate the most appropriate diagnosis.

6. Elaborate on Treatment Implications and Recommendations

The symptoms reported and reflected in elevations on the clinical syndrome scales (anxiety, depression, substance abuse, and so on) are those that will be most problematic and thus should be targeted as high priorities. However, these will also need to be understood within the context of the client's personality patterns and pathologies. Under each of the personality disorder scales, there are sections with relevant suggestions for treatment recommendations. These can be considered, along with other information, to expand on what would be the most appropriate interventions. Additional useful resources in this process would be Chapter 13 of this book ("Psychological Assessment and Treatment Planning"), Millon and Davis's (1996) *Disorders of Personality: DSM-IV and Beyond,* and Retzlaff's (1995) *Tactical Psychotherapy of the Personality Disorders: An MCMI-III-Based Approach.*

MODIFYING INDICES (VALIDITY SCALES)

The MCMI Modifying Indices are adequate at detecting random responding, fake bad, and fake good profiles. However, the detection rate appears lower than for the MMPI (Bagby, Gillis, Toner, & Goldberg, 1991) and, as with the MMPI, fake bad profiles are more accurately detected than fake good (defensive) profiles (Fals-Stewart, 1995; Millon, 1987). Using the decision rules for fake bad profiles, the rate of accurate detection runs between 48% and 92% (Bagby et al., 1991; Retzlaff, Sheehan, & Fiel, 1991). However, for severely disturbed clients, high scores on fake bad indices may be more indicative of high distress and a "cry for help" than an invalid profile (Wetzler & Marlowe, 1990). In contrast to the generally good detection rate for fake bad profiles, persons faking good (defensively) are only likely to be detected approximately 50% of the time (Retzlaff et al., 1991) and clients underreporting their substance abuse seem particular good at avoiding detection (Fals-Stewart, 1995). This means that the MCMI should be used with extreme caution in situations where individuals might be likely to underreport their psychopathology.

The most useful tool in making the above decisions related to validity is a careful consideration of the client's past and current level of functioning. Specifically, a person who may look like he or she is faking bad but whose history reveals a person who is dysfunctional, may be merely expressing distress. In contrast, a relatively highly functioning person with the same scores on modifying indices is much more likely to be faking bad. Conversely, a person with a potentially fake good profile but who also has a high level of functioning may be merely expressing actual confidence, assertiveness, and high self-esteem. In contrast, a person with a similar profile but a history of interpersonal, legal, and/or psychiatric history is much more likely to be underreporting psychopathology.

Validity Index (Scale V)

The MCMI-III Validity Index is comprised of three items (numbers 65, 110, 157) which, if endorsed as true, indicate absurd responses. As a result, endorsement of these items strongly suggests that a person has responded randomly. The manual states that one true response should be interpreted as indicating a profile of "questionable validity," and two or more endorsements can clearly be interpreted as an invalid profile. Presumably, the "questionable validity" option is given to suggest that the profile *may* still be valid in the event that the client has misread or randomly responded to only a few items (including one of the three on the Validity Index). This allows the possibility that most of the items were still responded to accurately. In contrast, Bagby et al. (1991) recommend that even one endorsed item be used to indicate an invalid profile. One caution: If a person did respond randomly, there is still a statistical chance that he or she may have gotten "lucky" and none of the three items was answered in a true direction, in which case detection on the Validity Index would be avoided. In addition, a person wishing to consciously fake responses would be able to notice the absurdity of answering true to any of the Validity Index questions and would answer them in such a way that they would not endorse scorable responses on the Validity Index.

Disclosure Index (Scale X)

The Disclosure Index was designed to measure whether a client's responses were open and revealing as opposed to defensive and secretive. If the MCMI-III raw score on the Disclosure Index is below 34, it most likely indicates a defensive underreporting of psychopathology. It may also mean that the person did not read or understand the questions correctly. A further interpretation is that the client is hesitant, reserved, and overconcerned with seeking social approval. However, low Disclosure Index scores on the MCMI-II were not found to be particularly sensitive because subjects requested to "fake good" still produced generally acceptable Disclosure Index scores (Retzlaff et al., 1991). This means that when clients do fake good extensively enough to produce a clearly low Disclosure Index, the profile can be considered to be invalid with a fair degree of certainty.

MCMI-III raw scores above 178 indicate that the individual has extensively exaggerated his or her symptoms. The reporting of symptoms would even exceed fairly disturbed psychiatric populations and therefore suggests an overreporting of symptoms. This is the only scale on the MCMI that is interpreted if either high or low. The other scales on the MCMI should only be interpreted if they are above the BR 75 cutoff.

Desirability Index (Scale Y)

Similar to the Disclosure Index, the Desirability Index is also a measure of defensive responding. Scores above BR 75 indicate the individual has presented in a manner that is unusually moral, interpersonally attractive, extremely emotionally stable, highly gregarious, organized, and with a high respect for the rules of society. Progressively higher scores suggest that the person is concealing crucial details regarding psychological or interpersonal difficulties. However, this is not a particularly good scale and should be interpreted with caution.

Debasement Index (Scale Z)

As the title of the scale suggests, the Debasement Index reflects the extent to which a person is describing himself or herself in negative, pathological terms. This might include feelings of being empty or angry, crying easily, having low self-esteem, possibly being self-destructive, and frequently feeling tense, guilty, and depressed. Thus, the Debasement Index measures characteristics opposite from those on the Desirability Index. They are rarely both elevated although, on occasion, someone who is unusually self-disclosing may have high scores on both. Scores above BR 85 indicate either a cry for help due to acute psychological distress or a fake bad profile. As with Desirability, this scale is not particularly effective and should be interpreted with caution.

CLINICAL PERSONALITY PATTERNS

Schizoid (Scale 1)

The core characteristic of persons with elevations on this scale is that they have little or no interest in other people. Their lives are spent as loners. They are detached, impersonal, passive, and distant, and have few if any friends. They rarely initiate conversation, are indifferent to other people, and rarely seek involvement with others. Within family, work, or social situations, they prefer to have a peripheral role. As a result, they frequently function on the margins of society. They have little drive to have their needs met, experience few erotic attachments, express little warmth, and are often asexual. Rarely do they experience very much depth of feeling (pleasure, sadness, anger). They are largely indifferent to praise or criticism from others. Their interpersonal distance is not based on a defense stemming from fear of rejection but is rather their natural and most comfortable way of functioning. They also lack vitality and are unanimated and almost robotlike in their movements. When they do communicate with others, it is in a vague, distant, unfocused manner. Often, the direction of their conversation loses its focus and whatever information is conveyed is delivered in a circuitous manner. As a result, others are likely to see them as strange or "spacey." They have little self-awareness or insight into the implications of interpersonal relationships. If they are involved in a committed or intimate relationship, a frequent spousal complaint is that there is insufficient closeness, sharing, and understanding.

An asset of this personality style is that these persons typically do not become particularly disturbed by anything. Although they are not particularly involved with or interested in others, when they do interact they are typically quite comfortable. Decision making is often easier for them because it is not complicated by emotional or interpersonal complications. They are also quite self-sufficient in that they are comfortable with spending extensive periods of time alone and may have a rich fantasy life. Their hobbies typically involve activities that require only minimal contact with other people.

Frequent Code Types

Clinical scales that are likely to be elevated along with Schizoid are Anxiety and Thought Disorder. This reflects the sometimes obsessive thinking of the schizoid along with the possibility that brief psychotic states might occur. Personality scales that are often elevated along with Schizoid are Avoidant, Passive-Aggressive (Negativistic), Dependent, and Compulsive. Each of these will add new variations onto the above description. A corresponding elevation on Avoidant suggests that these persons are not only uninterested in and unskilled at interpersonal relationships, but they are uncomfortable around others and fear rejection. However, behind their detachment may be a real desire to become involved. If Schizoid and *Avoidant* are both elevated, the possibility of problem use of alcohol should be investigated (check Alcohol and Drug Dependence). Elevations on the *Passive-Aggressive (Negativistic)* scale (along with Avoidant) underscore conflictual feelings and possible resentment toward the few interpersonal relationships they have. This resentment will center around a wish that someone will nurture and guide them (especially if Dependent is also elevated) along with fear that they might be rejected. This conflict will result in their frequently being moody and nervous. An elevation on *Dependent* (along with Avoidant) indicates that they feel less important and capable than others. As a result, they are submissive, humble, and congenial as a means of seeking acceptance and being cared for. When *Compulsive* is elevated, these persons will be disciplined, well organized, emotionally controlled, meticulous, dependable, and persistent. This is partially because they feel that emotions are threatening and confusing, and their strategy of working with this is to remain disciplined, self-restrained, and proper. They are typically overly polite and even ingratiating toward authority figures but, in contrast, may be somewhat disdainful toward subordinates.

Treatment Implications

The two major goals when working with persons with Schizoid elevations are to (a) encourage at least some increase in social interaction and (b) help them to enhance their ability to experience pleasure. However, these goals are difficult to achieve in a client who is neither likely to become particularly involved in the therapeutic relationship nor ready to place much value in exploration and insight. As a result, the prognosis is poor. In addition, many therapists are likely to feel that schizoids are not particularly rewarding to work with. Therapists must be prepared for long silences and a distant relationship. Yet, any relationship that does develop can be extremely important for the client. Problem solving should be directed at concrete, practical matters. Useful techniques might be audio/videotape feedback of their behavior, and cognitive monitoring and reorientation of their internal processes. On the other hand, operant conditioning might prove difficult because they have little capacity for external rewards. Similarly, insight might be unproductive because they are not particularly psychologically minded.

Avoidant (Scale 2A)

Both schizoids and avoidants live solitary, often isolated lives. However, schizoids are indifferent to relationships whereas avoidants desperately want to become accepted and involved with other people—a desire that is blocked by an intense fear of being rejected and humiliated. They warily scan their environment for threats and continually try to present themselves in as favorable a manner as possible. This is rarely successful in that they feel a continual sense of unease, disquiet, anxiety, and overreaction to minor events. Thus, they are frequently preoccupied with intrusive, fearful, and disruptive thoughts. They perceive themselves as socially inept, inferior, and inadequate, and they continually undervalue their achievements. In addition to fear and self-criticism, they frequently feel alone, empty, and isolated. To protect themselves from these fears, they restrict their social environments, constantly maintaining their distance and privacy. This is unfortunate because it undercuts future opportunities of enhancing relationships and places them in a solitary world where they are more likely to reactivate memories of past social rejections. In addition, they rely extensively on fantasy gratification of their needs for affection and anger. Given the above dynamics, they are quite likely to fulfill the formal criteria for a social phobia and are frequently depressed.

The positive side of avoidants is that they can be extremely sensitive to the needs and perspectives of others. They can potentially show considerable compassion and understanding, and can be emotionally responsive.

Frequent Code Types

Avoidants, along with Borderlines, are likely to experience a wide variety of Axis I-related disorders. As a result, it is quite common to see elevations in several of the clinical syndrome scales. Among the most frequent associated disorders are generalized anxiety, and phobic and social phobias (check Anxiety). Depression (check Dysthymia and Major Depression) and hypochondriacal syndromes and conversion disorders can also occur (check Somatoform). Personality pattern scales that can be elevated are Dependent, Schizoid, Passive-Aggressive (Negativistic), Narcissistic, and Antisocial. A corresponding elevation on *Dependent* augments the core dynamics of the avoidant in that the person has even stronger needs to not only become involved with others, but also be supported by and given guidance by them. Avoidant, in combination with *Schizoid,* adds the dimension of having a lack of awareness or even of interest in personal feelings. These persons are also likely to be detached, aloof, and apathetic, and they rarely develop strong emotional ties with others. They might have some acquaintances, but they are not likely to have any intimate friendships. Elevations on *Passive-Aggressive (Negativistic)* suggest moodiness and resentment combined with significant difficulty in trusting others. They might vacillate between being friendly and cooperative and then being hostile, which might be followed by apologies. Because they would feel uncomfortable with their anger, they might resort to covert expressions of hostility, such as passive obstructionism. Whereas many persons with avoidant characteristics have low self-esteem, avoidants with elevations on *Narcissistic* will have an inflated sense of importance, overestimating their own value. They will be unappreciative of others and will justify this attitude by perceiving themselves as special. Situations will be framed in such a way as to enhance their own self-worth, and they will describe themselves as intelligent, sophisticated, outgoing, and charming. However, their underlying style will be avoidant so that their sense of self-importance will be extremely flimsy and easily deflated. Elevations on *Antisocial* introduce to the avoidants' personality a competitive edge that might be expressed in hostile and exploitive behaviors. They would justify this by fears that others are trying to take advantage of them. They will usually describe themselves as self-reliant, strong, realistic, and assertive, and they exhibit a contemptuous attitude toward persons who do not have these qualities. In addition, they are likely to be impulsive, argumentative, guarded, reserved, intimidating, cold, and insensitive to the feelings of others.

Treatment Implications

Avoidants are among the most frequent clients in therapy. A potentially difficult issue is that they will reveal only the information they believe will not lead to rejection by the therapist. The central treatment task is to change these clients' self-image, but this will involve working with interpersonal behavior and helping to regulate their mood. Particularly useful techniques would be in vivo exposure based on a graded hierarchy, anxiety management training, cognitive reorientation to challenge thinking errors, assertiveness training, and possibly psychopharmacological interventions to deal with anxiety states and possible panic attacks. However, the most difficult challenge is to keep them in therapy long enough to achieve therapeutic gain. This would require carefully balancing support, empathy, and trust building while still encouraging them to experience situations that will challenge them to work on new behaviors and perceptions. Given that their high level of arousal would be the primary reason for their terminating prematurely, techniques of arousal reduction—emotional support, reassurance, relaxation, hypnosis, thought stopping, and supportive interpretation—would be particularly important to utilize. Typically, these clients will make significant therapeutic gains. One area to investigate is the possibility that they are using alcohol to medicate their anxiety. However, referral to AA might be difficult, given their avoidant style, so other forms of intervention should be considered.

Depressive (Scale 2B)

The depressive personality style involves not merely recurrent symptoms of depression, but an enduring pattern of thoughts, attitudes, behaviors, and self concepts related to depression. These clients perceive themselves as worthless, vulnerable, inadequate, unsuccessful, and guilty, and they frequently engage in self-criticism. Whenever possible, they will frame events in a defeatist, fatalistic manner. They have learned to expect ridicule and derision. Even extremely slight signs of indifference might be interpreted as contempt and condemnation. Others will perceive them as forlorn, somber, discouraged, and hopeless. Initially, their depressive behavior might elicit support and empathy from well-intentioned others. Eventually, however, they end up feeling deserted and abandoned because their interpersonal behavior is likely to either distance others or attract persons who will use their passivity and depression to exploit or otherwise control them. They rarely engage in active, assertive behavior to obtain reinforcement from others. Even though they crave love and support, they fail to act in ways that others will find attractive and gratifying. Sometimes their self-criticism is a tactic to diffuse the potential criticism of others and simultaneously solicit support and sympathy. As a result, their interpersonal style serves to further reinforce their depression, and they frequently end up feeling angry, resentful, and pessimistic. Depressive personality disorder can be distinguished from major affective disorder and dysthymia in that, with a depressive personality, there will be an early, extended onset (versus more rapid and intense) along with multiple personality traits consistent with depression.

Because Depressives are quite introspective, they have the potential for and the orientation toward developing depth of insight. In addition, they are emotionally responsive and often have depth of feeling. Their level of distress may also be used as an aid in motivating them to change.

Frequent Code Types

The most likely elevations on the clinical scales would be on Dysthymic Disorder, Major Depression, and possibly Bipolar: Manic. These would be natural extensions of the individual's overall depressive style. Considerable conceptual and clinical overlap with other personality scales is likely, resulting in frequent associated elevations on Schizoid, Avoidant, Passive-Aggressive (Negativistic), Self-Defeating (Masochistic), and Borderline. An associated elevation on *Schizoid* would introduce an apathetic, indifferent, self-sufficient element to the depressive style. Because they are more likely to be interested in inanimate objects than interpersonal relationships, developing an effective therapeutic working relationship would be difficult. Organizing and logically communicating thoughts will often be extremely difficult. If Depressive and *Avoidant* are both elevated, the depressive style will be characterized by anxiety and fear of interpersonal humiliation, which leads to isolation as they attempt to protect themselves. They will engage in extreme introspection and will have a sense of alienation from themselves. An elevation on *Passive-Aggressive (Negativistic)* will flavor the depression with anger, irritability, and sour grumbling. They will vacillate between being bitter and resentful toward others versus being intropunitive and self-deprecatory. Because they are uncomfortable with their anger and resentment, these feelings will typically be expressed in indirect ways, such as through obstinacy, procrastination, and inefficiency. There are clear similarities between Depressive and *Self Defeating* (Masochistic). Both of these scales emphasize behaviors that result in the person's not obtaining what he or she wants from life. However, elevation in both of these scales highlights active maneuvers that result in possibly undeserved blame and unjust criticism. These persons will present themselves as self-effacing, self-sacrificing, obsequious, and deserving of painful consequences. A *Borderline* and Depressive configuration emphasizes a serious difficulty with controlling affect and behavior. Cyclical variations of emotional constraint and criticism will be followed by impulsive outbursts, sometimes of a self-destructive nature. Accusations may be made that others have mistreated them. Their level of self-identity will be extremely weak, and sometimes they will have difficulty logically organizing their thoughts and emotions.

Treatment Implications

The major focus of intervention should be to work with their sense of helpless immobility and their belief that emotional pain is an inevitable life condition. Interventions related to interpersonal behavior, cognitive schemas, self concept, and expectations will often be essential. Specific techniques might include social skills and assertiveness training, cognitive interventions that challenge underlying assumptions, behavioral programs that enhance pleasure-related activities, and group involvement that combines support and encouragement for change. Initial contact should be characterized by support that seeks to satisfy some of the client's dependency needs without fostering further helplessness. Psychopharmacology might be considered but should not be an end in itself. Long-standing cognitions, modes of interacting with others, and self concept will persist even after medication might have removed some of the more symptomatic features of the disorder. Therapeutic challenges will involve preventing self-harm; preventing the client from proceeding too fast and possibly encountering failure and disillusionment; and preventing relapse. Relapse prevention can be enhanced by realistically advising that some recurrent difficulties are inevitable.

Dependent (Scale 3)

The core characteristic for persons with elevations on this profile is that they do not feel capable and competent to function independently and therefore create strong bonds with people whom they perceive as being able to lead and care for them. They will quickly create alliances and give up responsibility for decisions. Thus, they feel inadequate and insecure, and they have low self-esteem. A primary way in which they deal with these feelings is to identify with stronger people and define themselves in terms of these people. They are continually concerned with the possibility of losing friends. To maintain friendships, they will be extremely submissive and cooperative, and will cover up any unpleasant emotions out of fear that the emotions might alienate others. They therefore minimize objective problems, rarely disagree with others, and never take a strong position on an issue. Others will therefore perceive them as gullible, wishy-washy, humble, timid, docile, and passive. Internally, they have a limited range of competencies in reducing tension and stressors. Elevations on this scale are consistent with bulimia.

Often, dependent personalities are well liked because they are cooperative, compliant, and humble, and they value the opinions of others. They are also likely to be loyal, warm, tender, and noncompetitive. They attempt to develop and maintain lasting friendships and do so, in part, by defusing unnecessary conflict.

Frequent Code Types

The most frequent Axis I-related difficulty is likely to be an anxiety disorder (check Anxiety), which might include panic attacks, social phobias, and agoraphobic attacks often related to or triggered by fears of separation. Mood disorders would be represented by associated elevations on Dysthymia as well as Bipolar: Manic, and Major Depression might also be common. Frequent associated scale elevations on the personality scales include Avoidant, Schizoid (see section on Schizoid), Compulsive, Passive-Aggressive (Negativistic), Histrionic, and Self-Defeating. An associated elevation on *Compulsive* indicates that dependent characteristics are combined with seeking approval and nurturance from others by acting perfectionistic, disciplined, orderly, industrious, and persistent. They will be highly respectful and even ingratiating toward persons in positions of authority. Careful preparation will be made for future events. Due to their dependency and focus on details, they will likely have difficulty making decisions. Elevations on *Passive-Aggressive (Negativistic)* along with Dependent indicate that, although these persons seek out the guidance and leadership of others, they are also quite conflicted about these relationships. They may vacillate between appearing to cooperate and then feeling resentful and angry, which will lead to resistance toward others in power. Guilt will follow, but then the cycle is likely to repeat itself. High scores on *Histrionic* indicate that these clients will be active and outgoing in attempting to get others to notice and take care of them. To this end, they might appear charming, dramatic, seductive, and extroverted. They are often quite sensitive to the moods of others, but may have noteworthy difficulty and a feeling of emptiness when they have to act independently. Finally, when *Self-Defeating* is elevated with Dependent, it highlights these clients' poor self-esteem, based in part on having been in a series of relationships that have been painful. Even though they desperately want others to care for them, they present themselves in a negative and pessimistic manner. Eventually, they will undermine and sabotage the relationships that, on another level, they seek to create.

Treatment Implications

Dependents frequently seek treatment. Typically, rapport is quite easily established, especially if the therapist responds in an authoritative, comforting, and assertive manner. However, the greatest danger (or challenge) is that a relationship may be created in which the therapist becomes a rescuer, thereby reinforcing the dependent pattern. These clients may prefer the therapist to be directive, but a nondirective, Socratic method is more likely to encourage assertion and independence. An important goal would be to reduce their clinging patterns and, instead, encourage their interacting in a more direct, assertive manner. Specific techniques might include assertiveness training, anxiety reduction skills (deep breathing, muscle relaxation, meditation), role playing, group therapy (to explore their impact on others), and psychoanalytic techniques that can probe the origins of their dependent patterns.

Histrionic (Scale 4)

Histrionic persons are dramatic, colorful, and emotional. Their tolerance for boredom is extremely low, and they will constantly be seeking new situations. They typically become highly invested in situations or with friends, but, when the excitement ends, they reinvest their energy and interest elsewhere. They see themselves as charming, outgoing, and able to acquire the attention of other people. As a result, they make very good impressions in party-type situations, although sometimes they might be perceived as too loud, demanding, and uncontrollable. In addition, they might be exhibitionistic and seductive, placing excessive reliance on physical appearance. Because they react easily and spontaneously to new situations, it is easy for them to mingle with people and quickly establish friendships. However, behind these seemingly assertive and independent behaviors are strong needs for dependency. Whereas dependents seek the protection and guidance of others, histrionics also need the attention and support of others but seek it in an extroverted, overt manner rather than using more submissive methods. Behind histrionics' dramatics and high level of activity are often conflicted, painful feelings that they avoid focusing on. Thus, their activity allows them to skim the surface of these feelings. Dissociative techniques, including the development of conversion reactions, may even be used. Typically, they communicate in a global, general manner in which they make arbitrary judgments with little focus on the specifics of an event or concept.

Histrionics can be warm, colorful, interesting, engaging, and emotionally responsive; typically, they have a good sense of humor. They easily adapt to new situations and, at least superficially, appear to have little difficulty interacting with and becoming close with others.

Frequent Code Types

Because of their underlying feelings of dependency, histrionics are likely to experience separation anxieties or, as an expression of their fears of emptiness, agoraphobia (check Anxiety). Conversion symptoms or hypochondriasis might also be means of dramatically expressing their needs (check Somatoform), and their need for stimulus seeking may result in substance abuse (check Alcohol Dependence and Drug Dependence).

Possible associated elevations on personality scales include Dependent (see section on Dependent), Narcissistic, Passive-Aggressive (Negativistic), Antisocial, and Compulsive. Elevations on Somatoform might indicate conversions. An associated *Narcissistic* elevation along with Histrionic frequently occurs with and is quite consistent with Histrionic in that it exaggerates many of the self-centered qualities of the histrionics. They are also likely to emphasize how charming and capable they are and to belittle those who do not partake in reinforcing their own sense of self-importance. Their descriptions of their competence and exploits will often be exaggerated. They will continually indicate how they are special and worthy of more attention and praise than others. An associated elevation on *Passive-Aggressive (Negativistic)* is problematic in that the histrionics will not like to accept their own negative emotions, such as anger and resentment. As a result of this conflict, they will be moody, unpredictable, and emotionally reactive. They might overtly criticize or show disdain for others or, in contrast, express these feelings in a more indirect way, such as through obstructionism. Their attempts to repress and overcontrol their anger and resentment may sometimes culminate in explosive outbursts, followed by guilt and apologies. Similarly, an elevation on *Antisocial* creates conflict for these persons. They are highly dependent on others, but they also realize that their anger, disaffiliation, and resentment are likely to distance the very people whom they so much need. They might begin a relationship by being charming, friendly, and engaging, but eventually their antisocial feelings will become expressed in resentment, mistrust, and even anger. In extreme cases, they might fluctuate between overcontrol and occasional extreme emotional or even physical outbursts. They may also seek to cope with this conflict through passive-aggressive strategies. Their world is perceived as a competitive, potentially dangerous place, and, given these perceptions, they have similarly become competitive, tough realists who believe that this is the only means of coping. Elevations on *Compulsive* along with Histrionic also present a conflicted relationship in that part of the person wants to be unrestrained and emotional whereas another part believes in the importance of emotional overcontrol. These clients are likely to seek approval through being orderly, efficient, and dependable, and by dressing correctly. Often, they have difficulty integrating these two modes of adapting and may become tense and moody.

Treatment Implications

Histrionics are typically motivated to come to therapy because they have been through a time when they have been criticized and feel socially deprived. They will describe feeling empty, bored, lonely, and discontented. Because they are emotional, responsive, and friendly, and seek the support and approval of others, they are likely to become easily engaged in therapy. These qualities usually lead to an initial high level of motivation and a good prognosis. They are unlikely to develop severe or chronic forms of psychopathology. However, they usually only stay in therapy long enough to become stabilized and rarely engage in deeper levels of self-exploration. One of the primary goals is to reduce their overdramatization. A calm, objective, cognitive approach is often useful in achieving this goal. In addition, group or family interventions can be useful in enhancing and practicing improved interpersonal skills. Given their externalizing coping style, a behavioral approach combined with the development of specific skills is likely to be more effective than one attempting to develop extensive insight.

Narcissistic (Scale 5)

The central characteristic of individuals with elevations on this scale is that they have an exaggerated sense of their self-importance and competence. Because they perceive themselves as special, they are likely to assume that many of the conventional rules of living with people do not apply to themselves. In addition, they may feel that they deserve special favors without having to reciprocate the time and resources that are given to them. As a result, they are likely to be overrepresented among persons seeking workers' and other forms of legal compensation. Internally, they might be quite creative in developing plausible reasons for their self-centeredness, but, to others, these reasons might seem flimsy and transparent. Their fantasies typically involve immature, self-glorifying situations in which they are the center of attention because they are beloved, admired, successful, and physically attractive. In real life, failures are quickly rationalized and conflicts are minimized, and they are adept at enhancing their sense of pride. In building their image, they might depreciate the value of others to make themselves look superior by comparison. They might therefore appear arrogant, haughty, snobbish, pretentious, and conceited. They will present themselves as intelligent, sophisticated, outgoing, and charming, with an air of cool optimism and feigned tranquillity. Rarely will they express any self-doubt. Interpersonally, they are likely to be exploitive, autocratic, and insensitive to the needs and feelings of others. Thus, they are generally lacking in empathy. They constantly attempt to obtain admiration from others. If they are in situations where they are criticized, they might become quite competitive and aggressive toward those who criticize them, or they may react with contempt or indifference. If their narcissistic bubble is burst, they are at risk for becoming depressed and potentially involved in substance abuse.

They frequently make excellent first impressions and might even receive respect and affection from others. Typically, they carry themselves with dignity and have a good sense of humor. Others will often perceive them as being proud, independent, confident, and optimistic.

Frequent Code Types

Because narcissistic persons are prone to affective disorders and substance abuse, check relevant clinical scales (Bipolar: Manic, Dysthymia, Alcohol Dependence, Drug Dependence, Major Depression). Personality scales that are likely to be elevated include Avoidant (see section on Avoidant), Histrionic (see section on Histrionic), Antisocial, and Passive-Aggressive (Negativistic). Elevations on Narcissistic and *Antisocial* emphasize the self-centered, competitive, and possibly aggressive and intimidating character of these persons. They are likely to be hostile and exploitive and justify this conduct by pointing out the competitive and exploitive nature of other people. At times, they might become malicious, cruel, and abusive; at others times, they may be cheerful, gracious, and friendly. Because they fear the criticism and possible exploitiveness of others, they might frequently be guarded, resentful, and reserved. The combination of *Passive-Aggressive (Negativistic)* and Narcissistic places these persons in a difficult, conflicted position. They seek to perceive themselves as superior and special in relation to others, but they are also acutely aware of their limitations. Thus, they are likely to be apologetic, submissive, compliant, and cooperative on the one hand, but also hypersensitive, moody, resentful, and angry on the other. They will have marked difficulty in accepting criticism, combined with frequent mood changes.

Treatment Implications

Because attending therapy is an implicit admission of imperfections, it is unusual for narcissistic persons to initiate therapy themselves. When they do, it is usually because their narcissistic sense of superiority has been compromised through such events as divorce or loss of employment. Interpersonally, they are likely to remain aloof and often be competitive with the therapist. They might question how someone who is less talented than they are could possibly be of assistance. Alternatively, they might elevate and inflate the status of the therapist because their association with someone who is so accomplished can be used to bolster their own sense of self-esteem. The easiest tactic for returning them to their previous level of functioning is to encourage and support them in recounting their previous successes and achievements. However, this may do them a disservice in the long run because they will not learn new strategies of coping and relating. A particularly useful technique might be cognitive reorientation, in which they are helped to challenge the need to be perfect and desensitized to criticism. Group and family therapy might support them in achieving more realistic and adaptive interpersonal skills. Given that they are likely to deny imperfections and resist change, either paradoxical interventions or approaches that use nondirective or self-directed techniques are likely to produce the best outcomes.

Antisocial (Scale 6A)

The central theme for persons with elevations on this scale is competitiveness along with impulsive acting-out of antisocial feelings. Their actions are often hasty, short-sighted, imprudent, and generally ignore the consequences of their actions even to the extent of disregarding the safety of themselves and others. They can be interpersonally irresponsible in that they will violate the personal rights of others in occupational, marital, parental, or financial contexts. They can be expected to have legal difficulties because many persons with elevations on Antisocial engage in criminal activities. For others in this category, legal problems are often absent because they confine their acting-out to legal domains such as alcohol abuse, interpersonal insensitivity, unreliable work practices, and irresponsible sexual behavior. However, they do not conform to social norms and may even feel and express contempt toward these norms. They enjoy the feeling of not being confined by standard modes of conduct and will project the image of being free, flexible, unencumbered, and having little obligation to schedules, commitments, or persons. Unfortunately, this image is usually associated with a lack of: compassion, empathy, remorse, and charitableness. Frequent expressions of callous competitiveness are justified by their pointing out the exploitiveness of others, or otherwise conceptualizing the world as functioning according to the "law of the jungle." Because of these attitudes, they are mistrustful, suspicious, guarded, and reserved. They might also be aggressive, intimidating, cold, insensitive, or even cruel and malicious, thereby provoking fear. Those who are considered "weak" may be treated with contempt; or, their own malicious tendencies might be ascribed to others. When challenged, they are likely to become impulsively angry or resentful, vindictive, and vengeful.

At their best, antisocials can be gracious, charming, friendly, and cheerful. Some people might perceive them as interesting and exciting, at least in part, because they are not confined by the same rules of conduct and restraints that other people have.

Frequent Code Types

Check to see whether the clinical scales of Alcohol Dependence and Drug Dependence are elevated; given the impulsiveness and hedonism of antisocials, they are prone to substance abuse. Although generally free from anxiety, they can develop affective disorders, especially when being held accountable for antisocial acting-out (check Bipolar: Manic, Dysthymia, Major Depression). Associated personality scales that are frequently elevated include Avoidant (see section on Avoidant), Dependent, Narcissistic (see section on Narcissistic), Histrionic (see section on Histrionic), Compulsive, Passive-Aggressive (Negativistic), and Aggressive (Sadistic). High points on Antisocial and *Dependent* indicate that these persons are extremely conflicted because they perceive the world as a difficult, competitive place; yet at the same time, they feel that they need to rely on others for protection and guidance. They will be mistrustful, guarded, and reserved, and, even though they know that to function they need to be tough, they do not feel themselves capable of this stance. The combination of Antisocial and *Compulsive* is also a conflicted combination. These persons feel internally impulsive, but they believe in discipline, control, persistence, and dependability. Their typical strategy is to become emotionally overcontrolled, careful, and deliberate. Perceiving the world as competitive and potentially exploitive, they protect themselves with a strategy of hard work, self-restraint, thorough preparation, and being guarded and mistrustful. Others are likely to perceive them as emotionally distant, tough-minded, formal, perfectionistic, inflexible, and possibly indecisive. When *Passive-Aggressive (Negativistic)* is high along with Antisocial, the angry, resentful characteristics of the Antisocial are brought out; yet, the same individuals may desire the closeness and warmth that could be available in relationships. However, they perceive the world as a struggle in which most situations are framed in "win–lose" terms. Thus, they frequently override their need for affection by becoming tough-minded, competitive, and interpersonally superficial. They might excel in individualistic activities—some competitive sports, or sales positions, for example—but they would have difficulty working in situations that require loyalty and team coordination. The unusual combination of Antisocial and *Aggressive (Sadistic)* is noteworthy in that it indicates that any acting-out will be cruel, malicious, and callous. The elevation on Aggressive (Sadistic) indicates that the expression of antisocial feelings will be direct, overt, and abusive. Such persons will need to be treated with considerable caution.

Treatment Implications

Antisocials typically do not perceive the need for treatment and are most frequently referred either by the courts or because of threats from spouses that they will leave them. Once in therapy, they are likely to either openly defy therapist interventions or develop a facade of cooperation in the hope that they might be able to somehow exploit the situation. Therapists need to be cautious; they can potentially be conned by these clients, who would then perceive them as weak and not worthy of respect. The therapists may then run the risk of becoming angry, cynical, and punitive—and ineffective. Given that the antisocial's style is one of externally acting-out, the most appropriate interventions are ones that are directed toward changing specific forms of behavior with clear limits: behavior modification, behavioral contracting, and external monitoring of behavior. Antisocials are unlikely to be responsive to internalizing, insight-oriented interventions. In addition, because their arousal level will typically be low, techniques that increase arousal, distress, or even anxiety will serve to increase their level of motivation. A group context might work particularly well, because antisocials are more responsive to peer influence than to authority-directed influence. However, most interventions have not been demonstrated to be effective in changing their underlying personality structure. A more realistic goal is the reduction of specific targeted symptoms or behaviors, particularly their aggression, destruction, impulsiveness, and poor affect. Target behaviors might be framed within the context of change being in the client's self-interest.

Aggressive (Sadistic; Scale 6B)

Individuals scoring high on Aggressive are typically competitive, energetic, hardheaded, authoritarian, and socially intolerant. They are predisposed toward aggressive outbursts, which might be expressed in a callous manner with little awareness of the impact of their verbally or physically aggressive actions. In many ways, this can be seen as a further pathological variation of the antisocial personality. Being in control and exerting power perhaps to the point of intimidating others is a central means they use to achieve their goals. Humiliating their victims also serves to release their own psychological pain. Sometimes, they enter socially approved enforcing roles in which their expression of aggression will be disguised behind socially sanctioned rules (the strict disciplinarian school principal or overzealous police officer). They are relatively unaffected by pain and punishment and may act in a manner that is both reckless and daring. They have a tough-minded orientation, which might be expressed in a caustic and contemptuous attitude toward social events and is consistent with their being prejudiced, intolerant, and authoritarian. At their worst, they might express vicious, explosive, violent, and even brutal behavior. Noticeably absent will be a sense of shame, guilt, sentimentality, or internal conflicts. Individuals will be perceived as objects to manipulate and control. This attitude might be enhanced and justified if the victims can be considered members of disempowered, marginalized groups.

Positive aspects of persons with this profile are that they can effectively cope with challenges. They can be unflinching and daring which, if expressed in the right context, can be considered courageous. In reaching a goal, they are relatively unencumbered by subtle ambiguities that might make it difficult for other people to take action.

Frequent Code Types

Fortunately, elevations on Aggressive (Sadistic) are infrequent but, when they do occur, noteworthy elevations on other scales include Antisocial (see section on Antisocial), Narcissistic, Compulsive, and Paranoid. When Aggressive (Sadistic) is added to *Narcissistic,* it highlights that these individuals will not only have an inflated, unrealistic sense of themselves, but are likely to be openly hostile and destructive, which is not the case when Narcissistic is elevated by itself. Elevations on the *Compulsive* scale highlight a methodical and disciplined expression of aggression. A corresponding elevation on *Paranoid* indicates that these persons' cruelty might be self-justified by suspicions that others would like to exploit or even brutalize them.

Treatment Implications

This difficult-to-treat group almost never reports to therapy on their own initiative. Once in therapy, they are likely to belittle the therapist and may even be overtly hostile. A therapist who responds negatively is likely to be perceived as weak, and they will use this perception to discount therapist interventions. In addition, they typically lack insight into their behavior and can even be indifferent to the damage they inflict. Cognitive interventions are unlikely to be successful because their thought patterns are quite rigid. Potentially useful approaches might be anger and impulse management programs, developing assertive as opposed to hostile communications, and persuading them to see that changing some of their more problematic behavior is actually in their own self-interest.

Compulsive (Scale 7)

The core characteristics for persons with this elevation are conformity, discipline, self-restraint, and formality. They will strictly adhere to social norms and may even be upset by novel ideas, especially if they challenge established norms of conduct. They are conscientious, well prepared, righteous, and meticulous, and they perform well when required to work on a schedule. They typically work hard, sometimes to the exclusion of leisure activities. Their emotions and behavior are tightly controlled. Interpersonally, they are formal, moral, perfectionistic, and rigid. They are overrespectful and even ingratiating toward persons in authority. In contrast, they are likely to be demanding, perfectionistic, and even contemptuous of subordinates, insisting that they act in strict adherence to correct and preestablished rules and methods. Internally, they are rigidly controlled and will not allow themselves to experience any forbidden thoughts or impulses. Their world is constructed in terms of schedules, deadlines, rules, ethics, and prescribed forms of behavior. Although they perform well in structured, concrete working environments, they will have difficulty adjusting to changing work situations that require creative, spontaneous responses. Although the above strategies provide them with a high degree of control over their world and their inner impulses, the price they pay is a grim, tense, joyless life in which warm feelings and spontaneity are kept under tight control.

Positive qualities include loyalty, prudence, consistency, predictability, and a strong sense of duty. Often, they will be able to approach a difficult situation with maturity and competence. Within a work context, they are punctual, thorough, diligent, honest, and rarely make mistakes.

A defensive, fake good profile can produce an elevation on Compulsive. In these cases, the above scale interpretation should not focus on discipline and restraint but rather on the client's defensiveness.

Frequent Code Types

The most frequent comorbid clinical conditions (Axis I) are generalized anxiety disorders (check Anxiety scale) and depression, particularly of an agitated nature (check Dysthymia and, possibly, Major Depression scales). Compared to other personality disorders, compulsives tend to be a better defined population in that there is less over-lap with other personality disorders. Nonetheless, associated elevations can occur with Schizoid (see section on Schizoid), Dependent (see section on Dependent), Histrionic (see section on Histrionic), Antisocial (see section on Antisocial), Avoidant, and Narcissistic. Concurrent elevations on *Avoidant* indicate that these individuals would like to obtain the warmth and affection of others. However, they are extremely hesitant to do so because people are perceived as unpredictable and emotional. Both these aspects of relationships are experienced as risky and are likely to arouse significant anxiety. Compulsives have learned to minimize risk by becoming perfectionistic and relating in a distant, aloof manner. Elevations with Compulsive and *Narcissistic* suggest individuals who are confident, defensive, and unlikely to concede that they have made a mistake. They strongly rely on their own ideas and are likely to have difficulty accepting the advice, suggestions, and especially the orders of others. Individuals will perceive them as inflexible, formal, proper, and distant. As a result, they will have difficulty working in supportive team environments where mutual respect and consensus building are crucial factors.

Treatment Implications

Usually, compulsives lead controlled, predictable, and generally functional lives. However, when confronted with excessive change or important decisions, they may present to therapy with anxiety-related problems. In particular, these might be expressed in somatic complaints because they have a difficult time releasing internal tension. They view their world in a rigid, inflexible manner, and cognitive changes are difficult to achieve. Similarly, self-exploration is difficult; it is experienced as a violation of their "character armor" and their personal sense of privacy and conformity. In addition, self-exploration runs the risk of playing into their obsessiveness, so that change never actually occurs. One technique of breaking up their obsessive patterns is to help them access and experience their affect. Other strategies are to work with them to realize the irrationality of their patterns or to use paradoxical interventions (i.e., reframing perfection as actually allowing themselves to make mistakes). Usually, the first line of intervention is support combined with techniques of anxiety reduction: systematic desensitization, relaxation, emotional support, biofeedback, and possibly psychopharmacological agents. Any insight-related work should proceed cautiously and with considerable reassurance, so that their defenses are not challenged too quickly. Potentially problematic client–therapist transactions might be therapist boredom, power struggles, or therapist collusion with the client's compulsions in the form of endless but unproductive insights.

Passive-Aggressive (Negativistic; Scale 8A)

The core characteristic for clients with elevations in this scale is a mix of passive compliance combined with resentment and opposition. These clients usually act on these resentments in impulsive and erratic ways. Feeding their resentment is a sense that they have somehow gotten a raw deal in life and will inevitably be disappointed in relationships. However, they also feel that their resentment and anger are not acceptable emotions for them to have. As a result, guilt and conflict pervade their lives. This internal conflictual style also becomes externalized and creates problems in interpersonal relationships. They will be moody, complaining, and intermittently hostile. One moment they might be angry and stubborn, but the next moment they will feel guilty and apologetic. They are likely to express their negativism in indirect ways—procrastination, inefficiency, and contrary behavior that has the effect of undermining the happiness of others. They may also act on their resentment with caustic comments, complaining, and expressions of contempt toward others. One means of coping with these feelings is to deny them and, instead, attribute them to others. Another way is to conceptualize that the resentment and anger are justified because of the numerous reasons to be envious toward others, who are constantly seen as having things so much better. Their resulting chronic unhappiness is expressed through pessimism, disillusionment, and cynicism. Because they blame other people for their misfortunes, they have little insight into how their own behavior and attitudes cause others to reject them. However, when their attitudes and behaviors eventually lead to rejection by others, these clients feel demeaned, abandoned, unappreciated, and disillusioned. Thus, their difficulties are self-fulfilling and self-maintaining.

A further core conflict is a feeling that they would like to depend on others but this dependence is neither socially acceptable nor safe because others will inevitably exploit and disappointment them. Thus, they will seem moody and unpredictable as they ruminate over these contradictory feelings. They will often perceive relationships as a threat to their safety. To protect themselves, they will become superficially quite self-sufficient and independent.

At their best, persons with this elevation can be agreeable and friendly. They can also be flexible, changeable, emotionally responsive, and sensitive.

Frequent Code Types

Persons with this code type experience frequent rejection and are likely to experience depression (check Dysthymia and Major Affective Disorder). Their feeling that interpersonal situations are potentially dangerous is capable of producing chronic anxiety (check Anxiety), which might be expressed in indirect ways through psychophysiological disorders or conversions (check Somatoform). Concurrent elevations on personality scales include Schizoid, Avoidant, Dependent, Histrionic, Antisocial, Narcissistic, and Aggressive (Sadistic; check frequent code type descriptions for each one of these scales in previous sections).

Treatment Implications

The two major areas of intervention involve enabling passive-aggressives to be more consistent in their approach to life and to develop insight into the nature of their ambivalent style of responding. However, the therapeutic relationship itself is likely to be complicated by their ambivalence. Specifically, they desire caring and support by others but will perceive the development of such a relationship as a threat to their independence and will fear that it will end up with rejection and disappointment. As a result, they may erratically criticize their therapist or engage in passive resistance. Dealing with this potential difficulty through early behavioral contracting might be particularly useful in keeping these clients engaged in the therapy process. One concern related to clinical management is that their impulsiveness might involve suicide risk. This is especially problematic if they decompensate into an anxiety or depressive disorder. Family and marital interventions are likely to be extremely beneficial because passive-aggressive (negativistic) patterns are both initiated by and maintained by these systems. Formal programs of anger management and assertiveness training might also be quite helpful in developing greater control over impulses and learning more effective styles of communication. Their belief in future disappointments along with their dysfunctional thoughts of having been cheated by life can be worked on through cognitive interventions that challenge these assumptions. Because they are likely to be resistant, controlling clients, the use of either paradoxical directives or a combination of nondirective and client-directed techniques is likely to optimize outcome.

Self-Defeating (Scale 8B)

High elevations on Self-Defeating indicate aggrieved persons who continually place themselves in situations where they will be the victims. They present themselves as inferior, nonindulgent, self-effacing, or otherwise reluctant to accept pleasure and happiness. Somehow, pleasure is seen as something they do not deserve, and they feel that if they allow themselves to experience pleasure, further difficulties or other unpleasant consequences will follow. Anything positive is expressed with very little enthusiasm. Interpersonal relationships are characterized by these clients as being servile, self-effacing, self-sacrificing, or otherwise allowing or even encouraging others to exploit or mistreat them. This active involvement in creating situations in which they will be exploited differentiates these types of persons from other depressed clients. Close relationships are usually associated with disappointments and frustrations. Those who do try to support and help them are likely to be ignored or otherwise rendered ineffectual. One purpose of this response is to make themselves weak and harmless in an effort to discourage possible criticism and aggression from others and evoke guilt instead. In addition, their public displays of dejection initially produce both sympathy and a tacit permission to avoid unpleasant responsibilities. A further purpose is to keep their self-identity organized around being shamed, humbled, and debased. They may be so absorbed in their own suffering and misery that they have few resources for appreciating the dilemmas others might be in. Although superficially they might be sympathetic to others, underneath they are unempathic and distrustful. They will focus and ruminate on past failed relationships and disparage any personal achievements. This will result in their being anxious, apprehensive, mournful, anguished, and tormented.

Positive qualities are that, in comparison to disorders such as Schizoid, they are involved with and connected to people. Often, they can develop a good level of insight into their difficulties. In addition, their level of distress is likely to be sufficiently high that they can and will become engaged in therapy.

Frequent Code Types

The greatest risk for Self-Defeating persons is the development of depression (check Dysthymia and Major Affective Disorder). If anxiety is present, it will usually be diffuse and associated with fears of loss and abandonment. Hypochondriacal strategies might be grafted on to their aggrieved style as a means of channeling anxiety and obtaining support (check Somatoform). The most frequent associated elevations are with Dependent (see section on Dependent), Borderline (see section on Borderline), Depressive (see section on Depressive), and Avoidant. When Self-Defeating and *Avoidant* are both elevated, it suggests that these persons have found relationships sufficiently painful that they have withdrawn to the extent of rarely interacting and becoming relatively isolated. They would like to be involved with others, but that experience has simply proven to be too painful in the past.

Treatment Implications

The paradox of working with self-defeating persons is that the context of therapy is to make them happier; yet, on one level, they do not want to be happier. These clients might even try to provoke or at least frame situations in such a way that they feel rejected or humiliated by the therapist. To counter this tactic, a sufficient amount of support, understanding, and rapport must be established to work with these clients and make them understand that they do not necessarily have to suffer. Specific self-defeating behaviors need to be identified along with the circumstances that elicit them. Assertiveness training, to help clarify their rights and develop skills to stop exploitation, might be particularly helpful. These skills, and others, might be practiced within the context of role plays and/or couples therapy. Further examination of relationships and the part they play in them can occur both within individual therapy and through supportive group interaction.

SEVERE PERSONALITY PATHOLOGY

Schizotypal (Scale S)

The major characteristics of persons with elevations on Schizotypal are that they are eccentric, disorganized, and socially isolated. These difficulties will usually be of a long-term nature. Their eccentricities relate to peculiar mannerisms, strange clothes, and bizarre expressions. They will typically look drab, lifeless, apathetic, and joyless. They may engage in magical behavior and rituals in an attempt to neutralize "evil" thoughts, deeds, or omens. Often, there is little distinction between fantasy and reality. Their communication style is characterized by tangential comments, personal irrelevancies, and magical associations. As a result, they lead empty and meaningless lives in which they drift to and from various locations and sources of employment. Thus, they exist on the fringe of society. Some are detached and emotionally bland; others are more suspicious, anxious, and apprehensive. Because they are mistrustful and communicate poorly, their relationships usually make them quite uncomfortable. As a result, they develop few if any close friendships and prefer privacy and isolation. Usually, they lack the interest and energy to initiate social interaction. Internally, they have a deep sense of emptiness and meaninglessness, which sometimes is sufficiently severe to prompt a full schizophrenic episode. Their thought processes are scattered, autistic, and disorganized. They are likely to have experiences of depersonalization and dissociation. In summary, schizotypals are cognitively impaired in their ability to comprehend interpersonal motivations and communications.

Frequent Code Types

Diagnostically, schizotypals exist somewhere between the less severe schizoid disorder and the more severe schizophrenic disorders. However, there is conceptual and clinical overlap with both these disorders, so elevations on scales that measure these dimensions should be noted (check Schizoid, Thought Disorder, and Delusional Disorder). Accordingly, schizoid and schizophrenic disorders might coexist with schizotypal. The most likely associated elevations on personality scales are Schizoid, Avoidant, and Paranoid. The Schizoid and Avoidant elevations are important in distinguishing two subtypes of schizotypals. An elevation on Schizotypal in combination with *Schizoid* indicates a more passive, apathetic, detached expression of schizotypal characteristics. These persons will be deficient in their capacity to experience emotions, and extremely detached and indifferent toward others. In contrast, an associated elevation on *Avoidant* indicates a desire for personal contact, but these individuals will be more anxious and apprehensive, and will actively protect themselves by disengaging from others. If *Paranoid* is elevated along with Schizotypal, it highlights these clients' suspiciousness along with corresponding ideas of reference. Although their thoughts might be more organized because of the coherence provided by the paranoid content, they will still have the tangential thinking and eccentric behavior that are characteristic of persons with elevations on schizotypal.

Treatment Implications

The prognosis for Schizotypal is not good because of the ingrained, long-standing nature of their patterns and the difficulty of engaging them in the therapeutic process. Treatment goals should be tempered accordingly, with a focus on preventing further social isolation and deterioration. Changing these individuals' environment to encourage an increase in supportive interpersonal interaction might be particularly helpful. A further intervention might be to help them express and clarify their thoughts while simultaneously providing emotional support. Psychopharmacological agents might be useful both in helping to organize their thoughts as well as in reducing the likelihood of their acting on irrational impulses.

Borderline (Scale C)

The core features of individuals with elevations on this scale are instability and unpredictability of mood and behavior. One moment they might feel dejected and disillusioned; sometime later, feelings of euphoria will be followed by a phase of intense anger, irritability, and self-destructiveness—possibly even involving self-mutilation. Their self-destructiveness reflects a severely punishing conscience. In addition, much of their unstable behavior seems to be directed by internal factors rather than a reaction to environmental events. They will have marked mood swings, intermittent periods of depression, generalized anxiety, and intense emotional attacks on others, followed by apathy and dejection. Although these behaviors often create significant interpersonal difficulties, these clients are also extremely concerned with maintaining the care and emotional support of others. Even though they often elicit rejection, they strongly react to fears of abandonment. They might intermittently idealize people, but their ambivalence eventually gives way to devaluing and criticizing the same people they have previously idealized. Thus, their relationships are characterized by ambivalence, instability, and intensity. Underlying many of these behaviors is an extremely poorly developed sense of identity, which is at the core of their dissolution of controls. Their poorly defined sense of self might eventually give way to feelings of emptiness and to disorganized thoughts. Under stress, they might have transient psychotic episodes. However, these episodes will rarely be sufficient to be considered a formal thought disorder, and these clients will typically return fairly quickly to their previous levels of functioning.

Frequent Code Types

The symptomatology of borderlines can be extremely diverse; elevations may appear on any of the clinical scales. However, mood disorders (check Bipolar: Manic, Dysthymic, Major Depression) and substance abuse (check Alcohol Dependence and Drug Dependence) are among the most common complications. In many ways, borderlines can be conceptualized as exaggerations or extensions of the less dysfunctional personality disorders of self-defeating (masochistic), passive-aggressive (negativistic), dependent, histrionic, and/or narcissistic. As a result, elevations on one or more of the scales representing these constructs would be expected and would provide further information on these individuals' underlying dynamics and particular mode of expression. Because such a broad spectrum of behaviors is encompassed by the borderlines, this can be crucial information to attend to. One of the most frequent associated scale elevations is when Borderline is combined with *Passive-Aggressive (Negativistic)*, which emphasizes the conflicted aspect of the borderlines. These clients feel intense dependency, yet are anxious and extremely ambivalent about it. They also feel intense resentment and anger but simultaneously believe that such feelings are unacceptable. These intense polarities might naturally give way to both a disintegration of the sense of self as well as clearly unstable, unpredictable behavior. Another important combination is Borderline and *Self-Defeating*, which would highlight these clients' impulsive and self-destructive characteristics. Behind their unstable emotions and behavior would lie a strong underlying sense that they were not worthy of happiness but rather believe that they should be exploited and humiliated. Thus, the presence of depression and suicide would be an essential aspect of case management. Elevations on *Dependent* and Borderline emphasize these clients' low self-esteem, passivity, and apathy, combined with their need for someone else who will care for them and make decisions for them. A corresponding elevation on *Histrionic* would underscore these persons' dependency but, instead of being apathetic and passive, they would be outgoing, friendly, manipulative, and emotional. When their defenses are challenged, they might increase their activity and attention-seeking to intense levels, but if this strategy does not work, they may deteriorate into futility and self-destructiveness. When *Narcissistic* is elevated along with Borderline, it suggests that these individuals' self-inflated sense of importance has collapsed into feelings of shame, insecurity, emptiness, and self-condemnation.

Treatment Implications

Although borderlines are notoriously difficult to work with, they are also more amenable to change than many other personality-disordered individuals. The central, initial goal is to build sufficient rapport so that work can begin on stabilizing their erratic behavior and affect. This might involve a reality-oriented approach emphasizing such aspects as limit setting, sympathy, reassurance, advice, and insight regarding internal processes. Borderlines are capable of such a wide range of dysfunctional behaviors that knowing which one to address can sometimes be confusing. In addition, they are an unusually het-erogeneous group. For example, depression, anxiety, depersonalization, disorganized thoughts, fears of abandonment, self-destructiveness, and/or ambivalence may all be-come areas requiring attention. More than for most other client groups, building a strong therapeutic alliance is crucial in helping borderlines to adjust and cope with their many conflicted forms of acting and feeling. Because many borderlines resist authority-directed interventions, group therapy might be indicated since they are more likely to be responsive to peer influence.

Paranoid (Scale P)

The central issue for persons with elevations on Paranoid is suspiciousness and defen-siveness, combined with a feeling of superiority. They are constantly vigilant because they feel others will criticize or deceive them. Innocuous events will be perceived as insults or as the workings of a world in which others are trying to control or harm them. They will distort their world by interpreting events to fit their idiosyncratic views. Because they feel in frequent danger, they will be abrasive, touchy, hostile, and irritable. They are likely to feel bitter toward people who have been successful and to believe that their success has been achieved through dishonesty and possibly illegal ac-tivities. This process will involve denying their own shortcomings and attributing them to others. Although quick to notice and expand on minor faults in others, they will be ignorant of these same faults in themselves. These dynamics will be used as a means of establishing their own superiority in relation to others.

If high scorers on Paranoid perceive that anyone is trying to control or influence them, they will consider this a personal encroachment on their independence and will attack and humiliate the encroacher. As a result, they frequently induce fear and exas-peration in others. Unfortunately, their system of making sense of the world is self-fulfilling. People react negatively to their being mistrustful and even hostile, which provides evidence that indeed the world is a dangerous, insecure place. This pushes them progressively into a more insular world in which their thinking is extremely rigid. The rigidity and insularity are maintained because they depend on their own internal processes for both stimulation and reinforcement. They are terrified of being domi-nated and consider any sign of dependence an indication of weakness and inferiority. They insist on being the designers of their own fate and, in order to do so, need to be free from entanglements and obligations. Behind this separateness is a fear of losing their personal control and sense of autonomy. Thus, their extremely tightly organized and coherent personality and cognitive structure makes them feel emotionally and physically disconnected from others. In more extreme cases, these persons may have delusions of grandeur, ideas of reference, and intense fears of persecutory plots.

Frequent Code Types

Given the mistrust and fear expressed by many paranoids, anxiety is probably the most frequent Axis I complication (check Anxiety). Additional difficulties are likely to be obsessive-compulsive syndromes in which they engage in compulsive activities in an attempt to make their world "safe." In severe paranoid states, psychotic symptoms, expressed through delusions and hallucinations, may be present (check Delusional Disorder and Thought Disorder). Related elevations on personality scales include Narcissistic, Passive-Aggressive (Negativistic), Sadistic, and Avoidant. If *Narcissistic* is elevated, it suggests that, at some earlier stage, these clients' self-inflated sense of importance and superiority has been severely challenged. Paranoid processes become a means to resurrect these beliefs in a way that is further separated from reality and therefore requires more drastic measures. The result might be extravagant plans to defend the world from evil, create new societies, or solve insurmountable scientific problems. When an elevation in *Passive-Aggressive (Negativistic)* is associated with Paranoid, it represents an exaggeration of these persons' faultfinding, resentful, and discontented characteristics. These might be expressed as intense feelings of jealously or as claims that they are being cheated and misunderstood. Because their underlying negativism is unacceptable to themselves, they attribute it to the external world, thereby self-creating the world they are so afraid of. An elevation on both Paranoid and *Sadistic* suggests that these individuals' paranoia will be expressed in an authoritarian, controlling, intimidating, and belligerent manner. They are likely to ruminate over perceived past wrongs and develop callous plots of revenge. Elevations on *Avoidant* and Paranoid indicate that these clients are handling their fears and suspicions by becoming progressively more insular, reclusive, and isolated. Insularity helps to protect them from fears that others will be able to influence their thought processes. However, they will also feel extremely vulnerable and will have serious questions related to their self-esteem.

Treatment Implications

Although paranoid personalities have an intact, organized means of processing their world, they develop and maintain this perspective by insulating themselves from the influence of others and developing extremely rigid cognitive structures. Because therapy tries both to influence clients and to loosen habitual ways of perceiving the world, these people are difficult to work with. As a result, their prognosis is poor. Furthermore, submitting to therapy is an admission of weakness and of giving up self-sufficiency, and both situations are abhorrent to them. A therapist who is too friendly and empathic is likely to be perceived as being deceitful. In contrast, a therapist who is too distant or who challenges these clients' delusions will seem rejecting. Either approach may therefore invoke the clients' suspicions. The relationship requires a delicate balance. Trust needs to be slowly built up with gradual but careful encouragement to perceive events from several different perspectives.

CLINICAL SYNDROMES

Anxiety (Scale A)

High scores indicate clients are complaining of tension, difficulty relaxing, indecisiveness, and apprehension. Additional complaints include a highly sensitive startle response, hyperalertness, and fears related to the onset of poorly defined difficulties. Physiological complaints related to overarousal are also common. These might include insomnia, headaches, nausea, cold sweats, upset stomach, palpitations, excessive perspiration, and muscular aches. Anxiety may be either generalized or more focused, as in social situations or specific phobias. Inspection of responses to individual scale items can help to assess the degree of specificity of the anxiety.

Somatoform (Scale H)

Elevations reflect somatic complaints expressed in such areas as generalized pain, fatigue, multiple vague complaints, and/or preoccupation with health-related difficulties. However, these will typically represent psychological conflicts that are being expressed through physical means. If the clients have legitimate physical illnesses, they are likely to be unduly preoccupied and possibly exaggerating their difficulties. In other words, their difficulties will be overinterpreted to signify a major illness when the illness is actually relatively minor. Often, the complaints are expressed in a dramatic and/or vague manner. An important function of these complaints is to gain sympathy, attention, or medical reassurance. A careful medical history typically reveals a hypochondriacal pattern in which they will have been overutilizers of the healthcare system.

Bipolar: Manic (Scale N)

High scorers are likely to have mood swings that range from elation to depression. When elated, they will be restless and distractible, will have an exaggerated sense of self-esteem, and will be overly optimistic and impulsive. They will have a heightened and general sense of enthusiasm, along with unrealistic goals. Interpersonal relationships will have a demanding, intrusive, and pressured quality. There will be a reduced need for sleep, erratic mood shifts, and flightive ideas. Extreme elevations indicate a psychotic process characterized by delusions and possibly hallucinations.

Dysthymia (Scale D)

Elevations on Dysthymia reflect sadness, pessimism, hopelessness, apathy, low self-esteem, and guilt. These persons will continuously feel socially awkward, introverted, sad, useless, and filled with self-doubt. Discouragement and a preoccupation with their own inadequacy will also be present. They will have a sense of futility and may easily break into tears. Somatic complications might include insomnia, a poor appetite or habitual overeating, poor concentration, a continuous sense of feeling tired, and a marked loss of interest in pleasurable activities. Although they may have reduced effectiveness in competently undertaking daily activities, they will still remain involved in everyday life. Suicidal ideation might be present and should be investigated further. This, and other details related to the nature of the depression, can be further understood by noting the responses to particular items. Unless the Major Depression scale is markedly elevated, it is unlikely that the depression will be sufficiently severe to be considered psychotic.

Alcohol Dependence (Scale B)

Individuals scoring high on Alcohol Dependence are likely to have had a history of problem drinking. They may have tried to unsuccessfully curb or discontinue their drinking. High scorers are also likely to be having social, family, and/or occupational distress. However, the degree to which their drinking is problematic needs to be assessed in relation to other information on their level of functioning.

Drug Dependence (Scale T)

High scorers will have had a recurring history of difficulties with drug abuse. Also present will be a number of traits associated with drug-related difficulties: hedonism, impulsiveness, difficulty conforming to mainstream standards of behavior, self-indulgence, exploitiveness, and narcissistic personality characteristics. High scores are likely to have difficulty organizing daily life activities and will experience social, family, legal, and/or occupational distress.

Post-Traumatic Distress Disorder (Scale R)

Elevations on this scale suggest that these individuals have experienced an intense life-threatening event that has resulted in extreme fear, helplessness, and arousal. They have reacted by having uncontrolled, intrusive, and recurrent images or emotions related to the event(s): flashbacks, nightmares, or dissociative feelings that reactivate the event(s). Anxiety-related symptoms might include hypervigilance, hyperalertness, overreactive startle reactions, and a compulsive avoidance of circumstances that might be related to the trauma.

SEVERE SYNDROMES

Thought Disorder (Scale SS)

High scores on Thought Disorder suggest these persons have thoughts that are inconsistent, bizarre, fragmented, and disorganized. In addition, their behavior might be regressed, secretive, and incongruous, and they might be confused, withdrawn, and disoriented. Their affect is likely to be blunted, and they may report hallucinations. Possible diagnoses include schizophrenic, schizophreniform, and brief reactive psychosis.

Major Depression (Scale CC)

High scores suggest severe depression, to the extent that these individuals have difficulty with effective daily living. Psychological difficulties include a sense of hopelessness, suicidal ideation, pessimism, ruminating, and fear of the future. Somatic symptoms might include insomnia, poor concentration, psychomotor slowing or agitation, loss of appetite, weight loss, chronic fatigue, early morning awakening, and loss of sexual desire. They are also likely to feel worthless and to experience guilt. Some high scorers might express their symptoms in an irritable, whining manner, whereas others might be shy, passive, seclusive, and introverted.

Delusional Disorder (Scale PP)

Elevations on this scale indicate acutely paranoid states. These individuals will be characterized by irrational but interconnected delusions, persecutory thoughts, and grandiosity. They will be hyperalert to possible threats. The most frequent mood will be hostile suspiciousness, perhaps to the point of belligerence. They will feel mistreated, jealous, and betrayed.

RECOMMENDED READING

Choca, J. P., Shanley, L. A., & Van Denburg, E. (1996). *Interpretive guide to the Millon Clinical Multiaxial Inventory* (2nd ed.). Washington, DC: American Psychological Association.

Millon, T. (Ed.). (1996). *The Millon Inventories.* New York: Guilford.

Millon, T., & Davis, R. D. (1996). *Disorders of personality: DSM-IV and beyond.* New York: Wiley.

Retzlaff, P. D. (1995). *Tactical psychotherapy of the personality disorders: An MCMI-III-based approach.* Boston: Allyn & Bacon.

Chapter 8

THE CALIFORNIA PSYCHOLOGICAL INVENTORY

The California Psychological Inventory (CPI) is a self-administered, paper-and-pencil test comprised of 462 true-false statements. The test is designed for group administration, although it can also be given individually. Even though the test has been used to evaluate individuals between the ages of 12 and 70, it was mainly constructed for use with young adults having a minimum of a fourth-grade reading ability. The CPI items request information concerning an individual's typical behavior patterns, usual feelings and opinions, and attitudes relating to social, ethical, and family matters. The results are plotted on 20 scales and 3 vectors (factors) focusing on aspects of interpersonal relationships that are presented in everyday, commonsense descriptions.

The philosophical orientation of the CPI is based on an appreciation of enduring, commonly discussed personality variables that are relevant throughout different cultures. Thus, it uses such familiar commonsense terms as dominance, tolerance, and self-control, which Gough has referred to as "folk concepts." The value of using such common, easy-to-understand constructs is that they already have "functional validity." In other words, they have immediate cross-cultural relevance, are readily understood by a wide range of people, and have a high degree of power in predicting behavior. This is not to imply that untrained persons should be allowed to interpret the CPI, but rather that the test's roots and original constructs are based on conceptions of human behavior held by most people within most cultures. It is up to the skilled clinician to go beyond these common constructs and into a more subtle, broad, and integrated description of the person. Thus, the test does not have as its primary goal psychometric elegance, nor is it derived from any specific personality theory. The main focus or concern of the CPI involves practical usefulness and the development of descriptions that strive to be relevant, understandable, and accurate in terms of behavioral predictions.

The CPI, developed by Harrison Gough, was published in its original form in 1957. Although comments on the test have been mixed, most reviewers generally describe it in favorable terms. For example, Bolton (1992) concludes his review in the eleventh *Mental Measurements Yearbook* by stating that the "CPI is an excellent normal personality assessment device, more reliable than the manual advertises, with good normative data and outstanding interpretive information" (p. 139). It has been subjected to over 40 years of research and continuous improvement. The criticisms that have been directed at the CPI have stimulated extensive efforts toward refinement and improvement, including numerous studies on predictive validity, the development of alternate scales, and expanded normative data. Many of these improvements were incorporated into the 1987 revision. For these reasons, the CPI has become a respected and frequently used device in personality assessment, particularly in the areas of career development, personnel selection, interpersonal maladjustment, and prediction of antisocial behavior (McAllister, 1988; Van Hutton, 1990).

HISTORY AND DEVELOPMENT

The CPI was developed as an inventory to assess enduring interpersonal personality characteristics within a normal population. Gough published his original scales in 1948, but the first copyrighted edition of the initial 15 scales appeared in 1951. However, not until 1957 was a completed set of 18 scales published by Consulting Psychologists Press. It was further revised in 1987, at which time two new scales were included (empathy and independence), bringing the total number of scales to 20. These 20 scales measure such areas as social ascendancy, social image, intellectual stance, and conceptual interests. Three of these are validity scales that assess test-taking attitudes, including "fake bad" (Well-being/*Wb*), "fake good" (Good impression/*Gi*), and the extent to which highly popular responses are given (Communality/*Cm*).

The 1957 version of the CPI was derived from an original item pool of 3,500 questions. Of the 468 items that were eventually selected, 178 were identical to MMPI items, 35 were very similar, and the remaining 215 were developed specifically for the CPI. The items were selected on the basis of both empirical criterion keying and a rational approach in which questions were generated that, from a conceptual point of view, seemed to assess the characteristics the scales were trying to measure. These questions were then given to a sample group and accepted or rejected based on the extent of interitem correlation. However, the majority of the scales were not selected through the rational approach but rather through empirical criterion keying. Thus, series of questions, which had initially been developed rationally, were administered to different groups having specific, previously assessed characteristics that the scales were eventually intended to measure independently of these groups. Each group was selected through the use of a number of different criteria. For example, ratings, by friends and family, of an individual's degree of responsibility were used to select a person for inclusion in the sample group for the development of the scale on Responsibility. The Achievement via independence scale was based on college students' grade point averages; the Socialization scale used delinquents and nondelinquents; and Sociability involved the number of extracurricular activities that a student participated in. Items that were found to discriminate between the criterion group and a "normal" population (Responsibility, Sociability, and so on) were selected for initial inclusion in the scale.

It is important to emphasize that, similar to the MMPI items, the empirical relationships are more important than the "truth" of the content. For example, if a person in the group rated for responsibility answers "true" to the statement "I have never done anything hazardous just for the thrill of it," it does not matter whether he or she has actually performed hazardous behaviors for the thrill of it. The main consideration from a psychometric point of view is that he or she answers "true" to that question, which then indicates the item can be used to help differentiate responsible from nonresponsible persons.

The final step was to cross-validate the items with other populations to determine the extent to which the variable the scale was attempting to measure could be accurately assessed. Of the 18 original scales, 13 used empirical criterion keying, 4 used the rational approach, and the final one (Communality) cannot be easily categorized, although it primarily used a combination of the two techniques. The two new scales in the 1987 revision (Empathy and Independence) used a criterion keying approach to elicit and score items that already existed in the CPI.

Like the MMPI, the CPI scores are given a standard score (T score) with a mean of 50 and a standard deviation of 10. The 1957 scales were standardized on an original normative sample of 6,000 males and 7,000 females having a fairly wide range in age, socioeconomic status, and geographic area. The standardization for the 1987 revision was based on 1,000 males and 1,000 females who were selected from the CPI archives to be representative of the U.S. population in age, education, status, and other relevant variables. The 20 scales are arranged so that the first ones relate primarily to interactional, socially observable factors (Sociability, Social presence), the middle ones to more internal qualities (Responsibility, Self-control), and the final ones to "broadly stylistic variables related to different functional modes" (Intellectual efficiency, Flexibility; Gough, 1987). Interpretation is simplified in that higher-scale values are associated with traditionally more favorable qualities, and lower scores with more unfavorable qualities (Wallbrown & Jones, 1992). The exception to this is the final scale, F/M, which measures traditionally feminine and masculine characteristics. The scales form four groupings or classes that are based more on conceptual convenience than on any psychometrically pure procedures (Gough, 1987). The first class, containing six scales (*Do, Cs, Sy, Sp, Sa, In, Em*), is centered on poise, social ascendancy, and self-assurance. The second class relates more to a person's social image; it includes socialization, maturity, and responsibility, and contains a total of seven scales (*Re, So, Sc, To, Gi, Cm, Wb*). Class 3, which has only three scales (*Ac, Ai, Ie*), assesses the variables of a person's intellectual stance. The final class, also consisting of three scales (*Py, Fx, Fe*), measures conceptual abilities, such as intellectual and interest modes. Gough added three vectors or structural scales to the 1987 version. Rather than organizing these three scales conceptually, he developed them based on factor analysis to measure extraversion-introversion (externality-internality), norm-favoring versus norm-questioning, and degree of self-realization.

The CPI has been put to numerous uses since its initial development in 1957. Megargee (1972) reported that, when the test was first printed, researchers and practitioners used it for many of the more obvious purposes of a psychological test, such as the prediction of scholastic achievement, graduation from high school or college, and performance in specific areas, such as math and English. Later, its uses became much more diversified to the extent that work has now been done on managerial effectiveness, air traffic controllers, stock market speculators, the degree of creativity in such fields as architecture and mathematics, contraceptive practices, and performance in psychiatric residency programs. Furthermore, cross-cultural studies on validity have been performed in France, Israel, Italy, Japan, Poland, Switzerland, and Taiwan. Within the field of counseling, it has been used to predict response to therapy, to aid in the selection of a college major, to predict college GPA, and to predict the degree of success in such graduate education programs as medicine, dentistry, nursing, and education (see Gough, 1990, 1992; McAllister, 1988; Meyer & Davis, 1992; Van Hutton, 1990). Surveys of training programs indicate that it is the second most frequently taught objective personality test in clinical training programs (Piotrowski & Keller, 1984; Piotrowski & Zalewski, 1993), and, although it was actually used considerably less than many other instruments, it was still mentioned as being used by 21% of clinical psychologists (Watkins et al., 1995). From 1969 to 1973, it was also the second most frequently used assessment device with adolescents (LeUnes, Evans, Karnei, & Lowry, 1980). Computerized scoring and interpretation services are currently available, and several alternate scales have been developed. The manual accompanying the CPI was first published in 1957, but it was updated in 1969 and 1975. Along with a revision of the test itself, a new accompanying manual and administrators' guide was published in 1987 (Gough, 1957, 1975, 1987). All of this attests to the CPI's extensive diversity, popularity, and success.

COMPARISON WITH THE MMPI

Because there is similarity in both format and item content, comparisons between the CPI and MMPI are inevitable. Thorndike (1959) referred to the CPI as "the sane man's MMPI," and there are a number of clear similarities. The CPI uses more than one-third (194 of 462) of the MMPI's questions; a conversion is made from raw to standard scale scores with a mean of 50 and standard deviation of 10; and the final values are charted on a graph with peaks and valleys.

Despite these similarities, it is essential for any clinician using the CPI to also appreciate the significant conceptual and psychometric differences between the two tests. The general intent of the MMPI is to assess a person's intrapsychic processes and emotional distress as these relate to specific psychodiagnostic categories. Each of these categories has a group of internal dynamics surrounding it—for example, depression, which also includes apathy, lowered capacity for pleasure, and feelings of hopelessness and helplessness. The primary task of the MMPI is to identify either the presence or absence of these internal dynamics and to place the examinee in either a normal or one or more psychopathological categories. In contrast, the CPI focuses more on a normal population and is highly interpersonal in nature. In fact, there is a marked absence of symptom-oriented questions. Thus, the CPI is concerned with the presence or absence of specific interpersonal skills. In addition, the CPI avoids complex diagnostic nomenclature and instead emphasizes practical descriptions that are commonly used in most cultures.

From a psychometric perspective, the MMPI was originally developed from a bimodal distribution in which the main focus of the test was to be able to classify a specific client in either a pathological group or a normal one. The contrast groups were not high or low on a specific trait, but rather were high in pathology when compared with normals. For example, a group that was high in hysterical traits was contrasted not with a group of persons having superior health, but with individuals having only an average number of hysterical traits. In clinical assessment, members of the pathological group are considered to be anyone scoring greater than 2 standard deviations above the norm. As a result of this emphasis on differentiating pathological groups from "average" or normal groups, the interpretation of profiles within "normal" ranges (i.e., $T = 35$–64)

is uncertain and should be approached with caution. In contrast, the CPI uses a normal distribution within a standardized population. Furthermore, Gough used groups whose behavior was extreme on both high and low dimensions of the characteristic being measured. Thus, normal range scores of less than 2 standard deviations from the mean can be interpreted with a fairly high level of confidence. For example, a CPI score on Ac (Achievement via conformance) of $T = 60$ indicates a fairly high level of this particular attribute and a $T = 40$ score indicates a fairly low level. However, an MMPI T score of 60 on scale 8 (schizophrenia) does not indicate a relatively high degree of schizophrenia, nor does a T score of 40 indicate a low level. Thus, relatively normal profiles on the CPI not only are to be expected, but can also be interpreted successfully.

RELIABILITY AND VALIDITY

In general, the reliability and validity studies on the CPI compare favorably with those done on other personality inventories. Test-retest reliabilities for individual scales have ranged between a low reported median of .53 for Empathy to a high median of .80 for Self-control. The overall median reliability was reported to be .70 (Gough, 1987). Measures of internal consistency indicate that there is considerable variability among the test items, but, overall, the scale constructions are adequate. Internal consistency is lowest for the scales of Self-acceptance (.52), Capacity for status (.58), and Empathy (.58), and highest for vector 3 (Degree of self-realization; .85), vector 1 (Introversion-extraversion; .81), and Self-control (.80; Gough, 1987).

Factor-analytic studies have been reported for both a two-factor and a four-factor solution. In a general way, the factor structure suggests that elevations on CPI scales suggest personal adjustment whereas low scores indicate psychopathology (Higgins-Lee, 1990; Wallbrown & Jones, 1992). Megargee (1972) reported that the two factors of internal controls and interpersonal effectiveness accounted for a major portion of the variance on the original 1957 scales. Gough (1987) suggested four different factors for the 1987 revision. These included Extraversion (related to self-assurance, initiative, resourcefulness), Control (related to degree of rule-favoring, rule-following, conscientiousness, self-discipline), Flexibility (individuality, personal complexity, ingenuity, preference for change), and Consensuality (reliability, optimism, cooperation, agreeableness). These factors roughly corresponded with the three vectors or factor scorings that have been included in the 1987 revision. Vector 1 is a measure of introversion-extraversion, and vector 2 measures the extent to which a person is norm-favoring versus norm-doubting. Vector 3 provides an index of a person's psychological integration and self-realization.

The CPI has also been found to relate to most of the core five factors of personality (Neuroticism, Extraversion, Openness to experience, Agreeableness, and Conscientiousness). Both a conceptual and an empirical analysis found that four of these five factors correlated highly with different clusters of CPI scales (Deniston & Ramanaiah, 1993; McCrae, Costa, & Piedmont, 1993). For example, Openness to experience was found to correlate most strongly with Achievement via independence (.41) and Flexibility (.42), but also with Capacity for status (.38) and Social presence (.42; McCrae et al., 1993). However, the Agreeableness factor was only minimally represented on the CPI (Deniston & Ramanaiah, 1993; McCrae et al., 1993). This is despite a rational analysis of the CPI scales which would suggest that Agreeableness would be related to such scales as Socialization, Responsibility, Self-control, and Good impression. Despite this, the five-factor model was generally well represented on the CPI. This provides support that the CPI is measuring central aspects of personality and also suggests the possibility that future CPI scoring might include an option for scoring these factors (Bolton, 1992).

In line with Gough's practical orientation, the main work on validation has been predictive. Thus, Gough is less concerned with areas of psychometric elegance, such as whether the scales avoid overlap or measure psychometrically sound traits, than with the practical usefulness of the scales in providing accurate predictions. Specifically, persons scoring high on certain scales are more likely to be described in certain characteristic ways by those who know them. The scales themselves or the equations developed from various combinations of scales have also been able to predict a wide variety of different aspects of behavior. Many of the studies that have found useful levels of predictive validity are summarized later in this chapter, in the section on "Configural Interpretation."

ASSETS AND LIMITATIONS

The CPI focuses on diagnosing and understanding interpersonal behavior within normal populations. Instead of focusing on pathology, it assesses areas such as self-control, dominance, and achievement. However, even though its emphasis is on assessing normal variations, extreme scores can also provide important information about the specifics of a person's expression of maladjustment, particularly with regard to interpersonal relationships (Higgins-Lee, 1990; McAllister, 1988; Wallbrown & Jones, 1992). Whereas the MMPI is limited to use with primarily pathologically oriented populations, the CPI is appropriate for normal persons. Thus, it addresses issues that interest a great many people.

The main thrust of the research and construction of the CPI has been toward developing accurate, long- and short-term behavioral predictions. The focus is not so much on evaluating and predicting a specific, internal, unidimensional trait as on interpersonal behaviors and orientations. Gough (1968, p. 56) clarifies this by stressing that "a high score on a scale for social status does not mean that the individual has a 'trait' of high status; presumably, therefore, he may be already of high status, or possessed of those talents and dispositions that will lead him toward such attainment." Gough also stresses that certain interpersonal behaviors occur within specific contexts. For example, a person who scores high on "dominance" would be expected to assume control of a group requiring leadership. Thus, the longitudinal studies on the inventory have developed predictive strategies relating to such areas as graduating from high school (Gough, 1966), grades in college (Gough & Lanning, 1986), choice of major field in college (Goldschmid, 1967), predicting delinquent and criminal behavior (DeFrancisco & Taylor, 1993; Gough & Bradley, 1992), persistence among hospice volunteers (Lafer, 1989), creative potential (Gough, 1992), and police performance (Hargrave &

Hiatt, 1987). A number of special scales have been developed for assessing specific areas. These are available through the CPI computer-scored report and include Managerial Potential, Work Orientation, Leadership Potential Index, Social Maturity Index, and Creative Potential Index (see Gough, 1990; McAllister, 1988; Meyer & Davis, 1992). The test has generally proven to be a useful tool in the area of prediction and, as a result, has been particularly helpful in counseling high school and college students as well as in personnel selection (Meyer & Davis, 1992).

Because its basic concepts were derived from day-to-day social interaction, the CPI is relatively easily understood by a wide range of persons. Descriptions such as dominant, achievement-oriented, and self-controlled are generally straightforward and are therefore not easily misinterpreted by untrained professionals. In contrast, providing feedback to clients who have taken tests such as the MMPI or MCMI requires the clinician to rephrase psychiatric terminology into more approachable, easily understood "lay" terminology. Because the CPI relates to ongoing aspects of behavior, CPI interpretations are likely to have more immediacy, relevancy, and impact on persons receiving feedback from their test results. These "folk concepts" are generally found in all cultures and societies. Thus, Gough hoped that the inventory would have cross-cultural relevance and validity. Although some research has been conducted to test this hypothesis, more work still needs to be performed and subgroup norms should be applied when appropriate (Cross & Burger, 1982; Davis, Hoffman, & Nelson, 1990). Future research should be directed toward the relationship between CPI scores and race, socioeconomic status, and other demographic variables. Gynther (1978), in reviewing the literature on the CPI, stated that some of the research performed raises questions about Gough's assumption that the inventory has cross-cultural equivalence. He further questioned whether minorities produce valid results on the inventory. Although this issue is currently unresolved, studies that question the cross-cultural equivalence of the CPI are sufficient in number to advise that scores from persons of differing cultural backgrounds should be treated cautiously.

A number of predictive studies have been conducted from a research perspective, and several useful regression equations have been developed as aids in predicting behavior. However, extremely few studies have been performed to test the validity of predictions made by clinicians in actual practice (Gynther, 1978b). CPI-assisted clinical judgments may be generally accurate, but further empirical studies are needed to verify this. It is something of a contradiction that a test with an emphasis on practical usefulness has not been sufficiently evaluated within the clinical context. A further difficulty in developing accurate predictions is that few studies have been conducted to assess predictions of actual job performance. Most predictive studies have attempted to estimate such areas as future college attendance or grade point average in graduate programs. However, college attendance and grade point average do not necessarily correlate with later successful performance. For example, high medical school grades have not been found to correlate with later success as a physician (Loughmiller et al., 1970). This problem is certainly not unique to the CPI; it is a general issue with many similar tests, and it relates to a difficulty in establishing adequate and appropriate criteria. These issues suggest that test users should develop predictions based on test scores within limited and well-researched contexts. For example, if the CPI is being used to evaluate prospective medical students, it should be made clear that predictions are useful only with regard to the students' academic performance and not to their overall clinical skills or later success as physicians.

One major criticism which has been directed toward the CPI is the lack of factor analysis in the development of the different scales (Eysenck, 1985). Factor-analytic studies that have been conducted suggest that most of the variance can be accounted for by only two factors: (a) interpersonal effectiveness and (b) internal controls (Megargee, 1972). This conclusion is further supported in that many of the scales are highly correlated, are conceptually similar, and have extensive item overlap. Gough (1968) has responded by pointing out that the scales were designed to assess constructs that are in most people's minds on a daily basis. Any scale overlap, then, might accurately reflect the conceptual overlap in common folk concepts used on a daily basis, such as the self-control and high degree of socialization involved in responsible behavior. Even if many of the scales are quite similar, there is accumulating evidence that the scales measure what they were designed to measure. The lack of factor analysis is further corrected in that the 1987 version has included three different factor analytically derived scales that measure Extraversion-introversion (externality-internality), Norm-favoring versus norm-questioning, and Degree of self-realization (Gough, 1987). In addition, more recent factor-analytic studies indicate that four of the five core factors of personality are strongly represented in the CPI items and scales (McCrae et al., 1993; Walbrown & Jones, 1992).

A further limitation of the CPI is the insufficient number of studies undertaken on the meaning of pairs or triads of scales (Baucom, 1985). This may be partly due to the formidable number of possible CPI code types (compared with the MMPI's more manageable 45 possible combinations). In addition, many persons score within a relatively narrow range, which makes configural interpretation more difficult because clearly defined clusters of high and low scales are less likely (Shaw & Gynther, 1986). In contrast, extensive fruitful research has been conducted on two- and three-point codes for the MMPI. (Some of the work conducted on CPI code types is summarized later, in the section titled "Configural Interpretation.") Gough's more recent work on the three vectors (externality-internality, norm-favoring/norm-questioning, and realization) has also provided information regarding composite subscale or factor scores (see the section on "Structural Scale Interpretation"). In addition, McAllister (1988) has listed 132 different combinations of scale scores, of which 40 have empirical support and the remaining 92 are based on a combination of rational considerations and clinical experience. However, more research needs to be done on the many possible two- and three-point codes that could potentially be derived from the CPI.

In developing accurate clinical interpretations from the CPI, it is essential to consider the implications of such factors as the overall life situation of the examinee. For example, the profile of a 15-year-old on the CPI scale for Psychological mindedness (*Py*) has a meaning different from that of a person age 55. Another important consideration is the purpose for which the person believes he or she is being examined. A person who is taking the test in a conscious effort to receive a discharge from the military will be likely to bias his or her responses differently from a person seeking employment. It is also essential to look at overall patterns of scores rather than "single sign" indicators. Corresponding elevations on other scales can elaborate or modify the meaning they have for one another. Thus, clinicians should always keep in mind the implications of an examinee's overall life situation, age, education, perceived reason for assessment, and pattern of scores.

A final caution relates to the degree of comparability between the 1987 revision and the previous version. In the 1987 revision, the total number of items was reduced (from 468 to 462), some of the scale items were changed or deleted, and two new scales were added. Gough attempted to improve the old scales while still preserving their essential meanings. This is somewhat supported in that all correlations between the old and new scales were .91 or higher. Many of the prediction equations have been (and are being) updated. However, the new scales may be different in some yet-to-be-defined ways. Thus, it may be questionable whether the extensive research on the previous scales is also relevant for the new ones, and whether clinical interpretation of the new scales should be made in the same manner as the older ones. As more research on the 1987 revision continues, many of these questions can be progressively addressed and interpretations can be altered (or reinforced) accordingly.

The CPI, then, is an extremely useful test in the assessment of the interpersonal characteristics of relatively normal persons. It measures variables that interest a great number of people, thereby providing helpful behavioral predictions, and it uses routine, day-to-day interactional concepts. For these reasons, the CPI is extensively used in personnel selection and vocational guidance (Bolton, 1992; Gough, 1990; McAllister, 1988; Meyer & Davis, 1992). Significant limitations and cautions relate to limited validity studies in clinical settings, few empirical studies on the meaning of two- and/or three-point elevations, and the unknown (but continually emerging) comparability between the 1987 revision and the previous version.

INTERPRETATION PROCEDURES

Timing

The examiner should note the length of time it takes a person to complete the test. A person with an IQ within the normal range would be expected to complete the test in approximately one hour. If he or she takes 90 minutes or more, it suggests one of the following:

1. A major psychological disturbance such as severe depression or functional psychosis.
2. A low IQ combined with poor reading ability.
3. Cerebral impairment.

Tests that are completed in 20 minutes or less suggest:

1. An invalid profile.
2. An impulsive personality.
3. Both 1 and 2.

An alternative form of administration uses an oral or tape-recorded format, which can be particularly relevant for persons with unusually low reading skills. If time efficiency is important, two short forms are available. One is based on a factor-analytic strategy (Factor Analyzed Short Form; Burger, 1975) and the other is based on incorporating items repeated on the MMPI (Repeated Item Short Form; Schut, Hutzell, Swint, & Gaston, 1980).

Scoring

In scoring the profile, examiners should make sure that the correct scoring norms for the examinee's sex have been used. Examiners may also wish to extend the traditional scale information by using regression equations for such areas as high school achievement, parole success, or medical school performance (see the section on "Configural Interpretation," including Table 8–2). Alternate scales are also available and may be important in certain contexts.

Determining the Profile Validity

The CPI, like the MMPI, has built-in scales and relevant regression equations to detect invalid profiles. These features are important because Gough (1987) has estimated that, in large-scale testing situations, approximately 1.7% of all profiles will be invalid (.6% fake good, .4% fake bad, and .7% random answering).

An initial consideration in evaluating the profile validity is the number of items that have been left blank. If 30 or more spaces are blank, the test results may not be valid. The examiner should also make sure the subject has not marked a large number of questions (30 or more) as being both true and false. Another area that should be checked is the possibility of random answering. The subject may appear to have answered randomly simply because he or she misaligned the question numbers in the answer sheet and the test booklet, or may indeed have answered randomly in an attempt to hide his or her poor reading ability. A good indicator of random answering is a low score ($T = 29$ or less for males and 24 or less for females) on the Communality (Cm) scale.

Faking bad can usually be detected based on the presence of extremely low scores on Well-being (Wb; $T = 27$ or less for males and 31 or less for females) and Communality (Cm; $T = 29$ or less for males and 24 or less for females). A low score ($T = 39$ or less for males and 40 or less for females) on Good impression (Gi) is also frequently associated with faking bad, especially in the profiles of males. It should be stressed that a subject who fakes bad is not necessarily maladjusted. Rather, the specifics of his or her disorder cannot be evaluated because of the distorting effects of the person's need to create an impression of the seriousness of his or her problem. Thus, it is important to assess why the person is faking bad. Does it represent a "cry for help" in which suicide is a serious possibility, or is the person malingering due to numerous secondary gains?

To determine whether a subject is faking good, the most important scale to evaluate is Good impression (Gi). Fake good profiles will usually have high scores ($T = 69$ or more for males and 71 or more for females) on this scale, and it will most likely be a relative peak in comparison with the other scales. Usually, when a person is asked to fake good, all the scales with positive social connotations will be elevated but Gi will still be relatively higher than the others. Sometimes, it may be difficult to differentiate between someone who has a superior level of adjustment and a person who is faking good. The most significant consideration in making this distinction is the person's history. An individual with a history of poor adjustment combined with an unusually high *Gi* will probably be faking good, whereas a person with a history of good adjustment and a moderately high *Gi* will probably be expressing his or her superior level of adjustment.

The above critical-scale values for the three validity scales can generally serve as clinical tools to detect invalid profiles. However, Gough (1987), noting that a significant number of errors are still likely to occur, recommends a sequence of equations devised by Lanning (1989). The first step is to determine the probability of faking good by seeing whether the following equation (using CPI raw rather than standard scores for this and the other two equations) results in a score of 56.7 or greater:

$$\text{Fake good} = 44.67 + .15\,Do + .18\,Em + .35\,Gi - .11\,Wb - .13\,To - .12\,Fx.$$

Scores equal to or greater than 56.7 indicate a fake good profile. However, if scores are less than 56.7, the following equation should be calculated:

$$\text{Otherwise invalid} = 75.77 - .68\,Cm - .18\,Wb + .12\,Ac.$$

Scores on this equation are considered otherwise invalid if they are equal to or greater than 58.6, or normal if they are less than 58.55. To determine whether the profile is either random or fake bad, the following equation should be calculated:

$$\text{Random vs. Fake bad} = 41.95 + .13\,In + .22\,Gi - .06\,Cm + .14\,Py + .13\,Fx.$$

Scores equal to or greater than 50.00 indicate a randomly answered profile; a fake bad profile is indicated by scores less than 50.00. Use of the above decision tree is likely to significantly increase the accuracy of detecting invalid profiles when compared with clinical judgment based on single-scale evaluations. However, circumstances surrounding test administration still need to be taken into account before a final conclusion can be reached.

Profile Interpretation

After clinicians have determined that the test is valid, they should consider each of the following steps.

1. **Note the general patterns of elevations/lowerings.** Scores of $T = 50$ or more usually suggest a positive area of adjustment. Scales well below $T = 50$ indicate specific problem areas. However, the clinician must also interpret these scores within the overall context of assessment, taking into account such variables as the person's age, occupational level, cultural background, and educational level. For example, a high school student with an Intellectual efficiency (*Ie*) scale score of 60 represents a fairly high level of this characteristic, whereas the same score for a medical student represents a relatively low level when compared with his or her peers.

2. **Note the patterns of elevations/lowerings on different clusters and classes.**
After looking at possible areas of adjustment and maladjustment, the clinician can further evaluate the profile by examining the average elevations on the different clusters or
classes (Table 8–1) as organized by Gough (1987). For convenience, the clusters are
separated on the profile sheets by gray vertical lines. If most or all of the scales in a particular cluster are clearly above $T = 50$, then the qualities represented by the cluster are
areas of strength. In contrast, scores well below $T = 50$ represent areas of difficulty.

The clusters listed in Table 8–1 are organized according to conceptual similarity rather than statistically derived categories. In contrast, Gough (1987) also recommends examining the scales based on five factors that have been statistically
derived from more empirical relations. Factor 1 (*Do, Cs, Sy, Sp, Sa, In, Em*) indicates a
person's level of social poise and interpersonal effectiveness. Factor 2 (*Wb, Re, So, Sc,
To, Gi, Ac*) provides a general index of mental health, adjustment, and social conformity. The third factor (*Ai, Fx, To, Ie, Py*) includes scales that are characterized by assessing the extent to which a person can think and behave independently. The fourth
factor, comprised of scales *Cm, Re, So,* and *Wb,* measures the extent to which a person
adheres to social norms and expectations. High scorers (all above $T = 50$) are likely to
be conventional and place a high emphasis on doing and perceiving things correctly,
whereas low scorers (all below $T = 50$) will be more unconventional, individualistic,
and likely to perceive the world in more unusual ways. The fifth and final factor, comprised of Femininity/Masculinity, assesses a person's degree of aesthetic interests, dependency, and sensitivity. Clinicians can gain useful information by using either
Gough's clusters (classes) or the more empirically derived five factors.

In the 1987 revision of the CPI, Gough formalized aspects of the CPI factor
structure through the development and inclusion of three vectors. Each vector can be
used to obtain general descriptions of personality. The first vector describes the person's degree of introversion/extraversion, the second shows the degree to which the
person adheres to societal norms, and the third represents the extent to which the person has integrated and realized his or her personality. Scores on the first two vectors
can be used to categorize personality into various combinations of introversion/extra-
version and norm conformity (alphas, betas, gammas, deltas; see the next section,
"Structural Scales Interpretation").

3. **Evaluate the meaning of the scores on each individual scale.** Whereas the
different clusters, factors, or vectors provide general impressions for certain areas of

Table 8–1.   Cluster analysis

Cluster	Scales	Interpretation
1	Do, Cs, Sy, Sp, Sa, Em	Interpersonal effectiveness, style, and adequacy
2	Re, So, Sc, To, Gi, Cm, Wb	Intrapersonal controls, values styles, and beliefs
3	Ac, Ai, Ie	Intellectual stance, achievement, and academic ability
4	Py, Fx, F/M	Conceptual interests

functioning, the clinician can obtain more specific information by evaluating each scale individually. This involves looking at the relatively highest and lowest scales and developing a description of the dynamics involved with these scales. The meanings associated with specific high or low scores can be determined by considering the relevant scale descriptions (see the section on "The Individual Scales"). The general personality descriptions and discussions of the scales have been adapted and modified from the publications of Gough (1968, 1975, 1987), McAllister (1988), and Megargee (1972). Additional relevant material has also been included and is cited accordingly. The short list of most frequently used adjectives (provided at the end of the sections on high and low scores) is based on ratings reported by Gough (1987). The adjectives were included based on their occurring in two or more instances from within the different lists of ratings on the Adjective Check List made by peers, spouses, or CPI assessment staff.

4. **Note the scale configurations and calculate the regression equations.** Initial hypotheses can be further evaluated by consulting the section in this chapter dealing with typical scale configurations for different areas, including intellectual level, achievement, leadership, adjustment, and specific syndromes. This evaluation may also involve calculating and interpreting the regression equations, which are included in the section on "Configural Interpretations" and are summarized at the end of the chapter, in Table 8–2.

5. **Integrate the data into a profile description.** The final step in interpretation is to integrate all the data into a profile description. Essential here is the clinician's ability to assess the interactions between two or more scales. This suggests that, once a specific trend has been established, the clinician should elaborate on it by evaluating how the other scales change their meaning for the individual (cf. Heilbrun, Daniel, Goodstein, Stephenson, & Crites, 1962; McAllister, 1988; Meyer & Davis, 1992;

Table 8–2. Summary of CPI equations used for making predictions

---

1. Achievement (high school) = 20.116 + .317 Re + .192 So − .309 Gi + .227 Ac + .280 Ai + .244 Ie

2. Achievement (high school—using IQ) = .786 + .195 Re + .244 So − .130 Gi + .19 Ac + .179 Ai + .279 IQ

3. College attendance = 17.822 + .333 Do + .539 Cs − .189 Gi + .740 Ac

4. Achievement (Introduction to Psychology) = 35.958 − .294 Sy − .180 Sp + .185 Re − .189 Sc − .152 Gi − .210 Cm + .275 Ac + .523 Ai + .241 Ie + .657 Py

5. Male GPA = .16 SAT (Math) + .11 So − .19 Sp + .17 Fe

6. Female GPA = .25 SAT (Verbal) − .14 Sp + .06 Re + .20 Ac + .08 Fe

7. GPA = 30.60 − .26 Wb + .35 Re − .19 Gi + .39 Ai + .22 Ie + .36 Py

8. Teaching effectiveness = 14.743 + .334 So − .670 Gi + .997 Ac + .909 Py − .446 Fx

9. Medical promise = .794 Sy + .602 To + 1.114 Cm − .696 Cs

10. Dental performance = 29.938 − .110 Sp + .148 Re − .262 Gi + .727 Ac + .230 Py

11. Leadership (social) = 14.130 + .372 Do + .696 Sa + .345 Wb − .133 Gi + .274 Ai

12. Parole success = 45.078 − .353 Sp − .182 Sa + .532 So + .224 Sc

13. Social maturity = 25.701 + .408 Re + .478 So − .296 Gi

Webb, McNamara, & Rodgers, 1981). For example, dominance may be expressed in numerous ways, including rebellion, high achievement, leadership, or delinquency. Once these elaborations have been made within the test data, the clinician can seek outside confirmation through personal history, behavioral observations, and additional test data.

STRUCTURAL SCALE INTERPRETATION

The major addition to the 1987 revision was the development and inclusion of three structural scales. These three scales form what Gough (1987, 1990) has referred to as the cuboid model: a person's position can be conceptualized as existing in three-dimensional space. Each of the dimensions were based on a factor analysis of the different items on the CPI. The first theme or factor that seemed to emerge referred to elements of extraversion, self-confidence, assertive self-assurance, and social poise. Items measuring these dimensions were formerly used to develop a scoring for the first vector (or structural scale), which Gough (1987) referred to as *externality-internality*. The second factor was related more to the degree to which a person accepted societal norms and included such areas as social conformity, personal integrity, self-control, and disciplined effectiveness. Scoring for these qualities was formally developed into a second vector, which Gough (1987) referred to as *norm-favoring versus norm-questioning*. The third vector, labeled *realization,* assessed the degree to which a respondent has developed a sense of self-realization and psychological integration.

On the CPI profile sheet, the first two vectors (externality-internality and norm-favoring versus norm-questioning) are combined to place a person into one of four specific types (alpha, beta, gamma, delta) based on the interaction between vectors 1 and 2. The primary emphasis on structural scale interpretation is to understand the meaning associated with these four types. The third vector is used to provide additional meaning to these four types by considering the degree to which the person has managed to integrate them into a fully developed (self-realized) person. Vector 3 is rated on a scale between 1 and 7, where 1 represents no or little integration/realization and 7 represents an unusually high level. Gough (1987) describes these more specifically as 1 = poor, 2 = distinctly below average, 3 = below average, 4 = average, 5 = above average, 6 = distinctly above average, and 7 = superior.

Any interpretation of type should take into account both the extent to which the person has realized his or her type (vector 3) as well as the relative strength with which he or she represents the type. For example, an alpha combines qualities of extraversion and norm-favoring. These qualities would be far stronger if the person scored quite high on both extraversion and norm-favoring (vectors 1 and 2) than if he or she merely scored in the borderline areas. Specific interpretations and the implications of their degree of realization are described below and were derived from descriptions provided by Gough (1987) and Meyer and Davis (1992).

Alphas

Persons scoring in this quadrant tend to be highly extraverted and to adhere to societal norms. They will be good leaders in that they are task-focused and productive but are also interested in associating with others. Their social style may be somewhat manage-rial. Externally, they may be assertive and talkative, and they have high levels of achievement and social presence. If highly realized (note vector 3), alphas may be charismatic leaders and help to create social change. If undeveloped, they might be-come manipulative, self-centered, and concerned only with achieving their own ends regardless of consequences to others.

Betas

Betas combine qualities of both introversion and norm-favoring. Thus, they prefer ex-ternal structure and are generally most comfortable in the role of a follower. They will have a high degree of self-control, are highly dependable, conservative, value tradi-tions, and may place the needs of others before their own. If highly realized, they can be nurturant, represent ideal models of goodness, and convey conventional sources of wisdom. Poorly developed betas might be nonresponsive, overly conformist, inflexi-ble, constricted, and rigid.

Gammas

Gammas are extraverted and, at the same time, question traditional beliefs and values. Thus, they make their questions, beliefs, and challenges quite apparent. These are the skeptics and doubters and are often the persons who might try and change society. They perceive the world in highly individualistic ways but are still actively involved with others. Often, they might try to test limitations imposed on them and do so in a rebellious, self-dramatizing manner. At their best, gammas would be innovative, vi-sionary, perceptive, and imaginative. They are likely to be inventors, create new ideas, and push their field to new limits. If inadequately developed, they would be intolerant, belligerent, self-indulgent, rebellious, and disruptive.

Deltas

Persons scoring in this quadrant have qualities of introversion and also question tra-ditional values and beliefs. As a result, deltas will be highly reflective, somewhat de-tached, preoccupied, and possibly overly absorbed in their own fantasies and daydreams. They might prefer that others make decisions for them and, if extreme, may live primarily in their own private world. If fully developed, they might be highly imaginative, artistic, visionary, and innovative. However, they run the risk that their innovations may go unnoticed since they rarely make a production of their activities. If inadequately developed, deltas may be poorly organized, withdrawn, aloof, self-defeating, and at risk of decompensating.

THE INDIVIDUAL SCALES

1. Dominance (*Do*)

The *Do* scale measures areas of leadership ability and has become one of the most val-idated scales on the CPI. It includes verbal fluency, persuasiveness, and the extent to which a person is likely to take charge of a situation. Thus, high scorers are persistent in approaching a task and will usually take the initiative in interpersonal relationships. However, this description is more characteristic of the style in which high-scoring males express their dominance. High-scoring females express their dominance either by initiating attempts to choose a leader, or by being somewhat coercive, aggressive, or impatient. The contents of the items deal with social poise, confidence, verbal fluency, persuasiveness, and a sense of duty.

It should be stressed that the conditions in which leadership occurs are at least as important as the actual trait. This means that, when a situation arises requiring leadership, high scorers will usually become leaders rather than followers. More specifically, they are more likely to be the ones to set limits, and will become more assertive, goal-oriented, and clear and direct regarding their requests. They will adopt this role relatively comfortably and naturally. In contrast, low scorers experience discomfort when requested to take charge. They may be either more submissive, in which case they prefer to have others control and direct them, or merely socially isolated and introverted, in which case they do not want to control others but also do not want others to control them. They may even actively resist efforts that are made to control them.

High Do (T = 65 or More)

High scorers on *Do* are strong in expressing their opinions and in reaching their goals. This may range from being highly assertive, in which they are clear and direct in expressing their needs, to being aggressive, in which they are more forceful. They would rather take charge of a situation and can effectively do so because they have excellent abilities to plan and are self-confident when directing others. Persons high in dominance can use and develop the resources available to them and often express a sense of optimism. They are generally able to define their goals and work persistently to attain them. They would not be particularly compromising nor would they be the type of person to whom others would feel comfortable admitting their weaknesses. The most frequent adjectives used to describe them are dominant, confident, aggressive, assertive, outgoing, ambitious, and (having) initiative.

Moderate Do (T = 50–65)

Moderate *Do* scale scorers have the capacity for leadership but do not, under ordinary circumstances, seek opportunities to use this ability.

Moderately Low Do (T = 40–50)

With moderately low *Do,* people usually feel uncomfortable when leadership is required and much prefer being in the follower role. They are participants rather than organizers. Although some persons who are low in dominance are effective in relatively high leadership positions, they are uncomfortable with this aspect of their job, and usually have a democratic and participative style of decision making. However, most persons scoring low on *Do* experience a difficult time planning and, as a result, may sometimes appear reckless and impulsive. They are likely to believe and adhere to the beliefs of others and can therefore be easily influenced. Often, they have a difficult time making direct requests, and are usually seen as nonassertive. Low scorers, particularly females, are seen as submissive, shy, timid, and inhibited.

Low Do (T = 40 or Less)

Extremely low scores on *Do* suggest a general pattern of maladjustment (Gregory & Morris, 1978). These persons are likely to be socially withdrawn, insecure, and shy. They see themselves as having little or no leadership ability, and they dislike being directly responsible for either their own actions or the actions of others. They may be passive, require prodding, and attempt to avoid situations that are likely to produce tension and pressure. The adjectives most frequently used to describe these persons are shy, timid, submissive, withdrawn, quiet, retiring, unassuming, silent, and inhibited.

2. Capacity for Status (*Cs*)

An individual's capacity for status has been defined by Gough (1968, p.61) as equal to the "relative level of income, education, prestige, and power attained in [his or her] social-cultural milieu." This definition focuses on status as it has been achieved, but the *Cs* scale looks at status more as a trait associated with such features as ambition and self-assurance. The specific trait of capacity for status suggests that, eventually, a person will achieve and maintain a position of status. Thus, in creating the scale, Gough looked at the specific trait variables that would eventually lead to a higher status position. These traits include perseverance, self-direction, ambition, and self-confidence. Persons seeking status are usually willing to go through a fairly high degree of discomfort and personal change in order to achieve their goals. In the scale construction, there is some overlap of test items with Social presence (*Sp*), Intellectual efficiency (*Ie*), and Self-acceptance (*Sa*), indicating that Capacity for status also includes dimensions of social poise, efficiency, and self-confidence. The item content also reflects an absence of fears or anxieties, a high degree of social conscience, an interest in belonging to various groups, and an interest in literary and aesthetic activities.

High Cs (T = 60 or More)

Individuals with high scores on *Cs* scales are characterized as independent and imaginative; they will take advantage of opportunities that are presented to them. They will be highly self-directed, achievement-oriented, and able to respond to their environment in a manner designed to further their own goals. Their aspirations will be high, and they will have excellent verbal fluency. Extremely high scores suggest they will be overbearing, arrogant, and aristocratic, and will feel superior. The adjectives used most frequently to describe these high scorers are ambitious, confident, intelligent, versatile, enterprising, interests (are) wide, assertive, and (having) initiative.

Moderate Cs (T = 45–60)

As might be expected, moderate scorers are somewhat goal-oriented and relatively highly motivated to achieve. They are willing to change and adapt their lives to a certain extent, in their attempts to achieve status. They are also moderately ambitious and self-assured.

Moderately Low Cs (T = 35–45)

These individuals are minimally goal-oriented, but their general lack of self-direction is not sufficiently low to impair their level of functioning. They are unwilling to make many personal sacrifices in order to achieve power, prestige, or a higher income.

Low Cs (T = 35 or Less)

Persons who score extremely low on *Cs* usually have a low level of energy and are relatively rigid and inflexible. Their interests are extremely narrow, and they are likely to have little curiosity about their environment. They are usually resentful of their current position, an attitude that results in tension, restlessness, and depression. In the face of difficulties, they will usually give up easily and withdraw. Their thinking is commonplace, unimaginative, literal, and slow. The adjectives used most frequently to describe them are shy, timid, silent, quiet, simple, interests are narrow.

3. Sociability (Sy)

The Sociability scale was originally designed to measure the extent to which a person participates in social activities. It was later generalized to differentiate between a person who is outgoing, extraverted, and sociable versus one who is more introverted, withdrawn, and prone to avoid social visibility. There is a great deal of item overlap with Intellectual efficiency (*Ie*), Social presence (*Sp*), Self-acceptance (*Sa*), and, to a much lesser extent, Achievement via independence (*Ai*), Dominance (*Do*), Capacity for status (*Cs*), and Achievement via conformance (*Ac*). The questions deal with enjoyment of social interactions, a sense of poise, self-assurance in dealing with others, and interest in cultural and intellectual activities.

High Sy (T = 60 or More)

High scorers on *Sy* have some of the same traits as persons scoring high on Capacity for status (*Cs*), such as a greater sense of maturity and a wide range of interests. They are also described as outgoing, sociable, and confident. In general, they feel comfortable in social settings and can easily mix with others. They feel comfortable around large groups of people and would dislike working alone. They have well-developed social skills and generally make a good impression. The adjectives most frequently used to describe them are outgoing, sociable, confident, ambitious, aggressive, energetic, talkative, assertive, and enterprising.

Moderate Sy (T = 50–60)

Persons in this range have an average level of extraversion and are relatively comfortable in most social situations. Although they prefer to be around others, they do not, by any means, exclusively orient their lives in this direction.

Moderately Low Sy (T = 35–50)

Such persons are able to interact with groups of people without experiencing an excessive amount of discomfort, but they prefer to be alone. They feel somewhat anxious around strangers and strongly prefer to be with persons with whom they are already acquainted. Usually, they dislike being the center of attention.

Low Sy (T = 35 or Less)

Persons who score this low have a definite sense of awkwardness in social situations and frequently have bitter complaints about their lives. They have a marked lack of confidence in their social skills and, as a result, avoid most social encounters, especially in unfamiliar settings or with those they do not know. They might act in self-defeating ways, frequently perceive themselves as underachievers, and are prone to anxiety. The adjectives most frequently used to describe them are withdrawn, shy, retiring, quiet, timid, meek, quitting, reserved, and awkward.

4. Social Presence (*Sp*)

The Social presence scale was intended to serve as a measure of a person's degree of poise, self-confidence, verve, and spontaneity in social interactions. It especially assesses the extent to which the person is self-assured and assertive. Social presence is very similar to Sociability in that an individual scoring high on *Sp* is outgoing and extraverted, and enjoys being around other people. However, a person who is sociable does not necessarily also have social presence, even though this is often the case. Social presence implies not only that the person is sociable, but also that he or she has more of a need to have impact on others and is thus likely to be more verbally aggressive, irritable, and sarcastic. A person exerting social presence might manipulate and control others, especially by working on another person's defenses and self-deceptions. There is some overlap of items with Sociability (*Sy*), Self-acceptance (*Sa*), and, to a lesser extent, Capacity for status (*Cs*) and Intellectual efficiency (*Ie*). The primary content of the questions relates to a person's poise and the degree to which he or she enjoys social interactions.

High Sp (T = 65 or More)

High scorers are often described as being unconventional, spontaneous, witty, and perceptive. They are usually concerned with their own pleasure in interpersonal relationships and will often manipulate interactions in order to feel a sense of personal power. Thus, they not only like to be with other people, but also want to be in control. Their expression of ideas and their vocabulary are excellent, as are their social skills. They are often perceived as imaginative and socially relaxed, and they generally make a good impression. Extremely high scorers might be manipulative, highly energetic, and offended if people do not pay attention to them. The adjectives most frequently used to describe them are outgoing, confident, versatile, talkative, and adventurous.

Low Sp (T = 40 or Less)

High scorers are unconventional and uninhibited; low scorers are extremely cautious and concerned with proper etiquette. They feel that others should conform to set, predefined standards, and they disapprove of nonconforming behavior. Their view of what is correct or incorrect falls within relatively narrow limits. In their relationships with others, they emphasize cooperation rather than manipulation, and they are likely to be kind, appreciative, patient, and serious. However, kindness and appreciation are expressed only when the behavior of others falls within their definition of conventional. They would most likely feel anxious if expected to alter their routine. They are moralistic regarding the behavior of others, but also can be made to feel guilty regarding their own behavior. Extremely low scorers might lack energy, avoid being the center of attention, and feel uncomfortable when required to use their influence on others. The adjectives most frequently used to describe them are shy, withdrawn, retiring, silent, quiet, timid, and inhibited.

5. Self-Acceptance (*Sa*)

The Self-acceptance scale was intended to "assess factors such as a sense of personal worth, self-acceptance, and capacity for independent thinking and action" (Gough, 1969, p. 10). Furthermore, it was hoped that *Sa* could "identify individuals who would manifest a comfortable and imperturbable sense of personal worth, and who would be seen as secure and sure of themselves whether active or inactive in social behavior" (p. 10). Even though persons scoring high on Self-acceptance would be less likely to become upset, the *Sa* scale should not be used as an index of adjustment and is not related to the absence or presence of pathology. For example, a person might be high on Self-acceptance, yet still be rebellious and impulsive, and generally indulge in antisocial behavior. In fact, persons scoring extremely high on *Sa* are quite likely to be egocentric and indifferent, sometimes even to the point of narcissism. The scale questions have some overlap with Sociability (*Sy*), Social presence (*Sp*), and, to a lesser extent, Capacity for status (*Cs*). There is some negative overlap in which answers are scored in the opposite direction from Capacity for status (*Cs*). Thus, a number of statements deal with social poise and self-confidence. Additional areas of item content relate to an accepting attitude toward social prohibitions, attention to duty, consideration of others, and human frailties.

High Sa (T = 65 or More)

Individuals scoring high on *Sa* are comfortable with themselves, self-reliant, independent, and usually polished, sophisticated, enterprising, and self-seeking in social relations. They also have a clear sense of self-definition and are characterized as being self-confident and outgoing. However, *Sa* should not necessarily be tied with Sociability; Self-acceptance can be high regardless of the quantity of interaction with others. The scale is slightly correlated with hypomania, which has often been formulated as a defense against depression. Thus, extremely high scores may suggest an inflated sense of self-acceptance with underlying, but unacknowledged, feelings of self-criticism, pessimism, and hopelessness. The adjectives most frequently used to describe high scorers are outgoing, self-confident, talkative, ambitious, and assertive.

Moderate Sa (T = 50–65)

These persons have an average or somewhat above-average level of confidence, with a generally good sense of harmony and internal balance. They are somewhat adventurous and outgoing.

Moderately Low Sa (T = 35–50)

Moderately low scorers are somewhat low in self-confidence and have some significant doubts about themselves. For the most part, they can adequately cope with their lives, but they are prone to periods of insecurity and depression. One way in which they often attempt to adapt is through conformity and conventionality, which frequently has the desired effect of making their world safer and more predictable.

Low Sa (T = 35 or Less)

Such individuals have a pronounced lack of self-confidence. They are usually described as ordinary and have "flat" or unidimensional personalities. They achieve a moderate degree of safety in their world by withdrawing, quitting, and maintaining a relatively narrow range of interests. They are likely to have a strong sense of insecurity, are afraid to take risks, and have low levels of self-confidence. Although usually submissive and conventional, they may at times impulsively act-out in a reckless manner, almost as a form of rebellion against their largely self-imposed conventionality. The adjectives most frequently used to describe them are shy, withdrawn, retiring, silent, quiet, timid, and inhibited.

6. Independence (*In*)

The Independence scale is a new CPI scale (1987 revision) comprised of 30 items and originally developed by Kurtines (1974). It measures the extent to which a person strives toward vocational and interpersonal autonomy. Conceptually, it overlaps with Achievement via independence (*Ai*) in that they both assess the value a person places on working away from the restrictions, expectations, and influence of others. It also has similarities with Self-acceptance (*Sa*) because persons high in both *In* and *Sa* are likely to be self-assured and self-reliant. Similarities can also be found with *Sp* (both witty, animated) and *Do* (both like to be in control).

High In (T = 65 or More)

Persons scoring high on *In* are self-assured and confident, and they possess social presence. Their vocabulary is likely to be wide, and they are intelligent, self-reliant, witty, animated, and, as a result, likely to make a good impression. However, they are not necessarily affiliative and friendly. They are perceived as resourceful, confident, self-sufficient, and capable. If they believe in a concept, position, or fact, they will defend it without bending to external pressure. Interpersonally, they are likely to be dominant; vocationally, they have high needs for achievement, and they are willing to work to achieve higher status. They will also tend to be morally responsible and have high levels of self-control. They are most frequently described as confident, independent, aggressive, (having) initiative, and assertive.

Moderately High In (T = 55–65)

Moderately high scorers have many of the above characteristics in that they will be confident, goal-oriented, and able to rely on their own evaluations and directions. They are assertive and usually can deal effectively with others.

Low In (T = 30–45)

Low scorers need to rely on others for decisions and directions. They are likely to avoid conflict and competition, and they experience discomfort when they have to assert themselves. Assets include an excellent ability to cooperate and blend with the requirements and needs of others.

Extremely Low In (T = 30 or Less)

If persons score in the extremely low range, it suggests they are dependent and lack self-confidence. They will probably accept domination from others, partially because they feel uncomfortable when they must face uncertainty. Often, they will experience worry and anxiety and be reluctant to express their own ideas. Assets include tolerance, adaptability, generosity, and helpfulness. Adjectives used frequently to describe them are timid, shy, cautious, meek, submissive, unassuming, nervous.

7. Empathy (*Em*)

The 38-item Empathy scale was a new addition to the 1987 version and was originally developed by Greif and Hogan (1973). The central construct it attempts to measure is the degree to which a person perceives and can feel the inner experience of others. It also measures related abilities, including social skills, confidence, social presence, leadership, and extraversion. The major underlying themes to the scale are that "empathic persons are characterized by a patient and forbearing nature, by affiliative but socially ascendant tendencies, and by liberal and humanistic political and religious attitudes" (Greif & Hogan, 1973, p. 284).

High Em (T = 65 or Above)

High scorers are intuitive, perceptive, and verbally fluent. They have a wide range of interests and are usually perceived by others as interesting. In addition, they are highly creative, spontaneous, and able to use their imagination in a number of areas. They have social presence, are animated and witty, and make a good impression. Thus, they will be interpersonally effective, independent, and flexible. They are most frequently described as sociable, outgoing, versatile, spontaneous, interests (are) wide, confident, and humorous.

Moderately High Em (T = 55–65)

Moderately high scorers have some insight into the feelings and motives of others and are friendly, adaptable, and comfortable to be around.

Moderately Low Em (T = 30–45)

Persons with moderately low scores are typically slow to understand the feelings and motives of others. They are perceived as having narrow interests and as shy, withdrawn, narrow-minded, and conventional.

Very Low Em (T = 30 or Lower)

Extremely low scorers often feel bewilderment regarding the reasons others behave as they do. These individuals can often be insensitive, inconsiderate, shy, rigid, and unfriendly. Others find it difficult to please them. They are uncomfortable with uncertainty and, as a result, might cling to a rigid set of morals and narrow range of behaviors, often becoming authoritarian and ethnocentric. Their fathers were probably distant, cold, and taciturn. The adjectives most frequently used to describe them are shy, silent, interests (are) narrow, and conservative.

8. Responsibility (*Re*)

The intent of the *Re* scale was to assess the degree to which persons are "conscientious, responsible, dependable, [and] articulate regarding rules and order, and who believe life should be governed by reason" (Gough, 1968, p. 65). Although Responsibility is somewhat related to Sociability and Self-control, it also stresses that values and controls are well-defined and significant factors in a person's life. The person who is highly responsible will sacrifice his or her own needs for the benefit of the group. Such people accept the consequences of their behavior, are dependable and trustworthy, and have a sense of obligation to the larger social structure. They are not necessarily leaders, but they have a high sense of integrity and are committed to follow through on agreements they have made with others. In general, persons who express antisocial behavior score low on *Re*, whereas average or above-average scores are obtained by occupational groups in which responsible behavior and "attention to duty" are required. The *Re* scale is scored positively for items that reflect a high degree of commitment to social, civic, or moral values.

High Re (T = 60 or More)

High scorers respond well to tasks in which they are required to be conscientious, dependable, and reasonable. They will give up their own personal satisfactions for the sake of the group and will honor any commitments they have made. Their approach to problem solving is extremely rational and clear. Usually, they have strong religious beliefs and a clear sense of ethics, and are concerned with philosophical issues. Their work is productive because their aspiration levels are high and their work style is dependable and responsible. Their behavior is courteous, polite, alert, energetic, honest, and direct. If given a choice, they will seek additional information to reduce risk and generally prefer to avoid risky behaviors themselves (Weekes, 1993). The adjectives most frequently used to describe them are conscientious, responsible, dependable, thorough, industrious, and efficient.

Moderate Re (T = 40–60)

Such persons respond well to tasks in which they are required to be conscientious, dependable, and reasonable. Generally, they are not comfortable taking responsibility for the behavior of others, but they are seen by others as reasonably conscientious and straightforward.

Low Re (T = 40 or Less)

Individuals with scores this low show a lack of discipline and are usually rebellious and impulsive. They have difficulty budgeting their finances and are seen by others as restless and careless. Their perceptions are tied to their own personal biases, and they are mainly concerned with their own needs. They often behave in exploitive and immature ways. Their histories usually reveal that they had their first sexual encounters at an early age, they were underachievers in high school, they had considerable disagreements with their parents, they engaged in borderline delinquent behavior, and, often, their fathers were alcoholics. Their external behavior is typically crude, unpredictable, rebellious, nonconforming, and self-indulgent. Internally, they feel dissatisfied, moody, cynical, and distrustful. The adjectives most frequently used to describe them are rebellious, reckless, and pleasure-seeking.

9. Socialization (*So*)

The Socialization scale was originally called the "delinquency scale," and, as the name suggests, its intent was to assess the likelihood of antisocial behavior. The scoring was later reversed, the name was changed, and the scale gradually became a measure of an individual's social maturity, integrity, and rectitude. Probably Gough's favorite scale, it is based on his theory that antisocial behavior is the result of a role that certain individuals assume. There has been an extensive accumulation of literature on this scale, due at least in part to Gough's personal interest in it. The research indicates that the *So* scale has excellent concurrent, predictive, and cross-cultural validity, and is probably the most validated and most powerful scale on the CPI.

The Socialization scale was designed to measure the degree to which social norms are accepted and adhered to. An individual can score on a continuum from extremely well socialized to highly antisocial. The scale also estimates the probability that a person will engage in behavior considered incorrect within his or her culture. For example, the *So* scale has been able, with relative accuracy, to differentiate cheaters from noncheaters in a college population (Kipnis, 1968), and low *So* scores were related to a diagnosis of personality disorder (Standage, 1986, 1990). In addition, low scores were able to predict criminals who would reoffend (DeFrancesco & Taylor, 1993) and to differentiate between delinquents and nondelinquents (Gough & Bradley, 1992). Schizophrenics making violent suicide attempts were found to have particularly low scores on *So* (Seeman, Yesarage, & Widrow, 1985). The *So* scale has also differentiated high school dropouts from graduates (Gough, 1966; Hase & Goldberg, 1967). In a further study, Wernick (1955) demonstrated that 50% of the low scorers who were hired as temporary Christmas help stole from the store, and none proved to be a satisfactory worker. Several researchers have found a negative correlation between *So* scores and a past lack of family cohesiveness, a poor quality of parental care (Glueck & Glueck, 1950; Rosenquist & Megargee, 1969; Standage, 1986, 1990), and physical abuse (Barnett & Hamberger, 1992). In addition, low scorers reported having a dysphoric mood (Standage, 1990). Thus, many items included in the scale are designed to determine whether the examinees experienced warmth and satisfaction within their family relationships. Some of the items also reflect the presence or absence of pessimism regarding one's life and environment. The content of several other questions centers on whether examinees can properly evaluate the effects of their behavior as well as the extent to which they can be empathetic and sensitive to the feelings of others.

High So (T = 65 or More)

Persons scoring high on *So* are organized, adaptable, and efficient. They are highly dependable, but maintain this level of dependability by being cautious, self-controlled, and inhibited. In general, they are willing to trust others and express a fairly high level of optimism. They are often described as kind, honest, and practical, and they typically come from a stable, cohesive family environment where warmth and concern were freely expressed. Often, they were overprotected, and their current behavior is usually relatively conventional. Their external behavior is typically gentle, considerate, honest, tactful, well-organized, capable, and productive. Their values are conservative and, as a result, they behave in an ethically consistent manner. Internally, they feel optimistic, stable, and well controlled. They are most frequently described as reliable, organized, dependable, stable, and cooperative.

Moderate So (T = 50–65)

Individuals who score in this range are able to trust others and are generally accepting of the mores and rules established by society. They also tend to be inhibited and conventional, sometimes to the point of being overadapted, but not as much as those with higher *So* scores.

Moderately Low So (T = 30–45)

Individuals who score in the lower ranges of *So* are somewhat impulsive and unreliable, and often have a difficult time trusting others. They are not usually followers; rather, they frequently question the rules given to them and, in general, do not have a high degree of respect for society's prescribed forms of behavior. They will often express a moderate level of rebelliousness.

Low So (T = 30 or Less)

Such persons have a far greater likelihood of antisocial behavior and are usually unreliable, unconventional, rude, defensive, and impulsive. They reject past family ties, primarily because their past family life was filled with chaos and was unsatisfying. They were unhappy at home, experienced considerable friction with their parents, and were underachievers and sexually precocious. They experience a deep sense of alienation and have an extremely difficult time trusting people. They are likely to report having dysphoric moods. Scores below 25 are associated with personality disorders, especially borderlines and antisocial personality. Others see them as headstrong, unpredictable, deceitful, rebellious, and pleasure-seeking. Internally, they feel cynical and moody, and they often perceive that their lives are meaningless. The adjectives most frequently used to describe them are reckless, impulsive, rebellious, unconventional, bitter, restless, and suspicious.

10. Self-Control (*Sc*)

The original intent of the *Sc* scale was to measure the degree to which a person can self-direct his or her own behavior. More specifically, high scores suggest that a person can delay his or her behavior and redirect it in a clear, goal-oriented manner. Thus, a certain degree of similarity exists between Self-control and both Responsibility and Socialization. Gough (in Megargee, 1972) clarifies these concepts by stating that Responsibility reflects the "degree to which controls are understood," Socialization measures the "extent to which they influence a person's behavior," and Self-control assesses the "degree to which the individual approves of and espouses such regulatory dispositions" (pp. 65–66). Persons scoring high on *Sc* are self-directed and inhibited, and they withhold their expressions of emotions and behavior. Some types of persons who score extremely high on *Sc* are often overcontrolled to the extent that, for short periods of time, they lose control and become explosive (Megargee, 1966d; Megargee, Cook, & Mendelsohn, 1967). Individuals with low scores are impulsive and pleasure-seeking, have difficulty delaying their impulses, and are not good at evaluating the consequences of their behavior. Thus, both extremely high and extremely low scorers are similar in that they have significant problems dealing with the management of impulses; however, they use opposite strategies to cope with these impulses.

The primary overlap of items for *Sc* is with *Gi*. Several items are also scored in a direction opposite from *Sp* and *Sa*. Some of the most important items emphasize that thought and rationality are the primary determinants of behavior. Furthermore, high scorers usually endorse items that indicate they are taking precautions to avoid irrational behavior and are generally socially inhibited.

High Sc (T = 60 or More)

Persons who score high on *Sc* are considerate, self-denying, and dependable. They have a high need for precision and make every attempt to be reasonable. Other people perceive them as considerate, wholesome, and dependable, but also as stubborn, rigid, and overconforming. They avoid situations in which they might be tempted to act impulsively, are generally inhibited and lacking in spontaneity, and move slowly. Externally, their behavior is well organized, patient, capable, and fastidious. They are conservative and moralistic, and behave in an ethical, conscientious, and consistent manner. Internally, they usually feel optimistic but serious. The adjectives most frequently used to describe them are moderate, calm, quiet, conservative, conventional, and conscientious.

Moderate Sc (T = 45–60)

Such persons are fairly conventional and somewhat inhibited. They carefully consider the consequences of their behavior before acting. Others usually see them as reasonable and dependable, although somewhat lacking in spontaneity.

Moderately Low Sc (T = 30–45)

Persons scoring in this range sometimes act in a spontaneous, impulsive manner but can usually delay their behavior. Thus, their level of impulsiveness is insufficient to impair their interpersonal and work relationships.

Low Sc (T = 30 or Less)

Low scorers have a marked difficulty delaying their behavior, are hasty in making decisions, and are usually individualistic and self-seeking. Their impulsiveness may sometimes cause tension in group activities, and they often regret having acted in inappropriate ways. At times, they can seem extremely unrealistic and headstrong. They are prone to develop relationships quickly, which often readily become chaotic and confused. The background of these individuals usually reveals that they were sexually precocious and experienced considerable conflict with their parents. Academically, they were unhappy underachievers. Their external behavior is restless, excited, outgoing, rebellious, and unpredictable. They frequently perceive situations in sexual terms. They are most often described as impulsive, mischievous, restless, humorous, pleasure-seeking, and adventurous.

11. Good Impression (*Gi*)

Although *Gi* is mainly a validity scale designed to detect persons who are faking good, it also reflects the degree to which a person with a valid profile is concerned with creating a favorable impression on others. There is a fairly high degree of item overlap with Self-control (*Sc*), which suggests that an important component of creating a favorable impression is a good ability to delay impulses. Also, a number of items make fairly obvious statements concerning the person's level of functioning and amount of antisocial behavior; the extent to which he or she is goal-oriented; and whether he or she has complaints regarding personal failings. High scorers are prone to exaggerate their positive points and minimize their negative qualities. Furthermore, they state that they have a high level of confidence and self-assurance, and they minimize their anxieties or insecurities. They emphasize that they can adapt well to stress and that they have a stable personality. Finally, several items are related to the extent to which individuals behave in a socially approved manner and experience harmonious relationships with others.

The *Gi* scale has generally been successful in detecting invalid profiles. For example, Dicken (1960), by using a cutoff score of $T = 60$, was able to detect, in 79% of the cases, the profiles of persons attempting to make a favorable impression. With somewhat different criteria, only 3% of a total sample of profiles of mixed normal and fake good were incorrectly classified. In the same study, Dicken also demonstrated that even though persons were, in some of the cases, attempting to fake good on other scales, *Gi* still showed the greatest increase. This has practical importance because, even though a person might be attempting, for example, to exaggerate his or her level of responsibility, *Gi* would still be expected to increase. Thus, the use of *Gi* as a validity scale is not restricted to persons attempting to create a favorable impression in a global manner; it can be used to detect persons attempting to fake good along other specific dimensions as well. More precise and accurate classifications can be derived by using the equations devised by Lanning (1989). (See the earlier subsection, "Determining the Profile Validity.")

High Gi (T = 60 or More)

An examinee's personal history provides the best guide for determining whether a score in this range reflects a fake good profile or is more likely to indicate a person with an excellent level of adjustment. For example, an alcoholic with a high *Gi* is probably either consciously attempting to create a favorable impression or demonstrating the use of denial, which is often associated with that disorder. A further possibility for an extremely high *Gi* is that the person may be unaware of the impression he or she leaves with others and has an inflated self-image based on rigidly selective perceptions. The self-image of such persons would then likely be maintained by ignoring the feedback they receive from others and manipulating others to agree with the perceptions they have of themselves. They may be people-pleasers who will do anything to fit in and, as a result, will probably be liked but not respected by others. Gough (1987) recommends that the ideal cutoff score for detecting a fake good profile is $T = 69$ for males and $T = 71$ for females.

If the profile is only moderately high and has been determined to be valid, then the person is likely to be conventional, adaptable, self-denying, and capable of a high degree of empathy. These people are often oversensitive to the criticisms of others, and usually respond by attempting to change and adapt in order to gain approval. They feel it is important to please others and to be seen in a favorable light. Others usually see them as kind, warm, considerate, and patient. They will probably attempt to overcontrol their needs and be moralistic, but will try and adapt by becoming considerate and tactful. The adjectives most frequently used to describe them are calm, conventional, conservative, and moderate.

Moderate Gi (T = 45–60)

Persons with a moderate score on *Gi* are usually unselfish and concerned with making a favorable impression. They are able to take feedback from others and use it in a constructive way. Others perceive them as peaceable, trusting, understanding, and highly concerned with living up to their social responsibilities.

Moderately Low Gi (T = 30–45)

Moderately low scorers are only minimally concerned with the impression they make on others—to the extent that they are sometimes seen as insensitive. Feeling that they alone are the judges of their behavior, they rarely listen to the evaluations of others. They are often described as independent, witty, and occasionally temperamental and sarcastic.

Low Gi (T = 30 or Less)

Persons scoring in this range are typically arrogant, and they actively reject the judgments of others. They are even prone to exaggerate their negative behavior in a rebellious way, and then expect this behavior to be tolerated and even accepted. Others describe them as temperamental, cynical, sarcastic, and overly frank to the point of being disagreeable. This pattern usually has the effect of disrupting their interpersonal relationships. Their external behavior will typically be rebellious, undiplomatic, critical, nonconforming, unpredictable, and self-indulgent. They might come from conflict-ridden families in which the mother was nervous and dissatisfied. They are often perceived as insensitive and lacking the qualities of nurturance. Internally, they may often feel cynical, distrustful, and dissatisfied. Adjectives frequently used to describe them are temperamental, restless, and rebellious. Scores of *T* = 35 or less suggest a fake bad profile.

12. Communality (*Cm*)

The *Cm* scale is a validity scale originally designed to detect random answering. The questions are keyed in such a way that normal populations answer 95% of the questions in the keyed direction. Although the scale was not designed to measure personality variables, some personality indicators can tentatively be derived. This outcome is based mainly on the observation that the content of the items reflects the following areas: good socialization, conformity, optimism, denial of neurotic characteristics, and conventionality of behavior and attitudes. Gough points out that this is comparable to Popular responses on the Rorschach in that it reflects the degree to which examinees see their surroundings in ways that are similar to others' perceptions.

High Cm (T = 60 or More)

High scores suggest that the examinee adheres to highly conventional attitudes and is overly socialized, tending to see his or her world in a stereotyped manner. These individuals do not see themselves as particularly unique or special, and they are conscientious and serious. They are most frequently described as clear-thinking, planful, practical, and tactful.

Low Cm (T = 30 or Less)

A low score sometimes suggests that persons have chaotic, conflict-ridden family backgrounds. Their attitudes toward the world would typically be unusual and idiosyncratic. They might also be generally upset, poorly motivated, self-defeating, and frail, and they lack a sense of meaning in life. The adjectives most frequently used to describe them are reckless, distractible, unconventional, moody, and confused.

However, scores in this range primarily increase the likelihood that the test is of questionable validity, and scores below 20 almost always confirm that the profile is invalid. The ideal score for detecting a fake bad profile is $T = 29$ for males and $T = 24$ for females (see the earlier subsection on "Determining the Profile Validity").

13. Sense of Well-Being (*Wb*)

The scale for Well-being was originally developed to help recognize profiles in which the person was faking bad. Thus, it was initially referred to as the Dissimulation (*Ds*) scale. Fake bad profiles can usually be detected because they are significantly lower than even valid profiles for psychiatric patients. In contrast, persons who score high do not have a need to emphasize psychological or physical complaints. In fact, high scorers play down their worries and emphasize instead that they are enterprising and energetic, and they experience a sense of security. They are also likely to have effective interpersonal relations, a high level of mental health, and a sense of psychological and physical well-being. Low scorers usually have diminished health and experience difficulty meeting the daily demands of their environment. In general, the *Wb* scale has come to represent a rough estimate of a person's level of adjustment. However, it is more of a "state" scale than the others and is, therefore, somewhat changeable, depending on an individual's mood fluctuations.

The *Wb* scale has a low degree of item overlap with other scales because most of the questions were designed for exclusive use with this scale. The item content usually reflects a denial of various physical and psychological complaints. The second major content area reflects the extent to which a person is self-sufficient and independent.

High Wb (T = 55 or More)

Generally, high scorers on *Wb* have relaxed and satisfying interpersonal relationships, are able to trust others, and come from family backgrounds that were stable and supportive. They are dependable and responsible, and they value intellectual interests.

Usually, they are happily married and are stable, optimistic, and self-confident. The adjectives most frequently used to describe them are clear-thinking and capable.

Moderately Low Wb (T = 35–50)

Although persons scoring in this range generally feel that life is not going well, they continue to meet this perceived adversity with a sense of apathy and listlessness. They are often passive, awkward, and defensive.

Low Wb (T = 35 or Less)

With a further decrease in *Wb,* there is a corresponding exaggeration of the trends just discussed. These individuals are usually highly alienated and dissatisfied, and they experience a significant level of maladjustment. Characteristically, they are extremely distrustful in interpersonal relationships and have a tendency to dwell on real or imagined wrongs. Such people are seen by others as pessimistic, tense, restless, and moody. They feel their life lacks a sense of meaning and might cope by becoming absorbed in fantasy and daydreams. Individuals who use the test situation as a forum for complaining and for attempting to exaggerate their difficulties will often score in this range. The adjectives most frequently used to describe these persons are confused, bitter, and nagging.

The interpretation of extremely low *Wb* scores requires two considerations. First, the scale lowering may in part reflect a downward but temporary mood shift of a person who is only somewhat maladjusted—or even normal—most of the time. More important, an extremely low score suggests an invalid profile in which the examinee is faking bad (see the earlier subsection on "Determining the Profile Validity").

14. Tolerance (*To*)

The tolerance scale was designed to measure the degree to which persons are socially intolerant versus the extent to which they are accepting, permissive, and nonjudgmental in their social beliefs and attitudes. The content of most of the items focuses on openness and flexibility versus rigidity and dogmatism. Other content areas relate to an interest in intellectual and aesthetic activities, a level of trust, and a lack of hostility or resentment toward others. A person scoring high on Tolerance is also indicating that he or she is not alienated, does not feel isolated, rarely feels anxious, and is relatively poised and self-assured. There is a large variety of questions on this scale, but there is also a general lack of adequate validity studies. In fact, Tolerance is one of the poorer scales on the CPI, and its validity has even been questioned. Thus, interpretations based on this scale should be made cautiously and tentatively.

High To (T = 60 or More)

High scorers are likely to be intelligent, to have a wide range of interests, and to be socially tolerant. They are also able to trust others, and they may have a high degree of confidence and social poise. Furthermore, they are nonjudgmental, can easily accept divergent beliefs and values, and are forgiving, generous, and pleasant. They will typically have a wide vocabulary and varied interests. They are concerned with philosophical issues and can effectively understand and explain the core of many problems. They are likable and make a good impression because they are tolerant, permissive, and benevolent. Extremely high scorers might be overly trusting to the extent that they are naive and underestimate potential difficulties. They might also be so worried about potential confrontations that they have become overly adaptable and will fill any role in order to keep a situation peaceful. The adjectives most frequently used to describe them are fair-minded, insightful, clear-thinking, and interests (are) wide.

Moderate To (T = 45–60)

Moderate scorers are likewise somewhat nonjudgmental and open to the beliefs of others. They usually have a wide range of interests and are informal and independent.

Low To (T = 40 or Less)

Persons scoring in this range are likely to be judgmental and nonaccepting of the beliefs and values of others. This judgmental attitude tends to generalize into other areas of their lives so that, overall, they seem cold, smug, and stern. They are authoritarian and center their lives around a fixed and dogmatic set of beliefs. Furthermore, they are mannerly, fearful, arrogant, and sarcastic. If criticized, they will usually become extremely defensive, bitter, and rejecting. They are more likely to judge than to understand others. It is important for these individuals to exert power in relationships, and they may do so by becoming critical and outspoken, and by holding unrealistic expectations. Internally, they often feel moody, distrustful, cynical, and dissatisfied. The adjectives most frequently used to describe them are prejudiced, interests (are) narrow, and suspicious.

15. Achievement via Conformance (*Ac*)

The *Ac* scale involves not only an orientation toward achievement, but also a need for structure and organization as a means of channeling that achievement. This scale specifically relates to settings in which conformity is an asset, and it reflects the degree to which persons prefer to have their criteria of performance clearly specified by some outside source. The content of the items relates to how effectively examinees can perform within an academic setting and how high their relative levels of energy and efficiency are. High scorers also see themselves as being productive workers. Additional content areas relate to the extent to which the examinees are even-tempered, accept the rules of socially approved standards of behavior, and dislike frivolous, unconventional behavior.

The *Ac* scale has been one of the more thoroughly researched scales on the CPI, primarily because of its practical relevance for academic personnel. In a review of the literature, Megargee (1972) reports that it has good criterion validity and has been found to correlate significantly (.36 to .44) with grade point average (GPA) and general achievement in high school settings. The correlations are highest for high school performance and somewhat lower for college settings.

High Ac (T = 60 or More)

Persons scoring above 60 are typically persistent and industrious, especially when conforming to some external standard. They strongly prefer specificity and structure, and may even have a difficult time when structure is lacking, especially if a high *Ac* is accompanied by a low *Ai*. Such persons are usually responsible, capable, and ambitious, but they express these behaviors in a conservative, reserved, and obliging manner. Furthermore, they place a high degree of value on intellectual effort. They are most comfortable when working in highly organized settings, where they excel when given specific, well-defined criteria for performance. The adjectives most frequently used to describe them are responsible, organized, ambitious, persevering, efficient, and conscientious.

Moderately High Ac (T = 50–60)

Moderate scorers may question the need for structure and organization. Although they may prefer not to have structure, they can adequately function in a structured situation when required to do so. They are usually described as stable, optimistic, dependable, and responsible.

Low Ac (T = 35 or Less)

Persons in this range are rejecting of authority and regulations. Their rebellion may result in achievements far below their potential, because their energy is directed more toward rejecting external organization and rules than toward working within the limits imposed on them. Such persons are often characterized as intellectual rebels, especially if their Achievement via independence (*Ai*) scale is relatively high. When external demands for performance are placed on them, they may become disorganized and nonproductive. They will have difficulty committing themselves to organizations or people. The adjectives most frequently used to describe them are lazy, impulsive, reckless, rebellious, distractible, and mischievous.

16. Achievement via Independence (*Ai*)

Whereas *Ac* can be used to predict achievement in high school, *Ai* was designed to predict achievement in a college environment. Persons who are high in *Ai* succeed in settings that require creativity, self-actualization, and independence of thought. Gough (1968) has clarified this distinction by describing Achievement via conformance (*Ac*) as "form enhancing" whereas *Ai* is "form creating." *Ai* correlates significantly with college students' GPA (Gough & Lanning, 1986), yet there is only a low correlation with intelligence. Thus, students who have elevated *Ai* scales and who also achieve a high GPA do so mainly on the basis of a high need for achievement and only secondarily on the basis of intelligence. They are able to tolerate a high level of ambiguity and usually reject authoritarian or overly stringent regulations. In some cases, high *Ai* scores can predict achievement in situations in which originality and independence are rewarded. Persons with high scores are unwilling to accept conventional advice unquestioningly; they prefer to think for themselves. Also, some questions relate to the degree to which individuals appreciate activities involving the intellect. Other content areas attempt to assess their degree of adjustment and the extent to which they are concerned with the deeper aspects of interpersonal relationships.

High Ai (T = 60 or More)

Such persons prefer to work without rules and structures, and they usually feel restricted within a highly organized environment. They value creativity and originality, and they are self-motivated and rejecting of conventional standards of productivity. Their ability to produce and function is significantly impaired if a great deal of structure is required. They produce best and are most efficient when left to regulate their own behavior. Externally, they are verbally fluent, self-reliant, and capable of making a good impression. They have a wide range of interests, aspire to high goals, and are concerned with philosophical interests. The adjectives most frequently used to describe them are intelligent, clear-thinking, logical, foresighted, insightful, and interests (are) wide.

Moderate Ai (T = 40–50)

Persons scoring in this range are able to achieve based on their own self-direction but feel somewhat insecure when doing things completely on their own. Thus, they can work either with or without structure, but prefer a moderate degree of external organization. At times, they can be creative, but when they come to conclusions on their own, they still need external verification in order to feel comfortable.

Low Ai (T = 35 or Less)

Low scorers have difficulty trusting their own abilities, and this characteristic becomes more exaggerated as the scale score becomes lower. They require external definition in order to establish their self-concept, and they need others to specify their proper course of action. Because of their uncertainty and dependence on outside structure, these individuals are moderately anxious, depressed, and self-doubting. They are not intellectually inclined and tend to feel out of place in the world of abstract thinking. The adjectives most frequently used to describe them are confused and interests (are) narrow.

17. Intellectual Efficiency (*Ie*)

The *Ie* scale was originally called a "nonintellectual intelligence test" and was designed to measure personality traits that coincided with a high level of intellectual ability. High scorers on *Ie* tend to be competent and clear-thinking, and they make efficient use of the potential they possess. Thus, it is less an intelligence test than it is a measure of the degree to which persons make efficient use of their intelligence. There is a moderate amount of item overlap with Sociability (*Sy*), Achievement via independence (*Ai*), and Social presence (*Sp*). One important content area of the items relates to the degree to which a person enjoys and is interested in wide-ranging intellectual activities. Also, a number of questions relate to self-confidence and assurance. Other questions relate to good physiological functioning, positive relationships with others, and an absence of irritability and suspiciousness.

A number of representative and noteworthy validity studies have been performed on *Ie*. It is positively correlated with measures of intelligence (Gough, 1969), and members of an organization for persons with very high IQs (MENSA) scored significantly higher on Ie than the national norms (Southern & Plant, 1968). The scale has also been able to successfully identify future high school dropouts from students who later graduated (Gough, 1966). The autobiographies of high scorers reveal that they see themselves as well organized, efficient, and committed to pursuing intellectual and cultural activities (Hill, 1967).

High Ie (T = 60 or More)

Persons scoring high on *Ie* have a wide range of interests and an excellent ability to use their resources. They are capable and confident, have good planning abilities, and are independent, informal, and clear-thinking. Their vocabulary is wide, they are perceptive and verbally fluent, and they effectively understand subtle nuances of behavior. They value intellectual activities and have high aspirations. The adjectives most frequently used to describe them are intelligent, clear-thinking, alert, interests (are) wide, and (having) initiative.

Moderate Ie (T = 40–60)

Moderate scorers may still be highly competent, but they are likely to have some self-doubts regarding their intellectual capabilities.

Low Ie (T = 40 or Less)

Persons in this range may be insecure about their intellectual abilities, and they are likely to experience enough self-doubt to create a mild degree of depression and anxiety. They typically appear awkward, shallow, and suggestible. They might give up easily and feel uncomfortable with uncertainties. As an alternative interpretation, low scorers may merely be uninterested in intellectual activities, which is likely to be reflected in their choice of occupation. The latter interpretation would imply merely a lack of interest rather than self-doubt and insecurity. The adjectives most frequently used to describe individuals scoring low on *Ie* are confused, nervous, and interests (are) narrow.

18. Psychological Mindedness (*Py*)

The original intent of the *Py* scale was to identify persons who possess such insight into the behavior of others that they can accurately perceive others' inner needs and motivations. This scale focuses on an ability to figure other people out, and does not necessarily indicate people who are empathic and nurturing. To assess the degree of empathy of individuals, it would be necessary to consult additional scales, such as Empathy (*Em*), Sociability (*Sy*), and Well-being (*Wb*). However, as further research was done on *Py,* it became clear that it was more an indicator of persons interested in pursuing psychology from an academic perspective. In fact, Megargee (1972) concludes his literature review by stating that the *Py* scale has limited usefulness as an indicator of a person's ability to accurately perceive the inner needs and motivations of others. The content of the items relates to one's ability to concentrate, one's effectiveness in dealing with ambiguity, and one's degree of enjoyment in his or her occupation. Other content areas deal with an ability to stick with long-term goals and an acceptance of unconventional opinions.

High Py (T = 65 or More)

High scorers are interested in academic pursuits, especially in the area of research. They can be highly original and creative in their approaches to abstract problems. They place a high level of importance on obtaining recognition for their efforts, and they demonstrate perseverance, the ability to concentrate for long periods of time, and a high degree of satisfaction from their chosen profession. Other people often see them as independent, individualistic, preoccupied, and reserved. They are excellent in dealing with abstract situations but generally avoid concrete problem-solving situations. Extremely high scorers may be seen as distant, aloof, and detached. The most frequent adjectives used to describe them are logical, thorough, clear-thinking, foresighted, and interests (are) wide.

Low Py (T = 35 or Less)

Persons who score low on *Py* are generally not inclined toward research or scholarly activities. However, they are likely to be sociable, talkative, unassuming, and conventional. They usually accept the behavior and motivation of others at face value and are more comfortable with concrete situations. The adjectives most frequently used to describe them are simple and interests (are) narrow.

19. Flexibility (*Fx*)

The *Fx* scale was designed to assess the degree to which an individual is flexible, adaptable, and changeable in his or her thinking, behavior, and temperament. It was originally based on questions relating to rigidity, but as the scale construction evolved, the scoring was reversed and the name was changed from the Rigidity scale to the Flexibility scale. Other content areas relate to an ability to tolerate ambiguity, uncertainty, and impulsiveness, and a nonjudgmental, tolerant attitude toward moral and ethical formulas of right and wrong.

The validity studies in part agree with the intent of the scale in that they support the hypothesis that low-scoring individuals are somewhat rigid. However, there is little evidence to indicate that extremely high scores reflect a high degree of flexibility (Megargee, 1972). Gough (1975) suggests that scores in the higher ranges are curvilinear in that a moderately high score suggests that the person is relatively flexible, but with increasing elevation, a person becomes progressively more unstable and unpredictable. Megargee (1972) states that, given the weak evidence for the validity of this scale, especially for high *Fx,* it is one of the least valid scales on the CPI. Thus, any interpretations derived from it should be made with caution.

High Fx (T = 65 or More)

Persons having extremely high scores may feel rootless and are often emotionally unstable. Everything in their lives is open to question, including their sense of values and moral beliefs. Thus, it is difficult for them to internalize clear-cut standards. They can easily approach situations from a number of varying perspectives. This allows them to consider many alternatives but may create a disadvantage in that they have difficulty developing a clearly defined direction. Extremely high scorers might be volatile, distractible, restless, and poorly organized. The adjectives most frequently used to describe high scorers are logical, thorough, clear-thinking, foresighted, and interests (are) wide.

Moderate Fx (T = 50–65)

Moderate scorers are open to considering and experiencing alternative perspectives. They are nonjudgmental, intellectually flexible, original, and able to develop innovative ideas. They might also be independent, self-confident, and optimistic, and they value intellectual activities.

Moderately Low Fx (T = 35–50)

Persons scoring in this range prefer structure and like to have things clearly defined and specified. Although they can handle a certain degree of uncertainty, it usually creates discomfort. They are usually cautious and practical, and can be described as relatively rigid.

Low Fx (T = 35 or Less)

Low scorers generally dislike new ideas and experiences, and are continually seeking security. They have a strong need to control their thoughts and generally have a difficult time changing their decisions. They are usually rigid, stubborn, and defensive. Often, they have strong religious beliefs and are moralistic and conservative. Others perceive them as conscientious, serious, literal-minded, and overcontrolled. The adjectives most frequently used to describe them are organized, efficient, rigid, conservative, interests (are) narrow, conventional, and prejudiced.

20. Femininity/Masculinity (F/M)

The F/M scale was developed to assess the degree to which examinees were psychologically feminine or masculine, regardless of their actual sex. Its original intent was to detect significant conflicts over sexual identity, but this aspect of the scale has become progressively less emphasized. The scale is currently used to assess the extent to which individuals endorse beliefs, values, and occupations that are traditionally held either by males or by females. The intent of some items is fairly obvious, whereas the intent of other items is more subtle. Many items relate to traditional masculine or feminine roles. Additional content areas refer to a person's degree of restraint and impulsiveness, as well as the extent to which one is emotional during interpersonal relationships. McCrae et al. (1993) found that this was the only scale to correlate strongly (.45) with the core personality factor of Agreeableness. The items also reflect the degree to which a person is interested in politics, current affairs, and achievement. This scale has been well researched, and studies indicate it has a fairly high level of validity.

High F/M (T = 70 or More)

For males, scores within this range suggest the possibility of difficulties related to sexual identity. These males might also be highly introspective and have philosophical and aesthetic interests. Their interests might be wide ranging and their thought patterns unconventional. The adjectives most frequently used to describe them are nervous, worrying, weak, self-pitying, reflective, and sensitive.

Females with extremely high scores might be highly affiliative, dependent, and submissive, and they require continual reassurance. They might also be tolerant, permissive, giving, and oversensitive. Both male and female high scorers might use bodily symptoms to express anxiety and tension. The adjectives most frequently used to describe high-scoring females are warm, sympathetic, sentimental, and dependent.

Moderately High F/M (T = 60–70 or More)

Both males and females scoring within this range have significant needs for affiliation and dependency. They usually have a difficult time dealing with a high degree of autonomy, and they feel uncomfortable when independent action is required of them. They are highly sensitive and quite concerned with not hurting others.

Moderate F/M (T = 40–50)

Persons scoring within this range can deal effectively with autonomy and have an average need for dependency and affiliation. They are generally practical and self-sufficient but not to an exaggerated extent.

Moderately Low F/M (T = 40 or Less)

These persons are typically task-oriented, practical, and emotionally self-sufficient, with few dependency needs. They are often perceived as masculine, robust, tough, and even coarse.

Low-scoring males will generally fit the masculine stereotype in that they are described as masculine, emotionally independent, tough-minded, self-sufficient, and self-centered. They often have a clear, stable, internally consistent personality and adhere to conservative values. The adjectives most frequently used to describe low-scoring males are confident, independent, aggressive, and ambitious.

Females who score low will likewise be self-reliant, confident, independent, and deliberate. In addition, they might also be critical, distrustful, cynical, and outspoken. They tend to be motivated by power and have high aspirations for themselves. The adjectives most frequently used to describe moderately low-scoring females are strong, tough, and independent.

Low F/M (T = 30 or Less)

An F/M score this low suggests an exaggeration of the above trends and, in females, the likelihood of difficulties related to sexual identity.

CONFIGURAL INTERPRETATION

The following material on configural interpretation summarizes most of the empirical research on different code types. Regression equations have been included. (A summary of the equation appears at the end of the section, in Table 8–2.) The material is organized according to different topics (leadership, achievement, and so on). In contrast, McAllister (1988) has provided a listing of 132 code types arranged according to different patterns of low and high scale scores. Readers wanting to interpret scale scores can refer to McAllister (1988) or, alternatively, can use the topic listings below. They might also wish to make rational interpretations of patterns of scale scores by using the following sequence:

1. Note the high (generally above 60) and low (generally below 40) scale scores, and read the individual descriptions that correspond with these scores.

2. Write down key phrases that correspond with these single scales. The descriptions can be strengthened, weakened, or altered, according to their relative elevations or lowerings and their relationships with other scales.

3. Combine the descriptions to create a more integrated description of the person.

Intellectual Level

Megargee (1972) has reported that *To, Ac, Ai, Ie, Py,* and *Fx* are all related to an individual's intellectual level. Elevations ($T = 55$ or more) on all or most of these scales strongly indicate that the person has a high interest in intellectual activities and good overall intelligence. Consistently low scores on all or most of these scales reflect limited intellectual ability and give a strong indication that the person has a narrow range of interests. A narrowing of interests may, in part, be a response to an emotionally upsetting event either in the recent past or at a significant time during the person's earlier development.

The particular patterns of high and low scales can provide information on the specific expression of intelligence. For example, it might be noted whether individuals would be more likely to excel in structured (high *Ac*) or nonstructured (high *Ai*) environments (see the next subsection, "Achievement"). Similarly, an interpreter can note how tolerant, flexible, or efficient individuals might be.

Support for the CPI in measuring aspects of "social intelligence" lies in comparisons made with the Picture Arrangement and Comprehension subtests on the WAIS-R. Specifically, Comprehension has been found to be correlated with *Cs, Fx,* and *Cm,* and Picture Arrangement was similarly correlated with *Cs, Fx,* and *Fm* (Sipps, Berry, & Lynch, 1987). Sternberg et al. (1995) similarly found that CPI scores, in combination with measures of practical problem-solving abilities, could be used to increase predictions of work performance.

Achievement

Predicting and Assessing High School Achievement

The CPI is generally effective for detecting bright high school achievers. They typically have elevated scores on *Ie* and *Ai,* whereas underachievers are generally low on these scales. Bright achievers also have relatively high scores on *Re, So, To, Ac,* and *Py.* Persons who are high achievers but have average IQs have relatively high scores ($T = 55$ or more) on *Re* and *So* and, to a lesser extent, on *Wb, Ac,* and *Ie.*

A number of equations have been developed for use in predicting achievement of high school students (see Megargee, 1972). These equations are comprised of the weighted combinations of scales; when computed, they provide the best possible prediction of specific abilities. For predicting the achievement of both males and females with combined low, medium, and high IQs, the following equation is recommended:

1. Achievement (high school) $= 20.116 + .317\ Re + .192\ So - .309\ Gi + .227\ Ac + .280\ Ai + .244\ Ie.$

This equation correlates from .53 to .56 with overall high school GPA (Gough, 1964). If a student's IQ scores are available, the following equation is recommended:

2. Achievement (high school—using IQ) = .786 + .195 *Re* + .244 *So* − .130 *Gi* + .19 *Ac* + .179 *Ai* + .279 IQ.

Because *Ie* is a relatively inefficient measure of IQ, it has been excluded from this equation. Instead, the exact IQ is derived from formal intelligence test results. This equation raises the correlation with overall GPA to .68, which is significantly better than the typical .60 correlation found when using only IQ scores.

To evaluate whether students will drop out of high school or will graduate and continue on to college, social factors as measured by the CPI are at least as important as a student's intellectual ability. The primary scales used to predict high school graduation are *Re, Ac,* and, to a lesser extent, *Wb, To,* and *Ie,* all of which are usually significantly higher for students who graduate from high school than for students who are high school dropouts (Gough, 1964). High school students who later go on to college score significantly higher on *Re, Ac,* and *Ie* (Gough, 1968). The following formula correlates at a level of .52 with later college attendance for high school students (Gough, 1968):

3. College attendance = 17.822 + .333 *Do* + .539 *Cs* − .189 *Gi* + .740 *Ac.*

Predicting and Assessing College Achievement

Several studies have been conducted on the relative importance of single scale scores and combinations of scale scores in assessing college achievement. Significant correlations have been found among *Re, So, Ai,* and overall GPA (Hase & Goldberg, 1967). Further studies (Flaherty & Reutzel, 1965; Griffin & Flaherty, 1964) likewise stress the importance of *Re, So,* and *Ai* but also include *Ie* and *Cs.* In female samples, *Do* was significantly correlated with GPA as well (Flaherty & Reutzel, 1965). These scales are somewhat similar to those used to predict achievement in high school students, except that *Ai* becomes more significant for college populations and *Ac* decreases in relative importance. Also, the likelihood of later upward social mobility is correlated with *Cs* and college GPA.

Although positive correlations were found among the above single scales, the magnitude of these correlations was not extremely high: the highest correlation reached only .36 for males on *Ai.* Most other significant correlations ranged between .20 and .26. However, weighted combinations of scores produced higher correlations ranging from .35 to .54, depending on the type of population being assessed. Gough (1964) has found a .41 correlation between the following formula and grades for both males and females in introduction to psychology classes:

4. Achievement (Introduction to Psychology) = 35.958 − .294 *Sy* − .180 *Sp* + .185 *Re* − .189 *Sc* − .152 *Gi* − .210 *Cm* + .275 *Ac* + .523 *Ai* + .241 *Ie* + .657 *Py.*

Weighted combinations of scales in combination with SAT scores for males and females who were National Merit scholars were found to have a .32 and .23 correlation
with college GPA, respectively:

5. Male GPA = .16 SAT (Math) + .11 *So* − .19 *Sp* + .17 *Fe*.

6. Female GPA = .25 SAT (Verbal) − .14 *Sp* + .06 *Re* + .20 *Ac* + .08 *Fe*.

Although the correlations derived from these formulas are somewhat low, they are an
improvement on the use of SAT scores alone for this group.

Using a more general sample of college students' CPI scores to predict academic
performance, Gough and Lanning (1986) found that *Ai, Ie,* and *Py* correlated at the levels of .28, .25, and .23, respectively. Multiple regression analysis produced the following equation, which had a correlation with later course grades of .38 for males and .36
for females:

7. GPA = 30.60 − .26 *Wb* + .35 *Re* − .19 *Gi* + .39 *Ai* + .22 *Ie* + .36 *Py*.

Although the correlation was modest, it was able to predict academic performance
somewhat better than using SAT-V (.31 for males, .38 for females) and SAT-M (.30 for
males, .24 for females).

These rather modest correlations indicate that it is more difficult to predict performance for college students than for students attending high school. This can be traced
to the far greater number and complexity of variables involved in a college setting.
Both the selection of curricula and the student's motivation for attending college can
result from a variety of situations. Furthermore, significant changes have been made in
the curricula and admissions policies of colleges since the early equations (4, 5, and 6)
were developed. Finally, a student's lifestyle can be extremely varied. For example,
some students may be attempting to struggle through college with a part- or even a full-
time job, whereas others may be taking relatively few classes and are supported exclusively by their parents. All of these variables are beyond the scope of what can be
measured by a test such as the CPI. The practical implication for clinicians predicting
college GPA is to consider not only test scores but also as many of the other variables
as possible.

Achievement in Vocational Training Programs

Student Teaching

Several studies have been performed to assess the effectiveness of teachers in student-
teaching programs. Veldman and Kelly (1965) found that student teachers who were
rated highly by their supervisors scored significantly higher on *Ac, Cs, Do, Gi,* and *Py*
than those who were rated as less effective. Hill (1960) also emphasized the importance of *Ac* but did not find *Do* and *Py* to be important. A further study with a female
population again stressed the importance of *Ac* but also included *Re* and *Ie* as significant factors (Gough, Durflinger, & Hill, 1968). Although these studies consistently
emphasized the importance of *Ac,* none of the other individual scales was found to have

either consistent or large correlations with teaching effectiveness. However, Gough, Durflinger, and Hill (1968) found a moderate correlation of .44 between CPI scores and teacher effectiveness by using the following equation based on weighted scales:

$$8. \text{ Teaching effectiveness} = 14.743 + .334 \, So - .670 \, Gi + .997 \, Ac$$
$$+ .909 \, Py - .446 \, Fx.$$

Using this equation, they were able to predict with 65% accuracy the performance of student teachers.

Medical School

Several scales have been found to correlate positively with overall medical school GPA, including Sy (.35), To (.34), and Ie (.40; Gough & Hall, 1964). An equation based on weighted combinations of scores was found to correlate at a magnitude of .43 with both faculty ratings of students and GPA (Gough & Hall, 1964):

$$9. \text{ Medical promise} = .794 \, Sy + .602 \, To + 1.114 \, Cm - .696 \, Cs.$$

Dental School

Most studies using single-scale correlations with achievement in dental school have not produced significant correlations, although Kirk, Cumming, and Hackett (1963) did report a correlation of .28 between Ac and dental school GPA. Gough and Kirk (1970) also reported a .38 correlation with GPA by using the following equation based on weighted combinations of scales:

$$10. \text{ Dental performance} = 29.938 - .110 \, Sp + .148 \, Re - .262 \, Gi + .727 \, Ac + .230 \, Py.$$

Although this correlation is somewhat modest, it is higher than the Dental Aptitude Test's correlation of .29.

Seminary

Query (1966) performed a study on seminary students who were advised to discontinue and those who successfully completed the program. Although he did not develop any equations based on weighted scores, he did find that those who were unsuccessful tended to score higher on Sy and Sa.

Police and Military Training

Both Ie (Hogan, 1971) and Do (Hargrave, Hiatt, & Gaffney, 1986) have been found to be related to police effectiveness. Hogan (1971) found that Ie correlated .40 with ratings of effectiveness made by instructors during training, and it correlated .43 after one year in training when ratings were made by field commanders (Mills & Bohannon, 1980). Other noteworthy correlations with other scales were for Ac (.31), Ai (.33), and Sy (.45; Hogan, 1971). Hargrave et al. (1986) described the most effective deputies as sociable, outgoing, and gregarious, whereas effective traffic controllers were characterized by a high capacity for rewarding social interactions. The most effective persons in both these groups (deputies and traffic controllers) were relatively dominant (high *Do*), energetic (high *Ie*), competitive (high *Ac*), independent (high *Ai*), flexible (high *Fx*), and socially ascendant (high Class 1 scales; Hargrave et al., 1986). Mills and Bohannon (1980) somewhat similarly described effective officers who had been in the field a year or more as independent (high *Ai*), energetic (high *Ie*), and flexible (high *Fx*).

Pugh (1985) has pointed out that what determines successful police performance changes over time. During their training and first year of employment, the most effective officers were found to be those who were most able to obtain the trust of their coworkers and become accepted members of their department. After two years, their ability to strive for improvement (high *Cs*) became the best predictor. In contrast, the best predictors after 4.5 years of employment were qualities that indicated a person was stable, socially skilled, and responsible (high *Wb, Re, So*).

A study by Collins (1967) rated drill sergeants in a training program on the following criteria of success: academic grades, an assessment of leadership ability, final class standing, and a field test of combat skills. The only scale to correlate significantly was *Ie*. It is interesting to note that the scales stressing conformity (*Ac*) and dominance (*Do*) had no correlation. This is in contrast to the frequent stereotype of drill sergeants as authoritarian, rigid, conformist, and autocratic. It has also been found that women who were successful in Air Force basic training scored higher on all scales except *Sc, Cm, Py,* and *Fe* than those who were unsuccessful (Elliott, 1960). A different study found that successful students graduating from an Army language training program scored significantly higher on *Ai* and *Ie* but not *Ac* than those who were unsuccessful (Datel, Hall, & Rufe, 1965).

Achievement through Conformance versus Independence

A comparison between *Ac* and *Ai* can provide useful information regarding an individual's typical style or preference toward working. This can have important implications for helping a person make a career choice or understand existing job difficulties. If *Ai* is high (*T* = 50 or more) and significantly higher than *Ac* (10 or more), such persons usually place a high level of trust in their own judgments and conclusions, and are likely to reject conventional formulas. Their acceptance of decisions or ideas depends more on inward verification rather than a respect for, or adherence to, external standards. When left on their own, they are highly motivated to achieve, but they may feel restricted if placed in a structured environment. If *Ai* is exceptionally high (*T* = 65 or more), they may spend much of their time rejecting authority. This trend would be further exaggerated with high scores on *Do* and low scores on *Sy.* The result might be an almost obsessional quality in their thinking, characterized by strong themes of rebelliousness. In general, a significantly higher *Ai* than *Ac* is an excellent profile for authors, researchers, and persons in positions of independent leadership.

If *Ac* is high (*T* = 50 or more) and is significantly greater than *Ai* (10 or more), the opposite trend would be apparent. These persons would strongly prefer specificity and external structure. They would be more effective and feel more comfortable when "second in command," such as in a middle-management business position. An overall and generally effective combination occurs with high but evenly balanced scores on *Ai* and *Ac.* This suggests these individuals have the necessary flexibility both to work within a structured environment and to do effective work independently. The following is a listing of the descriptions given to persons scoring with different high and low combinations of *Ac* and *Ai* (Gough, 1968):

Ac High

idealistic	mannerly	intelligent	logical
cautious	shy	rational	interests (are) wide
praising	conscientious	realistic	inventive
nervous	inhibited	independent	active
helpful	dull	reasonable	stable

Ai Low ———————————————————————— Ai High

irresponsible	show-off	spunky	tolerant
careless	touchy	reckless	reliable
distrustful	undependable	unexcitable	courageous
disorderly	unstable	foresighted	distractible
indifferent	restless	frank	pleasure-seeking

Ac Low

Leadership and Managerial Style

The CPI has been extensively used within organizations to understand leadership and managerial style. Additional uses have been in team building, consulting with executives, personnel selection, individual development, and filling recently vacated positions with persons within the organization (succession planning). An excellent, practical, case-focused guide toward using the CPI in these areas has been developed by Meyer and Davis (1992). They emphasize that one of the crucial issues to understand is that a person's optimal performance in an organization depends not only on personality, but also on the degree to which an individual's personality fits into the direction the organization is headed, as well as on the organizational climate and culture. Thus, any interpretation of the CPI needs to take these factors into consideration. For example, an organization that is quickly undergoing extensive change will benefit from persons who will be flexible and adaptable, as might be reflected in high scores on the Flexibility scale. In some organizations, a consensus-building style will be most appropriate, and this might be suggested by high scores on Dominance, Tolerance, Empathy, and F/M but a lower score on Social presence. In a fast-paced, high-risk organization, this same style might be quite dysfunctional. Thus, any interpretation of CPI profiles needs to integrate test results with the specifics of the organization.

Relevant information on leadership and managerial style can often be found by carefully considering the CPI profile. One way of guiding the questions that can be asked regarding leadership is to consider the managerial competencies identified by Meyer and Davis (1992), which are summarized as follows:

Leadership orientation: drive for influence, method of working with others to achieve goals, negotiation skills, willingness to take charge, forceful versus low-key style, authoritative versus consensus-building style.

Problem solving: level of decisiveness, method of analyzing problems, extent to which others' input is used, cautiousness versus impulsivity, likelihood of considering a wide number of alternatives or holding to one or two options and arguing for them, creativity, and independence.

Achievement motivation: the extent or drive to achieve as well as the manner in which the person is likely to achieve, need for approval, need for recognition, achievement through independent efforts (form-creating) versus working with and under the direction of others (form-enhancing).

Interpersonal skills: social comfort, extent to which interaction is accepted or liked, awareness of interpersonal dynamics, concern and support for others, willingness to help and support others, tact, diplomacy, lack of abrasiveness, political astuteness.

Administrative skills: orientation toward planning, need for structure in organization and planning, attention to details, monitoring and controlling behavior, focus on short-term as well as long-term planning, degree to which work is approached in a systematic manner.

Adaptability: ability to cope with stress, self-reliance, ability to work within a wide number of contexts, tolerance of ambiguity, personal mastery, optimism, ability to be self-directed, possession of a wide number of adaptive behaviors.

Managers might vary on the extent to which they: need to take control, carefully consider all options in solving a problem, achieve individually or through conforming to some outside structure, are comfortable with their coworkers, are aware of details, and are flexible. The different high and low points on their CPI results can help with understanding and elaborating on the above differences in managerial style.

At the core of understanding a person's comfort and wish to lead is his or her level of dominance. Accordingly, the *Do* scale has consistently proven to be accurate in differentiating leaders from nonleaders. In discussing leadership, it is helpful to describe the difference between an executive leader who has been appointed and a social leader who has been elected. For both types of leaders, the *Do* scale is high. However, for the executive leader, there is considerably more variability among the other scales; the style of expressing leadership is more dependent on the condition the person is in, and the achievement scales are relatively more important than the other measurements (summarized in Megargee, 1972). This seems reasonable because the success of an executive leader is based more on his or her administrative and supervisory abilities than on his or her popularity. Social leadership is more likely to have a general elevation in factor 2 scales as well as an elevated *Do.*

For example, if *Do, Cs,* and *Sp* are the high points, the leader is likely to be socially charismatic, persuasive, at the center of attention, and energetic (Heilbrun, Daniel, Goodstein, Stephenson, & Crites, 1962). If *Do* is high along with *Sa* and *Ac,* the person will: have a high need for control, fear rejection, demand attention, dislike surprises, and emphasize clear structure (McAllister, 1988). If *Do* and *Ai* are the high points, these individuals will be independent achievers who may also be highly creative self-initiators (McAllister, 1988). Further interactions with *Do* can likewise be developed by taking into consideration the specific meanings of additional corresponding high and low scale scores.

Using a combination of weighted scales derived from social leaders in a high school environment, Gough (1969) was able to obtain a modest correlation of .34 between social leadership and weighted CPI scales:

11. Leadership (Social) = 14.130 + .372 *Do* + .696 *Sa* + .345 *Wb* − .133 *Gi* + .274 *Ai.*

In addition, a Leadership Potential Index and Managerial Potential scale have been developed and are a portion of the CPI computer report (see Gough, 1987; McAllister, 1988; Meyer & Davis, 1992).

Gough (1968) studied the relationship between *Do* and *Re* and found that the meaning of *Do* will be altered by the relative elevation of *Re*. If *Do* and *Re* are both high, a leader will be generally progressive, conscientious, and ambitious. In contrast, adjectives describing high *Do* persons with low *Re* indicate that they will be dominant in a more aggressive, rigid, and destructive way. The following is a list of adjectives used to describe various combinations of *Do* and *Re*:

Do High

touchy	dominant	dominant	ambitious
robust	strong	responsible	foresighted
cynical	tough	progressive	conscientious
hardheaded	aggressive	wise	formal
temperamental	opinionated	stern	alert

Re Low ————————————————————————————————— Re High

irresponsible	suggestible	quiet	calm
careless	foolish	peaceable	mild
unstable	pleasure-seeking	modest	gentle
apathetic	changeable	reserved	thoughtful
confused	lazy	cooperative	honest

Do Low

Executive Success

Success and effectiveness as an executive are frequently found in a profile in which $T = 60$ on *Do, Cs,* and *Sp*; $T = 40$–50 on *Sa, Re, So, Sc*; $T = 55$ or more on *Sy*; $T = 40$ or more on *Wb*; and $T = 50$ or less on *Gi* (in Webb et al., 1981). The most important variables are the indicated *T* scores on *Do, Cs, Sp, Sa, Re, So,* and *Sc*. This profile is common among business executives and managers. They are usually able to have others adapt to their plans, yet at the same time they are flexible enough to adapt to the demands that are placed on them. Although they are generally excellent leaders, they may create a certain degree of family discord by attempting to be too demanding and autocratic in the home. If this combination of scores is present for a person under 25 years of age, it can suggest a naive sense of overconfidence in which the person cannot effectively assess his or her personal limitations. However, this profile is generally a good predictor of later success in leadership positions.

Leadership and Empathy

If an individual has elevations on both *Do* ($T = 65$ or more) and *Gi* ($T = 60$ or more), he or she is likely to not only possess excellent leadership abilities, but also to demonstrate a concern with, and empathy for, others (Heilbrun et al., 1962). If *Gi* is low in relationship to *Do,* then the leadership style will usually be more critical, domineering, egotistical, and autocratic, with a decreased concern for creating and maintaining harmonious interpersonal relationships in the group. A low score on both *Gi* and *Do* will reflect a somewhat passive and withdrawn person who is socially inept and resentful, and whose passivity may be expressed in a shy seeking of approval from others.

Decision Making

The interaction between *Sa* and *Wb* reflects the degree to which the examinee turns to self or depends on others for decision making. If *Wb* is low and *Sa* is moderate to high, these persons will usually rely on their own self-evaluations and will feel that others are inferior and cannot be trusted. This may be because they are self-assured and independent, as reflected by a *Wb* that is only moderate to slightly low; or, they may only listen to their own judgments because they have a deep sense of alienation from and distrust of others, as reflected in a markedly low *Wb* and high *Sa.*

If *Wb* is moderate to high and *Sa* is low, these individuals will tend to believe that the judgment of others is superior to their own judgment. They may be still fairly accepting of themselves (only slightly low *Sa*) but think even more highly of others. Thus, they may have a high level of loyalty to people who are in superior positions, such as an employer or parent. Such persons may also have a poorly developed ability to accurately perceive the faults and limitations of others, and may have developed this loyalty in response to overprotective parents. A further possibility could be that they do not respect their own judgments and perceptions because they are lacking in their own resources.

With both *Sa* and *Wb* low, there are likely to be significant self-doubts. There may be an excessive level of dependency, fearfulness regarding one's own competence, and a corresponding resentment of one's continual dependency on others.

Clinical Assessment

For several reasons, the CPI has generally not proven to be as effective in the assessment of psychopathology as it has been in the educational and vocational areas. Primarily, the CPI was not designed for clinical assessment and thus relatively little research has been conducted in this area. In their organization and nature, the scales were not designed to differentiate among the various syndromes of pathology, nor do they provide information relating to a person's intrapsychic areas of functioning. Furthermore, devices such as the MMPI and MCMI are clearly superior for the evaluation of pathology.

Despite these limitations, the CPI can make some general as well as specific contributions. Even though it does not distinguish among the different patterns of pathology, general maladjustment is usually indicated by lowered profiles (Higgins-Lee, 1990). The CPI has also been effectively used to detect and assess criminal and delinquent individuals, which involves a more interpersonal or, more accurately, an individual versus societal type of conflict. Furthermore, the CPI is a good adjunct to more clinically oriented tests because it can assess the relative strengths in an otherwise pathological individual and answer questions relating to the type of educational and vocational programs this person might benefit from.

General Maladjustment

An individual's level of maladjustment is indicated by generally lowered profiles (Higgins-Lee, 1990), which are often accompanied by an elevation on *Fe* (Gough, 1969). A lowering of factor 1 scales (especially *Do, Re, So,* and *Sc*) is often a good indicator of poor adjustment, and men with low *Ac* and *Ie* are especially likely to be maladjusted (Stewart, 1962).

Personality Disorder

Persons with scores below 25 on the *So* scale are likely to have diagnoses of personality disorders, particularly those that are related to dramatic, emotional, or erratic behaviors (borderline, antisocial, histrionic, narcissistic; Standage, 1990; Standage, Smith, & Norman, 1988). However, if they score high on items related to "problem behaviors" (indicating denial of these problem behaviors) but low on items reflecting dysphoria and having had an unhappy childhood (thereby agreeing to these difficulties), then they would be unlikely to have alcohol or drug problems but may have difficulties with depression. The likelihood that they would have personality disorders would then be intermediate (Standage et al., 1988).

Vulnerability to Stress

Persons with a "V" formation in which *So* is low (*T* = 35 or less), with *Re* and *Sc* significantly higher (*T* = 40 or more), are likely to be defensive and susceptible to the effects of situational stress (in Webb et al., 1981). They usually come from chaotic, stress-filled families in which there were episodes of irrational parental abuse. Thus, they have learned that the world is a dangerous place and have developed a precarious balance in which they feel constantly on guard. They keep their emotions carefully controlled, continually attempt to avoid conflict, and feel they need to be constantly prepared to diffuse potentially stress-filled interactions. Their conformity to their environment is based not on an expectation of achieving positive rewards, but more on fear and an avoidance of negative consequences. These people may have occasional explosive outbursts in which they have an almost dissociative loss of control. This explosiveness is especially likely if their spouse is manipulative, insensitive, and exploitive. As the discrepancy between *So* and *Sc* increases, these dynamics become more pronounced.

Depression

The social ascendancy (Class 1) scales are generally lowered by depression, and a *T* score of 40 or less on *Sy, So, Wb,* and *Ie* is highly typical of depressed populations (Holliman & Montross, 1984). The scales that provided the best indicators of depression in males were *Sy, So,* and *Ie*; for females, the best discriminators were *Wb, So,* and *Ie* (Holliman & Montross, 1984). In most cases, the *Wb* scale is particularly important to notice, because a lowering on scales such as *Do, Cs, Sy, Sp,* and *Sa* might suggest merely a shy, unassertive, socially uninvolved person who is not necessarily depressed (McAllister, 1988). When the depression begins to lift and the person starts to have more optimism and a greater orientation to his or her environment, these scales generally increase. The mental and behavioral apathy often associated with depression can also be reflected by a lowering (*T* = 40 or less) in *Ac, Ai,* and *Ie*.

Psychosomatic Disorders

Although the CPI was not designed to diagnose psychosomatic disorders, it can assess certain personality characteristics that are consistent with individuals who are susceptible to this type of disturbance. Both male and female psychosomatics usually have lowered scores (*T* = 40 or less) on *Wb* and *Sc* and an elevation on *Cm* (Stewart, 1962). In addition, males often have a lowering on *Ie*. When the scores from male and female psychosomatics are compared with persons having behavior disorders, psychosomatics have a relatively higher *So* and *Cm*, with females also having a higher *Re* (Stewart, 1962). All of these scores suggest that psychosomatic patients have a significantly higher level of superego control and socialization. This agrees with most formulations of psychosomatic disorders that emphasize the suppression and repression of hostility and antisocial behavior as important predisposing factors. A pattern of psychosomatic disorders is especially likely if *Wb* has a *T* score of 35 or less, accompanied by an *Fe* of 60 or more. This pattern is associated with headaches, gastrointestinal upsets, or functional skin conditions. Such persons are likely to have moderately high needs for dependency, which are not being fulfilled, but they also tend to feel distrustful and alienated in their relationships with others.

Defense Mechanisms

Byrne (1964) has theorized that the two basic approaches to defense are either through repression or through sensitization. Whereas repressors attempt to avoid anxiety-arousing stimuli, sensitizers approach and attempt to control situations. Byrne, Golightly, and Sheffield (1965) found that high scorers on *Sy, Wb, Sc, To, Gi, Ac,* and *Ie* were more likely to use repression.

Certain types of assaultive offenders can usually be characterized as overcontrolled, but occasionally they drop all inhibitions and impulsively strike out (Megargee, 1964, 1965, 1966d). These persons score high on the "overcontrolled hostility" scale (OH) of the MMPI, and also have higher scores on *Sc* and *Gi* with a lowering on *Sa* (Megargee, Cook, & Mendelsohn, 1967). This gives further support to the view that *Sc* and *Gi* are associated with the use of repressive defenses.

Juvenile Delinquency and Criminal Behavior

The assessment of antisocial behavior with the CPI has been well researched, with generally useful findings. Both delinquents and criminals tend to have lower overall subscale scores, particularly on *Re* and *So* (Gough & Bradley, 1992; Laufer, Skoog, & Day, 1982). In addition, persons who scored in either the Gamma or Delta lifestyle categories (questioning of normative beliefs) were more likely to be delinquents than those in the Alpha or Beta categories (Gough & Bradley, 1992). However, level of self-realization or integration (score on vector 3) is important to consider in that delinquents and criminals had low levels of self-realization. In contrast, persons with high levels of self-realization were found to have a low level of criminal or delinquent behavior regardless of which of the four lifestyles they were in (Gough & Bradley, 1992).

Scores on *Wb, To,* and *Ac* are also likely to be somewhat lower (Gough, 1969). This pattern suggests that the social poise of delinquents is usually about the same as that of other persons their age, but in most other respects their behavior is definitely unconventional and they usually do not channel these differences into creative or intellectual areas. Mizushima and DeVos (1967) have found significant differences on the CPI between solitary delinquents who have lower scores on *Ie* and *Fe* and more socially oriented delinquents who have significantly higher scores on *Sy, Sp,* and *Sa.* They also found violent offenders to be higher on *Sp* and *Sa* but low on *Fe.* However, delinquents who committed extremely violent offenses were especially high on *Sc,* which supports Gough's theory that excessive overcontrol in certain individuals periodically breaks down, leading to assaultive behavior (Megargee, 1966d). In summarizing these data on delinquency, it is most important to consider lowerings in *Re* and *So.* Further information regarding the style of delinquency can be derived by the lowered *Ie* and *Fe* for solitary delinquents; higher *Sy, Sp,* and *Sa* for social delinquents; higher *Sp* and *Sa,* and low *Fe* for violent social delinquents; and outstandingly high *Sc* for extremely violent offenders who have periodic excessive losses of control.

The likelihood of successful parole for delinquents can, in part, be predicted. More successful parolees have higher scores on *Sp* and *Sa,* and less successful parolees have lower scores on *So* and *Sc* (Gough, Wenk, & Rozynko, 1965). Gough and his colleagues have developed the following regression equation to predict successful versus unsuccessful parolees:

12. Parole success $= 45.078 - .353\ Sp - .182\ Sa + .532\ So + .224\ Sc.$

Using this equation, Gough et al. (1965) were able to predict with 60% accuracy which of a population of California Youth Authority parolees would be successful and which parolees would later become recidivists.

Marital Violence among Males

Males who were found to be physically violent in their marriages generally had lower scores in ten of the CPI scales including *Re, So, Sc, To, Ac, Ai, Gi, Ie,* and *Py* (Barnett & Hamberger, 1992). Scales found to be particularly effective predictors were low scores on *Re, So,* and *Gi,* which suggests that maritally violent men have difficulties with a combination of impulsivity, problem solving, and intimacy.

Chemical Dependency

Kurtines, Hogan, and Weiss (1975) found that the possibility of potential or actual substance abuse, perhaps to the extent of actual addiction, is suggested by high *Sp* and *Sa* accompanied by low scores on *Re, So, Sc,* and *Wb.* In a college population, Goldstein

(1974) somewhat similarly found that students who used drugs were more likely than nonusers to have elevations on Capacity for status, Social presence, Self-acceptance, Psychological mindedness, and Flexibility. In contrast, nonusers scored higher on Well-being, Responsibility, Socialization, Self-control, Tolerance, Communality, Achievement via conformance, and Intellectual efficiency. The scale with the greatest ability to differentiate the two groups was Socialization, with users having a mean of 41.2 and nonusers having a mean of 52.1.

Social Maturity

The concept of social maturity includes *So,* but extends to areas other than that assessed by the *So* scale alone. Specifically, the person who is considered to be socially mature is not merely directed by blind conformance, but also has a high level of ethical standards that can even vary from the values held by the majority of people. He or she may, at times, feel a need to resist social pressure. Also, this person can accurately perceive the faults in a social system and will attempt to deal with them in a mature way. Thus, the socially mature person is clearly different from someone who is merely oversocialized or hypernormal. Gough (1966) developed the following multiple regression equation to assess social maturity using combined weighted scores:

$$13. \text{ Social maturity} = 25.701 + .408 \ Re + .478 \ So - .296 \ Gi.$$

A special Social Maturity scale has also been developed and is available as a portion of the CPI computer report (see Gough, 1987; McAllister, 1988).

   The CPI equations discussed in this section are summarized in Table 8–2 for quick reference.

RECOMMENDED READING

Gough, H. G. (1987). *California Psychological Inventory: Administrator's guide.* Palo Alto, CA: Consulting Psychologists Press.

McAllister, L. (1988). *A practical guide to CPI interpretation* (2nd ed.). Palo Alto, CA: Consulting Psychologists Press.

Megargee, E. I. (1972). *The California Psychological Inventory handbook.* San Francisco: Jossey-Bass.

Meyer, P., & Davis, S. (1992). *The CPI applications guide: An essential tool for individual, group, and organizational development.* Palo Alto: Consulting Psychologists Press.

Chapter 9

THE RORSCHACH

The Rorschach has traditionally been considered to be a projective test consisting of a set of ten bilaterally symmetrical inkblots. Subjects are requested to tell the examiner what the inkblots remind them of. The overall goal of the technique is to assess the structure of personality, with particular emphasis on how individuals construct their experience (cognitive structuring) and the meanings assigned to their perceptual experiences (thematic imagery; Weiner, 1994). Despite attacks from both within and outside the field of psychology, the Rorschach remains one of the most extensively used and thoroughly researched techniques (Durand, Blanchard, & Mindell, 1988; Watkins et al., 1995).

The central assumption of the Rorschach is that stimuli from the environment are organized by a person's specific needs, motives, and conflicts, and by certain perceptual "sets." This need for organization becomes more exaggerated, extensive, and conspicuous when subjects are confronted with ambiguous stimuli, such as inkblots. Thus, they must draw on their personal internal images, ideas, and relationships in order to create a response. This process requires that persons organize these perceptions as well as associate them with past experiences and impressions. The central thesis on which Rorschach interpretation is based is that the process by which persons organize their responses to the Rorschach is representative of how they confront other ambiguous situations requiring organization and judgment. Once the responses have been made and recorded, they are scored according to three general categories: (a) the "location," or the area of the inkblot on which they focused; (b) "determinants," or specific properties of the blot they used in making their responses (color, shape, and so on); and (c) the "content," or general class of objects to which the response belongs (human, architecture, anatomy, and so on). The interpretation of the overall protocol is based on the relative number of responses that fall into each of the above categories. Some systems also score for the extent to which subjects organize their response (organizational activity), the types of verbalizations, and the meaningful associations related to the inkblots.

Although these scoring categories may appear straightforward, the specifics of scoring and interpreting the Rorschach are extremely complex. Furthermore, attempts to develop a precise, universally accepted coding system have not been entirely successful, which creates some confusion and ambiguity in approaching the Rorschach technique itself (see Aronow, Reznikoff, & Moreland, 1995; Weiner, 1994). Although the primary scoring systems have some agreed-on similarities, there are also significant differences in the elements of these systems. These differences, in turn, reflect the complexity and ambiguity in the nature of the responses made to the cards. Thus, effective use of the Rorschach depends on a thorough knowledge of a scoring system, clinical experience, and adequate knowledge of personality and psychopathology.

The general purpose of this chapter is to provide an overview of administration, scoring, and interpretation using Exner's "Comprehensive System." Exner's system was selected because it is the most ambitious and psychometrically sound Rorschach system to date. Furthermore, the most frequently used scorings and interpretations from other systems have been included and integrated into Exner's approach.

Scoring for the Comprehensive System is quite complex, and only a brief overview can be covered in this chapter. Clinicians who wish to use precise scoring tables and criteria, as well as more extensive elaborations on interpretation, are encouraged to consult Exner and his colleagues' original works (Exner, 1990, 1991, 1993; Exner & Weiner, 1995). This chapter cannot stand as a substitute for Exner's work. Its major intent is to familiarize persons with the Rorschach in general and, more specifically, with Exner's approach to interpretation. This emphasis on interpretation rather than the technicalities of scoring is consistent with a recent survey noting that the main area where students experience insufficient training is in the actual interpretation and integration of results (Hilsenroth & Handler, 1995). In addition to students who are learning the system, persons who are already familiar with Exner's system might wish to consult sections of this chapter to obtain summaries of different scoring categories and interpretive hypotheses. This might be most appropriate for practitioners who use the Rorschach only occasionally. Finally, persons who use other scoring systems may wish to consult the different interpretive hypotheses as an aid to interpretation. This is theoretically possible because Exner incorporated the major approaches from other systems into his Comprehensive System. However, many minor variations are likely to occur between the Comprehensive System and other systems, so interpretations should be made with caution.

HISTORY AND DEVELOPMENT

Many inkblot-type tests and games had existed long before Rorschach published his original ten cards in 1921. For example, da Vinci and Botticelli were interested in determining how a person's interpretations of ambiguous designs reflected his or her personality. This theme was later considered by Binet and Henri in 1895, and by Whipple in 1910. A popular parlor game named Blotto, developed in the late 1800s, required players to make creative responses to inkblots. However, Rorschach developed the first extensive, empirically based system to score and interpret responses to a standardized set of cards. Unfortunately, Rorschach died at age 37, shortly after the publication of his major work, *Psychodiagnostik,* in 1921. His work was continued to a limited extent by three of his colleagues; Emil Oberholzer, George Roeurer, and Walter Morgenthaler.

The main approach used by Rorschach and other early developers of inkblot techniques was to note the characteristic responses of different types of populations. Thus, the initial norms were developed to help differentiate among various clinical and normal populations: mental retardates, normals, artists, scholars, and other specific subgroups with known characteristics. Rorschach primarily wanted to establish empirically based discriminations among different groups; he was only minimally concerned with the symbolical interpretation of contents. Many of his original concepts and scoring categories have been continued within current systems of analysis. For example, he noted that depressed, sullen patients seemed to give the fewest responses. Persons giving a large number of very quick responses were likely to be similarly "scattered" in their perception and ideation to nontest situations. He also considered the importance of long latencies (so-called "shock" responses), and hypothesized that they were related to a sense of helplessness and emotional repression.

Had Rorschach lived longer, the history and development of his test might have been quite different. Without the continued guidance and research from the "founding father," the strands of the Rorschach technique were taken up by persons who had quite different backgrounds from Rorschach and from one another. By 1957, five Rorschach systems were in wide use, the most popular being those developed by Beck and Klopfer. These two approaches came to represent polarized schools of thought and were often in conflict.

Beck (1937) adhered closely to Rorschach's format for coding and scoring. He continually stressed the importance of establishing strong empirical relationships between Rorschach codes and outside criterion measures. Beck emphasized that the response to the Rorschach involved primarily a perceptual-cognitive process in which the respondents structure and organize their perceptions into meaningful responses. This perceptual-cognitive process was likely to reflect their responses to their world in general. For example, persons who broke down their perceptions of an inkblot into small details were likely to behave similarly for perceptions outside the testing situation.

In contrast, Klopfer (1937) was closely aligned to phenomenology and the theories of personality developed by Freud and Jung. As a result, he emphasized the symbolical and experiential nature of a respondent's Rorschach contents. Thus, Klopfer believed that Rorschach responses were fantasy products triggered by the stimulus of the inkblots. For example, Rorschach responses that described threatening objects would suggest persons who perceive their world as similarly threatening. Although not as popular, additional systems developed by Piotrowski, Hertz, and Rapaport represented a middle ground between the two extremes taken by Beck and Klopfer.

With five distinct systems available, the Rorschach became not a unitary test but five different tests. Exner (1969) provided a comparative analysis of these different systems and later concluded that "the notion of *the* Rorschach was more myth than reality" (Exner, 1986, p. 19). He pointed out that none of the five systems used the same verbal instructions and only two of the systems required identical seating arrangements. More importantly, each systematizer developed his or her own format for scoring, which resulted in many differences regarding interpretation, the components required to calculate quantitative formulas, the meanings associated with many of the variables, and the interpretive postulates.

The wide range of often competing approaches resulted in numerous detrimental practices. A survey of practitioners by Exner and Exner (1972) indicated that 22% of all respondents had abandoned scoring altogether and, instead, based their interpretations on a subjective analysis of contents. Of those who did score, 75% used their own personalized integration of scores from a variety of systems. In addition, the vast majority did not follow any prescribed set of instructions for administration. With researchers using a variety of approaches, comparison of the results of different studies was difficult. Researchers in the early 1970s further reported difficulties in recruiting subjects, problems with experimenter bias that needed to be corrected by using multiple examiners, statistical complexities of data analysis, inadequate control groups, and insufficient normative data (Exner, 1993).

The general conclusion, based on the above findings, was that the research on and the clinical use of the Rorschach were seriously flawed, in part because of the lack of clarity inherent in having five different systems. Surveys and analysis of research conducted in the early 1970s by Exner and his colleagues concluded that, although all five systems included some empirically sturdy elements, they also included elements that had no empirical basis or elements for which negative findings were predominant.

To correct the difficulties with both the research and clinical use of the Rorschach, Exner and his colleagues began the collection of a broad normative database and the development of an integrated system of scoring and interpretation. Their initial step was to establish clear guidelines for seating, verbal instructions, recording, and inquiry by the examiner regarding the examinee's responses. The best features for scoring and interpretation, based on both empirical validation and commonality across systems, were adapted from each of the five different systems. A scoring category was included in the new system only after it had achieved a minimum .85 level for interscorer reliability. The final product was first published in 1974 as *The Rorschach: A Comprehensive System* and has since been released in second (1986) and third (1993) editions. A second volume relating to current research and interpretation has been released in two editions (Exner, 1978, 1991) and two editions of a volume on the assessment of children and adolescents have also been published (Exner & Weiner, 1982, 1995).

Exner's integration of the different Rorschach approaches into his Comprehensive System seems to have been largely successful. Most research studies over the past 15 years have used his system, and it has become by far the most frequently taught system in graduate training (Hilsenroth & Handler, 1995; Ritzler & Alter, 1986). His close adherence to empirical validation, combined with a large normative database, have served to increase its acceptance and status. Access to training and interpretive aids has been facilitated through numerous workshops, a scoring workbook, ongoing research publications, new editions of earlier volumes, and computer-assisted scoring and interpretation (Exner, 1984, 1986, 1993).

RELIABILITY AND VALIDITY

Debates regarding the psychometric adequacy of the Rorschach have created one of the greatest controversies in the history of psychology. From the beginning, the Rorschach was met with skepticism in the United States; yet, it developed a strong following. At one point, the Rorschach was the second most frequently used test, and, in the 1940s and 1950s, the name Rorschach was almost synonymous with clinical psychology. Despite this initial (and continuing) popularity, reviews have generally been quite critical. As early as 1954, Shaffer declared that the Rorschach could no longer be considered a promising instrument and, 11 years later, Dana (1965) somewhat prematurely concluded: "Indeed, we have come to the end of an era, preoccupation with the Rorschach as a test"

(p. 495). Jensen (1965) was even more critical when he recommended that "the Rorschach be altogether abandoned in clinical practice, and that students in clinical psychology not be required to waste their time learning the technique" (p. 509). Despite these attacks, by 1956 there were almost 2,000 publications pertaining directly to the Rorschach. This number was estimated to be 2,700 by 1969 (Exner, 1969) and had increased to 6,000 by 1982 (Kobler, 1983). Between 1982 and 1996, there were 1,300 additional publications.

Part of the difficulty in establishing the psychometric properties of the Rorschach has been in making meaningful comparisons across different studies. As Exner (1969, 1974, 1986, 1993) has repeatedly pointed out, there is not *a* Rorschach; rather, at least five different Rorschachs have been created around the five major systems. Reliability and validity studies performed on one system did not necessarily mean that the findings from these studies could be generalized to any of the other systems. However, reviewers have often acted as if there was only one Rorschach. Furthermore, many studies were poorly conducted. They were characterized by inadequate controls for age, sex, race, IQ, and socioeconomic status. In addition, many studies had extremely wide variations in the training required for scorers, insufficient protection from experimenter bias, poor validation criteria, and inadequate statistical models. These difficulties were amply demonstrated in that Exner (1986) and his associates found it necessary to discard 1,400 research studies of a total of 2,100 studies published prior to 1970.

Despite the above difficulties, estimates of reliability can be obtained by referring to meta-analytic reviews by Parker (1983b) and Parker, Hanson, and Hunsley (1988), in combination with data supplied by Exner (1983, 1993). Parker (1983b) analyzed 39 papers using 530 different statistical procedures published in the *Journal of Personality Assessment* between 1971 and 1980. He concluded that, overall, the Rorschach can be expected to have reliabilities in the low to middle .80s. During the development of the Comprehensive System, Exner gave particular attention to interscorer reliability in developing his different scoring categories. No category was included unless it achieved a minimum .85 level among different scorers, with most categories being higher (Exner, 1974, 1986, 1993). Test-retest reliabilities were somewhat more variable. Retesting of 25 variables over a one-year interval for a nonpatient group produced reliabilities ranging between .26 to .91 (Exner, 1986). A total of 20 of the variables had correlations above .72; 13 of them were between .81 and .89, and 2 were above .90. Exner has clarified that the five variables below .72 would all be expected to have had relatively low reliabilities because they related to changeable state (rather than trait) characteristics of the person. He also pointed out that the most important elements in interpretation are the quantitative formulas and Special Indices, all of which were among the higher reliabilities. Retesting for the same group over a three-year interval produced a similar but slightly lower pattern of reliability. In contrast, another group of nonpatient adults, retested over a much shorter (three-week) interval, had somewhat higher overall reliabilities than for either the one-year or three-year retestings (Exner, 1986).

Long-term retesting for children has not come close to the same degree of stability as for adults (Exner & Weiner, 1995). Exner (1986) clarifies that this low stability for test results is to be expected, given that children undergo considerable developmental changes. However, short-term retesting over 7-day (for 8-year-olds) and 3-week (for

9-year-olds) intervals did indicate acceptable levels of stability (Exner, 1986). Only 2 of 25 variables were below .70, with at least 7 above .90 and the remainder from .70 to .90. As with adults, the ratios and percentages demonstrated relatively high stabilities. Although acceptable short-term stability for young children's Rorschach variables was demonstrated, long-term stability was not found to occur until children reached the age of 14 years or older (Exner, Thomas, & Mason, 1985).

The primary focus of early validity studies was to discriminate empirically among different populations, based on: past observations of a particular group's responses to the Rorschach, the development of norms based on these responses, and comparisons of an individual's Rorschach responses with these norms. For example, a schizophrenic might have a relatively high number of poor-quality responses, or a depressed person might have very few human movement responses. In addition to this empirical discriminative validity, efforts have been made to develop a conceptual basis for specific responses or response patterns (Weiner, 1985, 1994). Thus, it has been conceptualized that schizophrenics have poor-quality responses because they do not perceive the world the way most people do; their perceptions are distorted and inaccurate, and their reality-testing is poor. A further approach, which was not extensively developed in the Comprehensive System (nor by Rorschach himself), was the validation of the latent meaning of symbolical content.

The above very general approaches have given rise to a surprisingly large number of specific scorings and interpretations, all of which have had various degrees of validation. Many of the early validity studies are difficult to evaluate because of the varying scoring systems and poor methodologies. In addition, most early studies depended on inadequate norms (especially for studies conducted on children, adolescents, and persons over 70). Test results might also have been significantly influenced by situational and interpersonal variables, such as seating, instructions, rapport, gender, and personality of the examiner (see review by Masling, 1992). It should then come as no surprise that, for every study supporting an interpretive hypothesis, there would often be another refuting the same hypothesis.

Establishing the validity of the Rorschach as a whole has been further complicated by the many scoring categories and quantitative formulas, each of which has varying levels of validity. Some interpretations have greater validity than others even within a specific category. For example, the number of human movement responses (M) has been used as an index of both creativity and fantasy. A review of the research by Exner (1993) indicates that M relates fairly clearly to fantasy in that it has been correlated with daydreaming, sleep/dream deprivation, dream recall, and total time spent dreaming, whereas associations between M and creativity have been weaker and more controversial. Validity might also depend on the context and population for which the test is used. For example, Exner (1993) reports that a depression index (DEPI) based on seven Rorschach combinations of scores was able to adequately discriminate depressed patients from controls. However, among adolescent populations, the depression index was unimpressive in distinguishing depressives from schizophrenics (Archer & Gordon, 1988; Ball, Archer, Gordon, & French, 1991). Additional validity data on specific scoring categories and formulas are included in the "Interpretation" section of this chapter. To more fully understand Rorschach validity, these data should be carefully read.

Probably the best way to provide a global index of validity is by combining the results from a large number of studies. The general consensus among several well-designed meta-analytic reviews was that, when rigorous, high-quality studies were analyzed, validity ranged from .40 to .50 (Atkinson, 1986; Atkinson, Quarington, Alp, & Cyr, 1986; Parker, 1983b, Parker et al., 1988; Weiner, 1996). However, interactions with type of scoring system, experience of the scorer, and type of population used were likely to have complicated the picture. More meta-analytic studies need to be conducted on both the global aspects of the Rorschach, the Comprehensive System, and more specific Rorschach scoring categories. Despite these difficulties, the above reviews suggest that, overall, the Rorschach has achieved levels of reliability and validity that are generally comparable to the MMPI and almost as high as the Wechsler scales.

One major factor that may serve to lower Rorschach validity is the meaning associated with, and the effects of, response productivity. Various interpretations have been associated with extremes of productivity, with low productivity suggesting defensiveness, depression, and malingering, and extremely high productivity suggesting high achievement or an obsessive-compulsive personality. However, response productivity has also been found to be closely tied to age, intellectual level, verbal aptitude, and amount of education. Norms have been provided for different ages (Exner, 1993; Exner & Weiner, 1995), which can be helpful in correcting for the effects of age. However, intellectual level, verbal aptitude, and amount of education can potentially confound the meanings associated with response productivity. A high number of responses does not necessarily represent traditional personality interpretations (obsessiveness, creativity, good impulse control), but might merely indicate a high level of verbal aptitude. Most early validity studies rarely took these factors into account. More importantly, the number of responses will not only affect interpretations related specifically to response productivity, but productivity will also affect many other areas of interpretation. For example, a low number of responses is likely to increase the relative number of responses based on the whole inkblot (W). In contrast, a high number of responses would be likely to increase the relative number of small detail (Dd) responses. Because interpretations are frequently based on the relative proportions of different scoring categories (calculated in quantitative formulas), the overall number of responses is likely to influence and possibly compromise the validity of the formulas. However, Exner (1993) has found that lengthy records generally did not result in different interpretations when compared with records from the same persons with average numbers of responses. Based on this finding, he has recommended that the number of responses should be limited if the person gives six or more responses to the first card or five or more responses to the second card (see "Administration," below). Protocols with an extremely low number of responses are therefore of questionable validity. Exner (1988) even recommends that brief protocols be discarded or a greater number of responses be obtained. A high number of responses also suggests caution, but this problem can be reduced by limiting the number of responses. This problem with the meaning of various numbers of responses largely led Holtzman to develop his alternate test (Holtzman Inkblot Test), in which subjects provide only one response for each inkblot in his series (Holtzman, 1988).

A further area of difficulty in establishing validity is that Exner cites extensive validity studies throughout his three volumes, but the majority of these studies were not done using his Comprehensive System. Comparability between the different studies and systems is frequently assumed or at least implied. Presumably, the studies he cites are those with relatively sound methodologies. However, these studies were frequently done at a time when norms were inadequate, interscorer reliability was questionable, and little concern was given to the possible confounding effects of age, intellectual level, education, and verbal aptitude. The development of the Comprehensive System itself was largely motivated by the deficiencies (and strengths) inherent in each of the earlier systems. More recently, there has been a greater proportion of studies that have used the Comprehensive System, which has helped to reduce this problem. Eventually, these newer studies based on the Comprehensive System will help clarify Rorschach validity without the possible contaminating effects of previous work that used other systems.

The main effort on Rorschach validity has been directed toward determining its ability to discriminate among different types of populations. The success of these differentiations has been somewhat equivocal (see Vincent & Harman, 1991). Although successful discriminations have sometimes been made, this is an important but limited form of validity. As Lanyon (1984) stresses, the Comprehensive System "still did not tackle [the] most urgent topic of external validity, one which continues to deny the Rorschach the status of scientific respectability" (p. 680). Little success has been achieved in making accurate predictions for such relevant areas as response to therapy, academic achievement, or spontaneous improvement in a clinical condition. Ideally, a test such as the Rorschach should not merely infer characteristics regarding the ways in which persons organize their perceptions of their world, but also should translate these inferences into understanding types of behaviors relevant to both clinicians and the subjects themselves.

ASSETS AND LIMITATIONS

The history of the Rorschach has been filled with controversy. Often, battle lines have been polarized into either "clinical loyalists" or "academic iconoclasts" (Parker, 1983b). Despite thousands of research studies, these positions have changed only minimally over the past 60 years. Atkinson (1986) has suggested that the controversial status of the Rorschach may be largely the result of sociocultural factors rather than actual scientific evidence. It is hoped that the Comprehensive System, along with meta-analytic reviews such as Parker et al. (1988), will eventually represent a middle ground that will satisfy hard-nosed empiricists and also will address areas relevant to clinicians.

Part of the reason the Rorschach has continued to have such high popularity is the number of attractive features associated with it. Perhaps part of its allure is the mystery it frequently seems to invoke. How could something as seemingly simple as ten inkblots reveal inner aspects of a person's personality? Such metaphors as "X rays of the mind" have certainly served to enhance its mystery and power. Often, a Rorschach protocol is perceived as something like a deep well, in that the skilled clinician can dip into it again and again, continually coming up with rich and valuable information. The practitioner is framed as a seer and an artist rather than a technician. Indeed, studies tend to support the belief that highly trained Rorschach experts can accurately describe a person's characteristics based on Rorschach responses (Karon, 1978). However, this accuracy has often been dependent more on intuition and clinical lore than on clearly validated interpretive rules.

One frequently noted asset is that the Rorschach is excellent at bypassing a person's conscious resistance and instead assesses a person's underlying, unconscious structure of personality. This asset might be particularly important if a person appears to have an adequate surface level of adjustment yet the clinician suspects there may be some underlying pathology. In contrast, a structured test, such as the MMPI, may have difficulty assessing these more hidden levels of pathology. It is precisely the difficulty in organizing the ambiguous Rorschach stimuli that is likely to bring out these latent levels of pathology. There is some support for this view in that persons with borderline psychopathology have relatively normal performance on structured tests. In contrast, they tend to show clear indications of thought disorder on the far less structured Rorschach (Edell, 1987). Similarly, a relatively hidden trait such as alexithymia has been found in psychosomatic patients, based on their Rorschach responses (Acklin & Bernat, 1987; Keltikangas-Jarvinen, 1986). Frank (1990) reviewed the existing literature and found that the Rorschach was sensitive to underlying schizophrenic processes even prior to their clinical expression.

A related asset is that the Rorschach has often been described as highly resistant to faking. It is argued that, because the true meanings of the Rorschach responses are unknown, the subject cannot easily invent faked responses. Some proponents have even stated that it is virtually impossible to fake a Rorschach. Like many other statements about the Rorschach, this has become quite controversial. Exner (1993) has presented material, from a theoretical and empirical perspective, suggesting that persons developing a Rorschach response go through a series of six stages, one of which is censorship. Subjects seem to come up with far more responses than they present to the examiner, and they select the ones they feel are most appropriate to reveal. Subjects who feel emotionally close to the examiner will tend to provide more responses and conceal less (Leura & Exner, 1978). This raises the possibility that they might also have enough control over their responses to effectively fake a protocol. Thus, responses might depend to a certain extent on social desirability, perceptual accuracy, the context of the assessment, and personal needs. Despite the possibility of censorship, which might potentially lead to undetected faking, Exner and Wylie (1975) have reported that only 1 student in 12 could simulate a schizophrenic profile, even though the students were familiar with protocols from actual schizophrenics. Specifically, malingerers were likely to have longer free associations (presumably because they were censoring and elaborating on their responses), relatively accurate perceptions, and highly dramatic and idiosyncratic responses (i.e., "That's too awful to look at"). Similarly, Frueh and Kinder (1994) found that persons who were malingering with posttraumatic stress disorder provided responses that were overly dramatic, relatively unrestrained, and indicative of an exaggerated sense of impaired reality testing. In contrast, Albert, Fox, and Kahn (1980) found that Rorschach experts did poorly when requested to blindly classify: protocols from normals who were requested to fake paranoid schizophrenia, normals taking a standard administration, and diagnosed paranoid schizophrenics. Computer analyses of the same protocols were likewise unsuccessful in effectively detecting faking (Kahn, Fox, & Rhode, 1988). Although this clearly challenges the unfakability of the Rorschach, the Albert et al. (1980) and Kahn et al. (1988) studies did not simulate the manner in which the Rorschach is likely to be used in clinical practice. Typically, practitioners have knowledge regarding the history of the person, context of the assessment, and behavioral observations, all of which potentially sensitize them to the possibility that a protocol might be faked. Consistent with this was the Frueh and Kinder (1994) study, which found that relevant behavioral observations were at least as important in detecting malingering as the actual scored protocols.

One clear asset of the Rorschach is its ease of administration. The cards can be easily handled, and the total administration time (including inquiry) is typically 50 minutes (Ball, Archer, & Imhof, 1994). In contrast to the relative ease of administration, scoring and interpretation are often quite complicated and time-consuming. Clinicians report that scoring usually takes 45 minutes and interpretation requires 50 minutes more (Ball et al., 1994). This means that, collectively, the entire procedure takes nearly 2.5 hours. However, computer-assisted scoring and interpretation would be expected to reduce significantly the time for both scoring and interpretation.

Alongside the advantages associated with the Rorschach, it has a number of limitations. Although both reliability and validity have generally reached adequate levels, validity is often quite variable across different scoring categories and formulas. Typically, multiple scores and formulas are derived from the Rorschach responses, some of which have relatively good validity and some of which are moderate, controversial, or even nonexistent. It is usually difficult for the average user to appreciate and take into account the disparate levels of validity when actually making his or her interpretations.

Because the Rorschach is one of the most complex psychological tests in current use, error can potentially be introduced from many different directions, including censorship by the subject, scoring errors (particularly for infrequently used scorings), poor handling of the subtleties of interpretation, incorrect incorporation of the implications of age or education, or possible examiner bias (illusory correlation, primacy effects, and so on). One temptation is to reduce the complexity of the data by using a single-sign approach rather than viewing each sign within the context of the overall configuration. Rorschach "elevations" are often subject to a number of possible interpretive hypotheses, so a single-sign approach is particularly open to error. Thus, interpretations must be continually checked and rechecked against the overall Rorschach configuration, additional test data, and the patient's history.

The complexity of the Rorschach also requires that potential users undergo extensive training. Each new scoring category and index that is introduced may add to this problem. In the past, graduate schools would sometimes provide a full-semester course on the Rorschach. Some authors, feeling that this is insufficient, have stated that the optimum amount of time is two full-semester courses devoted exclusively to the Rorschach (Hilsenroth & Handler, 1995), a curriculum that is currently difficult for many programs to justify. First, other tests clearly have superior psychometric properties. Second, the past 25 years have brought a significant increase in the roles and skills required of graduate students, including skills within the area of assessment (neuropsychology, behavioral assessment) as well as within other areas of clinical practice (family therapy, rehabilitation, new modes of intervention, treatment of chronic pain, and so on). Despite these increased requirements, the vast majority of training programs continue to expect trainees to have or to develop skills in the Rorschach (Piotrowski & Keller, 1984; Watkins et al., 1995). Specifically, heads of training programs expect students to have had an average of 22.3 hours of training in the Rorschach and to have given 6.4 administrations (Durand et al., 1988).

A further difficulty associated with the Rorschach is the previous lack of a single, standardized administration and scoring system. This is particularly important because numerous studies have clearly indicated that slight alterations in wording, rapport, and encouragement can significantly alter the numbers and types of responses. The numerous differences in administration and scoring will, it is hoped, be seen in the future as a historical aberration and will be corrected by wide acceptance of the Comprehensive System. However, belief that a single unified system will be accepted should be tempered by recent reviews indicating that between 25% and 33% of Rorschach courses do not use the Comprehensive System (Hilsenroth & Handler, 1995).

The Rorschach has often been considered to be of limited use with children, particularly children under the age of 14 years (Klein, 1986). Reliabilities have been found to be adequate for short-term assessments but clearly inadequate over a long-term basis. Thus, for purposes such as child custody decisions, where longer-term predictions are required, the Rorschach would be quite limited. Any use of the Rorschach for children should make clear that descriptions are only for the short term.

A final consideration, which has implications for both research and practice, is that the large number of variables is likely to produce spurious random significance. Wechsler subtest interpretation has attempted to correct for this possibility by carefully calculating the significance of subtest differences, including correction factors for the number of variables considered (see Chapter 5). In contrast, it is difficult to know when the numerous variables considered in the Rorschach might indicate "significance" simply because of random fluctuations of scores (i.e., a .05 level of significance would mean that "significance" would happen by chance in 1 of 20 variables considered). Rorschach interpreters must therefore take extra caution with their interpretations.

Thus, the Rorschach is difficult to evaluate because of its complexity, its frequent controversy, and the contradiction between its popularity and its reviews. The voluminous research associated with the Rorschach is often both an asset and a limitation. Sorting through the maze of sometimes contradictory findings is often difficult. Directing this wealth of research toward a clear understanding of the interpretive meanings associated with certain patterns of scores is especially difficult. The specific assets of the Rorschach are: potential wealth of information, simplicity of handling, ability to bypass conscious resistance, and possible resistance to faking. Significant weaknesses are: moderate and sometimes quite variable reliabilities and validities, previous lack of standardization, time required for scoring and interpretation, limited use with children, extensive time required for training, and possible introduction of error, especially spurious random significance as a result of the large number of areas considered.

ADMINISTRATION

Examiners should standardize their administration procedures as much as possible. This is particularly important because research has consistently indicated that it is relatively easy to influence a subject's responses. For example, saying the word "good" after each response can increase the overall number of responses on the Rorschach by as much as 50% (Hersen & Greaves, 1971). Similarly, examiners who were told that more experienced examiners elicited a greater proportion of human than animal responses actually produced this pattern from examinees, even though the examiners believed they were providing a standard administration (Exner, Leura, & George, 1976). These findings are consistent with the view that subjects will be particularly responsive to subtle influences when attempting to create clarity in an ambiguous situation such as projective testing. However, if the fluctuations in administration style are minor, they are unlikely to significantly influence a subject's responses (Phares, Stewart, & Foster, 1960; Williams, 1954). In general, examiners should minimize the variations in their administration procedures as much as possible. The following sequence of steps is recommended.

Step 1: Introducing the Respondent to the Technique

One of the most important goals an examiner must initially achieve is to allow the examinee to feel relatively comfortable with the testing procedure. Achieving this goal is complicated by the fact that tests in most cultures are associated with anxiety. Although, in some cases, an increase in anxiety may provide some information that cannot be obtained when the subject is relaxed, anxiety is usually regarded as a hindrance. Typically, anxiety interferes with a person's perceptions and with the free flow of fantasy, both of which are essential for adequate Rorschach responses. Thus, subjects should be as relaxed as possible. Their relaxation can be enhanced by giving a clear introduction to the testing procedure, obtaining personal history, answering questions, and generally avoiding any behavior that might increase the subjects' anxiety. In describing the test, examiners should emphasize relatively neutral words such as "inkblot," "interests," or "imagination," rather than potentially anxiety-provoking words such as "intelligence" or "ambiguous."

For the most part, any specific information regarding what subjects should do or say is to be avoided. The test situation is designed to be ambiguous, and examiners should avoid any statements that might influence the responses. If subjects push for more detailed information about what they should do or what their responses may mean, they should be told that additional questions can be answered after the test is completed.

Step 2: Giving the Testing Instructions

Although some Rorschach systematizers recommend that the subject tell the examiner "everything you see" (Beck, 1961), the Comprehensive System attempts to keep the task as ambiguous as possible. Thus, Exner (1993) recommends that the examiner hand the subject the first card and ask, "What might this be?"

Commentary on, or discussion of, the cards by the examiner should be avoided as much as possible. At times, it might be acceptable to briefly describe how the designs were made or, if questioned regarding what one is supposed to see, the examiner might state, "People see all sorts of things in the blots." Comments from the examiner that indicate the quantity or type of response, or whether the subject can turn the cards, should be strictly avoided. If the subject asks specific questions, such as the type of responses he or she is supposed to give or whether he or she can turn the cards, the examiner might reply that it is up to him or her to decide.

The main objective is to leave the subject maximum freedom to respond to the stimuli in his or her own manner. To enhance this, Exner (1993) strongly recommends that the subject and the examiner not be seated face-to-face, but rather side-by-side, to decrease the possible influence of the examiner's nonverbal behavior. The overall instructions and testing situation should be designed both to keep the task as ambiguous as possible and to keep examiner influence to a minimum.

Step 3: The Response (Association) Phase

Throughout the testing procedure, the basic conditions of step 2 should be adhered to as closely as possible. However, specific situations often arise as subjects are free-associating to the Rorschach designs. If a subject requests specifics on how to respond or asks the examiner for encouragement or approval, examiners should consistently reply that one can respond however one likes. The idea that there are no right or wrong answers might sometimes be mentioned.

The examiner should time the interval that begins when subjects first see the card and ends when they make their initial response, as well as the total time they spend with each card. These measurements can be helpful in revealing the general approach to the card and the possible difficulties in coming up with responses. Cards II, III, and V are generally considered relatively easy to respond to, and usually have shorter reaction times than Cards VI, IX, and X, which typically produce the longest reaction times (Meer, 1955). Because overt timing of subjects' responses is likely to produce anxiety, any recording should be done as inconspicuously as possible. It is recommended that, rather than using a stopwatch, the examiner should glance at a watch or clock and record the minute and second positions for the initial presentation, the first response, and the point at which the subject hands the card back to the examiner.

Exner (1988, 1993) has built in some safeguards to protect against unusually short or extremely long protocols. A client who produces an extremely brief protocol (fewer than fourteen responses) should be immediately retested and provided with a clearer request to provide more responses (Exner, 1993). If a client provides six or more responses to the first inkblot, the examiner should remove the inkblot. On all subsequent inkblots, the same procedure should be used whenever the client provides five or more responses. However, if fewer than six responses to the first inkblot are given, then no other limits on either the first inkblot or any later inkblots should be provided.

Exner (1993) stresses that all responses must be recorded verbatim. To simplify this process, most clinicians develop a series of abbreviations. A set of abbreviations used throughout all the Rorschach systems consists of the symbols (V, >, Λ, <) in which the peak indicates the angle of the card. It is also important to note any odd or unusual responses to the cards, such as an apparent increase in anxiety, wandering of attention, or acting-out on any of the percepts.

Step 4: Inquiry

The inquiry should begin after all ten cards have been administered. Its purpose is to collect the additional information required for an accurate scoring of the responses. It is intended to clarify the responses that have already been given, not to obtain new responses. The inquiry should not end until this goal has been accomplished. Exner (1993) recommends that the instructions for the inquiry should closely approximate the following:

> OK, we've done them all. Now we are going to go back through them. It won't take long. I want you to help me see what you saw. I'm going to read what you said, and then I want you to show me where on the blot you saw it and what there is that makes it look like that, so that I can see it too. I'd like to see it just like you did, so help me now. Do you understand? (p. 75)

Following closely the general theme of the overall administration, the inquiry should not influence the subject's responses. Thus, any questions should be as nondirective as possible. One should begin by merely repeating what the subject has said, and then waiting. Usually, the subject will begin to clarify his or her response. If this information is insufficient to clarify how to score the response, the examiner might become slightly more directive by asking, "What about it made it look like a [percept]?" The examiner should not ask, "Is it mainly the shape?" or "How important was the color?" These questions are far too directive and are worded in a way that can exert influence on the subject's descriptions of his or her responses. The examiner should consistently avoid leading the subject or indicating how he or she should respond. Particular skill is required when clarifying a determinant that has been unclearly articulated but merely implied.

The outcome of a well-conducted inquiry is the collection of information that is sufficient to decide on scoring for location and determinants. If, on the location, information based on the subject's verbal response is insufficient, the examiner should have the subject point to the percept. An additional feature of the inquiry is to test the subject's awareness of his or her responses. For example, does a strange percept represent coherent creativity, or does it reflect a lack of contact with the environment, with the subject perhaps having no awareness of the strangeness of his or her responses? The overall approach of the inquiry is to word questions in such a way as to be flexible without being too directive.

SCORING

The next step following administration is to code the different categories and calculate the different quantitative formulas in the structural summary. There is general agreement throughout the different Rorschach systems that these categories include location, determinants, content, and popularity. The Comprehensive System also includes 12 special scores for such responses as unusual verbalizations and aggressive movement. After these have been coded and tallied, a series of quantitative summaries, including six Special Indices, are created based on reorganizations of, and comparisons among, the scores on the different categories.

The following subsections merely list, outline, and define the scoring categories and quantitative summaries. To achieve accurate scoring, it would be necessary to consult Exner's scoring criteria (1993) or to implement his workbook (Exner, 1990, *A Rorschach*

Workbook for the Comprehensive System), which includes specific scoring criteria, tables, charts, and diagrams. The inclusion of specific scoring criteria is beyond the scope of this chapter. The focus here is on providing a key to interpretation that is concise, accountable, and clearly organized. The following definitions and the accompanying tables serve to outline and to briefly define the primary Rorschach factors.

Location

The location of the responses refers to the area of the inkblot that is used (Table 9–1). This can vary from the use of the entire blot (whole response) to the use of an unusual detail (Dd). Unusual details are defined as location responses made by less than 5% of subjects. Exner also specifies coding for Developmental Quality, which is determined by evaluating each location score in relation to its degree of integration. Table 9–2 presents the criteria used for scoring the respective Developmental Quality codes. Thus, each location response is given both a designation for the specific area of the blot and a symbol to indicate the quality of that response.

Determinants

Determinants refer to the style or characteristic of the blot to which the examinee responds, such as its shape, color, or texture (Table 9–3). The determinants also receive a scoring for their level of form quality (Table 9–4). The form quality scoring refers to how accurately the percept relates to the form of the inkblot. For example, an angel on Card I is considered to be an "ordinary" form quality response, which is empirically reflected in the fact that nonpsychiatric populations perceive it far more frequently than psychiatric patients. Initially, examiners should give a percept its appropriate classification regarding its determinants. This should then be followed by scoring the determinant for its relative form quality. Descriptions of the different form qualities are included in Table 9–4; however, for specific empirically derived form quality codings, examiners need to consult Exner's (1993) tables.

One relevant coding that should be added to all movement responses is the extent to which the movement is active versus passive. Active movement would include such

Table 9–1.   Symbols used for coding the location of Rorschach responses

Symbol	Definition	Criterion
W	Whole response	Where the entire blot is used in the response. All portions must be used.
D	Common detail response	A frequently identified area of the blot.
Dd	Unusual detail response	An infrequently identified area of the blot.
S	Space response	A white-space area is used in the response (scored only with another location symbol, as in WS, DS, DdS).

Source: From *The Rorschach: A Comprehensive System. Volume I: Basic Foundations* (3rd ed.), p. 94, by J. E. Exner, Jr., 1993, New York: John Wiley & Sons, Inc. Copyright © 1993 by John Exner, Jr. Reprinted with permission.

Table 9–2.   Symbols and criteria used for coding developmental quality

Symbol	Definition	Criterion
+	Synthesized response	Unitary or discrete portions of the blot are articulated and combined into a single answer. Two or more objects are described as separate but related. At least *one* of the objects involved must have a specific form demand, or be described in a manner that creates a specific form demand.
v/ +	Synthesized response	Unitary or discrete portions of the blot are articulated and combined into a single answer. Two or more objects are described as separate but related. None of the objects involved has a specific form demand, or is articulated in a way to create a specific form demand.
o	Ordinary response	A discrete area of the blot is selected and articulated so as to emphasize the outline and structural features of the object. The object reported has a natural form demand, or the description of the object is such as to create a specific form demand.
v	Vague response	A diffuse or general impression is offered to the blot or blot area in a manner that avoids the necessity of articulating specific outlines or structural features. The object reported has no specific form demand, and the articulation does not introduce a specific form demand for the object reported.

Source: From *The Rorschach: A Comprehensive System. Volume I: Basic Foundations* (3rd ed.), p. 99, by J. E. Exner, Jr., 1993, New York: John Wiley & Sons, Inc. Copyright © 1993 by John Exner, Jr. Reprinted with permission.

movements as "fleeing" or "lifting" whereas more passive movements might include "meditating" or "anchored." Whether a movement is active or passive is designated with either an "a" (for active) or a "p" (for passive) superscript. These are later scored and used for interpretation in the quantitative summaries (see "The Ideation Section," below).

In approximately 20% of all responses, more than one determinant is used to make a single response. These are referred to as *blends* and are designated by indicating the two (or more) determinants and placing a full stop (.) between them. The most important determinant is placed in front of the other determinant(s) and is considered the primary determinant. Less important determinants are placed after the primary one and are referred to as secondary or tertiary (if a third one is present).

A further score related exclusively to form determinants is the degree of Organizational Activity (Z) involved in creating the response. However, Organizational Activity is given only if at least one of the following three conditions is present:

1. A W response with codings of +, v/+, or o (Wv responses are not scored for Organizational Activity).

Table 9–3. Symbols and criteria for determinant coding

Category	Symbol	Criteria
Form	*F*	*Form answers.* To be used separately for responses based exclusively on form features of the blot, or in combination with other determinant symbols (except *M* & *m*) when the form features have contributed to the formulation of the answer.
Movement	*M*	*Human movement response.* To be used for responses involving the kinesthetic activity of a human, or of an animal or fictional character in humanlike activity.
	FM	*Animal movement response.* To be used for responses involving a kinesthetic activity of an animal. The movement perceived must be congruent to the species identified in the content. Animals reported in movement *not* common to their species should be coded as *M.*
	m	*Inanimate movement response.* To be used for responses involving the movement of inanimate, inorganic, or insensate objects.
Chromatic Color	*C*	*Pure color response.* To be used for answers based exclusively on the chromatic color features of the blot. *No* form is involved.
	CF	*Color-form response.* To be used for answers that are formulated *primarily* because of the chromatic color features of the blot. Form features *are* used, but are of secondary importance.
	FC	*Form-color response.* To be used for answers that are created mainly because of form features. Chromatic color is also used, but is of secondary importance.
	Cn	*Color naming response.* To be used when the colors of the blot or blot areas are identified by *name,* and with the intention of giving a response.
Achromatic Color	*C'*	*Pure achromatic color response.* To be used when the response is based exclusively on the gray, black, or white features of the blot, when they are clearly used as color. *No* from is involved.
	C'F	*Achromatic color-form response.* To be used for responses that are formulated *mainly* because of the black, white, or gray features, clearly used as color. Form features *are* used, but are of secondary importance.
	FC'	*Form-achromatic color response.* To be used for answers that are based *mainly* on the form features. The achromatic features, clearly used as color, are also included, but are of secondary importance.
Shading-Texture	*T*	*Pure texture response.* To be used for answers in which the shading components of the blot are translated to represent a tactual phenomenon, with no consideration to the form features.
	TF	*Texture-form response.* To be used for responses in which the shading features of the blot are interpreted as tactual, and form is used secondarily, for purposes of elaboration and/or clarification.
	FT	*Form-texture response.* To be used for responses that are based *mainly* on the form features. Shading features of the blot are translated as tactual, but are of secondary importance.

(continued)

Table 9–3. *(continued)*

Category	Symbol	Criteria
Shading-Dimension	*V*	*Pure vista response.* To be used for answers in which the shading features are interpreted as depth or dimensionality. *No* form is involved.
	VF	*Vista-form response.* To be used for responses in which the shading features are interpreted as depth or dimensionality. Form features are included, but are of secondary importance.
	FV	*Form-vista response.* To be used for answers that are based *mainly* on the form features of the blot. Shading features are also interpreted to note depth and/or dimensionality, but are of secondary importance to the formulation of the answer.
Shading-Diffuse	*Y*	*Pure shading response.* To be used for responses that are based exclusively on the light-dark features of the blot that are completely formless and do not involve reference to either texture or dimension.
	YF	*Shading-form response.* To be used for responses based primarily on the light-dark features of the blot. Form features are included, but are of secondary importance.
	FY	*Form-shading response.* To be used for responses that are based *mainly* on the form features of the blot. The light-dark features of the blot are included as elaboration and/or clarification and are secondary to the use of form.
Form Dimension	*FD*	*Form-based dimensional response.* To be used for answers in which the impression of depth, distance, or dimensionality is created by using the elements of size and/or shape of contours. *No* use of shading is involved in creating this impression.
Pairs & Reflections	(2)	*The pair response.* To be used for answers in which two identical objects are reported, based on the symmetry of the blot. The objects must be equivalent in all respects, but must *not* be identified as being reflected or as mirror images.
	rF	*Reflection-form response.* To be used for answers in which the blot or blot area is reported as a reflection or mirror image, because of the symmetry of the blot. The object or content reported has no specific form requirement, as in clouds, landscape, shadows, etc.
	Fr	*Form-reflection response.* To be used for answers in which the blot or blot area is identified as reflected or a mirror image, based on the symmetry of the blot. The substance of the response is based on form features, and the object reported has a specific form demand.

Source: From *The Rorschach: A Comprehensive System. Volume I: Basic Foundations* (3rd ed.), pp. 104–105, by J. E. Exner, Jr., 1993, New York: John Wiley & Sons, Inc. Copyright © 1993 by John Exner, Jr. Reprinted with permission.

Table 9–4.   Symbols and criteria for coding form quality

Symbol	Definition	Criterion
+	Superior-overelaborated	The unusually precise articulation of the use of form in a manner that tends to enrich the quality of the response without sacrificing the appropriateness of the form use. The + answer need not be original, but rather unique by the manner in which details are defined and by which the form is used and specified.
o	Ordinary	The obvious, easily articulated use of form features to define an object reported frequently by others. The answer is commonplace and easy to see. There is no unusual enrichment of the answer by overelaboration of the form features.
u	Unusual	A low-frequency response in which the basic contours involved are not significantly violated. These are uncommon answers that are seen quickly and easily by the observer.
−	Minus	The distorted, arbitrary, unrealistic use of form in creating a response. The answer is imposed on the blot structure with total, or near total disregard for the structure of the area being used in creating the response. Often, arbitrary contours will be created where none exists.

Source: From *The Rorschach: A Comprehensive System. Volume I: Basic Foundations* (3rd ed.), p. 152, by J. E. Exner, Jr., 1993, New York: John Wiley & Sons, Inc. Copyright © 1993 by John Exner, Jr. Reprinted with permission.

2. The response gives some sort of meaningful integration to two or more areas (either adjacent or nonadjacent).
3. The white space is given some sort of meaningful integration with other areas of the blot.

Specific converted weightings (ranging between 1 and 6.5) are given to integrative efforts for different types of responses and are provided in Exner (1993, p. 147). For example, the degree of organization required to integrate a whole response to Card I is considered to be much less (Z would only equal 1.0) than that required to integrate the much more fragmented details of Card X (Z would equal a much greater 5.5).

Content

The scoring of content is based on the type and quantity of specific subjects that examinees perceive in their responses. Each Rorschach system uses different lists of content categories, although they all agree on such basic contents as human, human detail, and animal. Table 9–5 provides a listing of Exner's content categories, with the symbol and criterion for each category.

When two or more content categories occur in the same response, they should both be coded and a comma should be placed between the two (or more) codings. If contents occur that are not on the list, they should be designated as idiographic (Id) and the unique name of the content should be written out.

Table 9–5. Symbols and criteria used for coding content

Category	Symbol	Criterion
Whole Human	H	Involving the percept of a whole human form. If the percept involves a *real* historical figure, such as Napoleon, Joan of Arc, etc., the content code Ay should be added as a secondary code.
Whole Human (fictional or mythological)	(H)	Involving the percept of a whole human form that is fictional or mythological, such as clowns, fairies, giants, witches, fairy-tale characters, ghosts, dwarfs, devils, angels, science fiction creatures that are humanoid, humanlike monsters.
Human Detail	Hd	Involving the percept of an incomplete human form, such as an arm, leg, fingers, feet, the lower part of a person, a person without a head.
Human Detail (fictional or mythological	(Hd)	Involving the percept of an incomplete human form that is fictional or mythological, such as the head of the devil, the arm of a witch, the eyes of an angel, parts of science-fiction creatures that are humanoid, and all masks.
Human Experience	Hx	Involving the percept of human emotion or sensory experience such as love, hate, depression, happiness, sound, smell, fear, etc. Most answers in which Hx is coded will also include the use of AB as a special score.
Whole Animal	A	Involving the percept of a whole animal form.
Whole Animal (fictional or mythological)	(A)	Involving the percept of a whole animal that is fictional or mythological, such as a unicorn, dragon, magic frog, flying horse, Black Beauty, Jonathan Livingston Seagull.
Animal Detail	Ad	Involving the percept of an incomplete animal form, such as the hoof of a horse, claw of a lobster, head of a dog, animal skin.
Animal Detail (fictional or mythological)	(Ad)	Involving the percept of an incomplete animal form that is fictional or mythological such as the wing of Pegasus, the head of Peter Rabbit, the legs of Pooh Bear.
Anatomy	An	Used for responses in which the content is skeletal, muscular, or of internal anatomy, such as bone structure, skull, rib cage, heart, lungs, stomach, liver, muscle fiber, vertebrae, brain. If the response involves a tissue slide, the code Art should be added as secondary.
Art	Art	Involving percepts of paintings, drawings, or illustrations, either abstract or definitive, art objects, such as statues, jewelry, chandelier, candelabra, crests, badges, seals, and decorations.

Table 9–5. *(continued)*

Category	Symbol	Criterion
Anthropology	*Ay*	Involving percepts that have a specific cultural or historical connotation such as totem, Roman helmet, Magna Carta, *Santa Maria,* Napoleon's hat, Cleopatra's crown, arrowhead, prehistoric axe.
Blood	*Bl*	Involving the percept of blood, either human or animal.
Botany	*Bt*	Involving the percept of any plant life such as bushes, flowers, seaweed, trees, or parts of plant life, such as leaves, petals, tree trunk, root.
Clothing	*Cg*	Involving the percept of any article of clothing such as, hat, boots, belt, necktie, jacket, trousers, scarf.
Clouds	*Cl*	Used specifically for the content cloud. Variations of this category, such as fog or mist, are coded *Na.*
Explosion	*Ex*	Involving percepts of a blast or explosion, including fireworks.
Fire	*Fi*	Involving percepts of fire or smoke.
Food	*Fd*	Involving the percept of any edible, such as fried chicken, ice cream, fried shrimp, vegetables, cotton candy, chewing gum, steak, a filet of fish.
Geography	*Ge*	Involving the percept of a map, specified or unspecified.
Household	*Hh*	Involving percepts of household items, such as bed, chair, lamp, silverware, plate, cup, glass, cooking utensil, carving knife, lawn chair, garden hose, rug (excluding animal skin rug, which is coded *Ad*).
Landscape	*Ls*	Involving percepts of landscape, such as mountain, mountain range, hill, island, cave, rocks, desert, swamp, or seascapes, such as coral reef or underwater scene.
Nature	*Na*	Used for a broad variety of contents from the natural environment that are not coded as *Bt* or *Ls,* such as sun, moon, planet, sky, water, ocean, river, ice, snow, rain, fog, mist, rainbow, storm, tornado, night, raindrop.
Science	*Sc*	Involving percepts that are associated with, or are the products of science or science fiction, such as microscope, telescope, weapons, rocket ships, motors, space ships, ray guns, airplane, ship, train, car, motorcycle, light bulb, TV aerial, radar station.

(continued)

Table 9–5.   *(continued)*

Category	Symbol	Criterion
Sex	*Sx*	Involving percepts of sex organs or activity of a sexual nature, such as penis, vagina, buttocks, breast (except if used to delineate a female figure), testes, menstruation, abortion, intercourse. *Sx* is usually scored as a secondary content. Primary contents are typically *H, Hd,* or *An.*
X-ray	*Xy*	Used specifically for the content of X-ray and may include either skeletal or organs. When *Xy* is coded, *An* is *not* included as a secondary code.

Source: From *The Rorschach: A Comprehensive System. Volume 1: Basic Foundations* (3rd ed.), pp. 158–159, by J. E. Exner, Jr., 1993, New York: John Wiley & Sons, Inc. Copyright © 1993 by John Exner, Jr. Reprinted with permission.

Popular Responses

Rorschach popular (P) scoring refers to the presence of frequently perceived responses. Although different systems have somewhat varying lists of populars, Exner (1993) has used, as the cutoff for inclusion as a popular, an occurrence at least once in every three protocols from nonpsychiatric populations. Exner's list of popular responses is detailed in Table 9–6.

Table 9–6.   Popular responses selected for the comprehensive system based on the frequency of occurrences of at least once in every three protocols given by nonpatient adult subjects and nonschizophrenic adult patients

Card	Location	Criterion	% Nonpatient Reporting	% Nonschizophrenic Reporting
I	*W*	Bat. The response always involves the whole blot.	48	38
I	*W*	Butterfly. The response always involves the whole blot.	40	36
II	*D*1	Animal forms, usually the heads of dogs, bears, elephants, or lambs; however, the frequency of the whole animal to this area is sufficient to warrant the scoring of *P.*	34	35
III	*D*1 or *D*9	Two human figures, or representations thereof, such as dolls and caricatures. The scoring of *P* is also applicable to the percent of a single human figure to area *D*9.	89	70

Table 9–6.   *(continued)*

Card	Location	Criterion	% Nonpatient Reporting	% Nonschizophrenic Reporting
IV	*W* or *D7*	A human or humanlike figure such as giant, monster, science fiction creature, etc.	53	41
V	*W*	Butterfly, the apex of the card upright or inverted. The whole blot *must* be used.	46	43
V	*W*	Bat, the apex of the card upright or inverted, and involving the whole blot.	36	38
VI	*W* or *D1*	Animal skin, hide, rug, or pelt. The *P* is also scored when a whole animal is given, provided reference is made to the back, skin, or hide.	87	35
VII	*D1* or *D9*	Human head or face, specifically identified as female, child, Indian, or with gender not identified. If *D1* is used, the upper segment (*D5*) is usually identified as hair, feather, etc. If the response includes the entire *D2* area, *P* is coded if the head or face is restricted to the *D9* area. If *Dd23* is included as part of the human form, the response is *not* coded as *P*.	59	47
VIII	*D1*	Whole animal figure. This is the most frequently perceived common answer, the content varying considerably, such as bear, dog, rodent, fox, wolf, and coyote. All are *P*. The *P* is also coded when the animal figure is reported as part of the *W* percept as in a family crest, seal, and emblem.	94	91
IX	*D3*	Human or humanlike figures such as witches, giants, science fiction creatures, monsters, etc.	54	24
X	*D1*	Spider with all appendages restricted to the *D1* area.	42	34
X	*D1*	Crab with all appendages restricted to the *D1* area. Other variations of multilegged animals are not *P*.	37	38

Source: From *The Rorschach: A Comprehensive System. Volume I: Basic Foundations* (3rd ed.), p. 24, by J. E. Exner, Jr., 1993, New York: John Wiley & Sons, Inc. Copyright © 1993 by John Exner, Jr. Reprinted with permission.

Special Scores

The Comprehensive System also includes 14 Special Scoring categories that were developed to take into account unusual characteristics of the response such as unusual verbalizations or inappropriate logic. These are listed, along with their definitions, in Table 9–7. A weighted sum of the first six categories (WSum6) is also required. The weightings are as follows: Deviant Verbalization (DV) = 1, Deviant Response (DR) = 3, Incongruous Combination (INCOM) = 2, Fabulized Combination (FABCOM) = 4,

Table 9–7.   Symbols and descriptions for special scores

Special Score (Symbol)	Description
Deviant Verbalization (DV)	*Verbalizations, associated with a response, that are odd and suggest some form of cognitive slippage has occurred, such as through neologisms or redundancies (i.e., "pair of two").
Deviant Response (DR)*	Responses that involve a longer segment of the response than verbalizations, such as through inappropriate phrases or circumstantial responses that are long, rambling, and unrelated to the inkblot.
Incongruous Combination (INCOM)*	Images that have been inappropriately merged into a single object.
Fabulized Combination (FABCOM)*	Implausible relationships between two or more portions of the inkblot.
Inappropriate Logic (ALOG)	Spontaneously offered justification of the response, using strained logic.
Contamination (CONTAM)*	Two or more impressions that have been inappropriately fused together.
Perseveration (PSV)	Providing either an identical or almost identical response two or more times in a row, or seeing the same object repeatedly ("There's that man again").
Confabulation (CONFAB)	Response related to only one detail of the inkblot but generalized to other portions.
Aggressive Movement (AG)	Any movement response that is clearly aggressive.
Cooperative Movement (COP)	Any movement response that is clearly cooperative.
Morbid Content (MOR)	Content is characterized by death or damage, or is designated as being dysphoric.
Abstractions (AB)	Symbolic representation is given to the content.
Personal (PER)	Reference to personal knowledge or experience is used to justify or clarify response.
Color Projection (CP)	Identification of an achromatic portion of an inkblot as being colored.

* These Special Scores are rated as either Level 1, indicating a mild to modest level of cognitive slippage, or Level 2, indicating that the level of cognitive slippage is moderate to severe.

Inappropriate Logic (ALOG) = 5, and Contamination (CONTAM) = 7. A weighted score is given each time the scoring is given. For example, three occurrences of Deviant Response (DR) would equal a sum weighted score of 9.

STRUCTURAL SUMMARY

After the examinee's responses have been coded according to locations, determinants, contents, populars, and special scorings, they are listed and rearranged into frequency summaries and quantitative formulas. The quantitative formulas are comprised of various ratios, percentages, and derivations. These formulas reflect the proportions of, and comparisons among, various Rorschach factors. After the quantitative formulas have been calculated, they become the primary focus on which Rorschach interpretations are made. Exner (1993) has categorized the formulas into a Core section followed by sections for Ideation, Affect, Mediation, Processing, Interpersonal, Self-Perception, and Special Indices (Depression Index, Obsessive Style Index, and so on). These sections provide a convenient way to thematically organize the different interpretations. The descriptions and their sequence closely follow those outlined by Exner (1993). The various scorings, frequencies, and formulas can be conveniently summarized on a commercially available record form that includes a *Structural Summary Blank* as well as a *Constellation Worksheet* for calculating the Special Indices.

The Core Section

The core section includes the frequencies for the total number of responses (R), the total number for each of the determinants, and the following nine quantitative formulas:

1. **Lambda (L):**

$$\frac{\text{F (number of responses having only Pure F determinants)}}{\text{R} - \text{F (total R minus Pure Form answers)}}$$

In calculating Lambda, only responses involving form are used (F, M, CF, and so on) and not determinants without form (C, C′, T, and so on).

2. **Experience Balance or Erlebnistypus (EB):** EB is the relationship between human movement responses and the weighted sum of the chromatic color responses. The ratio is expressed as Sum M : The Weighted Sum Color (WSumC). The Weighted Sum Color side of the ratio is calculated according to the following formula:

$$\text{WSumC} = (0.5) \times \text{FC} + (1.0) \times \text{CF} + (1.5) \times \text{C.}$$

All human movement responses are included in the formula, regardless of whether they are the major determinant of the response. Color naming responses are not included.

3. **Experience Actual (EA):**

Sum of Human Movement + Weighted Sum Color.

4. **Experience Pervasive (EBPer):** Experience Pervasive is calculated by dividing the larger number in the EB ratio by the smaller one. This is done only when a marked difference (style) is evident in the EB ratio. Exner (1993) clarifies this by stating that "if the value of EA is 10.0 or less, one side of the EB must be *at least two points* greater than the other side, or if the value of EA is more than 10.0, one side of the EB must be *at least* 2.5 points greater than the other" (p. 184).

5. **Experience Base (eb):** The Experience Base ratio compares all nonhuman movement determinants (FM + m) with the sum of all the shading and achromatic color determinants. It is summarized by the following ratio:

Sum FM + m : Sum All C′ + All T + All Y + All V.

6. **Experienced Stimulation (es):** This calculation merely requires adding together the two sides of the Experience Base ratio:

Sum of All Nonhuman Movement + Sum of All Shading or Achromatic Features

or

Sum (FM + m) + Sum (C′ + T + Y + V).

7. **The D Score (D):** This is determined by first subtracting es from EA (EA − es) and designating whether the resulting number is a plus or minus number. The resulting raw score can then be converted into a standard score by consulting a conversion table provided in Exner (1993, p. 185).

8. **Adjusted es (Adj es):** All but 1m and 1Y (this also includes FY and YF) are subtracted from es.

9. **Adjusted D Score (Adj/D):** This is simply calculated by subtracting Adj es from EA (EA − Adj es). This produces a raw score that is converted to a standard score by using the same conversion table used in calculating the standard score for D score (see Exner, 1993, p. 185).

The Ideation Section

This section consists of frequency data for M−, M, number of Level 2 responses, WSum6, and M with no FQ. In addition, there are three formulas:

1. **Active:Passive Ratio (a:p):** This is calculated by adding up the total number of active movement responses and comparing it with the total number of passive movement responses:

$$M^a + FM^a + m^a : M^p + FM^p + m^p$$

2. **M Active: Passive Ratio ($M^a : M^p$):** In contrast to the previous active: passive ratio, this ratio refers only to active or passive responses relating to human movement and is calculated by simply inserting the total number of active human movements on the left side of the ratio and the total number of passive human movements on the right side.

3. **The Intellectualization Index:** This is calculated by multiplying the total number of Abstract (AB) responses by 2, and adding the sum of Art and Ay responses according to the following formula:

$$2AB + (Art + Ay)$$

The Affect Section

Rorschach indicators of affect include frequency of Pure C, S, and CP, as well as three quantitative formulas:

1. **Form-Color Ratio [(FC : (CF + C)]:** This ratio indicates the total number of form-dominated chromatic color responses, as compared with the absolute number of color-dominant chromatic responses. To calculate this formula, each of the chromatic color determinants is weighted equally as 1. Cn determinants are also included on the left side of the ratio because they are considered color-dominant responses.

2. **Affective Ratio (Afr):** The Affective ratio is comprised of the total number of responses to the last three cards, compared with those given to the first seven cards, or:

$$\frac{\text{Sum of Responses to Last 3 Cards [Sum R(VIII + IX + X)]}}{\text{Sum of Responses to First 7 Cards [Sum R(I–VII)]}}$$

3. **Blends : R (Complexity Index):** This compares the total number of blend responses (entered on the left side of the ratio) with the total number of responses (R).

The Mediation Section

The mediation section includes the total number of Popular responses along with the following five percentages.

1. **Conventional Form (X + %):**

$$\frac{\text{Sum FQx + and o}}{R}$$

2. **Conventional Pure Form (F + %):**

$$\frac{\text{Sum F+ and Fo}}{\text{Sum F}}$$

3. **Distorted Form (X−%):**

$$\frac{\text{Sum FQ}-}{\text{R}}$$

4. **White Space Distortion (S−%):** The percentage for White Space Distortion is comprised of the total number of distorted form answers that have used the white space:

$$\frac{\text{Sum SQ}-}{\text{Sum FQx}-}$$

5. **Unusual Form (Xu%):** Unusual Form is a measure of the extent to which the contours of the inkblots have been used appropriately but unconventionally:

$$\frac{\text{Sum FQxu}}{\text{R}}$$

The Processing Section

This section includes three simple sets of frequency data—for Zf (total number of times an Organizational Activity response has occurred), DQ+ (Developmental Quality+), and DQv (Developmental Quality)—along with three ratios:

1. **Economy Index (W:D:Dd):** This index is developed by simply listing the total number of whole (W) responses on the left, the total number of D responses in the middle, and the total number of Dd responses on the right.

2. **Aspirational Ratio (W:M):** The ratio of W to M represents a comparison between the total number of whole responses (placed on the left side of the ratio) and the total number of human movement responses (placed on the right side).

3. **Processing Efficiency (Zd):** Processing Efficiency is a difference score. It is necessary to estimate what the Organizational Activity scores should be (Zest) by first summing the total number of times an Organizational Activity response occurred in a protocol (without taking into account the weightings) and then applying these values to a table provided by Exner (1993, p. 182). Next, the sum of all the weighted scores for Organizational Activity (ZSum) is calculated. Finally, Zest is subtracted from ZSum:

$$\text{ZSum} - \text{Zest.}$$

This allows an estimate of how much more Organizational Activity was actually used compared to how much would have been expected to be used, based simply on the total number of Organizational Activity occurrences (without their weightings).

The Interpersonal Section

This section is comprised of three sets of frequency calculations—for numbers of Cooperative Movements (COP), Aggressive Movements (AG), and primary and secondary Food contents (Fd)—plus four ratios:

1. **Isolation Index (Isolate/R):** Calculation of this index requires noting the total number of content responses for Botany (Bt), Clouds (Cl), Geography (Ge), Landscape (Ls), and Nature (Na). Contents for Clouds (Cl) and Nature (Na) are then multiplied by 2 and added to the number of responses for the rest of the contents. This sum is then divided by the total number of responses:

$$\frac{Bt + Cl + Ge + Ls + 2Na}{R}.$$

2. **Interpersonal Interest H:(H)+ Hd + (Hd):** The sum of responses that are Pure H is entered on the left side, and the sum of human interest contents—Hd and (Hd)—is entered on the right side.

3. **(H) + (Hd):(A) + (Ad):** This summarizes the frequencies of parenthesized (fictional/mythological) human and human detail responses and compares them with the total number of parenthesized (fictional/mythological) animal and animal detail responses.

4. **H + A:Hd + Ad:** This summarizes and compares the total number of whole human and animal contents with the total number of human detail and animal detail contents. Parenthesized human and animal contents are also included.

The Self-Perception Section

This section includes four frequency tallies for:

1. Sum of form-reflection and reflection-form responses (Fr + rF).
2. Total number of Form Dimension (FD) responses.
3. Total number of responses that have morbid content (MOR).
4. Sum of all responses that have content related to Anatomy (An) or X ray (Xy; primary or secondary).

The final component of this subsection is a ratio related to the number of pair responses:

1. **Egocentricity Index [3r + (2)/R]:** This index gives three times the weighting to reflection responses (r) compared to pair responses (2) and compares these to the total number of responses (R):

$$\frac{3 \times (Fr + rF) + Sum\ (2)}{R}.$$

Special Indices

Exner (1993) has developed the following six Special Indices:

1. Schizophrenia Index (SCZI).
2. Depression Index (DEPI).
3. Coping Deficit Index (CDI).
4. Suicide Constellation (S-CON).

  5. Hypervigilance Index (HVI).
  6. Obsessive Style Index (OBS).

The procedure for calculating these indices is more complex than for the other formulas and will not be covered in the present section. However, scoring criteria and cutoff scores can be found in Exner (1993, p. 189) and on the commercially available record form under a section designated as the *Constellations Worksheet*. Summaries of interpretive hypotheses for these indices are included in the next section of this chapter.

INTERPRETATION

The following description of interpretive information is meant to serve as a reference guide to alert Rorschach interpreters to a potentially wide range of possible interpretive hypotheses. Even though the format is as concise as possible, interpreters should be aware of the tremendous richness inherent in most Rorschach data. Effective interpreters should also have this richness reflected in the wide variety of possible interpretive hypotheses they generate. A mere labeling or simplistic "sign" approach should be avoided. Rather, clinicians must begin and end by continually being aware of the total overall configuration of the data. For example, the same number of C responses in two protocols can easily have quite different meanings, depending on the implications from, and interactions with, other aspects of the Rorschach data.

The typical sequence for Rorschach interpretation should follow the general conceptual model for testing developed by Maloney and Ward (1976) and discussed in Chapter 1. The model requires that clinicians initially take a propositional stance toward the protocol (phase 2). The purpose of this stage is to develop as many tentative hypotheses as possible, based on the quantitative data, verbalizations, and client history. The number and accuracy of these hypotheses will depend on the individual richness of the data as well as on the individual skill and creativity of the clinician. The final stage is the integration of the hypotheses into a meaningful and accurate description of the person (phase 4). This involves rejecting, modifying, or confirming previously developed hypotheses (phase 3). When this has been accomplished, clinicians can integrate the Rorschach interpretations into the overall report itself (phases 5, 6, and 7).

In the description of different interpretive hypotheses, continual reference is made to "high" and "low" scores. These relative weightings are based on extensive normative data that have been accumulated on the Rorschach. For comparisons of scores on individual protocols with normative ratings, clinicians can refer to Appendixes L and M, which provide means, standard deviations, and other relevant descriptive statistics for the different Rorschach factors and quantitative formulas.

The sequence of presenting interpretive information is first organized around specific scoring categories (Location, Determinants, Contents, Special Scorings). These are followed by scorings according to the different quantitative formulas (ratios, percentages, and derivations; Exner, 1993). Each listing of interpretive hypotheses is presented in the sequence given in the Structural Summary. In particular, the listing of the quantitative formulas begins with the Core section and then proceeds to the clusters of scores for Ideation, Affect, Mediation, Processing, Interpersonal, Self-Perception, and

Special Indices. These later groupings should provide a conceptually consistent means of organizing relevant interpretive material around functional domains, thereby enabling the different interpretations to be more easily integrated into the psychological report. For example, if a practitioner is interested in understanding issues related to interpersonal relationships, he or she can note the Rorschach data relevant to this area of functioning. Similarly, information related to dealing with affect can be noted in the section on affect. These interpretations can then be compared, contrasted, and modified with other assessment material on these dimensions. Table 9–8 outlines the different interpretive categories in the sequence in which they are presented for interpretation.

The process of reading through the many interpretations in the remainder of the chapter can potentially be tedious because of their sheer quantity. To deal with the quantity of interpretations, it is recommended that the practitioner initially skim over the different sections and interpretations. Next, a Rorschach protocol might be obtained through actually administering and scoring a Rorschach, requesting one from a colleague, or using one from one of Exner's books. The practitioner can then go through each of the different categories and generate hypotheses based on the client's results. The hypotheses can be integrated into a description of the person, based on domains measured by the Rorschach variables. This sequence would optimally make the information relevant and engaging as well as enhance the development of actual clinical skills.

Location

In general, the area of the inkblot to which examinees choose to respond is a reflection of the overall style in which they approach their world. This is especially true for the manner in which they confront uncertainties and ambiguities in their lives. For example, one person might perceive only the most obvious and concrete aspects of a situation, whereas another might avoid important aspects of a stimulus by focusing on small details and neglecting potentially more significant issues. An analysis of Rorschach locations does not provide information regarding why people approach their world in a certain manner; rather, it is limited to a description of their particular style.

Rorschach locations can be divided into usual and unusual features, depending on the area of the inkblot that is used. Frequently used locations, if they are within the normal number and of good quality, usually reflect good ties with reality, intelligence, ambition, good reasoning, and an ability to generalize. Unusual locations involving rarely used areas of the blot are associated with neurotic symptomatology, such as fears, anxiety, and obsessive or compulsive tendencies. An extreme use of unusual features may reflect more serious psychopathology (Exner, 1993).

Whole Response (W)

The whole response is related to the degree to which a person can interact in an efficient and active manner with his or her environment. This is particularly true if the quality and organization of the responses are good. Whereas whole responses occur with the greatest frequency in children from 3 to 4 years of age (Ames, Metraux, & Walker, 1971; Exner & Weiner, 1995), there is a gradual decline in later childhood and adolescence until 30% to 40% of normal adult responses are wholes. The average adult ratio of whole:detail is approximately 1:2 (refer also to interpretation of W:M and W:D:Dd formulas).

Table 9–8. Scoring and interpretive domains for the comprehensive system

Location

Whole Response (W)

Common Detail (D)

Unusual Detail (Dd)

Space (S)

Developmental Quality (DQ)

Determinants

Form (F)

Human Movement (M)

Animal Movement (FM)

Inanimate Movement (m)

Color Chromatic (C)

Color Achromatic (C')

Shading—Texture (T)

Shading—Dimension (Vista; V)

Shading—Diffuse (Y)

Form Dimension (FD)

Pairs (2) and Reflections (Fr)

Organizational Activity (Z)

Content

Human and Human Detail (H, Hd)

Animal and Animal Detail (A, Ad)

Anatomy and X Ray (An, Xy)

Food (Fd)

Popular Responses

Special Scores

Deviant Verbalizations (DV), Deviant
Responses (DR), Inappropriate Combination
(INCOM), Fabulized Combination
(FABCOM), Contamination (CONTAM),
and Inappropriate Logic (ALOG)

Perseveration (PSV)

Confabulation (CONFAB)

Aggressive (AG) and Cooperative Movement
(COP)

Morbid Content (MOR)

Abstractions (AB)

Personal (PER)

Color Projection (CP)

Ratios, Percentages, Derivations

Core Section—Seven sets of frequency data
(taken from previous sections plus number
of responses; FM, m, C', T, V, and Y); nine
quantitative formulas:

1. Lambda (L)
2. Experience Balance or Erlebnistypus
(EB)
3. Experience Actual (EA)
4. Experience Pervasive (EBPer)
5. Experience Base (eb)

6. Experienced Stimulation (es)
7. D Score (D)
8. Adjusted es (Adj es)
9. Adjusted D Score (Adj D)

Ideation Section—Five sets of frequency data
(taken from previous sections; M−, M,
number of Level 2 responses, WSum6, and
M with no FQ); three quantitative formulas:

1. Active:Passive Ratio (a:p)
2. M Active:Passive Ratio (M^a:M^p)
3. Intellectualization Index [2AB + (Art +
Ay)]

Affect Section—Three frequencies (taken from
previous sections; Pure C, S, and CP); three
quantitative formulas:

1. Form-Color Ratio [CF/(CF + C)]
2. Affective Ratio (Afr)
3. Complexity Index (Blends:R)

Mediation Section—One frequency (number of
Popular responses); five percentages:

1. Conventional Form (X+%)
2. Conventional Pure Form (F+%)
3. Distorted Form (X−%)
4. White Space Distortion (S−%)
5. Unusual Form (Xu%)

Processing Section—Three frequencies (taken
from previous sections; Zf, DQ+, DQv);
three formulas:

1. Economy Index
2. Aspirational Ratio (W:M)
3. Processing Efficiency (Zd)

Interpersonal Section—Three frequencies
(taken from previous sections; COP, AG, Fd);
four ratios:

1. Isolation Index (Isolate/R)
2. Interpersonal Interest [H:(H) + Hd +
(Hd)]
3. (H) + (Hd):(A) + (Ad)
4. H + A:Hd + Ad

Self-Perception Section—Four frequencies
(taken from previous sections; Fr + rF, FD,
MOR, An + Xy); one ratio:

1. Egocentricity Index [3r + (2)/R]

Special Indices

Schizophrenia Index (SCZI)

Depression Index (DEPI)

Coping Deficit Index (CDI)

Suicide Constellation (S-CON)

Hypervigilance Index (HVI)

Obsessive Style Index (OBS)

High W   Rorschach (1921) originally believed that a high number of W responses reflected a person's ability to organize and integrate his or her environment. However, subsequent research has modified this belief. W responses do reflect intellectual activity, but this activity can be understood only by looking at the quality of W responses (relative number of W+) and the relative complexity of responses (Exner, 1993; Exner & Weiner, 1995; Friedman, 1952). In considering the complexity of responses, it should be noted that W occurs with greatest frequency for Cards V, I, IV, and VI, and with lowest frequency for Cards X, IX, III, and VIII (Beck, 1945). Thus, W responses for the latter cards require significantly greater organizational activity. If good-quality responses and a high degree of organizing activity are both present, then a high number of W responses would reflect good synthesizing and abstracting abilities (Smith, 1981), ambition (Schachtel, 1966), good ties with reality (Abrams, 1955; Levitt & Truumaa, 1972), and excellent problem-solving abilities (Beck, 1961; Rossi & Neuman, 1961).

Low W   Low W responses can reflect depression (Beck, 1960; Rapaport, Gill, & Schafer, 1968) or anxiety (Eichler, 1951). If the frequency, quality, and complexity are low, then more serious levels of maladjustment (Exner, 1974) are indicated, such as intellectual deterioration possibly related to brain damage (Goldfried, Stricker, & Weiner, 1971) or mental retardation (Allison & Blatt, 1964).

Common Detail (D)

Rorschach (1921) originally conceptualized the D response as reflecting the degree to which a person perceives and reacts to the obvious aspects of a situation (Rorschach, 1921). This is supported by more recent normative data in which adult nonpsychiatric groups and outpatients gave 62% and 67% of their responses, respectively, as D, whereas inpatient nonschizophrenics and inpatient schizophrenics gave 46% and 47% of their responses, respectively, as D (Exner, 1974). D tends to be most frequent for Card X (Exner, 1993). Any interpretations relating to D should take into account the fact that a greater number of R will be likely to increase the relative proportion of D when compared with other locations (also refer to the W:D:Dd ratio).

High D   Often found in persons who overemphasize the concrete and obvious aspects of situations (Beck, 1961; Exner, 1993), high D requires less energy and less integration than making a W response. A high emphasis on D may further suggest that the person sacrifices the full use of his or her intellectual potential by merely focusing on the safe and obvious rather than probing into the more novel and unusual. This is sometimes reflected in the remitted schizophrenic who focuses on a relatively safe, conservative, and socially desirable response, which is suggested by pre- and post-treatment changes in D from 40% to 73%, respectively (Murillo & Exner, 1973).

Where D+ is high, an excellent level of developmental functioning and a concern with precision are likely (Goldfried et al., 1971). On the other hand, if D is high but the quality of responses is low, a severe level of maladjustment is indicated (Exner, 1974).

Low D   Persons under stress show a decrease in D and a corresponding increase in Dd (Exner, 1974). Furthermore, low D can reflect inadequate perceptual habits (Klopfer, Ainsworth, Klopfer, & Holt, 1956), which may suggest brain damage (Reitan, 1955b).

The proportion of D is lowest in young children and gradually increases with age (Ames, Metraux, Rodell, & Walker, 1974).

Unusual Detail (Dd)

The Dd response is considered to represent a retreat from a person's environment by focusing on details rather than either perceiving the whole situation or noticing the more obvious elements of the environment. A clinician would expect the number of Dd responses to comprise approximately 6% of the total R for a normal adult. However, Dd is frequently higher in the protocols of normal children and adolescents. For schizophrenics or severely impaired compulsives, the proportion of Dd can increase to 25% or more (Exner, 1974). When Dd is in good proportion to W and D, a healthy adjustment, in which a person combines initiative with an appropriate ability to withdraw, is reflected.

High Dd   Persons with high Dd scores reflect a need to pull back from the ambiguities that may be contained in a whole response. When high Dd occurs in schizophrenics, it suggests an attempt to narrow their perceptions of their environment in order to make these perceptions more congruent with their inner world (Exner, 1986). If Dd perceptions are combined with movement, the hypothesis that the person's thought processes are impairing his or her perceptions is given further support (Exner, 1986).

Compulsives use Dd to focus on the details of a situation in an attempt to reduce their anxiety and exert more control over their perceptions. Their thought processes are not flexible enough to take in a sufficient number of whole responses. This rigidity becomes more exaggerated as the overall number of Dd responses increases and the size of each perception decreases.

Space (S)

A high number of S responses (three or more) is associated with negativism, difficulty in handling anger, and oppositional tendencies (Exner, 1993). However, within normal populations, a moderate number of S responses probably does not relate to hostility (Martin, Pfaadt, & Makinister, 1983) but may suggest some contrariness that is adaptive (striving for independence, constructive self-assertion). This is especially true if form quality is good (Klopfer et al., 1956; Piotrowski, 1957). If S responses are high (three or more) and occur with poor form quality and/or poor primitive movements, a clinician should consider the presence of anger, hostility, and potential acting-out (Exner, 1993).

DQ+ and DQv

Developmental quality scores relate to a person's relative ability to analyze and synthesize information. A high DQ+ (above 9 or 10) is consistent with more intelligent, complex, and sophisticated persons. However, this greater complexity does not necessarily mean that the person is well adjusted or even that his or her cognitions are accurate (see Zd for an index of both efficiency and accuracy). A number of disorders are characterized by quite complex cognitive operations, yet they are not well adjusted. In contrast to DQ+, a higher proportion (three or more) of low Developmental Quality

(DQv) responses indicates persons who are immature and less sophisticated (children, neuropsychologically impaired, intellectually disabled; Exner, 1993).

Determinants

Because the majority of research has been done on the determinants, they are frequently seen as the core of the Rorschach data. An analysis of a person's determinant score shows the psychological activity that he or she engaged in while the response was being created. It examines his or her unique styles of perception and thinking, and how these interact with one another. In general, research has isolated specific details of the determinants that could possibly lure the clinician into a rigid and potentially inaccurate "single sign" approach. Again, a Rorschach interpreter should focus on the interaction among a large number of variables in order to modify, confirm, or reject tentative hypotheses derived from any single determinant score.

Form (F)

The amount of pure F in a protocol has generally been used to indicate the extent to which the person can remove affect from a situation. The presence of form in a response represents a certain degree of respect for the standards of the environment and reflects intact reasoning abilities. It is seen both as related to attention and concentration and as an index of affective control or delay (Exner, 1993). This is reflected in the fact that inpatient schizophrenics have a relatively higher percentage of Fu and F− responses than other groups (see Appendix L). However, schizophrenics have increases in pure F following treatment (Exner, 1993), and a higher level of pure F for schizophrenics is associated with a better prognosis (Exner & Murillo, 1977). The presence of a pure F response does not necessarily mean that no conflict is present, but rather that the person is able to suspend temporarily the affect associated with a conflict. Conversely, people in emotional turmoil are likely to produce a significantly lower number of pure form responses, reflecting their inability to remove their affect from their experience. (See also interpretations for Lambda and the percentages in the Mediation Section: X+%, F+%, X−%, S−%, Xu%.)

High Pure F   Persons with a high pure F score either are highly defensive and constricted (Leavitt & Garron, 1982) or merely demonstrate a good ability to deliberately suspend or control their affect (Beck, 1945; Klopfer et al., 1956). When a person is in a more defensive position, the number of pure F responses increases. For example, pure F increases in populations of recovering schizophrenics (Goldman, 1960), perhaps as a result of their attempting to cautiously give a socially acceptable answer in which they have to limit their affect. Also, pure F is higher among paranoid schizophrenics than among other types of schizophrenics (Rapaport et al., 1968), reflecting their greater degree of organization and caution. Pure F also increases for persons who have been given some prior knowledge of the purpose of the test (Henry & Rotter, 1956) or who are requested to respond as quickly as possible (Hafner, 1958).

After ECT, pure F is usually higher (Kelly, Marguilies, & Barrera, 1941), which corresponds with patients' subjective reports of decreased affect. Also, alcoholics give more pure F responses than do psychopaths (Buhler & LeFever, 1947), and Leavitt and Garron (1982) have found an increase in F% in the protocols of patients having both psychological disturbances and low back pain.

Low Pure F   If pure F is low, a person's level of turmoil is likely to be sufficiently high to prevent screening out his or her affective response to a situation. For example, acute schizophrenics who have difficulty reducing their level of affect have a low number of pure F responses (Exner & Murillo, 1973). Likewise, certain characterological disorders (Buhler & LeFever, 1947) and organic disorders, in which there is difficulty controlling impulses, both have a low number of pure F responses (Exner, 1974).

Human Movement (M)

Probably more research has been done on the M response than on any other Rorschach variable. Most of this research is consistent in viewing M as reflecting inner fantasies connected to the outside world. More specifically, M represents the bridging of inner resources with reality, or what might be described as "internalization of action" (Exner, 1993). M is also an inhibitor of outward behavior, even though that inhibition may be only temporary. It has been associated with creativity (Dudek, 1968; Hersh, 1962; Richter & Winter, 1966) and introverted thinking (Kunce & Tamkin, 1981), and there is a close relationship between M and daydreaming (Dana, 1968; Page, 1957). Schulman (1953) has shown M's relation to abstract thinking in that a high number of M responses reflects both an active inner process and a delay in expressing behavior. Thus, M can be generally understood as involving deliberate inner experience. In its positive sense, M can indicate good ego functioning, ability to plan, impulse control, and ability to withstand frustration. In a more negative vein, it can suggest an over-developed fantasy life.

While interpreting M, it is important to look carefully at the different components of the response. For example, does the movement involve conflict or cooperation? A high number of aggressive movements has been shown to reflect a person who is generally more aggressive and who typically perceives relationships as characterized by aggressiveness (Exner, 1983). The degree of passivity in the movement is also likely to suggest that the person has more dependent and passive behaviors external to the test situation (Exner & Kazaoka, 1978). Specific interests might be projected into the movement responses, such as the increased number of dance movements perceived in the protocols of physical education and dance students (Kincel & Murray, 1984). The clinician should also consider other data both from within the test and external to it. Further elaboration regarding M, especially as it relates to the person's degree of control of impulses, can be derived by referring to the EB and EA ratios.

High M   High M responses, especially if they are M+, have been reported by some authors to be associated with high IQ (Abrams, 1955; Goldfried et al., 1971); other authors have not found this relationship (Mason & Exner, 1984). An alternative hypothesis is that high M is associated with increased creativity (Dudek, 1968; Hersh, 1962; Richter & Winter, 1966). Dana (1968) has proposed that high M can represent any or all of several different psychological processes, including fantasy, an accurate sense of time, intellect, creativity, delay, and certain aspects of interpersonal relationships. Further studies include abstract thinking as an important correlate to M (Schulman, 1953) and to an introverted thinking orientation (Kunce & Tamkin, 1981). Because all of the above involve motor inhibition, high M can also indicate a capacity to delay impulses (Pantle, Ebner, & Hynan, 1994).

A relatively high number of M responses suggests that the individual is overly invested in his or her fantasy life, which might be similar to a "Walter Mitty syndrome." With a high number of M− responses, the person is likely to be deficient in social skills and to have poorly developed interpersonal relationships (Molish, 1967; Weiner, 1966) or even psychotic symptoms (Phillips & Smith, 1953). Schmidt and Fonda (1954), for example, have found a high number of M responses in manic patients.

Low M   In many respects, a low M response indicates the opposite of what is suggested by a high M. Persons, especially depressives, who have a difficult time using their inner resources, usually have low M scores (Ames, 1959; Beck, 1945; Exner, 1993). In addition, highly impulsive persons will usually have a low number of M (Pantle et al., 1994). Demented elderly patients have been found to produce a low number of movement responses of all types (Insua & Stella, 1986). Low M is also associated with inflexible persons who have difficulty accepting and adjusting to change (Alcock, 1963; Goldfried et al., 1971; Rapaport et al., 1968). This inflexibility can, at least in part, be explained by a low level of empathy and a lack of imagination (Klopfer et al., 1956; Piotrowski, 1960, 1969). Because successful psychotherapy involves both flexibility and a relatively active inner life, low M is indicative of a poor prognosis (Goldfried et al., 1971; Klopfer et al., 1956). Conversely, a high number of good-quality M responses are a positive prognostic indicator.

Animal Movement (FM)

Whereas human movement responses serve to mediate between the inner and outer environment, animal movement reflects more unrestrained emotional impulses in which there is less ego control. The impulses are more urgent, more conscious, and provoked by situations beyond the person's control. These observations are reflected in the higher number of FMs in children (Ames et al., 1971) and the aged (Klopfer et al., 1956), and they correlate positively with MMPI scales that measure irresponsibility, aggressiveness, and distractibility (Thompson, 1948). If persons are in situations in which they have little control, FM is likely to be increased. For example, FM has been found to increase in persons experiencing physical restraint (Exner, 1979), in chronic amphetamine users (Exner, Zalis, & Schumacher, 1976), and among prostitutes who were addicted to drugs (Exner, Wylie, Leura, & Parrill, 1977). Human movement responses involve delay; animal movements do not. FM responses correspond with persons who complain of "racing thoughts" and have too much on their minds (Exner, 1986, 1993).

High FM   A high number of FM responses suggests these persons are governed by their needs and urges. They generally have a difficult time delaying gratification and therefore rarely plan toward long-term goals (Exner, 1974). Typically, they will be highly defensive and will be using intellectualization, rationalization, regression, and substitution as their primary means of reducing anxiety (Haan, 1964). If the FM responses are aggressive, it is more likely that they will be assaultive (Sommer & Sommer, 1958). The general, overall theme of high FM responses is that thoughts or feelings are occurring beyond the person's control. The number of FM responses for children (8 to 16) is from 3.0 to 3.5, whereas adults have an average of approximately 3.5 (Exner, 1986).

Low FM   Low FM is found among persons who are overly inhibited in expressing their emotions and may deny their basic needs (Exner, 1993; Klopfer & Davidson, 1962). For example, Ames, Metraux, Rodell, and Walker (1974) have associated low FM with a decreased energy level in children.

Inanimate Movement (m)

Similar to FM, the number of inanimate movement responses also provides an index of the extent to which persons are experiencing drives or life events that are beyond their ability to control. The drives reflected by m threaten people's adjustment in that they are helpless to effectively deal with them (Klopfer et al., 1956). This helplessness is usually related to interpersonal activities (Hertz, 1976; Klopfer et al., 1956; Piotrowski, 1957, 1960). For example, Exner (1993) has found one or more m responses in the records of both inpatient and outpatient schizophrenics, and Piotrowski and Schreiber (1952) found no m scores in the records of successfully treated patients. The number of m responses is also more frequent with juvenile delinquents, to the extent that, by 16 years of age, they perceive an average of one per protocol (Majumber & Roy, 1962). The view that m represents threat from the external world is supported by the observation that sailors at sea produced significantly more m during a severe storm (Shalit, 1965). This is also consistent with the finding that normal subjects exposed to uncontrollable laboratory-induced stress (McCown, Fink, Galina, & Johnson, 1992) and those given amphetamines (Perry et al., 1995) had temporary increases in m. Similarly, paratroop trainees had an increase in m just before their first jump (Armbuster, Miller, & Exner, 1974) as did elective-surgery patients just prior to surgery (Exner, 1993). [See also the interpretation of experience base (eb).]

High m   The presence of m should serve as a warning sign to indicate a marked presence of conflict and tension. Subjects probably see themselves as surrounded by threatening persons and are unable to reconcile themselves with their environment. A related finding by Thomas and Duszynski (1985) is that the word "whirl" (or similar words) was found more frequently in the protocols of persons who later committed suicide. Although the use of these "whirl all" words may not have necessarily been formally scored as FM or m, there are clear similarities between these classes of responses. To gain a more complete understanding of the individual meaning of m, clinicians should investigate the possible resources and the characteristic means of resolving conflict by looking at M, sum C, frequency of D and S, and the accuracy of their perceptions as reflected in F+% and X+%.

Color Chromatic (C, CF, FC, Cn)

The manner in which color is handled reflects the style in which a subject deals with his or her emotions. If color dominates (C, CF, Cn), then affect is likely to be poorly controlled and disorganized. In such cases, affect is disruptive and the person could be expected to be emotional, labile, and overreactive. If the responses are more dominated by form (FC), affect will be more delayed, controlled, and organized. For example, it has been demonstrated that subjects who could effectively delay their responses in a problem-solving task had a higher number of FC responses in their protocols, whereas those who had difficulty delaying their responses had more CF and C responses (Gill, 1966; Pantle et al., 1994). They also found that a positive correlation exists between individuals having color-dominated responses and measurements of impulsiveness. However, if the number of color-dominated responses is used to determine impulsiveness, the implications of D scores, form quality, number of Y responses, and relative number of color-dominated responses (FC:CF + C) should also be taken into account. Furthermore, the chromatic cards produce a greater frequency of aggressive, passive, and undesirable contents than do the achromatic cards (Crumpton, 1956).

Adult nonpatients have between 1.5 to 2.5 times more form-dominated color than color-dominated responses [FC/(CF + C)]. This contrasts with the average patient group, which generally has an equal number of FC to CF + C responses (Exner, 1993). Pure C responses are also predominant in the protocols of very young children, as is color naming (*Cn*; Ames et al., 1974; Exner, 1986). (See also interpretation of the FC:CF + C formula.)

High C and Cn   Individuals with a high proportion of color-dominated responses typically have little regard for the adaptiveness of their expressions, and they discharge their emotions in an impulsive manner (Gill, 1966; Pantle et al., 1994). This suggests that higher cognitive abilities have been suspended or possibly overwhelmed by affective impulses. Stormant and Finney (1953) were able to differentiate between assaultive and nonassaultive patients based on the assaultive patients having a higher number of poor-quality color responses. Likewise, Townsend (1967) found a higher level of aggressiveness in adolescents who produced a greater-than-average number of CF responses combined with an absence of human movement. In general, a high number of color-dominant responses suggests that the person is more labile, suggestible (Linton, 1954; Mann, 1956; Steisel, 1952), sensitive, and irritable (Allen, 1954; Shapiro, 1960), and has difficulty delaying his or her responses during problem-solving tasks (Pantle et al., 1994).

Color naming suggests that the person is giving a concrete response to the stimuli, and the response is primitive and poorly conceptualized. Although research is inconclusive, color naming typically seems to occur in severe disorders for adults, such as organic impairment. This is somewhat supported in that some brain-damaged subjects show an increased interest in color and seem to be more "stimulus bound" in their perception of it (see Lezak, 1995; Stuss, Gow, & Hetherington, 1992). Color naming is not unusual in the protocols of young children, particularly if intellectually disabled (Exner & Weiner, 1995).

Low C and CF   A total absence of (or at least a very low frequency of) C and CF occurs more frequently with depressed or psychosomatic patients and those with a low level of spontaneity who consistently dampen and overcontrol their emotional expression (Costello, 1958; Exner, 1993). If other suicidal indicators are present, a low color-dominant protocol may give additional support to the presence of suicidal tendencies (Goldfried et al., 1971). Low C and CF responses from schizophrenics can be a good sign for successful treatment (Stotsky, 1952).

High FC   A moderately high number of FC responses can indicate a good level of integration between controlling emotions and appropriately expressing them (Beck, 1945; Klopfer et al., 1956; Pope & Scott, 1967). Typically, this level of FC responses indicates that individuals have the ability to develop good rapport with others (Allison, Blatt, & Zimet, 1968), low levels of anxiety (Greenwald, 1991), and a capacity to learn under stress (Phillips & Smith, 1953). The prognosis for therapy is good (Goldfried et al., 1971) because they can experience emotions yet also conceptualize and give form to the expression of these emotions. Beck (1945) has stated that a moderately high number of FC responses indicates that schizophrenia is unlikely. In children, it may reflect the effects of overtraining with a corresponding decrease in natural spontaneity (Klopfer et al., 1956; Shapiro, 1960). Within adult populations, it may also reflect overcompliance and a dependent personality (Schafer, 1954).

Low FC   Low FC suggests poor emotional control (Klopfer et al., 1956), which is likely to negatively affect interpersonal relationships (Piotrowski, 1957). Low FC can also indicate anxiety states (Rapaport et al., 1968) and gives support to a hypothesis of schizophrenia if other indicators of schizophrenia such as poor-quality responses are present (Beck, 1945; Thiesen, 1952).

Color Achromatic (C', C'F, FC')

Achromatic color responses constitute one of the least researched areas of the Rorschach. However, it has been suggested that C' responses reflect constrained, internal, and painful affects. In other words, there is a dampened emotional expressiveness in which the person is cautious and defensive. Exner (1993) has referred to C' as the psychological equivalent of "biting one's tongue, whereby emotion is internalized and consequently creates some irritation" (p. 386). Thus, it relates not only to painful emotions but also to affective constraint and defensiveness. Most Rorschach systematizers have consistently used C' as an index of depression. In considering the meaning of achromatic color responses, a clinician should look at the relative influence of form. If form is dominant (FC'), there is likely to be definition and organization to the affect, with a stronger ability to delay the behavior. On the other hand, dominant C' responses suggest the immediate presence of painful emotions.

The average number of achromatic color responses for nonpatients is 1.53. In contrast, depressives have an average of 2.16 and .83 for character disorders (Exner, 1993).

High C'   C' occurs most frequently among patients who constrain their emotions, such as psychosomatics, obsessive-compulsives, and depressives (Exner, 1991, 1993). The pain and constraint associated with these emotions may adversely affect these persons' overall level of adjustment. An absence of shading responses combined with a large proportion of C' responses has been suggested as predictive of suicidal gestures (Exner, 1974).

Shading—Texture (T, TF, FT)

Texture responses represent painful emotional experiences combined with needs for supportive interpersonal relationships (Beck, 1945, 1968; Klopfer et al., 1956). For example, recently divorced or separated subjects averaged 3.57 texture responses per protocol

(SD = 1.21) as compared with 1.31 for matched controls (SD = 0.96; Exner & Bryant, 1974). Persons with a high number of texture responses reach out, although they do so in a guarded and cautious manner (Hertz, 1976). If form plays a relatively insignificant role and texture is predominant, subjects tend to feel overwhelmed by painful experiences, which would probably be sufficiently intense to disrupt their ability to adapt. Conversely, if form dominates (FT), not only is the pain likely to be more controlled, but also the need for supportive contact from others would be of primary concern (Beck, 1968; Klopfer et al., 1956). Coan (1956) has suggested that a combination of movement and texture responses relates to inner sensitivity and empathy. If chromatic color and texture occur together, the subjects' behaviors would not only be less mature in seeking affection, but would also be more direct and unconstrained (Exner, 1974).

Responses in which texture dominates show an increase through childhood, reach a maximum by 15 years of age, and gradually subside over the next few years until a form-dominated texture response is most characteristic in late adolescence and adulthood (Ames et al., 1971). Nonpatient populations average 1 texture response per record, whereas psychiatric populations average 2 or more per record (Exner, 1993). They usually appear ten times more frequently on Cards IV and VI than on the other cards (Exner, 1993).

High T or TF   High scorers for T or TF are characterized as having intense needs for affection and dependency (Exner, 1993; Greenwald, 1991). Oversensitivity in personal relationships may result, to the extent that they may have a difficult time in reconciling the intensity of these needs with what they can realistically expect from their relationships. They are open to their environment, but they approach it with a cautious sensitivity.

Low T   The absence of any T responses may suggest an emotional "impoverishment" in which the person has ceased to look for meaningful emotional relationships (Exner, 1993). For example, inpatient depressives have the lowest average number of texture responses but the highest number of diffuse shading responses (Y; Exner, 1974). Likewise, psychosomatic patients give fewer T responses than other types of patients (Brown, 1953), which would correspond with their constrained expression of affect. In general, T, Y, and C' all represent an "irritating emotional experience" such as anxiety, tension, apprehension, and internal discomfort (Exner, 1993).

Shading—Dimension (Vista; V, VF, FV)

Rorschach systematizers have generally considered Vista responses, especially pure V, to represent a painful process of self-examination in which the person creates a sense of distance from self in order to introspect (Exner, 1993). This introspection usually involves depression and a sense of inferiority. However, if the V responses are dominated by form, introspection is still suggested but the process is unlikely to be emotionally painful. This is in contrast to the negative type of self-examination associated with pure V. Even a single pure V response in a Rorschach protocol can be an important indicator.

Within normal populations, V responses occur, on average, 0.26 per record. Depressed inpatients average 1.09, and schizophrenics and character disordered persons average 0.60 and 0.24, respectively (Exner, 1993). It is extremely rare for V to appear in the protocols of children, but it occurs at about the same rate among adolescents as it does for adults (Exner, 1993; Exner & Weiner, 1995).

High V   Pure V responses created by depressed patients indicate a deep level of self-critical introspection (Exner, 1993). Stutterers also produce more pure V responses (Light & Amick, 1956), as do alcoholics (Buhler & LeFever, 1947), reflecting the painful self-criticism that usually occurs in these patient groups. V responses have also been suggested as an index of suicidal risk and are an important part of Exner's Suicidal Constellation (Exner, 1991, 1993). Although shading (and combined color and shading) responses in themselves are probably ineffective in discriminating successful from nonsuccessful attempters, these responses may suggest a more stable suicidal trait (Hansell, Lerner, Milden, & Ludolph, 1988). However, Exner's Suicidal Constellation, comprised of 12 possible signs (high number of morbid responses, es greater than EA, and so on) with a cutoff of 8 or more, has been able to effectively discriminate persons who are serious suicidal risks (Exner, 1993).

Low V   The absence of V is usually a positive sign, and the presence of a single form-dominated V merely represents the ability to introspect (Exner, 1993). Although a certain degree of pain may be involved with the introspection, the more important fact is that the resulting information can be integrated and eventually used productively.

Shading—Diffuse (Y, YF, FY)

Klopfer et al. (1956) and Beck (1945) have described Y as representing a sense of helplessness and withdrawal, which is frequently accompanied by anxiety and is often a response to ambiguity. Beck (1945) further elaborated that subjects with a high number of Y responses are experiencing psychological pain and have resigned themselves to their situation. The same general rule for looking at the influences of form (F) in relation to Vista (V), texture (T), and color (C, C') also applies for shading-diffuse. When F is dominant, subjects are more able to delay their behavior, and their experience is more controlled, organized, and integrated. This ability to delay behavior also gives them time to mobilize their resources. When Y is dominant, there is a much greater sense of being overwhelmed. Although these individuals are characteristically withdrawn, any expression of pain and helplessness is direct. Because there is little ability to delay their impulses, they do not have enough time to mobilize their resources.

Within the general population, 86% of people give at least one Y (Y, YF, or FY) response. Schizophrenics give more Y responses than nonpatients and outpatients, and nonschizophrenic patients give twice the number of Y responses than normals do (Exner, 1993). To accurately understand the meaning of Y responses, the clinician should look for other indicators of coping. In particular, these might include the number and manner in which pure form is used, the quality of organization, and the number of human movement responses. If there is a high number of Y and these "coping indicators" are absent, the person is likely to be overwhelmed and will probably be unable to adapt or respond effectively (Exner, 1993).

High Y   A high number of Y is associated with anxiety (Beck, 1961; Klopfer & Davidson, 1962) and a constrained expression of emotions, even though the experience of these emotions may be direct (Salmon, Arnold, & Collyer, 1972). It is more frequent in the protocols of depressed patients and outpatients (Exner, 1978). High Y is also associated with a sense of resignation to life events and an attempt to create distance between oneself and the environment (Elstein, 1965). Y is higher in alcoholics (Buhler & LeFever, 1947) and increases during stress, such as prior to examinations (Ridgeway & Exner, 1980), surgery (Exner, Thomas, Cohen, Ridgeway, & Cooper, 1981), uncontrollable laboratory-induced stress (McCown et al., 1992), and situational crises (Exner, 1993). Because m and Y assess similar constructs, they should be considered together.

Low Y   Ambiguity is purposefully built into the test situation. Some Y, usually FY, can therefore be expected to occur in any protocol. Exner's (1993) normative group of adult nonpatients had an average of 0.57 Y responses (SD = 1.00), compared with 2.12 for schizophrenics (SD = 2.62), and 1.81 for depressives (SD = 1.40). The total absence of Y suggests an extremely indifferent attitude toward ambiguity (Exner, 1993).

Form Dimension

Form Dimension (FD) is unique to the Comprehensive System and was included because it seemed to be both an empirically distinct category and a source of some interpretive significance. The research that exists suggests that a high number of FD responses are related to introspection and self-awareness. For example, a relatively high number of FD responses have been found among persons who are introverted and are involved in the later phases of insight-oriented therapy, and among patients who have completed a wide number of other forms of therapy (Exner, 1993). FD responses occur more frequently among nonpatients (M = 1.16) than among other patient groups—including schizophrenics (M = 0.60) and depressives (M = 0.82)—and is particularly low among character disorders (M = 0.33; Exner, 1993).

High FD   High FD suggests that the person is introspective, self-aware, and able to delay and internalize behaviors. This introspection is not likely to be painful unless high FD is also associated with other indicators, particularly V, which would then suggest affective difficulties. A combination of high V and FD suggests the possibility of suicidal potential, which is reflected in its inclusion in the Comprehensive System's Suicide Constellation (Exner, 1993).

Pairs (2) and Reflections (rF and Fr)

Research on pairs and reflections has been linked both conceptually and empirically to relevant aspects of personality. Self-absorption is suggested if either of these categories is high (Exner, 1991, 1993). However, this does not necessarily mean that the individual will be pathological. For example, a high number of reflections were found among nonpatient persons in occupations that encourage a high level of self-worth, such as performing artists and surgeons (Exner, 1993). Whereas reflections occurred in only 7% of adult outpatients, they occurred in a full 20% of the protocols of character disorders and 75% of the records of antisocial groups (Exner, 1993). It is fairly common for children between the ages of 5 and 10 to have a high number of reflection (and pair) responses, but they usually decrease by adolescence, when individuals move to a less egocentric style of functioning (Exner, 1993; Exner & Weiner, 1995).

High Pairs (2) and Reflections (rF and Fr)   A high number of pairs and reflections suggests these persons are self-absorbed and have an inflated sense of self-worth. They might have an exaggerated sense of self-pride, with strong strivings toward status. If they are unable to achieve affirmation from their environment, they might become depressed and negativistic. This could potentially lead to difficulties in maintaining deep and meaningful relationships (Exner, 1991, 1993).

Organizational Activity (Z)

The relative extent to which a person efficiently and effectively organizes the disparate aspects of the inkblots will be reflected in the scoring for Organizational Activity. The possibility that Organizational Activity is conceptually related to intelligence is given some empirical support in that moderate correlations (.54) have been found with the Wechsler-Bellevue Full Scale IQ and an even higher correlation of .61 exists with the Wechsler Vocabulary subtest (see Exner, 1993). Adults and younger nonpatients will have frequencies of Organizational Activity ranging between 9 and 13 (Exner, 1993, 1995). Among psychiatric patients, lower organizational activity has been noted among depressed patients (Hertz, 1948). In contrast, quite high levels of organizational activity have been found among patients who projected organized delusions (Beck, 1945; see also the interpretation for Processing Efficiency, in the Processing Section, below).

High Zf (> 13)   High scores indicate that the degree of effort expended to process information is more extensive than required or expected. Thus, these persons may have a high level of intellectual striving in which they carefully and precisely work with their perceptions (Exner, 1993).

Low Zf (<9)   With scores of less than 9, it would be expected that the client expends less effort than needed or required to adequately process information.

Content

The different content categories are generally considered to contain information relating to a person's needs, interests, preoccupations, and social interactions. Positive correlations have been found between a large variety of contents and intelligence (Exner, 1986). Research has also shown that, whereas a high variety of contents is associated with intellectual flexibility, a low variety suggests intellectual constriction and rigidity. Persons' occupational interests are often represented in a higher number of contents relating to their specific career choice. For example, biologists and medical personnel usually give a higher number of anatomy responses than the general population (Exner, 1974). This may merely indicate that these persons have an interest in their career, but it could suggest they are overconcerned with their career to the extent that they neglect other areas of their lives, perhaps even impairing their overall level of adjustment. For example, biologists who see only nature contents may be using a preoccupation with their careers to withdraw from interpersonal relationships (Exner, 1974).

When interpreting Rorschach content, it is important to look at the variety of contents, the number of each content, and their overall configuration, as well as the implications other Rorschach factors may have for the meaning of the content scorings. It is usually essential to consider the age of the subject and to use age-appropriate norms. For example, children usually have significantly fewer human and human detail responses than adults, and the variety of their contents is also lower (Ames et al., 1974; Exner & Weiner, 1995). Another important step is to study contents relating to aggressiveness (fire, explosions, and so on), facial features, and orality. Although the focus of the Comprehensive System is on a quantitative approach to the Rorschach, symbolical considerations can also be extremely important in conducting a more qualitative analysis (see Aronow et al., 1995). The following section provides general information on the meaning associated with human and animal contents. Further interpretive material can be found in the interpretation of quantitative formulas relating to contents [see Intellectualization Index, Isolation Index, Interpersonal Index, (H) + (Hd):(A) + (Ad), and H + A:Hd + Ad].

Human and Human Detail [H, Hd, (H), (Hd)]

Human responses constitute one of the most thoroughly researched contents. Beck (1961), in general agreement with other researchers, has found that H and Hd gradually increase with age until the median for 10-year-old children is from 16% to 18%. This remains unchanged through adolescence and the overall adult proportion of 17% is eventually reached. Exner (1974) found that, whereas adult nonpatient H + Hd responses were 19% of the total adult outpatients' responses, schizophrenics had a lower total of 13%. He also demonstrated that the ratio of human to human detail (H:Hd) for nonpatients was 3:1. In contrast, schizophrenics' average ratio was approximately 1:1 and outpatients' ratio was 2:1. Molish (1967) suggests that when there is an increase in Hd compared with H, the subject is prone to use constricted defenses. Others have theorized that the increase suggests intellectualization, compulsiveness, and a preoccupation with the self that restricts the degree of contact with others (Klopfer & Davidson, 1962). Beck (1945) associated high Hd with anxiety, depression, and a low intellectual level. [See also the quantitative formulas for Interpersonal Index, (H) + (Hd):(A) + (Ad), H + A:Hd + Ad.]

High H   A high number of human contents occurs among individuals who have a wide-ranging interest in people (Beck, 1968), are more likely to have high self-esteem (Fisher, 1962), and possess greater intelligence (Beck, 1968; Rawls & Slack, 1968). A higher H content has been consistently found to be associated with a greater likelihood of successful psychotherapeutic treatment (Goldfried et al., 1971; Weiner & Exner, 1991). As might be expected, human responses are more frequent in the records of psychologists and anthropologists (Roe, 1952).

Low H   An unusually low number of H contents suggests a low level of empathy and a withdrawal from interpersonal relationships (Allison et al., 1968; Kahn & Giffen, 1960). The overall H% has been found to be lower for schizophrenics than for normals (Exner, 1993). The prognosis for successful psychotherapy with low H scorers is poor (Piotrowski & Bricklin, 1961), and if the low score is accompanied by a low number of M responses, their termination from therapy is likely to be abrupt, probably because a high level of anxiety is combined with a low intellectual level (Affleck & Mednick, 1959; Rapaport et al., 1968). The complete absence of human content is unusual and, with the exception of very young children, it is likely to indicate psychopathology characterized by difficulties with identity (Exner, 1978).

Animal and Animal Detail (A and Ad)

Most of the literature indicates that animal content is associated with the obvious aspects of adaptiveness and the most concrete features of reality testing (Draguns, Haley, & Phillips, 1967). Because animal contents are the easiest to perceive, their presence suggests that examinees are using routine and predictable ways of responding. Conversely, a low number of animal responses suggests highly individualistic persons who see their world in their own personal and unique ways.

Animal responses occur more frequently than any other content category and comprise 38% to 48% of the normal adult record (Beck, Rabin, Thieson, Molish, & Thetford, 1950; Cass & McReynolds, 1951; Wedemeyer, 1954), with a slightly higher amount for children (Beck, 1961). Schizophrenics and outpatients average 31% and 41%, respectively, whereas depressives score much higher, averaging 41% per protocol (Exner, 1974). Other studies have found that the percentage of A responses is low for manics (Kühn, 1963; Schmidt & Fonda, 1954) and high for alcoholics (Buhler & LeFever, 1947).

High A   High A suggests a predictable, stereotyped manner of approaching the world (Klopfer & Davidson, 1962; Levitt & Truumaa, 1972)—a manner often associated with depression and the use of constrictive and conforming defenses (Beck, 1945, 1960). There has been some evidence to suggest that high A responses are a sign of brain damage (Goldfried et al., 1971), but variables from without as well as within the test should be carefully considered before making this diagnosis.

Low A   Persons who are spontaneous, nonconforming, unpredictable, and of higher intelligence often have a low number of A responses (Allen, 1954; Kahn & Giffen, 1960).

Anatomy (An) and X Ray (Xy) (Body Concern)

Because An and Xy both measure concern with the body, they are considered together. Anatomy (An) responses have been well researched, and, along with human and animal contents, anatomy is one of the most frequently occurring responses (average of 0.6 for nonpatient adults). Anatomy content has an obvious connection with concern for the body, and the literature supports this connection in that it occurs more frequently for persons preparing to undergo elective surgery (Exner, Armbuster, Walker, & Cooper 1975) and among psychosomatic patients (Shatin, 1952). Anatomy responses also occur with greater frequency with the onset of psychological difficulties related to pregnancy (Zolliker, 1943). As might be expected, Anatomy responses occur more often in the protocols of biologists and persons with medical training (Dorken, 1954; Roe, 1952; Schactel, 1966). A review of the literature by Draguns et al. (1967) concluded that anatomy content can serve as an index of the degree of involvement persons have in their inner fantasy life or may reflect physical changes such as illness, puberty, or pregnancy. Exner (1993) has also suggested that anatomy content is associated with withdrawal from the environment and obsessive defenses.

The relative proportion of anatomy to Xy responses is an important consideration. Although anatomy responses are generally low for both psychiatric and nonpsychiatric groups, a combined anatomy and Xy score allows for a clearer differentiation between the two groups. Whereas the combined An and Xy responses for a nonpsychiatric group give an average of only 0.6 responses, outpatients give 1.5, schizophrenics give 1.4, and nonschizophrenic patients give 1.8 (which accounts for 9% of this last group's total number of responses; Exner, 1974). Xy responses have been found to be particularly high for schizophrenics with bodily delusions (average of 2.2) and depressed patients with concerns related to bodily functioning (1.7; Exner, Murillo, & Sternklar, 1979). Anatomy responses occur most frequently for Cards VIII and IX, and Xy responses are most frequent for Card I. Exner (1974) suggests that Xy responses reflect a concern with the self that is painful, but that these subjects are attempting to deal with this pain by distancing themselves from it or at least disguising their responses to it. On the other hand, anatomy responses reflect a process in which the person focuses more directly on the stress and there is a more direct emotional release.

A high number of An and Xy responses are associated with hypochondriasis (Carnes & Bates, 1971; Wagner, 1973) and psychosomatic conditions (Shatin, 1952). In congruence with these disorders, there are likely to be intellectualizing defenses (Allison et al., 1968), anxiety (Wagner, 1961), obsessive traits, and withdrawal (Exner, 1974). High An may also reflect a concern with physical functioning due to aging (Ames, Metraux, Rodell, & Walker, 1973) or career choice (Dorken, 1954), and it can reflect a greater-than-average level of narcissism in patients going through a physical rehabilitation program (Levi, 1951). Schizophrenic patients sometimes give an unusually high number (eight or more) of anatomy responses (Brar, 1970; Goldfried et al., 1971).

Food (Fd)

A high number (two or more) of food contents (primary or secondary) suggests dependency. High scorers would be expected to request extensive help and guidance from others, have difficulty making independent decisions, and be naive in their expectations of others (Exner, 1993).

Popular Responses

The number of popular responses reflects the subjects' degree of similarity to most people, the extent to which they conform to social standards, and the relative ease with which they can be influenced in interpersonal relationships. Persons who reject conventional modes of thinking give a significantly lower number of populars than those who are conforming and relatively conventional. With Exner's (1993) scoring system (see Table 9–6), the average number of P responses for nonpsychiatric subjects is 6.9 (SD = 1.39). Outpatients and nonschizophrenic patients, likewise, give approximately 7 per record, whereas inpatient schizophrenics give 4 or less, characterologically disordered persons give approximately 5, and depressives have slightly more than 5 (Exner, 1993).

High P   High P suggests that the subject is experiencing anxiety related to a fear of making mistakes and, therefore, clings to common perceptions as a way to achieve approval. These individuals can be described as conventional, overconforming, guarded, and, frequently, depressed (Exner, 1974; Levitt & Truumaa, 1972; Weiner, 1961).

Low P   The lowest number of P responses is given by inpatient schizophrenics, which is consistent with their poor contact with reality. They can be described as poorly adjusted, detached, aloof from their environment, and unable to see the world as others see it. Molish (1967) has suggested that if neurotic subjects, especially obsessive-compulsives, have low P, then the possibility of latent schizophrenia should be investigated. Patients diagnosed as having character disorders also have low P, which reflects their rejection of conventionality and their lack of conformity.

Because Populars are extremely common for Cards I, III, V, and VIII, an absence of them from these cards is significant in that it more strongly suggests the trends just discussed. However, the assumption that low P responses alone confirm maladjustment should be approached with caution. Low P subjects who have good form quality (F + % and X + %) and whose organizational activity is also good are likely to be creative individuals who are avoiding common or ordinary perceptions and want to extend their imagination. If organization and form quality are poor, there is a high likelihood that the psychopathological dimensions are more predominant.

Special Scores

Deviant Verbalization (DV), Deviant Responses (DR), Inappropriate Combination (INCOM), Fabulized Combination (FABCOM), Contamination (CONTAM), and Inappropriate Logic (ALOG)

The first six of the Special Scores were included in the Comprehensive System to detect the presence of cognitive slippage. Illogical, dissociated, fluid, or circumstantial thinking is particularly likely if there are any Level 2 scorings for the first four scores (Exner, 1991). This is consistent with the finding that virtually no Level 2 DV or DR responses occurred among nonpatients but fully 1.90 Level 2 DRs have been noted among schizophrenics (Exner, 1993). However, there is no specific interpretation for each of the six categories. Instead, they are used collectively to detect the presence and seriousness of cognitive distortions. The relative seriousness is indicated in part by the type of Special Score. Mild distortions are suggested by the presence of scores for DV (Level 1), INCOM (Level 1), or DR (Level 2), and moderate distortions are suggested by the presence of DV (Level 2), FABCOM (Level 1), INCOM (Level 2), and ALOG. The most serious degree of cognitive distortion is suggested if patients have Special Scores for DR (Level 2), FABCOM (Level 2), and CONTAM.

A further means of analyzing the first six Special Scores is by noting the relative elevation of WSUM6, which is simply a sum of the different weightings given to the Special Scores (see the section on "Scoring"). The WSUM6 for nonpatients is 3.2, indicating that normals do include at least some of the Special Score responses. In striking contrast are schizophrenics, who have a WSUM6 of nearly 45 (Exner, 1993). However, the presence of Special Scores does occur among children under 10 but gradually decreases during adolescence (Exner & Weiner, 1995). The general interpretation for the first six high Special Scores is that there is cognitive distortion. The interpretive hypothesis, especially with a high WSUM6, is that there is a serious disregard for reality, strained reasoning, faulty cause-and-effect relationships, loose associations, disorganized thinking, and poor ability to focus on tasks (Exner, 1991, 1993). This ability of the Rorschach to detect the bizarre and illogical processes of schizophrenia is probably one of its best validated features (Vincent & Harman, 1991), and there is some evidence that it is sensitive to these changes in thought processes even prior to their clinical manifestation (Frank, 1990).

Perseveration (PSV)

The presence of perseveration suggests some difficulty in cognitive shifting. Thus, the individual may have either a permanent or a temporary difficulty with rigidity or inflexibility in information processing or decision making (Exner, 1993).

Confabulation (CONFAB)

Confabulations are very rare but, when they do occur, they suggest serious intellectual dysfunction or alogical cognitive operations consistent with persons who are severely mentally retarded or brain damaged (Exner, 1993).

Aggressive (AG) and Cooperative Movement (COP)

It is useful to consider AG and COP together. If there is an absence of scores on either category, it suggests that the individual will be aloof, somewhat uncomfortable in social situations, and on the periphery of group situations. In contrast, if COP is high (two or more) and AG is low (zero or one), the person is likely to be perceived by others as trustworthy, cooperative, and easy to be around (Exner, 1993). It is also a favorable prognosis for psychotherapy. If COP is low (less than three or especially zero) and AG is high (greater than two), the person's interactions are likely to be forceful or even aggressive and hostile (Exner, 1993). Given the above interpretations, it might be speculated that high scores on both COP and AG would suggest some conflict regarding the appropriate and preferred mode of responding and would result in inconsistent interpersonal behaviors (i.e., passive aggressive interactions).

Morbid Content (MOR)

Although the presence of one MOR is not unusual in the records of nonpatients, two or more suggest pessimism, a negative self-image, and possible depression and is consistent with a diagnosis of PTSD (Weiner, 1996). If three or more MOR responses are present, it is both a strong indicator of depression and one of several indicators for suicide risk (see the Suicide Constellation; Exner, 1991, 1993). MOR content is likely to have unique meaning for the person and can often be interpreted symbolically and qualitatively.

Abstractions

The presence of one or more abstractions suggests intellectualizing defenses (see Intellectualization Index).

Personal (PER)

Scores of three or more suggest a defensive authoritarian stance in which the individual is insecure regarding challenges to his or her sense of self. Interpersonal difficulties may be experienced during attempts to get others to submit to his or her opinions (Exner, 1993).

Color Projection (CP)

This unusual response indicates persons who deny unpleasant emotions by creating false or substitute emotions instead. Thus, they have difficulty dealing with negative feelings and modulating their emotions, and they bend or even distort reality as a means of adapting (Exner, 1993). This scoring category should only be interpreted within the context of other indicators for processing and expressing affect (see the Affect Section).

Ratios, Percentages, Derivations

The quantitative formulas used to develop the different ratios, percentages, and derivations provide a more in-depth and complicated portrayal of the relationships among the locations, determinants, contents, populars, and special scores. These formulas provide some of the most important, reliable, and valid elements of interpretation. Their numbering and organization correspond with the numbers given to them in the previous listing of the quantitative formulas (see "Structural Summary").

The Core Section

The Core section provides information on the person's dominant personality style, particularly focusing on the level of stress the person is experiencing and how effectively the style allows him or her to tolerate stress. Of a total of 16 entries, 7 are frequency data providing summaries for total number of responses (R), animal movement (FM), inanimate movement (m), Achromatic color (C'), Shading—Texture (T), Shading—Dimension (V), and Shading—Diffuse (Y). Interpretive material for each of the last six categories can be found in previous sections; the first category, number of responses; (R), is detailed below. The nine quantitative formulas follow the interpretive material on number of responses.

Number of Responses Number of responses is not a quantitative formula (and is therefore not numbered). Rather, it is a simple sum of the total number of responses. In using Exner's set of instructions, the mean for the total number of responses for non-patient adults is 22.57, with a standard deviation of 5.54. However, different methods of administration can influence this number to a certain extent. For example, Ames, Metraux, Rodell, and Walker (1973) report an overall adult average of 26; Beck (1961) gives 32 for his adult mean; and both use instructions somewhat different from Exner's. Deviations from the normal range present the following possible interpretive hypotheses.

Low R (Adults, less than 17; Children, less than 15) A low number of R suggests defensiveness, constriction, organicity, depression, or attempted malingering (Exner, 1986). A clinician cannot confirm any of these hypotheses based solely on the occurrence of a low number of R, but they are raised as possibilities. To confirm these hypotheses, factors from both within and outside the test must be used. Protocols having less than 13 responses are not likely to be valid, and interpretations of the test, especially those based on the quantitative formulas, should be avoided (Exner, 1988, 1993). Examiners should either discard the protocol and interpret the verbal material clinically, or they should immediately retest the person and request that he or she include more responses.

High R (Greater Than 33)   A significantly higher-than-average number of responses suggests several possibilities, including an introversive character (Murstein, 1960; Wagner, 1971), above-average intelligence with a relatively high level of academic achievement (Beck, 1945; Goldfried et al., 1971), and a high degree of creativity (Adams, Cooper, & Carrera, 1963; Dana & Cocking, 1968; Raychaudhuri, 1971). It can also suggest good ego functioning, including the ability to plan ahead, adequate impulse control, and the ability to tolerate stress (Goldfried et al., 1971; Klopfer & Davidson, 1962). Among persons with psychopathology, high R is found among manics and obsessive-compulsives (Alcock, 1963; Beck, 1945, 1951; Pope & Scott, 1967).

A high number of R is likely to alter the meaning of specific formulas or render them useless. A higher proportion of D and Dd responses can be expected because the number of W responses is usually exhausted sooner. Pure F responses will also tend to increase in frequency, the number of Populars will increase, and there are usually relatively more R for Cards VIII and X, thus elevating the Affective Ratio (Afr). Thus, interpretations based on the quantitative formulas derived from a high number of R should be treated with appropriate caution.

1. ***Lambda [L; (Pure F:Non-Pure F)].***   The Lambda index was developed by Beck (1950) as an improvement on the F% that had been used by other Rorschach systematizers. The earlier F% used the total number of R as the denominator, whereas the Lambda uses the total number of non-pure F. The Lambda ratio is used as an overall index of the degree of responsiveness versus lack of responsiveness to stimuli (Exner, 1993, 1995). Thus, persons can range from highly constricted and withdrawn to completely emotionally flooded by their responses to stimuli. The Lambda for nonpatients is between 0.14 and 2.25, with a mean of .58. In contrast to this are schizophrenics (.05 to 29.00), depressives (.08 to 15.00), and character-disordered persons (0.015–16.00; Exner, 1993). The important factor with the above statistics is that psychiatric groups have a much wider range than normals. Thus, a maladjusted person may have a Lambda either greater than 0.99 or less than 0.32. The significance lies in Lambda's ability to provide specifics regarding the form this maladjustment takes. It is also important to look at other information within the test, such as form quality and Experience Balance, to obtain a more complete conceptualization of the meaning of L.

High L (L > .99).   Because pure F responses represent a withdrawal from experiencing a situation fully and an avoidance of perceiving all the possibilities that may be present, high L persons are likely to be conservative, insecure, and fearful of involvement (Exner, 1991, 1993). Such individuals have also been described as defensive, constricted (Klopfer et al., 1956; Piotrowski, 1957), unimaginative (Alcock, 1963; Levi, 1976), and anxious (Riessman & Miller, 1958; Singer, 1960). Levitt and Truumaa (1972) have demonstrated the association of high L with depression, guilt, and an increased potential for suicide. Lambdas of 1.20 or greater are found in persons who have an excessive degree of affective detachment, often screening out relevant information

(Exner, 1986, 1993). Thus, they avoid the complexities of a stimulus and often develop "tunnel vision" relating to certain ideas or perceptions. However, with adolescents, an interpretation that focuses on maladjustment should be made with caution because adolescents usually have a higher proportion of pure F responses (Ames et al., 1971; Exner, 1995).

Low L (L < .32). A low Lambda generally indicates that the person becomes overinvolved with stimuli to the extent that affect disrupts cognitive functioning (Exner, 1993). Low L scorers have also been described as having inadequate control over their emotions; their frequent, impulsive acting-out results in difficulty maintaining satisfactory interpersonal relationships (Allison et al., 1968; Exner, 1993; Klopfer & Davidson, 1972). Such people often have an impaired ability to attend to their environment (Alcock, 1963) and are often victims of their needs and conflicts (Exner, 1993). However, low Lambda might also be associated with persons who are achievement-oriented and who deal effectively with their environment (Exner, 1993). These characteristics are often suggested by other indicators in their protocols reflecting control and flexibility (average X+%, average number of Populars, good Organizational Activity, above-average W). This is consistent with the finding that increases in Lambda (along with decreases in es) have been associated with treatment improvement among children (Gerstle, Geary, Himelstein, & Reller-Geary, 1988).

2. ***Experience Balance or Erlebnistypus [EB; (M:C)].*** The Experience Balance formula or Erlebnistypus was originally devised by Rorschach and is the ratio between the sum of all M responses compared with the sum of all weighted color responses. Rorschach systematizers and researchers have come to view the Experience Balance ratio as the extent to which a person is internally oriented as opposed to being more externally directed and behaviorally responsive to outside stimuli. Although the EB ratio is usually relatively stable (Exner, Armbuster, & Viglione, 1978), it can temporarily change during times of stress or become more permanently altered during the course of successful psychotherapy (Exner, 1974; Exner & Sanglade, 1992). Although the EB ratio is usually stable for adults, there is considerable variability in children until midadolescence (Exner, Thomas, & Mason, 1985; Exner & Weiner, 1995). In an extensive literature review, Singer (1960) described the two sides of the ratio as representing dimensions of "constitutional temperament." These dimensions are introversives (higher M scores), who have a preference for internal experience, as opposed to extratensives (higher weighted C scores), who are more prone to activity and external expression. An introversive can more effectively delay his or her behavior, whereas the extratensive is more emotional and is likely to discharge his or her affect into some form of external behavior. Both types respond differently to stress and to problem-solving tasks (Exner, 1978). It should be emphasized that, in their moderate forms, neither is any more or any less effective than the other, nor is either more prone to psychopathology (Molish, 1967). [See also the interpretive meanings associated with M and C and the quantitative formulas dealing with either of these factors (EA, EBPer, D Score, Adjusted D Score, and W:M).]

Higher M (Introversives). Rorschach stated that persons with a relatively higher number of M responses were more oriented toward using their inner fantasy life. Thus, they are directed inward and use their inner experience to satisfy most of their basic needs. This is not so much an absolute necessity as it is a preference. In fact, these individuals may, on a more superficial level, even appear to be extraverted. Researchers have found them to be cautious, deliberate, submissive (Kurz, 1963; Rosenthal, 1962), and less physically active than persons scoring relatively higher on the C side of the ratio (Mukerji, 1969). They approach problem-solving tasks by internalizing the situation and mentally reviewing possible alternatives, and they engage in relatively few behaviors prior to reaching a solution (Exner, 1978).

Higher C (Extratensives). Persons who have relatively lower M responses and higher C responses (extratensives) tend to use external interactions as the most important means of satisfying their needs. They characteristically direct their energy toward the outside world. Extratensives are usually spontaneous and assertive, but also have difficulty delaying their responses (Alcock, 1963; Exner, Thomas, & Martin, 1980; Palmer, 1970). In children, higher C scores may represent a lack of self-assurance (Palmer, 1970). Extratensives are likely to approach problem-solving situations by experimenting with different behaviors (external trial and error) prior to achieving solutions (Exner, 1978).

M and C Equal (Ambients). If M and C are equal, individuals are more likely to be flexible during interpersonal relationships, but they are also less sure of themselves during problem solving and tend to vacillate (Exner, 1978). They usually need to verify every sequence in the solution of a problem at hand, and they do not profit as much from mistakes as either the introversive or the extratensive does (Exner, 1978). Whereas the latter types are more sure of which response style to employ in approaching an ambiguous situation, ambients have a liability when flexibility is required (Exner, 1978). Thus, ambients tend to be less consistent and efficient than either introversives or extratensives. Unusually high scores on both M and C suggest a manic condition (Beck, 1960; Singer, 1960).

3. *Experience Actual [EA; (M + C)].* Whereas the Experience Balance ratio emphasizes the assessment of a person's type, the Experience Actual indicates the "volume of organized activity" (Beck, 1960). The M side of the formula shows the extent to which persons are able to organize their inner lives, and the C side indicates the extent to which emotions are available. The emphasis here is that both the M and the C represent deliberate, organized activity, which is contrasted with the disorganization associated with nonhuman movement (FM, m) and the responses related to the gray-black features of the blot (T, V, Y).

For the most part, the adult ratio between M and C is remarkably stable (Exner, 1993), yet the sum of M and C can sometimes fluctuate on a daily basis, which theoretically parallels the effects of changes in mood (Erginel, 1972). After successful psychotherapy, particularly if long-term, M and C typically both increase (Exner & Sanglade, 1992; Weiner & Exner, 1991), indicating a greater increase in the degree of organization of the person's inner life and an availability of more emotions. In fact, Exner (1974) found that EA increases significantly more for patients who improved in therapy than for those who showed little or no improvement. Furthermore, persons who underwent long-term insight-oriented treatment showed much more of an increase in EA than those in a treatment that emphasized a combination of support and environmental manipulation (Exner, 1974). This is consistent with the goal of insight therapy, which focuses on helping patients to understand and organize their internal resources. The mean changes for children show a gradual increase (rarely more than 0.5) with each year from the ages of 5 to 13 (Exner, 1993). Although brief retesting for children has shown good stability, long-term retesting (nine months or more) has resulted in wide fluctuations (Exner, Thomas, & Mason, 1985; Exner & Weiner, 1995).

4. *Experience Pervasive (EBPer).* Because Experience Balance (M:WSumC) is a somewhat crude indicator of how pervasive or dominant the introversive or extratensive style is, Experience Pervasive was designed as a more refined means of indicating how dominant one of the two styles is. Thus, it is an extension of the interpretations described in Experience Balance. It is only calculated when a clear style is indicated, and it only takes on interpretive significance when the value of one style over the other is 2.5 or greater. When this occurs, it clearly indicates that one of the styles is quite pervasive, perhaps to the point of suggesting rigidity in problem-solving style (Exner, 1993).

5. *Experience Base [eb; (FM + m)/(Y + T + V + C')].* The Experience Base ratio was originally suggested by Klopfer et al. (1956) and later developed in its present form by Exner (1974, 1986). The nonhuman movement side of the ratio reflects tendencies to respond in ways that are not completely acceptable to the ego. These tendencies appear out of control, impinge on the individual, and are disorganized (Klopfer & Davidson, 1962). Although the tendencies and feelings may have originally been produced by outside sources, the resulting internal activity is not within the person's control. The opposite side of the ratio, which is a sum of the responses relating to the gray-black features of the blot, is a reflection of the pain and disharmony the person is feeling as a result of unresolved stress. The eb ratio indicates which of these two areas of functioning is more predominant. If the eb is small on both sides, it suggests that the person is not experiencing very much pain and that his or her needs are well organized. Usually, the values on either side of the ratio will range between one and three for nonpatients. If either side becomes greater than five, its interpretive meaning becomes more clear. [See also the additional interpretive meanings associated with material from the left side of the ratio (FM and m) and the right side (Y, T, V, and C).]

6. *Experienced Stimulation [es; (FM + m) + (C' + T + Y + V)].* Experienced Stimulation is the sum of the nonhuman movement responses and all responses relating to the gray-black features of the inkblot. These are all responses reflecting that the person's functioning is disorganized and that forces are acting on the person and he or she feels they are beyond control. Thus, the es sum is an index of a person's degree of disorganization and helplessness. Persons scoring high on es have a low frustration tolerance, and it is difficult for them to be persistent, even in meaningful tasks (Exner, 1978).

Important information can be obtained by comparing the amount of organization the person has (as represented by EA) with how much chaos and helplessness he or she experiences (as represented by es). Normal populations usually have a higher EA than es, whereas psychiatric populations have a higher es than EA (Exner, 1974). Exner (1978) has suggested that the ratio between EA and es can provide an index of the degree to which a person can tolerate frustration. Difficulty in dealing with frustration would be primarily due to high-scoring es persons' having a limited ability to process and mediate cognitive information (Wiener-Levy & Exner, 1981). As would be expected, a correlate of successful psychotherapy is that there is a decrease in es and a corresponding increase in EA, which suggests that at least some of the patient's activity has become more organized (Exner & Sanglade, 1992; Gerstle et al., 1988; Weiner

& Exner, 1991). This was supported by Exner (1974), who found that subjects rated as unimproved after therapy also showed little change in that their es still remained high in relationship to EA. In another study, Exner (1974) demonstrated that most persons in successful insight therapy had an increase in EA compared with es. This suggests that patients in successful insight therapy were able to either neutralize or reorganize the forces that were "acting on" them. In contrast, therapy emphasizing support or environmental manipulation produced no or little change in the es:EA ratio.

High es (11 or higher). High scores suggest low frustration tolerance, difficulty following through on tasks, disorganization, distractibility, and a sense of helplessness (Exner, 1978, 1986).

7. **D Score (D; EA − es).** The D Score is a further measure of the client's ability to tolerate stress. It is essentially a means of evaluating the degree of available resources the person has (EA) versus the amount of disorganized events that are occurring beyond the person's control (es). For example, veterans diagnosed with PTSD have been found to have low D Scores (Weiner, 1996).

Low D Score (−1 or lower). A low D Score indicates that es characteristics have relatively more weight than EA. The person is likely to feel overwhelmed and unable to deal with complex or ambiguous situations. His or her thoughts, affects, and behaviors might be impulsive and poorly focused (Exner, 1993, 1995). As the D Score becomes progressively lower, this trend is likely to become increasingly stronger. A sense of being overloaded, easily distracted, and limited psychological resources to deal with stress are characteristic.

High D Score (+0 or higher). A D score of 0 or higher indicates that the client can adequately deal with the current level of stress. Even if experiencing stress (high es), the relatively higher D Score indicates that he or she has adequate resources to cope effectively with this stress (Exner, 1993, 1995).

8. **Adjusted es (Adj es).** Because es includes measures of current stimuli impinging on the person (m and Y), a different, adjusted es that excluded m and Y was developed. This adjusted es represents the more chronic (rather than fluctuating) condition of the person (Exner, 1993). Thus, persons scoring high are likely to feel chronically overstimulated (i.e., racing thoughts, insomnia) and have difficulties organizing their thoughts. However, the main purpose of calculating Adjusted es is to enable the calculation of the Adjusted D Score.

9. **Adjusted D Score (Adj D).** Because the D Score includes measures of the current capacity to deal with stress, it may not provide a measure of the person's usual ability to modulate and control his or her behavior. This issue is particularly likely to be present for clients referred for evaluation, because the events surrounding a referral usually involve psychosocial difficulties. These situational uncontrollable stressful events are expressed on the Rorschach (and in the D Score) by the presence of m and Y responses (McCown et al., 1992). Adj es has had m and Y subtracted from it, so it theoretically removes the influence of current environmental stressors. What remains in the Adjusted D score is a measure of the person's typical or usual capacity to tolerate stress and to control behaviors (Exner, 1993, 1995).

Low Adj D (−1 or lower). These persons have fewer than average resources to adequately cope with stressful situations. They will function best in routine and predictable situations. Adapting to new situations will present difficulties in that they are prone to become distracted, disorganized, and impulsive. The above trends will be strengthened with progressively decreasing scores on Adj D.

High Adj D (+1 or higher). High scores on Adj D indicate a good ability to deal with stressful situations but not necessarily a well-adjusted person. For example, antisocial or paranoid personalities might have intricate systems of dealing with stress that are quite effective at reducing their anxiety levels; yet, they are clearly not well-adjusted persons. In addition, treatment might present difficulties. They may use their somewhat limited resources to distance themselves from the types of experiences that might potentially stimulate increased growth and awareness (Exner, 1993). In contrast, a certain amount of distress can be useful in motivating the client to change.

The Ideation Section

The Ideation section focuses on information related to how the client imposes mean-ingful organization onto his or her perceptions. It includes three quantitiative formulas (two ratios and an index) and frequency data for M−, M, number of Level 2 responses, WSum6, and M with no FQ (see the interpretation for each of these frequencies under the listings for human movement and Special Scores).

1. *Active:Passive Ratio (a:p). I*ndividuals who have a distinctly higher number of passive responses are likely to be correspondingly more passive in other situations. In contrast, a clearly higher number of active responses indicates a person who is more active in terms of thoughts and behaviors (see also the interpretation for M^a:M^p; Exner, 1974, 1993). However, the contrast or magnitude of differences must be quite clear, as indicated by one of the following conditions: 1. "sum of the values in the ratio is four and one value is zero," 2. "values in the ratio exceed four, and the value on one side of the ratio is no more than twice that of the other," or 3. "ratio ex-ceeds four, and the value on one side is two to three times greater than the value on the other side" (Exner, 1993, p. 475).

2. *M Active:Passive Ratio (M^a :M^p).* A further refinement of the a:p is to consider only the proportion of active and passive responses for human movement scorings. If the summed value of passive Ms (M^a) is greater than active Ms (M^p), it suggests a generally more passive orientation. For example, therapists' ratings of clients with a greater num-ber of passive Ms indicated that they made more requests for directions, seemed more helpless, and exhibited a relatively high number of silences (Exner, 1978). In addition, their daydreams had more passive themes (Exner, 1974) as did their TAT story endings (Exner, 1993).

3. *Intellectualization Index [2AB + (Art + Ay)].* Earlier research indicated that the presence of three or more summed scores for Abstraction (Ab) and Art (Art) suggests an excessive use of intellectualization (Exner, 1986). Both obsessives and paranoid schizo-phrenics were often found to have more than three combined Ab and Art frequencies in their protocols (Exner, 1986; Exner & Hillman, 1984), and both these groups are likely to use an intellectual approach to distance themselves from their emotions. This is in contrast to other patients and nonpatients who typically reported an average of approxi-mately one per protocol (Exner, 1986). The Intellectualization Index listed above is a more recent revision of the earlier simple sum of Ab and Art, but it also incorporates the new Special Score of Abstraction along with anthropology (Ay) (Exner, 1993).

High Intellectualization Index (Six or More). Although scores of four or more can indicate a trend toward intellectualization, scores of six or more are usually necessary to more strongly suggest this mode of defense. High scorers are likely to neutralize their emotions through analyzing things from an intellectual perspective. This might serve to deny or conceal the impact of affect. Their method of dealing with emotions will typically be quite circumspect and possibly unrealistic. Although this might provide them with a certain degree of control for moderate levels of affect, much higher levels of affect are likely to overwhelm them, quite possibly resulting in disorganization (Exner, 1993).

The Affect Section

The Affect Section provides information on how the person modulates and expresses affect. Because affect is most directly expressed on the Rorschach through color, the different frequencies and formulas are concerned with the various combinations of color with other types of Rorschach responses. Specifically, this section includes frequencies for Pure C, white spaces (S), color projection (CP), and three quantitative formulas.

The sum of C and Cn responses provides an index of the degree to which a person is likely to be overwhelmed by affective impulses. Among nonpatient adults, it is rare to have any C or Cn responses occurring in a protocol (M = 0.12, SD = 0.43), but this increases slightly for patient groups (see discussion in the section on interpretation of color). The degree to which a person uses white spaces (S) has been associated with the person's negativism, means of handling anger, and amount of oppositional tendencies (see interpretation section on white spaces). Color projection (CP), a rare response included as a Special Score, relates to a tendency for the individual to substitute alternative emotions in place of unacceptable unpleasant ones [in the interpretation section, see the discussion of color projection (CP)].

1. ***Form-Color Ratio [FC/(CF + C)].*** The ratio of form-dominated color responses to color-dominant responses provides a measure of the degree of control a person has over his or her impulses (also check D Score for a tendency to become overwhelmed by stress). If form is predominant (1.5 to 2.5 times greater), it suggests the person has good control over his or her impulses and experiences satisfying interpersonal relationships (Exner, 1969, 1974; Klopfer & Davidson, 1962). Exner (1978), for example, has found that schizophrenics who have FC responses greater than CF + C have a better response to psychotherapy and less likelihood of relapse. The high form suggests they can integrate an accurate, reality-oriented interpretation into their perceptions. However, if no or very few color-dominant responses (no CF + C) are present, the person will be overly constricted and will have little contact with his or her emotions (Exner, 1978, 1993). This is consistent with the finding that most psychosomatic patients, who are typically constricted, had ratios of 4:1 or greater (Exner, 1993). If the CF + C side of the ratio is relatively high (1:1), it suggests a weak control over one's impulses, which may be accompanied by impulsiveness (Pantle et al., 1994) or aggressive acting out, perhaps consistent with a narcissistic personality (Exner, 1969; Klopfer & Davidson, 1962). The perception of both internal and external events will typically be distorted and inaccurate, as will the responses to these events (Exner, 1974). The number of pure

C responses increases with pathological groups, as indicated by only 7% of nonpatients giving pure C responses in contrast to 45% of depressives, 32% of schizophrenics, and 27% of character-disordered patients (Exner, 1993).

2. *Affective Ratio [Afr; (R for Cards VIII, IX, X)/(R for Cards I-VII)].* Because the last three cards are chromatic and the first seven are primarily achromatic, the Affective Ratio indicates the extent to which affect (color) makes an impact on the person. Nonpatient adults usually show a mean Afr of .69 (SD = 0.16). However, it is relevant to consider Afr within the context of EB. Introversives (higher M side of EB), who primarily direct their experience inward, have Afr ranges between .50 and .80. In contrast, Extratensives (higher C side of EB) have Afr ranging between .60 and .95 (Exner, 1993). This means that it is useful to take EB scores into account when judging whether an Afr is high or low. Although the mean Afr for patient groups was not very different from that for nonpatients, the range was much higher for patients and the distribution was bimodal. This higher range among patient groups is consistent with the view that they are more likely to have difficulties with either undercontrolling or overcontrolling affect (Exner, 1993).

High Afr (Greater Than .85). A high Afr indicates an overresponsiveness to affect (Exner, 1974, 1993), reflecting that the person is more receptive to emotional inputs and more likely to respond immediately rather than delay behavior (Exner, 1993, 1995). It is also important to evaluate the FC/(CF + C) proportion to assess the degree of control the person has over his or her emotions. In other words, the Afr measures responsiveness, interest in, and degree of affect, whereas the FC/(CF + C) indicates the ability to control what affect is present.

Low Afr (Less Than .53). Persons with low Afr scores tend to withdraw from their emotions and, if they have an unusually low Afr, may attempt to exert an extreme amount of control over their affective responses (Exner, 1993, 1995). (To assess the possibility that they avoid emotions through intellectualization, note their scores on the Intellectualization Index.)

3. *Complexity Index (Blends:R).* Approximately 20% of all Rorschach responses involve blends. To create a blend response, the person must appreciate the complexity of the inkblot, which requires both analysis and synthesis. Exner (1993) has pointed out that the pure F response is the exact opposite of a blended response in that pure F requires attention to only the most simple, straightforward aspect of the stimulus. Usually, there will be one or more blends in a person's protocol. A complete absence of blends suggests narrowness and constriction. This is consistent with the finding that blends are less frequent in the protocols of depressives and persons with below-average intelligence (Exner, 1993). In contrast, an extremely high number of blends (eight or more) suggests an unusual amount of complexity, to the extent that the person may be overly burdened (Exner, 1993).

A thorough interpretation of blends also requires an understanding of their qualitative aspects. For example, a blend that includes color-dominated determinants implies that the person might be easily overwhelmed by affect, whereas the opposite would be true if the blend were form-dominated. The color-shading blend (combining color with C', Y, T, F, V) implies concern with painful, irritating, confusing emotional experiences, and it is associated with the protocols of depressives. Exner and Wylie (1977) found a moderate correlation with attempted suicide. Accordingly, this blend was included as one of several variables in Exner's (1993) Suicide Constellation. However, the presence of color-shading blends does not seem to be a sufficiently accurate predictor of suicide when used as a single sign (Hansell et al., 1988).

The Mediation Section

The Mediation section uses a series of indicators to measure the extent to which the client is oriented toward making conventional, acceptable responses versus more unique ones. If either one of these directions is extreme and rigid, it suggests difficulties in adapting. This section includes one simple frequency for the total number of Populars (see previous interpretation for Populars) along with the five percentages described below.

1. ***Conventional Form (X+%).*** X+% includes the form quality of all the responses in a protocol and, as such, tends to be less subject to distortions than F+% (see below). The X + % is essentially an indicator of the degree to which a person perceives things in a conventional, realistic manner. Most normal adults will have an X+% of 79% (SD = 8%; Exner, 1993). Normal children have a slightly lower mean, ranging between .67 and .78 (Exner & Weiner, 1995). An extremely high percentage (greater than 90%) means that persons will perceive their world in an overly conventional manner, to the extent that they might sacrifice their individuality. They are likely to be hypernormal, inflexible, rigid, and overly conventional (Exner, 1993). This is further supported by, and is consistent with, an elevated number of Populars. In contrast, lowerings in X+% (less than 70%) suggest persons who perceive their world in an unusual manner. This might be simply because they are highly committed to their individuality or, particularly if X+% is unusually low, it might suggest serious psychopathology. For example, schizophrenics have a mean X+% of only 40% (Exner, 1993). Thus, it is a critical indicator of schizophrenia, and an X+% of less than 50% is one of the five indicators on Exner's (1993) Schizophrenia Index.

2. ***Conventional Pure Form (F+%).*** F+% assesses the same dimension as X+% but is limited to a narrower number of responses because it involves only pure F responses rather than other scoring categories (C', Y, T, and V) that might have been combined with F. Thus, interpretation is similar to the interpretation of X+% but should be done more cautiously. It reflects a person's respect for the conventional aspects of reality and perceptual clarity. The Exner (1993) norms indicate schizophrenics have an F+% of only 42%, in contrast to the average of 71% among normals. In general, a low F+% might suggest limited intellectual endowment (Beck, 1961), organic impairment (Reitan, 1955b), or schizophrenia (Beck, 1968; Kahn & Giffen, 1960).

3. ***Distorted Form (X−%).*** In contrast to X+% (and F+%), X−% is a direct index of the degree to which a person has distorted perceptions of reality. The higher the X−%, the more likely that the person will have a significant level of impairment. For example, moderately high percentages (X−% = 20%) are found for depressives, and percentages of 37% are characteristic of schizophrenics (Exner, 1993). Any percentage above 20% suggests that the person will have difficulty, because he or she will have poor ties with reality and difficulty developing accurate abstractions.

4. ***White Space Distortion (S−%).*** Sometimes, X+% and F+% can be low and it might then be assumed that this is a result of a high number of form minus responses.

This assumption might then result in incorrect interpretations. One way of checking for this difficulty is to note the percentage of minus responses for the white space (S−). Instead of suggesting the sort of distortions suggestive of schizophrenia (see interpretations for F+% and X+%), a low S−% might be due to strong negativism or anger (Exner, 1993).

5. *Unusual Form (Xu%).* Xu% also provides a check for potentially incorrect interpretations derived from low X+% or F+% scores. There might be cases where X+% and F+% are low primarily as a result of a large proportion of unusual form (Fu) responses. Fu responses are unusual, but they still do not violate reality in the way that minus responses do, and thus they do not reflect severe pathology. In fact, a few Fu responses in a protocol can be a healthy sign that the person is capable of seeing his or her world in a novel manner. However, an overabundance of Fu responses suggests the person is highly committed to an unconventional orientation (Exner, 1993). Unless the environment is highly tolerant of such an orientation, he or she is likely to have numerous conflicts and confrontations.

The Processing Section

In addition to understanding clients' ideation and mediation, it is also important to assess the quality and efficiency by which they process information. Relevant frequency data are the overall amount of Organizational Activity (Zf; see interpretation under Organization Activity), DQ+, and DQv. In addition, three formulas offer further understanding of processing efficiency.

1. *Economy Index (W:D:Dd).* The W:D:Dd ratio compares the degree to which an individual attempts to create a more challenging response that requires a high degree of organization and motivation (W), rather than choosing a less demanding and easily perceived area (D or Dd). Normals and outpatients usually have a W:D ratio of 1:1.2 or even 1:1.8 (Exner, 1993). If a person includes a relatively large number of D responses, it suggests that he or she takes the least challenging and possibly least productive way out of a conflict situation. It could be assumed that his or her characteristic way of dealing with ambiguity is to withdraw from it and focus on the obvious. If W is predominant, the person is perhaps overdriven in his or her attempts to organize perceptions. If, with a high W, both the W and the D responses are of poor quality, it suggests that a person is withdrawn and unrealistically striving for perfection (Exner, 1974). However, when W and D responses are both of good quality, they more likely represent the successful intellectual efforts of a creative person (Exner, 1974).

2. *Aspirational Ratio (W:M).* The W:M ratio is a rough formula that, at the present time, is somewhat lacking in research. It can be generally understood by reconsidering that the W response is an indicator of the degree to which subjects aspire to effectively organize and conceptualize their environments. It is an effort to encompass and include a number of different details in one coherent response. However, determining whether subjects have the resources to actually accomplish an effective organization depends also on M. Although M represents the degree of investment subjects have in their fantasy lives, it also suggests how effectively they can bridge their inner resources with external reality and perform abstract thinking. Thus, the W:M ratio provides a rough comparison between a person's aspiration level, as represented by W,

and his or her actual capability, as represented by M (Exner, 1993). Because introversives have higher M values than extratensives and ambients, the relative value of EB needs to be taken into account in designating high or low W:M ratios. A high aspirational level is indicated if the W side of the ratio is greater than the following values: introversives, 1.5:1; ambients, 2.2:1; extratensives, 3:1 (Exner, 1993). However, scores with extremely high W components are common in children, which is consistent with the observation that children often underestimate the actual effort required to accomplish a goal (Exner, 1993, 1995). On the other hand, ratios where the right side (M) is clearly lower than the left (0.5:1 for introversives, and 1:1 for extratensives and ambients) suggest that these persons are extremely cautious and conservative in defining achievable goals (Exner, 1993). Their motivation to achieve might be low, which would involve their being cautious (not wishing to fail), conservative in defining their objectives, and economical in their expenditure of energy.

3. *Processing Efficiency (Zd)*. Although the frequency of Organizational Activity (Zf) along with the Economy Index (W:D) and the Aspirational Ratio (W:M) provide information on the motivation and effort that persons place into their perceptions, these indicators do not provide information related to quality or accuracy. In contrast, the Processing Efficiency (Zd) score provides an index not only of effort but also of ease and accuracy of processing. Individuals scoring high on Zd are considered to have an overincorporative style; they invest more effort and are more accurate in their perceptions and conclusions. This seems to be an enduring traitlike feature. In contrast, low scorers have an underincorporative style, which means that they process information in a more haphazard style, often neglecting relevant bits of information. This characteristic seems more amenable to change, as indicated by moves to a more overincorporative style following psychotherapy (Exner, 1978). A review of research on Zd (Exner, 1993) indicates that, consistent with theory, overincorporators (high Zd) have more extensive eye-scanning, make fewer errors on games, and are less likely to make guesses related to requests for factual information. In contrast, underincorporators (low Zd) make fewer eye movements while scanning, are more likely to make errors on games, and are more likely to make guesses related to factual information. Among children, low Zd scores occur among those diagnosed as hyperactive.

High Zd (> + 3). High scorers on Zd are more likely to be obsessive or perfectionistic but can also efficiently and accurately process information. They are likely to take care with their perceptions and continually check for accuracy. They exert more effort in information processing and are more confident in their abilities.

Low Zd (< − 3). Persons scoring low on Zd are more likely to be haphazard and to make impulsive decisions without fully taking into account all relevant aspects of a situation. Compared to high Zd scorers, they do not invest as much effort into actively working with their perceptions. They typically are uneasy with their information-processing ability and may question their efficiency at perceiving, integrating, and responding to information.

The Interpersonal Section

Even though the Rorschach does not obtain information regarding a person's actual environment or the other persons within that environment, it does provide information related to needs, attitudes, behavioral response sets, and coping styles, all of which are relevant to interpersonal relationships. The Interpersonal section lists several measures relevant to these domains, but several additional relevant measurements are not included in the Interpersonal section. Deficits in coping with the environment (including people) can be noted in the Coping Deficits Index (CDI); vigilance is suggested by elevations in the Hypervigilance Index (HVI); recent emotional loss is suggested by high scores on Texture (T); an active versus passive orientation can be determined by noting the Active:Passive Ratio (a:p); and measures of introversion-extroversion can be developed by working with the Experience Balance (Erlebnistypus; EB). Interpretive information can be derived by noting the descriptions under each of these indicators. The Interpersonal section itself lists a number of measures related to cooperativeness (COP), Aggressiveness (AG), and dependency (Food content; note the interpretive sections for COP, AG, and Fd), as well as four formulas related to degree of isolation (Isolation Index), level of interest in people (Interpersonal Interest), and conceptions of people.

1. *Isolation Index (Isolate:R).* Exner (1986) points out that the five contents (Botany, Clouds, Geography, Landscape, and Nature) used to develop the Isolation Index are all "nonhuman, nonsocial, inanimate, and usually static objects" (p. 406). If a high proportion of these contents (index score of .25 or greater) occurs in a person's protocol, it suggests the person may be withdrawn or alienated, or may at least have some difficulties related to social isolation (Exner, 1993). This seems to be true for children, adolescents, and adults (Exner, 1986, 1995). However, the above interpretations should not necessarily take on a pathological bias. A high score might merely represent less interest in people rather than a negative rejection and alienation from them.

2. *Interpersonal Interest [H:(H) + Hd + (Hd)].* The Interpersonal Interest ratio compares the amount of Pure Human responses with mythical/fictional and part human responses. Two of the human categories on the right side of the ratio relate to fictional/mythical descriptions. As such, they can be considered to represent the extent to which the individual bases his or her perceptions on real versus imaginary aspects of people. Adult and adolescent nonpatients usually give more Pure Human responses than (H) + Hd + (Hd) at a rate of approximately 3:2 (Exner, 1993, 1995). However, the means for the ratio are different for introversives (3:1) than for either extratensives or ambitents (1.3:1). In contrast, schizophrenics see a much higher proportion of fictional/mythical and part human responses (1.5:2; Exner, 1993). This low a level of Pure Human responses suggests that they are working from an unrealistic perception of themselves and others.

3. *(H) + (Hd):(A) + (Ad).* This ratio combines and compares aspects of parenthesized content. Exner (1986) has described it as an index of possible detachment from reality. The left side of the ratio is frequently higher than the right (1:0 or 2:1), but a higher right side or high combined total score (greater than three) can indicate significant misinterpretation and detachment from social interaction (Exner, 1986).

4. *H + A:Hd + Ad.* The general significance of human and animal responses has been discussed under the Contents section. However, the H + A:Hd + Ad ratio calls attention to the relative proportion of total whole human and animal versus the total human detail and animal detail responses. This is important to note because a high number of either human detail or animal detail responses is unusual. Nonpatient adults

will typically have a ratio of 4:1, whereas patients with clear paranoid features will have 50% or more of their responses on the right side. Although a high proportion of contents on the right side does not necessarily indicate paranoia, it does suggest that the person perceives his or her interactions with others in an unusual manner (Exner, 1986, 1993).

The Self-Perception Section

The Self-Perception Section includes information relevant to the relative assets and limitations of the clients as seen by the clients themselves. Of the five entries in this section, four are frequency tallies (Fr + rF, Form Dimension, Morbid content, and Anatomy/X ray responses) and there is one quantitative formula. The possibility of an inflated sense of self-worth can be noted by the relative number of Fr + rF responses, and the extent of introspective self-awareness can be noted by the number of Form Dimension Responses (see the interpretative sections for Fr + rF and Form Dimension). A negative self-concept can be indexed to the number of morbid contents, and an abnormal level of bodily concern can be noted by an unusually high number of Anatomy or X ray (see interpretation sections for Morbid content and Anatomy plus X Ray). There is only one quantitative formula for this section; it relates to the degree to which the person is self-absorbed.

1. *Egocentricity Index [3r + (2)/R].* The Egocentricity Index (EI) provides information related to whether the client has a sense of self-worth and further relates this to the extent that he or she is absorbed with self.

High EI (> .49). A certain level (index level of .40 to .45) of self-focusing and self-concern is associated with positive self-esteem (Exner, 1993). However, index scores above .49 suggest that the person has an overinflated sense of self-worth, which reflects underlying dissatisfaction. This may be expressed in part by neglect of aspects of the external world.

Low EI (< .32). In contrast to high EI, scores below .32 indicate that the person's self-worth is quite negative and he or she feels conflicted regarding a self-image. This may lead to mood fluctuations along with dysfunctional behaviors (Exner, 1993).

Special Indices

To increase the robustness and validity of various combinations of Rorschach measures, six Special Indices have been developed based on a composite of scores. For example, a number of different indicators of Schizophrenia are found throughout the Rorschach. These include a low number of high-quality form responses (X+%), the presence of one or more Level 2 Fabulized Combinations (FAB2), and more than one minus human movement response (M−). These, along with several other indicators, were combined to form the Schizophrenia Index (SCZI), which has been found to be a better discriminator of schizophrenia than any of the single scores (see Exner, 1991, 1993). A similar strategy was used for the other Special Indices. Collectively, they help to form a nucleus of indices to help with more specific types of diagnostic conditions. Exner (1993, p. 189) and the commercially available scoring forms have included Constellation Worksheets for calculating whether the Special Indices are positive.

1. *Schizophrenia Index (SCZI)*. SCZI scores above 4 suggest that many of the characteristics of schizophrenia will be present. They might include disordered thinking, inaccurate perception, interpersonal ineptness, and inadequate controls. However, a number of false positives have been noted using this cutoff, so diagnoses should be made with caution. More stringent cutoffs of 5 and 6 can be used to reduce the false positives problem. If still present, they should be used as fairly strong indicators of characteristics quite consistent with schizophrenia (Exner, 1991, 1993).

2. *Depression Index (DEPI)*. A DEPI value of 4 raises the possibility that the client is experiencing some depressive symptoms—fluctuations in moods, a sense of dissatisfaction, pessimism, and some mild vegetative symptoms (fatigue, insomnia, slowed thinking, anhedonia). Scores of 5, 6, or especially 7 are far more definitive and strengthen the likelihood of an affective disorder as reflected by an intensification of the above symptoms (Exner, 1991, 1993). However, the diagnosis of a specifically depressive disorder may not be warranted because depression is generic to a wide variety of disorders, particularly many of the personality disorders and schizophrenia. In addition, the term **depression** might be used to describe people who are emotionally distraught or are pessimistic, self-defeating, and lethargic, as well as those who feel a sense of futility when attempting to function competently in a complex society (Exner, 1993). Depressive symptoms as measured by DEPI may therefore relate to both a wide number of types of people as well as a wide range of possible diagnoses. In addition, research suggests that the DEPI does not seem to be effective when used to assess children or adolescent clients (Archer & Gordon, 1988; Ball et al., 1991).

3. *Coping Deficit Index (CDI)*. Clients with scores above 4 or 5 on the CDI are likely to have unsatisfying and somewhat meaningless interpersonal relationships, largely because they will find it difficult to effectively deal with everyday requirements (Exner, 1993). Their histories typically include social ineptness, poor success in interpersonal relationships, and times when they have felt overwhelmed by interpersonal demands. Effective moderate to long-term psychotherapy was found to result in decreases in CDI (Exner & Sanglade, 1992; Weiner & Exner, 1991).

4. *Suicide Constellation (S-CON)*. The Suicide Constellation is comprised of eleven variables that collectively are intended to detect persons at risk of attempting suicide. Retrodictive studies indicate that, using a cutoff score of 8, 80% of suicide attemptors were accurately identified (Exner, 1986, 1993). However, caution should be exercised in making final decisions. Some clients were incorrectly identified as not being suicidal and yet they later made attempts (false negative rate = 15%). Among depressed populations, a number of clients were incorrectly identified as being at risk of suicide when there was actually no or little risk (false positive rate among depressives = 10%; Exner, 1993).

5. *Hypervigilance Index (HVI)*. Originally, a series of indicators was isolated from patient protocols that seemed to differentiate paranoid-type patients (paranoid schizophrenics) from other patient groups. This was partially successful in that paranoid schizophrenics and paranoid personalities were correctly identified (88% and 90% respectively; Exner, 1993). Upon further investigation, it was found that HVI related more to the hypervigilant aspect of the paranoid style rather than paranoia itself. Thus, persons with positive indicators on HVI are likely to place a large amount of effort into maintaining a high state of preparedness. Motivating this is a sense that they

mistrust their environment and experience a chronic sense of vulnerability (Exner, 1993). Before initiating behaviors, they will carefully think through why and how they should express them. They are likely to be quite guarded regarding closeness in relationships and will initially respond to efforts at closeness with apprehension. As a result, they will only allow themselves to be close with others if they feel in control. They will generally be quite concerned with issues not only of emotional closeness, but also of personal space in general (Exner, 1993).

6. *Obsessive Style Index (OBS).* The Obsessive Style Index was developed by examining the records of clients who had been formally diagnosed as obsessive-compulsive to determine which Rorschach characteristics could distinguish them from other groups. Five characteristics were isolated and, using the designated criteria, they correctly identified 69% of obsessive-compulsives (Exner, 1993). If OBS is positive, it suggests persons who are perfectionistic, indecisive, and preoccupied with details, and who experience difficulty expressing emotion. They are likely to be cautious, conservative, conforming, and conventional (check for high Populars). They will process information extremely methodically and, when using the Zd index definition, are likely to be overincorporators (see interpretation for Zd). However, a positive index does not necessarily indicate psychopathology; rather, it shows a style of approaching the world and processing information. If this style is overly rigid, it can become dysfunctional, particularly when the person is under pressure or is required to achieve goals within a limited period of time (Exner, 1993).

RECOMMENDED READING

Exner, J. E. (1990). *A Rorschach workbook for the Comprehensive System* (3rd ed.). Asheville, NC: Rorschach Workshops.

Exner, J. E. (1991). *The Rorschach: A comprehensive system: Vol. 2. Current research and advanced interpretation* (2nd ed.). New York: Wiley.

Exner, J. E. (1993). *The Rorschach: A comprehensive system: Vol. 1. Basic foundations* (3rd ed.). New York: Wiley.

Exner, J. E., & Weiner, I. (1995). *The Rorschach: A comprehensive system: Vol. 3. Assessment of children and adolescents.* (2nd ed.). New York: Wiley.

Chapter 10

THE THEMATIC APPERCEPTION TEST

The Thematic Apperception Test (TAT) is a projective technique consisting of a series of pictures. The examinee is requested to create a story about what he or she believes is occurring in the situations or events depicted by the pictures. The test was originally published by Murray and his colleagues at the Harvard Psychological Clinic in 1938. Murray (1943) describes the TAT as a "method of revealing to the trained interpreter some of the dominant drives, emotions, sentiments, complexes, and conflicts of personality. Special value resides in its power to expose underlying inhibited tendencies which the subject is not willing to admit, or cannot admit because he is unconscious of them" (p. 1). It differs from either projective drawings or inkblot-type tests such as the Rorschach or Holtzman in that the TAT cards present more structured stimuli and require more organized and complex verbal responses. In addition, the TAT relies on more qualitative methods of interpretation and assesses the "here and now" features of an individual's life situation rather than the basic underlying structure of personality. Since its origin, the TAT has become one of the more extensively used psychological tools in clinical practice and has also served as a model for the development of similar techniques.

The TAT materials consist of 20 cards with ambiguous pictures on them. The examinee is instructed to make up a story that includes what is occurring in the picture: the thoughts and feelings of the characters, the events that led up to the situation, and the outcome of the story. The examiner can interpret the responses either quantitatively (using rating scales to measure intensity, duration, and frequency of needs) or qualitatively (evaluating the story themes using clinical judgment). The final results can be an important adjunct and supplement to other psychological tests because the TAT produces not only highly rich, varied, and complex types of information, but also personal data that theoretically bypass a subject's conscious resistances.

HISTORY AND DEVELOPMENT

The TAT was first conceptualized in a 1935 article by Christina Morgan and Henry Murray but was more fully elaborated in 1938 and 1943 (Morgan, 1995). Administrators were instructed to give all 20 cards in a given sequence in two separate sessions which, in total, could last up to two hours. The basic assumption was that unconscious fantasies could be revealed by interpreting the stories subjects told regarding ambiguous pictures. Examiners potentially gained access to things that a client was either unwilling to tell or unconscious of. Initially, it was believed that the material derived from the test could serve as an "X ray" of personality and would reveal basic themes that might otherwise take months of psychoanalysis to understand. The test immediately had an enthusiastic reception and quickly became used as both a clinical instrument and a research tool. By 1950, several books and over 100 articles were published either on or using it. The early research studies using the TAT investigated such areas as social attitudes, delinquency, abnormal personality, and variations in the use of language. By the late 1940s, many clinicians were using a limited number of cards and abbreviated scoring systems to reduce the time for administration and scoring. These different TAT systems were elaborated in Shneidman's (1951) *Thematic Test Analysis.* By 1971, over 1,800 articles had been written based on the TAT.

Despite continuing extensive research, the test is still not considered to have achieved a degree of standardization comparable to the MMPI/MMPI-2 or WAIS-R. There is no clear, agreed-on scoring and interpretive system, and controversy regarding the adequacy of its reliability and validity is ongoing. Most clinicians vary the methods of administration, especially regarding the number, sequence, and types of cards that are given (Haynes & Peltier, 1985; Keiser & Prather, 1990). As a result, the TAT is considered to be a highly impressionistic tool, with interpretation frequently coming from a combination of intuition and clinical experience. Yet the TAT continues to be extremely popular and ranks as the fourth most frequently used test by clinical psychologists (Piotrowski & Zalewski, 1993; Watkins et al., 1995). Fully 63% of psychologists reported using it with adolescent clients (Archer et al., 1991); 51% of them used it in juvenile forensic settings (Haynes & Peltier, 1985). Clinical psychologists have made it the second most frequently recommended projective test for clinical psychology trainees' competence (Watkins et al., 1995). Furthermore, it has been used in all the European countries, India, South Africa, China, South America, Asia, and the Soviet Union. The TAT (or TAT-type tests) has also been found to be the most frequently used assessment device for cross-cultural research (Retief, 1987).

A number of researchers were dissatisfied with the TAT because they wanted to study different populations (children, the elderly, minorities) and specific problem areas (frustration, stress, social judgment), or because they felt that the TAT produced negative, low-energy stories. These concerns stimulated numerous variations. The most common is the Children's Apperception Test (CAT; Bellak, 1954, 1986, 1993) designed for children between the ages of 3 and 10. Only 10 cards are given, and animals are depicted instead of humans. The rationale was that because children have shorter attention spans, they need fewer cards. It was also believed that they could more easily identify with pictures of animals rather than humans. Subsequently, another version of the CAT was developed depicting humans instead of animals (CAT-Human or CAT-H). The Gerontological Apperception Test (Wolk & Wolk, 1971) and the more frequently used Senior Apperception Test (SAT; Bellak, 1975, 1986, 1993; Bellak & Bellak, 1973) are designed for elderly populations and show pictures of elderly people involved in scenes more likely to concern them, such as depictions of loneliness and family conflicts. The Tell Me A Story Test (TEMAS; Costantino, Malgady, & Rogler, 1988), designed for use with minorities, includes 23 cards depicting Hispanic and Black characters in situations of interpersonal conflict. There is also a parallel version for nonminorities. Scoring is made for nine different personality functions (aggression, anxiety, and so on), and the scores have been found to effectively discriminate between minority outpatients and minority normal school children (Costantino, Malgady, Casullo, & Castillo, 1991; Costantino, Malgady, Rogler, & Tsui, 1988) as well as nonminority normals and clinical groups (Costantino, Malgady, Colon-Malgady, & Bailey, 1992).

Several TAT-type tests have been designed to study specific problem areas. The Rosenzweig Picture Frustration Study (Rosenzweig, 1976, 1977, 1978) was designed to more fully understand how persons perceive and deal with frustration. The Stress Tolerance Test is an older test that may begin to be used more frequently again in understanding how a subject responds to stressful scenes of combat (Harrower, 1986). More recently, Caruso (1988) developed a series of TAT-type cards to study the presence of and the dynamics involved in child abuse. Three sets of cards are available: (a) the basic set of 25 cards depicting scenes pulling for possible child abuse; (b) a 10-card set for neglect; and (c) 5 cards to assess attitudes toward different courtroom themes. The Family Apperception Test, comprised of 21 pictures of family interactions, is designed to assess family dynamics (Julian, Sotile, Henry, & Sotile, 1991). The Blacky Pictures Test (Blum, 1950, 1962, 1968) is another thematic-type test that is closely aligned to psychoanalytic theory. It presents children with pictures of a dog named Blacky who is involved in situations consistent with psychoanalytic theory, such as themes surrounding oral, anal, and phallic stages of development.

Ritzler, Sharkey, and Chudy (1980) have criticized the TAT for producing negative, low-energy stories and for containing outdated pictures that are difficult for persons to identify with. To counter this, they developed the Southern Mississippi TAT (SM-TAT) using pictures derived from the *Family of Man* (Steichen, 1955) photo collection. They report that using the SM-TAT pictures produces stories with more activity, greater emotional tone, and relatively few variations in thematic content (Sharkey & Ritzler, 1985). More importantly, the results derived from the SM-TAT were more effective in discriminating different pathological groups than the TAT. Depressives produced gloomy stories and psychotics demonstrated more perceptual distortions when compared with normals. A more recent but similar attempt is the 8-card Apperceptive Personality Test (APT), which has the advantages of an objective scoring system, a set sequence of card presentations, multiethnic pictures, and initial positive validity outcomes (Holmstrom, Karp, & Silber, 1994; Karp, Holmstrom, & Silber, 1989; Karp, Silber, Holmstrom, Banks, & Karp, 1992). Even though the SM-TAT and APT are more modern, are based on a more rigorous methodology, and demonstrate greater diagnostic validity, the long tradition and extensive research associated with the TAT may make it difficult to supplant, even with potentially better instruments.

In addition to the TAT's derivatives, a number of different approaches to scoring and interpreting the TAT itself have been developed. The original approach by Murray involves assessing which character in the story is the "hero" or focal figure, and then quantifying the relative intensity of each expressed need on a five-point scale. Murray also includes measuring the forces of the hero/heroine's environment (press), types of outcomes, basic themes (themas), and interests and sentiments of the hero/heroine. In addition to Murray's system, many variations have been developed by authors such as Arnold (1962), Bellak (1975, 1986, 1993), Chusmir (1985), Dana (1955), Eron (1950), McClelland (1971), Thomas and Dudek (1985), and Wyatt

(1947). The extensive diversity of different systems led Murstein, in his 1963 review of the TAT, to remark: "There would seem to be as many thematic scoring systems as there were hairs in the beard of Rasputin" (p. 23). Perhaps the strongest and most frequently updated system has been Bellak's (1975, 1986, 1993). His book on the TAT (*The TAT, CAT, and SAT in Clinical Use*) has undergone five editions and is perhaps the simplest and most frequently used of the available systems. As a result, his scoring method and his interpretive approach have been included in this chapter.

MURRAY'S THEORY OF PERSONALITY

The TAT is so integrally involved with Murray's concepts of personality that a survey of his basic theory is important. In constructing his theory, Murray emphasized the biological basis as well as the social and environmental determinants of behavior. He was also consistently aware of how individuals interact with their environment—how people are affected by external forces and how their unique set of needs, attitudes, and values influences their reaction to the world around them.

Perhaps more than any other theorist, Murray has analyzed and clarified the concept of *needs*. This has been the focus of his conceptual efforts, and the development of the TAT grew from his attempt to evaluate and assess the relative strength of individuals' specific psychological needs. Murray (1938) defined a need as:

> a construct which stands for a force . . . which organizes perception, apperception, intellectualization, connotation and action in such a way as to transform in a certain direction an existing, unsatisfying situation. Thus, it manifests itself by leading the organism to search for, or to avoid encountering, or when encountered, to attend and respond to certain kinds of press (environmental forces). . . . Each need is characteristically accompanied by a particular feeling or emotion and tends to use certain modes . . . to further its ends. (pp. 123–124)

A need can be either provoked by internal processes or, more frequently, the result of specific environmental events.

Although Murray distinguishes among different types of needs, the most important distinction is between primary or viscerogenic needs and secondary or psychogenic needs. Primary needs are linked to physiological events and are innate to each individual. They typically refer to physical satisfactions—the needs for air, water, food, or sex. Secondary needs, which are originally derived from primary needs, are acquired during the process of psychological development. They generally lack a strong connection to biological processes and are psychological in nature. Examples are: needs for affiliation, achievement, recognition, dominance, autonomy, and acquisition (see Table 10–1 for a complete listing).

Although it simplifies understanding to consider needs separately, in reality they do not function in isolation from one another. Rather, they interact with one another to create areas of mutual influence and effect. For example, needs may be in *conflict* with one another, as when a need for power is antagonistic to a need for affiliation, or a need for achievement is opposed to a need for pleasure. There may also be a *fusion* of needs,

Table 10–1. Murray's list of needs

A. Needs Motivated by Desire for Power, Property, Prestige, Knowledge, or Creative Achievement
1. n Achievement
2. n Acquisition
3. n Aggression
4. n Construction
5. n Counteraction
6. n Dominance
7. n Exposition
8. n Recognition
9. n Understanding

B. Needs Motivated by Affection, Admiration, Sympathy, Love, and Dependence
1. n Affiliation
2. n Deference
3. n Nurturance
4. n Sex
5. n Succorance

C. Needs Motivated by a Desire for Freedom, Change, Excitement, and Play
1. n Autonomy
2. n Change, Travel, Adventure
3. n Excitance, Dissipation
4. n Playmirth

D. Miscellaneous Needs
1. n Abasement
2. n Blame Avoidance
3. n Cognizance
4. n Harm Avoidance
5. n Passivity
6. n Rejection
7. n Retention
8. n Sentience

Source: Adapted from Murray (1938, pp. 152–226).

where separate needs such as power and achievement produce the same behaviors. Finally, there may be a *subsidization* of needs, where one need is subsidized by, or works for, another. For example, an individual may express a high degree of aggressiveness, which is actually working to support an underlying need for acquisition.

When Murray uses the term *need,* he refers to the significant determinants of behavior that reside in an individual. In contrast, *press* refers to the environmental determinants that elicit specific behaviors from an individual or constellate specific needs within him or her (see Table 10–2). "The press of an object is what it can do to the subject or for the subject—the power that it has to affect the well-being of the subject in one way or another" (Murray, 1938, p. 121). Murray conceptualizes press as either alpha or beta. Beta press refers to the individual's perceptions and interpretations of a specific aspect of the environment, and alpha press refers to the objective or real

Table 10–2.   Murray's list of press

A. Press of Deprivation
   1. p Acquisition
   2. p Retention

B. Press Descriptive of an Empty, Alien, or Rejecting Environment
   1. p Lack
   2. p Loss
   3. p Rejection
   4. p Uncongenial Environment

C. Press of Coercion and Restraint
   1. p Dominance
   2. p Imposed Task, Duty, Training

D. Press Descriptive of a Hostile, Aggressive Environment
   1. p Aggression

E. Press of Danger, Injury, Death
   1. p Affliction
   2. p Death of Hero
   3. p Physical Danger
   4. p Physical Injury

F. Press of Friendliness, Sympathy, Respect, Dependence, Love
   1. p Affiliation
   2. p Deference
   3. p Nurturance
   4. p Sex
   5. p Succorance

G. Miscellaneous Press
   1. p Birth of Offspring
   2. p Claustrum
   3. p Cognizance
   4. p Example
   5. p Exposition
   6. p Luck

Source: Adapted from Murray (1938, pp. 152–226).

aspects of that environment. Most behaviors are a direct result of beta press, but it is important to be aware of the wide discrepancies between an individual's subjective interpretation of the world and the world as it actually is. A striking example of such a discrepancy is the delusional systems of paranoid patients, who consistently distort external reality as a result of their inner psychological processes.

To conceptualize units of behavior that result from the interaction between needs and press, Murray developed the term *thema*. A thema is a small unit of behavior that can combine with other thema to form *serial thema*. An individual's *unity thema* is the pattern of related needs and press that gives meaning to the largest portion of his or her behavior. For example, a core and overriding feature of an individual might be rebelliousness or martyrdom. This may be sufficiently well organized and powerful to override even primary needs, as amply demonstrated in the case of a martyr who is willing

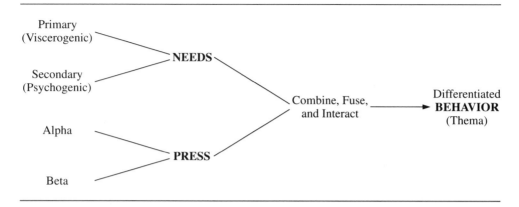

Figure 10–1.   Outline of Murray's theory of personality

to die for his or her beliefs. A unity thema is derived from early infantile experiences and, once developed, repeats itself in many forms during an individual's later life. It operates largely as an unconscious force, and Murray (1938) described it as "a compound of interrelated—collaborating or conflicting—dominant needs that are linked to press to which the individual was exposed on one or more particular occasions, gratifying or traumatic, in early childhood" (pp. 604–605). The TAT was designed to assess both small units of thema and the larger, core aspects of an individual's unity themas.

Figure 10–1 summarizes the basic elements of Murray's theory. These elements are relatively simple and straightforward, but the specific details are complicated and comprehensive. The details not only include an extensive enumeration of a wide variety of needs and press, but they take into account the complexities of their interactions.

In summary, Murray's theory is a listing and description of the various types of and interactions among different needs, not a comprehensive understanding of personality. Murray also focuses on motivational aspects of the person; tension reduction is the central theme to explain an individual's external behavior. Although these contributions are significant, the main achievement of Murray has been the development of the TAT, which is a direct result of his theories and has been used to provide support for them.

RELIABILITY AND VALIDITY

A subject's responses to the TAT involve complex, meaningful verbal material. Because of the complexity of this material, exact quantitative analysis is difficult, and interpretations are typically based more on a qualitative than a quantitative analysis of story content. Most methods of determining reliability therefore become problematic. However, some success in achieving adequate interscorer reliability has resulted from the development of quantitative scoring strategies and rating scales. This is especially true for the work of McClelland (1961) and Atkinson and Feather (1966), who developed complex scoring schemes for achievement, affiliation, and power. Interscorer reliability across different scoring systems has generally been found to be good, ranging between .37 and .90, with most reports in the higher ranges (Murstein, 1972). However, even though scorers can agree on the quantitative values assigned to different variables, these still constitute raw data and not conclusions. In other words, it remains questionable whether clinicians will make the same inferences regarding personality based on the quantitative scores. Good interscorer reliability relating to such areas as the weighting of different needs has been achieved, but agreement between the conclusions based on these scores has typically not been adequately demonstrated. A further complication is the fact that, in actual practice, clinicians rely primarily on intuitive clinical judgment, use different sets of instructions, and vary the number, type, and sequence of cards from one client to the next (Haynes & Peltier, 1985; Karp et al., 1992). Thus, reliability in clinical contexts is likely to be considerably lower than under experimental conditions.

Another difficulty in determining reliability lies in the wide variability among different stories. If test evaluators wish to determine the internal consistency of the TAT, they are confronted with the fact that the various cards are not comparable (Entwisle, 1972). They were designed to measure separate areas of a person's functioning. Thus, a strategy such as split half reliability is inappropriate. Not only are different stories in the same administration likely to be different, but so are the stories between two different administrations. Thus, measures of internal consistency have been (and would be expected to be) low (Entwisle, 1972). Likewise, when subjects were requested to tell different stories on different administrations, the test-retest reliabilities derived from quantitative scorings of various needs were low (Lindzey & Herman, 1955). In contrast, Lundy (1985) found that when subjects were requested to tell a similar story between one administration and the next, test-retest reliabilities achieved a respectable .56 (need for affiliation) and .48 (need for achievement). This suggests that the test-retest reliability of the TAT might be underestimated. However, the higher reliabilities found by Lundy (1985) might reflect merely the quality of memory rather than the stability of personality indices on the TAT (Kraiger, Hakel, & Cornelius, 1984).

Reviews of the TAT's validity have shown wide variability. Proponents of the test describe "impressive" and "strong" relationships, whereas critics have said that validity is "almost nonexistent." This disparity can be partially accounted for by differing interpretations of the data. One reviewer might be impressed by a correlation of .45 while another sees it as highly deficient. It would seem that not only is the TAT a projective test itself, but the research done on it likewise allows readers to project their biases, needs, and expectations onto the TAT. One factor that might help to explain the differences in results between studies is that the TAT has been found to be quite sensitive to the effects of instructions. Lundy (1988), for example, found that under conditions that were nonthreatening, neutral, and unstructured, there were moderate correlations between outside criterion measures and needs for achievement, affiliation, and power. When instructions were used that presented the TAT as a structured formal test or, especially, when any words were used that might have been interpreted as threatening (will "reveal imperfections" or "minor defects"), the correlations were nonsignificant. This suggests the interesting possibility that the wide variation in the findings of different studies may have been partially influenced by slight variations in instructions.

Studies attempting to determine criterion validity have shown a balance between positive and negative findings. One major problem lies in establishing agreed-on external criteria. If short-term overt behavior is used as the criterion, there is often little correspondence with test scores. For example, high aggression on TAT scores usually does not reflect the degree to which a person actually expresses aggressive behavior. However, it may still be valuable to understand a person's internal processes even though these are not outwardly expressed. When measures of needs on the TAT were compared with needs measured on tests such as the Edwards Personal Preference Schedule, Adjective Check List, and other forms of self-rated questionnaires, there was little correspondence (Megargee & Parker, 1968; Spangler, 1992). The above findings would seem to call into question the usefulness of TAT protocols. However, a number of positive findings between the TAT and outside criteria have also been reported. An early and frequently cited study by Harrison (1940) found that diagnosis by a trained clinician using the TAT was accurate 75% of the time when assessing broad diagnostic categories. Similarly, a correlation of .78 was found when comparing TAT inferences with data from hospital records. The most extensively studied constructs have been achievement, affiliation, and power (Lundy, 1988; Spangler, 1992), and these, too, have had varying degrees of success when they were compared with outside criteria. Examples of recent positive results include a high need for achievement being associated with greater social attractiveness (Teevan, Diffenderfer, & Greenfield, 1986), need for affiliation being positively correlated with a preference for an internally directed orientation to tasks (Schroth, 1987), and need for achievement being positively related to grade point average (although this might have been confounded by verbal fluency; Lindgren, Moritsch, Thurlin, & Mich, 1986). In addition, Coche and Sillitti (1983) reported that the presence of depressive themes on the TAT was correlated with measures of depression on the MMPI and Beck Depression Inventory. Maitra (1983) found that the fantasies of highly effective executives differed significantly from those of relatively ineffective executives in that the more effective executives had more original themes, expressed a broader range of interests, were more intellectual, and could see beyond the individual details of their work.

In a meta-analysis of 105 studies, Spangler (1992) concluded that, on average, TAT correlations of behavior (.19–.22) were slightly larger than correlations based on questionnaires (.13–.15). Although these correlations were quite low, the TAT and questionnaires were relatively more effective in different situations. The TAT produced quite high correlations (.66) when subjects were required to spontaneously initiate (*internally*) their own behavior in order to achieve some activity (moderate task risk, task completion, response to time pressure). In contrast, self-report questionnaires were low in making the above predictions, but relatively effective (.35) in predicting situations involving real-world behavior where social reinforcement (*external*) was present.

Like the studies on criterion validity, the work on construct validity has shown varying results. A representative confirmatory study provided support for the hypothesis that subjects who were experimentally frustrated produced subsequent stories in which the focal characters in the stories expressed increased aggression (Lindzey & Kalnins, 1958). Likewise, persons who had used marijuana prior to testing showed an increase in primary process content in their stories (West, Martindale, Hines, & Roth, 1983).

An important issue in the interpretation of criterion validity studies on the TAT and other projective devices is understanding the implications of different levels of interpretation. Klopfer (1983) summarized the earlier work of Leary (1957) by indicating that behavior can be based on outside observations (direct behavioral data, public communication), self-descriptions, or private symbolization. These three levels are often quite different from one another. For example, the observations by others are frequently quite discrepant from how a particular person perceives himself or herself. Likewise, a person's inner fantasy life (private symbolization) is often quite different from his or her public behavior. Projective tests such as the TAT primarily assess a person's inner life of private symbolization. McClelland, Koestner, and Weinberger (1989) have described the characteristics that the TAT measures as being *implicit* motives as opposed to more conscious self-attributions. Thus, the TAT measured motives and underlying themes that are physiologically and nonconsciously connected to the person, and they influence long- rather than short-term behaviors. This is supported in that TAT results do accurately predict long-term outcomes such as overall success in a person's career (Spangler, 1992). McClelland et al. (1989) even emphasize that it would be unreasonable for the TAT to correlate highly with immediate, conscious, short-term behavior because this is not what the TAT was designed to measure. Furthermore, it may not even be desirable for TAT data to relate to immediate external behavior because it is precisely this ability to access a person's inner life that makes projectives both unique and valuable. From a practical perspective, each clinician needs to evaluate the above issues and to establish the importance each places on having access to a person's inner world of private symbolization.

One argument against subjecting the TAT to strict psychometric scrutiny is that rigid objective studies do not represent the way in which the TAT is actually used in clinical practice. When experienced clinicians were requested to provide individual descriptions of persons based on TAT stories, the descriptions did tend to match independent descriptions based on case histories (Arnold, 1949; Harrison, 1940). However, even though the descriptions by individual clinicians were fairly accurate, there was usually little agreement among different clinicians evaluating the same person. It might be argued that, because of the complexity and richness of the material, each clinician was tapping into different (but still potentially valid) aspects of the same person. The poor interrater reliability might then be interpreted as not representing inaccuracy, but rather different approaches to the material, with each of these approaches having potentially relevant meanings for the client being evaluated.

ASSETS AND LIMITATIONS

Despite questions related to reliability and validity, the status of the TAT over the past 20 years has remained essentially unchanged (Archer et al., 1991; Lubin et al., 1985). It is still rated as the seventh most frequently used test, and it has produced the fourth largest number of research studies (behind the MMPI Wechsler-intelligence scales, and Rorschach). One reviewer has summarized the incongruity between its popularity and its questionable validity by stating that "there are still enthusiastic clinicians and doubting statisticians" (Adcock, 1965). In light of this controversy, it is especially important that clinicians fully understand the general assets and limitations involved with the TAT.

Like most projective techniques, the TAT is potentially a valuable tool. Theoretically, it offers access to the covert and deeper structures of an individual's personality. There is also less susceptibility to faking because the purpose of projective techniques is usually disguised, and the subject often slackens his or her conscious defenses while releasing unconscious material. However, because the TAT deals with verbally familiar material, there is a somewhat greater potential for the subject to bias and distort his or her responses when compared to other projective techniques. A further asset is the focus on the global nature of personality rather than on the objective measurement of specific traits or attitudes. These include not only emotional, motivational, and interpersonal characteristics, but also general intellectual level, verbal fluency, originality, and style of solving problems. Finally, there is ease of rapport. Most projective tests are regarded as intrinsically interesting and nonthreatening because there are no "wrong" answers. However, certain types of individuals might still feel quite anxious and insecure with the lack of structure of projective techniques.

In contrast to the above assets, the following general criticisms have been leveled at projective techniques and therefore must be considered when using the TAT. There has typically been difficulty establishing adequate internal consistency and test-retest reliability. Because inadequate normative data are generally lacking, clinicians often rely on clinical experience when they interpret the responses. The standardization in respect to administration and scoring is generally inadequate. Thus, the effectiveness of the technique is often more dependent on the clinician's individual skill than on the quality of the test itself. Most studies on projectives, as well as the results coming from individual assessments, are confounded by age, sex, intelligence, and reading ability (Klein, 1986). Projectives have also been shown to be quite sensitive to situational variables such as mood (McFarland, 1984), stress, sleep deprivation, and differences in instruction (Lundy, 1988). These variables can significantly alter test performance, thereby reducing the likelihood that stable aspects of personality are being measured. Finally, the validity studies on most projectives have been equivocal. In particular, several researchers have noted that there has been no increase in incremental validity when the TAT and most other projectives are used in a battery of tests (see Garb, 1984; Klein, 1986; Lanyon & Goodstein, 1982).

Although these general considerations must be understood when using projective techniques, a number of characteristics specific to the TAT should also be kept in mind. One important asset is that the responses it produces from clients (verbal stories) are familiar rather than hidden and mysterious. Even a relatively untrained person can appreciate the differing themes, moods, and perspectives portrayed in the stories. The experienced clinician also profits from this inherent familiarity or approachability of the test data.

A further asset of the TAT is its origin within an academic-humanistic environment. It is not closely aligned within any particular school of thought and therefore can be approached from, and interpreted by, a number of different theoretical orientations. Furthermore, the TAT was developed from the study of normal individuals rather than by case studies or normative comparisons with disordered populations. This orientation has evolved directly out of Murray's belief that the proper beginning point for understanding personality is the intensive and detailed study of normal persons.

The TAT potentially provides a comprehensive evaluation of personality, which has sometimes been referred to as a "wide-band" approach (Rabin, 1968). For example, among the comprehensive dimensions that the TAT can assess are: a person's cognitive style, imaginative processes, family dynamics, inner adjustment, emotional reactivity, general intelligence, and sexual adjustment (Bellak, 1993; Henry, 1956). The TAT also has some potential to evaluate such areas as creativity, level of affect, problem-solving skill, and verbal fluency. Thus, although the TAT is primarily concerned with providing insight into a person's fundamental needs and patterns of interaction, it can also give important information about a far wider range of areas. In particular, the TAT may bypass conscious resistance to provide themes that the person may not reveal upon direct questioning. For example, alcoholics who reported high levels of internal locus of control on direct self-report questionnaires, typically became highly externally oriented when locus of control was measured using a TAT-type instrument (Costello & Wicott, 1984). This might be interpreted as the TAT-type test bypassing their conscious denial and assessing a possibly more accurate, or at least different, level of private symbolization.

Although the TAT is potentially quite versatile, it is not self-sufficient. A number of authors have emphasized that the TAT yields optimal results only when included in a battery of tests (Anastasi, 1996) and/or as a type of structured clinical interview (Obrzut & Cummings, 1983). In contrast, some reviewers have pointed out that the TAT and other projective tests do not help increase incremental validity in structured conditions and may even serve to reduce it (Garb, 1984; Klein, 1986).

One unresolved dispute surrounding the TAT is the relationship between inner fantasies and overt behavior. It has been assumed by most projective test originators, including Murray, that fantasy productions can be used to predict covert motivational dispositions. However, it is questionable whether high fantasy productions in a certain area actually parallel overt behavior (Klinger, 1966; McClelland, 1966; Skolnick, 1966). In fact, fantasies may even serve to compensate for a lack of certain behaviors. It might be quite consistent for a highly repressed, overcontrolled person to have a high number of inner aggressive fantasies. In a 20-year longitudinal study of adolescents who obtained high TAT scores on need for achievement, the subjects were often *not* among those who subsequently showed upward social mobility. However, individuals who had shown upward social mobility typically obtained higher TAT need-for-achievement scores as adults. The interpretive significance here is that it might be better to see fantasy productions as samples of thoughts that may or may not accurately reflect overt behavior.

Practical difficulties associated with the TAT are: the extensive amount of training required to properly learn the technique, and its relative cost-effectiveness in terms of the time required for administration and scoring (Haynes & Peltier, 1985). Simply obtaining biographical information, asking direct questions during an interview, or using rating forms or questionnaires might give similar information in a simpler and quicker manner.

A further liability—one that is particularly relevant for the TAT—is the subjectivity involved in both scoring and interpretation procedures. Although the various scoring methods have attempted to reduce the degree of subjectivity, intuitive judgment necessarily plays a significant role. This results in part from an inadequate development of norms, and from the fact that the norms that have been created are only a rough approximation of common story themes (see "Typical Themes Elicited" below). Frequently, in clinical practice, each person develops his or her own individual intuitive norms, based on past experience. Thus, the clinician may have a general intuitive conception of what constitutes a "schizophrenic" or "narcissistic" story and will use this subjective schema during diagnostic or interpretive procedures. Reliance on clinical experience becomes indirectly encouraged both by the lack of precise normative data and, more importantly, by the belief that norms tend to decrease the richness and comprehensiveness of the material being studied. A possible source of bias is that, because clinicians work predominantly with pathology, their firsthand experience of the characteristic reactions of normal people on tests such as the TAT is limited. This may result in their overemphasizing the pathological features of stories and experiencing difficulty when assessing fairly well-adjusted persons.

ADMINISTRATION

General Considerations

The TAT was intended to be administered in an interpersonal setting in which subjects verbally respond to pictures presented to them. However, when the examiner is absent, responses may be taped or written out by the subject. The disadvantage of these latter procedures is that the subject's responses are often more contrived and clichéd, because more time is available to censor fantasy material.

The TAT materials consist of 20 cards on which ambiguous pictures are printed. The cards are numbered so that a total of 20 cards can be presented to four different groups: adult males, adult females, boys, and girls. The back of each card is coded with a number and/or letters to designate which sex and/or age group the card is intended for. A number without a letter indicates the card is to be administered to all subjects regardless of age or sex. A number with "M" or "F" designates that the card is intended for males or females, and "B" or "G" designates boys or girls, respectively. There may also be a number and either BM or GF, indicating the card is to be given to boys/males or girls/females.

There is some controversy as to whether all 20 cards should be administered or a shorter version of selected cards should be substituted. In actual practice, administration of between 8 and 12 cards is far more frequent (Bellak, 1993; Dana, 1985; Haynes & Peltier, 1985; Keiser & Prather, 1990). If fewer than 20 cards are administered, the selection of cards may be idiosyncratic to the patient's presenting problem or based on previous information derived from relevant history or other test data. For example, if depression and suicide are significant issues for the client, the examiner might administer cards 3BM, 13B, and 14, in an attempt to gather specific information regarding the dynamics of the client's condition. Specific cards may also be selected because they typically produce rich responses. Bellak (1993) recommends that the following standard sequence of 10 cards be administered to both females and males in this exact order: 1, 2, 3BM, 4, 6BM, 7GF, 8BM, 9GF, 10, and 13MF. He further recommends that an essential sequence of cards to be administered to any males consists of: 1, 2, 3BM, 4, 6BM, 7BM, 11, 12M, and 13MF. The essential cards for any females are the following sequence: 1, 2, 3, 3BM, 4, 6GF, 7GF, 9GF, 11, and 13MF. If a reduced number of cards is used, it may be preferable to give the cards in the sequence numbered on the back, although Murstein (1963) presents evidence to suggest that the stimulus value of the cards themselves overshadows any effects produced as a result of altered sequencing. Dana (1985) urges that if the TAT is the only means of assessment, or if the results of an assessment might be used in court proceedings, then all 20 cards should be administered, in two separate sessions, because rarely can a person continue for more than an hour without becoming fatigued and losing interest.

For research purposes, a slightly different listing of card frequencies has been found by Keiser and Prather (1990), who reviewed 26 studies that specified which of Murray's cards were used. The 10 most frequent cards were: 1, 2, 3BM, 3GF, 4, 5, 6BM, 6GF, 8BM, and 8GF.

During administration, the subject should be seated beside the examiner, with his or her chair turned away so that he or she cannot see the expressions on the examiner's face. Ideally, this creates a situation in which the subject is comfortable and relaxed, so that his or her imagination can freely respond to the cards. However, if some individuals do not feel comfortable when turned away from the examiner, they should be allowed to sit in a position that is more relaxing for them. Of primary importance are: establishing adequate rapport and keeping the subject comfortable and relaxed.

Instructions

Murray's original instructions from the TAT Manual (1943) are as follows:

> This is a test of imagination, one form of intelligence. I am going to show you some pictures, one at a time; and your task will be to make up as dramatic a story as you can for each. Tell what has led up to the event shown in the picture, describe what is happening at the moment, what the characters are feeling and thinking; and then give the outcome. Speak your thoughts as they come to your mind. Do you understand? Since you have fifty minutes for ten pictures, you can devote about five minutes to each story. Here is the first picture. (p. 3)

This set of instructions is suitable for adolescents and adults of average intelligence and sophistication. However, the instructions should be modified for children, adults with minimal education or intelligence, and psychotics. For these types of individuals, Murray (1943) suggests that the examiner state:

> This is a story-telling test. I have some pictures here that I am going to show you, and for each picture I want you to make up a story. Tell what is happening before and what is happening now. Say what the people are feeling and thinking and how it will come out. You can make up any story you please. Do you understand? Well, then, here is the first picture. You have five minutes to make up a story. See how well you can do. (pp. 3–4)

Such instructions may, of course, be modified, elaborated, or repeated to meet the individual needs of each subject. Lundy (1988) recommends that the instructions should be given in as neutral and nonthreatening a manner as possible, so that the person doesn't become defensive. Defensiveness is likely to reduce the validity of the results. Any references to the TAT as a "test" should be avoided. However, the instructions should clearly indicate that the client is to use some imagination and not merely provide a description of the pictures. Variations on the instructions should also emphasize the four requirements of the story structure:

1. Current situation.
2. Thoughts and feelings of the characters.
3. Preceding events.
4. Outcome.

The instructions, either in whole or in part, may be repeated at any time, particularly if the subject has given a story that is too short or too long, or if he or she has left out one or more of the four requirements. Hurley and Sovner (1985) suggest that the TAT can potentially be excellent for the evaluation of mentally retarded persons, but particular care needs to be taken to ensure that the instructions are concrete and explicit. The examiner may also want to check whether the instructions have been clearly understood. He or she may need to encourage the person at various times during the storytelling.

Procedure

Time

The time measured should begin when the picture is first presented and end when the subject begins his or her story. It is particularly important to notice any long pauses or hesitations. They may reflect a struggle with conflictual or anxiety-laden material.

Recording

A subject's complete responses should be recorded, along with any noteworthy behavioral observations: exclamations, stuttering, pauses, blushing, degree of involvement, and changes in voice inflection. Thus, the general purpose of recording is not only to develop a reproduction of the verbatim story content, but to assess how the person interacts with the picture. As mentioned previously, ongoing verbal involvement with the cards is the preferable form of administration. Having subjects write out their own stories allows time for critically evaluating and censoring their responses. There is no objection to the use of a tape recorder, although, under such conditions, it is helpful to have the examiner record noteworthy behavioral observations and obtain the clients' written consent.

Questioning and Inquiry

If a subject omits certain aspects of the story, such as the outcome or preceding events, the examiner should ask for additional information. This may take the form of questions, such as "What led up to it?" or "How does it end?" However, these requests for clarification or amplification should not be stated in such a way as to bias the stories or reveal the examiner's personal reaction. A more detailed inquiry may be undertaken either after the entire administration of the cards, or directly after each story. Murray recommends that the inquiry should occur only after the administration of all the cards. Sample inquiry questions may include: "What made you think of this story?" or "Do people you have mentioned in the story remind you of friends or acquaintances?" As with questioning, the inquiry should not be too forceful or it may produce defensiveness and withdrawal. The overall purpose of both the questioning and the inquiry is to produce an unhampered and free flow of the subject's fantasy material.

Order of Presentation

Usually, the cards should be administered according to their sequential numbering system. However, at times, the examiner may be interested in a specific problem and will alter the sequence to more effectively obtain information concerning that problem area. For example, if the clinician is particularly interested in problems relating to family constellation in a male subject, the examiner might include some of the female series involving sisters, girlfriends, or wives.

Use of the TAT (or CAT) with Children.

Instructions for children should, of course, be modified in accordance with their age and vocabulary. It is usually helpful to describe the test as an opportunity to tell stories or as an interesting game. In general, cards from the TAT should be based on the likelihood that children may easily identify with the characters. For use with children, the TAT cards that have the highest number of interpretable responses and the lowest number of refusals are, in order of usefulness: 7GF, 18GF, 3GF, and 8GF (Bellak, 1993). In contrast, the least helpful cards are: 19, 18BM, 11, and 12BG (Bellak, 1993).

The stories of children are relatively easily influenced by recent events experienced via television, comic books, and movies. Children also tend to project their problems and conflicts into a story in a more direct and straightforward manner than adults. Often, there is little hidden meaning or masking of the relationships involved.

TYPICAL THEMES ELICITED

At the present time, no formal normative standards have been developed for the TAT. However, Bellak (1993) has indicated that David Abrams and his colleagues are developing extensive norms for use with the Bellak scoring and interpretive system. Currently, the best substitute for extensive and objective norms is a well-developed knowledge of the typical stories elicited by each of the cards. This knowledge should be accompanied by an awareness of possible significant variations from the more frequent plots. These can serve to alert the examiner to unique, and therefore more easily interpretable, types of stories. Deviations from clichéd or stereotyped responses can be significant in that they may represent important areas of conflict, creative thinking, or important features of the subject's overall personality. If the clinician is equipped with expectations regarding typical versus unusual responses, it will enable him or her to (a) observe more easily specific attitudes toward the central problem; (b) notice gaps where the inquiry can begin; (c) assess which type of information the subject resists, as indicated by the use of noncommittal clichés; and (d) notice any deviation from the expected information that may contain significant and interpretable responses.

Murray's TAT cards and Bellak's original version of the CAT are described and discussed below. The descriptions of each TAT card that follow are divided into three sections:

1. Brief description of card.
2. Plots frequently encountered.
3. A general discussion of the significance and overall usefulness of the card.

The descriptions of each TAT card are this author's characterization of the scene's content; the CAT descriptions are from Bellak (1993, pp. 251–254). The discussion of each picture summarizes the work of Bellak (1993), Murray (1943), and Stein (1981).

Thematic Apperception Test (TAT)

Picture 1

1. **Description of Card.** A boy is sitting at a table looking at a violin placed on the table in front of him.
2. **Frequent Plots.** Typical stories emerging from this card revolve around either a self-motivated boy who is daydreaming about becoming an outstanding violinist, or a rebellious boy being forced by his parents, or some other significant authority figure, to play the violin.
3. **General Discussion.** This is often considered to be the most useful picture in the entire TAT (Bellak, 1993). It usually elicits stories describing how the subject deals with the general issue of impulse versus control, or, in a wider sense, the conflict between personal demands and external controlling agents. It also aids in providing information about the client's relationship with his or her parents, by making it relatively easy to see whether the parents are viewed as domineering, controlling, indifferent, helpful, understanding, or protecting (Bellak, 1993). This card frequently gives specific information regarding the need for achievement, and it is important to consider how any expressed achievement is accomplished.

Any variations from the frequent plots described should be taken into consideration. They are likely to provide important reflections of the subject's characteristic modes of functioning. For example, the attitude toward, and relationship with, any introduced figures, or their identification as parents or peers, should be given special attention. Also of importance are: the way in which the issue of impulse versus control is handled, any themes of aggression that might emerge, and, particularly, the specific outcome of the story.

Picture 2

1. **Description of Card.** Country scene with a woman holding a book in the foreground. In the background, a man is working a field while a woman watches.
2. **Frequent Plots.** Stories for this card often involve a young girl who is leaving the farm to increase her education or to seek opportunities that her present home environment cannot provide. Usually, the family is seen as working hard to gain a living from the soil. The family values often center on maintaining the status quo.
3. **General Discussion.** This picture usually provides an excellent description of family relations. As with Picture 1, various themes relate to autonomy from the family versus compliance with the status quo. This is one of the only cards in the series that presents the subject with a group scene and thus gives information relating to how the individual deals with the challenge of people living together. The card itself deals with a younger woman and an older male and female. Thus, it elicits stories dealing with

parent–child and heterosexual relationships. There is usually the added dimension of contrasting the new and the old, and demonstrating attitudes toward personal mobility and ambition. This card may elicit stories relating to competition by the younger daughter for the attention of both or one of the parents. In these stories, her rival is either a sibling, particularly an older female, or the other parent. The extent to which separations or alliances occur among the three figures represented can also be quite revealing. For example, the two women may be united against the male who is "merely a hired hand," or the older male and female may be united against the younger female. Within either of these possible formations, it is important to note the attributes of each person, and the patterns and styles of interaction. Because this card is relatively complex and has a large number of details, compulsive patients often spend an inordinate amount of time commenting and elaborating on the many small details.

Picture 3BM

1. **Description of Card.** A boy is huddled next to a couch. On the floor next to him is an ambiguous object that could be a set of keys or a revolver.

2. **Frequent Plots.** The stories usually center on an individual who has been emotionally involved with another person or who is feeling guilty over some past behavior he has committed. Drug abusers often perceive the person in the picture as an addict and interpret the "revolver" as a hypodermic needle.

3. **General Discussion.** This has been identified as one of the most useful pictures (Bellak, 1993; Keiser & Prather, 1990) because it concerns themes of guilt, depression, aggression, and impulse control. The manner in which the object on the left is seen and described often gives good information regarding problems concerning aggression. For example, if the object is described as a gun, is it used or intended to be used for intra-aggression (the subject is going to use it to do damage to self) or for extra-aggression (the subject has used it, or is going to use it, to harm another person)? If it is used for externally directed aggression, then what are the consequences, if any, for the focal figure as portrayed in the outcome? This picture is particularly important for depressed patients, whether male or female, because it can reveal important dynamics regarding the manner in which the depression developed and how it is currently being maintained. For example, denial of aggressive conflict may be represented by completely overlooking the gun or rendering it harmless by depicting it as a toy pistol or a set of keys. On the other hand, excessive hesitation and detailed consideration of what the object might be could represent a compulsive defense surrounding conflictual aggressive feelings. Because this picture contains a lone figure, attitudes toward the isolated self are often aroused. The picture might be particularly useful for drug abusers because it frequently brings out themes and attitudes toward overdosing, drug use, mechanisms for coping, self-destructive tendencies, and extent of social supports (Patalano, 1986).

Picture 3GF

1. **Description of Card.** A woman is standing next to an open door with one hand grabbing the side of the door and the other holding her downcast face.

2. **Frequent Plots.** As with Picture 3BM, the stories usually revolve around themes of interpersonal loss and contemplated harm directed internally because of guilt over past behavior.

3. **General Discussion.** The same general trends that hold for Picture 3BM are also true here, in that both pictures tend to bring out depressive feelings. Frequently, however, Picture 3BM brings out somewhat richer stories and allows both males and females to identify easily with the central figure.

Picture 4

1. **Description of Card.** A woman is grabbing the shoulders of a man who is turning away from her.

2. **Frequent Plots.** The primary task is to form some conceptualization as to why the woman is restraining the man. Often, the woman is seen as an advice-giving moral agent who is struggling with the more impulsive and irrational man. In approximately half the stories, the vague image of a woman in the background is brought into the story plot.

3. **General Discussion.** This picture typically elicits a good deal of information relating to the feelings and attitudes surrounding male–female relationships. Frequently, themes of infidelity and betrayal emerge, and details regarding the male attitude toward the role of women may be discussed. For example, the woman may be seen as a protector who attempts to prevent the man from becoming involved in self-destructive behavior, or as a siren who tries to detain and control him for evil purposes. Likewise, a woman's attitude toward past male aggressiveness and impulsiveness may be revealed.

A further area of interest is the vague image of a seminude woman in the background. This often provokes themes of triangular jealousy in which one or more characters have been betrayed. When this picture is described, it is important to note whether the woman is depicted as a sexually threatening person or is seen as being more benign.

Picture 5

1. **Description of Card.** A woman is looking into a room from the threshold of a door.

2. **Frequent Plots.** In the most frequent plot, a mother has either caught her child misbehaving or is surprised by an intruder entering her house.

3. **General Discussion.** This picture often reveals information surrounding attitudes about the subject's mother in her role of observing and possibly judging behavior. It is important to note how the woman is perceived and how the situation is resolved. Is she understanding and sympathetic? Does she attempt to invoke guilt? Or is she seen as severely restricting the child's autonomy? Sometimes, voyeuristic themes are discussed, including feelings related to the act of observing others' misbehavior. The examiner should note whether these feelings include guilt, anger, indifference, or fear, and the manner in which these feelings are resolved. Often, this card elicits paranoid fears of attack or intrusion by an outsider, represented by stories in which the woman is surprised by a burglar.

Picture 6BM

1. **Description of Card.** An elderly woman is standing parallel to a window. Behind her is a younger man with his face down. He is holding onto his hat.

2. **Frequent Plots.** This picture typically elicits stories of a son who is either presenting sad news to his mother, or attempting to prepare her for his departure to some distant location.

3. **General Discussion.** This picture is an extremely important one to include when testing males. It usually proves to be a rich source of information regarding attitudes and feelings toward their mother or maternal figures in general. Because the stories usually revolve around a young man striving for independence, the specific manner in which the subject depicts this struggle is important. Does the struggle include an exaggerated amount of guilt? Is there unexpressed or even overt anger toward the older woman? Or does the young man succumb to the woman's wishes? Of equal importance is the mother's reaction to her son's behavior. To what extent does she control him, and how? It is also of interest to note whether the subject accepts the traditional mother–son version, or whether he or she chooses to avoid discussing this relationship directly. If such an avoidance is evident, then how are mother–son themes depicted in other cards that may have elicited discussions of this area (i.e., picture 1 or 5)?

Picture 6GF

1. **Murray's Description.** A young woman sitting on the edge of a sofa looks back over her shoulder at an older man with a pipe in his mouth who seems to be addressing her.

2. **Frequent Plots.** The man is usually seen as proposing some sort of an activity to the woman, and the plot often includes her reaction to this suggestion.

3. **General Discussion.** This card was originally intended to be the female counterpart to Picture 6BM, and it was hoped that it, too, would elicit attitudes and feelings toward paternal figures. However, because the two figures are often seen as being somewhat equal in age, the card frequently does not accomplish its intended purpose. When clear father–daughter plots are not discussed, then the picture reflects the subject's style and approach to unstructured heterosexual relationships. For example, the subject may describe the woman as being startled or embarrassed or, on the other hand, may have her respond in a spontaneous and comfortable manner. It is important to note the manner in which the man is perceived by the woman. Is he seen as a seducer? Does he offer her helpful advice? Is he intrusive? Or is he perceived as a welcome addition? A person who mistrusts interpersonal relationships will typically create a story in which the man is intrusive and the woman's reaction is one of defensiveness and surprise. Subjects who are more trusting and comfortable usually develop themes in which the woman responds in a more accepting and flexible manner.

Picture 7BM

1. **Description of Card.** An older man is looking at a younger man who appears to be peering into space.

2. Frequent Plots. Stories usually describe either a father–son relationship or a boss–employee situation. Regardless of which of these variations is chosen, the older man is most frequently in the position of advising or instructing the younger one.

3. General Discussion. This card is extremely useful in obtaining information about authority figures and, more specifically, the subject's own father. The picture deals with hierarchical personal relationships and usually takes the form of an older, more experienced man interacting with a younger, less experienced one. Thus, the card can clearly show how the subject deals with external demands and attitudes toward authority.

Picture 7GF

1. Description of Card. A young girl is seated on a couch and is holding a doll in her hands. Behind her is an older woman who appears to be reading to her out of a book.

2. Frequent Plots. This picture is usually perceived as a mother and her daughter, with the mother advising, consoling, scolding, or instructing the child. Less frequently, there are themes in which the mother is reading to the child for pleasure or entertainment.

3. General Discussion. The intention here is to bring out the style and manner of mother–child interaction. When older women are the subjects, the picture often elicits feelings and attitudes toward children. Because both figures are looking away, either figure is sometimes perceived as rejecting the other. Thus, the card often elicits negative feelings and interactions, and it is important to note how these feelings are resolved, expressed, or avoided. Sometimes the older woman is described as reading a fairy story to the younger girl. Often, the most instructive data will then come from the fairy story itself.

Picture 8BM

1. Description of Card. A young boy in the foreground is staring directly out of the picture. In the background is a hazy image of two men performing surgery on a patient who is lying down.

2. Frequent Plots. Stories revolve around either ambition (the young man may have aspirations toward becoming a doctor) or aggression. Frequently, the aggressive stories relate to fears of becoming harmed or mutilated while in a passive state. Another somewhat less frequent theme describes a scene in which someone was shot and is now being operated on.

3. General Discussion. The picture can be seen as a thinly veiled depiction of a young man's oedipal conflicts, with concomitant feelings of castration anxiety and hostility. Thus, it is important to note what feelings the boy or other characters in the story have toward the older man performing the surgery. If the story depicts a need for achievement expressed by the younger man, it is also likely that he will identify with the older one and perhaps use him as an example. If this is the case, the details of how the identification takes place and specific feelings regarding the identification may be helpful.

Picture 8GF

1. **Description of Card.** A woman is sitting on a chair staring into space with her chin resting in her hand.
2. **Frequent Plots.** Because this picture is vague and nonspecific, extremely diverse plots are developed and there are no frequently encountered themes.
3. **General Discussion.** This picture is difficult to generalize about. Typically, it produces somewhat shallow stories of a contemplative nature.

Picture 9BM

1. **Description of Card.** Four men in a field are lying against one another.
2. **Frequent Plots.** Stories typically provide some explanation of why the men are there and frequently describe them either as homeless wanderers or as working men who are taking a much-needed rest.
3. **General Discussion.** This picture is particularly helpful in providing information about relations with members of the same sex. Are the men comfortable with one another? Is there any competitiveness? Is the central person in the story merely observing the four men, or is he one of the four men in the picture? Sometimes, homosexual tendencies or fears regarding such tendencies become evident in the story plot. Social prejudice surrounding attitudes toward "lazy," lower-class, or unemployed persons often becomes apparent, particularly when the men in the picture are seen as homeless.

Picture 9GF

1. **Description of Card.** A woman in the foreground is standing behind a tree, observing another woman who is running along a beach below.
2. **Frequent Plots.** Usually, the two women are seen as being in some sort of conflict, often over a man. Frequently, either in addition to this theme or in a separate story, the woman "hiding behind" the tree has done something wrong. It is very unusual to have a story in which cooperation between the women is the central plot.
3. **General Discussion.** This card basically deals with female peer relations and is important in elaborating on such issues as conflict resolution, jealousy, sibling rivalry, and competitiveness. Because the figure standing behind the tree is carefully observing the woman on the beach, stories may provide details surrounding paranoid ideation. At the very least, the dynamics of suspiciousness and distrust are usually discussed. Frequently, a man is introduced into the story, often in the role of a long lost lover whom one or both of the women are running to meet, or a sexual attacker, from whom the woman on the beach is attempting to escape.

Picture 10

1. **Description of Card.** One person is holding his or her head against another person's shoulder. The gender of the two persons is not defined.
2. **Frequent Plots.** Stories usually center around some interaction between a male and a female, and may involve either a greeting between the two or a departure.

3. **General Discussion.** This card often gives useful information regarding how the subject perceives male–female relationships, particularly those involving some degree of closeness and intimacy. It might be helpful to notice the relative degree of comfort or discomfort evoked by emotional closeness. A story of departure or of termination of the relationship may be reflective of either overt or denied hostility on the part of the subject. Sometimes, males will interpret the embrace as involving two males, which may suggest the possibility of a repressed or overt homosexual orientation.

Picture 11

1. **Description of Card.** On a road in a chasm, several figures are proceeding along a path toward a bridge. Above them and against the side of a cliff appears to be a dragon.

2. **Frequent Plot.** Typically, stories of attack and escape are elicited in which the subject takes into account the dragon, the path, and the obscure figures in the distance.

3. **General Discussion.** Because the form of this picture is quite vague and ambiguous, it is a good test of the subjects' imaginative abilities and their skill in integrating irregular and poorly defined stimuli. The picture also represents unknown and threatening forces, and reflects the manner in which the subjects deal with fear of attack. Thus, the examiner should take note of whether the characters in the story escape or instead become victims of their attackers. If they escape, how effective and coherent was the plan they devised to avoid danger? Were they instead saved by chance or "the forces of fate"? Subjects' stories can often suggest the degree to which they experience a sense of control over their environment and the course of their lives.

The dragon may be seen as coming out of the cliff and attacking people (representing aggressive forces in the environment), or as a protecting creature whom the characters are using for refuge and safety (a need for protection). Such themes can suggest aspects of the subjects' internal framework and mood. For example, when subjects report stories of "everything being dead," they give a strong indication of a depressive and extremely impoverished inner state.

Picture 12M

1. **Description of Card.** A man with his hand raised is standing above a boy who is lying on a bed with his eyes closed.

2. **Frequent Plots.** Stories center on illness and/or the older man's use of hypnosis or some form of religious rite on the younger, reclining figure.

3. **General Discussion.** The picture often elicits themes regarding the relationship between an older (usually more authoritative) man and a younger one. This can be significant in predicting or assessing the current or future relationship between the therapist and the client. The manner in which the older man is perceived is particularly important. Is he sympathetic and giving aid, or is he described in more sinister terms? Thus, the picture can represent specifics of the transference relationship and, as such, can be an aid in interpreting and providing feedback to the client regarding this relationship. It can also be used to predict a client's attitude toward, and response to, hypnotic procedures (White, 1941). Stories related to this picture may also represent

whether passivity is compatible with a subject's personality or is regarded with discomfort. In particular, subjects frequently reveal attitudes toward some external controlling force.

Picture 12F

1. **Description of Card.** A portrait of a woman is in the foreground; an older woman holding her chin is in the background.
2. **Frequent Plots.** Stories center on the relationship or specific communications between the two figures.
3. **General Discussion.** This picture elicits descriptions and conceptions of mother figures. The background figure is frequently seen as a mother-in-law who has a variety of evil qualities. Often, these negative qualities are feelings that the subject has toward his or her own mother but can indirectly, and therefore more safely, project onto the figure of a mother-in-law.

Picture 12BG

1. **Description of Card.** A country setting depicts a tree, with a rowboat pulled up next to it. No human figures are present.
2. **Frequent Plots.** Stories frequently center on themes of loneliness, peace, or enjoyment of nature.
3. **General Discussion.** With suicidal or depressed subjects, there may be an elaboration of feelings of abandonment and isolation—for example, someone has been lost or has fallen from the boat. More stable, adjusted subjects are likely to discuss the peace of being alone in the woods and perhaps of fishing or having gone fishing further down the stream.

Picture 13MF

1. **Description of Card.** A young man is standing in the foreground with his head in his arms. In the background is a woman lying in a bed.
2. **Frequent Plots.** The most frequent plot centers on guilt induced by illicit sexual activity. Themes involving the death of the woman on the bed and the resulting grief of the man, who is often depicted as her husband, are somewhat less frequent.
3. **General Discussion.** This picture is excellent for revealing sexual conflicts. In a general way, it provides information on a subject's attitudes and feelings toward his or her partner, particularly attitudes just prior to and immediately following sexual intercourse. Stories in which there are overt expressions of aggression or revulsion are significant variations and should be noted as relatively unusual. In particular, the relation between a subject's aggressive and sexual feelings is frequently portrayed.

Because this picture has a relatively large number of details, obsessive-compulsive personalities frequently spend an excessive amount of time describing and explaining these details. This approach may be particularly evident when the picture has a shock effect and may therefore create anxiety. The obsessive-compulsive's style of handling anxiety by externally focusing on detail is then brought out.

Picture 13B

1. **Description of Card.** A boy is sitting in the doorway of a log cabin.
2. **Frequent Plots.** Themes of loneliness and stories of childhood are often elicited. However, because the stimulus is somewhat vague, the content and the nature of these stories tend to be extremely varied.
3. **General Discussion.** This picture may help both adults and children to reveal attitudes toward introspection or loneliness. In adults, it frequently elicits reveries involving childhood memories.

Picture 13G

1. **Description of Card.** A girl is climbing a flight of stairs.
2. **Frequent Plots.** The plots are similar to Picture 13B, usually involving themes of loneliness and/or distant childhood memories.
3. **General Discussion.** This picture lacks the specificity and impact found in other TAT cards. It usually produces stories that are highly varied but lacking in richness and detail. Like Picture 13B, it can sometimes be useful in depicting a subject's attitude toward loneliness and introspection.

Picture 14

1. **Description of Card.** A person is silhouetted against a window.
2. **Frequent Plots.** This card produces themes of contemplation, wish fulfillment, or depression, or feelings related to burglary.
3. **General Discussion.** If a subject's presenting problem is depression, especially if there is evidence of suicidal ideation, this card, along with Picture 3BM, is essential. This type of subject often describes the figure in the picture and, more importantly, discusses the events, feelings, and attitudes that led up to the current self-destructive behavior. It becomes important to investigate, during the inquiry phase of examination, the particular methods and styles of problem solving that the story character has attempted or is attempting. Also significant are the character's internal dialogues and personal reactions as he or she relates to different life stresses.

This picture may also reveal the subject's aesthetic interests and personal philosophical beliefs or wish fulfillments. If a story involving burglary is depicted, it can be useful to consider the character's level of impulse control and guilt, or the consequences of his or her behavior. For example, is the character apprehended and punished for his or her behavior, or is he or she allowed to go free and enjoy the profits of his or her misdeeds?

Picture 15

1. **Description of Card.** A man is standing among tombstones with his hands clasped together.
2. **Frequent Plots.** Themes usually revolve around beliefs or events surrounding death and a hereafter.

3. **General Discussion.** Stories from Picture 15 reflect the subject's particular beliefs about, and attitudes toward, death and the dying process. For example, death may be viewed as a passive, quiet process, or, in contrast, it can be experienced as a violent, aggressive situation. If the subject is having an extremely difficult time coping with the death of a friend or relative, the themes on Picture 15 can provide useful information as to why this difficulty is being experienced. For example, the story may reveal a method of adjustment based on excessive denial and a seeming inability to engage in grieving, from which a lack of resolution results. The story might also indicate unexpressed and problematic anger directed toward the dead person, because of a sense of abandonment.

Picture 16

1. **Description of Card.** Blank card.
2. **Frequent Plots.** Stories from this card are highly varied. It frequently elicits narratives related to a person's life (current marital, family, and personal situation) and, to a lesser extent, idyllic, defensive, catastrophic, and achievement-oriented concerns.
3. **General Discussion.** Instructions for this card are: Imagine a picture and then tell a story about it. From subjects with vivid and active imaginations, this card often elicits extremely rich, useful stories, and the amount of detail and complexity in a person's stories has been found to correlate with different measures of creativity (Wakefield, 1986). The card does little to shape or influence the subject's fantasy material and can thus be seen as a relatively pure product of his or her unconscious. However, for anxious, resistant, or noncreative subjects, this card is often of little or no value because the stories are usually brief and lack depth or richness. In considering the story, it is helpful to note whether the depiction involves a scene that is vital and optimistic, or one that is desolate and flat. Kahn (1984) suggests that this card's value can be increased by repeating the instructions, which stress that the person must provide a complete story (preceding events, current situation, and outcome), and giving the card as the last one in a series. He further stresses that its value derives from both its total lack of structure and usefulness across different ages, ethnic backgrounds, and assessment goals.

Picture 17BM

1. **Description of Card.** A naked man is climbing up (or down) a rope.
2. **Frequent Plots.** Stories usually involve someone escaping from a dangerous situation or an athletic event of a competitive nature.
3. **General Discussion.** Because the card depicts a naked man, attitudes regarding the subject's personal body images are often revealed. They in turn may bring out themes of achievement, physical prowess, adulation, and narcissism. Possible homosexual feelings or anxiety related to homosexuality also becomes evident in the stories of some subjects. Stein (1981) has observed clinically that the direction in which the climber is going might reflect either an optimistic, positive outlook (indicated by his climbing up) or a pessimistic, negative one (reflected by a downward movement). However, correlations with self-report measures of optimism and self-efficacy have not supported this view (George & Waehler, 1994).

Picture 17GF

1. **Description of Card.** A female is standing on a bridge over water. Above the bridge is a tall building and behind the building the sun is shining from behind clouds.

2. **Frequent Plots.** A great variety of stories are elicited, although themes surrounding departure and social or emotional distance do occur with some frequency.

3. **General Discussion.** Attitudes toward a recent separation or the impending arrival of a loved one are sometimes described. This card can be particularly useful in cases of suicidal depression, where the figure on the bridge is perceived as contemplating jumping off, as a last attempt to resolve her difficulties. As with Pictures 3BM and 14, an inquiry into the specific difficulties the story character has encountered and the manner in which she has attempted to resolve these difficulties can often reflect the subject's manner and style of coping with his or her own difficulties. Personal reactions to, and internal dialogue involving, life stresses can also be extremely informative. However, some of this material is available only through a more detailed inquiry, after the initial story has been given.

Picture 18BM

1. **Description of Card.** A man dressed in a long coat is being grabbed from behind. Three hands are visible.

2. **Frequent Plots.** Typical themes involve either drunkenness on the part of the figure who is being supported by the three hands, or stories in which he is being attacked from behind.

3. **General Discussion.** This picture, more than any of the others, is likely to produce anxiety because of the suggestive depiction of invisible forces attacking the figure. Thus, it is important to note how the subject handles his or her own anxiety, as well as how the story character deals with his situation. Does the latter see himself as the victim of circumstance in which he is completely helpless? If so, how does he eventually resolve his feelings of helplessness? Is the helplessness a momentary phenomenon, or is it an ongoing personality trait? If the character is seen as the recipient of hard luck, then specifically what situation does the subject perceive as comprising hard luck? Exaggerated aggressiveness or attitudes toward addiction are also sometimes identified with this picture.

Picture 18GF

1. **Description of Card.** A woman has her hands around the throat of another woman. In the background is a flight of stairs.

2. **Frequent Plots.** Aggressive mother–daughter interactions or sibling relationships are often disclosed in response to this picture.

3. **General Discussion.** The manner in which the subject handles aggressive, hostile relationships with other women is the primary type of information this picture elicits. Particular note should be made of what types of events trigger this aggressiveness, and of the manner in which the conflict is or is not resolved. Does the

character submit passively, withdraw from the relationship, plot revenge, or negotiate change? Feelings of inferiority, jealousy, and response to being dominated are also often described. Although the representation of aggressiveness in the picture is quite explicit, subjects will occasionally attempt to deny or avoid this aggressiveness by creating a story in which one figure is attempting to help the other one up the stairs. This may point to general denial and repression of hostility on the part of the subject.

Picture 19

1. **Description of Card.** A surreal depiction of clouds and a home covered with snow.
2. **Frequent Plots.** Stories are highly varied because of the unstructured and ambiguous nature of the stimuli.
3. **General Discussion.** Because this is one of the more unstructured cards, the subject's ability to integrate disparate visual stimuli is tested. For certain subjects, the ambiguous nature of this picture can create anxiety and insecurity. The examiner can then observe how the subject handles his or her anxiety within the context of the story. Often, the stories produced deal with impersonal aggression from such forces as nature or the supernatural.

Picture 20

1. **Description of Card.** A hazy, nighttime picture of a man leaning against a lamp-post.
2. **Frequent Plots.** Stories range from the benign theme of a late evening date to more sinister circumstances, perhaps involving a gangster who is in imminent danger.
3. **General Discussion.** The picture often elicits information regarding a subject's attitudes toward loneliness, darkness, and uncertainty. Fears may be stated explicitly through gangster stories. As with Picture 18BM, the method of handling these fears and the examinee's response to physical danger should be noted.

Children's Apperception Test (CAT)

The following descriptions of, and typical responses to, pictures on the CAT are adapted from Bellak (1993, pp. 251–254).

Picture 1

1. **Bellak's Description.** Chicks seated around a table on which is a large bowl of food. Off to one side is a large chicken, dimly outlined.
2. **Discussion.** Stories typically revolve around concerns relating to eating or sibling rivalry. The sibling rivalry may center on who is the best behaved, what the consequences of this behavior are, and which one gets more to eat. To obtain useful information on this card, it is particularly important to decide which character the subject

identifies with. Food may be seen as reward for "good" behavior, or, conversely, when withheld, as punishment for "bad" behavior.

Picture 2

1. **Bellak's Description.** One bear is pulling a rope on one side, while another bear and a baby bear pull on the other side.

2. **Discussion.** Of particular importance in interpreting this picture is whether the bear who is helping the baby bear is seen as a male (father figure) or a female (mother figure). The struggle depicted can be seen either as a playful game of tug-of-war, or as a struggle involving a high degree of seriousness and aggression. For example, the loser(s) may end up falling off the edge of the rock and into a pool of dangerous animals. In the most recent revision of the CAT, the large bears were made equal in size, to avoid having the largest bear (previously depicted on the right) identified as the father.

Picture 3

1. **Bellak's Description.** A lion, with pipe and cane, sits in a chair; in the lower right corner, a little mouse appears in a hole.

2. **Discussion.** Because the lion is pictured with the characteristic symbols of authority (pipe and cane), this picture elicits attitudes and feelings toward father figures. It is important to note whether this figure is seen as benevolent and protecting, or dangerous and threatening. Sometimes, the subject will defensively attempt to minimize the threat of the lion by reducing him to a helpless cripple who needs a cane just to move around.

Most children notice the mouse in the hole and blend it into their stories. Because the mouse and the lion are frequently seen in adversary roles, it is important to note how the threatening presence of the lion is handled. Is the mouse completely under the control of the lion, and does it adapt by being submissive and placating? On the other hand, the mouse may be described as clever and manipulating, in order to trick and outsmart the lion. When subjects switch their identification back and forth between the lion and the mouse, some role confusion is suggested. This may be particularly true of enmeshed families or families in which the father is unable to set limits effectively.

Picture 4

1. **Bellak's Description.** A kangaroo who has a bonnet on her head is carrying a basket with a milk bottle. In her pouch is a baby kangaroo with a balloon; on a bicycle, there is a larger kangaroo child.

2. **Discussion.** As in Picture 1, this card elicits themes of sibling rivalry and, occasionally, themes revolving around a wish for regression, as demonstrated when the subject identifies with the baby kangaroo in the pouch. A regressive theme is particularly strong when a subject, who is in reality the oldest or middle child, identifies with the kangaroo in the pouch. On the other hand, a child who is actually the youngest may identify with the oldest kangaroo, thereby suggesting a strong need for autonomy and independence. On occasion, a theme of flight from danger may be introduced.

Picture 5

1. **Bellak's Description.** A darkened room contains a large bed in the background and a crib in the foreground in which there are two baby bears.

2. **Discussion.** Stories relating to attitudes and feelings about what occurs when parents are in bed are frequent responses to this card. They may involve such aspects as curiosity, conjecture, confusion, rejection, anger, and envy on the part of the children. Descriptions of the two bears in the foreground may also center on themes of sexual manipulation and mutual exploration.

Picture 6

1. **Bellak's Description.** A darkened cave shows two dimly outlined bear figures in the background and a baby bear lying in the foreground.

2. **Discussion.** This picture and Picture 5 elicit stories of parental bedtime activity. However, this picture tends to enlarge on and extend themes that have only begun to develop in Picture 5. Stories may also revolve around jealousy of the perceived intimacy between parents, or they may reflect possible feelings about masturbation on the part of the baby bear in the foreground.

Picture 7

1. **Bellak's Description.** A tiger with bared fangs and claws leaps at a monkey that is also leaping through the air.

2. **Discussion.** The subject will often discuss his or her fears of aggression and characteristic manner of dealing with it. At times, the anxiety produced by this picture may result in an unwillingness to respond to it at all. On the other hand, the subject's defenses may be either effective enough, or perhaps unrealistic enough, for him or her to transform the picture into a harmless story.

Picture 8

1. **Bellak's Description.** Two adult monkeys are sitting on a sofa drinking from tea cups. One adult monkey in the foreground is sitting on a hassock talking to a baby monkey.

2. **Discussion.** The subject often discusses his or her relative position and characteristic roles within the family. The description of the dominant monkey in the foreground as either a mother or a father figure should be noted as a possible indication of who has more control in the family. It is also significant to note how the dominant monkey is described. Is he or she threatening and controlling, or helpful and supportive?

Picture 9

1. **Bellak's Description.** A darkened room is seen through an open door from a lighted room. In the darkened one, there is a child's bed in which a rabbit sits up looking through the door.

2. **Discussion.** Typically, responses revolve around a subject's fears of darkness, possible desertion by parents, and curiosity as to what is occurring in the next room.

Picture 10

1. **Bellak's Description.** A baby dog is lying across the knees of an adult dog; both figures have a minimum of expressive features. The figures are set in the foreground of a bathroom.

2. **Discussion.** A child's attitudes and feelings about misbehavior and its resulting punishments are usually discussed in response to this card. In particular, his or her conceptions of right and wrong are often revealed. This picture is a good indicator of the child's degree of impulse control and his or her attitude toward authority figures when their role involves setting limits.

SCORING PROCEDURES

Since the publication of the original TAT Manual in 1943, there have been a number of alternate methods of scoring and interpretation. Whenever a large number of different approaches are given to explain a particular phenomenon, it is usually a strong indication that none of them is fully adequate and all of them have significant shortcomings. This is true of the many alternate interpretation methods for the TAT. Difficulty arises primarily because of the type of information that is under investigation. Fantasy productions involve extremely rich and diverse information, which is difficult to place into exact and specific categories. Even the selection of which categories to use is open to question. For example, Murray prefers a listing and weighting of the primary needs and press expressed in the stories, whereas Arnold (1962) emphasizes a restatement of the essential theme of the story on an interpretive level so as to highlight the basic meaning or moral. After deciding which method to use and evaluating the stories according to this method, the examiner is able to infer qualities of the subject's personality according to the categorization that is based on the specific method selected. Whether this final inference is valid and accurate is open to question and depends on a number of variables, including the skill and experience of the examiner, comparison with themes derived from other test data, and whether the state of the subject at the time of examination is representative of his or her usual orientation to the world.

For the purposes of this chapter, Bellak's (1954, 1993) method of interpretation will be described. It is fairly comprehensive, easy to score, relatively concise, frequently updated, and probably the most frequently used of the various systems. Bellak's approach involves a certain degree of quantification in that interpreters are requested to rate the stories along several areas, according to the different story styles and contents. The goal is not so much to achieve a diagnosis of the subject as to obtain a description of how the subject confronts and deals with basic universal life situations. Each of the stories can be conceptualized as a series of common social situations depicting interpersonal relations. The manner in which the person constructs what he or she believes is occurring in these situations reveals a dominant pattern of social behavior as well as internal needs, attitudes, and values (Bellak, 1993).

The specific scoring of the TAT cards can be organized on the Analysis Sheet for Use with the Bellak TAT Blank (see Figure 10–2). The same analysis sheet can be used with the CAT. The sheet provides a guide and frame of reference for TAT analysis that can be used later to organize and generate hypotheses about the person. It is intended to be used with a typical administration of 10 cards.

Using the long form of the scoring system, each one of the cards/stories is scored onto a single Analysis Sheet. The overall story themes and contents can then be analyzed by noting the common themes and unique features throughout the different sheets. A shorter form is also available, consisting of using the Analysis Sheet as shown in Figure 10–2, but simply having rows to the right of the 10 scoring categories to indicate the scoring for each card/story. Thus, 10 cards/stories might be scored in 10 consecutive rows to indicate Story No. 1, Story No. 2, and so on. At the end of this sequence is a Summary section, which the practitioner can use to organize conclusions. The summary categories are designated as follows:

1–3. Unconscious structure and drives of the subject (derived from scoring categories 1–3: Main Themes, Main Hero, and Main Needs and Drives of Hero).
  4. Conception of world.
  5. Relationship to others.
  6. Significant conflicts.
  7. Nature of anxieties.
  8. Main defenses used.
  9. Superego structure.
 10. Integration and strength of ego.

A table is also included (see Table 10–3), to provide a format for rating the person's ego functions. The combination of the summaries and ratings of ego functions serves as the actual interpretation of the TAT protocol. A short form is available from C. P. S., Inc. (see Figure 10–2 and Table 10–3), and variations on the short form and long forms are available from the Psychological Corporation.

For each of the scoring categories, practitioners should abbreviate their observations about the person. In some sections, practitioners are requested to indicate the levels of importance or strength for the person by putting one check ($\sqrt{}$—mere presence of characteristic), two checks ($\sqrt{}\sqrt{}$—moderate) or three checks ($\sqrt{}\sqrt{}\sqrt{}$—strong). The entire scoring and interpretation procedure typically takes a half-hour. The ten scoring categories are described in the following sections. An attempt has been made to summarize and clarify as much as possible the descriptions provided by Bellak (1993, pp. 75–99).

1. The Main Theme

This section requires the practitioner to restate the essential elements of the story. Each story may have one or more themes that need to be restated. The description of the main theme can vary in terms of its level of inference. On the one hand, it might be based on an observation and restatement of the client's story, staying as close as possible to the

1. **Main Theme:** (diagnostic level: if descriptive and interpretative levels are desired, use a scratch sheet or page 5)

2. **Main hero:** age_____ sex_____ vocation_____ abilities_____
   interests_____ traits_____ body image_____
   adequacy (√.√√.√√√)   and/or self-image_____

3. **Main needs and drives of hero:**
   a) behavioral needs of hero (as in story): _____
      implying: _____
   b) figures, objects, or circumstances *introduced*: _____

      implying need for or to: _____

   c) figures, objects or circumstances *omitted*: _____

      implying need for or to: _____

4. **Conception of environment (world) as:** _____

5. a) Parental figures   (m_____, f_____) are seen as _____
      and subject's reaction to a is _____
   b) Contemp. figures (m_____, f_____) are seen as _____
      and subject's reaction to b is _____
   c) Junior figures   (m_____, f_____) are seen as _____
      and subject's reaction to c is _____

6. **Significant conflicts:** _____

7. **Nature of anxieties:** (√)
      of physical harm and/or punishment _____
      of disapproval _____
      of lack or loss of love _____of illness or injury _____
      of being deserted _____of deprivation _____
      of being overpowered and helpless _____lonely_____
      of being devoured _____other _____

8. **Main defenses against conflicts and fears:** (✓)
      repression _____ reaction-formation _____ splitting _____
      regression _____ denial _____ introjection _____
      isolation _____ undoing _____
      rationalization _____ other _____

9. **Adequacy of superego as manifested by "punishment" for "crime" being:** ( )
      appropriate _____ inappropriate _____
      too severe (also indicated by immediacy of punishment) _____
      inconsistent _____ too lenient _____
      also: _____
      delayed initial response or pauses _____
      stammer _____ other manifestations of superego interference _____

10. **Integration of the ego, manifesting itself in:** (√.√√.√√√)
      Hero: adequate_____inadequate_____
      outcome: happy_____unhappy_____
               realistic_____unrealistic_____
      drive control_____
      thought processes as revealed by plot being: (√. √√. √√√)
      Stereotyped_____original_____appropriate_____
      complete_____incomplete_____inappropriate_____
      syncretic_____concrete_____contaminated_____
Intelligence_____
Maturational level_____
Organic Signs_____

Figure 10–2. Bellak TAT and CAT analysis sheet

Note: Reprinted with minor modification by permission of C.P.S., Inc., P.O. Box 83, Larchmont, NY 10538.

Table 10–3. Ego function assessment from TAT data

	I	II	III	IV	V	VI	VII	VIII	IX	X	XI	XII
	Reality Testing	Judgment	Sense of Reality	Regulat. & Cont. of Drives	Object Relat.	Thought Process.	ARISE	Defensive Functs.	Stimulus Barrier	Auton. Functs.	Synthet. Functs.	Mastery—Cmptnc.
13												
12												
11												
10												
9												
8												
7												
6												
5												
4												
3												
2												
1												

Ego functions

Psychotic range 1–6 Borderline range 4–8 Neurotic range 6–10 Normal range 8–13

Source: From *Ego Functions in Schizophrenics, Neurotics, and Normals* (p. 338) by L. Bellak, M. Murvich, and H. Gediman, 1973, New York: John Wiley & Sons, Inc. Copyright 1973 by C.P.S. Inc.

client's own words and experience of the story. On the other hand, practitioners may wish to move somewhat further away from the person's description of the story into a more *interpretive* or even *diagnostic* level. Elaboration on the story might even be developed by having the person free-associate to elements within the story. However, for persons who are learning the TAT or who use it infrequently, it is recommended that practitioners stay close to the client's own description. It should be as brief as possible and should aim to extract the essence of what has been described.

2. The Main Hero/Heroine

The hero/heroine is usually the person who is most frequently referred to in the story. More information is given on his or her feelings, beliefs, and behaviors than on those of any of the other characters. As a result, the client is assumed to be identifying with this person. In some stories, there might be a degree of uncertainty as to exactly who is the hero/heroine. The practitioner should infer that the story character who is most similar to the client in terms of age, sex, and other characteristics is the hero/heroine. In certain rare cases, there may be one or more heros/heroines. The Analysis Sheet further requests that the clinician rate the hero in terms of *interests, traits, abilities, adequacy,* and *body image.* The adequacy of the hero/heroine refers to an ability to complete tasks in a socially, emotionally, morally, and/or intellectually acceptable manner. This level of adequacy would be directly related to the ego strength of the hero/heroine—or, more inferentially, of the client. The body image refers to the style and qualities with which the body or body representation is depicted. Direct descriptions of the body are usually easy to interpret but a more indirect representation, such as certain symbolical features of the violin in TAT Picture 1, might also be included.

3. Main Needs and Drives of the Hero/Heroine

To more fully appreciate the wide variety of possible needs and drives of the hero, clinicians might wish to refer to Murray's list of needs (Table 10–1). The *behavioral needs* to be rated in the story refer to the most basic needs expressed in the client's story productions (i.e., affection, aggression, achievement). The descriptions of these needs are fantasy productions by the client and might reflect actual conscious needs as well as more disguised latent needs. The clinician might wish to simply state what the clearest and strongest of these needs are, or make inferences about the actual meaning of these needs for the client. For example, extreme nurturance expressed in the stories might indicate that the client demands nurturance from others, or, conversely, that this is a frequent need that he or she expresses. Another example might be extreme avoidance of aggression, which could suggest that the client has a high level of underlying aggression that is being denied.

Clinicians should also note any *figures, objects,* or *circumstances* that are *introduced* as well as any that have been *omitted* but perhaps should have been included. Particularly noteworthy omissions include: no mention of the rifle in Picture 8BM, the gun/keys in Picture 3BM, or the seminude in the background of Picture 4, or no sexual references to Picture 13MF. The implications of these inclusions/omissions should also be noted. For example, the inclusion of a relatively large number of weapons, food, and money might suggest high needs for aggression, nurturance, or financial success. The omission of important objects in the story productions might suggest some areas of repression, denial, or anxiety associated with the omitted objects.

4. The Conception of the Environment (World)

Clinicians may wish to review Murray's list of press (see Table 10–2) in order to more fully appreciate the variety of possible story descriptions related to the environment (press). Clinicians should summarize the most important and strongest of these conceptions of the environment. They might be alerted to this distinction by noting the number and strength of descriptive words such as *hostile, dangerous,* or *nurturing.* The summaries of conceptions of the world might include the overall meaning for the hero/heroine—for example, the environment is overly demanding, a wealth of opportunities, or something to be exploited and used.

5. Figures Seen as . . .

One of the main characteristics of the TAT stories is that they can be seen as "apperceptive distortions of the social relationships and the dynamic factors basic to them" (Bellak, 1993, p. 92). Thus, one of the cornerstones of TAT interpretation is understanding how the client views other persons, as represented in the story productions. This category attempts to elaborate on this by rating the hero/heroine's attitudes and behaviors toward *parental, contemporary* (age-related peers), and *junior figures*. For example, the level of aggressiveness of persons of the same gender might be noted, along with the response(s) of the hero/heroine (assertive, placating, hostile, withdrawing).

6. Significant Conflicts

The major conflicts within the hero/heroine should be noted by reviewing the client's current feelings and behaviors and assessing how congruent these are. In particular, clinicians should note any contrast between the *actual* feelings/behaviors and how the client *should* feel. For example, he or she might be trying to accomplish two incongruous goals such as need for achievement versus need for pleasure, or need for hostility versus need for affiliation. Other important conflicts might be between reality and fantasy, or aggression and compliance.

7. Nature of Anxieties

In addition to significant conflicts (above), clinicians should rate the nature and strength ($\sqrt{}$,$\sqrt{}\sqrt{}$,$\sqrt{}\sqrt{}\sqrt{}$) of the hero/heroine's anxieties in terms of fear of *physical harm and/or punishment, disapproval, lack or loss of love, illness or injury, being deserted, deprived, overpowered and helpless, devoured,* or *other.*

8. Main Defenses against Conflicts and Fears

The clinician is asked to rate the presence and strength of defenses against anxieties and conflicts. This helps to provide a description of the person's character structure. The strength of the defenses can be assessed by noting their frequency both within each story and among the different stories. For example, intellectualization occurring in six of the stories suggests a rigid and excessive defensive style. In contrast, the use of several different types of defenses suggests that the client has a much greater degree of variety and flexibility.

9. Adequacy of Superego as Manifested by "Punishment" for "Crime"

Clinicians are requested to rate the relative degree of appropriateness, severity, consistency, and extent of delay of any consequences for potentially punishable behavior. Particular note should be made of the relative strength and type of punishment compared to the seriousness of the "crime." For example, a harsh superego would be suggested when minor infractions by story characters result in imprisonment or even death. In contrast, a poorly developed superego would be suggested if little or no consequences occurred for a moderate or severe infraction. A section is also included for noting any relevant behavioral observations of the client, such as stammering or blushing, which could suggest an overly harsh superego.

10. Integration of the Ego

In general, the degree of ego integration is indicated by the quality with which the hero/heroine mediates between different conflicts. This is typically reflected in the effectiveness with which the main character can use interpersonal skills. Specific observations can be made regarding the adequacy, quality, effectiveness, flexibility, and style of problem solving. The overall quality (bizarre, complete, original, and so on) of the thought processes involved should also be rated.

Bellak provides a further unnumbered category for rating the client's intelligence. The traditional classifications of very superior, superior, high average, and so on, are used. An additional section allows an overall rating of the client's level of maturity.

In addition to the more traditional TAT areas described above, Bellak (1993) has provided scales for rating a client's 12 ego functions (I–XII in Table 10–3). These are based on both the total TAT stories the client has provided and on any relevant behavioral observations. A graph can be created by connecting the ratings summarized on Table 10–3. The 12 functions are briefly defined as follows.

I. Reality Testing

This variable rates the extent to which the client accurately perceives and relates to his or her external environment. It requires an accurate appraisal of both the physical environment and the social norms and expectations, as well as an accurate perception of inner reality testing and level of psychological sophistication. These can be partially assessed by noting the extent to which the client can articulate needs, feelings, values, and beliefs. Also included would be accuracy in perceiving time and place.

II. Judgment

What is the client's capacity for understanding a situation, particularly where interpersonal relationships are involved, and translating this understanding into an effective, coherent response? An appraisal of social and physical consequences as well as competent forward planning are involved.

III. Sense of Reality of the World and of the Self

Here, the clinician rates disturbances in the client's sense of self, such as dissociative experiences, depersonalization, and *déjà vu*. These will also relate to feelings of reality or unreality in the client's perceptions of the environment. In particular, how does this sense of reality/unreality relate to the degree to which the client feels that his or her body parts are well coordinated? Other aspects involved in the rating might be the degree of individuation versus differentiation, the sense of self-esteem, and the extent to which the self is experienced as distinct from others and the external world.

IV. Regulation and Control of Drives, Affects, and Impulses

How direct or indirect is the client's expression of impulses? Can they be appropriately and effectively controlled and delayed? How high a tolerance is there for frustration? Is the client undercontrolled or overcontrolled? Can he or she monitor drives and express them in a modified and adaptive manner? Each of these areas should be considered in order to make a final rating for this category.

V. Object Relations

To what extent are the client's relationships optimal in that they are appropriately relating to, committed to, and invested in others? What is the typical length of the relationships? What is their overall quality? Any distortions, and the degree to which the client gets his or her needs met, should be noted. How mature is the client and how free from maladaptive interpersonal patterns? To what extent is he or she overinfluenced or underinfluenced by others?

VI. Thought Processes

This category requires a rating of the general adequacy and coherence of the client's thought processes. Thus, careful attention should be given to the level of attention, concentration, memory, verbal ability, and abstract reasoning. Are there any distortions, delusions, or unusual associations? Is there clarity and integration in the thought processes? Is the thinking unrealistic, illogical, and characterized by the intrusion of primary process thinking? For example, obsessive-compulsives might be expected to describe minute details of the cards. In contrast, persons with Alzheimer's disease have been found to use fewer words. They merely describe the pictures rather than tell a story about them, and they lose track of the instructions (Johnson, 1994).

VII. ARISE (Adaptive Regression in the Service of the Ego)

Can the client temporarily lower his or her defenses to increase awareness and help with problem solving? This would allow for a relatively free expression of primary process thinking in which the client can approach self and others from different perspectives. Another concern is how adequately he or she can later reintegrate and reorganize the insights and new perspectives resulting from the lowered defenses. The task of responding to the TAT can be seen as an opportunity to allow for this temporary regression into fantasy activity, with the goal of helping to reveal, problem-solve, and understand aspects of self. Relevant questions might involve whether the client approaches the task easily or defensively. Are the story productions rich and creative, or constricted and defended? When they do enter into the fantasies, do they become lost and incoherent or are they able to organize the contents effectively?

VIII. Defensive Functioning

This category requires the clinician to rate the extent to which clients' defenses protect them from internal anxiety-provoking impulses and conflicts. Are they excessive, defective, adaptive/maladaptive? Overall, how successful are they? How much anxiety or depression does the person experience? The specific types and strengths of defenses have been summarized in Category 8 of the Analysis Sheet so that clinicians can refer to these previous summaries to obtain useful detail. However, this Category VIII differs in that it is more a global rating of defensive effectiveness, using all sources of information available to the clinician.

IX. Stimulus Barrier

The client's stimulus barrier refers to how reactive a person is to various events (high/low threshold). Is the person hypersensitive to minor criticisms or low levels of stress? Does he or she react to unpleasant situations with such responses as anger, aggression, assertiveness, withdrawal, disorganization, and/or victimization?

X. Autonomous Functioning

To what extent is the client disrupted by certain ideas, feelings, conflicts, or impulses? If the client feels disrupted, how much does this compromise his or her ability to work and socialize independently? Instead of functioning independently, does the client become highly dependent on others to cope, decide, and initiate what to do? In contrast, has he or she been able to develop autonomous behaviors such as adaptive habits, time management skills, or hobbies that help toward functioning relatively independently?

XI. Synthetic-Integrative Functioning

Clinicians must rate the client's ability to actively reconcile difficult needs and conflicts. Are important generalizations and similarities among different ideas, events, and persons perceived? Is there an ability to make necessary compromises between disparate areas of personality and/or interpersonal relationships? How adequately can these integrative abilities be used to work with contradictory behaviors, attitudes, values, and emotions?

XII. Mastery-Competency

This final category requires a rating of the client's overall sense of competency, especially as it relates to the outcome of different story themes. Information useful for this rating might come from a variety of different areas: ability to resolve conflict, quality of ego defenses, ego integrity, creative problem solving, relative degree of rigidity of defenses, self-efficacy, and degree to which the person has an internal versus external locus of control. One important consideration is whether the client's sense of competency is realistic, given his or her actual abilities and achievements. Some clients might either under- or overestimate their level of competency.

INTERPRETATION

When the scoring has been completed, it should be relatively easy to convert this information into a coherent description of the person. Indeed, the scoring and interpretation can often be considered to be the same task. At the very least, the scoring might require somewhat of an extension, to bring it into an interpretation. Bellak (1993) suggests that the three major levels of interpretation are: (a) the descriptive, (b) the interpretive, and (c) the diagnostic. The descriptive level is merely a short repeat of the story, as has been outlined in scoring category 1 of the Analysis Sheet. The interpretive level extends the descriptive level somewhat by an alteration of the descriptive level beginning with "If one . . . [does X, then the outcome will be Y]." For example, a descriptive "interpretation" to Card 1 might be: "Boy is practicing to increase his competence." The interpretive level would be "[If one] practices, then he or she will improve." The diagnostic level is a further extension in that an inference is made about the client. Thus, one might infer that, in the story for Card 1, "The client has a high need for achievement with a high level of self-efficacy."

The core features of the client can be organized in the summary section, which has been previously outlined and is included as part of Bellak's Short Form for scoring and interpretation. It is even possible for a report to be organized around the information noted on the 10 different scoring categories. These might be further integrated into the following three areas:

1. *Unconscious structure and needs:* Derived from categories 1 through 3.
2. *Conception of the world and perceptions of significant persons:* Derived from categories 4 and 5.
3. *Relevant dimensions of personality:* Derived from categories 6 through 10.

Further ratings can be noted for levels of intelligence and maturational level.

The above areas of description tend to be fairly abstract and inferential. One technique for balancing these abstract descriptions is to include actual story segments to illustrate the points or principles that are being described. This should effectively provide a more qualitative, concrete, and impactful description of the client

One useful interpretive consideration regarding the TAT stories is that approximately one-third of the stories are likely to be impersonal renditions or clichés of previously heard information. In the protocols of highly constricted, defensive clients, this proportion is likely to be even higher. As a result of the impersonal nature of these stories, it is usually difficult to infer the underlying determinants of personality. In contrast, some stories are extremely rich in that they reveal important core aspects of the client.

Yet another consideration is that, even though, for the most part, high, moderate, or low scores on the stories correspond to high, moderate, and low characteristics within the subject, this is not always the case. For example, Murray found that there was a negative correlation ($-.33$ to $-.74$) between n Sex on the TAT and n Sex expressed in overt behavior. Of final and particular note are the subject's current life situation and emotional state at the time of examination. One of the more important variables that can affect the emotional state of the subject, and therefore the test results, is the particular interaction between the subject and the examiner. A sensitive and accurate interpretation can be obtained only if the examiner takes into account the existence and possible influence of all these variables.

RECOMMENDED READING

Bellak, L. (1993). *The TAT, CAT, and SAT in clinical use* (5th ed.). New York: Grune & Stratton.

Spangler, W. D. (1992). Validity of questionnaire and TAT measures of need for achievement: Two meta-analyses. *Psychological Bulletin, 112,* 140–154.

Stein, M. (1981). *The Thematic Apperception Test: An introductory manual for its clinical use with adults* (2nd ed.). Springfield, IL: Charles C Thomas.

Chapter 11

PROJECTIVE DRAWINGS

Attempts to understand individuals from the interpretations they make of their world have a long, often honored history. Many different cultural traditions, including sections of the Hindu *Upanishads,* parables in the Bible, and stories in Sufiism discuss the importance of interpreting narrative information (Groth-Marnat, 1992; Vitz, 1990) . Utterances of Greek oracles were likewise open to a number of varying interpretations, depending on the personal needs and expectations of the listener. Similarly, interpretations of works of art have generally been considered to reveal something about the artist as well as his or her subject. As Hammer (1958) states, "When an artist paints a portrait, he paints two, himself and the sitter" (p. 8). Although intuitive methods of interpreting drawings have a history extending back many centuries, a more empirically based approach has only been popular within the past 30 or 40 years.

In the past, interpretation of drawings (and projective testing in general) drew heavily on psychoanalytic theory. One of the central assumptions of this procedure is that, because many important aspects of personality are not available to conscious self-report, questionnaires and inventories are of limited value. To obtain an accurate view of a person's inner world, one must somehow circumvent unconscious defenses and conscious resistances. From a psychoanalytic perspective, then, an indirect approach, such as through projective drawings, is essential. Through symbolical creation, an individual depicts important themes, dynamics, and attitudes. Psychoanalytic theory further assumes it is not only possible for this symbolical expression to occur, but a person's perceptions and responses to his or her world are actually determined by inner qualities and forces. These idiosyncratic expressions of inner dynamics are most likely to occur when a person is requested to interpret unstructured stimuli, such as might occur when the person draws something on a blank sheet of paper. This projection of inner aspects is most likely to involve anxiety-provoking images, feelings, thoughts, and memories. By externalizing onto the outside world, the person creates distance between self and the anxiety-provoking images, thereby temporarily reducing anxiety. An understanding of these projections can potentially reveal a person's inner predispositions, conflicts, and dynamics.

Projective drawings are expressive techniques in that they suggest aspects of the person while he or she is performing some activity. Other examples of expressive projective techniques are interpreting role plays, drama, or children's play, or understanding the latent meaning behind jokes. An extremely varied number of approaches can be used for expressive projective techniques in general as well as projective drawings themselves. Some clinicians request the subject to simply draw a picture of a person. Others might have the subject also draw a person of the opposite sex, a house, or a tree; or tell a story about his or her drawing; or use colored pencils or crayons.

The above discussion emphasizes the projective theory and use of drawings, but a parallel strand has clearly not aligned itself with either psychoanalysis or projective theory: the use of drawings to represent cognitive development and/or the perceptual and visuoconstructive difficulties associated with certain types of brain damage. Thus human-figure drawings can be viewed as functioning similarly to the Bender. Additional drawing techniques used in neuropsychology are drawings of complex designs, as in the Rey-Osterrith Complex Figure Test (Meyers & Meyers, 1996; Osterrith, 1944; Rey, 1941; Visser, 1992), or somewhat simpler drawings such as those of a bicycle, key, clock, Greek cross, or square (see Lezak, 1995).

Despite various criticisms, mainly directed at their projective use, drawings have continued to be highly popular. This popularity was especially prominent during the 1950s and 1960s, when psychoanalytic theory dominated. In 1961, Sundberg reported that projective drawings represented the second most popular test used in hospitals, clinics, and counseling centers. During the 1970s and especially the 1980s, their use declined in response to poor reviews regarding their validity, decreased belief in psychoanalytic theory, greater emphasis on situational determiners of behavior, and questions regarding their cost-effectiveness. Yet, drawing techniques are still ranked as among the ten most frequently used tests (Lubin et al., 1984, 1985; Piotrowski, 1984; Piotrowski & Zalewski, 1993; Watkins et al., 1995) and fully 41%, 33%, and 30% of psychologists assessing adolescents use, respectively, the Kinetic Family Drawing, Human Figure Drawing, and House-Tree-Person (Archer et al., 1991).

HISTORY AND DEVELOPMENT

The first formal development of a drawing technique for assessment was Goodenough's (1926) *Draw-A-Man Test.* She used it solely to estimate a child's cognitive abilities as reflected in the quality of the drawing. She assumed that the accuracy and number of details indicate the child's level of intellectual maturity. Points were given for the inclusion of different body parts, quality of lines, and connections. Although it has been used for children from the ages of 3–0 to 15–11, it has been found to be most accurate for ages 3–0 to 10–0. In 1963, Harris revised the Draw-A-Man by adding two new forms, a more detailed scoring system, and a much wider standardization. He suggested not only administering the draw-a-man portion, but including drawings of a woman and a drawing of the self. The new, extended point system had 73 scoring items for the drawing of the man (compared with Goodenough's 51), 71 items for drawings of the woman, and a 12-point quality scale, with 1 representing the lowest quality and 12 the highest. No scoring system was provided for the drawing of the self. The test was standardized on 2,975 boys and girls from ages 5 to 15, with 75 children in each age group. In a recently updated version of the Goodenough and Harris, Naglieri (1988) developed his *Draw A Person: A Quantitative Scoring System,* which similarly assesses the cognitive development of children between the ages of 5 and 17. His system uses clear scoring criteria and modern representative norms, and it allows conversion of scores into standard scores, percentiles, and age equivalents. His system has also included additional scoring and validity criteria for the detection of emotional disturbance (McNeish & Naglieri, 1993; Naglieri & Pfeiffer, 1992). To date, the most well-accepted and psychometrically sound uses of drawing techniques are those that have used drawings as measures of cognitive development.

Machover's (1949) *Draw-A-Person* (DAP) was the first to formally extend drawing techniques from tests of cognitive development and into personality interpretation based on projective testing theory. She developed a number of hypotheses based on clinical observation and intuitive judgments. For example, she speculated that the size of the drawings relates to the level of self-esteem and that placement on the page reflects the subject's mood and social orientation. During the administration phase, clients are given a blank sheet of paper and simply told to "draw a picture of a person." When they have completed the first drawing, they are given a new sheet of paper and requested to "draw a person of the opposite sex." An inquiry phase is often recommended, in which the subject answers specific questions about the persons in the drawings, such as what their mood is, their interests, or what makes them angry. Koppitz (1968, 1984) later extended the developmental and personality aspects of human figure drawings by creating objective scoring systems for developmental level and emotional indicators. More recently, an adult scoring and interpretation system by Mitchel, Trent, and McArthur (1993) has been developed as a screening device for cognitive impairment caused by psychopathology, neuropsychological dysfunction, or mental retardation.

Concurrent with Machover's early work, Buck (1948) developed the *House-Tree-Person* (HTP). He theorized that, in addition to the significance attributed to human-figure drawings, people similarly attach meaning to houses and trees. Jolles (1952, 1971) further expanded the HTP by recommending three different administrations. First, the client is requested to make pencil (achromatic) drawings, then to answer questions regarding his or her drawings, and, finally, to make another series of drawings using crayons (chromatic). One variation of the above is to have the client draw the house, tree, and person all on one sheet of paper; another is to draw the house, tree, and person separately on three sheets of paper. Some examiners also have the subject draw a person of the same sex and of the opposite sex (the HTPP). The Kinetic House-Tree-Person is a more recent variation in which the subject is requested to make the person in the drawing "doing something" (Burns, 1987). A further development is Van Hutton's (1994) quantitative scoring system for the House-Tree-Person (and Draw-A-Person), which focuses on indicators of child abuse among children.

To assess interpersonal relationships, several variations of projective drawings have involved the client depicting groups of significant people in his or her environment. For example, Hulse (1951) developed the *Draw-A-Family* (DAF), in which subjects draw a picture of their whole family. He recommended interpreting the drawings globally (mood, overall quality) as well as descriptively (relative size of figures, proximity to one another, line pressure, shading). Very few validity studies were performed on the DAF, although Wright and McIntyre (1982) have developed an objective scoring system that is a useful and reliable indicator of depression. In addition, Spigelman, Spigelman, and Englesson (1992) concluded that the drawings of children from divorced families were more likely to omit their siblings, portray family conflict, and separate family members from one another, when compared with the drawings of children from nondivorced families. One criticism of the DAF is that it produces stiff and static figures and, as a result, is of limited usefulness in assessing the more fluid, ongoing aspects of family relations. To counter this, some clinicians recommend the *Kinetic Family Drawing* test (KFD; Burns, 1982; Burns & Kaufman, 1972), in which clients are requested to draw their whole family "doing something." The resulting drawings are assumed to be better than the DAF at revealing a person's perceptions and attitudes toward his or her ongoing family dynamics. The KFD has been used in the evaluation of therapy for abused children, diabetics, children with perceptual-motor delay, and family relationships, and in making cross-cultural comparisons. In a somewhat similar vein, the *Kinetic School Drawing* (KSD; Knoff & Prout, 1985; Prout & Phillips, 1974) requests a child to draw a picture in which he or she is doing something in school. It is designed to complement the KFD (Knoff & Prout, 1985) and provide information regarding the self, teacher, and peers, and, when used with the KFD, to understand how the school and home environment interact. A qualitative analysis of the drawing is usually recommended (Sarbaugh, 1982), although quantitative ratings have been found to correlate with school achievement (Prout & Celmer, 1984).

Currently, the most frequently used version of any of the above drawing techniques is the Draw-A-Person (DAP). Within clinical settings, quantitative scoring systems for cognitive development, emotional disturbance, impulsiveness, or cognitive impairment are rarely used, despite their greater levels of reliability and validity. Unfortunately, clinicians are far more likely to use intuitive judgments based on clinical experience and assumed isomorphy between the characteristics of the drawing and the client's outside environment (Smith & Dumont, 1995). Most of these intuitive interpretations, especially those based on single-sign interpretations, have not been found to be valid (Kahill, 1984; Roback, 1968; Swenson, 1968). This difficulty is largely attributable to a combination of assumed relationships between drawings and psychological factors; a lack of any unified administration, scoring, or interpretation; and the complexity, diversity, and richness of the drawings themselves. However, the more recent development of several formal and relatively psychometrically sound systems may mean that clinicians will rely on these approaches more frequently (see Mitchell et al., 1993; Naglieri, 1988; Van Hutton, 1994).

RELIABILITY AND VALIDITY

Establishing the reliability and validity of projective drawings presents special challenges, given the fluctuating conditions between one administration and the next; the underlying, often difficult-to-prove (or disprove) assumptions behind the procedure; and the frequent richness and complexity of the productions. Several rigorous analyses of the psychometric properties of projective drawings have generally failed to demonstrate that the drawings are valid indicators of personality (Motta, Little, & Tobin, 1993; Roback, 1968; Smith & Dumont, 1995; Stawar & Stawar, 1989). However, other results have been more encouraging and have provided at least partial support for some of the hypotheses (Kahill, 1984; Koppitz, 1968, 1984; Naglieri, 1988; Swenson, 1968). The greatest success has been achieved when drawings are used as a rough measure of intellectual maturation; moderate success has been achieved in making global ratings (level of adjustment, impulsiveness, anxiety); but little success has been recorded in assessing specific aspects of personality by using single signs or making specific differential diagnoses.

One important issue in determining reliability and validity is that, typically, there is wide variation between one drawing and the next, particularly regarding content. A child might draw a picture of a cowboy during one administration and an astronaut during the next. Although it is easy to subject global ratings of such areas as overall drawing quality to test-retest or interrater reliability, the specific contents can be expected to show wide variation. As would then be expected, test-retest reliabilities based on global quantitative ratings using the Naglieri (1988) and other similar DAP guidelines have found moderate to good reliabilities ranging between .60 and .89, with a mean of .74. In contrast, test-retest of contents would be expected to be low. Interrater reliabilities have been quite high, with the drawing of the man being .92 and the drawing of the woman, .93 (Naglieri, 1988). Further studies on interrater reliability on adult DAPs have likewise been respectable. In general, interrater reliabilities of structural/formal content and of global ratings have usually been greater than .80 (Kahill, 1984).

Whereas some success has been achieved in establishing adequate reliability, attempts to demonstrate adequate validity have been more problematic. The greatest success has been achieved by using quantitative scoring categories, such as those provided by Harris (1963) and Naglieri (1988). Accurate discriminations have been made in determining the ages of different children who are between 5 and 17 years old, moderate to low correlations (ranging between .22 and .63) have been found between DAP scores and intelligence (Tramill, Edwards, & Tramill, 1980), and low to moderate correlations have been found with academic achievement (Naglieri, 1988). Thus, when quantitative scorings (number of details, overall quality) are made of children's (5 to 17 years) drawings, the DAP does seem to be a useful nonverbal device for screening cognitive ability. This is especially true for children in the lower ranges of intelligence (Scott, 1981).

Global ratings based on multiple signs or overall impressions (bizarreness, quality) have produced mixed results. For example, distinctions among diagnostic groups have not been successful when ratings were of the drawing's bizarreness (Cauthen, Sandman, Kilpatrick, & Deabler, 1969), body disturbance (Carlson, Tucker, Harrow, & Quinlan, 1971), or Koppitz's emotional indicators (Norford & Barrakat, 1990; Rubin, Ragins, Schacter, & Wimberly, 1979; Tharinger & Stark, 1990). In contrast, overall DAP scores have correlated with such areas as scores on a self-concept scale (Ottenbacher, 1981), a modified Halstead-Reitan organicity scale (McLachlan & Head, 1974), and indicators of the presence of sexual abuse (Van Hutton, 1994; Waldman, Silber, Holmstrom, & Karp, 1994).

The most controversial area of projective drawings has been their use for the assessment of specific personality characteristics (see Chapman & Chapman, 1967; Kahill, 1984; Machover, 1949; Smith & Dumont, 1995; Swenson, 1968). The original basis for interpreting the drawings was developed from clinical experience combined with psychoanalytic theory. For example, Machover (1949) hypothesized that drawing the opposite-sex figure indicated possible homosexuality or at least confusion regarding sexual identity. However, most empirical research has failed to support this interpretation. No differences have been found in the proportion of opposite-sex drawings made first by lesbians (Hassell & Smith, 1975; Janzen & Coe, 1975) or by homosexuals of both sexes (Roback, Langevin, & Zajac, 1974), nor in scores on the MMPI Mf scale (Gravitz, 1969), or the Wellesley Sex Role Orientation Scale (Teglasi, 1980). Another hypothesis, by Hammer (1954, 1958), states that persons who placed their drawings on the left side of the page were more likely to be impulsive. However, no relationship was found for persons who emphasized left-sided placement and Pd (psychopathic deviance) scores on the MMPI (Dudley, Craig, Mason, & Hirsch, 1976) or between delinquent and nondelinquent adolescents (Montague & Prytula, 1975).

Early reviews of research rarely supported the validity of projective drawings in personality assessment (Suinn & Oskamp, 1969; Swenson, 1968). Klopfer and Taulbee (1976) lamented the expenditure of so much energy on research that had produced so few encouraging results. Some authors have thus suggested that drawing techniques be considered not so much a formal test but rather a way to increase understanding of the client based on client/clinician interaction related to the drawing, or to help access important life experiences (Chantler, Pelco, & Martin, 1993; Hartman, 1992; Klopfer & Taulbee, 1976; Stawar & Stawar, 1989).

A somewhat more recent review of adult human-figure drawings, by Kahill (1984), found varying levels of support for different aspects of projective drawing interpretations. In keeping with previous reviews, most of the hypotheses derived from specific aspects of drawings (eyes, ears, line pressure, and so on) were either not supported or were mixed. Global ratings of the overall drawing were somewhat more successful in discriminating level of adjustment. In particular, ratings of overall quality were related to levels of adjustment (Maloney & Glasser, 1982). In fact, ratings of overall quality have accounted for most of the variance in global ratings in general (Lewinsohn, 1965; Shaffer, Duszynski, & Thomas, 1984). However, this may be confounded by artistic ability and training, which have rarely been controlled in the studies. Kahill (1984) concludes by suggesting that:

> . . . rather than making futile attempts to turn itself into a scientific instrument, figure [drawing] should more properly take its place as a rich and potentially valuable clinical tool that can provide working hypotheses and a springboard for discussion with the patient. (p. 288)

ASSETS AND LIMITATIONS

One difficulty in evaluating projective drawings is that most published studies were conducted either by enthusiastic psychoanalytically oriented clinicians or by highly critical, empirically based researchers. The clinicians often give, as verification for their findings, anecdotes and clinical experience, or they selectively present primarily supportive research. In contrast, empirically oriented reviewers have seriously criticized projective drawings, particularly when the interpretations are based on specific signs (ears, hair, edging, and so on). However, these reviewers have rarely been appreciative of the assumptions, procedures, and flexibility inherent in a holistic and interactive psychoanalytic approach. It is an exception when a reader is given a balanced perspective that combines consensually supported empirical research with an appreciation of working with unconscious processes.

An added difficulty is that many of the interpretive hypotheses have either not been fully investigated or, in the investigations that have been done, have been flawed. In particular, many early studies did not consider the importance of base rates in evaluating the significance of interpretations. For example, if the group studied was comprised of persons in psychotherapy, and their drawings were said to indicate low self-esteem or high levels of anxiety, then there would be a high chance of being correct simply because a relatively large proportion of persons in psychotherapy experience these difficulties. Base rates have also not been included for the presence of specific characteristics of drawings, such as the frequency of enlarged heads, persons drawn without clothes, or the inclusion of guns or knives. Furthermore, few studies have taken into account a number of factors that can considerably influence drawings: a person's artistic skill, the testing situation, intelligence, previous experience with similar situations, characteristics of the examiner, and test-taking attitudes.

Some proponents have suggested that projective drawings are relatively culture-free (Hammer, 1985; Oakland & Dowling, 1983), but others have challenged this assumption. For example, Sundberg and Ballinger (1968) have noted the differences in content that are likely to occur in the drawings of Nepalese as compared with American children. Similarly, drawings of children from tropical regions might be likely to include more outdoor settings, a greater number of palm (as opposed to pine) trees, fewer chimneys, and possibly less clothing. Thus, interpretations need to take these types of influences into account. Other features of drawings do seem to be universal, such as the observation that the number of details increases with age (Gonzales, 1982; Groves & Fried, 1991).

One major criticism of projective drawings is the frequent subjectivity involved in their interpretation. This happens primarily when interpretations are made from intuitive judgments based on assumed isomorphy between the drawings and the person or his or her world (i.e., shrunken figure equals a shrunken ego; see Smith & Dumont, 1995). It might be speculated that subjectivity is doubled, in that not only might the client subjectively project portions of self into the drawing, but the interpreter might project self into his or her interpretations. For example, Hammer (1968) has noted that interpretations of clients have been related to characteristics of the interpreters themselves (e.g., more hostile clinicians produced a greater number of "hostile indicators" in the drawings).

Chapman and Chapman (1967) suggested that reliance on incorrect but repeatedly used interpretations may be caused by what they refer to as "illusory correlation." They demonstrated this by providing college undergraduates with human-figure drawings accompanied by specific validated interpretive statements. They were thus clearly taught the "correct" interpretations. They were then given a list of six personality statements and requested to list the drawing characteristic associated with the statements. Despite the previous instruction, students listed aspects of the drawings based not on their previous learning, but on invalid yet intuitively derived associations (i.e., suspiciousness being reflected by overworking the eyes). Perhaps the most disturbing aspect of the study was that the intuitive interpretations from the students corresponded closely with impressionistic interpretations by trained clinicians. This illusory correlation has been found even when subjects were asked to guard against it (Waller & Keeley, 1978) and is stronger when attempting to process large amounts of information (Lueger & Petzel, 1979). Similarly, Smith and Dumont (1995) used a simulated case review and found that psychologists used the same sorts of unvalidated, intuitive interpretive guidelines as nonpsychologists. These findings, combined with poor research results, suggest that clinical lore may be based more on common sense than on validated hypotheses. In fact, interpreters may even ignore research data in favor of intuitively appealing interpretations that are unsupported or even contradicted by empirical literature.

A number of additional, more specific limitations have also been directed toward the projective use of drawings. No agreed-on interpretation or scoring systems exist, and there is a wide number of variations on administration. In many cases, the catalogs used for interpretation are arranged in a way that allows them to be mistaken as test manuals with empirically established interpretations. The misinformed reader might thus make incorrect interpretations based on these seductively listed interpretive hypotheses. This problem is further compounded in that some of the manuals have been reprinted without taking into account a balanced review of relevant research. Thus, many "interpretations" are still included, even though they quite clearly have been found to be invalid. Finally, the quality of standardization groups for the different systems is quite variable. The above factors are all likely to significantly alter both the drawings themselves and the interpretations resulting from them.

Given the largely unencouraging empirical research, explanations need to be provided for the continued popularity of projective drawings. Proponents stress that the drawings are simple, easy procedures that can be administered quickly, require few materials, and are found to be enjoyable by most participants. In addition, the drawings can often be used to generate a large number of hypotheses relating to a person's self-concept, ego ideal, perceptions of persons of the opposite sex, level of adjustment, impulsiveness, anxiety, contact with reality, and conflict areas. Because responses are supposed to depend on a person's inner organizing abilities, the drawings theoretically provide an index of the nature and quality of these organizational processes. Furthermore, drawing techniques can be used with children within a wide age range. Because drawings are nonverbal, they can be used with clients who have poor verbal skills, such as the intellectually disabled, non-English-speaking clients, persons with reading/learning difficulties, or those who are withdrawn, evasive, or defensive. Administration can be done either individually or in groups. Not only can the results from projective drawings be easily integrated into psychological reports, but they can be used to indicate change as a result of psychotherapy.

In terms of the practical, day-to-day types of concerns encountered by clinicians, the above-mentioned assets of projective drawings are significant. However, each clinician who plans to use projective drawings should consider whether these assets are sufficient to counter the difficulties related to their psychometric properties. Clinicians who want a clear, valid, foolproof means of assessing personality will be disappointed. In contrast, practitioners who are comfortable with a more intuitive, metaphorical, tentative, and interactive approach for generating hypotheses and facilitating interaction will find projective drawings to be a useful tool.

ADMINISTRATION

Regardless of the different variations in administration, instructions are kept to a minimum. This helps to maintain the ambiguity of the situation, thereby increasing the likelihood that significant aspects of personality will be projected onto the drawings. Clients should be seated in a comfortable position, with sufficient room to freely move their arms while completing the drawings. They are provided with a single sheet of 8.5 × 11-inch unlined paper and, if an achromatic drawing is desired, a sharp No. 2 pencil with an eraser. If chromatic drawings are desired, clients should be provided with crayons, colored pencils, or different-colored felt-tip pens. If the DAP is given, they are simply requested to "Draw a picture of a person." Once the first drawing is completed, subjects are given another 8.5 × 11-inch, unlined sheet of paper and requested to "Draw a person of the opposite sex." If the "self" version is also administered, they would be requested to "Draw a picture of yourself." Some administrators suggest that no other instructions be given; others recommend that the person also be told to take his or her time and draw the best drawing possible. Later in the chapter, in a subsection titled "Cognitive Maturity," the somewhat more precise set of instructions using a three-person (Man, Woman, and Self) format is recommended, according to the guidelines provided by Naglieri (1988, pp. 23–24).

Administrations other than the DAP would require instructions similar to the general instructions for the draw-a-person test. For example, one variation of the HTP recommends that the client be requested to "Draw a picture that includes a house, a tree, and a person," or, for kinetic drawings, to "Draw a picture of your family (or persons in school) doing something." After the drawing has been completed, the clinician should note the client's name, age, and date, and should number the drawings according to the order in which they were completed.

Sometimes, clients complain that they are poor artists. This might be countered with the observation that, for most people, artistic ability stops when they are about 10 years of age and most people are not particularly good artists. Furthermore, it might be stressed that this is not a test of artistic ability but they should still do the best they can. Occasionally, clients will request specific guidelines, such as how big to make the person, what sex the person should be, or what the person in the drawing should be doing. The examiner should simply state that it is up to them. If they draw a stick figure, they should be given a new sheet of paper and requested to draw a more complete person. Some examiners recommend that, if subjects draw only the top half or quarter of a person, they should also be given a new sheet of paper and requested to draw a complete person.

One option is to include an inquiry phase, in which the client might be requested to tell a story about the person in the drawing. This story can then be used to aid future interpretations. More specific questions might be asked, to have subjects indicate what the person in the drawing is thinking or feeling, what makes him or her happy or sad, or what his or her interests are. If only the DAP is administered, the examiner might only select and ask the questions relevant to the person drawing(s). Some examiners might want clients to associate to and interpret the significance of their drawings. The clients themselves are thereby being used as consultants to help with the interpretations. This latter procedure is likely to be most successful for clients who have a good level of insight and are fairly appreciative of internal psychological processes.

During the administration, the examiner should note any relevant behaviors: clients' level of confidence or hesitancy, whether the procedure increases anxiety, the degree of playfulness, impulsiveness, or conscientiousness, or repeated or excessive erasures.

The most appropriate variation on administration will depend on the purpose of assessment as well as the personal preference of the practitioner. In general, the most research and therefore the most strategies available for interpretation can be found with human-figure drawings. However, if a clinician would like to obtain information about family, school, or work, then variations such as the Kinetic Family Drawing or Kinetic School Drawing might be administered. Different authors argue the relative usefulness of different variations. For example, Burns (1987) has argued for and provided examples of the advantages of the Kinetic House-Tree-Person over the regular House-Tree-Person. Similarly, Sarrell, Sarrell, and Berman (1981) have emphasized that the Draw-A-Person is good at uncovering attitudes toward the person's sexuality and body image.

GENERAL INTERPRETIVE CONSIDERATIONS

Interpretation of drawing techniques varies on a continuum ranging from objective scoring to an intuitive, impressionistic analysis. Objective scoring is based primarily on specific details or patterns of details that occur in the drawings. These might include scoring for such factors as cognitive maturity, impulsiveness, neuropsychological deficit, or overall level of adjustment. However, it is frequent in clinical practice to take a more flexible, impressionistic approach that might begin with considering the overall feel of the drawing, proceeding to standard interpretations of specific signs, and integrating the hypotheses derived from these steps within the context of information obtained from other sources.

Some clinicians prefer to base their interpretations on interactions with their clients, in which both the client and the therapist confer to establish the individual meaning of the drawings. In this more interactive approach, the drawings can be used as a tool for focusing on the inner experience of the client in order to either expand the depth of assessment or accomplish therapeutic goals, such as resolving difficulties, uncovering unconscious patterns, or facilitating catharsis.

Interpretation by means of quantitative scoring provides clear results that can be empirically supported. In contrast, more impressionistic approaches often produce questionable results because of various types of clinician bias (illusory correlation, primacy/recency effects, halo effects, and so on) combined with the generally poor psychometric properties of the test itself. The advantage of an impressionistic approach lies in its flexibility, which potentially allows practitioners to discover unique aspects of the person that might be missed by an objective approach, and enables the development of a deeper level of rapport between the client and clinician. However, the accuracy of this approach varies tremendously, based on the individual skill of the clinician and/or various conditions surrounding test administration and interpretation.

The Body Image Hypothesis

The most central assumption behind projective interpretation of human-figure drawings is that they represent the artist or at least some aspect of the artist. All other interpretations (head size, nudity, sex of first-drawn figure) revolve around this central assumption. Some of the numerous studies made to test this hypothesis have been supportive. For example, a moderate relationship was found between human-figure drawings by adolescent males and judges' ratings of the boys' physical characteristics (Van

Dyne & Carsleadon, 1978). Similarly, obese subjects drew larger figures than did persons with normal weight (Bailey, Shinedling, & Payne, 1970), and schizophrenics who had undergone training in movement and creative expression had increased scores using the Goodenough-Harris criteria (Rosenthal & Beutal, 1981). Similarly, subgroups of females who would be expected to have extra concern with their bodies have been found to reflect these concerns in their human-figure drawings. These subgroups included pubertal girls, who were found to give more explicit representation to breasts (Reirdan & Koff, 1980); sexually abused females, who were likely to express concern over sexual characteristics on their drawings (Chantler et al., 1993; Van Hutton, 1994); and pregnant women, who were more likely to draw breasts and nude and/or distorted figures (Tolor & Digrazia, 1977).

The results of both the research on the body image hypothesis and the drawings themselves should be interpreted cautiously, because the projection of the self onto the drawings is likely to be complicated and multifaceted. Clients might even draw a figure that is opposite to their actual self if they have "decided" to portray an unrealistic ego ideal. Central to the problem is the difficulty in determining what constitutes a "true" view of a person's body image:

> Is it a photograph, or a verbal self-description, or is the body image a function of the interaction between a person's physical appearance and his self-concept? Or is it something else, or some combination of something else? The question is, of course, unanswerable. (Swenson, 1968, p. 23)

Thus, the projection of the self should not be defined in narrow terms. It might be subjects' actual self, their ideal self, or their feared self, or it might represent their perception of other people in their environment.

Age Considerations

Some reviewers have concluded that the primary factor involved in children's drawings is cognitive maturity (see the Goodenough-Harris and Naglieri scoring criteria) and that personality or emotional states are relatively minor. In contrast, others believe that, because children have fewer defenses than adults, they are more likely to create drawings that are strong, direct, and clear expressions of their emotional states. Regardless of which position is correct, it is essential to understand the expected versus the unusual features of the drawings produced by persons from different age groups. For example, it's normal for 5-year-olds not to draw feet, hair, or necks, which means their absence should not be considered clinically significant.

Koppitz (1968) summarized the items that are expected in 86% to 100% of the drawings of children from ages 5 to 12 (see Table 11–1). For example, Table 11–1 shows that it is normal for 86% to 100% of 5-year-olds to include a head, eyes, nose, mouth, and so on. Only 15% of this age group fail to include these features; their omission may suggest that the child is mentally immature. In addition, Table 11–1 includes unusual or "exceptional items" that are included by only 15% of this age group. For example, a 5-year-old who includes such features as a knee, elbow, or two lips might be indicating either superior mental ability or perhaps some special concern with the area

Table 11–1. Expected and exceptional items on human-figure drawings of boys and girls ages 5 to 12

Item	Age 5 Boys	Age 5 Girls	Age 6 Boys	Age 6 Girls	Age 7 Boys	Age 7 Girls	Age 8 Boys	Age 8 Girls	Age 9 Boys	Age 9 Girls	Age 10 Boys	Age 10 Girls	Ages 11 and 12 Boys	Ages 11 and 12 Girls
N =	128	128	131	133	134	125	138	130	134	134	109	108	157	167
Expected Items														
Head	X	X	X	X	X	X	X	X	X	X	X	X	X	X
Eyes	X	X	X	X	X	X	X	X	X	X	X	X	X	X
Nose	X	X	X	X	X	X	X	X	X	X	X	X	X	X
Mouth	X	X	X	X	X	X	X	X	X	X	X	X	X	X
Body	X	X	X	X	X	X	X	X	X	X	X	X	X	X
Legs	X	X	X	X	X	X	X	X	X	X	X	X	X	X
Arms	X	X	X	X	X	X	X	X	X	X	X	X	X	X
Feet			X	X	X	X	X	X	X	X	X	X	X	X
Arms 2 dimension							X		X		X		X	X
Legs 2 dimension													X	X
Hair				X		X	X	X	X	X	X	X	X	X
Neck								X		X	X	X	X	X
Arm down														X
Arms at shoulder														
2 clothing items												X		
Exceptional Items														
Knee	X	X	X	X	X	X	X	X	X	X	X	X	X	
Profile	X	X	X	X	X	X	X	X	X	X		X		
Elbow	X	X	X	X	X	X	X	X	X					
Two lips	X	X	X	X	X	X	X		X		X			
Nostrils	X	X	X	X	X		X		X					
Proportions	X	X	X	X	X									
Arms at shoulder	X	X	X	X										
4 clothing items	X	X	X	X										
Feet 2 dimension	X	X	X											
Five fingers	X													
Pupils	X													

Source: Data from *Psychological Evaluation of Children's Human Figure Drawings* (p. 189), by E. Koppitz, 1968, New York: Grune & Stratton, Inc. Reproduced with permission.

of the body that has been depicted. Thus, the table can be used to determine which features of a child's drawings are normal versus unusual for children of different ages. The more formal Naglieri scoring system, used to determine a child's cognitive maturity, can supplement Table 11–1 and is summarized in the section on objective scoring.

Although most change and variety occur in the drawings of young children as they go through various developmental stages, some patterns have also emerged in the drawings of adolescents and the elderly. Adolescence is frequently a time of experimentation and exaggerated behaviors, which are often reflected in drawings. For example, Saarni and Azara (1977) found it was fairly typical for adolescent males to have more extreme expressions of gender identity (huge muscles, dominant expressions), more hostile-aggressive features, and greater bizarreness. In contrast, drawings by female adolescents were more likely to have features suggesting insecurity-lability and to be more ambiguous and childlike. Thus, interpretations should take these features into account so that the drawings of adolescents are interpreted differently from the drawings of adults that contain these features. There is also some suggestion that the elderly are more likely to make relatively fragmented, incongruous, absurd, and primitive drawings (Gilbert & Hall, 1962).

The Healthy Drawing

Clinical psychology and psychiatry frequently show a bias toward focusing on problem areas. Frequently, little attention is paid to the person's strengths, resources, and areas of positive growth. This bias is clearly seen in the psychoanalytic interpretation of projective material. Most interpretive guides to projective drawings generally make a passing reference to the importance of adjustment and then quickly proceed into a long list of features suggesting pathology. Often, the implied assumption is that, if no pathological features are identified, then the drawing is probably from a healthy, well-adjusted person. Morena (1981) originally reviewed the literature relating to healthy drawings and summarized different features found in drawings that suggest positive self-esteem, confidence, security, well-functioning interpersonal relations, openness to self and environment, clarity regarding sexual orientation, and ability to organize self and life effectively. Out of this original listing, two quantitative scoring systems were developed for human-figure drawings and the house-tree-person test (Groth-Marnat & Roberts, in press). Global ratings were used, based on recommendations made by previous reviewers, the lack of success in validating single signs (Kahill, 1984; Roback, 1968), and the finding that the overall quality of drawings (or lack of it) is the single most important underlying factor in determining level of psychological functioning (Shaffer, Duszynski, & Thomas, 1984). However, neither global ratings comprised of overall numbers of indicators nor single signs were found to correlate with traditional measures of self-esteem and positive self-concept within a university student population. Tharinger and Stark (1990) similarly found that a quantitative scoring system did not relate to measures of self-esteem. However, they did find that a more impressionistic qualitative rating of human-figure drawings did correlate (.43) with positive self-esteem. These ratings were based on the relative "humanness" of the design, an ability to interact with the world, a sense of well being, and the absence of a "hollow, vacant, or stilted" feel to the figure.

Interpretive Procedure

The following four steps are recommended as a sequence to follow when interpreting projective drawings. These steps combine options for both objective scoring and a more impressionistic approach. Individual practitioners may wish to vary their reliance on objective or impressionistic strategies based on personal preference (need for empirically valid interpretations, comfort with metaphorical approaches) or on the needs defined by the context of the assessment itself (as a prelude to therapy, high validity demanded by a legal assessment, relative richness of the drawings, time constraints).

1. *Objective scoring.* Practitioners can score for one or more of the objective scoring systems included in the following section (cognitive maturity, maladjustment and emotional disturbance, impulsiveness, and assessment of cognitive impairment). This approach (a) will provide relatively valid interpretations while alerting the clinician to specific, relevant details in the drawing, and (b) is in keeping with the conclusions of virtually all objective reviewers of projective drawings, who have recommended global ratings and objective scoring as the preferred method of interpretation.

2. *Overall impression.* After a specific scoring has been calculated, the clinician can step back from the drawing and consider it as a whole (Handler, 1985; Morena, 1981): What is its overall mood, general message, or feel? What does it convey about the client's view of the world, self-concept, attitude toward his or her body, perception of the opposite sex, or receptivity in interpersonal relationships? In this highly intuitive process, practitioners attempt to place themselves in the position of the client and see the client's world from the perspective suggested by the drawing(s). There is evidence that such a global impressionistic approach is more effective than quantitative systems in differentiating children with mood disorders from normal controls (Tharinger & Stark, 1990). Accuracy, using this approach, has been found to be related to persons who were high in empathy, intuition, flexibility, and creativity, and who were sensitive to interpersonal relations (Burley & Handler, 1970). This is emphasized by Hammer (1968) who states that "in the hands of some students, projective drawings are an exquisitely sensitive tool" but for others who use a stilted, rigid approach, the interpretations are "like disconnected phones" (p. 385).

3. *Consideration of specific details.* When a global consideration has been made, clinicians can make a rational analysis of the different details in the drawing, as outlined in the later section, "Interpretation of Specific Signs." This analysis might include the meaning associated with unusual aspects or features, such as the size of the drawing, detailing, line quality, or breast emphasis. However, this detailed analysis should be made cautiously because very few individual signs have received clear empirical support. Even the strongest proponents of projective drawings stress that one of the worst violations of working with drawings is to make rigid, single-sign interpretations. For example, Handler (1985) advises that clinicians should not ask what a specific sign *means* but rather what it *could mean.*

4. *Integration.* The final step is to take the information obtained in steps 1 through 3 and integrate it into a wider context derived from interview data, personal records, and other test results. For example, if the person scored high on Oas's (1984) measures of impulsiveness, did he or she also score high on measures of impulsiveness on the

MMPI (primarily, scales 4 and 9)? Likewise, do measures of neuropsychological deficit found on the human-figure drawings correspond with the person's history and/or neuropsychological indicators on the Bender (see Chapter 12)? The final phase, then, is one of reality testing, which is intended to increase the incremental validity of assessment data.

INTERPRETATION THROUGH OBJECTIVE SCORING

The four representative scoring systems discussed below have been selected because they are relatively psychometrically sound and easily scored, and they represent clearly different types of information. The section on cognitive maturity uses administration instructions provided by Naglieri (1988). The remaining three sections should follow the standard instructions for the DAP, described in the Administration section.

Cognitive Maturity

The Goodenough-Harris (Harris, 1963) and Naglieri (1988) scoring systems provide an adequate method for screening children to determine their level of cognitive maturity. Goodenough (1926) originally assumed that the skills needed for making a drawing require the child to make relevant discriminations related to that object. Children must not only accurately perceive the object, but also must organize their response into a systematic, meaningful pattern. The degree of complexity of their response (the drawing) can serve as an index of their ability to form complex concepts. Research has generally provided some support for this belief (Koppitz, 1968, 1984; Naglieri, 1988; Sitton & Light, 1992). Complexity is measured by the number of relevant details included in the drawings. The following discussion outlines the Naglieri system (*The Draw A Person: A Quantitative Scoring System*), which is preferred over the Goodenough-Harris system because it provides well-developed, modern norms, its standard scores are related to half- and quarter-year intervals, and it uses objective, reliable scoring criteria. All information on administration, scoring criteria, norms, and interpretation is included in a clear, well-developed manual. The previous summary of the Naglieri system indicated that reliability was good (test-retest = .74; interrater = .93 to .95) and validity was adequate. In particular, the scale has been able to accurately discriminate between children of different ages (5 to 17). It has also been found to have low to moderate correlations with nonverbal intelligence (.31) and achievement on reading (.24) and math (.21; Naglieri, 1988). Despite the correlations with intelligence and achievement, the scale should not be used as a substitute for a formal intelligence test. It is, however, most appropriate as a rapid screening device.

Administration should follow these guidelines provided by Naglieri (1988, pp. 23–24):

> I'd like you to draw some pictures for me. First I'd like you to draw a picture of a man. Make the very best picture you can. Take your time and work very carefully, and I'll tell you when to stop. Remember, be sure to draw the whole man. Please begin.

After 5 minutes (or sooner, if the child has finished), supply a new piece of paper and say:

This time I want you to draw a picture of a woman. Make the very best picture you can. Take your time and work very carefully, and I'll tell you when to stop. Be sure to draw the whole woman. Please begin.

Again, allow 5 minutes for completion. When either the time has elapsed or the child indicates the drawing is finished, supply a new sheet of paper and say:

Now I'd like you to draw a picture of yourself. Be sure to draw the very best picture you can. Take your time and work very carefully, and I'll tell you when to stop. Be sure to draw your whole self. Please begin.

Again, allow 5 minutes, unless the drawing is completed sooner. With the above administration instructions, three drawings are used and scored. Using the three drawings, Naglieri found an increase in reliability compared with a one- or two-drawing format.

Naglieri (1988) has provided scoring criteria, a scoring chart, and a scoring record form. Each item was selected based on its ability to make age-related discriminations. The result is a system comprised of 14 criteria containing a total of 64 items (see Table 11–2). Tables and procedures are provided to convert a child's raw scores into standard scores with a mean of 100 and standard deviation of 15. The resulting scores can be used as an index of the child's level of cognitive maturity (Sitton & Light, 1992), which is roughly correlated with intelligence and achievement scores. If a child scores within either the quite low or quite high range (greater than one or two standard deviations above the mean), further investigation may be needed to explore the reason.

Maladjustment and Emotional Disturbance

Several researchers have noted that global ratings are the major area in which the DAP has been found to have adequate reliability and validity. This is congruent with reviewers of the DAP, such as Roback (1968) who has stated that the most probable clear future for the DAP is as a "rough screening device [to determine] gross level of maladjustment" (p. 17). Several studies have included overall ratings based on global

Table 11–2. Scoring criteria for the Draw-A-Person: A quantitative scoring system

1. Arms*	8. Hair
2. Attachment	9. Head
3. Clothing	10. Legs
4. Ears	11. Mouth
5. Eyes	12. Neck
6. Feet	13. Nose
7. Fingers	14. Trunk

Source: Adapted from Naglieri (1988).

* Each of the 14 criteria is further divided into specific items such as presence of the item, one or more specific details, and a bonus point for superior performance. This results in a total of 64 items.

subjective impressions (bizarreness, creativity, quality), number of details present, or quantitative scoring of one or more characteristics of the drawing. For example, Tharinger and Stark (1990) found that qualitative, impressionistic ratings of the degree of health versus psychopathology were able to differentiate persons with mood disorders more effectively than formal scoring systems. This finding is consistent with Shaffer et al.'s (1984) comparisons of different scoring systems, which indicated that most of the variance could be accounted for by the general factor of drawing quality.

Maloney and Glasser (1982) reviewed the literature on DAP signs that indicate maladjustment and developed a list of nine easily scored characteristics that they judged most able to discriminate between adults with difficulties. These are listed, along with scoring criteria, in Table 11–3. All the indicators except Transparency and Vertical Imbalance of Stance were able to discriminate between normal persons and different patient groups. The most accurate discriminators were Head Simplification and Body Simplification, followed by Poor Overall Quality, Sexual Differentiation, and Distortion (indicators 5, 6, 7, 9, and 3, respectively). Overall interrater reliabilities ranged from .78 to .30. The lowest levels were for Vertical Imbalance of Stance (.39) and Sexual Elaboration (.30). Discriminations between normal persons and psychiatric patients were most accurately made using Head Simplification, Body Simplification, Distortion, and Poor Overall Quality (indicators 5, 6, 3, and 7, respectively). These indicators occurred either rarely or not at all in the drawings of normals. Head Simplification, Body Simplification, Sexual Differentiation, and Sexual Elaboration (indicators 5, 6, 8, and 9, respectively) occurred more frequently in the drawings of psychiatric psychotic patients than in those of psychiatric nonpsychotics (few or no indicators). Mentally retarded persons had the highest number of indicators (except 9, Sexual Elaboration) of any of the groups except psychotics.

Table 11–3. DAP indicators for maladjustment

1. Omissions: Significant details of the drawing not included (no feet, legs, arms, etc.).

2. Transparency: Body parts can be seen through (arms, legs, clothes, etc.) or internal organs (heart, stomach, etc.) can be seen inside the body.

3. Distortion: Parts of the person are clearly drawn out of proportion (huge or elongated arms, tiny head, etc.), relevant portions of the body are not connected, body parts are connected to the wrong areas.

4. Vertical Imbalance of Stance: Person is clearly tilted to one side.

5. Head Simplification: Head is overly simple, primitive, or basic (similar or the same as a stick figure).

6. Body Simplification: (as in item 5).

7. Poor Overall Quality: The overall quality of the drawing as a whole, same as artistic quality, accuracy of depiction, related to number of details. The rating is impressionistic and rated on a scale from 1 (poor) to 9 (excellent).

8. Sexual Differentiation: Clarity to which the person resembles either a male or a female. Likewise rated on a scale from 1 (undifferentiated) to 9 (clearly differentiated).

9. Sexual Elaboration: Amount of details related to sex (breasts, penises, excessive makeup, etc.).

Source: Adapted from Maloney and Glasser (1982).

The above data strongly suggest that an increase in psychopathology is associated with a greater number of the indicators summarized by Maloney and Glasser (1982). However, specific meanings associated with these signs are less clear. They might indicate overall maladjustment, a relation to cognitive maturity/sophistication, a general but nonspecific disturbance, or, quite possibly, anxiety. (The first six indicators were derived from Handler's (1967) 21 anxiety indicators.) Clinicians are best advised to use the nine indicators as a global screening device for the presence of maladjustment and to determine the specific meaning of any maladjustment based on other test and/or interview data.

Naglieri, McNeish, and Bardos (1991) have developed a somewhat similar 55-item system to screen for general emotional disturbance among children ages 6 through 17 (*Draw-A-Person: Screening Procedure for Emotional Disturbance,* DAP:SPED). The DAP:SPED was developed using an actuarial approach. It was standardized using the same group (ages 6 to 17) as for Naglieri's (1988) more cognitive-based system, and it provides scores that can be presented as standard scores or percentile equivalents. Interrater reliabilities ranged between .91 to .94, internal consistency ranged between .71 to .76, and ethnic differences were minimal. Initial results suggest that a general clinical sample and a sample of students in special education produced higher scores on the DAP:SPED than normal controls (McNeish & Naglieri, 1993; Naglieri & Pfeiffer, 1992). However, high scores only discriminated the two groups slightly better than a random classification (Cohen, Swerdlik, & Phillips, 1996). High scores suggest that students should be evaluated further to confirm the presence of emotional difficulties and introduce greater detail into their expression.

Impulsiveness

Impulsiveness is a disorder of attention involving behavior that is typically inappropriate to the situation and occurs with little self-reflection or awareness. In contrast, the previous indicators for maladjustment are more clearly identified with anxiety. Anxiety and impulsiveness are generally different constructs, and they are likely to have different expressions on the DAP. Probably, a moderate level of anxiety serves to place controls on impulsiveness so that one might even expect a negative correlation between anxiety and impulsiveness.

Various impulsive versus nonimpulsive (reflective) measures have been identified on the DAP. The most extensive and successful formulation was developed by Oas (1984). The study was unusual for DAP research in that it controlled for drawing ability, IQ, age, drugs, organicity, and motivation. Using Oas's scoring system (see Table 11–4), it was possible to accurately discriminate adolescents who were independently rated as impulsive from those independently rated as nonimpulsive. The impulsive adolescents had higher total DAP indicators (M = 3.4, SD = 1.5) than nonimpulsives (M = 1.4, SD = 1.0). Likewise, impulsive adolescents in school had a significantly higher number of indicators (M = 4.2, SD = 1.3) than nonimpulsive adolescents in school (M = 1.6, SD = 1.1). The best discriminators for identifying impulsive (versus nonimpulsive) adolescents (ages 12 to 18) were: short completion time, aggressive content, overall drawing quality, discontinuity (difficulty connecting lines), general omission of important details, specific omissions, poor proportion, and inadequately drawn

Table 11–4.   DAP indicators of impulsivity and nonimpulsivity

Impulsive:	Nonimpulsive:
1. Completion time*	1. Symmetry
2. Aggression*	2. Detailing[†]
3. Overall quality*	3. Completion time[†]
4. Discontinuity*	4. Placement
5. Omissions*	5. Sketching[†]
6. Specific omissions*	6. Erasures
7. Proportion*	7. Size
8. Size increase	8. Gender identification
9. Neck	9. Eye emphasis[†]
10. Stance	10. Right side
11. Shoulders	11. Perspective
12. Poor planning	12. Mouth detail[†]
13. Left side	13. Shading[†]

Source: Adapted from Oas (1984).

* Best discriminators for identifying impulsiveness.

[†] Best discriminators for identifying nonimpulsiveness.

shoulders. Using discriminant function analysis for the 13 different impulsive and 13 nonimpulsive indicators, 93% of hospitalized impulsives and 97% of impulsives in school were correctly identified.

Oas (1984) also listed DAP indicators that were more characteristic of reflective (nonimpulsive) adolescents. The best discriminators were aspects of the drawings that required a delay of impulses and conscientiousness. These included detailing, a longer completion time, sketching, emphasis on the eyes, mouth details, and shading (see Table 11–4 and Appendix N). However, specific details should not be considered separately but rather should be placed into the overall context of the total number of impulsive versus nonimpulsive indicators. For clinical purposes, a cutoff of three impulsive indicators and five nonimpulsive indicators can be used.

Assessment of Cognitive Impairment

A number of drawing tests have been developed for the assessment of cognitive impairment. These tests are based on the observation that brain damage interferes with the complex integration of the spatial, perceptual, and motor responses required to accurately reproduce drawings. Specifically, right-hemisphere lesions have been associated with clients who have difficulty maintaining the overall gestalt of the drawing. This results in distortions in the perspective or proper proportion of the drawing. For most persons, left-hemisphere lesions will also result in drawing difficulties because the left hemisphere provides directions or commands to the right hand to correctly reproduce the design. Thus, drawings from persons with left-hemisphere lesions are likely to get the overall proportion correct, but might omit significant details (Lezak,

1995). A variety of visuographic and visuoconstructive tasks have been developed for the assessment of neuropsychological impairment (see Chapter 12). It would be logical to assume that similar efforts had been conducted to identify central nervous system indicators on the DAP.

Some guidelines have been suggested by McLachlan and Head (1974), who reviewed the literature and developed a list of 15 possible indicators for organicity. Only 5 of these indicators were found to have significant correlations with an outside criterion measure (Halstead-Reitan Neuropsychological Test Battery's Impairment Index). The resulting *Projective Impairment Rating Scale* (see Table 11–5) is scored on a three-point scale, with ratings given for an indicator not being present (0), present on one drawing (1), or present on both drawings (2). The scale scores thus range from 0 to 10. Interjudge reliabilities for total score and each of the five indicators were high (.79 to .95), as was split-half reliability (.89). Validity was low for each of the individual indicators (.31 to .37), but a moderate correlation was found between the summed scores and Reitan's Impairment Index (.50). A cutoff score of between 7 and 8 was recommended for identifying neuropsychological deficit. Although the above findings are modest, these indicators might serve as a brief screening device for identifying neuropsychological impairment. However, the same cautions that apply to the Bender are likely to be at least as relevant when using the DAP for identifying neuropsychological impairment: low sensitivity to subtle levels of impairment, overlap with emotional indicators, and difficulty identifying left-hemisphere dysfunction (see Chapter 12, assets and limitations for the Bender).

Table 11–5. DAP indicators of organicity and correlations with validity measures

Indicator	Correlation with Impairment Index
1. Figure off balance.	.37
2. Major detail missing (on head: eyes, nose, mouth, ears, or hair; on body: arm, leg, or torso; on extremities: foot, hand, or fingers. Do not score as missing if hands drawn behind back; score if figure runs off page).	.31
3. Gross body distortions (other than head and extremities; e.g., square-shaped or pear-shaped bodies, lack of symmetry, legs smaller than arms, discrepancy between sizes of arms and legs, arms unequal, distended belly).	.46
4. Weak synthesis (poor integration of arms, legs, head, neck with torso, arm "stuck on"/dislocated at wrong place; limb or body displaced).	.37
5. Poor motor control (line destruction: bending a straight line more than one-quarter inch, dashed or dotted line, jagged lines, and so on).	.35
Sum of Projective Impairment Index (obtained by adding scores on the above 5 indicators)	.50

Mitchell et al. (1993) developed a more detailed, 74-item system for identifying cognitive impairment. Quantitative scores can be calculated for Impairment, Distortion, Simplification, and an Organic Factors Index. Interrater reliability ranged between .42 and .77; internal consistency was .83 for a modified Impairment Index scale, .77 for the Distortion scale, and .85 for the Simplification scale. The scale was standardized on a sample of 800 persons comprised of normal controls (N = 100) and various patient groups (depressed, antisocial, manic, paranoid, schizophrenic, organic, mentally retarded; N = 100 in each group). Validity was suggested in that the Impairment score was significantly related to patient group membership, with scale performance accounting for 27% of the variance. Classification rate using the Impairment and Organic Factor Index scales resulted in 72% accuracy in differentiating controls, psychiatrics, and organics (including mental retardation). The distinction between schizophrenics and organics achieved a similar 75% correct classification rate. The following descriptions provide a general guide to interpretation:

- *Impairment scale:* Scores from 56 to 70 indicate moderate to severe impairment; scores above 70 are in the severely impaired range. However, elevations are not specific to central nervous system dysfunction but may reflect cognitive impairment related to psychopathology as well. The authors specify that scores in the severe range (above standard scores of 70) are likely to reflect organic conditions rather than psychopathology.
- *Distortion scale* (comprised of items such as arms that are clearly of unequal length): Moderate to severe elevations (56 to 70) suggest that basic elements of the design have been altered because of cognitive disturbance, and this becomes more pronounced as scores enter the severe range (above 70). As with the Impairment scale, elevations can suggest either psychopathology or neuropsychological deficit, with more organic conditions suggested by the scores in the higher elevations. One of the main purposes of this scale is to provide a differentiation between performances caused by simplifying the designs versus actually distorting them.
- *Simplification scale* (comprised of items such as squares or circles for body parts): In contrast to scores on Distortion, an elevation on the Simplification scale is more likely to originate from mentally retarded clients. High scores (especially above 70) are strongly suggestive of this condition.
- *Organic Factor Index* (derived from subtracting the Simplification raw score from the Distortion raw score): A score of 4 or more on the Organic Factors Index suggests an organic condition; scores below 4 suggest mental retardation. As with the Distortion and Simplification scales, the Organic Factor Index provides a further tool to distinguish between mental retardation and cognitive impairment due to other conditions.

INTERPRETATION OF SPECIFIC SIGNS

The hypotheses described in this section are those that, based on the three major reviews of the literature (Kahill, 1984; Roback, 1968; Swenson, 1968), have produced at least some support. Research between 1984 and 1996 has also been consulted. The criterion for inclusion was that, at the very least, an equal number of studies had to support the hypothesis, compared with the number that failed to support it. In addition to the mere number of supportive versus nonsupportive studies, the quality and relevance of the studies were taken into account. Hypotheses that were clearly not supported are listed at the end of the section.

Before attempting interpretations of specific details, clinicians should observe a number of cautions. Most of the research has produced conflicting results for even the best of these signs. Swenson (1968) explains the widely varying results as being consistent with the moderate to low reliabilities associated with both the occurrence of these signs (test-retest reliability) and the low agreement found when scoring them (interrater reliability). From a practical perspective, this means any interpretation should be made tentatively. In particular, Handler's (1985) advice to ask what a specific sign *could* mean rather than what it *does* mean should be heeded. Interpreters should also keep in mind the possibility that a sign may take on specific meaning for a client and thereby lead to an idiosyncratic interpretation for that person, even though the sign may not be sufficiently supported in any normative sense. Clinicians who are comfortable with a more interactive, metaphorical approach might find the interpretation of specific signs to be a rich source of information about the client. At the same time, clinicians should be aware of the limitations and possible errors associated with clinical judgment (see Chapter 1). A final caution: The vast majority of the research on specific interpretive signs has been done on adults and adolescents. Thus, the use of personality assessment for children's drawings should be approached with extreme caution, especially because the drawings of children may relate more to cognitive ability than to personality (Swenson, 1968). Even when aspects of children's drawings do relate to personality, it would be difficult to separate this relationship from the effects of cognitive ability.

Interpretation of Structure and Form

Size

Machover (1949) hypothesized that the relative size of a drawing is related to a person's level of self-esteem and energy. She speculated that extremely small, miniaturized drawings reflect low self-concept, depression, and lack of energy. Moderately large drawings suggest higher levels of energy and self-esteem. If the drawing is extremely large, this suggests compensatory inflation, which is consistent with persons having energy levels characteristic of manics or persons with delusions of grandeur. If a male draws a much larger female figure than a male figure, Machover (1949) further hypothesized that the person may be dominated by his mother or a mother-type figure, and/or may have difficulties with sexual identity. Empirical research has produced inconsistent results but there has been moderate support for the view that size reflects varying levels of self-esteem, mood, anxiety level, and relative degree of self-inflation (Fox & Thomas, 1990; Kahill, 1984; Mitchell et al., 1993; Paine, Alves, & Tubin, 1985).

Detailing

Hammer (1954), Handler (1985), and Machover (1949) have all suggested that inclusion of an excessive number of details is consistent with persons who handle anxiety by becoming more obsessive. Thus, the number of details has been used as a rough index not only of anxiety but also of the style by which the person attempts to deal with his or her anxiety. In contrast, a noteworthy lack of detail suggests withdrawal and a reduction of energy. A low number of details may also be consistent with persons who are mentally deficient, hesitant, or merely bored with the task (Kahill, 1984; Mitchell et al., 1993).

Line Characteristics

The line used to draw the figure can be conceptualized as the wall between the person's environment and his or her body (Machover, 1949). It can thus reflect the person's degree of insulation, vulnerability, or sensitivity to outside forces. Thick, heavily reinforced lines might be attempts to protect the self from anxiety-provoking forces, and faint, sketchy, thin lines might conversely represent insecurity and anxiety (Kahill, 1984; Mitchell et al., 1993).

Shading

Machover (1949) and Hammer (1954, 1958) have hypothesized that shading represents anxiety. The specific area that is shaded is likely to suggest concern regarding that area. Thus, a person who is self-conscious about his or her facial complexion might provide a high amount of shading on the face, or a person with concern regarding his or her breasts might similarly include more shading in this area (Burgess & Hartman, 1990; Kahill, 1984; Van Hutton, 1994). However, this interpretation should be made cautiously: a lack of shading in specific areas does not mean that there is no anxiety regarding those areas. Shading might also represent adaptation and adjustment in the drawings of persons who are merely trying to increase the quality of their drawing by emphasizing its three-dimensional aspect.

Distortion

Distortion in drawings occurs when the overall drawing or specific details are drawn in poor proportion, are disconnected, or are placed in inappropriate locations on the body. Hammer (1958) hypothesized that mild distortions reflect low self-concept, anxiety, and poor adjustment, and excessive distortions are characteristic of persons who have experienced a severe emotional upheaval. This has become one of the most strongly supported hypotheses (Chantler et al., 1993; Kahill, 1984; Roback, 1968; Swenson, 1968). In addition, distortion might occur as the result of neuropsychological deficit (see Chapter 12).

Chromatic Drawings

Some variations on administration suggest that, in addition to pencil drawings, the person should be requested to draw a person in color by using crayons or felt-tip pens. Hammer (1969b) suggested that the use of colors would be more likely to reveal emotionally charged and primitive aspects of the person, particularly if he or she is under stress or pressure. Although this has been supported by two studies, it has so far not been fully researched.

Hypotheses Not Supported

A number of traditional personality hypotheses related to the structure and form of drawings have clearly not been supported. These include placement on the page, stance, perspective (where the person in the drawing is viewed from), number of erasures, omissions, degree of symmetry, and presence of transparencies.

Interpretation of Content

Sex of First-Drawn Figure

The body image hypothesis states that not only do clients identify with the figure they have drawn, but this identification is likely to be strongest for the subject they choose to draw first. Based on this hypothesis, Machover (1949) and Hammer (1954) suggested that persons with clear gender identity will make the first drawing the same sex as themselves and persons with sexual-identity confusion will more often draw a member of the opposite sex. Later researchers and theorists have indicated that this relationship is more complex (Houston & Terwilliger, 1995). For example, Handler (1985) has suggested that, although gender confusion is a possibility, drawing the same-sex person first might also indicate additional issues such as a strong attachment to/dependence on a person of the opposite sex, greater awareness of/interest in persons of the opposite sex, or a poor self-concept.

Over the past 40 years, the hypothesis that clients with sexual-identity confusion will draw the opposite-sex person first has been tested by over 28 studies. The general consensus is that minimal support has been established. For example, in an early review, Brown and Tolor (1957) reported that 85% to 95% of a population of normal college males drew the same sex first as opposed to 75% to 92% of homosexuals. Although the percentage was slightly lower for homosexuals, the overlap between the two groups was sufficiently high to indicate that an unacceptably high rate of inaccuracies would occur if this were used to discriminate the two groups. Kahill (1984) reports that most of the studies in her review investigating the more general distinction of sex-role identification or sex-role conflict have likewise not found significant relationships. The hypothesis is further complicated in that children quite frequently draw the opposite sex first but this frequency gradually decreases in teenagers. By late adolescence, individuals draw opposite-sex persons first in percentages that approximate those of adults. Specifically, a large-scale university survey found that 92% of men and only 64% of females drew the same sex first (Zaback & Waehler, 1994). This suggests that any interpretations of females or children should be made with the knowledge that drawings in which the opposite sex is drawn first occur quite frequently within these groups. In addition to age and biological gender influencing masculinity/femininity of drawings, the degree to which a person identifies with masculine, feminine, or androgenous characteristics can also influence gender attributes of the drawings (Aronof & McCormick, 1990). Houston and Terwilliger (1995) summarize that gender-related details of drawings can be influenced by biological gender of the subject, culturally defined attitudes about gender, gender-role attitudes, or emotionally toned attitudes toward sexuality. The above discussion is provided because sex of the first-drawn figure is one of the classic interpretive signs in human-figure drawings. However, the complexity of factors influencing the occurrence and expression of this sign clearly indicates that interpretations based on it should be considered with caution and flexibility.

Mouth and Teeth

Intuitively, it might be conjectured that the manner in which subjects depict a figure's mouth reveals their attitudes toward processing things from the world or how they express themselves verbally. Specifically, Machover (1949) hypothesized that emphasis on the mouth suggests either an immature personality with oral characteristics, or verbal aggression. Although an emphasis on the mouth has not been found to be related to immature oral characteristics, there is some indication that the presence of teeth in combination with a slash representing the mouth suggests verbal (but not physical) aggression (see Kahill, 1984).

Breasts

Breast emphasis was theorized to occur in the drawings of emotionally and psychosexually immature males (Machover, 1949). However, breast emphasis in male drawings has been found in both normal and disturbed persons, so pathology should be inferred cautiously. In drawings by females, breast emphasis has been found to occur more frequently in drawings by pubescent girls (Reirdan & Koff, 1980) and pregnant women (Tolor & Digrazia, 1977). In addition, emphasis on sexual characteristics (including breasts) has been found more frequently among children who have been sexually abused (Burgess & Hartman, 1990; Hibbard & Hartman, 1990; Van Hutton, 1994)

Nudity/Clothing

Hammer (1954) hypothesized that drawings of underclothed persons indicate "body narcissism" and possibly a person who is self-absorbed to the point of being schizoid. On a more global level, it might be a general sign of maladjustment particularly related to sexual difficulties among children (Van Hutton, 1994). Although it has received some support, this interpretation is complicated in that either nudity or lack of clothing is sometimes found in the drawings of normals and frequently occurs in the drawings of artists. Specific populations who would be expected to have bodily concerns have likewise been found to draw a high proportion of nude figures. This includes 58% of the DAPs from pregnant women, 60% of those who have recently given birth, and 60% of those with gynecological problems (Tolor & Digrazia, 1977).

Hypotheses Not Supported

The majority of the hypotheses relating to content of human-figure drawings have clearly not been given support. This is partially due to the idiosyncratic meanings associated with many of the contents as well as the low reliabilities of these signs. Interpretations related to specific contents that have not been supported include those related to the head, head size, face, facial expressions, hair, facial features (eyes, ears, lips, nose), neck, contact features (arms, hands, legs, feet, toes), trunk, shoulders, anatomy indicators (internal glands, genitals), hips/buttocks, waistline, and clothing details (buttons, earrings, heels, belt).

THE HOUSE-TREE-PERSON TEST

The House-Tree-Person test (HTP) was originally developed by Buck (1948) and Buck and Hammer (1969), who reasoned that, in addition to human-figure drawings, drawings of houses and trees were also likely to be associated with relevant aspects of the person. Houses, trees, and persons are all familiar objects, are likely to be accepted objects for drawing, and will produce a greater number of associations than most other, more neutral objects. The HTP potentially has advantages over the DAP. Not only does it include human-figure drawings, but the greater variety of objects drawn is likely to produce a greater number of areas for interpretation. If the house, tree, and person are all drawn on one sheet of paper, as recommended by Burns and Kaufman (1972) and Burns (1987), then the picture often results in an integrated, interactional story.

The early developers of the HTP tended to rely heavily on traditional psychoanalytic theory, as represented by the following discussion of chimneys by Handler (1985):

> [I]f a subject suffers from psychosexual conflicts, the chimney, by virtue of its structural design and its protrusion from the body of the house is susceptible to receive the projection of the subject's inner feelings about his phallus. (p. 137)

However, Burns (1987), as well as many other practitioners, have emphasized a more humanistic and/or Jungian approach.

The disadvantage of the HTP (and other drawing techniques included later in this chapter) is that it tends to lack the extensive research base associated with the more traditional DAP. As such, the HTP is even less of a standardized, empirically based test than the DAP. The HTP (and Draw-A-Family, Kinetic Family Drawing, and so on) tends to appeal to, and be used more extensively by, clinicians attracted to intuitive, interactive, and metaphorical approaches. In many ways, it is similar to dream interpretation in that it relies heavily on the client's and/or therapist's associations to the drawings. Often, the meaning is derived primarily from interactively engaging the client. A large number of art therapists tend to use this and related techniques for assessment and as a prelude to and technique for therapy (Neale, Rosal, & Rosal, 1993; Oster & Gould, 1987).

The empirical research that has been done with the HTP provides some support. Buck (1966) found quite high correlations (.70–.75) between the Wechsler-Bellevue and a quantitative scoring system for the HTP. A more recent study found somewhat lower but still quite respectable correlations between the WAIS-R and Buck's quantitative scoring system (Heiberger, Abell, & Johnson, 1994). The highest correlations were found with the Performance IQ (.43), somewhat lower correlations were found with the Full Scale IQ (.32), and, as might be expected, there was no correlation with the Verbal IQ. Van Hutton (1994) has provided a somewhat different quantitative investigation by using the HTP to assess child abuse among children. She initially reviewed the empirical and clinical literature on drawings related to child abuse and developed the following four scales: Preoccupation with Sexually Relevant Concepts (SRC), Aggression and Hostility (AH), Withdrawal and Guarded Accessibility (WGA), and Alertness for Danger, Suspiciousness, and Lack of Trust (ADST). Raters agreed on each of the items within these scales 93% of the time. The scale that most clearly differentiated normal controls from emotionally disturbed and from those who had been sexually abused was the Preoccupation with Sexually Relevant Concepts. It is suggested that this scale is sensitive to the presence of sexual abuse (rather than merely emotional disturbance in general). The Aggression and Hostility scale was, similarly, a specific discriminator among the three groups for males but not for females. The Withdrawal and Guarded Accessibility scale differentiated normals from the generally emotionally disturbed and those who had been sexually abused, but was not successful in distinguishing between general emotional disturbance and sexual abuse. The Alertness for Danger, Suspiciousness, and Lack of Trust scale was not an effective discriminator. Despite the above quite encouraging results, Cohen and Phelps (1985) did not find the HTP effective in detecting and assessing for child abuse.

Administration

The administration of the HTP tends to be similar to that of the DAP, except that the person is requested to draw a house, a tree, and a person on separate sheets of paper. Typically, the order of drawings is given in the above sequence because the house and the tree are believed to be easier and less threatening to draw than the person. Some clinicians prefer to have the client draw "a person" for the first human figure and then a second one that is to be "a person of the opposite sex." These can then be scored and interpreted in the same way as DAP drawings. The sheet of paper on which the house is to be drawn should be given to the client with the longer side horizontal; the pages intended for the tree and person(s) should be presented with the longer side vertical. The client should be requested to draw as good a picture as possible. The first set of drawings is done with a pencil. Some clinicians prefer to have the sequence repeated in a chromatic version, with clients using crayons or felt-tip pens.

An efficient variation recommended by Burns and Kaufman (1970, 1972) is to have the person draw all three objects on the same sheet of paper. Burns (1987) later included a kinetic version (Kinetic House-Tree-Person; KHTP) using the following set of instructions:

> Draw a house, a tree, and a whole person on this piece of paper [and show] some kind of action. Try to draw a whole person, not a cartoon or stick person. (p. 5)

This version is time-efficient and often produces an energetic, integrated story. Usually, less detail is included on the individual objects derived from the HTP (or HTP variations), so the procedures and database used for scoring and interpreting the DAP cannot be employed.

General Interpretative Considerations

A number of theoretical and somewhat speculative approaches are used to interpret the HTP. Most of these interpretive guidelines do not have much empirical validation but are included here to provide an overview of associations that might be helpful in interacting with clients and their drawings in order to develop potentially useful hypotheses. The following hypotheses or associations are derived from traditional publications on the HTP (see Bolander, 1977; Buck, 1948, 1966; Burns, 1987; Hammer, 1954, 1958, 1985; Jolles, 1971). One hypothesis considers the house, tree, and person as representing different aspects of the self. The house represents the part of the self that is concerned with the body (the "house" one lives in) as well as nurturance, stability, and a sense of belonging. The tree is more concerned with a person's sense of growth, vitality, and development. The relative size and quality of these two figures might reveal attitudes and feelings toward these aspects of the client's situation. The person depicted in the drawing is a more direct representation of the self, but the relative size and proximity of the person (if all three objects are drawn on one page) in relationship to the house and the tree can reveal how different aspects of the self relate to one another. For example, if different objects are touching, it may suggest that the client is having difficulty separating or untangling different aspects of his or her life.

A similar theoretical view maintains that the house represents the client's mother whereas the tree represents his or her father. The placement of the person (self), then, might indicate how close the client feels to one or both parents. The person might be distant from both parents, caught in the middle (pulled, mediating, supporting), or closer to one than the other. If the client's parents are experiencing conflict or are separated/ divorced, then the house and the tree might be drawn on separate sides of the paper. If one "parent" is significantly larger than the other, the disparity might reflect greater power and dominance on the part of the larger one.

Burns (1987) suggests that the order in which the objects are drawn reflects the relative degree of importance of each object (aspect of the person, parent). Drawing the tree first indicates that a client is primarily concerned with growth, development, or issues of life and death. The meaning can be made clearer by considering the details of the tree itself. Is it harmonious, balanced, and healthy, or is it dead and decaying? If the house is drawn first, the primary concern will most likely be with a sense of belonging, nurturance, or concern with the body and its needs. Again, the way in which the house is drawn will provide more specific information on this aspect of the person. Is the house depicted as a nurturing and open place, is it a prison, is it dominating, or is it primarily a place to symbolize success and power? Likewise, the drawing of the person provides more direct information about the client. Is the depiction hidden or open, does it demonstrate success and power, or a degree of concern with the body and its needs? If the person is drawn first and is depicted as quite large relative to the other objects, this might suggest preoccupation with the self, which is consistent with a person who is self-absorbed, perhaps to the point of narcissism or hedonism. If someone other than the artist is drawn, it might suggest extreme interest in or even obsession with the person depicted. Other possibilities are intense love, hate, hero worship, or perhaps unfinished grieving for a deceased family member.

The meaning of the structure and form (line pressure, shading, detailing, and so on) of the HTP/KHTP is similar to interpretations for the DAP. However, interpretations should be made with more caution because the greater number of drawings and the greater complexity of the task (when all objects are drawn on the same page) may result in some differences.

Interpretation of Content

The following summary of content features includes classic interpretations available in the literature. The material on HTP person drawings refers the reader to the previous discussion of the DAP. The more specific material on the house and tree is derived from the work of Bolander (1977), Buck (1948, 1966), Burns (1987), Jolles (1971), and Hammer (1954, 1958, 1985). Other authors are cited in the text as their research is discussed. Most of this material is based on clinical experience and theories of the unconscious, so it should not be considered empirically validated. Caution is particularly recommended, given that the majority of content interpretations on the DAP have not turned out to be supported by research even when they have been extensively investigated. The following material is included here in an attempt to provide clinicians with useful leads they can pursue through interactions with their clients as well as through integrating these leads within the context of interview data and other test results. Client/therapist interaction with the drawing might begin with an open-ended question, such as asking the client what is occurring in the picture.

House

The symbolism of the house has been subject to several different interpretations. It might be perceived as a symbol of the self, where different portions of the house represent different aspects of the self (the roof as fantasy life, or windows and doors as interpersonal accessibility). It might also represent the body. In addition, the home is usually the place where nurturing and a sense of security occur, so it might suggest attitudes toward these qualities as well as attitudes toward home life in general. Because many of these qualities are traditionally expressed by a person's mother, the house might also express the client's attitude toward his or her actual mother or, more generally, toward "mothering." The first and most general approach toward interpreting the house is to note the general mood, level of warmth, or accessibility of the house. Is it humble and simple or large and ostentatious? Is it covered with numerous details or is it sparse and empty? If details are included, what do they contribute to the general feel of the house? Is the house accessible or closed? Does it dominate the picture or is it small and placed to one corner of the page? An extremely small house suggests rejection of the home life; an extremely large and dominating house might reflect a view of the home as overly restrictive and controlling.

Once the general feel of the house is determined, the clinician can focus on more specific details. The *roof* (and the attic within) is often considered to represent either someone's fantasy life or intellectual side. An extremely large roof suggests the person is highly withdrawn and extremely involved with an inner world of fantasy. If windows are drawn in the roof, the person might tend to view the environment through a world of fantasy images. The absence of a roof suggests a highly constricted, concrete orientation. For example, mentally retarded persons often draw a single line to represent the roof.

The *walls* represent the person's relative degree of ego strength. Crumbling or disintegrating walls might reflect a disintegration of personality, exaggerated reinforcement of the walls might suggest a fear of disintegration in which added protection is needed, and transparent walls (although frequent in young children) might indicate poor reality testing.

The *door and windows* are the portions of the house that relate to the outside world. Small, bolted-up, barred windows or doors suggest that the person might be shy, withdrawn, and inaccessible, or possibly suspicious or even hostile. This is further exaggerated if the doors and windows are entirely missing. An open door and/or many windows suggest strong needs for contact with others. However, if the indicators of openness are overdone, the person might be highly dependent. Very large windows, especially in the bedroom or bathroom, suggest exhibitionism. The absence of windows on the HTP, in combination with several other features such as enlarged heads, absence of feet, and extremely geometric figures, have frequently been found in the drawings of abused children (Blain, Bergner, Lewis, & Goodstein, 1981).

A *chimney* can relate either to a person's availability and warmth, or to the degree of power and masculinity he or she feels. A missing chimney suggests passivity or a lack of psychological warmth in the person's home life. Whereas normal amounts of smoke accentuate warmth in the home, an excessive amount of smoke suggests inner tension, pent-up aggression, emotional turbulence, and conflict. However, interpretations of chimneys need to take into consideration biasing factors, such as geography (e.g., tropics) and season (summer versus winter).

In addition to the house itself, many clients include a number of accessories to the house, the most frequent of which is a *pathway*. Pathways that are wide and lead directly to the door suggest the client is accessible, open, and direct. In contrast, the absence of a pathway indicates the client may be closed, distant, and removed. Pathways that are long and winding may reflect someone who is initially aloof but can later warm up and become accessible. If the pathway is extremely wide, the client might initially express a superficial sense of friendliness but later become aloof and distant. The presence of *fences* suggests defensiveness. If many irrelevant *details* are included, the client might be indicating strong needs to exercise a high degree of structure over his or her environment, perhaps because of an inner sense of insecurity.

Tree

Initially, a general impression of the tree can be obtained by noting its overall feel and tone. Based on this impression, an idea of the relationship the person has with his or her environment can be obtained. How full, balanced, harmonious, open, and integrated does the tree look? If the tree is withered by the environment, it might reflect a person who has been broken by external stress. A tree with no branches suggests the person has little contact with people.

In addition to the general impression derived from the tree, clinicians can look at its specific features. As the center and most vital part of the tree, the *trunk* can be seen as representing inner strength, self-esteem, and intactness of personality. The use of faint, sketchy lines to represent the trunk indicates a sense of vulnerability, passivity, and insecurity. These same concerns might also be represented by shading on the trunk, or lines that are heavily reinforced (defensiveness) or perforated. Scars or knotholes suggest traumatic experiences, and the age when the trauma occurred can often be determined by the relative height of the scar or knothole (i.e., a knothole halfway up the trunk, drawn by a 10-year-old, suggests the trauma occurred at age 5). Very thin trunks suggest a precarious level of adjustment. If the *bark* on the trunk is heavily drawn, it suggests anxiety; bark that is extremely carefully drawn might reflect a rigid, compulsive personality. If the tree or tree trunk is *split down the middle,* a severe disintegration of the personality is suggested.

The branches and root structure typically symbolize different aspects of the person. The *branches* function as a means by which the tree extends itself out into and relates to its environment. They reflect a person's growth and degree of perceived resources. If the branches are moving upward, the person might be ambitious and "reaching" for opportunities, whereas downward-reaching (weeping willow) branches suggest low levels of energy. Branches that are cut represent a sense of being traumatized, and dead branches indicate feelings of emptiness and hopelessness. Tiny branches suggest that the person experiences difficulty getting attention from his or her environment, and small new branches might represent either new personal growth or psychological immaturity. If a *tree house* is drawn in the branches, the person might be expressing a need to escape from a threatening environment.

In contrast to the branches, the *roots* reflect the degree to which someone is settled and secure. The roots refer to the person's hold on reality but also reflect a relationship to past issues. If a person is having a difficult time "getting a grip on life," the roots might be small and ineffective, or the drawing might compensate by making them piercing and talonlike. Dead roots indicate emptiness and anxiety consistent with obsessive-compulsives, especially if there is excessive detailing in other areas.

Person

If the client is instructed to draw objects on separate sheets of paper, then the task and resulting production are quite similar to the DAP. As a result, similar interpretive principles can be used, including objective scoring and interpretation of content. However, some caution should be exercised in that the human-figure drawings come after the drawings of the house and tree, and the resulting fatigue might cause slight changes in the content and style of the drawings (e.g., less detail, lighter line pressure). If all three objects are requested to be drawn on the same page, the human figure is likely to be significantly smaller than for a regular DAP test. Differences would be even further accentuated if the client/artist is requested to draw the person "doing something" (KHTP). Interpretations of the human figure should therefore be made with great caution. A preferred approach would be to focus on the theme(s) expressed in the drawing and the placement of the different objects/persons, and to engage the client in associating with the drawing.

Signs of Adjustment on the HTP

The signs of health on the HTP, which are somewhat similar to signs of health on the DAP, have been conceptualized and listed by Burns (1987). In a psychologically "healthy" drawing, the house would be depicted as a place of happiness and would contain signs of warmth and openness (a pathway to the door, accessible appearance of doors and windows). It should also have a sense of wholeness and integration and contain the presence of homelike objects (pets, toys, flowers). The tree would be depicted as full, whole, and harmonious, and would appear to move upward and outward. The branches would also be expected to look nourished and healthy and be continuous rather than broken. Most of the healthy characteristics from the DAP also apply to the person(s) drawn on the HTP. All essential details should be included, the person(s) should be grounded, and the figure's appearance would be open, moderately symmetrical, and accepting. If the house, tree, and person are all drawn on the same page, a healthy person would be expected to integrate the three objects into a coherent interaction. The objects would be neither too separate and distant nor overly enmeshed and colliding into one another. Their size and placement, while expressing individual differences between one client and the next, would be appropriate. Such a description is intuitively appealing, but an initial study to verify the use of a composite rating of healthy indicators among university students did not correlate with measures of self-esteem or positive self-concept (Groth-Marnat & Roberts, in press). Further studies might be conducted using different correlates and a wider range of subject level of adjustment (healthy normals compared with inpatient or outpatient populations).

FAMILY DRAWINGS: THE DRAW-A-FAMILY AND KINETIC FAMILY DRAWING TESTS

The DAP and, to a lesser extent, the HTP/KHTP focus on individual dynamics. However, many persons involved in assessment and therapy have been interested in understanding the structure of and relationships within families. As with previously discussed drawing techniques, family drawings provide a less threatening means of revealing this information than direct questioning. This is particularly true for children and adolescents, who usually have greater difficulties than adults in articulating how they feel about relationships. Family drawings were originally suggested by Appel (1931) and Wolff (1942), but later were more fully developed as the Draw-A-Family Test (DAF) by Hulse (1951) and Harris (1963). The technique gained considerable popularity in the 1960s and 1970s with the increased development and use of family therapy.

Administration involves giving the person a paper, pencil, and eraser and requesting him or her to "Draw a picture of your family" (Harris, 1963). After the individual has completed the drawing, he or she is requested to identify the different persons in the drawings. These are labeled, and the artist/client's name and the date the drawing was made are noted on the drawing.

General interpretive procedures are similar to those for the HTP. Initially, a holistic appraisal of the drawing is made by noting such features as its mood or tone. This is followed by an assessment of the meaning behind the size and placement of the figures. Usually, this assessment provides information about the way in which the person fits in with the family. Emotional closeness is reflected by the relative physical proximity of the figures on the page. A father whom no one can get close to might be placed in the corner, away from the other family members. A client who feels rejected might place himself or herself quite far apart from other family members or on the back of the page or might even omit himself or herself entirely. The larger figures and those drawn first are likely to be perceived by the client as more important and powerful than figures drawn smaller or last. As with the DAP, the structure and formal properties of the drawing might indicate such features as anxiety, hesitancy, or confidence. For example, a family member who provokes anxiety in the artist/client might be drawn with a greater amount of shading.

A more recent and quite popular variation of the DAF is Burns and Kaufman's (1970, 1972) Kinetic Family Drawing (KFD). The authors have criticized the DAF as producing fairly rigid, low-energy, noninteractive drawings, and have attempted to correct this result by requesting that the client draw his or her family "doing something." These instructions are usually supplemented by asking the client to include himself or herself in the drawing. After completing the drawing, the client is requested to describe it and/or to tell a story about it. This aids the interpreter by clarifying the interactions, characters, and underlying message of the drawing.

As in the DAF, the interpreter should note the order in which each figure is drawn, as well as the size and placement, and any indicators of anxiety (shading, line pressure, erasures). It is important to note the type of activity the family is involved with. A passive activity, such as watching television, might reflect that the family has a low level of energy and that family members rarely communicate. Placing the parents at opposite ends of the table during a depiction of eating might indicate that the parents are perceived as being emotionally distant. To facilitate KFD interpretation, Burns and Kaufman (1972) provide scoring through means of an Analysis Grid, which focuses on the different placement of the figures. The following interpretive hypotheses are derived primarily from the implications of different dimensions of the grid. Sometimes, different figures in the drawings are depicted in a *precarious position,* which suggests that the client feels a sense of inner tension in or toward the person. Placing a person in the *corner,* or in the *back,* or *omitting* the person altogether suggests the artist/client perceives the person as emotionally distant from the family or perhaps the artist/client has a wish to make this the case (as in intense sibling rivalry). If an individual in the drawing is *elevated,* the client perceives the person to be in a position of dominance, power, or status in the family. *Extended arms* suggest that the figure is controlling (and characteristically controls) his or her environment. If a person is *doing something different,* this individual might be different (exceptional, rejected, eccentric) in real life. *Fire* or *light* might represent positive feelings between persons. In contrast, placing a *wall* or *barrier* between people suggests interpersonal distance. Feelings of insecurity and anxiety might be represented by *heavy, dark clouds,* and *underlining* might serve to compensate for a sense of instability.

Several different objective scoring systems have been devised for use with the DAF or KFD. Each of these has produced varying degrees of success related to interscorer reliability, concurrent validity, and sensitivity to changes in the client's clinical condition. For example, Wright and McIntyre (1982) developed a scale comprised of 15 items, including such variables as poor organization, small figures, self drawn small relative to other figures, separation of self from others, lack of detail, poor sexual differentiation, low energy expressed by self and family, and a large amount of empty space. The presence of these (and other) items accurately discriminated between depressed and normals and also demonstrated sensitivity to improvement. Interscorer reliabilities for the different scoring systems have been quite good (ranging between 87% to 95% agreement), but test-retest reliabilities have been low, partially because of the greater degree of change found in children (Handler & Habenicht, 1994). Overall validity has been somewhat variable. For example, several studies found that a greater degree of isolation of self in the drawings has been able to identify children with difficulties (Raskin & Bloom, 1979; Sayed & Leaverton, 1974). This is consistent with Spigelman et al. (1992), who used objective ratings to compare the DAFs of children from divorced versus intact families and found that children from divorced families separated figures in the drawings more frequently, omitted other siblings (boys' drawings only), depicted more negative expressions (boys' drawings only), drew less positive depictions of the parents, and drew more figures with concealed hands and/or feet. Another study found that sexually abused adolescents drew KFDs that were either very sexual or quite asexual (Rogers, 1984). In contrast, McGregor (1979) and Stawar and Stawar (1989) did not find that the KFD was able to make useful discriminations between normal and clinical populations. This is consistent with most KFD studies, particularly those that used single signs or groupings of signs; they have not been particularly effective at distinguishing among different groups (Handler & Habenicht, 1994).

One well-designed study by Tharinger and Stark (1990) was consistent with many earlier studies of the KFD in that it did not find that a formally developed KFD scoring system was effective in distinguishing normal children from those with mood disorders. However, a more impressionistic, qualitative global appraisal of the relative degree of health versus psychopathology (rated on a scale from 1 to 5) did differentiate between normal children and those with mood disorders (but not those with anxiety disorders). This qualitative appraisal involved an integration of the following characteristics: relative accessibility of family members, degree to which family members seemed engaged with one another, appropriateness of the underlying structure, and relative "humanness" of the family figures. A similar global and impressionistic rating of the degree to which the family appeared to be one that would be nice to live in found that the less desirable families occurred more frequently among children who had been sexually abused. However, there was no indication in the study of whether this finding was specific to child abuse or was a more general sign for a wide variety of emotional disturbance. The success, as well as the clinical utility of Tharinger and Stark's (1990) more global approach using the integrative ability of the practitioner, has led some authors to encourage further research in this direction rather than continuing the more reductionistic sign approach (Cook, 1991; Handler & Habenicht, 1994).

MISCELLANEOUS PROCEDURES

The most frequently used projective drawings are the DAP, HTP/KHTP, and DAF/KFD. However, other noteworthy procedures include additional kinetic techniques, drawings produced by groups, and spontaneous drawings. Following Burns and Kaufman's (1970, 1972) initial emphasis that the persons in the drawings should "do something," similar techniques have been used for different settings, including school, business, politics, and religion. The most fully developed is Prout and Phillip's (1974) Kinetic School Drawing (KSD), in which the person is requested to draw people at school "doing something." Scoring and interpretation are similar to the KFD. Elements considered are: whether clients include or exclude themselves from the drawing, the distance between themselves and the teacher, types of interactions, and number of peers included. Although interpretations are mainly based on clinical impression, correlations have been found between elements in the drawings considered favorable to school and academic achievement (Prout & Celmer, 1984). Knoff and Prout (1985) emphasize that the KSD can be effectively complemented by the KFD and have attempted to integrate both these methods of data collection in their Kinetic Drawing System (Knoff & Prout, 1985).

Other projective drawing variations have been developed for use with groups. Members of the group might be requested to make their own drawings in the presence of each other, or all might participate, as a group, in the creation of a single drawing. One possibility is to provide felt-tip pens and a large piece of paper in the center of the group, request members to draw designs, and every few minutes rotate the page. Kwiatkowska (1978) has emphasized family drawings and suggests that each family member work on his or her own drawing. However, there is opportunity to interact because the easels are arranged in a circle, with each member seated inside the circle so that he or she can easily observe what the other family members are doing. Observations and later interpretations can be made of both the group interaction while the drawings were being created as well as the drawings themselves. Some groups or families make clear, smooth decisions; others develop conflict when members try to control what the others do. Group members might also become quite territorial about their drawing or portion of the drawing, and defend it from encroachment by others. Typically, the method of interaction within the drawing session highlights typical patterns that occur outside the session.

Another technique is to have clients draw a picture of an island, with the suggestion that they include all the things they might need if they were to live on that island. The objects they choose to include and the manner in which each object is depicted can help to identify dominant themes and values in clients' lives. More free-form options are to have clients draw how they are feeling or how they perceive a specific situation such as birth, death, conflict, or happiness. The most unstructured approach is to observe spontaneous drawings.

Any of the above techniques can use many of the approaches for interpretation described for the more formal methods (DAP, HTP, etc.). Interpreters might look at the feel, tone, mood, or quality of a drawing and should consider the significance of the line quality, size of the figures and their relative placement to one another, themes, or contents. Such interpretations might vary in terms of the amount of interaction between the artist/client and interpreter, and might be influenced by the theoretical orientation of the interpreter.

RECOMMENDED READING

Burns, R. C. (1987). *Kinetic House-Tree-Person Drawings (KHTP)*. New York: Brunner/Mazel.

Handler, L. (1985). The clinical use of the Draw-A-Person Test (DAP). In C. S. Newmark (Ed.), *Major psychological assessment instruments*. Newton, MA: Allyn & Bacon.

Kahill, S. (1984). Human-figure drawings in adults: An update of the empirical evidence, 1962–1982. *Canadian Psychology, 25,* 269–292.

Mitchell, J., Trent, R., & McArthur, R. (1993). *Human Figure Drawing Test: An illustrated handbook for clinical interpretation and standardized assessment of cognitive impairment.* Los Angeles: Western Psychological Services.

Naglieri, J. A. (1988). *Draw A Person: A quantitative scoring system.* San Antonio, TX: The Psychological Corporation.

Oster, G. D., & Gould, P. (1987). *Using drawings in assessment and therapy.* New York: Brunner/Mazel.

Van Hutton, V. (1994). *House-Tree-Person and Draw-A-Person as measures of abuse in children: A quantitative scoring system.* Odessa, FL: Psychological Assessment Resources.

Chapter 12 ———————————————————————————————

SCREENING AND ASSESSING FOR NEUROPSYCHOLOGICAL IMPAIRMENT

An important role in clinical practice is screening and assessing for the presence of possible neuropsychological impairment. Craig (1979) found that fully 30% of referrals to psychologists in general neuropsychiatric settings requested information related to central nervous system (CNS) involvement. A similar proportion of CNS-related referrals would be likely to occur in general medical, particularly neurological, settings. Information derived from these sorts of assessments might serve as an early warning sign that, if positive, would then result in a more in-depth medical or neuropsychological assessment and/or further monitoring of the patient. Examples of the types of situations where screening might be important would be among substance-abusing populations, persons exposed to neurotoxic substances, or elderly populations where the distinction between depression and organically based dementia might be crucial. Additional situations might occur with a school psychologist who is trying to understand why a student is performing poorly, workers' compensation cases where brain damage might be suspected, or screening for brain damage among psychiatric populations. Each of these situations would require that the assessing clinician be sensitive to the expression of brain impairment, methods of assessing for it, and the patterns of behavioral and test results which would suggest the presence of such impairment.

This chapter provides introductory knowledge and strategies for screening for CNS involvement. It also provides strategies for assessing different domains of neuropsychological functioning. These domains, and the recommended tests used to assess them, are listed in Table 12–1. While assessing these domains according to the recommended procedures will still not entail a full neuropsychological assessment, it will provide considerably more depth than that obtained from simple screening instruments. The chapter therefore follows the trend in neuropsychology toward greater sophistication of instruments and away from simple screening procedures. It is also based on the belief that general clinical psychologists will be expected to become increasingly familiar with the rapidly developing field of clinical neuropsychology. The coverage is as comprehensive as possible within the space limitations of a single chapter. Initially, it may seem somewhat technical. However, it is expected that, when clinicians actually work with the instruments and integrate them into a report, they will internalize the information and find it practical.

When appraising clients with suspected CNS involvement, it is important to appreciate that the behavioral manifestation of such involvement is extremely heterogeneous. Some brain-damaged persons might have specific signs such as aphasia, neglect

Table 12–1.   Recommended screening battery for neuropsychological impairment

Function and Test	Estimated Time for Tests Not Covered Elsewhere
Visuoconstructive Abilities	
Bender (Standard or Background Interference Procedure)*	5**
Block Design, Object Assembly	
Free Drawing Procedures (Draw-A-Person, etc.)	
Mental Activity (Attention and Speed of Information Processing)	
Trail Making*	3
Digit Span	3
Arithmetic	
Digit Symbol	
Memory and Learning	
Rey Auditory Verbal Learning Test*	12
Bender memory*	2
Digit Symbol, Information	
Verbal Functions and Academic Skills	
Controlled Oral Word Association (FAS)	10
Information, Vocabulary, Comprehension	
Similarities (Arithmetic)	
Motor Performance	
Finger Tapping*	5
Executive Functions	
(Behavioral observations, reports by significant others)	
Emotional Status	
Minnesota Multiphasic Personality Inventory (MMPI-2/MMPI-A)	
Beck Depression Inventory (BDI)	
Total estimated additional time:	50

* Indicates tests unique to Chapter 12.
** Times given only for tests not covered in previous chapters so clinicians will have an estimate of the additional time(s) beyond the standard core battery.

of a portion of their visual field, or word-finding difficulties. In contrast, others might have widespread impairments such as a general lowering of cognitive abilities or difficulty regulating their behavior. Deficits might also range in their expression between being extremely subtle to being quite severe. The practical implication of this is that any one screening test for neuropsychological impairment is likely to assess for a narrow range of abilities. If a client has deficits outside this range, then the test will not be sensitive to that particular area of difficulties. The result will be a high number of false negatives. Indeed, this problem has plagued most screening devices. For example, a test such as the Bender Gestalt is primarily a test of visuoconstructive abilities. Clients with a wide range of other difficulties are likely to perform quite well on the

Bender Gestalt with the resulting danger that the clinician might erroneously conclude they were not organically impaired.

The presence of false negatives (or false positives) depends in part on the "narrowness" versus the "width" of the test. For example, a test that measures a specific function such as ability to name objects is quite narrow in its focus. Clients who do poorly on such a test would most likely be experiencing neuropsychological impairment (true positives). However, there will also be many persons who, despite being neuropsychologically impaired, will do quite well on such a test and may be misclassified as normal (false negatives). This is because most neuropsychologically impaired persons do not experience object-naming difficulties. The sign of object naming thus is too specific. If another test is used that casts a wider net by using more general indicators (concrete thinking, impaired immediate memory, distractibility), then not as many persons with neuropsychological impairment will be missed (few false negatives). However, there will be many people labeled as being brain damaged who are not (many false positives). This is likely to be particularly true for severe psychiatric patients. Indeed, neuropsychological tests have had a notoriously difficult time distinguishing psychotics, especially chronic schizophrenics, from brain-damaged persons since they often appear quite similar on test performance (Mittenberg et al., 1989; Yozawitz, 1986).

This difficulty does not invalidate the use of psychological tests for neuropsychological assessment. However, it does highlight the importance of being aware of their limitations and being clear on what they do measure. It also suggests that, instead of using one or two tests, a clinician reviewing neuropsychological impairment ideally should use a number of different tests that assess a wide number of domains. These domains might include tests for mental activity (attention and speed of information processing), visuoconstructive abilities, memory and learning, verbal functions including academic skills, executive functions (observing, directing, and regulating behavior), motor performance, and emotional status. Accordingly, the emphasis in this chapter is to present a series of brief assessment techniques that can be used to screen for as well as provide greater depth into the assessment of neuropsychological impairment. In addition, readers will be referred to tests in other sections of the book that are relevant for assessing a client's neuropsychological status (primarily portions of the Wechsler Intelligence scales). The result will be a relatively brief assessment battery that would not be expected to add more than an additional hour to a usual core test battery (WAIS-R/WISC-III, MMPI-2, etc.). The recommended tests will also familiarize students and professionals with some of the more frequently used neuropsychological procedures. However, this group of tests still does not assess a sufficiently wide number of areas to be considered a comprehensive neuropsychological battery.

The two general strategies in neuropsychological assessment are a qualitative or pathognomonic sign approach and the use of quantitative cutoff scores. The pathognomonic sign approach assumes the existence of distinctive behaviors indicative of brain damage. Rotations or perseverations are examples of such signs. Additional ones might be aphasias, line tremor, distortions of drawings, difficulty with serial subtraction, clang responses (i.e., ponder meaning "to pound"), neglecting a portion of a visual field (visual neglect), or difficulty distinguishing whether a stimulus is either on the right or left when they are stimulated at the same time (suppressions on bilateral simultaneous stimulation). In contrast to the sign approach are the use of cutoff scores which optimally separate a person's performance into either a brain-damaged or normal range. These are a frequent feature of the Halstead Reitan Neuropsychological Test Battery (HRNTB; Jarvis & Barth, 1994; Reitan & Wolfson, 1993). For example, the Trail Making Test (Part B) requires examinees to connect a sequence of alternating numbers and letters until a section marked "End" is reached. Times greater than 40 seconds for Part A and 91 seconds for Part B indicate performances in the impaired range. Sometimes a combination of both approaches is used. This can be seen on the Bender Gestalt, which requires examinees to draw a series of designs that are presented to them. Clinicians typically note the presence of pathognomonic signs such as poor closure or line tremor but also score different aspects of the drawing to develop a quantitative rating. Scores above a certain level indicate impaired performances.

Similar to other psychological tests, moderator variables such as age, education, premorbid intelligence, and sometimes ethnicity are related to neuropsychological test performance. For example, using the standard cutoff score of 91 seconds on Trail Making B will result in unacceptably high numbers of misclassifications in the impaired range if used with persons over the age of 70. It has thus been recommended that cutoff scores for determining impairment should use norms corrected for age, education, and gender. These are available in Heaton, Grant, and Mathews (1991) *Comprehensive Norms for an Expanded Halstead-Reitan Battery* and are planned for inclusion in D'Elia, Boone, and Mitrushina's *Handbook of Normative Data for Neuropsychological Assessment* (anticipated publication in 1997). However, a significant controversy is that the preceding norms have been developed using normal populations, where it has been established that age and education significantly influence level of performance. In contrast, Reitan and Wolfson (1995) have argued and presented preliminary evidence that the impact of brain damage is sufficiently strong to minimize or even negate the influence of age and education. Their data, however, relate to their global index (General Neuropsychological Scale; GNDS) based on a composite score of 42 variables rather than the individual tests that Heaton et al. (1991) have presented (and will be included by D'Elia and his colleagues). As a result, the impact of age and education for neuropsychologically impaired clients on the individual tests is still unclear. Future research will no doubt work to clarify this controversy and provide further guidelines for practitioners.

HISTORY AND DEVELOPMENT

Neuropsychological assessment as a well-defined discipline began in the 1950s with the work of Halstead, Reitan, and Goldstein in the United States, Rey in France, and Luria in the Soviet Union. Within the United States, the experimental and statistical orientation of American psychology was reflected in test design and use. Norms were refined and used for comparison with an individual patient's performance. Optimal cutoff scores were developed to distinguish impaired from normal performances. In particular, the Halstead Reitan Neuropsychological Test Battery grew out of an original 27 tests that Ward Halstead selected in the belief that they measured cerebral functioning based on "biological intelligence." He reduced these to 10 tests, and Reitan (1955a) later reduced these to 7. Cutoff scores were developed on these tests, and based on the proportion of tests in the impaired range, an Impairment Index could be calculated.

Early success was achieved with the HRNTB in distinguishing not only the presence of brain damage, but also the location and nature of the lesion (Reitan, 1955a). During the days before sophisticated neuroradiological techniques, this was extremely useful information. These efforts emerged into an emphasis on what has sometimes been referred to as the three L's of neuropsychology: Lesion detection, Localization, and Lateralization. In contrast, there was a relative neglect in the study of diffuse impairment in favor of the stronger emphasis on focal involvement.

Concomitant with the developments in the United States was the work of Alexander Luria in the Soviet Union and Rey in France. They relied extensively on close patient observation and in-depth case histories. They were not so much interested in what score a person might have obtained but rather why the individual performed in a certain manner. Their work has epitomized the flexible pathognomonic sign or qualitative approach. Rather than developing a series of quantitatively oriented tests with optimal cutoff scores, Luria emphasized a series of "procedures" that he believed would help the client to express relevant behavioral domains. As such, his approach relied far more heavily on clinician expertise and observation than formal psychometric data. Although somewhat controversial (see Adams, 1980), these procedures have more recently been formalized and standardized into the Luria Nebraska Neuropsychological Battery (Golden, Purisch, & Hammeke, 1985).

From these early beginnings, two distinct strategies of approaching neuropsychological assessment emerged. One was the comprehensive battery approach epitomized by Halstead and Reitan and formalized into the Halstead Reitan Neuropsychological Test Battery and the other was a more flexible, qualitative, hypothesis testing strategy as represented by Goldstein and Luria. Each of these approaches has different strengths and weaknesses (see Bauer, 1995; Jarvis & Barth, 1994; McDonald, 1996; Russell, 1995). The battery approach has the advantages of assessing both strengths and weaknesses for a broad spectrum of behaviors, is easier to use for research, is more extensively normed and researched, can be administered by trained technicians, and is easier for students to learn. Its disadvantages are that it is typically quite time consuming, may overlook the underlying reasons for a client's specific test score, and is more difficult to tailor toward the unique aspects of the client and referral question. The contrasting qualitative hypothesis-testing approach has the advantages that it can be tailored to the specifics of the client and referral question, emphasizes the processes underlying a client's performance rather than a final score, and is quite time efficient. Measurements of a client's strengths, weaknesses, or certain reasons for ambiguous responses can be pursued in more depth according to decisions made by the examiner. Weaknesses frequently attributed to this approach are that, in practice, it focuses on a client's weaknesses, relies too extensively on clinician expertise, is more difficult to research, is not as extensively researched, and provides a narrower slice of a client's domains of functioning.

Despite the preceding somewhat polarized description, two trends indicate an integration of the quantitative psychometric and the qualitative hypothesis-testing strategies. The first is the development of objective, in-depth, computerized scoring systems that can help clinicians understand the underlying qualitative processes a client makes in responding to test items (i.e., scoring for the California Verbal Learning Test; Delis, Kramer, Kaplan, & Ober, 1987). The second, is that, in practice, most neuropsychologists use a combination of the strategies. This is illustrated by Benton's (1992) support for a "flexible-fixed" battery comprising a relatively short "fixed" or core battery combined with additional flexible tests that could be selected based on the uniqueness of the client and specifics of the referral questions.

Concurrent with the development of the early testing procedures and batteries, there was also an emphasis on brief screening instruments. The Bender Visual Motor Gestalt, or simply the Bender Gestalt, was one of the earliest of these. It was first developed by Lauretta Bender in 1938 and comprises nine designs that a client is requested to reproduce. A similar but more complex visuoconstructive test was originally devised by Rey in 1941 and expanded by Osterrith in 1944 (Osterrith, 1944; Rey, 1941). It has since become refined and referred to as the Rey-Osterrith Complex Figure Test (Meyers & Meyers, 1996; Visser, 1992). Subjects are first requested to complete the drawing while it is directly in front of them and then requested to make a second reproduction of the drawing from memory. Rey also developed the Rey Auditory-Verbal Learning Test (Rey, 1964) which screens for difficulties with immediate memory span. Clients are instructed to recall a series of words that are read to them and then repeat back as many of the words as possible. A final example of an early screening test for attentional difficulties is the Stroop procedure (Jensen & Rohwer, 1966; Stroop, 1935). This test presents clients with a series of names of colors but written in different color ink from the written name of the color given. For example, the name green might be written in red ink. The client is then requested to read through the list and give the name of the color of the ink (i.e., red) rather than merely reading the word (i.e., green).

A frequent goal of many of the early screening tests was to differentiate between organic versus functional difficulties. Thus a referral question was sometimes expressed in terms of "ruling out organicity" or to "differentiate between organic versus functional causes." More recently, the appropriateness of this goal, and the assumptions behind it, have been questioned. Leonberger (1989) has pointed out that there has been a gradual disintegration of the distinction between many functional and organic disorders. For example, early conceptualizations of schizophrenia considered it to be functional. In contrast, current research supports strong biochemical and structural correlates in a substantial proportion of schizophrenics (Heinrichs, 1993; Raz & Raz, 1990; Weinberger & Berman, 1988). A second factor is that advances in neuroradiological and other neurologically oriented techniques have greatly refined the diagnosis of brain damage. As a result, the use of neuropsychological techniques in diagnosis has become deemphasized. In contrast, referrals from neurologists and psychiatrists are more likely to request information regarding the nature of already identified lesions.

A further change over time has been that, rather than focusing on measurement, there has been greater emphasis on application (Ponsford, 1988). Thus it is no longer sufficient merely to state that a client is experiencing cognitive deficits in certain areas. Instead, answers to more functionally relevant questions are being required such as the client's employability, responsiveness to rehabilitation, and the need for certain environmental supports (Sbordone & Long, 1996). This can be clarified by considering the differences between "impairment" versus "disability." Impairment typically reflects normative comparisons and test data. In contrast, the functionally relevant term "disability" more closely takes into account the context of the client including his or her circumstances, environment, and interests. A client might be statistically in the impaired range on tests requiring sequencing. If he or she was a computer programmer, this problem would render the person quite disabled. In contrast, another client with different interests may not be particularly disabled by this problem. There are increasing expectations on clinicians to work with both the test data and the specifics of the client to translate the impact of any test-related impairment on the level to which the individual might be disabled. This may also require using methods of analysis other than psychological tests such as the ratings of relatives, ward observation charts, and simulations (Knight & Godfrey, 1996; Ponsford, 1988).

Consistent with these points is that more recent emphasis has not so much been on measuring "organicity" or "brain damage," but rather on assessing different functions or domains. This might include attention, short-term memory, or visuoconstructive abilities. Thus "brain sensitive" screening tests should not be considered to be tests of brain damage but rather tests of certain functions that *may* be consistent with CNS involvement. This means that, instead of using single tests, neuropsychological assessment ideally should use several instruments to examine a number of different domains. This emphasis is reflected in this chapter through the presentation and elaboration of a number of short, easily administered tests that cover a wide range of the person's abilities. There have also been a number of formally developed screening and short assessment batteries by other authors. Wysocki and Sweet (1985) developed a seven-test battery composed of Trail Making, finger-tapping speed, drawing a Greek cross, the Pathognomonic Scale of the Luria-Nebraska Neuropsychological Battery, the Stroop, and the Logical Memory and Visual Reproduction subtests of the Wechsler Memory Scale. Total administration time is approximately 60 minutes. Another representative screening system is the BNI Screen for Higher Cerebral Functions (Prigatano, Amin, & Rosenstein, 1992a, 1992b). Its purpose is to determine whether patients are capable of taking other neuropsychological tests; it evaluates their level of self-awareness, provides qualitative information regarding cognitive functioning, and assesses a wide range of cerebral functions. The entire procedure typically takes 10 to 15 minutes to complete. There have also been two abbreviated versions of the Halstead Reitan Battery by Golden (1976) and Erickson, Caslyn, and Scheupbach (1978).

In addition to these procedures, several short batteries have been developed for reviewing possible neuropsychological impairment with specific types of disorders. Batteries for the evaluation of neurotoxicity are the California Neuropsychological Screening Battery (Bowler, Thakler, & Becker, 1986), Pittsburgh Occupation Exposureal Test (Ryan, Morrow, Parklinson, & Branet, 1987), and the Individual Neuropsychological Testing for Neurotoxicity Battery (Singer, 1990). Similar to the previous screening batteries, each of these uses a combination of previously developed tests such as Trail Making and portions of the WAIS-R. Assessment and monitoring of some of the more important domains of dementia might be achieved with the *CERAD Battery* (Morris et al., 1989) or the *Dementia Assessment Battery* (Corkin et al., 1986). A similar specialized battery for detecting the early signs of AIDS-related dementia is the *NIMH Core Neuropsychological Battery* (Butters et al. 1990).

INTERVIEWING FOR BRAIN IMPAIRMENT

While tests can be quite useful, the strongest tool for a clinician is still a clear, thorough, and well-informed history. One of the major factors guiding such a history is understanding the types of behavior that are likely to reflect neuropsychological impairment. Table 12–2 provides a summary of possible behavior changes indicative of impaired brain processes. While the presence of one of these is not sufficient in and of itself to diagnose pathology, several of them would suggest such a process. An additional tool in extracting the range of possible symptoms is a checklist of potential areas of difficulties that the client can easily complete. This might be informally developed by a clinician through simply listing all potentially problematic behaviors such as difficulties with memory, hearing, depression, or confusion. Alternatively, a checklist is commercially available to allow clients to detail the full range of their symptoms (*Neuropsychological Symptom Checklist;* Schinka, 1983). Any items a client endorses can be further explored in the interview to determine when the symptoms began as well as their frequency, intensity, and duration.

A family history should focus on some of the general areas previously outlined in Chapter 3. The family history for neurological and/or psychiatric complaints should receive particular attention. A family history that includes conditions with a known or suspected genetic component such as schizophrenia, early onset Alzheimer's disease, Huntington's chorea, or hypertension should alert the clinician that similar processes may be occurring with the client. The presence of any early deaths in the family, learning disabilities, or mental retardation would also be important to consider. Since some types of clients have difficulty recalling detailed information, relevant family members might be contacted to help obtain, elaborate, or verify information.

Prenatal and early personal history are also important areas for consideration. The client's prenatal environment might have involved relevant events such as his or her mother being exposed to pesticides, solvents, dyes, drugs, or alcohol. Complications during pregnancy and birth should also be considered such as low birth weight, forceps birth, premature birth, or difficulties related to any anesthetics used. Early developmental milestones including the age at which the client sat upright, walked, and talked should be noted and verified with an outside source. Academic history is particularly helpful in determining the person's premorbid level of functioning. Favorite and worst subjects, grades obtained, and highest level of education are all significant. Assessing for possible attentional or learning difficulties is also essential. School records often provide useful information, especially when objective, outside support is required to support a client's claims.

A client's occupational history helps establish his or her premorbid level of functioning and social functioning. Each occupation requires certain skills that might have implications in interpreting test results. For example, test scores indicating average verbal skills would mean something quite different for an unskilled laborer than for a successful attorney. Average scores might be consistent with the former but could very well reflect impairment for the latter. It also might be relevant to note whether the person's occupation has resulted in exposure to potentially neurotoxic substances such as organic solvents, insecticides, lead, or mercury. If so, the occupational precautions used and occurrence of all incidents would need to be determined.

Table 12–2.   Behavior changes that are possible indicators of a pathological brain process

Functional Class[1]	Symptoms and Signs	Functional Class[1]	Symptoms and Signs
Speech and language	Dysarthria Dysfluency Marked change in amount of speech output Paraphasias Word-finding problems	Visuospatial abilities	Diminished or distorted ability for manual skills (e.g., mechanical repairs, sewing) Spatial disorientation Impaired spatial judgment Right-left disorientation
Academic skills	Alterations in reading, writing, calculating, and number abilities (e.g., poor reading comprehension, frequent letter or number reversals in writing)	Emotional	Diminished emotional control with temper outbursts, antisocial behavior Diminished empathy or interest in interpersonal relationships without depression
Thinking	Perseveration of speech or action components Simplified or confused mental tracking, reasoning, concept formation		Affective changes without known precipitating factors (e.g., lability, flattening, inappropriateness)
Motor	Lateralized weakness or clumsiness Problems with fine motor coordination Tremors		Personality changes without known precipitating factors Increased irritability without known precipitating factors
Perception	Diplopia or visual field alterations Inattention (usually left-sided; may be perceptual and/or in productions) Somatosensory alterations (particularly lateralized or confined to one limb)	Comportment[2]	Altered appetites and appetitive activities (eating, drinking, play, sex) Altered grooming habits (overly fastidious, careless) Hyper- or hypoactivity Social inappropriateness

Source: Adapted from Howieson and Lezak, 1991. Copyright 1991 by American Psychiatric Association Press.

[1] Many emotionally disturbed persons complain of memory deficits that typically reflect their self-preoccupations, distractibility, or anxiety rather than a dysfunctional brain. Thus memory complaints in themselves are not good indicators of neuropathology.

[2] These changes are most likely to have neuropsychological relevance in the absence of depression, but they can be mistaken for depression.

Knowing current and past interests and hobbies can develop a more complete portrayal of the person.

A review of the client's medical history and any available medical records should be obtained from the client as well as from relevant persons close to the client. The central focus of such a review is to attempt to determine whether the current symptoms can be accounted for based on this history. A person might have had a recent head injury but inferring that his or her symptoms are partially or wholly the result of this injury might be more difficult. The history might include previous head injuries, high fevers, learning disabilities, or exposure to neurotoxic substances. Any history of a head injury should include details as to the last memory he or she had before the injury, recall of the injury itself, the length of time the person was unconscious, and the first memory following the injury. Any behavioral changes (irritability, poor memory, confusion) should be carefully documented. Further relevant medical complications might include history of high fevers (103+ F) or significant infectious diseases (meningitis, encephalitis, HIV/AIDS), thyroid dysfunction, diabetes, epilepsy, hypoxia, suicide attempts, hypertension, or neurosurgery for such complications as tumors or aneurisms. If any neurosurgery was performed, then details should be obtained related to anesthetic use, complications, possible loss of consciousness, psychosocial changes following the surgery, and the nature and duration of these changes. Headaches, especially if accompanied by neuropsychological complaints, might suggest a tumor or a vascular disorder. Drug and alcohol use also needs to be carefully documented along with possible changes in prescription or nonprescription medication. Any current or past psychiatric difficulties might also complicate a client's presentation of neuropsychological symptoms.

Any neuropsychological history should provide a careful documentation of present complaints and current overall life situation. Each symptom should be described along with its onset, frequency, duration, intensity, and any changes over time. Asking the client when the symptom first appeared and how it has changed over time frequently can access much of this information. For example, the abrupt onset of neuropsychological complaints with no clear-cut trauma suggests a cerebral vascular accident. In contrast, gradual change might suggest a dementing condition or a slow-growing tumor. Discrete, temporary symptoms suggest transient ischemic attacks. A complicating factor is that clients will vary in relation to their awareness of symptoms. Some might be preoccupied with them, others might be indifferent, while still others might be aware of some difficulties but relatively unaware of others. This would then require that the interviewer refer to medical records and relevant persons in the client's life. This would be especially important in conditions such as dementia or frontal lobe impairment where clients might be both unaware of their deficits and inaccurate regarding details of their personal history (desRosiers, 1992; Gilley et al., 1995). A client's sexual functioning can often reveal relevant information related to neuropsychological status. Changes in sexual desire might be related to certain medications, growth of tumors in strategic areas, affective disorders, infectious diseases, exposure to neurotoxins, or head injuries (especially with frontal lobe involvement). It is also wise for clinicians to investigate the psychosocial factors that might be related to symptoms. Stress, depression, and family turmoil might either cause or serve to exacerbate "neuropsychological" symptoms such as concentration, memory, confusion, and irritability (Burt, Zembar, & Niederehe, 1995). Finally legal complications might be intricately entangled with symptoms. This is especially true for cases involving litigation or workers' compensation.

Whereas the preceding suggestions represent a variety of areas that can be explored flexibly, several structured interviews and questionnaire formats are currently available. The *Neuropsychological History Questionnaire* (Wolfson, 1985) is an easily completed, 37-page, comprehensive series of questions to be answered by the client. It includes such topics as referral information, academic history, medical and general history, and present status compared with preinjury/preillness status. The *Neuropsychological Status Examination* (Schinka, 1983) includes a similar organization of topics but is a semi-structured interview in which most of the questions are asked by the interviewer. The *Neuropsychological Status Examination* also includes the previously mentioned *Neuropsychological Symptom Checklist,* which provides a brief self-report of symptoms, which can be used to assist the interview. Additional useful tools might be brief, simple rating forms such as the *Mini-mental State* (Folstein, Folstein, & McHugh, 1975), *Neurobehavioral Rating Scale* (Levin et al., 1987) or *Patient Competency Rating* (Prigatano, 1986). Any of these structured formats requires an examiner to integrate the information into the unique characteristics of the client and relevant test data.

TESTS FOR SCREENING AND ASSESSING FOR NEUROPSYCHOLOGICAL IMPAIRMENT

The criteria for including the tests in this section are that they are brief, well researched, psychometrically sound, frequently used, and collectively provide an overview of a broad range of neuropsychological functioning (see Table 12–1). This selection of tests is similar to recommendations made by other authors for batteries of screening or brief assessment instruments (see Berg, Franzen, & Wedding, 1987; Kane, 1991; Lezak, 1995; Wysocki & Sweet, 1985). A number of the instruments listed in Table 12–1 have already been extensively described within a more general testing context elsewhere in the book (WAIS-R/WISC-III, MMPI/MMPI-2/MMPI-A, BDI, Human Figure Drawing). This chapter will highlight their use in neuropsychological assessment. In contrast to these more general tests, other tests listed in Table 12–1 are highly specific to neuropsychological assessment and have not been described elsewhere (Bender Gestalt, Trail Making, Rey Auditory Verbal Learning, Controlled Oral Word Association, finger tapping). Accordingly, the chapter will provide details about their history and development, psychometric properties, and interpretation. The Bender Gestalt is given particular emphasis due to its versatility, extensive research base, and frequency of use (Lacks, 1982; Watkins, 1995).

The various tests in this chapter (see Table 12–1) are organized around domains (visuoconstructive abilities, mental activity, etc.) rather than merely the names of the tests. This increases the likelihood that clinicians will focus on relevant abilities of the client rather than being test oriented. It thus makes it easier to organize relevant topics for inclusion in the psychological report. However, it should be stressed that none of these tests are pure measures of those abilities, which means that clinicians should be cautious in regarding them as such. For example, previous discussions of Digit Symbol (Chapter 5) have stressed that it involves not only attention and speed of information processing but also rote learning, sequencing, and high test-taking motivation. It is then incumbent on the examiner to work with all sources of information to determine the most accurate meanings underlying test scores.

A further important caution and limitation of the chapter is that, while a number of relevant domains have been included, the full assessment of these domains should not be assumed. For example, a number of memory functions have still not been assessed even when all the tests listed in the "Memory and Learning" section have been given. Thus, a person with memory and learning impairments might still be misclassified as normal. The procedures in this chapter should not be considered to be a full neuropsychological evaluation, but the recommended tests can provide far more information than the practitioner can obtain merely using one or two screening instruments.

Even though the recommended procedures in this chapter do not entail a full neuropsychological interpretation, the results can be helpful in making tentative predictions about the current level of functioning of the client, degree of adjustment, and likely response to rehabilitation, employment, or interpersonal relationships. These uses are partially supported in that cognitive tests can often be quite accurate in making such predictions (Acker, 1990; Sbordone & Long, 1996; Vilkki et al., 1994). However, practitioners must be careful to avoid overgeneralization. For example, standard intelligence test scores have not been found to predict psychosocial recovery following closed-head injury with suspected frontal lobe involvement (Vilkki et al., 1994). In contrast, three tests of mental flexibility and mental programming (such as the Stroop procedure) were good predictors. Furthermore, Heaton, Chelune, and Lehman (1981) found that MMPI scores were better predictors of level of disability than cognitive abilities based on neuropsychological test performance. These representative areas of research emphasize the importance of taking into account measures of psychosocial functioning as well as taking a flexible approach to test administration and interpretation.

TESTS OF VISUOCONSTRUCTIVE ABILITIES

The accurate construction of objects involves intact visual perception along with effective visuospatial and visuomotor abilities. Each one of these three areas (perceptual, spatial, motor) might have disturbances that could make visual construction more difficult. Benton (1979) has listed these as follows:

1. *Visuoperceptual Disturbances.* Impaired discrimination of complex stimuli, visual recognition, color recognition, figure-ground differentiation, visual integration.
2. *Visuospatial Disturbances.* Impaired localization of points in space, topographic orientation, neglect of part of a person's visual field, difficulties with direction and distance.
3. *Visuomotor Disturbances.* Defective eye movement, assembling, graphomotor performance.

For some patients, these disturbances might occur together whereas with others they might occur separately. A patient might have excellent visuoperceptual abilities but still have significant problems making accurate constructions. At other times, poor perception would lead to or occur in combination with poor constructional abilities. In addition, the ability to draw and assemble objects can be quite variable for a particular patient, whose ability to assemble objects might be intact (as in Block Design) but whose drawings of human figures or simpler designs might be quite poor.

Each one of the three disturbances is also likely to have somewhat different neuroanatomical pathways. The practical implication is that any inferences regarding localization of lesion should not be made by merely taking into consideration a person's overall score on a particular visuoconstructive test. Although overall scores are of limited use, important information and the implications for localization can be derived more appropriately from a careful observation of how the client approaches the task and the types of errors the person makes. In general, patients with lesions in their right hemispheres tend to approach visuoconstructive tasks in a fragmented, piecemeal fashion in which they often lose the overall gestalt of the design. In contrast, left hemisphere lesion patients are likely to duplicate the overall gestalt of the design but often omit important details of the drawing. Further information on behavioral observations and error types is provided in the sections on interpreting the specific tests of visuoconstructive abilities.

The tests that are recommended and described here should provide clinicians with a good overview of visuoconstructive functions. The Bender Gestalt is a simple, straightforward task that has been extensively researched and frequently used in clinical practice. The Bender Gestalt might be further supplemented with a free drawing task such as a Human Figure Drawing or a House-Tree-Person. Other somewhat simpler drawing tasks have also been frequently used such as drawing a clock, bicycle, or Greek cross. Whereas these tasks involve drawing, the Block Design task requires assembling (rather than drawing) designs with the added factor of a time limit.

The Bender Visual Motor Gestalt Test

The Bender Visual Motor Gestalt Test (Bender, 1938), usually referred to as the Bender Gestalt or simply the Bender, has been extensively used as a screening device for neuropsychological impairment by assessing a client's visuoconstructive abilities. It consists of nine designs that are sequentially presented to subjects, with the request that they reproduce them on a blank, $8\frac{1}{2}$-by-11-inch sheet of paper. The subject's designs are then rated on their relative degree of accuracy and overall integration.

Although the Bender Gestalt has most frequently been used as a screening device for brain damage, its research and clinical applications extend well beyond this area. Within child populations, it has been used to screen for school readiness, predict school achievement, diagnose reading and learning problems, evaluate emotional difficulties, and study developmental disabilities. It has also been used as a nonverbal intelligence test (see reviews in Koppitz, 1975; Sattler, 1992). For adults and adolescents, the Bender Gestalt has proved useful in the assessment of brain damage (see Lacks, 1984; Marley, 1982) and as a projective test for the assessment of various personality functions (see Hutt, 1985; Oas, 1984; Rossini & Kaspar, 1987). Thus, the Bender Gestalt, whose task appears simple at first glance, has given rise to a surprisingly diverse and flexible number of clinical and research uses. The diversity of the Bender Gestalt and the amount of interest it has engendered have also resulted in a variety of administration procedures, scoring guidelines, and interpretation systems. Its popularity can be partially accounted for in that it is brief, economical, flexible, nonthreatening, nonverbal, and extensively researched.

Despite equivocal reviews and ambiguous research findings, the Bender Gestalt has consistently been one of the five or six most frequently used tests. Watkins et al. (1995) found that, overall, it was the sixth most frequently used test among clinical psychologists. This is consistent with other studies on test usage dating back to 1969. A survey of psychologists offering speciality neuropsychological services found that the Bender Gestalt was ranked sixth in terms of frequency with the five highest rated tests being the Wechsler intelligence tests, Wechsler Memory Scales, Trail Making, MMPI, and the Wide Range Achievement Test (Guilmette, Faust, Hart, & Arkes, 1990). An indication of the extensive research and clinical interest in the Bender Gestalt is that well over 1,100 studies were listed in the eleventh edition of the *Mental Measurements Yearbook* (1992).

A wide number of scoring systems for adults and children have been developed for the Bender Gestalt, each having various advantages and disadvantages. One of the earliest and most widely accepted scoring systems for adults was developed by Pascal and Suttell (1951). Although this system is widely cited in research studies, it has not gained wide acceptance in clinical settings, primarily due to its complexity and time inefficiency. Another early adult system was developed by Hutt in the 1940s and later formally published in 1960 (Hutt & Briskin, 1960). Although his interest in the Bender Gestalt was primarily for projective personality assessment, he also listed "12 essential discriminators of intracranial damage" (Fragmentation, Closure Difficulty, etc.). Lacks (1984) adapted this system and provided a detailed scoring manual along with substantial empirical support. In contrast to the Pascal and Suttell (1951) system, it is straightforward and time efficient, typically taking three minutes or less to score. Studies using her system have reported diagnostic accuracies of from 64% to 84% with a mean of 77% (Lacks, 1984; Lacks & Newport, 1980). The system is limited to persons 12 years of age or older.

A system for children was developed by Koppitz (1963, 1975). She carried out an extensive standardization of 1,104 children from kindergarten through fourth grade. Her system provides measures of both developmental maturation and neuropsychological impairment. She cautions that, for a diagnosis of brain damage, the examiner needs not only to consider the child's scores, but also to observe the time required to complete the test, the amount of space used, and the child's behavior and relative degree of awareness about his or her errors. The original Koppitz system was developed for relatively young children since the scores of children over the age of 10 no longer correlate with either intelligence test results or age. In addition, after the age of 10 most individuals obtain nearly perfect scores. However, more recent research has indicated that the Koppitz system can be used for adolescents between the ages of 12 and 18 although the relation with age is not nearly as strong as with younger children (McIntosh, Belter, Saylor, Finch, & Edwards, 1988; Shapiro & Simpson, 1995). The Koppitz interpretive guidelines are summarized later in this section. A detailed scoring manual can be found in Appendix A of Koppitz's book, *The Bender Gestalt Test for Young Children* (1975).

Whereas the use of the Bender Gestalt in screening for brain dysfunction has been generally accepted, its use in personality assessment has been questionable. Single-sign indicators have rarely been found to be valid. For example, "edging" (consistently draw-ing the designs along the edge of the paper) has not generally been found to indicate per-sonality variables (Holmes, Dungan, & Medlin, 1984; Holmes & Stephens, 1984). Likewise, projective interpretations that rely heavily on psychoanalytic theory and clin-ical lore have neither been generally accepted nor sufficiently validated (Sattler, 1985, 1992). However, global ratings that typically sum a series of indicators (size increases, collisions, scribbling, etc.) have had greater validity. For example, accurate discrimina-tions have been made for impulsivity by comparing total scores for impulsive versus non-impulsive indicators (Oas, 1984). Likewise, Koppitz (1975) has listed emotional indicators that have been found to be good predictors of the general presence of psycho-pathology when three or more are present (Koppitz, 1975; Rossini & Kaspar, 1987). Thus, the Bender Gestalt has generally been found to be valid in predicting the absence or presence of psychopathology based on clusters of indicators rather than on single signs. With the possible exception of impulsivity and anxiety, the Bender Gestalt is probably ineffective in identifying specific personality characteristics or specific psy-chiatric diagnoses.

Although the Bender Gestalt has a good track record of achievements, a number of cautions and limitations surround its use. The test has often been described as "assess-ing" brain damage, yet it is perhaps more accurate to say that it is a "screening" device for brain damage. It does not provide in-depth information about the specific details and varieties of such damage. In fact, the Bender Gestalt is limited to relatively severe forms of brain damage, especially in the right parietal region of the right hemisphere (Black & Bernard, 1984; Filskov, 1978). Thus, a patient may have significant lesions or subtle deficits that could easily go undetected if a traditional scoring of the Bender Gestalt were the sole method used to assess the presence of cerebral impairment (Delaney, 1982). It is more correct to say, then, that the Bender Gestalt is a screening device for generalized impairment and/or right parietal involvement.

One difficulty in interpreting Bender Gestalt performance is that a certain degree of overlap often exists between emotional and organic indicators on the Bender Gestalt. For example, one of the better indicators for organic impairment is the pres-ence of difficulties with overlapping, which has been found in the Bender Gestalt records of 45% of patients with organic impairment. However, Lacks (1984) also found that overlapping difficulties occurred in the records of 26% of persons with personal-ity disorders and 26% of those with psychosis. The degree of overlap occurring in the scores of different populations has led some reviewers (Dana, Field, & Bolton, 1983; Sattler, 1985) to seriously question the clinical usefulness of the Bender Gestalt. From a clinical practice perspective, this means that practitioners should not rely on single indicators such as overlapping or rotations, but rather use optimal cutoff scores to help determine the presence of organicity. If single signs are attended to, they should be used tentatively to formulate hypotheses or to provide qualitative descriptions of spe-cific difficulties in performance.

A further difficulty with the Bender Gestalt is the absence of a commonly ac-cepted and verified scoring and interpretation system. The result is that different re-search studies have often used different systems, which makes it somewhat difficult to compare their conclusions. Clinicians generally begin by learning a system of scor-ing and interpretation, but end up with their own unique, subjective approach based on clinical impressions (Robiner, 1978). Although this may be a highly workable, flexible approach, disagreements between "experts" can occur due to their differences in approaching the designs. Another difficulty in depending on clinical impressions is continued, unwarranted reliance on unsubstantiated and possibly incorrect clinical "lore." Lacks (1984) has argued for the use of formal scoring by presenting evidence that clinicians could increase their diagnostic accuracy for organic impairment on the average of 10% to 15% by using a brief, easily learned, objective scoring system.

Reliability and Validity

Reliabilities across the Lacks adaptation and the Koppitz system have been generally acceptable. Using the Lacks adaptation of the Hutt system, interscorer reliability for the 12 organic signs has been found to range between .98 to .95 (Lacks & Newport, 1980). Test-retest reliabilities over a 3- to 12-month interval were .79 for protocols from neuropsychiatric patients, .66 for patients with Alzheimer's disease, and from .57 to .63 for older adults (Lacks, 1984).

Interscorer reliabilities for the Koppitz system have been found to be excellent (.88 and .96), although test-retest reliabilities over a four-month interval were somewhat low (.58 to .66; Koppitz, 1975; Neale & McKay, 1985). Overall, the test-retest reliabilities for the Koppitz (1975) system range from .53 to .90 (*Mdn r* = .77), depending on age and time between retesting (Koppitz, 1975; Neale & McKay, 1985). The test-retest reliabilities for the total number of errors was .83, but reliabilities for specific errors (distortion, rotation, integration, perseveration) were too low to be dependable. Thus the major focus should be on the total-error score rather than the specific features of the reproductions.

In many studies, the Bender Gestalt has been able to demonstrate its ability to discriminate brain-damaged from non-brain-damaged populations (Hain, 1964; Lacks, 1984; Marley, 1982). Studies using the Lacks adaptation have reported diagnostic accuracies of from 64% to 84% with a mean of 77% (Lacks, 1984; Lacks & Newport, 1980). Its diagnostic accuracy has been questioned, however, when used to assess subtle neuropsychological deficits, such as among many epileptics (Delaney, 1982), or when a differentiation is attempted between functional psychotic patients and brain-damaged patients (Hellkamp & Hogan, 1985). The differentiation between brain-damaged and psychiatric patients has been found to be particularly difficult when distinguishing severely disturbed chronic schizophrenics from brain-damaged patients. However, this distinction may be inappropriate because schizophrenia is being progressively more conceptualized as an organically based disorder. Further studies have found that Bender Gestalt performance has been able to differentiate Alzheimer's patients from controls as well as reflect the progression of the disease (Storandt, Botwinick, & Danzinger, 1986). Similarly, Bender Gestalt scores were able to predict the extent to which head trauma patients could function independently (Acker & Davis, 1989).

The hit rate with the Lacks adaptation compares favorably with other Bender Gestalt scoring systems. Under equal conditions, the Lacks adaptation had an 84% hit rate, whereas the Pauker was 79% and Hain was 71% and, when only scoring for rotations, the hit rate was 63% (Lacks & Newport, 1980). The Lacks adaptation also has a lower rate of false negatives than either the Hain or Pauker systems. In addition, the

Lacks adaptation compares favorably with the Halstead Reitan composite impairment index, which has a hit rate of 84% for identifying organic impairment (Dean, 1982; Reitan, 1974). Despite these similarities in diagnostic hit rates, the Bender Gestalt takes only three to eight minutes to administer, whereas the tests specific to the Halstead Reitan can take up to three to four hours. For screening purposes, the Bender Gestalt has a clear advantage simply due to its greater time efficiency. However, the Halstead Reitan, when used in combination with the WAIS-R, provides detailed information on a wide range of cognitive strengths and weaknesses.

The validity of Koppitz's (1975) developmental system depends primarily on the purpose for which it is used. Validity is fairly good as an index of perceptual-motor development since error scores decrease with age, between the ages of 5 and 9 (Koppitz, 1963, 1975). Concurrent measures of visual-motor perception also suggest a moderate level of validity based on correlations with the Developmental Test of Visual Motor Integration (*Mdn r* = .65) and the Frostig Developmental Test of Visual Perception (*Mdn r* = .47; Breen, 1982; Wright & DeMers, 1982). Correlations with intelligence and academic achievement have been low to moderate (Koppitz, 1975; Lesiak, 1984; Vance, Fuller, & Lester, 1986). For example, correlations with the WISC-R performance subtests ranged from .51 (Block Design) to .08 (Coding; Redfering & Collings, 1982), which suggests that the quality of Bender Gestalt performance is moderately related to ability to perform well on Block Design but not on Coding. Moderate correlations (.57) have also been found between the K-ABC Simultaneous Scale and Bender Gestalt error scores (Haddad, 1986). Significant correlations have been reported between the degree of mental retardation and the number of errors (Andert, Hustak, & Dinning, 1978), as well as between first graders' Bender Gestalt scores and their level of performance in reading and arithmetic (Ackerman, Peters, & Dykman, 1971; Koppitz, 1958a). However, these correlations are sufficiently low so that the Bender Gestalt should not be used as a substitute for a formal intelligence test or a standardized test of academic achievement.

Administration

When administering the Bender Gestalt, the examiner presents the cards one at a time and clients are asked to copy each design with a number 2 pencil on a single, blank, 8½-by-11-inch sheet of white paper that has been presented to the client in a vertical position. If a client breaks the graphite on the pencil, a sharpened backup pencil should be available. Pencils should include erasers. The following verbal directions are taken from Hutt (1977) and are recommended as a standard procedure:

> **I am going to show you these cards, one at a time. Each card has a simple drawing on it. I would like you to copy the drawing on the paper, as well as you can. Work in any way that is best for you. This is not a test of artistic ability, but try to copy the drawings as accurately as you possibly can. Work as fast or as slowly as you wish.**
> (p. 64)

Each design should be placed directly in front of the client, one at a time. After the person has completed it, the next one should be presented until the entire nine designs have been reproduced. No comments or additional instructions are to be given while clients are completing the drawings. If clients ask specific questions, they should be given a noncommittal answer, such as, "Make it look as much like the picture on the card as you can." If clients begin to count the dots on Design 5, the examiner may say, "You don't have to count the dots, just make it look like the picture." If they persist, this may show perfectionistic or compulsive tendencies, and the behavioral observation should be considered when evaluating the test results and formulating diagnostic impressions. Although examinees are allowed to pick up the cards, they are not allowed to turn them unless they are in the process of completing their drawing. If it looks as if they have turned the design and are beginning to copy it in the new position, the examiner should straighten the card and state that it should be copied from this angle. As many sheets of paper may be used as desired, although clients are presented with only one sheet initially. There is no time limit, but it is important to note the length of time required to complete the test, since this information may be diagnostically significant.

When clients have completed their drawings, they should be asked to write their names and the date on the paper. No instructions are included as to where this information should be placed and, if asked, it should be clarified that it is up to him or her (Lezak, 1995). A somewhat simpler variation of the preceding instructions may be given to children.

In addition to the standard procedure for using the Bender Gestalt, a memory task is often diagnostically useful. Clients, immediately after having first copied the designs during the standard administration, are asked to reproduce as many designs as possible from memory. This variation provides an assessment of their level of short-term, visual-motor recall. Typically, adult brain-injured subjects will not be able to recall the designs as well as persons who are non-brain-injured (Lyle & Gottesman, 1976). Tolor (1956) found that organic patients could only recall an average of 3.69 designs, whereas convulsive (epileptic) patients and patients with psychological difficulties successfully recalled an average of 5.5 and 5.53 of the designs accurately. These norms were quite similar to those later reported by other authors (Hutt, 1985; Lyle & Gottesman, 1976; Schraa, Jones, & Dirks, 1983). The recall method has not been found to be successful for the screening of children (Kopptiz, 1975). A further variation for memory assessment is to present clients with each design for five seconds, remove it, and then have them reproduce it from memory. A difficulty with the memory procedures is that administration has not been standardized and scoring criteria have not been developed for what should be considered an accurate level of recall. Thus clinicians need to rely on clinical judgment frequently resorting to such methods as giving half credit for partially recalled designs.

An important addition to Bender Gestalt administration procedures for adolescents and adults is the Background Interference Procedure (BIP; Canter, 1963, 1966, 1976; Heaton, Beade, & Johnson, 1978). This requires the subject to first complete a standard administration and then complete the Bender Gestalt designs on a specially designed sheet of paper that contains a confusing array of curved, intersecting lines. Subjects are not allowed to turn either the card or the paper. Scoring is based on the Pascall and Suttell system. It has been demonstrated that brain-damaged patients show significant decrements in their BIP performance compared with their performances using a standard administration (Canter, 1966, 1971, 1976; Norton, 1978; Pardue, 1975). This is in contrast to functionally disordered patients and normals who typically do not show significant differences between the two administration procedures. A review of 94 studies by Heaton, Beade, and Johnson (1978) indicated that, overall, it had a median 84% correct classification rate in differentiating organic and psychiatric patients.

Interpretation Guidelines: Adults

This section will provide general guidelines for organic as well as emotional indicators. Quantitative scoring of organic indicators can be obtained by using the "Detailed Scoring Instructions" in Chapter 8 of Lacks (1984, pp. 83–110). The results can be summarized and tabulated on the "Bender Gestalt Test Scoring Summary" included in both Lacks (1984, p. 110) and Table 12–3.

Often the style and manner of drawing, including behavioral observations, can help to develop hypotheses related to personality characteristics. Such observations can be as important as the drawings themselves and provide a context in which to understand the examinee's approach to the task. For example, drawing times between different groups have been found to vary. Times for character disorders average 3.5 minutes, 4.5 for schizophrenics, 5.8 for depressives, 6.25 for organics (Armstrong, 1965), and 7 to 9.75 minutes for adults with intellectual disabilities (Andert, Hustak, & Dinning, 1978). Next, the examiner can evaluate general features of the drawing, such as line quality, organization, size, and number of erasures. The meaning of these responses can then be interpreted within the context of results from the quantitative scoring, history, and other relevant test data. For example, a person with no indications of organicity who takes a greater than average length of time (5 minutes or more), has a high number of erasures, and has a sketchy line quality might be expressing a general trait of hesitancy and self-doubt. Another person with documented brain damage who also takes a greater than average time but insists on counting each dot precisely may be attempting to compensate for his or her impairment by developing obsessive behaviors.

The quantitative method of scoring adult Bender Gestalts using the Lacks adaptation of the Hutt-Briskin scoring system is a relatively brief and straightforward procedure. The 12 "essential discriminators of intracranial damage" outlined in the Lacks

Table 12–3. Scoring checklist for the Lacks indicators of organicity

———	1. Rotation
———	2. Overlapping difficulty
———	3. Simplification
———	4. Fragmentation
———	5. Retrogression
———	6. Perseveration
———	7. Collision or collision tendency
———	8. Impotence
———	9. Closure difficulty
———	10. Motor incoordination
———	11. Angulation difficulty
———	12. Cohesion
———————	Time greater than 15 minutes

Total score ———————

Test diagnosis ——————

Source: Adapted from Lacks (1984).

adaptation were originally derived from Hutt and Briskin (1960). Descriptions and examples of each of these categories are included in Lacks's (1984) Detailed Scoring Instructions. A computer program is also available to assist with scoring and interpretation of protocols (Lacks, 1996). A brief description of the categories follows. When relevant research is available, some of the descriptions are also accompanied by a brief discussion.

1. ***Rotation: Severe.*** Using the Lacks (1984) system, rotations are scored when there is a change in the orientation of the axis of the figure ranging from 80 to 180 degrees. Mirror imaging of the figure is included as part of the scoring for rotations. Other scoring systems have been more lenient in defining a rotation as a reorientation of 45 or more degrees, but Lacks (1984) scores rotations of 45 to 80 degrees as "Angulation Difficulty" (see description of Angulation Difficulty).

Research on past systems has found that rotations occur most frequently on Designs 3 (28% of the instances) and A (17%), and least frequently on Designs 6 (2%), 2 (5%), and 1 (6%; Freed, 1966). Rotations occur both for organics and nonorganic psychiatric patients, such as hospitalized persons with intellectual disabilities (Silverstein & Mohan, 1962), and for schizophrenics (Hutt, 1985; Mermelstein, 1983). Thus, differentiated diagnosis between the two groups cannot be made based on the presence of rotations, or any other single sign. Lacks (1984) has reported that 26% of persons with organic dysfunction made rotations, whereas only 13% of psychotics and 9% of personality disordered patients did. It has been noted that organics produce more spontaneous rotations, but they also have more difficulty in creating a rotation when specifically requested to do so (Royer & Holland, 1975). This suggests that assessment of the relative difficulty a person experiences in making deliberate rotations may have relevance for differential diagnosis. The primary mental functions associated with rotations are impaired attention, limited capacity for new learning (Marley, 1982), and disorientation (Mermelstein, 1983). As with other visuographic disabilities, the most likely area of the brain to be affected is the parietal lobe (Black & Bernard, 1984). Although Bender Gestalt rotations can occur with either right or left hemisphere lesions, the incidence is about twice as frequent for right hemisphere patients as for left (Diller et al., 1976).

2. ***Overlapping Difficulty.*** If a client has difficulty drawing portions of figures that should overlap, then overlapping difficulty should be scored. This might include failing to draw portions which are supposed to overlap, simplifying the figure in the area they overlap, or sketching or redrawing overlapping portions.

3. ***Simplification.*** Simplification is scored when the figure is drawn in a simplified or easier form. Note that simplification is only scored if the figure is drawn in a simpler but not a maturationally more primitive form. If a more maturationally primitive figure is drawn, then it is scored for Retrogression (see description of Retrogression). Examples of simplification include drawing very simplified figures, making circles for dots (Design 1), drawing parts that should overlap as being separate (Designs 6 and 7), and making parts that should join as being ⅛ inch or more apart (Designs A, 4, 5, or 8).

4. ***Fragmentation.*** Scoring for fragmentation should occur if the figure is broken up into different parts sufficiently to destroy the actual gestalt of the design.

5. ***Retrogression.*** Scoring for retrogression is made when the figure is drawn in a more primitive gestalt than the actual stimulus figure. Examples include making loops

for circles (Design 2), dashes for dots (Design 1), or making a square instead of a diamond (Designs A and 8).

6. *Perseveration.* Within the more general neurological and psychiatric literature, perseveration refers to the continuation of a response well beyond the required number expected. On the Bender Gestalt, Lacks (1984) describes two types of perseverative errors. Type A, or interdesign perseveration, occurs when there is the "inappropriate substitution of the features of a preceding stimulus, such as replacing the circles of Figure 2 with the dots of Design 1 . . ." (p. 96). Type B, or intradesign perseverations, occur when the client continues to draw a figure beyond the limits specified by the stimulus. This might occur if 14 or more dots are drawn for Design 1 or 13 or more columns of circles for Design 2. The presence of perseverations is scored if either Type A or Type B perseverations are present.

Since the general behavior of perseveration has been extensively discussed as being an important feature of some patients who are organically or psychiatrically impaired, it has similarly been researched in relation to Bender Gestalt responses. Although perseveration has been found to exist both in schizophrenic and organic populations (see Tolor & Brannigan, 1980), it is more strongly associated with organicity (Hain, 1964; Lacks, 1984; Lerner, 1972). Lacks (1984) reported that perseveration occurred in 56% of the protocols of brain-damaged patients, whereas only 31% of personality disordered persons and 32% of psychotics had perseverations on their protocols. Thus it is not a particularly effective discriminator between organics and other patient groups.

The presence of perseveration suggests impaired executive abilities in which the person may have deficits in initiating, inhibiting, sequencing, and monitoring his or her behavior. To confirm this, check with family members to determine the extent to which the client requires prompting, supervision, and coaching. Behavioral observations during the testing can also be extremely helpful.

Marley (1982) has expanded the definition of perseveration and divided it into three different types. While each type is considered an indicator of organic impairment, she also associated different areas of mental functioning with each one. Marley's Type A perseveration occurs when numbers, letters, or other shapes are substituted for those elements found in the original Bender Gestalt design. This suggests a loosening of associations, impaired planning, diminished attention, poor concentration, and a difficulty with immediate and delayed memory. It is characteristic of dementia and is associated with frontal, frontotemporal, or bilateral involvement. Type B perseveration occurs when additional elements are drawn into Designs 1, 2, 3, and 5 or when additional curves are included in Design 6 (the same as the Lacks adaptation's definition of perseveration). Possible areas of mental functioning are an inability to shift-set, dissociation from the task, diminished attention, poor concentration, concrete thinking, and perseverating behavior outside the testing situation. This is characteristic of dominant hemisphere temporal involvement. The final form of scorable perseveration (Type C) occurs when the examinee redraws his or her design without any effort to erase or cross out the previous one. This can be the result of impaired concentration, intermittent confused ideation, difficulty with planning, and impaired visual-motor functions. Type C perseveration is characteristic of cortical impairment in the parieto-occipital areas of the dominant hemisphere. These findings represent possibilities for determining the nature of cognitive impairments and the location of lesions, which may either support other data or point out future directions to explore.

7. ***Collision or Collision Tendency.*** Scoring for collision is given when the figure is drawn so that it overlaps or collides with another figure.

8. ***Impotence.*** Impotence occurs when clients realize they have drawn the figure incorrectly but appear unable to correct the error. This may be reflected in either their verbal acknowledgment of difficulty or through repeated unsuccessful attempts to draw it accurately. Lacks (1984) found that impotence was a good discriminator between organics and other groups. Whereas 24% of her sample of organics experienced impotence, it was only found in 2% of the records of personality disorders and 4% of psychotics.

9. ***Closure Difficulty: Marked and Persistent.*** This category is scored when the client "shows repeated difficulty in getting parts of figures to join that should join" (Lacks, 1984, p. 39); for example, closing circles and hexagrams or difficulty joining the two portions of Design A. This was the most frequent error among Lacks's (1984) population of organics, with 79% of them demonstrating closure difficulties. The percentages were also fairly high for psychotics (53%) and personality disorders (55%) indicating that, although this scoring category occurred frequently among organics, it was still not an effective discriminator in and of itself.

10. ***Motor Incoordination.*** Lacks (1984) defines this category as "irregular (tremorlike) lines, especially with heavy pressure." This category has been found to fairly effectively discriminate between Lacks's (1984) samples of subjects with personality disorders, psychosis, and organic dysfunction. Fully 55% of organics had motor incoordination, whereas it occurred in only 24% of personality disordered subjects and 13% of psychotics.

11. ***Angulation Difficulty.*** Angulation difficulty is scored when there is "severe difficulty in reproducing the angulation of figures" (Lacks, 1984, p. 106). This category is only scored for either Design 2 or 3. For example, Design 2 might be tilted or rotated 45 to 80 degrees (more than 80 degrees would be scored as a Rotation). Lacks (1984) found that angulation difficulty occurred in 41% of her sample of organics but only in the records of 15% of personality disorders and 18% of psychotics.

12. ***Cohesion.*** Cohesion is scored when there are "isolated decreases or increases in size of figures" (Lacks, 1984, p. 108). For example, cohesion is present when the right portion of Figure A is decreased by more than $\frac{1}{3}$ of the size of the portion on the left side.

Once a protocol has been scored using Lacks's (1984) Detailed Scoring Instructions, a clinician can then check to see if the examinee's score falls within the brain-damaged range. Lacks (1984, 1996) gives the normal range as 0 to 4 and the optimum cutoff for organic impairment as 5 or more errors (see Table 12–4). The clinical utility of the Lacks adaptation for the Bender Gestalt can be evaluated by its ability to differentiate organic populations from normals and psychiatric populations other than organics. The hit rate must exceed the typical base rate of 20% to 30% organics and 20% to 30% schizophrenics found in most psychiatric settings. Lacks (1984) presents evidence that it is unusual for nonorganic persons to have 5 or more essential discriminators (error categories). Table 12–4 indicates that 74% to 96% of nonorganics scored

Table 12–4.   Percentile distributions of Hutt-Briskin total scores for various comparison groups

Number of Errors	Nonpatient Adults ($N = 495$)	Nonpatient Older Adults ($N = 334$)	Nonorganic Psychiatric Inpatients ($N = 264$)	Organic Psychiatric Inpatients ($N = 85$)
0	20	5	3	0
1	51	17	10	0
2	75	35	31	4
3	87	52	55	9
4	96	74	74	18
5	98	85	85	51
6	99	92	93	71
7	100	96	96	80
8		99	99	87
9		99	100	95
10		100		99
11				100
12				

Source: The cutoff score for organic dysfunction is 5 or more errors. From *Bender Gestalt Screening for Brain Dysfunction,* by P. Lacks, p. 52. Copyright © 1984 by John Wiley & Sons, Inc. Reprinted by permission of John Wiley & Sons, Inc.

less than 5, whereas only 18% of diagnosed organics did. Using a cutoff score of 5 or more indicators results in a hit rate for accurately identifying organics that ranges from 82% to 86% (Lacks, 1984; Lacks & Newport, 1980). McIntosh et al. (1988) suggest that the Lacks adaptation can also be used for adolescent populations from age 12 to 16 by using a similar cutoff score.

Whereas some of the scoring categories described earlier were relatively more effective at discriminating between organics and other patient groups, none of them should be used as single signs in and of themselves. The only clearly validated approach is to use cutoff scores. However, the presence of some of the different scoring categories, along with relevant behavioral observations, can be used to form tentative hypotheses concerning client functioning. In particular, there are often qualitative differences in the performance of persons with lesions in different areas of the brain. Whereas right hemisphere patients are more likely to make errors related to visuospatial abilities (e.g., rotations, asymmetry, fragmentation, unrecognizable drawings, unjoined lines), persons with left hemisphere lesions often make drawings that are shaky (line tremors) and smaller in size, with rounded corners and missing parts (oversimplification; Filskov, 1978). However, the Bender Gestalt is still more likely to miss patients who have left hemisphere lesions.

Emotional Indicators

The more serious indicators outlined by the different scoring systems (impotence, motor incoordination, angulation difficulty) are most characteristic of brain-damaged populations. However, these can also occur in the protocols of emotionally disturbed persons. Distinguishing between the two categories of disorders based on Bender Gestalt responses can often be difficult. This is further complicated because organically impaired persons will almost always have emotional responses to their deficits. It is often difficult, if not impossible, to differentiate precisely the extent to which their current problems are organic as opposed to functional. Related to this is that schizophrenics may have a far greater number of abnormal neurological signs than was previously believed (Heinrichs, 1993; Weinberger & Berman, 1988), which again makes a precise division into organic versus nonorganic categories difficult and sometimes inappropriate.

A consideration of the Bender Gestalt cards themselves reveals that the same card may have different meanings for different persons. Thus, two persons may make the same response to a card for different reasons. For example, a rotation may result from a neurologically based processing deficit in one person, but for another it may result from a functionally based sense of disorientation.

Various attempts have been made to list possible emotional indicators on the Bender Gestalt. For example, Hutt (1985) developed a Psychopathology Scale composed of 17 indicators. However, many of these indicators overlap with scoring categories for organic impairment. Additional researchers have attempted to identify different categories associated with specific emotional states. The following three emotional states have been found to have empirical relationships with clusters of Bender Gestalt responses.

Anxiety and Depression   Anxiety and depression can be characterized as a person's withdrawal from and narrowing of his or her contact with the world in an attempt to create security. Bender Gestalt responses from either anxious or depressed persons likewise reflect a constriction of the designs (Johnson, 1973; White & McGraw, 1975). In addition to constricted placement, depressed or anxious persons also decrease the overall size of their reproductions and make their lines in a sketchy, hesitant manner (Clawson, 1962; Hutt & Briskin, 1960). The possibility of suicidal behavior is raised if, in addition to constricted, hesitantly drawn designs, the examinee also encounters difficulty maintaining Design 2 in a horizontal position (Leonard, 1973) and draws Design 6 penetrating into the open semicircular areas of Design 5 (Sternberg & Levine, 1965).

Rao and Potash (1985) found that persons who were typically relaxed (low trait anxiety) had few size distortions (larger or smaller) under nonstress conditions, but when placed in an anxiety-provoking situation, they did create size distortions. In contrast, persons who were ordinarily anxious (high trait anxiety) had size distortions during normal conditions but actually had few size distortions during an anxiety-provoking situation. Thus, anxiety and size distortions on the Bender Gestalt may interact with both situational variables (level of stress) and personality characteristics (trait anxiety).

Impulsivity   Persons who frequently engage in acting-out behavior have a low tolerance for restraint or inhibition, difficulty in completing an exacting task, and a tendency to comply with requests in a superficial manner. If the Bender Gestalt task is conceptualized as an exacting task requiring some degree of self-discipline, then acting-out persons would be expected to express their impulsiveness within this context. Oas (1984) found that impulsivity was likely to be characteristic of the person if five or more of the following indicators were present:

- Short time for completion.
- Poor overall quality.
- Discontinuing the task.
- Omissions.
- Collisions.
- Transformations.
- Size increases.
- Angle changes.
- Poor planning.
- Perseveration.
- Scribbling.
- Aggression.

A composite score of these categories had a hit rate of 79% for discriminating impulsive from nonimpulsive adolescents, with 4.8 as a mean score for impulsives ($SD = 2.0$) and 2.3 as a mean for nonimpulsives ($SD = 1.4$). In contrast to impulsives, persons with good impulse control were most likely to take significantly longer to complete the task, more likely to have better, overall quality of their designs, and were more likely to count relevant details of the designs. The study was noteworthy in that it controlled for a wide number of variables, including IQ, age, drawing ability, organicity, and motivation.

A somewhat similar listing of acting-out signs reported by McCormick and Brannigan (1984), but derived from previous authors (Brown 1965; Hutt, 1969; Koppitz, 1968, 1975), included:

- Figures spread widely on the page.
- Progressive increase in figure size.
- Overall increase in figure size.
- Collisions.
- Dashes for dots or circles.
- Circles for dots.
- Dots for circles.
- Excessively heavy line.
- Second attempt.
- Acute angulation.

McCormick and Brannigan (1984) found that a composite score on these signs was significantly related to adolescent acting-out behavior. Specific signs were that the presence of collisions was related to unethical behavior and that the creation of circles for dots was associated with inability to delay impulses.

Schizophrenia   Both acting out and anxiety or depression are usually less severe levels of disturbance than a psychotic disorder such as schizophrenia. As the severity of a functional disorder increases, the Bender Gestalt responses will be more likely to resemble the responses of organically impaired persons. For example, the presence of hallucinations for schizophrenics has also been found to cause greater disruption in the selective perception required to draw the Bender Gestalt designs. Thus, schizophrenics reporting hallucinations will have significantly greater errors on their Bender Gestalt responses than nonhallucinating schizophrenics (Rockland & Pollin, 1965). The following specific indicators have been identified by various authors as being associated with schizophrenia: confused sequence, concreteness, fragmentation, overlapping and crossing difficulty, perseveration, severe difficulties with closure, spontaneous elaborations, embellishments, or doodling, expansion in size, extreme crowding, and collisions (Hutt, 1985; Hutt & Gibby, 1970; Lacks, 1984).

To differentiate organic impairment from schizophrenia, the best approach is to use information from both the patient's history and test scores. There are also several distinguishing signs related to the Bender Gestalt. First, schizophrenics are more adept than organics at creating deliberate distortions. Second, schizophrenics are somewhat less likely to have the serious indicators of organicity and will probably have fewer of them. For example, in Lacks's (1984) sample of psychotics, impotence, motor incoordination, angulation difficulty, retrogression, and fragmentation occurred in the records of organics far more frequently than in those of psychotics. Finally, clinicians can use Canter's Background Interference Procedure (1966), which tends to decrease the performance of organics but not psychotics (Canter, 1976; Heaton, Beade, & Johnson, 1978).

Interpretation Guidelines: Children

The Developmental Bender Gestalt Test scoring system (Koppitz, 1963, 1975) is the dominant system used for children. The primary focus is on understanding children's visual-motor abilities as they relate to developmental maturation. Koppitz (1963, 1975) also lists typical errors associated with emotional indicators and brain damage, but places these within the context of what would be expected for a particular individual having a specified chronological age. Bender Gestalt protocols are scored based on the presence of 30 mutually exclusive items. Composite scores can thus range from 0 to 30. The system is relatively easy to learn. The following section is primarily a summary of Koppitz's approach and provides general interpretative guidelines based on indicators for developmental maturation, organicity, visual-motor perception difficulties, and emotional indicators.

The specific scoring criteria developed by Koppitz (1963, 1975) for developmental level can be found in Appendix B of *The Bender Gestalt for Young Children* (Volume 2, 1975). Table 12–5 in the present chapter summarizes the scoring criteria. A different set of scoring criteria for emotional indicators has also been developed by Koppitz and appears in *The Bender Gestalt Test for Young Children* (1963). To obtain specific scores, clinicians should consult these criteria and use the outline in Table 12–5 as a scoring guide. Both texts by Koppitz (1963, 1975) include important guidelines, cautions, and reviews of research, and clinicians are encouraged to consult these for further elaboration and discussion.

The Bender Gestalt can provide information about a child's perceptual maturity, degree of emotional adjustment, or extent of neuropsychological impairment. A particular clinician may wish to assess only one of these areas, or may consider them all. However,

Table 12–5. Summary and scoring sheet for Koppitz developmental scoring system

Design		Type of Error	Check if Present
A	1a	Distortion of shape	_____
	1b	Disproportion	_____
	2	Rotation	_____
	3	Integration	_____
1	4	Circles for dots	_____
	5	Rotation	_____
	6	Perseveration	_____
2	7	Rotation	_____
	8	Row added, omitted	_____
	9	Perseveration	_____
3	10	Circles for dots	_____
	11	Rotation	_____
	12a	Shape test	_____
	12b	Lines for dots	_____
4	13	Rotation	_____
	14	Integration	_____
5	15	Circles for dots	_____
	16	Rotation	_____
	17a	Shape test	_____
	17b	Lines for dots	_____
6	18a	Angles in curves	_____
	18b	Straight line	_____
	19	Integration	_____
	20	Perseveration	_____
7	21a	Disproportion	_____
	21b	Incorrect angles	_____
	22	Rotation	_____
	23	Integration	_____
8	24	Incorrect angles	_____
	25	Rotation	_____

if all the areas are considered, it is crucial to be cautious of the possible overlap among them since many of the signs occur throughout the different scoring guidelines.

A suggested sequence in approaching the Bender Gestalt is to initially develop a global impression of the relative quality of the reproductions as a whole. It is also important to note any relevant behavioral observations made while the child is completing the designs. These observations might include such areas as the child's level of confidence, awareness of errors, completion time, and any comments that are made. The clinician might then look at specific features of the drawings, including figure size, placement, line quality, order and organization of the designs, distortions, erasures, reworking, omissions, and any other unusual treatment. Finally, objective scoring can be made for developmental maturity, organicity, visual-motor perception, and emotional difficulties.

Developmental Maturation , As is true with all areas of development, visual-motor perception skills increase with the growth of the child. Although children mature at different rates, the following guidelines developed by Bender (1938) and outlined by Clawson (1962) describe the typical pattern of visual-motor development.

Typical patterns of reproduction:

Age

2   Has not developed the skills necessary to reproduce the designs with any degree of accuracy but is able to keep pencil on paper and make scribbles, dots, and dashes.

3   Ability to draw loops, lines, arcs, and circles.

4   Can arrange circles or loops in a horizontal left-to-right direction.

5   Figures characterized by having a square appearance; can create many different designs; crosses horizontal and vertical lines.

6   Can create a relatively accurate reproduction of the Bender Gestalt designs since visual perception is more mature and can be integrated with kinesthetic and tactual perception. Designs A, 1, 4, and 5 are likely to be particularly accurate.

7   Good ordering of designs, relatively accurate reproduction of oblique lines. Subparts to Designs A and 8 are joined. There are no major additions to the child's drawing ability beyond the age of 7, but there is an increasing number of successful reproductions, greater combinations of basic forms, and more refinement in techniques.

8   Accuracy in joining subparts and making dots, and an improvement in the contours on curved figures. Design 2 is drawn with vertical rather than oblique columns, Design 3 has columns of arcs instead of angles; figure is accurate except for an obliqueness in vertical support.

9   Less frequent occurrence of rotations; subtle improvement in the detail of the designs, no longer tends to draw the designs vertically.

10   Accurate hexagons drawn for Design 7; subparts correctly joined; oblique columns drawn for Design 2.

11   All designs reproduced accurately with correct sequence, organization, and size.

Visual examples of the preceding maturational guidelines are provided in Appendix O. The table in Appendix O lists the relevant ages in the left-hand column and the specific designs on the top row. The percentage in each box represents the percentage of persons from a particular age group who produce an accurate reproduction of the designated design. As can be seen, the percentage of accurate reproductions gradually increases for Design A until the age of 11, at which time 95% of all children produce an accurate design. A clinician can develop a rough indication of the person's maturational level by referring to the visual norms included in Appendix O.

A more specific rating of developmental level can be determined for children from 5 to 12 by scoring with the criteria developed by Koppitz (1975) and outlined in Table 12–5. However, the decrease in errors with age is not even and steady but rather decreases rapidly around age 8. This results in a skewed distribution, with most of the errors occurring between the ages of 5 to 8 (Taylor, Kaufman, & Partenio, 1984). Thus, it should not be considered developmental past the age of 8 or 10. If there is a significant lag between the child's chronological age and the level at which he or she reproduces the Bender Gestalt designs, the possible causes should be explored with a more complete evaluation of the protocol as well as a review of other relevant data.

Indicators for Organicity.   When screening for neuropsychological impairment using the Bender Gestalt, it is important to be aware that many of the indicators for central nervous system (CNS) involvement are also indicators for emotional disturbance. This raises the serious possibility of misclassification. Thus, the results of the Bender Gestalt alone are rarely sufficient to make a differential diagnosis between neuropsychological impairment and emotional disturbance; additional information is needed to determine both the nature and cause of the individual's problems.

The error categories described in this section have been reported in the literature to be significant indicators of neuropsychological impairment both for children and for adults. Although the presence of these errors may indicate impairment, even if none of these factors are present, the person may still be suffering a neuropsychological impairment. Conversely, a poor Bender Gestalt performance may reflect a variety of factors, only one of which is neuropsychological impairment. The most common errors associated with organicity are fragmentation or omission of parts of a design, closure problems, distortion of figures, rotations of all or part of a design, perseveration within one design or from one design to another, and substitution of lines for dots. The presence of only one of these is rarely likely to indicate neuropsychological impairment. However, the likelihood of organic deficit increases with the presence of several indicators.

The assessment of neuropsychological impairment using the Bender Gestalt requires a number of important considerations and cautions. Perhaps the most clear and specific indicator is a score greater than one standard deviation above the mean normative score for a given age group (see Table 12–6). However, alternate considerations should still be made. The high score might be the result of emotional factors, poor motivation, fatigue, a poor understanding of the instructions, or developmental delay. A high score that is due to developmental delay may merely reflect individual differences in the rate of maturation. The possibility then exists that significant improvement might occur with increased age. Koppitz (1975) points out that there is little to be gained by scoring for both developmental level and brain damage since they are both equally effective in detecting neuropsychological impairment. This overlap between the two scoring guidelines also underlies the difficulty in differentiating between developmental delay and a more pathological injury to the brain.

When using the indicators of brain injury described and listed in Table 12–7, clinicians should note the overall number of indicators. An abbreviated list of nine indicators follows and can be used as a brief reference and summary. Whereas normal

Table 12–6. Distribution of Bender test mean scores and standard deviations

Age Group	1964 Normative Sample*			1974 Normative Sample[†]		
	N	Mean	SD	N	Mean	SD
5–0 to 5–5	81	13.2	3.8	47	13.1	3.3
5–6 to 5–11	128	10.2	3.8	130	9.7	3.4
6–0 to 6–5	155	8.0	3.8	175	8.6	3.3
6–6 to 6–11	180	6.4	3.8	60	7.2	3.5
7–0 to 7–5	156	5.1	3.6	61	5.8	3.3
7–6 to 7–11	110	4.2	3.4	47	4.6	2.8
8–0 to 8–5	62	3.4	3.1	53	4.2	2.5
8–6 to 8–11	60	2.7	2.8	60	3.0	2.5
9–0 to 9–5	65	2.2	2.5	78	2.8	2.2
9–6 to 9–11	49	1.8	2.2	47	2.3	2.1
10–0 to 10–5	27	1.5	1.8	76	1.9	1.9
10–6 to 10–11	31	1.2	1.5	68	1.8	1.8
11–0 to 11–11				73	1.4	1.4

Source: From *The Bender Gestalt Test for Young Children, Vol. 2: Research and Applications 1963–1973,* by E. M. Koppitz, Grune & Stratton, 1975. Reprinted with permission.

* $N = 1104$; socioeconomic cross section: 98% white, 2% nonwhite.
[†] $N = 975$; socioeconomic cross section: 86% white, 8.5% black, 1% Oriental, 4.5% Mexican-American and Puerto Rican.

children from the ages of 5 to 8 might be expected to make some of these errors, persons above the age of 8 or 9 should be expected to have few or no errors (Taylor, Kaufman, & Partenio, 1984). If four or more of the following characteristics are present, then CNS impairment is a strong possibility:

1. Simplification of two or more figures to a level three or more years below the child's chronological age.
2. Collision of a figure with another figure or a reproduction in which a figure runs off the edge of the paper.
3. Fragmentation of one or more figures.
4. Rotation of one or more figures 90 degrees or more.
5. Incorrect number of units in three or more figures.
6. Perseveration from figure to figure of one type or more.
7. Tremulous line quality.
8. Lines instead of dots.
9. Drawing a straight line when a curved one is indicated.

Visual-Motor Perception Difficulties   Difficulties in visual-motor perception might be caused by emotional factors, developmental delay, CNS complications, or a combination of all of these. Often, it will be the task of the clinician to understand both the underlying causes of the visual-motor difficulties and the manner in which these difficulties affect the child. The specific pattern of effects can be noticed by observing the child's

Table 12–7.   Bender indicators of brain injury for children 5 to 10 years of age*

Extra or Missing Angles

Figure A   Significantly[†] more often in BI at all age levels.

Figure 7   Common in BI and NBI through more frequently in BI at all age levels; *no* BI drew correct angles before age 8.

Figure 8   Common in BI and NBI through age 6, significant[†] for BI thereafter.

Angels for Curves

Figure 6   Common in BI and NBI but significantly[†] more often in BI at all age levels; *all* BI drew angels up to age 7.

Straight Line for Curves

Figure 6   Rate but highly significant[‡] for BI when present.

Disproportion of Parts

Figure A   Common in BI and NBI through age 6, significant[†] for BI thereafter.

Figure 7   Common in BI and NBI through age 7, significant[†] for BI thereafter.

Substitution of Five Circles for Dots

Figure 1   Present in BI and NBI but significantly[†] more often in BI at all ages.

Figure 3   Present in BI and NBI through age 6, significant[†] for BI thereafter.

Figure 5   Present in BI and NBI through age 8, significant[†] for BI thereafter.

Rotation of Design by 45°

Figures 1, 4, and 8   Highly significant[‡] for BI at all age levels.

Figures A and 5   Significant[†] for BI at all age levels.

Figure 7   Present in BI and NBI through age 6, significant[†] for BI thereafter.

Figure 3   Present in BI and NBI through age 7, significant[†] for BI thereafter.

Figure 2   Present in BI and NBI through age 8, significant[†] for BI thereafter.

Failure to Integrate Parts

Figures A and 4   Significant[†] for BI at all age levels.

Figure 6   Rare but significant[†] for BI at all age levels.

Figure 7   Common for BI and NBI through age 6, significant[†] for BI thereafter.

Omission or Addition of Row of Circles

Figure 2   Common in BI and NBI through age 6, highly significant[‡] for BI thereafter.

Shape of Design Lost

Figure 3   Present in BI and NBI through age 5, significant[†] for BI thereafter.

Figure 5   Rare and does *not* differentiate between BI and NBI at any age.

Line for Series of Dots

Figures 3 and 5   Rare but highly significant[‡] for BI at all age levels.

Perseveration

Figures 1, 2, and 6   Common in BI and NBI through age 7, highly significant[‡] for BI thereafter.

Source: From *The Bender Gestalt Test for Young Children,* by E. M. Koppitz, New York: Grune & Stratton, 1963. Reprinted with permission.

* BI = brain-injured; NBI = non-brain-injured.

† Significant = occurring more often, but not exclusively, in BI group.

‡ Highly significant = occurring almost exclusively in BI group.

behavior during the test as well as the type and severity of errors on the reproductions of the designs. Some children might have primary difficulties with rotations, which might reflect mirror reversals involved with other tasks, such as reading. In contrast, other children might have difficulties in sequencing, which could be suggested by a poorly confused sequence in the reproduction of their Bender Gestalt designs. This qualitative analysis of Bender Gestalt protocols should always be conducted within the context of additional material in the client's history as well as other test data.

Sometimes children have learned to compensate for visual-motor difficulties caused by CNS complications. As a result, their actual Bender Gestalt reproductions might be relatively accurate. This compensation is particularly likely if an injury is not too extensive, there was above-average premorbid intelligence, the location of the lesion is not too critical, and the injury has not been recently acquired. If children have achieved an adequate level of compensation, then their actual Bender Gestalt reproductions might be quite accurate. Clinicians can sometimes detect the possible presence of brain damage by becoming sensitized to a wide range of possible compensatory mechanisms. Koppitz (1975) has listed some of these:

- Excessive length of time for completion.
- "Anchoring" designs by placing a finger on them as they attempt to reproduce them.
- Reproducing a design from memory after first glancing at it.
- Checking and rechecking the number of dots yet still being uncertain regarding the correct number that should be included.
- Rotating either the sheet of paper or the Bender Gestalt card itself as an aid in reproducing the design.
- Designs that are quickly and impulsively drawn and then corrected with extreme difficulty.
- Expressions of dissatisfaction with the poorly reproduced designs followed by repeated efforts to correct them.

It is sometimes useful to attempt to determine whether a child's poor Bender Gestalt reproductions are the result of inadequate reception (difficulty in visual perception) or inadequate expression (difficulty in reproducing that which might have been accurately perceived). This distinction can sometimes be determined by asking the child to evaluate the accuracy of the drawing he or she has made. Children who feel that their poorly reproduced drawings are accurate will most likely have receptive difficulties and possibly difficulties with expression. If they recognize that their drawings were done poorly, this suggests their problem might be primarily expressive. Even though they might be aware of the inaccuracy of their drawings, they would be expected to have extreme difficulty in correcting the inaccuracies.

Emotional Indicators   The most clearly supported use of the Bender Gestalt is as a screening device for neuropsychological impairment and as an index of developmental delay. However, it has also been used as a projective device to measure various personality functions (Clawson, 1959; Koppitz, 1963, 1975; Reichenber & Raphael, 1992;

Rossini & Kaspar, 1987). This usage has been most successful when cutoff scores have been established for various indicators of emotional difficulties. However, often children with visual-motor difficulties due to developmental delay also have numerous emotional indicators. Despite this, a significant number of cases have several emotional indicators without necessarily having scores that indicate developmental delay. In these cases, the emotional indicators assess different levels of functioning. As Koppitz (1975) summarizes, "Not all youngsters with poor Developmental Bender Gestalt test scores necessarily have emotional problems, nor do all children with Emotional Indicators on their Bender Gestalt records inevitably show malfunctioning or immaturity in the visual-motor area" (p. 83).

Koppitz (1963, 1975) has listed 12 emotional indicators and developed a scoring manual for 10 of these, which she includes in her 1963 text. Each indicator has specific interpretive hypotheses associated with it. However, these specific hypotheses have not received sufficient empirical support, so any interpretation based on these indicators should be speculative. In contrast, far greater success has been achieved at predicting such difficulties as psychopathology, acting out, and anxiety by using summed totals of indicators (McCormick & Brannigan, 1984; Oas, 1984; Rossini & Kaspar, 1987). Koppitz (1975) recommended using three or more indicators as the cutoff for inferring emotional difficulties. She reports that over 50% of children with three indicators were emotionally disturbed and 80% with four or more indicators had serious emotional problems. Any person with three or more indicators should be given a more complete evaluation to determine the nature and extent of possible difficulties. It is likely that a high number of persons with less than three indicators may still have significant difficulties and yet might be misclassified as normal. Rossini and Kaspar (1987) suggest that one indicator is not uncommon for normal controls; children with adjustment problems often have two to three, and three or more indicators are typical among behavior-disordered children. Thus, they recommend a more conservative approach: Two or more indicators suggest psychopathology. Although the total number of indicators has been used to successfully distinguish psychotic from neurotic levels of psychopathology in children (McConnel, 1967), it has not been successful in discriminating difficulties within nonclinical samples of schoolchildren (Gregory, 1977).

Koppitz (1963) originally listed 10 emotional indicators and later expanded these to 12 in her 1975 update of her system. Rossini and Kaspar (1987) found that the following three emotional indicators were given strong support:

1. Confused order.
2. Large size.
3. Box around design.

The following five indicators were found less frequently in Rossini and Kaspar's (1987) control group of normals. Although they did not relate significantly to psychopathology, their less frequent occurrence in the normal controls suggested some possible relationship with emotional difficulty:

4. Expansion.
5. Fine line.

6. Careless overwork (or heavily reinforced lines).

7. Second attempts (without correcting the original).

8. Small size.

The following four indicators did not relate to psychopathology in Rossini and Kaspar's (1987) sample, but have been found to be indicators by other researchers:

9. Wavy line.

10. Dashes for circles.

11. Increased size.

12. Elaboration.

Quite possibly, indicators 4 to 12 may relate to types of pathology other than the adjustment and behavior disorders used in Rossini and Kaspar's (1987) sample of 7- to 10-year-olds. Also, older populations (e.g., adolescents) having emotional problems might be more likely to have a wider variety of emotional indicators. Future research may eventually refine Koppitz's 12 indicators and identify those that have been demonstrated to be the most powerful predictors.

Block Design and Object Assembly

Both Block Design and Object Assembly are sensitive to lowering due to any type of organic impairment but are especially sensitive to damage in the right parietal region (Golden, 1979; Lezak, 1995). An advantage of both subtests is that careful behavioral observation can help the practitioner more fully understand a client's deficits. Clients with perceptual difficulties will do poorly primarily because they will distort and misperceive the design with a frequent sense of disorientation. These difficulties are more consistent with right parietal lesions. In contrast, patients with left parietal lesions will be able to correctly perceive the overall gestalt of the design, but their problem-solving style may be confused and simplified. Other clients might be able to understand the task and perceive it correctly, but still experience difficulty in actually completing the task. This dissociation between intent and actually being able to make the blocks do what they want is formally referred to as constructional dyspraxia. Sometimes clients with a concrete orientation to problem solving will do quite poorly on Block Design since it requires a certain degree of abstraction. In contrast, Object Assembly deals with more concrete objects with the result that these same persons might perform relatively better on it. Additional interpretive details can be found by consulting the relevant sections on these subtests in Chapter 5.

Human Figure Drawings and Other Free Drawing Tasks

Whereas the preceding tests (Bender Gestalt, Block Design, Object Assembly) are visuoconstructive tasks within a structured situation, free drawing (visuographic) tasks are far less structured. Clients must initiate, organize, and monitor their activity to a greater extent. As such, they add a new dimension to the more structured Bender

Gestalt and Wechsler subtest tasks. Draw-A-Person administration procedures, scoring criteria, and interpretative guidelines for neuropsychological impairment can be found in Chapter 11. In addition to the Draw-A-Person, quality of drawings can be assessed with drawings from the House-Tree-Person, drawings of bicycles, clocks, or the more simpler drawings of a square or Greek cross. Formal scoring criteria and norms can be found for bicycle and house drawings in Lezak (1995, pp. 584–585).

MENTAL ACTIVITIES (ATTENTION AND SPEED OF INFORMATION PROCESSING)

The maintenance of an optimum amount of mental activity involves a complex variety of functions related to filtering, selecting, focusing, shifting, and tracking. Since there is typically a huge amount of available information to attend to, a person must be able to filter this potential information and attend to only the most relevant sources. Any irrelevant information must be ignored. This filtering, selecting, and focusing process is still not sufficient in and of itself. Unless a person can shift attention, he or she will have difficulty functioning. Attention must strike a balance and neither be overly focused nor too ready to shift. An individual who becomes too focused will express this symptomatically in perseverations. Such persons will then experience difficulty shifting their attention to a new task and will therefore be likely to continue with a behavior beyond the point in which it is adaptable. Conversely, people who shift their focus too readily will express this symptomatically in distractibility.

Due to the complexity and interrelationship of attention with other tasks, it is quite sensitive to the effects of CNS complications. It is thus one of the most frequently reported disturbances associated with cerebral impairment (Lezak, 1989). The most basic form of assessment for attentional deficits is through simple reaction time tasks. For example, reaction time has been found to be sensitive to the effects of head trauma (Zomeren & Brouwer, 1990), solvent exposure (Groth-Marnat, 1993) and the early impact of dementia (Teng, Chui, & Saperia, 1990). As attentional tasks become more complex, they become progressively more sensitive to the impact of neuropsychological dysfunction. Thus, not only do the tests in this subsection require simple attention, but clients must also effectively filter out irrelevant stimuli and shift their attention. The Trail Making test requires them to sequence their responses and, on Trail B, they must shift their attention back and forth from numbers to letters, and scan the page while still maintaining the correct sequence of responses. To further assess for attentional difficulties, clinicians can note performances on Arithmetic, Digit Span, Digit Symbol, and Symbol Search (WISC-III only) (see Chapter 5 for interpretation of these subtests). The result should be a relatively thorough overview of attention and related functions.

Trail Making Test

The Trail Making Test (Army Individual Test, 1944; Reitan & Wolfson, 1993) is an easily administered, widely used test that requires a client to draw lines connecting consecutively numbered circles (Part A; Figure 12–1) followed by a similar task in which they

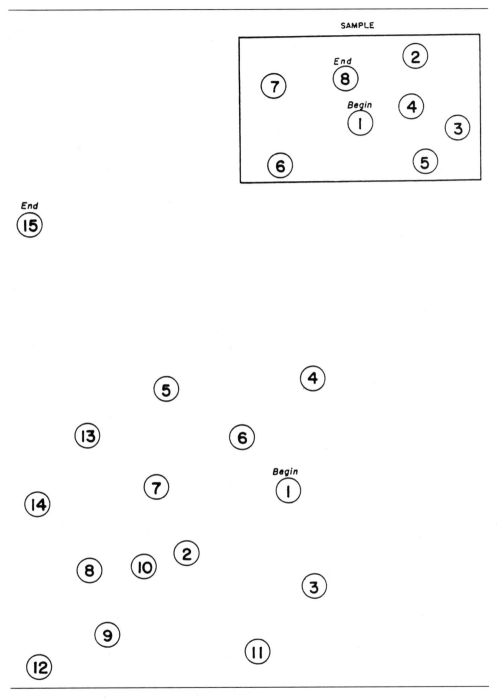

Figure 12–1.   Trail Making Part A. Note that Part A and the sample have been reduced and they are ordinarily on separate 8½″ × 11″ sheets of paper.

draw lines connecting alternating numbered and lettered circles (Part B; see Figures 12–1 and 12–2). Scores are based on the total time it takes to complete Part A and the total time it takes to complete Part B. It is part of the comprehensive Halstead Reitan Neuropsychological Test Battery but is frequently used as a component of other comprehensive or screening batteries. It was originally developed by U.S. Army psychologists and is considered to be in the public domain. It can thus be reproduced without obtaining permission. Alternate forms have been developed (Trails C and D; McCracken & Franzen, 1992), which can be used for retesting when it would be important to minimize increases in performance due to practice effects (Dye, 1979).

Trail Making is frequently listed under tests assessing orientation and attention (Lezak, 1995). However, it involves a series of skills related to attention including complex scanning, coordination, visuomotor tracking, speed of information processing, and motivation (Gaudino, Geisler, & Squires, 1995; Shum et al., 1990). Consistent with this is that Trail Making has loaded most heavily on both "visuospatial sequencing" and "rapid visual search" factors (desRosiers & Kavanagh, 1987). A client completing the task must understand the symbolic importance of the numbers and letters, effectively scan the page, accurately identify the next stimulus to respond to, and perform these functions in a relatively fast manner. Left hemisphere abilities are most likely required to understand and correctly sequence the numbers and letters, and right hemisphere abilities are required to visually scan the page. Doing this in an accurate and quick manner is likely to reflect an intact integration of these abilities. Although Part A has sometimes been used to reflect left hemisphere functioning and Part B to reflect right hemisphere abilities, this lateralization of functions should not be made (Gaudino, 1995; Reitan & Wolfson, 1993; Wedding, 1979). In contrast, Trail Making should more accurately be considered to reflect the overall integrity of general brain functioning.

Reliability and Validity

Most reports of reliability have been above .60 with some being in the .90s (Lezak, 1995; Spreen & Strauss, 1991). Reliability for a group of healthy adults over a 6- to 12-month interval was .78 for Part A and .67 for Part B (Lezak, 1982). However, there is considerable variability among different populations. For example, neuropsychiatric patients having vascular disorders had a test-retest reliability of .94 for Part A (Goldstein & Watson, 1989). Similarly, epileptics had test-retest reliabilities over a 6- to 12-month retesting period ranging between .78 and .89 for Part A and .39 and .87 for Part B (Dodrill & Troupin, 1975). The lowest overall reliabilities were found for schizophrenics who only had a reliability of .36 on Part A (Goldstein & Watson, 1989).

Trail Making, like other tests that load heavily on attention, is quite sensitive to the effects of CNS deficits. In particular, Trail Making has been effectively used to detect the early stages of dementia as well as track the progressive decline in abilities during the course of dementia (Botwinick, Storandt, Berg, & Boland, 1988; Greenlief, Margolis, & Erker, 1985). There is also slowing of Trail Making performance following head injury with greater slowing reflecting the severity of the injury (Leninger et al., 1990). Performance on Trail Making has also been used to effectively monitor the improvement of head-injured patients over time (Stuss, Stethem, Hugenholtz, & Richard, 1989). Prigatano (1983) found significantly slower performances on Trail B for clients with mild hypoxemia compared with matched controls. Ecological validity

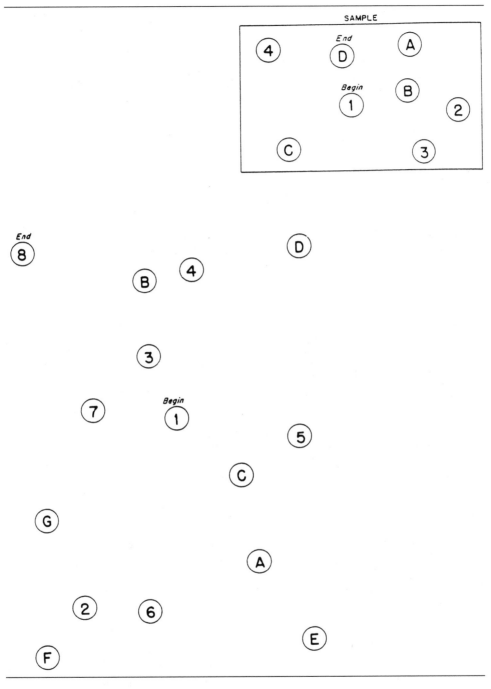

Figure 12–2.   Trail Making Part B. Note that Part B and the sample have been reduced and they are ordinarily on separate 8½″ × 11″ sheets of paper.

for Trail Making is suggested in that scores were able to predict the extent to which moderately to severely head-injured patients could function independently (Acker & Davis, 1989).

An important consideration with Trail Making is the extent to which it can effectively distinguish between severe psychiatric conditions such as schizophrenia and brain damage. Crockett et al. (1988) found that Trail Making scores could differentiate between psychiatric clients, general medical patients, and patients with neuropsychological impairment. Whereas emotional factors seem to lower Trail Making performance, they rarely lower it as much as brain damage (Gass & Daniel, 1990). Thus the MMPI, particularly any elevations on Scales 6 (Paranoia), 7 (Psychasthenia), and 8 (Schizophrenia), can be used to determine the extent to which emotional factors might be involved in poor Trail Making performance. However, some authors have cautioned that, in a number of cases, Trail Making performance has had difficulty distinguishing between psychiatric and brain-damaged patients (Norton, 1978). This is conceptually consistent with the view that attentional difficulties can be disrupted not only by brain damage, but also by conditions such as anxiety and depression.

Administration

The task for Trail Making requires clients to accurately connect the correct sequence of numbers and letters by drawing a line from one to the next as quickly as possible. The client should be seated comfortably at a table and supplied with a pencil. The correct sequence of the test (practice samples followed by Trails A and then Trails B; see Figures 12–1 and 12–2) is then given to them. If a client makes an error, then the examiner needs to detect this error as quickly as possible and then place the client's pencil back to the preceding (correct) circle as soon as possible. If a client intended to touch a circle but did not quite do so, this should not be counted as an error, but the client should be requested to actually touch or preferably enter the circle during future trials. The following instructions have been adapted from Reitan and Wolfson (1993, pp. 279–288) and Spreen and Strauss (1991, pp. 321–323):

> *Practice Sample for Part A.* Place the practice sample for Part A (see Figure 12–1) directly in front of the client. Point to the sheet and say, **On this page are some numbers. Begin at number 1** (point to circle 1), **and draw a line from 1 to 2** (point to circle 2), **2 to 3, 3 to 4, and so on in order, until you reach the end** (point to the circle designated as "End"). **Draw the lines as fast as you can. Do not lift the pencil from the paper. Ready, begin!**
>
> If the client makes an error on practice sample A (or Part A itself), you can provide the following explanations depending on the type of error made:
>
> • **You started with the wrong circle. This is where you start** (point to circle 1).
> • **You skipped this circle** (point to the one skipped). **You should go from number 1 to 2, 2 to 3** (point to each circle), **and so on until you reach the circle marked END** (point).
> • **Please keep the pencil on the paper, and continue right on to the next circle.**
>
> If the client still cannot complete the practice sample, then take the erasure of the pencil, place his or her hand around it, and guide the person through the trail with the erasure on the page. Then turn the pencil around with the point facing downward and say **Now you**

try it. Put your pencil point down. Remember begin at number one and draw a line from one to two, two to three, three to four (point to each of the numbers), **and so on, in order until you reach the circle marked END. Ready, Begin!**

When clients have difficulty, repeat the instructions until they can demonstrate that they understand what is required. If they still cannot complete or cannot adequately understand the task, then discontinue the test. However, if the client completes the task correctly, then immediately go on to Part A of the test.

Say, **On this page are numbers from 1 to 25. Do this the same way. Begin at number 1 and draw a line from 1 to 2, 2 to 3, 3 to 4** (point to each circle with the designated number in it) **and so on, in order, until you reach the end** (point to the circle designated END). **Remember to work as fast as you can. Ready, begin!**

Begin timing as soon as the instructions have been given. If a client makes an error, point out the error immediately, guide the person's pencil back to the prior (and correct) circle, and have him or her continue the test from this point. Do not discontinue timing while you are correcting the client. The error is taken into account only in that it increases the time it takes to complete the entire Part A task. After completing Part A, note the final time and say, **That's fine. Now we'll try another one.** Then proceed immediately to the practice sample for Part B.

Practice Sample for Part B. Place the practice sample page (see Figure 12–2) directly in front of the client and say, **On this page are some numbers and letters. Begin at 1** (point to 1) **and draw a line from 1 to A** (point to circle A), **A to 2** (point to circle 2), **2 to B** (point to circle B), **B to 3** (point to circle 3), **3 to C** (point to circle C), **and so on, in order, until you reach the end** (point to the circle indicated as END). **Remember first you have a number** (point to circle 1) **then a letter** (point to circle A), **then a number** (point to 2), **then a letter** (point to B), **and so on. Draw the line as fast as you can. Ready, begin!**

If the client makes a mistake on practice sample B (or Part B itself) you can, based on the type of error, provide the following instructions:

- **You started with the wrong circle. This is where you start** (point to circle 1).
- **You skipped this circle** (point to the circle that was skipped). **You should go from circle 1 to A, A to 2, 2 to B, B to 3** (point to each of the correct circles) **and so on until you reach the circle marked END** (point to the circle indicated as END).
- **You only went as far as this circle** (point to the last circle the person went to). **You should have gone to the circle marked END** (point to the circle indicated as END).
- **Please keep the pencil on the paper, and go right on to the next circle.**

If the client still cannot complete the practice sample, then take the erasure of the pencil and, with the person's hand around it, guide him or her through the trail with the erasure on the page. Then turn the pencil around with the point facing downward and say **Now you try it. Remember you begin at number 1 and draw a line from 1 to A, A to 2, 2 to B, B to 3, and so on until you reach the circle marked END** (point to each one of the circles to clarify which one is being referred to). **Ready, begin!** If the client completes the practice sample or can demonstrate adequate understanding of the procedure, then immediately go on to Part B.

Say, **Now let's try this one. On this page are both numbers and letters. Do this the same way. Begin at number 1 and draw a line from 1 to A, A to 2, 2 to B, B to 3, 3 to C, and so on in order** (point to each one of the circles as it is being referred to), **until you reach the end. Remember, first you have a number, then a letter, then a number, then**

a letter, and so on, until you reach the end. Do not skip around, but go from one circle to the next in the proper order. Draw the lines as fast as you can. Do you have any
questions? Ready, begin!

Begin timing as soon as the directions for Part A and B have been completed. Parts A
and B are scored separately with the scoring ending as soon as the client completes
each of the two parts. Scoring for each part is the total number of seconds it takes to
complete each task. Any errors should be noted and written down as an additional interpretive consideration.

Interpretation

While scores on Trail Making can generally be considered to assess abilities associated with attention, it is often difficult to determine more specifically which related
skills are involved. The clearest factor loadings indicate the importance of speed of
visual search and visuospatial sequencing (desRosiers & Kavanagh, 1987). Additional areas to consider are level of motivation, depression, poor coordination, or
conceptual confusion. Often behavioral observations and types of errors can be
quite useful in refining the meanings of low or high scores. Some errors, particularly
among head-injured patients, might reflect impulsivity in that they jump ahead to
an incorrect number/letter (Lezak, 1989b). Perseverative errors might be reflected
in difficulty alternating between numbers and letters in Trails B. Scores can be
used clinically to make inferences related to the presence of scanning and tracking
problems.

The interpretive guidelines indicate that low scores reflect that the patient has difficulty dealing with more than one stimulus at a time and maintaining a flexible mental orientation. Since flexible thinking is important in everyday activities, it suggests
the person will have difficulty working effectively in employment settings and, if
scores are sufficiently low, living independently. Particular difficulties might develop
when the person is attempting to perform tasks requiring divided attention (performing more than one task at the same time). This is likely to be particularly true for low
Trails B scores. In general, since Trails B is a more complex task, it is both more sensitive to impairment and more useful in making inferences regarding a client's level of
functioning.

Low Trail Making scores further suggest that a client has a more general difficulty
with executive functions related to initiating, inhibiting, sequencing, and monitoring his
or her behavior. Relevant behavioral observations to note would be difficulty initiating
behavior unless specifically directed to do so, impulsiveness as suggested by beginning
behavior without being requested to do so, or perseverations. The clinician should also
interview family members to determine the extent of coaching or prompting that the
client requires and the extent to which he or she can function independently.

Reitan and Wolfson (1993) provide a general classification of scores for Trails A
with the normal range being 0–39, mildly impaired 40–51, and moderate to severe
impairment being 52 or more. Normal Trails B performances range between 0 and
85, mild impairment 86–120, and moderate to severe impairment is 121 or more.
However, since Trail Making is influenced by age, education, and intelligence, most
authors recommend using scores corrected for age and education (Heaton et al.,

Table 12–8. Trails test: Time in seconds (on Parts A and B) for normal control subjects at different age levels

Percentile	15–20 Years (n = 108)		20–39 Years (n = 275)		40–49 Years (n = 138)		50–59 Years (n = 130)		60–69 Years (n = 120)		70–79 Years (n = 90)	
	A	B	A	B	A	B	A	B	A	B	A	B
90	15	26	21	45	18	30	23	55	26	62	33	79
75	19	37	24	55	23	52	29	71	30	83	54	122
50	23	47	26	65	30	78	35	80	35	95	70	180
25	30	59	34	85	38	102	57	128	63	142	98	210
10	38	70	45	98	59	126	77	162	85	174	161	350

Source: Data extrapolated from Davies (1968), based on a representative British (Liverpool) sample; Fromm-Auch & Yeudall (1983); and Kennedy (1981). From *A Compendium of Neuropsychological Tests: Administration, Norms, and Commentary* (p. 326) by Otfried Spreen and Esther Strauss. Copyright © 1991 by Oxford University Press, Inc. Reprinted by permission.

1991; Spreen & Strauss, 1991). Since age has the most influence on performance, Table 12–8 presents age-related norms developed by several authors and compiled by Spreen and Strauss (1991). This set of norms has the advantage of conveniently presenting percentiles so that low scores (especially under the 10th percentile) can be easily determined. However, education correlates .19 for Trails A and .33 for Trails B (Bornstein, 1985) so level of education should be noted and taken into account when making interpretations.

Digit Span, Arithmetic, Digit Symbol (and Symbol Search)

The Freedom from Distractibility Factor on the WAIS-R/WISC-III comprises Digit Span, Arithmetic, and sometimes Digit Symbol. Each one of these subtests requires subjects to pay careful attention to the task. Digit Symbol (and, to a lesser extent, Arithmetic) also assesses speed of information processing (as does the WISC-III Symbol Search subtest). Digit Span also is a fairly good measure of immediate auditory memory for simple information and Digit Symbol also involves ability to remember, process, and learn. As a result, they have been included as measures of these functions in the section on Learning and Memory. More extensive interpretive guidelines, including relevant neuropsychological issues, can be found in Chapter 5.

One option for extending the sensitivity of Digit Symbol is to administer the quite similar Symbol Digit Modalities Test (SDMT; Smith, 1982). However, SDMT is different in that the symbols are printed on the test form and the client must write in the numbers (the opposite occurs for Digit Symbol). In addition, SDMT includes not only a written presentation of the task but also an oral administration. The test is quite sensitive to a wide range of cerebral dysfunction, is particularly effective in discriminating depression from dementia (Smith, 1982), and is sensitive to the effects of head injuries (Ponsford & Kinsella, 1992). The reason for using it in addition to Digit Symbol is that SDMT appears to be a more sensitive indicator of cerebral dysfunction as indicated by instances in which Digit Symbol was normal, whereas SDMT was in the impaired range (Smith, 1982).

MEMORY AND LEARNING

The types and procedures of memory and learning are complex (see Bauer, Tobias, & Valenstein, 1993). Aspects of these processes might include sensory memory, short-term memory, rehearsal, long-term memory, consolidation, recall, recognition, and forgetting. In addition, memory and learning can be divided into two major subsystems: declarative memory, which refers to learning about information, objects, and events; and procedural or implicit memory, which refers to automatic, habitual responses. Each of these subdivisions has somewhat different anatomical structures. Additional useful subdivisions of memory are verbal versus spatial, automatic versus effortful, and semantic versus episodic. Studies of brain-lesioned patients indicate that memory can be further divided into extremely specific subareas based on such functions as sensory modality (verbal, tactile, auditory, etc.), type of material (verbal, motor skill, etc.), or content of information (numbers, letters, pictures, names, faces, etc.; Bauer et al., 1993; Schacter, 1990). For the practitioner, providing a truly comprehensive evaluation of memory functions is a daunting task.

Fortunately, a more limited number of memory domains can usually provide practitioners with an overview of the general intactness of memory. These include (1) the extent to which the subject can acquire and retain new material; (2) how quickly material is forgotten; (3) the extent to which competing information interferes with learning; (4) the degree of specificity or generality of the deficit; (5) the stability or fluctuation of the deficits over time (Walsh, 1994). Ideally, these domains should include measurements of both visual and verbal material.

Despite the complexity and multifactorial structure of learning and memory, a number of relatively comprehensive memory batteries have been developed. Among the oldest and certainly the most frequently used (Butler et al., 1991; Watkins et al., 1995) is the Wechsler Memory Scale (WMS; Wechsler, 1945, 1974) and, more recently, the Wechsler Memory Scale-Revised (WMS-R; Wechsler, 1987). The revised WMS (WMS-R) has 9 subtests, assesses both verbal and visual-spatial functions, includes a delayed recall component, and takes approximately 45 minutes to administer. Additional relatively comprehensive batteries include the Rivermead Behavioural Memory Test (Wilson, Cockburn, & Baddeley, 1985), Memory Assessment Scales (Williams, 1991), and the Denman Neuropsychology Memory Scale (Denman, 1984).

One important distinction is between attention versus memory and learning. In some ways, this distinction is inappropriate in that attention is a necessary prerequisite for learning to occur. A person who is easily distracted will not effectively learn and remember relevant information or events. Attention is therefore closely linked to learning. However, in other ways they do represent distinct functions. In particular, it is important to distinguish whether a person is capable of learning but is easily distracted, or whether, even under circumstances in which the person fully attends to a task, he or she still cannot learn very efficiently. This sometimes happens when clients state that they have a memory problem but, despite their symptom description, they perform learning and memory tasks quite well under the ideal circumstances that often characterize assessment procedures. In contrast, real-world situations frequently mean that they will need to exclude a number of distractions and carry on two or more activities simultaneously. Under these conditions, they might have distinct difficulties dividing their attention and therefore might not be able to learn and remember particularly effectively.

Interviewing them regarding situations in which they do versus don't remember effectively might help the practitioner to understand this issue better. In addition, their test performances would be expected to be lower on tasks that load more heavily on attention (Trails B, Arithmetic, Digit Span, serial sevens or serial threes) than those that are more pure tests of learning (Rey Auditory Verbal Learning Test, repeating paragraphs/stories, Bender Gestalt memory).

A good beginning place to assess memory is in the interview. Details regarding such basic information as personal, family, educational, and employment history can be pursued. Interviewers might request dates when the client began or finished employment or education, parent's or children's birthdays, or details related to medical history. Some of this information might be compared with more objective sources to determine its accuracy. In addition, behavioral observations such as pauses, expressions of uncertainty, or confusion might suggest difficulties with retrieval.

Current research consistently indicates that there is a mild to moderate relationship between memory impairment and depression. An extensive meta-analysis by Burt et al. (1995) found that memory impairment was most clearly associated with inpatients (vs. outpatients) and mixed bipolar and unipolar patients (vs. purely unipolar). In addition, negative affective information was more likely to be remembered accurately than material with a positive or neutral emotional tone. However, memory impairments were also present among populations of schizophrenics and mixed groups of psychiatric patients but not among either patients diagnosed with anxiety disorders or substance abuse. Interestingly, the association between memory and depression was stronger among younger than older persons. This is probably because early-onset depression is likely to be more severe and younger persons have a greater amount of memory to lose (greater "ceiling" and "floor") than older persons (narrower range between ceiling and floor). Despite these findings, it should also be stressed that the link between memory impairment and depression should not be exaggerated. In comparison with dementia, the proportion of variance accounted for by depression is relatively small.

The tests recommended in this subsection provide a useful slice of memory functions relevant to populations with CNS deficits. The WAIS-R/WISC-III subtests of Digit Span, Digit Symbol, and Information include potentially valuable information related to learning and memory. In addition, the Rey Auditory Verbal Learning test is a relatively brief, well researched, frequently used individually administered test that assesses short-term verbal memory, the ability of the client to learn new material, the extent to which interference disrupts learning, and the ability to recognize information that might have been previously learned. As the name suggests, however, it is verbally oriented. To include at least some visual spatial memory assessment, the memory version of the Bender Gestalt is recommended. If a more thorough assessment of visual spatial memory is required, clinicians might consider the Benton Visual Motor Retention Test (Benton, 1974), the three visual portions of the WMS-R (Visual Reproduction, Figural Memory, and Visual Paired Associates), or the Rey-Osterrith Complex Figure Test (Meyers & Meyers, 1996; Osterrith, 1944; Rey, 1941; Spreen & Strauss, 1991).

Rey Auditory Verbal Learning Test

The Rey Auditory Verbal Learning Test (RAVLT; Rey, 1964; Spreen & Strauss, 1991) uses a simple format in which the client is requested to remember a list of 15 unrelated words (List A) repeated over five different trials. The client is then presented with another list of 15 unrelated words (List B) which serves to potentially interfere with previous learning, followed by a request to recall as many of the words from the original list as possible. After a 30-minute delay, the client is again requested to recall words from the original list (List A), following which he or she is requested to recognize as many words as possible in a list that includes words from the original list. The result is that a wide diversity of functions can be assessed. These include short-term auditory verbal memory, rate of learning, learning strategies, retroactive and proactive interference, presence of confabulation or confusion in memory processes, retention of information, and differences between learning and retrieval. The entire procedure takes 10 to 15 minutes.

A number of variations of the RAVLT are available. Alternative lists have been developed should examiners wish to conduct follow-up evaluations and avoid the difficulties of practice effects. These lists are available for the original list (List A), interference list (List B) as well as the longer lists used for the recognition task. Although several authors have developed such lists, most of them are summarized in Lezak (1995, pp. 439, 441). In addition, Shapiro and Harrison (1990) have developed four alternative sets of lists which have been found to be equivalent to the original RAVLT. Some examiners prefer to vary the length of delayed recall and recognition tasks so that, instead of being presented 30 minutes later, a period of several hours or even days is allowed to elapse. For testing children, a simpler Children's Auditory Verbal Learning Test (CAVLT; Talley, 1990) is available that uses the same format as the RAVLT but is commercially available with a manual, scoring keys, and set of children's norms (Talley, 1990). Another commercially available variation of the RAVLT is the California Verbal Learning Test (CVLT; Delis, Kramer, Kaplan, & Ober, 1987). Instead of the RAVLT's list of unrelated words, the CVLT uses more conceptually consistent items that might be found in a typical shopping list. While scoring can be quite complex, there is a computer program to help with calculating some of the more elaborate scores. The test is well normed and has been found sensitive to such important clinical areas as the early effects of Alzheimer's disease and the differential diagnosis between various types of dementias (Massman, Delis, Butters, Dupont, & Gillin, 1992).

A potential problem with the RAVLT is that there has never been a definitive manual published on its use and interpretation. As a result, different sets of instructions and scoring procedures have been developed and used by different authors. Some authors recommend a 20-minute delay, whereas others recommend a 30-minute delay. The verbatim instructions also vary between authors and several different sets of norms have been developed. Options for scoring also vary considerably. There has been no systematic research to determine if these variations in format, instructions, and scoring make a difference in terms of such clinically relevant outcomes as level of impairment or diagnosis. It is hoped that a clear, well-developed RAVLT manual will be developed, which will become the standard for research and clinical use.

Reliability and Validity

Test-retest reliability of the RAVLT over a one-year interval was a somewhat moderate .55 (Snow, Tierney, Zorzitto, Fisher, & Reid, 1988). The highest reliability was .70 for the total number of words recalled for the five trials of List A. In contrast, the lowest reliability was .38 for recall of List B (Snow et al., 1988). The importance of using alternate forms is highlighted by the finding that practice effects for the same form over a 6- to 12-month retesting period were small but significant (1–2 words per trial; Crawford, Stewart, & Moore, 1989; Lezak, 1982). In contrast, no differences were found when alternate forms were used (Crawford et al., 1989).

Consistent with expectations, patients with left hemisphere damage have been found to have lower performances than those with damage to the right hemisphere (Ivnik, Sharbrough, & Laws, 1988; Miceli, Caltagirone, Gainotti, Masullo, & Silveri, 1981). In addition, the RAVLT has been found to be sensitive to the effects of different memory disorders. Heavy drinkers scored poorly on the RAVLT even if they did not have signs of neurologically related disease (Jackson, Fox, Waugh, & Tuck, 1987). As would be expected, Korsakoff's patients did consistently poorly on each of the five trials but, when presented with a recognition format after each of the first five trials, their performances increased (Janowsky, Shimamura, & Squire, 1989). In a similar administration format, frontal lobe patients had poor recall over the five trials of List A, but when requested to recognize which words had been on the list using a recognition list, their performances were near normal (Janowsky et al., 1989). This suggests that their difficulties were mainly due to retrieving, organizing, and keeping track of the answers related to any potentially learned material rather than to their not having learned it. Finally, patients in the early stages of Alzheimer's disease showed a slow learning curve in which they only recalled an average of 6 of the 15 words following the fifth trial of List A (Mitrushina, Satz, & Van Gorp, 1989). They also had far more words intruding between the A and B Lists than other diagnostic groups (Bigler, Rosa, Schultz, Hall, & Harris, 1989; Mitrushina et al., 1989). When the disease progressed to a moderate level, the number of words recalled for the fifth trial dropped to approximately 5 and for severe cases only an average of 2.6 words were recalled (Tierney et al., 1994).

Further support comes from correlations ranging between .50 to .65 between RAVLT factor groupings and other learning instruments (MaCartney-Filgate & Vriezen, 1988). A factor analytic study with normals indicated that the tests measured the functions of acquisition, storage, and retrieval (Vakil & Blachstein, 1993).

Administration

Word lists and a scoring format can be found in Appendix P. The following set of instructions are derived from guidelines and verbatim instructions provided primarily by Lezak (1983, 1995, pp. 438–440) and, to a lesser extent by Spreen and Strauss (1991, pp. 150–151). The reliance on Lezak's instructions is emphasized since most research studies specify that they have relied on her guidelines. For Trial 1, examiners should state:

> **I am going to read a list of words. Listen carefully, for when I stop, you are to repeat back as many words as you can remember. It doesn't matter in what order you repeat them. Just try to remember as many words as you can.**

Each word in List A should be read with a one-second interval between the words. No feedback should be given regarding whether or not they have given correct responses, repeated words, or included words not on the list. However, clients can be encouraged for their efforts on this, as well as additional trials. The order in which the words are recalled can be indicated by numbering them on the scoring sheet.

Once the client indicates that he or she is unable to think of additional words, Trial 2 for List A can be given with the following instructions:

> **Now I am going to read the same list again, and once again, when I stop, I want you to tell me as many words as you can remember, *including words you said the first time*. It doesn't matter in what order you say them. Just say as many words as you can remember, whether or not you said them before.**

Trials 3–5 are also given again using the words from List A and following the preceding instructions. Again a one-second interval between each word should be provided. Each of these trials should only be initiated after the client has indicated he or she cannot recall any words from the list that has just been read.

After completing Trial 5 for List A, the examiner should then begin Trial 6 (and using List B) by saying:

> **Now I am going to read a second list of words. This time, again, you are to say back as many words of this second list as you can remember. Again, the order in which you say the words does not matter. Just try to remember as many as you can.**

Immediately after the client indicates being unable to recall additional words from List B, begin Trial 7 by requesting that he or she recall as many words as possible from the previous list (List A). Note that List A is not read to the person prior to this request.

After an interval of 30 minutes, begin Trial 8 by requesting the client to repeat as many words as possible from the original list of words (List A). Again, the list should not be read to the person. Directly after the client indicates being unable to think of additional words, begin Trial 9 by providing them with the recognition list of 50 words listed at the bottom of Appendix P. This list contains all the words in both Lists A and B (indicated as either A or B). In addition, words that are semantically similar to words on Lists A or B (coded as SA or SB respectively) are included plus words that are phonemically similar to words on lists A and B (coded as PA and PB respectively). In some cases, words are both semantically and phonemically similar and are indicated as either SPA or SPB.

Any incorrect responses can be coded using the following designations: R for words that are repeated, RC if repeated but then self-corrected, RQ if the client has repeated the word but indicates being unsure if this has occurred or not, and E for words that are not on the list. This coding can provide clinicians with a quick review of the types of errors made.

A wide number of different scoring categories have been developed (see Geffen, Moar, O'Hanlon, Clark, & Geffen, 1990; Ivnik et al., 1990). To keep the scoring and interpretation procedures manageable, the following list describes the most useful and frequently used scores:

1. *Immediate Memory.* Score for Trial 1; based on the total number of words correctly recalled from word List A immediately following the first trial (scoring for the next four trials is also based on the total number of words correctly recalled after being presented with word List A on successive occasions).

2. *Best Learning.* Score for Trial 5; based on the total number of words correctly recalled from word List A immediately following the fifth trial.

3. *Total Learning.* Sum of the total number of words correctly recalled for Trials 1–5.

4. *Proactive Interference.* Score for Trial 6; based on the total number of words correctly recalled from List B immediately following the sixth trial.

5. *Retroactive Interference.* Score for Trial 7; based on the total number of words correctly recalled from List A (directly following Trial 6 and without having word List A repeated).

6. *Delayed Recall.* Score for Trial 8; based on the total number of words correctly recalled following a 30-minute delay and without having word List A repeated.

7. *Recognition.* Score for Trial 9; based on the total number of words correctly recalled when presented with the recognition list.

Norms for each of the seven scoring categories are included in Appendix Q. However, clinicians skilled in the use of the RAVLT can increase the variety of information by noting such additional features as the number and types of words that intrude between Lists A and B or assessing the relative extent to which words at the beginning of a list are more likely to be recalled than those at the end of a list (primacy versus recency effect).

Interpretation

Since there are a number of different scoring categories, it is difficult to easily summarize normative results. One representative norm is that for *immediate memory*; healthy adult males aged 16 to 70+ correctly recalled between 6.9 and 3.6 words depending on their age grouping. This same group correctly recalled between 12.5 and 8.2 words for the *best learning* trial (total number of words recalled for Trial 5 of List A), and between 11.2 and 6.2 words were recalled for *retroactive interference* (total number of words correctly recalled from List A following the administration of the Interference Trial for List B). While there is some variation between different normative groups, the preceding values are roughly similar to other norms provided by different authors (Geffen et al., 1991; Ivnik et al., 1990; Lezak, 1995; Spreen & Strauss, 1991; Vakil & Blachstein, 1993). To provide a contrast, moderately impaired Alzheimer's disease patients only recalled 2.7 ($SD = 2.1$) words for *immediate recall,* 5.3 ($SD = 3.4$) words for *best learning,* and 1.8 ($SD = 3.0$) words for *retroactive interference* (Tierney et al., 1994).

Normative studies have found RAVLT performance gradually declines with age, with a more pronounced decline after the age of 70 (Geffen et al., 1990; Savage & Gouvier, 1992). In addition, females score better than males on many of the RAVLT scoring categories. As a result, any interpretative procedures should use age- and gender-related norms. In contrast, education and intelligence have been found to have relatively little influence on RAVLT performance (Ryan, Rosenberg, & Mittenbery, 1984; Savage & Gouvier, 1992; Weins, McMinn, & Crossen, 1988) and are thus less important considerations.

Hypotheses related to client functioning can be derived from considering level of performance on the different scoring categories listed in Appendix Q. For example, immediate or short-term memory can be assessed by noting scores on the *immediate memory* scoring category. Similarly, the degree to which new learning interferes with past learning can be inferred by noting the level of performance on the scoring category for *retroactive interference*. However, practitioners must use caution when making these inferences. Although the RAVLT has been successful in both identifying patients with memory disorders and even distinguishing between these disorders, insufficient validity studies have been done to investigate the validity of more specific interpretations. For example, it is tempting to interpret low scores on Trial 7 as indicating that the person is particularly susceptible to retroactive interference. However, this interpretation has not been systematically investigated. In addition, the reliability of some of the scores, particularly recall for List B, is quite low (Snow et al., 1988). This means that interpretations based on scores derived from recall of List B (Trial 6/Proactive Interference) should be made with considerable caution.

A client's learning curve is a useful index. Normal persons under the age of 70 will usually remember between 6 to 8 words on Trial 1 and this slowly increases to between 12 and 14 words for the final trial (Trial 5). In contrast, if little or no learning has occurred, few additional words will be recalled by Trial 5. Moderately impaired Alzheimer's and Parkinson patients recall an average of 2.7 and 2.9 words for Trial 1, and their performances increased only to an average of 5.3 words each by Trial 5 (Tierney et al., 1994). Another potentially useful pattern is that sometimes brain-damaged patients can do as well as normal healthy persons on the first trial but have difficulty increasing their recall much beyond this original performance. A further pattern is that normal persons typically show a primacy effect in which they recall more words from the first part of the list as well as a recency effect in which they recall more words from the end of the list (those words heard most recently). Clients with memory impairments who are struggling with the material are more likely to have a recency effect without a corresponding primacy effect.

A useful comparison is to note the difference in performance between the first recall for List A (Trial 1; *immediate memory*) and the (first) recall for List B (Trial 6; *proactive interference*). Usually the number of words recalled for Trial 6 will only be about one word less than for Trial 1. If Trial 6 is lower than Trial 1 by two to three words or more, it suggests that the person has difficulty "freeing up" abilities to attend to new learning (proactive interference). This hypothesis is further strengthened if words from List A "intrude" into the words recalled from List B (as requested on Trial 6).

One qualitative difference between patients with Alzheimer's disease versus those with depression is a greater number of intrusions between lists of words for the Alzheimer's patients (Burt et al., 1995; Ober, Koss, Friedland, & Delis, 1985). This represents a general trend among Alzheimer's patients to be liberal in their responses resulting in more intrusion errors as well as more false positives on recognition type tasks (Gainotti & Marra, 1994). In contrast, depressed patients tend to be conservative in their responses. A further distinction is that depressed patients tend to do relatively poorly on immediate memory tasks but are able to consolidate the information such that their delayed recall is relatively good. In contrast, Alzheimer's patients do more poorly on delayed than on immediate recognition indicating primary difficulties in consolidating and retaining the information (Burt et al., 1995). Further differences between these two groups are that depressed persons have more variable performances, whereas Alzheimer's patients are more consistent in performance; and the level of concentration among depressed persons is adequate, whereas it is quite likely to be deficient among Alzheimer's patients (see desRosiers, 1992).

Similar to the difficulty with intrusions between Lists A and B, interference due to the new task of having to learn List B (in Trial 6) can be noted by comparing the difference between performance on Trial 7 (recall of the previously learned List A as measured by score on *retroactive interference*) and performance on Trial 5 (recall of List A after five trials as measured on score for *best learning*). Usually the number of words recalled on Trial 7 will be approximately one word less for a normal performance. A lowering of two to four words or more suggests that the task of learning List B has interfered with the previously learned List A.

One way to organize patterns of scores is to group them around the following RAVLT memory factors of acquisition, storage, and retrieval (Vakil & Blachstein, 1993):

- Acquisition:
  Immediate memory.
  Proactive interference.
- Retrieval:
  Delayed recall.
  Retroactive interference.
  Best learning.
- Storage.
- Recognition.

The preceding clustering should provide a more theoretically and psychometrically sound analysis of memory than merely using individual scoring categories. In addition, it can help specify the various strengths and weaknesses of a particular client's memory functions. For example, the previous information on depression and memory indicates that depressed patients would be slow to acquire the information since their attention and motivation is typically poor. In contrast, Alzheimer's patients would also have some difficulties in acquiring the information, but their storage would be particularly poor in that they would make a considerable number of errors in recognizing previous words from the different lists.

Digit Span, Digit Symbol, Information

An important source of memory functions can be found throughout various sections of the WAIS-R/WISC-III. Digit Span involves the assessment of both attention (and thus its inclusion in the "Mental Activities" section) and short-term memory. Digit Symbol similarly requires intact attention and short-term memory, but also requires the person to effectively rote-learn simple nonverbal material. In contrast to the short-term emphasis of Digit Span and Digit Symbol, Information allows an examiner to assess the extent of remote memory. It is usually difficult, however, to distinguish between lack of knowledge and retrieval difficulties. One way to assess this is to note whether the client's level of knowledge is clearly discrepant with his or her level of education (e.g., a person with a university education who doesn't know the capital of a major country). Another strategy is based on the relative ease by which material can be recognized as opposed to recalled. Thus, clients might be presented with multiple-choice questions (available as part of the WAIS-RNI; Kaplan et al., 1991) in which a greater recognition result suggests that they once knew the material but had a difficult time retrieving it during the standard recall instructions. The hypothesis that retrieval is a difficulty for a client should be supported by a corresponding relatively low score on the RAVLT Retrieval Factor (composed of scores on Delayed Recall, Retroactive Interference, and Best Learning).

Bender Gestalt (Memory Administration)

A very general idea of visual memory can be obtained by requesting the client to draw as many of the Bender Gestalt designs as possible directly after completing the last Bender Gestalt design with the standard procedure (see discussion, p. 551). A more detailed assessment of visual memory can also be obtained through additional more extensive procedures (visual memory portions of the Wechsler Memory Scale-Revised, Rey-Osterrith Complex Figure, Benton Visual Motor Retention).

VERBAL FUNCTIONS AND ACADEMIC SKILLS

Disturbances of verbal functions are frequently associated with brain damage, particularly when the damage is to the left hemisphere. As a result, any review of neuropsychological functions needs to assess verbal functions as well as the academic skills that are frequently associated with these verbal abilities. The most common disturbances are the aphasias (impaired speech, writing, or understanding spoken or written language) and problems with speech production. These disorders can involve extremely diverse difficulties including poor articulation, loss of verbal fluency, word-finding difficulty, poor repetition of words or sentences, loss of grammar and syntax, misspoken words (paraphasias), poor auditory comprehension, reading difficulties, and impaired writing (Goodglass & Kaplan, 1983).

As a result of the variety of these disorders, a neuropsychological screening and initial review as recommended in this chapter can only assess a relatively small number of them. For a full assessment of aphasic and related disorders, several comprehensive batteries are available, including the Boston Diagnostic Aphasia Examination (Goodglass & Kaplan, 1983), Communicative Abilities in Daily Living (Holland, 1980), and the Multilingual Aphasia Examination (Benton & Hamsher, 1989). In contrast to these formal, comprehensive batteries, Lezak (1995) recommends an informal and general clinical review of six major functions as follows:

1. *Spontaneous Speech.* Observe how clients initiate, articulate, and organize their speech.
2. *Speech Repetition.* Ask clients to repeat words, phrases, and sentences. In particular, this might include repeating difficult words such as "Massachusetts" or "Methodist Episcopal" (see Reitan & Wolfson's, 1993, Aphasia Screening Test) to assess for disorders of articulation.
3. *Speech Comprehension.* Request that they answer simple questions (e.g., is a ball square?) or obey simple commands (e.g., point to specific objects, put their hand on their chin).

4. *Naming*. Ask clients to name common objects, colors, letters, and actions.

5. *Reading*. Have clients read aloud; for comprehension, have them explain what they have read.

6. *Writing*. Request that the subject copy, write to dictation, and compose a sentence.

Choosing which tasks to give can be based on the hypotheses derived from other information related to the client (symptom checklist, medical history, etc.). The relative difficulty of the tasks can similarly be tailored to additional information regarding client symptoms and behaviors. For example, it would be neither necessary nor appropriate to request that a client with mild deficits obey simple commands or name common objects.

The following recommended tests emphasize five of the Wechlser scales that load most strongly on verbal and academic abilities: Information, Comprehension, Similarities, Vocabulary, Arithmetic. Each of these contributes somewhat different types of information (see discussions in Chapter 5). The Controlled Oral Word Association test (COWA; Benton & Hamsher, 1989; Spreen & Strauss, 1991) was selected since word fluency and word finding are frequent complaints among brain-damaged populations (Benson, 1993). Available evidence indicates that the COWA can effectively identify these complaints (Benton, 1968; Murdoch, Chenery, Wilks, & Boyle, 1987; Parks et al., 1988). In addition, it does not require any equipment, is easily administered, short, frequently used, and has good psychometric properties including excellent normative data (see Benton & Hamsher, 1983; Lezak, 1995; Spreen & Strauss, 1991).

The Boston Naming Test has similar assets and might also be considered for screening and assessment. Somewhat similar to the COWA, it assesses disturbances in word finding and word naming. Clients are requested to look at pictures of objects and provide their names (tree, abacus, etc.). Research has indicated that it can effectively identify word naming and finding difficulties (Margolin, Pate, Friedrich, & Elia, 1990; Morris et al., 1989; Spreen & Strauss, 1991; Storandt et al., 1986) and, due to its sensitivity to the early effects of dementia, a shortened version has been included in the CERAD battery (Morris et al., 1989). Clinically, naming difficulties might be noted during the course of an interview or somewhat more formally by noting difficulties in naming different objects in Picture Completion. These observations might suggest a more thorough assessment with the Boston Naming Test.

The most frequently used educational achievement battery in clinical neuropsychology (Butler et al., 1991) is the Wide Range Achievement Test, which is now available in its third edition (WRAT-III; Jastak & Wilkinson, 1994). The battery is easy to administer, covers a wide range of ages (12–75 years), and provides scores for Spelling, Reading, and Arithmetic. These can each be conveniently portrayed as school grade equivalents, standard scores, or percentiles. However, it assesses a fairly narrow range of abilities within these domains and thus should only be used as a crude screening instrument.

Controlled Oral Word Association

The Controlled Oral Word Association test (COWA; Benton & Hamsher, 1989; Spreen & Strauss, 1991) simply requests that a client say as many words as possible beginning with a certain letter and within a certain time limit. The COWA has also been variously referred to as Word Fluency or, more frequently, simply the FAS Test since the letters F, A, and S are the ones which are most commonly used. A similar and much earlier version was developed by Thurstone (1938), who used written word production, and Newcomb (1969), who recommended alternating between colors and birds. It has also been included in the much longer Neurosensory Center Comprehensive Examination for Aphasia (Spreen & Benton, 1977) as well as the Iowa Screening Battery for Mental Decline (Eslinger, Damasio, & Benton, 1984) and the Multilingual Aphasia Examination (Benton & Hamsher, 1989).

The skills involved are that the client must both freely produce words, yet also monitor their previous responses. A factor analysis indicated that it loaded most strongly (.62) on "abstract mental operations" which makes it similar to such tasks as oral spelling, mental calculations, and digit span type tests (Snow et al., 1988). Somewhat differently, Kavanagh (1987) found that it loaded primarily on a "verbal knowledge" factor thereby making it closer to tests such as Vocabulary and those that contribute to a person's overall Verbal IQ.

Reliability and Validity

Test-retest reliability for adults over a 19–42 day retesting interval was .88 (desRosiers & Kavanagh, 1987), whereas this dropped to .70 for older adults with a much longer retesting interval of one year (Snow et al., 1988). Due to the clarity of scoring (number of words recalled), interscorer reliability was almost perfect.

COWA scores are sensitive to a variety of CNS impairments, and the patterns of performance conform to what is known regarding brain function. Lesions to the frontal (especially left) lobes have been found to most noticeably produce word fluency difficulties that are reflected in lower COWA performance (Miceli et al., 1981; Perret, 1974). The lowest overall word fluency scores have been with bilateral frontal lesions (Benton, 1968). Dementing patients have also shown lowerings in word fluency (Murdoch et al., 1987) although COWA scores have not been able to effectively differentiate between patients with dementia and those who are elderly and depressed (Hart, Kwentus, Taylor, & Hamer, 1988). In addition, patients with right hemisphere damage (excluding right frontal) have not been found to be impaired on COWA (Cavalli, De Renzi, Faglioni, & Vitale, 1981).

Administration

Instructions provided by Spreen and Strauss (1991) are as follows:

> **I will say a letter of the alphabet. Then I want you to give me as many words that begin with that letter as quickly as you can. For instance, if I say "B," you might give me "bad," "battle," "bed." I do not want you to use words that are proper names such as "Boston," "Bob," or "Brylcreem." Also, do not use the same word again with a different ending such as "eat" and "eating." Any questions?** (pause) **Begin when I say the letter. The first letter is "F." Go ahead.**

As soon as the instructions have been given, the examiner should begin timing. One minute should be allowed for each of the different trials for the letters F, A, and S.

Indicate when each of the three trials is completed by saying **Fine** or **Good.** If, after initially producing only a few words, the client becomes silent, encourage the person to continue trying to produce additional words. This might require providing a brief synopsis of the instructions. Write down all words in the order in which they were produced. The score is the sum of all admissible words across the three trials. Inadmissible words (i.e., proper nouns, wrong words, repetitions) should not be counted for the final score.

Interpretation

While scoring COWA is straightforward, performance is considerably influenced by education, age, and, to a lesser extent, gender. Specialized norms need to be consulted (see Appendix R) and interpretations made taking these demographics into account.

High scores (relative to age and education) suggest that the person has good verbal knowledge (check Vocabulary and Similarities) and is competent in dealing with abstract mental operations (check Arithmetic and Digit Span). Low scores suggest the person has difficulties in these areas. However, the meaning of a low score can be refined by considering the patterns of other test scores along with relevant behavioral observations. If the client demonstrates difficulties with naming objects such as struggling with some of the visual stimuli on Picture Completion, then word finding and naming (agnosia) might be the primary impairment. It is possible for verbal fluency difficulties and visual naming deficits to occur separately (Benson, 1993). On the other hand, a client who has low scores on tests of attention (Arithmetic, Digit Span, Trail Making, and possibly Digit Symbol) may be having difficulties with distractibility and may be unable to maintain a focus on the task. Alternatively, mental inflexibility might be the major reason for lowered performance on these tests. This might be assessed by noting the presence of any perseverations or lack of flexibility as noted on poor performances with Trails B.

Vocabulary, Information, Comprehension, Similarities, Arithmetic

Both Vocabulary and Information are heavily dependent on past learning, require good verbal abilities, and are relatively resistant to deterioration (Lezak, 1995). Thus they provide good measures of an individual's general verbal abilities. In addition, both these subtests are associated with activation of the left temporal lobe (Chase et al., 1984). Qualitative responses, especially on Vocabulary, can be quite useful and include clang responses, idiosyncratic associations, or confabulations. Comprehension measures a person's common sense, judgment, and practical reasoning. As such, it is not as dependent on past education as Vocabulary and Information. Since the questions are open-ended and require the client to exercise judgment, the qualitative responses to the different items can be quite useful in understanding the client's reasoning processes. In contrast to the more crystallized abilities of Vocabulary and Information, Similarities is more of a fluid task and is also more sensitive to left hemisphere lesions (Warrington, James, & Maciejewski, 1986), especially to the left frontal (Rzechorzek, 1979) and bilateral frontal regions (Rao, 1990). It is also quite sensitive to the presence and progression of dementia (Hart, Kwentus, Taylor, & Hamer, 1988).

Whereas the above Wechsler subtests primarily assess verbal abilities, Arithmetic is somewhat different in that it also has a very strong memory and attentional component as well as mathematical and verbal components. Thus it comprises a number of different interacting abilities. Low scores do not necessarily mean that the client has low mathematical abilities, especially if other tasks loading heavily on attention and concentration are also low. However, if a person's verbal and attentional abilities are intact, then scores are much more likely to indicate the level of a person's mathematical abilities based partially on his or her past academic background. More detailed discussions of each of the preceding subtests can be found in Chapter 5.

TESTS OF MOTOR ABILITY

Measurements of motor abilities can frequently be used to assess for subtle motor impairment as well as make inferences regarding lateralization of lesions. The expected difference is that the dominant hand will be 10% stronger and faster than the nondominant hand. Differences of 20% or more have frequently been used to infer lesions contralateral to the side of weakness/slowing (Reitan & Wolfson, 1993). While these inferences tend to hold true when several different measures are used (Bornstein, 1986; Thompson, Heaton, Mathews, & Grant, 1987), measurements by a single test need to be treated with caution. Equal levels of dexterity as measured by finger-tapping speed occur relatively frequently among normal populations. Conversely, differences between finger-tapping speeds occur relatively frequently such that, if a 20% discrepancy is used for finger-tapping speed among left-handed persons, then 18% are misclassified as having lateralized hemisphere dysfunction (Thompson et al., 1987). Localization (including lateralization) also needs to be treated cautiously due to the variety of locations that might produce right-left motor discrepancies. Since a test such as finger tapping requires planning and initiation of behavior (executive functions), it might be impaired due to anterior frontal or even subcortical involvement. Alternatively, impairment might be due to damage in the motor strip or perhaps to coordinative dysfunction from cerebellar damage. Thus, the following test(s) should be used for hypothesis generation rather than diagnosis.

Finger Tapping Test

The Finger Tapping Test (FTT) is an essential component of the Halstead Reitan Neuropsychological Test Battery (Reitan & Wolfson, 1993). It was originally referred to as the Finger Oscillation Test and, in some sources, is still referred to by that name. While some coordination is required, it is primarily a test of simple motor speed. Clients are requested to initially tap their dominant index finger for five consecutive 10-second trials. The procedure is then repeated for their nondominant index finger. Their performances are measured on a recording device (available from Reitan Neuropsychology Laboratory, Lafayette Instruments, or Western Psychological Services). The score is simply their average number of taps in a 10-second interval. The two average scores (for dominant and nondominant fingers/hands) are compared with one another to see if there are wide discrepancies; normative comparisons can also be made.

Reliability and Validity

Test-retest reliability for normal controls over a 10-week interval was quite high (male $r = .94$, female $r = .86$; Gill et al., 1986). A longer retesting interval of 6 months for another group of normals still revealed relatively good reliabilities of .71 for the dominant hand and .76 for the nondominant hand (Ruff & Parker, 1993). A mixture of clinical samples (vascular disease, head trauma, alcoholics, schizophrenics) for a mean 2-year retesting interval similarly showed good reliabilities ranging between .64 and .87 (Goldstein & Watson, 1989).

One of the main rationales for the FTT is that it should reflect CNS dysfunction contralateral to the finger with slowed tapping speed. This has been generally supported (Brown et al., 1989; Finlayson & Reitan, 1980; Reitan & Wolfson, 1993; Ross et al., 1990). However, lateralized damage might still occur without being reflected in lowered speed, particularly if the damage is in the posterior cortex (Reitan & Wolfson, 1993).

Administration

Clients are instructed to tap as rapidly as they can with their index finger on a small lever. Recording begins with their dominant finger/hand for a 10-second trial. This is repeated over five trials with a mandatory rest of two to three minutes after the third trial. This procedure is then repeated for their nondominant hand. Never alternate trials between dominant and nondominant hands; all five trails should be given first for the dominant, and then for the nondominant hand. The following instructions adapted from Reitan and Wolfson (1993, p. 232) should be given to the client:

> **Now we are going to do a test to see how fast you can tap. We will use this little key here** (indicate the key to the client) **and I want you to tap just as fast as you can, using the forefinger of your right** (or left, depending on which is dominant) **hand.**
>
>   **When you tap, be sure to use a finger movement; do not move your whole hand or arm. When you tap this key, you will have to remember to let the key come all the way up and click each time, or else the number on the dial won't change.** (Demonstrate how the lever works and tap it for five or six seconds.)
>
>   **Now you move the board to a comfortable position for your hand and try it for practice.**
>
>   After a brief period of practice, say:
>   **That was fine. Remember to tap as rapidly as you possibly can.**
>   Make sure that the client understands the instructions and then say:
>   **Do you have any questions? . . . All right. Ready—Go!** At the end of the 10-second trial say, **Stop!** Then repeat this procedure for another four trials. After the client has completed the procedures with the dominant hand, repeat for the nondominant hand.

Several additional considerations are relevant. First, examiners must take care to start the stopwatch as soon as the client begins tapping. Similarly, the timing must cease as soon as the 10-second interval is finished. If clients continue to tap after the examiner says "stop," then the number of taps should be noted and subtracted from their score. Second, be sure that only the index finger does the tapping. Any extraneous movements of the hand or arms should be discouraged. This can be best accomplished by instructing the client to keep the heel of the hand on the base of the tapping board or table.

Interpretation

Averaged scores for dominant and nondominant hands can be interpreted using two different approaches. The first is to assess the discrepancy between performance on the dominant versus nondominant hands. Usually, there is a 10% faster performance for the dominant as opposed to the nondominant hand. If the discrepancy appears considerably wider than expected, then brain damage contralateral to the lowered hand is suspected. Reitan and Wolfson (1993, p. 387) provide the following categories based on dividing the nondominant hand by the dominant hand and subtracting this from 1.0:

.12 (or less)–.18   normal
.19–.26   mild to moderate impairment
.27 (or more)   severe impairment

Diffuse impairment may cause a general lowering in both hands that would make a lateralized effect unlikely to occur. This may mean that it would be most appropriate to note the relative degree of lowering without reference to lateralized differences. To interpret this second strategy, Bornstein, Paniak, and O'Brien (1987) recommend the following cutoff scores for impaired performances:

males   dominant hand ≤ 32
          nondominant hand ≤ 31
females   dominant hand ≤ 26
          nondominant hand ≤ 21

A caution relevant to both approaches is that some clients will have developed considerable abilities on one side of the body (e.g., musicians who have well-developed nondominant hand strength and coordination) and examiners should take this into account in their interpretations.

EXECUTIVE FUNCTIONS

Executive functions involve a person's ability to effectively regulate and direct self-behavior. These functions can be further subdivided into volition, planning, purposive action, and effective performance (Lezak, 1995). For example, patients experiencing significant executive impairments might exist in a semivegetative state in which they rarely initiate much activity although other cognitive abilities might be quite intact. Other patients with executive difficulty may have little awareness of their impact on others and thus will be unable to effectively direct or regulate their social behavior. While frontal lobe damage is most typically implicated with executive deficits, damage to subcortical, especially thalamic regions or the more diffuse damage caused by anoxia or organic solvents can also produce executive impairment.

Despite the importance of executive abilities, they can be overlooked during formal psychological assessment. This is partially because executive functions can be impaired even though other cognitive functions appear quite intact. As a result, a clinician might look at cognitive test scores such as a composite IQ and erroneously conclude that a patient has made a good or even full recovery. There are even anecdotal reports of patients' IQs actually increasing after frontal lobe damage even though they became quite impaired due to a loss of executive abilities. A further reason for failure to assess executive functions is that no tests are specifically designed to accomplish this purpose. Even tests that have claimed to assess frontal abilities, such as the Austin Mazes, have been questioned regarding their ability to accurately perform this task (Bowden & Smith, 1994). Finally, since much formal assessment is a structured situation in which the examiner directs the patient to do certain things, the patient's ability to self-initiate might be overlooked. This presents examiners with the dilemma that they must "structure" an unstructured situation in which patients can demonstrate the extent, style, and manner they would initiate, develop, plan, and monitor their own behavior. A final assessment issue is that frequently depression can produce some of the same behaviors (i.e., apathy, flat affect, lack of direction) that occur with executive loss stemming from brain damage. A clinician might therefore erroneously conclude that the executive dysfunctions were the result of depression rather than brain damage (or vice versa).

Because of these concerns, strategies to assess executive functions are through various combinations of interview, behavioral observations, and brief informal clinical tests (see Hall & Sbordone, 1993). Interviews with patients might focus on their articulation of future goals along with their descriptions of recreational activities. Typically, patients with executive difficulties will provide little detail about these areas. If they do provide detail, it may be primarily based on reciting their goals and activities prior to the injury. This means that interviewers will need to establish what their present activities and goals are and, in particular, what they have done recently to pursue these goals. Interviewers might also establish the extent to which they can realistically pursue these goals, anticipate and plan relevant activities, develop alternative plans, and give direction to actually putting these plans into action. Since poor executive functions will frequently be accompanied by lack of awareness, it might be essential to interview family members who have had a chance to observe the patient on a daily basis. Thus the client's descriptions can be compared with more objective external descriptions.

Within the actual examination itself, various types of behavior can provide information. Does the patient initiate and direct any activity or does he or she tend to be relatively passive? Are there unusual social behaviors (e.g., poor grooming, discussion of irrelevant tangents, inappropriate jokes) that suggest poor awareness of his or her social impact? The examiner must determine whether such behaviors developed postinjury or were premorbid characteristics. Planning abilities might be estimated based on how well such patients organize their human figure drawings, blocks on Block Design, Bender Gestalt drawings, or their stories on the TAT. Perseverations suggest poor mental flexibility and difficulty monitoring their behavior and are a component of executive functions; the patient may make too many dots on the Bender Gestalt, have difficulty making mental shifts on Trails B, or find it difficult to understand changes in test stimuli (e.g., slow to understand the requirements of the RAVLT). Since poor executive functions also include difficulty attending to stimuli while simultaneously performing other tasks, low scores on the Wechsler Freedom from Distractibility factor or Bannatyne's Sequencing might also reflect poor executive abilities (Wielkiewicz, 1990).

A number of informal clinical tests might also help to determine possible executive impairments. For example, the patient might be requested to continue the pattern of a drawing that has various repetitive but alternating small shapes (three circles, two squares, one triangle and then to repeat this sequence several times; see Goldberg & Bilder, 1987). A similar "chain of command" type test would be to have the patient tap the desk with the fist, then tap it with the palm, and then repeat this pattern several times. A slightly more complicated task might be as follows: the examiner taps his or her foot once, then the patient taps a foot twice. Alternatively, the examiner may tap a foot twice, while then the patient is instructed to tap once (see Lezak, 1995). None of these procedures have formal scoring; instead the examiner must determine, based on observation, whether or not the patient had relative difficulty with all or any of the activities. Although no single strategy in this section will be sufficient to identify executive impairments, collectively they will help to ensure that this critical domain of functioning is included in a client's assessment.

EMOTIONAL STATUS AND LEVEL OF ADJUSTMENT

While measures of cognitive and behavioral abilities are important, a client's emotional status and relative level of adjustment are also of considerable relevance (Knight & Godfrey, 1996). This information is useful for at least three types of situations. First, clinicians might be trying to decide whether abnormal cognitive test results are due primarily to CNS involvement or emotional factors. If emotional functioning was relatively normal, but the individual still had cognitive deficits, this more strongly implicates CNS involvement. On the other hand, if a client is quite depressed, then the depression, not organic factors, might be the primary reason for a symptom such as slowed information processing. Second, a clinician might need to know the extent to which emotional reactions are complicating organic impairment. A client with organically based confusion is likely to have this further exacerbated by such reactions as depression. Third, predictions often need to be made related to a person's overall level of functioning. While level of cognitive deficit is useful, personality and emotional factors have often been found to be better predictors of psychosocial adjustment and rehabilitation outcome (Fordyce, Roueche, & Prigatano, 1983; Heaton et al., 1978).

A wide variety of emotional and personality domains are relevant to neuropsychological impairment. On one end of the spectrum are the negative reactions of anxiety, depression, irritability, emotional lability, suspiciousness, and aggression. At the opposite end are euphoria, emotional flatness, placidity, and naivete (Prigatano, 1987). Other important areas might be level of self-awareness, interpersonal insensitivity, behavioral rigidity, empathy, and self-centeredness. A common cluster of changes associated with frontal lobe damage is limited self-awareness, impulsivity, concreteness, and poor social awareness (Stuss et al., 1992). The presence or absence of each of these symptoms will have importance for diagnosis, treatment planning, short- and long-range predictions, and feedback to the client and their families.

The assessment of personality and adjustment can be accomplished through a variety of different strategies. The interview might include contrasting the client's descriptions of difficulties with those provided by friends and family. This can help to determine whether and the extent to which a client overestimates or denies any deficits (Prigatano, 1992). This also provides an opportunity to obtain descriptions of a client's premorbid characteristics as well as the extent and quality of the person's social supports. Rating instruments designed for use specifically with neuropsychological populations include *Patient Competency Rating* (Prigatano, 1986), *Neurobehavioral Rating Scale* (Levin et al., 1987), and the *Neuropsychology Behavior and Affect Profile* (Nelson et al., 1989). In addition, traditional scales including the MMPI/MMPI-2 and BDI have been extensively used. The MMPI/MMPI-2 in particular has the advantage that it provides an index of both stable or trait type characteristics (social nonconformity, shyness) along with more changeable symptom features (depression, anxiety).

The MMPI/MMPI-2/MMPI-A and Neuropsychological Impairment

Possible roles for the MMPI/MMPI-2/MMPI-A among neuropsychologically impaired populations are to differentiate between persons who are organically versus nonorganically impaired and to provide information related to persons with known organic complaints. Within differential diagnosis, the MMPI/MMPI-2 can often be effectively used to exclude/include complicating psychiatric disturbances. For example, a client who presents with a variety of subtle neurological signs but also has a pronounced conversion V on the MMPI/MMPI-2 is more likely to have his or her symptoms based on a somatoform disorder as opposed to organic factors. This hypothesis is further strengthened if medical records indicate that the client characteristically produces similar symptoms when under stress.

The MMPI/MMPI-2 has not been particularly successful in producing either an "organic" profile or in localizing known lesions (Farr & Martin, 1988; Gass & Ansley, 1995; Lezak, 1995) even though some code types, such as 28/82, occur more frequently among brain-damaged groups. They do not occur frequently enough, however, to be diagnostic of CNS involvement. One study found that the 123 code type ("neurotic triad") was the most frequent to occur but only did so in 11.2% of a brain-damaged sample (Wooten, 1983). Theoretically and clinically, this makes sense because brain damage is not a unitary phenomenon. It is heterogeneous and is likely to be considerably influenced by a particular client's premorbid personality and style of coping. As a result, a wide diversity of profiles would be expected to (and do) occur among brain-damaged groups.

Despite this heterogeneity, there are individual items that seem to be endorsed more frequently among persons with CNS complications. Many of the items relate to such symptoms as fatigue, weakness, sensorimotor symptoms, distractibility, and paralysis and are more likely to occur among brain-damaged populations. Thus some of the scales might be inflated not so much because of psychiatric disturbance, but because of organically based neuropsychological impairment. As a result, clinicians may incorrectly infer, or at least exaggerate, the extent of psychiatric disturbance among brain-damaged populations. To compensate for this, a variety of correction factors have been developed for various brain-damaged populations. These include patients with closed head injury (Gass, 1991), cerebrovascular disease (Gass, 1992), and multiple sclerosis (Meyerink, Reitan, & Selz, 1988). Most of these items are derived from Scales 1, 2, 3, and 8 so that, unless these correction factors are used, clinicians should be somewhat cautious about making interpretations based on elevations on these scales. This caution should be balanced by being aware of and sensitive to the subgroup of brain-damaged persons who have poor awareness of their psychiatric and neuropsychological deficits. Given their minimization of difficulties, they might produce quite normal MMPI/MMPI-2/MMPI-A profiles despite significant pathology.

In summary, the MMPI/MMPI-2 has usually not been effective in diagnosing the presence or location of brain-damage, although it can be useful in assessing the current adjustment of brain-damaged persons. This might be due to psychopathology that preceded the brain damage, organically based personality changes resulting from the injury, a person's individual reaction to the damage, or a combination. Thus, with the preceding guidelines and cautions, clinicians are referred to Chapter 6 for more specific interpretations of MMPI/MMPI-2/MMPI-A profiles.

Beck Depression Inventory (BDI)

The BDI can provide a brief, easily administered assessment of a client's level of depression (see Chapter 4). When working with neuropsychological populations, there is some indication that stroke patients may have somewhat elevated scores due to endorsing items with somatic content (e.g., item 20 related to somatic preoccupation; Gordon, Hibbard, Egelkos, & Riley, 1991). This might reflect the physiological effects of the stroke rather than actual psychiatric complications. In contrast, Levin, Llabre, and Weiner (1988) demonstrated that Parkinson patients are more likely to have endorsed the BDI somatic items due to endorsing actual psychiatric disturbance rather than to the somatic impact of Parkinson's disease. However, the BDI has relatively less somatically related items and more items related to cognitive and affective domains than a scale such as the Hamilton Rating Scale for Depression (Brown et al., 1995). As a result, the BDI would be preferable in that scores would be less likely to be incorrectly inflated due to medical conditions. For assessing depression among elderly persons, the Geriatric Depression Inventory (Brink et al., 1982) may be preferable since it was standardized and validated on this population and has relatively fewer items related to somatic concerns (Olin, Schneider, Eaton, Zemansky, & Pollock, 1992).

RECOMMENDED READING

Gass, C. S., & Ansley, J. (1995). Personality assessment of neurologically impaired patients. In J. Butcher (Ed.), *Clinical personality assessment: Practical approaches* (pp. 192–210). New York: Oxford University Press.

Hutt, M. L. (1985). *The Hutt adaptation of the Bender-Gestalt Test* (4th ed.). New York: Grune & Stratton.

Koppitz, E. M. (1963, 1975). *The Bender Gestalt Test for young children* (Vols. 1 & 2). New York: Grune & Stratton.

Lacks, P. (1984). *Bender-Gestalt screening for brain dysfunction.* New York: Wiley.

Lezak, M. (1995). *Neuropsychological assessment* (3rd ed.). New York: Oxford University Press.

Chapter 13

PSYCHOLOGICAL ASSESSMENT AND TREATMENT PLANNING

The ultimate goal of psychological assessment is to help solve problems by providing information and recommendations relevant to making the optimum decisions related to the client. This involves integrating a wide variety of information related to diagnosis including specifics of the problem, client resources, a client's personal characteristics, and environmental circumstances. Practitioners must then work with this information to make recommendations related to treatment setting (inpatient/outpatient), intensity (frequency and duration), goals, mode (individual, group, family), and specific strategies and techniques. The sheer number of these variables can make assessment a daunting task. Thus the focus of this chapter will be to provide a framework for systematically organizing assessment results for planning treatment that is most likely to enhance outcome.

The following format for organizing results and developing treatment plans has been guided by several principles and values. Whenever possible, empirically supported information has been provided. This is possible using the knowledge derived from the fairly extensive body of research currently available. In fact, treatment that ignores the procedures indicated by current research runs the risk of not offering clients the most effective treatments available. At the same time, it is acknowledged that clinical experience and judgment will inevitably need to interact with the research, assessment results, and the uniqueness of the client to generate the best treatment plan. A further guiding principle underlying this chapter is that the format is both sequential and systematic. It is sequential in that typically a series of decisions confront clinicians beginning with such areas as how restrictive interventions should be and ending with such issues as specific techniques of therapy and methods of relapse prevention. Finally, the number of variables considered has been reduced to those that seem most relevant, easily manageable, and best supported by research.

Developing effective recommendations requires a number of knowledge and skill areas beyond merely test interpretation. One of the more important ones relates to general case management. This requires practitioners to survey the general case issues, focus on the most salient features, and make recommendations accordingly. This should include noting how restrictive treatment should be which would be directly related to the severity of the problem and whether the patient is likely to present a danger to self or others. After reviewing these considerations, practitioners need to be aware of the resources available in the community and make recommendations to the most appropriate one(s). This might include treatment in a specific inpatient setting or referral to such areas as an outpatient clinic, medical facility, suicide prevention center, Alcoholics

Anonymous, or behavioral medicine unit. Decisions also need to be made related to the frequency and duration of treatment. Practitioners should also be able to assess and provide recommendations on how to optimize a client's environment. For example, assessing the client's level of social support might help either in encouraging the person to use available supports or in enhancing only partially adequate supports. Environments might also be changed to increase social interaction or decrease the likelihood of relapse.

Practitioners can and should be able to deliberately tailor their responses toward specific characteristics and circumstances of the client. While this might seem self-evident, many therapists typically provide the same or at least similar interventions for all their clients. Frequently, these interventions are based on the specific school of therapy the therapist is most familiar with (e.g., uses cognitive therapy for every client who comes in for treatment). Research has demonstrated, however, that whereas cognitive behavior therapy can be effective for patients with externalizing coping styles, a supportive, self-directive method is more effective for patients with internalizing styles of coping (Barber & Muenz, in press; Beutler et al., 1991). A further assumption frequently found in clinical lore is that empathy is an essential ingredient of all effective therapy. Despite this, controlled studies indicate suspicious clients with low motivation do poorly when psychotherapists are empathic, involved, and accepting (Beutler, Crago, & Arizmendi, 1986). These examples, and many others, indicate that therapists need to have relational flexibility and a broad range of skills. In contrast, providing clients with a narrow range of possible interventions not only may reduce treatment effectiveness, but also may raise a question of ethics in that the best interventions are not being provided for them. Recommendations and interventions should, as much as possible, be guided by research since clinical lore can sometimes be misleading.

This brief introduction to treatment planning is not intended to minimize either the tremendous impact that the quality of the treatment relationship has on outcome, or of the importance of clinical experience. The overall quality of the therapeutic relationship accounts for at least as much of the outcome variance as specific techniques (Blatt, Zuroff, Quinlan, Pilkonis, 1996; Norcross, 1993). Well-defined techniques, however, are often easier to specify and control than the more general quality of the relationship. In addition, techniques that match a client's needs and expectations are likely to enhance the quality of the working relationship. For example, relationship quality is likely to deteriorate if a therapist tries highly directive techniques with quite defensive clients (Beutler, Sandowicz, Fisher, & Albanese, 1996). In addition, clinical experience will always be crucial in integrating a diverse range of client information into an optimum set of recommendations. While this process should be generally guided by available research, the specifics of a particular case might be sufficient to alter or even negate the generalities suggested by research data alone. Thus research findings and clinical information should ideally be in an active interplay such that they optimize each other's strengths and minimize their respective weaknesses.

DEVELOPMENT AND APPROACHES TO TREATMENT PLANNING

One of the central concerns for researchers and clinicians refining treatment planning has been efforts to understand how and why therapeutic interventions do or don't work. Similar to the debates on intelligence, researchers and clinicians can be divided into "splitters" who have focused on the impacts of specific techniques or "lumpers" who have been more concerned with the common, nonspecific ingredients that facilitate change. A further related theme is the identification of relevant client domains or behaviors needing change and matching these with appropriate interventions. The general purpose of assessment in this process is to identify the most relevant client characteristics or symptom behaviors and match these with optimal interventions. Paul Gordon (1967) ambitiously stated this agenda with a question: "*What* treatment, by *whom,* is most effective for *this* individual with *that* specific problem, and under *which* set of circumstances?" (p. 44).

Ancient traditions of mental health were fully aware of the importance of tailoring interventions toward the specifics of the client. For example, the Vedas discuss the differential effects of telling appropriate metaphors to clients according to their needs. Similarly, Sufism has had a well-developed tradition of storytelling designed to create specific impacts on the participants (Groth-Marnat, 1992). As early as 1919, Freud was concerned with matching patients to different types of psychotherapy. Classical psychoanalysis was recommended for patients who were quite psychologically minded. In contrast, clients who were considered "unanalyzable" due to a lack of psychological sophistication were referred for psychoanalytic psychotherapy that focused on direct suggestion rather than extensive insight and in-depth self-exploration.

Throughout the 1950s and 1960s, an extremely diverse number of therapies were developed. Each one provided a different theoretical model for causation and a wide variety of techniques. Part of what stimulated these developments was the hope that a series of techniques would prove successful in treating certain types of problems. Examples of such techniques included systematic desensitization for phobias or interpreting the transference as a tool in resolving past interpersonal conflicts. Within the psychosomatic literature, it was believed that certain disorders (e.g., asthma) were the result of specific types of conflicts (e.g., suppressed dependency needs). Resolving these specific conflicts, it was hoped, would similarly remove the relevant symptoms. This extensive variety and specificity has led to the development of over 400 different types of psychotherapies, only a few of which have been subjected to any degree of empirical investigation.

Psychological assessment during the 1950s and 1960s closely paralleled the particular school of therapy it was aligned with. Since many assessment procedures were both used within a medical context and relied on projective techniques, they accordingly reflected a psychoanalytic perspective. The goal, then, was to list a patient's symptoms along with a dynamic interpretation of the conflicts believed to be causing these symptoms. The specificity of treatment planning was deemphasized in favor of detailed descriptions of inner dynamics. It was assumed that, by describing these conflicts, the therapist would then know better how to proceed. During the 1960s and 1970s, the competing schools of behaviorism and humanism developed their own modes of assessment either based on specifying target behaviors and the antecedent events leading to these behaviors, or attending to the ongoing experience of the client. In either case, the value of traditional psychometric procedures was not only deemphasized but even criticized and abandoned.

Understandably, there was considerable competition between the different therapies as to which one was most effective. In 1952, Eysenck stimulated considerable controversy with his verdict that psychotherapy (particularly psychoanalysis) was no more effective than placebo. In contrast, he concluded that behavior therapy has demonstrated positive outcomes above and beyond merely placebo effects (Eysenck, 1994). Much of the ensuing research became a horse race in which proponents of particular schools wanted to demonstrate the superiority of the chosen therapeutic mode that they had received training in for so many years. The classic and much cited summary study of therapeutic outcome was Smith, Glass, and Miller's (1980) meta-analysis, which concluded that all of the evaluated therapies were effective. They also found greater effect sizes for those therapies with a progressively narrow focus than for those with a wider focus. For example, techniques such as systematic desensitization and hypnosis, which typically target a narrow band of behavior (elimination of a phobia, habit modification), were found to have greater impact than client-centered therapy, with its more general goal of personal growth. However, the differences between the various therapies were not extensive, which led many reviewers of the field to agree with Luborsky, Singer, and Luborsky's (1975) earlier verdict that "Everybody has won and all must have prizes" (often referred to as the "dodo bird" verdict). This is supported by more recent, methodically well-designed studies that have demonstrated little or no differential outcomes between different therapies when targeted at the same problems (Anderson & Lambert, 1995; Patterson, 1989; Seligman, 1995). For example, current high-quality research has found that randomly assigned manualized cognitive-behavioral versus psychodynamic-interpersonal interventions for depression had similar effectiveness on therapeutic outcome (Gallagher-Thompson & Steffen, 1994; Shapiro et al., 1994).

The preceding studies, along with responses to these findings, have significant implications for treatment planning. One category of response has been to investigate the non-specific features of therapy common to all systems (see Patterson, 1989). Underlying this response is the hope that these nonspecific factors would explain the general equivalence of outcomes across therapies. The earliest formal conceptualization was a 1957 description of "necessary and sufficient conditions of therapeutic change" by Rogers (1957/1992). These included genuineness, unconditional positive regard, and accurate empathy. A somewhat similar nonspecific formulation was also proposed by Frank (1973), who emphasized that successful therapy involved providing the client with hope, overcoming demoralization, and creating a corrective emotional experience involving benevolent persuasion. This nonspecific focus provides a contrast to the more directive, technique-oriented approaches. In particular, the nonspecific explanations place considerable emphasis on the quality of the therapeutic relationship above and beyond mere technique. The implications for assessment and treatment planning are that the technical aspect of assessment (formal tests) recedes in importance compared with the quality of the relationship (Luborsky, 1994). Formal testing may even be perceived as interfering with the development of a positive therapeutic relationship. In addition, the specificity of treatment recommendations is also deemphasized. What still remains, however, are basic case management issues (restrictiveness, format, and intensity of treatment) and enhancing aspects of the relationship that are likely to maximize outcome (i.e., matching client expectations, being perceived as trustworthy and credible).

A second general strategy has collectively been referred to as differential therapeutics. This approach focuses on refining intervention techniques based on specific diagnoses combined with additional information related to aspects of the problem (see

Barlow, 1993; Frances, Clarkin, & Perry, 1984). The general function of assessment in differential therapeutics is to diagnosis and evaluate the specifics of a disorder as carefully as possible. Techniques believed to be most effective in optimizing outcome are tailored and directed toward a symptom or symptom cluster. This model closely parallels and draws on procedures used in medicine, which similarly rely on accurate diagnosis prior to applying the optimal treatment.

The above approach has had varying degrees of success. Probably the most noteworthy of these successes has been the development of specific targeted interventions for clusters of anxiety-related symptoms (Barlow, 1988; Beck & Zebb, 1994; Steketee, 1994). In particular, Barlow, Craske, Cerny, and Klosko (1989) have developed a specific targeted treatment for panic disorder that has been found to be effective for 80% to 100% of those who completed the program. In addition, it has been found to provide clearly superior outcomes then pharmacotherapy (Gould, Otto, & Pollack, 1995). The treatment involves a combination of muscle relaxation, cognitive restructuring, and exposure to internal sensations linked to training in breathing. Interventions for social phobia and social anxiety have also shown differential effectiveness over other forms of treatment. Such programs involve restructuring cognitions, simulations of feared situations, and homework assignments in which the clients gradually exposes themselves to actual anxiety-related situations (Hope & Heimberg, 1993). Finally, differentially effective interventions for obsessive-compulsive disorder have primarily centered around gradual exposure to the anxiety-related situations along with strategies to prevent the occurrence of the compulsive behaviors (Riggs & Foa, 1993).

While most of the anxiety disorders have indicated the advantage of using interventions targeted directly at the subtype of disorder (diagnosis), less success has been achieved for specific interventions in the treatment of depression. The extent of vegetative symptoms, presence of manic episodes (bipolar), and presence of suicidal risk have implications for type of medication and restrictiveness of treatment. However, research has so far not been able to clearly identify the best psychosocial intervention for depression (Gallagher-Thompson & Steffen, 1994; Rude, 1986; Shapiro et al., 1994) although some have argued for the differential effectiveness of cognitive behavioral approaches (see Antonuccio, Danton, & DeNelsky, 1995). Researchers have also had difficulty demonstrating differential effectiveness for specific psychosocial interventions for schizophrenia, sleep disorders, sexual disturbances, generalized anxiety disorder, and personality disorders (Beutler & Crago, 1986; Brown, O'Leary, & Barlow, 1993).

A third general response has been to consider the nonequivalence of therapeutic outcomes to be the result of insufficiently explored client characteristics (see Beutler, 1979). This would mean that some types of clients do quite well when provided with a certain type of therapy and others, given the same therapy, will do quite poorly. If those clients who did poorly could have been identified and provided with different strategies, they might have made significant therapeutic gains using an alternate approach. However, the averaged scores on outcome studies using heterogeneous populations have obscured these potentially relevant client differences. The strategy, then, has been to thoroughly research a wide variety of client characteristics to determine which ones can be used to predict differential response to therapy. Over 200 of these characteristics have been suggested, of which 100 have been subjected to empirical investigation (Garfield, 1994). The result has been that, over the past 15 years, there has been increasing delineation and use of the most empirically validated characteristics for systematic treatment planning (Beutler & Clarkin, 1990; Beutler, Consoli, & Williams, 1994; Gaw & Beutler, 1995; Norcross & Beutler, in press). Reviews of this strategy have indicated that, under optimal matching conditions, up to 64% of the outcome variance can be accounted for (Beutler, 1983, 1989; Berzins, 1977). In contrast, providing therapeutic techniques without considering predisposing client characteristics has only been found to account for 10% of the outcome variance (Beutler, 1989). The implication for assessment is that predisposing client characteristics can and should be used to identify relevant dimensions. Furthermore, these dimensions should then be used to develop optimum treatment plans. This emphasizes both the technical and clinical aspects of assessment as well as the specificity of treatment recommendations. This does not negate the importance of common factors (caring, empathy, respect, etc.), but systematic treatment selection can potentially add to the effects of these common factors.

In addition to the preceding three general strategies, a variety of specific attempts have emerged to provide guidelines for prescriptive matching of client characteristics with therapeutic interventions. Ideally, the *DSM* should be useful in developing treatment plans in a similar manner as occurs for specific disease entities in general medicine. Generally, however, this has not been the case. Although some of the diagnostic categories have implications for different forms of somatic interventions (i.e., antidepressants for depressive disorders), they generally are not particularly helpful for designing psychosocial interventions (Beutler, 1989). In an effort to more clearly identify the full array of relevant domains for intervention, Lazarus (1973) suggested that clinicians analyze a patient's **B**ehaviors, **A**ffects, **S**ensory experiences, **I**magery, **C**ognitions, **I**nterpersonal relationships, and need for **D**rugs (BASIC-ID; see Chapter 4). A somewhat different perspective has been taken by authors who believe that the various stages of therapy or change are crucial to consider in tailoring interventions. Prochaska and DiClemente (1984, 1992) encouraged practitioners to tailor their interventions around the stages of precontemplation, contemplation, preparation, action, and maintenance. Beitman (1987) has somewhat similarly emphasized interventions tailored toward the following phases of treatment: (1) engagement or relationship building, (2) exploration of patterns in the client's responses, (3) the initiation of personal and/or interpersonal change, and (4) preparation for termination.

Within a behavioral medicine context, Wickramasekera (1995) has developed a high-risk model for identifying and assessing clients likely to have somatizing complaints. This includes predisposing factors consisting of either very high or very low hypnotizability, neuroticism (level of sympathetic reactivity), and catastrophizing cognitions. Precipitating factors relate to major life changes or minor hassles, and client factors that are likely to serve as buffers include level of social support and coping ability. Treatment can then be tailored toward the patterns of scores on these client dimensions.

A further strategy has been to determine the factors involved in creating optimal matches between therapist and client. In some ways, similarity between client and therapist has been found to be advantageous, particularly for such dimensions as age, gender, and ethnicity (Beutler & Clarkin, 1990). Similarity is also likely to enhance the value placed on interpersonal treatment goals, friendship, and social recognition (Arizmendi, Beutler, Shanfield, Crago, & Hagaman, 1985; Talley, Strupp, & Morey, 1990). In contrast, dissimilarity between patient and client predicted better outcomes when therapists who valued a high level of autonomy worked with clients who had a high need for attachment and dependence. Conversely, therapists who were highly oriented toward attachment and dependency did better with clients who were highly self-sufficient and autonomous (Jacobson, Follette, & Pagel, 1986).

Beutler and his colleagues (Beutler, 1979; Beutler & Clarkin, 1990) have developed a model of treatment selection based primarily on the identification of relevant client characteristics. This approach relies on systematically identifying these characteristics and making recommendations based on empirically and clinically established relationships with treatment outcomes. These characteristics include problem severity, motivational distress, problem complexity, level of resistance, coping style, and stages of change. This model, along with stages of change, will be emphasized in the remainder of this chapter. The rationale for using this model is that it closely adheres to empirically validated research, utilizes many of the assessment techniques discussed in previous chapters, follows a clear sequence of decision making, and is comprehensive while detailing a manageable number of variables.

The relevance and urgency of working with empirically validated methods of treatment planning is likely to significantly increase in the future. A powerful factor fueling this urgency is the current managed care movement, which will increasingly demand that both assessment procedures and interventions demonstrate their cost-effectiveness (Austad & Hoyt, 1992; Groth-Marnat & Edkins, 1996; Groth-Marnat, Edkins, & Schumaker, 1995). As a result, there is increasing pressure to demonstrate that assessment can quickly identify client problems, facilitate optimal treatment recommendations, and demonstrate the effectiveness of actual interventions. These "tools of the trade" must be able to provide these services in a way that has been demonstrated to be cost-effective. At the present time, the cost-effectiveness of assessment is not yet available but will most likely be forthcoming in the near future (see Butcher, in press). Future research should clarify when assessment is and is not cost-effective and, in particular, demonstrate that assessment results can be used to save money by quickly and effectively developing a treatment plan and thereby avoiding misplaced and possibly ineffective or unnecessarily long treatment.

A SYSTEMATIC APPROACH TO TREATMENT SELECTION

When a practitioner is confronted with a client, relevant information needs to be acquired, and based on this information, a series of decisions and recommendations should be developed. Beutler and Clarkin (1990) have identified six patient dimensions and related these to different types of decisions (see Table 13–1). The first of these relates to *problem severity* and has clear implications for general case management. Issues include the relative restrictiveness of therapy (inpatient/outpatient), whether medication should be considered, the intensity of treatment (duration and frequency), and what should be the immediate goals. The other five dimensions relate more to specific techniques of intervention than to general case management. *Motivational distress* can be used to guide

Table 13–1.   Systematic steps in treatment planning

Variable	Treatment Considerations
1. Problem severity	Restrictiveness (inpatient/outpatient) Intensity (duration and frequency) Medical vs. psychosocial intervention Prognosis Urgency of achieving goals
2. Motivational distress	Increase/decrease arousal
3. Problem complexity	Narrow symptom focus vs. resolution of thematic unresolved conflicts
4. Resistance	Supportive, nondirective, or paradoxical vs. structured, directive interventions
5. Coping style	Behavioral symptom oriented vs. structured, directive interventions
6. Problem-solving phase	Understanding, exploration, and awareness vs. overt behavioral or interpersonal change

Source: Adapted from Beutler & Gaw (1995).

clinicians as to whether the client's level of arousal should be increased or decreased. The relative *complexity* of a client's problem is important in considering whether the focus of treatment should be on specific, discrete, environmentally related symptoms, or more internal, chronic areas of conflict. In addition, level of *resistance* (reactance) of the client has implications for how directive interventions should be, and *coping style* can help guide whether interventions should be on changing external behavior or directed at more internal insight-oriented levels of change. A final, sixth domain developed by Prochaska and DiClemente (1984, 1992) relates to tailoring interventions based on the *problem-solving phase* (stage of change) the client is in.

Each of these dimensions can be assessed with a combination of formal tests, interview data, behavioral observations, and relevant history. The following descriptions of these dimensions includes a section on describing the construct followed by methods of assessment and different treatment implications based on the information derived from assessment. Relevant research to support important themes is cited but, given the often immense volume of possible literature, it is not possible to provide an exhaustive listing of citations. Practitioners can use the following dimensions to organize their assessment procedures as well as to guide treatment interventions.

PROBLEM SEVERITY

A pressing problem related to any assessment is an evaluation of the severity of the problem. The core issue is to assess the extent to which the patient's problem interferes with his or her ability to effectively deal with everyday social, occupational, and intrapersonal requirements. This might have a direct relationship to the client's ability to cope, ego strength, level of insight, and chronicity of symptoms. An important variable is the extent to which the person has adequate levels of environmental support particularly in the form of a strong family or a secure form of employment. These external means of support can often modify the impact of other forms of stressors. In many cases, problem severity will relate to the extent to which the client is subjectively distressed. In many instances, however, subjective distress does not relate to the presence of severe problems. Examples include antisocial personalities who create suffering for others but do not feel particularly distressed themselves and schizoid personalities who are functioning on the fringes of society but do not feel particularly worried about their marginal status and level of dysfunction. The major distinction is that problem severity is reflected in objective indicators of impairment. In contrast, subjective distress does not necessarily mean that the person will also be impaired based on objective indicators.

There are numerous formal and informal assessment procedures for assessing problem severity. Beutler and his colleagues (Beutler, Wakefield, & Williams, 1994; Gaw & Beutler, 1995) have summarized the relevant assessment dimensions to include the following:

- A problem that interferes with the client's ability to function during the interview.
- Poor concentration during assessment tasks.
- Distraction by minor events.
- General incapacity to function.
- Difficulty interacting with the clinician.
- Multiple impaired areas of performance in the client's daily life.

A Mental Status Examination is a structured means of obtaining useful information related to problem severity.

One of the more useful psychometric indications of problem severity is the presence of generally elevated scales on the MMPI-2/MMPI-A. Problem severity is especially likely if elevations are found on scales on the right side of the profile (Paranoia, Schizophrenia, Hypomania). High Beck Depression Inventory (BDI) scores (30 or above) also suggest a high level of incapacity. Suicide level should always be assessed if the patient is depressed. Specific signs to alert the clinician to suicide risk are relevant critical items on the MMPI-2/MMPI-A (check critical items listed under Depressed Suicidal Ideation in Appendix K) or items 2 and 9 on the BDI. General elevations on the MCMI scales also suggest a high level of problem severity, particularly if elevations occur on the Severe Personality Pathology or Severe Syndrome scales. The multiaxial *DSM-IV* system also provides methods for summarizing information relevant to estimating problem severity. Severity can be generally assessed by the specific type of diagnoses and is likely to be more severe if there are diagnoses on both Axis I and Axis II. There is also a continuum of severity ranging from the mild adjustment disorders to the more severe disorders in the psychotic domain (schizophrenia, bipolar). In addition, the *DSM-IV* Global Assessment of Functioning specifically requests clinicians to provide an assessment of the level of functioning over the past year on a scale between 1 and 100.

Several noteworthy instruments that have not been covered in previous chapters can also provide useful indices of problem severity. A high number of reported problems

(T above 63) on the Brief Symptom Inventory (BSI; Derogatis, 1992) suggests high problem severity as does high scores (T above 55) on the Trait Anxiety scale of the State-Trait Anxiety Inventory (STAI; Speilberger, Gorsuch, Lusene, Vagg, & Jacobs, 1983).

High Level of Problem Severity

High levels of problem severity have implications for the following five areas: restrictiveness of treatment, intensity of interventions (duration and frequency), use of medical/somatic versus psychosocial interventions, prognosis, and the urgency of achieving initial goals. Severe problems, particularly if the client is suicidal or cannot function in daily activities may require immediate inpatient care. Examples of diagnoses that may require inpatient care include bipolar mood disorders, psychotic conditions, major depression with suicidal intentions, acute substance abuse requiring detoxification, and some organic conditions which have resulted in significant decompensation. Initial treatment on an inpatient basis might later be reduced to partial hospitalization once the condition has become stabilized. Initial treatment for inpatients might need to be intensive. Outpatient interventions would be appropriate for the vast majority of clients whose problems are of mild to moderate severity (e.g., adjustment reactions, mild to moderate depression) and have greater resources.

The intensity of treatment (duration and frequency) will vary from client to client based primarily on problem severity. Greater duration of treatment is generally suggested for the following types of patients:

- Those with more serious diagnoses (e.g., borderline personality).
- Poor premorbid functioning.
- External stress seemingly of minor importance in the development and maintenance of the disorder.
- Aged between 25 and 50 years.
- Client expectation that change will take time, and the technique used will be exploratory and insight oriented.

In contrast, Perry (1987) has summarized the following indicators for short duration:

- An acute disorder (e.g., adjustment disorder, acute reactive psychosis).
- External stress that seems to be of primary causal significance.
- Good premorbid level of functioning.
- Clients who expect change to occur quickly.
- Symptom-oriented focus of treatment, or crisis intervention.
- Structured, directive, and active interventions.
- Person who is either child/adolescent or elderly.

For some conditions, intermittent brief therapy throughout the lifespan at critical junctures might be an appropriate recommendation. At times, it might be appropriate to recommend no treatment, particularly if the person might have a negative response (e.g., some borderlines), no response (e.g., some antisocial personalities), spontaneous improvement (e.g., normal grief), or strongly respond to suggestions that they will improve rapidly with no treatment (Perry, 1987). Additional characteristics contraindicating psychotherapy might be a client associating emotional pain with the change process, suspiciousness toward the therapist, and the client's need for control (Mohr, 1995).

Conditions such as schizophrenia, bipolar disorder, or severe anxiety states might require medical intervention (pharmacotherapy, electroconvulsive therapy) to enable clients to function well enough to become engaged in psychosocial or environmental interventions. Markers for such interventions might include poor orientation to time and place, poor short-term memory, marked confusion, clearly inappropriate mood, or low level of intelligence. Past clinical and research evidence has suggested severe and/or endogenous depression responds better to pharmacotherapy, whereas situationally caused mild and moderate depression responds better to psychosocial interventions. In contrast, the preponderance of current evidence indicates that both severe and endogenous depressions, as well as mild to moderate depression, can be treated at least as effectively with psychotherapy but without the potential for problematic side effects (Antonuccio et al., 1995; Free & Oei, 1989; Garvey, Hollon, & DeRubeis, 1994; McLean & Taylor, 1992; Simons & Thase, 1992). A clearer indication for antidepressant medication is a high number of vegetative symptoms (e.g., fatigue, insomnia, loss of appetite; Preston, O'Neal, & Talaga, 1994). Similar decision processes can be made for anxiety, psychotic, and bipolar disorders (see Preston et al., 1994).

To make prognostic judgments requires considering and integrating a diverse amount of information with particular reference to diagnosis, chronicity, subjective distress, and client resources (employment, abilities, social support). Research on prognosis is somewhat contradictory. On the one hand, it might be argued that a person with a severe problem will have difficulty overcoming it since it has progressed to such an extensive level. On the other hand, problem severity may represent an extreme level in a fluctuating condition so that the person is likely to spontaneously return to an improved level of functioning. In addition, the potential magnitude of change is likely to be greater since the person has so much room for potential improvement. One guideline is that a high degree of psychiatric symptoms associated with the presence of somatic complaints (headaches, irritable bowel syndrome) is likely to suggest a poor prognosis (Blanchard, Schwarz, Neff, & Gerardi, 1988; Jacob, Turner, Szekely, & Eidelman, 1983). In contrast, patients presenting with severe levels of general anxiety and ambulatory depression typically do quite well with either psychosocial or pharmacological interventions (Elkin et al., 1989). Specific diagnosis can also be important considerations since some diagnoses are likely to have poorer prognoses than others. For example, schizoid and antisocial personalities have difficulty engaging in productive therapy although certain Axis I conditions related to these personality types can often be targeted and effectively treated. It is a rule of thumb that the greater the chronicity of the disorder, the more difficult it will be to treat. A final principle in prognosis is that clients with low levels of social support are not as likely to improve as those with high support (Billings & Moos, 1986; Moos, 1990).

Finally, severe problems suggest that the urgency of treatment is greater and should be focused around working with the symptomatic areas causing the client the greatest distress. Less severe problems mean that the urgency of change is less and the goals can change and be negotiated over time.

Low Level of Problem Severity

In contrast to the previously described treatment considerations, low problem severity suggests that treatment can be in an unrestricted setting (outpatient) and of relatively low frequency and duration. Psychosocial interventions will be more likely to be the predominant form of intervention and there will be less urgency to rapidly define and achieve specific, symptom-oriented goals.

MOTIVATIONAL DISTRESS

Motivational distress relates to the degree to which the person subjectively experiences his or her problem and is manifest primarily in heightened anxiety, confusion, or depression. A moderate level of subjective distress is useful because it motivates a client to become involved with change. It can lead to cognitive improvements including enhanced memory, faster performance, and higher intellectual efficiency. If a client's distress becomes too high, however, it will be disruptive and result in deteriorated ability to function. The person will then have difficulty appropriately processing information and concentrating. This will interfere with the problem solving and behavioral experimentation required in therapy. A client whose level of subjective distress is too low will have difficulty becoming engaged in actively working to change behavior. Thus, there is an optimum window of distress that clinicians should try to achieve (Beutler et al., 1994; Gaw & Beutler, 1995).

While there is some overlap with problem severity and motivational distress, there are also a number of differences. As was discussed previously, problem severity relates to objective indicators of impairment, whereas motivational distress is more an internal, subjective phenomenon. In addition, motivational distress can be quite changeable and may be controlled by environmental events. A client's level of motivational distress needs to be monitored from session to session or even within each session. A further contrast exists in the range and types of decisions relevant to either problem severity or motivational distress. Issues relevant to problem severity require wide-ranging decisions related to treatment setting (inpatient/outpatient), prognosis, treatment intensity (duration and frequency), and the general goals of intervention. The treatment implications of motivational distress are much narrower in that they provide guidance on whether arousal should be increased or decreased.

Frequent review of interview data, including behavioral observations and relevant history, is one of the best methods of monitoring a client's distress levels. Specific indicators of high distress include the following (Beutler et al., 1994; Gaw & Beutler, 1995):

- Motor agitation.
- High emotional arousal.
- Poor concentration.
- Unsteady voice.
- Autonomic symptoms.
- Hyperventilation.
- Hypervigilance.

- Excited affect.
- Intense feelings.

In contrast, low levels of distress are indicated by:

- Reduced motor activity.
- Poor emotional investment in treatment.
- Low energy level.
- Blunted or constricted affect.
- Slow speech.
- Unmodulated verbalizations.
- Absence of symptoms.

MMPI-2/MMPI-A scales that are especially sensitive to subjective distress are F, 2 (Depression), and 7 (Psychasthenia). Collectively, these are frequently referred to as the "distress scales" (see descriptions under F scale, Scales 2 and 7, and the 27/72 code type in Chapter 6). However, motivation to change might be undermined if scales related to denial, resistance, and defensiveness are elevated (L and K as well as 3/Hysteria). A poor prognostic sign is a low 7 (Psychasthenia) with elevations on other scales suggesting psychopathology. This suggests that the client might be unrealistically relaxed regarding his or her difficulties or has given in to the inevitably of the problems.

Assessment devices not covered in the preceding chapters that might be sensitive to a client's level of motivational distress are the Brief Symptom Inventory (BSI) and the State-Trait Anxiety Inventory (STAI). A high level of distress is suggested if the Global Severity Index on the BSI is above 63 or the State Anxiety Score is in the top quartile.

High Motivational Distress

If subjective distress is quite high, an immediate goal is to reduce the anxiety level. This would be particularly urgent if the distress is sufficiently high to result in a significant disruption in the ability to cope. A wide variety of psychosocial techniques are available but are characterized by being supportive, structured, and designed to enhance relaxation. If a client's arousal is primarily expressed through physiological signs, then techniques targeted at this level are warranted and might include the following:

- Progressive muscle relaxation.
- Hypnotically assisted physiological relaxation.
- Guided imagery.
- Biofeedback.
- Aerobic exercise.
- Graded exposure.

Arousal that is more socially or cognitively related might be most effectively reduced through the following techniques:

- Meditation.
- Reassurance.
- Emotional support.
- Cathartic discharge.
- Supportive challenging of dysfunctional cognitions.
- Time management.
- Thought stopping.

Pharmacotherapy might be useful but should be accompanied by learning new coping skills so that medication can be discontinued as soon as possible. The newly acquired coping skills will then decrease the likelihood of relapse once the medication has been discontinued.

Low Motivational Distress

Clients with low motivational distress are likely to be associated with involuntary referrals. Experiential strategies can confront clients with the impact and consequences of their difficulties and are likely to increase distress to a level that makes them more open to changing their behavior. Possible techniques are:

- Two-chair work.
- Symptom exaggeration.
- Experiential role plays.
- Confrontation.
- Family therapy initially focusing on the impact of client behavior on family members.
- Overt practice.
- Predicting the recurrence of symptoms.
- Discussing painful memories.
- Accessing affective responses.
- Directed imagery.
- Interpretation of the transference.
- Interpretation of resistance.

PROBLEM COMPLEXITY

Some clients present with problems, such as simple phobias, that are narrow, focused, and either reinforced by or elicited by the environment. In contrast, other clients present problems of a diverse, complex nature. These problems are likely to be pervasive, enduring, and occur in many contexts. Instead of being focused around one or two specific behaviors, they involve diverse themes. A review of past relationships will typically reveal that these themes have been enacted with persons in intimate relationships or who were in positions of authority. Examples might include passive-aggressive interactions with authority figures, conflicts between dependency and independence in intimate relationships, or consistently creating problematic relationships by choosing incompatible partners (e.g., alcoholics) despite the availability of more appropriate persons. These themes can be considered reenactments of internal, unresolved conflicts. While the overt goal of becoming involved with such relationships is to somehow resolve the conflicts and achieve a certain level of gratification, the result is usually further suffering. For these sorts of problems the level of intervention needs to be quite different from problems that are narrow and symptomatic.

Problem complexity can be differentiated from problem severity in several ways. Whereas problem severity refers to level of impairment, problem complexity refers to underlying thematic patterns in the person's life that may or may not result in a high level of impairment. For example, a client may be functioning at a fairly high level (low problem severity) but still be quite troubled by chronic dissatisfactions in his or her relationships. These dissatisfactions may be the result of complex themes related to difficulties dealing with anger or issues related to dependency. Such themes may pervade not only one or two primary relationships, but most of the people the person comes into contact with. Whereas severe problems might be quite directly caused and reinforced by the environment (e.g., habits, reactions to stress), a complex problem is likely to be strongly related to internal unseen events. Furthermore, complex problems are likely to involve personality patterns and spread across a wide variety of domains.

Problem complexity is more difficult to measure than most of the other factors relevant for treatment planning, in part because it is more theoretically bound. Clinicians from psychodynamic perspectives are far more likely to frame client difficulties as centering around symbolic, underlying, complex themes, whereas behaviorally oriented practitioners will describe problems in narrower, concrete, environmentally oriented language. Although there is no clear resolution to this dilemma, three main features can be used to indicate problem complexity. The first is the presence of several problem domains or diagnoses (comorbidity), and the second is the presence of pervasive or recurrent patterns and themes of problem behaviors. A third feature suggesting a complex problem is the presence of a personality disorder or at least a personality style suggestive of a personality disorder. Beutler and his colleagues (Beutler et al., 1994; Gaw & Beutler, 1995) have summarized indicators of problem complexity based on the following background information and behavioral observations:

- Behaviors are repeated as themes across unrelated situations.
- Behaviors are ritualized efforts to resolve underlying interpersonal or dynamic conflicts.
- Interactions seem primarily related to past rather than present relationships.
- Suffering rather than gratification is the result of the repetitive behavior.
- Problems are symbolic expressions of underlying unresolved conflicts.

In contrast, noncomplex problems are more often characterized by being:

- Situation-specific.
- Transient.
- Based on inadequate knowledge or skills.

- Having a direct relationship to initiating events.
- Stemming from chronic habits.

Another reason problem complexity is more difficult to assess is that there are no clear, well-defined instruments. However, some inferences can be made from existing tests. In particular, elevations on the MCMI personality scales are likely not only to suggest the presence of a complex problem, but also to provide information related to personality themes. The presence of a personality disorder as defined by *DSM-IV* criteria further suggests a complex problem. Additional information can be derived from themes noted in TAT story content or from the client's organization of his or her responses to the Rorschach. Both of these instruments can be quite useful in articulating how a client copes with his or her emotions, responds to stress, resolves conflicts, relates interpersonally, and defends against anxiety. Finally, the MMPI-2/MMPI-A can help clarify not only a client's symptom pattern, but also the dynamic interplay between the symptoms, coping strategies, likely patterns in interpersonal relationships, and overall personality structure. A chronic problem is indicated if Scales 1 (Hypochondriasis) and 2 (Depression) are both above 65 but Scale 1 is clearly higher (5–10 points or more) than 2. Problem chronicity is also suggested if both Scales 7 (Psychasthenia) and 8 (Schizophrenia) are above 65 but Scale 8 is clearly higher (5–10 points or more) than 7 (see Chapter 6).

High Problem Complexity

Complex problems are likely to respond best to broad treatments that are directed toward resolving long-standing underlying conflicts and changing patterns of interpersonal relationships. Depending on the problem, specific techniques might include:

- Two-chair work.
- Group or family therapy exploring patterns of responses.
- Dream work.
- Cathartic discharge.
- Enacting opposite patterns of how the client typically behaves.
- Exploring thematic patterns in behavior and relationships.
- Interpreting the transference.
- Interpreting resistance.
- Free association.

Low Problem Complexity

Noncomplex problems can be effectively treated by targeting specific symptoms, antecedents that elicit these symptoms, and consequences that maintain them. Depending on the problem, specific techniques might include:

- Behavioral contracting.
- Social skills training.
- Graded exposure.

- Reinforcement of target behaviors.
- Contingency management.
- Challenging dysfunctional cognitions.
- Practicing alternative cognitions.
- Practicing new self-statements.
- Self-monitoring.
- Paradoxical strategies.
- Counterconditioning.
- Relaxation.
- Deep muscle relaxation.
- Biofeedback.

RESISTANCE LEVEL

Clients vary on the extent to which they are accepting and responsive to treatment versus being resistant and oppositional. This resistance is frequently a defense against what they perceive as others attempting to exert or intrude on their sense of control. Those who are most resistant are likely to have a constellation of traits including need for control, hostility, impulsivity, and direct avoidance (Dowd & Wallbrown, 1993). They may also have difficulty taking feedback and lack empathy. In addition to the preceding trait perspective, resistance can also be a state. The defensive or reactant state usually occurs when the client feels as if his or her freedom is somehow being threatened (Brehm & Brehm, 1981). Persons who are prone to be resistant are more likely to feel that they have a continual lack of personal control. As a result, they may compensate for this and establish a sense of control by acting in ways that oppose what is being requested or demanded of them. This is most likely to occur when the threatened area of freedom is important to the person and the individual making the request is doing so in an authoritative fashion such as through instruction, confrontation, directives, or structured techniques. Such a structured, directive approach can potentially result in actual increases in client dysfunction. Understandably, highly reactant clients are likely to have a poorer prognosis than those who are more responsive and receptive.

Clinical indicators that may suggest high resistance include the following (Beutler et al., 1994; Gaw & Beutler, 1995):

- Extreme need to maintain autonomy.
- Opposes external influences.
- Dominant.
- Anxious oppositional style.
- History of interpersonal conflict.
- Poor response to previous treatment.
- Refuses to accept therapist interpretations.
- Does not complete homework assignments.

In contrast, a low level of resistance is suggested by the following:

- Seeks direction.
- Submissive to authority.
- Open to experience.
- Accepts therapist interpretations.
- Agrees to and follows through with homework assignments.
- Indicates a tolerance to events beyond his or her control.

Although the MMPI-2/MMPI-A and MCMI-III do not have pure measures of resistance, elevations on some of the scales might be consistent with high resistance. Specifically, high scores on L and K are likely to have oppositional styles as would elevations on 6 (Paranoia) and possibly 1 (Hypochondriasis). Beutler et al. (1991) have used a combination of the MMPI research scales for anxiety (Taylor Manifest Anxiety Scale) and social desirability (Edwards Social Desirability Scale) as a measure of resistance. MCMI-III elevations on scales for Narcissistic, Negativistic (Passive/Aggressive), Paranoid, Aggressive/Sadistic, and Compulsive also suggest a defensive, oppositional person. In contrast, elevations on Dependent and Histrionic suggest a more responsive, compliant style. The most frequently used pure measure of resistance (reactance) is Dowd, Milne, and Wise's (1991) Therapeutic Reactance Scale with scores above 68 indicating sufficient resistance/reactance to have implications for treatment planning.

High Resistance

Strong empirical relationships have been found between positive treatment outcome and the use of nondirective, supportive, self-directed interventions for resistant clients (Beutler et al., 1991; Beutler et al., 1996; Beutler & Clarkin, 1990; Norcross & Beutler, in press). Specific techniques might include:

- Self-monitoring.
- Therapist reflection.
- Support and reassurance.
- Indirect hypnotic techniques (indirect suggestion, metaphor).
- Supportive interpretation of transference.

In addition, paradoxical techniques have been found to be particularly effective with reactant clients and might include:

- Encouraging relapse.
- Prescribing that no change occur.
- Exaggeration of the symptom.

This is most likely to be true if resistance levels are quite high as might be reflected in scores above 84 (top 75%) on the Therapeutic Reactance Scale (Beutler et al., 1996; Debord, 1989; Dowd & Wallbrown, 1993; Horvath & Goheen, 1990).

Low Resistance

Clients who are responsive and compliant are likely to achieve the most gains when therapists use a more directive, structured approach (Beutler et al., 1991; Beutler et al., 1996; Gaw & Beutler, 1995; Horvath & Goheen, 1990). Specific techniques might include:

- Behavior contracting.
- Contingency management.
- Graded exposure.
- Direct hypnotic suggestion.
- Stimulus control.
- Cognitive restructuring.
- Developing alternative client self-statements.
- Directed imagery.
- Advice.
- Thought stopping.
- Therapist interpretation.

COPING STYLE

Theory, research, and clinical observations indicate that client coping style varies on a continuum between externalization to internalization. Externalizers cope with their problems by impulsively acting out, externalizing blame, attributing the cause of their difficulties to bad luck or fate, and actively attempting to avoid their problems. They are not psychologically minded and, as a result, do not respond well to insight. In contrast, internalizers are more prone to blame themselves based in part on the perception that they do not have the sufficient skills or abilities to overcome their difficulties. Accordingly, they tend to experience more subjective distress than externalizers. To cope with this distress, they are likely to attempt to understand their difficulties in more depth.

Clinical indicators for externalization based on history and behavioral observations include the following (Beutler et al., 1994; Gaw & Beutler, 1995):

- Projection.
- Blaming others for their problems.
- Paranoia.
- Low frustration tolerance.
- Extroversion.
- Unsocialized aggression.
- Manipulation of others.
- Distraction through seeking stimulation.
- Somatization with a focus on seeking secondary gains.

In contrast, internalizers are more likely to have the following characteristics:

- Introversion.
- Intellectualization.
- Constricted or overcontrolled emotions.
- Denial.
- Repression.
- Reaction formation.
- Minimizing difficulties.
- Social withdrawal.
- Somatization with symptoms related to the autonomic nervous system.

MMPI-2/MMPI-A assessment of externalization for clinical populations can be made by finding the sum of T scores on 4 (Psychopathic Deviance), 6 (Paranoia), and 9 (Mania) and then comparing this with the sum of T scores on the internalization measures of 2 (Depression), 7 (Psychasthenia), and 0 (Social Introversion). If the sum of externalization $(4 + 6 + 9)$ is greater than internalization $(2 + 7 + 0)$, the client can be considered an externalizer. Conversely, if the internalizing sum $(2 + 7 + 0)$ is greater than the sum for externalization $(4 + 6 + 9)$, then the client is likely to internalize conflicts and stress (Beutler et al., 1991). Note that the preceding ratio has been designed for use with clinical populations who will have at least some elevations on the MMPI-2/MMPI-A scales. For depressed patients, greater sensitivity can be achieved by calculating the sum of T scores for Scales 4 (Psychopathic Deviance) and 6 (Paranoia) which should be above 125 to fulfill the criteria for having an externalizing coping style.

Several additional measures might also provide useful information related to coping style. Low scores on the CPI socialization scale suggest an externalizing coping style whereas high scores suggest a person who is more responsive and compliant (internal). The MCMI scales of Histrionic, Antisocial, Aggressive/Sadistic, and Paranoid conceptually suggest externalizing styles. In contrast, Avoidant, Depressive, Dependent, and Compulsive seem consistent with more internalizing styles of coping.

High Externalizers

Clients using externalizing coping strategies have better treatment outcomes when behavioral, symptom-oriented interventions or specific techniques for building skills are used. In contrast, they do relatively poorly with techniques that attempt to enhance awareness and create insight (Beutler et al., 1991; Beutler & Clarkin, 1990; Kadden, Cooney, Getter, & Litt, 1990). Techniques that are likely to be effective with externalizers include:

- Social skills enhancement.
- Assertiveness training.
- Group interventions.
- Anger management.
- Graded exposure.

- Reinforcement.
- Contingency contracting.
- Behavioral contracting.
- Questioning dysfunctional beliefs.
- Practicing alternate thinking.
- Stimulus control.
- Thought stopping.
- Counterconditioning.
- Relaxation.

High Internalizers

High internalizers benefit the most from techniques that emphasize the development of insight and the development of emotional awareness (Beutler et al., 1991; Beutler & Clarkin, 1990; Kadden et al., 1990). Specific techniques might include:

- Cathartic discharge.
- Therapist-directed imagery.
- Dream interpretation.
- Direct instruction.
- Outside reading (bibliotherapy).
- Interpreting transference reactions.
- Interpreting resistance.
- Two-chair work.

PROBLEM-SOLVING PHASE

Clients undergo a series of steps during the process of change. Accordingly, any client referred for evaluation may be at a different stage in the change process. Some individuals might be simply considering the possibility of change but have not yet struggled with the specifics of how to accomplish it. This might be particularly true for involuntary referrals who are resistant and experiencing a low level of motivational distress. On the other extreme might be a client who has already taken a number of clear steps for change but is seeking help to prevent relapse. According to the stage of change, a client might require somewhat different approaches. However, considering stage of change may not be relevant for disability, medical, or many court assessments (e.g., personal injury) since facilitating change may not be part of the referral question. In these cases, assessment of the current level of functioning or differential diagnosis becomes the main focus of the report.

The stages of change are likely to be quite variable. One person might pass through the different stages quite rapidly and another who is perhaps more ambivalent or less directed might have been considering the possibility of change for years. During the process of successful therapy, it would be expected that the client will have undergone all the different stages at some point. As a result, practitioners need to be continually aware of possible changes in the stage of change and adapt their interventions accordingly. In addition, a client might have several problem areas, especially if the problem is complex, and each area might be at a different stage in the change process. This variability requires a flexible approach depending on which area is being addressed.

Prochaska and DiClemente (1984, 1992) have described the following five stages in the change process: precontemplation, contemplation, preparation, action, and maintenance. Each stage will have a different set of tasks that must be accomplished prior to proceeding to the next stage. The first three stages are processes that occur prior to any actual change or actual attempts at concrete change. In the *precontemplation* stage, people have little intention of changing behavior or attitudes. They might be vaguely aware that change needs to occur but, for the most part, they are underaware of the possible importance of change. In contrast, other people they relate with can clearly see the need for change. As a result, these clients are likely to be referred or seek treatment when the legal-justice system threatens to punish them, a spouse threatens to leave them, parents threaten to disown them, or an employer threatens to dismiss them. Under these conditions, change is only likely to proceed if there is either continual outside pressure, or the actual client internalizes the need for change. When individuals begin to more seriously consider change they can be considered to be in the *contemplation* stage. At this point they are aware that they have a problem and are concerned with how coping with the problem might best be accomplished. However, they have not yet committed themselves to the process. In the *preparation* stage, they have become more committed to change, which is represented by their intent to take action in the near future. This intent may also be accompanied by the possible presence of minor experiments with new behaviors. Because they are not yet clear on how best to accomplish their intended change, they may need help considering all relevant options and choosing the optimal strategy for implementing the change.

The final two steps in the change process focus on actually implementing the change and ensuring that it is maintained. *Action* is the point at which clients actually change their environment, attitudes, or behavior. Often this requires a considerable amount of time and energy and, as a result, individuals must be highly committed. Changes at this point are most clearly visible to others. The preceding preparatory and contemplative processes should not be underestimated, however, since they are crucial in determining the relative success of any change. During the *maintenance* stage individuals work to consolidate change and prevent relapse.

The following interview questions can help determine the stage of change: Do you intend to change in the near future? Are there current changes you are going through? Have you made changes? Are you currently working to prevent relapse? These questions might also be incorporated into an intake form (Prochaska, Norcross, & DiClemente, 1994). It may be necessary to probe or otherwise obtain clarification to clearly determine the stages of change. Formal assessment of the stages of change can also be made on the 32-item Stages of Change Scale (McConnaughy, Prochaska, & Velicer, 1983).

Research has generally supported the clinical utility and predictive validity of tailoring interventions according to the different stages of change. This research has primarily focused on problems such as addictive behaviors, weight control, sunscreen use, and exercise acquisition (Prochaska, DiClemente, & Norcross, 1992; Prochaska, Rossi,

& Wilcox, 1991). Further research needs to be conducted to determine its applicability for a wider range of problem areas. Within the areas researched, there is evidence that tailoring interventions toward the stage of change can optimize treatment outcome (Pallonen et al., 1994; Prochaska et al., 1992).

- *Precontemplation Stage.* This is often, although not necessarily, consistent with involuntary referrals. As a result, resistance level may be high and motivational distress low, such that interventions would need to be made accordingly (e.g., increase arousal; use nondirective, supportive techniques; paradoxical interventions). Since these clients might feel ambivalent about treatment, it would be crucial to spend time building rapport and discussing areas that work or don't work in their lives.

- *Contemplation and Preparation Stages.* As in the previous stage, enhancing the relationship would be particularly important. Providing understanding and awareness would also be crucial. This should include exploring the interpersonal or behavioral patterns of the client, reasons for and against changing and the different strategies for creating change. An inventory of client strengths or resources and weaknesses might also be useful. The first three stages might be most consistent with humanistic or psychodynamic approaches that stress insight, exploration, value clarification, novel experiences, and clarification of personal goals.

- *Action Stage.* A wide variety of specific, concrete techniques might be used. The selection of these techniques will in part be dependent on such areas as problem severity, problem complexity, motivational distress, and resistance. Specific strategies can be implemented that might involve changes in concrete behavior, patterns of interpersonal relationships, self-statements, or ways of experiencing the world. Cognitive or behavioral techniques might be most effective at this point, particularly stimulus control, graded exposure, cognitive restructuring, role plays, social skills training, or counterconditioning.

- *Maintenance Stage.* At this point, the therapist can become like a coach or a consultant who advises and encourages the client. A crucial consideration would be how relapse is most likely to occur and to develop countermeasures to prevent these situations from occurring or at least to minimize their impact over a longer period. Specific techniques might include stimulus control, social contracting, enhancing social support, anger management, or a behavioral contract requiring the person to take preventive measures if relapse seems likely.

The preceding six dimensions are intended to be logically consistent as well as manageable. To facilitate the organization of relevant client dimensions, a software program should be available in the near future (Beutler & Williams, in press). The use of the model might be particularly crucial during training for new clinicians or skill enhancement of more experienced ones. With practice, it is likely that many of the features will become progressively more internalized perhaps requiring less formal assessment. A briefer, more clinical assessment of the dimensions may also be required when short-term interventions (e.g., crisis intervention) are the only options available.

As further research provides more precise definitions of empirical relationships, additional dimensions will likely be included. There may also be further integration with both differential therapeutics and therapist-client matching. Each of these developments will bring clinicians closer to Gordon's (1967) previously stated ultimate goal of combining the best treatment with the optimal mix of therapist, client, problem, and context.

RECOMMENDED READING

Beutler, L. E., & Berren, M. R. (1995). *Integrative assessment of adult personality.* New York: Guilford.

Beutler, L. E., & Clarkin, J. F. (1990). *Systematic treatment selection: Toward targeted therapeutic interventions.* New York: Brunner/Mazel.

Beutler, L. E., & Williams, O. (in press). *A software package for treatment planning.* Minneapolis, MN: New Standards Incorporated.

Butcher, J. N. (Ed.). (in press). *Objective psychological assessment in managed health care: A practitioner's guide.* New York: Oxford University Press.

Maruish, M. E. (Ed.). (1994). *The use of psychological testing for treatment planning and outcome assessment.* Hillsdale, NJ: Erlbaum.

Chapter 14

THE PSYCHOLOGICAL REPORT

The psychological report is the end product of assessment. It represents the clinician's efforts to integrate the assessment data into a functional whole so that the information can help the client solve problems and make decisions. Even the best tests will be useless unless the data from them is explained in a manner that is relevant and clear, and meets the needs of the client and referral source. This requires clinicians to not merely give test results, but to also interact with their data in a way that will make their conclusions useful in answering the referral question, making decisions, and helping to solve problems.

An evaluation can be written in several possible ways. The manner of presentation used depends on the purpose for which the report is intended as well as on the individual style and orientation of the practitioner. The format provided in this chapter is merely a suggested outline that follows common and traditional guidelines. It includes methods for elaborating on such essential areas as the referral question, behavioral observations, relevant history, impressions (interpretations), and recommendations. This format is especially appropriate for evaluations that are problem oriented and that offer specific prescriptions for change. Additional alternatives for organizing the report are to use a letter format, give only the summary and recommendations, focus on a specific problem, summarize the results test by test, write directly to the client, or provide client descriptions around a particular theory of personality. The sample evaluations vary somewhat from the suggested format, although they usually still include the essential categories of information that will be discussed in this chapter.

One general style to avoid is sometimes referred to as a "shotgun" report (Tallent, 1992, 1993). This provides a wide variety of often fragmented descriptions in the hope that some useful information can be found within. The shotgun approach is usually vague, stereotyped, and overinclusive. The recommendations for treatment are often neither specific nor practical. The most frequent cause of a shotgun report is a referral question that is too general, vague, and therefore poorly understood. In contrast, the "case-focused" report centers on the specific problems outlined by the referring person. It reveals unique aspects of the client and provides specific accurate descriptions, rather than portraying stereotypes that may also be overly "theory linked" or "test linked." Furthermore, the recommendations for treatment are both specific and practical. The general approach of the case-focused report is not so much *what* is to be known, but rather *why* different types of information are important for the purposes of the report.

The creation of a case-focused report involves understanding and applying several basic principles. First, the report should use action-oriented language rather than metapsychological abstractions. This means the client's ongoing behaviors and likely personality processes should be described in relation to different situations. Harty (1986) indicates that the use of "action-language" links the person with specific behaviors, forces reports to address specific therapeutic issues, and conveys a better understanding of the client's active role in the testing situation. Second, the recommendations in a case-focused report need to directly relate to what specifically can be done for this client within his or her particular environment. They may apply to such areas as occupational choice, psychotherapy, institutional programs, or additional evaluation. In certain types of referrals, however, especially clients self-referred for psychotherapy, an important goal may be to help them increase their level of personal insight. In these cases, a wider description of the client that includes a number of different topics might be more appropriate than the narrower, problem-solving approach. Also, there should be a focus on that which differentiates one person from another. This means avoiding discussions of what is average about the client, and emphasizing instead what stands out and is unique to this individual. Further, there is a current trend, consistent with the case-focused approach, toward deemphasizing diagnosis and etiology. There is rather an emphasis on current descriptions of the person that are tied to specific behaviors. In certain cases, especially within a medical setting, the clinician may still need to provide diagnoses in addition to behaviorally oriented descriptions. Another consideration is that a case-focused report should be written with an awareness of the point of view of the intended readers. This includes taking into consideration their level of expertise, their theoretical or professional orientation, the decisions they are facing, and the possible interpretations they are likely to make of the information.

A final point is that the quality and usefulness of a report is typically enhanced if the practitioner is knowledgeable about the area or type of issue the client is experiencing. Such knowledge helps to increase the depth of the interpretations and provides relevant information or a general "map" of the problem area that can be used to help ensure that all relevant aspects have been covered. Importantly, background knowledge on the problem area provides relevant information on a range of interventions as well as the effectiveness of these interventions. For example, knowledge regarding depression means that the practitioner will be aware of its causes, variety of ways in which it is expressed, options for interventions, and when further assessment is indicated (for suicide potential). Often consulting a well written, up-to-date chapter will provide sufficient information. Within the clinical area, useful resources are Barlow's (1993) *Clinical Handbook of Psychological Disorders* (2nd ed.), Meyer's (1993) *The Clinician's Handbook* (3rd ed.), Kaplan and Sadock's (1996) *Comprehensive Textbook of Psychiatry* (6th ed.), or Bellack and Hersen's (1990) *Handbook of Comparative Treatment for Adult Disorders*. Persons doing neuropsychological reports might consult Lezak's (1995) *Neuropsychological Assessment* or Heilman and Valenstein's (1993) *Clinical Neuropsychology* (3rd ed.). Educational reports might benefit from reading relevant sections in Hoghughi's (1992) *Assessing Child and Adolescent Disorders: A Practice Manual* or Walker and Roberts' (1992) *Handbook of Clinical Child Psychology*. A particularly useful resource when doing vocational assessments is Lowman's (1991) *The Clinical Practice of Career Assessment: Interests, Abilities, and Personality*.

GENERAL GUIDELINES

Style

The style or "flavor" of a report will be influenced primarily by the training and orientation of the examiner. The clinician can choose from four general report-writing approaches: literary, clinical, scientific, and professional (Ownby, 1987; Tallent, 1992, 1993). Each style has unique strengths, and all have a number of liabilities. The literary approach uses everyday language, is creative, and often dramatic. Although it can effectively capture a reader's attention and provide colorful descriptions, it is often imprecise and prone to exaggeration.

The clinical approach focuses on the pathological dimensions of a person. It describes the client's abnormal features, defenses, dynamics involved in maladjustment, and typical reactions to stress. The strength of the clinical approach is that it provides information about areas in need of change and alerts a potential practitioner to likely difficulties during the course of treatment. However, such a report tends to be one-sided in that it may omit important strengths of the person. The result is likely to be more a description of a "patient" than a person. Such a maladjustment bias is a frequent difficulty in clinical psychology and results in a distorted, unrealistic view of the client. Although most clinical reports should describe a person's problem areas, these problem areas should be given appropriate emphasis within the context of the client's relevant strengths and resources.

The scientific approach to report writing emphasizes normative comparisons, tends to be more academic, and to a lesser extent, relates to the nature of a client's pathology. The scientific style differs from the other two approaches chiefly in its reference to concepts, theories, and data. It looks at and describes test findings in an objective, factual manner. Thus, there might be frequent references to test data, normative comparisons, probability statements, and cutoff scores to be used for decision making. A scientific approach is likely to discuss the person by addressing different, often isolated, segments of personality. Thus, such areas as a client's cognitive, perceptual, and motivational abilities may be described as discrete and often unrelated functions. Although the scientific approach is objective and factual, it has been criticized for violating the unity of personality. Many readers, particularly those from other disciplines (Sandy, 1986; Tallent & Reiss, 1959b, 1992), do not respect or empathize with scientific evaluations and perceive them as cold, distant, and overly objective. Purely data-oriented evaluations can potentially do the profession a disservice by reinforcing the view that an assessment is like a laboratory test rather than a professional consultation with a clinician. Furthermore, a focus on factual data may not address the practical decisions the client and referral source are facing.

In actual practice, it is unusual to find a pure example of a literary, clinical, or scientific report. Clinicians will generally draw from all three approaches but will typically emphasize one. An important part of effective report writing is the ability to evaluate the assets and limitations of each style, and to maintain a flexible orientation toward appropriately combining them. In any one report, there may be a need to use creative literary descriptions, elaborate on different pathological dimensions, or provide necessary scientific information. Again, the key is to avoid the pitfalls associated with specializing in any one of these styles and to emphasize instead their relative strengths.

Ownby (1987) stresses that the most important style to use in report writing is what he refers to as a "professional style." This is characterized by short words that are of common usage and that have precise meanings. Grammatically, writers should use a variety of sentence constructions and lengths to maintain the reader's interest. The paragraphs should be short and should focus on a single concept. Similar concepts should be located close to one another in the report. Whereas Hollis and Donna (1979) urge writers to use short words, short sentences, and short paragraphs, the *Publication Manual of the American Psychological Association* (1994) recommends varying the lengths of sentences and paragraphs. The result should be a report that combines accuracy, clarity, integration, and readability.

Presenting Test Interpretations

Clinicians generally prefer to orient their reports around specific hypotheses or different relevant domains, or adhere to interpreting the data test by test. The hypothesis-oriented model focuses heavily on answering specific questions asked by the referral source. The report tends to be highly focused, well integrated, and avoids any extraneous material. For example, if a referral source asks whether person X is brain damaged, then all the interpretations based on the test data are directed toward answering whether this hypothesis is supported.

A domain-oriented report discusses the client in relation to specific topics such as cognitive abilities, interpersonal relationships, vocational abilities, or sexuality. This approach is comprehensive, indicates the client's strengths and weaknesses, and typically gives the reader a good feel for the person as a whole. The referral question is still answered but is addressed by responding to specific domains relating to the referral question. Readers tend to prefer and better comprehend integrated reports written by addressing functional domains rather than test scores (Wiener, 1985). The weakness of domain-oriented reports lies in the potential to provide too much information, thus overloading the reader.

Occasionally, a report will be organized by presenting the results of each test, one at a time (WAIS-R, Bender, MMPI, etc.). This approach clarifies where the data came from and enables the reader to more clearly understand how the clinician made his or her inferences. This advantage is offset by some significant disadvantages. The emphasis on tests can distract the reader and tends to reduce the client from a person to a series of test numbers. This is reflected in that readers of reports, regardless of their theoretical or disciplinary background, do not respond well to this style of report writing (Tallent 1992, 1993; Tallent & Reiss, 1959a, 1959b). A test-by-test presentation also reflects a failure to integrate the data and further suggests that the practitioner has neither adequately conceptualized relevant dynamics nor fully understands the area under investigation (Wolber & Carne, 1993). It also encourages the belief that an examiner is a technician who merely administers tests rather than a clinician who uses multiple sources of information to answer referral questions and help people solve problems they are facing. As a result, it is strongly recommended that an integrated, rather than a test-by-test style be used (Beutler & Berron, 1995; Ownby, 1987; Sattler, 1992; Tallent, 1992, 1993; Wolber & Carne, 1993; Zuckerman, 1991).

Topics

There is an extremely wide range of topics or domains that clinicians may decide to discuss in their reports. These topics serve as conceptual tools that enable report writers to give form and direction to the information they are trying to communicate. Possible topics include intellectual functioning, vocational aptitudes, conflicts, interpersonal relationships, cognitions, suicidal potential, defenses, behavior under stress, impulsiveness, or sexuality. Often, an adequate case-focused report can be developed by describing just a few of these topics. For example, a highly focused report may elaborate on one or two significant areas of functioning, whereas a more general evaluation may discuss seven or eight relevant topics. Table 14–1 is a representative list of topics that may be considered for inclusion in an evaluation. This list is by no means complete but can provide a general guide for the wide range of possible topics from which a report writer can choose.

Deciding What to Include

The general purpose of a psychological evaluation is to provide information that will be most helpful in meeting the needs of the client. Within this context, the clinician must strike a balance between providing too much information and providing too little, and between being too cold and being too dramatic. As a general rule, information should only be included if it serves to increase the understanding of the client. For example, descriptions of a client's appearance should be oriented toward such areas as his or her level of self-esteem or anxiety. Such information as the types of clothing the person is wearing or color of his or her eyes or hair are generally not relevant. Likewise, an elaboration of family dynamics should be helpful in understanding such areas as a child's current behavioral problems or lack of academic motivation.

The basic guidelines for deciding what to include in a report relate to the needs of the referral setting, background of the readers, purpose of testing, relative usefulness of the information, and whether the information describes unique characteristics of the person. Once these general guidelines have been taken into account, the next step is to focus on and organize the information derived from the tests. For example, if a general review of aspects of personality is the purpose of the report, then a clinician can look at each test to determine what information it can provide. Ownby (1987, 1990) recommends using a worksheet with the domain or topic for consideration in the left column, a review of relevant data in the next, followed by a list of possible constructs, diagnoses or conclusions, and, finally, recommendations. This enables the practitioner to extract relevant data from the mass of assessment data and to organize conclusions and recommendations in preparation for report writing. An example of a portion of such a worksheet is included in Figure 14–1.

A further general rule is that information should focus on the client's unique method of psychological functioning. A reader is concerned not so much with how the client is similar to the average person as in what ways he or she is different. A common

Table 14–1.   Examples of general personality topics around which a case presentation may be conceptualized

Achievement	Intellectual controls
Aggressiveness	Intellectual levels
Antisocial tendencies	Interests
Anxieties	Interpersonal relations
Aptitudes	Interpersonal skills
Attitudes	Lifestyle
Aversions	Molar surface behavior
Awareness	Needs
Background factors	Outlook
Behavioral problems	Perception of environment
Biological factors	Perception of self
Cognitive functioning	Personal consequences of behavior
Cognitive skills	Placement prospects
Cognitive style	Psychopathology
Competency	Rehabilitation needs
Cognitive factors	Rehabilitation prospects
Conflicts	Sentiments
Content of consciousness	Sex
Defenses	Sex identity
Deficits	Sex role
Developmental factors	Significant others
Diagnostic considerations	Situational factors
Drives, dynamics	Social consequences of behavior
Emotional cathexes	Social role
Emotional controls	Social stimulus value
Emotivity	Social structure
Fixations	Special assets
Flexibility	Subjective feeling states
Frustrations	Symptoms
Goals	Treatment prospects
Hostility	Value system
Identity	Vocational topics

Source: From *Psychological Report Writing* (3rd ed.), p. 120, by N. Tallent, 1988, Englewood Cliffs, NJ: Prentice-Hall. Copyright 1988 by Prentice-Hall, Inc. Reprinted by permission.

error in psychological reports is the inclusion of generalized statements that are so vague they could apply to the majority of the population. Several researchers (Snyder, 1974; Sundberg, 1955; Ulrich, Stachnik, & Stainton, 1963) have studied the frequency, manner, and types of vague, generalized statements that individuals are likely to unconditionally accept as applying to themselves even though these statements were randomly selected. For example, Sundberg (1955) administered a "personality" test to a group of students and gave them all identical "interpretations" based on universal or stereotyped personality descriptions composed of 13 statements, such as:

- You have a great need for other people to like and admire you.
- You have a tendency to be critical of yourself.

Topic	Data	Constructs	Conclusions	Recommendations
Appropriateness for therapy	Distractible High MMPI scale 9 Resisted Interpretations Low Digit Span & Digit Symbol Changes topic during discussion of difficult areas	Possible anxiety Low sequencing ability Mildly inflated ideation Irritable Use of denial Oppositional/ high resistance	Mild manic state and significant use of denial	1. Weekly individual psychotherapy: focus on insight regarding decisions; supportive; nondirector or paradoxical approach 2. Possible referral for medication

Figure 14–1.   Worksheet for organizing a topic for a psychological report

- You have a great deal of unused capacity you have not turned to your advantage.
- While you have some personality weaknesses, you are generally able to compensate for them.
- At times you have serious doubts as to whether you have made the right decision or done the right thing.

Virtually all students used in the study reported that the evaluation statements were accurate descriptions of themselves. Other studies suggest that, not only were students unable to discriminate between fictitious and genuine feedback (Dies, 1972), but they may even have preferred generalized fictitious results, particularly if they were framed within a positive context (Merrens & Richards, 1970; Mosher, 1965). This uncritical acceptance of test interpretations might be even further encouraged when objective-appearing, computer-generated interpretations are used (Groth-Marnat & Schumaker, 1989; O'Dell, 1972; Rubenzer, 1992). Klopfer (1960) has referred to this uncritical acceptance of universally valid statements as the "Barnum effect," in reference to Phineas Barnum's saying, "There is a fool born every minute." Although "universal statements" may add to the "subjective" validity of the report when read by the client, such statements should be avoided in favor of stressing the person's essential uniqueness.

Once the data, conclusions, and recommendations have been outlined, the next step is to decide on the manner in which to present them. This involves clear communication about the relative degree of emphasis of the results, type of report, proper use of terminology, and the extent to which the raw data will be discussed.

Emphasis

Careful consideration should be given to the appropriate emphasis of conclusions, particularly when indicating the relative intensity of a client's behavior. General summaries may be given, such as "this client's level of depression is characteristic of inpatient populations," or the relative intensity of certain aspects of a client's disorder may be more specifically discussed. To continue with the example of depression, a clinician may discuss the client's cognitive self-criticisms, degree of slowed behavior, extent of social support, level of social skills, or suicidal potential. In addition to discussing and giving the appropriate degree of emphasis to a client's pathology, his or her psychological strengths need to be compared with his or her relative weaknesses. Furthermore, the report should not discuss areas of minor relevance unless they somehow relate to the purpose of the evaluation. To achieve proper emphasis, the examiner and the referral source must clarify and agree on the purpose of the evaluation. Only after this has been accomplished can the examiner decide whether certain information should be elaborated in-depth, briefly mentioned, or deleted.

When clinicians present their conclusions, it is essential that they indicate their relative degree of certainty. Is a specific conclusion based on an objective fact, or is the clinician merely presenting a speculation? For example, the statement "John scored in the dull normal range of intelligence" is an objective fact. However, even in this case, examiners may want to give the standard error of measurement to provide an estimate of the probable range of scores. If only mild supporting data is available or if clinicians are presenting a speculation, then phrases such as "it appears . . . ," "tends to . . . ," or "probably . . ." should be used. This is especially important when clinicians are attempting to predict a person's behavior, because the predicted behavior has not yet been observed. It may be useful for clinicians to indicate that their predictions cannot be found directly in the tests themselves, but rather represent inferences that have been made based on the test data. There should be a clear distinction between what the client did, and what he or she anticipates doing. If a statement made in a report is a speculation, then it should be clearly indicated that the statement has only a moderate or small degree of certainty. Whenever a speculation is included, it should be relevant to the referral question.

Improper emphasis can reflect an incorrect interpretation by the examiner, and this misinterpretation is then passed down to the reader. Clinicians sometimes arrive at incorrect conclusions because their personal bias results in selective perception of the data. Thus, clinicians can develop an overly narrow focus with which they overlook potentially relevant data. Personal bias may result from such factors as a restrictive theoretical orientation, incorrect subjective feelings regarding the client, or an overemphasis on pathology. Inaccurate conclusions can also result from attempts to please the referral source or from interpretations based on insufficient data. The reader may also be likely to misinterpret the conclusions if the report is generally overspeculative or if speculations are not specified as such but, rather, are disguised as assertions. If speculations are overly assertive, this may not only lead the reader to develop incorrect conclusions, but the report may also become overly authoritative and dogmatic, perhaps leading readers to become irritated and skeptical.

Misinterpretations can also result from vague and ambiguously worded sentences that place incorrect or misleading emphasis on a client's behavior. A statement such as "the client lacks social skills" is technically incorrect because the client must have some social skills, although these skills may be inadequate. A more correct description would be to state that the client's social skills are "poorly developed" or "below average." Likewise, a statement such as "the client uses socially inappropriate behavior" is subject to a myriad of interpretations. This could be rephrased to include more behaviorally oriented descriptions, such as "frequently interrupts" or "would often pursue irrelevant tangents." One technique of emphasizing results is to place the most relevant sections in bold. For example, the major identified symptoms, most important findings, and the major recommendations could all be placed in bold. This enables persons reading the report to more easily absorb the most salient features. In addition, they can easily relocate major points that have been made. However, this technique should be used sparingly since readers can become fairly easily saturated with too much bold print. This means that, instead of placing entire paragraphs or sentences in bold, only key phrases should be given this method of emphasis.

The areas, extent, and method of emphasis will significantly contribute to the conclusions of a report. However, responsibility for a report's conclusions rests on the clinician. This responsibility should not and cannot be transferred to the tests themselves. To take this a step further, decisions made about a person should never be in the hands of tests, which may even have questionable validity in certain contexts. Rather, conclusions and decisions regarding people should always be in the hands of responsible persons. Thus, the style of emphasizing results should reflect this. Phrases such as "test results indicate . . ." may give the impression that the examiner is trying to hide behind and transfer responsibility for his or her statements onto the tests. Not only is this not where the responsibility should be, but the reader may develop a lack of confidence in the clinician. If clinicians feel uncertain about a particular area, then they should either be clear about this uncertainty or, if they cannot personally stand by the results, they should exclude the results from the report.

Use of Raw Data

When writing the impressions and interpretation section, a report writer should generally avoid adhering too closely to the raw data. For certain purposes, however, it may be useful to include raw data or even to describe the tests themselves. Test descriptions allow untrained persons to know specific behaviors the client engaged in rather than merely the final inferences. For, example, a report may include a description such as "Mr. A had an average level of recall for short-term visual information, as indicated by his being able to accurately recall and reproduce five out of a possible nine geometric designs that he had previously worked with for five minutes." This sentence provides a more behaviorally referenced description than one like "Mr. A had an average level of recall as measured on the Bender memory." Thus, a test description is apt to give the reader a more in-depth, precise, and familiar reference regarding the subject's abilities. In addition to the test descriptions themselves, test responses can serve to make the description behavior specific and to balance high-level abstractions with concrete responses. For example, a clinician might discuss a client's impulsiveness and include illustrative items on the MMPI, such as:

38. During one period when I was a child I engaged in petty thievery. (True)

205. At times it has been impossible for me to keep from stealing or shoplifting. (True)

In discussing the same issue, a clinician could also include a portion of a TAT story that illustrates a similar point:

> . . . so he took the violin and, without even thinking about it, threw it into the fire and ran outside.

It is crucial to stress that the purpose of providing raw data and behavioral descriptions is to enrich and illustrate the topic and not to enable the reader to follow the clinician's line of reasoning or document the inferences that have been made. In developing inferences, clinicians must draw on a wide variety of data. They cannot possibly discuss all the patterns, configurations, and relationships they used to come to their conclusions. Any attempt to do so would necessarily be overly detailed, cumbersome, and incomplete. Statements such as, "In considering the pattern of elevated Scales 4 and 9 on the MMPI, it is safe to conclude . . ." are unnecessary and rarely contribute to a report's overall usefulness. In certain types of reports, such as those for legal purposes, it might be helpful to include some raw data, not so much to repeat the thinking process of the clinician but more to substantiate that the inferences are data based, to provide a point of reference for discussing the results, and to indicate what assessment procedures were used.

Terminology

Several arguments have been made in determining whether to use technical or nontechnical language in psychological reports. It might be argued that technical terminology is precise and economical, increases the credibility of the writer, and can communicate concepts that are impossible to convey through nontechnical language. However, a number of potential difficulties are often encountered with the use of technical language. One of the more frequent problems involves the varying backgrounds and levels of sophistication of the persons reading the report. The most frequent readers of reports include teachers, administrators, judges, attorneys, psychiatrists, and social workers, most of whom do not have the necessary background to interpret technical terminology accurately. Even psychologists with different theoretical persuasions may be apt to misinterpret some of the terms. Take, for example, the differing uses of "ego" by Freud, Jung, and Erikson. Also, the term "anxiety" might have several different categories of use. Although technical words can undoubtedly be precise, their precision is only helpful within a particular context and with a reader who has the proper background. Generally, reports are rated as more effective when the material is described in clear, basic language (Berry, 1975; Ownby, 1990; Sandy, 1986; Tallent, 1993; Weiner, 1987). Even among readers who have the proper background to understand technical terms, many prefer a more straightforward presentation (Ownby, 1990; Tallent, 1992, 1993; Tallent & Reiss, 1959c). Technical terms also run the danger of becoming nominalisms in which, by merely naming the phenomenon, persons develop an illusory sense of understanding more than is actually the case. Terms like "immature" or "sadistic" cover a great deal of information because they are so general, but they say nothing about what the person is like when he or she is behaving in these maladaptive ways. They also do not adequately differentiate one person from the next and are frequently ambiguous. Furthermore, technical terms are often used inappropriately (e.g., a person who is sensitive and cautious in interpersonal relationships is labeled "para-noid," or "compulsive" is used to describe someone who is merely careful, conscientious, and effective in dealing with details).

Klopfer (1960) provides an excellent and still relevant rationale for using basic English rather than technical terminology. First, and perhaps most important, the use of basic English allows the examiner, through his or her report, to communicate with and affect a wide audience. This is particularly important since the number and variety of persons who read reports is much greater now than 20 or 30 years ago. Furthermore, basic English is more specific and descriptive of an individual's uniqueness, whereas technical terms tend to deal with generalities. Terms such as "sadomasochistic" and "hostile" do not provide essential information about whether the person is assaultive or suicidal. Finally, the use of basic English generally indicates that the examiner has more in-depth comprehension of the information he or she is dealing with and can communicate this comprehension in a precise, concrete manner. Klopfer (1960) stresses that any description found in a psychological report should be comprehensible to any literate person of at least average intelligence. The first four are his examples of translating technical concepts into basic English (Klopfer, 1960):

"Hostility toward the father figure" becomes "the patient is so fearful and suspicious of people in positions of authority that he automatically assumes an aggressive attitude toward them, being sure that swift retaliations will follow. He doesn't give such people an opportunity to demonstrate their real characteristics since he assumes they are all alike."

"The patient projects extensively" becomes "the patient has a tendency to attribute to other people feelings and ideas originating within himself regardless of how these other people might feel."

"The defenses the patient uses are . . ." becomes "the methods characteristically employed by the patient for reducing anxiety are . . ."

"Empathy" becomes "the patient can understand and sympathize with the feelings of others, since she finds it relatively easy to put herself in their place." (pp. 58–60)

"The client is hostile and resistant" may be changed to include a behavioral description; "when the client entered the room she stated, 'My Dad said I had to come and that's the only reason I'm here' " or "later on in the testing she made several comments such as 'This is a stupid question.' "

The general principle involved in the preceding examples is to translate high-level abstract terms into basic English that provides useful, concrete behavioral descriptions.

Ownby (1987, 1990) recommends combining any conclusion or generalization with specific behaviors or test observations. Recommendations should also be directly linked with the relevant behaviors/generalizations, either in the same place or in the recommendations section. For example, instead of saying a client is "depressed," a writer might state, "The client's behavior, which included self-criticism and occasional crying, suggested he was depressed." Linking generalizations with clear concrete descriptions tends to create reports that are perceived to be relatively credible and persuasive (Ownby, 1986, 1990). If this process is followed, descriptions will be less subject to misinterpretation, less ambiguous, and more likely to convey the unique characteristics of the client. Although abstract technical terms can at times be important components of a psychological report, they should be used sparingly and only when clearly appropriate.

This particularly means carefully considering the background of the persons who will be reading the report. Sandy (1986) even recommends having the clinician collaborate with the relevant recipients of the report, including the client, so that the final report is descriptive rather than interpretive and the readers are not passive recipients of the "higher" wisdom of the psychologist.

Content Overload

There are no specific rules to follow in determining how much information to include in a report. A general guideline is to estimate how much information a reader can realistically be expected to assimilate. If too many details are given, the information may begin to become poorly defined and vague and, therefore, lack impact or usefulness. When clinicians are confronted with a great variety of data from which to choose, they should not attempt to include it all. A statement such as "The client's relative strengths are in abstract reasoning, general fund of knowledge, short-term memory, attention span, and mathematical computation" is likely to overload the reader with too many details. The clinician should instead focus on and discuss only those areas that are most relevant to the purpose of the report.

Feedback

During the earlier days of psychological assessment, examiners often kept the results of psychological assessments carefully concealed from the client. There was often an underlying belief that the results were too complex and mysterious for the client to adequately understand. In contrast, current practices are to provide the client with clear, direct, and accurate feedback regarding the results of an evaluation (Pope, 1992).

The change toward providing feedback to clients has been motivated by several factors. First, regulations have supported a growing list of consumer rights, including the right to various types of information. Second, it might be perceived as a violation if the client did not receive feedback regarding the results of testing after he or she had been subjected to several hours of assessment. Even the most secure of clients might easily feel uncomfortable knowing a report with highly personal information might be circulated and used by persons in power to make decisions about the client's future. Such practices could understandably result in suspicion and irritation on the part of the public. Third, examiners cannot safely assume that the original referral source will provide feedback to the client. Even if the referral source does provide feedback, there is no guarantee that the information will be provided in an appropriate manner. Thus, the responsibility for providing feedback will ultimately be on the clinician. Finally, there is increasing evidence that providing clients with test feedback can result in significant therapeutic benefits (Finn & Tonsager, 1992; Gass & Brown, 1992).

The extent to which a clinician providing feedback will allow the client to actually read all or portions of the report will vary. The rationale for allowing the client to actually read the report is that doing so enables the client to experience the product of assessment in a direct manner. It also enables a practitioner to explain any areas that are unclear. A significant difficulty is that the client might misinterpret various portions of the report, especially IQ scores and diagnosis. For this reason, most clinicians paraphrase and elaborate on selected portions of the report. This increases the likelihood that clients will readily understand the most important material and will not be overloaded with too much content.

The likelihood of providing effective feedback can be enhanced by following several guidelines. Initially, the rationale for assessments should be explained and any misconceptions should be corrected. One particularly important misconception is that sometimes clients mistakenly fear that the purpose of assessment is to evaluate their sanity. Practitioners must also select the most essential information to be conveyed to the client. To a large extent, this will involve clinical judgment. Important considerations include the client's ego strength, life situation, stability, and receptiveness to different types of material. Typically, three to four general and well-developed areas will represent an optimum amount of information. The information that is provided should be carefully integrated into the overall context of the person's life. This integration might be enhanced by providing concrete behavioral examples, reflecting on aspects of the client's behavior, referring to relevant aspects of the client's history, or paraphrasing and expanding on a client's self-descriptions. A useful technique is to have the client evaluate the relevance and accuracy of the information. The client might also be requested to give his or her own examples of the trait or pattern of behavior described in the report. Such a collaboration with the client helps the clinician to determine how well the client has understood the feedback. Underlying any feedback should be an attempt to provide the information in a clear, intelligible manner. Commonplace language should be used instead of psychological jargon. It is also important to take into account the client's level of intelligence, education, vocabulary, and level of psychological sophistication. Feedback should not only be a neutral conveyance of data but should also be a clinical intervention. The information should provide the client with new perspectives and options, and should aid in the client's own problem solving.

One possibility is to prepare a personalized report designed specifically for the client. This forces the practitioner to write in a clear, straightforward style. Such reports are more likely to emphasize adaptation rather than pathology. In addition, clear recommendations tend to be emphasized. The optimal communication style is an informal letter written to and for the client ("I am writing to communicate the findings of our psychological assessment . . ."). There are currently a number of computerized reports available directed toward providing the client with feedback. There also seems to be a trend for additional resources to include interpretations directed toward the client such as Lewak et al.'s (1990) *Therapist Guide to the MMPI & MMPI-2: Providing Feedback and Treatments*. These sources should not be seen as substitutes for a dynamic interaction with a client, but as adjuncts for enhancing this process.

FORMAT FOR A PSYCHOLOGICAL REPORT

Even though no single, agreed-on format exists, every report should integrate old information as well as provide a new and unique perspective on the person. Old information should include identifying information (name, birthdate, etc.), reason for referral, and relevant history. New information should include assessment results, impressions, summary/conclusions, and recommendations. At the top of the report, practitioners should indicate its confidential nature by writing "Confidential Psychological Evaluation." A suggested outline is as follows:

Name:
Age (date of birth):
Sex:
Ethnicity:
Date of Report:
Name of Examiner:
Referred by:
   I. Referral Question
  II. Evaluation Procedures
 III. Behavioral Observations
 IV. Background Information
   V. Test Results
 VI. Impressions and Interpretations
VII. Recommendations

Although this outline represents a frequently encountered format, there are many variations. Some practitioners prefer to include the client's marital status, occupational status, and handedness (for neuropsychological reports) at the top of the report along with the other demographic information. Other practitioners prefer to exclude the test results section or include additional sections on diagnosis, case formulation, or summary. Still others like to include subheadings within the "Impressions and Interpretation" section (cognitive functioning and ideation, coping style, affect/mood/emotional control). Sometimes it might be more appropriate to eliminate all or most of the headings and write the report directly to the referral source in a letter format ("Dear Dr. Jones, . . ."). The sample reports included at the back of this chapter have purposely been chosen to demonstrate a variety of different formats in diverse styles and contexts. Each practitioner needs to develop both the format and style that most effectively meets their client's and referral source's needs. In addition, different assessment contexts will require different styles and areas of focus. Medical contexts typically prefer quite brief reports (2–3 single-spaced pages), whereas legal reports often provide much more detail and tend to be considerably longer (5–10 pages or more). A report within a psychology clinic would typically be from 4 to 6 single-spaced pages.

Referral Question

The "Referral Question" section provides a brief description of the client and a statement of the general reason for conducting the evaluation. In particular, this should include a brief description of the nature of the problem. If this section is adequately completed, it should give an initial focus to the report by orienting the reader to what will follow and to the types of issues that will be addressed. This section should begin with a brief, orienting sentence that includes essential information about the client.

("Mr. Smith is a 35-year-old, white, married male with a high school education who presents with complaints of depression and anxiety.") Such a sentence clearly and succinctly introduces the client. Alternatively, such a sentence might be the first sentence in the "Background Information" section. A necessary prerequisite for this section is that the clinician has developed an adequate clarification of the referral question. The purpose of testing should be stated in a precise and problem-oriented manner. Thus, phrases such as "the client was referred for a psychological evaluation" or "as a requirement for a class project" are inadequate in that they lack focus and precision. It is helpful to include both the specific purpose of the evaluation and the decisions facing the referral source. Whenever possible, the reason for referral should be discussed directly with the referring person, and it may sometimes be necessary or useful to discuss the rationale for testing the client. Examples of general reasons for referral include:

- Intellectual evaluation: routine, intellectually disabled (retarded), gifted.
- Differential diagnosis, such as the relative presence of psychological (functional) difficulties versus organic impairment.
- Assessment of the nature and extent of brain damage.
- Evaluation as a component of and to provide recommendations for vocational counseling.
- Evaluation of appropriateness for, possible difficulties encountered, and optimal approach in psychotherapy.
- Personal insight regarding difficulties with interpersonal relationships.
- Evaluation as an aid in client placement.

These represent general referral questions that, in actual situations, would still require further clarification especially regarding the decisions facing the referral source. The key should be to find out what the referring person really wants from the report. This may require reading beneath the surface of the referral question(s) and articulating possible hidden agendas and placing the referral question into a wider context than the presenting problem. An effective referral question should accurately describe the client's and the referral source's current problems. In the report itself, the question(s) should then be answered in the summary of the report, and the recommendations should be relevant to the client's problem.

Evaluation Procedures

The report section that deals with evaluation procedures simply lists the tests and other evaluation procedures used but does not include the actual test results. Usually, full test names are included along with their abbreviations. Later in the report, the abbreviations can be used, but the initial inclusion of the entire name provides a reference for readers who may not be familiar with test abbreviations. For legal evaluations or other occasions in which precise details of administration are important, it is important to include the date on which different tests were administered and the length of time required to complete each one. For most routine evaluations, however, this degree of detail is not recommended. It may also be important to include whether a clinical interview or mental status examination was given and, if so, the degree of interview structure and the amount of time required for the interview or examination. Evaluation procedures may not necessarily be restricted to testing and interviews with the client. Often evaluation will include a review of relevant records such as medical reports, nursing notes, military records, police records, previous psychological or psychiatric reports, or educational records. Additional material might come from interviews with individuals such as spouses, children, parents, friends, employers, physicians, lawyers, social workers, or teachers. If any of these sources are used, their dates and, if relevant, who wrote them should be included. This section might end with a statement summarizing the total time required for the evaluation.

Behavioral Observations

A description of the client's behaviors can provide insight into his or her problem and may be a significant source of data to confirm, modify, or question the test-related interpretations. These observations can be related to a client's appearance, general behavioral observations, or examiner-client interaction. Descriptions should be tied to specific behaviors and should not represent a clinician's inferences. For example, instead of making the inference that the client was "depressed," it is preferable to state that "her speech was slow and she frequently made self-critical statements such as 'I knew I couldn't get that one right.'"

Relevant behavioral observations made during the interview include physical appearance, behavior toward the task and examiner, and degree of cooperativeness. A description of the client's physical appearance should focus on any unusual features relating to facial expressions, clothes, body type, mannerisms, and movements. It is especially important to note any contradictions, such as a 14-year-old boy who acts more like an 18-year-old or a person who appears dirty and disheveled but has an excellent vocabulary and high level of verbal fluency. The behaviors the client expresses toward the test material and the examiner often provide a significant source of information. These may include behaviors that reflect the person's level of affect, manifest anxiety, presence of depression, or degree of hostility. The client's role may be as an active participant or generally passive and submissive; he or she may be very much concerned with his or her performance or relatively indifferent. The client's method of problem solving is often a crucial area to note, and may range from careful and methodical to impulsive and disorganized. It is also important to pay attention to any unusual verbalizations that the client makes about the test material. The level of cooperation expressed by the client should be a factor in assessing the validity of the test results. This is especially important for intelligence and ability tests, since a necessary prerequisite is that the client be alert and attentive, and put forth his or her best effort. It may also be important to note events prior to testing, such as situational crises, previous night's sleep, or use of medication. If there are situational factors that may modify or bring into question the test's validity, they should be noted with statements like, "The test results should be viewed with caution since . . ." or "The degree of maladjustment indicated on the test scores may represent an exaggeration of the client's usual level of functioning due to conditions surrounding the test administration." Often, the most important way to determine test validity in relationship to the client is through a careful look at the client's behaviors relating to the tests and his or her life situation prior to testing.

Sattler (1988, 1992) has developed a "behavior and attitude checklist" comprising 10 major categories that can be rated on a 7-point scale (see Figure 14–2). The examiner may wish to use this checklist as a tool to help focus on areas that might be significant to mention or discuss. It is important to emphasize that other crucial behaviors may occur that are not covered in the checklist and that still require discussion.

Behavioral observations should usually be kept concise, specific, and relevant. If a description does not develop some insight about the person or demonstrate his or her uniqueness, then it should not be included. Thus, if a behavior is normal or average, it will usually not be important to discuss other than to briefly mention that the person had, for example, an average level of cooperation, alertness, or anxiety. The focus, then, should be on those client behaviors that create a unique impression. The relative length of this section will vary from a few brief sentences to considerably longer depending on the amount of relevant information the clinician has noticed. The relative importance of this section in relationship to the overall report will likewise be extremely varied. Sometimes, this section can be almost as important as the test results, whereas at other times it might consist of a few minor observations.

Clinicians who prefer behavioral assessment procedures might wish to emphasize the behavioral observation section by providing more in-depth descriptions of relevant antecedents. Also, consequent events surrounding the problem behavior itself might be evaluated in relationship to their onset, duration, frequency, and intensity. Specific strategies of behavioral assessment include narrative descriptions, interval recording, event recording, ratings recordings, and self-report inventories (see Chapter 4).

At the end of the Behavioral Observations section, it is customary and appropriate to include a statement indicating the validity of the assessment procedures. For example, it might state something like "given the consistency and detail of the client's responses, the client's high level of motivation, and validity indicators on the MMPI-2, the assessment appears to be an accurate assessment of this person's current level of functioning."

Background Information

The write-up of a client's background information should include aspects of the person's history that are relevant to the problem the person is confronting and to the interpretation of the test results. The history, along with the referral question, should also place the problem and the test results into the proper context. In accomplishing these goals, the clinician does not need to include a long, involved chronology with a large number of details, but rather should be as succinct as possible. Some practitioners even urge that the background information section should be kept to one concise paragraph, particularly in medical settings where there is considerable emphasis on conciseness. In selecting which areas to include and which to exclude, a clinician must continually evaluate these areas in relationship to the overall purpose of the report. It is difficult to specify precise rules since each individual will be different. Furthermore, each clinician's own personal and theoretical orientation will alter the types of information he or she feels are significant. Whereas one clinician may primarily describe interpersonal relationships, another may focus on intrapsychic variables, birth order, early childhood events, or details about the client's present situation and environment. The key is to maintain a flexible orientation so that the interviewer will be aware of the most significant elements in the client's

Behavior and Attitude Checklist

Client's name: _____   Examiner: _____

Age: _____   Date of report: _____

Test(s) administered: _____   Date of examination: _____

IQ: _____   Grade: _____

Instructions: Place an X on the appropriate line for each scale.

I. Attitude toward examiner and test situation:

   1. cooperative   __:__:__:__:__:__   uncooperative

   2. passive   __:__:__:__:__:__   aggressive

   3. tense   __:__:__:__:__:__   relaxed

   4. gives up easily   __:__:__:__:__:__   does not give up easily

II. Attitude toward self:

   5. confident   __:__:__:__:__:__   not confident

   6. critical of own work   __:__:__:__:__:__   accepting of own work

III. Work habits:

   7. fast   __:__:__:__:__:__   slow

   8. deliberate   __:__:__:__:__:__   impulsive

   9. thinks aloud   __:__:__:__:__:__   thinks silently

   10. careless   __:__:__:__:__:__   neat

IV. Behavior:

   11. calm   __:__:__:__:__:__   hyperactive

V. Reaction to failure:

   12. aware of failure   __:__:__:__:__:__   unaware of failure

   13. works harder after failure   __:__:__:__:__:__   gives up easily after failure

   14. calm after failure   __:__:__:__:__:__   agitated after failure

   15. apologetic after failure   __:__:__:__:__:__   not apologetic after failure

VI. Reaction to praise:

   16. accepts praise gracefully   __:__:__:__:__:__   accepts praise awkwardly

   17. works harder after praise   __:__:__:__:__:__   retreats after praise

VII. Speech and language:

   18. speech poor   __:__:__:__:__:__   speech good

   19. articulate language   __:__:__:__:__:__   inarticulate language

   20. responses direct   __:__:__:__:__:__   responses vague

   21. converses spontaneously   __:__:__:__:__:__   only speaks when spoken to

   22. bizarre language   __:__:__:__:__:__   reality-oriented language

VIII. Visual-motor:

   23. reaction time slow   __:__:__:__:__:__   reaction time fast

   24. trial-and-error   __:__:__:__:__:__   careful and systematic

   25. skillful movements   __:__:__:__:__:__   awkward movements

IX. Motor:

   26. defective motor coordination   __:__:__:__:__:__   good motor coordination

X. Overall test results:

   27. reliable   __:__:__:__:__:__   unreliable

   28. valid   __:__:__:__:__:__   invalid

Figure 14–2.   Behavior and attitude checklist

Source: From *Assessment of Children* (3rd ed.), p. 92, by J. M. Sattler, 1988, 1992, San Diego: Author. Copyright 1992 by Jerome M. Sattler, Publisher. Reprinted by permission.

life. In general, the end product should include a good history of the problem, along with such areas as important life events, family dynamics, work history, personal interests, daily activities, and past and present interpersonal relationships (see Table 3–1 from Chapter 3).

When describing a client's background, it is important to specify where the information came from ("The client reported that . . ."). This is particularly essential when there may be some question regarding the truth of the client's self-reports or when the history has been obtained from multiple sources.

Usually, a history will begin with a brief summary of the client's general background, including age, sex, family constellation, education, health, and a restatement of the problem. The first sentence might read something like, "Mary Smith is a 48-year-old, white, divorced female, with a high school education, who presents complaints of nervous tension, insomnia, and depression." As pointed out previously, this type of sentence may alternatively be included as the first sentence in the "Referral Question" section. This can be followed by sections describing family background, personal history, medical history, history of the problem, and current life situation.

The extent to which a clinician decides to pursue and discuss a client's family background is subject to a great degree of variability. The primary purpose of such information is to help determine causal factors, what variables might help maintain relevant behaviors, and the extent to which the family should be used as either a focus of systemic intervention or as social support. At a minimum, a brief description of the client's parents is warranted; this may include whether they are separated/divorced and alive/deceased, and their socioeconomic level, occupation, cultural background, and health status. Sometimes, it is important to include information about the emotional and medical backgrounds of parents and close relatives, since certain disorders occur with greater frequency in some families than in the overall population. A description of the general atmosphere of the family is often helpful, including the client's characteristic feelings toward family members and his or her perceptions of their relationships with each other. Descriptions of common family activities and whether the family was from an urban or a rural environment might also be included. If one or both parents died while the client was young, the clinician can still discuss the speculations the client has about his or her parent(s) and can describe the significant persons for the client as he or she was growing up.

The client's personal history can include information from infancy, early childhood, adolescence, and adulthood. Each stage has typical areas to investigate and problems to be aware of. The information from infancy will usually either represent vague recollections or be secondhand information derived from parents or relatives. Thus, it may be subject to a great deal of exaggeration and fabrication. If possible, it may be helpful to have details verified by additional sources, such as through direct questioning of parents or examination of medical records. The degree of contact with parents, toilet training, family atmosphere, and developmental milestones may all be important areas to discuss. Since physical and psychological difficulties often are related and occur simultaneously, including a client's early medical history is sometimes helpful. The most significant tasks during childhood are the development of peer relationships and adjustment to school. What was the quality of the client's early friendships? How much time did the client spend with others? Were there any fights or rebellious acting out? Was the client basically a loner or did he or she have a large number of friends? Did the person join clubs and have group activities, hobbies, or extracurricular interests? In the academic area, it may be of interest to note the usual grades, best or worst subjects, and whether the client skipped or repeated grades. Furthermore, what was his or her relationship with parents, and did the parents restrict activities or allow relative freedom? During adolescent years, clients typically face further academic, psychological, and social adjustments to high school. Of particular importance are their reactions to puberty and early heterosexual relationships. Did they have difficulties with sex role identity, abuse drugs or alcohol, or rebel against authority figures? The adult years center around occupational adjustment and establishing marital and family relationships. During early adulthood, what were clients' feelings and aspirations regarding marriage? What were their career goals? Did they effectively establish independence from parents? As adulthood progressed, were there any significant changes in the quality of their close relationships, employment, or expression of sexuality? What activities did they engage in during their leisure time? As clients age, they face challenges in adapting to their declining abilities and limitations, and developing a meaningful view of their lives.

Although the personal history can help place the problem in its proper context and explain certain causative factors, it is usually essential to spend some time focusing directly on the problem itself. Of particular importance are the initial onset and the nature of the symptoms. From the time when the client first noticed these symptoms, have there been any changes in frequency, intensity, or nature? Furthermore, were there any previous attempts at treatment, and if so, what was the outcome? In some reports, the history of the problem will be the longest and most important part of the history section.

The family and personal histories usually reveal information relating to the predisposing cause of a client's difficulties, whereas the history of the problem often provides an elaboration of the precipitating and reinforcing causes. To complete this picture, the clinician also has to develop a sense of the factors currently reinforcing the problem. This requires information relating to the client's life situation. Significant areas may be the client's life stresses, including changes that he or she is confronting. Also, what are the nature of and resources provided by his or her family and work relationships? Finally, it is important to understand the alternatives and decisions that the client is facing.

Sometimes, an evaluation needs to assess the possible presence and nature of organic impairment. In many cases, the history is of even greater significance than test results and often the most valuable information a psychologist can provide to a referring medical practitioner is a thorough history. Thus, the history needs to be complete and must address a number of areas that are not ordinarily covered in personality evaluations. Several interview aids have been commercially developed to help ensure that most relevant areas are covered (see Chapter 12). If the person reports having had a head injury, it is important to note the length of time the client was unconscious (if at all), whether he or she actually remembers getting hit, the last memory before the injury and the first thing he or she clearly remembers following the injury. In all neuropsychological assessments, a crucial area is to establish the person's premorbid level of functioning. This may mean obtaining information on his or her grade point average in high school or college, sending for any relevant records (e.g., previous IQ results), previous highest level of employment, and personal interests or hobbies. Often it may be necessary to verify the client's previous level of functioning from outside sources, such as from parents or employers. In determining the probable cause of brain impairment, it may be difficult to rule out other possibilities, such as exposure to toxic substances, strokes, high fevers, or other episodes of head trauma. Areas of current functioning that need to be addressed might include memory problems, word-finding difficulties, weakness on one side of the body, alterations in gait, loss of consciousness, and unusual sensations. Previous assessments with CT/MRI scans, EEGs, or neurological physical exams would also be important to obtain. Even though these medical records might be able to identify the site and size of a lesion, it is still the work of the psychologist to describe what the person is doing as a result of these lesions. It might also be important to obtain current or past information regarding drug intake, especially recent alterations in prescriptions since these might effect psychological functioning. The interview data and neuropsychological test results from a psychologist should ideally be combined with and complement medical records, such as CT scans and neurological exams. Although the preceding topics are by no means exhaustive, they represent some of the more important areas to consider when taking a history related to possible neuropsychological deficit.

Although the quantity of such information may seem immense, the history format described here is only a general guideline. At times, it may be appropriate to ignore many of the areas mentioned earlier and focus on others. In condensing the client's history into the report, it is important to avoid superfluous material and continually question whether the information obtained is relevant to the general purpose of the report. Again, some practitioners might prefer to restrict the length of this section to a single paragraph. Furthermore, it is typically not useful to include material that is already in the possession of the referral source. This may be perceived as needless duplication and could result in the history section becoming needlessly long.

Test Results

For certain reports, it may not be necessary to list test scores. Some practitioners even prefer to completely exclude actually giving test scores since it might give the report the impression of being too data/test oriented. However, it is usually recommended that at some point test scores be included especially in legal reports or when professionals who are knowledgeable about testing will be reading the report. If practitioners feel that including this section in the report itself is too test/data oriented or serves to unnecessarily "clutter" the report, then the test data, perhaps including the actual profiles, might be inserted in an appendix. This could then be noted and the reader referred to the appendix in the evaluation procedures section. Intelligence test scores are traditionally listed first and, for the Wechsler scales, should include Verbal IQ, Performance IQ, and Full Scale IQ, along with the subtests and their scaled scores. Subtests that have been found to be significant strengths should be indicated with an "S" next to the subtest score and significant weaknesses should be indicated with a "W." This is often followed by Bender results, which may simply be summarized by a statement like: "Empirically not in the organic range, although there were difficulties organizing the designs and frequent erasures." MMPI-2/MMPI-A results are often listed with the validity scales given first, followed by scales ordered from highest to lowest. They can also be listed in the order in which they appear on the profile sheet. Any standardized test results (MMPI-2, MMPI-A, CPI, etc.) should always be referred to by their T (or other standardized) scores and *not* the raw scores. Whereas it is fairly straightforward to list the objective and intelligence test scores, it is considerably more difficult to adequately describe the scores on projective tests. The Rorschach summary sheet can be included, but the results from projective drawings and the TAT are usually omitted. Should a clinician wish to summarize projective drawings, a brief statement is usually sufficient, such as "human figure drawings were miniaturized and immature, with the inclusion of two transparencies." Likewise, TAT "scores" can be summarized by a brief statement of the strongest needs and press, and a mention of the most common themes encountered in the stories.

Impressions and Interpretations

This section can be considered to be the main body of the report. It requires that the main findings of the evaluation be presented in the form of integrated hypotheses. The areas discussed and the style of presentation will vary according to the personal orientation of the clinician, the purpose of testing, the individual being tested, and the types of tests administered. One format that should be encouraged is to discuss the material by different integrated topics rather than test by test. This provides a more coherent presentation of the information. Klopfer (1960) recommends using a grid with the topics for consideration in the left column (derived from Table 14–1) with the assessment results in the top row. This enables the practitioner to list the essential findings in the appropriate box where the topic and the method of assessment intersect. When actually writing the "Impressions and Interpretations" section of the report, the clinician can then review all findings within a particular topic and summarize them on the report. An example of such a grid is given in Figure 14–3. The

Topics	Evaluation Procedures				
	Interview	WAIS-R	MMPI-2	BDI	Rorschach
Validity of results					
Cognitive functioning					
Emotional controls					
Interpersonal relations					
Diagnostic impression					
Recommendations					

Figure 14–3.   Sample grid of personality characteristics by tests administered
Source: Modified from Klopfer, W. G., *The Psychological Report: Use and Communication of Psychological Findings,* p. 36, by W. G. Klopfer, 1960, New York: Grune & Stratton, Copyright 1960 by Grune & Stratton. Reprinted by permission.

list of assessment methods is dependent on which tests the examiner administered, but the topics can be chosen and arranged according to which areas the clinician would like to focus on.

All inferences made in the "Impressions and Interpretations" section should be based on an integration of the test data, behavioral observations, relevant history, and additional available data. The conclusions and discussion may relate to such areas as the client's overt behavior, self-concept, family background, intellectual abilities, emotional difficulties, medical disorders, school problems, or interpersonal conflicts. A client's intellectual abilities often provide a general frame of reference for a variety of personality variables. For this reason, a discussion of the client's intellectual abilities usually occurs first. Although this should include a general estimate of the person's intelligence as indicated by IQ scores, it is also important to provide a discussion of more specific abilities. This discussion may include an analysis of such areas as memory, problem solving, abstract reasoning, concentration, and fund of information. If the report is to be read by persons who are familiar with test theory, it may be sufficient to include IQ scores without an explanation of their normative significance. In most reports, it is helpful to include the IQ scores as well as the percentile ranking (see Appendix A) and general intellectual classification (high average, superior, etc.; see Table 5–1). Some examiners may even prefer to omit the actual IQ scores in favor of including only percentile rank and general classification. This can be useful in cases where persons reading the report might be likely to misunderstand or misinterpret unexplained IQ scores. Once a general estimate of intelligence has been made, it should, whenever possible, be followed by a discussion of the client's intellectual strengths and weaknesses. This may involve elaborating on the meaning of the difference between Verbal IQ and Performance IQ or a discussion of subtest scatter. In addition, it can be useful to compare the client's potential level of functioning with his or her actual performance. If there is a wide discrepancy between these two, then reasons for this discrepancy should be offered. For example, the client may be underachieving due to anxiety, low motivation, emotional interference, or perceptual processing difficulties. Practitioners may also wish to discuss additional noncognitive areas of intellectual assessment. This might include the extent to which the person prefers to achieve through independent activities versus within a structured environment, the level of motivation, or, the relative intellectual efficiency or hardiness. Cognitive assessments in psychiatric contexts might include any bizarre associations, degree to which their thinking is organized, or how concrete or abstract their thought processes are.

Whereas a discussion of intellectual abilities is relatively clear and straightforward, the next sections are frequently more difficult to select. There is an extremely wide number of possibilities to choose from, many of which have been listed in Table 14–1. Some practitioners recommend including set topics. These typically include the client's level of emotional functioning (affect and mood), interpersonal style and orientation, and intrapersonal or intrapsychic functioning (Beutler, 1995b; Wolber & Carne, 1993). A neuropsychological evaluation might divide the impression and interpretation into such areas as memory, language functions, executive abilities, awareness of deficits, sensory/perceptual functions, and personality. One rationale for not having a preset list of topics to discuss is that the topics should be based primarily on the referral question. This allows the practitioner to flexibly organize the topics based on the context of the report and the needs of the referral source and client. If the referral question is clearly focused on a specific problem, then it may only be necessary to elaborate on two or three topics. A referral question that is more general may require a wider approach in which six or more areas are discussed.

Some of the more common and important topics are the client's level of psychopathology, dependency, hostility, sexuality, interpersonal relationships, diagnosis, and behavioral predictions. A client's level of psychopathology refers to the relative severity of the disturbances he or she is experiencing. It is important to distinguish whether the results are characteristic of normals, outpatients, or inpatients, and whether the difficulties are long term or a reaction to current life stresses. Does the client use behaviors that are adaptive or those that are maladaptive and self-defeating? Within the area of ideation, are there persistent thoughts, delusions, hallucinations, loose associations, blocking of ideas, perseveration, or illogical thoughts? It may also be important to assess the adequacy of the client's judgments and relative degree of insight. Can the person effectively make plans, understand the impact he or she has on others, and judge the appropriateness of his or her behavior? To assess the likelihood of successful therapy, it is especially important to assess the client's level of insight. This includes assessing the person's ability to think psychologically, awareness of his or her own changing feelings, understanding of the behaviors of others, and ability to conceptualize and discuss relevant insights.

Usually, a client's greatest conflicts will center on difficulties with dependency, hostility, and sexuality. In discussing a client's dependency, it is important to discuss the strength of these needs, the typical roles played with others, and present or past significant relationships. In what ways does the client defend him- or herself against, or cope with, feelings of dependency? This evaluation may include a discussion of defense mechanisms, thoughts, behaviors, feelings, or somatic responses as they relate to dependency. The relative intensity of a client's hostility is also important. Is the expression of hostility indirect, or is it direct in the form of either verbal criticisms or actual assaultive behavior? If the expression of hostility is covert, it may be the result of such factors as fear of loss of love, retaliation, or guilt. When the client does feel anger, what are his or her characteristic defenses against these feelings? For example, some clients might express opposite behaviors, with overly exaggerated concern for others, or they might direct the anger inward by developing physical aches and pains that serve as self-punishment for having aggressive impulses. They may also adapt through such means as extreme suspiciousness of others, which has been created by denying their hostility and attributing it to others. A discussion of a client's sexuality usually involves noting the relative intensity of his or her urges and the degree of anxiety associated with the expression of those urges. Does the client inhibit his or her sexuality due to a belief that it is dirty, experience anxiety over possible consequences, or associate it with aggressiveness? Defenses against sexual urges may be handled in ways similar to hostility, such as by performing the opposite behavior through extreme religiosity or celibacy, or by denying the feelings and attributing them instead to others. On the other hand, clients may impulsively act out their sexual urges, at least in part out of a need to obtain self-affirmation through sexual contact. Clinicians may want to discuss the dynamics involved in any unusual sexual practices.

Discussing clients' characteristic patterns and roles in interpersonal relationships can also be extremely useful. These can often be discussed in relationship to the dimensions of submissiveness/dominance and love/hate, or the extent to which they orient themselves around the need to be included, control others, or seek affection. Is their style of communicating typically guarded or is it open and self-disclosing to the extent that they can discuss such areas as painful feelings and fears? Can they deal with the specifics of a situation or are they usually vague and general? Do they usually appear assertive and direct, or passive and indirect? Finally, it is often important to determine the extent to which they are perceptive about interpersonal relationships and their typical approaches toward resolving conflict.

It may also be appropriate to include descriptions of vocational goals and aptitudes. This is becoming increasingly important in educational reports, especially for students with special educational needs, such as those who are handicapped (Levinson, 1987; Luckasson et al., 1992; Schalock et al., 1994). Many of the tests covered in this text can help in assessing a person's strengths and weaknesses, but practitioners may also need to include further assessment devices, such as the Self Directed Search, Strong-Campbell Interest Inventory or Kuder Occupational Interest Survey.

A frequent consideration is whether the client's difficulties will continue or, if currently absent, recur. If the client's future prospects are poor, then a statement of the rationale for this conclusion should be given. For example, if a clinician predicts that the response to treatment will be poor, then he or she should explain that this is due to such factors as a strong need to appear hypernormal, poor insight, and a high level of defensiveness. Likewise, favorable predictions should include a summary of the client's assets and resources, such as psychological mindedness, motivation to change, and social supports. If difficulties are likely to be encountered during the course of treatment, then the nature and intensity of these difficulties should be discussed. The prediction of suicidal potential, assaultive behavior, child abuse, or criminal behavior is essential in certain types of reports. Often the tests themselves are not useful in predicting these behaviors. For example, one of the best ways of predicting suicidal potential is to evaluate the client's past history, current environment, personal resources, and degree of suicide intent (see Stelmachers, 1995). However, research indicates that many predictions of behavior, such as dangerousness, are subject to error (Hall, 1984; Megargee, 1995; Ziskin & Faust, 1995). This is especially true for long-term predictions. Clinicians should thus exercise appropriate caution in making predictions and not exceed the bounds of reasonable certainty.

Sometimes clinicians may wish to include a separate section on diagnosis. However, whether to include a *DSM-IV* (or *ICD-10;* World Health Organization, 1990) diagnosis has been an area of some controversy. Some clinicians feel that labels should be avoided since they may result in self-fulfilling prophecies, be overly reductionistic, and allow clients to avoid responsibility for their own behavior. Other objections to diagnosis stem from researchers who feel that many of the terms are not scientifically valid (Rosenhan, 1973; Ziskin & Faust, 1995), are not particularly useful in planning interventions (Beutler, 1989) or from psychiatrists who feel that it should be primarily their role to provide diagnoses (Tallent & Reiss, 1959c). If a clinician does decide to give a diagnosis, he or she must first have a clear operational knowledge of the diagnostic terms. He or she should also include the client's premorbid level of adjustment, and the severity and frequency of the disturbance. Instruments such as the Structured Clinical Interview for the *DSM-IV* (SCID; Spitzer et al., 1990), Structured Interview for *DSM-IV* Personality (SIDP) or Anxiety Disorders Interview Schedule (Brown et al., 1994) might help to increase the reliability of diagnosis. It is also important to include the possible causes of the disorder. A discussion of causes should not be simplistic and one-dimensional but rather should appreciate the complexity of causative factors. Thus, causes may be described from the perspective of primary, predisposing, precipitating, and reinforcing factors. Clinicians may also discuss the relative significance of biological, psychological, and sociocultural variables.

One option is to include a summary paragraph at the end of the "Impressions and Interpretations" section. The purpose of the summary is to restate succinctly the primary findings and conclusions. This requires that the practitioner select only the most important issues and that he or she be careful not to overwhelm the reader with needless details. If the summary is included at the end of the section, there is no need to summarize the entire report but only the major interpretations. However, some practitioners prefer to include a separate "Summary and Recommendations" section at the end of the entire report. In this case, the section should summarize the entire report and include the recommendations. Either location is acceptable; the choice can be based on the clinician's personal preference and the needs of the report as suggested by the referral question(s) and background of the readers.

Recommendations

The ultimate practical purpose of the report is contained in the recommendations since they suggest what steps can be taken to solve problems. Such recommendations should be clear, practical, and obtainable, and should relate directly to the purpose of the report. The best reports are those that help the referral source and/or the client to solve the problems they are facing (Ownby, 1990; Pryzwansky & Hanania, 1986; Tallent, 1992, 1993). To achieve this report-writing goal, the clinician must clearly understand the problem, the best alternatives for remediation, and the resources available in the community. One practical implication is that writers can improve their reports by becoming as familiar as possible with the uses to which their reports will be applied. An effective report must answer the referral question and also have decisional value. Once these factors have been carefully considered, recommendations can be developed. Decisions related to recommendations occur on three different levels (Beutler, 1995b). First, decisions need to be made related to the *setting or context* (outpatient, day hospital, halfway house, inpatient, new work environment, change in schools/classes). Second, consideration needs to be given to *developing a relationship* with the client (degree of resistance, level of insight, interpersonal style, empathy, etc.). Finally, decisions need to be made about *specific intervention procedures* (systematic desensitization, emotional support, vocational training, rehabilitation, special education, etc.).

Practitioners and researchers alike have become increasingly interested in tailoring the results of assessment towards optimal client interventions (see Chapter 13). For example, Beutler and Clarkin (1990) provide strong empirical support that planning interventions around problem complexity, problem severity, motivational distress, coping styles, and level of resistance (reactance) can increase the effectiveness of treatment outcomes. Additional relevant variables include the stage of change (Prochaska & DiClemente, 1992), hypnotic responsiveness (Groth-Marnat, 1991), neuroticism, level of stress (Wickramasekera, 1995), level of abstract versus concrete thinking, and ego strength. Outcome research for particular types of problems (anxiety, sexual dysfunction, etc.) frequently indicate that certain interventions are more effective than others. Especially relevant are the specific causes and expression of a disorder. For example, depression can result from and be maintained by a variety of factors including irrational cognitions, poor social skills, grief, stress, poor interpersonal relations, medical illnesses, substance abuse, medications, and faulty biological mechanisms. The relative contribution of each of these causes has important implications for optimally tailoring client interventions. By considering each of these areas, the practitioner can develop optimal specific, targeted recommendations.

One clear finding is that reports are typically rated most useful when their recommendations are highly specific rather than general (Brandt & Giebink, 1968; Ownby, 1990; White, Nielsen, & Prus, 1984). Thus, a recommendation that states "the client should begin psychotherapy" is not as useful as a statement of the need for "individual therapy focusing on the following areas: increased assertiveness, relaxation techniques for reducing anxiety, and increased awareness of the self-defeating patterns he creates in relationships." Likewise, a recommendation for "special education" can be improved by expanding it to "special education two hours a day, emphasizing exercises in auditory sequencing and increasing immediate recall for verbally relevant information." However, caution should be exercised when providing specific recommendations in some contexts since some health professionals may feel that developing treatment recommendations is primarily their responsibility or perhaps should be made by the overall treatment team (Tallent, 1993; Tallent & Reiss, 1959a). Once the report, with its recommendations, has been submitted, continued contact should be made with the readers(s) to make sure the report has not been filed and forgotten. Even the best report will not be functional unless the recommendations are practical, obtainable, and actually put into action.

SAMPLE REPORTS

The sample reports in this section are from the more common settings in which clinicians work and consult. The dimensions in which the reports vary are:

- Format.
- Extent to which history rather than test data is emphasized.
- Types of tests used.
- Degree to which they include a variety of descriptions rather than being case focused with a relatively limited range of topics.

Within each setting, specific questions have been presented along with decisions that must be made related to the client. The different reports illustrate how the clinician has integrated the test data, client's history, and behavioral observations to handle these questions. The reports were selected to illustrate a wide diversity in format, length, type of setting, referral question, and type of tests used.

The first report was developed for a psychiatric setting and was intended to be read by professional mental health personnel. For this reason, there is some use of technical language and a focus on developing a detailed, traditional *DSM-IV* diagnosis. What is noteworthy in the handling of the test data is that the bulk of the discussion relating to test interpretation revolves around projective test findings (Rorschach, TAT, projective drawing). Furthermore, much of the projective data is used in a qualitative, content-oriented manner. This was achieved by providing actual verbatim responses, which give a more colorful and rich portrayal of the client's thought processes than could be achieved through quantitative scores. For example, some of the TAT stories are written out to illustrate attitudes toward the client's parents and how the client perceives and attempts to cope with his inner sense of "evilness."

The evaluation written for a legal context approaches the client from a variety of angles. It tries to fit the presenting problem into material derived from behavioral observations during the interview; discusses his reaction to the charges, family relationships, and interests; and reviews relevant aspects of test data. This noteworthy diversity of approaches also helps to develop a complete picture of the person. The psychological test results represent just one source of data. There are also additional features to the structure of the report. Initially, there is a personal letter format directed to the referral source. When a report is being directed to a primary referral person, an opening letter tends to make the report more personal, thereby enhancing the likelihood of good rapport between the clinician and the referring person. The section summarizing the report is placed at the end and given considerable emphasis. This section integrates information not only from psychological tests, but also from other sources. Furthermore, the recommendations are included in, and closely tied to, the summary.

The third sample is from an educational context and is the most case focused of the reports. It mainly discusses the intellectual strengths and weaknesses of the client, and connects these in a general way with her social development. For the most part, the report avoids a discussion of personality dynamics because these were not requested by the referral source. Furthermore, her history indicated that the client's level of interpersonal adjustment was good. The most important part of the report is the recommendations. These are given the most discussion, and are as specific and concrete as possible. Once the client's cognitive weaknesses are documented in the section on interpretation and impressions, the main thing her parents and teachers need to know is what specific measures can be taken to work with these weaknesses.

The final report was written within a general psychology clinic and was intended for use by mental health professionals. As a result, some technical language is used primarily in the form of a formal *DSM-IV* diagnosis. The major feature of the report is the extensive development of a detailed treatment planning for psychotherapeutic intervention. This plan was developed based on the model detailed in Chapter 13. The recommendations are eclectic in orientation and assume that the treating practitioner can effectively use a number of techniques from a variety of theoretical orientations. Another feature of the report is that psychological test data has not been included. Specifically, there is no "Test Results" section. This is because some, if not many practitioners believe that the inclusion of detailed test results is both unnecessary and results in "cluttering" up the report with distracting detail. It is rather assumed that the referral source is most interested in the integration of the overall assessment along with the relevant recommendations.

THE PSYCHIATRIC SETTING*

NAME: Robert
DATE OF BIRTH: 2/5/81
DATES OF EVALUATION: 3/14/95

IDENTIFYING INFORMATION

Robert M. is a 14-year-old high school student admitted to the psychiatric unit at Monte Hospital on March 10, 1995, for his second psychiatric hospitalization. He was referred for an interview and psychological testing by Harold Smith, MD, to estimate his intelligence, differential diagnosis, behavioral dynamics, and potential for adjustment.

PRESENTING PROBLEM

Robert stated that he was in the hospital "for family problems." (What kind?) "Just not getting along. Not being able to work out at home." He said these problems started two years ago when "my mom put me into a private school, and I got kicked out" for "doing wrong things. Inappropriateness." Reportedly, on March 9, 1995, Robert consumed a large quantity of alcohol, became acutely intoxicated and was agitated, belligerent, combative, tearful, and yelled obscenities. His family took him to Monte hospital where tests revealed a blood alcohol level of .24 without indication of other drugs. Seemingly, he consumed this near lethal dose of alcohol in response to his hatred and fear of his parents.

BACKGROUND INFORMATION

The following information was obtained from Robert, who was a restless and dubious historian, from his hospital chart, and from a March 12, 1995, telephone conversation with Dr. Smith.

Robert was born and raised in San Francisco County and his biological parents remain married. The father, approximately age 40, is a career Air Force person with a rank unknown to Robert. He said his father teaches machine maintenance and attends college. He described his father as "a mean, violent, cruel person." (How does he show this?) "He used to hit me." (What would cause him to do that?) "Sometimes when I did something wrong." (Like what?) "Anything, any little thing, sometimes." He said he was hit with objects such as "a belt, sticks, spoons, forks, knives. Any object a lot of times." He said the most significant injuries he suffered during such beatings were "large blood blisters on my hand." He said he never suffered an injury that required medical attention but that he did ask his father's permission to remain out of school to conceal the marks from his peers. He said his father refused the request.

---

*Report contributed by Tom MacSpeiden, PhD.

Robert's mother is approximately age 35 and a business secretary. Asked to describe her, he said, "I don't know. I guess she's mean. That's what I think. Is it my opinion?" (Yes. Mean in what way?) "Verbal abuse, yelling, screaming." (What causes her to do this?) "Anything, like my father. Frustration." (How does she react when your father hits you?) "She doesn't do anything. She lets him."

Robert is the oldest of three siblings with a brother, age 13, and a sister, age 10. Both siblings live in the home and attend school. "My brother's a little strange. Very silly and inappropriate for his age." He said his brother shows these characteristics when he "runs around naked, talks real strange like he's on an acid trip when he's not." He said his brother excels in school and has never received counseling or psychotherapy. Regarding the sister, "She's fine."

Medically, Robert believes he experienced an uneventful gestation and delivery. Regarding unusual illnesses or accidents, he said that at age 10 or 11 he broke either his wrist or his thumb during horseplay with friends and that the break healed without limitation. He said that at a later age he could not recall he broke his finger and wrist in horseplay and that he had broken such bones approximately four or five times. He said that otherwise his health has been good.

Asked about unusual events in his life before starting school, Robert said, "I can't remember that far back." He said he enrolled at Rutledge Elementary School at the usual age where he remained in regular classes through the sixth grade. He earned primarily "C's," and related to his peers "well." He said he also related to his teachers "well." He said he had no behavioral problems in elementary school and that his life was uneventful.

For the seventh grade, Robert was placed in a Roman Catholic school "because during the sixth grade they felt I was failing, not doing my work, taking too much leisure time." He said he remained at the Catholic school until the last month of the school year when he was expelled because of frequent misbehavior. Initially, he said he could not remember what act led to the expulsion but later said, "I lit a firecracker in class." (In your opinion, why did you do that?) "Rebelling." (Against?) "Parents. It was also for fun." (Why were you rebelling against them?) "Cause I didn't want to go to that school. I wanted to go to public school." (Why?) "Because I had gone to a public school for six years, and all my friends were going there."

Robert said he remained home without attending school until the following fall, September 1994, when he enrolled in the eighth grade at Franklin Junior High School to remain in regular classes until entering Monte Hospital. In the eighth grade his marks were "failing, no, below standard." (Why were they so low?) "Because I had started using alcohol, drugs. I don't know. I don't know if that's the reason." (Why did you start using drugs?) "I don't know that, the reason why." He said he was introduced to alcohol and other drugs by his age peers. He estimated that he was intoxicated approximately 30 times during the eighth grade, usually at home with friends while his parents were out. The only street drug used was marijuana. He said his parents did not know about his substance misuse but complained about his grades. "They wanted me to bring them up, but I started failing even more." He said otherwise there were no unusual events during the eighth grade.

Last September, Robert enrolled in the ninth grade. Then, "I started hanging out with more friends that drank and used more drugs," but he misused only alcohol and marijuana. He said he was intoxicated "a few times a week" and misused marijuana "maybe four or five times a week." He said that otherwise his life was uneventful until he entered Monte Hospital for the first time during Christmas vacation because "I was dead drunk." He said he remained hospitalized three days, until "the doctor thought I should be discharged." A week later, he returned to Monte Hospital for his current hospitalization.

Asked about his future plans in life, Robert said, "I haven't made any. I want to live with my grandparents, but they're not going to let me." He said his mother and his treating psychiatrist were against this plan because "they think I'm running away from my problems."

PSYCHOLOGICAL IMPRESSIONS

Robert was seen on the Delta unit at Monte Hospital on March 12, 1995. He presented himself looking his stated age and adequately nourished as a pubescent male with somewhat disheveled dark blond hair parted approximately on the right side, a fair facial complexion with mild acne and dressed in a white T-shirt, a blue and white plaid long-sleeved shirt in poor repair and new appearing Levi's. A cross-shaped earring dangled from his left ear. At the beginning of the interview and multiple times thereafter, Robert asked when the evaluation would end. At one point, this examiner asked what Robert would do after the evaluation was completed, and Robert said he would go to his room to lie down because he was tired. He had a depressed facial expression, but was physically agitated and demonstrated considerable motor overflow although he remained continuously seated in his chair. During the intelligence testing, he seemed to exert effort until a task became difficult whereupon he became disheartened and reduced his effort. During the projective testing, he was brief and hurried to complete the tasks. There were no indications of delusions or hallucinations, and he was oriented in all three spheres. His hygiene was adequate. He was alert, and both recent and remote memory appeared intact.

Robert was administered the Wechsler Intelligence Scale for Children-3rd ed. (WISC-III), Rorschach, Thematic Apperception Test (TAT), Bender Visual Motor Gestalt Test (Bender) and Draw-A-Family Test.

On the WISC-III, Robert obtained a Verbal IQ of 91, a Performance IQ of 84 and a Full Scale IQ of 86. His Verbal scaled scores ranged from 7 to 10 without significant deviation from the Verbal mean. Similarly, his Performance scaled scores ranged from 6 to 10. Verbally he functioned at the 27th percentile and in the average range. In terms of perceptual motor performance he functioned at the 14th percentile and in the low average range. Overall he functioned intellectually at the 18th percentile and in the low average range. His performance is probably a conservative reflection of his intellectual capacity which may be as high as the high average range.

The structure of Robert's personality was difficult to estimate from his limited 14 Rorschach responses but appears nonpsychotic. Because of his limited responses, his ratios and percentages should be interpreted with caution. He uses repression and denial excessively in an attempt to exclude unacceptable impulses and fantasies from consciousness ($F = 92\%$). Nonetheless, Robert has difficulty seeing those things in the environment seen by most persons (Populars = 1) and at times gravely distorts his perceptions ($X + \% = 65\%$). These distortions are not frequent and are most likely to occur when he is emotionally stimulated. Because of his rigid defense posture, he currently has few energies available ($M + C = 2.0$). He attempts to enhance control by denying emotional stimuli (Sum $C = 0$), and generally when expressing emotion has adequate control ($FC:CF + C = 1:0$). Because of his rigidity, his aspirations exceed his ability to perform ($W:M = 7:0$), and there was no indication of whether he prefers to accomplish more in fantasy or more in action ($EB = 1:1$). Because of his excessive repression and denial, his depression is not obvious since he does not easily respond to emotional material ($Afr = .60$). For his age, his interests are somewhat narrow and immature ($A = 64\%$).

The content of Robert's personality projected in his Rorschach responses is a perception of himself as confused and disorganized, much as he projected in his first response to Card I: "A star. A messed up star. Someone drew it wrong." As noted in his Rorschach scores, he attempts to deny emotional stimuli to enhance control, a mechanism typified in his rejection of Cards VIII and IX, the first of three highly chromatic and therefore affectively stimulating cards. When presented with Card VIII, he responded in approximately two seconds, "I see nothing in this. I don't see anything." His response to Card IX was similar. On Card X he used the whole of the blot as "an insect," a response that had negative form level. Curiously, he saw on each of the first five Rorschach cards the percept of "insect." Such perseveration is often found among neurologically damaged persons although it appears more likely in Robert's case a product of anxiety which limited his ability to structure the amorphous blot material much beyond an unspecified insect.

The content of Robert's personality projected in his TAT responses is a painful perception of himself as evil, a perception that may have resulted in part from his already overly punitive superego receiving further stimulation while he was enrolled in a parochial school for the seventh grade. This content was suggested by his cryptic response to Card 2, a man plowing with a horse in the background, a pregnant woman standing to one side near a tree, and a girl in the foreground holding books:

Past, going, gone to a church school. Present, leaving home. Future, death. (Death in what way?) Starvation.

Robert views his internal anger and violence as undeniable indicators of his evilness, an evilness from which he can escape by drowning it along with himself in alcohol. Vivid were his responses to Cards 8BM, a primitive surgical scene with a boy standing in the foreground and a gun to one side; and 13MF, a bare-breasted woman lying on a bed and a man standing with one hand to his forehead:

8BM   Past, Vietnam War. Present, remembering. Future, death of a heart attack. (What was he remembering?)

The people being cut up in the Vietnam War.

13MF   Past, alcoholic. Present, wife died. Future, death from alcohol. (Why did the wife die?) Kidney disease.

Alternatively he conceptualizes continuing to live with the evil within him without death, as projected in his response to Card 15, a figure standing among tombstones:

Past, possessed with evil. Present, trying to destroy the evil. Future, living with evil. (What was the evil?) The devil.

He believes that were he to continue living with his evil he would represent a danger to other persons. This content was typified in his response to Card 7BM, a younger and older man in conversation:

Past, jail. Present, courtroom. Future, jail. (Why was he in jail?) Murder.

Robert believes that in the past he was unwanted by a significant other. This awareness instilled in him the belief he was lacking in some way. When someone now offers him acceptance, he rejects it although he hopes he will be able to accept it at some point in the future.

On the Bender, all figures were completed with relative accuracy, and there were no indications of a neurological dysfunction affecting Robert's perceptual motor control. There were several indicators of impulsivity including overlapping, poor planning, and poor overall quality (see Figure 14–4).

Asked to draw a picture of his family, Robert drew from left to right persons he later labeled verbally as "Dad," "Sister," and "Mom." Above these three and along the upper margin of the page from left to right he drew "Me" and "Brother" (see Figure 14–5).

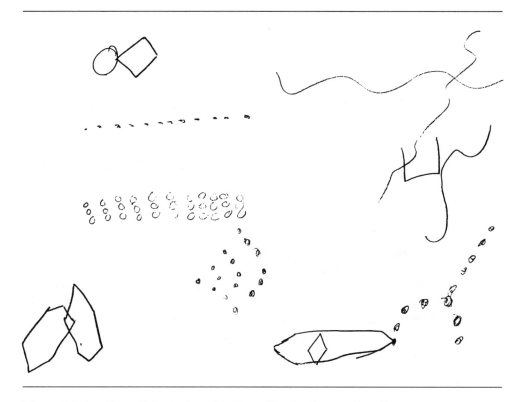

Figure 14–4.   Case: Robert. Age: 14. *Note:* **Size has been reduced.**

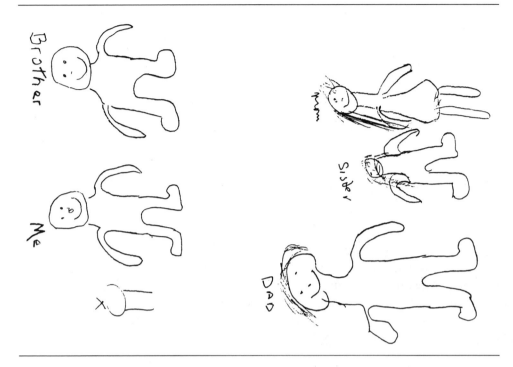

Figure 14–5.   Case: Robert. Age: 14. *Note:* **Size has been reduced.**

The drawing projects Robert's perception of him and his brother as separate from the parents and sister, much as he indicated during the interview when he said, "My brother's a little strange"; and clearly he views himself as somewhat strange. Not surprisingly, he perceives the father as powerful and his mother as significantly weaker than his father.

SUMMARY

Robert functions intellectually in the low average range although his endowment may be in the high average range and is currently reduced by his mental condition. He does not suffer from a neurological dysfunction affecting his perceptual motor control. His personality structure is nonpsychotic but exceedingly rigid and characterized by repression and denial such that he fails to see those things in the environment seen by most persons and has few energies available. He attempts to enhance control by denying emotional stimuli and generally can maintain control when responding emotionally. When highly stimulated emotionally, however, he gravely distorts his perceptions. With his rigid defense structure, he has few energies available to gratify his aspirations but is capable of concealing overt indications of depression such as tearfulness and significant withdrawal. When he is consuming disinhibiting chemicals such as alcohol, his behavioral and emotional expressions are far less controlled.

Robert has at least a vague awareness he is "messed up." It is probable he was highly critical of himself prior to enrollment in the Roman Catholic school. There he may have been overly scrupulous when interpreting moral teachings, and his already punitive superego became self-destructive. He may have felt most guilty about the commandment to honor parental figures. He came to view himself as anathema. He believes his alternatives are to continue living with the believed devil inside him with the probability he will eventually murder someone or alternatively to end his life to escape the internal evil and avoid harming others. Not unexpectedly, death is frightening to him and presently he flirts with self-destruction by poisoning himself with alcohol.

DIAGNOSTIC IMPRESSIONS [*DSM-IV*]

AXIS I	300.40	Dysthymia, Secondary Type, Early Onset
	303.90	Alcohol Dependence, Moderate
	305.20	Cannabis Abuse
AXIS II	V71.09	No Developmental or Personality Disorder Diagnosed
AXIS III		No Physical Condition or Disorder Diagnosed
AXIS IV		Psychosocial Stressors: Perception of himself as intrinsically evil and unlovable, believed rejection by parents, effects of drug misuse, failure to adjust socially and psychiatric hospitalization. Severity: 4-Severe [Admixture of acute events and enduring circumstances]
AXIS V		Global Assessment of Functioning [GAF]: Current GAF: 35 Highest GAF past year: 50

RECOMMENDATIONS

A more complete social history would be useful in determining the major factors contributing to Robert's strong negative self-image. Although it is unlikely Robert's father is as abusive as Robert describes him, some series of events have led Robert to view his father as unaccepting and unacceptable. A combination of family psychotherapy on a weekly basis and continuing individual psychotherapy with Robert are the treatments of choice. Initially, Robert will find individual treatment threatening and consequently may gain more in the family sessions. As he progresses in treatment, he will profit more from the individual sessions. Without treatment, he is a significant danger to himself and could end his life in suicide.

THE LEGAL CONTEXT

Dear Mr. Hamlin,

I would like to thank you for your kind referral of Mr. Jones. As you know, he is a 27-year-old white, unmarried male with a 10th-grade education who has been charged with assault and inflicting grievous bodily injury. I interviewed Mr. Jones on December 12 and 15, 1995, and administered the Wechsler Adult Intelligence Scale-Revised (WAIS-R), Bender, Bender Memory, Minnesota Multiphasic Personality Inventory-2 (MMPI-2), Draw-A-Person, Incomplete Sentences, and Rorschach. He was dressed casually, appeared somewhat nervous, and he was slow to respond.

My understanding is that you would like me to evaluate Mr. Jones in order to develop a greater understanding of his recent legal difficulties. I further understand that, in the past, there have been other similar charges and you would like to have a description of what psychological factors might have been involved. In addition, you would like to have an estimate of his intelligence, possible presence of brain impairment, level of alcohol-related difficulties, and recommendations for counseling.

CURRENT SITUATION

Mr. Jones lives with his parents and several younger brothers and sisters. He is the third in a family of seven. His father works as a packer for a pharmaceutical company and his mother is a waitress. Mr. Jones is employed as a meat packer at a nearby factory. He dislikes the work because he feels it is boring and would prefer to work outside. However, he is committed to continuing his employment at the factory until he finds other work that is more satisfactory. He has few friends and is apparently somewhat of a loner. Although he has had a relationship with a woman when he was between the ages of 20 and 24, he is not, and has not for some time, been involved with anyone else. He expresses some bitterness over the ending of this relationship since her family felt he was not "good enough." His primary activities are watching videos, fishing, and occasionally socializing. He stated that he is currently not drinking at all because his doctor and his attorney told him not to. Mr. Jones describes his life as being routine and meaningless, yet he has a difficult time conceptualizing what things he could do to improve his life or change himself.

BACKGROUND

Mr. Jones was born in and has lived in Smallport all his life with the exception of several months in two small, nearby cities. He was an extremely limited historian regarding his early years, stating that he was unable to recall any memories prior to the age of 13. He was also unable to conceptualize or describe his relationship with his parents or their relationship with one another. When pushed for specifics he simply but nondefensively stated "they're alright." It was as if he drew a blank when he either tried to describe family relationships or childhood experiences. In school, he stated that "I wasn't much good at anything," and described his favorite subjects as motor mechanics, woodworking, and sheet metal work. Occasionally he was referred to the principal for creating problems.

Mr. Jones' prior convictions include a previous assault (1988) and willful damage, resisting arrest, and escape (1990). In describing the cause of previous fights, he stated that when someone teased him "I go off me head" and elaborated that "I can't stop meself from doing it." During these situations in which he loses control, he reported that he often doesn't even know who it is he's attacking. The loss of control usually lasts for several minutes and is almost always associated with drinking. When questioned why he feels he is so "touchy," he stated that there are two types of people, those who "take it" and "those that don't" and that he was one of those that "don't take it." He expressed a desire to change and when asked how, he stated that he should develop patience.

On April 5, 1992, he was in an automobile accident in which his "head went through the windshield." There was apparently no loss of consciousness and few posttraumatic sequalae other than a headache for approximately 24 hours. Shortly after the accident, he began drinking excessively, sometimes as much as 6 to 7 bottles of wine a day. This apparently resulted in physiological dependence for which he was treated by Dr. Welby. His drinking was characterized by a loss of control, preoccupation with drinking, morning drinking, and blackouts. He has never been to an AA meeting nor has he received other forms of psychological counseling. Although not currently drinking, he states that if he were to have 2 to 3 beers he would be unable to stop until completely intoxicated.

REACTION TO THE CHARGES

Mr. Jones appears genuinely remorseful regarding the incident he has been charged for and wishes he could somehow undo the damage he has caused. He feels both empathy and concern. However, he maintains that it was the other person's fault since the other person called him a "gutless wonder" in front of the whole bar. In fact, his overall perception of his fights and his life in general is that he is a victim and really has little control over what happens to himself. However, for the few brief moments when he is assaulting someone, it's as if he gains some sort of brief sense of power and control over his life. Most of the time he responds to life in a relatively passive, conforming manner.

TEST RESULTS

WAIS-R: Full Scale IQ   = 74
           Verbal IQ   = 83
           Performance IQ = 65

Information	6	Digit Symbol	6
Comprehension	7	Picture Completion	3
Arithmetic	7	Block Design	4
Similarities	6	Picture Arrangement	5
Digit Span	10	Object Assembly	5
Vocabulary	8		

MMPI:	L	42	5	58
	F	68	6	45
	K	44	7	60
	1	52	8	50
	2	80	9	32
	3	60	0	75
	4	74		

Bender: Empirically not in the organic range (although there were dashes rather than dots, minor distortion of designs, difficulty making smooth curves; see Figure 14–6).

Bender Memory: 4 designs recalled

Draw-A-Person: Absence of pupils, large heads (see Figures 14–7 and 14–8)

Rorschach: (data available on request)

INTERPRETATION AND IMPRESSIONS

Mr. Jones obtained a Full Scale IQ of 74, Verbal IQ of 83, and Performance IQ of 65. Overall, this places him in the 4th percentile when compared with his age-related peers. Relative mental strengths were in short-term memory for numbers and visual material in which he scored in the average range. In contrast, relative weaknesses were

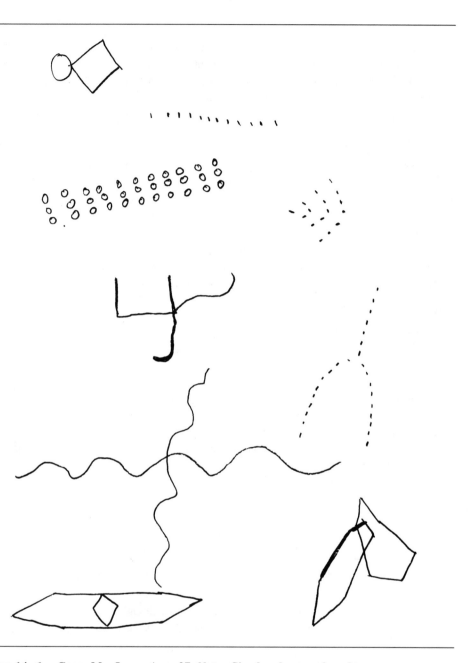

Figure 14–6.   Case: Mr. Jones. Age: 27. *Note:* **Size has been reduced.**

in problem solving for visual tasks and distinguishing relevant from irrelevant details in his environment. In other words, he frequently has difficulty accurately perceiving relevant aspects of what is occurring around him. Furthermore, his perceptions are fairly rigid since he experiences difficulty sorting out his world and flexibly coming up with different possibilities. These difficulties or rigidities in perception are likely to be exaggerated either under stress or after consuming alcohol. Thus, when someone

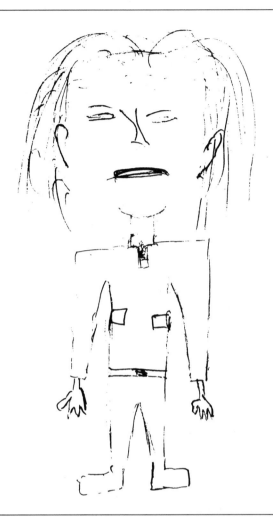

Figure 14–7. Case: Mr. Jones. Age: 27. *Note:* **Size has been reduced.**

provokes him, he is fairly bound by the external situation and has difficulty developing an inner sense of directedness to free himself from outer events.

A general review of Mr. Jones' personality indicates a man who is usually cooperative and concerned with his behavior but who also has periods of impulsiveness and is highly self-critical. However, he is not by any means psychotic. His thoughts are coherent, he has the ability to form adequate relationships with others, and perceives his world without any exaggerated distortions. He typically feels a marked sense of distance between himself and his world. His level of depression is particularly noteworthy and I believe he is a mild to moderate suicide risk. In fact, he has made several previous suicide gestures and stated that he wouldn't want to live anywhere where there was a gun. The following sample of responses to several questions on the MMPI are noteworthy:

I certainly feel useless at times. (True)

I cry easily. (True)

Figure 14–8.   Case: Mr. Jones. Age: 27. *Note:* **Size has been reduced.**

I usually feel that life is worthwhile. (False)

Sometimes I feel I must injure myself. (True)

In dealing with his emotional world, he attempts to gain some control over it by ignoring most feelings he has. He accomplishes this by observing the most obvious features of his environment but blocks out or denies many of his emotions or relevant emotion-laden memories. For example, he was unable to give any description of his relationship with his family nor could he come up with any childhood memories prior to the age of 13. When he does experience emotions, however, they are likely to overwhelm him such as during episodes of either crying or anger.

In understanding his aggressiveness, it is important to stress that he would by no means plot or anticipate retaliation against somebody. He lacks the inner directedness this would require and does not have a brooding sense of suspicion. Furthermore, he feels remorse and concern for those he has hurt. What does trigger off his aggressiveness is a combination of alcohol and being "swept away" by the controlling events in his world. In these conditions, guilt does occur but usually too late to control his behavior. This is further complicated by his usual style of blocking out his emotions so that, when they do occur, they overwhelm him. Thus he is typically unaware of his underlying sense of hostility unless actually acting out these feelings.

In the past, alcohol has significantly complicated Mr. Jones' life and, at time, he has apparently consumed large quantities. Several of the important warning signs for alcoholism are present including blackouts, morning drinking, and a loss of control. He currently states that if he were to have 2 or 3 beers he would have to continue drinking more and more until fully intoxicated. Given his level of depression, I would say that an important motivation for his drinking is as a form of "self-medication." Without some form of intervention, his potential for future alcohol-related problems is moderately high.

Neuropsychologically, Mr. Jones demonstrates some "soft" neurological signs of mild brain impairment. He has difficulty pronouncing certain words, a poor ability to reproduce designs, and his general spatial abilities were significantly lower than his verbal skills. In fact, given Mr. Jones' educational and occupational background, one would expect that his verbal abilities should be lower than his performance abilities and yet the opposite is true. One possibility for these impairments was injury from the automobile accident on April 5, 1985. However, the history surrounding the injury and the limited number of posttraumatic sequalae argue against this. It is more likely that some form of earlier head injury or an accumulation of injuries might have caused these deficits. I would speculate that there would be some mild dysfunction in the right parietal and left temporal regions as a result of static lesions to these areas. However, the focus of the testing was not to assess brain impairment so that the above must necessarily be speculative in nature.

SUMMARY AND RECOMMENDATIONS

Mr. Jones was a cooperative but somewhat isolated 27-year-old white male who, at the time of evaluation, was depressed and, in the past, has experienced alcohol-related difficulties. Although stating that he lost control of himself during the incident for which he was referred, he is by no means psychotic and understands the reasons and implications for his behavior. He does not have a criminal mentality. In other words he feels guilt regarding his behavior, concern for his victims, and is unlikely to make any long-term plans to either harm another person, or commit some premeditated criminal act. He is not by any means inner directed but experiences himself as controlled by external events. This is further complicated and exaggerated by alcohol and the fact that he attempts to block out uncomfortable emotions to the extent that when his environment triggers them, they are overwhelming. In addition, there is a mild to moderate suicide risk, definite potential for future alcohol-related problems, and some soft neurological signs suggesting a mild level of brain impairment.

The key to working with Mr. Jones would be to focus on teaching him to be more inner directed and to structure his environment, or at least his perception of his environment, in such a way as to not trigger his aggression. Effective counseling must include clear limits, a change in environment, warm support, and continual contact. In particular, Mr. Jones would require concrete suggestions since his capacity for insight-oriented counseling is quite limited. He should enter the type of counseling that focuses on building his self-esteem and developing clear alternatives on how he might improve his life. If given probation, this should be accompanied by the requirement that he attend AA meetings and receive supportive counseling. He is currently experiencing a sufficient amount of psychological turmoil so that he is motivated to change. However, without some sort of intervention, there is a high risk of increasing alcohol-related problems and further, probably debilitating, levels of depression. Some long-term legal leverage over his future behavior should be maintained for supervision and monitoring of progress.

THE EDUCATIONAL SETTING

NAME: M. K.
DATE OF BIRTH: February 8, 1983
DATE OF EXAMINATION: May 12, 1992
EXAMINED BY: G. G-M.

REFERRAL QUESTION
M. was referred by her mother for a psychological evaluation to assess her current level of functioning. An evaluation had become of particular importance since a decision was imminent regarding continued placement in her special education class as opposed to mainstreaming. Furthermore, the last psychological evaluation that had been performed on M. was over two years ago, and Mrs. K. requested a follow-up evaluation to assess possible improvement, stability, or deterioration in M.'s cognitive abilities.

EVALUATION PROCEDURES
M. was administered the Wechsler Intelligence Scale for Children-Revised (WISC-R), the Bender Visual Motor Gestalt Test (Bender), and the House-Tree-Person Test (H-T-P).

BEHAVIORAL OBSERVATIONS
M. appeared neatly dressed, and was cooperative and friendly throughout the testing procedure. When confronted with more difficult tasks, she would at times discontinue trying to perform as best as she could. However, for the most part, she gave the tasks her best efforts, and the test results appear to be an accurate assessment of her current level of functioning.

RELEVANT HISTORY
M. is a right-handed female, 9 years and 3 months of age, with a history of delayed development resulting from a hypothyroid condition that was diagnosed and treated when she was 5 years old. She is currently living with her natural parents, and her older sister Susan (17) also lives with the family.

Mrs. K. reported that during her pregnancy with M., she was consistently under a doctor's care. There were no unusual features at birth, and she stated that M.'s early developmental milestones were normal. Between the ages of 2 and 4, Mr. and Mrs. K.

noticed a gradual but progressive slowness in M.'s behavior. During the end of her fourth year, this pattern became more pronounced, and she was referred to a physician who diagnosed and treated her.

Her parents have responded to her condition with conscientiousness and support. She was assessed at the Speech, Hearing, and Neurosensory Center and treated for a period of six months. She has been enrolled in a special education class in school following a psychological evaluation performed by Dr. Lewis of the Los Angeles Union School District on August 15, 1990. He diagnosed her as being educable mentally retarded and summarized his report by stating that M. is "functioning with apparent developmental delays in many areas. She has significant cognitive difficulties along with severe academic deficiencies. Her ability to participate in a regular education program is extremely limited at this time" (p. 5). She was placed in a learning handicapped program including speech therapy and a special education class. An important aspect of her overall program with regard to her interpersonal development was that all her social activities took place with a regular first-grade class. Her interpersonal adjustment in these activities has been described by her mother as good. Her mother reported that in most areas she has seen a great deal of improvement over the past year. M.'s parents are currently interested in developing the most suitable academic and social placement for her, as well as what assets and limitations she may have for the future.

TEST RESULTS

WISC-R: Full Scale IQ   = 70
         Verbal IQ   = 73
         Performance IQ = 71

Subscale Scores		Subscale Scores	
Information	5	Picture Arrangement	1
Comprehension	7	Picture Completion	10
Digit Span	3	Block Design	5
Arithmetic	3	Object Assembly	7
Similarities	8		
Vocabulary	8		

BENDER: Impaired; lack of closure, distortions, difficulty making dots, rotations, perseverations (see Figure 14–9).

BENDER MEMORY: Two designs recalled.

HOUSE-TREE-PERSON: Disorganized, immature (see house, Figure 14–10).

INTERPRETATION AND IMPRESSIONS

M. scored in the borderline range of intelligence on the WISC-R with a Full Scale IQ of 70, a Performance IQ of 71, and a Verbal IQ of 73, which places her in the second percentile when compared with her age-related peers. These scores are roughly equivalent to those taken by Dr. Lewis on August 9, 1990. Relative strengths were in the areas of ability to distinguish relevant from irrelevant details in her environment (10, within normal range), ability to conceptualize the similarity between one object or event and another (8), and vocabulary (8). Relative but pronounced weaknesses were in tasks requiring sequencing and a sustained attention span. This suggests that her overall social and verbal skills are nearly within normal limits, whereas her academic abilities, particularly in reading, writing, and arithmetic, are moderately impaired.

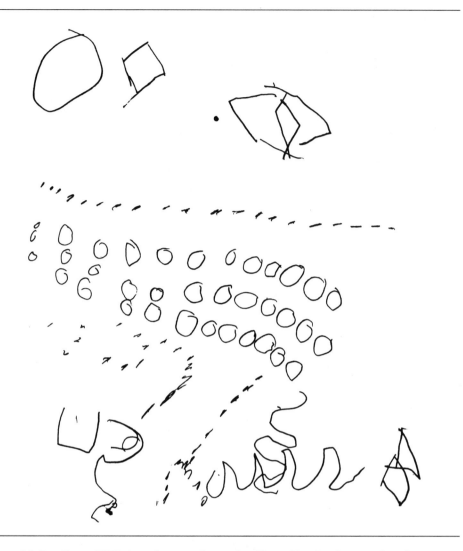

Figure 14–9.   Case: M.K. Age: 9 years, 3 months. *Note:* **Size has been reduced.**

M.'s performance on the Bender was in the impaired range and characterized by difficulties with closure, distortions of the designs, producing dashes instead of dots, rotations, and perseverations. This suggests that she is definitely lagging in her visual-motor abilities when compared with her age-related peers and may have difficulty organizing the spatial information in her environment. Drawings of her house, tree, and person, although of appropriate size and good line pressure, were likewise disorganized and generally more like that of someone 6 years of age rather than 9.

In summary, M.'s performance is consistent with generalized impairment to both cerebral hemispheres. Her relative strengths are that she has normal abilities in noticing the relevant details in her environment, as well as good comprehension and vocabulary. In other words, she has made a good adjustment in learning how to deal with her environment, which reflects the impact that speech therapy and her special education

Figure 14–10. **Case: M.K. Age: 9 years, 3 months.** *Note:* **Size has been reduced.**

program have had on her. Weaknesses, on the other hand, are in the academic areas, particularly attention, mathematical computation, sequencing, and visual organization. In these areas, her abilities have stayed relatively the same during the past two years. Although she has progressed academically, she has done so at a rate consistent with a child having an IQ of 70.

RECOMMENDATIONS

1. Continued placement in special education classes emphasizing sequencing, math, memory training, visual organization, and sustained attention.

2. Social activities should be designed to increase or maintain social contacts with age-related peers in the normal school program. This is particularly important since M.'s social-verbal skills are close to normal, and contact with children in the normal school program would provide her with normal role models. On the

other hand, her academic abilities are certainly well below most children, and placement in a normal program would be likely to create turmoil and a sense of inferiority.

3. Home tutoring emphasizing drill and repetition is recommended, in addition to what the school provides.

4. M. should have follow-up psychological assessment every 12 to 24 months since, as she gets older, the precision of measurements increases, and continual evaluations of her level of progress or stability can be made to aid in further academic or interpersonal recommendations.

THE PSYCHOLOGY CLINIC*

NAME: A. G.
DATE OF BIRTH: May 30, 1925
DATE OF EXAMINATION: December 12, 1995
CASE #: 96-041
SEX: Female
ETHNICITY: European American
REFERRED BY: Dr. M.

REFERRAL QUESTION
This 70-year-old, divorced woman was referred for psychological evaluation by Dr. M. who specified that the patient suffered from agoraphobia and requested assistance in identifying effective treatment for her condition. A. G., on the other hand, indicated that she had had agoraphobia in the past, but described her current problem as one of motivation rather than panic or fear. She asserted that she is currently not immobilized nor is she extremely anxious when she travels. She attributes her restrictive lifestyle to the absence of "energy" and "motivation" to travel and engage in social activities. She acknowledged an "underlying apprehension" that arises when she is scheduled to leave home, however, resulting in her putting off her departure as long as possible. Once she actually goes out, she reported that she remains anxious until she returns home.

The current evaluation was designed to clarify the nature of the problem, to develop treatment plans, and, if indicated, to initiate a treatment program.

EVALUATION PROCEDURES
By prior arrangement, A. G. completed the Life History Questionnaire prior to her intake interview on 12/12/95. She was unable to complete additional testing during the intake because of "discomfort" and "apprehension" about making the drive home. She was therefore rescheduled with the request that she complete the rest of the paper-and-pencil materials over the course of the next two weeks.

During the total assessment sessions she was evaluated using the following procedures:

Life History Questionnaire (12/12/95)

Clinical Interview (12/12/95)

*Report contributed by Larry Beutler, PhD, Combined Clinical/Counseling/School Program, Graduate School of Education, University of California, Santa Barbara.

Structured Clinical Interview for *DSM-IV* (SCID; 12/22/95)

State-Trait Anxiety Inventory (STAI)-(12/13/95)

Millon Clinical Multiaxial Inventory-III (MCMI-III; 12/13/95)

Personal Attitude Inventory (Dowd Therapeutic Reactance Scale; 12/13/95)

Beck Depression Scale (BDI; 12/13/95)

Beck Hopelessness Scale (BDI; 12/13/95)

MMPI-2 (12/21/95)

Sarason Social Support Questionnaire (SSQ; 1/2/95)

RELEVANT HISTORY

History of Presenting Problem. This 70-year-old, Jewish woman identifies three major symptom clusters that have been problematic for her: agoraphobia, panic attacks, and dissociation. She has a long history of panic attacks without agoraphobia, dating to age 12. The first panic episode occurred when she was babysitting for a family friend. She suddenly hyperventilated, began experiencing heart palpitations, and became afraid that she was going to die. She ran into the street yelling for help, but no one heard her or tried to assist her. The situation was resolved by exerting "self-control."

After her initial panic attacks began, they gradually increased to a frequency of about once per week throughout her teenage years. To protect herself from feared panic and what she perceived as possible death, she frequently slept with her parents and confined herself to known places and locations. At their worst, panic attacks involved physical symptoms such as nausea, shortness of breath (hyperventilation), and dizziness, as well as cognitive symptoms such as fears of losing her mind, dying, of being overwhelmed, and unspecified danger. However, she learned to control these symptoms over time by avoiding such activities as going out, driving, and socializing with groups. These efforts have been successful in that A. G. reported that she had been asymptomatic for agoraphobia and panic for 31 years.

She currently reports that she has become apprehensive about travel and social activity, but the symptoms are confined to initial anticipatory anxiety, gastrointestinal distress, and headaches but with no heart palpitations, shortness of breath, or fainting. She prevents more extensive symptoms by avoiding travel and through a variety of distraction procedures. When she begins to experience the onset of panic, she calls someone or begins to read an interesting book. Her contacts with other people at these times do not include a disclosure of or discussions about the panic, but are reported to be simply methods to involve herself with others and to take her mind off her feelings.

She reported that the current symptoms are mild in intensity and include a general distaste of travel, an inability to get comfortable with being out alone, and a general heightened sense of vulnerability and apprehension until she is able to return home. She continues to avoid night travel and avoids being alone, if possible, to prevent the associated anxiety.

Since 1986, several dissociative episodes have occurred, which she believes were precipitated by her decision to openly acknowledge her homosexual orientation. The first instance followed a sexual encounter with her current partner, during a vacation. After the sexual act, the client experienced an apparent fugue state. She became disoriented, was unable to recall such personal information as that her parents were deceased, and engaged in distraught communication with her lover about "why am I here." The episodes have subsequently recurred several times: They come on suddenly and without warning and she subsequently has no memory for the events. They uniformly follow a lesbian sexual encounter, and if her partner remains with her during this period (sometimes up to several hours), the fears gradually subside. However, after these dissociative states she reported having a sense of helplessness, hopelessness, confusion, headaches, and nausea that sometimes lasted for several days. She has been able to successfully avoid these episodes by not engaging in sexual activities for nearly six years.

History of Treatment. Ms. G. was first treated and hospitalized in 1965 because of agoraphobia. There have been no subsequent hospitalizations. However, she has entered into two treatment relationships, in the years since. Her current medication is managed by a psychiatrist who is treating her with Xanex, Tagamet, and Paxil. She reported that since being on the medication she has been excessively sleepy and has a difficult time staying awake during the day. She also has experienced an increase in stomach difficulties and diarrhea. She was also treated for a short time in 1985 by an internist and psychiatrist. At that time, she was given tricyclic antidepressants. These drugs produced hallucinations and were discontinued shortly after initiation.

A review of this woman's symptom history also reveals that she has had substantial periods of time in which she has been asymptomatic for fugue states, panic attacks, and agoraphobia. She reported that between August 1994 and June 1995 she was the "best ever." She was able to travel alone, found life enjoyable, and experienced no episodes of discomfort or fear. More recently, she has gradually become more depressed and dysphoric as well as fearful, although there was no obvious precipitator for these feelings.

Family Background. A. G. was raised in a middle-class, Jewish family. She was the oldest of two children, having a brother who is one and a half years her junior. The family always maintained at least a superficial religious identity and a facade of happiness. However, she reported that behind this facade there were significant underlying family conflicts. Religion has always been a source of conflict for her as has her sexual orientation. Moreover, she reported a long family history of mental illness and interpersonal conflict. While she described her parents as emotionally stable, both her parents' families have histories of psychiatric disorders. Her mother was the oldest of 9 children; an uncle died in a halfway house with a diagnosis of schizophrenia, another was diagnosed as having bipolar disorder, and still another was diagnosed as having depression. On her father's side, at least one uncle is reported to have had a major depression that was treated with antidepressants.

In her own personal history, A. G. reported that she always felt confused about her sexual orientation. At age 17, she received a proposal of marriage. She declined but he persisted, and she went to live with an uncle to escape his advances. He pursued her and finally, against her "better judgment," talked her into marriage. The newlyweds moved to Metroville to be with her family, but problems persisted and they separated after about a year. By that time, she had given birth to a daughter. She moved in with her parents, but long-standing conflicts with her mother became more frequent. When her husband contested and prevented the culmination of the divorce, A. G. moved out of the family home and went to work, leaving her daughter with her mother. A. G. blamed her parents for her failed marriage and refused further contact. She did not see or speak with her daughter for two years.

After a period of estrangement from parents and daughter, the patient was contacted by her attorney, who informed her that A. G.'s mother could no longer raise the baby. Her husband was also informed, demanded that A. G. reconcile with him to raise the child. A. G. agreed to do so if they would move to Betterville to make a fresh start. Shortly after moving, A. G.'s husband became disillusioned and returned to Metroville leaving her to raise the child. It was very shortly thereafter that she acknowledged to herself that she was a lesbian. She subsequently engaged in a series of brief lesbian affairs, and adopted a "secret life" in which she prevented her parents and husband from an awareness of this emerging sexual orientation.

Still being unable to raise her daughter and work, the client gave up the child to a foster family for temporary care. After a few years, she initiated an effort to again assume care of the child. Concerned about raising the child within a lesbian relationship, she accepted the proposal of marriage from a man who knew about her lesbian lifestyle. He, nonetheless, agreed to adopt the child and allowed her to continue her lesbian affairs. Their marriage lasted 23 years and produced two sons. Although unsatisfied with her dual life, she waited until her youngest son graduated from high school before she left the marriage and began to pursue lesbian relationships exclusively and openly. She met her current lover in 1986. This relationship continues to be close even though they ceased sexual contact approximately six years ago in order to prevent dissociative episodes.

A. G. reported being close to her brother when she was young, but that relationship became disrupted during their teenage years. At that time, he had more problems with their parents then she and, due to these conflicts, A. G.'s parents left all their money to her rather than to her brother. However, she had come to feel alienated from him and subsequently refused to share her inheritance. In spite of having become quite wealthy, he became resentful of her refusal to share the inheritance and cut off all relationships with her. In the past few years she has tried unsuccessfully to reestablish this relationship. He has indicated his willingness to "forgive" her, but denies any desire for a continuing relationship.

Medical History. A. G.'s medical history is unremarkable. She currently takes Tagamet for stomach distress and Xanex for anxiety. Aside from some loss of hearing and psychophysiological symptoms, she acknowledges no significant medical problems.

Validity and Reliability of Assessment. Throughout the evaluation, A. G. was articulate, introspective, and cooperative. While acknowledging discomfort in talking about her sexual orientation and religious feelings, she was quite forthcoming when questioned directly. A valid MMPI-2 profile along with her willingness to cooperate and introspect suggest that the current evaluation presents a valid picture of her current level of functioning.

INTERPRETATION AND IMPRESSIONS

While a formal assessment of intellectual level was not undertaken, both A. G.'s verbal conceptual skills and oral presentation suggest at least average and probably bright normal intellectual performance. Her ideation is dominated by preoccupation with ways to avoid uncomfortable feelings along with concerns with physical symptoms. Collectively, this results in mild impairment to her cognitive efficiency. Her verbal processes are organized, circumstantial, and occasionally dominated by topics about which she has pressing concerns but they reflect no disorganization, no memory impairment, and moderately well developed associative and abstract reasoning processes. While she is oriented in all three spheres and manifests no significant mental impairment, she notes having always been concerned with the potential loss of mental functions.

A. G. denies dysphoria, depression, and anxiety. She complains of poor sleep, loss of energy, and lack of motivation. Formal assessment confirms the presence of vegetative signs (increased appetite, variable sleep, social withdrawal, loss of interest, reduced libido), consistent with the presence of mild to moderate depression without subjective dysphoria. Trait anxiety levels are within the normal range for her age, and subjective depression is only mild, with the dominant symptoms being psychophysiological. Her affect is appropriate, though somewhat variable. Affective responsivity is both dysthymic and blunted.

Ms. G.'s mood disturbance reflects a chronic condition, against which she has constructed a variety of rigid and brittle defenses. She is excessively sensitive to environmental signals of threat and, at the least suggestion of emotional arousal, engages in both direct and cognitive avoidance patterns. The result is that she prevents the intensification or even emergence of feelings that might overwhelm her. While protecting her somewhat from subjective sensations of anxiety and dysphoria, A. G.'s defenses are not sufficiently strong to prevent the emergence of a variety of secondary symptoms. Denial, phobic avoidance in the face of anticipatory cues, self-criticism, compartmentalization, and somatization are among her most frequently used defenses. As threat intensifies, her fragile denial deteriorates, and both somatization and direct avoidance predominate. Thus, acute stress evokes a variety of stress-related somatic symptoms and phobic behaviors that provide expression for her denial of anxiety and depression.

A. G. experiences ambivalent personality organization, with moderate disturbances to her functional adaptation. Her dominant conflicts involve strong needs for dependency, counterbalanced by equally strong strivings for self-definition. Her coping style involves both passive and active efforts to reconcile these strong drives. Thus, while she seeks approval and confirmation from others, even to the point of excessive subservience in which she gives up personal strivings, this is frequently a futile effort to ensure the presence of other people in her life. Indeed, these efforts are usually designed to compensate for a host of covert rebellious and angry impulses and by overt efforts to be autonomous and self-guided. Thus, efforts to achieve self-fulfillment and autonomy are followed by guilt, self doubt, and shame in which fear and withdrawal dominate. These latter symptoms, however, may be so demanding of attention that they are the functional equivalent of interpersonal anger, hurt, and resentment. Thus, her pattern of phobic anxiety and dissociation has led to sexual withdrawal and physical dependency. This may both allow an indirect expression of anger and yet also be a compromise between asocial impulses and needs for approval. Unfortunately, this compromise also includes low self-regard, and restricted mobility. Another consequence of this pattern is the current low level of available others to provide support. In spite of this, A. G.'s satisfaction with the level of interpersonal support available from her significant other is good and suggests the availability of this individual as a support in any treatment program.

DIAGNOSTIC IMPRESSION

| Axis   I | 300.22 | Agoraphobia without recent panic disorder (by history) |

| | 296.3 | Rule out Major Depressive Disorder, recurrent |

The diagnosis of Anxiety Disorder is based on history rather than current symptomatology. A major differential question has to do with the relevant salience of Major Depression versus Anxiety Disorder.

| Axis II | None |

| Axis III | Rule out gastrointestinal disorder |

| Axis IV | None |

| Axis V | Problems related to social environment—social isolation, restriction of friendships, lifecycle transitions |

| Axis VI | Past year: 80
 Current: 62 |

RECOMMENDATIONS

Overall, the foregoing confirms the presence of a complex and long-standing problem founded more in dynamic and early developing interpersonal expectations and conflicts than in symptom-contingent events. However, this is not meant to discount the importance and debilitating nature of the patient's symptom picture, nor the need to give it direct attention in treatment. The dynamic nature of the associated conflicts, and their role in maintaining systemic dysfunction in her relationships with significant others, suggests the need to combine a symptom-focused treatment along with efforts to resolve fundamental conflicts. These core conflicts seem to be largely founded in postpubescent strivings to resolve needs for autonomy and dependency. The initial focus of treatment should be on reducing territorial apprehension, with a concomitant increase in social involvement and independent functioning. Once there is initial symptomatic improvement, further interventions should focus on A. G.'s pattern of rebelliousness which seems to be intertwined with self-incrimination, guilt, and withdrawal. In particular, this might emphasize confirming both needs for autonomy and acceptance along with greater insight into this pattern.

A. G.'s level of functional impairment is moderate. Numerous areas of functioning are affected and this, coupled with the chronicity of the condition, suggests the need for long-term treatment. However, the level of defense and personal control is sufficient and the level of subjective despair and hopelessness is within a range that suggests outpatient care is appropriate. There is no evidence of direct risk to self or others. Anxiolytic or antidepressant medications are contraindicated due to her relative degree of control over her symptoms combined with the high potential for somatic side effects. Individual treatment may allow a more selective and intensive focus on problematic behaviors and prevent the operation of direct avoidance of discomfort than would the less intensive nature of group treatment.

A. G.'s level of distress is well contained, being in the average or even below-average range for patients who seek treatment. While her distress increases significantly when exposed to immediate threat, she quickly compensates and is so well versed at avoidance that she may experience difficulty sustaining sufficient motivation for therapy. Thus, interventions that confront or expose her to feared and avoided circumstances may be helpful to desensitize her to anxiety as well as to increase her level of motivation to continue treatment.

A. G.'s coping style vacillates between being primarily impulsive and externalizing, to being self-critical and internalizing. This pattern of cyclic coping suggests the need to address her problems at both a behavioral and an insight level. When her impulses and direct avoidance dominate, behavioral strategies should be emphasized. During phases in which she is more introspective and self-blaming, insight-oriented interventions are likely to be more effective. Given the unsustaining nature of her subjective distress, abreactive and sensate focused, cathartic interventions may prove to be especially helpful during these more introspective phases.

Finally, A. G. manifests a pattern of superficial compliance and more covert resistance to the directives of helpgivers. Thus, special attention should be given to developing a trusting relationship. Even if this is achieved, however, she would still be expected to undermine direct suggestions and specific assignments. The most effective approaches, then, would be collaborative interventions emphasizing clear behavioral change, contingency contracting, or paradoxical interventions such as symptom prescription and "no-change" directives. Particular attention may be given to predicting the exacerbation of physical and phobic symptoms following intense sessions since these sessions may mobilize her resistant impulses in an asymptomatic direction.

Collectively, the symptomatic aspects of the patient's fears and phobias may be susceptible to a combination of structured exposure procedures cognitive restructuring and interoceptive awareness (Craske & Barlow, 1993). These procedures circumvent patient resistance by virtue of their reliance on self-monitoring, as well as being both symptom and behaviorally focused. The more thematic and dynamic aspects of A. G.'s problem may be addressed by initiating work that specifically mobilizes her anxiety in motivational directions. Confrontation with feared material, along with the use of such procedures as two-chair work and imaginal reliving of unsettling relationships may be helpful. Imaginal confrontation might be initiated with images and memories of disapproving parents, children, and other significant others, the goals of which may be to help her tolerate discomfort and disapproval. The procedures outlined by Daldrup et. al. (1988, *Focused Expressive Psychotherapy,* Guilford Press) for working with the overcontrolled patient may also be particularly helpful.

RECOMMENDED READING

Klopfer, W. G. (1983). Writing psychological reports. In A. Walker (Ed.), *The handbook of clinical psychology: Theory, research and practice.* Homewood, IL: Dow Jones-Irwin.

Tallent, N. (1993). *Psychological report writing* (4th ed.). Englewood Cliffs, NJ: Prentice-Hall.

Zuckerman, E. L. (1993). *The clinician's thesaurus three: A guidebook for wording psychological reports* (3rd ed.). Pittsburgh: Three Wishes Press.

Appendix A

Percentile Rankings for Wechsler Deviation IQs

IQ	Percentile Rank	IQ	Percentile Rank	IQ	Percentile Rank
155	99.99	118	88	81	10
154	99.98	117	87	80	9
153	99.98	116	86	79	8
152	99.97	115	84	78	7
151	99.97	114	82	77	6
150	99.96	113	81	76	5
149	99.95	112	79	75	5
148	99.93	111	77	74	4
147	99.91	110	75	73	4
146	99.89	109	73	72	3
145	99.87	108	70	71	3
144	99.83	107	68	70	2
143	99.79	106	66	69	2
142	99.74	105	63	68	2
141	99.69	104	61	67	1
140	99.62	103	58	66	1
139	99.53	102	55	65	1
138	99	101	53	64	1
137	99	100	50	63	1
136	99	99	47	62	1
135	99	98	45	61	.47
134	99	97	42	60	.38
133	99	96	39	59	.31
132	98	95	37	58	.26
131	98	94	34	57	.21
130	98	93	32	56	.17
129	97	92	30	55	.13
128	97	91	27	54	.11
127	96	90	27	53	.09
126	96	89	23	52	.07
125	95	88	21	51	.05
124	95	87	19	50	.04
123	94	86	18	49	.03
122	93	85	16	48	.03
121	92	84	14	47	.02
120	91	83	13	46	.02
119	90	82	12	45	.01

Appendix B

Conversion Formulas* and Difference Scores* for Determining Magnitude (.05 level) of Fluctuations for Wechsler Adult Intelligence Scale-Revised (WAIS-R) Factor Scores and Additional Groupings

Factor or Additional Grouping	Conversion Formula $(M = 100, SD = 15)^{\dagger}$	Difference[‡] Score (.05) Ages 16–19	Difference[‡] Score (.05) Ages 20–74
WAIS-R Factors			
Verbal Comprehension	$1.4(I+V+C+S)+44$	8	7
Perceptual Organization	$2.0(PC+BD+OA)+40$	11	9
Freedom from Distractibility	$2.8(DSp+A)+44$	11	9
Bannatyne's Categories			
Spatial	$2.0(PC+BD+OA)+40$	11	10
Verbal Conceptualization	$1.9(V+C+S)+43$	9	8
Sequential	$2.1(DSp+A+DSy)+37$	11	9
Acquired Knowledge	$1.9(I+V+A)+43$	8	7
ACID Profile	$1.6(A+Dy+I+DSp)+36$	11	9
Horn Groupings			
Fluid Intelligence	$1.1(DSp+S+PC+BD+OA)+34$	9	9
Crystallized Intelligence	$1.4(I+V+C+S)+44$	7	6
Retention	$2.0(I+DSp+A)+40$	9	7

[†] Age-corrected subtest scores must be used in formulas to calculate standard scores.

[‡] Difference scores are based on subtracting the standard score on a particular factor/grouping from the mean of all standard scores within that grouping. The ACID profile uses the Full Scale IQ as its comparison mean.

---

* Formulas and difference scores are from Kaufman (1990).

Appendix C

Conversion Formulas* and Difference Scores* for Determining Magnitude (.05 level) of Fluctuations for Wechsler Intelligence Scale for Children (3rd ed.; WISC-III) Factor Scores and Additional Groupings

Factor or Additional Grouping	Conversion Formula $(M = 100, SD = 15)^{\dagger}$	Difference Score $(.05)^{\ddagger}$ Mean for All Ages
WISC-III Factors		
Verbal Comprehension	(see Wechsler, 1991, Table A.5,	9.1
Perceptual Organization	A.6, and A.7, pp. 255–257)	10.4
Freedom from Distractibility		11.5
Processing Speed		12
Bannatyne's Categories		
Spatial	2.0(PC+B+OA) + 40	10
Verbal Conceptualization	1.9(V+C+S) + 43	8.5
Sequential	2.3(DSp+A+Coding) + 31	12
Acquired Knowledge	1.9(I+V+A) +43	8.5
SCAD Profile	1.7(SS+C+A+DSp) + 32	9.5
Horn Groupings		
Fluid Intelligence	1.3(S+A+PA+BD+OA) + 34	8.5
Crystallized Intelligence	1.3(I+S+V+C+PA) + 35	9
Achievement	0.85(I+S+A+V+C+PA) + 49	8.5

† Age-corrected scores must be used in formulas to calculate standard scores.

‡ Difference scores are calculated by subtracting the standard score on a factor/grouping from the mean of all standard scores within that grouping. The SCAD profile uses the Full Scale IQ as its comparison mean.

---

* Formulas (excluding the WISC-III factors) are from Kaufman (1994) and difference scores for the factor scores are from Naglieri (1993) and difference scores for the additional groupings were calculated from tables provided by Kaufman (1994).

Appendix D

Directions for Completing Appendixes D1 and D2: (Worksheets for Determining Magnitude of WAIS-R and WISC-III Subtest Fluctuations)

The following directions allow examiners to determine whether subtests fluctuate at a statistically significant level from the full scale, verbal, or performance means. The four steps in this process are numbered to correspond to the numbered (1–4) sections of the worksheet.

1. Decide whether it is appropriate to use either the full scale mean (based on all 11 WAIS-R subtests or the 10–13 WISC-III subtests) or the verbal and/or performance subtest means. If there is a significant discrepancy between Verbal and Performance IQs (12 points or more to be significant at the .05 level), then calculate the mean subtest scores separately for the verbal and for the performance scales. If Verbal and Performance IQ scores are not significantly different (e.g. less than 12 points), then calculate the mean for all subtests used to develop the Full Scale IQ.

2. Write down the relevant verbal, performance, or full scale mean(s) in the "Mean" column. Calculate the magnitude of any potentially discrepant subtests by noting the difference between the age-corrected subtest scores (Step 1) and the relevant means. Record the differences in the "Difference" column.

3. To determine whether the difference is significant, note whether the magnitude of the difference is greater than the value indicated for a specific subtest. For example, if, upon initial appraisal, the WAIS-R Information subtest looked as if it might be a significant strength, then it would first need to be decided whether the full scale mean or verbal mean would be the most appropriate to use. Then Information would need to be greater than or equal to the full scale mean by a value of 2.6 points, or if the verbal mean was calculated, then the difference would need to be greater than or equal to 2.4. However, be aware that these are average values calculated for all age groups across the standardization samples. Some age groups may require different values in order to achieve significance at the set values. This is especially important for the WISC-III where the youngest samples typically have a wider range of error and thus require greater values to achieve significance (see Wechsler, 1991, Table 5.2 for greater precision across different age groups).

4. All subtests that achieved significance should be indicated as either a strength ("S" indicated on the profile sheet) or a weakness ("W"). If a subtest is neither a strength nor a weakness, then leave the section blank.

Subtest	1. Age-corrected Subtest Scores			2. Mean	Difference	3. Score required for difference to be significant (.05 level)*			4. Strength or Weakness
	Full Scale	V	P			Full Scale	V	P	
I						2.6	2.4		
DSp						3.4	2.9		
VB						1.9	1.8		
A						3.1	2.8		
C						3.3	2.9		
S						3.4	3		
PC						3.4		3	
PA						3.8		3.2	
BD						2.8		2.5	
OA						4.1		3.5	
DSy						3.5		3	
MEAN									

Appendix D1.   Worksheet for determining magnitude (.05) of Wechsler Adult Intelligence Scale—Revised (WAIS-R) subtest fluctuations

* Data are from Silverstein (1982a).

Subtest	1. Subtest Scores			2. Mean	Difference	3. Score required for difference to be significant (.05 level)*			4. Strength or Weakness
	Full Scale	V	P			Full Scale (12 subtests; excluding Mazes)	V	P (excluding Mazes)	
I						3.4	3		
S						3.6	3.1		
A						3.9	3.3		
VB						3	2.7		
C						4	3.4		
DSp						3.3	2.9		
PC						3.9		3.5	
Coding						3.9		3.4	
PA						4		3.6	
BD						3.1		2.9	
OA						4.5		3.9	
SS						4		3.6	
MEAN									

Appendix D2.   Worksheet for determining magnitude (.05) of Wechsler Intelligence Scale for Children (3rd ed.; WISC-III) subtest fluctuations

*Data are from Wechsler (1991).

Appendix E

Guidelines for Hypothesizing Subtest Strengths and Weaknesses

Instructions

To complete Appendixes E1, E2, and E3, you will need to determine values for examinee's subtests based on whether they are *significantly above, above, equal to, below,* or *significantly below* their relevant mean score. Which mean score to use (Full Scale, Verbal, Performance) and what the means are have already been determined in Level IIIa (and for Appendix D). For Appendix E1, use the verbal mean if there was a significant difference between Verbal and Performance IQ; otherwise use the mean for all the subtests administered. Similarly for Appendix E2, use the performance mean if there was a significant difference between Verbal and Performance IQs. For Appendix E3, use verbal means when determining values for verbal subtests and performance means when determining values for performance subtests if there was a significant discrepancy between Verbal and Performance IQ. If there was not a significant difference between Verbal and Performance IQs, then use the mean for the total number of subtests administered. Note that for the WAIS-R, only *age-corrected scores should be used;* in contrast, the WISC-III has these included in the scoring.

To complete Appendixes E1, E2, and E3, work through the following steps:

1. Designate the following values in the columns directly under the subtests:
   a. *Significantly Above.* Place a "+ +" in the ability-related boxes in the column(s) under each subtest abbreviation that has been determined to be a significant (.05) strength (see Level IIIa). For example, if someone had a significant strength in Picture Arrangement, then all the boxes directly under Picture Arrangement should have + + placed in them.
   b. *Above.* Place a "+" in the ability-related boxes under each subtest that is greater than 1 scaled score above the relevant mean (but lower than the magnitude required to be significantly above the relevant subtest means).
   c. *Equal to.* Place a "0" in each ability-related box with subtest scores between 1 subtest score above and 1 subtest score below the mean.
   d. *Below.* Place a "−" in each ability-related box with subtest scores 1 subscale score below the relevant mean (but not lower than the magnitude required to be significantly above the relevant mean).
   e. *Significantly below.* Indicate weaknesses by placing a "− −" in the ability-related boxes under each subtest that has been determined to be a significant weakness (see Level IIIa).

2. The next step is to decide whether a hypothesized ability is actually a relative strength (or weakness). The basic strategy is that if a strength (or weakness) is to be accepted, then other subtests measuring the same ability should also be high (or low if weaknesses are being determined). However, this is made somewhat

more complicated in that there are various numbers of ability boxes in the rows to the right of the ability descriptions. For example, in the first ability listing (Verbal Memory) there are three boxes in the row to the right. Similarly, there are three boxes in the next ability listing (Verbal Conceptualization). However, others have only one box to the right of the ability and others have up to eight. The number of these boxes needs to be taken into account when deciding whether to accept or reject a hypothesized strength or weakness. The following decision rules are recommended:

One Box. In some cases, there are abilities that are specific to a certain subtest and therefore have only one ability related to them. If this ability is determined to be a significant strength (++), then the hypothesized ability is strengthened. For example, in the ability described as "Practical knowledge and judgment related to conventional standards of behavior," only the Comprehension subtest is indicated as being the subtest that measures this area. Thus, consideration of whether or not other subtests were above, equal to, or below the mean is obviously not possible. However, these *subtest specific abilities* should be interpreted with caution with additional outside support provided whenever possible (behavioral observations, relevant history).

Two Boxes. To accept a hypothesized strength comprised of a composite of two subtests, one box must be significantly (as determined in Level IIIa) above the mean (++) and the other must also be above the mean (+), although not necessarily significantly above the mean. To accept a hypothesized weakness, the opposite logic would apply in that one box would need to be significantly below the mean (− −) and the other would need to be below the mean (− or − −).

Three to Four Boxes. To accept strengths comprised of composites of three or four subtests, one ability box must be designated as significantly above the relevant mean (++), another must be above the mean (+ or ++), and while it is *preferable* for the third and fourth to be above the mean, one or both are permitted to be at the mean (but none must be below the mean). Again, the opposite logic would be used to accept or reject relative weaknesses.

Five or More Boxes. To accept a hypothesized strength comprising of five or more subtests, at least one of the ability boxes must be a significant strength (++). The rest of the boxes need to be designated as above (+ or + +) or equal (0) to the relevant mean with the exception that one can be below the mean (−) and it is even permissible for it to be significantly below the mean (− −) assuming that most of the other subtests are above the mean. The opposite logic would be used to accept or reject a relative weakness.

3. Examiners should indicate on the far right any strength that has been accepted by writing an "S"; similarly a "W" should be written if it is a weakness. For example, a person who had a significantly high Picture Arrangement score would have had a "++" placed in the ability-related box for sequencing. If other subtests measuring sequencing (Arithmetic, Digit Span, Digit Symbol, Symbol Search) also had average and/or above average scores (with one being permissible in the below average range), then this would support the hypothesis that good Sequencing was the (or at least one of the) relative cognitive strengths resulting in

an elevated score on Picture Arrangement. The higher the corroborating scores from the other subtests also relating to sequencing, the stronger the support that sequencing is the relevant ability. However, note that in most cases abilities will be found to be neither strengths nor weaknesses and thus the box on the far right will need to be left blank.

4. Examiners should work through Steps 1–3 only for those abilities in subtests found to be either significantly high or significantly low based on calculations in Level IIIa.

Ability	Verbal Subtests						Strength or Weakness
	I	DSp	V	A	C	S	
Verbal Memory (with Little Verbal Expression)			▓		▓	▓	
Verbal Conceptualization (Concept Formation)	▓	▓		▓			
Fund of Information		▓		▓			
Abstract Verbal Reasoning	▓	▓					
Auditory Short-Term Memory	▓		▓		▓		
Auditory Sequencing	▓		▓		▓		
Verbal Comprehension		▓					
Acquired Knowledge		▓			▓	▓	
Retention			▓		▓	▓	
Language Development and Word Knowledge	▓	▓		▓		▓	
Computational and Numerical Skill	▓						
Practical Knowledge and Judgment Related to Conventional Standards of Behavior	▓	▓	▓	▓		▓	
Amount of Benefit from Old Learning or Schooling, Intellectual Curiosity, Range of Interests		▓			▓		
Long-Term Memory		▓			▓	▓	
Complex Verbal Expression	▓	▓	▓				
Simple Verbal Expression			▓		▓	▓	

Appendix E1.   Guidelines for determining subtest strengths and weaknesses (verbal)

Ability	Performance							Strength or Weakness
	PC	PA	BD	OA	DSy coding	SS (WISC-III)	Mazes (WISC-III)	
Visual Organization					■	■		
Visual-Motor Coordination	■	■						
Visual Perception & Processing of Abstract Information	■	■		■			■	
Visual Perception & Processing of Meaningful Stimuli			■		■	■	■	
Nonverbal Reasoning	■		■		■	■	■	
Reproduction of Models	■	■		■				
Simultaneous Processing of Visual-Spatial Information		■			■	■	■	
Visual Sequencing	■		■	■	■			
Visual Closure		■	■		■	■		
Visual Memory		■	■		■	■		
Synthesis	■				■	■		
Trial and Error Learning	■	■			■	■	■	
Visual-Spatial Reasoning (Concept Formation)	■				■	■		
Perceptual Organization/ Spatial Ability		■			■	■		
Speed of Processing Information	■							
Planning Ability and Anticipation of Consequences	■		■	■	■			

Appendix E2.   Guidelines for determining subtest strengths and weaknesses (performance)

Ability	Performance							Strength or Weakness
	PC	PA	BD	OA	DSy coding	SS (WISC-III)	Mazes (WISC-III)	
Analysis of Whole into Component Parts		�▨		▨	▨	▨	▨	
Anticipation of Relationships among Parts	▨		▨		▨	▨	▨	
Clerical Speed and Accuracy	▨	▨	▨	▨			▨	
Visual Short-Term Memory	▨	▨	▨	▨			▨	
Spatial Visualization	▨	▨			▨	▨	▨	
Speed of Visual Search	▨	▨	▨	▨	▨		▨	

Appendix E2.   (continued)

Ability	Verbal					
	I	DSp	V	A	C	S
General Ability		■				
Social Comprehension	■	■	■	■		■
Abstract Reasoning	■	■	■	■		
Attention & Concentration	■		■		■	
Sequencing	■				■	■
Fluid Intelligence	■				■	
Crystallized Intelligence		■	■	■		
Achievement		■				
Immediate Rote Learning and Recall	■		■	■	■	■
Alertness & Recognition of Relevant from Irrelevant Details	■	■	■	■		
Alertness to Day-to-Day World		■	■			■
Ability to Evaluate Past Experience; Social Judgment	■	■	■	■		■
Flexibility of Thinking	■		■	■	■	■
Ability to Evaluate Information	■		■	■		■
Short-Term Memory (Visual or Auditory)	■		■	■		■

Appendix E3:   Guidelines for determining subtest strengths and weaknesses—using verbal and performance scales combined

Performance							Strength or Weakness
PC	PA	BD	OA	DSy coding	SS (WISC-III)	Mazes (WISC-III)	

Appendix E3.   (continued)

Appendix F

Wechsler Adult Intelligence Scale—Revised (WAIS-R) Profile Sheet

Name _____   Date _____   Birth Date _____   Age _____   Grade _____   School _____

School District _____   Examiner _____   VERBAL IQ _____   PERFORMANCE IQ _____   FULL SCALE IQ _____

INDEX SCORES: Verbal Comprehension _____   Perceptual Organization _____   Freedom from Distractibility _____   Processing Speed _____

Verbal Scales: Ability to work with abstract verbal symbols; perceptual skills included (auditory)

Subtest	5	6	7	8	9	10	11	12	13	14	15	16	17	18	19	SUBTEST ABILITIES*
Information	·	·	·	·	·	·	·	·	·	·	·	·	·	·	·	Remote memory; experience and education; cultural background
Digit Span	·	·	·	·	·	·	·	·	·	·	·	·	·	·	·	Concentration; immediate auditory memory
Vocabulary	·	·	·	·	·	·	·	·	·	·	·	·	·	·	·	Education background; general verbal intelligence; range of ideas
Arithmetic	·	·	·	·	·	·	·	·	·	·	·	·	·	·	·	Concentration; numerical reasoning; school learning
Comprehension	·	·	·	·	·	·	·	·	·	·	·	·	·	·	·	Practical knowledge and social judgment; common sense
Similarities	·	·	·	·	·	·	·	·	·	·	·	·	·	·	·	Verbal concept formation; logical and abstract reasoning

Performance Scale: Ability to work in concrete situation; perceptual skills included (visual)

Subtest	5	6	7	8	9	10	11	12	13	14	15	16	17	18	19	SUBTEST ABILITIES*
Picture Completion	·	·	·	·	·	·	·	·	·	·	·	·	·	·	·	Verbal concentration; ability to visually differentiate essential information
Picture Arrangement	·	·	·	·	·	·	·	·	·	·	·	·	·	·	·	Planning ability and foresight; ability to assess nonverbal social interactions
Block Design	·	·	·	·	·	·	·	·	·	·	·	·	·	·	·	Visual-motor coordination; spatial problem solving; concentration
Object Assembly	·	·	·	·	·	·	·	·	·	·	·	·	·	·	·	Visual-motor organization; seeing relationships of parts to wholes
Digit Symbol	·	·	·	·	·	·	·	·	·	·	·	·	·	·	·	Visual-motor speed; ability to learn rote tasks

* Subtest abilities should be considered as hypotheses in need of confirmation through comparisons with other subtests as well as outside sources.

Appendix G

Wechsler Intelligence Scale for Children (3rd ed.; WISC-III) Profile Sheet

Name _____   Date _____   Birth Date _____   Age _____   Grade _____   School _____

School District _____   Examiner _____   VERBAL IQ _____   PERFORMANCE IQ _____   FULL SCALE IQ _____

INDEX SCORES: Verbal Comprehension _____   Perceptual Organization _____   Freedom from Distractibility _____   Processing Speed _____

Verbal Scales: Ability to work with abstract verbal symbols; perceptual skills included (auditory)

	5	6	7	8	9	10	11	12	13	14	15	16	17	18	19	SUBTEST ABILITIES*
Information	·	·	·	·	·	·	·	·	·	·	·	·	·	·	·	Remote memory; experience and education; cultural background
Similarities	·	·	·	·	·	·	·	·	·	·	·	·	·	·	·	Concentration; immediate auditory memory
Arithmetic	·	·	·	·	·	·	·	·	·	·	·	·	·	·	·	Education background; general verbal intelligence; range of ideas
Vocabulary	·	·	·	·	·	·	·	·	·	·	·	·	·	·	·	Concentration; numerical reasoning; school learning
Comprehension	·	·	·	·	·	·	·	·	·	·	·	·	·	·	·	Practical knowledge and social judgment; common sense
Digit Span	·	·	·	·	·	·	·	·	·	·	·	·	·	·	·	Verbal concept formation; logical and abstract reasoning

Performance Scale: Ability to work in concrete situation; perceptual skills included (visual)

	5	6	7	8	9	10	11	12	13	14	15	16	17	18	19	SUBTEST ABILITIES*
Picture Completion	·	·	·	·	·	·	·	·	·	·	·	·	·	·	·	Verbal concentration; ability to visually differentiate essential information
Picture Arrangement	·	·	·	·	·	·	·	·	·	·	·	·	·	·	·	Planning ability and foresight; ability to assess nonverbal social interactions
Block Design	·	·	·	·	·	·	·	·	·	·	·	·	·	·	·	Visual-motor coordination; spatial problem solving; concentration
Object Assembly	·	·	·	·	·	·	·	·	·	·	·	·	·	·	·	Visual-motor organization; seeing relationships of parts to wholes
Coding	·	·	·	·	·	·	·	·	·	·	·	·	·	·	·	Visual-motor speed; ability to learn rote tasks
Symbol Search	·	·	·	·	·	·	·	·	·	·	·	·	·	·	·	Short-term memory; attention and concentration
Mazes (optional)	·	·	·	·	·	·	·	·	·	·	·	·	·	·	·	Planning and foresight in following a visual pattern

* Subtest abilities should be considered as hypotheses in need of confirmation through comparisons with other subtests as well as outside sources.

Appendix H

Interpretive Rationales, Implications of High and Low Scores, and Instructional Implications for Wechsler Scales and Factor Scores.

Ability	Background Factors	Possible Implications of High Scores	Possible Implications of Low Scores	Instructional Implications
Full Scale				
General intelligence Scholastic aptitude Academic aptitude Readiness to master a school curriculum	Natural endowment Richness of early environment Extent of schooling Cultural opportunities Interests Rate of motor activity Persistence Visual-motor organization Alertness	Good general intelligence Good scholastic aptitude Readiness to master a school curriculum	Poor general intelligence Poor scholastic aptitude Not ready to master school curriculum	Focus on language development activities Focus on visual learning activities Develop concept formation skills Reinforce persistence
Verbal Scale or Verbal Comprehension Factor				
Verbal comprehension Application of verbal skills and information to the solution of new problems Verbal ability Ability to process verbal information Ability to think with words	Natural endowment Richness of early environment Extent of schooling Cultural opportunities Interests	Good verbal comprehension Good scholastic aptitude Possession of knowledge of the cultural milieu Good concept formation Readiness to master school curriculum Achievement orientation	Poor verbal comprehension Poor scholastic aptitude Inadequate understanding of the cultural milieu Poor concept formation Bilingual background Foreign background Not ready to master school curriculum Poor achievement orientation	Stress language development activities Use verbal enrichment activities Focus on current events Use exercises involving concept formation

686

Ability	Background Factors	Possible Implications of High Scores	Possible Implications of Low Scores	Instructional Implications
Performance Scale or Perceptual Organization Factor				
Perceptual organization Ability to think in terms of visual images and manipulate them with fluency, flexibility, and relative speed Ability to interpret or organize visually perceived material against a time limit Nonverbal ability Ability to form relatively abstract concepts and relationships without the use of words	Natural endowment Rate of motor activity Persistence Visual-motor organization Alertness	Good perceptual organization Good alertness to detail Good nonverbal reasoning ability Good persistence Good ability to work quickly and efficiently Good spatial ability	Poor perceptual organization Poor alertness to detail Poor nonverbal reasoning ability Limited persistence Poor ability to work quickly and efficiently Poor spatial ability	Focus on visual learning activities Focus on part-whole relationships Use spatial-visual tasks Encourage trial-and-error activities Reinforce persistence Focus on visual planning activities Improve scanning techniques
Freedom from Distractibility				
Ability to sustain attention Short-term memory Numerical ability Encoding ability Ability to use rehearsal strategies Ability to shift mental operations on symbolic material Ability to self-monitor	Natural endowment Ability to passively receive stimuli	Good ability to sustain attention Good short-term memory Good numerical ability Good encoding ability Good use of rehearsal strategies Good ability to shift mental operations on symbolic material Good ability to self-monitor	Difficulty in sustaining attention Distractibility Anxiety Short-term retention deficits Encoding difficulties Poor rehearsal strategies Difficulty in rapidly shifting mental operations on symbolic material Inadequate self-monitoring skills	Develop attention skills Develop concentration skills Focus on small, meaningful units of instruction

Source: From *Assessment of Children* (3rd ed.), pp. 856–857, by J. M. Sattler, 1988, San Diego: Author. Copyright © 1988 by Jerome M. Sattler, Publisher. Entire table reprinted with permission of the publisher and author.

Interpretive Rationale, Implications of High and Low Scores, and Instructional Implications for the Processing Speed Factor (WISC-III only)

Ability	Background Factors	Possible Implications of High Scores	Possible Implications of Low Scores	Instructional Implications
Clerical speed and accuracy	Rate of motor activity	Good processing speed	Poor processing speed	Use visual-motor scanning exercises, such as having child look at two or more objects and decide if they are the same or different, or detect words embedded in a group of letters
Visual scanning and tracking	Motivation	Good perceptual discrimination ability	Poor perceptual discrimination ability	
Visual perception and processing of abstract info		Good attention and concentration	Distractibility	
Speed of mental operation		Sustained energy or persistence	Visual defects	
Psychomotor speed		Good motivation or desire for achievement	Lethargy	
Attention and concentration skills			Poor motivation	
Visual short-term memory				
Visual-motor coordination				
Cognitive flexibility				

Source: Note from Sattler (1992, p. 1177).

Appendix I

Suggested Remediation Activities for Combinations of Wechsler Subtests

Subtests	Ability	Activities
Information, Vocabulary, and Comprehension	General knowledge and verbal fluency	(1) Review basic concepts, such as days of the week, months, time, distances, and directions; (2) have children report major current events by referring to pictures and articles from magazines and newspapers; (3) teach similarities and differences of designs, topography, transportation, etc.; (4) have children make a scrapbook of pictures of animals, buildings, etc.; (5) introduce words, dictionary work, abstract words; (6) have children repeat simple stories; (7) have children explain how story characters are feeling and thinking.
Similarities and Vocabulary	Verbal conceptual	(1) Use show-and-tell games; (2) have children make a scrapbook of classifications, such as of animals, vehicles, and utensils; (3) have children match abstract concepts; (4) have children find commonality in dissimilar objects; (5) review basic concepts such as days of the week, months, time, directions, and distances.
Digit Span, Arithmetic, Picture Completion, and Picture Arrangement	Attention and concentration	(1) Have children arrange cards in a meaningful sequence; (2) have children learn telephone number, address, etc.; (3) use spelling word games; (4) use memory games; (5) have children learn days of week, months of year; (6) use mathematical word problems; (7) use dot-to-dot exercises; (8) have children describe details in pictures; (9) use tracing activities; (10) use Tinker Toys.
Block Design and Object Assembly	Spatial-visual	(1) Have children identify common objects and discuss details; (2) use guessing games involving description of a person, place, or thing; (3) have children match letters, shapes, numbers, etc.; (4) use jigsaw puzzles; (5) use block-building activities.
Coding, Digit Symbol, Block Design, Object Assembly, Animal House, and Mazes	Visual-motor	(1) Use paper-folding activities; (2) use finger-painting activities; (3) use dot-to-dot exercises; (4) use scissor-cutting exercises; (5) use sky-writing exercises; (6) have children string beads in patterns; (7) use pegboard designs; (8) use puzzles (large jigsaw pieces); (9) have children solve a maze; (10) have children follow a moving object with coordinated eye movements; (11) use tracing exercises (e.g., trace hand, geometric forms, and letters); (12) have children make large circles and lines on chalkboard; (13) have children copy from patterns; (14) have children draw from memory.

Source: From *Assessment of Children* (3rd ed.), by J. M. Sattler, 1988, San Diego: Author, pp. 856–857. Copyright © 1988 by Jerome M. Sattler, Publisher. Reprinted with permission of the publisher and author.

Appendix J

Directions for Hand Scoring the Minnesota Multiphasic Personality Inventory (MMPI-2) Validity and Clinical Scales

1. Separate the Scale 5 *(Mf)* scoring keys by sex to correspond with the gender of the person who has taken the test.

2. Items that have been either omitted or double marked should be crossed out with a colored pen, counted as cannot say (?) responses, and the raw score (total number) should be entered on the profile sheet indicated to the right of "? Raw Score."

3. The scoring keys for the validity and clinical scales are then placed over the "softcover answer sheet." The total number of marked items are counted to determine the raw scores for each of the scales. Items marked with a colored pen to designate they are cannot say (?) responses are ignored. The raw scores for each of the scales are entered in the designated sections on the profile sheet. Examiners should make sure that the gender indicated on the profile sheet matches the gender of the examinee.

4. Before plotting the profile, *K* corrections need to be added to the raw scores for *Hs, Pd, Pt, Sc,* and *Ma.* This is done by first calculating the appropriate fractions of *K* (.5K to *Hs*; .4K to *Pd*; 1K to *Pt*; 1K to *Sc*; and .2K to *Ma*). This can be easily done by using the box to the far left of the profile sheet designated as "Fractions of *K*." The raw score of *K* that was derived from scoring *K* can be located in the far left column of the "Fractions of *K*" box. The three numbers to the right of the raw score of *K* are the correct fractions of *K*. For example, if a raw score for *K* was 15, then .5K, .4K, and .2K would be 8, 6, and 3 respectively. The correct fractions of *K* can then be added to the raw scores for *Hs, Pd,* and *Ma.* *Pt* and *Sc* both have a full *K* correction added to them.

5. When *K* corrections have been added to *Hs, Pd, Pt, Sc,* and *Ma,* the raw scores can then be plotted on the profile sheet. This can be done by noting the lower scale labels (*L, F, K, Hs* + .5K, etc.) and finding the correct raw score on the profile sheet directly above them. These raw scores can then be marked with a dot, circle, or cross. When they have all been marked, a line can be made connecting the three validity scales and the 10 clinical scales. The T scores can be found by lining up the raw scores with the correct T scores on either the far right or the far left of the profile sheet (designated as "T or Tc"). For example, a raw score of 25 on Scale 1 *(Hs)* converts to a T score of 80.

Appendix K

Koss-Butcher Critical Items*

Acute Anxiety State

2(2)[†] I have a good appetite. (F)

3(3). I wake up fresh and rested most mornings. (F)

5(5). I am easily awakened by noise. (T)

10(9). I am about as able to work as I ever was. (F)

15(13). I work under a great deal of tension. (T)

28(29). I am bothered by an upset stomach several times a week. (T)

39(43). My sleep is fitful and disturbed. (T)

59(72). I am troubled by discomfort in the pit of my stomach every few days or oftener. (T)

140(152). Most nights I go to sleep without thoughts or ideas bothering me. (F)

172(186). I frequently notice my hand shakes when I try to do something. (T)

208(230). I hardly ever notice my heart pounding and I am seldom short of breath. (F)

218(238). I have periods of such great restlessness that I cannot sit long in a chair. (T)

223(242). I believe I am no more nervous than most others. (F).

301(337). I feel anxiety about something or someone almost all the time. (T)

444(506). I am a high-strung person. (T)

463(543). Several times a week I feel as if something dreadful is about to happen. (T)

469(555). I sometimes feel that I am about to go to pieces. (T).

Threatened Assault

37(39). At times I feel like smashing things. (T)

85(97). At times I have a strong urge to do something harmful or shocking. (T)

134(145). At times I feel like picking a fistfight with someone. (T)

213(234). I get mad easily and get over it soon. (T)

389(381). I am often said to be hotheaded. (T)

---

* Source for MMPI-2 numbers is Butcher, Dahlstrom, Graham, Tellegen, & Kaemmer (1989), and for MMPI numbers is Koss and Butcher (1973). Items are from *Minnesota Multiphasic Personality Inventory,* Copyright © the University of Minnesota 1942, 1943 (renewed 1970, 1989). Reproduced by permission of the publisher.

[†] Item numbers are according to the MMPI-2 with the numbers in parentheses indicating the numbers in the MMPI Group Form. All wording is according to the MMPI-2.

Mental Confusion

24(27).	Evil spirits possess me at times. (T)
31(328).	I find it hard to keep my mind on a task or job. (T)
32(33).	I have had very peculiar and strange experiences. (T)
72(50).	My soul sometimes leaves my body. (T)
96(66).	I see things or animals or people around me that others don't see. (T)
180(168).	There is something wrong with my mind. (T)
198(184).	I often hear voices without knowing where they come from. (T)
299(335).	I cannot keep my mind on one thing. (T)
311(345).	I often feel as if things are not real. (T)
316(349).	I have strange and peculiar thoughts. (T)
325(356).	I have more trouble concentrating than others seem to have. (T)

Depressed Suicidal Ideation

9(318).   My daily life is full of things that keep me interested. (F)
38(41).   I have had periods of days, weeks, or months when I couldn't take care of things because I couldn't "get going." (T)
65(76).   Most of the time I feel blue. (T)
71(84).   These days I find it hard not to give up hope of amounting to something. (T)
75(88).   I usually feel that life is worthwhile. (F)
92(104).   I don't seem to care what happens to me. (T)
95(107).   I am happy most of the time. (F)
130(142).   I certainly feel useless at times. (T)
146(158).   I cry easily. (T)
215(236).   I brood a great deal. (T)
233(259).   I have difficulty starting to do things. (T)
273(301).   Life is a strain for me much of the time. (T)
303(339).   Most of the time I wish I were dead. (T)
306(252).   No one cares much what happens to you. (T)
388(379).   I very seldom have spells of the blues. (F)
411(418).   At times I think I am no good at all. (T)
454(526).   The future seems hopeless to me. (T)
485(418).   I often feel that I'm not as good as other people. (T)
506.   I have recently considered killing myself. (T)
518.   I have made lots of bad mistakes in my life. (T)
520.   Lately I have thought a lot about killing myself. (T)
524.   No one knows it but I have tried to kill myself. (T)

Situational Stress Due to Alcoholism

125(137).   I believe that my home life is as pleasant as that of most people I know. (F)
264(215).   I have used alcohol excessively. (T)
487.   I have enjoyed using marijuana. (T)

489.   I have a drug or alcohol problem. (T)
502.   I have some habits that are really harmful. (T)
511.   Once a week or more I get high or drunk. (T)
518.   I have made lots of bad mistakes in my life. (T)

Persecutory Ideas

17(16).   I am sure I get a raw deal from life. (T)
42(35).   If people had not had it in for me, I would have been much more successful. (T)
99(110).   Someone has it in for me. (T)
124(136).   I often wonder what hidden reason another person may have for doing something nice for me. (T)
138(121).   I believe I am being plotted against. (T)
144(123).   I believe I am being followed. (T)
145(157).   I feel that I have often been punished without cause. (T)
162(151).   Someone has been trying to poison me. (T)
216(197).   Someone has been trying to rob me. (T)
228(200).   There are persons who are trying to steal my thoughts and ideas. (T)
241(265).   It is safer to trust nobody. (T)
251(278).   I have often felt that strangers were looking at me critically. (T)
259(284).   I am sure I am being talked about. (T)
314(347).   I have no enemies who really wish to harm me. (F)
333(364).   People say insulting and vulgar things about me. (T)
361(293).   Someone has been trying to influence my mind. (T)

Appendix L

Descriptive Statistics for 700 Adult Nonpatients

Variable	Mean	SD	Min	Max	Freq	Median	Mode	SK	KU
R	22.67	4.23	14.00	38.00	700	23.00	23.00	0.54	1.37
W	8.55	1.94	3.00	20.00	700	9.00	9.00	1.28	8.87
D	12.89	3.54	0.00	22.00	698	13.00	14.00	−0.38	1.02
Dd	1.23	[1.70]	0.00	15.00	452	1.00	0.00	3.89	22.18
S	1.47	[1.21]	0.00	10.00	600	1.00	1.00	2.44	11.43
DQ+	7.31	2.16	2.00	13.00	700	7.00	6.00	0.27	−0.39
DQo	13.64	3.46	5.00	34.00	700	14.00	15.00	0.95	4.67
DQv	1.30	[1.26]	0.00	6.00	477	1.00	0.00	0.93	0.38
DQv/+	0.41	[0.66]	0.00	2.00	219	0.00	0.00	1.35	0.53
FQx+	0.90	0.92	0.00	5.00	427	1.00	0.00	1.21	2.26
FQxo	16.99	3.34	7.00	29.00	700	17.00	17.00	0.04	0.52
FQxu	3.25	1.77	0.00	13.00	667	3.00	3.00	0.94	3.37
FQx−	1.44	1.04	0.00	6.00	605	1.00	1.00	0.95	0.93
FQxNone	0.09	[0.33]	0.00	3.00	58	0.00	0.00	4.00	18.52
MQ+	0.55	0.73	0.00	3.00	297	0.00	0.00	1.23	1.02
MQo	3.52	1.89	0.00	8.00	693	3.00	3.00	0.46	−0.60
MQu	0.20	0.45	0.00	2.00	123	0.00	0.00	2.23	4.31
MQ−	0.03	[0.19]	0.00	2.00	22	0.00	0.00	5.90	36.99
MQNone	0.01	[0.11]	0.00	1.00	8	0.00	0.00	9.21	83.11
SQual−	0.18	[0.49]	0.00	3.00	102	0.00	0.00	3.16	11.29
M	4.31	1.92	1.00	9.00	700	4.00	3.00	0.51	−0.74
FM	3.70	1.19	1.00	9.00	700	4.00	4.00	−0.05	0.46
m	1.12	0.85	0.00	4.00	530	1.00	1.00	0.51	0.32
FC	4.09	1.88	0.00	9.00	690	4.00	5.00	0.31	−0.13
CF	2.36	1.27	0.00	6.00	670	2.00	3.00	0.40	−0.12
C	0.08	[0.28]	0.00	2.00	51	0.00	0.00	3.73	14.14
Cn	0.01	[0.08]	0.00	1.00	5	0.00	0.00	11.73	135.98
Sum Color	6.54	2.52	1.00	12.00	700	7.00	5.00	−0.04	−0.79
WSumC	4.52	1.79	0.50	9.00	700	4.50	3.50	0.02	−0.69
Sum C'	1.53	[1.25]	0.00	10.00	551	1.00	1.00	1.32	5.24
Sum T	1.03	[0.58]	0.00	4.00	620	1.00	1.00	1.35	5.39
Sum V	0.26	[0.58]	0.00	3.00	137	0.00	0.00	2.39	5.54
Sum Y	0.57	[1.00]	0.00	10.00	274	0.00	0.00	4.08	28.70
Sum Shading	3.39	2.15	0.00	23.00	689	3.00	3.00	3.03	20.65
Fr + rF	0.08	[0.35]	0.00	4.00	47	0.00	0.00	6.06	49.54
FD	1.16	[0.87]	0.00	5.00	553	1.00	1.00	1.00	2.57
F	7.99	2.67	2.00	19.00	700	8.00	8.00	0.65	1.21

Source: From *The Rorschach: A Comprehensive System I: Basic Foundations* (2nd ed.), pp. 260–262, by J. E. Exner, Jr. Copyright © 1993 by John E. Exner, Jr. Reprinted by permission of John Wiley & Sons, Inc.

Note: Standard deviations shown in brackets indicate that the value is probably unreliable and/or misleading because the variable is nonparametric.

Variable	Mean	SD	Min	Max	Freq	Median	Mode	SK	KU
(2)	8.68	2.15	1.00	14.00	700	8.00	8.00	0.06	0.63
3r + (2)/R	0.40	0.09	0.03	0.79	700	0.38	0.33	0.42	2.59
Lambda	0.58	0.26	0.14	2.25	700	0.56	0.50	2.23	9.91
Fm + m	4.82	1.51	1.00	10.00	700	5.00	5.00	0.27	0.30
EA	8.83	2.18	2.00	14.50	700	9.00	9.50	−0.30	0.15
es	8.20	2.98	3.00	31.00	700	8.00	7.00	1.90	10.18
D Score	0.04	1.08	−10.00	2.00	244	0.00	0.00	−3.29	24.95
AdjD	0.20	0.87	−5.00	2.00	272	0.00	0.00	−1.11	6.04
a (active)	6.48	2.14	2.00	13.00	700	6.00	6.00	0.57	−0.09
p (passive)	2.69	1.52	0.00	9.00	659	2.00	2.00	0.54	0.26
M^a	3.04	1.59	0.00	7.00	679	3.00	2.00	0.45	−0.38
M^p	1.31	0.94	0.00	5.00	568	1.00	1.00	0.59	0.34
Intellect	1.56	1.29	0.00	6.00	546	1.00	1.00	0.78	0.25
Zü	11.81	2.59	5.00	23.00	700	12.00	12.00	0.27	1.47
Zd	0.72	3.06	−6.50	9.50	644	0.50	−1.00	0.48	0.09
Blends	5.16	1.93	1.00	12.00	700	5.00	5.00	0.04	−0.37
Blends/R	0.23	0.09	0.04	0.67	700	0.23	0.26	0.76	1.55
Col-Shd Bld	0.46	[0.69]	0.00	3.00	252	0.00	0.00	1.45	1.66
Afr	0.69	0.16	0.27	1.29	700	0.67	0.91	0.40	0.30
Populars	6.89	1.39	3.00	10.00	700	7.00	8.00	−0.47	−0.13
X + %	0.79	0.08	0.50	1.00	700	0.80	0.80	−0.23	1.17
F + %	0.71	0.17	0.25	1.00	700	0.71	1.00	−0.24	−0.24
X − %	0.07	0.05	0.00	0.43	605	0.05	0.04	1.86	8.97
Xu%	0.14	0.07	0.00	0.37	667	0.14	0.15	0.17	0.41
S − %	0.08	[0.23]	0.00	1.00	102	0.00	0.00	2.93	7.99
Isolate/R	0.20	0.09	0.00	0.47	689	0.19	0.16	0.39	−0.23
H	3.40	1.80	0.00	9.00	694	3.00	3.00	0.90	0.30
(H)	1.20	0.98	0.00	4.00	499	1.00	1.00	0.41	−0.35
HD	0.69	0.89	0.00	7.00	348	0.00	0.00	2.06	8.03
(Hd)	0.14	0.35	0.00	2.00	99	0.00	0.00	2.14	2.95
Hx	0.01	[0.11]	0.00	1.00	8	0.00	0.00	9.21	83.11
All H Cont	5.42	1.63	1.00	11.00	700	5.00	6.00	0.23	−0.10
A	8.18	2.04	3.00	15.00	700	8.00	7.00	0.43	0.17
(A)	0.17	[0.47]	0.00	3.00	95	0.00	0.00	3.27	12.22
Ad	2.21	[1.18]	0.00	9.00	665	2.00	2.00	1.14	4.65
(Ad)	0.05	[0.26]	0.00	2.00	33	0.00	0.00	5.14	28.41
An	0.42	[0.65]	0.00	4.00	244	0.00	0.00	1.54	2.46
Art	0.91	0.83	0.00	4.00	448	1.00	1.00	0.50	−0.41
Ay	0.34	[0.48]	0.00	2.00	236	0.00	0.00	0.78	−1.09
Bl	0.15	[0.40]	0.00	2.00	96	0.00	0.00	2.64	6.55
Bt	2.48	1.29	0.00	6.00	652	3.00	3.00	−0.02	−0.47
Cg	1.29	0.93	0.00	4.00	572	1.00	1.00	0.62	0.12
Cl	0.15	[0.38]	0.00	2.00	102	0.00	0.00	2.32	4.54
Ex	0.13	[0.34]	0.00	1.00	93	0.00	0.00	2.17	2.71
Fi	0.42	[0.67]	0.00	2.00	221	0.00	0.00	1.33	0.44
Food	0.23	[0.50]	0.00	2.00	136	0.00	0.00	2.11	3.65

(continued)

Variable	Mean	SD	Min	Max	Freq	Median	Mode	SK	KU
Ge	0.04	[0.21]	0.00	2.00	25	0.00	0.00	5.74	35.68
Hh	0.93	0.85	0.00	4.00	458	1.00	1.00	0.76	0.32
Ls	0.89	0.78	0.00	3.00	460	1.00	1.00	0.45	−0.50
Na	.038	[0.60]	0.00	2.00	222	0.00	0.00	1.34	0.72
Sc	0.91	[0.97]	0.00	6.00	411	1.00	0.00	1.25	2.99
Sx	0.07	[0.39]	0.00	5.00	30	0.00	0.00	8.41	85.78
Xy	0.03	[0.18]	0.00	2.00	17	0.00	0.00	7.25	57.98
Idio	1.85	1.29	0.00	7.00	599	2.00	2.00	0.75	1.08
DV	0.70	[0.79]	0.00	4.00	373	1.00	0.00	1.12	1.20
INCOM	0.52	[0.65]	0.00	4.00	323	0.00	0.00	1.39	3.56
DR	0.15	[0.38]	0.00	2.00	103	0.00	0.00	2.30	4.44
FABCOM	0.17	[0.41]	0.00	2.00	111	0.00	0.00	2.27	4.43
DV2	0.01	[0.10]	0.00	1.00	7	0.00	0.00	9.87	95.70
INC2	0.00	[0.07]	0.00	1.00	3	0.00	0.00	15.21	229.99
DR2	0.00	[0.04]	0.00	1.00	1	0.00	0.00	26.46	700.00
FAB2	0.02	[0.13]	0.00	1.00	12	0.00	0.00	7.46	53.74
ALOG	0.04	[0.22]	0.00	2.00	29	0.00	0.00	5.23	29.28
CONTAM	0.00	0.00	0.00	0.00	0	0.00	0.00	—	—
Sum6 Sp Sc	1.62	1.26	0.00	7.00	564	1.00	1.00	0.73	0.35
Sum6 Sp Sc2	0.03	[0.18]	0.00	1.00	23	0.00	0.00	5.25	25.66
WSum6	3.28	2.89	0.00	15.00	564	3.00	0.00	1.07	1.15
AB	0.15	[0.40]	0.00	2.00	98	0.00	0.00	2.57	6.17
AG	1.18	1.18	0.00	5.00	466	1.00	1.00	1.04	0.62
CFB	0.00	0.00	0.00	0.00	0	0.00	0.00	—	—
COP	2.07	1.52	0.00	6.00	555	2.00	2.00	0.25	−0.84
CP	0.02	[0.14]	0.00	1.00	13	0.00	0.00	7.15	49.23
MOR	0.70	[0.82]	0.00	4.00	356	1.00	0.00	1.03	0.60
PER	1.05	1.00	0.00	5.00	478	1.00	1.00	1.38	3.27
PSV	0.05	[0.22]	0.00	1.00	34	0.00	0.00	4.21	15.76

Appendix M

Descriptive Statistics for 1,390 Nonpatient Children and Adolescents by Age

Age	5		6		7		8	
Variable	Mean	SD	Mean	SD	Mean	SD	Mean	SD
R	17.64	1.44	18.91	0.98	19.93	1.25	18.73	2.46
W	9.97	1.65	10.79	1.17	10.33	2.01	10.03	1.01
D	7.10	2.61	7.94	1.01	9.09	2.86	7.00	1.28
Dd	0.58	[0.65]	0.30	[0.46]	0.82	[0.32]	1.70	[0.84]
S	1.40	[1.14]	0.79	[0.76]	1.44	[1.06]	1.73	[0.58]
DQ+	5.47	1.43	4.42	0.59	6.48	0.80	6.80	1.74
DQo	10.72	2.07	11.31	1.35	11.15	0.98	11.27	1.40
DQv	1.37	[0.62]	2.54	[1.19]	1.63	[0.58]	0.90	[0.62]
DQv/+	0.09	[0.29]	0.45	[0.64]	0.28	[0.45]	0.17	[0.25]
FQX+	0.00	0.00	0.00	0.00	0.00	0.00	0.00	0.00
FQXo	11.54	2.50	13.39	1.22	14.37	1.46	13.22	1.83
FQXu	3.59	1.96	4.01	1.29	2.08	0.69	3.47	1.37
FQX−	1.46	0.64	0.94	0.50	1.99	1.27	1.72	0.76
FQXNone	0.87	[0.62]	0.74	[0.48]	1.10	[0.30]	0.43	[0.48]
MQ+	0.00	0.00	0.00	0.00	0.00	0.00	0.00	0.00
MQo	1.13	0.34	1.96	0.75	2.51	1.16	3.12	1.62
MQu	0.38	0.66	0.00	0.00	0.56	0.34	0.20	0.40
MQ−	0.19	[0.39]	0.23	[0.67]	0.45	[0.22]	0.07	[0.25]
MQNone	0.00	[0.00]	0.00	[0.00]	0.00	[0.00]	0.00	[0.00]
S−	0.91	[0.69]	0.42	[0.78]	0.12	[0.32]	0.13	[0.34]
M	1.70	1.00	1.96	0.75	3.02	1.22	3.38	1.85
FM	5.00	0.95	4.52	0.81	5.92	1.20	4.72	1.37
m	0.78	0.80	1.40	1.48	1.06	0.40	0.57	0.50
FM + m	5.78	1.19	5.92	0.99	6.08	1.14	5.28	1.56
FC	0.71	0.46	1.11	1.09	2.17	0.93	1.80	0.84
CF	3.02	1.41	3.51	0.94	3.19	0.98	2.73	0.78
C	0.67	[0.62]	0.94	[0.48]	0.99	[0.30]	0.43	[0.48]
Cn	0.00	[0.00]	0.06	[0.09]	0.00	[0.00]	0.00	[0.00]
FC + CF + C + Cn	4.40	1.10	5.56	1.63	6.15	1.39	4.87	0.72
WGSum C	4.38	1.09	5.02	1.42	4.97	1.14	4.13	0.77
Sum C'	0.63	[0.48]	0.58	[0.50]	1.25	[0.86]	1.30	[0.89]
Sum T	0.83	[0.48]	0.83	[0.22]	0.93	[0.78]	1.08	[0.60]
Sum V	0.00	[0.00]	0.00	[0.00]	0.00	[0.00]	0.00	[0.00]
Sum Y	0.36	[0.33]	0.54	[0.48]	0.23	[0.42]	0.92	[0.85]
SumShd	1.77	0.97	1.95	0.88	2.48	1.12	2.90	1.47
Fr + rF	0.38	[0.45]	0.28	[0.40]	0.30	[0.39]	0.33	[0.48]
FD	0.28	[0.63]	0.48	[0.68]	0.13	[0.70]	0.53	[0.34]
F	6.98	1.26	5.77	1.47	7.62	1.60	6.98	1.64
PAIR	9.08	1.96	9.61	1.79	9.73	1.94	7.97	1.19
3r(2)/R	0.69	0.14	0.67	0.15	0.65	0.12	0.62	0.12
LAMBDA	0.86	0.15	0.79	0.17	0.79	0.16	0.77	0.27
EA	5.08	1.34	6.98	1.42	7.48	1.04	7.51	1.45
es	7.04	1.14	7.87	1.00	8.56	1.67	8.18	2.51
D	−0.24	0.43	−0.41	0.59	−0.53	0.67	−0.22	0.64
AdjD	−0.20	0.40	−0.21	0.41	−0.47	0.58	−0.15	0.61
a (active)	6.28	0.95	6.03	1.27	6.97	1.24	6.73	1.63
p (passive)	1.20	1.37	1.85	1.90	3.03	1.28	1.93	1.30
Ma	1.42	0.67	0.98	0.84	2.82	0.87	3.12	1.66
Mp	0.28	0.45	0.99	1.35	0.20	0.40	0.37	0.45

Source: Standard Deviations shown in brackets indicate that the value is probably unreliable and/or misleading and should not be used to estimate expected ranges. Ordinarily, these variables should not be included in most parametric analyses.

Note: Adapted from Exner (1986).

(continued)

Age	5		6		7		8	
Variable	Mean	SD	Mean	SD	Mean	SD	Mean	SD
Intellect	0.17	0.38	0.96	0.51	0.27	0.44	0.46	0.98
Zf	10.08	2.18	10.15	1.44	11.51	1.46	11.27	1.49
Zd	−1.13	2.60	−1.38	2.20	−1.04	2.41	−0.70	1.93
Blends	2.86	1.92	2.16	0.49	5.11	0.65	4.88	1.03
Col Shd Bl	0.18	[0.56]	0.44	[0.64]	0.36	[0.64]	0.30	[0.40]
Afr	0.88	0.13	0.87	0.26	0.79	0.09	0.69	0.09
Popular	4.66	1.69	5.02	1.43	4.75	0.79	5.68	0.80
X + %	0.67	0.10	0.71	0.07	0.74	0.09	0.69	0.07
F + %	0.84	0.13	0.74	0.25	0.66	0.17	0.59	0.07
X − %	0.09	0.04	0.11	0.07	0.12	0.07	0.10	0.04
Xu%	0.23	0.10	0.18	0.09	0.14	0.08	0.20	0.06
S − %	0.49	[0.46]	0.25	[0.67]	0.15	[0.14]	0.06	[0.15]
Isolate	0.17	0.06	0.24	0.08	0.25	0.05	0.23	0.04
H	2.19	0.50	2.63	1.14	1.87	0.79	1.87	1.03
(H)	1.46	0.50	0.78	0.50	1.64	0.88	1.47	0.62
Hd	0.36	0.48	0.64	0.62	0.38	0.49	0.27	0.45
(Hd)	0.46	0.57	0.23	0.63	0.74	0.87	1.20	0.55
Hx	0.00	[0.00]	0.00	[0.00]	0.00	[0.00]	0.00	[0.00]
All H Cont	4.00	1.15	4.28	0.68	4.63	0.89	4.80	1.92
A	10.69	2.32	8.24	0.96	9.26	0.77	9.27	1.45
(A)	0.37	[0.48]	0.30	[0.46]	1.18	[0.81]	1.73	[0.58]
Ad	0.71	[0.60]	0.95	[0.22]	0.68	[0.79]	0.33	[0.48]
(Ad)	0.00	[0.00]	0.00	[0.00]	0.05	[0.22]	0.13	[0.34]
An	0.37	[0.49]	0.33	[0.50]	0.37	[0.48]	0.20	[0.40]
Art	0.17	0.38	0.96	0.51	0.10	0.30	0.59	0.64
Ay	0.00	[0.00]	0.00	[0.00]	0.17	[0.37]	0.10	[0.35]
Bl	1.13	[0.46]	0.25	[0.44]	0.48	[0.45]	0.33	[0.48]
Bt	0.28	0.45	1.52	0.60	2.11	0.56	1.45	0.65
Cg	3.73	1.35	1.02	0.70	1.15	0.36	1.80	1.18
Cl	0.58	[0.74]	0.11	[0.32]	0.38	[0.57]	0.13	[0.34]
Ex	0.22	[0.51]	0.20	[0.40]	0.41	[0.64]	0.43	[0.34]
Fi	0.22	[0.51]	0.64	[0.48]	0.48	[0.50]	0.33	[0.48]
Fd	0.41	[0.53]	0.58	[0.50]	0.20	[0.40]	0.20	[0.40]
Ge	0.00	[0.00]	0.05	[0.22]	0.00	[0.00]	0.00	[0.00]
Hh	0.71	0.65	1.26	0.55	1.45	0.88	0.45	0.36
Ls	2.68	0.63	1.27	0.78	1.21	0.93	0.93	0.25
Na	0.36	[0.51]	0.81	[0.75]	0.96	[0.77]	0.80	[0.40]
Sc	0.52	[0.43]	0.69	[0.57]	1.54	[1.14]	2.45	[0.62]
Sx	0.00	[0.00]	0.00	[0.00]	0.00	[0.00]	0.00	[0.00]
Xy	0.00	[0.00]	0.00	[0.00]	0.00	[0.00]	0.00	[0.00]
Idio	0.14	0.35	0.15	0.36	0.53	0.59	0.53	0.62
DV	1.16	[1.05]	0.26	[0.24]	1.39	[0.49]	1.33	[0.71]
INCOM	1.96	[0.70]	2.35	[0.48]	1.39	[0.58]	2.07	[0.45]
DR	0.11	[0.21]	0.78	[0.56]	0.46	[0.63]	0.47	[0.62]
FABCOM	0.89	[0.57]	0.58	[0.50]	0.49	[0.46]	0.55	[0.89]
DV2	0.00	[0.00]	0.00	[0.00]	0.00	[0.00]	0.07	[0.25]
INC2	0.09	[0.29]	0.15	[0.36]	0.29	[0.57]	0.13	[0.34]
DR2	0.09	[0.29]	0.00	[0.00]	0.10	[0.34]	0.00	[0.00]
FAB2	0.22	[0.42]	0.20	[0.45]	0.08	[0.26]	0.13	[0.34]
ALOG	0.61	[0.50]	0.64	[0.48]	0.48	[0.49]	0.73	[0.45]
CONTAM	0.00	0.00	0.00	0.00	0.01	0.09	0.00	0.00
Sum6 Sp Sc	6.88	2.01	6.63	1.38	5.92	1.25	6.15	1.96
Sum6 Sp Sc2	0.40	[0.58]	0.72	[0.98]	0.18	[0.26]	0.33	[0.48]
WSum6	14.88	4.68	13.30	5.03	12.18	4.66	14.33	5.12
AB	0.00	[0.00]	0.00	[0.00]	0.00	[0.00]	0.00	[0.00]
AG	1.23	0.67	0.30	0.56	1.20	0.40	0.93	0.58
CFB	0.00	0.00	0.00	0.00	0.00	0.00	0.00	0.00
COP	1.08	0.52	2.40	0.54	1.57	0.59	1.93	1.01
CP	0.23	[0.81]	0.18	[0.30]	0.00	[0.00]	0.08	[0.40]
MOR	0.78	[0.75]	0.60	[0.57]	1.64	[0.58]	1.13	[0.34]

Age	9		10		11		12	
Variable	Mean	SD	Mean	SD	Mean	SD	Mean	SD
PER	0.18	0.41	0.23	1.06	2.22	0.57	0.33	0.48
PSV	0.63	[0.48]	0.64	[0.77]	0.54	[0.50]	0.46	[0.78]
R	20.53	2.46	20.97	1.92	21.29	2.43	21.40	2.05
W	10.33	1.57	9.52	0.87	9.61	0.95	8.79	1.85
D	9.00	1.28	10.10	1.48	10.01	1.31	10.85	1.96
Dd	1.20	[0.84]	1.35	[0.44]	1.67	[1.13]	1.76	[1.11]
S	1.73	[0.58]	1.48	[0.70]	1.75	[0.68]	1.92	[0.76]
DQ+	6.40	1.94	7.68	0.96	8.07	1.22	8.16	1.90
DQo	11.67	1.80	12.07	1.78	12.08	2.14	12.12	1.07
DQv	1.61	[0.65]	0.53	[0.50]	0.64	[0.88]	1.03	[0.26]
DQv/+	0.45	[0.65]	0.38	[0.28]	0.50	[0.69]	0.38	[0.38]
FQX+	0.26	0.31	0.30	0.50	0.21	0.38	0.30	0.54
FQXo	14.22	1.83	15.80	1.98	15.83	1.40	15.34	2.32
FQXu	3.49	1.37	2.95	0.79	3.18	1.26	3.77	0.89
FQX−	2.04	0.76	1.58	1.03	2.20	1.87	1.95	1.04
FQXNone	0.38	[0.48]	0.13	[0.34]	0.18	[0.27]	0.43	[0.26]
MQ+	0.00	0.00	0.08	0.21	0.11	0.45	0.10	0.30
MQo	3.12	1.62	3.23	1.48	3.59	1.38	3.21	1.52
MQu	0.20	0.40	0.25	0.44	0.33	0.47	0.67	0.51
MQ−	0.37	[0.25]	0.17	[0.37]	0.20	[0.40]	0.22	[0.41]
MQNone	0.00	[0.00]	0.00	[0.00]	0.00	[0.00]	0.02	[0.13]
S−	0.13	[0.34]	0.12	[0.32]	0.31	[0.46]	0.57	[0.62]
M	3.12	1.85	3.65	1.63	4.12	1.67	4.21	2.06
FM	4.22	1.47	5.53	1.46	4.48	1.21	5.02	1.66
m	0.67	0.58	1.08	0.28	1.00	0.89	1.00	0.45
FM + m	5.64	1.86	6.62	1.40	5.48	1.21	6.02	1.70
FC	1.89	0.86	2.55	0.96	2.93	0.95	2.87	1.17
CF	2.79	0.78	3.68	1.29	3.43	1.13	3.14	1.40
C	0.43	[0.48]	0.13	[0.34]	0.28	[0.27]	0.39	[0.13]
Cn	0.00	[0.00]	0.00	[0.00]	0.00	[0.00]	0.00	[0.00]
FC + CF + C + Cn	4.15	0.72	6.37	1.50	6.44	1.39	6.03	2.29
WGSum C	5.13	1.07	5.16	1.25	4.02	1.15	4.05	1.78
Sum C'	1.16	[0.79]	0.79	[0.85]	1.06	[0.71]	1.08	[0.88]
Sum T	0.97	[0.63]	0.98	[0.39]	0.94	[0.47]	0.88	[0.32]
Sum V	0.00	[0.00]	0.02	[0.13]	0.00	[0.00]	0.07	[0.36]
Sum Y	0.83	[0.85]	0.43	[0.65]	0.85	[0.70]	1.01	[0.67]
SumShd	2.96	1.27	1.83	1.32	2.85	1.10	3.74	1.37
Fr + rF	0.42	[0.43]	0.35	[0.36]	0.21	[0.41]	0.20	[0.13]
FD	0.63	[0.34]	0.67	[0.58]	0.91	[0.84]	1.48	[0.83]
F	9.14	1.84	6.38	2.04	6.70	2.37	5.84	1.65
PAIR	8.97	1.69	9.62	1.36	9.90	1.08	9.09	1.89
3r(2)/R	0.57	0.12	0.54	0.07	0.53	0.04	0.54	0.08
LAMBDA	0.81	0.37	0.49	0.23	0.68	0.22	0.66	0.58
EA	8.25	1.95	8.81	1.36	8.14	1.37	8.26	2.38
es	8.60	2.59	8.45	1.90	8.33	1.72	8.97	2.59
D	−0.18	0.54	−0.15	0.44	−0.09	0.29	−0.21	0.53
AdjD	−0.10	0.41	−0.12	0.49	−0.06	0.34	−0.11	0.67
a (active)	6.26	1.23	7.15	1.37	7.89	1.42	6.53	1.45
p (passive)	2.51	1.40	3.27	0.66	2.79	1.60	4.00	2.01
Ma	2.72	1.36	2.82	1.09	2.81	1.01	2.47	0.80
Mp	0.27	0.45	0.98	0.83	1.38	1.33	1.73	1.60
Intellect	1.03	0.98	0.53	0.56	0.77	0.65	1.05	0.59
Zf	11.16	1.54	13.52	1.19	13.70	1.22	13.14	1.96
Zd	0.40	2.03	−0.13	2.32	0.60	2.74	1.67	2.11
Blends	4.38	1.23	5.80	1.05	6.04	1.41	6.67	2.29
Col Shd Bl	0.90	[0.56]	0.42	[0.13]	0.00	[0.00]	0.05	[0.22]
Afr	0.79	0.13	0.63	0.09	0.62	0.09	0.65	0.11
Popular	5.78	0.63	6.07	0.84	6.06	0.86	6.22	1.10

(continued)

Age	9		10		11		12	
Variable	Mean	SD	Mean	SD	Mean	SD	Mean	SD
X + %	0.74	0.09	0.76	0.08	0.75	0.08	0.75	0.09
F + %	0.70	0.08	0.55	0.14	0.54	0.16	0.54	0.11
X − %	0.09	0.06	0.08	0.06	0.10	0.07	0.10	0.05
Xu%	0.17	0.07	0.15	0.05	0.15	0.05	0.15	0.04
S − %	0.06	[0.15]	0.12	[0.14]	0.11	[0.19]	0.27	[0.28]
Isolate	0.16	0.05	0.19	0.03	0.20	0.05	0.15	0.04
H	2.87	1.03	2.47	1.12	2.80	1.27	3.38	1.64
(H)	1.32	0.61	1.48	0.74	1.51	0.66	1.24	0.84
Hd	0.57	0.40	0.25	0.47	0.52	0.66	0.59	0.69
(Hd)	0.74	0.58	0.85	0.36	0.87	0.33	0.78	0.41
Hx	0.00	[0.00]	0.00	[0.00]	0.00	[0.00]	0.13	[0.34]
All H Cont	5.50	1.62	5.05	1.64	5.70	1.80	6.00	2.56
A	8.28	1.59	8.92	1.18	8.58	1.25	7.70	1.29
(A)	0.73	[0.68]	1.20	[0.77]	1.00	[0.83]	0.47	[0.50]
Ad	0.53	[0.98]	1.35	[1.08]	1.54	[0.95]	1.97	[0.45]
(Ad)	0.23	[0.39]	0.07	[0.25]	0.16	[0.36]	0.36	[0.54]
An	0.36	[0.60]	0.67	[0.57]	0.73	[0.64]	1.14	[0.60]
Art	0.32	0.71	0.53	0.56	0.56	0.50	0.92	0.28
Ay	0.13	[0.28]	0.23	[0.41]	0.21	[0.59]	0.03	[0.18]
Bl	0.33	[0.48]	0.60	[0.59]	0.44	[0.57]	0.26	[0.44]
Bt	1.45	0.65	2.17	0.74	2.10	0.67	1.52	0.65
Cg	1.84	1.08	1.48	1.03	1.60	0.99	1.90	1.06
Cl	0.16	[0.39]	0.08	[0.28]	0.16	[0.24]	0.22	[0.13]
Ex	0.26	[0.54]	0.08	[0.28]	0.23	[0.17]	0.47	[0.38]
Fi	0.69	[0.68]	0.75	[0.44]	0.85	[0.36]	0.57	[0.26]
Fd	0.18	[0.46]	0.53	[0.50]	0.64	[0.48]	0.37	[0.34]
Ge	0.00	[0.00]	0.00	[0.00]	0.10	[0.27]	0.02	[0.13]
Hh	0.59	0.36	0.60	0.49	0.81	0.46	0.88	0.32
Ls	0.93	0.59	1.00	0.45	1.28	0.61	1.36	0.60
Na	0.70	[0.48]	0.30	[0.46]	0.35	[0.48]	0.10	[0.35]
Sc	1.55	[0.72]	2.85	[0.40]	2.96	[0.36]	2.47	[0.87]
Sx	0.00	[0.00]	0.00	[0.00]	0.00	[0.00]	0.02	[0.13]
Xy	0.00	[0.00]	0.00	[0.00]	0.09	[0.29]	0.06	[0.12]
Idio	0.63	0.42	0.08	0.28	0.06	0.34	0.15	0.51
DV	1.01	[0.61]	1.03	[0.61]	1.21	[0.41]	1.21	[0.55]
INCOM	1.37	[0.75]	1.35	[0.51]	1.44	[0.63]	1.35	[0.57]
DR	0.67	[0.72]	0.18	[0.28]	0.22	[0.32]	0.44	[0.43]
FABCOM	1.05	[0.89]	0.65	[0.48]	0.46	[0.48]	0.46	[0.53]
DV2	0.07	[0.21]	0.00	[0.00]	0.00	[0.00]	0.02	[0.16]
INC2	0.11	[0.59]	0.23	[0.43]	0.12	[0.32]	0.17	[0.56]
DR2	0.00	[0.00]	0.02	[0.13]	0.03	[0.17]	0.02	[0.16]
FAB2	0.05	[0.39]	0.02	[0.09]	0.00	[0.00]	0.04	[0.20]
ALOG	0.61	[0.49]	0.47	[0.48]	0.28	[0.43]	0.41	[0.68]
CONTAM	0.00	0.00	0.00	0.00	0.00	0.00	0.00	0.00
Sum6 Sp Sc	5.95	2.16	5.15	1.20	4.36	1.16	4.06	0.95
Sum6 Sp Sc2	0.27	[0.51]	0.09	[0.44]	0.15	[0.36]	0.27	[0.68]
WSum6	13.06	4.72	10.22	3.79	8.93	3.04	8.86	3.85
AB	0.00	[0.00]	0.08	[0.28]	0.21	[0.39]	0.05	[0.22]
AG	1.37	0.78	1.57	0.62	1.42	0.57	1.08	0.66
CFB	0.00	0.00	0.00	0.00	0.00	0.00	0.00	0.00
COP	2.03	1.14	1.73	0.84	1.56	0.50	1.93	0.53
CP	0.00	[0.00]	0.00	[0.00]	0.00	[0.00]	0.00	[0.00]
MOR	0.87	[0.64]	0.75	[0.62]	0.72	[0.57]	0.67	[0.37]
PER	1.16	0.78	0.75	0.44	0.88	0.53	0.93	0.36
PSV	0.26	[0.61]	0.05	[0.22]	0.09	[0.25]	0.03	[0.18]
R	21.20	3.30	21.72	3.36	21.94	4.21	22.89	5.16

Age	13		14		15		16	
Variable	Mean	SD	Mean	SD	Mean	SD	Mean	SD
W	8.57	2.15	8.92	2.19	8.87	2.20	8.96	2.37
D	11.15	3.09	11.13	3.16	11.42	3.66	11.91	3.74
Dd	1.46	[1.66]	1.67	[1.70]	1.65	[1.31]	2.02	[1.82]
S	1.33	[1.16]	1.32	[1.09]	1.44	[1.31]	1.24	[1.23]
DQ+	7.70	2.54	7.81	2.55	7.88	2.02	7.94	2.04
DQo	12.40	2.02	12.69	2.06	12.67	3.62	13.12	3.47
DQv	0.45	[0.99]	0.58	[1.01]	0.75	[1.29]	0.89	[1.35]
DQv/+	0.24	[0.57]	0.65	[0.58]	0.14	[0.42]	0.84	[0.53]
FQX+	0.20	0.59	0.14	0.50	0.36	0.70	0.54	0.83
FQXo	15.24	3.04	15.17	3.09	16.35	3.34	16.43	3.36
FQXu	3.27	1.53	3.27	1.56	3.08	1.57	3.19	1.56
FQX−	2.00	1.42	1.84	1.25	1.60	0.91	1.58	0.91
FQXNone	0.07	[0.32]	0.02	[0.53]	0.04	[0.25]	0.06	[0.26]
MQ+	0.13	0.43	0.11	0.44	0.25	0.57	0.35	0.64
MQo	3.23	1.66	3.21	1.66	3.54	2.01	3.50	2.01
MQu	0.54	0.66	0.51	0.67	0.44	0.52	0.37	0.50
MQ−	0.14	[0.51]	0.13	[0.50]	0.12	[0.32]	0.09	[0.29]
MQNone	0.02	[0.13]	0.00	[0.00]	0.00	[0.00]	0.00	[0.00]
S−	0.52	[0.81]	0.39	[0.82]	0.38	[0.57]	0.34	[0.55]
M	4.14	2.24	4.06	2.24	4.35	2.17	4.31	2.13
FM	4.42	1.94	4.35	1.96	4.82	1.73	4.58	1.66
m	1.25	0.94	1.27	0.96	1.17	0.78	1.14	0.80
FM + m	5.67	2.10	5.62	2.14	5.99	1.78	5.72	1.78
FC	2.95	1.72	2.93	1.76	3.14	1.14	3.43	1.34
CF	2.70	1.50	2.70	1.53	2.85	1.53	2.78	1.45
C	0.07	[0.26]	0.10	[0.27]	0.03	[0.16]	0.04	[0.20]
Cn	0.00	[0.00]	0.00	[0.00]	0.02	[0.13]	0.01	[0.12]
FC + CF + C + Cn	5.73	2.61	5.71	2.67	6.04	2.01	6.26	2.08
WGSum C	4.29	1.94	4.29	1.98	4.47	1.68	4.56	1.66
Sum C′	1.20	[0.89]	1.11	[0.91]	1.63	[1.35]	1.15	[1.27]
Sum T	0.97	[0.51]	0.99	[0.52]	1.06	[0.51]	1.02	[0.48]
Sum V	0.14	[0.48]	0.13	[0.50]	0.18	[0.49]	0.19	[0.51]
Sum Y	1.02	[0.81]	0.88	[0.84]	1.30	[1.27]	1.04	[1.21]
SumShd	3.34	1.44	3.10	1.47	4.17	2.55	3.44	2.35
Fr + rF	0.45	[0.23]	0.38	[0.43]	0.50	[0.45]	0.48	[0.41]
FD	1.27	[0.87]	1.24	[0.87]	1.33	[0.97]	1.31	[0.93]
F	6.90	2.52	6.96	2.56	6.48	2.71	6.85	2.69
PAIR	8.64	2.30	8.59	2.34	9.10	2.00	9.04	2.00
3r(2)/R	0.49	0.10	0.47	0.10	0.44	0.10	0.43	0.09
LAMBDA	0.67	0.61	0.67	0.62	0.65	0.22	0.65	0.21
EA	8.43	2.69	8.34	2.70	8.82	2.34	8.87	2.23
es	9.01	3.01	8.92	3.06	9.16	3.40	9.21	3.29
D	−0.09	0.82	−0.09	0.84	−0.45	1.39	−0.31	1.31
AdjD	0.10	0.84	0.09	0.86	−0.25	1.07	−0.11	1.04
a (active)	6.23	1.89	6.20	1.92	6.99	1.73	6.82	1.71
p (passive)	3.61	2.11	3.49	2.07	3.36	1.93	3.22	1.89
Ma	2.49	1.30	2.59	1.32	2.58	1.44	2.62	1.42
Mp	1.67	1.44	1.49	1.36	1.77	1.46	1.69	1.38
Intellect	1.22	0.95	1.23	0.97	1.04	0.83	1.14	0.93
Zf	12.64	3.02	12.56	3.06	12.68	2.59	12.61	2.64
Zd	1.37	2.27	1.27	2.26	1.03	2.96	1.12	2.96
Blends	5.81	2.43	5.74	2.46	6.34	2.16	6.11	2.13
Col Shd Bl	0.16	[0.37]	0.17	[0.38]	0.22	[0.51]	0.24	[0.50]
Afr	0.69	0.15	0.69	0.16	0.65	0.18	0.65	0.17
Popular	6.19	1.34	6.02	1.17	6.33	1.23	6.46	1.27

(continued)

Age	13		14		15		16	
Variable	Mean	SD	Mean	SD	Mean	SD	Mean	SD
X + %	0.76	0.11	0.76	0.12	0.78	0.07	0.78	0.07
F + %	0.61	0.18	0.69	0.18	0.62	0.18	0.74	0.18
X − %	0.10	0.07	0.09	0.07	0.07	0.05	0.07	0.05
Xu%	0.16	0.07	0.16	0.07	0.14	0.06	0.14	0.06
S − %	0.20	[0.28]	0.19	[0.28]	0.18	[0.27]	0.16	[0.27]
Isolate	0.16	0.06	0.16	0.06	0.15	0.07	0.16	0.07
H	3.09	1.72	3.00	1.71	3.42	1.96	3.39	1.94
(H)	1.25	1.02	1.23	1.03	1.04	0.90	1.07	0.89
Hd	0.68	0.83	0.67	0.85	0.57	0.82	0.59	0.81
(Hd)	0.56	0.53	0.56	0.54	0.54	0.50	0.46	0.50
Hx	0.00	[0.00]	0.00	[0.00]	0.00	[0.00]	0.00	[0.00]
All H Cont	5.59	2.46	5.46	2.44	5.57	2.28	5.51	2.12
A	7.96	1.81	7.97	1.85	7.98	1.96	8.04	1.97
(A)	0.37	[0.49]	0.39	[0.49]	0.36	[0.55]	0.32	[0.54]
Ad	2.00	[0.81]	2.00	[0.83]	2.08	[1.20]	2.11	[1.15]
(Ad)	0.00	[0.00]	0.23	[0.41]	0.05	[0.30]	0.07	[0.33]
An	0.84	[0.69]	0.84	[0.71]	0.43	[0.79]	0.41	[0.79]
Art	0.85	0.48	0.85	0.50	0.85	0.63	0.83	0.68
Ay	0.11	[0.31]	0.15	[0.32]	0.14	[0.34]	0.19	[0.41]
Bl	0.19	[0.39]	0.20	[0.40]	0.22	[0.41]	0.21	[0.43]
Bt	1.74	0.98	1.73	1.00	1.68	0.82	1.87	1.03
Cg	1.62	1.10	1.55	1.08	1.47	1.11	1.39	1.06
Cl	0.05	[0.23]	0.06	[0.23]	0.09	[0.35]	0.11	[0.36]
Ex	0.09	[0.29]	0.09	[0.29]	0.12	[0.32]	0.31	[0.32]
Fi	0.76	[0.54]	0.75	[0.55]	0.69	[0.52]	0.39	[0.57]
Fd	0.42	[0.52]	0.30	[0.53]	0.30	[0.51]	0.31	[0.52]
Ge	0.04	[0.19]	0.04	[0.19]	0.01	[0.09]	0.01	[0.12]
Hh	1.07	0.81	1.08	0.83	0.89	0.60	0.91	0.67
Ls	1.10	0.97	1.06	0.97	1.12	0.71	1.07	0.74
Na	0.22	[0.50]	0.23	[0.50]	0.12	[0.35]	0.17	[0.41]
Sc	1.97	[1.14]	1.93	[1.15]	1.70	[1.34]	1.51	[1.31]
Sx	0.07	[0.42]	0.08	[0.43]	0.11	[0.44]	0.11	[0.41]
Xy	0.00	[0.00]	0.04	[0.20]	0.04	[0.19]	0.04	[0.19]
Idio	0.78	1.14	0.82	1.16	1.09	1.47	1.31	1.45
DV	1.01	[0.70]	0.98	[0.69]	0.98	[0.70]	0.99	[0.71]
INCOM	1.07	[0.79]	1.05	[0.79]	0.88	[0.74]	0.83	[0.75]
DR	0.30	[0.66]	0.29	[0.66]	0.13	[0.33]	0.14	[0.37]
FABCOM	0.42	[0.71]	0.44	[0.72]	0.23	[0.46]	0.21	[0.44]
DV2	0.02	[0.13]	0.02	[0.14]	0.03	[0.16]	0.02	[0.14]
INC2	0.22	[0.60]	0.12	[0.60]	0.01	[0.09]	0.01	[0.12]
DR2	0.04	[0.19]	0.03	[0.17]	0.01	[0.09]	0.01	[0.08]
FAB2	0.07	[0.32]	0.08	[0.33]	0.04	[0.19]	0.04	[0.19]
ALOG	0.34	[0.19]	0.11	[0.19]	0.05	[0.26]	0.05	[0.25]
CONTAM	0.00	0.00	0.00	0.00	0.00	0.00	0.00	0.00
Sum6 Sp Sc	2.94	1.46	2.89	1.38	2.27	1.36	2.22	1.34
Sum6 Sp Sc2	0.34	[0.77]	0.14	[0.38]	0.08	[0.27]	0.08	[0.27]
WSum6	7.54	6.99	7.42	7.14	4.71	3.33	4.57	3.23
AB	0.13	[0.33]	0.13	[0.34]	0.03	[0.16]	0.06	[0.25]
AG	1.18	0.91	1.30	0.92	1.14	0.91	1.20	0.99
CFB	0.00	0.00	0.00	0.00	0.00	0.00	0.00	0.00
COP	1.84	1.22	1.75	1.14	1.54	0.97	1.60	1.10
CP	0.02	[0.13]	0.00	[0.00]	0.00	[0.00]	0.00	[0.00]
MOR	0.49	[0.74]	0.61	[0.75]	0.54	[0.83]	0.58	[0.81]
PER	1.05	0.89	1.01	0.81	0.92	0.65	0.96	0.72
PSV	0.04	[0.21]	0.03	[0.12]	0.04	[0.19]	0.04	[0.20]

Appendix N

Scoring Criteria for Impulsive and Nonimpulsive Variables on the Draw-A-Person (DAP)*

Impulsive Variables The DAP impulsivity score for each subject is the total number of Impulsive variables scored. A variable is scored when it meets the scoring criteria listed under each individual for both male and female drawings. The maximum DAP-impulsivity score is 13.

1. *Completion time* Completion time decreases with impulsivity. One point is scored if the total drawing time for each figure is less than five minutes (median completion time for adolescents is between five and ten minutes).

2. *Aggression* Appearance of certain features suggesting acting-out tendencies. One point is scored for the appearance of at least one of each of the following: teeth, knife, gun, bomb, stick fingers, blood, appearance of aggressive movement (striking, hitting, or kicking an object), or club.

3. *Overall quality* The quality of the drawings is poor as defined by the Harris (1963) or Koppitz (1968) scoring system. Scores of less than 36 are scored one *SD* less than the group mean score of normal adolescent drawings according to Harris (1963) and Harris and Pinder (1974).

4. *Discontinuity* Impulsives have difficulty connecting lines on drawings. One point is scored for overlapping lines that would normally be connected to give shape and form to at least two of the following parts: head, trunk, neck, arm, leg, foot.

5. *Omissions* Impulsives leave out important aspects of the human figure such as head, arms, legs, etc. One point is scored for omission of at least one of the following missing body parts: head, trunk, neck, hand, arm, leg, foot, hair, all fingers. Not scored if hands behind back.

6. *Specific omissions* Impulsives leave out the pupils, fingers, and nose. One point is scored for omission of either pupil or either eye, any finger or either hand, or nose.

7. *Proportion* Impulsives are unconcerned with proportionality of drawing. One point is scored if at least one of the following items are drawn with either no proportion or out of proportion according to items in Harris (1963): Head (Item 48), Trunk (Item 47), Face (Item 50), Arms (Items 51, 52), Legs (Items 53).

8. *Size Increase* Impulsives are expansive in their drawings. One point is scored for a figure drawn in excess of either six inches in height or three inches in width of trunk.

---

* Adapted from Oas, 1984.

9. *Neck* Impulsives tend to leave out or else draw the neck proportionately large. One point is scored if neck is omitted or one point is scored if neck is longer than $2/3$ the length of the head.

10. *Stance* Impulsive subjects draw figures with stances slanted or widened. One point is scored if legs are drawn 22.5 degrees or greater in distance from body midline.

11. *Shoulders* Impulsives do not take the time to draw square shoulders. One point is scored if shoulders are improperly attached or not drawn squarely as defined by Harris (1963, p. 281).

12 *Poor planning* Impulsives do not plan their actions. One point is scored if any part of drawing is cut off by the side of the page it is drawn on or if any part of the figure is redrawn without erasure.

13. *Left side* Impulsives tend to draw toward the left side of the page. One point is scored if midline of the figure is more than one inch to left of center of page.

Nonimpulsive Variables The DAP nonimpulsivity score for each subject is the total number of nonimpulsive variables scored. A variable is scored when it meets the criteria listed under each individual for both the male and female drawings. The maximum DAP non-impulsivity score is 13.

1. *Symmetry* One point is scored if drawing has "a symmetrical quality" or appearance such that at least three of the following pairs of body parts are each drawn at the same angle and opposite position in space from the body midline: arms, legs, eyes, ears, feet.

2. *Detailing* One point is scored for the presence of at least five of the following items: earrings, necklace, ring, bracelet, broach, shoelaces, hairstyles, eyeglasses, pants, belt, shirt, dress, buttons, zipper, shoes, pockets, makeup, or socks.

3. *Completion time* One point is scored if total drawing time for each figure is at least eight minutes.

4. *Placement* One point is scored if at least $3/4$ of drawing measured from top of head to bottom of feet is on the lower half of the page.

5. *Sketching* One point is scored for sketching used to give form to any of the following body parts: arm, leg, trunk, head.

6. *Erasures* One point is scored for complete erasure and subsequent redrawing of any of the following body parts: foot, leg, trunk, hand, arm, finger, head, facial features, handheld objects, other objects, or complete figure.

7. *Size* One point is scored if drawing is less than four inches in length from head to foot or less than two inches in length in width of torso.

8. *Gender identity* One point is scored if opposite sex of subject is drawn first.

9. *Eye emphasis* One point is scored for presence of at least two of the following: glasses, eyebrows, eyelashes, large eyes, cornea detail, shaded eyes, pupils.

10. *Right side* One point is scored if figure is drawn one inch or further to the right of the midline of the page.

11. *Perspective* One point is scored for either a side-view or rearview perspective of complete figure or head.

12. *Mouth detail* One point is scored if mouth is drawn with both lips depicted in two dimensions.

13. *Shading* One point is scored for shading used to give form or color to at least two of the following body parts of clothing: foot, hand, trunk, arm, eye, mouth, leg, neck, shirt, pants, or dress.

Appendix O

Maturational Guidelines for Bender Gestalt Designs

	Figure A	Figure 1	Figure 2	Figure 3	Figure 4	Figure 5	Figure 6	Figure 7	Figure 8
Adult	100%	25%	100%	100%	100%	100%	100%	100%	100%
11 yr	95%	95%	65%	60%	95%	90%	70%	75%	90%
10 yr	90%	90%	60%	60%	80%	80%	60%	60%	90%
9 yr	80%	75%	60%	70%	80%	70%	80%	65%	70%
8 yr	75%	75%	75%	60%	80%	65%	70%	65%	65%
7 yr	75%	75%	70%	60%	75%	65%	60%	65%	60%
6 yr	75%	75%	60%	80%	75%	60%	60%	60%	75%
5 yr	85%	85%	60%	80%	70%	60%	60%	60%	75%
4 yr	90%	85%	75%	80%	70%	60%	65%	60%	60%
3 yr		←————Scribbling————→							

706

Appendix P

Rey Auditory-Verbal Learning Test Scoring Sheet

RAVLT Scoring Sheet

Name _____

Date _____

Examiner _____

(Note: Do not re-read List A for Recall Trial 7 or 8)

List A	Recall Trials 1	2	3	4	5	List B	Recall Trials 6	7	8	9*	
drum						desk					drum
curtain						ranger					curtain
bell						bird					bell
coffee						shoe					coffee
school						stove					school
parent						mountain					parent
moon						glasses					moon
garden						towel					garden
hat						cloud					hat
farmer						boat					farmer
nose						lamb					nose
turkey						gun					turkey
color						pencil					color
house						church					house
river						fish					river
#correct:											

Scoring Categories:

1. Immediate Memory (score for Trial 1)   _____
2. Best Learning (score for Trial 5)   _____
3. Total Learning (sum of the scores for Trials 1–5)   _____
4. Proactive Interference (score for Trial 6)   _____
5. Retroactive Interference (score for Trial 7) _____
6. Delayed Recall (score for Trial 8)   _____
7. Recognition (score for Trial 9)   _____

* Trial 9: Determine the number of words correctly/incorrectly recognised from the following recognition list.

bell (A)	home (SA)	towel(B)	boat (B)	glasses (B)
window (SA)	fish (B)	curtain (A)	hot (PA)	stocking (SB)
hat (A)	moon (A)	flower (SA)	parent (A)	shoe (B)
barn (SA)	tree (PA)	color (A)	water (SA)	teacher (SA)
ranger (B)	balloon (PA)	desk (B)	farmer (A)	stove (B)
nose (A)	bird (B)	gun (B)	rose (SPA)	nest (SPB)
weather (SB)	mountain (B)	crayon (SA)	cloud (B)	children (SA)
school (A)	coffee (A)	church (B)	house (A)	drum (A)
hand (PA)	mouse (PA)	turkey (A)	stranger (PB)	toffee (PA)
pencil (B)	river (A)	fountain (PB)	garden (A)	lamb (B)

Note: (A) words from list A; (B) words from list B; (S) word with a semantic association to a word on list A or B as indicated; (P) word phonemically similar to a word on list A or B.

Appendix Q

Norms for the Rey Auditory Verbal Learning test based on Age and Gender

RAVLT Scores by Age: Males

Scoring Category			16–19 (13)	20–29 (10)	30–39 (10)	40–49 (11)	50–59 (11)	60–69 (10)	70+ (10)
	(n)								
1. Immediate Memory:	Trial 1 (List A)	M	6.9	8.4	6.0	6.4	6.5	4.9	3.6
		SD	(1.8)	(1.2)	(1.8)	(1.8)	(2.0)	(1.1)	(0.8)
	2		9.7	10.8	8.0	9.0	8.6	6.4	5.7
			(1.7)	(1.9)	(2.4)	(2.3)	(2.0)	(1.2)	(1.7)
	3		11.5	11.3	9.7	9.8	10.1	8.0	6.8
			(1.2)	(1.6)	(2.7)	(2.0)	(1.6)	(2.6)	(1.6)
	4		12.8	12.2	10.9	11.5	10.7	8.5	8.3
			(1.5)	(1.8)	(2.8)	(1.9)	(1.9)	(2.7)	(2.7)
2. Best Learning	5		12.5	12.2	11.4	10.9	11.8	8.9	8.2
			(1.3)	(2.2)	(2.6)	(2.0)	(2.6)	(2.0)	(2.5)
3. Total Learning	Total		53.2	54.9	46.0	47.5	47.6	36.7	32.6
			(5.4)	(7.0)	(10.9)	(8.3)	(8.5)	(8.4)	(8.3)
4. Proactive Interference	Trial 6 (Distractor List B)		6.9	6.5	5.3	6.1	5.0	4.9	3.5
			(1.9)	(1.8)	(1.6)	(2.1)	(2.3)	(1.6)	(1.3)
5. Retroactive Interference	Trial 7 (Retention)		11.2	11.1	9.7	9.7	9.6	7.2	6.4
			(1.6)	(1.7)	(2.3)	(2.5)	(2.9)	(2.8)	(1.7)
6. Delayed Recall	Trial 8 (Delayed Recall)		11.3	10.6	10.4	10.5	10.0	7.1	5.6
			(1.7)	(2.4)	(2.3)	(2.7)	(2.6)	(3.8)	(2.6)
7. Recognition	Trial 9 (Recognition List A)		14.4	14.2	13.5	14.2	13.9	12.4	11.5
			(0.9)	(0.8)	(1.5)	(1.0)	(0.9)	(2.8)	(2.6)

Age Groups

Adapted from Geffen et al. (1990).

RAVLT Scores by Age: Females

Scoring Category				Age Groups						
	(n)		16–19 (13)	20–29 (10)	30–39 (10)	40–49 (11)	50–59 (11)	60–69 (10)	70+ (10)
		Trial								
1. Immediate Memory	1 (List A)	M	7.8	7.7	8.0	6.8	6.4	6.0	5.6
		SD	(1.9)	(1.0)	(2.0)	(1.5)	(1.5)	(2.2)	(1.4)
	2		10.5	10.5	10.8	9.4	8.2	9.0	6.9
			(2.0)	(2.0)	(2.1)	(1.5)	(2.4)	(2.0)	(2.1)
	3		12.3	12.2	11.5	11.4	10.2	10.8	8.9
			(1.2)	(2.3)	(1.7)	(1.7)	(2.1)	(2.0)	(1.9)
	4		12.5	12.0	12.9	11.7	11.1	11.3	10.1
			(1.7)	(1.6)	(1.3)	(2.1)	(1.9)	(1.4)	(1.9)
2. Best Learning	5		13.3	12.9	12.7	12.8	11.6	11.9	10.1
			(1.5)	(1.5)	(1.3)	(1.4)	(2.1)	(1.6)	(1.2)
3. Total Learning	Total		56.5	55.3	55.9	52.1	47.6	49.0	41.6
			(6.0)	(6.6)	(6.3)	(7.1)	(7.7)	(7.1)	(6.6)
4. Proactive Interference	Trial 6 (Distractor List B)		7.7	7.9	6.5	5.2	4.6	5.3	4.2
			(1.3)	(2.0)	(1.5)	(1.3)	(1.9)	(1.1)	(1.9)
5. Retroactive Interference	Trial 7 (Retention)		11.9	11.6	12.1	11.1	9.9	9.8	7.8
			(2.5)	(2.5)	(1.9)	(2.4)	(2.8)	(1.6)	(1.8)
6. Delayed Recall	Trial 8 (Delayed Recall)		11.4	11.0	12.2	11.1	10.2	10.3	8.3
			(2.5)	(2.0)	(2.5)	(2.3)	(2.7)	(2.3)	(2.1)
7. Recognition	Trial 9 (Recognition List A)		13.8	14.4	14.2	14.4	13.7	13.8	13.6
			(2.0)	(0.8)	(1.7)	(0.8)	(1.1)	(1.1)	(2.0)

Appendix R

Controlled Word Association: Normative Data for Males and Females Stratified by Age

		Age Groups				
		15–20 (N = 62)	21–25 (N = 73)	26–30 (N = 48)	31–40 (N = 42)	15–40 (N = 225)
Males						
Oral						
"F"	M	13.82	14.99	15.65	16.83	15.15
	SD	4.36	4.37	4.42	4.04	4.41
"A"	M	12.48	13.33	13.08	14.50	13.26
	SD	3.87	4.89	3.41	3.66	4.13
"S"	M	15.87	16.63	16.54	18.10	16.67
	SD	4.52	4.97	4.70	4.89	4.80
Sum of 3 trials	M	42.17	44.95	45.27	49.43	45.08
	SD	6.82	6.29	5.34	5.61	5.90
Written						
"F"	M	13.85	14.09	14.82	15.37	14.42
	SD	3.65	3.44	3.83	3.90	3.69
"A"	M	12.06	13.22	12.62	13.83	12.88
	SD	3.24	3.47	4.03	3.57	3.57
"S"	M	14.81	15.46	15.65	16.03	15.42
	SD	3.34	3.89	3.95	3.43	3.66
Sum of 3 trials	M	40.72	42.77	43.09	45.23	42.72
	SD	6.14	6.16	6.46	6.01	6.21
Females						
Oral						
"F"	M	13.60	15.14	15.25	17.25	15.03
	SD	4.29	3.90	5.16	3.64	4.31
"A"	M	11.93	13.44	13.19	14.50	13.11
	SD	3.82	4.24	3.71	2.85	3.88
"S"	M	15.93	16.31	14.75	18.44	16.29
	SD	4.31	4.94	2.91	5.72	4.68
Sum of 3 trials	M	41.46	44.89	43.20	50.19	44.43
	SD	6.71	6.86	6.27	6.43	5.73
Written						
"F"	M	14.40	15.03	15.09	15.67	14.94
	SD	3.97	3.12	4.48	3.06	3.57
"A"	M	13.00	13.69	13.64	15.00	13.66
	SD	3.15	3.51	2.58	4.29	3.41
"S"	M	15.88	16.52	15.09	17.17	16.21
	SD	3.27	4.36	2.84	3.21	3.65
Sum of 3 trials	M	42.75	45.24	43.83	47.85	44.64
	SD	6.33	6.32	6.03	5.79	6.20

Source: Subjects in this sample had relatively high education levels. Subjects with education levels below grade 12 usually achieve 4–5 words less on the sum score. From *A Compendium of Neuropsychological Tests: Administration, Norms, and Commentary* (p. 222) by Otfried Spreen and Esther Strauss. Copyright © 1991 by Oxford University Press, Inc. Reprinted by permission. [Data from Yendall, Fromm, Reddon, and Stefanyk (1986).]

Supplement

Wechsler Adult Intelligence Scale-III Supplement

The Wechsler Adult Intelligence Scale-III (WAIS-III; Wechsler, 1997a) became available in August 1997 and was developed to revise the earlier (1981) WAIS-R. The primary reason for the revision was to update the norms. Additional reasons included extending the age range, modifying items, developing a higher IQ "ceiling" and "floor," decreased reliance on timed performance, developing Index/factor scores, creating linkages to other measures of cognitive functioning/achievement, and extensive testing of reliability and validity (see Table S–1). Despite these changes, many of the traditional features of the WAIS-R have been maintained including the six Verbal subtests and the five Performance subtests (although Object Assembly has been turned into an optional test and Digit Symbol has been renamed Digit Symbol-Coding). This still enables practitioners to calculate the Full Scale, Verbal, and Performance IQs. An added feature of the WAIS-III has been the inclusion of three new subtests that enable the calculation of four Index scores. Thus the WAIS-III is not merely a renormed "facelift," but also enables the clinician to do more with the different test scores. This might involve being able to assess persons with either greater age or IQ ranges as well as linking scores with the Wechsler Memory Scales or calculating both IQ as well as Index/factor scores.

The most obvious feature of the WAIS-III is the inclusion of three new subtests: Symbol Search, Matrix Reasoning, and Letter-Number Sequencing. Symbol Search is essentially an upward extension of the WISC-III subtest of the same name. It is primarily a speeded test that presents clients with a set of symbols they visually scan.

Table S–1. Major Changes on the WAIS-III

Addition of three new subtests: Symbol Search (adapted from WISC-III), Matrix Reasoning, Letter Number Sequencing.

Inclusion of four Index (factor) scores: Verbal Comprehension, Perceptual Organization, Working Memory (Freedom from Distractibility), Processing Speed.

Extension of the upper age range (89 for the WAIS-III versus only 74 for the WAIS-R).

Higher ceiling (IQ of 155) and floor (IQ of 45).

Integration with the Wechsler Memory Scales-III including sharing the Digit Span and Letter-Number Sequencing subtests (and also some integration with the Wechsler Individual Achievement Test for 16–19-year-olds).

Use of "reversal" items which are very easy ("low end") items given in reverse order if the recommended starting items are missed.

Subtest scaled scores and profiling based on age-related norms (rather than the 20–34-year-old reference group used for the WAIS-R).

Minor changes: Numerous small changes in administration and scoring, Object Assembly is an optional subtest and is not used to calculate either the IQ or Index scores, two optional procedures (Incidental Learning and Copy) on Digit Symbol-Coding to determine whether performance was mainly due to visual memory or processing speed.

They are requested to answer whether or not any of the first two symbol clusters also appear in the next cluster of five symbols. In contrast to the emphasis on speed in Symbol Search, Matrix Reasoning is an untimed test that requires examinees to solve a visuospatial task requiring abstract reasoning. The examinee is shown a configuration of designs in a matrix that has a section which is missing. They are then required to indicate which of five additional designs would be the correct one to complete the matrix. The final new subtest, Letter-Number Sequencing, emphasizes attention and working memory. The examinee must recall and properly rearrange numbers and letters. This is done by the examiner reading a list of numbers and letters that are mixed together. The examinee must attend to these and respond by rearranging first the numbers by numerical order, and then the letters in alphabetical order.

The advantage of having added the above three subtests is that it allows the examiner to calculate not only the traditional Verbal and Performance IQs, but also four Index (or factor) scores. The Index scores enable a more detailed understanding of the examinees' relative strengths and weaknesses than merely the Verbal and Performance IQs. However, slightly different combinations of subtests are needed to provide the Index as opposed to the Verbal/Performance IQs (see Table S–2). It should be noted that Object Assembly, which has always been the weakest of the Wechsler subtests, has now been made optional and is recommended for use as a substitute if another performance subtest has been "spoiled."

These additions and arrangement of subtests represent the most obvious changes on the WAIS-III. Although not as obvious, its restandardization also represents a major development. The sample was comprised of 2,450 adults between the ages of 16 and 89. Each of the 13 age groups was comprised of 200 participants with the exception of the 80–84 and 85–89 age groups which contained 150 and 100 participants, respectively. Gender and ethnicity closely correspond to the 1995 U.S. Census data. This included a slightly greater number of women than men at the higher age levels to represent the greater proportion of females in this group. Whites, African Americans, and Hispanics were also represented within each age band according to the 1995 Census data. The sample was selected from all geographical regions in the United States and stratified to represent the different educational levels within each age group.

Table S–2. WAIS-III Subtests Used for Calculating IQs and Indexes

Subtests used to calculate Full Scale Verbal and Performance IQs:

Verbal IQ	Vocabulary, Similarities, Arithmetic, Digit Span, Information, Comprehension, Letter-Number Sequencing
Performance IQ	Picture Completion, Digit Symbol-Coding, Block Design, Matrix Reasoning, Picture Arrangement, Symbol Search, Object Assembly

Subtests used to calculate Indexes:

Verbal Comprehension	Vocabulary, Similarities, Information
Perceptual Organization	Picture Completion, Block Design, Matrix Reasoning
Working Memory	Arithmetic, Digit Span, Letter-Number Sequencing
Processing Speed	Digit Symbol-Coding, Symbol Search

One of the difficulties with the WAIS-R was the use of the age group between 20–34 as a reference group to compare the performance of all other age groups. These comparisons were reflected on the profiles plotted for each client. Thus, when superficially appraising the profiles (and not taking into account age-related corrections), older persons would often look as if they had performed quite poorly. This was unfortunate in that some practitioners compared the subtest scores of older groups by contrasting them with this reference group and incorrectly inferred relative weaknesses or even impairment. For example, the mean on Digit Symbol for the age group 70–74 was 5.5. On the surface, the average healthy 70–74-year-old might therefore appear to be in the impaired range (Palmer, Boone, Lesser, & Wohl, 1998). Ryan, Paolo, and Brungardt (1990) have noted that the average performance subscale score for individuals 75–79 was 1.5 subscale points lower than the mean of the reference group. In contrast to the performance subtests, the verbal subtests are not as likely to decrease with age (Sattler & Ryan, 1998). The WAIS-III has corrected for this at the subtest level by not using the 20–34 age group as the reference. Thus, each age group is compared with their age-related peers on their subscale scores. These subscale scores are also used to calculate both IQ and Index scores. Importantly, the profile which depicts the various subtest scores is represented using these age-corrected scores.

RELIABILITY AND VALIDITY

The reliabilities for the WAIS-III are generally quite high and roughly comparable to, but slightly higher than, the WAIS-R (see Table S–3). Areas of note are that average split-half reliability for the Full Scale IQ is .98, Verbal IQ is .97, and Performance IQ is .94. The Index reliabilities were similarly quite high with a Verbal Comprehension of .96, Perceptual Organization of .94, Working Memory of .93, and a Processing Speed of .87. The somewhat lower reliability for the Processing Speed Index is primarily due to their only being two subtests (Digit Symbol-Coding and Symbol Search) used to calculate this index. It should also be noted that, since these two subtests are speeded tests, it was not appropriate to use split-half reliability and test-retest reliability was calculated instead. The subtest reliabilities were, as expected, somewhat lower. The highest reliabilities were for Vocabulary (.93) and Information (.91) with the lowest for Object Assembly (.70) and Picture Arrangement (.74). Average test-retest reliability over a 2 to 12 week interval (M = 34.6 days) was generally comparable, although slightly lower, than the above split-half reliabilities.

While the above test-retest reliabilities indicate a high degree of temporal stability, there is still some degree of improvement on retesting due to practice effects. The Full Scale IQ was found to increase by 3.2 to 5.7 points, the Verbal IQ increased 2.0 to 3.2 points, and the Performance Scale increased 3.7 to 8.3 points. These increases are not only statistically significant, but may have clinical significance when making inferences about the extent to which real improvement/deterioration has occurred for a particular client. This is particularly important when interpreting either specific performance subtests or scores derived from the performance subtests (i.e. Performance IQ, Processing Speed). Thus, a client who has a Performance IQ increase of 8–10 point on retesting may not really be improving in their everyday functions, but

Table S–3. Average Reliability Coefficients (r) and Standard Error of Measurements (SEM) for WAIS-III IQs, Indexes, and Subtests[a]

IQ/Index/Scale	Average Split-Half r	Average Test-Retest r[b]	Average SEM[c]
Full Scale IQ	.98	.96	2.30
Verbal IQ	.97	.96	2.55
Performance IQ	.94	.91	3.75
Verbal Comprehension	.96	.95	3.01
Perceptual Organization	.93	.88	3.95
Working Memory	.88	.89	3.84
Processing Speed	.88	.89	5.13
Vocabulary	.93	.91	.79
Similarities	.86	.83	1.12
Arithmetic	.88	.86	1.05
Digit Span	.90	.83	.94
Information	.91	.94	.91
Comprehension	.84	.81	1.21
Letter-Number Sequencing	.82	.75	1.30
Picture Completion	.83	.79	1.25
Coding (Digit Symbol)	.84[d]	.86	1.19
Block Design	.86	.82	1.14
Matrix Reasoning	.90	.77	.97
Picture Arrangement	.74	.69	1.53
Symbol Search	.77[d]	.79	1.43
Object Assembly	.70	.76	1.66

[a]Data derived from Wechsler (1997b); averages were derived from combining all age groups from the standardization sample.
[b]Test-retest reliability interval ranged between 2 to 12 weeks (M = 34.6 days, N = 394 participants).
[c]SEM values are reported in IQ/Index units for the IQs and Index scores and scaled-score units for the subtests.
[d]For Digit Symbol-Coding and Symbol Search, test-retest r3eliability coefficients are reported.

will merely be demonstrating practice effects. Research with the WAIS-R indicates that these practice effects can occur up to 9 months later even among head injured patients (see p. 148). However, these retest gains have also been found to diminish with age (Ryan et al., 1990).

Since extensive validity studies exist for the WAIS-R, one of the most important initial steps in WAIS-III validation has been to determine the comparability between the two tests. Comparability would be expected given that the two versions share 70% of their items. As expected, correlations were found to be a quite high of .94, .86, and .93 for the Verbal, Performance, and Full Scale IQs respectively (Wechsler, 1997b). This suggests that the WAIS-III measures essentially the same constructs as the WAIS-R. Noteworthy high correlations between the different subtests were .90 for Vocabulary, .83 for Information, and .82 for Digit Span. In contrast, relatively low correlations were found for Picture Completion (.50), Picture Arrangement (.63), and Object Assembly (.69). Correlations between the WAIS-III and WISC-III for a group of 16-year-olds were also quite high (VIQ = .88, PIQ = .78, FSIQ = .88). The Index scores were somewhat more variable (Verbal Index = .87, Perceptual Organization Index = .74, Working Memory = .50, Processing Speed = .79). The low correlation for Working Memory is most likely due to the WAIS-III including the new Letter-Number Sequencing subtest. In contrast, the WISC-III uses only Arithmetic and Digit Span to determine the Working Memory Index. The above sets of correlations indicate a mostly high level of correspondence between the WAIS-III and WAIS-R as well as the WAIS-III and WISC-III.

The WAIS-III has also been found to correlate highly with several standard ability measures (Wechsler, 1997b). The Standard Progressive Matrices test is an untimed, nonverbal test and, as such, the WAIS-III correlations between the Performance IQ and Perceptual Organization Index were moderately high (.79 and .65, respectively). In contrast (and consistent with the construct that the Standard Progressive Matrices is both untimed and nonverbal), the correlation with the Processing Speed Index was low (.25). The correlation between the WAIS-III and Stanford Binet-IV was .88. Further high to moderate correlations (typically in the high .60s to .70s) were found between the WAIS-III and the Wechsler Individual Achievement Test (Wechsler, 1997b). While beyond the scope of this review, correlations have also supported expected associations with measures of attention and concentration, memory, language, fine motor speed/dexterity, spatial processing, and executive functioning (Wechsler, 1997b).

Since the Wechsler Memory Scales-III (WMS-III) and WAIS-III have been more closely linked, it is important to evaluate the extent and manner they were related (Wechsler, 1997b). Correlations between the WAIS-III IQ/Index scores and WMS-III Index scores have generally ranged from .33 to .77 (Wechsler, 1997b, p. 124). The VIQ was found to correlate moderately with both the WMS-III Verbal Memory Index (.71) and Visual Memory Index (.73). However, somewhat low correlations were found between the WAIS-III PIQ and WMS-III visual immediate (.39) and visual delayed (.44) scores. The strongest correlation was between WAIS-III Working Memory and WMS-III Working Memory (.82), which is expected given that they share the Digit Span and Letter-Numbering subtests (Wechsler, 1997b, p. 93). The above pattern of correlations between the WAIS-III and standard tests of intelligence, achievement, and memory provide support for the convergent and divergent validity of the WAIS-III.

Factor analysis of the WAIS-III has supported the presence of g in that most subtests correlate with each other, as well as with the FSIQ at least to a moderate extent (Wechsler, 1997b). Support for the division between verbal and performance subtests is also present in that the verbal subtests have distinctly higher correlations with VIQ than PIQ. Finally, dividing subtests into four Indexes is supported by current theories of intelligence as well as factor analytic procedures (Sattler & Ryan, 1998; Wechsler, 1997b).

A variety of clinical populations have patterns of deficits in learning, cognition, and memory. It would thus be expected that the WAIS-III would be sensitive to these patterns. This was somewhat supported in that the mean WAIS-IQ and Index scores for Alzheimer's disease patients were lower than expected when compared with their age-related peers. Comparisons among the Index scores indicated differential cognitive abilities in that the mean Verbal Comprehension Index was relatively higher (93.0) than either the Processing Speed (M = 79.6) or Perceptual Organization (M = 84.8). However, it would have been expected that the Working Memory Index would have been somewhat lower than the mean of M = 87.2 given the considerable memory complaints among this population. A variety of other neurological disorders (Huntington's disease, Parkinson's disease, traumatic brain injury) found somewhat similar patterns to those with Alzheimer's disease in that verbal abilities were relatively spared (relatively higher VIQ and Verbal Comprehension Index) whereas Processing Speed was lowest. This indicates that the WAIS-III is sensitive to the difficulties these patient populations have with rapidly processing and consolidating information.

Whereas the mean IQ scores for clients diagnosed with ADHD did not differ from the standardization sample, the mean Working Memory Index scores were 8.3 points lower than their Verbal Comprehension Index scores (Wechsler, 1997b). Similarly, subjects diagnosed with learning disabilities were found to have IQ scores within the normal range (Wechsler, 1997b). However, pronounced discrepancies on Index scores were found. Mean Verbal Comprehension scores were 7 points higher than Working Memory scores for reading disabled subjects and 13 points higher for math disabled subjects. A subgroup (47.7%) of persons with reading disabilities had at least 15 point higher mean Verbal Comprehension than Working Memory scores. Discrepancies were further reflected in that mean Perceptual Organization scores were 7 points higher than Processing Speed scores for both math and reading disabled groups. The ACID profile (lower **A**rithmetic, **C**oding, **I**nformation, **D**igit Span) was also found in that 24% of learning disabled subjects expressed a partial ACID profile and 6.5% expressed a pronounced ACID profile. However, the Verbal Comprehension/Working Memory and Perceptual Organization/ Processing Speed discrepancies seemed to more strongly reflect the patterns of cognitive strengths and weaknesses than the ACID profile. The above data indicate that the WAIS-III accurately reflected the patterns of deficits related to known characteristics of various clinical and psychoeducational groups.

ASSETS AND LIMITATIONS

Since the WAIS-III is similar to the earlier WAIS-R, it also has many of the same advantages. Specifically, it is familiar to both researchers and practitioners, scores can help practitioners develop relevant hypotheses, most of the subtests are relatively easy to administer, and the manual provides clear instructions, concise tables, and excellent norms. Various aspects of cognitive functioning can often be determined by noting the patterns of Index and subtest scores. The WAIS-III (like the WAIS-R) can also be used to infer personality variables. This can be accomplished by noting relevant behavioral observations, patterns of subtest scores, and qualitative responses to various items. The WAIS-III has the further advantage of excellent standardization and has been co-normed with measures of memory (WMS-III) and achievement (Wechsler Individual Achievement Test).

Perhaps the greatest asset of the WAIS-III is the increased number of options for assessing the various components of a client's cognitive functioning. In addition to the standard Verbal and Performance IQs, the four Index (factor) scores provide further precision regarding relative cognitive strengths and weaknesses. These Indexes are based on solid theoretical and empirical grounds. Since greater detail can be obtained from the Index scores, this reduces the need to interpret individual subtests. This is particularly advantageous since interpretation of individual subtests, and even many patterns of subtests, has received criticism (Glutting, McDermott, Watkins, Kush, & Konold, 1997; McDermott, Fantuzzo, & Glutting, 1989). However, should practitioners chose to interpret various patterns of subtests, calculations can be made on the WAIS-III Record Form and in accordance with guidelines provided in the *WAIS-III Administration and Scoring Manual* (pp. 60–62). Once these calculations have been made, the manual includes tables to determine whether or not subtest fluctuations are significantly different from means of verbal, performance, or total subtests (see Table B.3, pp. 208–209).

These guidelines and procedures should help discourage clinicians from the dubious practice of interpreting subtest patterns by using a brief clinical appraisal of the profiles and making interpretations without either determining whether the differences are significant or hypothesis testing to ensure that the patterns are conceptually consistent. Similar tables are also provided for determining whether or not IQ and Index scores represent significant fluctuations across the various age ranges (see Table B.1, p. 205 in the *WAIS-III Administration and Scoring Manual*).

As was mentioned previously, one of the unwieldy and potentially problematic features of the previous WAIS-R was subtest interpretation for persons in the older age ranges. Although various age group comparisons were incorporated into calculations for the IQs, they were not incorporated into the standard procedure for calculating and profiling the subtests. In contrast, the WAIS-III has nicely incorporated age-related comparisons into the calculation and profiling of the subtests. Thus, a subtest profile portrays the client's strengths and weaknesses compared to persons within their own age group. The WAIS-III has also increased the age by which subtest comparisons can be made by including persons up to the age of 89.

One criticism of the previous WAIS-R is that it did not adequately measure extreme ranges of intelligence. In response to this, the WAIS-III has lowered its floor to 45 and increased its ceiling to 155. In contrast, the WAIS-R ceiling was 150 and the floor varied between 45 to 51 depending on the age range. Assessing the lower ranges of intelligence with the WAIS-III is also facilitated by using "low end" or "reversal" (since they are given in the reverse order) items which are extremely easy. These reversal items are given only if one or both of the two starting items are missed.

Scoring the various items on the subtests is generally clear and is guided by criteria in the manual. However, items on Similarities, Comprehension, and Vocabulary may result in client responses which are sometimes ambiguous. As a result, clinical judgment might be used resulting in possible discrepancies between scorers. A further potential difficulty is that when supplementary subtests are substituted for regular subtests, it is unclear how these supplementary subtest scores will affect the three IQ or Index scores. As a result, supplementary subtests should only be given under unusual circumstances such as when one of the regular subtests have been "spoiled."

The reliability of the WAIS-III is clearly outstanding and represents a slight improvement on the WAIS-R. Since the WAIS-III is a relatively newly published test, little is known about its validity other than the material that is published in the manual (and reviewed previously). However, the basic structure of the WAIS-III is primarily the same as the WAIS-R. As a result, much of the extensive and highly supportive research on the WAIS-R is also transferable to the WAIS-III. Of particular interest will be the emerging research on the new features of the WAIS-III such as the Working Memory and Processing Speed Indexes along with the new subtests of Symbol Search, Matrix Reasoning, and Letter-Number Sequencing. A further agenda for research will be to more closely examine the ecological validity of both the WAIS-III IQs/Indexes as well as its specific subtests. This is a pressing issue given that referral questions are increasingly related to clients' everyday levels of functioning (i.e., ability to function independently, extent of disability, everyday aspects of memory; Groth-Marnat & Teal, 1998; Sbordone & Long, 1996).

The WAIS-III has continued the traditional measurement of intelligence as represented by the Stanford Binet scales and the earlier versions of the Wechsler scales. Although their revisions have provided such features as updated norms and Index scores (especially the inclusion of Working Memory and Processing Speed), the theories underlying and essential construction of these scales have remained relatively unchanged for well over 50 years. This is despite numerous developments in both theory and measurement. These include Luria's PASS (**P**lanning-**A**ttention-**S**uccessive-**S**equencing; Luria, 1980) model, Gardner's independent competencies (Gardner, 1993), various theories on emotional intelligence (Bar-on, 1998), and common sense problem solving (Sternberg, Wagner, Williams, & Horvath, 1995). Thus, one criticism of the WAIS-III is that it has not responded to more current views on intelligence (Sternberg & Kaufman, 1998). It remains to be seen whether newer models and assessment tools will have much of an impact on either assessing intelligence or especially the frequency to which the Wechsler scales will be used in this process.

INTERPRETIVE CONSIDERATIONS

The WAIS-III has the distinct advantage that many of the detailed procedures outlined in Chapter 5 (pp. 157–172) have been conveniently incorporated into the standard procedures on the WAIS-III Record Form and *WAIS-III Administration and Scoring Manual*. However, the same general successive five-level interpretive procedures detailed in Chapter 5 for the other Wechsler scales and outlined in Table 5–2 (p. 158) is still recommended. In addition, each of the general interpretive principles and cautions described on pages 158–159 are also important. Particular care should be taken during clerical procedures since these procedures are more numerous for the WAIS-III than the WAIS-R. A number of specific considerations relevant for the WAIS-III are described below and numbered according to the five-level successive procedures.

Level 1. The Full Scale IQ

Interpretation of the Full Scale IQ is essentially the same as for the WAIS-R. However, the lowest IQ classification (69 and below) has been changed from Mentally Retarded on the WAIS-R to the more neutral term of Extremely Low on the WAIS-III (see Table 2.3, p. 25 in the *WAIS-III Administration and Scoring Manual*). In addition, practitioners might wish to use Table 3.4 (p. 54) in the *WAIS-III-WMS-III Technical Manual* to determine the Standard Error of Measurement of the Full Scale IQ according to various age groups. This will then provide readers of interpretations with an approximation of the likely range of error around the Full Scale IQ. Table 3.4 can also be used to determine the standard error of measurements for the Verbal/Performance IQs, Index scores, and each of the different subtests.

Level II: Verbal-Performance IQs, Index Scores, and Additional Groupings

The same general procedures and considerations described in Chapter 5 (pp. 160–168) for Level II interpretations also apply for the WAIS-III. However, there are specific procedures built in to the WAIS-III which facilitate this process. On the Record Form itself there is a Discrepancy Analysis Page which provides a form for calculating whether or not (and at what level) the Verbal IQ, Performance IQ, and four Index scores are discrepant from each other. This means that much of the detailed instruction provided for Level II interpretation in Chapter 5 (pp. 160–168) is now unnecessary.

The interpretation for Verbal and Performance IQs are essentially the same as for previous versions of the Wechsler intelligence scales. In order to facilitate interpreting the Index scores a brief summary of what subtests are included along with possible Index interpretations are included below.

- *Verbal Comprehension Index* (VCI; Vocabulary, Similarities, Information). This is a purer, more refined measure of verbal comprehension than the Verbal IQ. This has been achieved by excluding the Digit Span and Arithmetic subtests which focus primarily on attention and working memory. VCI reflects a person's acquired verbal-related knowledge and verbal reasoning.
- *Perceptual Organization Index* (POI; Picture Completion, Block Design, Matrix Reasoning). POI measures nonverbal, fluid reasoning, visual-motor integration, and attention to detail. POI is less a measure of processing speed than Performance IQ since only one of the subtests (Block Design) emphasizes speeded performance.
- *Working Memory Index* (WMI; Arithmetic, Digit Span, Letter-Numbering Sequencing). This Index has frequently been referred to as the Freedom from Distractibility factor and thus the previously given interpretations under this title are also relevant (pp. 162–163). Each of the tasks require that the client attend to oral information that is presented to them, hold and process the information in memory, and develop a response (similar to a mental scratch pad). WMI is a measure of concentration, attention, short-term memory, and number facility. Good performance also requires abilities often ascribed to "executive functioning" including intact sequencing, making successful mental shifts, and the ability to monitor one's processes and responses. WMI is also comprised of those subtests most easily disrupted by anxiety. Optimal performance also requires a high level of motivation so that this index will be particularly low if clients lose interest in the test due to such factors as fatigue or boredom.
- *Processing Speed Index* (PSI; Digit Symbol-Coding, Symbol Search). By including an upward extension of the WISC-III's Symbol Search, the WAIS-III similarly saw the emergence of the PSI. It measures the mental and motor speed with which

a person can solve visual-spatial problems. It also requires them to plan, organize, and develop relevant strategies. Either poor motivation, or an overly reflective problem-solving style can lower performance on this Index.

One issue is that the WAIS-III procedures make comparisons and establish the significance of discrepancies *between all possible combinations of Indexes* (i.e., VCI-POI, VCI-WMI). In contrast, the method detailed in Chapter 5 (pp. 162–168) calculates discrepancies based on differences from a *mean* developed from the three (WAIS-R) or four (WISC-III) Index/factor scores. Given that the WAIS-III makes comparisons between all possible combinations of Index scores, this procedure (rather than comparisons with various means) should be followed at this time. Thus, interpretations should be made based on discrepancies between different pairs of indexes. For example, a significantly higher Verbal Comprehension than Perceptual Organization Index suggests that the person's verbal reasoning and acquired knowledge are higher *relative* to their nonverbal, visual-motor, fluid abilities.

The usual method for determining whether or not Verbal-Comprehension or Index discrepancies should be interpreted is to note whether the discrepancies are significant (determined from Table B.1 in the manual). As has been noted, however, significant discrepancies can occur fairly frequently (see pp. 161, 169). The frequency (base rate) occurence of Verbal-Performance and Index discrepancies can be noted on Table B.2 in the manual. These base rate figures provide percentages of how frequently differences occurred in the standardization sample. It should be clarifed that the cumulative percentages shown in these tables are for differences in both direction. They do not distinguish, for example, whether the Verbal is higher than the Performance IQ or vice versa. This means that practitioners should divide the cumulative percentages by 2 to find the frequency for a specific discrepancy (Sattler & Ryan, 1998). Thus, if a Verbal IQ is 28 points higher than a Performance IQ, it is not only quite significant (.01 level), but it is also very unusual in that it occurred in only 1.5% (3% divided by 2) of the standardization sample. However, even if a discrepancy is not particularly unusual but is still statistically significant, it may still have interpretive meaning for the individual client.

A further issue is that interpretations based on Index discrepancies is still somewhat speculative and should be made cautiously. For example, it would seem reasonable to conclude that if WMI was significantly lower than POI, a client will also show relatively superior abilities in everyday performance on visual, nonverbal tasks than mathematical skills or other abilities requiring a high degree of concentration. It might be further predicted that they would do better in professions requiring interacting with visual-spatial materials (fine art, architecture) or interpersonal relations (interviewing, public relations) than ones requiring a high level of concentration and sequencing (air traffic controller, computer programmer, scientist). However, such interpretations need to be made by taking into consideration all additional relevant data as well as relying on forthcoming research.

Bannatyne's categories (see pp. 164–166) can be developed based on relative scores on Spatial (Picture Completion + Block Design + Object Assembly and possibly Matrix Reasoning), Verbal Conceptualization (Vocabulary + Comprehension + Similarities), Sequential (Digit Span + Arithmetic + Digit Symbol-Coding and probably Letter-Number Sequencing), and Acquired Knowledge (Information + Vocabulary

+ Arithmetic) abilities. Subtest scores should be used and the means determined for each of the different categories. These means can then be used to develop hypotheses related to the client's relative strengths and weaknesses (Groth-Marnat, in press). Note that WAIS-III formulas for establishing standard scores and values for determining discrepancies are not yet available. In addition, the inclusion of Matrix Reasoning and Letter-Number Sequencing into Bannatyne's factors is conceptually consistent with these subtests but should be considered speculative at this time.

The ACID (**A**rithmetic, **C**oding-Digit Symbol, **I**nformation, **D**igit Span) profile can also be calculated and has been found to reflect WAIS-III patterns among some learning disabled persons (Wechsler, 1997b). Given that Symbol Search has been included in the WAIS-III, it would be reasonable to assume that adult learning disabled persons would also have a lowered *SCAD profile*. The SCAD profile can be determined by noting whether subtest scores on **S**ymbol Search, **C**oding (Digit Symbol-Coding), **I**nformation, and **D**igit Span are relatively lower than other subtests. It should be noted that, since Letter-Number Sequencing requires extensive sequencing and attentional abilities, this subtest might either be included along with the other SCAD subtests, or replace one of the existing ones. Formulas for establishing standard scores and values for determining discrepancies are not yet available. Formulas for determining the *Horn* groupings are also not available and therefore cannot be calculated at this time.

Level III. Interpreting Subtest Variability

The Score Conversion on the WAIS-III Record Form conveniently provides instructions for determining the relative strengths and weaknesses of subtests. The statistical significance and frequency of these differences can be found in Table B.3 (pp. 208–209) of the *WAIS-III Administration and Scoring Manual*. Note that practitioners are given the option of calculating these differences based either on the total of all subtests given (for 11, 13, or 14 subtests) or to use either the means derived from all verbal (6 or 7) or all performance (5 or 7) subtests. The general rule should be that if there is a significant (.05) discrepancy between Verbal and Performance IQs (9 points or more), the means for verbal and performance subtests should be calculated separately. A large Verbal-Performance discrepancy indicates that the client's IQ is not a unitary factor and thus comparisons of subtests should be made reflecting these different components of their IQs.

Once it has been determined that a subtest represents either a significant strength or weakness, the next step is to develop and test hypotheses related to the meaning behind the subtest fluctuations. Procedures for this process are detailed in the Level IIIb procedures (pp. 170–171) and in Appendix E (pp. 677–683). A complication is that there are three new WAIS-III subtests and two of these subtests (Letter-Number Sequencing and Matrix Reasoning) are not included on the tables in Appendix E. Since Symbol Search was included in the WISC-III, it has already been included in Appendix E and can be used in establishing WAIS-III strengths/weaknesses related to this subtest. In order to compensate for the absence of Letter-Numbering Sequencing and Matrix Reasoning, a listing of the abilities for these two subtests are included in Figures S–1 and S–2 and should be added to the relevant portions of Appendix E.

The Wechsler intelligence scale subtests vary in the extent they measure factors specific to the subtest versus a more general factor common to all the subtests. The degree of subtest specificity also varies according to age. Subtests with a relatively high degree

	Subtest	
Ability	L-NS[a]	MR[b]
Verbal Memory		░
Auditory Short Term Memory		░
Auditory Sequencing		░
Retention		░
Visual Organization		░
Visual Perception		░
Nonverbal Reasoning		░
Simultaneous Processing of Visual-Spatial Information		░
Visual Sequencing	░	
Visual-Spatial Reasoning (Concept Formation)	░	
Perceptual Organization/ Spatial Ability	░	
Analysis of Whole into Component Parts	░	

[a] L-N S abilities should be included and used as part of the hypothesis testing for the Verbal Subtests (Appendix E1, p. 679).

[b] MR abilities should be included and used as part of the hypothesis testing for the Performance Subtests (Appendix E2, pp. 680–681).

Figure S–1.   Listing of abilities measured by Letter-Number Sequencing and Matrix Reasoning to be used for hypothesis testing either Verbal (Appendix E1) or Performance (Appendix E2) subtests

of specificity can be more safely interpreted. The WAIS-III subtests with the highest degree of specificity across all age groups are Arithmetic, Digit Span, Information, Digit Symbol-Coding, Block Design, Matrix Reasoning, and Picture Completion. The remaining seven subtests (Vocabulary, Similarities, Comprehension, Letter-Number Sequencing, Picture Arrangement, Symbol Search, and Object Assembly) do not have adequate

Ability	Subtest	
	L-NS	MR
Attention and Concentration		░
Sequencing		░
Fluid Intelligence		
Alertness to Day-to-Day World		
Short Term Memory		░
General Ability	░	
Abstract Reasoning	░	
Ability to Evaluate Information	░	

[a] Both L-NS and MR should be used with Appendix E3 (pp. 682–683).

Figure S–2.   Listing of abilities for Letter-Number Sequencing and Matrix Reasoning to be used for hypothesis testing with combined Verbal and Performance abilities (Appendix E3)[a]

specificity for some of the ages (see Sattler & Ryan, 1998). As a result, interpretation needs to be made either not at all or with considerable caution.

A further approach to understanding the meaning of subtest scores is through alternative administration or scoring procedures (Kaplan, Fein, Morris, & Delis, 1991; Kaplan & Gallagher, in press). Specifically, the WAIS-III has included optional procedures for scoring Digit Span and optional administration and scoring procedures for Digit Symbol-Coding. The Digit Span optional scoring is based on research and clinical observation indicating that Digits Forward and Digits Backwards may require different cognitive processes. This is because Digits Backwards requires more concentration and is also potentially aided by a person internally visualizing the numbers as an aid to reversing them. Thus, Digits Backwards is more sensitive to deterioration and is also more likely to be lowered by either right hemisphere or diffuse damage (Lezak, 1995; Rudel & Denckla, 1974; Swierchinsky, 1978). In contrast, Digits Forward is quite stable. As a general rule, a discrepancy of five or more digits in favor of Digits Forward indicates the presence of organic deficit. However, it is important to both formally record the discrepancies, as well as make comparisons with age-related groups. On the Discrepancy Analysis Page of the Record Form there is a section to record the longest Digit Span Forward, longest Digit Span Backward, and to calculate the difference between the two. Age-related comparisons of difference scores (DS Forward minus DS Backward) can be found on Table B.7 of the *WAIS-III Administration and Scoring Manual*.

Digit Symbol-Coding has been the focus of both concern and investigation since it involves so many different abilities (Kaplan et al., 1991). This makes it particularly difficult to determine why a person might have done poorly. Two important possibilities for poor performance are that the person had either poor memory for the material, or their speed of processing was low. Thus, the WAIS-III has two optional procedures to determine which (or both) of these might be responsible. The first assesses memory by having the person recall as many of the symbols as possible by first pairing the symbols with numbers (but with no cueing from the symbols; Pairing). The second procedure has the person write down as many of the symbols as possible on a blank sheet of paper during a 90-second interval. It is thus a simple measure of raw speed.

Level IV and V. Intrasubtest Variability and Qualitative Analysis

These two levels can proceed according to the previous guidelines (p. 172).

COMPARISONS BETWEEN SCORES ON THE WAIS-R AND THE WAIS-III

The WAIS-III is somewhat more difficult than the WAIS-R. Specifically, the WAIS-III Full Scale I.Q. was 2.9 points lower than a comparison group who had been given the WAIS-R (Wechsler, 1997b). The WAIS-III Performance IQ had a considerably lower 4.8 IQ point difference whereas the Verbal IQ was somewhat more comparable with a much smaller difference of 1.2 points lower. This means that clinicians need to take this into account when making comparisons between clients who were previously given the WAIS-R but have more recently been given the WAIS-III. The lower WAIS-III scores for the overall Performance IQ and specific performance subtests suggests particular caution in making inferences between these two sets of test scores. This will have particular implications when making inferences related to premorbid IQ, level of deterioration, or degree of impairment.

DESCRIPTION OF NEW WAIS-III SUBTESTS

The following information on the new WAIS-III subtests is based on material provided in the *WAIS-III Administration and Scoring Manual* and the *WAIS-III-WMS-III Technical Manual*. The descriptions will be expanded and refined as further research on these subtests begins to emerge.

Letter-Number Sequencing:

   Auditory short-term memory

   Sequencing ability

   Concentration and attention

A good performance on Letter-Number Sequencing suggests that the person has good sequencing, attention, and concentration. It requires them to attend to a series of letters and numbers that have been read to them, hold them in their memory, manipulate them into a new order, and repeat the new sequence. When combined with Arithmetic and Digit Span, it forms the Working Memory Index but it is not used to calculate any of the IQs. Letter-Number Sequencing (along with Digit Span) is a subtest which is also included on the Wechsler Memory Scale-III.

Psychometrically, Letter-Number Sequencing is good to adequate. Test-retest reliability has been found to range between .70 to .80, the SEM is 1.30, and it has a factor loading of .62 with the Working Memory Index.

Matrix Reasoning:

   Visual spatial reasoning

   Abstract reasoning

High scores on Matrix reasoning suggest good visual information processing and nonverbal abstract reasoning skills. It is combined with Picture Completion and Block Design to form the Perceptual Organization Index. Matrix Reasoning is untimed and is therefore useful for persons from older age groups who might do poorly on some of the other timed tests. It also does not penalize those who have a reflective, cautious problem solving style. Matrix Reasoning is relatively culture free and requires only a minimal amount of visual motor-coordination since the subject merely points to the correct response. Conceptually, Matrix Reasoning is similar to the Halstead Reitan Category Test and Raven's Progressive Matrices. However, future studies will need to determine the nature and degree of correspondence between these measures.

One of the rationales for Matrix Reasoning was to develop a visual-spatial subtest with good psychometric properties which could replace the psychometrically poor Object Assembly subtest. In many ways this has been realized in that Matrix Reasoning has been found to have test retest stabilities ranging from .75 to .81, SEM of .97, a correlation with the Full Scale IQ of .75, and a factor loading of .61 on the Perceptual Organization Index. It is one of the best performance subtest measure of g (52% of its variance can be attributed to g). In contrast, Object Assembly has poorer psychometric properties with particular concerns related to its lack of stability (SEM = 1.66). As a result Object Assembly is now an optional WAIS-III subtest.

Symbol Search:

   Speed of visual search

   Speed of processing information

   Planning

Encoding of information in preparation for further processing

Visual-motor coordination

Learning ability

Symbol Search is an upward extension of the WISC-III subtest of the same name. As a result, it measures essentially the same areas and was similarly intended to be as pure a test as possible of information processing speed. High scores indicate that the individual can rapidly absorb information as well as integrate and respond to this information. High scores also suggest good visual-motor coordination, short-term visual memory, planning, general learning, and a high level of attention and concentration. In contrast, low scores suggest slow mental processes, visual perceptual difficulties, and difficulties with short-term visual memory. It might also reflect poor motivation, anxiety, or a reflective, perfectionistic, or obsessive problem-solving style. Digit Symbol-Coding combines with Symbol Search to form the Processing Speed Index.

Symbol Search is psychometrically a relatively good subtest. Test-retest reliability over a 2 to 12 week interval ranged between .74 to .80 with the SEM being 1.43. However, the SEM does suggests that it is somewhat unstable from one testing to the next. It has a factor loading with Processing Speed of .63 and is a fair measure of g (49% of its variance can be attributed to g).

SHORT FORMS

The average time to administer the 11 standard WAIS-III subtests is 75 minutes (60–90 minute range). Since clinical samples often present with special needs, administration time typically takes a longer average of 91 minutes (range of 54 to 136 minutes; Ryan, Werth, & Lopez, 1998).

Various short forms can considerably shorten the administration time. As has been discussed previously (see pp. 200–203) these short forms can be selected based on psychometric considerations, type of clinical information which is needed, or special client characteristics (i.e. handicapped, non-english background). The best combinations based on their psychometric properties are described below and are derived from Sattler and Ryan (1998).

Best Two- and Three-Subtest Short Forms

As with the WAIS-R and WISC-III, Vocabulary and Block Design make an excellent two subtest short form. They represent one verbal and one performance subtest, are both good measures of g, their combined reliability is .93, and their validity coefficient is .88. Vocabulary and Matrix Reasoning also make a good combination in that they are both good measures of g, and their combined reliabilities and validities are .93 and .88 respectively. The best triad is Vocabulary, Information, and Block Design in that they are all good measures of g and the combined reliabilities and validities are .95 and .90 respectively.

Best Four Subtest Short Form

The two best four subtest short forms are comprised of (a) Information, Arithmetic, Picture Completion, and Block Design and (b) Information, Arithmetic, Picture Completion, and Matrix Reasoning. Each of these combinations provides valuable clinical and diagnostic information and their reliabilities and validities are both above .95 and .92 respectively.

Seven Subtest Short Form

A strategy described previously for the WAIS-R (p. 202) is to use the seven shortest subtests. This reduces the administration time by 50% and still provides estimates of the Verbal, Performance, and Full Scale IQs. Sattler and Ryan (1998) report that using this short form with the WAIS-III still results in a quite high reliability of .96.

References

Abrams, E. (1955). Prediction of intelligence from certain Rorschach factors. *Journal of Clinical Psychology, 11,* 81–83.

Achenbach, T. M. (1978). The Child Behavior Profile: I. Boys aged 6–11. *Journal of Consulting and Clinical Psychology, 46,* 478–488.

Achenbach, T. M., & Edelbrock, C. S. (1979). The Child Behavior Profile: II. Boys aged 12–16 and girls 6–11 and 12–16. *Journal of Consulting and Clinical Psychology, 47,* 223–233.

Achenbach, T. M., & Edelbrock, C. S. (1983). *Manual for the Child Behavior Checklist and Revised Child Behavior Profile.* Burlington, VT: University of Vermont, Department of Psychiatry.

Acker, M. B. (1990). A review of the ecological validity of neuropsychological tests. In D. E. Tupper & K. D. Cicerone (Eds.), *The neuropsychology of everyday life: Assessment and basic competencies* (pp. 19–55). Boston: Kluwer Academic.

Acker, M. B., & Davis, J. R. (1989). Psychology test scores associated with late outcome head injury. *Neuropsychology, 3,* 1–10.

Ackerman, P. T., McGrew, M. J., & Dykman, R. A. (1987). A profile of male and female applicants for a special college program for learning disabled students. *Journal of Clinical Psychology, 43,* 67–78.

Ackerman, P. T., Peters, J. R., & Dykman, R. A. (1971). Children with specific learning disabilities: Bender Gestalt Test findings and other signs. *Journal of Learning Disabilities, 4,* 437–446.

Acklin, M. W., & Bernat, E. (1987). Depression, alexithymia, and pain prone disorder: A Rorschach study. *Journal of Personality Assessment, 51,* 462–479.

Adams, H., Cooper, G., & Carrera, R. (1963). The Rorschach and the MMPI: A concurrent validity study. *Journal of Projective Techniques, 27,* 23–24.

Adams, K. M. (1980). In search of Luria's battery: A false start. *Journal of Consulting and Clinical Psychology, 48,* 511–516.

Adams, R. L., Smigielski, J., & Jenkins, R. L. (1984). Developments of a Satz-Mogel short form of the WAIS-R. *Journal of Consulting and Clinical Psychology, 52,* 908.

Adcock, C. J. (1965). Thematic Apperception Test: A review. In O. K. Buros (Ed.), *The sixth mental measurements yearbook* (Vol. 1, pp. 533–535). Highland Park, NJ: Gryphon Press.

Affleck, D. C., & Mednick, S. A. (1959). The use of the Rorschach test in the prediction of the abrupt terminator in individual psychotherapy. *Journal of Consulting Psychology, 23,* 125–128.

Ager, A. (Ed.). (1991). *Microcomputers and clinical psychology: Issues, applications, and future developments.* New York: Wiley.

Ahern, S., & Beatty, J. (1979). Pupillary responses vary during information-processing with scholastic aptitude test score. *Science, 205,* 1289–1292.

Akutagawa, D. A. (1956). *A study in construct validity of the psychoanalytic concept of latent anxiety and a test of projection distance hypothesis.* Unpublished doctoral dissertation, University of Pittsburgh, Pittsburgh, PA.

Albert, N., & Beck, A. T. (1975). Incidence of depression in early adolescence: A preliminary study. *Journal of Youth and Adolescence, 4,* 301–307.

Albert, S., Fox, H. M., & Kahn, M. W. (1980). Faking psychosis on the Rorschach: Can expert judges detect malingering? *Journal of Personality Assessment, 44,* 115–119.

Alcock, T. (1963). *The Rorschach in practice.* Philadelphia: J.B. Lippincott.

Alessi, G. J. (1980). Behavioral observation for the school psychologist: Responsive-discrepancy model. *School Psychology Review, 9,* 31–45.

Alker, H. A. (1978). Minnesota Multiphasic Personality Inventory: A review. In O. K. Buros (Ed.), *The eighth mental measurements yearbook* (Vol. 1, pp. 931–935). Highland Park, NJ: Gryphon Press.

Allen, J. J., Iacono, W. G., & Danielson, K. (1992). The identification of concealed memories using the event-related potential and implicit behavioral measures: A methodology for prediction in the face of individual differences. *Psychophysiology, 29,* 504–522.

Allen, R. M. (1953). *Introduction to the Rorschach technique.* New York: International Universities Press.

Allen, R. M. (1954). *Elements of Rorschach interpretation.* New York: Harper & Row.

Allen, S. R., & Thorndike, R. M. (1995). Stability of the WAIS-R and the WISC-III factor structure using cross-validation of covariance structures. *Journal of Clinical Psychology, 51,* 645–657.

Allison, J., & Blatt, S. J. (1964). The relationship of Rorschach whole responses to intelligence. *Journal of Projective Techniques, 28,* 255–260.

Allison, J., Blatt, S. J., & Zimet, C. N. (1968). *The interpretation of psychological tests.* New York: Harper & Row.

Allison, J., Blatt, S. J., & Zimet, C. N. (1988). *The interpretation of psychological tests* (2nd ed.). New York: Harper & Row.

Alnacs, R., & Torgerson, S. (1989). Clinical differentiation between major depression only, major depression with panic disorder, and panic disorder: Childhood personality, and personality disorder. *Acta Psychiatrica Scandinavica, 79,* 370–377.

Amabile, T. M. (1983). *The social psychology of creativity.* New York: Springer-Verlag.

Ambrosini, P. J., Metz, C., Prabucki, K., & Lee, J. (1989). Videotape reliability of the third revised edition of K-SADS. *Journal of the American Academy of Child and Adolescent Psychology, 28,* 723–728.

American Association on Mental Deficiency (AAMD). (1973). *Manual on terminology and classification in mental retardation* (Rev. ed.). H. J. Grossman (Ed.), Special Publication Series No. 2, 11+. Washington, DC: Author.

American Education Research Association, American Psychological Association, & National Council on Measurement in Education. (1985). *Standards for educational and psychological testing.* Washington, DC: American Psychological Association. *American Journal of Psychiatry, 146,* 200–205.

American Psychiatric Association. (1980). *Diagnostic and statistical manual of mental disorders* (3rd ed.). Washington, DC: American Psychiatric Association.

American Psychiatric Association. (1987). *Diagnostic and statistical manual of mental disorders* (3rd ed., rev.). Washington, DC: American Psychiatric Association.

American Psychiatric Association. (1994). *Diagnostic and statistical manual of mental disorders* (4th ed.). Washington, DC: American Psychiatric Association.

American Psychological Association. (1967). *Casebook on ethical standards of psychologists.* Washington, DC: American Psychological Association.

American Psychological Association. (1981). *Ethical principals of psychologists.* Washington, DC: American Psychological Association.

American Psychological Association. (1985). *Standards for educational and psychological tests.* Washington, DC: American Psychological Association.

American Psychological Association. (1986). *Guidelines for computer-based test interpretations.* Washington, DC: American Psychological Association.

American Psychological Association. (1987). General guidelines for providers of psychological services. *American Psychologist, 42,* 7.

American Psychological Association. (1988). *Computer use in psychology.* Washington, DC: American Psychological Association.

American Psychological Association. (1992). Ethical principles of psychologists and code of conduct. *American Psychologist, 47,* 1597–1611.

American Psychological Association. (1994). *Publication manual of the American Psychological Association* (4th ed.). Washington, DC: Author.

Ames, L. B. (1959). Further check on the diagnostic validity of the Ames danger signals. *Journal of Projective Techniques, 23,* 291–298.

Ames, L. B., & Gillespie, C. (1973). Significance of Rorschach modified by responses to other projective tests. *Journal of Personality Assessment, 37,* 316–327.

Ames, L. B., Learned, J., Metraux, R., & Walker, R. N. (1952). *Child Rorschach responses.* New York: Hoeber.

Ames, L. B., Metraux, R. W., Rodell, J. L., & Walker, R. N. (1973). *Rorschach responses in old age* (Rev. ed.). New York: Brunner/Mazel.

Ames, L. B., Metraux, R. W., Rodell, J. L., & Walker, R. N. (1974). *Child Rorschach responses: Developmental trends from two to ten years* (Rev. ed.). New York: Brunner/Mazel.

Ames, L. B., Metraux, R. W., & Walker, R. N. (1971). *Adolescent Rorschach responses: Developmental trends from ten to sixteen years* (2nd ed.). New York: Brunner/Mazel.

Anastasi, A. (1967). Psychologists and psychological testing. *American Psychologist, 22,* 297–306.

Anastasi, A. (1982). *Psychological testing* (5th ed.). New York: Macmillan.

Anastasi, A. (1988). *Psychological testing* (6th ed.). New York: Macmillan.

Anastasi, A. (1996). *Psychological testing* (7th ed.). New York: Macmillan.

Anastopoulos, A. D., Spisto, M. A., & Maher, M. C. (1994). The WISC-III Freedom from Distractibility Factor: Its utility in identifying children with Attention Deficit Hyperactive Disorder. *Psychological Assessment, 6,* 368–371.

Anderson, E. M., & Lambert, M. J. (1995). Short-term dynamically oriented psychotherapy: A review and meta-analysis. *Clinical Psychology Review, 15,* 503–514.

Anderson, S., & Harthorn, B. H. (in press). The recognition, diagnosis, and treatment of mental disorders by primary care physicians. *Medical Care.*

Anderson, S., & Messick, S. (1974). Social competency in young children. *Developmental Psychology, 10,* 282–293.

Anderson, T. K., Cancelli, A. A., & Kratochwill, T. R. (1984). Self-reported assessment practices of school psychologists: Implications for training and practice. *Journal of School Psychology, 22,* 17–29.

Anderson, V., & Gilandas, A. (1994). Neuropsychological assessment of learning disability: Linking theoretical and clinical perspectives. In S. Toyz, D. Byrne, & A. Gilandas (Eds.), *Neuropsychology in clinical practice* (pp. 128–161). New York: Academic Press.

Andert, J. N., Hustak, T., & Dinning, W. D. (1978). Bender-Gestalt reproduction times for retarded adults. *Journal of Clinical Psychology, 34,* 927–929.

Andreasen, N. C., Flaum, M., Swayze, V., O'Leary, D. S., Alliger, R., Cohen, G., Ehrhandt, J., & Yuh, W. T. C. (1993). Intelligence and brain structure in normal individuals. *American Journal of Psychiatry, 150,* 130–134.

Andrews, L. W., & Gutkin, T. B. (1991). The effects of human versus computer authorship on consumers's perceptions of psychological reports. *Computers in Human Behavior, 7,* 311–317.

Antonuccio, D. O., Danton, W. G., & DeNelsky, G. Y. (1995). Psychotherapy versus medication for depression: Challenging the conventional wisdom with data. *Professional Psychology: Research and Practice, 26,* 574–585.

Appel, K. E. (1931). Drawings by children as aids in personality studies. *American Journal of Orthopsychiatry, 1,* 129–144.

Appelbaum, A. S., & Tuma, J. M. (1982). The relationship of the WISC-R to academic achievement in a clinical population. *Journal of Clinical Psychology, 38,* 401–405.

Apperson, L. J., Mulvey, E. P., & Lidz, C. W. (1993). Short-term clinical prediction of assaultive behavior: Artifacts of research methods. *American Journal of Psychiatry, 150,* 1374–1379.

Apter, A., Bleich, A., Plutchik, R., Mendelsohn, S., & Tyrano, S. (1988). Suicidal behavior, depression, and conduct disorder in hospitalized adolescents. *Journal of the American Academy of Child and Adolescent Psychiatry, 27,* 696–699.

Aram, D. M., & Ekelman, B. L. (1986). Cognitive profiles of children with early onset unilateral lesions. *Developmental Neuropsychology, 2,* 155–172.

Archer, R. P. (1984). Use of the MMPI with adolescents: A review of salient issues. *Clinical Psychology Review, 4,* 241–251.

Archer, R. P. (1987). *Using the MMPI with adolescents.* Hillsdale, NJ: Erlbaum.

Archer, R. P. (1992). Review of the Minnesota Multiphasic Personality Inventory-2. In J. J. Kramer & J. C. Conoley (Eds.), *Eleventh mental measurements yearbook* (pp. 558–562). Lincoln, NE: Buros Institute of Mental Measurements.

Archer, R. P. (1992). *MMPI-A: Assessing adolescent psychopathology.* Hillsdale, NJ: Erlbaum.

Archer, R. P., & Gordon, R. (1988). MMPI and Rorschach indices of schizophrenic and depressive diagnosis among adolescent inpatients. *Journal of Personality Assessment, 52,* 276–287.

Archer, R. P., Gordon, R., Giannetti, R. A., & Singles, J. M. (1988). MMPI scale clinical correlates for adolescent inpatients. *Journal of Personality Assessment, 52,* 707–721.

Archer, R. P., Griffin, R., & Aiduk, R. (1995). MMPI-2 clinical correlates for ten common codes. *Journal of Personality Assessment, 65,* 391–407.

Archer, R. P., & Jacobson, J. M. (1993). Are critical items "critical" for the MMPI-A? *Journal of Personality Assessment, 61,* 547–556.

Archer, R. P., Maruish, M., Imhof, E. A., & Piotrowski, C. (1991). Psychological test usage with adolescent clients: 1990 survey findings. *Professional Psychology: Research and Practice, 22,* 247–252.

Archer, R. P., Pancoast, D. L., & Klinefelter, D. (1989). A comparison of MMPI code types produced by traditional and recent adolescent norms. *Psychological Assessment, 1,* 23–29.

Arizmendi, T. G., Beutler, L. E., Shanfield, S., Crago, M., & Hagaman, R. (1985). Client-therapist similarity and psychotherapy outcome: A microscopic approach. *Psychotherapy: Theory, Research, and Practice, 22,* 16–21.

Armbuster, G. L., Miller, A. S., & Exner, J. E. (1974). *Rorschach responses of parachute trainees at the beginning of training and shortly before their first jump.* Workshop Study No. 201 (unpublished), Rorschach Workshops.

Armstrong, R. G. (1965). A re-evaluation of copied and recalled Bender-Gestalt reproductions. *Journal of Projective Techniques and Personality Assessment, 29,* 134–139.

Armstrong, R. G., & Hauck, P. A. (1960). Correlates of the Bender-Gestalt scores in children. *Journal of Psychological Studies, 11,* 153–158.

Army Individual Test Battery. (1944). *Manual of directions and scoring.* Washington, DC: War Department, Adjutant General's Office.

Arnaud, S. (1959). A system for deriving quantitative Rorschach measures of certain psychological variables for group comparisons. *Journal of Projective Techniques, 23,* 311–400.

Arnold, M. B. (1949). A demonstration analysis of the TAT in a clinical setting. *Journal of Abnormal and Social Psychology, 44,* 97–111.

Arnold, M. B. (1962). *Story sequence analysis: A new method of measuring and predicting achievement.* New York: Columbia University Press.

Aronof, D. N., & McCormick, N. B. (1990). Sex, sex role identification, and college students projective drawings. *Journal of Clinical Psychology, 46,* 460–466.

Aronow, E., Reznikoff, M., & Moreland, K. L. (1995). The Rorschach: Projective technique or psychometric test? *Journal of Personality Assessment, 64,* 213–228.

Arrindell, W. A. (1980). Dimensional structure and psychopathology correlates of the Fear Survey Schedule (FSS-III) in a phobic population: A factorial definition of agoraphobia. *Behavior Research and Therapy, 18,* 229–242.

Arrindell, W. A., Emmelkamp, D. M. G., & van der Ende, J. (1984). Phobic dimensions: I. Reliability and generalizability across samples, gender, and nations. *Advances in Behavior Research and Therapy, 6,* 207–254.

Arvey, R. D., & Campion, J. E. (1982). The employment interview: A summary and review of recent research. *Personnel Psychology, 35,* 281–322.

Association for Measurement and Evaluation in Guidance. (1984). *Guide to microcomputer software in testing and assessment.* Washington, DC: American Association for Counseling and Development.

Atkinson, L. (1986). The comparative validities of the Rorschach and MMPI: A meta-analysis. *Canadian Psychology, 27,* 238–347.

Atkinson, J. W., & Feather, N. T. (Eds.). (1966). *A theory of achievement motivation.* New York: Wiley.

Atkinson, L. (1986). The comparative validities of the Rorschach and the MMPI: A meta-analysis. *Canadian Psychology, 27,* 238–347.

Atkinson, L., Bowman, T. G., Dickens, S., Blackwell, J., Vasarhelyi, J., Szep, P., Dunleary, B., MacIntyre, R., & Bury, A. (1990). Stability of Wechsler Adult Intelligence Scales-Revised factor scores across time. *Psychological Assessment, 2,* 447–450.

Atkinson, L., Quarington, B., Alp, I. E., & Cyr, J. J. (1986). Rorschach validity: An empirical approach to the literature. *Journal of Clinical Psychology, 42,* 360–362.

Austad, C. S., & Berman, W. H. (1991). *Psychotherapy and managed health care: The optimal use of time and resources.* Washington, DC: American Psychological Association.

Ax, A. F. (1953). The physiological differentiation between fear and anger in humans. *Psychosomatic Medicine, 15,* 433–442.

Axelrod, B. N., Woodward, J. L., Schretlen, D., & Benedict, R. H. B. (1996). Corrected estimates of WAIS-R short form reliability and standard error of measurement. *Psychological Assessment, 8,* 222–223.

Baer, J. S., Holt, C. S., & Lichtenstein, E. (1986). Self-efficacy and smoking re-examined: Construct validity and clinical utility. *Journal of Consulting and Clinical Psychology, 54,* 846–852.

Baer, J. S., & Lichtenstein, E. (1988). Classification and prediction of smoking relapse episodes: An exploration of individual differences. *Journal of Consulting and Clinical Psychology, 56,* 104–110.

Baer, R. A., Wetter, M. W., & Berry, D. T. R. (1992). Detection of underreporting of psychopathology on the MMPI: A meta-analysis. *Clinical Psychology Review, 12,* 509–525.

Baer, R. A., Wetter, M. W., Nichols, D. S., Greene, R., & Berry, D. T. (1995). Sensitivity of MMPI-2 validity scales to underreporting of symptoms. *Psychological Assessment, 7,* 419–423.

Bagby, R. M., Buis, T., & Nicholson, R. A. (1995). Relative effectiveness of the standard validity scales in detecting fake-bad and fake-good responding: Replication and extension. *Psychological Assessment, 7,* 84–92.

Bagby, R. M., Gillis, J. R., & Rogers, R. (1991). Effectiveness of the Millon Clinical Multiaxial Inventroy Validity Index in the detection of random responding. *Psychological Assessment, 3,* 285–287.

Bagby, R. M., Gillis, J. R., Toner, B. B., & Goldberg, J. (1991). Detecting fake-good and fake-bad responding on the Millon Clinical Multiaxial Inventory-II. *Psychological Assessment, 3,* 496–498.

Bagby, R. M., Rogers, R., & Buis, T. (1994). Detecting malingering and defensive responding on the MMPI-2 in a forensic inpatient sample. *Journal of Personality Assessment, 62,* 191–203.

Bailey, W. J., Shinedling, M. M., & Payne, I. R. (1970). Obese individuals' perception of body image. *Perceptual and Motor Skills, 31,* 617–618.

Baker, L. L., & Jessup, B. A. (1980). The psychophysiology of affective verbal and visual information processing in depression. *Cognitive Therapy and Research, 4,* 135–148.

Bakker, C., Bakker-Rabdau, M., & Breit, S. (1978). The measurement of assertiveness and aggressiveness. *Journal of Personality Assessment, 42,* 277–284.

Baldwin, M. V. (1950). A note regarding the suggested use of the Bender-Gestalt Test as a measure of school readiness. *Journal of Clinical Psychology, 6,* 412.

Ball, J. D., Archer, R. P., Gordon, R. A., & French, J. (1991). Rorschach Depression Indices with children and adolescents: Concurrent validity findings. *Journal of Personality Assessment, 57,* 465–476.

Ball, J. D., Archer, R. P., & Imhof, E. A. (1994). Time requirements of psychological testing: A survey of practitioners. *Journal of Personality Assessment, 63,* 239–249.

Bamgbose, O., Smith, G. T., Jesse, R. C., & Groth-Marnat, G. (1980). A survey of the current and future directions of professional psychology in acute general hospitals. *Clinical Psychologist, 33,* 24–25.

Bandura, A. (1986). *Social foundations of thought and action: A social cognitive theory.* Englewood Cliffs, NJ: Prentice-Hall.

Bank, L., & Patterson, G. R. (1992). The use of structural equation modeling in combining data from different types of assessment. In J. C. Rosen & P. McReynolds (Eds.), *Advances in psychological assessment* (Vol. 8, pp. 41–74). New York: Plenum Press.

Bannatyne, A. (1974). Diagnosis—a note on recategorization of the WISC scaled scores. *Journal of Learning Disabilities, 7,* 272–273.

Barber, J., & Muenz, L. R. (in press). The role of avoidance and obsessiveness in matching patients to cognitive and interpersonal psychotherapy: Empirical findings from the Treatment for Depression Collaborative Research Program. *Journal of Consulting and Clinical Psychology.*

Barber, T. X., & Silver, M. J. (1968). Fact, fiction and the experimenter bias effect. *Psychological Bulletin Monograph Supplement, 70,* 1–29.

Barlow, D. H. (1988). *Anxiety and its disorders: The nature and treatment of anxiety and panic.* New York: Guilford.

Barlow, D. H. (Ed.). (1993). *Clinical handbook of psychological disorders* (3rd ed.). New York: Guilford Press.

Barlow, D. H., Craske, M. G., Cerny, J. A., & Klosko, J. S. (1989). Behavioral treatment of panic disorder. *Behavior Therapy, 20,* 261–282.

Barnett, O. W., & Hamberger, L. K. (1992). The assessment of maritally violent men on the California Psychological Inventory. *Violence and Victims, 7,* 15–28.

Bar-on, R. (1998). *BarOn emotional quotient inventory (EQ-i-tm): Technical manual.* Toronto, Canada: Multi-Health Systems.

Barona, A., Reynolds, C., & Chastain, R. (1984). A demographically based index of premorbid intelligence for the WAIS-R. *Journal of Consulting and Clinical Psychology, 26,* 74–75.

Barrios, B. A., & Hartman, D. P. (1988). Fears and anxieties in children. In E. J. Mash & L. G. Terdel (Eds.), *Behavioral assessment of childhood disorders* (2nd ed.). New York: Guilford Press.

Bartlett, J. A., Schleifer, S. J., Johnson, R. L., & Keller, S. E. (1991). Depression in inner city adolescents attending an adolescent medicine clinic. *Journal of Adolescent Health, 12,* 316–318.

Basham, R. B. (1992). Clinical utility of the MMPI research scales in the assessment of adolescent acting out. *Psychological Assessment, 4,* 483–492.

Baucom, D. H. (1980). Independent CPI masculinity and femininity scales: Psychological correlates and a sex role typology. *Journal of Personality Assessment, 44,* 262–271.

Baucom, D. H. (1985). Review of the California Psychological Inventory. In J. V. Mitchel (Ed.), *The ninth mental measurements yearbook.* Highland Park, NJ: Gryphon Press.

Bauer, R. M. (1995). The flexible battery approach to neuropsychological assessment. In R. D. Vanderploeg (Ed.), *Clinician's guide to neuropsychological assessment* (pp. 259–290). Hillsdale, NJ: Erlbaum.

Bauer, R. M., Tobias, B., & Valenstein, E. (1993). Amnesic disorders. In K. M. Heilman & E. Valenstein (Eds.), *Clinical neuropsychology* (3rd ed.). New York: Oxford University Press.

Beck, A. T. (1967a). *The diagnosis and management of depression.* Philadelphia: University of Pennsylvania Press.

Beck, A. T. (1967b). *Depression: Clinical, experimental, and theoretical aspects.* New York: Harper & Row.

Beck, A. T., & Beck, R. W. (1972). Screening depressed patients in family practice: A rapid technique. *Postgraduate Medicine, 52,* 81–85.

Beck, A. T., Rial, W. Y., & Rickels, K. (1974). Short form of depression inventory: Cross-validation. *Psychological Reports, 34,* 1184–1186.

Beck, A. T., Rush, A. J., Shaw, B. F., & Emery, G. (1979). *Cognitive therapy of depression.* New York: Guilford Press.

Beck, A. T., Steer, R. A., & Garbin, M. (1988). Psychometric properties of the Beck Depression Inventory: Twenty-five years of evaluation. *Clinical Psychology Review, 8,* 77–100.

Beck, A. T., Ward, C. H., Mendelson, M., Mock, J., & Erbaugh, J. (1961). An inventory for measuring depression. *Archives of General Psychiatry, 4,* 561–571.

Beck, H. S. (1955). A study of the applicability of the H-T-P to children with respect to the drawn house. *Journal of Clinical Psychology, 11,* 60–63.

Beck, H. S. (1959). A comparison of convulsive organics, non-convulsive organics, and non-organic public school children. *American Journal of Mental Deficiency, 63,* 866–875.

Beck, J. G., & Heimberg, R. G. (1983). Self-report assessment of assertive behavior: A critical analysis. *Behavior Modification, 7,* 451–487.

Beck, J. G., & Zebb, B. J. (1994). Behavioral assessment and treatment of panic disorder: Current status, future directions. *Behavior Therapy, 25,* 581–611.

Beck, J. S. (1994). *Cognitive therapy: Basics and beyond.* New York: Guilford.

Beck, S. J. (1937). Introduction to the Rorschach method: A manual of personality study. *American Orthopsychiatric Association Monograph, 1.*

Beck, S. J. (1945). *Rorschach's test: A variety of personality pictures* (Vol. 2). New York: Grune & Stratton.

Beck, S. J. (1951). The Rorschach test: A multi-dimensional test of personality. In H. H. -Anderson & G. Anderson (Eds.), *An introduction to projective techniques.* Englewood Cliffs, NJ: Prentice-Hall.

Beck, S. J. (1960). *The Rorschach experiment.* New York: Grune & Stratton.

Beck, S. J. (1961). *Rorschach's test: Basic processes* (Vol. 1). New York: Grune & Stratton.

Beck, S. J. (1968). Reality, Rorschach and perceptual theory. In A. I. Rabin (Ed.), *Projective techniques in personality assessment.* New York: Springer.

Beck, S. J., & Molish, H. B. (1967). *Rorschach's test. Vol. II: A variety of personality pictures* (2nd ed.). New York: Grune & Stratton.

Beck, S. J., Rabin, A. I., Thieson, W. C., Molish, H. B., & Thetford, W. N. (1950). The normal personality as projected in the Rorschach test. *Journal of Psychology, 30,* 241–298.

Beier, E. G. (1966). *The silent language of psychotherapy.* New York: Aldine.

Bellack, A. S., & Hersen, M. (Eds.). (1988). *Behavioral assessment: A practical handbook* (3rd ed.). New York: Pergamon.

Bellack, A. S., Hersen, M., & Turner, S. M. (1979). Relationship of roleplaying and knowledge of appropriate behavior to assertion in the natural environment. *Journal of Consulting and Clinical Psychology, 47,* 670–678.

Bellak, L. (1954). *The Thematic Apperception Test and the Children's Apperception Test in clinical use.* New York: Grune & Stratton.

Bellak, L. (1975). *The TAT, CAT, and SAT in clinical use* (3rd ed.). New York: Grune & Stratton.

Bellak, L. (1986). *The TAT, CAT, and SAT in clinical use* (4th ed.). New York: Grune & Stratton.

Bellak, L. (1993). *The TAT, CAT, and SAT in clinical use* (5th ed.). New York: Grune & Stratton.

Bellak, L., & Bellak, S. S. (1973). *Manual: Senior apperception test.* Larchmont, NY: C.P.S.

Bellak, L., & Hurvich, M. S. (1966). A human modification of the Children's Apperception Test (CAT-H). *Journal of Projective Techniques and Personality Assessment, 30,* 228–242.

Bellak., L., Hurvich, M., & Gediman, H. (1973). *Ego functions in schizophrenics, neurotics, and normals.* New York: Wiley.

Bem, D., & Funder, D. C. (1978). Predicting more of the people more of the time: Assessing the personality of situations. *Psychological Review, 85,* 485–501.

Bender, L. (1938). *A visual motor gestalt test and its clinical uses.* Research Monograms No. 3. New York: American Orthopsychiatric Association.

Bender, L. (1970). Use of the visual motor Gestalt test in the diagnosis of learning disabilities. *Journal of Special Education, 4,* 29–39.

Benedict, R. H., Schretlen, D., & Bobholz, J. H. (1992). Concurrent validity of three WAIS-R short forms in psychiatric inpatients. *Psychological Assessment, 4,* 322–328.

Ben-Porath, Y. S., & Butcher, J. (1989). The psychometric stability of rewritten MMPI items. *Journal of Personality Assessment, 53,* 645–653.

Ben-Porath, Y. S., Butcher, J. N., & Graham, J. (1991). Contribution of the MMPI-2 content scales to the differential diagnosis of schizophrenia and major depression. *Psychological Assessment, 3,* 634–640.

Ben-Porath, Y. S., Hostetler, K., Butcher, J. N., & Graham, J. R. (1989). New subscales for the MMPI-2 Social Introversion (Si) Scale. *Psychological Assessment, 1,* 169–174.

Ben-Porath, Y. S., McCulley, E., & Almagor, M. (1993). Incremental validity of the MMPI-2 content scales in the assessment of personality and psychopathology by self-report. *Journal of Personality Assessment, 61,* 557–575.

Ben-Porath, Y. S., Slutsky, W. S., & Butcher, J. N. (1989). A real-data simulation of computerized adaptive administration of the MMPI. *Psychological Assessment: A Journal of Consulting and Clinical Psychology, 1,* 18–22.

Benson, D. F. (1993). Aphasia. In K. M. Heilman & E. Valenstein (Eds.), *Clinical neuropsychology* (3rd ed., pp. 17–36). New York: Oxford University Press.

Benton, A. L. (1968). Differential behavioral effects in frontal lobe disease. *Neuropsychologia, 6,* 53–60.

Benton, A. L. (1974). *The Revised Visual Retention Test* (4th ed.). New York: Psychological Corporation.

Benton, A. L. (1979). Visuoperceptive, visuospatial, and visuoconstructive disorders. In K. M. Heilman & E. Valenstein (Eds.), *Clinical neuropsychology* (pp. 186–232). New York: Oxford University Press.

Benton, A. L. (1992). Clinical neuropsychology: 1960–1990. *Journal of Clinical and Experimental Neuropsychology, 14,* 407–417.

Benton, A. L., & Hamsher, K. (1983). *Multilingual Aphasia Examination.* Iowa City: AJA Associates.

Benton, A. L., & Hamsher, K. (1989). *Multilingual Aphasia Examination.* Iowa City, Iowa: AJA Associates.

Berg, F. W., Franzen, M., & Wedding, D. (1987). *Screening for brain impairment.* New York: Springer.

Bergin, A. E. (1971). The evaluation of therapeutic outcomes. In A. E. Bergin & S. L. Garfield (Eds.), *Handbook of psychotherapy and behavior change.* New York: Wiley.

Bernstein, L. (1956). The examiner as an inhibiting factor in clinical testing. *Journal of Consulting Psychology, 20,* 287–290.

Berry, K. K. (1975). Teacher impressions of psychological reports on children. *Journal of Pediatric Psychology, 3,* 11–14.

Berry, T. R., Baer, R. A., & Harris, M. J. (1991). Detection of malingering on the MMPI: A meta-analysis. *Journal of Personality Assessment, 11,* 585–598.

Berzins, J. I. (1977). Therapist-patient matching. In A. S. Guzman & A. M. Razin (Eds.), *Effective psychotherapy: A handbook of research* (pp. 222–251). New York: Pergamon.

Beutler, L. E. (1979). Toward specific psychological therapies for specific conditions. *Journal of Consulting and Clinical Psychology, 47,* 882–897.

Beutler, L. E. (1983). *Eclectic psychotherapy: A systematic approach.* New York: Pergamon.

Beutler, L. E. (1989). Differential treatment selection: The role of diagnosis in psychotherapy. *Psychotherapy, 26,* 271–281.

Beutler, L. E. (1995a). The clinical interview. In L. E. Beutler & M. R. Berren (Eds.), *Integrative assessment of adult personality* (pp. 96–120). New York: Guilford.

Beutler, L. E. (1995b). Integrating and communicating findings. In L. E. Beutler & M. R. Berren (Eds.), *Integrative assessment of adult personality* (pp. 25–64). New York: Guilford.

Beutler, L. E., & Berren, M. R. (Eds.). (1995). *Integrative assessment of personality.* New York: Guilford.

Beutler, L. E., & Clarkin, I. F. (1990). *Systematic treatment selection: Toward targeted therapeutic interventions.* New York: Brunner/Mazel.

Beutler, L. E., Consoli, A. J., & Williams, R. E. (1994). Integrative and eclectic therapies in practice. In B. Bongar & L. E. Beutler (Eds.), *Foundations of psychotherapy: Theory, research, and practice* (pp. 264–269). New York: Oxford University Press.

Beutler, L. E., & Crago, M. (1986). Strategies and techniques of prescriptive psychotherapeutic intervention. In R. E. Hales & A. J. Francis (Eds.), *American Psychiatric Association Annual Review* (Vol. 6, pp. 378–397). Washington, DC: American Psychiatric Press.

Beutler, L. E., Crago, M., & Arizmendi, T. G. (1986). Therapist variables in psychotherapy process and outcome. In S. L. Garfield & A. E. Bergin (Eds.), *Handbook of psychotherapy and behavioral change* (3rd ed., pp. 257–310). New York: Wiley.

Beutler, L. E., Engle, D., Mohr, D., Daldrup, R. J., Bergan, J., Meredith, K., & Merry, W. (1991). Predictors of differential response to cognitive, experential, and self-directed psychotherapeutic procedures. *Journal of Consulting and Clinical Psychology, 59,* 1–8.

Beutler, L. E., Karacan, I., Anch, A. M., Salis, P., Scott, F. B., & Williams, R. (1975). MMPI and MIT discriminators of biogenic and psychogenic impotence. *Journal of Consulting and Clinical Psychology, 43,* 899–903.

Beutler, L. E., Sandowicz, M., Fisher, D., & Albanese, A. L. (1996). Resistance in psychotherapy: What can be concluded from empirical research. *In Session: Psychotherapy in Practice, 2,* 77–86.

Beutler, L. E., Wakefield, P., & Williams, R. E. (1994). Use of psychological tests/instruments for treatment planning. In M. Maruish (Ed.), *Use of psychological testing for treatment planning and outcome assessment* (pp. 55–74). Hillsdale, NJ: Erlbaum.

Beutler, L. E., & Williams, O. (in press). *A software package for treatment planning.* Minneapolis, MN: New Standards Incorporated.

Beutler, L. E., Williams, R. E., Wakefield, P. J., & Entwistle, S. R. (1995). Bridging scientist and practitioner perspectives in clinical psychology. *American Psychologist, 50,* 984–994.

Bigler, E. D., Rosa, L., Schultz, F., Hall, S., & Harris, J. (1989). Rey Auditory Verbal Learning and Rey-Osterrieth Complex Figure Design Test performance in Alzheimer's diseases and closed head injury. *Journal of Clinical Psychology, 45,* 277–280.

Billings, A. G., & Moos, R. H. (1986). Psychosocial processes of remission in unipolar depression: Comparing depressed patients with matched community controls. *Journal of Consulting and Clinical Psychology, 3,* 314–325.

Billingslea, F. Y. (1948). The Bender-Gestalt: An objective scoring method and validating data. *Journal of Clinical Psychology, 4,* 1–27.

Binet, A., & Simon, T. (1908). The development of infant intelligence. *The Annals of Psychology, 14,* 1–94.

Binet, A., & Simon, T. (1916). *The development of intelligence in children* (E. S. Kit, Trans.). Baltimore: Williams & Wilkins.

Birchler, G. R. (1989). Review of behavioral assessment. A practical handbook (3rd ed.). *Behavioral Assessment, 11,* 384–388.

Black, F. W., & Bernard, B. A. (1984). Constructional apraxia as a function of lesion locus and size in patients with focal brain damage. *Cortex, 20,* 111–120.

Blaha, J., & Wallbrown, F. H. (1984). Hierarchical analyses of the WISC and WISC-R: Synthesis and clinical implications. *Journal of Clinical Psychology, 40,* 556–571.

Blaha, J., & Wallbrown, F. H. (1996). Hierarchical factor structure of the Wechsler Intelligence Scale for Children-III. *Psychological Assessment, 8,* 214–218.

Blain, G. H., Bergner, R. M., Lewis, M. L., & Goodstein, M. A. (1981). The use of objectively scorable House-Tree-Person indicators to establish child abuse. *Journal of Clinical Psychology, 37,* 667–673.

Blakey, W. A., Fantuzzo, J. W., Gorsuch, R. L., & Moon, G. W. (1987). A peer-mediated competency-based training package for administering and scoring the WAIS-R. *Professional Psychology, 18,* 17–20.

Blakey, W. A., Fantuzzo, J. W., & Moon, G. W. (1985). An automated competency-based model for teaching skills in the administration of the WAIS-R. *Professional Psychology, 16,* 641–647.

Blanchard, E. B., Schwarz, S. P., Neff, D. F., & Gerardi, M. A. (1988). Prediction of outcome from the self-regulatory treatment of irritable bowel syndrome. *Behavior Research and Therapy, 26,* 187–190.

Blatt, S. J., & Allison, J. (1968). The intelligence test in personality assessment. In A. I. Rabin (Ed.), *Projective techniques in personality assessment* (pp. 421–460). New York: Springer.

Blatt, S. J., Zuroff, D. C., Quinlan, D. M., & Pilkonis, P. A. (1996). Interpersonal factors in brief treatment of depression: Further analysis of the National Institute of Mental Health treatment of depression collaborative research program. *Journal of Consulting and Clinical Psychology, 64,* 162–171.

Blau, T. (1984). *The psychologist as expert witness.* New York: Wiley.

Blum, G. S. (1950). *The Blacky pictures and manual.* New York: Psychological Corp.

Blum, G. S. (1962). A guide for research use of the Blacky pictures. *Journal of Projective Techniques, 26,* 3–29.

Blum, G. S. (1968). Assessment of psychodynamic variables by the Blacky Pictures. In P. McReynolds (Ed.), *Advances in psychological assessment* (Vol. 1, pp. 150–168). Palo Alto, CA: Science & Behavior Books.

Blum, L. H., Davidson, H. H., & Fieldsteel, N. D. (1975). *A Rorschach workbook.* New York: International Universities Press.

Boerger, A. R. (1975). *The utility of some alternative approaches to MMPI scale construction.* Doctoral dissertation, Kent State University, Kent, OH.

Bolander, K. (1977). *Assessing personality through tree drawings.* New York: Basic Books.

Boll, T. J. (1974). Behavioral correlates of cerebral damage in children age 9–14. In R. M. Reitan & L. A. Davison (Eds.), *Clinical neuropsychology: Current status and application.* Washington, DC: V. H. Winston & Sons.

Boll, T. J. (1981). The Halstead-Reitan neuropsychological battery. In S. B. Filskov & T. J. Boll (Eds.), *Handbook of clinical neuropsychology* (pp. 577–607). New York: Wiley.

Bolton, B. (1992). Review of the California Psychological Inventory, revised edition. In J. J. Framer & J. C. Conely (Eds.), *Eleventh mental measurements yearbook* (pp. 558–562). Lincoln, NE: Buros Institute of Mental Measurements.

Bonarius, H. (1984). Prediction or anticipation: Some implications of personal construct psychology for professional practice. *Jyvaskyla Studies in Education: Psychology and Social Research, 54,* 190–206.

Boone, D. E. (1990). Short forms of the WAIS-R with psychiatric inpatients: A comparison of techniques. *Journal of Clinical Psychology, 46,* 197–200.

Borkowski, J. G. (1985). Signs of intelligence: Strategy, generalization and metacognition. In S. R. Yussen (Ed.), *The growth of reflection in children* (pp. 105–144). Orlando, FL: Academic Press.

Bornstein, P. H., Bridgewater, C. A., Hickey, J. S., & Sweeney, T. M. (1980). Characteristics and trends in behavioral assessment: An archival analysis. *Behavioral Assessment, 2,* 125–133.

Bornstein, R. A. (1983). Verbal I.Q.—Performance I.Q. discrepancies on the Wechsler Adult Intelligence Scale-Revised in patients with unilateral or bilateral cerebral dysfunction. *Journal of Consulting and Clinical Psychology, 51,* 779–789.

Bornstein, R. A. (1985). Normative data on selected neuropsychological measures from a nonclinical sample. *Journal of Clinical Psychology, 41,* 651–659.

Bornstein, R. A. (1986). Normative data on intermanual differences on three tests of motor performance. *Journal of Clinical and Experimental Neuropsychology, 8,* 12–20.

Bornstein, R. A., & Matarazzo, J. D. (1982). Wechsler VIQ versus PIQ differences in cerebral dysfunction: A literature review with emphasis on sex differences. *Journal of Clinical Neuropsychology, 4,* 319–334.

Bornstein, R. A., Suga, L., & Prifitera, A. (1987). Incidence of verbal I.Q.—performance I.Q. discrepancies at various levels of education. *Journal of Clinical Psychology, 43,* 387–389.

Borus, J. F., Howes, M. J., Devins, N. P., & Rosenberg, R. (1988). Primary health care providers' recognition and diagnosis of mental disorders in their patients. *General Hospital Psychiatry, 10,* 317–321.

Botwinick, J., Storandt, M., Berg, F. W., & Boland, S. (1988). Senile dementia of the Alzheimer type: Subject attrition and testability in research. *Archives of Neurology, 45,* 493–496.

Bowden, S. C., & Smith, L. C. (1994). What does the Austin Maze measure? *Australian Psychologist, 29,* 34–37.

Bowler, R. M., Thakler, C. D., & Becker, C. E. (1986). California Neuropsychological Screening Battery (CNC/BI & II). *Journal of Clinical Psychology, 42,* 946–955.

Bradway, K., Lion, E., & Corrigan, H. (1946). The use of the Rorschach in a psychiatric study of promiscuous girls. *Rorschach Research Exchange, 9,* 105–110.

Brandt, D. (1982). Comparison of various WISC-R summary scores for a psychiatric sample. *Journal of Clinical Psychology, 38,* 830–837.

Brandt, H., & Giebink, J. (1968). Concreteness and congruence in psychologists' reports to teachers. *Psychology in the Schools, 5,* 87–89.

Brar, H. S. (1970). Rorschach content responses of East Indian psychiatric patients. *Journal of Projective Techniques and Personality Assessment, 34,* 88–94.

Braun, P. R., & Reynolds, D. J. (1969). A factor analysis of a 100-item fear survey inventory. *Behavior Research and Therapy, 7,* 399–402.

Brawman-Mintzer, O., Lydiard, R. B., Emmanuel, N., Payeur, R., Johnson, M., Roberts, J., Jarrell, M. P., & Ballenger, J. C. (1993). Psychiatric comorbidity in patients with generalized anxiety disorder. *American Journal of Psychiatry, 150,* 1216–1218.

Brayfield, A. H. (Ed.). (1965). Testing and public policy. *American Psychologist, 20,* 857–1005.

Breen, M. J. (1982). Comparison of educationally handicapped student's scores on the Revised Developmental Test of Visual-Motor Integration and Bender-Gestalt. *Perceptual and Motor Skills, 54,* 1227–1230.

Brehm, S. S., & Brehm, J. W. (1981). *Psychological reactance: A theory of freedom and control.* New York: Wiley.

Brenda, G. L., & Waehler, C. A. (1994). The ups and downs of TAT Card 17BM. *Journal of Personality Assessment, 63,* 161–172.

Brennan, M., & Reichard, S. (1943). Use of the Rorschach test in predicting hypnotizability. *Bulletin of the Menninger Clinic, 7,* 183–187.

Brenner, O. C., & Bertsch, T. M. (1983). Do assertive people prefer merit pay? *Psychological Reports, 52,* 595–598.

Brewin, C. R. (1985). Depression and causal attributions: What is their relation? *Psychological Bulletin, 98,* 297–309.

Brewin, C. R. (1996). Theoretical foundations of cognitive-behavior therapy for anxiety and depression. *Annual Review of Psychology, 47,* 33–57.

Bricklin, H. (1984). *Bricklin Perceptual Scales.* Furlong, PA: Village Publishing Center.

Brink, T. L., Yesavage, J. A., Owen, L., Heersema, P. H., Adey, M., & Rose, T. L. (1982). Screening tests for geriatric depression. *Clinical Gerontology, 1,* 37–43.

Brodsky, S. L. (1972). Shared results and open files with the client. *Professional Psychology, 3,* 362–364.

Brooker, B. H., & Cyr, J. J. (1986). Tables for clinicians to use to convert WAIS-R short forms. *Journal of Clinical Psychology, 42,* 982–986.

Brooks, B. L., & Hosie, T. W. (1984). Assumptions and interpretations of the SOMPA in estimating learning potential. *Counselor Education and Supervision, 23,* 290–299.

Broughton, R. (1984). A prototype strategy for construction of personality scales. *Journal of Personality and Social Psychology, 47,* 1334–1346.

Brown, C., Schulberg, H. C., & Madonia, M. J. (1995). Assessing depression in primary care practice with the Beck Depression Inventory and the Hamilton Rating Scale for Depression. *Psychological Assessment, 7,* 59–65.

Brown, D., & Tolor, A. (1957). Human figure drawings as indicators of sexual identification and inversion. *Perceptual and Motor Skills, 7,* 199–211.

Brown, F. (1953). An exploratory study of dynamic factors in the content of the Rorschach protocol. *Journal of Projective Techniques, 17,* 251–279.

Brown, F. G. (1965). The Bender-Gestalt and acting out. In L. E. Apt & S. L. Weissman (Eds.), *Acting out: Theoretical and clinical aspects.* New York: Grune & Stratton.

Brown, F. G. (1979). The SOMPA: A system of measuring potential abilities. *School Psychology Digest, 8,* 37–46.

Brown, G. G., Spicer, K. B., & Robertson, W. M. (1989). Neuropsychological signs of lateralized arteriovenous malformations: Comparisons with ischemic stroke. *The Clinical Neuropsychologist, 3,* 340–352.

Brown, L. (1990). Taking account of gender in the clinical assessment interview. *Professional Psychology, 21,* 12–17.

Brown, T. A., DiNardo, P. A., & Barlow, D. H. (1994). *Anxiety Disorders Interview Schedule for DSM-IV.* Albany, NY: Graywind Publications.

Brown, T. A., O'Leary, T. A., & Barlow, D. H. (1993). Generalized anxiety disorder. In D. H. Barlow (Ed.), *Clinical handbook of psychological disorders* (2nd ed, pp. 127–188). New York: Guilford.

Brown, W. R., & McGuire, J. M. (1976). Current assessment practices. *Professional Psychology, 7,* 475–484.

Buck, J. N. (1948). The H-T-P technique, a qualitative and quantitative scoring manual. *Journal of Clinical Psychology, 4,* 317–396.

Buck, J. N. (1966). *The House-Tree-Person technique: Revised manual.* Beverly Hills, CA: Western Psychological Services.

Buck, J. N., & Hammer, E. F. (Eds.). (1969). *Advances in House-Tree-Person Techniques: Variations and applications.* Los Angeles: Western Psychological Services.

Buhler, C., & LeFever, D. (1947). A Rorschach study on the psychological characteristics of alcoholics. *Quarterly Journal of Studies on Alcoholism, 8,* 197–260.

Burger, G. K. (1975). A short form of the California Psychological Inventory. *Psychological Reports, 37,* 179–182.

Burgess, A. W., Flint, J., & Adsheed, H. (1992). Factor structure of the Wechsler Adult Intelligences Scale-Revised (WAIS-R): A clinical sample. *British Journal of Clinical Psychology, 31,* 336–338.

Burgess, A. W., & Hartman, C. R. (1990). Children's drawings. *Child Abuse and Neglect, 17,* 161–168.

Burley, T., & Handler, L. (1970). *Creativity, empathy, and intuition in DAP interpretation.* Unpublished manuscript.

Burns, R. C. (1970). *Kinetic Family Drawings (KFD): An introduction to understanding children through kinetic drawings.* New York: Brunner/Mazel.

Burns, R. C. (1982). *Self-growth in families: Kinetic Family Drawings (KFD): Research and application.* New York: Brunner/Mazel.

Burns, R. C. (1987). *Kinetic House-Tree-Person (KHTP).* New York: Brunner/Mazel.

Burns, R. C., & Kaufman, S. H. (1970). *Kinetic Family Drawings (KFD): An introduction to understanding children through kinetic drawings.* New York: Brunner/Mazel.

Burns, R. C., & Kaufman, S. H. (1972). *Action, styles, and symbols in Kinetic Family Drawings (KFD).* New York: Brunner/Mazel.

Buros, O. K. (Ed.). (1978). *Eighth mental measurements yearbook.* Highland Park, NJ: Gryphon Press.

Burt, D. B., Zembar, M. J., & Niederehe, G. (1995). Depression and memory impairment: A meta-analysis of the association, its pattern, and specificity. *Psychological Bulletin, 117,* 285–305.

Butcher, J. N. (1979). Use of the MMPI in personnel selection. In J. N. Butcher (Ed.), *New developments in the use of the MMPI.* Minneapolis: University of Minnesota Press.

Butcher, J. N. (1985). Current developments in MMPI use: An international perspective. In C. D. Speilberger & J. N. Butcher (Eds.), *Advances in personality assessment* (Vol 4, pp. 83–94). Hillsdale, NJ: Erlbaum.

Butcher, J. N. (1987). *Computerized psychological assessment: A practitioner's guide.* New York: Basic Books.

Butcher, J. N. (1990). *The MMPI-2 in psychological treatment.* New York: Oxford University Press.

Butcher, J. N. (Ed.). (in press). *Objective psychological assessment in managed health care: A practitioner's guide.* New York: Oxford University Press.

Butcher, J. N., Ball, B., & Ray, E. (1964). Effects of socioeconomic level on MMPI differences in Negro-white college students. *Journal of Consulting Psychology, 11,* 83–87.

Butcher, J. N., & Clark, L. A. (1979). Recent trends and application. In J. N. Butcher (Ed.), *New developments in the use of the MMPI.* Minneapolis: University of Minnesota Press.

Butcher, J. N., Dahlstrom, W. G., Graham, J. R., Tellegen, A., & Kaemmer, B. (1989). *Manual for administration and scoring: MMPI-2.* Minneapolis: University of Minnesota Press.

Butcher, J. N., Graham, J. R., Williams, C. L., & Ben-Porath, Y. S. (1990). *Development and use of the MMPI-2 content scales.* Minneapolis: University of Minnesota Press.

Butcher, J. N., & Hostetler, K. (1990). Abbreviating MMPI item administration: What can be learned from the MMPI for the MMPI-2? *Psychological Assessment, 2,* 12–21.

Butcher, J. N., & Pancheri, P. (1976). *A handbook of cross-national MMPI research.* Minneapolis: University of Minnesota Press.

Butcher, J. N., & Pope, K. S. (1989). *MMPI-2: A practical guide to psychometric, clinical, and ethical issues.* Unpublished manuscript.

Butcher, J. N., & Williams, C. L. (1992). *Essentials of MMPI-2 and MMPI-A interpretation.* Mineaopolis: University of Minnesota Press.

Butcher, J. N., Williams, C. L., Graham, J. R., Archer, R. P., Tellegen, A., Ben-Porath, Y. S., & Kraemmer, B. (1992). *MMPI-A (Minnesota Multiphasic Personality Inventory-Adolescent): Manual for administration, scoring, and interpretation.* Minneapolis: University of Minnesota Press.

Butler, M., Retzlaff, P., & Vanderploeg, R. (1991). Neuropsychological test usage. *Professional Psychology, 22,* 510–512.

Butters, N., Grant, I., Haxby, J., Judd, L. L., Martin, A., McClelland, J., Pequegnat, W., Schacter, D., & Stover, E. (1990). Assessment of AIDS-related cognitive changes: Recommendations of the NIMH Workgroup on neuropsychological assessment approaches. *Journal of Clinical and Experimental Neuropsychology, 12,* 963–978.

Byerly, E. C., & Carlson, W. A. (1982). Comparison among inpatients, outpatients, and normals on three self-report depression inventories. *Journal of Clinical Psychology, 38,* 797–804.

Byrne, D. (1964). Repression-sensitization as a dimension of personality. In B. A. Mohrer (Ed.), *Progress in experimental personality research* (Vol. 1). New York: Academic Press.

Byrne, D., Golightly, C., & Sheffield, J. (1965). The repression-sensitization scale as a measure of adjustment: Relationship with the CPI. *Journal of Consulting Psychology, 29,* 585–589.

Cacioppo, J. T., Glass, C. R., & Merluzzi, T. V. (1979). Self-statements and self-evaluations: A cognitive response analysis of heterosocial anxiety. *Cognitive Therapy and Research, 3,* 249–262.

Caldwell, A. B. (1969). *MMPI critical items.* Unpublished Mimeograph (available from Caldwell Report, 1545 Sawtelle Blvd., Suite 14, Los Angeles, CA 90025).

Caldwell, A. B. (1988). *MMPI supplemental scale manual.* Los Angeles: Caldwell Report.

Caldwell-Colbert, A. T., & Robinson, W. L. (1984). Utilization and predicted trends of behavioral inventories. *Journal of Behavioral Assessment, 6,* 189–196.

Calvin, J. (1975). *A replicated study of the concurrent validity of the Harris subscales for the MMPI.* Unpublished doctoral dissertation, Kent State University, Kent, OH.

Campione, J. C., & Brown, A. L. (1978). Toward a theory of intelligence: Contributions from research with retarded children. *Intelligence, 2,* 279–304.

Canter, A. (1963). A background interference procedure for graphomotor tests in the study of deficit. *Perceptual and Motor Skills, 16,* 914.

Canter, A. (1966). A background interference procedure to increase sensitivity of the Bender-Gestalt Test to organic brain disorder. *Journal of Consulting Psychology, 30,* 91–97.

Canter, A. (1971). A comparison of the background interference procedure effect in schizophrenic, non-schizophrenic, and organic patients. *Journal of Clinical Psychology, 27,* 473–474.

Canter, A. (1976). *The Canter background interference procedure for the Bender-Gestalt Test: Manual for administration, scoring, and interpretation.* Nashville, TN: Counselor Recordings and Tests.

Carkhuff, R. R. (1969). *Helping and human relations. I: Selection and training. II: Practice and research.* New York: Holt, Rinehart & Winston.

Carlson, J. G. (1982). Some concepts of perceived control and their relationship to bodily self-control. *Journal of Biofeedback and Self-Regulation, 7,* 341–375.

Carlson, K., Tucker, G., Harrow, M., & Quinlan, D. (1971). Body image and mental illness. In I. Jakab (Ed.), *Psychiatry and art: Vol. 3. Conscious and unconscious expressive art.* Basel, Switzerland: Karger.

Carnes, G. D., & Bates, R. (1971). Rorschach anatomy response correlates in rehabilitation of failure subjects. *Journal of Personality Assessments, 35,* 527–537.

Cartwright, R. D. (1986). Affect and dream work from an information processing point of view. *Journal of Mind and Behavior, 7,* 411–428.

Caruso, K. R. (1988). *Manual for the Projective Storytelling Cards.* Sarasota, FL: Professional Resource Exchange.

Carvajal, H., Gerber, J., Hewes, P., & Weaver, K. A. (1987). Correlations between scores on Stanford-Binet IV and Wechsler Adult Intelligence Scale-Revised. *Psychological Reports, 56,* 189–190.

Cass, W. A., & McReynolds, P. A. (1951). A contribution to Rorschach norms. *Journal of Consulting and Clinical Psychology, 15,* 178–183.

Cattell, R. B. (1963). Theory of fluid and crystalized intelligence: A critical experiment. *Journal of Educational Psychology, 54,* 1–22.

Cattell, R. B., Eber, H. W., & Tatsuoka, M. M. (1970). *Handbook for the Sixteen Personality Factor Questionnaire.* Champaign, IL: Institute for Personality and Abilities Testing.

Cauthen, N. R., Sandman, C. A., Kilpatrick, D. G., & Deabler, H. L. (1969). DAP correlates of Sc scores on the MMPI. *Journal of Projective and Personality Assessment, 33,* 262–264.

Cavalli, M., De Renzi, E., Faglioni, P., & Vitale, A. (1981). Impairment of right brain-damaged patients on a linguistic cognitive task. *Cortex, 17,* 545–556.

Cella, D. (1984). The modified WAIS-R: An extension and revision. *Journal of Clinical Psychology, 40,* 801–804.

Chambers, W. J., Puig-Antich, J., Hirsch, M., Paez, P., Ambrosini, P. J., Tabrizi, M. A., & Davies, M. (1985). The assessment of affective disorders in children and adolescents by semistructured interview: Test-retest reliability of the Schedule for Affective Disorders and Schizophrenia for School Age, Present Episode Version. *Archives of General Psychiatry, 42,* 696–702.

Chantler, J. R., Pelco, L., & Martin, P. (1993). The psychological evaluation of sexual abuse using the Louisville Behavior Checklist and Human Figure Drawing. *Child Abuse and Neglect, 17,* 271–279.

Chapman, L. J., & Chapman, J. P. (1967). Genesis of popular but erroneous psychodiagnostic observations. *Journal of Abnormal Psychology, 72,* 193–204.

Chappell, P. A., & Steitz, J. A. (1993). Young children's human figure drawings and cognitive development. *Perceptual and Mortor Skills, 76,* 611–617.

Chase, T. N., Fedio, P., Foster, N. L., Brooks, R., DiChio, G., & Mansi, L. (1984). Wechsler Adult Intelligence Scale performance. Cortical localization by fluorodeoxyglucose F18-positive emmision tomography. *Archives of Neurology, 41,* 1244–1247.

Cheung, F. M. (Ed.). (1986). *The Chinese Minnesota Multiphasic Personality Inventory: Research and applications* [Occasional paper no. 12]. Hong Kong: The Chinese University of Hong Kong, Centre for Hong Kong Studies.

Cheung, F. M., & Song, W. (1989). A review on the clinical applications of the Chinese MMPI. *Psychological Assessment, 1,* 230–237.

Cheung, F. M., Zhao, J., & Wu, C. Y. (1992). Chinese MMPI profiles among neurotic patients. *Psychological Assessment, 4,* 214–218.

Choca, J., Shanley, L. A., Peterson, C. A., & Van Denburg, E. (1990). Racial bias and the MCMI. *Journal of Personality Assessment, 54,* 479–490.

Choca, J. P., Shanley, L. A., & Van Denburg, E. (1992). *Interpretive guide to the Millon Clinical Multiaxial Inventory.* Washington, DC: American Psychological Association.

Choca, J. P., Shanley, L. A., & Van Denburg, E. (1996). *Interpretive guide to the Millon Clinical Multiaxial Inventory* (2nd ed.). Washington, DC: American Psychological Association.

Choca, J. P., Van Denburg, E., Bratu, M. E., & Meaghur, S. (1995, March). *Personality changes of psychiatric patients with aging.* Paper presented at the midwinter meeting of the Society for Personality Assessment, Denver, CO.

Chojnacki, J. T., & Walsh, W. B. (1992). The consistency of scores and configural patterns between MMPI and MMPI-2. *Journal of Personality Assessment, 59,* 276–289.

Chusmir, L. H. (1985). Short-form scoring for McClelland's version of the TAT. *Perceptual and Motor Skills, 61,* 1047–1052.

Cicchetti, D. V. (1994). Guidelines, criteria, and rules of thumb for evaluating normed and standardized assessment instruments in psychology. *Psychology Assessment, 6,* 284–290.

Ciminero, A. R., Calhoun, K. S., & Adams, H. E. (Eds.). (1977). *Handbook of behavioral assessment.* New York: Wiley-Interscience.

Clark, C. G., & Miller, H. L. (1971). Validation of Gilberstadt and Duker's 8-6 profile type on a black sample. *Psychological Reports, 29,* 259–264.

Clark, M. E. (1996). MMPI-2 Negative treatment indicators content and content component scales: Clinical correlates and outcome prediction for men with chronic pain. *Psychological Assessment, 8,* 32–38.

Clawson, A. (1959). The Bender Visual Motor Gestalt Test as an index of emotional disturbance in children. *Journal of Projective Techniques, 23,* 198–206.

Clawson, A. (1962). *The Bender Visual Motor Gestalt for children: A manual.* Beverly Hills, CA: Western Psychological Services.

Clopton, J. R. (1978a). A note on the MMPI as a suicide predictor. *Journal of Consulting and Clinical Psychology, 46,* 335–336.

Coan, R. (1956). A factor analysis of Rorschach determinants. *Journal of Projective Techniques, 20,* 280–287.

Coche, E., & Sillitti, J. A. (1983). The Thematic Apperception Test as an outcome measure in psychotherapy. *Psychotherapy: Theory, Research, and Practice, 20,* 41–46.

Cohen, J. (1959). The factorial structure of the WISC at ages 7–6, 10–6, and 13–6. *Journal of Consulting Psychology, 23,* 285–299.

Cohen, R. J., Swerdlik, M. E., & Phillips, S. M. (1996). *Psychological testing and assessment: An introduction to tests and measurement.* Mountain View, CA: Mayfield.

Cojnacki, J. T., & Walsh, W. B. (1992). The consistency of scores and configural patterns between the MMPI and MMPI-2. *Journal of Personality Assessment, 59,* 278–289.

Colby, F. (1989). Usefulness of the K correction in MMPI profiles of patients and non-patients. *Psychological Assessment, 1,* 142–145.

Colligan, R. C., & Offord, K. P. (1989). The aging MMPI: Contemporary norms for contemporary teenagers. *Mayo Clinic Proceedings, 64,* 3–27.

Collins, D. J. (1967). Psychological selection of drill sergeants: An exploratory attempt in a new program. *Military Medicine, 132,* 713–715.

Cone, J. D. (1977). The relevance of reliability and validity for behavioral assessment. *Behavior Therapy, 8,* 411–426.

Cone, J. D. (1978). The behavioral assessment grid (BAG): A conceptual framework and taxonomy. *Behavior Therapy, 9,* 882–888.

Conoley, J. C., & Impara, J. C. (Eds.). (1995). *The twelfth mental measurements yearbook.* Lincoln: University of Nebraska Press.

Conoley, J. C., & Kramer, J. J. (Eds.). (1989). *The tenth mental measurements yearbook.* Lincoln: University of Nebraska Press.

Cook, K. (1991). Integrating kinetic family drawings into Adlerian life-style interviews. *Individual Psychology: Journal of Adlerian Theory, Research, & Practice, 47,* 521–526.

Cook, M. L., & Peterson, C. (1986). Depressive irrationality. *Cognitive Therapy and Research, 10,* 293–298.

Cooney, N. L., Kadden, R. M., & Litt, M. D. (1990). A comparisons of methods assessing sociopathy in male and female alcoholics. *Journal of Studies on Alcohol, 51,* 42–48.

Cooper, H. M., & Rosenthal, R. (1980). Statistical versus traditional procedures for summarizing research findings. *Psychological Bulletin, 87,* 442–449.

Cooper, J. O., Heron, T. B., & Heward, W. L. (1987). *Applied behavior analysis.* Columbus, OH: Merrill.

Cooper, W. H. (1981). Ubiquitous halo. *Psychological Bulletin, 90,* 218–244.

Cooper, Z., & Fairburn, C. G. (1987). The eating disorder examination: A semistructured interview for the assessment of the specific psychopathology of eating disorders. *International Journal of Eating Disorders, 6,* 136–141.

Corcoran, K., & Fischer, J. (1994). *Measures for clinical practice: A sourcebook* (2nd ed.). (Vols. 1–2). New York: Macmillan.

Cordoni, B. K., O'Donnell, J. P., Ramaniah, N. V., Kurtz, J., & Rosenshein, K. (1981). Wechsler Adult Intelligence Scale patterns for learning disabled young adults. *Journal of Learning Disabilities, 14,* 404–407.

Cormier, W. H., & Cormier, L. S. (1990). *Interviewing strategies for helpers* (3rd ed.). Monterey, CA: Brooks-Cole.

Coryell, W. H., Akiskal, H. S., Leon, A. C., Winokur, G., Masur, J. D., Mueller, T. I., & Keller, M. B. (1994). The time course of nonchronic major depressive disorder. *Archives of General Psychiatry, 51,* 405–410.

Costa, P. T., Zonderman, A. B., Williams, R. B., & McRae, R. R. (1985). Content and comprehensiveness of the MMPI: An item factor analysis in a normal adult sample. *Journal of Personality and Social Psychology, 48,* 925–933.

Costantino, G., & Malgady, R. G. (1983). Verbal fluency of Hispanic, Black and White children on TAT and TEMAS, a new thematic apperception test. *Hispanic Journal of Behavioral Sciences, 5,* 199–206.

Costantino, G., Malgady, R. G., Casullo, M. M., & Castillo, A. (1991). Cross-cultural standardization of the TEMAS in three Hispanic subcultures. *Journal of Behavioral Sciences, 13,* 48–62.

Costantino, G., Malgady, R. G., Colon-Malgady, G., & Bailey, J. (1992). Clinical utility of the TEMAS with nonminority children. *Journal of Personality Assessment, 59,* 433–438.

Costantino, G., Malgady, R. G., & Rogler, L. H. (1988). *Technical manual: TEMAS thematic apperception test.* Los Angeles: Western Psychological Services.

Costantino, G., Malgady, R. G., Rogler, L. H., & Tsui, E. C. (1988). Discriminant analysis of clinical outpatients and public school children by TEMAS: A thematic apperception test for Hispanics and Blacks. *Journal of Personality Assessment, 52,* 670–678.

Costello, C. G. (1958). The Rorschach records of suicidal patients. *Journal of Projective Techniques, 22,* 272–275.

Costello, E. J., Benjamin, R., Angold, A., & Silver, D. (1991). Mood variability in adolescence: A study of depressed and nondepressed comorbid patients. *Journal of Affective Disorders, 23,* 199–212.

Costello, E. J., Edelbrock, C. S., & Costello, A. J. (1985). Validity of the NIMH Diagnostic Interview Schedule for Children: A comparison between psychiatric and pediatric referrals. *Journal of Abnormal and Child Psychology, 13,* 579–595.

Costello, E. J., Edelbrock, C. S., Duncan, M. K., & Kalas, R. (1984). *Testing of the NIMH Diagnostic Interview Schedule for Children (DISC) in a clinical population. Final report to the*

Center for Epidemiological Studies, National Institute for Mental Health. Pittsburgh: University of Pittsburgh.

Costello, R. M., & Wicott, K. A. (1984). Impression management and testing for locus of control in an alcoholic sample. *International Journal of the Addictions, 19,* 45–56.

Cox, F. N., & Sarason, S. B. (1954). Test anxiety and Rorschach performance. *Journal of Abnormal and Social Psychology, 49,* 371–377.

Craig, P. L. (1979). Neuropsychological assessment in public psychiatric hospitals: The current state of the practice. *Clinical Neuropsychology, 1,* 1–7.

Craig, R. J. (1993). *Psychological assessment with the Millon Clinical Multiaxial Inventory (II): An interpretive guide.* Odessa, FL: Psychological Assessment Resources.

Craig, R. J. (1995). Clinical diagnoses and MCMI codetypes. *Journal of Clinical Psychology, 51,* 352–360.

Crary, W. G., & Johnson, C. W. (1981). Mental status examination. In C. W. Johnson, J. R. Snibbe, & L. A. Evans (Eds.), *Basic psychopathology: A programmed text* (2nd ed., pp. 56–57). Lancaster, PA: MTP Press.

Craske, M. G., & Barlow, D. H. (1993). Panic and agoraphobia. In D. H. Barlow (Ed.), *Clinical handbook of psychological disorders,* 1–47. New York: Guilford.

Crawford, J. R., & Allan, K. M. (1996). WAIS-R subtest scatter: Base rate data from a healthy UK sample. *British Journal of Clinical Psychology, 35,* 235–247.

Crawford, J. R., Stewart, L. E., & Moore, J. W. (1989). Demonstration of savings on the AVLT and development of a parallel form. *Journal of Clinical and Experimental Neuropsychology, 11,* 975–981.

Crenshaw, D. A., Bohn, S., Hoffman, M., Matheus, J. M., & Offenbach, S. G. (1968). The use of projective methods in research: 1947–1965. *Journal of Projective Techniques and Personality Assessment, 32,* 2–9.

Crockett, D., Tallman, K., Hurwitz, T., & Kozak, J. (1988). Neuropsychological performance in psychiatric patients with or without documented brain dysfunction. *International Journal of Neuroscience, 41,* 71–79.

Cronbach, L. J. (1978). Black Intelligence Test of Cultural Homogeneity: A review. In O. K. Buros (Ed.), *The eighth mental measurements yearbook* (Vol. 1, p. 250). Highland Park, NJ: Gryphon Press.

Crookes, T. G. (1984). A cognitive peculiarity specific to schizophrenia. *Journal of Clinical Psychology, 40,* 893–896.

Cross, D. T., & Burger, G. (1982). Ethnicity as a variable in responses to California Psychological Inventory items. *Journal of Personality Assessment, 46,* 155–158.

Crowne, D. P., & Marlowe, D. (1964). *The approval motive: Studies in evaluative dependence.* New York: Wiley.

Crumpton, E. (1956). The influence of color on the Rorschach test. *Journal of Projective Techniques, 20,* 150–158.

Culbertson, F. M., Feral, C. H., & Gabby, S. (1989). Pattern analysis of Wechsler Intelligence Scale for Children-revised profiles of delinquent boys. *Journal of Clinical Psychology, 45,* 651–660.

Culkin, J., & Perrotto, R. S. (1985). Assertiveness factors and depression in a sample of college women. *Psychological Reports, 57,* 1015–1020.

Cummings, N. A. (1991). The somatizing patient. In C. A. Austad & W. A. Berman (Eds.), *Psychotherapy in managed care: The optimal use of time and resources* (pp. 234–237). Washington, DC: American Psychological Association.

Cunningham, T. R., & Thorp, R. G. (1981). The influence of settings on accuracy and reliability of behavioral observation. *Behavioral Assessment, 3,* 67–78.

Dahlstrom, W. G. (1969). Recurrent issues in the development of the MMPI. In J. N. Butcher (Ed.), *MMPI: Research developments and clinical applications.* New York: McGraw-Hill.

Dahlstrom, W. G. (1980). Altered versions of the MMPI. In W. G. Dahlstrom & L. Dahlstrom (Eds.), *Basic readings on the MMPI: A new selection on personality measurement* (pp. 386–393). Minneapolis: University of Minnesota Press.

Dahlstrom, W. G., Lachar, D., & Dahlstrom, L. E. (1986). *MMPI patterns of American minorities.* Minneapolis: University of Minnesota Press.

Dahlstrom, W. G., & Welsh, G. S. (1960). *An MMPI handbook: A guide to use in clinical practice and research.* Minneapolis: University of Minnesota Press.

Dahlstrom, W. G., Welsh, G. S., & Dahlstrom, L. E. (1972). *An MMPI handbook: Vol. 1. Clinical Interpretation.* Minneapolis: University of Minnesota Press.

Dahlstrom, W. G., Welsh, G. S., & Dahlstrom, L. E. (1975). *An MMPI handbook: Vol. 2. Research developments and applications.* Minneapolis: University of Minnesota Press.

Daldrup, F. J., Beutler, L. E., Engle, D., & Greenberg, L. S. (1988). *Focused expressive psychotherapy: Freeing the overcontrolled patient.* New York: Pergamon.

Dana, R. H. (1955). Clinical diagnosis and objective TAT scoring. *Journal of Abnormal and Social Psychology, 50,* 19–24.

Dana, R. H. (1965). Review of the Rorschach. In O. K. Buros (Ed.), *Sixth mental measurements yearbook* (pp. 492–495). Highland Park, NJ: Gryphon.

Dana, R. H. (1968). Six constructs to define Rorschach M. *Journal of Projective Techniques and Personality Assessment, 32,* 138–145.

Dana, R. H. (1982). *A human science model for personality assessment with projective techniques.* Springfield, IL: Charles C. Thomas.

Dana, R. H. (1984). Personality assessment: Practice and teaching for the next decade. *Journal of Personality Assessment, 48,* 46–57.

Dana, R. H. (1985). Thematic Apperception Test (TAT). In C. S. Newmark (Ed.), *Major psychological assessment instruments* (pp. 89–134). Newton, MA: Allyn & Bacon.

Dana, R. H., & Cocking, R. R. (1968). Cue parameters, cue probabilities, and clinical judgment. *Journal of Clinical Psychology, 24,* 475–480.

Dana, R. H., Field, K., & Bolton, B. (1983). Variations of the Bender-Gestalt Test: Implications for training and practice. *Journal of Personality Assessment, 47,* 76–84.

Das, J. P., & Naglieri, J. A. (1994). *Das-Naglieri Cognitive Assessment System—Standardization Test Battery.* Chicago: Riverside Press.

Das, J. P., Naglieri, J. A., & Kirby, J. R. (1994). *Assessment of cognitive processes: The PASS theory of intelligence.* Boston, MA: Allyn & Bacon.

Datel, W. E., Hall, F. D., & Rufe, C. P. (1965). Measurement of achievement motivation in army security agency foreign language candidates. *Educational and Psychological Measurement, 25,* 539–545.

Davies, A. (1968). The influence of age on Trail Making performance. *Journal of Consulting and Clinical Psychology, 24,* 96–98.

Davis, G. L., Hoffman, R. G., & Nelson, K. S. (1990). Differences between Native Americans and whites on the California Psychological Inventory. *Psychological Assessment, 2,* 238–242.

Davis, W. E., Beck, S. J., & Ryan, T. A. (1973). Race-related and education related MMPI profile differences among hospitalized schizophrenics. *Journal of Clinical Psychology, 29,* 478–479.

Dawes, R. M., & Corrigan, B. (1974). Linear models in decision making. *Psychological Bulletin, 81,* 95–106.

Deabler, H. L. (1969). The H-T-P in group testing and as a screening device. In J. N. Buck & E. F. Hammer (Eds.), *Advances in the House-Tree-Person Technique: Variations and applications.* Los Angeles: Western Psychological Services.

Dean, R. S. (1982). Neuropsychological assessment. In T. Kratochwill (Ed.), *Advances in school psychology* (Vol. 2). Hillsdale, NJ: Erlbaum.

Debord, J. B. (1989). Paradoxical interventions: A review of the recent literature. *Journal of Counseling and Development, 67,* 394–398.

DeFrancesco, J. J., & Taylor, J. (1993). A validation on the revised socialization scale of the California psychological Inventory. *Journal of Psychopathology and Behavioral Assessment, 15,* 53–56.

Delaney, R. C. (1982). Screening for organicity: The problem of subtle neuropsychological deficit and diagnosis. *Journal of Clinical Psychology, 38,* 843–846.

Delatte, J. G., & Hendrickson, N. J. (1982). Human figure drawing size as a measure of self-esteem. *Journal of Personality Assessment, 46,* 603–606.

Delay, J., Pichot, P., Lemperiere, T., & Mirouze, R. (1963). Classification of depressive states: Agreement between etiology and symptomatology: 2. Results of Beck's Questionnaire. *Encephale, 52,* 497–505.

Del Greco, L., Breitbach, L., & McCarthy, R. H. (1981). The Rathus Assertiveness Schedule modified for early adolescents. *Journal of Behavioral Assessment, 3,* 321–328.

Del Greco, L., Breitbach, L., Rumer, S., McCarthy, R. H., & Suissa, S. (1986). Further examination of the reliability of the Modified Rathus Assertiveness Schedule. *Adolescence, 21,* 483–485.

D'Elia, L. F., Boone, K. B., & Mitrushina, A. M. (in press). *Handbook of normative data for neuropsychological assessment.* New York: Oxford University Press.

Delis, D. C., Kramer, J. H., Kaplan, E., & Ober, B. A. (1987). *California Verbal Learning Test: Adult Version.* San Antonio, TX: The Psychological Corporation.

Deniston, W. M., & Ramanaiah, N. V. (1993). California Psychological Inventory and the five-factor model of personality. *Psychological Reports, 73,* 491–496.

Denman, S. (1984). *Denman Neuropsychology Memory Scale.* Charleston, SC: S. B. Denman.

Derogatis, L. R. (1992). *BSI: Administration, scoring, and procedures manual-II* (2nd ed.). Baltimore: Clinical Psychometric Research.

desRosiers, G. (1992). Primary or depressive dementia: Clinical features. *International Journal of Geriatric Psychiatry, 7,* 629–638.

desRosiers, G., & Kavanagh, D. (1987). Cognitive assessment in closed head injury: Stability, validity, and parallel forms for two neuropsychological measures of recovery. *International Journal of Clinical Neuropsychology, 9,* 162–173.

Detterman, D. K. (1994). Intelligence and the brain. In P. A. Vernon (Ed.), *The neuropsychology of individual differences* (pp. 35–57). New York: Academic Press.

Dibner, A. S., & Korn, E. J. (1969). Group administration of the Bender-Gestalt test to predict early school performance. *Journal of Clinical Psychology, 49,* 822–834.

Dicken, C. F. (1960). Simulated patterns on the California Psychological Inventory. *Journal of Counseling Psychology, 7,* 24–31.

DiClemente, C. (1986). Self-efficacy and the addictive behaviors. *Journal of Social and Clinical Psychology, 4,* 302–315.

Dies, R. R. (1972). Personal gullibility or pseudodiagnosis: A further test of the "fallacy of personal validation." *Journal of Clinical Psychology, 28,* 47–50.

Diller, L., Ben-Yishay, Y., Gertsman, L. J., Goodkin, R., Gordon, W., & Weinberg, J. (1976). *Studies in cognition and rehabilitation in hemiplegia* (Rehabilitation Monograph, No. 50). New York: New York University Medical Center, Institute of Rehabilitation Medicine.

Dimatteo, M. R., & Taranta, A. (1976). Nonverbal communication and physician-patient rapport: An empirical study. *Professional Psychology, 10,* 540–547.

Dixon, W. E., & Anderson, T. (1995). Establishing covariance continuity between the WISC-R and the WISC-III. *Psychological Assessment, 7,* 115–117.

Dobbins, C., & Russell, E. W. (1990). Left temporal lobe brain damage pattern on the Wechsler Adult Intelligence Scale. *Journal of Clinical Psychology, 46,* 863–868.

Dodrill, C. B., & Troupin, A. S. (1975). Effects of repeated administration of a comprehensive neuropsychological battery among chronic epileptics. *Journal of Nervous and Mental Diseases, 161,* 185–190.

Donahue, D., & Sattler, J. M. (1971). Personality variables affecting WAIS scores. *Journal of Consulting Psychology, 36,* 441.

Donnelly, E. F., & Murphy, D. L. (1974). Primary affective disorder: Bender-Gestalt sequence of placement as an indicator of impulse control. *Perceptual and Motor Skills, 38,* 1079–1082.

Dorken, H. A. (1954). A psychometric evaluation of 68 medical interns. *Journal of the Canadian Medical Association, 70,* 41–45.

Dougherty, T. W., Ebert, R. J., & Callender, J. C. (1986). Policy capturing in the employment interview. *Journal of Applied Psychology, 71,* 9–15.

Dove, A. (1968). Taking the Chitling Test. *Newsweek, 72,* 51–52.

Dowd, E. T., Milne, C. R., & Wise, S. L. (1991). The Therapeutic Reactance Scale: A measure of psychological reactance. *Journal of Counseling and Development, 69,* 541–545.

Dowd, E. T., & Wallbrown, F. (1993). Motivational components of client reactance. *Journal of Counseling and Development, 71,* 533–538.

Draguns, J. G., Haley, E. M., & Phillips, L. (1967). Studies of the Rorschach content: A review of the research literature: Part 1. Traditional content categories. *Journal of Projective Techniques and Personality Assessment, 31,* 3–32.

Drake, L. E. (1946). A social I.E. scale for the MMPI. *Journal of Applied Psychology, 30,* 51–54.

Dritschel, B. H., Williams, K., & Cooper, P. J. (1991). Cognitive distortions among women experiencing bulimic episodes. *International Journal of Eating Disorders, 10,* 547–555.

DuAlba, L., & Scott, R. L. (1993). Somatization and malingering for workers' compensation applicants: A cross-cultural MMPI study. *Journal of Clinical Psychology, 49,* 913–917.

Dudek, S. Z. (1968). M and active energy system correlating Rorschach M with ease of creative expression. *Journal of Projective Techniques and Personality Assessment, 32,* 453–461.

Dudley, H. K., Craig, E. M., Mason, M., & Hirsch, S. M. (1976). Drawings of the opposite sex: Continued use of the Draw-A-Person test and young state hospital patients. *Journal of Adolescence, 5,* 201–219.

Durand, V. M. (1990). *Severe behavior problems: A functional communication training approach* (pp. 80–82). New York: Guilford.

Durand, V. M., Blanchard, E. B., & Mindell, J. A. (1988). Training in projective testing: Survey of clinical training directors and internship directors. *Professional Psychology: Research and Practice, 19,* 236–238.

Duthie, B., & Vincent, K. R. (1986). Diagnostic hit rates of high point codes for the Diagnostic Inventory of Personality and Symptoms using random assignment, base rates, and probability scales. *Journal of Clinical Psychology, 42,* 612–614.

Dye, O. A. (1979). Effects of practice on Trail Making performance. *Perceptual and Motor Skills, 48,* 296.

Earls, R., Reich, W., Jung, K. G., & Cloninger, C. R. (1988). Psychopathology in children of alcoholic and antisocial parents. *Alcoholism: Clinical and Experimental Research, 12,* 481–487.

Edelbrock, C., Costello, A. J., Duncan, M. K., Kales, R., & Conover, N. C. (1985). Age differences in the reliability of the psychiatric interview of the child. *Child Development, 56,* 265–275.

Edell, W. S. (1987). Role of structure in disordered thinking in borderline and schizophrenic disorders. *Journal of Personality Assessment, 51,* 23–41.

Edwards, A. L. (1957). *The social desirability variables in personality assessment and research.* New York: Dryden Press.

Edwards, A. L. (1964). Social desirability and performance on the MMPI. *Psychometrika, 29,* 295–308.

Edwards, D. W., Morrison, T. L., & Weissman, H. N. (1993). The MMPI and MMPI-2 in an outpatient sample: Comparisons of code types, validity scales, and clinical scales. *Journal of Personality Assessment, 61,* 1–18.

Egeland, B. R. (1969). Examiner expectancy: Effects on the scoring of the WISC. *Psychology in the Schools, 6,* 313–315.

Eichler, R. M. (1951). Experimental stress and alleged Rorschach indices of anxiety. *Journal of Abnormal and Social Psychology, 46,* 169–177.

Eisdorfer, C. (1963). The WAIS performance of the aged: A retest evaluation. *Journal of Gerontology, 18,* 169–172.

Elashoff, J., & Snow, R. E. (Eds.). (1971). *Pygmalion revisited.* Worthington, OH: C.A. Jones.

Elion, V. H., & Megargee, E. I. (1975). Validity of the MMPI Pd scale among black males. *Journal of Consulting and Clinical Psychology, 43,* 166–172.

Elkin, I., Shea, T., Watkins, J. T., Imber, S. D., Sotsky, S. M., Collins, J. F., Glass, D. R., Pilkonis, P. A., Leber, W. R., Docherty, J. P., Feister, S. J., & Parloff, M. B. (1989). National Institute of Mental Health treatment of depression collaborative research program. *Archives of General Psychiatry, 46,* 971–982.

Elliot, L. L. (1960). *WAF performance on the California Psychological Inventory* (Wright Air Development Division Technical Note 60-218). Lackland AFB, San Antonio, TX: Air Research and Development Command.

Ellis, M. V., Robbins, E. S., Schult, D., Ladny, N., & Baker, J. (1990). Anchoring errors in clinical judgments: Type I error, adjustment or mitigation. *Journal of Counseling Psychology, 37,* 343–351.

Elstein, A. A. (1965). Behavioral correlates of the Rorschach shading determinant. *Journal of Consulting Psychology, 29,* 231–236.

Embretson, S. (1986). Intelligence and its measurement: Extending contemporary theory to existing tests. In R. J. Sternberg (Ed.), *Advances in the psychology of human intelligence* (Vol. 3, pp. 335–368). Hillsdale, NJ: Erlbaum.

Endicott, J., & Spitzer, R. L. (1978). A diagnostic interview: The schedule for affective disorders and schizophrenia. *Archives of General Psychiatry, 35,* 837–844.

Enelow, A. J., & Wexler, M. (1966). *Psychiatry in the practice of medicine.* New York: Oxford University Press.

Engel, R., & Fay, W. H. (1972). Visual evoked responses at birth, verbal scores at three years, and I.Q. at four years. *Developmental Medicine and Child Neurology, 14,* 283–289.

Entwisle, D. R. (1972). To dispel fantasies about fantasy-based measures of achievement motivation. *Psychological Bulletin, 77,* 377–391.

Eppinger, M. G., Craig, P. L., Adams, R. L., & Parsons, O. A. (1987). The WAIS-R Index for estimating premorbid intelligence: Cross-validation and clinical utility. *Journal of Consulting and Clinical Psychology, 55,* 86–90.

Equal Employment Opportunity Commission (EEOC). (1970). Guidelines on employee selection procedures. *Federal Register, 35,* 12333–12336.

Erginel, A. (1972). On the test-retest reliability of the Rorschach. *Journal of Personality Assessment, 36,* 203–212.

Erickson, R. C., Caslyn, D. A., & Scheupbach, C. S. (1978). Abbreviating the Halstead-Reitan Neuropsychological Test Battery. *Journal of Clinical Psychology, 42,* 946–955.

Eron, L. D. (1950). A normative study of the Thematic Apperception Test. *Psychological Monographs, 64,* 315.

Eslinger, P. J., Damasio, A. R., & Benton, A. L. (1984). *The Iowa Screening Battery for Mental Decline.* Iowa City: University of Iowa.

Exner, J. E. (1961). The influence of achromatic color in Cards IV and VI of the Rorschach. *Journal of Projective Techniques, 25,* 38–41.

Exner, J. E. (1969). *The Rorschach systems.* New York: Grune & Stratton.

Exner, J. E. (1974). *The Rorschach: A comprehensive system* (Vol. 1). New York: Wiley.

Exner, J. E. (1978). *The Rorschach: A comprehensive system: Vol. 2. Current research and advanced interpretations.* New York: Wiley.

Exner, J. E. (1979). *The effects of voluntary restraint on Rorschach retests.* Workshops Study No. 258 (unpublished), Rorschach Workshops.

Exner, J. E. (1983). Rorschach assessment. In I. B. Weiner (Ed.), *Clinical methods in clinical psychology* (2nd ed.). New York: Wiley.

Exner, J. E. (1984). *A computer program to assist in Rorschach interpretation* (Rev. ed.). Bayville, NY: Rorschach Workshops.

Exner, J. E. (1986). *The Rorschach: A comprehensive system: Vol. 1. Basic foundations* (2nd ed.). New York: Wiley.

Exner, J. E. (1988). Problems with brief Rorschach protocols. *Journal of Personality Assessment, 52,* 640–647.

Exner, J. E. (1990). *A Rorschach workbook for the Comprehensive System* (3rd ed.). Asheville, NC: Rorschach Workshops.

Exner, J. E. (1991). *The Rorschach: A comprehensive system: Vol. 2. Current research and advanced interpretation* (2nd ed.). New York: Wiley.

Exner, J. E. (1993). *The Rorschach: A comprehensive system: Vol. 1. Basic foundations* (3rd ed.). New York: Wiley.

Exner, J. E. (1995). *The Rorschach: A comprehensive system: Vol. 3. Assessing children and adolescents.* New York: Wiley.

Exner, J. E., Armbuster, G. L., & Viglione, D. (1978). The temporal stability of some Rorschach features. *Journal of Personality Assessment, 42,* 474–482.

Exner, J. E., Armbuster, G. L., Walker, E. J., & Cooper, W. H. (1975). *Anticipation of elective surgery as manifest in Rorschach records.* Workshops Study No. 213 (unpublished), Rorschach Workshops.

Exner, J. E., & Bryant, E. L. (1974). Rorschach responses of subjects recently divorced or separated. Workshops Study No. 206 (unpublished), Rorschach Workshops.

Exner, J. E., & Exner, D. E. (1972). How clinicians use the Rorschach. *Journal of Personality Assessment, 36,* 403–408.

Exner, J. E., & Hillman, L. (1984). A comparison of content distributions for the records of 76 paranoid schizophrenics and 76 nonparanoid schizophrenics. Workshops Study No. 293 (unpublished), Rorschach Workshops.

Exner, J. E., & Kazaoka, K. (1978). *Dependency gestures of 16 assertiveness trainees as related to Rorschach movement responses.* Workshops Study No. 261 (unpublished), Rorschach Workshops.

Exner, J. E., Leura, A. V., & George, L. M. (1976). A replication of the Masling study using four groups of new examiners with two seating arrangements and ride evaluation. Workshops Study No. 256 (unpublished), Rorschach Workshops.

Exner, J. E., & Murillo, L. G. (1973). Effectiveness of regressive ECT with process schizophrenics. *Diseases of the Nervous System, 34,* 44–48.

Exner, J. E., & Murillo, L. G. (1977). A long-term follow up of schizophrenics treated with regressive ECT. *Diseases of the Nervous System, 38,* 162–168.

Exner, J. E., Murillo, L. G., & Sternklar, S. (1979). *Anatomy and X-ray responses among patients with body delusions or body problems.* Workshops Study No. 257 (unpublished), Rorschach Workshops.

Exner, J. E., & Sanglade, A. A. (1992). Rorschach changes following brief and short term therapy. *Journal of Personality Assessment, 59,* 59–71.

Exner, J. E., Thomas, E. A., Cohen, J. B., Ridgeway, E. M., & Cooper, W. H. (1981). Stress indices in the Rorschachs of patients recovering from myocardial infarctions. Workshops Study No. 286 (unpublished), Rorschach Workshops.

Exner, J. E., Thomas, E. A., & Martin, L. S. (1980). *Alterations in G. S. R. and cardiac and respiratory rates in introversives and extratensives during problem solving.* Workshops Study No. 272 (unpublished), Rorschach Workshops.

Exner, J. E., Thomas, E. E., & Mason, B. (1985). Children's Rorschachs: Descriptions and prediction. *Journal of Personality Assessment, 49,* 13–20.

Exner, J. E., & Weiner, I. B. (1995). *The Rorschach: A comprehensive system: Vol. 3. Assessment of children and adolescents* (2nd ed.). New York: Wiley.

Exner, J. E., & Wylie, J. R. (1975). *Attempts at simulation of schizophrenia-like protocols by psychology graduate students* (Workshops Study No. 211, unpublished). Bayville, NY: Rorschach Workshops.

Exner, J. E., & Wylie, J. R. (1977). *Some Rorschach data concerning suicide. Journal of Personality Assessment, 41,* 339–348.

Exner, J. E., Wylie, J. R., Leura, A. V., & Parrill, T. (1977). Some psychological characteristics of prostitutes. *Journal of Personality Assessment, 41,* 474–485.

Exner, J. E., Zalis, T., & Schumacher, J. (1976). *Rorschach protocols of chronic amphetamine users.* Workshops Study No. 233 (unpublished), Rorschach Workshops.

Eysenck, H. J. (1976). Behavior therapy; dogma or applied science? In M. P. Feldman & A. Broadhurst (Eds.), *Theoretical and experimental bases of the behavior therapies.* New York: Wiley.

Eysenck, H. J. (1985). Review of the California Psychological Inventory. In J. V. Mitchell (Ed.), *The ninth mental measurements yearbook* (pp. 252–253). Highland Press, NJ: Gryphon Press.

Eysenck, H. J. (1994). The outcome problem in psychotherapy: What have we learned? *Behavior Research and Therapy, 32,* 477–495.

Eysenck, H. J., & Barrett, P. (1985). Psychophysiology and measurement of intelligence. In C. R. Reynolds & V. L. Wilson (Eds.), *Methodological and statistical advances in the study of individual differences* (pp. 1–49). New York: Plenum Press.

Fals-Stewart, W. (1995). The effect of defensive responding by substance-abusing patients on the Millon Clinical Multiaxial Inventory. *Journal of Personality Assessment, 64,* 540–541.

Fantuzzo, J. W., Blakey, W. A., & Gorsuch, R. L. (1989). *WAIS-R: Administration and Scoring Training Manual.* San Antonio, TX: The Psychological Corporation.

Fantuzzo, J. W., & Moon, G. W. (1984). Competency mandate: A model for teaching skills in the administration of the WAIS-R. *Journal of Clinical Psychology, 40,* 1053–1059.

Farr, S. P., & Martin, P. W. (1988). Neuropsychological dysfunction. In R. L. Greene (Ed.), *The MMPI: Use with special populations* (pp. 214–245). San Diego: Grune & Stratton.

Fauschingbauer, T. R., & Newmark, C. S. (1978). Short forms of the MMPI. Lexington, MA: Heath.

Faust, D. (1991). Forensic neuropsychology: The art of practicing a science that does not yet exist. *Neuropsychology Review, 2,* 205–231.

Faust, D., & Ziskin, J. (1989). Computer-assisted psychological evaluation as legal evidence: Someday my prints will come. *Computers in Human Behavior, 5,* 23–36.

Faust, D., Ziskin, J., & Hiers, J. B. (1991). *Brain damage claims: Coping with neuropsychological evidence* (Vol. 1–2). Los Angeles: Law and Psychology Press.

Feighner, J. P., Robins, E., Guze, S. B., Woodruff, R. A., Winokur, G., & Munoz, R. (1972). Diagnostic criteria for use in psychiatric research. *Archives of General Psychiatry, 26,* 57–63.

Feingold, A. (1983). The validity of the Information and Vocabulary Subtests of the WAIS for predicting college achievement. *Educational and Psychological Measurement, 43,* 1127–1131.

Feldman, S. E., & Sullivan, D. S. (1971). Factors mediating the efforts of enhanced rapport on children's performance. *Journal of Consulting and Clinical Psychology, 36,* 302.

Fernandez-Ballesteros, R., & Staats, A. W. (1992). Paradigmatic behavioral asssessment, treatments, and evaluation: Answering the crisis in behavioral assessment. *Advances in Behavior Research and Therapy, 14,* 1–27.

Field, K., Bolton, B., & Dana, R. H. (1982). An evaluation of three Bender-Gestalt scoring systems as indicators of psychopathology. *Journal of Clinical Psychology, 38,* 838–842.

Filskov, S. B. (1978). *The prediction of impairment from figure copying.* Paper presented at the Southeastern Psychological Association Convention, Atlanta, GA.

Finer, E., Beebe, D. W., & Holmbecke, G. N. (1994). *An evaluation of the BDI general distress at zero scores.* Paper presented to the 102nd annual American Psychological Association Convention, Los Angeles, CA.

Finlayson, M. A. J., & Reitan, R. M. (1980). Effect of lateralized lesions on ipsilateral and contralateral motor functioning. *Journal of Clinical Neuropsychology, 2,* 237–243.

Finn, S. E. (1982). Base rates, utilities, and the *DSM-III*: Shortcomings of fixed rule systems of psychodiagnostics. *Journal of Abnormal Psychology, 48,* 294–302.

Finn, S. E., & Tonsager, M. E. (1992). Therapeutic effects of providing MMPI-2 test feedback to college students awaiting therapy. *Psychological Assessment, 4,* 278–287.

Finney, B. C. (1951). Rorschach test correlates of assaultive behavior. *Journal of Projective Techniques, 15,* 250–254.

First, M. B., Frances, A., Widiger, T. A., Pincus, H. A., & Davis, W. W. (1992). *DSM-IV* and behavioral assessment. *Behavioral Assessment, 14,* 297–306.

First, M. B., Gibbon, M., Williams, J. B., & Spitzer, R. L. (1995). *Users manual for the Mini-SCID (for DSM-IV-version 2).* North Tonewanda, NY: Multi-Health Systems/American Psychiatric Association.

First, M. B., Gibbon, M., Williams, J. B., & Spitzer, R. L. (1996). *Users manual for the Auto SCID-II (for DSM-IV)*. North Tonewanda, NY: Multi-Health Systems/American Psychiatric Association.

First, M. B., Spitzer, R. L., Gibbon, M., & Williams, J. B. W. (1995). The Structured Clinical Interview for DSM III-R Personality Disorders (SCID-II): Description. *Journal of Personality Disorders, 9,* 83–91.

Fischer, S. C., & Turner, R. M. (1978). Standardization of the Fear Survey Schedule. *Journal of Behavior Therapy, 9,* 129–133.

Fisher, D., & Thornton, D. (1993). Assessing risk of re-offending in sexual offenders. *Journal of Mental Health, 150,* 1374–1379.

Fisher, S. (1962). Relationship of Rorschach human percepts to projective descriptions with self reference. *Journal of Projective Techniques, 26,* 231–233.

Flaherty, M. R., & Reutzel, G. (1965). Personality traits of high and low achievers in college. *Journal of Educational Research, 58,* 409–411.

Flaugher, R. L. (1978). The many definitions of test bias. *American Psychologist, 33,* 671–679.

Flaugher, R. L., & Schrader, W. B. (1978). *Eliminating differentially difficult items as an approach to test bias (RB-78-4)*. Princeton, NJ: Educational Testing Service.

Flynn, P. M., McCann, J. T., & Fairbank, J. A. (1995). Issues in the assessment of personality disorder and substance abuse using the Millon Clinical Multiaxial Incentory (MCMI-II). *Journal of Clinical Psychology, 51,* 415–421.

Follette, W. C., & Hayes, S. C. (1992). *Behavioral assessment in the DSM era. Behavioral Assessment, 14,* 293–295.

Folstein, M. F., Romanoski, A. J., Nestadt, G., Chahal, R., Merchant, A., Shapiro, S., Kramer, M., Anthony, J., Gruenberg, E. M., & McHugh, P. R. (1985). Brief report on the clinical reappraisal of the Diagnostic Interview Schedule carried out at the Johns Hopkins site of the Epidemiological Catchment Area Program of the NIMH. *Psychological Medicine, 15,* 809–814.

Folstein, M. F., Folstein, S. E., & McHugh, P. R. (1975). "Mini-mental state." *Journal of Psychiatric Research, 12,* 189–198.

Fordyce, D. J., Roueche, J. R., & Prigatano, G. P. (1983). Enhanced emotional reactions in chronic head trauma patients. *Journal of Neurology, Neurosurgery, and Psychiatry, 46,* 620–624.

Foster, S. L., Bell-Dolan, D. J., & Burge, D. A. (1988). Behavioral observation. In A. S. Bellack & M. Hersen (Eds.), *Behavioral assessment* (3rd ed., pp. 119–160). New York: Pergamon.

Foster, S. L., & Cone, J. D. (1995). Validity issues in clinical assessment. *Psychological Assessment, 7,* 248–260.

Fox, T. J., & Thomas, G. V. (1990). Children's drawings of an anxiety-eliciting topic: Effect on the size of the drawing. *British Journal of Clinical Psychology, 29,* 71–81.

Frances, A., Clarkin, J., & Perry, S. (1984). *Differential therapeutics in psychiatry*. New York: Brunner-Mazel.

Frank, G. (1990). Research on the clinical usefulness of the Rorschach: 1. The diagnosis of schizophrenia. *Perceptual and Motor Skills, 71,* 573–578.

Frank, J. D. (1973). *Persuasion and healing: A comparative study of psychotherapy* (Rev. ed.). Baltimore: Johns Hopkins University Press.

Frederiksen, N. (1986). Toward a broader conception of human intelligence. *American Psychologist, 41,* 445–452.

Free, M. L., & Oei, T. P. S. (1989). Biological and psychological processes in the treatment and maintenance of depression. *Clinical Psychology Review, 9,* 653–688.

French, C. C., & Beaumont, J. G. (1987). The reaction of psychiatric patients to computerized assessment. *British Journal of Clinical Psychology, 26,* 267–278.

Friedman, H. (1952). Perceptual regression in schizophrenia: An hypothesis suggested by the use of the Rorschach test. *Journal of Genetic Psychology, 81,* 63–98.

Friedman, H. S., & Booth-Kewley, S. (1987). The "Disease-prone personality": A meta-analytic view of the construct. *American Psychologist, 42,* 539–555.

Fromm-Auch, D., & Yeudall, L. T. (1983). Normative data for the Halstead-Reitan neuropsychological tests. *Journal of Clinical Neuropsychology, 5,* 221–238.

Frueh, B. C., & Kinder, B. N. (1994). The susceptibility of the Rorschach inkblot test to malingering of combat-related PTSD. *Journal of Personality Assessment, 62,* 280–298.

Fuchs, D., & Fuchs, L. S. (1986). Test procedure bias: A meta-analysis of examiner familiarity effects. *Review of Educational Research, 56,* 243–262.

Fuld, P. A. (1983). Psychometric differentiation of the dementias: An overview. In B. Reisberg (Ed.), *Alzheimer's disease: The standard reference* (pp. 201–210). New York: The Free Press.

Fuld, P. A. (1984). Test profile of cholingeric dysfunction and of Alzheimer's-type dementia. *Journal of Clinical Neuropsychology, 6,* 380–392.

Fuller, G. B., & Chagnon, G. (1962). Factors influencing rotation in the Bender Gestalt performance of children. *Journal of Projective Techniques, 26,* 36–46.

Futch, E. J., & Lisman, S. A. (1977, December). *Behavioral validation of an assertiveness scale: The incongruence of self-report behavior.* Paper presented at the annual meeting of the Association for Advancement of Behavior Therapy, Atlanta, GA.

Fyer, A. J., Endicott, J., Manuzza, S., & Klein, D. F. (1985). *Schedule of Affective Disorders and Schizophrenia-Lifetime version* (modified for the study of anxiety disorders). New York: New York State Psychiatric Institute, Anxiety Disorder Clinic.

Gainotti, G., & Marra, C. (1994). Some aspects of memory disorders clearly distinguish dementia of the Alzheimer's type from depressive pseudo-dementia. *Journal of Clinical and Experimental Neuropsychology, 16,* 65–78.

Galassi, J. P., & Galassi, M. D. (1979). Modification of heterosocial skills deficits. In A. S. - Bellack & M. Hersen (Eds.), *Research and practice in social skills.* New York: Plenum.

Gallagher-Thompson, D., & Steffen, A. M. (1994). Comparative effects of cognitive-behavioral and brief psychodynamic psychotherapies for depressed family caregivers. *Journal of Consulting and Clinical Psychology, 62,* 543–549.

Gallucci, N. T. (1994). Criteria associated with clincial scales and Harris-Lingoes subscales of the Minnesota Multiphasic Personality Inventory with adolescent inpatients. *Psychological Assessment, 6,* 179–187.

Gambrill, E. D. (1977). *Behavior modification.* San Francisco: Jossey-Bass.

Gambrill, E. D., & Richey, C. A. (1975). An assertion inventory for use in assessment and research. *Behavior Therapy, 6,* 550–561.

Garb, H. N. (1984). The incremental validity of information used in personality assessment. *Clinical Psychology Review, 4,* 641–655.

Garb, H. N. (1989). Clinical judgment, clinical training, and professional experience. *Psychological Bulletin, 105,* 387–396.

Garb, H. N. (1992). The trained psychologist as expert witness. *Clinical Psychology Review, 12,* 451–467.

Garb, H. N. (1994a). Judgment research: Implications for clinical practice and testimony in court. *Applied & Preventive Psychology, 3,* 173–183.

Garb, H. N. (1994b). Toward a second generation of statistical prediction rules in psychodiagnostics and personality assessment. *Computers in Human Behavior, 10,* 377–394.

Garcia, J. (1981). The logic and limits of mental aptitude testing. *American Psychologist, 36,* 1172–1180.

Gardner, H. (1983). *Frames of mind: The theory of multiple intelligences.* New York: Basic Books.

Gardner, H. (1993). *Multiple intelligences: The theory in practice.* New York: Basic Books.

Garfield, S. L. (1994). Research on client variables in psychotherapy. In A. E. Bergin & S. L. Garfield (Eds.), *Handbook of psychotherapy and behavior change* (4th ed., pp. 190–228). New York: Wiley.

Garvey, M. J., Hollon, S. D., & DeRubeis, R. J. (1994). Do depressed patients with higher pretreatment stress levels respond better to cognitive therapy than imiprimine? *Journal of Affective Disorders, 32,* 45–50.

Gass, C. S. (1991). MMPI-2 interpretation and closed-head injury: A correction factor. *Psychological Assessment, 3,* 27–31.

Gass, C. S. (1992). MMPI-2 interpretation of patients with cerebrovascular disease: A correction factor. *Archives of Clinical Neuropsychology, 7,* 17–27.

Gass, C. S., & Ansley, J. (1995). Personality assessment of neurologically impaired patients. In J. Butcher (Ed.), *Clinical personality assessment: Practical approaches* (pp. 192–210). New York: Oxford University Press.

Gass, C. S., & Brown, M. C. (1992). Neuropsychological test feedback to patients with brain dysfunction. *Psychological Assessment, 4,* 272–277.

Gass, C. S., & Daniel, S. K. (1990). Emotional impact on Trail Making Test performance. *Psychological Reports, 67,* 435–438.

Gaudino, E. A., Geisler, M. W., & Squires, N. K. (1995). Construct validity in the Trail Making Test: What makes Part B harder? *Journal of Clinical and Experimental Neuropsychology, 17,* 529–535.

Gaw, K. F., & Beutler, L. E. (1995). Integrating treatment recommendations. In L. E. Beutler & M. R. Berren (Eds.), *Integrative assessment of adult personality* (pp. 280–319). New York: Guilford.

Geer, J. H. (1965). The development of a scale to measure fear. *Behavior Research and Therapy, 3,* 45–53.

Geffen, G., Moar, K. J., O'Hanlon, A. P., Clark, C. R., & Geffen, L. B. (1990). Performance measures of 16- to 86-year-old males and females on the Auditory Verbal Learning Test. *The Clinical Neuropsychologist, 4,* 45–63.

Geiselman, R. E., Woodward, J. A., & Beatty, J. (1982). Individual differences in verbal memory performance: A test of alternative information processing models. *Journal of Experimental Psychology: General, 111,* 109–134.

George, B. L., & Waehler, C. A. (1994). The ups and downs of TAT card 17BM. *Journal of Personality Assessment, 63,* 167–172.

Gerstle, R. M., Geary, D. C., Himelstein, P., & Reller-Geary, L. (1988). Rorschach predictors of therapeutic outcome for inpatient treatment of children: A proactive study. *Journal of Clinical Psychology, 44,* 277–280.

Gibbs, R. W., & Beitel, D. (1995). What proverb understanding reveals about how people think. *Psychological Bulletin, 118,* 133–154.

Gibertini, M. Brandenberg, N. A., & Retzlaff, P. D. (1986). The operating characteristics of the Millon Clinical Multiaxial Inventory. *Journal of Personality Assessment, 50,* 554–567.

Gilbert, J. (1969). *Clinical psychological tests in psychiatric and medical practice.* Springfield, IL: Charles C. Thomas.

Gilbert, J., & Hall, M. (1962). Changes with age in human figure drawings. *Journal of Gerontology, 17,* 397–404.

Gill, D. M., Reddon, J. R., Stefanyk, W. O., & Hans, H. S. (1986). Finger tapping: Effects of trials and sessions. *Perceptual and Motor Skills, 62,* 675–678.

Gill, H. S. (1966). Delay of response and reaction to color on the Rorschach. *Journal of Projective Techniques and Personality Assessment, 30,* 545–552.

Gilley, D. W., Wilson, R. S., Fleischmann, D. A., Harrison, D. W., Goetz, C. G., & Tanner, C. M. (1995). Impact of Alzheimer's-type dementia and information source on the assessment of depression. *Psychological Assessment, 7,* 42–48.

Gilmore, D. C., Beehr, T. A., & Love, K. G. (1986). Effects of applicant sex, applicant physical attractiveness, and type of job on interview decisions. *Journal of Occupational Psychology, 59,* 103–109.

Glass, C. R., Merluzzi, T. V., Biever, J. L., & Larsen, K. H. (1982). Cognitive assessment of social anxiety: Development and validation of a self-statement questionnaire. *Cognitive Therapy and Research, 6,* 37–55.

Glueck, S., & Glueck, E. (1950). *Unravelling juvenile delinquency.* New York: Common Wealth Fund.

Glueckauf, R. L., Sechrest, L. B., Bond, G. R., McDonel, E. C. (Eds.). (1993). *Improving assessment in rehabilitation and health*. London: Sage.

Glutting, J. J., McDermott, P. A., Watkins, M. M., Kush, J. C., & Konold, T. R. (1997). The base rate problem and its consequences for interpreting children's ability profiles. *School Psychology Review, 26*, 176–188.

Gocka, E. (1965). [American Lake norms for 200 MMPI scales]. Unpublished raw data.

Goldberg, E., & Bilder, R. M. (1987). The frontal lobes and heirarchical organization of cognitive control. In E. Perecman (Ed.), *The fronal lobes revisited*. New York: IRBN Press.

Goldberg, L. R. (1965). Diagnosticians versus diagnostic signs: The diagnosis of psychosis versus neurosis from the MMPI. *Psychological Monographs, 79*, No. 602.

Golden, C. J. (1976). The identification of brain damage by an abbreviated form of the Halstead-Reitan Neuropsychological Battery. *Journal of Clinical Psychology, 32*, 821–826.

Golden, C. J. (1979). *Clinical interpretation of objective psychological tests*. New York: Grune & Stratton.

Golden, C. J., Purisch, A. D., & Hammeke, T. A. (1985). *Luria-Nebraska Neuropsychological Battery: Forms I and II* (Manual). Los Angeles: Western Psychological Services.

Goldfried, M. R. (1982a). On the history of therapeutic integration. *Behavior Therapy, 13*, 572–593.

Goldfried, M. R. (1982b). *Behavioral assessment: An overview*. In A. S. Bellack, M. Hersen, & A. E. Kazdin (Eds.), *International handbook of behavior modification and therapy*. New York: Pergamon.

Goldfried, M. R. (1983). A behavior therapist looks at reapproachment. *Journal of Humanistic Psychology, 23*, 97–107.

Goldfried, M. R., Stricker, G., & Weiner, I. B. (1971). *Rorschach handbook of clinical and research application*. Englewood Cliffs, NJ: Prentice-Hall.

Goldman, R. D. (1960). Changes in Rorschach performance and clinical improvement in schizophrenia. *Journal of Consulting Psychology, 24*, 403–407.

Goldman, R. D., & Hartig, L. (1976). The WISC may not be a valid predictor of school performance for primary grade minority children. *American Journal of Mental Deficiency, 80*, 583–587.

Goldschmid, M. L. (1967). Prediction of college majors by personality tests. *Journal of Counseling Psychology, 14*, 302–308.

Goldstein, G., & Watson, J. R. (1989). Test-retest reliability of the Halstead-Reitan Battery and the WAIS in a neuropsychiatric population. *The Clinical Neuropsychologist, 3*, 265–272.

Goldstein, J. W. (1974). Motivations for psychoactive drug use among students. In B. Kleinmuntz (Ed.), *Readings in the essentials of abnormal psychology* (pp. 371–375). New York: Harper & Row.

Goncalves, A. A., Woodward, M. J., & Millon, T. (1994). The Millon Clinical Multiaxial Inventory-II. In M. Maruish (Ed.), *The use of psychological testing for treatment planning and outcome assessment* (pp. 161–184). Hillsdale, NJ: Erlbaum.

Gonzales, E. (1982). A cross-cultural comparison of the developmental items of five ethnic groups in the southwest. *Journal of Personality Assessment, 46*, 26–31.

Goodenough, F. (1926). *Measurement of intelligence by drawings*. New York: World Book.

Goodglass, H., & Kaplan, E. (1983). *Boston Diagnostic Aphasia Examination (BDAE)*. Philadelphia: Lea and Febiger. Distributed by Psychological Assessment Resources.

Gordon, N. G., & Swart, E. C. (1973). A comparison of the Harris-Lingoes subscales between the original standardization population and an inpatient Veterans Administration hospital population. *Newsletter for Research in Mental Health and Behavioral Sciences, 15*, 28–31.

Gordon, W. A., Hibbard, M. R., Egelkos, S., & Riley, E. (1991). Issues in the diagnosis of post-stroke depression. *Rehabilitation Psychology, 36*, 71–87.

Gottlieb, A., & Parsons, O. (1960). A coaction compass evaluation of Rorschach determinants in brain damaged individuals. *Journal of Consulting Psychology, 24*, 54–60.

Gough, H. G. (1987). *California Psychological Inventory: Administrator's guide*. Palo Alto, CA: Consulting Psychologists Press.

Gough, H. G. (1948). A new dimension of status: I. Development of a personality scale. *American Sociological Review, 13,* 401–409.

Gough, H. G. (1952). Identifying psychological femininity. *Educational and Psychological Measurement, 12,* 427–439.

Gough, H. G. (1957). *California Psychological Inventory Manual*. Palo Alto, CA: Consulting Psychologists Press.

Gough, H. G. (1964). Academic achievement in high school as predicted from the California Psychological Inventory. *Journal of Educational Psychology, 65,* 174–180.

Gough, H. G. (1965). Cross-cultural validation of a measure of asocial behavior. *Psychological Reports, 17,* 379–387.

Gough, H. G. (1966). Graduation from high school as predicted from the California Psychological Inventory. *Psychology in the Schools, 3,* 208–216.

Gough, H. G. (1968). An interpreter's syllabus for the California Psychological Inventory. In P. McReynolds (Ed.), *Advances in psychological assessment* (Vol. 1, pp. 55–79). Palo Alto, CA: Science and Behavior Books.

Gough, H. G. (1975). *Manual for the California Psychological Inventory* (Rev. ed.). Palo Alto, CA: Consulting Psychologists Press.

Gough, H. G. (1990). The California Psychological Inventory. In C. E. Watkins & V. L. Campbell (Eds.), *Testing in counseling practice* (pp. 37–62). Hillsdale, NJ: Erlbaum.

Gough, H. G. (1992). Assessment of creative potential in psychology and the development of a creative temperament scale for the CPI. In J. C. Rusen & P. McReynolds (Eds.), *Advances in psychological assessment* (Vol 8, pp. 225–257). New York: Plenum.

Gough, H., & Bradley, P. (1992). Delinquent and criminal behavior as assessed by the revised California psychological Inventory. *Journal of Clinical Psychology, 48,* 298–308.

Gough, H. G., Durflinger, G. W., & Hill, R. E., Jr. (1968). Predicting performance in student teaching from the California Psychological Inventory. *Journal of Educational Psychology, 52,* 119–127.

Gough, H. G., & Hall, W. B. (1964). Prediction of performance in medical school from the California Psychological Inventory. *Journal of Applied Psychology, 48,* 218–226.

Gough, H. G., & Kirk, B. A. (1970). Achievement in dental school as related to personality and aptitude variables. *Measurement and Evaluation in Guidance, 2,* 225–233.

Gough, H., & Lanning, K. (1986). Predicting grades in college from the California Psychological Inventory. *Educational and Psychological Measurement, 46,* 205–213.

Gough, H. G., Wenk, E. A., & Rozynko, V. V. (1965). Parole outcome as predicted from the CPI, the MMPI, and a Base Expectancy Table. *Journal of Abnormal Psychology, 70,* 432–441.

Gould, J. (1982). A psychometric investigation of the standard and short form Beck Depression Inventory. *Psychological Reports, 51,* 1167–1170.

Gould, R. A., Otto, M. W., & Pollack, M. H. (1995). A meta-analysis of treatment outcome for panic disorder. *Clinical Psychology Review, 15,* 819–844.

Grace, W. C., & Sweeny, M. E. (1986). Comparison of the P > V sign on the WISC-R and WAIS-R in delinquent males. *Journal of Clinical Psychology, 42,* 173–176.

Graham, F. K., & Kendall, B. C. (1960). Memory-For-Designs Test: Revised general manual. *Perceptual and Motor Skills, 11*(Monograph suppl. no. 2-VIII), 147–188.

Graham, J. R. (1978). A review of some important MMPI special scales. In P. McReynolds (Ed.), *Advances in psychological assessment* (Vol. 4, pp. 311–331). San Francisco: Jossey-Bass.

Graham, J. R. (1987). *The MMPI: A practical guide* (2nd ed.). New York: Oxford University Press.

Graham, J. R. (1993). *MMPI-2: Assessing personality and psychopathology* (2nd ed.). New York: Oxford University Press.

Graham, J. R., & Lilly, R. S. (1984). *Psychological testing*. Englewood Cliffs, NJ: Prentice-Hall.

Graham, J. R., & McCord, G. (1985). Interpretation of moderately elevated MMPI scores for normal subjects. *Journal of Personality Assessment, 49,* 477–484.

Graham, J. R., Smith, R. L., & Schwartz, G. F. (1986). Stability of MMPI configurations for psychiatric inpatients. *Journal of Consulting and Clinical Psychology, 49*, 477–484.

Graham, J. R., Watts, D., & Timbrook, R. E. (1991). Detecting fake-good and fake-bad MMPI-2 profiles. *Journal of Personality Assessment, 57*, 264–267.

Graham, P., & Rutter, M. (1968). The reliability and validity of the psychiatric assessment of the child: II. Interview with the parent. *British Journal of Psychiatry, 114*, 581–592.

Gravitz, M. A. (1968). The height of normal adult figure drawings. *Journal of Clinical Psychology, 24*, 75.

Gravitz, M. A. (1969). Direction of psychosexual interest and figure drawing choice. *Journal of Clinical Psychology, 25*, 311.

Grayson, H. M. (1951). *A psychological admissions testing program and manual.* Los Angeles: Veterans Administration Center.

Green, B. F. (1978). In defense of measurement. *American Psychologist, 33*, 664–670.

Green, S. B., & Kelley, C. K. (1988). Racial bias in prediction with the MMPI for a juvenile delinquent population. *Journal of Personality Assessment, 52*, 263–275.

Greenbaum, P. F., Prange, M. E., Friedman, R. M., & Silver, S. E. (1991). Substance abuse prevalence and comorbidity with other psychiatric disorders among adolescents with severe emotional disorders. *Journal of the Academy of Child and Adolescent Psychology, 30*, 575–583.

Greenbaum, R. S. (1955). A note on the use of the Word Association Test as an aid to interpreting the Bender-Gestalt. *Journal of Projective Techniques, 19*, 27–29.

Greene, R. L. (1987). Ethnicity and MMPI performance: A review. *Journal of Consulting and Clinical Psychology, 55*, 497–512.

Greene, R. L. (Ed.). (1988). *The MMPI use with special populations.* San Diego: Grune & Stratton.

Greene, R. L. (1988). The relative efficiency of F-K and the obvious and subtle scales to detect overreporting of psychopathology on the MMPI. *Journal of Clinical Psychology, 44*, 152–159.

Greene, R. L. (1989). *The MMPI: An interpretive manual* (2nd ed.). New York: Grune & Stratton.

Greene, R. L. (1991). *The MMPI-2/MMPI: An interpretive manual.* Boston: Allyn & Bacon.

Greene, R. L., & Clopton, J. R. (1994). Minnesota Multiphasic Personality Inventory-2. In M. Maruish (Ed.), *The use of psychological testing for treatment, planning and outcome assessment* (pp. 137–159). Hillsdale, NJ: Erlbaum.

Greene, R. L., Weed, N. C., Butcher, J. N., Arredono, R., & Davis, H. G. (1992). A cross validation of MMPI-2 substance abuse scales. *Journal of Personality Assessment, 58*, 405–410.

Greenlief, C. L., Margolis, R. B., & Erker, G. J. (1985). Application of the Trail Making Test in differentiating neuropsychological impairment of elderly persons. *Perceptual and Motor Skills, 61*, 1283–1289.

Greenwald, D. F. (1991). Personality dimensions reflected by the Rorschach and the 16PF. *Journal of Clinical Psychology, 47*, 708–715.

Gregory, M. L. (1977). Emotional indicators on the Bender Gestalt and the Devereux Child Rating Scale. *Psychology in the Schools, 14*, 433–437.

Gregory, R. J. (1987). *Adult intellectual assessment.* Boston: Allyn & Bacon.

Gregory, R., & Morris, L. (1978). Adjective correlates for women on the CPI scales: A replication. *Journal of Personality Assessment, 42*, 258–264.

Greif, E. B., & Hogan, R. (1973). The theory and measurement of empathy. *Journal of Counseling Psychology, 20*, 280–284.

Gresham, F. M. (1984). Behavioral interviews in school psychology: Issues in psychometric adequacy and research. *School Psychology Review, 13*, 17–25.

Griffin, M. L., & Flaherty, M. R. (1964). Correlation of CPI traits with academic achievement. *Educational and Psychological Measurement, 24*, 369–372.

Grillo, J., Brown, R. S., Hilsabeck, R., Price, J. R., & Lees-Haley, P. (1994). Raising doubts about claimes of malingering: Implications of relationships between MCMI-II and MMPI-2 performances. *Journal of Clinical Psychology, 50*, 651–655.

Groff, M., & Hubble, L. (1981). Recategorized WISC-R scores of juvenile delinquents. *Journal of Learning Disabilities, 14,* 515–516.

Gross, A. M. (1990). An analysis of measures and design strategies in research in behavioral therapy: Is it still behavioral? *The Behavior Therapist, 13,* 203–209.

Grossman, F. M. (1983). Percentage of WAIS-R standardization sample obtaining verbal-performance discrepancies. *Journal of Consulting and Clinical Psychology, 51,* 641–642.

Grossman, F. M., & Johnson, K. M. (1982). WISC-R Factor scores as predictors of WRAT performance: A multivariate analysis. *Psychology in the Schools, 19,* 465–468.

Groth-Marnat, G. (1985). Evaluating and using psychological testing software. *Human Resource Management Australia, 23,* 16–21.

Groth-Marnat, G. (1988). A survey of the current and future direction of professional psychology in acute general hospitals in Australia. *Australian Psychologist, 23,* 39–43.

Groth-Marnat, G. (1991). Hypnotizability, suggestibility, and psychopathology: An overview of research. In J. F. Schumaker (Ed.), *Human suggestibility: Advances in theory, research, and application* (pp. 219–234). New York: Routledge.

Groth-Marnat, G. (1992). Past cultural traditions of therapeutic metaphor. *Psychology: An International Journal of Human Behavior, 29,* 1–8.

Groth-Marnat, G. (1993). Neuropsychological effects of styrene exposure: A review of current literature. *Perceptual and Motor Skills, 77,* 1139–1149.

Groth-Marnat, G. (1995). *The Rey Auditory Verbal Learning Test: A manual for administration, scoring, and interpretation* (Tech. and Res. Rep.). Perth: Curtin University of Technology, Research Center for Applied Psychology.

Groth-Marnat, G. (in press). The Wechsler intelligence scales—WISC-III and WAIS-III. In A. S. Kaufman & N. L. Kaufman (Eds.), *Learning disabilities: Psychological assessment and evaluation.* New York: Cambridge University Press.

Groth-Marnat, G., & Edkins, G. (1996). Professional psychologists in general health care settings: A review of the financial efficacy of direct treatment interventions. *Professional Psychology: Research and Practice, 27,* 161–174.

Groth-Marnat, G., Edkins, G., & Schumaker, J. F. (1995). Psychologists in disease prevention and health promotion: A review of the cost-effectiveness literature. *Psychology, 32,* 127–135.

Groth-Marnat, G., & Roberts, L. (in press). Indicators of psychological health on Human Figure Drawings and the House Tree Person: A search for concurrent validity. *Journal of Clinical Psychology.*

Groth-Marnat, G., & Schumaker, J. (1989). Computer-based psychological testing: Issues and guidelines. *American Journal of Orthopsychiatry, 59,* 257–263.

Groth-Marnat, G., & Teal, M. (1998). *Ecological validation of the WAIS-R Block Design subtest: Ability to predict everyday spatial performance.* Paper presented at the annual meeting of the American Psychological Association, San Francisco, CA.

Groves, J. R., & Fried, P. A. (1991). Developmental items on Children's Human Figure Drawings: A replication and extension of Koppitz to younger children. *Journal of Clinical Psychology, 47,* 140–148.

Guilford, J. P. (1967). *The nature of human intelligence.* New York: McGraw-Hill.

Guilford, J. P. (1988). Some changes in the structure-of-intellect model. *Educational and Psychological Measurement, 48,* 1–4.

Guilford, J. P., & Zimmerman, W. S. (1956). *The Guilford-Zimmerman Temperament Survey.* Beverly Hills, CA: Sheridan Psychological Services.

Guilmette, T. J., Faust, D., Hart, K., & Arkes, H. R. (1990). A national survey of psychologists who offer neuropsychological services. *Archives of Clinical Neuropsychology, 5,* 373–392.

Gulas, I., McClanahan, L. D., & Poetter, R. (1975). Phobic response factors from the Fear Survey Schedule. *Journal of Psychology, 90,* 19–25.

Gynther, M. D. (1978). The California Psychological Inventory: A review. In O. K. Buros (Ed.), *The eighth mental measurements yearbook* (Vol. 1, pp. 733–737). Highland Park, NJ: Gryphon Press.

Gynther, M. D. (1979). Aging and personality. In J. N. Butcher (Ed.), *New developments in the use of the MMPI* (pp. 240–256). Minneapolis: University of Minnesota Press.

Gynther, M. D., & Green, S. B. (1980). Accuracy may make a difference, but does a difference make for accuracy?: A response to Pritchard and Rosenblatt. *Journal of Consulting and Clinical Psychology, 48,* 268–272.

Gynther, M. D., & Shimkuras, A. M. (1966). Age and MMPI performance. *Journal of Consulting Psychology, 30,* 118–121.

Haaga, D. A., Dyck, M. J., & Ernst, D. (1991). Empirical status of cognitive theory of depression. *Psychological Bulletin, 110,* 215–236.

Haan, N. (1964). An investigation of the relationships of Rorschach scores, patterns and behaviors to coping and defense mechanisms. *Journal of Projective Techniques and Personality Assessment, 28,* 429–441.

Haas, A. P., Hendin, H., & Singer, P. (1987). Psychodynamic and structured interviewing: Issues of validity. *Comprehensive Psychiatry, 28,* 40–53.

Hackbarth, S. G., Murphy, H. D., & McQuary, J. P. (1991). Identifying sexually abused children by using Kinetic Family Drawings. *Elementary School Guidance & Counseling, 25,* 255–260.

Haddad, F. A. (1986). The performance of learning disabled children on the Kaufman Assessment Battery for Children and the Bender-Gestalt Test. *Psychology in the Schools, 23,* 342–345.

Hafner, A. J. (1958). Response time and Rorschach behavior. *Journal of Clinical Psychology, 14,* 154–155.

Hain, J. D. (1964). The Bender Gestalt Test: A scoring method for identifying brain damage. *Journal of Consulting Psychology, 28,* 34–40.

Hall, C. (1983, December 6). Psychiatrist's computer use stirs debate. *The Wall Street Journal,* 35, 39.

Hall, H. V. (1984). Predicting dangerousness for the courts. *American Journal of Forensic Psychiatry, 5,* 77–96.

Hall, H. V., Catlin, E., Boissevain, A., & Westgate, J. (1984). Dangerous myths about predicting dangerousness. *American Journal of Forensic Psychology, 2,* 173–193.

Hall, H. V., & Sbordone, R. J. (Eds.) (1993). *Disorders of executive function.* Winter Park, FL: PMD Publishers.

Halpern, F. (1951). The Bender Visual Motor Gestalt Test. In H. H. Anderson & G. L. Anderson (Eds.), *An introduction to projective techniques* (pp. 324–340). New York: Prentice-Hall.

Halpern, F. (1955). Rotation errors made by brain-injured and familial children on two visual motor tests. *American Journal of Mental Deficiency, 59,* 485–489.

Halstead, W. C. (1961). Biological intelligence. In J. J. Jenkins & D. G. Paterson (Eds.), *Studies in individual differences* (pp. 661–668). New York: Appleton-Century-Crofts.

Hammen, C. L. (1978). Depression, distortion, and life stress in college students. *Cognitive Therapy and Research, 2,* 189–192.

Hammen, C. L., & Krantz, S. (1976). Effect of success and failure on depressive cognitions. *Journal of Abnormal Psychology, 85,* 577–586.

Hammen, C. L., & Mayol, A. (1982). Depression and cognitive characteristics of stressful life-event types. *Journal of Abnormal Psychology, 91,* 165–174.

Hammer, E. F. (1954). A comparison of H-T-P's of rapists and pedophiles. *Journal of Projective Techniques, 18,* 346–354.

Hammer, E. F. (1958). *The clinical application of projective drawings.* Springfield, IL: Charles C. Thomas.

Hammer, E. F. (1960). The House-Tree-Person (H-T-P) drawings as a projective technique with children. In A. I. Rabin & R. Haworth (Eds.), *Projective techniques with children.* New York: Grune & Stratton.

Hammer, E. F. (1968). Projective drawings. In A. I. Rabin (Ed.), *Projective techniques in personality assessment* (pp. 366–393). New York: Springer.

Hammer, E. F. (1969a). The use of the H-T-P in a criminal court: Predicting acting out. In J. N. Buck & E. F. Hammer (Eds.), *Advances in the House-Tree-Person technique: Variations and applications* (pp. 267–295). Los Angeles: Western Psychological Services.

Hammer, E. F. (1969b). Hierarchical organization of personality and the H-T-P, achromatic and chromatic. In J. N. Buck & E. F. Hammer (Eds.), *Advances in the House-Tree-Person technique: Variations and applications.* Los Angeles: Western Psychological Services.

Hammer, E. F. (1985). The House-Tree-Person Test. In C. S. Newmark (Ed.), *Major psychological assessment instruments* (pp. 135–164). Newton, MA: Allyn & Bacon.

Hammill, D. D. (1990). On learning disabilities: An emerging consensus. *Journal of Learning Disabilities, 23,* 74–84.

Handelsman, M. M., & Galvin, M. D. (1988). Facilitating informed consent for outpatient psychotherapy: A suggested written format. *Professional Psychology: Research & Practice, 19,* 223–225.

Handler, L. (1967). Anxiety indexes in the Draw-A-Person Test: A scoring manual. *Journal of Projective Techniques, 31,* 46–57.

Handler, L. (1985). The clinical use of the Draw-A-Person Test (DAP). In C. S. Newmark (Ed.), *Major psychological assessment instruments* (pp. 165–216). Newton, MA: Allyn & Bacon.

Handler, L., & Habenicht, D. (1994). The Kinetic Family Drawing technique: A review of the literature. *Journal of Personality Assessment, 62,* 440–464.

Hansell, A. G., Lerner, H. D., Milden, R. S., & Ludolph, P. (1988). Single-sign Rorschach suicide indicators: A validity study using a depressed inpatient population. *Journal of Personality Assessment, 52,* 658–669.

Hanson, R. K., Hunsley, J., & Parker, K. C. H. (1988). The relationship between WAIS subtest reliability, "g" loadings, and meta-analytically derived validity estimates. *Journal of Clinical Psychology, 44,* 557–562.

Hargrave, G. E., & Hiatt, D. (1987). Law enforcement selection with the interview, MMPI, and CPI: A study of reliability and validity. *Journal of Police Science and Administration, 15,* 110–117.

Hargrave, G. E., Hiatt, D., & Gaffney, T. W. (1986). A comparison of MMPI and CPI test profiles for traffic officers and deputy sheriffs. *Journal of Police Science and Administration, 14,* 250–258.

Hargrave, G. E., Hiatt, D., Ogard, E. M., & Karr, C. (1994). Comparison of the MMPI and MMPI-2 for a sample of peace officers. *Psychological Assessment, 6,* 27–32.

Harper, R. G., Wiens, A. N., & Matarazzo, J. D. (1978). *Nonverbal communication: The state of the art.* New York: Wiley.

Harrell, T. H., Honaker, L. M., & Parnell, T. (1992). Equivalence of the MMPI-2 with the MMPI in psychiatric patients. *Psychological Assessment, 4,* 460–465.

Harris, D. B. (1963). *Children's drawings as measures of intellectual maturity.* New York: Harcourt, Brace, & World.

Harris, D. B., & Pinder, G. D. (1974). The Goodenough-Harris Drawing Test as a measure of intellectual maturity of youths 12–17: U.S. *Vital and Health Statistics, 11,* 46.

Harris, R. E., & Lingoes, J. C. (1955/1968). *Subscales for the MMPI: An aid to profile interpretation.* Department of Psychiatry: University of California.

Harris, R., & Lingoes, J. (1968). *Subscales for the Minnesota Multiphasic Personality Inventory* (mimeographed materials). Ann Arbor: University of Michigan, Department of Psychology.

Harrison, R. (1940). Studies in the use and validity of the Thematic Apperception Test with mentally disordered patients. II: A quantitative validity study. III: Validation by blind analysis. *Character and Personality, 9,* 122–133, 134–138.

Harrower, M. (1986). The Stress Tolerance Test. *Journal of Personality Assessment, 50,* 417–427.

Hart, K. J., & Ollendick, T. H. (1985). Prevalence of bulimia in working and university women. *American Journal of Psychiatry, 142,* 851–854.

Hart, R. P., Kwentus, J. A., Taylor, J. R., & Hamer, R. M. (1988). Productive naming and memory in depression and Alzheimer's type dementia. *Archives of Clinical Neuropsychology, 3,* 313–322.

Hartman, D. E. (1992). Neuropsychological toxicity. In A. E. Puente & R. J. McCaffrey (Eds.), *Handbook of neouropsychological assessment: A biopsychosocial perspective* (pp. 485–507). New York: Plenum Press.

Hartshorne, H., & May, M. A. (1928). *Studies in deceit.* New York: Macmillan.

Harty, M. K. (1986). Action language in the psychological test report. *Bulletin of the Menninger Clinic, 50,* 456–463.

Hase, H. D., & Goldberg, L. R. (1967). Comparative validity of different strategies of constructing personality inventory scales. *Psychological Bulletin, 67,* 231–248.

Hassell, J., & Smith, E. W. L. (1975). Female homosexuals' concept of self, men, and women. *Journal of Personality Assessment, 39,* 154–159.

Hathaway, S. R., & McKinley, J. C. (1940). A Multiphasic Personality Schedule (Minnesota): I. Construction of the schedule. *Journal of Psychology, 10,* 249–254.

Hathaway, S. R., & McKinley, J. C. (1943). *Manual for the Minnesota Multiphasic Personality Inventory.* New York: Psychological Corporation.

Hathaway, S. R., & Monachesi, E. D. (1963). *Adolescent personality and behavior: MMPI patterns of normal, delinquent, dropout, and other outcomes.* Minneapolis: University of Minnesota Press.

Haverkamp, B. E. (1993). Confirmatory bias in hypothesis testing for client-identified and counselor self-generated hypotheses. *Journal of Counseling Psychology, 40,* 303–315.

Hawkins, S. A., & Hastie, R. (1990). Hindsight: Biased judgments of past events after the outcomes are known. *Psychological Bulletin, 107,* 311–327.

Hayes, S. C., Nelson, R. O., & Jarrett, R. B. (1987). The treatment utility of assessment: A functional approach to evaluating assessment quality. *American Psychologist, 42,* 963–974.

Haynes, J. P., & Howard, R. C. (1986). Stability of WISC-R scores in a juvenile forensic sample. *Journal of Clinical Psychology, 42,* 534–537.

Haynes, J. P., & Peltier, J. (1985). Patterns of practice with the TAT in juvenile forensic settings. *Journal of Personality Assessment, 49,* 26–29.

Haynes, S. N. (1991). Clinical applications of psychophysiological assessment: An introduction and overview. *Psychological Assessment, 3,* 307–308.

Haynes, S. N. (1995). Introduction to the special section in chaos theory and psychological assessment. *Psychological Assessment, 7,* 3–4.

Haynes, S. N., & O'Brien, W. H. (1988). The gordian knot of *DSM-III-R* use: Integrating principles of behavior classification and complex causal models. *Behavioral Assessment, 10,* 95–106.

Haynes, S. N., Richard, D. C. S., & Kubany, E. S. (1995). Content validity in psychological assessment: A functional approach to concepts and methods. *Psychological Assessment, 7,* 238–247.

Haynes, S. N., & Uchigakivchi, P. (1993). Incorporating personality trait measures in behavioral assessment. *Behavior Modification, 14,* 297–306.

Haynes, S. N., & Wilson, C. C. (1979). *Behavioral assessment: Recent advances in methods, concepts and applications.* San Francisco: Jossey-Bass.

Heaton, R. K., Beade, L. E., & Johnson, K. L. (1978). Neuropsychological test results associated with psychiatric disorders in adults. *Psychological Bulletin, 85,* 141–162.

Heaton, R. K., Grant, I., & Mathews, C. G. (1991). *Comprehensive norms for an expanded Halstead-Reitan Battery.* Odessa, FL: Psychological Assessment Resources.

Hebb, D. O. (1972). *Textbook of psychology* (3rd ed.). Philadelphia: W.B. Saunders.

Hedlund, J. L., Sletten, I. W., Evenson, R. C., Altman, H., & Cho, D. W. (1977). Automated psychiatric information systems: A critical review of Missouri's Standard System of Psychiatry (SSOP). *Journal of Operational Psychiatry, 8,* 5–26.

Heflinger, C. A., Cook, V. J., & Thackrey, M. (1987). Identification of mental retardation by the System of Multicultural Pluralistic Assessment: Nondiscriminatory or nonexistent? *Journal of School Psychology, 25,* 177–183.

Heiberger, A. M., Abell, S. C., & Johnson, J. E. (1994, August). *Cognitive assessment with the House-Tree-Person drawings: An empirical study.* Paper presented at the annual convention of the American Psychological Association, Los Angeles, CA.

Heiby, E. M. (1995). Assessment of behavioral chaos with a focus on transitions in depression. *Psychological Assessment, 7,* 10–16.

Heilbrun, A. B. (1961). Male and female personality correlates of early termination in counseling. *Journal of Counseling Psychology, 8,* 31–36.

Heilbrun, A. B., Daniel, J. L., Goodstein, L. D., Stephenson, R. R., & Crites, J. O. (1962). The validity of two-scale pattern interpretation on the California Psychological Inventory. *Journal of Applied Psychology, 46,* 409–416.

Heilman, K. M., & Valenstein, E. (1993). *Clinical neuropsychology.* New York: Oxford University Press.

Heimberg, R. G. (1994). Cognitive assessment strategies and the measurement of outcome of treatment for social phobia. *Behavior Research and Therapy, 32,* 269–280.

Heimberg, R. G., Harrison, D. F., Goldberg, L. S., Desmarais, S., & Blue, S. (1979). The relationship of self-report and behavioral assertion in an offender population. *Journal of Behavior Therapy and Experimental Psychiatry, 10,* 283–286.

Heinrichs, R. W. (1993). Schizophrenia and the brain: Conditions for a neuropsychology of madness. *American Psychologist, 48,* 221–233.

Hellkamp, D. T., & Hogan, M. E. (1985). Differentiation of organics from functional psychiatric patients across various I.Q. ranges using the Bender-Gestalt and Hutt scoring system. *Journal of Clinical Psychology, 41,* 259–264.

Helmes, E., & Reddon, J. R. (1993). A perspective on development in assessing psychopathology: A critical review of MMPI and MMPI-2. *Psychological Bulletin, 113,* 453–471.

Helzer, J. E., & Robins, L. N. (1988). The Diagnostic Interview Schedule: Its development, evolution and use. *Social Psychiatry and Psychiatric Epidemiology, 23,* 6–16.

Helzer, J. E., Robins, L. N., Croughan, J. L., & Welner, A. (1981). Renard Diagnostic Interview: Its reliability and procedural validity with physicians and lay interviewers. *Archives of General Psychiatry, 38,* 393–398.

Helzer, J. E., Robins, L. N., McEvoy, L. F., Spitznagel, E. L., Stolzman, R. K., Farmer, A., & Brockington, I. F. (1985). A comparison of clinical and Diagnostic Interview Schedule diagnoses: Physician re-examination of lay-interviewed cases in the general population. *Archives of General Psychiatry, 42,* 657–666.

Helzer, J. E., Spitznagel, E. L., & McEvoy, L. (1987). The predictive validity of lay Diagnostic Interview Schedule diagnoses in the general population: A comparison with physician examiners. *Archives of General Psychiatry, 44,* 1069–1077.

Henderson, M., & Furnham, A. (1983). Dimensions of assertiveness: Factor analysis of five assertion inventories. *Journal of Behavior Therapy and Experimental Psychiatry, 14,* 223–231.

Henderson, N. B., & Engel, R. (1974). Neonatal visual evoked potentials as predictors of psychoeducational tests at age seven. *Developmental Psychology, 10,* 269–276.

Hendrickson, A. E., & Hendrickson, D. E. (1980). The biological basis for individual differences in intelligence. *Personality and Individual Differences, 1,* 3–33.

Henry, B., Moffitt, T. E., Caspi, A., Langley, J., & Silva, P. A. (1994). On the "remembrance of things past": A longitudinal evaluation of the retrospective method. *Psychological Assessment, 6,* 92–101.

Henry, E. M., & Rotter, J. B. (1956). Situational influences on Rorschach responses. *Journal of Consulting Psychology, 20,* 457–462.

Henry, W. E. (1956). *The analysis of fantasy: The Thematic Apperception Test in the study of personality.* New York: Wiley.

Herjanic, B., & Campbell, W. (1977). Differentiating psychiatrically disturbed children on the basis of a structured interview. *Journal of Abnormal Child Psychology, 51,* 127–134.

Herjanic, B., Herjanic, M., Brown, F., & Wheatt, T. (1975). Are children reliable reporters? *Journal of Abnormal Child Psychology, 3,* 41–48.

Herjanic, B., & Reich, W. (1982). Development of a structured psychiatric interview for children: Agreement on diagnosis comparing child and patient interviews. *Journal of Abnormal Psychology, 10,* 325–336.

Hersen, M. (1988). Behavioral assessment and psychiatric diagnosis. *Behavioral Assessment, 10,* 107–121.

Hersen, M., & Bellack, A. S. (1976). *Behavioral assessment: A practical handbook.* New York: Pergamon.

Hersen, M., & Bellack, A. S. (Eds.). (1988a). *Dictionary of behavioral assessment techniques.* New York: Pergamon.

Hersen, M., & Bellack, A. S. (1988b). DSM-III and behavioral assessment. In A. S. Bellack & M. Hersen (Eds.), *Behavioral assessment: A practical handbook* (3rd ed., pp. 67–84). New York: Pergamon.

Hersen, M., & Greaves, S. T. (1971). Rorschach productivity as related to verbal performance. *Journal of Personality Assessment, 35,* 436–441.

Hersh, C. (1962). The cognitive functioning of the creative person: A developmental analysis. *Journal of Projective Techniques, 26,* 193–200.

Hertz, M. R. (1943). Personality patterns in adolescence as portrayed by the Rorschach ink blot method: IV. The "Erlebnistypus." *Journal of General Psychology, 29,* 3–45.

Hertz, M. R. (1948). Suicidal configurations in Rorschach records. *Rorschach Research Exchange, 12,* 3–58.

Hertz, M. R. (1960). The organization activity. In M. Rickers-Ovsiankina (Ed.), *Rorschach psychology* (pp. 25–57). New York: Wiley.

Hertz, M. R. (1976). Detection of suicidal risks with the Rorschach. In M. Abt & S. L. Weissman (Eds.), *Acting out: Theoretical and clinical aspects* (2nd ed.). New York: Aronson.

Hertz, M. R., & Paolino, A. (1960). Rorschach indices of perceptual and conceptual disorganization. *Journal of Projective Techniques, 24,* 310–388.

Herzog, D. B., Keller, M. B., Sacks, N. R., Yeh, C. J., & Lavori, P. W. (1992). Psychiatric comorbidity in treatment-seeking anorexics and bulimics. *Journal of the American Academy of Child and Adolescent Psychiatry, 31,* 810–818.

Hibbard, R. A., & Hartment, G. L. (1990). *Journal of Clinical Psychology, 46,* 211–219.

Higgins, R. L., Alonso, R. R., & Pendleton, M. G. (1979). The validity of roleplay assessments of assertiveness. *Behavior Therapy, 10,* 655–662.

Higgins-Lee, C. (1990). Low scores on California psychological Inventory as predictors of psychopathology in alcoholic patients. *Psychological Reports, 67,* 227–232.

Hill, A. H. (1967). Use of a structured autobiography in the construct validation of personality scales. *Journal of Consulting Psychology, 31,* 551–556.

Hill, R. E., Jr. (1960). Dichotomous prediction of student teaching excellence employing selected CPI scales. *Journal of Educational Research, 53,* 349–351.

Hilsenroth, M. J., & Handler, L. (1995). A survey of graduate students' experiences, interests, and attitudes about learning the Rorschach. *Journal of Personality Assessment, 64,* 243–257.

Hinkle, J. S. (1994). Practitioners and cross-cultural assessment: A practical guide to information and training. *Measurement and Evaluation in Counseling and Development, 27,* 103–115.

Hirschenfang, S. A. (1960b). A comparison of WAIS scores of hemiplegic patients with and without aphasia. *Journal of Clinical Psychology, 16,* 351.

Hishinuma, E. S., & Yamakawa, R. (1993). Constructional and criterion related validity of the WISC-III for exceptional students and those at risk. In B. A. Braken & R. S. McCullum (Eds.). Wechsler Intelligence Scales for children: 3rd ed. Brandon VT: Clinical Psychology Publishing Company.

Hoffman, B., Choca, J., Gutman, D., Shanley, L., & Van Denburg, E. (1989, August). *Personality changes with aging in male psychiatric patients.* Paper presented at the 97th Annual Convention of the American Psychological Association, New Orleans, LA.

Hoffman, H., Loper, R. G., & Kammeier, M. L. (1974). Identifying future alcoholics with MMPI alcoholism scales. *Quarterly Journal of Studies on Alcohol, 35,* 490–498.

Hoffman, R. G., & Nelson, K. (1988). Cross-validation of six short forms of the WAIS-R in a healthy geriatric sample. *Journal of Clinical Psychology, 44,* 950–952.

Hogan, A. E., Quay, H. C., Vaughn, S., & Shapiro, S. K. (1989). Revised Behavior Problem checklist: Stability, prevalence, and incidence of behavior problems in kindergarten and first grade. *Psychological Assessment, 1,* 103–111.

Hogan, R. (1971). Personality characteristics of highly rated policemen. *Personnel Psychology, 24,* 679–686.

Hogan, R., Hogan, J., & Roberts, B. W. (1996). Personality measurement and employment decisions: Questions and answers. *American Psychologist, 51,* 469–477.

Hogan, R., & Kurtines, W. (1975). Personological correlates of police effectiveness. *Journal of Psychology, 92,* 289–295.

Hogan, R., & Nicholson, R. (1988). The meaning of personality test scores. *American Psychologist, 43,* 621–626.

Hoge, R. D., Andrews, D. A., Robinson, D., & Hollett, J. (1988). The construct validity of interview-based assessments in family counseling. *Journal of Clinical Psychology, 44,* 563–571.

Hoghughi, M. (1992). *Assessing child and adolescent disorders: A practice manual.* London: Sage.

Holland, A. L. (1980). *Communicative Abilities in Daily Living. A test of functional communication for aphasic adults.* Austin, TX: Pro-Ed.

Holliman, N. B., & Montross, J. (1984). The effects of depression upon responses to the California Psychological Inventory. *Journal of Clinical Psychology, 40,* 1373–1378.

Hollis, J. W., & Donna, P. A. (1979). *Psychological report writing: Theory and practice.* Muncie, IN: Accelerated Development.

Hollon, S. D., & Kendall, P. C. (1980). Cognitive self-statements in depression: Development of an automatic thoughts questionnaire. *Cognitive Therapy and Research, 4,* 383–395.

Holmes, C. B., Dungan, D. S., & Medlin, W. J. (1984). Reassessment of inferring personality traits from Bender-Gestalt drawing styles. *Journal of Clinical Psychology, 40,* 1241–1243.

Holmes, C. B., & Stephens, C. L. (1984). Consistency of edging on the Bender-Gestalt, Memory for Designs, and Draw-A-Person Tests. *The Journal of Psychology, 117,* 269–271.

Holmstrom, R. W., Karp, S. A., & Silber, D. E. (1994). Prediction of depression with the Apperceptive Personality Test. *Journal of Clinical Psychology, 50,* 234–237.

Holt, R. R. (1970). Yet another look at clinical and statistical prediction: Or is clinical psychology worthwhile? *American Psychologist, 25,* 337–349.

Holtzman, W. H. (1988). Beyond the Rorschach. *Journal of Personality Assessment, 52,* 578–609.

Honaker, L. M. (1988). The equivalency of computerized and conventional MMPI administration: A critical review. *Clinical Psychology Review, 8,* 561–577.

Hope, D. A., & Heimberg, R. G. (1993). Social phobia and social anxiety. In D. H. Barlow (Ed.), *Clinical handbook of psychological disorders* (pp. 99–136). New York: Guilford.

Horn, J. L. (1985). Remodeling old models of intelligence. In B. Wolman (Ed.), *Handbook of intelligence* (pp. 267–300). New York: Wiley.

Horn, J. L., & Cattell, R. B. (1966). Refinement and test of the theory of fluid and crystalized intelligence. *Journal of Educational Psychology, 57,* 253–270.

Horowitz, M. J. (1985). *Report of the program on conscious and unconscious mental processes of the John D. and Catherine T. MacArthur Foundation.* University of California—San Francisco, CA.

Horvath, A. O., & Goheen, M. D. (1990). Factors mediating the success of defiance- and compliance-based interventions. *Journal of Consulting and Clinical Psychology, 37,* 363–371.

Houston, A. N., & Terwilliger, R. (1995). Sex, sex roles, and sexual attitudes: Figure gender in the Draw-A-Person test revisited. *Journal of Personality Assessment, 65,* 343–357.

Houts, P. L. (Ed.). (1977). *The myth of measurability.* New York: Hart.

Howieson, D. B., & Lezak, M. D. (1991). The neuropsychological evaluation. In S. C. Yudofsky & R. E. Hales (Eds.), *American Psychiatric Press textbook of neuropsychiatry* (2nd ed.). Washington, DC: American Psychiatric Press.

Hoyt, M. F. (1994). Single session solutions. In M. Hoyt (Ed.), *Constructive therapies* (pp. 140–159). New York: Guilford.

Huettner, M. I. (1994). Neuropsychology of language and reading development. In P. A. Vernon (Ed.), *The neuropsychology of individual differences* (pp. 9–34). New York: Academic Press.

Hulse, W. C. (1951). The emotionally disturbed child draws his family. *Quarterly Journal of Child Behavior, 3,* 152–174.

Humphrey, D. H., & Dahlstrom, W. G. (1995). The impact of changing from the MMPI to the MMPI-2 on profile configurations. *Journal of Personality Assessment, 64,* 428–439.

Hunsley, J., Hanson, R. K., & Parker, K. C. H. (1988). A summary of the reliability and stability of MMPI scales. *Journal of Clinical Psychology, 44,* 44–46.

Hunter, J. E. (1986). Cognitive ability, cognitive aptitudes, job knowledge, and job performance. *Journal of Vocational Behavior, 29,* 340–362.

Hurley, A. D., & Sovner, R. (1985). The use of the Thematic Apperception Test in mentally retarded persons. *Psychiatric Aspects of Mental Retardation Reviews, 4,* 9–12.

Hutt, M. L. (1985). *The Hutt adaptation of the Bender-Gestalt Test* (4th ed.). New York: Grune & Stratton.

Hutt, M. L., & Briskin, G. J. (1960). *The clinical use of the revised Bender-Gestalt Test.* New York: Grune & Stratton.

Hutt, M. L., & Gibby, R. G. (1970). *An Atlas for the Hutt adaptation of the Bender-Gestalt Test.* New York: Grune & Stratton.

Hyler, S. E., Skodol, A. E., Andrew, E., Kellman, H. D., & Oldham, J. M. (1990). Validity of the Personality Diagnostic Questionnaire-Revised: Comparison with two structured interviews. *American Journal of Psychiatry, 147,* 1043–1048.

Iacono, W. G. (1991). Psychophysiological assessment of psychopathology. *Psychological Assessment, 3,* 309–320.

Ingram, R. E., Kendall, P. C., Siegle, G., Guarino, J., & McLaughlin, S. C. (1995). Psychometric properties of the Positive Automatic Thoughts Questionnaire. *Psychological Assessment, 7,* 495–507.

Insua, A. M., & Stella, M. (1986). Psychometric patterns on the Rorschach of healthy elderly persons and patients with suspected dementia. *Perceptual and Motor Skills, 63,* 931–936.

Ireland-Galman, M., Padilla, G., & Michael, W. (1980). The relationship between performance on the mazes subtest of the Wechsler Intelligence Scale for Children-Revised (WISC-R) and speed of solving anagrams with simple and difficult arrangements of letter and order. *Educational and Psychological Measurement, 40,* 513–524.

Iverson, G. L., Franzen, M. D., & Hammond, J. A. (1995). Examination of inmate's ability to malinger on the MMPI-2. *Psychological Assessment, 7,* 115–117.

Ivnik, R. J., Malec, J. F., Smith, G. E., Tangalos, E. G. et al. (1992). Mayo–s older Americans normative studies: Updated WAIS-R norms for ages 56 to 97. *Clinical Neuropsychologist, 6,* 293–297.

Ivnik, R. J., Malec, J. F., Tangalos, E. G., Peterson, R. C., Kokmen, E., & Kurland, L. (1990). The Auditory-Verbal Learning Test (AVLT): Norms for ages 55 years and older. *Psychological Assessment, 2,* 304–312.

Ivnik, R. J., Sharbrough, F. W., & Laws, E. R. (1988). Anterior temporal lobectomy for the control of partial complex seizures: Information for counseling patients. *Mayo Clinic Proceedings, 63,* 783–793.

Jackson, D. N. (1986). The process of responding in personality assessment. In A. Anglietner & J. S. Wiggins (Eds.), *Personality assessment via questionnaire: Current issues in theory and measurement* (pp. 123–142). Berlin: Springer-Verlag.

Jackson, M., Fox, G. A., Waugh, M., & Tuck, R. R. (1987). The Rey Auditory Verbal Learning Test: A follow-up study on alcoholics with and without neurological disease. *Australian Drug and Alcohol Review, 6,* 71–76.

Jacob, R. G., Turner, S. M., Szekely, B. C., & Eidelman, B. H. (1983). Predicting outcome of relaxation therapy in headaches: The role of "depression." *Behavior Therapy, 14,* 457–465.

Jacobson, N. S., Folette, W. C., & Pagel, M. (1986). Predicting who will benefit from behavioral marital therapyh. *Journal of Consulting and Clinical Psychology, 54,* 518–522.

Janowsky, J. S., Shimamura, A. P., & Squire, L. R. (1989). Source memory impairment in patients with frontal lobe lesions. *Neuropsychologia, 27,* 1043–1056.

Jansky, J., & de Hirsch, K. (1972). *Preventing reading failure.* New York: Harper & Row.

Janzen, W. B., & Coe, W. C. (1975). Clinical and sign prediction: The Draw-A-Person and female homosexuality. *Journal of Clinical Psychology, 31,* 757–765.

Jarman, R. F., & Das, J. P. (1977). Simultaneous and successive synthesis and intelligence. *Intelligence, 1,* 151–169.

Jarvis, P. E., & Barth, J. (1994). *The Halstead-Reitan Neuropsychological Battery: A guide to interpretation and clinical application.* Odessa, FL: Psychological Assessment Resources.

Jastak, S., & Wilkinson, G. (1984). *Wide Range Achievement Test* (Rev. ed.). Wilmington, DE: Jastak Assessment Systems.

Jastak, S., & Wilkinson, G (1994). *Wide Range Achievement Test* (3rd ed.). San Antonio, TX: The Psychological Corporation.

Jencks, S. F. (1985). Recognition of mental distress and diagnosis of mental disorder in primary care. *Journal of the American Medical Association, 253,* 1903.

Jensen, A. R. (1965). Review of the Rorschach. In O. K. Buros (Ed.), *The sixth mental measurements yearbook* (pp. 501–509). Highland Park, NJ: Gryphon Press.

Jensen, A. R. (1969). How much can we boost I.Q. and scholastic achievement? *Harvard Educational Review, 39,* 1–23.

Jensen, A. R. (1972). *Genetics and education.* New York: Harper & Row.

Jensen, A. R. (1984). The black-white difference on the K-ABC: Implications for future tests. *Journal of Special Education, 18,* 377–408.

Jensen, A. R., & Reynolds, C. R. (1982). Race, social class, and ability patterns on the WISC-R. *Personality and Individual Differences, 3,* 423–438.

Jensen, A. R., & Rohwer, W. D. (1966). The Stroop Color-Word Test: A review. *Acta-Psychologica, 25,* 36–93.

Johnson, D. L., & Danley, W. (1981). Validity: Comparison of the WISC-R and SOMPA estimated learning potential scores. *Psychological Reports, 49,* 123–131.

Johnson, J. H. (1973). Bender-Gestalt constriction as an indicator of depression in psychiatric patients. *Journal of Personality Assessment, 37,* 53–55.

Johnson, J. H., Null, C., Butcher, J. M., & Johnson, K. N. (1984). Replicated item level factor analysis of the full MMPI. *Journal of Personality and Social Psychology, 47,* 105–114.

Johnson, J. L. (1994). The Thematic Apperception Test and Alzheimer's Disease. *Journal of Personality Assessment, 62,* 314–319.

Johnson, J. W. (1977). Technology in mental health in the 21st century. In J. B. Sidowski & T. A. Williams (Eds.), *Technology in Mental Health Care Delivery Systems* (pp. 140–156). Norwood, NJ: Ablex.

Johnson, J. W. (1984). An overview of psychological testing. In M. D. Schwartz (Ed.), *Using computers in clinical practice* (pp. 131–134). New York: Haworth Press.

Johnson, J. W., & Mihal, W. L. (1973). The performance of blacks and whites in computerized versus manual testing environments. *American Psychologist, 28,* 694–699.

Johnson, J. W., & Williams, T. A. (1977). Using on-line computer technology to improve service response and decision-making effectiveness in a mental health admitting system. In J. B. Sidowski & T. A. Williams (Eds.), *Technology in mental health care delivery systems* (pp. 237–249). Norwood, NJ: Ablex.

Johnson, M. H., Margo, P. A., & Stern, S. L. (1986). Use of the SADS-C as a diagnostic and symptom severity measure. *Journal of Consulting and Clinical Psychology, 54,* 546–551.

Jolles, I. A. (1952). *A catalogue for the qualitative interpretation of the H-T-P.* Beverly Hills, CA: Western Psychological Services.

Jolles, I. A. (1969). The use of the H-T-P in a school setting. In J. N. Buck & E. F. Hammer (Eds.), *Advances in the House-Tree-Person technique: Variations and applications.* Beverly Hills, CA: Western Psychological Services.

Jolles, I. A. (1971). *A catalogue for the qualitative interpretation of the H-T-P.* Beverly Hills, CA: Western Psychological Services.

Jones, M. C. (1924). The elimination of children's fears. *Journal of Experimental Psychology, 7,* 382–390.

Jones, R. G. (1969). A factored measure of Ellis's Irrational Belief System. *Dissertation Abstracts International, 29,* 4379B-4380B. (University Microfilms No. 69–64, 43).

Jongsma, A. E., & Peterson, L. M. (1995). *The complete psychotherapy treatment planner.* New York: Wiley.

Julian, A., Sotile, W. M., Henry, S. H., & Sotile, M. O. (1991). *Technical manual: The Family Apperception Test.* Beverly Hills: Western Psychological Services.

Kadden, R. M., Cooney, N. L., Getter, H., & Litt, M. D. (1990). Matching alcoholics to coping skills or interactional therapies: Post-treatment results. *Journal of Consulting and Clinical Psychology, 57,* 698–704.

Kagan, J., Moss, H. A., & Siegel, I. E. (1963). Psychological significance of styles of conceptualization. *Monographs of the Society for Research in Child Development, 28,* 73–124.

Kahill, S. (1984). Human figure drawings in adults: An update of the empirical evidence, 1967–1982. *Canadian Psychology, 25,* 269–290.

Kahn, M. W. (1984). The usefulness of the TAT blank card in clinical practice. *Psychotherapy in Private Practice, 2,* 43–50.

Kahn, M. W., Fox, H., & Rhode, R. (1988). Detecting faking on the Rorschach: Computer versus expert clinical judgment. *Journal of Personality Assessment, 52,* 516–523.

Kahn, R. L., & Cannell, C. F. (1961). *The dynamics of interviewing: Theory, technique, and cases.* New York: Wiley.

Kahn, T. C., & Giffen, M. B. (1960). *Psychological techniques in diagnosis and evaluation.* New York: Pergamon.

Kallingal, A. (1971). The prediction of grades for black and white students at Michigan State University. *Journal of Educational Measurement, 8,* 263–265.

Kamin, L. J. (1974). *The science and politics of I.Q.* Hillsdale, NJ: Erlbaum.

Kamphaus, R. W. (1993). *Clinical assessment of children–s intelligence: A handbook for professional practice.* Boston: Allyn & Bacon.

Kane, R. L. (1991). Standardized and flexible batteries in neuropsychology: An assessment update. *Neuropsychology Review, 2,* 281–337.

Kane, R. L., & Kay, G. G. (1992). Computerized assessment in neuropsychology: A review of tests and test batteries. *Neuropsychology Review, 3,* 1–117.

Kanfer, F. H., & Grimm, L. G. (1977). Behavioral analysis: Selecting target behaviors in the interview. *Behavior Modification, 4,* 419–444.

Kanfer, F. H., & Saslow, G. (1969). Behavioral diagnosis. In C. M. Franks (Ed.), *Behavior therapy: Appraisal and status.* New York: McGraw-Hill.

Kaplan, E., Fein, D., Morris, R., & Delis, D. (1991). *WAIS-R as a neuropsychological instrument.* San Antonio, TX: The Psychological Corporation.

Kaplan, E., & Gallagher, R. (in press). The Wechsler intelligence scales. In G. Groth-Marnat (Ed.), *Neuropsychological assessment in clinical assessment: A practical guide to test interpretation and integration.* New York: Wiley.

Kaplan, H. I., & Sadock, B. J. (1996). *Comprehensive textbook of psychiatry* (6th ed.). Washington, DC: American Psychiatric Press.

Kaplan, R. M., & Saccuzzo, D. P. (1989). *Psychological testing: Principles, applications, and issues* (2nd ed.). Pacific Grove, CA: Brooks Cole.

Kaplan, R. M., & Sacuzzo, D. P. (1993). *Psychological testing: Principles, applications, and issues* (3rd ed.). Pacific Grove, CA: Brooks Cole.

Kareken, D. A., & Williams, J. M. (1994). Human judgement and estimation of premorbid intellectual function. *Psychological Assessment, 6,* 83–91.

Karon, B. P. (1978). Projective tests are valid. *American Psychologist, 33,* 764–765.

Karp, S. A., Holstrom, R. W., & Silber, D. E. (1989). *Manual for the Apperceptive Personality Test (APT).* Orland Park. IL: International Diagnostic Systems.

Karp, S. A., Silber, D. E., Holstrom, R. W., Banks, V., & Karp, J. (1992). Outcomes of Thematic Apperceptive Test and Apperceptive Personality Test stories. *Perceptual and Motor Skills, 74,* 479–482.

Katz, L., Goldstein, G., Rudisin, S., & Bailey, D. (1993). A neuropsychological approach to the Bannatyne recategorization of the Wechsler Intelliegence Scales in adults with learning disabilities. *Journal of Learning Disabilities, 26,* 65–72.

Kaufman, A. S. (1975). Factor analysis of the WISC-R at eleven ages between $6\frac{1}{2}$ and $16\frac{1}{2}$ years. *Journal of Consulting and Clinical Psychology, 43,* 135–147.

Kaufman, A. S. (1976a). Verbal-performance I.Q. discrepancies on the WISC-R. *Journal of Consulting and Clinical Psychology, 44,* 739–744.

Kaufman, A. S. (1976b). A new approach to the interpretation of test scatter on the WISC-R. *Journal of Learning Disabilities, 9,* 160–168.

Kaufman, A. S. (1979). *Intelligent testing with the WISC-R.* New York: Wiley.

Kaufman, A. S. (1983). Test review: WAIS-R. *Journal of Psychoeducational Assessment, 1,* 309–319.

Kaufman, A. S. (1990). *Assessing adolescent and adult intelligence.* Boston: Allyn & Bacon.

Kaufman, A. S. (1994). *Intelligent testing with the WISC-III.* New York: Wiley.

Kaufman, A. S., & Horn, J. L. (1994). *Age changes on tests of fluid and crystallised ability for females on the Kaufman Adolescent and Adult Intelligence Test (KAIT) at ages 17 to 94 years.* Manuscript submitted for publication.

Kaufman, A. S., Kaufman, J. C., Balgopal, R., & McLean, J. E. (1996). Comparison of three WISC-III short forms: Weighing psychometric, clinical, and practical factors. *Journal of Clinical Child Psychology, 25,* 97–105.

Kaufman, A. S., Kaufman, J. C., Ramaswamy, B., & McLean, J. E. (1996). Comparison of three WISC-III short forms: Weighing psychometric, clinical, and practical factors. *Journal of Clinical Child Psychology, 25,* 97–105.

Kaufman, A. S., & Kaufman, N. L. (1983). *Interpretive manual for the Kaufman Assessment Battery for Children.* Circle Pines, MN: American Guidance Service.

Kaufman, A. S., & Kaufman, N. L. (1993). *Manual for the Kaufman Adolescent and Adult Intelligence Test (KAIT).* Circle Pines, MN: American Guidance Service.

Kaufman, A. S., McLean, J. E., & Reynolds, C. R. (1988). Sex, race, residence, region, and education differences on the 11 WAIS-R subtests. *Journal of Clinical Psychology, 44,* 231–248.

Kaufman, A. S., Reynolds, C. R., & McLean, J. E. (1989). Age and WAIS-R intelligence in a national sample of adults in the 20- to 74-years age range: A cross-sectional anaysis with educational level controlled. *Intelligence, 13,* 225–253.

Kavale, K. A., & Forness, S. R. (1984). A meta-analysis of the validity of Wechsler Scale profiles and recategorizations: Patterns or parodies? *Learning Disability Quarterly, 7,* 136–156.

Kazdin, A. E. (1988). The diagnosis of childhood disorders: Assessment issues and strategies. *Behavioral Assessment, 10,* 67–94.

Kearney, P., Beatty, M. J., Plax, T. G., & McCroskey, J. C. (1984). Factor analysis of the Rathus Assertiveness Schedule and the Personal Report of Communication Apprehension: 24. Replication and extension. *Psychological Reports, 54,* 851–854.

Kehoe, J. F., & Tenopyr, M. L. (1994). Adjustment in assessment scores and their usage: A taxonomy and evaluation of methods. *Psychological Assessment, 6,* 291–303.

Keiller, S., & Graham, J. R. (1993). The meaning of low scores on the MMPI-2 clinical scales of normal subjects. *Journal of Personality Assessment, 61,* 211–223.

Keiser, R. E., & Prather, E. N. (1990). What is the TAT? A review of ten years of research. *Journal of Personality Research, 55,* 800–803.

Keith, T. Z., Fehrmann, P. G., Harrison, P. L., & Pottebaum, S. M. (1987). The relation between adaptive behavior and intelligence: Testing alternative explanations. *Journal of School Psychology, 25,* 31–43.

Keller, J. (1955). The use of a Bender-Gestalt maturation level scoring system with mentally handicapped children. *American Journal of Orthopsychiatry, 25,* 563–573.

Kelly, D., Marguilies, H., & Barrera, S. (1941). The stability of the Rorschach method as demonstrated in electroconvulsive therapy cases. *Rorschach Research Exchange, 5,* 44–48.

Kelly, E. L., & Fiske, D. W. (1951). *The prediction of performance in clinical psychology.* Ann Arbor: University of Michigan Press.

Keltikangas-Jarvinen, L. (1986). Concept of alexithymia: I. The prevalence of alexithymia in psychosomatic patients. *Psychotherapy and Psychosomatics, 44,* 132–138.

Kendall, P. C., & Hollon. (Eds.). (1981). *Assessment strategies for cognitive-behavioral interventions.* New York: Academic Press.

Kennedy, K. J. (1981). Age effects on Trail Making Test performance. *Perceptual and Motor Skills, 52,* 671–675.

Keogh, B. K., & Smith, C. (1961). Group techniques and a proposed scoring system for the Bender-Gestalt Test with children. *Journal of Clinical Psychology, 17,* 172–175.

Kerns, L. L. (1986). Falsifications in the psychiatric history: A differential diagnosis. *Psychiatry, 49,* 13–17.

Keyser, D. J., & Sweetland, R. C. (Eds.). (1985). *Test critiques* (Vol. 1). Kansas City: Test Corporation of America.

Kincel, R. L., & Murray, S. C. (1984). Kinesthesias in perception and the experience type: Dance and creative projection. *British Journal of Projective Psychology and Personality Study, 29,* 3–7.

Kinder, B. N. (1994). Where the action is in personality assessment. *Journal of Personality Assessment, 62,* 585–588.

Kipnis, D. (1968). Social immaturity, intellectual ability, and adjustive behavior in college. *Journal of Applied Psychology, 52,* 71–80.

Kirk, B. A., Cumming, R. W., & Hackett, H. H. (1963). Personal and vocational characteristics of dental students. *Personnel and Guidance Journal, 41,* 522–527.

Kitson, D. L., & Vance, H. B. (1982). Relationship of the Wechsler Intelligence Scale for Children-Revised and the Wide Range Achievement Test for a selected sample of young children. *Psychological Reports, 50,* 981–982.

Klassen, D., & O'Connor, W. A. (1989). Assessing the risk of violence in released mental patients: A cross-validation study. *Psychological Assessment, 1,* 75–81.

Klein, R. G. (1986). Questioning the usefulness of projective psychological tests for children. *Journal of Developmental and Behavioral Pediatrics, 7,* 378–382.

Kleinmuntz, B. (1990). Why we still use our heads instead of formulas: Toward an integrative approach. *Psychological Bulletin, 107,* 296–310.

Kleinmuntz, B., & Szucko, J. J. (1984). Lie detection in ancient and modern times: A call for contemporary scientific study. *American Psychologist, 39,* 766–776.

Kline, R. B., Snyder, J., & Castellanos, M. (1996). Lessons from the Kaufman Assessment Battery for Children (K-ABC): Toward a new cognitive assessment model. *Psychological Assessment, 8,* 7–17.

Klinefelter, D., Pancoast, D. L., Archer, R. P., & Pruitt, D. L. (1990). Recent adolescent MMPI norms: T score elevation comparisons to Marks and Briggs. *Journal of Personality Assessment, 54,* 379–389.

Klinger, E. (1966). Fantasy need achievement as a motivational construct. *Psychological Bulletin, 66,* 291–308.

Klopfer, B. (1937). The present status of the theoretical development of the Rorschach method. *Rorschach Research Exchange, 1,* 142–147.

Klopfer, B., Ainsworth, M. D., Klopfer, W. G., & Holt, R. R. (1956). *Developments in the Rorschach technique* (Vol. 2). Yonkers, NY: World Book.

Klopfer, B., & Davidson, H. (1962). *The Rorschach technique: An introductory manual.* New York: Harcourt, Brace, Jovanovich.

Klopfer, W. G. (1960). *The psychological report.* New York: Grune & Stratton.

Klopfer, W. G. (1983). Writing psychological reports. In A. Walker (Ed.), *The handbook of clinical psychology: Theory, research, and practice.* Homewood, IL: Dow Jones-Irwin.

Klopfer, W. G., & Taulbee, E. S. (1976). Projective tests. *Annual Review of Psychology, 27,* 543–567.

Knight, R. G., & Godfrey, H. P. D. (1996). Psychosocial aspects of neurological disorders: Implications for research in neuropsychology. *Australian Psychologist, 31,* 48–51.

Knoff, H. M., & Prout, H. T. (1985). The Kinetic Drawing System: A review and integration of the kinetic family and school drawing techniques. *Psychology in the Schools, 22,* 50–59.

Kobler, F. (1983). The Rorschach test in clnical practice. *Interdisciplinaria, 4,* 131–139.

Kobler, F. J., & Stiel, A. (1953). The use of the Rorschach in involutional melancholia. *Journal of Consulting Psychology, 17,* 365–370.

Koch, C. (1952). *The tree test.* New York: Grune & Stratton.

Kolb, L. C. (1977). *Modern clinical psychiatry* (9th ed.). Philadelphia: W.B. Saunders.

Koppitz, E. M. (1958a). Relationships between the Bender-Gestalt Test and the Wechsler Intelligence Scale for Children. *Journal of Clinical Psychology, 14,* 413–416.

Koppitz, E. M. (1958b). The Bender-Gestalt Test and learning disturbance in young children. *Journal of Clinical Psychology, 14,* 292–295.

Koppitz, E. M. (1960a). Teacher's attitude and children's performance on the Bender-Gestalt Test and human figure drawings. *Journal of Clinical Psychology, 16,* 204–208.

Koppitz, E. M. (1960b). The Bender-Gestalt Test for children: A normative study. *Journal of Clinical Psychology, 16,* 432–435.

Koppitz, E. M. (1962a). Diagnosing brain damage in young children with the Bender-Gestalt Test. *Journal of Consulting Psychology, 26,* 541–546.

Koppitz, E. M. (1962b). *The Bender Gestalt Test with the Human Figure Drawing Test for young school children.* Columbus, OH: Department of Education.

Koppitz, E. M. (1963). *The Bender Gestalt Test for Young Children* (Vol. 1). New York: Grune & Stratton.

Koppitz, E. M. (1965). Use of the Bender Gestalt Test in elementary school. *Skolepsykologi, 2,* 193–200.

Koppitz, E. M. (1968). *Psychological evaluation of children's human figure drawings.* Yorktown Heights, NY: The Psychological Corporation.

Koppitz, E. M. (1975). *The Bender Gestalt Test for Young Children: Vol. 2. Research and Applications 1963–1973.* New York: Grune & Stratton.

Koppitz, E. M. (1984). *Psychological evaluation of human figure drawings by middle school pupils.* New York: Grune & Stratton.

Koppitz, E. M., Mardis, V., & Stephens, T. (1961). A note on screening school beginners with the Bender Gestalt Test. *Journal of Educational Psychology, 52,* 80–81.

Koss, M. P. (1979). MMPI item content: "Recurring issues." In J. N. Butcher (Ed.), *New developments in the use of the MMPI* (pp. 3–38). Minneapolis: University of Minnesota Press.

Koss, M. P., & Butcher, J. N. (1973). A comparison of patient's self report with other sources of clinical information. *Journal of Personality Assessment, 7,* 225–236.

Koss, M. P., Butcher, J. N., & Hoffman, N. (1976). The MMPI critical items: How well do they work? *Journal of Consulting and Clinical Psychology, 44,* 921–928.

Kostlan, A. (1954). A method for the empirical study of psychodiagnosis. *Journal of Consulting Psychology, 18,* 83–88.

Kovess, V., & Fournier, L. (1990). The DISSA: An abridged self administered version of the DIS. *Social Psychiatry and Psychiatric Epidemiology, 25,* 170–186.

Kraiger, K., Hakel, M. D., & Cornelius, E. T. (1984). Exploring fantasies of TAT reliability. *Journal of Personality Assessment, 48,* 365–370.

Kramer, J. H. (1993). Interpretation of individual subtest scores on the WISC-III IQ and index scores. *Psychological Assessment, 5,* 193–196.

Kramer, J. J., & Conoley, J. C. (Eds.). (1992). *The eleventh mental measurements yearbook.* Lincoln, NE: Buros Institute of Mental Measurements.

Kratochwill, T. R. (1985). Selection of target behaviors in behavioral consultation. *Behavior Assessment, 7,* 49–61.

Krug, S. E. (1988). *Psychware sourcebook, 1987–1988.* Kansas City, MO: Test Corporation of America.

Krug, S. E. (1993). *Psychware sourcebook* (4th ed.). Kansas City, MO: Test Corporation of America.

Kühn, R. (1963). Über die kritische Rorschach-Forschung and einige ihrer Ergebnisse. *Rorschachiana, 8,* 105–114.

Kunce, J. T., & Tamkin, A. S. (1981). Rorschach movement and color responses and MMPI social extraversion and thinking introversion personality types. *Journal of Personality Assessment, 45,* 5–10.

Kurtines, W. (1974). Autonomy: A concept reconsidered. *Journal of Personality Assessment, 38,* 243–246.

Kurtines, W., Hogan, R., & Weiss, D. (1975). Personality dynamics of heroin use. *Journal of Abnormal Psychology, 84,* 87–89.

Kurz, R. B. (1963). Relationship between time imagery and Rorschach human movement responses. *Journal of Consulting Psychology, 29,* 379–382.

Kwiatkowska, H. Y. (1978). *Family therapy and evaluation through art.* Springfield, IL: Charles C. Thomas.

Lachar, D., & Wrobel, T. A. (1979). Validation of clinician's hunches: Construction of a new MMPI critical item set. *Journal of Consulting and Clinical Psychology, 47,* 277–284.

Lacks, P. (1982). Continued popularity of the Bender-Gestalt Test: Response to Bigler and Ehrfurth. *Professional Psychology, 13,* 677–680.

Lacks, P. (1984). *Bender-Gestalt screening for brain dysfunction.* New York: Wiley.

Lacks, P. (1996). *Bender Gestalt Screening for Brain Dysfunction.* [Computer software]. Odessa, FL: Psychological Assessment Resources.

Lacks, P., & Newport, K. (1980). A comparison of scoring systems and level of scorer experience on the Bender-Gestalt test. *Journal of Personality Assessment, 44,* 351–357.

Lafer, B. (1989). Predicting performance and persistance in hospice volunteers. *Psychological Reports, 65,* 467–472.

Lamb, D. G., Berry, D. T., Wetter, M., & Baer, R. A. (1994). Effects of two types of information on malingering of closed head injury on the MMPI-2: An analog investigation. *Psychological Assessment, 6,* 8–13.

Lanning, K. (1989). Detection of invalid response patterns on the California Psychological Inventory. *Applied Psychological Measurement, 13,* 45–56.

Lanyon, B. P., & Lanyon, R. I. (1980). *Incomplete Sentences Task: Manual.* Chicago: Stoelting.

Lanyon, R. I., & Goodstein, L. D. (1982). *Personality Assessment* (2nd ed.). New York: Wiley.

Lapouse, R., & Monk, M. A. (1958). An epidemiologic study of behavior characteristics of children. *American Journal of Public Health, 48,* 1134–1144.

Lapouse, R., & Monk, M. A. (1964). Behavior deviations in a representative sample of children: Variations by sex, age, race, social class, and family size. *American Journal of Orthopsychiatry, 34,* 436–446.

Larrabee, G. J. (1986). Another look at VIQ-PIQ scores and unilateral brain damage. *International Journal of Neuroscience, 29,* 141–148.

La Rue, A., & Janvik, L. R. (1987). Cognitive function and prediction of dementia in old age. *International Journal of Aging and Human Development, 25,* 78–89.

Laufer, W. S., Skoog, D. K., & Day, J. M. (1982). Personality and criminality: A review of the California Psychological Inventory. *Journal of Clinical Psychology, 38,* 562–573.

Lawrence, S. B. (1984). *Lawrence Psychological-Forensic Examination (Law-PSI).* San Bernadino, CA: Lawrence Psychological Center.

Lazarus, A. A. (1973). Multimodel behavior therapy: Treating the "BASIC ID." *The Journal of Nervous and Mental Diseases, 156,* 404–411.

Lazarus, A. A. (1989). *The practice of multi-modal therapy.* Baltimore: Johns Hopkins University Press.

Leahy, J. M. (1992). Validity and reliability of the Beck depression inventory-short form in a group of adult bereaved females. *Journal of Clinical Psychology, 48,* 64–67.

Leary, T. (1957). *Interpersonal diagnosis of personality.* New York: Ronald Press.

Leavitt, F., & Garron, G. C. (1982). Rorschach and pain characteristics of patients with low back pain and "conversion V" MMPI profiles. *Journal of Personality Assessment, 46,* 18–25.

Leckliter, I. N., Matarazzo, J. D., & Silverstein, A. B. (1986). A literature review of factor analytic studies of the WAIS-R. *Journal of Clinical Psychology, 42,* 332–342.

Lee, J. A., Moreno, K. E., & Sympson, J. B. (1986). The effects of mode of test administration on test performance. *Educational and Psychological Measurement, 46,* 467–473.

Lefebvre, M. F. (1981). Cognitive distortions and cognitive errors in depressed and low back pain patients. *Journal of Consulting and Clinical Psychology, 49,* 517–525.

Lefkowitz, J., & Fraser, A. W. (1980). Assessment of achievment and power motivation of blacks and whites, using a black and white TAT with black and white administrators. *Journal of Applied Psychology, 65,* 685–696.

Leninger, B. E., Gramling, S. E., & Farrell, A. D. (1990). Neuropsychological deficits in symptomatic minor head injury patients after concussion and mild concussion. *Journal of Neurology, Neurosurgery, and Psychiatry, 53,* 293–296.

Leon, G. R., Gillum, B., Gillum, R., & Gouze, M. (1979). Personality stability and change over a 30-year period—middle age to old age. *Journal of Consulting and Clinical Psychology 47,* 517–524.

Leonard, C. V. (1973). Bender-Gestalt as an indicator of suicidal potential. *Psychological Reports, 32,* 665–666.

Lerner, E. A. (1972). *The projective use of the Bender-Gestalt Test.* Springfield, IL: Charles C. Thomas.

Lesiak, J. (1984). The Bender Visual Motor Gestalt Test: Implications for the diagnosis and prediction of reading achievement. *Journal of School Psychology, 22,* 391–405.

Lesser, G. S., Fifer, G., & Clark, D. H. (1965). Mental abilities of children from different social class and cultural groups. *Monographs of the Society for Research in Child Development, 30,* Serial No. 102.

LeUnes, A., Evans, M., Karnei, B., & Lowry, N. (1980). Psychological tests used in research with adolescents, 1969–1973. *Adolescence, 15,* 417–421.

Leura, A. V., & Exner, J. E. (1978). Structural differences in the records of adolescents as a function of being tested by one's own teacher. (Workshops Study No. 265, unpublished). Bayville, NY: Rorschach Workshops.

Levi, J. (1951). Rorschach patterns predicting success or failure in rehabilitation of the physically handicapped. *Journal of Abnormal and Social Psychology, 46,* 240–244.

Levi, J. (1976). Acting out indicators on the Rorschach. In L. Abt & S. Weissman (Eds.), *Acting out* (2nd ed.). New York: Aronson.

Levin, B. E., Llabre, M. M., & Weiner, W. J. (1988). Parkinson's disease and depression: Psychometric properties of the Beck Depression Inventory. *Journal of Neurology, Neurosurgery, and Psychiatry, 51,* 1401–1404.

Levin, H. S., High, W. M., Goethe, K. E., Sisson, R. A., Overall, J. E., Rhoades, H. M., Eisenberg, H., Kalisky, Z., & Gray, H. E. (1987). The Neurobehavioral Rating Scale: Assessment of the behavioral sequalae of head injury by the clinician. *Journal of Neurology, Neurosurgery, and Psychiatry, 50,* 183–193.

Levine, D. (1981). Why and when to test: The social context of psychological testing. In A. I. Rabin (Ed.), *Assessment with projective techniques* (pp. 553–580). New York: Springer.

Levinson, E. M. (1987). Incorporating a vocational component into a school psychological evaluation: A case example. *Psychology in the Schools, 24,* 254–264.

Levitt, E. E. (1957). Results of psychotherapy with children: An evaluation. *Journal of Consulting Psychology, 21,* 189–196.

Levitt, E. E. (1963). Psychotherapy with children: A further evaluation. *Behavioral Research and Therapy, 1,* 45–51.

Levitt, E. E. (1980). *Primer on the Rorschach technique.* Springfield, IL: Charles C. Thomas.

Levitt, E. E., & Gotts, E. E. (1995). *The clinical application of MMPI special scales* (2nd ed.). Hillsdale, NJ: Erlbaum.

Levitt, E. E., & Truumaa, A. (1972). *The Rorschach technique with children and adolescents: Applications and norms.* New York: Grune & Stratton.

Lewak, R. W., Marks, P. A., & Nelson, G. E. (1990). *Therapist guide to the MMPI & MMPI-2.* Muncie, IN: Accelerated Development.

Lewinsohn, P. M. (1965). Psychological correlates of overall quality of figure drawings. *Journal of Consulting Psychology, 29,* 504–512.

Lezak, M. D. (1982). *The test-retest stability and reliability of some tests commonly used in neuropsychological assessment.* Paper presented at the 5th European conference of the International Neuropsychological Society, Deauville, France.

Lezak, M. D. (1983). *Neuropsychological assessment* (2nd ed.). New York: Oxford University Press.

Lezak, M. D. (1989a). *Assessment of the behavioral consequences of brain injury:* Vol. 7. *Frontiers of clinical neuroscience.* New York: Alan R. Liss.

Lezak, M. D. (1989b). Assessment of psychosocial dysfunctions resulting from head trauma. In M. D. Lezak (Ed.), *Assessment of the behavioral consequences of head trauma:* Vol. 7. *Frontiers of clinical neuroscience.* New York: Alan R. Liss.

Lezak, M. D. (1995). *Neuropsychological assessment* (3rd ed.). New York: Oxford University Press.

Lichtenstein, S., & Fischoff, B. (1977). Do those who know more also know more about how much they know? *Organizational Behavior and Human Performance, 20,* 159–183.

Lick, J., Sushinsky, L., & Malow, R. (1977). Specificity of Fear Survey Schedule items and the prediction of avoidance behavior. *Behavior Modification, 1,* 195–203.

Light, B. H., & Amick, J. (1956). Rorschach responses of normal aged. *Journal of Projective Techniques, 20,* 185–195.

Lightfoot, S. L., & Oliver, J. M. (1985). The Beck Inventory: Psychometric properties in university students. *Journal of Personality Assessment, 49,* 434–436.

Lindgren, H. C., Moritsch, B., Thurlin, E. K., & Mich, G. (1986). Validity studies of three measures of achievement motivation. *Psychological Reports, 59,* 123–136.

Lindsay, D. S., & Read, J. D. (1995). "Memory work" and recovered memories of childhood sexual abuse: Scientific evidence and public and professional issues. *Psychology, Public Policy, and Law, 1,* 846–908.

Lindzey, G., & Herman, P. S. (1955). Thematic Apperception Test: A note on reliability and situational validity. *Journal of Projective Techniques, 19,* 36–42.

Lindzey, G., & Kalnins, D. (1958). Thematic Apperception Test: Some evidence bearing on the "hero assumption." *Journal of Abnormal and Social Psychology, 57,* 76–83.

Linton, H. B. (1954). Rorschach correlates of response to suggestion. *Journal of Abnormal and Social Psychology, 49,* 75–83.

Lipsitt, P. D., Lelos, D., & McGarry, A. L. (1971). Competency for trial: A screening instrument. *American Journal of Psychiatry, 128,* 137–141.

Lipsitz, J. D., Dworkin, R. H., & Erlenmeyer-Kimling, L. (1993). Wechsler Comprehension and Picture Arrangment subtests and social adjustment. *Psychological Assessment, 5,* 430–437.

Lison, S., & Van der Spuy, H. I. J. (1977). *Cross-national MMPI research: Group personality in South Africa.* Unpublished manuscript, University of Capetown, Capetown, South Africa.

Little, K. B., & Shneidman, E. S. (1959). Congruencies among interpretations of psychological test and anamnestic data. *Psychological Monographs, 73,* (6, Whole No. 476).

Little, S. G. (1992). The WISC-III: Everything old is new again. *School Pychology Quarterly, 7,* 136–142.

Lockshin, S. B., & Harrison, K. (1991). Computer-assisted assessment of psychological problems. In A. Ager (Ed.), *Microcomputers and clinical psychology: Issues, applications, and future developments* (pp. 47–63). New York: Wiley.

Loehelin, J. C. (1989). Partitioning environmental and genetic contributions to behavioral development. *American Psychologist, 10,* 1285–1292.

Loenberger, L. T. (1989). The question of organicity: Is it still functional? *Professional Psychology: Research and Praqctice, 20,* 411–414.

Loftus, E. F. (1993). The reality of repressed memories. *American Psychologist, 48,* 518–537.

Loosli-Usteri, M. (1929). The Rorschach test applied with different groups of children between 10–13 years. *Archives of Psychology, 22,* 51–106.

Loranger, A. W. (1988). *Personality Disorder Examination (PDE) manual.* Yonkers, NY: DV Communications.

Loughmiller, G. C., Ellison, R. L., Taylor, C. W., & Price, P. B. (1970). Predicting career performances of physicians using the autobiographical inventory approach. *Proceedings of the American Psychological Association, 5,* 153–154.

Louks, J., Hayne, C., & Smith, J. (1989). Replicated factor structure of the Beck Depression Inventory. *The Journal of Nervous and Mental Diseases, 177,* 473–479.

Lovell, V. R. (1967). The human use of personality tests: A dissenting view. *American Psychologist, 22,* 383–393.

Lowman, R. L. (1991). *The clinical practice of career assessment: Interests, abilities and personality.* Washington, DC: American Psychological Association.

Lubin, B., Larsen, R. M., & Matarazzo, J. D. (1984). Patterns of psychological test usage in the United States: 1935–1982. *American Psychologist, 39,* 451–454.

Lubin, B., Larsen, R. M., Matarazzo, J. D., & Seever, M. (1985). Psychological test usage patterns in five professional settings. *American Psychologist, 40,* 857–861.

Lubin, B., Larsen, R. M., Matarazzo, J. D., & Seever, M. (1986). Selected characteristics of psychologists and psychological assessment in five settings: 1959–1988. *Professional Psychology: Research and Practice, 17,* 155–157.

Lubinski, D., & Benbow, C. P. (1995). An opportunity for empiricism. *Contemporary psychology, 40,* 935–940.

Luborsky, L. (1994). Therapeutic alliances as predictors of psychotherapy outcomes: Factors explaining predictive success. In A. O. Horvath & L. S. Greenberg (Eds.), *The working alliance: Theory, research, and practice* (pp. 38–50). New York: Wiley.

Luborsky, L., Singer, B., & Luborsky, L. (1975). Comparative studies of psychotherapies. *Archives of General Psychiatry, 32,* 995–1008.

Lucas, R. W., Mullin, P. J., Luna, C. B., & McInroy, D. C. (1977). Psychiatrists and a computer as interrogators of patients with alcohol-related illnesses: A comparison. *British Journal of Psychiatry, 131,* 160–167.

Lucio, E., Reyes-Lagunes, I., Scott, R. L. (1994). MMPI-2 for Mexico: Translation and adaption. *Journal of Personality Assessment, 63,* 105–116.

Luckasson, R., Coulter, D. L., Polloway, E. A., Reiss, S., Schalock, R. L., Snell, M. E., Spitalnik, D. M., & Stark, J. A. (1992). *Mental retardation: Definition, classification, and systems of support.* Washington, DC: American Association on Mental Retardation.

Lueger, R. L., & Petzel, T. P. (1979). Illusory correlation in clinical judgement: Effects of amount of information to be processed. *Journal of Consulting and Clinical Psychology, 47,* 1120–1121.

Lukin, M. E., Down, E. T., Plake, B. S., & Kraft, R. G. (1985). Comparing computerized versus traditional psychological assessment. *Computers in Human Behavior, 1,* 49–58.

Lundy, A. (1985). The reliability of the Thematic Apperception Test. *Journal of Personality Assessment, 49,* 141–145.

Lundy, A. (1988). Instructional set and Thematic Apperception Test Validity. *Journal of Personality Assessment, 52,* 309–320.

Luria, A. R. (1973). *The working brain.* New York: Basic Books.

Luria, A. R. (1980). *Higher cortical functions in man* (2nd ed.). New York: Basic Books.

Lyle, O. E., & Gottesman, I. I. (1976). Premorbid psychometric indicators of the gene for Huntington's disease. *Journal of Consulting and Clinical Psychology, 45,* 1011–1022.

Mabe, L., & West, C. (1982). Validity of self evaluation of ability: A review and meta-analysis. *Journal of Applied Psychology, 67,* 280–296.

MaCartney-Filgate, M. S., & Vriezen, E. R. (1988). Intercorrelation of clinical tests of verbal memory. *Archives of Clinical Neuropsychology, 3,* 121–126.

Machover, K. (1949). *Personality projection in the drawings of the human figure.* Springfield, IL: Charles C. Thomas.

Maitra, A. K. (1983). Executive effectiveness: Characteristic thematic phantasy. *Managerial Psychology, 4,* 59–68.

Majumber, A. K., & Roy, A. B. (1962). Latent personality content of juvenile delinquents. *Journal of Psychological Research, 1,* 4–8.

Maloney, M. P., & Glasser, A. (1982). An evaluation of the clinical utility of the Draw-A-Person Test. *Journal of Clinical Psychology, 38,* 183–190.

Maloney, M. P., & Ward, M. P. (1976). *Psychological assessment: A conceptual approach.* New York: Oxford University Press.

Malpass, R. S., & Kravitz, J. (1969). Recognition for faces of own and other race. *Journal of Personality and Social Psychology, 13,* 330–334.

Mann, L. (1956). The relation of Rorschach indices of extratension and introversion to a measure of responsiveness to the immediate environment. *Journal of Consulting Psychology, 20,* 114–118.

Margolin, D. I., Pate, D. S., Friedrich, F. J., & Elia, E. (1990). Dysnomia in dementia and in stroke patients: Different underlying cognitive deficits. *Journal of Clinical and Experimental Neuropsychology, 12,* 597–612.

Margolin, G., Hattem, D., John, R. S., & Yost, K. (1985). Perceptual agreement between spouses and outside observers when coding themselves and a stranger dyad. *Behavioral Assessment, 7,* 235–247.

Marks, I. M., & Mathews, A. M. (1979). Brief standard self-rating for phobic patients. *Behavior Research and Therapy, 17,* 263–267.

Marks, P. A., Seeman, W., & Haller, D. L. (1974). *The actuarial use of the MMPI with adolescents and adults.* Baltimore: Williams & Wilkins.

Marley, M. L. (1982). *Organic brain pathology and the Bender Gestalt Test: A differential diagnostic scoring system.* New York: Grune & Stratton.

Martin, J. D., Pfaadt, N. K., & MaKinister, J. G. (1983). Relationship of hostility and white space responses on the Rorschach. *Perceptual and Motor Skills, 57,* 739–742.

Marton, P., Churchard, M., Kutcher, S., & Korenblum, M. (1991). Diagnostic utility of the Beck Depression Inventory with adolescent psychiatric outpatients and inpatients. *Canadian Journal of Psychiatry, 36,* 428–431.

Maruish, M. (1990, Fall). Psychological assessment: What will be its role in the future? *Assessment Applications, 5,* 1–10.

Maruish, M. (Ed.). (1994). *Use of psychological testing for treatment planning and outcome assessment.* Hillsdale, NJ: Erlbaum.

Masling, J. (1992). The influence of situation and interpersonal variables in projective testing. *Journal of Personality Assessment, 59,* 616–640.

Mason, B., & Exner, J. E. (1984). *Correlations between WAIS subtests and nonpatient adult Rorschach data.* Workshops Study No. 289 (unpublished), Rorschach Workshops.

Massman, P. J., & Bigler, E. D. (1993). A quantitative review of the diagnostic utitiity of the WAIS-R Fuld Profile. *Archives of Clinical Neuropsychology, 8,* 417–428.

Massman, P. J., Delis, D. C., Butters, N., Dupont, M., & Gillin, N. (1992). The subcortical dysfunction model of memory deficits in depression: Neuropsychological validation in a subgroup of patients. *Journal of Clinical and Experimental Neuropsychology, 14,* 687–706.

Matarazzo, J. D. (1965). The interview. In B. B. Wolman (Ed.), *Handbook of clinical psychology* (pp. 403–450). New York: McGraw-Hill.

Matarazzo, J. D. (1972). *Wechsler's measurement and appraisal of adult intelligence* (5th ed.). Baltimore: Williams & Wilkins.

Matarazzo, J. D. (1986). Computerized clinical psychological test interpretations: Unvalidated plus all mean and no sigma. *American Psychologist, 41,* 14–24.

Matarazzo, J. D. (1990). Psychological assessment versus psychological testing: Validation from Binet to the school, clinic, and courtroom. *American Psychologist, 45,* 999–1017.

Matarazzo, J. D., Carmody, T. P., & Jacobs, L. D. (1980). Test-retest reliability and stability for the WAIS: A literature review with implications for clinical practice. *Journal of Clinical Neuropsychology, 2,* 89–105.

Matarazzo, J. D., Daniel, M. H., Prifitera, A., & Herman, D. O. (1988). Inter-subtest scatter in the WAIS-R standardization sample. *Journal of Clinical Psychology, 44,* 940–950.

Matarazzo, J. D., & Herman, D. O. (1984). Base rate data for the WAIS-R: Test-retest stability and VIQ-PIQ differences. *Journal of Clinical Neuropsychology, 6,* 351–366.

Matarazzo, J. D., & Prifitera, A. (1989). Subtest scatter and premorbid intelligence: Lessons from the WAIS-R standardization sample. *Psychological Assessment, 1,* 186–191.

Mauger, P. A. (1972). The test-retest reliability of persons: An empirical investigation utilizing the MMPI and the personality research form. *Dissertation Abstracts International, 33,* 2816B.

May, A. E., Urquhart, A., & Tarran, J. (1969). Self-evaluation of depression in various diagnostic and therapeutic groups. *Archives of General Psychiatry, 21,* 191–194.

Mayman, M. (1959). Style, focus, language, and content of an ideal psychological test report. *Journal of Projective Techniques, 23,* 453–458.

Maziade, M., Roy, A. A., Fournier, J. P., Cliche, D., Merette, C., Caron, C., Garneau, Y., Montgrain, N., Shriqui, C., Dion, C., Nicole, L., Potvin, A., Lavallee, J. C., Pires, A., & Raymond, V. (1992). Reliability of best-estimate diagnosis in genetic linkage studies of major psychoses. *American Journal of Psychiatry, 149,* 1674–1686.

McAllister, L. (1988). *A practical guide to CPI interpretation* (2nd ed.). Palo Alto, CA: Consulting Psychologists Press.

McCann, J. T. (1991). Convergent and discriminant validity of the MCMI-II and MMPI personality disorder scales. *Psychological Assessment, 3,* 9–18.

McCarthy, D. A. (1972). *Manual for the McCarthy Scales for Children's Abilities.* New York: Psychological Corporation.

McCathie, H., & Spence, S. H. (1991). What is the revised Fear Survey for children measuring? *Behavior Research and Therapy, 29,* 495–502.

McClelland, D. C. (1961). *The achieving society.* Princeton, NJ: Van Nostrand.

McClelland, D. C. (1966). Longitudinal trends in the relation of thought to action. *Journal of Consulting Psychology, 30,* 479–483.

McClelland, D. C. (1971). *Assessing human motivation.* New York: General Learning Press.

McClelland, D. C., Koestner, P., & Weinberger, J. (1989). How do self-attributed and implicit motives differ? *Psychological Review, 96,* 690–702.

McConnaughy, E. A., Prochaska, J., & Velicer, W. (1983). Stages of change in psychotherapy: Measurement and sample profiles. *Psychotherapy: Theory, Research, and Practice, 20,* 368–375.

McConnell, O. L. (1967). Koppitz's Bender Gestalt in relation to organic and emotional problems in children. *Journal of Clinical Psychology, 23,* 370–374.

McCormick, I. A. (1984). A simple version of the Rathus Assertiveness Schedule. *Behavioral Assessment, 7,* 95–99.

McCormick, T. T., & Brannigan, G. G. (1984). Bender-Gestalt signs as indicants of anxiety, withdrawal, and acting-out behaviors in adolescents. *Journal of Psychology, 118,* 71–74.

McCown, W., Fink, A. D., Galina, H., & Johnson, J. (1992). Effects of laboratory-induced controllable and uncontrollable stress on Rorschach variables m and Y. *Journal of Personality Assessment, 59,* 564–573.

McCracken, L. M., & Franzen, M. D. (1992). Principal-components analysis of the equivalence of alternate forms of the Trail Making Test. *Psychological Assessment, 4,* 235–238.

McCrae, R. R., Costa, P. T., & Piedmont, R. L. (1993). Folk Concepts, natural language, and psychological constructs: The California Psychological Inventory and the five-factor model. *Journal of Personality Assessment, 61,* 1–25.

McCreary, C. P. (1976). Trait and type differences among male and female assaultive and nonassaultive offenders. *Journal of Personality Assessment, 40,* 617–621.

McCurry, S. M., Fitz, A. G., & Terri, L. (1994). Comparison of age-extended norms for the Wechsler Adult Intelligence Scale-Revised in patients with Alzheimer's disease. *Psychological Assessment, 6,* 231–235.

McCusker, P. J. (1994). Validation of Kaufman, Ishikuma, and Kaufman-Packer's Wechsler Adult Intelligence Scale-Revised short forms on a clinical sample. *Psychological Assessment, 6,* 246–248.

McDermott, P. A., Fantuzzo, J. W., & Glutting, J. J. (1989). Just say no to subtest analysis: A critique on Wechsler theory and practice. Conference on Intelligence: Theories and Practice (Memphis, TN). *Journal of Psychoeducational Assessment, 8,* 514–517.

McDermott, P. A., Fantuzzo, J. W., & Glutting, J. L. (1990). Just say no to subtest analysis: A critique on Wechsler theory and practice. Conference on Intelligence: Theories and Practice (1990 Memphis, TN). *Journal of Psychoeducational Assessment, 8,* 290–302.

McDermott, P. A., Fantuzzo, J. W., Glutting, J. J., Watkins, M. W., & Baggaley, M. (1992). Illusions of meaning in the ipsative assessment of children's abilities. *Journal of Special Education, 25,* 504–526.

McDonald, S. (1996). Hypothesis testing in neuropsychology in context: Another response to the neuropsychology debate. *Australian Psychologist, 31,* 73–75.

McFall, R. M., & Lillesand, D. V. (1971). Behavior rehearsal with modeling and coaching in assertive training. *Journal of Abnormal Psychology, 77,* 313–323.

McFarland, R. A. (1984). Effects of music upon emotional content of TAT stories. *Journal of Psychology, 116,* 227–234.

McFie, J. (1960). Psychological testing in clinical neurology. *Journal of Nervous and Mental Disease, 131,* 383–393.

McFie, J. (1969). The diagnostic significance of disorders of higher nervous activity syndromes related to frontal, temporal, parietal, and occipital lesions. In P. J. Vinken & G. W. Bruyn (Eds.), *Handbook of clinical neurology* (Vol. 4). New York: American Elsevier.

McGregor, J. P. (1979). Kinetic Family Drawing Test: A validity study. *Dissertation Abstracts International, 40,* 927–928.

McIntosh, J. A., Belter, R. W., Saylor, C. F., Finch, A. J., & Edwards, G. L. (1988). The Bender-Gestalt with adolescents: Comparison of two scoring systems. *Journal of Clinical Psychology, 44,* 226–230.

McKay, M. F., & Neale, M. D. (1985). Predicting early school achievement in reading and handwriting using major "error" categories from the Bender-Gestalt Test for young children. *Perceptual and Motor Skills, 60,* 647–654.

McKnight, D. L., Nelson, R. O., Hayes, S. C., & Jarrett, R. B. (1984). Importance of treating individually-assessed response classes in the amelioration of depression. *Behavior Therapy, 15,* 315–335.

McLachlan, J. F. C., & Head, V. B. (1974). An impairment rating scale for human figure drawings. *Journal of Clinical Psychology, 30,* 405–407.

McLean, P., & Taylor, S. (1992). Severity of unipolar depression and choice of treatment. *Behavior Research and Therapy, 30,* 443–451.

McNeish, T. J., & Naglieri, J. A. (1993). Identification of individuals with serious emotional disturbance using the Draw A Person: Screening procedure for emotional disturbance. *The Journal of Special Education, 27,* 115–121.

McNemar, Q. (1974). Correction to a correction. *Journal of Consulting and Clinical Psychology, 42,* 145–146.

McReynolds, P. (1989). Diagnosis and clinical assessment: Current status and major issues. *Annual Review of Psychology, 40,* 83–108.

Meehl, P. E. (1954). *Clinical versus statistical prediction: A theoretical analysis and a review of the evidence.* Minneapolis: University of Minnesota Press.

Meehl, P. E. (1965). Seer over sign: The first good example. *Journal of Experimental Research in Personality 1,* 27–32.

Meer, B. (1955). The relative difficulty of the Rorschach cards. *Journal of Projective Techniques, 9,* 43–59.

Megargee, E. I. (1964). *Undercontrol and overcontrol in assaultive and homicidal adolescents* (Doctoral dissertation, University of California, Berkley, 1964). University Microfilms, No. 64-9923.

Megargee, E. I. (1965). Assault with intent to kill. *Trans-Action, 2,* 27–31.

Megargee, E. I. (1966a). Estimation of CPI scores from MMPI protocols. *Journal of Clinical Psychology, 22,* 456–458.

Megargee, E. I. (1966b). *Research in clinical assessment.* New York: Harper & Row.

Megargee, E. I. (1966c). The Edwards SD Scale: A measure of dissimulation or adjustment? *Journal of Consulting Psychology, 30,* 566.

Megargee, E. I. (1966d). Undercontrolled and overcontrolled personality types in extreme antisocial aggression. *Psychological Monographs, 80,* No. 611.

Megargee, E. I. (1972). *The California Psychological Inventory handbook.* San Francisco: Jossey-Bass.

Megargee, E. I. (1995). Assessing and understanding aggressive and violent patients. In J. Butcher (Ed.), *Clinical personality assessment: Practical approaches* (pp. 395–409). New York: Oxford University Press.

Megargee, E. I., Cook, P. E., & Mendelsohn, G. A. (1967). Development and evaluation of an MMPI scale of assaultiveness in overcontrolled individuals. *Journal of Abnormal Psychology, 72,* 519–528.

Megargee, E. I., & Mendelsohn, G. A. (1962). A cross-validation of twelve MMPI indices of hostility and control. *Journal of Abnormal Psychology, 65,* 431–438.

Megargee, E. I., & Parker, G. V. (1968). An exploration of the equivalence of Murrayan needs as assessed by the Adjective Check List, the TAT, and the Edwards Personal Preference Schedule. *Journal of Clinical Psychology, 24,* 47–51.

Mehrabian, A. (1972). *Nonverbal communication.* Chicago: Aldine-Atherton.

Melzack, R. (1975). The McGill Pain Questionnaire: Major properties and scoring methods. *Pain, 1,* 277–299.

Mendez, F. (1978). *Adult Neuropsychological Questionnaire.* Odessa, FL: Psychological Assessment Resources.

Merbaum, M., & Hefetz, A. (1976). Some personality characteristics of soldiers exposed to extreme war stress. *Journal of Consulting and Clinical Psychology, 44,* 1–6.

Mercer, J. R. (1979). In defense of racially and culturally non-discriminatory assessment. *School Psychology Digest, 8,* 89–115.

Mercer, J. R., & Lewis, J. F. (1978). *System of multicultural pluralistic assessment.* San Antonio, TX: The Psychological Corporation.

Mermelstein, J. J. (1983). The relationship between rotation on the Bender-Gestalt Test and ratings of patient disorientation. *Journal of Personality Assessment, 47,* 490–491.

Merrens, M. R., & Richards, W. S. (1970). Acceptance of generalized versus "bona fide" personality interpretation. *Psychological Reports, 27,* 691–694.

Messick, S. (1984). Assessment in context: Appraising student performance in relation to instructional quality. *Educational Research, 13,* 3–8.

Messick, S. (1995). Validity of psychological assessment: Validation of inferences from persons' responses and performances as scientific inquiry into score meaning. *Psychological Assessment, 7,* 741–749.

Meyer, P., & Davis, S. (1992). *The CPI applications guide: An essential tool for individual, group, and organizational development.* Palo Alto, CA: Consulting Psychologists Press.

Meyer, R. G. (1993). *The clinician's handbook: Integrated diagnostics, assessment and intervention in adult and adolescent psychopathology.* Needham Heights, MA: Allyn & Bacon.

Meyerink, L. H., Reitan, R. M., & Selz, M. (1988). The validity of the MMPI with multiple sclerosis. *Journal of Clinical Psychology, 44,* 764–769.

Meyers, J. E., & Meyers, K. R. (1996). *Rey Complex Figure Test and Recognition Trial: A Professional Manual.* Odessa, FL: Psychological Assessment Resources.

Miceli, G., Caltagirone, C., Gainotti, G., Masullo, C., & Silveri, M. C. (1981). Neuropsychological correlates of localized cerebral lesions in non-aphasic brain-damaged patients. *Journal of Clinical Neuropsychology, 3,* 53–63.

Michael, C. C., & Funabiki, D. (1985). Depression, distortion, and life stress: Extended findings. *Cognitive Therapy and Research, 9,* 659–666.

Miller, C., Knapp, S. C., & Daniels, C. W. (1968). MMPI study of Negro mental hygiene clinic patients. *Journal of Abnormal Psychology, 73,* 168–173.

Miller, H. R., Streiner, D. L., & Parkinson, A. (1992). Maximum liklihood estimates of the ability of the MMPI and the MCMI personality disorder scales and the SIDP to identify personality disorders. *Journal of Personality Assessment, 59,* 1–13.

Miller, I. W., III, & Norman, W. H. (1986). Persistance of depressive cognitions within a subgroup of depressed inpatients. *Cognitive Therapy and Research, 10,* 211–224.

Miller, L. (1993, January/February). Toxic torts: Clinical neuropsychological and forensic aspects of chemical and electrical injuries. *Journal of Cognitive Rehabilitation, 11,* 6–18.

Millon, T. (1969). *Modern psychopathology: A biosocial approach to maladaptive learning and functioning.* Philadelphia: Saunders.

Millon, T. (1977). *Millon Clinical Multiaxial Inventory.* Minneapolis, MN: National Computer Systems.

Millon, T. (1985). The MCMI provides a good assessment of *DSM-III* disorders. The MCMI-II will prove even better. *Journal of Personality Assessment, 49,* 379–391.

Millon, T. (1987). *Manual for the MCMI-II* (2nd ed.). Minneapolis, MN: National Computer Systems.

Millon, T. (1992). Millon Clinical Multiaxial Inventory: I & II. *Journal of Counseling and Development, 70,* 422–426.

Millon, T. (1994). *Manual for the MCMI-III.* Mineapolis, MN: National Computer Systems.

Millon, T. (1996). *The Millon Inventories.* New York: Guilford.

Millon, T., & Davis, R. D. (1996). *Disorders of personality: DSM-IV and beyond.* New York: Wiley.

Mills, C. J., & Bohannon, W. E. (1980). Personality characteristics of effective state police officers. *Journal of Applied Psychology, 65,* 680–684.

Milne, D. (1984). Improving the social validity and implementation of behavior therapy training for psychiatric nurses using a patient-centred learning format. *British Journal of Clinical Psychology, 23,* 313–314.

Mirza, L. (1977). *Multiple administration of the MMPI with schizophrenics.* Unpublished manuscript, Fountain House, Pakistan.

Mischel, W. (1968). *Personality and assessment.* New York: Wiley.

Mishra, S. P., Ferguson, B. A., & King, P. V. (1985). Research with the Wechsler Digit Span subtest: Implications for assessment. *School Psychology Review, 14,* 37–47.

Mitchell, J. V. (Ed.). (1985). *The ninth mental measurements yearbook.* Highland Park, NJ: Gryphon Press.

Mitchell, J., Trent, R., & McArthur, R. (1993). *Human Figure Drawing Test: An illustrated handbook for clinical interpretation and standardized assessment of cognitive impairment.* Los Angeles: Western Psychological Services.

Mitchell, R. E., Grandy, T. G., & Lupo, J. V. (1986). Comparison of the WAIS and the WAIS-R in the upper ranges of I.Q. *Professional Psychology: Research and Practice, 17,* 82–83.

Mitrushina, M., & Satz, P. (1995). Base rates of the WAIS-R intersubtest scatter and VIQ-PIQ discrepancy in normal elderly. *Journal of Clinical Psychology, 51,* 70–78.

Mitrushina, M., Satz, P., & Van Gorp, W. (1989). Some putative cognitive precursors in subjects hypothesized to be at-risk for dementia. *Archives of Clinical Neuropsychology, 4,* 323–333.

Mittenberg, W., Hammeke, T. A., & Rao, S. M. (1989). Intrasubtest scatter on the WAIS-R as a pathognomonic sign of brain injury. *Psychological Assessment, 1,* 273–276.

Mizes, J. S., & Christiano, B. A. (1994). Assessment of cognitive variables relevant to cognitive behavioral perspectives on anorexia nervosa and bulimia nervosa. *Behavior Research and Therapy, 33,* 95–105.

Mizushima, K., & De Vos, G. (1967). An application of the California Psychological Inventory in a study of Japanese delinquency. *Journal of Clinical Psychology, 71,* 45–51.

Mohr, D. C. (1995). The role of proscription in psychotherapy. *Psychotherapy, 32,* 187–193.

Molish, H. B. (1967). Critique and problems of the Rorschach. A survey. In S. J. Beck & H. B. Molish (Eds.), *Rorschach's Test: Vol. 2. A variety of personality pictures* (2nd ed., pp. 45–48). New York: Grune & Stratton.

Montague, D. J., & Prytula, R. E. (1975). Human figure drawing characteristics related to juvenile delinquents. *Perceptual and Motor Skills, 40,* 623–630.

Moon, G. W., Blakey, W. A., Gorsuch, R. L., & Fantuzo, J. W. (1991). Frequent WAIS-R administration errors: An ignored source of inaccurate measurement. *Professional Psychology, 22,* 256–258.

Moon, G. W., Fantuzzo, J. W., & Gorsuch, R. L. (1986). Teaching WAIS-R administration skills: Comparison of the MASTERY model to other existing clinical training modalities. *Professional Psychology, 17,* 31–35.

Moore, A. D., Stanbrook, M., Hawryluk, G. A., Peters, L. C., Gill, D. D., & Hymans, M. M. (1990). Test-retest stability of the Wechsler Adult Intelligence Scale-Revised in the assessment of head-injured patients. *Psychological Assessment, 2,* 98–100.

Moos, R. H. (1990). Depressed outpatients' life contexts, amount of treatment, and treatment outcome. *Journal of Nervous and Mental Disease, 178,* 105–112.

Moreland, K. L., Eyde, L. D., Robertson, G. J., Primoff, E. S., & Most, R. B. (1995). Assessment of test user qualifications: A research-based measurement procedure. *American Psychologist, 50,* 14–23.

Morena, D. (1981). The healthy drawing. In G. Groth-Marnat & D. Morena (Eds.), *Handbook of psychological assessment* (pp. 80–85). Unpublished manuscript.

Morey, L. C., Blashfield, R. K., Webb, W. W., & Jewell, J. (1988). MMPI scales for *DSM-III* personality disorders: A preliminary validation study. *Journal of Clinical Psychology, 44,* 47–50.

Morgan, C. D., & Murray, H. A. (1935). A method for investigating fantasies. *AMA Archives of Neurology and Psychiatry, 34,* 389–406.

Morgan, W. G. (1995). Origin and history of the Thematic apperception Test Images. *Journal of Personality Assessment, 65,* 237–254.

Morganstern, K. P. (1988). Behavioral interviewing. In A. S. Bellack & M. Hersen (Eds.), *Behavioral assessment: A practical handbook* (3rd ed., pp. 86–118). New York: Pergamon.

Morris, J. C., Heyman, A., Mohs, R. C., Hughes, J. P., van Belle, G., Fillenbaum, G., Mellits, E. D., Vlark, C., & the CERAD investigators. (1989). The Consortium to Establish a Registry for Alzheimer's Disease (CERAD): Part 1. Clinical and neuropsychological assessment of Alzheimer's disease. *Neurology, 39,* 1159–1165.

Morrison, J. (1993). *The first interview: A guide for clinicians.* New York: Guilford.

Morrison, R. L. (1988). Structured interviews and rating scales. In A. S. Bellack & M. Hersen (Eds.), *Behavioral assessment: A practical handbook* (3rd ed., pp. 252–277). New York: Pergamon.

Morrow, L. A., Furman, J. M. R., Ryan, C. M., & Hodgson, M. J. (1988). Neuropsychological deficits associated with verbatim abnormalities in solvent exposed workers. *The Clinical Neuropsychologist, 2,* 272–273.

Mosher, D. L. (1965). Approval motive and acceptance of personality-test interpretations which differ in favorability. *Psychological Reports, 17,* 395–402.

Motta, R., Little, S., & Tobin, M. (1993). The use and abuse of human figure drawings. *School Psychology Quarterly, 8,* 162–169.

Mueller, H. H., Dash, V. N., Matheson, D. W., & Short, R. H. (1984). WISC-R subtest patterning of below average, average, and above average I.Q. children: A meta-analysis. *Alberta Journal of Educational Research, 30,* 68–85.

Mukerji, M. (1969). Rorschach indices of love, aggression, and happiness. *Journal of Projective Techniques and Personality Assessment, 33,* 526–529.

Mulvey, E. P., & Lidz, C. W. (1995). Conditional prediction: A model for research on dangerousness to others in a new era. *International Journal of Psychiatry and the Law, 18,* 129–143.

Munley, P. H. (1991). Confidence intervals for the MMPI-2. *Journal of Personality Assessment, 57,* 52–60.

Murdoch, B. E., Chenery, H. J., Wilks, V., & Boyle, R. S. (1987). Language disorder in dementia of the Alzheimer's type. *Brain and Language, 31,* 122–137.

Murillo, L. G., & Exner, J. E. (1973). The effects of regressive ECT with process schizophrenics. *American Journal of Psychiatry, 130,* 269–273.

Murray, H. A. (1938). *Explorations in personality.* New York: Oxford University Press.

Murray, H. A. (1943). *Thematic Apperception Test manual.* Cambridge, MA: Harvard University Press.

Murstein, B. I. (1960). Factor analysis of the Rorschach. *Journal of Consulting Psychology, 24,* 262–275.

Murstein, B. I. (1963). *Theory and research in projective techniques (Emphasizing the TAT).* New York: Wiley.

Murstein, B. L. (1972). Normative written TAT responses for a college sample. *Journal of Personality Assessment, 36,* 104–147.

Myers, P. I., & Hammill, D. D. (1982). *Learning disabilities: Basic concepts, assessment practices, and instructional strategies.* Austin, TX: Pro-Ed.

Nagle, R. J., & Bell, N. L. (1995). Clinical utility of Kaufman's "amazingly" short forms of the WAIS-R with educable mentally retarded adolescents. *Journal of Clinical Psychology, 51,* 396–400.

Naglieri, J. A. (1980). A comparison of McCarthy General Cognitive Index and WISC-R I.Q. for educable mentally retarded, learning disabled, and normal children. *Psychological Reports, 47,* 591–596.

Naglieri, J. A. (1988). *Draw A Person: A quantitative scoring system.* San Antonio, TX: The Psychological Corporation.

Naglieri, J. A. (1993). Pairwise and ipsative comparisons of WISC-III IQ and index scores. *Psychological Assessment, 5,* 113–116.

Naglieri, J. A., & Kaufman, A. S. (1983). How many factors underlie the WAIS-R? *Journal of Psychoeducational Assessment, 1,* 113–119.

Naglieri, J. A., McNeish, T. J., & Bardos, A. N. (1991). *Draw-A-Person: Screening Procedure for Emotional Disturbance.* Austin, TX: Pro-Ed.

Naglieri, J. A., & Pfeiffer, S. I. (1992). Performance of disruptive behavior disordered and normal samples on the Draw A Person: Screening Procedure for Emotional Distrubance. *Psychological Assessment, 4,* 156–159.

National Institute of Mental Health. (1991). *NIMH Diagnostic Interview Schedule for Children, Version 2.3.* Rockville, MD: Author.

Neale, E. L., Rosal, M., & Rosal, M. L. (1993). What can art therapists learn from the research on projective techniques for children? A review of the literature. *The Arts in Psychotherapy, 20,* 37–49.

Neale, M. D., & McKay, M. F. (1985). Scoring the Bender-Gestalt Test using the Koppitz Developmental System: Interrater reliability, item difficulty, and scoring implications. *Perceptual and Motor Skills, 60,* 627–636.

Neisser, U., Boodoo, G., Bouchard, T. J., Boykin, A. W., Brody, N., Ceci, S. J., Halpern, D. F., Loehelin, J. C., Perloff, R., Sternberg, R. J., & Urbina, S. (1996). Intelligence: Knowns and unknowns. *American Psychologist, 51,* 77–101.

Nelson, L. D., Satz, P., Mitrushina, M., Van Gorp, W., Cicchetti, D., Lewis, R., & Van Lancker, D. (1989). Development and validation of the Neuropsychology Behavior and Affect Profile. *Psychological Assessment, 1,* 266–272.

Nelson, R. E. (1977). Irrational beliefs in depression. *Journal of Consulting and Clinical Psychology, 45,* 1190–1191.

Nelson, R. E., & Maser, J. D. (1988). The *DSM-III* and depression: Potential contributions of behavioral assessment. *Behavioral assessment, 10,* 45–66.

Nevo, B. (1985). Face validity revisited. *Journal of Educational Measurement, 22,* 287–293.

Nevo, B., & Sfez, J. (1985). Examinee's feedback questionnaires. *Assessment and Evaluation in Higher Education, 10,* 236–249.

Newcombe, F. (1969). *Missle wounds of the brain.* New York: Oxford University Press.

Newmark, C. S., & Thibodeau, J. R. (1979). Interpretive accuracy and empirical validity of abbreviated forms of the MMPI with hospitalized adolescents. In C. S. Newmark (Ed.), *MMPI: Clinical and research trends.* New York: Praeger.

Nezu, A. M., & Nezu, C. M. (1993). Identifying and selecting target problems for clinical intervention: A problem-solving model. *Psychological Assessment, 5,* 254–263.

Nicholi, A. M. (1978). History and mental status. In A. M. Nicholi (Ed.), *The Harvard guide to modern psychiatry.* Cambridge, MA: Harvard University Press.

Nisbett, R. E., & Wilson, T. D. (1977). Telling more than we can know: Verbal reports on mental processes. *Psychological Review, 84,* 231–259.

Nobo, J., & Evans, R. G. (1986). The WAIS-R Picture Arrangement and Comprehension subtests as measures of social behavior characteristics. *Journal of Personality Assessment, 50,* 90–92.

Norcross, J. C., & Beutler, L. E. (in press). Determining the therapeutic relationship of choice in brief therapy. In J. N. Butcher (Ed.), *Objective psychological assessment in managed health care: A practitioner's guide.* New York: Oxford University Press.

Norford, B. C., & Barrakat, L. P. (1990). The relationship of human figure drawings to aggressive behavior in preschool children. *Psychology in the Schools, 27,* 318–324.

Norman, R. D. (1966). A revised deterioration formula for the Wechsler Adult Intelligence Scale. *Journal of Clinical Psychology, 22,* 287–294.

Norton, J. C. (1978). The Trail Making Test and Bender Background Interference Procedure as screening devices. *Journal of Clinical Psychology, 34,* 916–922.

Norton, R., & Warnick, B. (1976). Assertiveness as a communication construct. *Human Communication Research, 3,* 62–66.

Nottingham, E. J., & Mattson, R. E. (1981). A validation study of the competency screening test. *Law and Human Behavior, 5,* 329–335.

Oakland, T. D. (1980). An evaluation of the ABIC, pluralistic norms, and estimated learning potential. *Journal of School Psychology, 18,* 3–11.

Oakland, T. D., & Dowling, L. (1983). The Draw-A-Person Test: Validity properties for nonbiased assessment. *Learning Disabilities Quarterly, 6,* 526–534.

Oas, P. (1984). Validity of the Draw-A-Person and Bender Gestalt Tests as measures of impulsivity with adolescents. *Journal of Consulting and Clinical Psychology, 52,* 1011–1019.

Ober, B. A., Koss, E., Friedland, R. P., & Delis, D. C. (1985). Processes of verbal memory failure in Alzheimer-type dementia. *Brain and Cognition, 4,* 90–103.

Obrzut, J. E., & Cummings, J. A. (1983). The projective approach to personality assessment: An analysis of thematic picture techniques. *School Psychology Review, 12,* 414–420.

O'Dell, J. P. (1972). Barnum explores the computer. *Journal of Consulting and Clinical Psychology, 38,* 270–273.

Oei, T. P. S., Moylan, A., & Evans, L. (1991). Validity and clinical utility of the Fear Questionnaire for anxiety-disorder patients. *Psychological Assessment, 3,* 391–397.

Office of Science and Technology. (1967). *Privacy and behavioral research.* Washington, DC: U.S. Government Printing Office.

Office of Strategic Services Staff. (1948). *Assessment of men.* New York: Holt, Rinehart & Winston.

O'Leary, A. (1985). Self-efficacy and health. *Behavior Therapy and Research, 23,* 437–451.

Olin, J. T., Schneider, L. S., Eaton, E., Zemansky, M. F., & Pollock, V. E. (1992). The Geriatric Depression Scale and the Beck Depression Inventory as screening instruments in an older adult outpatient population. *Psychological Assessment, 4,* 190–192.

Ollendick, T. H. (1978). *The Fear Survey Schedule for Children-Revised.* Unpublished manuscript, Indiana State University, Terre Haute.

Ollendick, T. H. (1983). Reliability and validity of the revised fear survey schedule for children (FSSC-R). *Behavior Research and Therapy, 21,* 685–692.

Orne, M. T. (1962). On the social psychology of the psychological experiment: With particular reference to demand characteristics and their implications. *American Psychologist, 17,* 766–783.

Osato, S. S., van Gorp, W. G., Kern, R. S., Satz, P., & Steinman, L. (1989). The Satz-Mogel Short form of the WAIS-R in an elderly, demented population. *Psychological Assessment, 1,* 339–341.

Oster, G. D., & Gould, P. (1987). *Using drawings in assessment and therapy.* New York: Brunner/Mazel.

Osterrith, P. A. (1944). Le test de copie d'une figure complexe. *Archives de Psychologie, 30,* 206–356; translated by J. Corwin & F. W. Byslma (1993), *The Clinical Neuropsychologist, 7,* 9–15.

Othmer, E., & Othmer, S. C. (1994). *The clinical interview using DSM-IV. Vol. 1. Fundamentals.* Washington, DC: American Psychiatric Press.

Ottenbacher, K. (1981). An investigation of self concept and body image in the mentally retarded. *Journal of Clinical Psychology, 37,* 415–418.

Overholser, J. C. (1989, August). *Temporal stability of the MCMI personality disorder scales.* Paper presented at the 97th annual convention of the American Psychological Association, New Orleans, LA.

Ownby, R. L. (1986). *A study of the expository process model (EPM) with clinical and counseling psychologists.* Manuscript submitted for publication.

Ownby, R. L. (1987). *Psychological reports: A guide to report writing in professional psychology.* Brandon, VT: Clinical Psychology.

Ownby, R. L. (1990). A study of the expository process model in mental health settings. *Journal of Clinical Psychology, 46,* 366–371.

Ownby, R. L., & Wallbrown, F. H. (1983). Evaluating school psychological reports: Part I. A procedure for systematic feedback. *Psychology in the Schools, 20,* 41–45.

Page, H. A. (1957). Studies in fantasy-daydreaming frequency and Rorschach scoring categories. *Journal of Consulting Psychology, 21,* 111–114.

Paine, P., Alves, E., & Tubin, P. (1985). Size of human figure drawings and Goodenough-Harris scores of pediatric oncology patients: A pilot study. *Perceptual and Motor Skills, 60,* 911–914.

Pallonen, U. E., Leskinen, L., Prochaska, J. O., & Willey, C. J. (1994). A 2-year self-help smoking cessation manual intervention among middle-aged Finnish men: An application of the transtheoretical model. *Preventive Medicine, 23,* 507–514.

Palmer, J. O. (1970). *The psychological assessment of children.* New York: Wiley.

Palmer, B. W., Boone, K. B., Lesser, I. M., & Wohl, M. A. (1998). Base rates of "impaired" neuropsychological test performance among healthy older adults. *Archives of Clinical Neuropsychology, 13,* 503–511.

Paludi, M. A. (1978). Machover revisited: Impact of sex-role orientation on sex sequence on the Draw-A-Person Test. *Perceptual and Motor Skills, 47,* 713–714.

Pancoast, D. L., & Archer, R. P. (1988). MMPI adolescent norms: Patterns and trends across 4 decades. *Journal of Personality Assessment, 52,* 691–706.

Pantle, M. L., Ebner, D. L., & Hynan, L. S. (1994). The Rorschach and the assessment of impulsivity. *Journal of Clinical Psychology, 50,* 633–638.

Pardue, A. M. (1975). Bender-Gestalt test and background interference procedure in discernment of organic brain damage. *Perceptual and Motor Skills, 40,* 103–109.

Parker, K. (1983a). Factor analysis of the WAIS-R at nine age levels between 16 and 74 years. *Journal of Consulting and Clinical Psychology, 51,* 302–308.

Parker, K. (1983b). A meta-analysis of the reliability and validity of the Rorschach. *Journal of Personality Assessment, 47,* 227–231.

Parker, K. C. H., Hanson, R. K., & Hunsley, J. (1988). MMPI, Rorschach, and WAIS: A meta-analytic comparison of reliability, stability, and validity. *Psychological Bulletin, 103,* 367–373.

Parks, C. W. (1982). *A multi-dimensional view of the imagery construct: Issues of definition and assessment.* Unpublished manuscript.

Parks, C. W., & Hollon, S. D. (1988). Cognitive assessment. In A. S. Bellack & M. Hersen (Eds.), *Behavioral assessment: A practical handbook* (3rd ed., pp. 161–212). New York: Pergamon.

Parks, R. W., Loewenstein, D. A., Dodrill, K. L., Barker, W. W., Yoshii, F., Chang, J. Y., Emran, A., Apicella, A., Sheramata, W. A., & Duara, R. (1988). Cerebral metabolic effects of a verbal fluency test: A PET scan study. *Journal of Clinical and Experimental Neuropsychology, 10,* 565–575.

Pascal, G. R., & Suttell, B. J. (1951). *The Bender Gestalt Test: Quantification and Validity for Adults.* New York: Grune & Stratton.

Patalano, F. (1986). Drug abusers and Card 3BM of the TAT. *Psychology: A Quarterly Journal of Human Behavior, 23,* 34–36.

Patterson, C. H. (1989). Foundations for a systematic eclectic psychotherapy. *Psychotherapy, 26,* 427–435.

Pauker, J. D. (1976). A quick-scoring system for the Bender-Gestalt: Interrater reliability and scoring validity. *Journal of Clinical Psychology, 32,* 86–89.

Payne, F. D., & Wiggins, J. S. (1972). MMPI profile types and the self-reports of psychiatric patients. *Journal of Abnormal Psychology, 79,* 1–8.

Pennington, B. F. (1991). *Diagnosing learning disorders: A neuropsychological framework.* New York: Guilford.

Perret, E. (1974). The left frontal lobe of man and the suppression of habitual responses in verbal categorical behavior. *Neuropsychologia, 12,* 323–330.

Perry, N. W., McCoy, J. G., Cunningham, W. R., Falgout, J. C., & Street, W. J. (1976). Multivariate visual evoked response correlates of intelligence. *Psychophysiology, 13,* 323–329.

Perry, S. W. (1987). The choice of duration and frequency for outpatient psychotherapy. In R. E. Hales & A. J. Frances (Eds.), *American Psychiatric Association annual review* (Vol. 6, pp. 398–412). Washington, DC: American Psychiatric Press.

Perry, W., Sprock, J., Schaible, D., McDougall, A., Minassian, A., Jenkins, M., & Braff, B. (1995). Amphetamine use on Rorschach measures in normal subjects. *Journal of Personality Assessment, 64,* 456–465.

Persons, J. B., Mooney, K., & Padesky, C. A. (1995). Interrater reliability of cognitive behavioral case formulations. *Cognitive Therapy and Research, 19,* 21–34.

Pfeifer, C., & Sedlacek, W. (1971). The validity of academic predictors for black and white students at a predominantly white university. *Journal of Educational Measurement, 8,* 253–261.

Phares, E. J., Stewart, L. M., & Foster, J. M. (1960). Instruction variation and Rorschach performance. *Journal of Projective Techniques, 24,* 28–31.

Phillips, L., & Smith, J. (1953). *Rorschach interpretation: Advanced technique.* New York: Grune & Stratton.

Piaget, J. (1950). *The psychology of intelligence.* New York: Harcourt, Brace & World.

Pickford, R. W. (1963). *Pickford Projective Pictures.* London: Tavistock.

Piedmont, R. L., Sokolove, R. L., & Fleming, M. Z. (1989a). On WAIS-R Difference Scores in a psychiatric population. *Psychological Assessment, 1,* 155–159.

Piedmont, R. L., Sokolove, R. L., & Fleming, M. Z. (1989b). An examination of some diagnostic strategies involving the Wechsler intelligence scales. *Psychological Assessment, 1,* 181–185.

Piersma, H. L. (1986). The stability of the Millon Clinical Multiaxial Inventory for psychiatric patients. *Journal of Personality Assessment, 50,* 193–197.

Pilowsky, I., Spence, N., Cobb, J., & Katsikitis, M. (1984). The Illness Behavior Questionnaire as an aid in clinical assessment. *General Hospital Psychiatry, 6,* 123–130.

Piotrowski, C. (1984). The status of projective techniques: Or, "Wishing won't make it go away." *Journal of Clinical Psychology, 40,* 1495–1502.

Piotrowski, C., & Keller, J. W. (1984). Psychodiagnostic testing in APA-approved clinical psychology programs. *Professional Psychology: Research and Practice, 15,* 450–456.

Piotrowski, C., & Keller, J. W. (1989a). Psychological testing in outpatient mental health facilities: A national study. *Professional Psychology: Research and Practice, 20,* 423–425.

Piotrowski, C., & Keller, J. W. (1989b). Use of assessment in mental health clinics and services. *Psychological Reports, 64,* 1298.

Piotrowski, C., Sherry, D., & Keller, J. W. (1985). Psychodiagnostic test usage: A survey of the Society for Personality Assessment. *Journal of Personality Assessment, 49,* 115–119.

Piotrowski, C., & Zalewski, C. (1993). Training in psychodiagnostic testing in APA-approved PsyD and PhD clinical training programs. *Journal of Personality Assessment, 61,* 394–405.

Piotrowski, Z. A. (1937). The Rorschach ink-blot method in organic disturbances of the central nervous system. *Journal of Nervous and Mental Disorders, 86,* 525–537.

Piotrowski, Z. A. (1957). *Perceptanalysis.* New York: Macmillan.

Piotrowski, Z. A. (1960). The movement score. In M. Rickers-Ovsiankina (Ed.), *Rorschach psychology* (pp. 49–58). New York: Wiley.

Piotrowski, Z. A. (1969a). A Piotrowski interpretation. In J. E. Exner (Ed.), *The Rorschach systems.* New York: Grune & Stratton.

Piotrowski, Z. A. (1969b). Long-term prognosis in schizophrenia based on Rorschach findings: The LTPTI. In D. V. Sira Sankar (Ed.), *Schizophrenia, current concepts and research* (pp. 84–103). Hicksville, NY: PJD.

Piotrowski, Z. A., & Bricklin, B. A. (1961). A second validation of a long-term prognostic index for schizophrenic patients. *Journal of Consulting Psychology, 25,* 123–128.

Plenk, A. M., & Jones, J. (1967). An examination of the Bender-Gestalt performance of three and four year olds and its relationship to Koppitz scoring system. *Journal of Clinical Psychology, 23,* 367–370.

Polyson, J., Norris, D., & Ott, E. (1985). The recent decline in TAT research. *Professional Psychology: Research and Practice, 16,* 26–28.

Ponsford, J. (1988). Neuropsychological assessment: The need for a more pragmatic approach. *Australian Psychologist, 23,* 349–360.

Ponsford, J., & Kinsella, G. (1992). Attentional deficits following closed head injury. *Journal of Clinical & Experimental Neuropsychology, 16,* 822–838.

Pope, B. (1979). *The mental health interview: Research and application.* New York: Pergamon.

Pope, B., & Scott, W. H. (1967). *Psychological diagnosis in clinical practice.* New York: Oxford University Press.

Pope, K. S. (1992). Responsibilities in providing psychological test feedback to clients. *Psychological Assessment, 4,* 268–271.

Pope, K. S., Butcher, J. N., & Seelen, J. (1993). *The MMPI, MMPI-2 and MMPI-A in court: A practical guide for expert witnesses and attorneys.* Washington, DC: American Psychological Association.

Porges, S. W., & Fox, N. A. (1986). Developmental psychophysiology. In M. G. H. Coles, E. Donchin, & S. W. Porges (Eds.), *Psychophysiology: Systems, processes and applications.* New York: Guilford.

Porter, E. H. (1950). *An introduction to therapeutic counseling.* Boston: Houghton-Mifflin.

Preston, J., O'Neal, J. H., & Talaga, M. C. (1994). *Handbook of clinical psychopharmacology for therapists.* Oakland, CA: New Harbinger.

Prifitera, A., & Dersh, J. (1993). Base rates of WISC-III diagnostic subtest patterns among normal, learning disabled, and ADHD samples. In B. A. Bracken & R. S. McCallum (Eds.), *Journal of Psychoeducational Assessment monograph series, advances in psychoeducational assessment: Wechsler Intelligence Scale for Children* (3rd ed., pp. 43–55). Greentown, TN: Psychoeducational Corporation.

Prigatano, G. P. (1983). Neuropsychological test performance in mildly hypoxemic patients with chronic obstructive pulmonary disease. *Journal of Consulting and Clinical Psychology, 51,* 108–116.

Prigatano, G. P. (1986). *Neuropsychological rehabilitation after brain injury.* Baltimore: The Johns Hopkins University Press.

Prigatano, G. P. (1987). Personality and psychosocial consequences after brain injury. In M. Meir, A. Benton, & L. Diller (Eds.), *Neuropsychological rehabilitation* (pp. 335–378). New York: Plenum.

Prigatano, G. P. (1992). Personality disturbance associated with traumatic brain injury. *Journal of Consulting and Clinical Psychology, 60,* 360–368.

Prigatano, G. P., Amin, K., & Rosenstein, L. D. (1992a). *Manual for the BNI Screen for Higher Cerebral Functions.* Phoenix, AZ: Barrow Neurological Institute.

Prigatano, G. P., Amin, K., & Rosenstein, L. D. (1992). Validity studies of the BNI Screen for Higher Cerebral Functions. *BNI Quarterly, 9,* 2–9.

Pritchard, D. A., & Rosenblatt, A. (1980). Reply to Gynther and Green. *Journal of Consulting and Clinical Psychology, 48,* 273–274.

Prochaska, J. O. (1991). Prescribing to the stage and level of phobic patients. *Psychotherapy, 28,* 463–468.

Prochaska, J. O., & DiClemente, C. S. (1984). *The transtheoretical approach: Crossing the traditional boundaries of therapy.* Homesood, IL: Dow Jones-Irwin.

Prochaska, J. O., & DiClemente, C. C. (1992). The transtheoretical approach. In J. C. Norcross & M. R. Goldfried (Eds.), *Handbook of psychotherapy integration* (pp. 300–334). New York: Basic.

Prochaska, J. O., DiClemente, C. C., & Norcross, J. C. (1992). In search of how people change: Applications to addictive behaviors. *American Psychologist, 47,* 1102–1114.

Prochaska, J. O., & Norcross, J. C. (1994). *Systems of psychotherapy: A transtheoretical analysis* (3rd ed.). Pacific Grove, CA: Brooks/Cole.

Prochaska, J. O., Norcross, J. C., & DiClemente, C. C. (1994). *Changing for good.* New York: William Morrow.

Prochaska, J. O., Rossi, J. S., & Wilcox, N. S. (1991). Change processes and psychotherapy outcome in integrative case research. *Journal of Psychotherapy Integration, 1,* 103–120.

Prokop, C. K. (1988). Chronic pain. In R. L. Greene (Ed.), *The MMPI: Use with specific populations* (pp. 22–49). San Diego: Grune & Stratton.

Prout, H. T., & Celmer, D. S. (1984). School drawings and academic achievement: A validity study of the Kinetic School Drawing technique. *Psychology in the Schools, 21,* 176–180.

Prout, H. T., & Phillips, D. D. (1974). A clinical note: The Kinetic School Drawing. *Psychology in the Schools, 11,* 303–306.

Pruitt, J. A., Smith, M. C., Thelen, M. H., & Lubin, B. (1985). Attitudes of academic clinical psychologists toward projective techniques: 1968–1983. *Professional Psychology: Research and Practice, 16,* 781–788.

Pryzwansky, W. B., & Hanania, J. S. (1986). Applying problem-solving approaches to school psychological reports. *Journal of School Psychology, 24,* 133–141.

Pugh, G. (1985). The California Psychological Inventory and police selection. *Journal of Police Science and Administration, 13,* 172–177.

Puig-Antich, J., & Chambers, W. (1978). *The schedule for affective disorders and schizophrenia for school aged children.* New York: New York State Psychiatric Institute.

Quay, H. C., & Peterson, D. R. (1987). *Manual for the Revised Behavior Problem Checklist.* Miami, FL: Authors (at University of Miami).

Quereshi, M. Y., & Erstad, D. (1990). A comparison of WAIS and WAIS-R for ages 61–91 years. *Psychological Assessment 2,* 293–297.

Query, W. T. (1966). CPI factors and success of seminary students. *Psychological Reports, 18,* 665–660.

Quill, T. E. (1985). Somatization disorder: One of medicine's blind spots. *Journal of the American Medical Association, 254,* 3075–3079.

Quillan, J., Besing, S., & Dinning, D. (1977). Standardization of the Rathus Assertiveness Schedule. *Journal of Clinical Psychology, 33,* 418–422.

Rabin, A. I. (1968). *Projective techniques in personality assessment: A modern introduction.* New York: Springer.

Rabin, A. I., & Beck, S. J. (1950). Genetic aspects of some Rorschach factors. *American Journal of Orthopsychiatry, 20,* 595–599.

Ramos, M. C., & Die, A. H. (1986). The WAIS-R Picture Arrangement subtest: What do scores indicate? *Journal of General Psychology, 113,* 251–261.

Rao, A. V., & Potash, H. M. (1985). Size factors on the Bender-Gestalt test and their relationship to trait anxiety and situationally induced anxiety. *Journal of Clinical Psychology, 41,* 834–838.

Rao, S. M. (1990). Neuroimaging correlates of cognitive dysfunction. In S. M. Rao (Ed.), *Neurobehavioral aspects of multiple sclerosis* (pp. 118–135). New York: Oxford University Press.

Rapaport, C., Gill, M., & Schafer, J. (1946). *Diagnostic psychological testing* (Vol. 2). Chicago: Year Book Publishers.

Rapaport, C., Gill, M., & Schafer, J. (1968). *Diagnostic psychological testing* (Vol. 1). (Rev. ed.). Chicago: Year Book Publishers.

Raskin, L. M., & Bloom, A. S. (1979). Kinetic Family Drawings by children with learning disabilities. *Journal of Pediatric Psychology, 4,* 247–251.

Rathus, S. A. (1972). An experimental investigation of assertive training in a group setting. *Journal of Behavior Therapy and Experimental Psychiatry, 3,* 81–86.

Rathus, S. A. (1973). A 30-item schedule for assessing assertive behavior. *Behavior Therapy, 4,* 398–406.

Rathus, S. A., & Nevid, J. S. (1977). Concurrent validity of the 30-item assertiveness schedule with a psychiatric population. *Behavior Therapy, 8,* 393–397.

Rawls, J. R., & Slack, G. K. (1968). Artists versus non-artists: Rorschach determinants and artistic creativity. *Journal of Projective Techniques and Personality Assessment, 32,* 233–237.

Raychaudhuri, M. (1971). Relation of creativity and sex to Rorschach M responses. *Journal of Personality Assessment, 35,* 27–36.

Raz, S., & Raz, N. (1990). Structural brain abnormalities in the major psychosis: A quantitative review of the evidence from computerized imaging. *Psychological Bulletin, 108,* 93–108.

Reddon, J. R., Marceau, R., & Jackson, D. D. (1982). An application of singular value decomposition to the factor analysis of MMPI items. *Applied Psychological Measurement, 6,* 275–283.

Redfering, D. L., & Collings, J. (1982). A comparison of the Koppitz and Hutt techniques of Bender-Gestalt administration correlated with WISC-R performance scores. *Educational and Psychological Measurement, 42,* 41–47.

Reich, J. H., & Noyes, R. (1987). A comparison of *DSM-III* personality disorders in acutely ill panic and depressed patients. *Journal of Anxiety Disorders, 1,* 123–131.

Reich, W., Herjanic, B., Welner, Z., & Gandhy, P. R. (1982). Development of a structured psychiatric interview for children: Agreement on diagnosis comparing parent and child. *Journal of Abnormal Child Psychology, 10,* 325–326.

Reich, W., Shayka, J. J., & Taibleson, C. (1991a). *Diagnostic Interview for Children and Adolescents (DICA-RC): Child version.* St. Louis, MO: Washington University.

Reich, W., Shayka, J. J., & Taibleson, C. (1991b). *Diagnostic Interview for Children and Adolescents (DICA-RP): Parent version.* St. Louis, MO: Washington University.

Reich, W., Shayka, J. J., & Taibleson, C. (1991c). *Diagnostic Interview for Children and Adolescents (DICA-RA): Adolescent version.* St. Louis, MO: Washington University.

Reich, W., Shayka, J. J., & Taibleson, C. (1991d). *Diagnostic Interview for Children and Adolescents (DICA-RA): Adolescent version.* St. Louis, MO: Washington University.

Reichenberg, N., & Raphael, A. R. (1992). *Advanced psychodiagnostic interpretation of the Bender Gestalt Test.* New York: Praeger.

Reilly, T. P., Drudge, O. W., Rosen, J. C., Loew, D. E., & Fischer, M. (1985). Concurrent and predictive validity of the WISC-R, McCarthy Scales, Woodcock-Johnson, and academic achievement. *Psychology in the Schools, 22,* 380–382.

Reirdan, J., & Koff, E. (1980). Representation of the female body by early and late adolescent girls. *Journal of Youth and Adolescence, 9,* 339–346.

Reiss, S., Peterson, R. A., Gursky, D. M., & McNally, R. J. (1986). Anxiety sensitivity, anxiety frequency, and the prediction of fearfulness. *Behavior Research and Therapy, 24,* 1–8.

Reitan, R. M. (1955a). Certain differential effects of left and right cerebral lesions in human adults. *Journal of Comparative and Physiological Psychology, 48,* 474–477.

Reitan, R. M. (1955b). Validity of the Rorschach test as a measure of the psychological effects of brain damage. *Archives of Neurology and Psychiatry, 73,* 445–451.

Reitan, R. M. (1974a). Methodological problems in clinical neuropsychology. In R. M. Reitan & L. A. Davison (Eds.), *Clinical neuropsychology: Current status and applications.* New York: Wiley.

Reitan, R. M. (1974b). Psychological effects of cerebral lesions in children of early school age. In R. M. Reitan & L. A. Davison (Eds.), *Clinical neuropsychology: Current status and applications* (pp. 53–90). Washington, DC: V. H. Winston & Sons.

Reitan, R. M., & Davison, L. A. (Eds.). (1974). *Clinical neuropsychology: Current status and applications.* New York: Halsted Press.

Reitan, R. M., & Wolfson, D. (1985). *The Halsted-Reitan Neuropsychological Battery: Theory and clinical interpretation.* Tucson, AZ: Tucson Neuropsychological Press.

Reitan, R., & Wolfson, D. (1992). *Neuropsychological education of older children.* South Tucson, AZ: Neuropsychology Press.

Reitan, R. M., & Wolfson, D. (1993). *The Halstead-Reitan Neuropsychological Test Battery: Theory and clinical interpretation.* Tucson, AZ: Neuropsychology Press.

Reitan, R., & Wolfson, D. (1995). Influence of age and education on neuropsychological test results. *The Clinical Neuropsychologist, 9,* 151–158.

Reschley, D. J. (1981). Psychological testing in educational classification and placement. *American Psychologist, 36,* 1094–1102.

Research and Education Association. (1981). *Handbook of psychiatric rating scales.* New York: Author.

Retief, A. (1987). Thematic apperception testing across cultures: Tests of selection versus tests of inclusion. *South African Journal of Psychology, 17,* 47–55.

Retzlaff, P. D. (1995). *Tactical psychotherapy of the personality disorders: An MCMI-III-based approach.* Boston: Allyn & Bacon.

Retzlaff, P. D. (in press). MCMI-III Diagnostic validity: Bad test or bad validity study. *Journal of Personality Assessment.*

Retzlaff, P. D., Lorr, M., & Hyer, L. (1989). *An MCMI-II item-level component analysis: Personality and clinical factors.* Unpublished manuscript.

Retzlaff, P. D., Sheehan, E. P., & Fiel, A. (1991). MCMI-II report style and bias: Profile and validity scales analysis. *Journal of Personality Assessment, 56,* 478–486.

Rey, A. (1941). Psychological examination of traumatic encephalopathy. *Archives de Psychologie, 28,* 286–340; sections translated by J. Corwin & F. W. Bylsma (1993), *The Clinical Neuropsychologist,7,* 4–9.

Rey, A. (1964). *The clinical exam in psychology.* Paris: Presses Universitaires de France.

Reynolds, C. R. (1986). Wide Range Achievement Test (WRAT-R), 1984 edition. *Journal of Counseling and Development, 64,* 540–541.

Reynolds, C. R., Chastain, R. L., Kaufman, A. S., & Mclean, J. E. (1987). Demographic charactersitics and IQ among adults: Analysis of the WAIS-R standardization sample as a function of the stratification variables. *Journal of School Psychology, 25,* 323–342.

Reynolds, C. R., & Ford, L. (1994). Comparative three-factor solutions of the WISC-III and WISC-R at 11 age levels between 6½ and 16½ years. *Journal of School Psychology, 9,* 553–570.

Reynolds, C. R., & Gutkin, T. B. (1979). Predicting the premorbid intellectual status of children using demographic data. *Clinical Neuropsychology, 1,* 36–38.

Reynolds, C. R., & Hartlage, L. (1979). Comparison of WISC and WISC-R regression lines for academic prediction with black and white referred children. *Journal of Consulting and Clinical Psychology, 47,* 589–591.

Richter, R. H., & Winter, W. D. (1966). Holtzman ink-blot correlates of creative potential. *Journal of Projective Techniques and Personality Assessment, 30,* 62–67.

Rickers-Ovsiankina, M. A. (1977). *Rorschach psychology.* New York: Robert E. Krieger.

Ridgeway, E. M., & Exner, J. E. (1980). *Rorschach correlates of achievement needs in medical students under an arousal state.* Workshops Study No. 274 (unpublished), Rorschach Workshops.

Riessman, F., & Miller, S. M. (1958). Social class and projective tests. *Journal of Projective Techniques, 22,* 432–439.

Riggs, D. S., & Foa, E. B. (1993). Obsessive compulsive disorder. In D. H. Barlow (Ed.), *Clinical handbook of psychological disorders* (2nd ed., pp. 189–239). New York: Guilford.

Riskind, J. H., Beck, A. T., Berchick, R. J., Brown, G., & Steer, R. A. (1987). Reliability of *DSM-III* diagnoses for major depression and generalized anxiety disorder using the Structured Clinical Interview for *DSM-III. Archives of General Psychiatry, 44,* 817–820.

Rissetti, F., Butcher, J. N., Agostini, J., Elgueta, M., Gaete, S., Marguilies, T., Morlans, I., & Ruiz, R. (1979). *Translation and adaptation of the MMPI in Chile: Use in a university student health service.* Paper given at the 14th Annual Symposium on the Recent Developments in the Use of the MMPI, St. Petersburg, FL.

Ritzler, B. A., & Alter, B. (1986). Rorschach teaching in APA-approved clinical graduate programs: Ten years later. *Journal of Personality Assessment, 50,* 44–49.

Ritzler, B. A., Sharkey, K. J., & Chudy, J. F. (1980). A comprehensive projective alternative to the TAT. *Journal of Personality Assessment, 44,* 358–362.

Roback, H. B. (1968). Human figure drawings: Their utility in the clinical psychologist's armamentarium for personality assessment. *Psychological Bulletin, 70,* 1–19.

Roback, H. B., Langevin, R., & Zajac, Y. (1974). Sex of free choice figure drawings by homosexual and heterosexual subjects. *Journal of Personality Assessment, 38,* 154–155.

Robiner, W. (1978). *An analysis of some of the variables influencing clinical use of the Bender-Gestalt.* Unpublished manuscript, Washington University, St. Louis, MO.

Robins, L. N., & Helzer, J. E. (1994). The half life of a structured interview: The NIMH Diagnostic Interview Schedule (DIS). *International Journal of Methods in Psychiatric Research, 4,* 95–102.

Robins, L. N., Helzer, J. E., Cottler, L. B., & Goldring, E. (1989). *NIMH Diagnostic Interview Schedule, Version III-Revised,* St. Louis, MO: Washington University School of Medicine.

Robins, L. N., Helzer, J. E., Croughan, J. L., & Ratcliff, K. S. (1981). National Institute of Mental Health Diagnostic Interview Schedule. *Archives of General Psychiatry, 38,* 381–389.

Robins, L. N., Helzer, J. E., Ratcliff, K. S., & Seyfried, W. (1982). Validity of the Diagnostic Interview Schedule, version II: *DSM-III* diagnoses. *Psychological Medicine, 12,* 855–870.

Rockland, L. H., & Pollin, W. (1965). Quantification of psychiatric mental status. *Archives of General Psychiatry, 12,* 23–28.

Rodenhauser, P., & Fornal, R. E. (1991). How important is the mental status examination? *Psychiatric Hospital, 22,* 256–262.

Rodgers, D. A. (1972). The MMPI: A review. In O. K. Buros (Ed.), *Seventh mental measurements yearbook* (Vol. 1, pp. 243–250). Highland Park, NJ: Gryphon Press.

Roe, A. (1952). Analysis of group Rorschachs of psychologists and anthropologists. *Journal of Projective Techniques, 16,* 212–242.

Rogers, C. R. (1957/1992). The necessary and sufficient conditions of therapeutic personality change. *Journal of Consulting and Clinical Psychology, 60,* 827–832.

Rogers, C. R. (1961). A process conception of psychotherapy. In C. R. Rogers (Ed.), *On becoming a person.* Boston: Houghton Mifflin.

Rogers, R. (1984). *Rogers Criminal Responsibility Assessment Scales.* Odessa, FL: Psychological Assessment Resources.

Rogers, R. (1995). *Diagnostic and structured interviewing: A handbook for psychologists.* Odessa, FL: Psychological Assessment Resources.

Rogers, R., Bagby, R. M., & Chakraborty, D. (1993). Feigning schizophrenic disorders on the MMPI-2: Detection of coached simulators. *Journal of Personality Assessment, 60,* 215–226.

Romancyzk, R. G., Kent, R. N., Diament, C., & O'Leary, K. D. (1973). Measuring the reliability of observational data: A reactive process. *Journal of Applied Behavior Analysis, 6,* 175–186.

Rorschach, H. (1941). *Psychodiagnostics.* (Hans Huber Verlag, Transl.). Bern: Bircher. (Original work published 1921)

Rosen, B. M., Bahn, A. K., & Kramer, M. (1964). Demographic and diagnostic characteristics of psychiatric clinic patients in the U.S.A., 1961. *American Journal of Orthopsychiatry, 34,* 455–468.

Rosenhan, D. L. (1973). On being sane in insane places. *Science, 179,* 250–257.

Rosenquist, C. M., & Megargee, E. I. (1969). *Delinquency in three cultures.* Austin: University of Texas Press.

Rosenthal, M. J. (1962). Some behavior correlated to the Rorschach experience-balance. *Journal of Projective Techniques, 26,* 442–446.

Rosenthal, M. J. (1989). Towards selective and improved performance of the mental status examination. *Acta Psychiatrica Scandinavica, 80,* 207–215.

Rosenthal, M. J., & Beutell, N. J. (1981). Movement and body-image: A preliminary study. *Perceptual and Motor Skills, 53,* 758.

Rosenthal, R. (1966). *Experimenter effects in behavioral research.* New York: Appleton-Century-Crofts.

Rosenthal, R., & Fode, K. L. (1963). The effects of experimenter bias on the performance of the albino rat. *Behavioral Science, 8,* 183–189.

Rosenthal, R., & Jacobson, L. (1968). *Pygmalion in the Classroom.* New York: Holt, Rinehart and Winston.

Rosenzweig, S. (1976). *Manual for the Rosenzweig Picture-Frustration Study, Adolescent Form.* St. Louis: Author.

Rosenzweig, S. (1977). *Manual for the Children's Form of the Rosenzweig Picture-Frustration (P-F) Study.* St. Louis: Rana House.

Rosenzweig, S. (1978). *Adult Form Supplement to the Basic Manual of the Rosenzweig Picture Frustration (P-F) Study.* St. Louis: Rana House.

Ross, L. D. (1977). The intuitive psychologist and his shortcomings: Distortions in the attribution process. In L. Berkowitz (Ed.), *Advances in experimental social psychology* (Vol. 10). New York: Academic Press.

Rossi, A., & Neuman, G. (1961). A comparative study of Rorschach norms: Medical students. *Journal of Projective Techniques, 25,* 334–338.

Rossini, E. D., & Kaspar, J. C. (1987). The validity of the Bender-Gestalt emotional indicators. *Journal of Personality Assessment, 51,* 254–261.

Roth, D. L., Hughes, C. W., Mankowski, P. G., & Crosson, B. (1984). Investigation of validity of WAIS-R short forms for patients suspected to have brain impairment. *Journal of Consulting and Clinical Psychology, 52,* 722–723.

Rotter, J. B., & Rafferty, J. E. (1950). *Manual: The Rotter Incomplete Sentences Blank.* New York: Psychological Corporation.

Rourke, B. P. (Ed.). (1991). *Neuropsychological validation of learning disability subtypes.* New York: Guilford.

Royer, F. L., & Holland, T. R. (1975). Rotations of visual design in psychopathological groups. *Journal of Consulting and Clinical Psychology, 43,* 346–356.

Rubenzer, S. (1992). A comparison of traditional and computer generated psychological reports in an adolescent inpatient setting. *Journal of Clinical Psychology, 48,* 817–827.

Rubin, J. A., Ragins, N., Schacter, J., & Wimberly, F. (1979). Drawings by schizophrenics and non-schizophrenic mothers and their children. *Art Psychotherapy, 6,* 163–175.

Rude, S. R. (1986). Relative benefits of assertion or cognitive self-control treatment for depression as a function of proficiency in each domain. *Journal of Consulting and Clinical Psychology, 54,* 390–394.

Rudel, R. G., & Denckla, M. B. (1974). Relation of forward and backward digit repetition to neurological impairment in children with learning disabilities. *Neuropsychologia, 12,* 109–118.

Ruegg, R. G., Ekstrom, D. E., Evans, D. L., & Golden, R. N. (1990). Introduction of a standardized report form improves the quality of mental status examination reports by psychiatric residents. *Academic Psychiatry, 14,* 157–163.

Ruff, R. M., & Parker, S. B. (1993). Gender and age-specific changes in motor speed and eyehand coordination in adults: Normative values for the Finger Tapping and Grooved Pegboard Tests. *Perceptual and Motor Skills, 76,* 1219–1230.

Rushton, J. P. (1994). The equalitarian dogma revisited. *Intelligence, 19,* 263–280.

Russell, E. W. (1972). Effect of acute lateralized brain damage on a factor analysis of the Wechsler-Bellevue intelligence test. *Proceedings of the 80th Annual Convention of the American Psychological Association, 7,* 421–422.

Russell, E. W. (1979). Three patterns of brain damage on the WAIS. *Journal of Clinical Psychology, 35,* 611–620.

Russell, E. W. (1995). The cognitive-metric, fixed battery approach to neuropsychological assessment. In R. D. Vanderploeg (Ed.), *Clinician's guide to neuropsychological assessment* (pp. 211–258). Hillsdale, NJ: Erlbaum.

Ryan, C. M., Morrow, L., Parklinson, D., & Branet, E. (1987). Low level lead exposure and neuropsychological functioning in blue collar males. *International Journal of Neuroscience, 36,* 29–39.

Ryan, J. J. (1981). Clinical utility of a WISC-R short form. *Journal of Clinical Psychology, 37,* 389–391.

Ryan, J. J., Georgemiller, R. J., Geisser, M. E., & Randall, D. M. (1985). Test-retest stability of the WAIS-R in a clinical sample. *Journal of Clinical Psychology, 41,* 552–556.

Ryan, J. J., Georgemiller, R., & McKinney, B. (1984). Application of the four-subtest WAIS-R short form with an older clinical sample. *Journal of Clinical Psychology, 40,* 1033–1036.

Ryan, J. J., Nowak, T., & Geisser, M. E. (1987). On the comparability of the WAIS and WAIS-R: Review of the research and implications for clinical practice. *Journal of Psychoeducational Research, 5,* 15–30.

Ryan, J. J., Paolo, A. M., & Brungardt, T. M. (1990). Standardization of the Wechsler adult intelligence scale—revised for persons 75 years and older. *Psychological Assessment, 2,* 404–411.

Ryan, J. J., Paolo, A. M., & Brungardt, T. M. (1993). Factor analysis of the Wechsler Adult Intelligence Scales-Revised for persons 75 years and older. *Professional Psychology: Research and Practice, 21,* 177–181.

Ryan, J. J., Paolo, A. M., & Smith, A. J. (1992). Wechsler Adult Intelligence Scale-Revised intersubtest scatter in brain damaged patients: A comparison with the standardization sample. *Psychological Assessment, 4,* 63–66.

Ryan, J. J., & Rosenberg, S. J. (1983). Relationship between the WAIS-R and Wide Range Achievement Test in a sample of mixed patients. *Perceptual and Motor Skills, 56,* 623–626.

Ryan, J. J., Rosenberg, S. J., & Mittenberg, W. (1984). Factor analysis of the Rey Auditory Verbal Learning Test. *The International Journal of Clinical and Experimental Neuropsychology, 5,* 249–253.

Ryan, J. J., Werth, T., & Lopez, S. J. (1998). *Administration time estimates for WAIS-III subtests, scales, and short forms in a clinical sample.* Unpublished manuscript.

Rzechorzek, A. (1979). Cognitive dysfunctions resulting from unilateral frontal lesions in man. In M. Molloy, G. V. Stanley, & K. W. Walsh (Eds.), *Brain impairment: Proceedings of the 1978 Brain Impairment Workshop.* Melbourne: University of Melbourne, Australia.

Saarni, C., & Azara, V. (1977). Developmental analyses of human figure drawings in adolescence, young adulthood, and middle age. *Journal of Personality Assessment, 41,* 31–38.

Sacuzzo, D. P., & Lewandowski, D. G. (1976). The WISC as a diagnostic tool. *Journal of Clinical Psychology, 32,* 115–124.

Sales, J., & Miller, P. (1994). *Psychology in litigation and legislation.* Washington, DC: American Psychological Association.

Salmon, R., Arnold, J. M., & Collyer, Y. M. (1972). What do the determinants determine: The internal validity of the Rorschach. *Journal of Personality Assessment, 36,* 33–38.

Sanchez, V., & Lewinsohn, P. M. (1980). Assertive behavior and depression. *Journal of Consulting and Clinical Psychology, 48,* 119–120.

Sandy, L. R. (1986). The descriptive-collaborative approach to psychological report writing. *Psychology in the Schools, 23,* 395–400.

Sanford, R. N. (1939). *Thematic Apperception Test-Directions for administration and scoring.* Cambridge, MA: Harvard Psychological Clinic (mimeographed).

Sarbaugh, M. E. A. (1982). Kinetic Family Drawing-School (KD-S) technique. *Illinois School Psychologists' Association Monograph Series, 1,* 1–70.

Sarrel, P., Sarrel, L., & Berman, S. (1981). Using the Draw-A-Person (DAP) Test in sex therapy. *Journal of Sex & Marital Therapy, 7,* 163–183.

Sartorius, N., Goldberg, D., de Girolamo, G., Costa de Silva, J. A., Lecrubier, Y., & Wittchen, U. (Eds.). (1990). *Psychological disorders in medical settings.* Toronto, Canada: Hogrefe & Huber.

Sattler, J. M. (1973a). Examiners scoring style, accuracy, ability, and culturally disadvantaged children. In L. Mann & D. Sabatino (Eds.), *The first review of special education* (Vol. 2). Philadelphia: J. S. E. Press.

Sattler, J. M. (1973b). Racial experimenter effects. In K. S. Miller & R. M. Dreger (Eds.), *Comparative studies of blacks and whites in the United States* (pp. 8–32). New York: Seminar Press.

Sattler, J. M. (1980). Learning disabled children do not have a perceptual organization deficit: Comments on Dean's WISC-R analysis. *Journal of Consulting and Clinical Psychology, 48,* 254–255.

Sattler, J. M. (1982). *Assessment of children's intelligence and special abilities* (2nd ed.). Boston: Allyn & Bacon.

Sattler, J. M. (1985). Review of the Hutt Adaptation of the Bender-Gestalt Test. In J. V. Mitchell (Ed.), *The ninth mental measurements yearbook* (Vol. 1, pp. 184–185). Highland Park, NJ: Gryphon Press.

Sattler, J. M. (1992). *Assessment of children* (3rd ed. rev.). San Diego: Author.

Sattler, J. M., & Atkinson, L. (1993). Item equivalence across scales: The WPPSI-R and WISC-III. *Psychological Assessment, 5,* 203–206.

Sattler, J. M., & Gwynne, J. (1982). White examiners generally do not impede the intelligence test performance of black children: To debunk a myth. *Journal of Consulting and Clinical Psychology, 50,* 196–208.

Sattler, J. M., Hillix, W. A., & Neher, L. A. (1970). Halo effect in examiner scoring of intelligence test responses. *Journal of Consulting and Clinical Psychology, 34,* 172–176.

Sattler, J. M., & Ryan, J. J. (1998). *Assessment of children, revised and updated third edition, WAIS-III supplement.* San Diego: Jerome Sattler.

Sattler, J. M., & Winget, B. M. (1970). Intelligence testing procedures as affected by expectancy and I.Q. *Journal of Clinical Psychology, 26,* 446–448.

Satz, P., & Mogel, S. (1962). An abbreviation of the WAIS for clinical use. *Journal of Clinical Psychology, 18,* 77–79.

Savage, R. M., & Gouvier, W. D. (1992). Rey Auditory-Verbal Learning Test: The effects of age and gender, and norms for delayed recall and story recognition trials. *Archives of Clinical Neuropsychology, 1,* 407–414.

Saxe, L., Dougherty, D., & Cross, T. (1985). The validity of polygraph testing. *American Psychologist, 40,* 355–366.

Sayed, A. J., & Leaverton, D. R. (1974). Kinetic Family Drawings of children with diabetes. *Child Psychiatry and Human Development, 5,* 40–50.

Sbordone, R. J., & Long, C. J. (Eds.). (1996). *Ecological validity of neuropsychological testing.* Odessa, FL: Psychological Assessment Resources.

Schactel, E. G. (1966). *Experimental foundations of Rorschach's test.* New York: Basic Books.

Schacter, D. (1990). Perceptual representation systems and implicit memory: Toward a resolution of the multiple systems debate. In A. Diamond (Ed.), *Developmental and neural basis of higher cognitive function* (pp. 233–268). New York: Annals of the New York Academy of Science.

Schafer, R. (1954). *Psychoanalytic interpretation in Rorschach testing.* New York: Grune & Stratton.

Schalock, R. L., Stark, J. A., Snell, M. E., Coulter, D. L., Polloway, E. A., Luckasson, R., Reiss, S., & Spitalnik, D. M. (1994). The changing conception of mental retardation: Implications for the field. *Mental Retardation, 32,* 181–193.

Scherer, M. W., & Nakamura, C. Y. (1968). A fear survey schedule for children (FSS-FC): A factor analytic comparison with manifest anxiety. *Behavior Research and Therapy, 6,* 173–182.

Schinka, J. A. (1983). *Neuropsychological Status Examination.* Odessa, FL: Psychological Assessment Resources.

Schmidt, F. L., Ones, D. S., & Hunter, J. E. (1992). Personnel selection. *Annual Review of Psychology, 43,* 627–670.

Schmidt, H. O., & Fonda, C. P. (1954). Rorschach scores in the manic state. *Journal of Psychology, 38,* 427–437.

Schorr, D., Bower, G. H., & Kiernan, R. (1982). Stimulus variables in the Block Design task. *Journal of Consulting and Clinical Psychology, 50,* 479–487.

Schraa, J. C., Jones, N. F., & Dirks, J. E. (1983). Bender-Gestalt recall: A review of the normative data and related issues. In J. N. Butcher & C. D. Spielberger (Eds.), *Advances in personality assessment* (Vol. 2, pp. 125–138). Hillsdale, NJ: Erlbaum.

Schretlen, D., Benedict, R. H. B., & Bobholz, J. H. (1994). Composite reliability and standard errors of measurement for a seven sub-test short form of the Wechsler Adult intelligence Scale-Revised. *Psychological Assessment, 6,* 188–190.

Schroth, M. L. (1987). Relationships between achievement-related motives, extrinsic conditions, and task performance. *Journal of Social Psychology, 127,* 39–48.

Schulman, I. (1953). *The relation between perception of movement on the Rorschach test and levels of conceptualization.* Unpublished doctoral dissertation, New York University, New York.

Schultz, C. B., & Sherman, R. H. (1976). Social class, development, and differences in reinforcer effectiveness. *Review of Educational Research, 46,* 25–59.

Schut, B., Hutzell, R. R., Swint, E. B., & Gaston, C. D. (1980). CPI short form incorporating MMPI shared items: Construction, cross validation, and comparison. *Journal of Clinical Psychology, 36,* 940–944.

Schwab-Stone, M., Fisher, P., Piacentini, J., Shaffer, D., Davies, M., & Briggs, M. (1993). The Diagnostic Interview Schedule for Children-Revised version (DISC-R): II. Test-retest reliability. *Journal of the American Academy of Child and Adolescent Psychiatry, 32,* 651–657.

Schwartz, G. E. (1982). Testing the biopsychosocial model: The ultimate challenge facing behavioral medicine? *Journal of Consulting and Clinical Psychology, 50,* 1040–1053.

Schwartz, L., & Levitt, E. E. (1960). Short forms of the WISC for children in the educable, non-institutionalized mentally retarded. *Journal of Educational Psychology, 51,* 187–190.

Schwartz, R. M., & Garamoni, G. L. (1989). Cognitive balance and psychopathology: Evaluation of an information processing model of positive and negative states of mind. *Clinical Psychology Review, 9,* 271–294.

Schwartz, S., & Wiedel, T. C. (1981). Incremental validity of the MMPI in neurological decision-making. *Journal of Personality Assessment, 45,* 424–426.

Scott, L. H. (1981). Measuring intelligence with the Goodenough-Harris Drawing Test. *Psychological Bulletin, 89,* 483–505.

Seamons, D. T., Howell, R. J., Carlisle, A. L., & Roe, A. V. (1981). Rorschach simulation of mental illness and normality by psychotic and nonpsychotic legal offenders. *Journal of Personality Assessment, 45,* 130–135.

Seeman, K., Yesarage, J., & Widrow, L. (1985). Correlations of self-directed violence in acute schizophrenics with clinical ratings and personality measures. *Journal of Nervous and Mental Diseases, 173,* 298–302.

Seiber, K. O., & Meyers, L. S. (1992). Validation of the MMPI-2 social introversion subscales. *Psychological Assessment, 4,* 185–189.

Seligman, M. E. P. (1995). The effectiveness of psychotherapy: The Consumer Reports study. *American Psychologist, 50,* 965–974.

Seligman, M. E. P., Abramson, L. Y., Semmel, A., & von Baeyer, C. (1979). Depressive attributional style. *Journal of Abnormal Psychology, 88,* 242–247.

Semeonoff, B. (1976). *Projective techniques.* New York: Wiley.

Sewitch, T., & Kirsch, I. (1984). The cognitive content of anxiety: Naturalistic evidence for the predominance of threat-related thoughts. *Cognitive Therapy and Research, 8,* 49–58.

Shaffer, D., Schwab-Stone, M., Fisher, P., Cohen, P., Piacentini, J., Davies, M., Connors, C. K., & Regier, D. (1993). The Diagnostic Interview Schedule for Children-Revised version (DISC-R): I. Preparation, field testing, interrater reliability, and acceptability. *Journal of the American Academy of Child and Adolescent Psychiatry, 32,* 643–650.

Shaffer, J. W., Duszynski, K. R., & Thomas, C. B. (1984). A comparison of three methods for scoring figure drawings. *Journal of Personality Assessment, 48,* 245–254.

Shalit, B. (1965). Effects of environmental stimulation on the M, FM, and m response to the Rorschach. *Journal of Projective Techniques and Personality Assessment, 29,* 228–231.

Shapiro, D. A. (1956). Color-response and perceptual passivity. *Journal of Projective Techniques, 20,* 52–69.

Shapiro, D. A. (1960). Perceptual understanding of color response. In M. Rickers-Ovsiankina (Ed.), *Rorschach psychology* (pp. 89–103). New York: Wiley.

Shapiro, D. A., Barkham, M., Rees, A., Hardy, G. E., Reynolds, S., & Startup, M. (1994). Effects of treatment duration and severity of depression on the effectiveness of cognitive-behavioral and psychodynamic-interpersonal psychotherapy. *Journal of Consulting and Clinical Psychology, 62,* 522–534.

Shapiro, D. M., & Harrison, D. W. (1990). Alternative forms of the AVLT: A procedure and test of form equivalency. *Archives of Clinical Neuropsychology, 5,* 405–410.

Shapiro, M. B., Field, J., & Post, F. (1981). An inquiry into the determinants of a differentiation between elderly "organic" and "non-organic" psychiatric patients on the Bender-Gestalt Test. *Journal of Mental Science, 103,* 364–374.

Shapiro, P. N., & Penrod, S. (1986). Meta-analysis of facial identification studies. *Psychological Bulletin, 100,* 139–156.

Shapiro, S. K., & Simpson, R. G. (1995). Koppitz scoring system as a measure of Bender-Gestalt performance in behaviorally disturbed adolescents. *Journal of Clinical Psychology, 51,* 108–112.

Sharkey, K. J., & Ritzler, B. A. (1985). Comparing diagnostic validity of the TAT and a new picture projective test. *Journal of Personality Assessment, 49,* 406–412.

Shatin, L. (1952). Psychoneurosis and psychosomatic reactions: A Rorschach contrast. *Journal of Consulting Psychology, 16,* 220–223.

Shaw, D. S., & Gynther, M. (1986). An attempt to obtain configural correlates for the California Psychological Inventory. *Psychological Reports, 59,* 675–678.

Sheehan, P. W., Ashton, R., & White, K. (1983). Assessment of mental imagery. In A. A. Sheikh (Ed.), *Imagery: Current theory, research, and application* (pp. 189–221). New York: Wiley.

Sheppard, D., Smith, G. T., & Rosenbaum, G. (1988). Use of the MMPI subtypes in predicting completion of a residential alcoholism treatment program. *Journal of Consulting and Clinical Psychology, 4,* 590–596.

Sherman, E. M. S., Strauss, E., Spellacy, F., & Hunter, M. (1995). Construct validity of WAIS-R: Neuropsychological test correlates in adults referred for evaluation of possible head injury. *Psychological Assessment, 7,* 440–444.

Shneidman, E. S. (Ed.). (1951). *Thematic test analysis.* New York: Grune & Stratton.

Shorkey, C. L., Reyes, E., & Whiteman, V. L. (1977). Development of the rational behavior inventory: Initial validity and reliability. *Educational and Psychological Measurement, 37,* 527–534.

Shrauger, J. S., & Osberg, T. M. (1981). The relative accuracy of self-predictions and judgments of others in psychological assessment. *Psychological Bulletin, 90,* 322–351.

Sieber, K. O., & Myers, L. S. (1992). Validation of the MMPI-2 Social Introversion Subscales. *Psychological Assessment, 4,* 185–189.

Siegler, R. S., & Richards, D. D. (1982). The development of intelligence. In R. J. Sternberg (Ed.), *Handbook of Intelligence* (pp. 897–971). New York: Cambridge University Press.

Sigel, I. E. (1963). How intelligence tests limit understanding of intelligence. *Merrill-Palmer Quarterly, 9,* 39–56.

Silverstein, A. B. (1967). Validity of WISC short forms at three age levels. *California Mental Health Research Digest, 5,* 253–254.

Silverstein, A. B. (1982a). Pattern analysis as simultaneous statistical inference. *Journal of Consulting and Clinical Psychology, 50,* 234–240.

Silverstein, A. B. (1982b). Two- and four-subtest short forms of the Wechsler Adult Intelligence Scale-Revised. *Journal of Consulting and Clinical Psychology, 50,* 415–418.

Silverstein, A. B. (1990). Short forms of individual intelligence tests. *Psychological Assessment, 2,* 3–11.

Silverstein, A. B., & Mohan, P. J. (1962). Bender-Gestalt figure rotations in the mentally retarded. *Journal of Consulting Psychology, 26,* 386–388.

Simon, W. E. (1969). Expectancy effects in the scoring of vocabulary items: A study of scorer bias. *Journal of Educational Measurement, 6,* 159–164.

Simons, A. D., & Thase, M. E. (1992). Biological markers, treatment outcome, and 1 year follow-up in endogenous depression: Electroencephalographic sleep studies and response to cognitive therapy. *Journal of Consulting and Clinical Psychology, 60,* 392–401.

Singer, J. L. (1960). The experience type: Some behavioral correlates and theoretical implications. In M. Rickers-Ovsiankina (Ed.), *Rorschach psychology.* New York: Wiley.

Singer, R. M. (1990). *Neurotoxicity guidebook.* New York: Van Nostran Reinhold.

Sipps, G. J., Berry, G. W., & Lynch, E. M. (1987). WAIS-R and social intelligence: A test of established assumptions that uses the CPI. *Journal of Clinical Psychology, 43,* 499–504.

Sitton, R., & Light, P. (1992). Drawing to differentiate: Flexibility in young children's human figure drawings. *British Journal of Developmental Psychology, 10,* 25–33.

Sivec, H. J., Hilsenroth, M. J., & Lynn, S. J. (1995). Impact of simulating borderline personality disorder on the MMPI-2: A costs-benefit model employing base rates. *Journal of Personality Assessment, 64,* 295–311.

Skolnick, A. (1966). Motivational imagery and behavior over twenty years. *Journal of Consulting Psychology, 30,* 463–478.

Slate, J. R., & Hunnicutt, L. C. (1988). Examiner errors on the Wechsler scales. *Journal of Psychoeducational Assessment, 6,* 280–288.

Slate, R. J., Jones, C. H., & Murray, R. A. (1991). Teaching administration and scoring of the Wechsler Adult Intelligence Scale Revised: An empirical evaluation of practice administrations. *Professional Psychology, 22,* 375–379.

Smith, A. (1982). *Symbol Digit Modalities Test (SDMT). Manual* (Rev.). Los Angeles: Western Psychological Services.

Smith, A. (1983). Clinical psychological practice and principles of neuropsychological assessment. In C. E. Walker (Ed.), *Handbook of clinical psychology: Theory, research, and practice.* Homewood, IL: Dorsey Press.

Smith, C. E., & Keogh, B. K. (1962). The group Bender-Gestalt as a reading readiness screening instrument. *Perceptual and Motor Skills, 15,* 639–645.

Smith, C. P., & Graham, J. R. (1981). Behavioral correlates for the MMPI standard F scale and the modified F scale for black and white psychiatric patients. *Journal of Consulting and Clinical Psychology, 49*(3), 455–459.

Smith, D., & Dumont, F. (1995). A cautionary study: Unwarranted interpretations of the Draw-A-Person test. *Professional Psychology: Research and Practice, 26,* 298–303.

Smith, G. T., & McCarthy, D. M. (1995). Methodological considerations in the refinement of clinical assessment instruments. *Psychological Assessment, 7,* 300–308.

Smith, M. L., Glass, G. V., & Miller, T. L. (1980). *The benefits of psychotherapy.* Baltimore: Johns Hopkins University Press.

Smith, N. M. (1981). The relationship between the Rorschach whole response and level of cognitive functioning. *Journal of Personality Assessment, 45,* 13–19.

Smith, R. E., & Sarason, I. G. (1975). Social anxiety and the evaluation of negative interpersonal feedback. *Journal of Consulting and Clinical Psychology, 43,* 429.

Snow, W. G., Tierney, M. C., Zorzitto, M. L., Fisher, R. H., & Reid, D. W. (1988). One year test-retest reliability of selected tests in older adults [abstract]. *Journal of Clinical and Experimental Neuropsychology, 10,* 60.

Snyder, C. R. (1974). Acceptance of personality interpretations as a function of assessment procedures. *Journal of Consulting and Clinical Psychology, 42,* 150.

Snyder, W. V. (1945). An investigation of the nature of nondirective psychotherapy. *Journal of General Psychology, 33,* 139–223.

Snyderman, M., & Rothman, S. (1987). Survey of expert opinion on intelligence and aptitude testing. *American Psychologist, 42,* 137–144.

Sommer, R., & Sommer, D. (1958). Assaultiveness and two types of Rorschach color responses. *Journal of Consulting Psychology, 22,* 57–62.

Southern, M. L., & Plant, W. T. (1968). Personality characteristics of very bright adults. *Journal of Social Psychology, 75,* 119–126.

Spangler, W. D. (1992). Validity of questionnaire and TAT measures of need for achievement: Two meta-analyses. *Psychological Bulletin, 112,* 140–154.

Sparrow, S. S., Balla, D. A., & Cicchetti, D. V. (1984). *Vineland Adaptive Behavior Scales.* Circle Pines, MN: American Guidance Service.

Spearman, C. (1927). *The abilities of man: Their nature and measurement.* New York: Macmillan.

Spielberger, C. D., Gorsuch, R. L., Lushene, R., Vagg, P. R., & Jacobs, G. A. (1983). *Manual for the State-Trait Anxiety Inventory.* Palo Alto, CA: Consulting Psychologists Press.

Spielberger, C. D., & Piotrowski, C. (1990). Clinician's attitudes toward computer-based testing. *The Clinical Psychologist, 43,* 60–63.

Spigelman, G., Spigelman, A., & Englesson, I. (1992). Analysis of family drawings: A comparison between children from divorce and nondivorce families. *Journal of Divorce & Remarriage, 18,* 31–54.

Spiker, D. G., & Ehler, J. G. (1984). Structured psychiatric interviews for adults. In G. Goldstein & M. Hersen (Eds.), *Handbook of psychological assessment* (pp. 291–304). New York: Pergamon.

Spinks, P. M. (1980). An item and factor analysis of the FSS (III). *Personality and Individual Differences, 1,* 363–370.

Spirito, A., Faust, D., Myers, B., & Bechtel, D. (1988). Clinical utility of the MMPI in the evaluation of adolescent suicide attempters. *Journal of Personality Assessment, 52,* 204–211.

Spitz, H. H. (1986). Disparities in mentally retarded person's I.Q.'s derived from different intelligence tests. *American Journal of Mental Deficiency, 90,* 588–591.

Spitzer, R. L., Endicott, J., & Cohen, J. (1974). Constraints on the validity of computer diagnosis. *Archives of General Psychiatry, 31,* 197–203.

Spitzer, R. L., Endicott, J., & Robins, E. (1978). Research diagnostic criteria: Rationale and reliability. *Archives of General Psychiatry, 35,* 773–782.

Spitzer, R. L., & Williams, J. B. W. (1983). *Instruction manual for the structured clinical interview for DSM-III (SCID).* New York: New York State Psychiatric Institute, Biometrics Research Department.

Spitzer, R. L., Williams, J. B. W., & Gibbon, M. (1987). *Structured clinical interview for DSM-III-R (SCID).* New York: State Psychiatric Institute.

Spitzer, R. L., Williams, J. B. W., Gibbon, M., & First, M. B. (1990). *Structured Clinical Interview for DSM-III-R Personality Disorders (SCID-II).* Washington, DC: American Psychiatric Press.

Spreen, O., & Benton, A. L. (1977). *Neurosensory Center Comprehensive Examination for Aphasia (NCCEA)* (Rev. ed.). Victoria, Canada: University of Victoria, Neuropsychology Laboratory.

Spreen, O., & Strauss, E. (1991). *A compendium of neuropsychological tests.* New York: Oxford University Press.

Spruill, J. (1991). A comparison of the Wechsler Adult Intelligence Scale-Revised with the Stanford-Binet Intelligence Scale (4th Edition) for mentally retarded adults. *Psychological Assessment, 3,* 133–135.

Spruill, J., & Beck, B. (1988). Comparison of the WAIS and the WAIS-R: Different results for different I.Q. groups. *Professional Psychology: Research and Practice, 19,* 31–34.

Staats, A. W. (1970). Intelligence, biology, or learning? Competing conceptions with social consequences. In H. C. Haywood (Ed.), *Social-cultural aspects of mental retardation: Proceedings of the Peabody-NIMH Conference* (pp. 246–277). New York: Appleton-Century-Crofts.

Standage, K. (1986). Socialization scores in psychiatric patients and their implications for the diagnosis of personality disorders. *Canadian Journal of Psychiatry, 31,* 138–141.

Standage, K. (1990). A classification of respondents to the CPI Socialization scale: Associations with diagnosis and other clinical variables. *Personality and Individual Differences, 11,* 335–341.

Standage, K., Smith, D., & Norman, R. (1988). A classification of respondents to the CPI Socialization Scale: Associations with psychiatric diagnosis and implications for research. *Personality and Individual Differences, 9,* 231–236.

Stawar, T. L., & Stawar, D. E. (1989). Kinetic Family Drawings and MMPI diagnostic indicators in adolescent psychiatric inpatients. *Psychological Reports, 65,* 143–146.

Steer, R. A., Beck, A. T., Brown, G., & Berchick, R. (1987). Self-reported depressive symptoms differentiating recurrent-episode major-depression from dysthymic disorders. *Journal of Clinical Psychology, 43,* 246–250.

Steer, R. A., Beck, A. T., & Garrison, B. (1986). Applications of the Beck Depression Inventory. In N. Sartorius & T. A. Ban (Eds.), *Assessment of depression* (pp. 121–142). Geneva, Switzerland: World Health Organization.

Steichen, E. (1955). *Family of man.* New York: Simon & Schuster.

Stein, L. A. R., Graham, J. R., & Williams, C. L. (1995). Detecting fake-bad MMPI-A profiles. *Journal of Personality Assessment, 65,* 415–427.

Stein, M. (1981). *The Thematic Apperception Test: An introductory manual for its clinical use with adults* (2nd ed.). Springfield, IL: Charles C. Thomas.

Steinberg, M. (1993). *Interviewer's guide to the Structured Clinical Interview for DSM-IV Dissociative Disorders (SCID-D).* Washington, DC: American Psychiatric Press.

Steisel, I. M. (1952). The Rorschach test and suggestibility. *Journal of Abnormal and Social Psychology, 47,* 607–614.

Steketee, G. (1994). Behavioral assessment and treatment planning with obsessive compulsive disorder: A review emphasizing clinical application. *Behavior therapy, 25,* 613–633.

Stelmachers, Z. T. (1995). Assessing suicidal clients. In J. Butcher (Ed.), *Clinical personality assessment: Practical approaches* (pp. 367–379). New York: Oxford University Press.

Sternberg, D., & Levine, A. (1965). An indicator of suicidal ideation on the Bender Visual-Motor Gestalt Test. *Journal of Projective Techniques and Personality Assessment, 29,* 377–379.

Sternberg, R. J. (Ed.). (1982). *Handbook of human intelligence.* New York: Cambridge University Press.

Sternberg, R. J. (1985). *Beyond I.Q.: A triarchic theory of human intelligence.* New York: Cambridge University Press.

Sternberg, R. J. (1992). Metaphors of mind underlying the testing of intelligence. In J. C. Rosen & P. McReynolds (Eds.), *Advances in Psychological Assessment* (Vol. 8, pp. 1–39). New York: Plenum Press.

Sternberg, R. J. (1994a). Commentary: Reforming school reform: Comments on *Multiple intelligences: The theory in practice. Teachers College Record, 95,* 561–569.

Sternberg, R. J. (1994b). *Personality and Intelligence*. Cambridge, England: Cambridge University Press.

Sternberg, R. J., & Kaufman, J. C. (1998). Innovation and intelligence testing: The curious case of the dog that didn't bark. *European Journal of Psychological Assessment, 12,* 175–182.

Sternberg, R. J., & Lubart, T. I. (1996). Investing in creativity. *American Psychologist, 51,* 677–688.

Sternberg, R. J., Wagner, R. K., Williams, W. M., & Horvath, J. A. (1995). Testing common sense. *American Psychologist, 50,* 912–927.

Stewart, L. H. (1962). Social and emotional adjustment during adolescence as related to the development of psychosomatic illness in adulthood. *Genetic Psychology Monographs, 65,* 175–215.

Stoloff, M. L., & Couch, J. V. (Eds.). (1992). *Computer use in psychology: A directory of software* (3rd ed.). Washington, DC: American Psychological Association.

Storandt, M., Botwinick, J., & Danzinger, W. L. (1986). Longitudinal changes: Patients with mild SDAT and matched health controls. In L. W. Poon (Ed.), *Handbook for clinical memory assessment of older adults.* Washington, DC: American Psychological Association.

Stormant, C. T., & Finney, B. C. (1953). Projection and behavior: A Rorschach study of assaultive mental hospital patients. *Journal of Projective Techniques, 17,* 349–360.

Stotsky, B. A. (1952). A comparison of remitting and non-remitting schizophrenics on psychological tests. *Journal of Abnormal and Social Psychology, 47,* 489–496.

Strasberg, D. S., Tilley, D., Bristone, S., & Oei, T. P. (1992). The MMPI and chronic pain: A cross-cultural view. *Psychological Assessment, 4,* 493–497.

Streiner, D. L., & Miller, H. R. (1990). Maximum liklihood estimates of the accuracy of four diagnostic techniques. *Educational and Psychological Measurement, 50,* 653–662.

Stroop, J. R. (1935). Studies of interference in serial verbal reactions. *Journal of Experimental Psychology, 18,* 643–662.

Stroup, A., & Manderscheid, R. (1977). CPI and 16PF second-order factor congruence. *Journal of Clinical Psychology, 33,* 1023–1026.

Strub, R. L., & Black, F. W. (1977). *The mental status examination in neurology.* Philadelphia, PA: F. A. Davis.

Strub, R. L., & Black, F. W. (1993). *The Mental Status Examination in neurology* (3rd ed.). Philadelphia, PA: F. A. Davis.

Strupp, H. H. (1958). The psychotherapist's contribution to the treatment process. *Behavioral Science, 3,* 34–67.

Stukenberg, K. W., Dura, J. R., Kiecolt-Glaser, J. K. (1990). Depression screening scale validation in an elderly, community-dwelling population. *Psychological Assessment, 2,* 134–138.

Sturgis, E., & Gramling, S. (1988). Psychophysiological assessment. In A. S. Bellack & M. Hersen (Eds.), *Behavioral assessment: A practical handbook* (3rd ed., pp. 213–251). New York: Pergamon.

Stuss, D. T., Gow, C. A., & Hetherington, C. R. (1992). "No longer Gage": Frontal lobe dysfunction and emotional changes. *Journal of Consulting and Clinical Psychology, 60,* 349–359.

Stuss, D. T., Stethem, L. L., Hugenholtz, H., & Richard, M. T. (1989). Traumatic brain injury: A comparison of three clinical tests, and analysis of recovery. *Clinical Neuropsychologist, 3,* 145–156.

Suinn, R. M., & Oskamp, S. (1969). *The predictive validity of projective measures: A fifteen year evaluative review of research* (Chap. 8). Springfield, IL: Charles C. Thomas.

Sundberg, N. D. (1955). The acceptability of "fake" versus "bona fide" personality test interpretations. *Journal of Abnormal and Social Psychology, 50,* 145–147.

Sundberg, N. D. (1961). The practice of psychological testing in clinical services in the United States. *American Psychologist, 16,* 79–83.

Sundberg, N., & Ballinger, T. (1968). Nepalese children's cognitive development as revealed by drawings of man, woman, and self. *Child Development, 39,* 969–985.

Sutter, E. G., & Bishop, P. C. (1986). Further investigation of the correlations among the WISC-R, PIAT, and DAM. *Psychology in the Schools, 23,* 365–367.

Suzuki, L. A., Meller, P. J., & Ponterotto, J. G. (Eds.). (1996). *Handbook of multicultural assessment: Clinical, psychological, and educational applications.* Englewood Cliffs, NJ: Prentice-Hall.

Swartz, M. S., Blazer, D. G., George, L. K., Winfield, I., Zakris, J., & Dye, E. (1989). Identification of borderline personality with the NIMH Diagnostic Interview Schedule. *American Journal of Psychiatry, 146,* 200–205.

Sweetland, R. C., & Keyser, D. J. (1991) *Tests: A comprehensive reference for assessment in psychology, education, and business* (2nd ed.). Kansas City: Test Corporation of America.

Swensen, W. M., Pearson, J. S., & Osborne, D. (1973). *An MMPI source book: Basic item, scale, and pattern data on 50,000 medical patients.* Minneapolis: University of Minnesota Press.

Swenson, C. H. (1968). Empirical evaluations of human figure drawings: 1957–1966. *Psychological Bulletin, 70,* 20–44.

Swierchinsky, D. (1978). *Manual for the adult neuropsychological evaluation.* Springfield, IL: Charles C. Thomas.

Sylvester, C. E., Hyde, T. S., & Reichler, R. J. (1987). The Diagnostic Interview for Children and the Personality Inventory for children in studies of children at risk for anxiety disorders or depression. *Journal of the American Academy of Child and Adolescent Psychiatry, 26,* 668–675.

Szasz, T. (1987). Justifying coercion through religion and psychiatry. *Journal of Humanistic Psychology, 27,* 158–174.

Taft, R. (1955). The ability to judge people. *Psychological Bulletin, 52,* 1–23.

Tallent, N. (1992). *The practice of psychological assessment.* Englewood Cliffs, NJ: Prentice-Hall.

Tallent, N. (1993). *Psychological report writing* (4th ed.). Englewood Cliffs, NJ: Prentice-Hall.

Tallent, N., & Reiss, W. J. (1959a). Multidisciplinary views on the preparation of written psychological reports: I. Spontaneous suggestions for content. *Journal of Clinical Psychology, 15,* 218–221.

Tallent, N., & Reiss, W. J. (1959b). Multidisciplinary views on the preparation of written psychological reports: II. Acceptability of certain common content variables and styles of expression. *Journal of Clinical Psychology, 15,* 273–274.

Tallent, N., & Reiss, W. J. (1959c). Multidisciplinary views on the preparation of written psychological reports: III. The trouble with psychological reports. *Journal of Clinical Psychology, 15,* 444–446.

Talley, J. L. (1990). *Children's Auditory Verbal Learning Test.* Odessa, FL: Psychological Assessment Resources.

Talley, P. F., Strupp, H. S., & Morey, L. C. (1990). Matchmaking in psychotherapy: Patient-therapist dimensions and their impact on outcome. *Journal of Consulting and Clinical Psychology, 58,* 182–188.

Tanaka-Matsumi, J., & Kameoka, V. A. (1986). Reliabilities and concurrent validities of popular self-report measures of depression, anxiety, and social desirability. *Journal of Consulting and Clinical Psychology, 54,* 328–333.

Tasto, D. L. (1977). Self-report schedules and inventories. In A. R. Ciminero, K. S. Calhoun, & H. E. Adams (Eds.), *Handbook of behavioral assessment.* New York: Wiley.

Taylor, M. A. (1981). *The neuropsychiatric mental status examination.* Jamaica, NY: Spectrum.

Taylor, M. A. (1993). *The neuropsychiatric guide to modern everyday psychiatry.* New York: Free Press.

Taylor, R. L., Kauffman, D., & Partenio, I. (1984). The Koppitz developmental scoring system for the Bender-Gestalt: Is it developmental? *Psychology in the Schools, 21,* 425–428.

Taylor, R. L., Sternberg, L., & Partenio, I. (1986). Performance of urban and rural children on the SOMPA: Preliminary investigation. *Perceptual and Motor Skills, 63,* 1219–1223.

Teevan, R. C., Diffenderfer, D., & Greenfield, N. (1986). Need for achievement and sociometric status. *Psychological Reports, 58,* 446.

Teglasi, H. (1980). Acceptance of the traditional female role and sex of the first person drawn on the Draw-A-Person test. *Perceptual and Motor Skills, 51,* 267–271.

Tellegen, A., & Ben-Porath, Y. S. (1992). The new uniform T scores for the MMPI-2: Rationale, derivation, and appraisal. *Psychological Assessment, 4,* 145–155.

Tellegen, A., & Ben-Porath, Y. S. (1993). Code-type comparability of the MMPI and MMPI-2: Analysis of recent findings and criticisms. *Journal of Personality Assessment, 61,* 489–500.

Temp, G. (1971). Test bias: Validity of the SAT for blacks and whites in thirteen integrated institutions. *Journal of Educational Measurement, 8,* 245–251.

Teng, E. L., Chui, H. C., & Saperia, D. (1990). Senile dementia: Performance on a neuropsychological test battery. *Recent advances in Cardiovascular Disease, 11,* 27–34.

Terman, L. M. (1916). *The measurement of intelligence.* Boston: Houghton Mifflin.

Terman, L. M., & Merril, M. A. (1960). *Stanford-Binet Intelligence Scale.* Boston: Houghton Mifflin.

Terman, L. M., & Miles, C. C. (1936). *Sex and personality: Studies in masculinity and femininity.* New York: McGraw-Hill.

Terrell, F., Taylor, J., & Terrell, S. L. (1978). Effects of types of social reinforcement on the intelligence test performance of lower-class black children. *Journal of Consulting and Clinical Psychology, 46,* 1538–1539.

Tharinger, D. J., & Stark, K. (1990). A qualitative versus quantitative approach to evaluating the Draw-A-Family and Kinetic Family Drawing: A study of mood- and anxiety-disorder children. *Psychological Assessment, 2,* 365–375.

Thiesen, J. W. (1952). A pattern analysis of structural characteristics of the Rorschach test in schizophrenia. *Journal of Consulting Psychology, 16,* 365–370.

Thomas, A. D., & Dudek, S. Z. (1985). Interpersonal affect in Thematic Apperception Test responses: A scoring system. *Journal of Personality Assessment, 49,* 30–36.

Thomas, C. B., & Duszynski, K. R. (1985). Are words of the Rorschach predictors of disease and death? The case of "whirling." *Psychosomatic Medicine, 47,* 201–211.

Thompson, G. M. (1948). MMPI correlates of movement responses on the Rorschach. *American Psychologist, 3,* 348–349.

Thompson, L. L., Heaton, R. K., Mathews, C. G., & Grant, I. (1987). Comparison of preferred and nonpreferred hand performance on four neuropsychological tasks. *The Clinical Neuropsychologist, 1,* 324–334.

Thompson, R. J. (1981). The diagnostic utility of Bannatyne's recategorized WISC-R scores with children referred to a developmental evaluation center. *Psychology in the Schools, 18,* 43–47.

Thorndike, R. L. (1959). The California Psychological Inventory: A review. In O. K. Buros (Ed.), *Fifth mental measurements yearbook.* Highland Park, NJ: Gryphon Press.

Thorndike, R. L. (1968). Review of Pygmalion in the classroom by R. Rosenthal & L. Jacobson. *American Educational Research Journal, 5,* 708–711.

Thurstone, L. L. (1938). Primary mental abilities. *Psychometric Monographs,* No. 1.

Thweatt, R. C., Obrzut, J. F., & Taylor, H. D. (1972). The development and validation of a soft-scoring system for the Bender Gestalt. *Psychology in the Schools, 9,* 170–174.

Thyer, B. A., Tomlin, P., Curtiss, G. C., Cameron, O. G., & Nesse, R. (1985). Diagnostic and gender differences in the expressed fears of anxious patients. *Journal of Behavior Therapy and Experimental Psychiatry, 16,* 111–115.

Tierney, M. C., Nores, A., Snow, W. G., Fisher, R. H., Zorzitto, M. L., & Reid, D. W. (1994). Use of the Rey Auditory Verbal Learning Test in differentiating normal aging from Alzheimer's and Parkinson's dementia. *Psychological Assessment, 6,* 129–134.

Timbrook, R. E., & Graham, J. R. (1994). Ethnic differences on the MMPI-2. *Psychological Assessment, 6,* 212–217.

Todd, A. L., & Gynther, M. D. (1988). Have MMPI Mf scale correlates changed in the past 30 years? *Journal of Clinical Psychology, 44,* 505–510.

Todd, J., Coolidge, F., & Satz, P. (1977). The Wechsler Adult Intelligence Scale discrepancy index: A neuropsychological evaluation. *Journal of Consulting and Clinical Psychology, 45*, 450–454.

Tolor, A. (1956). A comparison of the Bender Gestalt test and the digit-span test as measures of recall. *Journal of Consulting Psychology, 20*, 305–309.

Tolor, A., & Brannigan, G. C. (1980). *Research and clinical applications of the Bender-Gestalt Test.* Springfield, IL: Charles C. Thomas.

Tolor, A., & Digrazia, P. V. (1977). The body image of pregnant women as reflected in their human figure drawings. *Journal of Clinical Psychology, 34*, 537–538.

Tolor, A., & Schulberg, H. C. (1963). *An evaluation of the Bender-Gestalt Test.* Springfield, IL: Charles C. Thomas.

Tombaugh, T. N., McDowell, I., Kristjansson, B., & Hubley, A. M. (1996). Mini-mental state examination (MMSE) and the Modified MMSE (3MS): Psychometric comparison and normative data. *Psychological Assessment, 8*, 48–59.

Tomlin, P., Thyer, B. A., Curtis, R. N., Cameron, O., & Wright, P. (1984). Standardization of the Fear Survey Schedule based upon patients with *DSM-III* anxiety disorders. *Journal of Behavior Therapy and Experimental Psychiatry, 15*, 123–126.

Townsend, J. K. (1967). The relation between Rorschach signs of aggression and behavioral aggression in emotionally disturbed boys. *Journal of Projective Techniques and Personality Assessment, 31*, 13–21.

Tramill, J., Edwards, P., Tramill, J. (1980). Comparison of the Goodenough-Harris Drawing Test and the WISC-R for children experiencing academic difficulties. *Perceptual and Motor Skills, 50*, 543–546.

Tranel, D. (1994). The release of psychological data to nonexperts: Ethical and legal considerations. *Professional Psychology: Research and Practice, 25*, 33–38.

Truax, C. B., & Carkhuff, R. R. (1967). *Toward effective counseling and psychotherapy.* New York: Aldine.

Tsushima, W. T., & Onorato, V. A. (1982). Comparison of MMPI scores of white and Japanese-American medical patients. *Journal of Clinical and Consulting Psychology, 50*, 150–151.

Tucker, R. K., Weaver, R. L., Duran, R. L., & Redden, E. M. (1983). Criterion-related validity of three measures of assertiveness. *Psychological Record, 33*, 361–370.

Tukey, J. W. (1977). *Exploratory data analysis.* Reading, MA: Addison-Wesley.

Turk, D., & Salovey, P. (1985). Cognitive structures, cognitive processes, and cognitive behavior modification. *Cognitive Therapy and Research, 9*, 19–33.

Turpin, G. (1991). The psychophysiological assessment of anxiety disorders: Three-systems measurement and beyond. *Psychological Assessment, 3*, 366–375.

Ullman, L. P., & Krasner, L. A. (1965). *Case studies in behavior modification.* New York: Holt, Rinehart & Winston.

Ulrich, L. P., & Trumbo, D. (1965). The selection interview since 1949. *Psychological Bulletin, 63*, 100–116.

Ulrich, R. E., Stachnik, T. J., & Stainton, N. R. (1963). Student acceptance of generalized personality interpretations. *Psychological Reports, 13*, 831–834.

Urban, W. H. (1963). *The Draw-A-Person Catalogue for Interpretive Analysis.* Los Angeles: Western Psychological Services.

Vakil, E., & Blachstein, H. (1993). Rey Auditory Verbal Learning Test: Structure analysis. *Journal of Clinical Psychology, 49*, 883–890.

Vance, B., Fuller, G. B., & Lester, M. L. (1986). A comparison of the Minnesota Perceptual Diagnostic Test Revised and the Bender-Gestalt. *Journal of Learning Disabilities, 19*, 211–214.

Vandiver, T., & Sheer, K. J. (1991). Temporal stability of the diagnostic interview schedule. *Psychological Assessment, 3*, 277–281.

Van Dyne, W. T., & Carsleadon, T. G. (1978). Relationships among three components of self-concept and same-sex and opposite-sex human figure drawings. *Journal of Clinical Psychology, 34*, 537–538.

Vane, J. R. (1981). The Thematic Apperception Test: A review. *Social Psychology Review, 1,* 319–336.

Vane, J. R., & Guarnaccia, V. J. (1989). Personality theory and personality assessment measures: How helpful to the clinician? *Journal of Clinical Psychology, 45,* 5–19.

van Gorp, W. G., Tulin, S. J., Evans, G., & Satz, P. (1990). Incidence of the WAIS-R Fuld profile in HIV-1 infection. *Journal of Clinical and Experimental Neuropsychology, 12,* 807–811.

Van Hutton, V. (1990). Test review: The California Psychological Inventory. *Journal of Consulting and Development, 69,* 75–77.

Van Hutton, V. (1994). *House-Tree-Person and Draw-A-Person as measures of abuse in children: A quantitative scoring system.* Odessa, FL: Psychological Assessment Resources.

Veldman, D. J., & Kelly, S. J. (1965). Personality correlates of a composite criterion of teaching effectiveness. *Alberta Journal of Educational Research, 11,* 702–707.

Verma, S. K., Wig, N. N., & Shaw, D. K. (1962). Validity of Bender Gestalt Test in Indian psychiatric patients. *Indian Journal of Applied Psychology, 9,* 65–67.

Vernon, P. A. (Ed.). (1987). *Speed of information-processing and intelligence.* Norwood, NJ: Ablex.

Vernon, P. E. (1950). *The structure of human abilities.* London: Methuen.

Vernon, P. E. (1961). *The structure of human abilities* (2nd ed.). London: Methuen.

Vernon, P. E. (1964). *Personality assessment: A critical survey.* London: Methuen.

Vilkki, J., Ahola, K., Holst, P., Ohman, J., Servo, A., & Heiskanen, O. (1994). Prediction of psychosocial recovery after head injury with cognitive tests and neurobehavioral ratings. *Journal of Clinical and Experimental Neuropsychology, 16,* 325–338.

Vincent, K. R., Castillo, I., Hauser, R., Stuart, H. J., Zapata, J. A., Cohn, C. K., & O'Shanick, G. J. (1983). MMPI code types and *DSM-III* diagnosis. *Journal of Clinical Psychology, 39,* 829–842.

Vincent, K. R., & Harman, M. J. (1991). The Exner Rorschach: An analysis of its clinical validity. *Journal of Clinical Psychology, 47,* 596–599.

Visser, R. S. H. (1992). *Manual for the Complex Figure Test.* Amsterdam: Swets & Zeitlinger.

Vitz, P. C. (1990). The use of stories in moral development: New psychological reasons for an old education model. *American Psychologist, 45,* 709–720.

Vogel, S. A. (1990). Gender differences in intelligence, language, visual-motor abilities and academic achievement in students with learning disabilities: A review of the literature. *Journal of Learning Disabilities, 23,* 44–52.

Vogt, A. T., & Heaton, R. L. (1977). Comparison of WAIS indices of cerebral dysfunction. *Perceptual and Motor Skills, 45,* 607–615.

Wade, T. C., & Baker, T. B. (1977). Opinions and use of psychological tests: A survey of clinical psychologists. *American Psychologist, 32,* 874–882.

Wade, T. C., Baker, T. B., & Hartman, D. P. (1979). Behavior therapist's self-reported views and practices. *The Behavior Therapist, 2,* 3–6.

Wagner, E. E. (1961). The interaction of aggressive movement responses and anatomy responses on the Rorschach in producing anxiety. *Journal of Projective Techniques, 25,* 212–215.

Wagner, E. E. (1971). Structural analysis: A theory of personality based on projective techniques. *Journal of Personality Assessment, 37,* 5–15.

Wagner, E. E. (1973). Diagnosis of conversion hysteria: An interpretation based on structural analysis. *Journal of Personality Assessment, 37,* 5–15.

Wagner, E. E., & Flamos, O. (1988). Optimized split-half reliability for the Bender Visual Motor Gestalt Test: Further evidence for the use of the maximization procedure. *Journal of Personality Assessment, 52,* 454–458.

Wagner, R. (1949). The employment interview: A critical review. *Personnel Psychology, 2,* 17–46.

Wagner, R. K., & Sternberg, R. J. (1991). *Tacit knowledge inventory for managers.* San Antonio, TX: Psychological Corporation.

Wakefield, J. F. (1986). Creativity and the TAT blank card. *Journal of Creative Behavior, 7,* 127–133.

Waldman, T. L., Silber, D. E., Holmstrom, R. W., & Karp, S. A. (1994). Personality character-istics of incest survivors on the Draw-A-Person Questionnaire. *Journal of Personality Assessment, 63,* 97–104.

Walker, C. E., & Roberts, M. C. (1992). *Handbook of child psychology* (2nd ed.). New York: Wiley.

Walker, N. W., & Myrick, C. C. (1985). Ethical considerations in the use of computers in psychological testing and assessment. *Journal of School Psychology, 23,* 51–57.

Wallbrown, F. H., & Jones, J. A. (1992). Reevaluating the factor structure of the revised California Psychological Inventory. *Educational and Psychological Measurement, 52,* 379–386.

Waller, N. G., & Waldman, I. D. (1990). A re-examination of the WAIS-R factor structure. *Psychological Assessment, 2,* 139–144.

Waller, R. W., & Keeley, S. M. (1978). Effects of explanation and information feedback on the illusory correlation phenomenon. *Journal of Consulting and Clinical Psychology, 46,* 342–343.

Walsh, K. (1987). *Neuropsychology* (2nd ed.). Edinburgh, England: Churchill-Livingston.

Walsh, K. (1994). Neuropsychological assessment of patients with memory disorders. In S. Toyz, D. Byrne, & A. Gilandis (Eds.), *Neuropsychology in clinical practice* (pp. 107–127). New York: Academic Press.

Ward, L. C. (1990). Prediction of verbal, performance and full-scale IQs from seven subtests of the WAIS-R. *Journal of Clinical Psychology, 46,* 436–440.

Ward, L. C. (1991). A comparison of the MMPI and the MMPI-2. *Psychological Assessment, 3,* 688–690.

Ward, L. C., & Ryan, J. J. (1996). Validity and time savings in the selection of short forms of the Wechsler Adult Intelligence Scale-Revised. *Psychological Assessment, 8,* 69–72.

Warrington, E. K., James, M., & Maciejewski, C. (1986). The WAIS as a lateralizing and localizing diagnostic instrument. *Neuropsychologia, 24,* 223–239.

Watkins, C. E. (1986). Validity and usefulness of WAIS-R, WISC-R, and WPPSI short forms: A critical review. *Professional Psychology Research and Practice, 17,* 36–43.

Watkins, C. E. (1991). What have surveys taught us about the teaching and practice of psychological assessment. *Journal of Personality Assessment, 56,* 426–437.

Watkins, C. E., Campbell, V. L., Nieberding, R., & Hallmark, R. (1995). Contemporary practice of psychological assessment by clinical psychologists. *Professional Psychology: Research and Practice, 26,* 54–60.

Watkins, C. E., Edinger, J. D., & Shipley, R. H. (1986). Validity of a WAIS-R screening instrument (Satz-Mogel) for medical inpatients. *Rehabilitation Psychology, 31,* 103–109.

Watkins, J. T., & Rush, A. J. (1983). Cognitive response test. *Cognitive Therapy and Research, 7,* 425–435.

Watson, C. G., Thomas, D., & Anderson, P. E. D. (1992). Do computer-administered Minnesota Multiphasic Personality Inventories underestimate booklet-based scores? *Journal of Clinical Psychology, 48,* 744–748.

Watson, D., & Friend, R. (1969). Measurement of social-evaluative anxiety. *Journal of Consulting and Clinical Psychology, 33,* 448–457.

Watson, J. B., & Raynor, R. (1920). Conditioned emotional reactions. *Journal of Experimental Psychology, 3,* 1–14.

Watzlawick, P., Beavin, J. H., & Jackson, D. D. (1966). *Pragmatics of human communication.* New York: Norton.

Waugh, K. W., & Bush, W. J. (1971). *Diagnosing learning disorders.* Columbus, OH: Merrill.

Webb, J. T., McNamara, K. M., & Rodgers, D. A. (1981). *Configural interpretation of the MMPI and CPI.* Columbus, OH: Ohio Psychology Publishing.

Wechsler, D. (1949). *Manual for the Wechsler Intelligence Scale for Children.* New York: Psychological Corporation.

Wechsler, D. (1955). *Manual for the Wechsler Adult Intelligence Scale.* New York: Psychological Corporation.

Wechsler, D. (1958). *The measurement and appraisal of adult intelligence* (4th ed.). Baltimore: Williams & Wilkins.

Wechsler, D. (1967). *Manual for the Wechsler Preschool and Primary School of Intelligence.* New York: Psychological Corporation.

Wechsler, D. (1974). *Wechsler Memory Scale manual.* San Antonio, TX: The Psychological Corporation.

Wechsler, D. (1981). *Manual for the Wechsler Adult Intelligence Scale-Revised.* New York: Psychological Corporation.

Wechsler, D. (1987). *Wechsler Memory Scale-Revised manual.* San Antonio, TX: The Psychological Corporation.

Wechsler, D. (1989). *Manual for the Wechsler Preschool and Primary Sale of Intellience-Revised (WPPSI-R).* San Antonio, TX: Psychological Corporation.

Wechsler, D. (1991). *Manual for the Wechsler Intelligence Scale for Children* (3rd. ed.). New York: Psychological Corporation.

Wechsler, D. (1997a). *WAIS-III Administration and Scoring manual.* San Antonio, TX: Psychological Corporation.

Wechsler, D. (1997b). *WAIS-III/WMS-III technical manual.* San Antonio, TX: Psychological Corporation.

Wechsler, D. (1945). A standardized memory scale for clinical use. *Journal of Psychology, 19,* 87–95.

Wedding, D. (1979). *A comparison of statistical, actuarial, and clinical models used in predicting presence, lateralization, and type of brain damage in humans.* Unpublished doctoral dissertation, University of Hawaii, Honolulu.

Wedding, D., & Faust, D. (1989). Clinical judgment and decision making in neuropsychology. *Archives of Clinical Neuropsychology, 4,* 233–265.

Wedemeyer, B. (1954). Rorschach statistics on a group of 136 normal men. *Journal of Psychology, 37,* 51–58.

Weed, L. L. (1968). Medical records that guide and teach. *New England Journal of Medicine, 278,* 593–600.

Weed, N. C., & Butcher, J. N. (1992). The MMPI-2. Development and research issues. In J. C. Rosen & P. McReynolds (Eds.). *Advances in psychological assessment,* (Vol.8, pp. 131–163). New York: Plenum Press.

Weed, N. C., Butcher, J. N., Ben-Porath, Y. S., & McKenny, T. (1992). New measures for assessing alcohol and drug abuse with the MMPI-2: The APS and AAS. *Journal of Personality Assessment, 58,* 389–404.

Weed, N. C., Butcher, J. N., & Williams, C. L. (1994). Development of MMPI-A Alcohol/Drug problem scales. *Journal of Studies on Alcohol, 55,* 296–302.

Weekes, B. (1993). Criterion related validity of the responsibility scale of the California Psychological Inventory. *Psychological Reports, 73,* 315–320.

Weinberg, R. A. (1989). Intelligence and IQ: Landmark issues and great debates. *American Psychologist, 44,* 98–104.

Weinberger, D. R. (1987). Implications of normal brain development for the pathogenesis of schizophrenia. *Archives of General Psychiatry, 44,* 660–669.

Weinberger, D. R., & Berman, K. F. (1988). Speculation on the meaning of cerebral metabolic hypofrontality in schizophrenia. *Schizophrenia Bulletin, 14,* 157–163.

Weiner, I. B. (1961). Cross-validation of a Rorschach checklist associated with suicidal tendencies. *Journal of Consulting Psychology, 25,* 312–315.

Weiner, I. B. (1966). *Psychodiagnosis in schizophrenia.* New York: John Wiley.

Weiner, I. B. (1977). Approaches to Rorschach validation. In M. A. Rickers-Ovsiankira (Ed.), *Rorschach Psychology.* Huntington, NY: Robert E. Krieger.

Weiner, I. B. (1986). Conceptual and empirical perspectives on the Rorschach assessment of psychopathology. *Journal of Personality Assessment, 50,* 472–479.

Weiner, I. B. (1994). The Rorschach Inkblot Method (RIM) is not a test: Implications for theory and practice. *Journal of Personality Assessment, 62,* 498–504.

Weiner, I. B., & Exner, J. E. (1991). Rorschach changes in long-term and short-term psychotherapy. *Journal of Personality Assessment, 56,* 453–465.

Weiner, I. B. (1996). Some observations on the validity of the Rorschach Inkblot method. *Psychological Assessment, 8,* 206–213.

Weins, A. N., McMinn, M. R., & Crossen, J. R. (1988). Rey Auditory-Verbal Learning Test: Development of norms for healthy young adults. *Clinical Neuropsychologist, 2,* 67–87.

Weissman, A., & Beck, A. T. (1978, November). *Development and validation of the Dysfunctional Attitude Scale (DAS).* Paper presented at the 12th annual meeting of the Association for the Advancement of Behavior Therapy, Chicago, IL.

Weissman, H. N. (1992, August 18). MMPI and MMPI-2 comparisons in an outpatient population. Paper presented at the 100th Annual Convention of the American Psychological Association, Washington, DC.

Welch, G., Hall, A., & Walkey, F. (1990). The replicable dimensions of the Beck Depression Inventory. *Journal of Clinical Psychology, 46,* 817–827.

Wellbrown, F. H., & Jones, J. A. (1992). Reevaluating the factor structure of the revised California Psychological Inventory. *Educational and Psychological Measurement, 52,* 379–386.

Weller, N. G., & Weldman, I. D. (1990). A reexamination of the WAIS-R factor structure. *Psychological Assessment, 2,* 139–144.

Weller, R. A., Penick, E. C., Powell, B. J., Othmer, E., Rice, A. S., & Kent, T. A. (1985). Agreement between two structured psychiatric diagnostic interviews: DIS and the PDI. *Comprehensive Psychiatry, 26,* 157–163.

Wenger, M. A. (1966). Studies of autonomic balance: A summary. *Psychophysiology, 2,* 173–186.

Wernick, R. (1955, September 12). The modern-style mind reader. *Life,* 95–108.

Wertheimer, M. (1923). Studies in the theory of Gestalt psychology. *Psychological Forsch, 41,* 301–350.

West, A., Martindale, C., Hines, D., & Roth, W. T. (1983). Marijuana-induced primary process content in the TAT. *Journal of Personality Assessment, 47,* 466–467.

Westling, B. E., & Ost, L. (1995). Cognitive bias in panic disorder patients and changes after cognitive-behavioral treatments. *Behavior Research & Therapy, 33,* 585–588.

Wetter, M., Baer, R. A., Berry, D. T., Robinson, L. H., & Sumpter, J. (1993). MMPI-2 profiles of motivated fakers given specific symptom information: A comparison to matched patients. *Psychological Assessment, 5,* 317–323.

Wetter, M. W., & Deitsch, S. E. (1996). Faking specific disorders and temporal response consistency on the MMPI-2. *Psychological Assessment, 8,* 39–47.

Wetzler, S. (1989). *Measuring mental illness: Psychometric measurement for clinicians.* Washington, DC: American Psychiatric Press.

Wetzler, S. (1990). The Millon Clinical Multiaxial Inventory (MCMI): A review. *Journal of Personality Assessment, 55,* 445–464.

Wetzler, S., & Marlowe, D. (1990). "Faking bad" on the MMPI, MMPI-2 and Millon-II. *Psychological Reports, 67,* 1117–1118.

Wetzler, S., & Marlowe, D. (1992). What they don't tell you in the test manual: A response to Millon. *Journal of Counseling & Development, 70,* 427–428.

Wheeler, L., & Reitan, R. M. (1962). Presence and laterality of brain damage predicted from responses to a short aphasia screening test. *Perceptual and Motor Skills, 15,* 783–799.

White, G. W., Nielsen, L., & Prus, J. S. (1984). Head start teacher and aide preferences for degree of specificity in written psychological recommendations. *Professional Psychology: Research and Practice, 15,* 785–790.

White, R. B., Jr., & McGraw, R. K. (1975). Note on the relationship between downward slant of Bender figures 1 and 2 and depression in adult psychiatric patients. *Perceptual and Motor Skills, 40,* 152.

White, R. W. (1941). An analysis of motivation in hypnosis. *Journal of General Psychology, 24,* 145–162.

White, S., & Edelstein, B. (1991). Behavioral assessment and investigatory interviewing. *Behavioral Assessment, 13,* 245–264.

Whitworth, R. H., & McBlaine, D. D. (1993). Comparison of the MMPI and MMPI-2 administered to Anglo- and Hispanic-American university students. *Journal of Personality Assessment, 61,* 19–27.

Wickham, T. (1978). *WISC patterns in acting-out delinquents, poor readers, and normal controls.* Unpublished doctoral dissertation, United States International University, San Diego, CA.

Wickramasekera, I. E. (1988). *Clinical behavioral medicine.* New York: Plenum Press.

Wickramasekera, I. E. (1995). A model of people at high risk to develop chronic stress-related somatic symptoms: Some predictions. *Professional Psychology: Research and Practice, 17,* 437–447.

Wickramasekera, I. E. (1995). Somatization: Concepts, data, and predictions from the high risk model of threat perception. *Journal of Nervous and Mental Diseases, 186,* 15–23.

Widiger, T. A., & Frances, A. (1987). Interviews and inventories for the measurement of personality disorders. *Clinical Psychology Review, 7,* 49–75.

Widiger, T. A., & Kelso, K. (1983). Psychodiagnosis of Axis II. *Clinical Psycholology Review, 3,* 491–510.

Widiger, T. A., Williams, J., Spitzer, R., & Francis, A. (1985). The MCMI as a measure of *DSM-III. Journal of Personality Assessment, 49,* 366–378.

Wielkiewicz, R. M. (1990). Interpreting low scores on the WISC-R Third Factor: It's more than distractibility. *Psychological Assessment, 2,* 91–97.

Wiener, J. (1985). Teacher's comprehension of psychological reports. *Psychology in the Schools, 22,* 60–64.

Wiener-Levy, D., & Exner, J. E. (1981). The Rorschach Comprehensive System: An overview. In P. McReynolds (Ed.), *Advances in psychological assessment* (Vol. 5). San Francisco: Jossey-Bass.

Wiens, A. N. (1976). The assessment interview. In I. B. Weiner (Ed.), *Clinical methods in psychology* (pp. 3–60). New York: Wiley.

Wiens, A. N. (1983). The assessment interview. In I. B. Weiner (Ed.), *Clinical methods in psychology* (pp. 3–57). New York: Wiley.

Wiggins, J. S. (1966). Substantive dimensions of self-report in the MMPI item pool. *Psychological Monographs, 80,* No. 630.

Wiggins, J. S. (1971). Content scales: Basic data for scoring and interpretation. Unpublished raw data.

Wiggins, J. S. (1973). *Personality and prediction: Principles of personality assessment.* Reading, MA: Addison-Wesley.

Wiggins, N., & Kohen, E. S. (1971). Man versus model of man revisited: The forecasting of graduate school success. *Journal of Personality and Social Psychology, 19,* 100–106.

Williams, A. F., McCourt, W. F., & Schneider, L. (1971). Personality self-descriptions of alcoholics and heavy drinkers. *Quarterly Journal of Studies on Alcohol, 32,* 310–317.

Williams, C. L., & Butcher, J. N. (1989a). An MMPI study of adolescents: I. Empirical validity of the standard scales. *Psychological Assessment, 1,* 251–259.

Williams, C. L., & Butcher, J. N. (1989b). An MMPI study of adolescents: II. Verification and limitations of code type classifications. *Psychological Assessment, 1,* 260–265.

Williams, J. B. W., Gibbon, M., First, M. B., Spitzer, R. L., Davies, M., Borus, J., Howes, M. J., Kane, J., Pope, H. G., Rounsaville, B., Wittchen, H. U. (1992). The Structured Clinical Interview for *DSM-III-R* (SCID): II. Multisite test-retest reliability. *Archives of General Psychiatry, 49,* 630–636.

Williams, J. M. (1991). *Memory Assessment Scales.* Odessa, FL: Psychological Assessment Resources.

Williams, M. H. (1954). The influence of variations in instructions on Rorschach reaction time. *Dissertation Abstracts, 14,* 2131.

Williams, R. L. (1974). Scientific racism, and I.Q.: The silent mugging of the black community. *Psychology Today, 7,* 32–41.

Williamson, D. A., Davis, C. J., & Prather, R. C. (1988). Assessment of health-related disorders. In A. S. Bellack & M. Hersen (Eds.), *Behavioral assessment: A practical handbook* (3rd ed., pp. 396–440). New York: Pergamon.

Wilson, B. A., Cockburn, J., & Baddeley, A. (1985). *The Rivermead Behavioral Memory Test.* Gaylord, MI: National Rehabilitation Services.

Wilson, T. E., & Evans, I. M. (1983). The reliability of target behavior selection in behavioral assessment. *Behavioral Assessment, 5,* 33–54.

Wing, J. K., Cooper, J. E., & Sartorius, N. (1974). *Description and classification of psychiatric symptoms.* Cambridge, England: Cambridge University Press.

Wirt, R. D., Lachar, D., Klinedinst, J. K., & Seat, P. D. (1977). *Multidimensional description of child personality: A manual for the Personality Inventory for Children.* Los Angeles: Western Psychological Services.

Witmer, J. M., Bornstein, A. V., & Dunham, R. M. (1971). The effects of verbal approval and disapproval upon the performance of third and fourth grade children of four subtests of the Wechsler Intelligence Scale for Children. *Journal of School Psychology, 9,* 347–356.

Witt, J. C., & Elliott, S. N. (1983). Assessment in behavioral consultation: The initial interview. *School Psychology Review, 12,* 42–49.

Wittchen, H., Semler, G., & von Zerssen, D. (1985). A comparison of two diagnostic methods. *Archives of General Psychiatry, 42,* 667–684.

Wolber, G. J., & Carne, W. F. (1993). *Writing psychological reports: A guide for clinicians.* Sarasota, FL: Professional Resource Press.

Wolff, W. (1942). Projective methods for personality analysis of expressive behavior in preschool children. *Character & Personality, 10,* 309–330.

Wolfson, D. (1985). *Neuropsychological History Questionnaire.* Tucson, AZ: Reitan Neuropsychology Laboratory.

Wolk, R., & Wolk, R. B. (1971). *Manual: Gerontological Apperception Test.* New York: Behavioral Publications.

Wolpe, J., & Lang, P. J. (1964). A fear survey schedule for use in behavior therapy. *Behavior Research and Therapy, 2,* 27–30.

Wolpe, J., & Lang, P. J. (1969). *Fear Survey Schedule.* San Diego, CA: Educational and Industrial Testing Service.

Wolpe, J., & Lang, P. J. (1977). *Manual for the Fear Survey Schedule.* San Diego, California: EdITS.

Wolpe, J., & Lazarus, A. (1966). *Behavior therapy techniques.* New York: Pergamon.

Wong, M. R. (1984). MMPI scale five: Its meaning or lack thereof. *Journal of Personality Assessment, 48,* 279–284.

Woodcock, R. W. (1990). Theoretical foundations of the WJ-R measures of cognitive ability. *Journal of Psychoeducational Assessment, 8,* 231–258.

Woodcock, R. W., & Johnson, M. B. (1989). *Woodcock-Johnson Tests of Cognitive Ability: Standard and supplemental batteries.* Allen, TX: DLM/Teaching Resources.

Woodruff, R. A., Goodwin, D. W., & Guze, S. B. (1974). *Psychiatric diagnosis.* New York: Oxford University Press.

Woody, R. W. (Ed.). (1980). *Encyclopedia of clinical assessment* (Vol. 1). San Francisco: Jossey-Bass.

Wooten, A. J. (1983). MMPI profiles among neuropsychology patients. *Journal of Clinical Psychology, 39,* 392–406.

World Health Organization (1990). *The ICD-10 classification of mental and behavioural disorders: Clinical description and diagnostic guidelines.* Geneva, Switzerland: Author.

Wright, D., & DeMers, S. T. (1982). Comparison of the relationship between two measures of visual-motor coordination and academic achievement. *Psychology in the Schools, 19,* 473–477.

Wright, J. H., & McIntyre, M. P. (1982). The family drawing depression scale. *Journal of Clinical Psychology, 38,* 853–861.

Wurtz, R. G., Sewell, T. E., & Manni, J. L. (1985). The relationship of estimated learning potential to performance on learning task and achievement. *Psychology in the Schools, 22,* 293–302.

Wyatt, F. (1947). The scoring and analysis of the Thematic Apperception Test. *Journal of Psychology, 24,* 319–330.

Wyndowe, J. (1987). The microcomputerized Diagnostic Interview Schedule: Clinical use in an out-patient setting. *Canadian Journal of Psychiatry, 32,* 93–99.

Wysocki, J. J., & Sweet, J. J. (1985). Identification of brain-damaged schizophrenic, and normal medical patients using a brief neuropsychological screening battery. *International Journal of Clinical Neuropsychology, 7,* 40–44.

Yeudall, L. T., Fromm, D., Reddon, J. R., & Stefanyk, W. O. (1986). Normative data stratified by age and sex for 12 neuropsychological tests. *Journal of Clinical Psychology, 42,* 918–946.

Yossef, S., Slutsky, W. S., & Butcher, J. N. (1989). A real-data simulation of computerized and adaptive administration of the MMPI. *Psychological Assessment, 1,* 18–22.

Yozawitz, A. (1986). Applied neuropsychology in a neuropsychiatric center. In I. Grant & K. M. Adams (Eds.), *Neuropsychological assessment of neuropsychiatric disorders.* New York: Oxford University Press.

Yudin, L. W. (1966). An abbreviated form of the WISC for use with emotionally disturbed children. *Journal of Consulting Psychology, 30,* 272–275.

Zaback, T. P., & Waehler, C. A. (1994). Sex of human figure drawings and sex-role orientation. *Journal of Personality Assessment, 62,* 552–558.

Zedeck, S., Tziner, A., & Middlestadt, S. E. (1983). Interviewer validity and reliability: An individual analysis approach. *Personnel Psychology, 36,* 355–370.

Zigler, E., & Farber, E. A. (1985). Commonalities between the intellectual extremes: Giftedness and mental retardation. In F. D. Horowitz & M. O'Brien (Eds.), *The gifted and talented: Developmental perspectives* (pp. 387–408). Washington, DC: American Psychological Association.

Zilmer, E. A., Bell, J. D., Fowler, P. C., Newman, A. C., & Stutts, M. L. (1991). Wechsler Verbal-Performance I.Q. discrepancies among psychiatric inpatients: Implications for subtle neuropsychological dysfunctioning. *Archives of Clinical Neuropsychology, 6,* 61–71.

Zilmer, E. A., Waechtler, C., Harris, B., Khan, F., & Fowler, P. C. (1992). The effects of unilateral and multifocal lesions on the WAIS-R: A factor analytic study of stroke patients. *Archives of Clinical Neuropsychology, 7,* 29–40.

Ziskin, J., & Faust, D. (1995). *Coping with psychiatric and psychological testimony* (4th ed.). Marina del Rey, CA: Law and Psychology Press.

Zolliker, A. (1943). Schwangerschaftsdepression and Rorschach'scher formdeutversuch. *Schweiz Archeives Neurologie und Psychiatri, 53,* 62–78.

Zomeren, A. H., van, & Brouwer, W. H. (1990). Attentional deficits after closed head injury. In B. G. Deelman, R. J. Saan, & A. H. van Zomeren (Eds.), *Traumatic brain injury: Clinical, social, and rehabilitation aspects.* Amsterdam: Swets & Zeitlinger.

Zotter, D. L., & Crowther, J. H. (1991). The role of cognitions in bulimia nervosa. *Cognitive Therapy and Research, 15,* 413–426.

Zuckerman, E. L. (1991). *The clinician's thesaurus: A guidebook for wording psychological reports and other evaluations* (2nd ed.). Pittsburgh, PA: Three Wishes Press.

Zuckerman, E. L., & Guyett, I. P. R. (1992). *The paperwork office: The tools to make your small psychotherapy practice work ethically, legally, profitably—forms, guidelines, and resources.* Pittsburgh, PA: Three Wishes Press.

Author Index

Vane, J. R., 29
Van Gorp, W. G., 195, 202, 579, 593
Van Hutton, V., 344, 346, 503, 509, 521, 523, 524, 533
Van Lancker, D., 593
Vasarhelyi, J., 149
Vaughn, S., 44
Veldman, D. J., 382
Vernon, P. E., 26, 136, 137, 138
Viglione, D., 444
Vilkki, J., 545
Vincent, K. R., 56, 217, 304, 400, 441
Visser, R. S. H., 500, 539
Vitale, A., 586
Vitz, P. C., 499
Vlark, C., 540, 585
Vogt, A. T., 189
Von Baeyer, C., 119
Vriezen, E. R., 579

Wade, T. C., 107
Waechtler, C., 190
Waehler, C. A., 483, 522
Wagner, E. E., 439, 443
Wagner, R. K., 69, 72, 138, 143, 718
Wakefield, J. F., 483
Wakefield, P., 603, 606, 609
Wakefield, P. J., 7, 611
Waldman, I. D., 162
Waldman, T. L., 503
Walker, C. E., 620
Walker, N. W., 65
Walker, R. N., 423, 426, 429, 430, 431, 433, 437, 438, 439, 442, 444
Walkey, F., 125
Wallbrown, F. H., 136, 151, 162, 196, 345, 347, 348, 350, 611, 612
Wallbrown, W. A., 28
Waller, N. G., 162
Waller, R. W., 505
Walsh, K., 183, 576
Walsh, W. B., 216
Ward, C. H., 74, 124
Ward, L. C., 201, 202, 216
Ward, M. P., 3, 22, 24, 33, 80, 422
Warnick, B., 129
Warrington, E. K., 587
Watkins, C. E., 3, 6, 7, 200, 202, 205, 301, 346, 393, 402, 459, 500, 547, 576
Watkins, J. T., 119, 605
Watkins, M. M., 169, 717
Watson, C. G., 53, 65
Watson, D., 120
Watson, J. B., 102
Watson, J. R., 570, 589
Watts, D., 232, 235, 236, 238
Watzlawick, P., 69
Waugh, K. W., 189
Waugh, M., 579

Weaver, K. A., 152
Weaver, R. L., 106
Webb, J. T., 356, 386, 389
Webb, W. W., 217
Wechsler, D., 147, 148, 150, 154, 156, 159, 161, 162, 168, 169, 176, 183, 184, 189, 204, 576, 674, 711, 714, 715, 716, 721, 724
Wedding, D., 26, 28, 544, 570
Wedemeyer, B., 438
Weed, L. L., 103, 218, 298
Weekes, B., 265
Weinberg, J., 553
Weinberg, R. A., 132, 140, 204
Weinberger, D. R., 539, 557
Weinberger, J., 467
Weiner, I. B., 182, 393, 394, 396, 397, 398, 399, 423, 425, 428, 429, 431, 432, 437, 438, 439, 443, 434, 435, 437, 438, 439, 440, 441, 443, 444, 445, 446, 447, 451, 456, 457
Weiner, W. J., 594
Weins, A. N., 581
Weiss, D., 391
Weissman, A., 119
Weissman, H. N., 216, 225, 262, 263
Welch, G., 125
Weller, R. A., 95
Welner, A., 7, 89, 96
Welsh, G. S., 212, 213, 214, 223
Wenger, M. A., 123
Wenk, E. A., 391
Wernick, R., 366
Werth, T., 726
West, A., 466
West, L., 23
Westgate, J., 41, 42
Westling, B. E., 118
Wetter, M. W., 232, 238
Wetzler, S., 3, 63, 310, 312, 317
Wexler, M., 87
White, G. W., 645
White, K., 121
White, R. B., 557
White, R. W., 480
White, S., 72
Whiteman, V. L., 120
Whitworth, R. H., 220
Wickham, T., 199
Wickramasekera, I. E., 39, 600, 645
Wicott, K. A., 469
Widiger, T. A., 8, 60, 101, 103, 304, 310
Widrow, L., 266
Wiedel, T. C., 23, 215
Wielkiewicz, R. M., 163, 176, 192, 196, 591
Wiener-Levy, D., 446
Wiens, A. N., 70, 78
Wiggins, J. S., 29, 286
Wilcox, N. S., 617

Wilkinson, G., 585
Wilks, V., 585, 586
Willey, C. J., 617
Williams, C. L., 18, 63, 210, 211, 217, 218, 220, 222, 223, 224, 225, 232, 248, 262, 286, 292, 296
Williams, J. B., 75
Williams, J. B. W., 97, 310, 644
Williams, J. M., 27, 194, 576
Williams, M. H., 404
Williams, O., 617, 618
Williams, R. B., 213
Williams, R. E., 7, 600, 603, 606, 609, 611
Williams, R. L., 57
Williams, T. A., 70
Williams, W. M., 138, 143, 718
Williamson, D. A., 103
Wilson, B. A., 576
Wilson, R. S., 543
Wilson, T. D., 118
Wilson, T. E., 110
Wimberly, F., 503
Winfield, I., 95
Wing, J. K., 71
Winget, B. M., 48
Winokur, G., 89, 92
Winter, W. D., 428
Wirt, R. D., 43
Wise, S. L., 612
Witmer, J. M., 47
Witt, J. C., 110
Wittchen, U., 39
Wohl, 713
Wolber, G. J., 622, 623, 641
Wolff, W., 530
Wolfson, D., 8, 39, 65, 173, 175, 176, 183, 185, 186, 187, 191, 192, 537, 544, 568, 570, 572, 574, 584, 588, 590
Wolk, R. B., 459
Wolpe, J., 126, 127, 129
Wong, M. R., 248
Woodcock, R. W., 138, 143, 167
Woodruff, P. A., 89
Woodruff, R. A., 89
Woodward, J. A., 123, 140
Woodward, J. L., 202
Woody, R. W., 5
Wooten, A. J., 593
Wright, D., 550
Wright, J. H., 501, 531
Wrobel, T. A., 296
Wu, C. Y., 210, 217, 220
Wurtz, R. G., 58
Wyatt, F., 460
Wylie, J. R., 401, 429, 450
Wyndowe, J., 94
Wysocki, J. J., 540, 544

Yamakawa, R., 184
Yeh, C. J., 91

Subject Index

Note: The bold numbers indicate primary information.

Ethical practice of assessment,
46–55
communicating test results,
53–54
competencies in using, 51–53
developing a professional
relationship, 47–48
integration and use of results,
53
invasion of privacy, 48
inviolacy, 50
labeling and restriction of
freedom, 50
test security, 54
*Ethical Principles of
Psychologists and Code of
Conduct,* 47, 50
Ethnicity and test performance,
55–60, 143–144, 218–220
Evaluating psychological tests,
9–22
norms, 11–12
practical considerations, 11
reliability, 12–17
standardization, 11–12
theoretical orientation, 10
validity, 17–25
Event recording, 115–117
Examiner expectations, 48
Executive Functions, 574, 588,
590–592
Exner's Comprehensive System,
393–457
Expressive techniques, 495
Externalizing coping style,
613–615
Extratensives (Rorschach),
444–445
Extraversion-introversion, *see*
Introversion-extraversion

Face validity, 18
Factor analysis, 21
Faking bad, 42, 232, 234–236,
314, 317–319, 344, 353,
369–372
Faking good, 232–236, 314,
317–319, 344, 352,
369–372
Family of Man, 460
FAS test, *see* Controlled Oral
Word Association test
Fear Survey Schedule, 126–128
Fear Survey Schedule for
Children, 126–128
Revised Fear Survey Schedule
for Children (FSSC-R),
126
Feedback of test results,
53–54
Finger tapping, 540, 544,
588–590
administration, 589–590
interpretation, 590
reliability and validity, 589
Five Factor model, 347–348

Fluid *vs.* crystallized
intelligence, 139–140, 149,
164, 167–168, 587,
672–673
Focal lesions, 173, 181
Frostig Developmental Test of
Visual Perception, 550
Fuld profile, 194–195

Gambrill Assertion Inventory,
129
Gender-Role Scales (GM/GF),
299
General Behavior Inventory,
308
Generalized Neuropsychological
Scale (GNDS), 537
General medical setting, 38–40
Gerontological Apperception
Test, 459
Geriatric Depression Inventory,
594
Gifted children, 198–199
Goodenough-Harris Drawing
Test, 57, 500–501. *See also*
Draw-A-Person; Projective
drawing
*Guidelines for Computer-Based
Test Interpretations,* 47, 66
*Guidelines for Test User
Qualifications,* 66

Hain system for scoring the
Bender, 549
Halo effects, 26
Halstead Reitan
Neuropsychological Test
Battery, 8, 518, 537, 540,
550, 570, 588
Hamilton Rating Scale for
Depression, 125, 594
*Handbook of Behavioral
Assessment,* 103
Harris and Lingoes content
scales, 205, 228, 292–295,
672–673
Head injury, *see* Traumatic head
injury
Healey Picture Completion, 147
"Hold" *vs.* "no-hold" tests, 189
Holtzman Inkblot Test, 899
Homosexuality, 247–250,
277–278, 479, 483–484,
503, 522
Hostility, *see* Aggression
House-Tree-Person (HTP), 3, 6,
523–533, 568, 661–663
administration, 525
interpretation of content,
526–529
interpretive considerations,
525–526
signs of adjustment, 529–530
Human figure drawings, *see*
Draw-A-Person; Projective
drawings

Hutt-Briskin scoring system,
547–550, 552
Hypnosis, 480–481
Hypochondriasis, 240–241,
263–266, 340, 438–439
Hysteria, 243–245, 264–266,
268–269, 276–277,
325–326

Idiot savants, 135
Illness Behavior Questionnaire,
60
Illusory correlation, 505–506
Imagery (clinical assessment
of), 121
Impulsivity, indicators of:
Bender, 548
CPI, 365–368, 390–391
MCMI, 328–331
MMPI, 243–245, 274,
281–282, 627
projective drawings,
516–517, 703–705
TAT, 474, 628
WAIS-R/WISC-R, 162–163,
173, 188
Impulsivity and
neuropsychology, 592–593
Incomplete Sentences Test, 43,
653
Incremental validity, 22–44,
469
Individual Neuropsychological
Testing for Neurotoxicity
Battery, 540
Information-processing
approaches to intelligence,
142–144
Information variance, 89
Insanity, 41–42
Insomnia, 283–284
Intellectual disability, 197–198,
550, 660–664. *See also*
Mental retardation
Intelligence, **132–204,** 671
bias, 55–60, 143
classifications, 155–156, 160
correlates of, 144–145
definitions, 132–144
developmental theory,
140–142
deviation IQ, 135, 154,
160–161
ethnicity, 42–47, 143
fluid *vs.* crystallized
intelligence, 139–140,
672–673
global factor (g) *vs.* specific
factor (s), 135–138
hierarchical model, 136–137
information processing
approaches, 142–144
meaning of IQ scores,
153–155, 671
multiple intelligences
(Gardner), 136